W9-AYC-922

SIXTH EDITION

ORGANIZATIONAL BEHAVIOR

SIXTH EDITION

ORGANIZATIONAL BEHAVIOR

Don Hellriegel
Texas A & M University

John W. Slocum, Jr.
Southern Methodist University

Richard W. Woodman
Texas A & M University

WEST PUBLISHING COMPANY
St. Paul   New York   Los Angeles   San Francisco

PRODUCTION CREDITS
Copyediting: Marilynn Taylor
Text Design: Wendy Calmenson, The Book Company
Composition: Carlisle Communications
Artwork: Alexander Teshin and Associates
Cover Design: John Rokusek
Cover Image: David Bishop

COPYRIGHT © 1976, 1979,
1983, 1986, 1989,   By WEST PUBLISHING COMPANY
COPYRIGHT © 1992   By WEST PUBLISHING COMPANY
                         610 Opperman Drive
                         P.O. Box 64526
                         St. Paul, MN 55164-0526

Library of Congress Cataloging-in-Publication Data

Hellriegel, Don.
    Organizational behavior / Don Hellriegel, John W. Slocum, Jr.,
Richard W. Woodman.— 6th ed.
      p. cm.
    Includes index.
    ISBN 0-314-92684-4 (hard)
    1. Organizational behavior.   I. Slocum, John W.   II. Woodman,
Richard W.   III. Title.
HD58.7.A44   1992
658 — dc20   91-31812
                                                    CIP

To Jill, Kim, and Lori (DH)
Christopher, Bradley, and Jonathan (JWS)
David and Anna (RWW)

CONTENTS

PART II: INDIVIDUAL PROCESSES   73

◆ CHAPTER 3: PERSONALITY AND ATTITUDES   74

◆ CHAPTER 4: PERCEPTION AND ATTRIBUTION   102

◆ CHAPTER 5: INDIVIDUAL PROBLEM-SOLVING STYLES   138

CHAPTER 6: LEARNING AND REINFORCEMENT
168

CHAPTER 7: WORK MOTIVATION
202

PART III: INTERPERSONAL AND GROUP PROCESSES   309

◆ **CHAPTER 10: DYNAMICS WITHIN GROUPS**   310

◆ **CHAPTER 11: DYNAMICS BETWEEN GROUPS**   350

CHAPTER 12: LEADERSHIP   382

CHAPTER 13: INTERPERSONAL COMMUNICATION   426

CHAPTER 16: POWER AND POLITICAL BEHAVIOR   532

CHAPTER 17: JOB DESIGN   564

CHAPTER 18: ORGANIZATION DESIGN   596

PREFACE

The 1980s brought tremendous changes in the world. Governments altered in fundamental ways, the Berlin Wall came down, and the world's work force became a culturally diverse one. Some previously successful organizations were suddenly faced with pressures to innovate and change their ways in order to remain successful. The restructuring of organizations around the world put pressures on many managers to alter how they managed their people and organizations. These changes often required them to develop new insights and practices.

One major goal of the sixth edition of *Organizational Behavior* is to present a realistic and complete picture of people working in organizations. As we did in the last two editions, we have included an Across Cultures section in each chapter that enables the reader to see problems and issues from other perspectives. Managers must learn to compete for resources, negotiate contracts, influence behaviors, and conduct business with a diverse group of employees and customers. These Across Cultures sections permit the reader to see how management concepts and practices are applied in other parts of the world.

A theme introduced in Chapter 1 and carried throughout the book is that successful employees and managers should understand how various management concepts and approaches can be applied in an organization. Given this theme, each chapter opens with a Preview Case that details a problem or issue that is addressed by the content of that chapter. Current research is provided as a foundation for practical applications.

A second goal of the sixth edition is to present the readers with true-to-life problems and issues that illustrate the concepts and models in the chapter. The In Practice sections that appear in each chapter are about problems and issues that managers and employees have faced in hospitals, manufacturing plants, insurance companies, and other organizations. Many chapters contain diagnostic questionnaires that make topics "come alive" for readers by providing them with insights into their own experiences or behaviors.

xx   PREFACE

The third goal for *Organizational Behavior,* sixth edition, is to help readers who study this book to:

- Develop a clear and meaningful understanding of the field of organizational behavior.
- Acquire insights and knowledge concerning the behavior of culturally diverse individuals and groups in work settings.
- Develop an appreciation for how managers design their organizations.
- Develop a foundation to guide them in their choice of relevant concepts and models to use in diagnosing and implementing an effective solution to a problem.
- Experience first-hand some of the problems and issues that employees and managers face on a daily basis in many organizations.

NEW MATERIAL IN THIS EDITION

The sixth edition includes important new subject matter, as well as additional learning approaches. We have reorganized the book to more clearly focus on four key areas of organizational behavior: the individual, interpersonal and group processes, organizational processes, and individual and organizational change.

Reviewers encouraged us to introduce a new chapter on "Learning about Organizational Behavior" (Chapter 2). This chapter helps readers decide how to design a research project to address important questions facing them and their organization. Not all designs will yield reliable and valid data that managers and other employees can use to make a decision.

We have expanded our materials on goal-setting and reward systems by introducing another new chapter, "Goal-Setting and Performance Enhancement" (Chapter 8). Included in this chapter is information on goal-setting, as well as on performance-appraisals and types of reward systems that managers can choose to increase employees' performance and sustain it over time.

We also have expanded our coverage of managing a culturally diverse work force and ethics. Managing a culturally diverse work force is a major factor in organizations. Rather than singling it out in any one chapter, we continuously introduce this theme in many chapters. Our coverage of ethics has grown, and now ethical problems and issues facing employees and managers are included in many chapters.

Positive reactions to the experiential exercises in earlier editions encouraged us to change and add new ones. In all cases, new exercises were chosen to reinforce major sections of a chapter.

The In Practice sections have been well received by students and instructors. These present actual managerial problems and issues that reinforce the concepts and models presented in the chapter. They appear where the concept or model is discussed in the text. All chapters have at least three

In Practice sections, and more than 80 percent of these are new to this edition.

We have added new management cases and exercises at the end of all chapters. Special care was taken to choose new cases and exercises that will aid the readers' understanding of the materials presented in the chapter. Other end-of-chapter features that aid reader understanding and comprehension are a list of key words and concepts and discussion questions that can be used for written assignments or class discussion.

We also have changed the integrated cases. Two of the more popular cases have been retained, and others added. The new cases focus on ethics, managing a culturally diverse work force, and self-managed work groups.

Finally, the materials in each chapter have been expanded and updated. A sampling of the new materials include social learning theory, mentoring, charismatic and attributional leadership, wellness programs, quality of work life, information technologies, goal setting and performance, self-managed teams, electronic brainstorming, communication networks, negotiations in conflict management, network organizations, ethical intensity, lateral thinking method, cognitive moral development, globalization, the exchange process in power relationships, computer-integrated manufacturing, and continuous improvement programs. The list of references at the end of each chapter provides current sources for students who desire additional materials on each subject.

FRAMEWORK OF THIS EDITION: FIVE MAJOR PARTS

This book is organized around four major issues facing employees and managers: understanding people, managing people in groups, designing organizations to be more effective, and changing the organization and employees' behaviors to respond to pressures from customers, competitors, and others. This order has been followed in response to many reviewers who have found it easier to discuss materials that focus on why and how people behave and then on understanding groups. As in the fifth edition, this material is integrated but in a manner that allows instructors to change the sequence of materials as they prefer.

Part I—The Introduction consists of two chapters. Chapter 1 discusses the changing nature of the work force and what this means for organizations. It also discusses what managers do and how they accomplish their roles in organizations. Chapter 2 develops the theme that managers and other employees need to know how to design and conduct some basic research programs in their organizations to improve their organization's effectiveness.

Part II—Individual Processes includes seven chapters that focus on factors that influence an individual's behavior. Separate chapters are included on personality and how attitudes are formed (Chapter 3); the factors that influence a person's perceptual processes (Chapter 4); how a person's problem-solving style influences how he or she makes decisions, motivates, and communicates with others (Chapter 5); how employees learn (Chapter 6); what motivates employees (Chapter 7); evaluating and rewarding behavior (Chapter 8); and stress, including methods of coping with stress (Chapter 9).

Part III—Interpersonal and Group Processes focuses on group behavior and interpersonal communications. It is organized into five chapters. What happens within groups is the focus of Chapter 10, while Chapter 11 looks at what can happen between groups in an organization. The nature of leadership and how a leader can influence groups and individuals to achieve organizational goals are the central themes of Chapter 12. Chapter 13 illustrates the influence of communication openness, networks, and media. We close this section with Chapter 14, which focuses on ways that people manage conflict and negotiate effectively with others.

Part IV—Organizational Processes includes five chapters. Chapter 15 describes organizational culture and how culture influences employee attitudes and behaviors. Power and political behavior are the focuses of Chapter 16. In Chapter 17, we examine how the design of employees' jobs can influence their productivity and job satisfaction. Chapter 18 considers the factors that influence the design of organizations and the range of design options. We conclude this part with Chapter 19 on decision making, including an extensive discussion of ethical decision making.

Part V—Individual and Organizational Change has three chapters that focus on change. Chapter 20 addresses how organizations socialize new employees and describes the career paths that most employees will take. Chapter 21 examines organizational change, including pressures for and resistance to change. Chapter 22 concludes the book with a discussion of approaches that managers and employees have actually used to change their organization.

SUPPLEMENTS AVAILABLE

A variety of supplementary materials are available for use with this book. These include:

- The third edition of *Organizational Behavior: Experience and Cases*, written by Dorothy Marcic. This book contains experiential exercises and cases that closely parallel material presented in *Organizational Behavior*, sixth edition.

- A *student study guide* prepared by Roger Roderick. This contains learning objectives, chapter outlines, practice questions, and a programmed study supplement to *Organizational Behavior*.

- An *instructor's resource guide* by Patricia Fandt. It contains lecture resource materials; transparency masters; answers to all discussion questions, end-of-chapter case questions, and end-of-book case questions; and suggestions for films and videotapes that correspond to topics covered in the book.

- A *test manual* by Patricia Fandt. It contains over fourteen hundred true-or-false and multiple-choice questions.
- A set of four-colored *transparency acetates* from the instructor's resource guide.
- *Westtest*, a computer-based test bank.

All of these supplements are available from West Publishing Company.

ACKNOWLEDGEMENTS

We would like to express our appreciation to the following individuals whose suggestions led to improvements in the sixth edition of *Organizational Behavior:*

Royce L. Abrahamson	Southwest Texas State University
Reginald Beal	University of Wisconsin-Whitewater
Charles Capps	Sam Houston State University
James W. Carr	West Georgia College
Tupper Causey	Wilfred Laurier University
J. Gregory Chachere	Northeast Louisiana University
Gene Deszca	Wilfred Laurier University
Robert Isaac	University of Calgary
Steven Meisel	LaSalle University
Herff L. Moore	University of Central Arkansas
Kevin Mossholder	Auburn University
Ivan Perlaki	East Tennessee State University
Afzalur Rahim	Western Kentucky University
David A. Tansik	University of Arizona
Cheryl Tromley	Fairfield University
Robert J. Vandenberg	Georgia State University

We continue to enjoy a fine working relationship with the people of West Publishing Company. In particular, we want to thank the following individuals for their excellent support and help with this book: Dick Fenton, acquisitions editor; Esther Craig, developmental editor; Tom Modl, production editor; and Ann Hillstrom, promotion manager. In addition, Marilynn J. Taylor, our copy editor, did her usual superior job.

For their able help with the many critical tasks of manuscript preparation, we would like to thank Argie Butler and Johnny Rodriguez of Texas A & M University and Billie Boyd of Southern Methodist University. We are also grateful to Dean Benton Cocanougher of Texas A & M, as well as President Ken Pye and Provost Ruth Morgan of Southern Methodist University for their personal support and encouragement. Our thanks to them for creating and supporting an environment that made this book possible.

Finally, we want to express a special debt to our colleagues and friends at Southern Methodist University and Texas A & M University for creating the community of scholars that encourages and sustains our professional development.

Don Hellriegel
Texas A & M University

John W. Slocum, Jr.
Southern Methodist University

Richard W. Woodman
Texas A & M University

PART I

INTRODUCTION

CHAPTER 1:

MANAGERS AND ORGANIZATIONAL BEHAVIOR

LEARNING OBJECTIVES

When you have finished studying this chapter, you should be able to:

- Discuss how the changing demographics of the work force and changes in organizations will affect employees.
- State how managers spend their time during a day.
- Describe the roles that managers play.
- Define three approaches to studying organizational behavior.
- Explain how using contingency concepts in studying organizational behavior will help you as a manager.

OUTLINE

SANDRA KURTZIG SEEKS TO REVIVE ASK'S ENTREPRENEURIAL SPIRIT

When Sandra Kurtzig quit as president and chief executive officer of ASK Computer Systems in 1984, she never intended to return to the company that she founded in 1972. She wanted to take time off to be with her two sons, travel, and write a book about her experiences. But in 1989, she returned to bring back the entrepreneurial spirit that the company had lost. Since then, she has redesigned products, gotten rid of ineffective managers, recruited new managers with entrepreneurial backgrounds, and subtly changed the culture of ASK. Employees even say the food and beer at the "Friday bash" have improved.

In 1972, Kurtzig quit as marketing specialist for General Electric and founded ASK computer with her husband. She started with a single customer and two thousand dollars. Doing all of the work in the spare bedroom of their home, she designed a program that would help small manufacturing companies run an entire plant. The program was an instant success, and by 1981, the company's sales were over $67 million. Today, that spare bedroom has grown into a $200 million-a-year corporation with more than one thousand employees and fifty-five offices worldwide.

The success at ASK reflects her managerial skills. She constantly meets with fellow workers and closely involves them in ASK's operations. She plows back monies into new product development. She believes in delegating responsibilities to people and giving them room to make decisions. She has employees rate the job performances of division managers. Those division managers rated highly get rewarded with greater responsibility and bonuses. Most of those who receive low ratings are not with the company much longer. She attends as many company meetings as possible to observe and follow what is happening and foster team spirit. She has no qualms about going directly to people, bypassing the hierarchy of managers. She is also working on ASK's next generation of products, making them simpler to use and compatible with different types of computers and data bases. ASK is also increasing its efforts to sell its products for a variety of computer systems, including those made by IBM and Sun Microsystems, Inc. To position the company in a new global manufacturing market, she has established offices in Europe and Asia.[1]

As Sandra Kurtzig found out, managing is a difficult task. Although ASK is now a very successful company, it still faces difficult problems. During her absence, new competitors entered the information systems market that ASK had at one time dominated. Oracle Corporation, an aggressive seller of data-based software, has taken away some of ASK's market share with new products and a fancy advertising slogan, "Kiss Your ASK Goodbye." ASK has not aggressively developed products for the emerging workstation market but has instead focused on creating products for the minicomputer market. Kurtzig has boosted funds for new products from 10 percent of the research and development budget to 50 percent. Finally, she is spending time on the road with customers trying to reassure them that ASK is now back on track and will have competitive products.

When Kurtzig left ASK in 1985, Ronald Braniff took over. Braniff had excellent managerial experience and was a member of Kurtzig's top management team. For a while, things went well enough. Over the next four years, profits grew, but in 1989, sales flattened. More telling, the company had no new products on line. It had been living off old software packages created when Kurtzig was running the company. One way to understand what happened at ASK is to consider the **organizational iceberg** in Figure 1.1. Using the organizational iceberg, let's analyze ASK. The formal aspects were the same under Braniff as under Kurtzig:

- Goals: To make a profit, be a responsible member of the community, show growth in sales and profits each year, and remain a leader in information systems for manufacturing firms.
- Technology: Software to design the information systems, engineers to design and test new products, and so on.

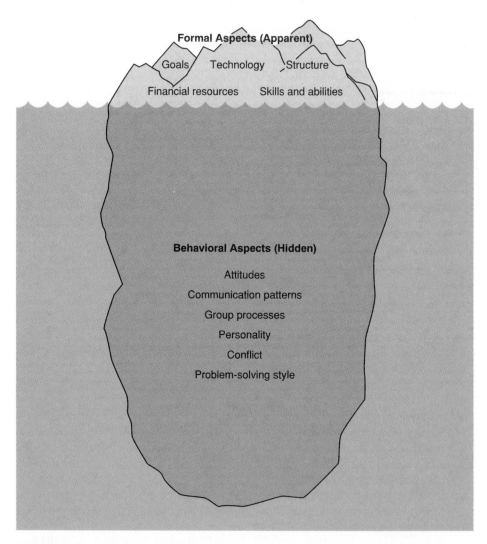

FIGURE 1.1   Organizational Iceberg

- Structure: The departments (finance, marketing, research and development, sales) and the division of labor (president, vice-president, department managers, assistant department managers), and so on.

- Financial resources: The current assets and liabilities, shareholders' equity, and the like.

- Skills and abilities: The technical skills of employees and their managerial skills, such as interpersonal relations, communications, and leadership.

Even all this knowledge would not reveal why the company did not prosper under Braniff's leadership. The answer probably lies with his approach to those aspects of the organization and management below the tip of the iceberg—the behavioral aspects of performance. Kurtzig said that Braniff simply was not a visionary leader. Others indicated that he was cool, unapproachable, and distant from employees, a direct contrast to Kurtzig's warm and open style.

There are no easy or complete answers as to why people and organizations do not always function smoothly. Braniff was hand-picked by Kurtzig to run ASK, and still he floundered. Your study of organizational behavior should provide you with a systematic way to better understand the behavior of people in organizations. **Organizational behavior** is the study of human behavior, attitudes, and performance within organizational settings. It is an interdisciplinary field, drawing concepts from social and clinical psychology, sociology, cultural anthropology, industrial engineering, and organizational psychology.

Why should you study organizational behavior? Most people who study organizational behavior are or will be employees in organizations. Organizational behavior should help you become a better employee. It should help you diagnose, understand, and explain what is happening around you in your job.

The study of organizational behavior is similar to the study of botany. People who do not work with trees find it enjoyable and refreshing to be able to identify and describe trees around them and to know their history, important differences among them, and the role trees play in our ecological system. For a manager at International Paper, however, who is responsible for cutting trees in a forest, the value of botany is even more important. This manager needs to understand how many and what kinds of trees to cut down for certain kinds of woods and the relationships between tree size and wood volume, age and wood quality, and the like.

In a very real sense, organizational behavior can prepare people to become better employees and managers by providing insights into how and why individuals act as they do. Recall that Sandra Kurtzig thought that she was leaving her company in good hands. In a short time, ASK was in trouble. Perhaps she should have diagnosed the situation more closely before leaving the organization. Some of the issues she might have considered include:

- How will my leaving affect the bottom line of ASK?

- How will Ronald Braniff's style and leadership affect the running of the organization?

- Will people's enthusiasm for ASK change after I leave?
- Is the organization structured properly?
- Should I consult with members of my staff about my decision to leave before I make it, or should I just make it myself?

Effective managers try to find answers to these and many similar questions. They also try to understand how their behavior affects others in their organization. In the chapters that follow, we present information that will help you answer such questions and to become more aware of the importance of behavior (both overt and covert) in an organizational setting, including your own behavior.

CHANGING WORLD OF WORK

Let's consider what it will be like to be an employee in the year 2000 in a U.S. organization. The entire work force for the year 2000 has already been born, and over two-thirds of these people in this group are already working in organizations. Each group—the newcomers and those already working in organizations—present unique concerns. We have broadly classified two issues facing managers: the changing nature of the work force and the changing nature of organizations.

The Work Force

Fewer people will be entering the U.S. job market by the turn of the century than at any time in the past. Once the massive baby boom generation (those born between 1946 and 1961) started entering the work force, organizations could be highly selective about whom to choose.[2] By the late 1970s, about three million people per year within the age group of 18 to 24 were entering organizations. In 1990, there were only 1.3 million new workers between those ages, and by 1995, there will be about 1.3 million fewer workers in that age group. The labor force will be increasing at a slower rate than at any time since the 1930s. This slow growth will impact U.S. productivity. When the size of the labor force is steadily increasing, lower productivity can be overcome by the sheer increase in the numbers of individuals working. But with fewer new employees entering the work force, organizations must foster increased productivity in each worker in order for productivity to increase.

Skill Level   The skill level of entry-level employees presents another challenge. When the labor supply was high, organizations could easily be selective, retaining the skilled and not hiring the undereducated. Already, many organizations are having difficulty in recruiting new entry-level workers and have had to invest money and time in training those selected to acquire basic skills, such as simple math and writing. The present concern with the level of literacy and basic skills will be compounded by the fact that in the years to come, an increase in skill level will be needed to perform many jobs. Computer software can check the spelling of words, but it cannot proofread for meaning and context. As robots take over routine assembly line work from people, jobs will open up for troubleshooting and monitoring computerized equipment. It should not be surprising then that U.S. organizations spent over $220 billion in 1990 for on-the-job training.[3]

What skills will managers in the year 2000 need? This question was asked of several thousand managers.[4] Their answers are shown in Table 1.1. We have broken the managerial skills down into four types. **Conceptual skills** refer to an individual's ability to understand how his or her organization is affected by competitors and how each department of the organization is related to others. **Technical skills** refer to an individual's ability to apply specific methods, procedures, and techniques to a problem. **Interpersonal skills** include the ability to lead, motivate, manage conflict, and work with others. **Communication skills** refer to the individual's ability to send and receive information, thoughts, feelings, and attitudes.

The skills that managers in the year 2000 will need to learn and use more effectively lie heavily in interpersonal and communication competen-

---

TABLE 1.1 Importance of Managerial Skills Now and in theYear 2000

Managerial Skill	Examples	Now	Year 2000
Conceptual	Strategy formulation	68%	78%
	Conveys strong sense of vision	75%	98%
	Plans for management succession	56%	85%
	International economics and politics	10%	19%
Interpersonal	Ethical behaviors	74%	85%
	Human resource management	41%	53%
	Reassigns or terminates unsatisfactory employees	34%	71%
Technical	Computer literacy	3%	7%
	Marketing and sales	50%	48%
	Production	21%	9%
Communication	Communicates frequently with customers	41%	78%
	Communicates frequently with employees	59%	89%
	Handles media and public speaking	16%	13%
	Sensitivity to individuals in different cultures	10%	40%

Sources: Adapted from L. B. Korn, "How the Next CEO Will Be Different," *Fortune,* May 22, 1989, 157–161; B. Dumaine, "What Leaders of Tomorrow See," *Fortune,* July, 3, 1989, 48–62; D. Anderson, "Building Tomorrow's Leaders," *GE Plastics.* January 1, 1990, 14–15.

cies. Managers, customers, and employees who have different values, goals, and ethical principles from yours could pose many challenges for you. Throughout this book, we present *Management Cases and Exercises* designed to help you learn these new skills.

Gender   Women accounted for 60 percent of the total growth of the U.S. work force between 1970 and 1985, and they are expected to make up a similar percentage of new entry-level employees between 1991 and 2000. Many of these women have children. In fact, one of the fastest growing segments of the labor market is mothers with infants.[5]

The influx of women with children into the work force is having a tremendous impact on the workplace. The increase of dual-career couples has brought a growing concern over balancing the demands of work and the family. A survey of the Society for Human Resource Management reported that only 10 percent of U.S. organizations provide for child care assistance, although nearly 50 percent are considering some form of such assistance for employees. In addition, dual-career couples are no longer able to frequently relocate with the assumption that one spouse is free to follow the other. Organizations are now forced to engage in joint career management decisions in which spousal employment opportunities must be carefully considered.

There is considerable evidence that women face a glass ceiling in management. The **glass ceiling** refers to a barrier so subtle that it is transparent, yet so strong that it prevents women and minorities from moving up in the management ranks.[6] A recent study of the Fortune 500, the Fortune Service 500, and the 190 largest health care organizations in the United States found that less than 4 percent of these organizations had women in top management positions. One result is that some women are bailing out of large organizations. Women started their own organizations at six times the rate for men during the 1980s.[7] Of the one hundred leading corporate women identified in a *Business Week* survey in 1980, nearly one-third had left their corporate jobs for other pursuits ten years later.

Race/ethnicity   It is projected that a third of the newcomers into the work force between now and the year 2000 will be minority group members. Those future workers are today's minority children, more than half of whom are being raised in poverty by a single parent. As a result, these new workers will be coming from school systems that have not been able to adequately prepare them for organizational life. Since many new jobs will require higher education and skill levels, training for skills will be of critical importance to minority groups. There also is evidence that minority members face the glass ceiling. For example, only one black heads a Fortune 1000 company, and less than 4 percent of top management positions are held by African-Americans, Asians, and Hispanics.[8]

Promotion   The U.S. work force is aging along with the baby boomers. Between 1990 and 2000, the number of persons aged 35 to 47 will increase by 38 percent, while the number between 48 and 53 will increase by 67 percent. In the past, these workers have been less likely to relocate or train for new occupations than younger workers. This tremendous expansion in the number of middle-aged workers will also mean increased competition for fewer high-level management jobs. In 1987, one person in twenty was promoted into a top management position; in 2001, the ratio is expected to be one in fifty. The traditional lure of promotion as an incentive to keep people working hard appears to be threatened. The lower odds of promotion within an organization may also lead talented people to become more entrepreneurial and seek to form businesses themselves rather than working for others.[9] Sandra Kurtzig of ASK Computers, Steve Jobs of Next, Debbi Fields of Mrs. Fields' Cookies, and Michael Dell of Dell Computer Company, among others, are talented people who have chosen to start their own businesses rather than work their way up the corporate ladder.

Retirement Although mandatory age-based retirement has been banned since 1986, the trend toward early retirement is increasing. Many experts feel, however, that to maintain adequate staffing, older men and women will be needed on the job longer. Increased attention to career planning and retirement issues will be required of all managers.

Organizational Revolution

Just as the work force is changing, so, too are organizations. Let's briefly review some of the revolutionary changes in organizations.

Mergers/Downsizing It is estimated that more than 15 million workers have been affected by mergers.[10] Mergers often bring significant changes in top management. Nearly half of the top managers in an acquired company leave within one year of the merger, and almost 75 percent leave within three years.

One of the results of the merger mania that swept through U.S. organizations in the latter part of the 1980s is downsizing. **Downsizing** is the process of letting people go in an attempt to improve efficiency and the organization's competitive position. A survey by the American Management Association showed that almost 40 percent of the one thousand organizations surveyed planned to reduce their work force by downsizing.[11] In downsizing, the central question is how best to accomplish this reduction. Options typically include natural attrition, layoffs, early retirement packages, and shortened work weeks, among others. Each of these options have different financial costs to the organization. Organizations must also be aware that there are concerns among the "survivors," as well as those who are forced to leave. Managers of survivors are frequently faced with employees who report a loss of identity or purpose, high levels of anxiety about their personal life, emotional problems within their families, and an obsession with self-survival. As one manager stated, "People were spending a lot of time worrying about their stock and personal futures rather than doing their work."

Expanding Service Organizations The focus of many of tomorrow's organizations will be on service and not manufacturing. In 1990, the service sector accounted for more than 68 percent of the U.S. gross national product and 71 percent of its employment. Service organizations have grown so rapidly that they accounted for nearly 90 percent of all new, nonfarm jobs created in the past thirty years.[12]

Global Challenge   North American organizations are a part of a global economy. Some experts believe that more than one-third of these organizations' profits are derived from international business, along with one-sixth of the jobs. Managers will be asked to understand the complex nature of their organization's political environment in different countries and learn how it can affect decisions they will make at home. To meet these challenges, U.S. and Canadian organizations are forming business alliances with foreign corporations. Ford's reengineered Escort line of cars was developed with Mazda, which provided many design and production features. For many managers, this means that they will have to work closely with individuals who have different values and ways of doing their job. Staffing these businesses with managers who are flexible and can handle different styles and management philosophies will become more important.[13]

Use of Technology   Managers have begun to design their organizations in order to take advantage of advances in computer-based information systems. It has been estimated that about 16 million employees now work out of their homes instead of going to an office.[14] The prospect of "electronic offices" will continue to expand as computers link people together without them meeting face-to-face. This raises a serious problem in how to effectively motivate and lead people whom you do not manage on a face-to-face basis.

Managerial Challenge

The challenge for managers of the future is going to be to simultaneously deal with a newly diversified work force characterized by changing attitudes and values and with changing organization structures in order to maintain their competitiveness. As the work force continues to diversify, you will need to be especially attuned to potentially different expectations of these groups. The organization in the year 2000 will be a rich melting pot of people of various backgrounds, cultures, and expectations, rather than a homogenized one as it has been in the past.

How can we help you with this challenge? One way is by providing frameworks and concepts that will give you insights into these challenges. One of the first ways to accomplish this is to focus on the basic characteristics of managerial work.

BASIC CHARACTERISTICS OF MANAGERIAL WORK

Few of the thousands of books and articles written about managers tell us anything about what managers actually do.[15] They give us the impression that managers spend most of their time reading reports in their air-conditioned offices, trying to get to the airport to catch the 5:30 plane, entertaining important customers, and solving complicated problems. Studies of top managers suggest that they seldom stop thinking about their jobs. Four nights out of five are spent working for the company. One night is spent at the office, another entertaining business associates. On other nights, when the manager does go home, it is not to a place of rest and relaxation but to a place that serves as a branch office for more work.

This work schedule, while freeing some time at work for the manager, creates stress in most family situations. Moreover, tightly scheduled workdays, frequent travel, and simultaneous demands exert considerable pressures on managers. It is not uncommon for many managers to work fifty-five to sixty hours or longer each week. John Flavin, co-owner of Optigraphics, a firm that makes baseball and football cards and sells them under the tradename of Sportflics, starts his days between 5:00 A.M. and 5:30 A.M. with a three-mile walk. His day ends fourteen hours later. Before he gets to his office, he reads the morning newspaper and finishes paperwork that he did not get to the night before. By 8 A.M., he and his top management team meet to discuss production problems that might have arisen on the night shift (midnight to 8 A.M.) and financial matters. During lunch, he either dines with people from the baseball and/or football world to make sure that all players will be available for trading cards next season or eats in his office alone to get more work done. Should Flavin have any free time, it is taken up by subordinates who drop in to chat about personal and/or company matters. His advice is constantly sought.

One reason that managers work at such a fast pace is that managerial work is open-ended. Engineers can point to a bridge and know that the project is finished. Computer programmers can make a system work and know that their job on it is completed. However, the manager's job is fast-paced, continuous action. The manager is constantly responsible for the success or failure of the organization, and there are few guidelines that enable him or her to say, "My job is finished."

Managerial work has five basic characteristics: (1) hard work in a variety of tasks; (2) preference for nonroutine tasks; (3) use of communication media; (4) involvement in communication networks; and (5) a blend of rights and duties.

Hard Work in a Variety of Tasks

Many jobs require specialization and concentration. A machine operator may require forty hours to machine a part. A computer programmer may need a month to write programs to handle the materials flow of the purchasing department. A certified public accountant may need a month to audit the books of an organization. In contrast, a manager's job is often characterized by variety, brevity, and fragmentation. One study found that first-line managers averaged 583 different job problems a day (about one every 48 seconds). As a result, these managers had little time to plan.

A top manager's day might include processing mail, listening to a subordinate explain a consumer group's boycott of the organization's services or products, attending a meeting with other community leaders to discuss how to handle the local water shortage, or listening to another manager complain about the lack of office space. During the day, the manager may attend a ceremonial luncheon for an employee who is retiring after forty-five years with the organization or discuss the loss of an important contract with the purchasing manager. Constant interruptions and a variety of tasks characterize a manager's day, and an effective manager must be able to shift gears quickly and frequently. According to one vice-president in charge of a finance division, "I change hats every ten minutes. I act as a tax specialist for a while, a manager for the next few minutes, then a banker, a personnel specialist, and so on."

A manager's actions are brief, and most tasks take less than ten minutes. Telephone calls average about six minutes (they are brief and to the point), unscheduled meetings about twelve minutes, and routine desk work (dictating letters, reading the *Wall Street Journal,* and so on) about fifteen minutes. Few managers have time to do more than merely skim long reports and memos.

Managers frequently leave meetings before they are over and interrupt subordinates and others to discuss problems. One study found that a manager worked undisturbed for as long as twenty-three minutes only twelve times in thirty-five days.

Preference for Nonroutine Tasks

Managers move toward the active elements in their work. They delegate to subordinates the more routine tasks, such as handling the mail or reviewing long reports. Managers constantly seek new and "hot" information, which they learn from unscheduled meetings, telephone calls, gossip, and speculation. These are important parts of managers' sources of information. When they receive this type of information, they give it top priority. Deborah Cannon, vice president of NCNB Bank, sets aside a couple of two-hour periods each week to "free-think" in her office. During this time, subordinates can come in for quick conversations to handle unscheduled business.

Routine reports may not contain the latest information. Managers may pay little, if any, serious attention to them. Although most managers have to write routine reports as part of their jobs, few take the time to study those written by others. Top managers are especially concerned with what is happening today and what is likely to happen tomorrow.

Managers work in a stimulus-response environment: they respond to the immediate situation. Jim Steffel, division manager of Fleet Line Trucking, has to make fast decisions when an eighteen-wheeler spills its cargo on an interstate highway. Is the driver okay? Is there personal or property damage? Which wrecking service is nearby? Is the cargo hazardous? Has the owner of the cargo been notified? Is the cargo insured? As soon as he handled that situation, another arose: his chief financial officer handed in her resignation to go into business for herself—effective immediately. His immediate concern shifted to determining whether the books were up-to-date and correct and whether there was an assistant he could promote into this position.

Use of Communication Media

Managers communicate in five ways: mail (documented communication), telephone calls (verbal communication), scheduled and unscheduled meetings (formal person-to-person communication), and tours (visual and informal verbal communication). Basic differences exist among these means of communication.

Mail communication is described by formality, long delays in feedback, and little opportunity for give-and-take. "E-mail," or **electronic mail,** uses text editing to transmit written information quickly, inexpensively, and efficiently. Messages are sent at the sender's convenience, transmitted in seconds, and read at the reader's convenience. The messages often appear and disappear on PC display screens and leave no hard copies behind. Regardless of the type of mail, it is a processing chore that has to be done but not enjoyed. Managers can dispose of more than thirty pieces of mail per hour by just skimming over inconsequential pieces, such as solicitations and acknowledgments. Nearly 90 percent of all mail communications does not deal with "live" action. Most managers tend not to use it and ignore most of what they get.

Managers prefer verbal communication. As shown in Figure 1.2, 78 percent of all managerial time is spent in verbal communication: in meetings, on the telephone, and during tours. Telephone calls and unscheduled meetings are typically short. Together, they account for nearly an hour and a half per day that managers spend communicating verbally. Managers use the telephone and unscheduled meetings when they know the other party well and have to send information quickly. Using these forms of communication, managers quickly give and receive a great deal of "live" information. This is one of the ways that Sandra Kurtzig found was very effective in running ASK. When problems suddenly arise, unscheduled meetings can be called and telephone calls made to straighten things out. Maury Gerard of

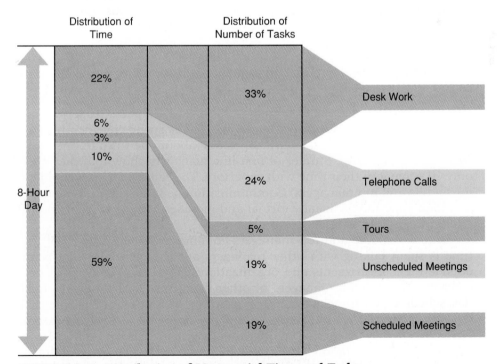

FIGURE 1.2 Distribution of Managerial Time and Tasks

Ciba-Geigy tries to build some leeway into his day by generally refusing to schedule formal meetings early in the morning. So between 8:00 A.M. and 10:30 A.M., he returns phone calls, dictates letters, skims mail, and tries to handle "hot" issues. Roberta Rocheferd, staff vice president at Northwest Airlines, knows that 25 percent of her time each day will be spent with customers, but she doesn't know which customers she'll spend that time with. It depends on which ones face important issues affecting their dealings with the airline at any particular time.

Distribution of Managerial Time and Tasks

Managers tend to hold scheduled meetings when (1) a large amount of information needs to be sent; (2) when information must be communicated to others who are not well-known to a manager; and (3) when scheduling a meeting is the only way to bring together all the people who need the information.

Tours—walking through the building and chatting with employees—give managers a unique opportunity to get out of the office and talk informally with people. Although many managers use tours infrequently, they are a good way to talk with individuals about their work and stress priorities for the organization. To reinforce and stimulate development of new software, when Kurtzig walks through ASK's research and development department, she asks employees what new software they are working on. While on tour, she also expresses her congratulations on a recent marriage, birth, graduation, or other employee achievements.

In sum, communication is a manager's work. Managers do not do research, admit patients to a hospital, or write computer programs. Managers are senders and receivers of information—information that is essential to decision making.

Involvement in Communication Networks

Because managers prefer verbal communication, they are the center of communication networks that include subordinates, peers, superiors, and people outside the organization. Managers usually spend considerably more time with subordinates than with superiors (about one-third to one-half of their time on the job). Studies of first-line managers show that they spend only 10 percent of their time with superiors. The same appears to hold true for middle and top managers. Communication between first-line managers and their superiors is usually formal and includes routine written and verbal reports, such as status reports.

Who do middle and top managers communicate with? Much of their time is spent talking with other managers at their own level and people outside their departments and organizations. These managers must be in constant contact with managers of other departments about plans, facilities, schedules, customer problems, market opportunities, and people problems. Contacts outside the organization include those with trade associations, consultants, lawyers, underwriters, suppliers, government agencies, and consumer associations. Each of these groups provides special information for managers. For example, the National Industrial Distributors Association keeps its members abreast of the latest legislation pending in Congress, union problems, and new product development.

Blend of Rights and Duties

What rights do managers have, and what duties do they perform? According to Peter F. Drucker:

> "The manager has the task of creating a true whole that is larger than the sum of its parts. . . . One analogy is the conductor of a symphony orchestra, through whose effort, vision, and leadership, individual parts that are so much noise by themselves become the living whole of music. But the conductor has the composer's score; the conductor is only the interpreter. The manager is both composer and conductor."[16]

Thus, Drucker portrays the manager as a person who brings order out of chaos. There are times when managers are unable to control their tasks: the telephone rings, the calendar pad shows a long list of meetings, subordinates drop in with personal or organizational problems, and other unexpected situations arise.

Managers have two important rights. First, they can influence their long-term commitments. However, once they are committed, many of their tasks will then be planned by others. For example, a manager can decide whether to join the board of directors of the local United Way campaign. Once the decision to do so is made, the manager has the duty to attend board meetings and spend other time on board business. Managers develop their own information channels and control the use of their time to a large extent through the key decisions they make.

Second, managers take advantage of their duties. The retirement ceremony for an employee at Citicorp provides Milt Reisman, vice president for human resources, the opportunity to collect information from those in attendance. Also, during the short ceremony, Reisman can say a few words about important company issues. An effective manager seizes every opportunity to speak, to lobby for a cause, to short-circuit potential problems, and to kill stories in the rumor mill.

It should be clear by now that managers spend most of their time communicating verbally; the frequency of interaction with others changes for different managerial levels; the importance of "hot" and "grapevine" information increases with managerial level; and managerial work is hectic and fragmented, requiring the ability to shift continually from person to person and from problem to problem.

MANAGERIAL ROLES

According to Henry Mintzberg, there are ten different managerial roles. We define a **role** as an organized set of behaviors. Figure 1.3 shows that these ten roles fall into three major categories: interpersonal, informational, and decisional.[17]

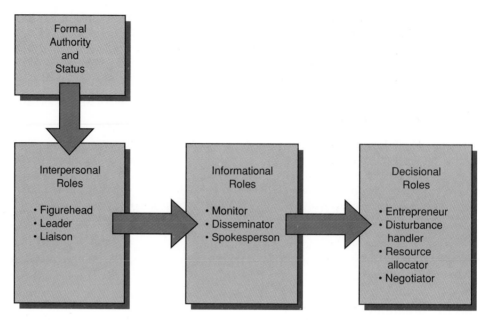

FIGURE 1.3   Managerial Roles

Before we discuss these roles, we need to point out that (1) every manager's job consists of some combination of roles; (2) the roles played by managers often influence the five basic characteristics of managerial work; (3) the roles are described separately to aid in understanding them, but in practice, they are highly integrated; and (4) the importance of these roles can vary considerably according to managerial level (first-line, middle, and top).

Interpersonal Roles

Interpersonal roles refer to relationships with others and flow directly from a manager's formal authority. The **figurehead role** includes handling of symbolic and ceremonial tasks for the department or organization. The president who greets a touring dignitary, the mayor who gives a key to the city to a local hero, the first-line manager who attends the wedding of a machine operator, the sales manager who takes an important customer to lunch—all these managers are performing ceremonial duties that are important to the organization's success. These duties may not appear to be important, but managers are expected to perform them. They show that managers care about employees, customers, and others who deserve recognition.

The **leadership role** involves directing and coordinating the tasks of subordinates in order to accomplish organizational goals. Some aspects of the leadership role have to do with staffing, such as hiring, promoting, and firing. Other aspects concern motivating subordinates to be sure that organizational goals are consistent with employees' job-related needs. Still other aspects of the leadership role involve controlling the tasks of subordinates and probing for problems that need managerial attention.

The **liaison role** is concerned with the development of information sources, both inside and outside the organization. It involves dealing with clients, government officials, members of boards of directors, suppliers, and others. In performing the liaison role, the manager gathers information from others that can affect the organization's success. In effect, the liaison role helps to build the manager's information system and is closely related to the monitor informational role.

Informational Roles

Through their **informational roles,** managers build a network of contacts. These contacts enable managers to receive and send vast amounts of information. Managers obtain and process this information through three informational roles.

In the **monitor role,** the manager seeks and receives information. Managers are like radar systems, scanning the setting for information that may affect their department's or organization's performance. Remember that a large part of the information received is verbal, often from gossip and hearsay. The monitor role often enables the manager to be the best-informed person in the organization.

In the **disseminator role,** the manager shares and distributes information to others in the organization. Sometimes this information is passed along as privileged information, meaning that, unless the manager passed it along, other managers and employees would not have access to it. Informing subordinates is often difficult and time consuming—but necessary.

Finally, in the **spokesperson role,** the manager makes official statements to outsiders through speeches, reports, television (such as Lee Iacocca's ads for buying American-made Chrysler cars and Jeeps instead of Japanese imports), and other media. In this case, if the manager says it, the company says it.

Decisional Roles

The purpose of information in an organization is to help people decide. As the person in charge of a department or an entire organization, the manager often commits the organization to new courses of action. **Decisional roles** actually commit the organization or a department to courses of action. A manager can play four different roles as decision maker.

In the **entrepreneur role,** the manager seeks to improve the department and organization by initiating projects or identifying needed changes. Ken Olsen, president and chief executive officer at Digital Equipment Corporation (DEC), plays an important entrepreneurial role within that company. To keep in touch with the latest ideas and thoughts, Olsen asks for proposals from middle and first-level managers. He constantly floats ideas around in the company and encourages others to do the same. There are few barriers to prevent someone with a good idea from going anywhere in the organization to make it happen. Many employees have flexible hours and can work through computer modems from the homes. Many call DEC an entrepreneur's paradise.

The entrepreneurial role is not confined to those working within the organization. Often times, a successful entrepreneur is someone who starts his or her own organization. Manual A. Villafaña, chief executive officer of

Helix BioCore, Inc., is one such person. He has started four different businesses because, once things get too routine, he longs for the challenge of getting another company off the ground. Helix BioCare manufactures proteins secreted by the cells of mammals. These proteins can be used to treat a wide variety of diseases, including leukemia and other cancers, diabetes, and arthritis.[18]

In the **disturbance handler role,** the manager resolves conflicts between subordinates or departments. In some cases, such as a strike, work stoppage, or the bankruptcy of a supplier, managers need to resolve conflicts between organizations. Even the best of managers cannot always anticipate or prevent such disturbances. Effective managers learn how best to handle them when they do occur. Poor managers not only confront these unforeseeable problems but also those that are preventable.

In the **resource allocator role,** the manager is responsible for deciding who will get which resources and how much they will get. These resources may include budgeted or extra funds, equipment, personnel, and access to the manager's time. A manager must continually make choices as to how resources will be distributed. Should money be spent for painting walls or for new furniture? What proportion of the budget should be earmarked for advertising and for improving the existing services? Should a second shift be added, or should the company pay overtime to handle new orders?

Closely linked to the resource allocator role is the **negotiator role.** In the negotiator role, the manager represents a department or the company in bargaining with others. For example, a purchasing manager negotiates with suppliers for lower costs and faster delivery times, and a sales manager negotiates a price reduction to keep a major customer happy. These negotiations are an integral part of a manager's job because only managers have the information needed to decide and the authority necessary to commit the organization to a course of action.

Summary of Roles

Ten managerial roles add up to one manager. A manager who does not perform all ten roles probably is not performing as well as possible. Nevertheless, a manager may perform some roles more ably and vigorously than others, depending on personal background and style, managerial level, type of organization, and career path.

Every nation has a heritage that has created certain cultural expectations about the roles of manager and subordinate. What one culture encourages as participatory management, another may see as managerial incompetence. What one values as employee initiative and leadership, another may consider selfish and destructive to group harmony. Thus, nothing is carved in stone about the way managers and subordinates are supposed to act. Managers must understand why people behave as they do.

In this chapter's Across Cultures, we look at how managers from several countries play the three major roles—interpersonal, informational, and decisional. We have not singled out any one country but have tried to give you some feel for how managers in several countries act.

GETTING THE BEST FROM MANAGERS IN DIFFERENT CULTURES

INTERPERSONAL ROLES

In some countries, authority is inherited; that is, key positions are filled from certain families. In other countries, a manager may command respect by virtue of position, age, or expertise.

In Mexico, machismo is important. In Germany, polish, decisiveness, and breadth of knowledge give a manager power. In Asia, the Arab world, and Latin America, a manager needs to be warm and personal. Managers often demonstrate this approach by appearing at birthday parties, soccer matches, and other social events and by walking through work areas, recognizing employees by name, talking to them, and listening to their concerns. In China, it is important for the managers to drop in periodically for social visits with workers, inquiring about their health and morale without discussing specific work problems. Without singling out any person, managers thus compliment the work group.

In the United States and Canada, subordinates might normally have a give-and-take discussion and present a recommendation to their manager. Subordinates in the previously mentioned countries would expect their manager to give them instructions. A U.S. manager who tries to get German workers to make a group decision may be told: "No, let the foremen decide."

DECISIONAL ROLES

U.S. and Canadian managers have been told to involve employees in making decisions that affect them, that is, participation strengthens commitment to the goals and values of the firm and improves performance. Conversely, French, Italian, Indian, and German managers believe that rigid controls and strict obedience to authority are needed to obtain high job performance, that is, subordinates are not expected to try to in-

fluence their manager. These managers believe that subordinates want strong managers and that subordinates do not question the actions of their superiors.

INFORMATIONAL ROLES

In Japan, many workers are identified by the organization for which they work. Their attention and energies are focused on the organization—their personal life is their company life, and their company's future is their future. Compared to U.S. and Canadian employees, who tend to be job-oriented rather than company-oriented, the Japanese tend to be better informed about their organization's business and more ready to take steps to help others within the organization.

Latin Americans, on the other hand, tend to work for an individual, not the job or organization. They strive for personal power. Relationships and loyalties are much more personalized than in North America. Managers can obtain high performance only by effectively gathering information and working through individual members of a group.

In the United States and Canada, competition is often the name of the game: everyone wants a winner. In other countries, competition in the workplace means that everyone loses. In Greece, managers say: "Two Greeks will do badly what one will do well." Greek teams work well only when a strong leader is available to set goals and settle conflicts. The leader often acts as a spokesperson and transmits information to others.

In the United States and Canada, a subordinate is supposed to accept criticism of performance as valuable feedback. In other countries, such criticism might be a big mistake. To Arabs, Africans, Asians, and Latin Americans, preservation of dignity or "face" is an all-important value. Those who lose self-respect dishonor both themselves and their families. Public criticism is intolerable.[19]

APPROACHES TO ORGANIZATIONAL BEHAVIOR

Many of the concepts and ideas we use to try to understand the behavior of individuals and groups in organizations are based on knowledge from the behavioral sciences. The **behavioral sciences** represent a systematic body of knowledge drawn from sociology, psychology, and anthropology that helps us to understand why and how people behave as they do. We will apply important concepts from the behavioral sciences to explain individual and group behaviors within organizations and how managerial actions can affect these behaviors. As you will discover, there are no simple solutions to organizational behavior issues and problems. Seldom is there one best answer or the ideal organization.

The key to understanding behavior in organizations is knowing what to look for and what to look at. We can begin by looking at an entire organization, or we can begin by looking at small parts of the organization, such as individuals, work teams, and departments. However, examining one part of an organization is not enough; eventually, we must also know something about how that part relates to other parts and to the whole.

Traditional Approach

Originally, managers thought that there was only one way to manage people because all organizations were the same, managerial tasks were identical, and all employees' jobs were similar. Although these beliefs may have been valid to some extent during the early 1900s, such approaches now are considered to be overly simplistic and, in fact, incorrect. The **traditional approach** to organizational behavior emphasized the development of principles that were appropriate to all organizations and managerial tasks. These *universal principles* were generally prescriptive: there was only one way to manage organizations and employees. That perception began to change with Frederick W. Taylor, Elton Mayo, F. J. Roethlisberger, and Douglas McGregor, who sought to develop concepts that would increase managers' understanding of behavior. Their work was the beginning of a more modern and realistic approach to human resources management.

Taylor Frederick W. Taylor advocated the scientific management of factory production, using time-and-motion studies, standard parts, and standard processes, among other scientific and efficiency techniques.[20] (We describe his approach in more detail in Chapter 17.) Taylor observed production operations to determine how they could be performed most efficiently. He believed in a system of rewards and punishments based on performance and output. Taylor also advocated setting up a system of management controls so first-line managers would have to deal only with the exceptional and not have to personally supervise routine tasks.

Mayo and Roethlisberger In the 1920s and 1930s, Elton Mayo and F. J. Roethlisberger of Harvard University applied their knowledge of sociology to industrial experiments at Western Electric Company's Hawthorne

Plant.[21] (In Chapter 10, we discuss how the structure of the group affects its members' behavior.) Their work showed that an organization should be viewed as a social system and that the social setting could influence workers' behaviors more than management's rules. The result of their experiments emphasized that workers are not simple tools. They are a rather complex set of personalities interacting in a group situation that is often difficult for managers to understand. Mayo and Roethlisberger believed that instead of trying to improve employee job performance according to Taylor's principles of scientific management, managers could improve performance by humanizing the work situation. Thus, managers should adopt participative leadership styles and pay attention to the social setting in which employees work.

McGregor   In 1960, Douglas McGregor introduced a powerful perspective of the behavior of employees in organizations.[22] This perspective has been labeled *Theory X and Theory Y.* Before proceeding, take a few minutes and complete the questions in Table 1.2

Theory X implies an autocratic approach to managing people. According to Theory X, most people dislike work and try to avoid it if possible. People are not willing to make a 100-percent effort because they are lazy. They have little ambition and will avoid responsibility if they can. They are self-centered, indifferent to organizational needs, and resistant to change. The ordinary rewards given by organizations are not enough to overcome employees' dislike for work. Thus, the only way that management can get a high level of performance is to coerce, control, and threaten employees. Some managers deny that they hold this view of people, but their actions prove that Theory X represents their view of employees.

Theory Y implies a humanistic and supportive approach to managing people. According to Theory Y, people are not lazy. If employees are lazy, this behavior grew out of their experiences with organizations. If management were to provide the proper environment to release the employees' potential, work would become as natural to them as play or rest. People will exercise self-direction and self-control to achieve goals to which they have become committed. Therefore management's role is to provide an environment in which this potential can be released at work.

McGregor argued that management had been following an outmoded set of assumptions about people. Management continued to adhere to Theory X assumptions, when the facts were that people's behavior more nearly matches the set of assumptions in Theory Y. Managers did not recognize that most employees have at least some Theory Y potential for growth. Consequently, their policies and practices failed to develop it. As a result, many people did not regard work as an opportunity for growth and fulfillment. Thus McGregor stressed that management needed to adopt a new theory, Theory Y, for working with people.

Systems Approach

The traditional approach to understanding behavior is to assume that people do things for simple (uncomplicated) reasons. The tendency to think only in causal terms is an example of simple reasoning. For example, the automobile accident was "caused" by driver carelessness or by dangerous

TABLE 1.2   **Management Beliefs Questionnaire**

Complete the following questionnaire. Indicate your agreement or disagreement with each of the eight statements by a check mark on the scale below each statement. Determine the appropriate score by noting the points for the response you made to each statement. For example, if your response to Question 1 was strongly agree, you would give yourself five points; disagree is worth two points; and so on. Add the eight scores together.

1.   The average human being prefers to be directed, wishes to avoid responsibility, and has relatively little ambition.

Strongly Agree (5)	Agree (4)	Undecided (3)	Disagree (2)	Strongly Disagree (1)

2.   Most people can acquire leadership skills regardless of their particular inborn traits and abilities.

Strongly Agree (5)	Agree (4)	Undecided (3)	Disagree (2)	Strongly Disagree (1)

3.   The use of rewards (for example, pay and promotion) and punishment (for example, failure to promote) is the best way to get subordinates to do their work.

Strongly Agree (5)	Agree (4)	Undecided (3)	Disagree (2)	Strongly Disagree (1)

4.   In a work situation, if the subordinates can influence you, you lose some influence over them.

Strongly Agree (5)	Agree (4)	Undecided (3)	Disagree (2)	Strongly Disagree (1)

continues

road conditions or by some other single factor. However, if we were to make a list—and it would be a long one— of "single causes" of automobile accidents, it would clearly show that many, if not all, the items on the list could play some role in any one accident.If the single-cause assumption of the traditional approach is inadequate, an obvious substitute is the assumption that events are caused by many complex and interrelated forces. To establish conditions that would reduce the frequency of automobile accidents, we would have to study the primary factors associated with accidents and their interrelationships. The **systems approach** emphasizes the interrelatedness of parts and suggests the importance of interpreting a single part (person, work group, department, or organization) only in the context of the whole. The idea of a system assumes multiple causation and complex interrelationships: everything is related to everything else. You should think of or-

---

TABLE 1.2 *continued*

5.   A good leader gives detailed and complete instructions to subordinates, rather than giving them merely general directions and depending on their initiative to work out the details.

| Strongly Agree (5) | Agree (4) | Undecided (3) | Disagree (2) | Strongly Disagree (1) |

6.   Individual goal setting offers advantages that cannot be obtained by group goal setting, because groups do not set high goals.

| Strongly Agree (5) | Agree (4) | Undecided (3) | Disagree (2) | Strongly Disagree (1) |

7.   A superior should give subordinates only the information necessary for them to do their immediate tasks.

| Strongly Agree (5) | Agree (4) | Undecided (3) | Disagree (2) | Strongly Disagree (1) |

8.   The superior's influence over subordinates in an organization is primarily economic.

| Strongly Agree (5) | Agree (4) | Undecided (3) | Disagree (2) | Strongly Disagree (1) |

☐ Total Score   *Scoring Key:* A score of more than 32 points indicates a tendency to manage others according to the principles in Theory X. A score of less than 16 points indicates a tendency to manage others according to the principles in Theory Y. A score somewhere between 16 and 32 indicates flexibility in the management of others.

Source: Adapted from M. Haire, E. Ghiselli, and L. Porter, *Managerial Thinking: An International Study,* Appendix A. Copyright © 1966 by John Wiley & Sons, Inc. Reprinted with permission of John Wiley & Sons, Inc.

ganizations as numerous subsystems, such as work flows, reward structures, communication networks, and role structures. All of these subsystems, functioning together, are what we commonly refer to as an organization. This approach leads to a different understanding of organizational behavior than that presented by the traditional approach.[23]

The basic elements of a systems approach—inputs, a transformation process, and outputs—are shown in Figure 1.4. **Inputs** are the physical, human, financial, and information resources that an organization uses to produce goods and services. The **transformation process** is the technology that the organization uses to transform (change) inputs into outputs. **Outputs** include the goods and services that the organization offers to its customers or clients. Outputs also include wastes. **Feedback** is knowledge of results, which influences the selection of inputs for the next cycle of the

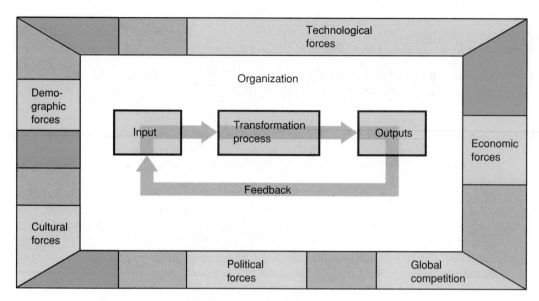

FIGURE 1.4   Basic Systems Concepts

process. The environment surrounding the organization includes the political, social, and economic forces that affect its goals and effectiveness.
In a university, inputs include students, faculty, alumni gifts, foundation
support, research grants, buildings, and the like. The faculty and administrators use the transformation process—teaching and other educational
services—to change the student into an educated person. Different faculty
members use different transformation processes to achieve their department's and university's goals. For example, work experience, case teaching, lectures, and experiential exercises are some of the methods that
faculty members use to teach. The output of the system is an educated
person.

Contingency Approach

The **contingency approach** is based on the belief that there is no one way
of managing that is best in all situations.[24] It rejects the notion that universal principles can be applied to managing behavior in organizations. Further, it means that no situation falls into a neatly defined classification.
Thus, each situation must be analyzed separately and then managed accordingly. However, principles can give managers insight in a vague, general
way. They have their place in the contingency approach and are used when
the situation calls for them.

Before reading further, please respond to the statements in Table 1.3. If
you answered maybe/sometimes to all the questions, you already have a
good idea of the meaning of the contingency approach. For example, satisfied workers are not always the most productive. The satisfaction they derive from their jobs may come primarily from the work group, co-workers,
and the ability to form friendships at work, all of which have very little to do
with performance. Bureaucratic organizations, such as McDonald's, the

---

TABLE 1.3   Contingency Quiz

Instructions: Answer each of the following questions by checking yes, no, or maybe/sometimes.

	Yes	No	Maybe/Sometimes
1. Satisfied workers are more productive workers than dissatisfied workers.	_____	_____	_____
2. Adding a piece-rate pay system to a job where the employee is already intrinsically motivated to work will be best in the long run for management.	_____	_____	_____
3. Bureaucracy is inefficient and is a bad way to organize.	_____	_____	_____
4. Workers should participate in decisions that concern them.	_____	_____	_____
5. Workers want challenging jobs.	_____	_____	_____
6. Cohesive work groups are more productive than noncohesive work groups.	_____	_____	_____
7. Organizational structures should be very flexible and readily changed to achieve maximum productivity.	_____	_____	_____
8. Leaders should use styles that are person-oriented rather than task-oriented.	_____	_____	_____
9. The behavior observed in an organization is the result of the total of all the personalities in it.	_____	_____	_____
10. Cohesiveness among group members will result in better group decision making than will a lack of cohesiveness.	_____	_____	_____

Internal Revenue Service, the U.S. Postal Service, and Anheuser-Busch are efficient because they perform routine tasks. Regulations characteristic of bureaucratic organization serve to increase an organization's effectiveness when their customers, suppliers, and regulatory bodies are relatively stable. Daily changes in McDonald's menu, for example, would make it a much less efficient operation. Moreover, not all workers want challenging jobs. Some only want jobs that pay well, require little thinking, provide security, and offer good fringe benefits (for example, vacation time, sick days, paid holidays, and life/medical insurance). Workers have been known to turn down promotions that would challenge them to think creatively on a new job.

Advantages of the Contingency Approach The contingency approach advocates selecting a management response from among various alternatives, based on the characteristics of the specific situation. It holds that the key to becoming a successful manager is the ability to diagnose a situation correctly.

According to the contingency approach, the nature of the organization's environment, its size, its technology, the character of its markets, its legal charter, its personnel, and other factors not only confront the organization with problems but simultaneously offer opportunities. Thus organizations should adapt to situations. The contingency approach holds that different kinds of structures, reward systems, and change strategies are appropriate responses to different situations.

An advantage of using the contingency approach comes from the recognition that an organization's environment is constantly changing. Managers must recognize and adapt to changes occurring both inside and outside the organization. For example, managers who assume a stable market for their goods and services will not be successful very long. Let's read how managers have learned to diagnose the situation and change their behaviors to fit the situation.

IN PRACTICE

BEST WESTERN HOTELS

Ronald A. Evans is doing fine as the new president of Best Western Hotels. He is a conservative executive who will delegate responsibility, watch budgets, and facilitate slow, controlled growth. His style is democratic, and he is quick to respond to the wishes of motel operators.

Executives at Best Western are pleased with the change that occurred when Robert T. Hazard, Jr., resigned as president. Hazard was a strong-minded leader who forced rapid expansion from 1974 to 1980, increasing the chain from 800 to 2,597 hotels. Hazard seemed involved in everything down to picking out the color of tablecloths. The installation of expensive new programs, such as a supersophisticated reservation system, did not pay off. The disagreements between Hazard and motel operators resembled open warfare.

The curious thing is that Hazard left Best Western to become chief executive at Quality Inns International, Inc. Observers indicate he is doing well there. Quality Inns had just finished a period of cost cutting and decline in order to survive and is now ready for an ambitious building program. Hazard has increased the number of franchise units from 345 to 750, refurbished many of the hotels, and revamped the computerized reservation system. Every one of Hazard's initiatives has been received enthusiastically by the board of directors.

Why is Evans doing so well at Best Western and Hazard so well at Quality Inns? After all, Hazard had to leave Best Western. The answer lies partly with the person and partly with the situation. In the early years of Hazard's tenure at Best Western, the organization was ready for growth. Best Western needed to take advantage of the trend toward motor hotels. Strong, top-down leadership was the way to succeed. But as Best Western matured, the situation demanded a different style. Maintaining orderly growth and a profitable operation became more urgent than rapid growth. Thus, the democratic style of Evans suited the new situation at Best Western.

The same is true at Quality Inns. Quality Inns went through a period of decline to avoid bankruptcy and was ready to dive into a rapid growth period. An autocratic leader who pushes new ideas was the right leader in this situation. Quality Inns needed to move forward or lose its share of the market.

The executive shuffle between Best Western and Quality Inns illustrates the importance of the situation. Hazard's leadership style was appropriate when it fit a high-growth situation. Other leadership styles were better for a situation of carefully controlled growth. Contingencies, such as the environment and the need for growth, had significant impact on company profitability. The situation, not just leadership style, influenced performance.[25]

The basic concepts of the contingency approach are more difficult to grasp than the traditional principles of management. They do, however, help managers to develop a more thorough understanding of complex situations and increase the probability that they will take action that is appropriate and yields the intended results. An old Chinese proverb perhaps best summarizes this advantage:

> Give a person a fish, and you feed that person for a day; teach a person to fish, and you feed that person for life.

The contingency approach enables managers to diagnose each situation so that they can manage it effectively. We want to teach you to fish, not simply to give you fish.

FUNDAMENTAL CONCEPTS OF ORGANIZATIONAL BEHAVIOR

One purpose of this book is to present as clearly as possible the basic knowledge we have about the behavior of people in organizations. Students of physics or accounting learn certain fundamental principles. The law of gravity is the same in Dallas, Paris, and Singapore; a hydrogen atom in New York is the same as a hydrogen atom in Los Angeles. An account receivable is carried on the books of a company in Seattle the same way it is carried on the books of a company in Atlanta. A cash transaction credit and debit are the same in Boston as they are in Phoenix. These hard-and-fast rules do not exist for people and their behavior in organizations. Nevertheless, four fundamental concepts can help in understanding the behavior of employees and managers in most situations.

Basics of Human Behavior

One of the primary concepts of psychology is that people are different from each other. From birth, each person is unique, and experiences in life increase the differences among people. This means that managers can get the best performance from employees by treating them as individuals.

Both internal and external factors shape a person's behavior on the job. Some of the internal factors that affect a person's behavior are learning ability, motivation, perception, attitudes, and personality. We discuss these factors in more detail in Part II. Among the external factors that affect a person's behavior are the organization's reward system, organizational politics, group behavior, managerial leadership styles, and organizational structure. We examine these factors in Parts III, IV, V, and VI.

Situational Perspectives

For years, behavioral scientists have stressed that individual behavior is a function of the interaction between the personal characteristics of the individual and the situation. To understand a person's behavior in a work-related situation, we must analyze the pressures that the situation places on the person. For example, what are the situational factors affecting the success of Domino's Pizza? Some of the most important ones are Americans' love of pizza, Domino's ability to deliver within thirty minutes, the availability of part-time delivery people, and the top management's willingness to reward employees for doing their jobs well.

Specifying all the factors in a situation is complex and can be very time-consuming. The contingency approach should be used to identify and diagnose only the significant factors involved. The components of a specific situation—organizational structure, peer group pressures, leadership, job-related stress, organizational politics—are examined, and the significant ones are analyzed.

Organizations as Social Systems

People in organizations have both psychological and social needs. They have needs for approval, status, and power, and they play various roles (interpersonal, informational, and decision making). Since individuals' behavior is influenced by their groups, managers may be able to use groups to improve performance and also to satisfy employees' needs for belonging. An example is United Parcel Service's (UPS) policies of providing a common eating area for all employees and having no reserved parking spots.

Interaction between Structure and Process

Accomplishing something in organizations often involves knowing who to see and how to present an idea to that person. **Structure** refers to how people are grouped within an organization. For example, the basic UPS structure is the service center. Packages are delivered to customers from each service center by drivers. Each service center has the responsibility for making its own deliveries on time. **Process** refers to how the tasks of the organization are carried out. Decision making, leadership, communication, motivation, and conflict-resolution practices are processes. To give you an idea of how structure and process work together and to help you understand why people behave as they do in organizations, consider how Herman J.

Russell, chairman of H. J. Russell & Company of Atlanta, uses these concepts to run his company.

HERMAN J. RUSSELL

Herman J. Russell is the chairman of a construction and engineering firm in Atlanta, Georgia. With sales of over $133 million, it ranks fourth in the nation among minority-owned firms. His firm has been responsible for building parts of Atlanta's rapid-rail stations, a new terminal at Atlanta's Hartsfield International Airport, as well as numerous other buildings in the southeastern United States.

With thirty-five years of well-managed, uninterrupted growth under his belt, Russell attributes his success to finding good people. He believes in paying good salaries and fringe benefits. These are needed to attract outstanding people. Once he has recruited the best people, he makes them feel a part of the organization. He constantly walks around the firm's various construction sites to talk with the people actually doing the job. He asks them for their advice. He says, "I like it to be known that I care and that I'm not someone sitting in an ivory tower." Since his firm is typically engaged in several large projects at any one time, he has learned to delegate tasks to others and not second-guess them. He lets project managers monitor the progress of their projects and then compares their progress against the goals of the owner and the progress his firm has made toward reaching these goals.

His organization is structured to give project managers a high degree of autonomy. But decisions about what projects to undertake are usually made by him and his partners in joint ventures. "Real joint ventures are going to have total participation," he says. "It is one of the finest ways to learn new techniques. What I have learned from the joint ventures is that people are most important."[26]

ORGANIZATIONAL BEHAVIOR: A FRAMEWORK

The framework for understanding the behavior of employees in organizations consists of four basic components: (1) individual processes; (2) interpersonal and group processes; (3) organizational processes; and (4) individual and organizational change processes. The relationships among these components, as well as the important dimensions of each, are shown in Figure 1.5. These relationships are much too dynamic—in terms of variety and change—to describe them by stating "laws." As we analyze each component and its dimensions, the dynamics and complexities of organizational behavior will become more understandable.

Let's look, for example, at what happens when a company suddenly decides to move its headquarters. In 1990, Exxon did just that, announcing

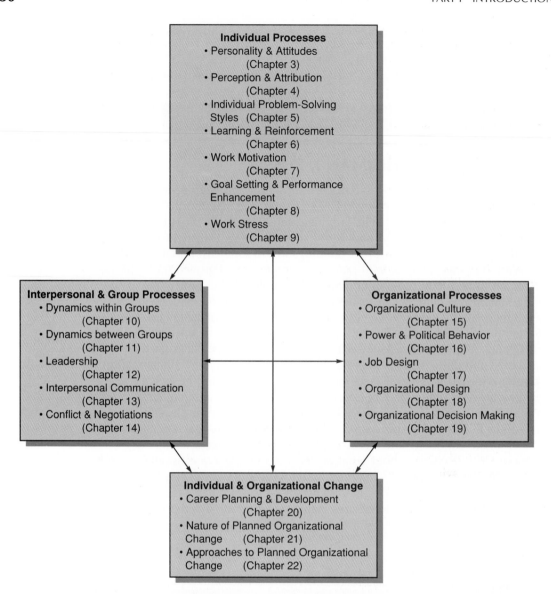

FIGURE 1.5   **Framework for Understanding Organizational Behavior**

that it was moving its corporate headquarters from New York City to Irving, Texas. Managers would be asked to relocate during 1991. Whether a manager was interested in moving became contingent on three factors: environment, behavior, and consequences.

First, a manager's perception of general economic conditions (the business environment) in the oil industry might make a difference in the decision to relocate. Was the industry experiencing growth, maintaining stability, or declining—and did the manager want to stay in the industry? The decision to relocate could also depend on the number of other job possibilities available to the manager. If the job market in New York City were tight, a manager might not have much to choose from and be more willing to relocate. On the other hand, if finding another job in New York City were reasonably certain, the manager might decide to change jobs, rather than relocate.

Second, the behaviors of managers would likely change if they moved. For example, many managers commuted sixty to ninety minutes each way in New York City. Living in Irving would dramatically reduce commuting time. The extra time would allow managers to spend more time with their families and in leisure activities. On the other hand, Irving was not seen as offering the excitement, challenge, and ethnic diversity of New York City. Since Exxon's headquarters had been in New York City for decades, managers' families and their relatives had grown accustomed to sharing holidays, birthdays, and other special events. The move to Irving would dramatically reduce the opportunity for those relocating to see other family members and longtime friends. Such social interaction could be extremely important for some people.

Third, the consequences of any action must be understood in terms of a particular environment. At Exxon, if a manager was near retirement age, had grown children, and could take early retirement, the decision not to relocate would be more feasible. Conversely, for those who had been with the company for only ten to fifteen years and could not find a comparable job in New York City, the decision not to relocate would likely have far different consequences.

Individual Processes

Each person makes assumptions about the people with whom he or she works, supervises, or spends time in leisure activities. These assumptions, to some extent, influence a person's behavior toward others. Effective managers understand what affects their own behavior before attempting to influence the behavior of others. (In Chapters 3 through 9, we focus on the behavior of individuals.)

Individual behavior is the foundation of organizational performance. Understanding individual behavior, therefore, is crucial for effective management, as illustrated in the Best Western Hotel account. Each individual is a physiological system composed of a number of subsystems—digestive, nervous, circulatory, and reproductive—and a psychological system composed of a number of subsystems—attitudes, perceptions, learning capabilities, personality, needs, feelings, and values. In this book, we concentrate on the individual's psychological system.

Because organizational effectiveness depends on individual performance, managers must have more than a passing knowledge of the determinants on individual performance. In Chapter 3, we examine how personality and attitudes can affect an individual's behavior on the job. An individual's capacity to learn depends on perception, which we discuss in Chapter 4. Because each person gives his or her own meaning to a situation, different individuals view the same situation differently. How various managers use data to make decisions is the focus of Chapter 5. We present a framework for studying the effects of decisions on subordinates' motivation and commitment to the organization.

Managers communicate many decisions to employees through the organization's reward system. In Chapter 6, we indicate ways that managers can use rewards to encourage or inhibit employee behaviors. Most managers agree that there are a number of ways to motivate others, and motivation is extremely important because it is tied so closely to performance. In Chapter 7, we explain how behavior is stimulated, sustained, and stopped in organizations. In Chapter 8, we examine how goal-setting and performance enhancement techniques have been successfully used by managers to increase performance. The existence of organizationally sponsored health promotion activities, such as exercise programs and alcohol and substance abuse counseling, are often started to relieve stress. Chapter 9 focuses on work-related stress and how managers and organizations are attempting to cope with it.

Interpersonal and Group Processes

Being inherently social, people generally do not choose to live or work alone. We are born into a group called a family and would likely not survive without it. Almost all our time is spent interacting with others in groups: we worship in groups; we work in groups; we play in groups. Our personal identity is derived from the way in which we are perceived and treated by other group members. Thus, skills in group dynamics are vital to all managers. Recall that managers spend more than two-thirds of their working day in meetings (Figure 1.2).

Many organizational goals can be achieved only with the cooperation of others. The history of such organizations as Red Cross, PepsiCo, Girl Scouts, Westinghouse, Kodak, and Xerox is the history of organized groups created to find ways of improving the quality of life, and to satisfy the needs of their employees and customers. The productivity resulting from effective group action makes the development of group skills one of the most essential aspects of managerial training. Furthermore, membership in productive and cohesive groups is essential to maintaining psychological health throughout a person's life.

Being an effective group member means understanding the dynamics of what happens in and between groups. We discuss methods of increasing group effectiveness in Chapters 10 and 11. Group members must be skillful in eliminating most barriers to the accomplishment of the group's goals, in solving problems, in maintaining productive interaction among group members, and in overcoming obstacles to developing a more effective group.

Management today needs leaders who have the ability to integrate employee goals with organizational goals. The ability of organizations to achieve their goals depends on the degree to which their leaders' ability and style enable them to control, influence, and act effectively. In Chapter 12, we examine how leaders influence others and choose their own leadership style.

Since most managers spend considerable time dealing with others, Chapter 13 focuses on interpersonal communications. How managers communicate with superiors, peers, and subordinates either can help build them into an effective team or lead to low morale and lack of commitment. Often times, groups and/or individuals within groups are in conflict with each other over a variety of issues. Managing conflict is carried out through a process of negotiation. Chapter 14 explains why conflict arises and how employees can effectively negotiate ways to resolve them.

Organizational Processes

Individuals enter organizations to work, to earn money, and to pursue their own career goals. The process by which the individual learns of the organization's expectations is through the organization's culture (Chapter 15). It is the important set of shared assumptions and understandings about how things really work in the organization, that is, which policies, practices, and norms are really important. Newcomers have to understand the organization's culture in order to be accepted and become successful. Some organizations use formal programs, whereas others simply rely on co-workers to guide the newcomer in what to do and not do in the organization.

Not all behaviors are aimed at improving the organization's performance. Power and political behavior (Chapter 16) are realities of organizational life. Employees and managers use power to accomplish goals and, in many cases, to strengthen their own positions in the organization. A person's success or failure in using or reacting to power is largely determined by his or her understanding of power, knowing how and when to use it, and being able to predict its probable effects on others.

To work effectively, all employees must have a clear understanding of their jobs and the organization's structure. In Chapter 17, we describe the process of job design by which managers define jobs, work methods, and relationships among jobs at various levels. The technology utilized by the organization has a tremendous impact on the design of managerial and nonmanagerial jobs alike.

Organization design (Chapter 18) refers to the overall structure of the organization. An organization chart presents a simplified view of authority, responsibility, and functions within an organization. However, organizational structures are far more complex than can be depicted on such a chart. Major features of this chapter include identification of factors that influence the design of an organization and presentation of some typical organization designs.

The world of managerial decision making is not particularly orderly or totally within the control of managers. Chapter 19 focuses on the factors, both internal and external, that affect a manager's ability to make decisions. We also explore the phases of decision making and ethical dilemmas faced by managers when making a decision.

Individual and Organizational Change

Most individuals look to an organization for opportunities to be involved in satisfying work throughout their careers. In Chapter 20, we emphasize that a career consists of both attitudes and behaviors over a long period of time. How people react to organizational events, such as relocation, promotion, demotion, or firing, is related to their personality, career stage, and career alternatives. For example, a single person in her twenties and living in New York City might react quite differently to the Exxon relocation to Irving, Texas, than a person who has young school-age children and wants to leave behind the problems of big-city life.

The management of change involves adapting an organization to the demands of the environment and modifying the actual behaviors of employees. If employees do not change their behaviors, the organization cannot change. A manager must consider many things when undertaking organizational change, including the types of pressures being exerted on the organization to change, the kinds of resistance to change that are likely to be encountered, and the person or persons who should implement change. We present a general model of organizational change in Chapter 21 and discuss five basic managerial strategies for achieving change in Chapter 22. These strategies are:

- People approaches—using behavioral science techniques to involve employees in diagnosing organizational problems and planning actions to correct them.
- Technological approaches—changing the methods by which work is accomplished.
- Structural approaches—rearranging organizational authority, responsibility, and decision making.
- Task approaches—redesigning individuals' jobs.
- Strategy approaches—changing the organization's intended courses of action to attain its goals or the selection of new goals.

SUMMARY

In this chapter, we described the typical managerial job characteristics, some of the problems facing employees, and how behavioral science concepts can improve individual effectiveness. The five basic characteristics of managerial work are (1) hard work in a variety of tasks; (2) a preference for nonroutine activities; (3) use of communication media; (4) involvement in communication networks; and (5) a blend of rights and duties.

To accomplish their work, managers perform ten different roles. These can be grouped into three broad categories: interpersonal, informational, and decisional. Through the interpersonal roles of figurehead, leader, and liaison, managers exercise their formal authority within the system. The monitor, disseminator, and spokesperson roles enable managers to establish and maintain a network of personal contacts, which they use to give and receive a wide range of information. Information is, of course, the basic input to the managers' decisional roles. As decision makers, managers are entrepreneurs, disturbance handlers, resource allocators, and negotiators.

Three approaches to the study of organizational behavior are the traditional approach, the systems approach, and the contingency approach. The traditional approach focuses on developing principles, such as Theory X and Theory Y, that can be applied to all situations. The systems approach emphasizes the interrelatedness of factors that influence behaviors. The contingency approach is not based on a fixed set of principles, although proven management principles have been developed for particular situations. Rather, the contingency approach looks at interrelationships because each individual and group is dependent on others. The contingency approach is based on four fundamental concepts: (1) people are different; (2) behavior is a function of the personal characteristics of the individual, as well as the characteristics of the situation; (3) organizations are social systems; and (4) both structure and process variables influence employee behaviors.

The four major components of organizational behavior are (1) individual processes; (2) interpersonal and group processes; (3) organizational processes; and (4) individual and organizational change.

Key Words and Concepts

Behavioral sciences	Liaison role
Communication skills	Monitor role
Conceptual skills	Negotiator role
Contingency approach	Organizational behavior
Decisional roles	Organizational iceberg
Disseminator role	Outputs
Disturbance handler role	Process
Downsizing	Resource allocator role
Electronic mail	Role
Entrepreneur role	Spokesperson role
Feedback	Structure
Figurehead role	Systems approach
Glass ceiling	Technical skills
Informational roles	Theory X
Inputs	Theory Y
Interpersonal roles	Traditional approach
Interpersonal skills	Transformation process
Leadership role	

Discussion Questions

1. Why is it difficult to understand why people behave as they do?

2. How will the predicted changes in the work force affect your behavior in your first job?

3. The popular business press, *Wall Street Journal, Business Week, Fortune,* and *Forbes,* is filled with tales about organizations downsizing in an attempt to improve their competitive position. Do you think that downsizing is really an answer?

4. What management skills will you need to become an effective manager? How will you learn these skills?

5. Schedule an appointment with a manager. Ask the manager how he or she spends the day. How does the manager set priorities? What are his or her biggest time wasters? From listening to the manager, what did you learn about how managers spend their time?

6. How might employees react to managers who use Theory X? What was Sandra Kurtzig's management philosophy? How do you know this?

7. How does using the contingency approach help you understand what happened at ASK Computer Systems?

8. In what ways does a manager's culture affect his or her behaviors?

9. How might the study of organizational behavior help managers in Germany restore the productivity levels of employees who for years labored under the communist regime in East Germany?

10. James Osborne, national commander of the Salvation Army, said, "We have limited resources, which means that we have to manage them even better to achieve the best results." Isn't this true for any manager? What resources are most critical for organizations entering the next decade?

◆ MANAGEMENT CASES AND EXERCISES

DEBBI FIELDS OF MRS. FIELDS' COOKIES

When she was still in her twenties, Debbi Fields was one of the most successful entrepreneurs in the United States. She is now the president of the world's largest and best-known chocolate chip cookie company, Mrs. Fields' Cookies. She got into the business by accident. Her husband, Randy, was a financial consultant whose clients could not resist her cookies that she set out in his office. When Debbi Fields decided to turn her baking skill into a business, a banker who liked her cookies lent her fifty thousand dollars to open her first store in Palo Alto, California, in August 1977.

By 1987, her chain had 543 stores in six countries, including Japan and Australia. Sales were over $100 million. She also bought La Petite Boulangerie, a nationwide bakery chain of one hundred stores, from PepsiCo. The strategy was to add the La Petite stores to the Mrs. Fields' chain by combining the products of both stores. The combination stores are about three times larger than the older cookie stores, and they sell cookies, soups, bagels, and sandwiches. Store re-dos run from ten to forty thousand dollars each. However, the early sales returns from these have been promising. Each store, on average, has sales that exceed $540,000, almost 10 percent more than projected. By 1990, Debbi Fields plans to have thirty-seven in operation.

Consumers reportedly like the stores because the menu items are healthy and inexpensive. Sandwiches, such as oriental chicken salad and albacore tuna, are about four dollars each. Each store has the same high-quality that has made her cookie stores famous.

How does she manage her cookie stores to maintain high quality and still maintain her long-standing rule that cookies out of the oven more than two hours cannot be sold (these are usually given away to charities)? The secret is her management system. Debbi Fields maintains direct contact with all stores hourly by computer. Each store manager uses a computerized "day planner." The computer tracks sales data from each store, hour by hour and product by product. Based on these figures and the historical sales figures in the day planner, the computer program calculates the number of customers and sales volume needed each hour in order to meet daily sales projections. It also indicates how many batches of cookie dough to mix and when to mix them to meet anticipated demand and minimize leftovers.

As the day progresses, electronic cash registers automatically feed data into the company's computer in Park City, Utah. If sales are down at certain stores, it then tells the managers of those stores to try several promotional tactics, such as giving away free cookies, to lure more people into the stores. If a store manager wants to communicate with Debbi Fields, the manager calls up the Form-Mail program, types the message, and the next morning, it is on Debbi Fields' desk. She promises an answer, from her or her staff, within forty-eight hours. Randy Fields believes that this system permits Debbi to influence managers directly and helps to keep store managers close to their customers.

Four important managerial chores are handled on the computer. First, it helps the store manager schedule his or her crew. The store manager simply plugs sales projections for the next two weeks into a scheduling program. The program calculates the number of people with each skill who will be needed during each hour. Second, it helps the manager interview job applicants, who sit at a keyboard and answer the questions posed to them on a computer screen. Based on the answers given by past applicants who were hired, the computer program identifies candidates that are likely to succeed or fail. Third, the computer helps the manager maintain a personnel file on each employee. The manager enters the person's data in a file maintained at headquarters. The computer issues paychecks, reminds the store manager that an employee's performance appraisal is due, and continually updates certain employee records. Last, the computer schedules the maintenance of the store's equipment. If a piece of equipment breaks down, the store manager enters the appropriate information into the company's computer, which then tells the store manager which vendor to contact to fix the equipment and the approximate cost. When the equipment has been repaired, the computer issues a check to the vendor.

Even with these systems, in late 1987 and early 1988, things started to fall apart. Debbi Fields learned that too many of her stores were too close together and others were simply not in the right locations. In 1988, she closed ninety-seven stores, and the company lost $19 million. She found out that running specialty stores was very difficult and much different than running cookie stores.

In 1988, Debbi Fields began to hire professional managers to help her. They told her that she would have to remove herself from the day-to-day running of the business to focus on making the company a great specialty retailer. With her new managerial role, she expanded her product line by developing Mrs. Fields' Bakeries. The bakeries offer muffins, bread, sandwiches, and soups. She plans to open around two hundred fifty in the early 1990s. She also entered into an agreement with Marriott Hotels to open sixty cookie stores on its property before 1995. This deal puts her stores into prime real estate to which they did not have access before.

In her new role, Debbi Fields has more time to read every comment card sent by customers, several hundred a month, and now spends nine months a year personally visiting her stores and meeting local managers.[27]

QUESTIONS

1. How would you characterize Debbi Fields' work?

2. What managerial role(s) did she play?

3. Using the contingency approach, describe the factors affecting her organization. Why has she been effective?

CLARIFYING WORK VALUES

Below are listed ten work values that can be fulfilled in organizations. Please rank order these according to which values you want your job to fulfill. The value you want most to fulfill in your career should be ranked 1, the value you next most want to fulfill should be ranked 2, and so on, until the last value is ranked 10.

_____ Accomplishment
_____ Equality
_____ Happiness
_____ Independence
_____ Power
_____ Recognition
_____ Responsibility
_____ Security
_____ Self-respect
_____ True friendships

Consider the value you ranked first. List some examples of ways in which this value could be fulfilled in an organization.

Why do you feel this value is the most important to fulfill in an organization?

References

1. Adapted from Gupta, U. ASK Co-Founder Is Proving You Can Go Home Again. *Wall Street Journal,* May 30, 1990, B-2; Pitta, J. Mommy Track Revised. *Forbes,* March 19, 1990, 158–159; Cole, D. The Entrepreneurial Self. *Psychology Today,* June 1989, 60–63; Shao, M. The Founder Is Back, but So Far, ASK Isn't. *Business Week,* October 12, 1990, 132.

2. Offermann, L. R., and Gowing, M. K. Organizations of the Future. *American Psychologist,* 1990, *45,* 95–108.

3. Hamilton, M. H. Employing New Tools to Recruit Workers. *Washington Post,* July 10, 1990, H1 and H3.

4. Kron, L. B. How the Next CEO Will Be Different. *Fortune,* May 22, 1989, 157–161; Dumaine, B. What Leaders of Tomorrow See. *Fortune,* July 3, 1989, 48–62; Kraut, A. I., Pegrego, P. R., McKenna, D. D., and Dunnette, M. D. The Role of the Manager: What's Really Important in Different Management Jobs. *Academy of Management Executive,* 1989, *3,* 286–293.

5. Morrison, A. M., and VonGlinow, M. A. Women and Minorities in Management. *American Psychologist,* 1990, *45,* 200–208.

6. Morrison, A. M., White, R. P., Van Velsor, E., and the Center for Creative Leadership. *Breaking the Glass Ceiling: Can Women Reach the Top of America's Largest Corporations?* Reading, MA: Addison-Wesley, 1987; VonGlinow, M. A., and Kryczkowska-Mercer, A. Women in Corporate America: A Caste of Thousands. *New Management,* Summer 1988, *6,* 36–42.

7. Bowen, D. D., and Hisrich, R. D. The Female Entrepreneur: A Career Develop Perspective. *Academy of Management Review,* 1986, *11,* 393–407.

8. Johnston, W.B. Global Workforce 2000: The New Labor Market. *Harvard Business Review,* March-April 1991, 115–129.

9. Bardwick, J. M. *The Plateauing Trap.* New York: American Management Association, 1986.

10. Ivancevich, J. M., and Stewart, K. A. Appraising Management Talent in Acquired Organizations. *Human Resource Planning,* 1989, *12(2),* 141–154; Nienstedt, P. R. Effectively Downsizing Management Structures. *Human Resource Planning,* 1989, *12(2),* 155–165.

11. Leana, C. R., and Feldman, D. C. When Mergers Force Layoffs: Some Lessons about Managing the Human Resource Problems. *Human Resource Planning,* 1989, *12(2),* 123–140; Feldman, D. C., and Leana, C. R. Managing Layoffs: Experiences at the Challenger Disaster Site and the Pittsburgh Steel Mills. *Organizational Dynamics,* Summer 1989, 52–65.

12. Offermann, L. R., and Gowing, M. K. Organizations of the Future. *American Psychologist,* 1990, *45,* 95–108.

13. Lei, D., and Slocum, J. W., Jr. Global Strategic Alliances. *Organizational Dynamics,* Winter 1991, 44–53.

14. Turnage, J. J. The Challenge of New Workplace Technology for Psychology. *American Psychologist,* 1990, *45,* 171–178.

15. Mintzberg, H. *The Nature of Managerial Work.* New York: Harper and Row Publishers, 1973; Stewart, R. Studies of Managerial Jobs and Behavior: The Ways Forward. *Journal of Management Studies,* 1989, *26,* 1–10.

16. Drucker, P. F. *Management: Tasks, Responsibilities and Problems.* New York: Harper and Row, 1973, 398.

17. Mintzberg, H. *The Nature of Managerial Work.*

18. Main, J. The Golden Age for Entrepreneurs. *Fortune,* February 12, 1990, 120–125.

19. Adapted from Copeland, L., and Griggs, L. Getting the Best from Foreign Employees. *Management Review,* June 1986, 19–26; Jackofsky, E. F., Slocum, J. W., Jr., and McQuaid, S. J. Cultural Values and the CEO: Alluring Companions? *Academy of Management Executive,* 1988, *2,* 39–49.

20. Taylor, F. W. *The Principles of Scientific Management.* New York: Harper and Brothers, 1911.

21. Roethlisberger, F. J., and Dickson, W. *Management and the Worker.* Cambridge: Harvard University Press, 1939; Sonnenfeld, J. A. Shedding Light on the Hawthorne Studies. *Journal of Occupational Behaviour,* 1985, *6,* 111–130.

22. McGregor, D. M. *The Human Side of the Enterprise,* 2nd ed. New York: McGraw-Hill, 1985.

23. Hellriegel, D., and Slocum, J. W., Jr. *Management,* 6th ed. Reading, MA: Addison-Wesley, 1992.

24. Fry, L. W., and Smith, D. A. Congruence, Contingency and Theory Building. *Academy of Management Review,* 1987, *12,* 117–132; Kazanjian, R. K., and Drazin, R. Implementing Internal Diversification: Contingency Factors for Organization Design Choices. *Academy of Management Review,* 1987, *12,* 324–354.

25. Adapted from Matching Managers to a Company's Life Cycle. *Business Week,* February 23, 1981, 62; Quality Inns: Reading for Fast-Track Growth. *Business Week,* February 23, 1981, 70–74; Romeo, P. Growth's the Word at Quality Inn's Annual Convention. *Hotel and Motel Management,* November 1981, 1 ff; Wolff, C. More Growth Abroad Seen for Best Western, *Hotel and Motel Management,* November 1988, A2 ff.

26. Adapted from Shaw, R., Herman J. Russell. *SKY,* August, 1990, 41–47.

27. Adapted from Morrow, D. Not By Cookies Alone. *American Way,* September, 1990, 29–33; Riehman, T. Mrs. Fields' Secret Ingredient. *INC.,* October 1987, 65–72.

CHAPTER 2

LEARNING ABOUT ORGANIZATIONAL BEHAVIOR

LEARNING OBJECTIVES

When you have finished studying this chapter, you should be able to:

* State the three steps in the scientific approach.
* Give the conditions for well and poorly designed research projects.
* Describe the four research designs commonly used in organizational research.
* Describe ways that individuals can gather data for a research project.
* State three ethical dilemmas that individuals could face when carrying out their research in organizations.

OUTLINE

DRUG TESTING AT WARNER CORPORATION

President Ronald Reagan's 1987 Commission on Organized Crime requested that all U.S. corporations test employees for drug use. The commission felt that this was needed because of the increased use of illegal drugs within all elements of society, the reluctance of employers to report known or suspected drug usage of former employees for fear of a lawsuit, and employer liability for the negligent hiring of employees. Illegal drugs cost organizations up to an estimated $100 billion a year. Drug abuse leads to higher absenteeism, shoddy products, workplace accidents, and skyrocketing insurance costs.

Tom Warner runs the Warner Corporation, a $16 million plumbing, heating, and air conditioning repair company with 220 employees and fifteen locations in the Washington, D.C., area. After reading these statistics, he wondered if drugs were not behind some of the odd behavior around the company—why, for example, some people were especially accident prone, or why others just seemed to drift with no ambition or motiva-

tion. Warner was also concerned that his workers often worked in customers' houses when nobody was home. An addict with an expensive cocaine habit could steal customers blind, or a stoned plumber could torch an entire house by mistake.

With all that in mind, Warner initiated a company-wide drug-testing program. All employees, including managers, were required to sign consent forms indicating that they understood the new policy and agreed to urinalysis. Any employees who tested positive for drugs would be discharged immediately. They could be rehired after a year, however, if they were not on drugs and agreed to ongoing random testing.

What has been the result? It costs twelve thousand dollars a year for the drug testing. Warner figures that he saves $385,000 per year in decreased worker's compensation claims, car accidents, auto insurance premiums, absenteeism, and training costs for new employees. He also believes that customers are better satisfied with his company's work because of its higher quality and reliability.[1]

$\mathbf{T}$he problems facing Tom Warner are not unlike those faced by many other managers. The idea of testing for illegal drugs might seem like a good one, but it raises questions. Some people say that drug abuse, like alcoholism, is a disease and the way to handle it is through rehabilitation, not by firing people. Others say that an employee's right to privacy is violated by drug testing. Still others question whether random testing is fair to all employees. Tom Warner also wondered whether to test employees when managers had probable cause. But what does probable cause mean?

This chapter will help you learn how to investigate these and other problems in organizational behavior. We provide frameworks for thinking about issues and applying sound research methodologies to solve them. For example, an understanding of research methodology would help Tom Warner determine if his procedure would produce reliable and valid test results. How confident can we be in saying that his program alone produced the $385,000 savings?

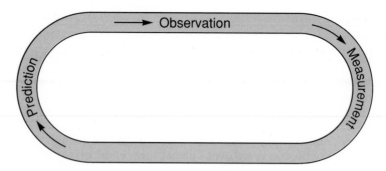

FIGURE 2.1   The Scientific Approach

THE SCIENTIFIC APPROACH

Good management involves the ability to understand job-related problems and to make valid predictions about employee behavior. The key to this is understanding the **scientific approach,** a method for seeking out and analyzing information in a systematic and unbiased manner.[2] Figure 2.1 illustrates the three basic steps of the scientific approach: observation, measurement, and prediction. These steps are so basic that most people, without even realizing it, use them in their everyday living. The Fleet Line Transportation Company is but one example of successful use of the scientific approach, applied in this instance to understand a costly employee turnover problem.

IN PRACTICE

FLEET LINE TRANSPORTATION COMPANY

Jim Steffel, president of Fleet Line Transportation Company, was trying to figure out what was wrong. He had set a goal of $52 million in sales revenue in 1990. To reach this goal, he needed 550 drivers in his fleet's operation. During 1989, driver turnover was nearly 45 percent. Steffel knew that unless he and his assistant, Joyce Haggard, could devise a plan to reduce turnover to 15 percent a year, it would be impossible to achieve the sales goal. He and Haggard guessed that it cost the company $550 to recruit and train a driver who could handle the company's eighteen-wheelers. If the company could reduce turnover by 30 percent, it would save a considerable amount of money.

Steffel and Haggard thought that they should first call the drivers who had quit and ask them why they had left. Was it for more money, shorter trips, more time at home, or what? While Haggard was making these inquiries, Steffel arranged for drivers to stop by his office in groups of five or six and chat about the problems they were having as employees. Steffel also arranged his busy schedule to spend time at major truck stops around Chicago, where he listened to what other truck-ers were saying about Fleet Line and other truck companies. During these sessions, he observed the drivers' responses to questions about pay, time off to go home, fuel charges, equipment malfunctions, and how long it took for them to get paid. Steffel and Haggard also visited with several of the firm's largest customers and chatted with their shipping managers about Fleet Line's drivers' ability to deliver quality services.

After several weeks of gathering these data, Jim Steffel and Joyce Haggard felt that they had heard most of the drivers' complaints. To see if these complaints were real, Haggard devised a measurement system to determine the actual number of times a driver got home, whether the drivers were able to drive about eleven thousand miles a month, whether the drivers were paid on time, and whether the drivers were taking advantage of fuel and equipment purchases from company-run truck stops throughout the country. From these measurements, Steffel and Haggard were able to identify those drivers who had profiles that matched those who had left the company and those who had stayed. This enabled them to predict the type of driver that would probably leave the firm. Those drivers who left Fleet Line (1) had a higher number of injury accidents; (2) had less total outside income; (3) delivered fewer loads; (4) made less money; and (5) ran more unloaded miles. In hiring new drivers, Steffel and Haggard now were able to focus more clearly on those factors that lead to high turnover than they could have before their study.[3]

This In Practice illustrates the three basic steps of the scientific approach and some of its other important features. For example, Steffel and Haggard observed the drivers in several different situations, rather than focusing on a single example of performance. If managers base conclusions about a person's performance solely on observations made at one time or in one particular situation, they may wrongly conclude that a worker is either a high or low performer. For example, one employee might have been observed to be late for a customer pickup, but her reports were accurate and on time. The driver might have gotten to the customer late simply because she had a poor connection with the dispatcher and went to the wrong customer. The scientific approach encourages managers to study all the events that could affect an individual's performance. A thorough study—not just a one-shot observation of a study of a few isolated incidents—is needed. The scientific approach also requires a systematic test of assumptions. A careful testing of assumptions about an apparent problem may reveal that it does not exist or is less or more serious than initially assumed. The scientific approach guards against preconceptions or personal bias by requiring as complete an assessment of the problem or issue as resources permit.

PREPARATION OF RESEARCH DESIGNS

A **research design** is a plan, structure, and strategy of investigation developed to obtain answers to one or more questions.[4] The *plan* is the researcher's overall program for the research. It includes a list of everything the manager will do from the start until the final analysis of the data and submission of the report. The plan should identify the types of data to be collected, sample populations, research instruments, methods of analysis, tentative target completion dates, and the like. The *structure* is an outline of the specific variables to be measured. Diagrams can be used to show how the variables—and their assumed relationships—are to be examined during the research. If we want to examine students' learning in a class, for example, the structure might indicate an assumed direct relationship between student evaluations of faculty performance and academic achievement. The *strategy* presents the methods to be used to validate the data, to achieve research objectives, and to resolve the problems that will be encountered in the research. In Tom Warner's study, for example, strategic issues would focus on how to validly measure the presence of illegal drugs and employee behavior. Other strategic questions might be: What happens if employees do not show up for their urinalysis test on the scheduled date? What if another test, such as a hair analysis or pupillary-reaction, is more reliable and valid? What statistical tests will be used to measure the degree of association between presence of illegal drugs in an employee's system and the employee's behavior?

Purposes of Research Designs

A research design has two major purposes: to provide answers to questions and to provide control for nonrelevant effects that could influence the results of the study.[5] Investigators devise research designs to obtain answers to questions as objectively, accurately, and economically as possible. The design determines what observations to make, how to make them, and how to analyze them. A **nonrelevant effect** is anything the investigator has little control over but that could affect the results. In the Fleet Line example, nonrelevant effects might include a recession where drivers need work but stay home because they have no other driving jobs or bad weather that forces them to stay off the road.

Fundamentals of Research Designs

Rarely does a research design satisfy all the criteria associated with the scientific approach, but managers should strive to satisfy as many as possible in choosing their design. The ultimate findings of a poorly conceived research design may be invalid or have limited applicability. The ultimate product of a well-conceived design is more likely to be valid and receive serious attention.

Hypothesis The design of a research project typically provides for the collection of data about a hypothesis in such a way that inferences of a causal relationship between an independent (causal) variable and a dependent (effect) variable can legitimately be drawn. A **hypothesis** is a statement about the relationship between two or more variables. It asserts that a particular characteristic or occurrence of one of the factors (the

independent variable) determines the characteristic or occurrence of another factor (the **dependent variable**). Hypotheses that Tom Warner at Warner Corporation may have stated include the following:

- Employees who use illegal drugs are more likely to steal from customers and do shoddy work than employees who do not use illegal drugs.

- Spending twelve thousand dollars a year testing for the presence of illegal drugs will be less costly than not testing for these drugs.

- Customers will use the services of organizations whose employees are drug-free more frequently than organizations who cannot pledge drug-free employees.

We often make a hypothesis and then investigate to determine whether the facts support or disprove it. A cause-and-effect relationship often is not easy to establish; yet all of us informally pose hypotheses daily in making decisions. With this in mind, let us examine the basics of an experimental design.

Experimental Design   Some types of research designs provide more convincing grounds for drawing causal inferences than do others. The concepts of causality and experimental designs are complex. A thorough analysis of them is beyond the scope of this book. We will limit this discussion to key points that are essential to an understanding of the requirements for an adequate research design. We use the example of physical fitness and wellness programs in organizations to introduce these key points.

In the past fifteen years, U.S. and Canadian businesses have become increasingly aware of the importance of physical fitness and wellness in the workplace.[6] The estimated cost for medical treatment and loss of worker productivity for all diseases is more than $150 billion per year.[7] The tremendous growth of work site health programs has partially resulted from the belief that an organization should take some of the responsibility for the welfare of its most valuable asset, its employees. Organizations sponsoring fitness and wellness programs include Fortune 500 companies, public safety agencies (such as fire and police departments), insurance providers, federal and state agencies, manufacturing organizations, and communications industries.

Many organizations have adopted one of three levels of fitness and wellness programs to control costs and maintain a healthier workforce.[8] Level I programs consist of efforts aimed at making individuals aware of specific consequences of unhealthful habits. These programs may include newspapers, health fairs, screening sessions, posters, flyers, and classes. Level II programs involve life-style changes by providing specific programs (for example, strength training or back training) that last a minimum of eight to twelve weeks or are available to employees on an ongoing basis. These programs use motivation techniques (see Chapters 6 and 7) and direct participation of the employee to achieve a long-term effect through the formation of new habits. Level III programs are designed to create an environment that assists individuals in maintaining healthy life-styles and behaviors. A Level III program typically assists participation in a healthy life-style by providing a fitness center, including equipment, space, and locker facilities, at the work site, making healthy food (for example, low-cholesterol items) available in lounges and cafeterias, and removing un-healthy temptations (for example, candy and cigarettes) from the work-place.

Johnson and Johnson (J&J) wanted to test the hypothesis that employ-ees who participated in Level III fitness and wellness programs would have lower health costs than employees who participated in Level I or II pro-grams.[9] Johnson and Johnson believed that the Level III approach, with its constant reinforcing messages, would change the health-related behaviors of employees more permanently than Level I or II programs. The change in work environment brought about by a participation in Level III programs would also provide a positive reinforcement for employees to change their behaviors. In the experimental setting, more than eleven thousand employ-ees were divided into two groups. All agreed to participate in either a Level I and II or Level III program for thirty months. Initial analysis of the groups indicated that medical costs and other factors, such as age, gender, and marital status prior to the experiment, were about the same. After thirty months, J&J concluded that employees participating in Level III programs had fewer admissions to hospitals, visited doctors less, and were absent from work less than employees who had participated in Level I and II programs.

Two groups are always used in an experiment. The **experimental group**—in the J&J case, employees who participated in Level III fitness programs—is exposed to the treatment, or the independent variable. The **control group**—employees in the Level I and II fitness programs—is not exposed to the treatment. After a thirty-month period, J&J was then able to compare the medical and performance data on employees in the experi-mental and control groups. Since Level III participants reported fewer med-ical expenses and higher performance, J&J concluded that employees who had participated in Level III fitness programs were better-performing em-ployees than those who did not take Level III training.

Johnson and Johnson randomly chose employees to participate in this experiment. In this **random selection,** each person had an equal chance of being selected. One way to obtain a random selection involves assigning each person a number and then consulting a table of random numbers. Another way is to flip a coin for each person; heads are members of the control group; tails are members of the experimental group. Random se-lection ensures that any experimenter's preconceptions or biases do not influence the choice of who participates in either the control or the exper-imental group. Each person has the same chance as any other person to be assigned to either group.

Another way of selecting people to participate is matching. In **match-ing,** people must be determined to be equal in all aspects that are consid-ered relevant to the experiment. For example, in the J&J example, employ-ees could be matched on the basis of their length of tenure with the company, the level of their job, prior medical costs, marital status, age, educational level, and the like. The employees who fit the same profile would then be divided into experimental and control groups (quite possibly by random selection).

The use of a control group permits investigators to rule out other causes for improvement in job performance. Significant other possible causes include:

- Natural maturing or development. Whether or not employees attended the program, day-to-day experiences that have nothing to do with that training could affect their performance.

- The influence of the measurement process itself. If employees felt that they were being studied, they might respond differently than if they felt that they were not being studied.

- Contemporaneous events other than the exposure of the employees to the program. Events that occurred during the training that were completely uncontrollable by the researcher might affect employees' performance.

Employees could decrease their medical expenses during the experimental period (that is, thirty months) whether they attended a Level III fitness program or not. However, if this maturing process could be assumed to be the same in the experimental and control groups and if it could be assumed that the effect of the fitness program was not due to any extraordinary circumstances, the effects of maturation could be ruled out when comparing the two groups.

If the employees felt like guinea pigs in the experiment or if they felt that they were being tested and had to make a good impression, the measurements obtained could distort the experimental results. (Variations in experimental designs can be used to take the effects of the measuring process into account but are too complex to discuss here.)

Contemporaneous events may also affect the outcome of the experiment but cannot be controlled by the researcher in advance. For example, while employees were participating in the fitness programs, a feature story in the *Wall Street Journal* indicated that the surgeon general of the United States believed that all employees should engage in regular, vigorous exercise. The article also said that prior to exercising, employees should have a health screen and receive medical encouragement to maintain a regular exercise program. The story indicated that those employees who regularly exercised had lower medical expenses and were more productive than those who did not exercise regularly. If the story was read by most of Johnson and Johnson's employees in either fitness program, they might start exercising regardless of whether they were enrolled in Level III fitness programs. Like maturational effects, however, if such an event affected the experimental group and control group in the same way, this common effect would not be important enough to cause differences between the two groups.

The following story about sugar and ants was told by Mark Twain. After reading it, name the independent and dependent variables.

IN PRACTICE

SUGAR AND ANTS

I constructed four miniature houses of worship—a Mohammedan mosque, a Hindu temple, a Jewish synagogue, a Christian cathedral—and placed them in a row. I then marked fifteen ants with red paint and turned them loose. They made several trips to and fro, glancing in at the places of worship but not entering.

I then turned loose fifteen more painted blue; they acted just as the red ones had done. I now gilded fifteen and turned them loose. No change in the result; the forty-five traveled back and forth in a hurry persistently and continuously visiting each fane but never entering. This satisfied me that these ants were without religious prejudices—just what I wished; for under no other conditions would my next and greater experiment be valuable. I now placed a small square of white paper within the door of each fane; and upon the mosque paper I put a pinch of putty, upon the temple paper a dab of tar, upon the synagogue paper a trifle of turpentine, and upon the cathedral paper a small cube of sugar.

First I liberated the red ants. They examined and rejected the putty, the tar, and the turpentine, then took to the sugar with zeal and apparent sincere conviction. I next liberated the blue ants, and they did exactly as the red ones had done. The gilded ants followed. The preceding results were precisely repeated. This seemed to prove that ants destitute of religious prejudice will always prefer Christianity to any other creed.

However, to make sure, I removed the ants and put putty in the cathedral and sugar in the mosque. I now liberated the ants in a body, and they rushed tumultuously to the cathedral. I was very much touched and gratified and went back in the room to write down the event; but when I came back, the ants had all apostatized and gone over to the Mohammedan communion.

I saw that I had been too hasty in my conclusions and naturally felt rebuked and humbled. With diminished confidence, I went on with the test to the finish. I placed the sugar first in one house of worship, then in another, till I had tried them all.

With this result: whatever church I put the sugar in, that was the one the ants straightway joined. This was true beyond a shadow of doubt, that in religious matters, the ant is the opposite of man, for man cares for but one thing: to find the only true Church; whereas the ant hunts for the one with the sugar in it.

TYPES OF RESEARCH DESIGNS

There are many different types of research designs, and numerous textbooks have been written on the subject.[10] There is a growing recognition that managers and others need a basic knowledge of certain research methods in order to understand the contributions and limitations of research in organizational behavior. A discussion of these should temper the tendency to rush into cause-and-effect solutions to problems that frequently confront all of us.

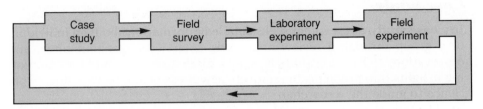

Note: A logical sequence of research might follow the above diagram.

FIGURE 2.2   Relationships of Research Designs

Managers should familiarize themselves with the similarities and differences among several research designs so that they can select the most efficient designs for the problem at hand. Managers should select the design that will do the most complete job, which depends on:

- The kinds of information the design provides.
- The purity of the data; that is, how confident the investigator can be about inferences based on the findings.
- The amount of time and money required and available to perform the research.
- The kinds of resources needed by the investigator and organization in order to use the design.

Instead of scientifically considering these and other issues, people often select a research design, become comfortable with it, and then apply it in situations where its usefulness is limited. Unfortunately, prior habits, experiences, and biases often play a significant role in determining one's choice of research design. Instead of becoming solely interested in, say, laboratory experiments or field surveys, you should understand and appreciate the usefulness of all the available research designs.

The four most common types of research design are the case study, the field survey, the laboratory experiment, and the field experiment. They may be interrelated in many ways, and Figure 2.2 suggests one type of relationship. Although other feedback loops are possible (for example, field survey to case study, laboratory experiment to field survey, and case study to laboratory experiment), the rationale for the sequence shown in Figure 2.2 is appealing because:

- A case study of an organization may identify one or more important variables that a researcher can then investigate by means of a field survey.
- The major relationships uncovered in the field survey may leave unanswered questions concerning the dynamics and the cause-and-effectrelationships among the important variables that can be pursued in a laboratory experiment.
- If the laboratory experiment yields a relationship of general significance to theory or practice, the investigator can then explore the importance of the relationship in a field experiment.

Case Study

In a **case study,** a researcher seeks detailed information about an individual or a group through a review of records, interviews, questionnaires, and observations.[11] The case study is a particularly useful method for stimulating insights into problems in relatively new areas where there is little experience to guide the researcher.

Three distinctive features of the case study make it an important tool for stimulating new insights. First, the researcher can adopt an attitude of alert receptivity, of seeking rather than testing. The factors being studied guide the investigator, who is not limited to the testing of existing hypotheses. Second, the case study is intense. The researcher attempts to obtain sufficient information to characterize and explain the unique aspects of the case being studied and other cases with which it shares common factors. Third, the case study relies on the researcher's ability to draw together many diverse bits of information into a unified interpretation.

If the investigator gives careful attention to these three key features, the case study can be an effective research technique for the analysis of organizational behavior. It is highly adaptable to many problems found in organizations, such as in obtaining the reactions of a newcomer to an established work group. A newcomer to a group tends to be sensitive to social customs and practices that members probably take for granted. For example, a six-person work group loses one member because of retirement, and a newcomer to the plant fills this vacancy. The social practices of the group (for example, lunch breaks, kidding each other while working, and the bowling league) and its production standard (no more than one hundred axles per day) must be communicated to this newcomer. In the analysis of the newcomer's reactions, the depth that can be attained through the case study is its major advantage.

The investigator must also consider the limitations of the case study. The method's most prominent disadvantage is that generalizing the results of one case study to other cases is not usually practical or logical. That is, only rarely can two cases be meaningfully compared in terms of essential characteristics (for example, growth potential, number of employees, location, number of products made, levels of hierarchy, and technology used to manufacture the goods). Therefore, case studies can rarely be repeated exactly or their findings applied validly to other settings.

A further disadvantage is that a case study does not usually lend itself to a systematic investigation of cause-and-effect relationships. Although a case study extending over time can offer the opportunity to determine changes, the range of variations observed in the case study may be too limited for practical cause-and-effect analysis. Case studies, therefore, may not yield definitive proof or rejection of a hypothesis; however, they frequently provide many clues and insights for further investigation.

Field Survey

In a **field survey,** data are collected through interviews or a questionnaire from a sample of people selected to represent the group under examination. Using a sample avoids the expensive and time-consuming procedure of taking a census, or a complete accounting of every person in the group being studied.[12]

The intent of a field survey is to gather information—to discover how people feel and think—and not to change or influence the respondents. You may be familiar with the ABC-Lou Harris Poll. This field survey asks people to express their opinions about such topics as the economy, presidential decisions, and proposed legislation in Congress. Each person in the sample is asked the same series of questions. A field survey generally requires a large number of people in its sample in order to draw valid conclusions. Of those initially selected to be sampled, many fail to respond: typically, only about 20 percent to 30 percent of the people who receive a questionnaire fill it out. Their answers are combined in an organized way from which the researchers draw conclusions and state the results.

The field survey is not the best research design for obtaining some kinds of data; its use is limited to data about things of which the respondents are consciously aware. If people's unconscious motivations are important, an in-depth personal interview would be more productive.

Problems with inferring cause-and-effect relationships also arise in the field study. Consider an analysis of the relationships between job satisfaction, leadership styles, and performance. Does job satisfaction lead to higher performance, and then do leaders change their personal style? Or is leadership related to job satisfaction, which is then associated with high performance? Because of the large number of unmeasured variables usually involved in a field survey, questions concerning causal relationships among the variables remain unanswered.

Laboratory Experiment

Compared with the case study and the field survey, the laboratory experiment increases the ability of the investigator to establish cause-and-effect relationships among the variables.[13] By conducting an experiment in an artificial setting, the investigator can create and control the exact conditions desired.

The essence of the **laboratory experiment** is to manipulate one or more independent variables and observe the effects on one or more dependent variables. For example, an autocratic leader tells one group of three blindfolded subjects to build a tower as high as possible with Tinker Toys. A democratic leader asks another group of blindfolded subjects to perform the same task. The dependent variable is the height of the tower; the independent variable is leadership style.

The laboratory setting permits the investigator to closely control the conditions under which the experiment is carried out. Laboratory experiments are very useful when the conditions required to test a hypothesis are not practically or readily obtainable in natural situations and when the situations can be replicated under laboratory conditions. For example, Chili's restaurants has built a challenge course to demonstrate how team work can improve managerial effectiveness. The challenge course consists of fifteen constructed low events, such as having members of a group all exchange places while standing on a horizontal telephone pole suspended six inches off the ground, and eight high elements, such as a sixty-foot-high climbing and rappeling tower. By manipulating the types of challenges facing the group, Jan Beatty, the director of the course, can determine the effects on team effectiveness, cooperation, and commitment.

There are several disadvantages in using the laboratory research design. For practical reasons, college students are the most common source of subjects in studies of organizational behavior. However, it is difficult to justify their use to represent actual managers involved in decision-making processes. Many students are young, transient, have not yet occupied positions of responsibility, and do not depend on the successful completion of a task under laboratory conditions for their livelihood. Therefore, to what populations and treatment variables can the laboratory results of experiments using students be generalized? Simulating many of the properties of organizational structure and process in the laboratory can be extremely difficult.

Another problem with the laboratory experiment is that much of the work undertaken in the laboratory deals with phenomena that cannot be reproduced in or applied to real-life situations. A firm could not readily restructure its organizational hierarchy to fit an ideal model. Even if it found and could hire the "perfect" personnel, the changeover would likely result in serious morale and productivity problems. Conversely, many behavioral problems in organizations cannot be isolated to permit their examination under laboratory conditions. Investigators thus tend to focus narrowly on problems that can be addressed in the laboratory setting. Ideally, laboratory experiments should be derived from studies in real-life situations, and results should be continually checked against them.

Field Experiment

A **field experiment** is an attempt to apply the laboratory method to ongoing real-life situations. The field experiment permits the researcher to manipulate one or more independent variables in an organization. The researcher can study the changes in the dependent variables and can infer the direction of causality with some degree of confidence.[14]

The subjects in a field experiment ordinarily know that they are under investigation, so the investigator must adopt procedures that will decrease the possibility of subjects changing their behavior simply because they are being observed. Compared with the laboratory experiment, the field experiment provides the investigator with fewer controls.

Let's read how Prudential Insurance Company used a field experiment to determine the success of its general fitness program. After reading this In Practice, you should be able to state the independent and dependent variables, the purpose of the field experiment, and the hypothesis.

IN PRACTICE

PRUDENTIAL INSURANCE COMPANY FITNESS PROGRAM

Prudential Insurance Company started a general fitness program for 190 white-collar workers who were engaged in sedentary jobs. The program was designed to provide participants with a healthy work environment. The company provided a smoke-free office, an on-site fitness center with an instructor, and low-cholesterol food in the cafeteria and removed candy and cigarette machines from the office, among other things. The study, which used a control group of 190 nonexercisers, was conducted over a five-year period. It included employees who were employed for at least one year prior to and one year after participation in the study. The participants' level of cardiorespiratory fitness (aerobic capacity) was determined by performance on a treadmill exercise test prior to the field experiment. Each individual was classified in one of five fitness categories (low to high) as defined by the American Heart Association in relation to that person's age, gender, and aerobic activity. The results of the study showed that the percentage of individuals in the experimental group who were classified in the low and fair fitness categories decreased from 57 percent to 33 percent. These individuals moved into the average, good, and high fitness categories. The proportion of the participants in the high and good categories increased from 16 percent to 39 percent. There were no changes in categories for participants who were in the control group.

In addition to the marked improvement in the level of fitness of the employees in the experimental group, their average sick days dropped 20 percent when compared to their previous year's sick days before entry into the program. When these days were converted to dollars, the experimental group showed a 32 percent reduction in costs one year after entry into the program. Similarly, their major medical costs dropped by 46 percent during a period when the health care costs of the nation as a whole increased by 13.9 percent. Over the duration of the study, the medical costs for those in the control group rose by 29 percent. The annual disability and major medical costs savings per participant in the experimental group were $353.88, compared to the fitness program's cost of $120.60 per participant.[15]

Comparison of Research Designs

Each of the four types of research design has both strong and weak points. By selecting one, the researcher must often forgo some of the advantages of the alternative. A few aspects of the major designs are summarized and compared below.[16]

Realism   A major advantage of doing research in a natural setting, such as in a field experiment within an organization, is the ability to increase the level of realism. The researcher can be somewhat confident that the employees are behaving under natural and ongoing conditions. This is an advantage over the laboratory setting, which typically involves artificial conditions. However, the investigator in the field loses the ability to manipulate the independent variable or variables as freely as in the laboratory.

Scope   Case studies and field surveys usually have a broad scope and incorporate many variables of interest to the investigator. Laboratory experiments, by their nature, are the most limited in scope, and a field experiment is often an expansion of a laboratory experiment.

Precision   Research undertaken in the laboratory setting is usually more precise than research in the field. In the laboratory, the use of multiple measures of the same variable or variables under controlled conditions allows the researcher to obtain more accurate information about the variables than do other strategies. The use of videotape, for example, permits the investigator to record an entire experiment and then study it at a later time, examining such things as styles of behavior, motives, and gestures.

Control   Investigators hope to control the experimental situation so that events being observed will be related to the causes that are hypothesized and not to some unknown, unrelated events. The laboratory experiment allows researchers to reproduce a situation repeatedly, so that they do not have to rely on a single observation for their conclusions. By replicating a study, predictions about cause-and-effect relationships can be refined from "sometimes" to, say, "ninety-five times out of one hundred." The laboratory experiment also avoids many factors present in the field over which the investigator has little control (personnel changes or employees forgetting to fill out the questionnaire, for example). However, the results obtained from ideal circumstances may not fit the real situation.

Cost   Research designs differ in their relative costs and in the kinds of resources they require. Designs vary in initial setup costs, that is, in the time and resources needed to plan and initiate a study. They also vary in the cost per case for additional samples. For example, a laboratory experiment has relatively low setup costs, requires relatively few kinds of resources, and costs relatively little for additional subjects. The resources required can be found in most colleges. Because of high costs, field experiments and surveys tend to be carried out by large research organizations rather than by a researcher and a few assistants. These designs require a large number of subjects and computation facilities to analyze the data.

Summary   All research designs have both strengths and weaknesses. Too much has been written about the reasons for one strategy being weak or one strategy being better than others: no one strategy is best in every case. It is far more important to study how each of the research designs differs from and is complementary to the others. Rather than search for the ideal, effective investigators select the research design that is best for their purposes and circumstances at the time, use all the strengths of that design, and limit or offset its weaknesses whenever possible.

DATA COLLECTION METHODS

Managers observe and gather data all day, every day. Some data they reject, some they store away, and some they act on. The problem with this ordinary method of data gathering, as opposed to scientific data gathering, is that day-to-day observations of behavior are frequently unreliable or biased by personal attitudes or values. Also, the sample of behaviors observed is often limited and does not truly represent typical behavior; hence, it is not a good basis for generalizations. It is easy to understand why erroneous conclusions frequently are drawn from observations of human behavior.

The quality of research depends not only on the adequacy of the research design but also on the adequacy of the data-collection methods used. The investigator can collect data in a number of ways: by interviews, questionnaires, observation, nonreactive measures, or qualitative methods.[17] The rules for using these data-collection methods to make statements about the relevant subject matter may be built into the data-collecting technique, or they may be developed during the investigator's study.

Interviews

The interview is one of the oldest and most often used methods for obtaining information.[18] It relies on the willingness of people to communicate. Asking someone a direct question can save considerable time and money if the respondent is willing to talk and the answer is honest.

An interview's quality depends heavily on the mutual trust and goodwill established between the interviewer and the respondent. A trained interviewer builds these relationships early in the interview, so that more of the data will be useful. One way to build trust is to assure the respondent that all answers will be confidential. In addition, an interviewer must be a good listener in order to hold the attention of the respondent.

On the other hand, the interview method has several major shortcomings. First, people may be unwilling to provide certain types of information readily in a face-to-face situation. Employees, for example, may be unwilling to express negative attitudes about a superior when the interviewer is from the human resources department. Getting employees to talk openly—even to an outsider—and answer questions about their jobs, other individuals, and the organization is a difficult task because trust is necessary for this to happen. Thus, the importance of establishing trust cannot be overstated. The second shortcoming of this method is that interviews take time, which costs money. Third, to achieve reliability, interviewers must be well-trained and must present questions in a way that ensures validity. Interviewers must eliminate personal biases. Their questions must be tested in advance of the actual interviews for hidden biases. Fourth, the questions asked by the interviewer place limitations on the answers that respondents will freely give.

Questionnaires

Questionnaires are sets of written items to which the subject is asked to respond. This is probably the most frequently used data-gathering device.[19] A questionnaire may measure the respondent's attitudes, opinions, or demographic characteristics or even two or all three of these variables.

Because of the wide variety of variables that questionnaires can measure, thousands of kinds of questionnaires are used to measure variables such as job satisfaction, need fulfillment, company satisfaction, job stress, leadership style, values, vocational interest, and so on.

Developing a questionnaire is more of an art than a science. Such factors as the research budget, the purpose of the study, and the nature of the population to be sampled must be answered before a sound decision can be

tionnaire in Table 2.1 has been used to measure the degree of sexual harassment in offices. Prior to designing this questionnaire, the investigators actually observed the eight behaviors that are measured in this questionnaire. They asked managers if these behaviors were considered to be sexual harassment. Once these eight behaviors were identified, the investigators had to select a scale to measure the extent to which these behaviors actually occurred. They chose structured scales to indicate the extent to which individuals think that sexual harassment exists in their office. Complete the questionnaire in Table 2.1 to determine how much sexual harassment you have observed in your college or university.

Observation

We all observe the actions of others. On the basis of these observations, we infer others' motivations, feelings, and intentions. A major advantage of the observation method is that it focuses attention on the behavior of individuals rather than relying only on their verbal or written expressions. By looking at behavior, the observer can study the entire person or group. The total behavior of the person or group studied becomes the primary interest of the researcher.

A major problem with the observation method is inherent in the observers. They must digest the information derived from the observation and then make inferences from what they have observed. However, these inferences often are incorrect. Suppose, for example, that a person intensely dislikes college football because of its violence, the corruption in recruiting of athletes, and the emphasis on winning. This individual's previously formed personal biases may well invalidate any personal observations and inferences he or she might make after watching a game.

In this chapter's Across Cultures, a researcher observed the behaviors of Asian and American chief executive officers (CEOs) to determine if they behaved differently from each other and whether these differences could be attributed to their cultural heritages. According to T. Fujisawa, the cofounder of Honda, "Japanese and American management practices are 95 percent the same and differ in all important respects."[21] Before reading this Across Cultures, we will briefly mention several important aspects of cultures in Japan and Korea so that you can more accurately interpret the results.

Fundamental to the Japanese culture is that one part of society affects other parts. Thus, the balance and harmony among all groups must be maintained. It is important for all employees to have trust in their co-workers. Trust takes time to develop. Corporate loyalty is extremely important. The Japanese managers almost always use analytical thought patterns that are extremely concrete, detached from the subjective, and often reflective. For example, when a new employee is hired by the stock brokerage house of Sumitomo Corporation, they are expected to live in the corporation's Tokyo headquarters, which is a dorm. All freshman, as they are called, receive a meager salary. According to a manager at this firm, "All new employees are blank sheets. I look forward to seeing what kind of Sumitomo manager they will become." Individuals are highly aware of their specific place within society and their place is determined by the corporation's image and power.

TABLE 2.1   Sexual Harassment in the Workplace

We would like you to describe the environment in which you work. By environment, we mean daily routines that shape employees' behaviors. Make your descriptions as objectively and factually accurate as possible without regard to whether you like or dislike your job. Please use the following scales and circle the one that best describes your description of practices that occur in your place of work (or where you have worked).

1. Would you say that joking or talking about sexual matters at your workplace happens:
    1. Frequently
    2. Occasionally
    3. Sometimes
    4. Not at all

2. Where you work, how much social pressure is there for women to flirt with men?
    1. A lot
    2. Some
    3. None

3. Where you work, how much social pressure is there for men to flirt with women?
    1. A lot
    2. Some
    3. None

4. How much of a problem at your place of work do you consider sexual harassment to be?
    1. A major problem
    2. A problem
    3. Can't say
    4. A minor problem
    5. No problem

5. How many women dress to appear sexually attractive to men at work?
    1. Most
    2. Many

continues

Korean organizations reflect several important cultural themes of that country.[22] First, large diversified organizations—such as Lucky Gold Star, Hyundai, Samsung—are controlled by the families who founded them. The Korean cultural tradition places responsibility on the eldest son to inherit most family property and assume decision-making responsibility. Second, decision making is done by the founder following the principles of Confucius. One of these principles is that decisions should balance the needs of the organization and the harmony of the group. Third, there are close ties between organizations and the government. The government uses its power to give organizations preferential loans and interest rates.

With this brief background of these two cultures, read this chapter's Across Cultures. When you are finished, you should be able to trace aspects of various management practices to these cultures.

TABLE 2.1 *continued*

       3.   Some

       4.   Hardly any

       5.   No women do this

6.   How many men dress to appear sexually attractive to women at work?

       1.   Most

       2.   Many

       3.   Some

       4.   Hardly any

       5.   No men do this

7.   How many women present themselves in sexually seductive ways to men at work in your office?

       1.   Most

       2.   Many

       3.   Some

       4.   Hardly any

       5.   No women do this

8.   How many men present themselves in sexually seductive ways to women at work?

       1.   Most

       2.   Many

       3.   Some

       4.   Hardly any

       5.   No women do this

Scoring:

   Add up your total points. The lower the score, the more likely sexual harassment practices are occurring in your place of work.

Source: Adapted from B. A. Gutek, A. M. Konrad, and A. G. Cohen, Predicting Social-Sexual Behavior at Work: A Contact Hypothesis. *Academy of Management Journal,* 1990, 33, 560–577.

Nonreactive Measures

If we want to know something about someone, we might turn to nonreactive sources for our information instead of asking or observing that person directly. **Nonreactive measures** do not require the cooperation of the person. Company records provide investigators with valuable data on absenteeism, turnover, grievances, performance ratings, and demographics. In some cases, these sources may yield more accurate data than that obtained by directly questioning the employee. Nonreactive measures have the advantage of being inconspicuous because they are generated without the person's knowledge of their use. For example, radio dial settings can be used determine the listener appeal of different radio stations. A Dallas automobile dealer estimates the popularity of different radio stations by having

◆ *ACROSS CULTURES*

ASIAN AND AMERICAN MANAGERIAL BEHAVIORS

This study analyzed and compared two basic aspects of the managerial behavior performed by American, Japanese, and Korean managers. First, we observed whether the management activity was performed alone or involved others. Work performed alone included such activities as desk work and telephone communications. Work that involved others included scheduled and unscheduled meetings. Second, the amount of time managers spent accomplishing the fundamental activities of desk work, telephone communications, and meetings was organized into three time periods: short (less than nine minutes), medium (from nine minutes to an hour), and long (more than one hour). Seven Korean managers were observed for twenty-five days, and eight Japanese managers were observed for twenty-four days. (Data from American managers were gathered by Henry Mintzberg and were reported in Chapter 1 in this book [see pages 11–15]). The researchers recorded, on a checklist, how long the behavior lasted and the type of behavior.

The data in Table 2.2 indicate the major findings of this study. There are several important differences. First, all managers spend most of their time working with others. Seldom do managers have time to spend by themselves at work. Second, how managers spend their time varies considerably. Japanese and Korean managers spend very small amounts of time (14 percent and 10 percent of the total, respectively) working in segments of less than nine minutes, whereas Americans spend 49 percent of their time working in short-duration periods. Ten percent of American managers' time is spent on tasks lasting more than an hour, while Japanese and Korean managers spend 44 percent and 42 percent, respectively, of their time in prolonged activities.

A major implication of these findings is that Asian managers function as social leaders. They spend time cultivating social relationships that might increase their effectiveness in the future and bind employees to the organization. The Asian manager is seen as a spokesperson of the organization. Ritualistic ceremonies and courtesies must be observed

continues

mechanics record the radio dial position on all cars brought in for service. The dealer then uses these data to select radio stations to carry his advertising. The wear on library books, particularly on the corners where the pages are turned, offers another example of a nonreactive measure librarians can use to learn the popularity of a book.

Qualitative Methods

Qualitative methods are measures used by investigators to describe and clarify the meaning of naturally occurring events in organizations. These methods are, by design, open-ended and interpretative. Qualitative data are rarely quantifiable; thus, the researcher's interpretation and description are significant in a qualitative study.

Qualitative methods use the experience and intuition of the investigator to describe the organizational processes and structures that are being studied.[24] The type of data collected requires the qualitative researcher to become very close to the situation or problem studied. For example, a qualitative method used for years by anthropologists is known as ethnography.[25]

continued

and cannot be hurried without taking offense. The key to learning the process of decision making and collecting information is to understand how Asians make decisions. This process, according to Asian managers, means sixteen-hour days, six days a week.

Real decision making often occurs at unscheduled meetings at sushi bars and on the golf course. Their longer meetings do not imply that they are less efficient; it may be just the opposite. Since Asian executives spend less total time in meetings starting up and winding down, more time is spent on problem solving.[23]

TABLE 2.2   Asian and American Managerial Behaviors

Managerial Behavior	Percent of Time Spent on Each Activity		
	Korean	*Japanese*	*American*
Working Alone	22%	25%	28%
Group Work	78%	75%	72%
Total	100%	100%	100%
Duration of Behavior	Percent of Time Spent in Activities Lasting for Each Division		
	Korean	*Japanese*	*American*
Less than 9 minutes	10%	14%	49%
9 to 60 minutes	48%	42%	41%
More than 60 minutes	42%	44%	10%
Total	100%	100%	100%

Source: Adapted from R. H. Doktor, Asian and American CEOs: A Comparative Study. *Organizational Dynamics*, Winter 1990, 53-54.

Ethnography requires the investigator to study the organization for long periods of time as a participant observer. That is, the investigator becomes part of the situation being studied in order to feel what it is like for the people in that situation. The investigator thus becomes totally immersed in the situation. One researcher studying a big city police department accompanied police officers on their daily duties. Thus, this person was able to informally interview police officers, read important police documents, use nonreactive methods to gather other data, and, as a result, provide vivid descriptions of what police work was really like.[26]

Criteria for Data Collection

Any data-collection method used to measure attitudes or behaviors must meet three important requirements: reliability, validity, and practicality.

Reliability The accuracy of measurement and the consistency of results determine **reliability,** which is one of the most important characteristics of any good data-collection method.[27] A bathroom scale would be worthless if you stepped on it three times in sixty seconds and got a different reading each time. Similarly, a questionnaire would be useless if the scores obtained on successive administrations were not consistent. Consistently different scores by the same individual at different times reflects low reliability, unless something happened (experimental change) between each time to warrant the change.

Control normally is the only prerequisite for high reliability. So long as the directions for a data-collection method are clear, the environment is comfortable, and ample time is given for the subject to respond, the method should give reliable results. Furthermore, all data-collection methods, except those utilizing nonreactive sources, are affected to some degree by random changes in the subject—such as fatigue, distraction, or emotional strain. These conditions can also affect the researcher's reliability, especially in the observation method. Finally, changes in the setting, such as unexpected noises or sudden changes in weather, can also affect reliability of the data collected.

Validity   Even a reliable data-collection method is not necessarily valid. **Validity** is the degree to which a test or questionnaire actually measures what it claims to measure. Validity is an evaluation, not a fact. It is usually expressed in broad terms such as high, moderate, or low, instead of precise quantities or numbers.[28] A method can reliably measure the wrong variables. For example, a low score on a math test denies a job to a potential machine repairer. The test may have reliably measured the applicant's abstract math ability. It may not, however, be a valid measure of the applicant's actual manual skill at repairing machines.

The validity of many psychological tests used by firms in employee selection is being questioned. The U.S. Equal Employment Opportunity Commission insists that the use of tests that cannot be validated be discontinued. Tests that are not valid are worse than useless: they are misleading and dangerous. Often such tests have been used—either consciously or unwittingly—to discriminate against certain minority or ethnic groups. Those who challenge the use of drug testing in the hiring process question not their reliability but their validity.

Practicality   Do not underestimate the importance of **practicality,** the final requirement of a good data-collection method. Questionnaires, interviews, and other data-collection methods should be acceptable to both management and the employees who are asked to participate. Unions and various civil rights groups have raised questions about what management has the right to know. In the case of testing for drugs, the question of who has the right to know the results of the tests is critical. Most organizations maintain confidentiality by recording positive tests on only the doctor's records. Some organizations, such as IBM and Kodak, have adopted the following practical plan to test for the presence of illegal drugs in their new hires. First, all applicants are notified of the screening test and procedures on the physical examination form. This states what kinds of tests, such as hair analysis or urinalysis, will be used. Second, the applicant is not permitted to change a test date after he or she appears at the doctor's office and realizes that drug testing is part of the physical examination. Third, in the event of a positive test, the test is repeated using the same sample in order to ensure validity. Samples are kept in the doctor's office for 180 days in case of a lawsuit. Fourth, all records are confidential. Only the applicant knows the results of these tests. Where employees are unionized, the union must approve the data-collection method. The use of a planning committee consisting of representatives from each management level and the unions can increase widespread acceptance. The investigator can consider the viewpoints of these groups in deciding on the data-collection method to be used. The method chosen should also involve easy accessibility by the participants and test administrators in order to save time and money and to minimize disruption of the organization's normal operations.

Let's look at how one large corporation, Shell Canada, used a combination of data-collection methods and a sound research design to implement its high-involvement change program at its oil refinery in Sarnia, Ontario. The example suggests that issues of research design must be addressed early in a change program. Considerable follow-up is needed to assure that the program changes persist. These and other types of organizational change programs will be discussed in Chapter 22.

IN PRACTICE

QUALITY OF WORK LIFE AT SHELL CANADA

Several years ago, after studying how to improve the work life of its employees, a Shell Canada task force recommended creating a high-involvement plant for its Sarnia, Ontario, refinery. A joint labor-management team was established and asked for its input on how to improve the conditions at this plant. No changes were planned for Shell's other oil refineries.

For two years, this joint labor-management team gathered data from employees and managers. They interviewed all employees and asked them to complete a variety of questionnaires that tapped various aspects of their work.

After gathering these data for two years, the team recommended that self-regulating teams operate each one of the three shifts. To gain a sense of pride in their team, members of each team attend a thirty-two-hour self-management training program. During this program, members are instructed in how to select other employees to join their team, how to lead group meetings, and how to develop appropriate group norms. A full-time management person was hired to help employees form effective teams and to help team members deal with issues as they arose. Members of these teams have the skills to perform all jobs at the plant during their shift. Employees are paid on a skill-based pay plan. Under this plan, employees are paid depending on their skill in or knowledge of the various jobs. Employees are taught these skills by team members. Everyone was encouraged to reach the top rate. There are no job classifications for employees and few status differences (for example, parking spaces or eating areas) between employees and managers. A flexible work schedule allows free weekends for some employees in a plant that runs twenty-four hours a day every day of the year. Team members are responsible for scheduling themselves to work.

If there are disagreements within the team and/or between a team and management, a formal review board listens to the disagreement and makes a decision that binds both parties. This board consists of a representative from each team, a team leader, an operations manager, and the union vice president.

What have been the results? According to Shell, the Sarnia plant is one of the most profitable refineries in the Shell Canadian system. It has fewer employee problems, such as absenteeism, lateness, and sick days, and higher productivity than other plants have.[29]

ETHICS IN RESEARCH

Investigators who obtain data from the general public, students, or employees must deal with the ethical and legal obligations they have to their subjects. Generally, there are three types of ethical issues that face managers and researchers:

- Misrepresentation and misuse of data
- Manipulation
- Value and goal conflict

Misrepresentation and Misuse of Data

Misrepresentation and misuse of data are widespread problems. The issue for the investigator is to decide between fully representing all available information to the people involved or sharing just some of these data. Oftentimes it is easy for a manager to gather data about a department's performance under the guise of asking about a competitor's performance. People might talk freely about this and give the manager information regarding the department. What happens, however, if a higher-level manager asks for that information?

Many organizations use computer monitoring to watch a person's performance. **Computer monitoring** refers to the collection of detailed, minute-by-minute information on employee performance through computers for management's use. Oftentimes computer monitoring is sold to employees as a way to help them improve their performance and gain valuable rewards, such as prizes and/or bonus checks. An estimated seven million workers currently are being monitored electronically, often without their knowledge.[30] These include employees who work at computer terminals in data-processing services bureaus, insurance, airlines, telemarketing, and telephone service. Many managers in these organizations, however, collect these data to discipline employees who talk too long on the phone with customers, make personal calls, and the like.

In laboratory experiments, investigators sometimes present false statements or attribute true statements to false sources. The code of ethics of the American Psychological Association states, "Only when a problem is significant and can be investigated in no other way is the psychologist justified in giving misinformation to research subjects."[31] Many researchers feel an ethical obligation to inform the subjects of any false information presented as soon as possible after terminating the research.

The U.S. Department of Health, Education, and Welfare issued an extensive report recommending research requirements intended to protect human subjects. One requirement is that a committee must conduct objective and independent reviews of research projects and activities involving the use of human subjects when federal funds are involved. Most universities, for example, have an independent review committee composed of various directors of research from the colleges within the university. Each member arrives at a decision based on professional judgment as to whether the research will place the participating subjects at risk. If a majority of the review committee members feel that the procedure employed will not put the subjects at risk, the committee will approve the proposal. After this approval, each subject must sign an agreement of informed consent. The basic elements of informed consent include:

- A fair explanation of the procedures to be followed, including those that are experimental.
- A description of the study.
- A description of the benefits to be expected.
- An offer to answer any inquiries concerning the procedures.
- An announcement that the subject is free to withdraw consent and to discontinue participation in the activity at any time.

When the investigators have completed the research, they should make available an abstract of the report to all interested subjects who took part in the study.

Manipulation

Manipulation arises in decision making involving the exercise of a person's free will. Basically, manipulation occurs when the investigator requires employees to do something that is against their personal values. Shell's experiment in its Sarnia Canada plant was voluntary, but what if employees did not want to go along with the experiment or had lost pay because their productivity did not increase as planned?

Value and Goal Conflicts

The third major issue is that of value and goal conflicts. We opened this chapter with a story of Tom Warner's decision to test all employees for illegal drugs. One of his concerns was that this action violated employees' personal freedom to use drugs if they so desire. The American Civil Liberties Union and other organizations protest the use of such testing unless the organization can show probable cause. Does the fact that employees are behaving differently give managers the right to test for illegal drugs in the blood system of these employees?

Many organizations are employing undercover security agents to stem the flow of employee theft. Employee theft is estimated to cost organizations more than $40 billion a year.[32] One of the common tactics used by undercover agents is **entrapment,** the process of luring an individual into performing an illegal act. What are the ethical implications of such procedures? You may recall the trial of Marion Barry, the former mayor of Washington, D.C. He claimed that government agents used entrapment tactics to arrest him and that these violated his rights as a citizen. What do you think?

Whistle-blowing has become a household word in the past few years. **Whistle-blowing** refers to a person (usually a member of the organization) turning in the organization for wrongdoing.[33] According to legislation passed in many states, the whistle-blower is supposed to be protected from management retaliation. Oftentimes, however, the whistle-blower's career is ruined by management. Top management has been known to distort the person's complaint as enthusiastic tattling and reassign the individual to a job that is out of the mainstream of the organization. For example, a Pratt and Whitney auditor was involuntarily transferred after he reported that the contractor had overcharged the Defense Department for spare parts.[34] Similarly, within three days of assuming the chair of the Tennessee Parole Board, Marie Raggshianti discovered evidence that state officials were taking kickbacks in exchange for the release of convicted felons from prison. After she informed the media, her life was threatened and she was subjected to defamatory remarks by managers in her organization as well as in the news media.[35]

SUMMARY

The research methods that investigators find useful in the study of organizational behavior are based on the scientific method, which consists of systematic observation, measurement, and prediction. This approach involves testing a hypothesis, which is a tentative statement that links one or more independent and dependent variables. The four most commonly used research designs to test hypotheses are case studies, field surveys, laboratory experiments, and field experiments. Each method has advantages and disadvantages. Case studies provide insights, but they cannot be used to prove or disprove anything. Field surveys, which are the most widely used research design, enable researchers to collect information about employees, but cause-and-effect relationships cannot be determined from them. Laboratory and field experimentation are superior for determining cause-and-effect relationships. Laboratory experiments offer the greatest control for the investigator but are less generalizable to other situations.

Most organizational behavior research uses one of four methods to collect data: interviews, questionnaires, observations, and nonreactive sources. The investigator must select the most effective method for answering the research question. The method selected should be reliable, valid, and practical. The way data are collected is very important. Ethical practices, trust, and confidentiality are important considerations in organizational behavior research.

Key Words and Concepts

Case study	Matching
Computer monitoring	Nonreactive measures
Control group	Nonrelevant effect
Dependent variable	Practicality
Entrapment	Qualitative methods
Ethnography	Random selection
Experimental group	Reliability
Field experiment	Research design
Field survey	Scientific approach
Hypothesis	Sexual harassment
Independent variable	Validity
Laboratory experiment	Whistle-blowing

Discussion Questions

1. What are some research design problems that Tom Warner, in the Preview Case, should have considered before making his statement about saving the company money through the drug-testing policy? How confident are you that these savings can be attributed to this testing program?

2. What are ethical issues faced by most investigators?

3. How do managers gain knowledge about the behavior of employees in their organization?

4. What problems do field experiments pose for managers and others?

5. Prudential Insurance Company designed a field experiment to evaluate the effectiveness of its fitness program. What other type of research design might Prudential investigators have used to evaluate the effectiveness of the program?

6. Why is validity important for managers?

7. If Jim Steffel and Joyce Haggard at Fleet Line Transportation Company wanted to use qualitative research methods to study turnover at their firm, how would they design their study?

8. Why should an investigator use both a control and an experimental group?

9. What do you think are some of the research problems related to conducting a field survey in another country?

10. What are some potential ethical problems in Johnson and Johnson's fitness program? How would you resolve these problems if you were a manager at Johnson and Johnson?

SAWYER GAS COMPANY

A $12 million, Jacksonville-based corporation, Sawyer Gas provides propane gas, appliances, and heating and air conditioning services from its seven locations throughout northeastern Florida. Its drug-testing program has evolved over a decade, beginning the day in 1980 when company president Charles Sawyer got word that one of his three thousand-gallon propane trucks was lying upside down in a ditch. When he arrived, the driver was in a rescue van. Stepping inside, Sawyer suspected instantly that his driver was high. The man admitted he had been smoking marijuana. "If we had one who was doing it, we probably had others," Sawyer recalls thinking. "So we had a town meeting, so to speak, of all the employees and asked what we should do about it. Our own people suggested that we start testing."

Immediately, the company decided to screen applicants for drugs. Sawyer turned to an outside polygraph specialist, who quizzed job applicants about whether they had used drugs. At that time, it was legal to use polygraphs for such purposes. Some 60 percent of the prospects flunked. As word spread that Sawyer Gas tested for drugs, the number of job seekers dropped. Sawyer lost no sleep over that—at least the ones getting through were clean. He broadened the testing program to include all employees, even himself. Polygraph tests were mandated annually and after any accident or injury occurred.

But testing alone, Sawyer knew, did not attack the root of the problem. Education, he decided, was the answer. He wanted to deal not just with today's workers but also with their children. They, after all, were the future work force.

So in 1987, Sawyer and his wife, Joanne, looked around for materials they could use to teach their employees about the dangers of drugs. Together, over time, they distilled and fashioned all the information into a comprehensive drug-education program. They called it "Knowledge Is Power."

"It's a very unintimidating, very positive type of education," Sawyer explains. "It never says don't do drugs because it harms your company. Instead, it's a program to teach our people the signs of drug use, the paraphernalia used, what to watch for in both their fellow employees and their families."

The Sawyers kicked off the program in October 1988, assembling the entire company—160 strong—at a local hotel. They had charts and videos and pictures of narcotics, as well as tips on drug detection. The local sheriff made a presentation of his own. Crack had infiltrated Jacksonville, he informed the group, and the drug was quite popular among the area's teenagers.

"That knocked me off my chair," recalls office manager Pat DeWitt. "I was sitting there thinking about my kids"—two daughters who were teenagers at the time. "I figured that they must be around drugs all the time."

Sawyer's program is run by his seven branch managers. Once a year, they hold drug-education classes for their subordinates. Every new employee must take the class in the first three months on the job. The three sessions, with three short videos and workbook exercises, last about one hour each. The instruction is done on company time, and participation is mandatory. "It's all directed at employees and their environment," says general manager J. N. "Sandy" Kicliter. "We stress in the handouts that they share the information with their families."

Two years into the program, Sawyer is confident that his managers and supervisors are proficient at detecting drug abusers. They have learned to watch for danger signals—slipshod work habits, paperwork errors, dilated pupils.

"The way to get to most people about drugs is in the workplace," Sawyer says. "I think every business in the country has a responsibility to have a drug-free work force. Because when you reach those parents, you're reaching their kids. Every time you educate an employee, you're educating three to ten other people."

In Jacksonville, at least, that philosophy is catching on. Last fall, Sawyer, a member of the executive board of the Jacksonville Chamber of Commerce, solicited six thousand dollars from each of twenty-two local companies. Those companies became the sponsors of an upgraded version of Sawyer's Knowledge Is Power program called "Put Drugs Out of Business." Each of the sponsors was supplied with kits for its own programs, and Sawyer bought a Put Drugs Out of Business T-shirt for each of his employees. The program has been adopted by more than six hundred companies. The cost is $100 to chamber members and $295 to nonmembers. Any profit goes to the chamber. The Jacksonville chamber owns the program and is making it available nationally.

When Congress outlawed polygraph testing of employees in 1988, Sawyer switched to urinalysis. He screens all applicants. Additionally, all employees and managers are automatically tested once a year and after any accident, no matter how minor. Supervisors, moreover, can request a urinalysis for anyone anytime they are suspicious. Refusal to submit to the test is considered a positive test and grounds for discharge. No one gets a second chance.

"We make a flat statement—if you do drugs, go somewhere else," says Kicliter. "We are not a rehabilitative employer. We might, however, consider the reapplication of a good employee who's gone through rehabilitation and can demonstrate that he's been clean for at least a year."

Since 1980, about fifteen employees have tested positive. Sawyer has not had to fire a single one. "They have quit immediately," he says. "They don't even want to talk to you about it." In the past year, only one employee has tested positive—for marijuana after an accident. Sawyer will bet heavy odds, he says, that his crew is now drug-free or close to it. And his employees are the program's biggest backers, he says.

There has been, however, an undercurrent of loss of privacy. "Some of the younger guys resent it," says Hollis Williams, a 34-year-old pipe fitter.

"They think their personal life should be their own business. But if you have nothing to hide, it's no problem. If you are going to have any kind of decent job these days, you're going to have to go through drug testing here or someplace else. To tell you the truth, I'm all for it. We have guys driving propane trucks and looking for gas leaks—that's sensitive work."

In quantifying results, Sawyer says that the company's accident rate has declined dramatically both in numbers and severity since the program began. Worker's compensation claims have declined, saving the company approximately $75,000 annually in insurance costs, and absenteeism has declined by 64 percent over the same period.

"This program costs me peanuts," says Sawyer. "Last year, I spent $1,500 on drug testing. The only other cost is the time the employees spend in class. It's not an expense as much as an investment. And it's the most positive thing our company has ever done."[36]

QUESTIONS

1. What kind of research design would you choose to evaluate the effectiveness of Sawyer Gas Company's drug program? Why?

2. What kind(s) of data might you gather to evaluate the effectiveness of Sawyer's educational program? How would you gather these data?

3. What are some research design limitations to the Sawyer Gas Company program?

4. What are some ethical dilemmas facing Charles Sawyer?

HOW CORNING GLASS IS FACING GLOBAL COMPETITION

In the 1980s, millions of workers watched helplessly as imports took their jobs and their futures, leaving them only unwanted lower-skill jobs and wrecked communities. What Corning Glass did in its Blacksburg, Virginia, plant was to form links between education, training, and work reforms to change this plant into a global competitor.

Opening the plant in 1989, Corning decided to use multiskilled, team-based production crews. These crews faced challenging jobs instead of simple, repetitive ones. This means that Corning has chosen to compete in global markets on the basis of a highly skilled, well-paid work force, rather than cutting wages or farming out manufacturing to low-wage nations around the world. Corning sorted through more than 8,000 applications and hired 150 employees with the best problem-solving abilities and a willingness to work in a team setting. Corning invested extensive training in technical and interpersonal skills. In the first year of production, 25 percent of all hours worked were devoted to training, at a cost of about $750,000.

Corning believes that U.S. workers must learn new ways to work. At Blacksburg, for example, employees put in shifts of twelve and a half hours in alternating three-day and four-day weeks. The workers are divided into fourteen-member teams. They make managerial decisions, discipline co-workers for shoddy production, and are required to learn three skill modules or lose their job within two years. The plant has only two levels of management: the plant manager and two "line leaders" who advise teams but do not supervise them. As a result, Corning reduced the number of job classifications from forty-seven to four to enable production workers to rotate jobs upon learning new skills.

Has it been worth it? A team with interchangeable skills can retool a line to produce a different type of product in only ten minutes, six times faster than workers at its other plant making a similar product. To be competitive in a global marketplace, the plant must constantly change product lines. That is the reason why the Blacksburg plant turned a $2 million profit in its first eight months, instead of losing $2.3 million as projected.[37]

QUESTIONS:

1. Design a research project that would enable Corning to determine if the plant's success could be attributed to its operating structure alone.

2. What kind(s) of data might you want to gather for your research project? How would you gather these?

3. What are some limitations of carrying out your research project?

References

1. Adapted from D. L. Gebhardt and C. E. Crump. Employee Fitness and Wellness Programs in the Workplace. *American Psychologist*, 1990, 2, 262–272; F. J. Tasco and A. J. Gajda. Substance Abuse in the Workplace. *Compensation and Benefits Management*, Winter 1990, 140–144; J. Finegan. Coping with Drugs. *INC.*, November 1990, 120–136; K. R. Murphy, G. C. Thornton, III, and D. H. Reynolds. College Students' Attitudes toward Employee Drug Testing Programs. *Personnel Psychology*, 1990, 43, 615–632.

2. J. P. Campbell, R. L. Daft, and C. L. Hulin. *What to Study*. Beverly Hills, Calif.: Sage Publications, 1982. A. M. Pettigrew. Longitudinal Field Research on Change: Theory and Practice. *Organization Science*, 1990, 1, 267–292.

3. Personal interview by John Slocum with Jim Steffel and Joyce Haggard, November 1990.

4. T. Cook and D. T. Campbell. The Design and Conduct of Quasi-Experiments and True Experiments in Field Settings. In M. Dunnette (ed.). *Handbook of Industrial Psychology*. Chicago: Rand McNally, 1976, 223–326.

5. E. Stone. *Research Methods in Organizational Behavior*. Glenview, Ill.: Scott-Foresman, 1978.

6. J. D. Blair and M. D. Fotter. *Challenges in Health Care Management*. San Francisco: Jossey-Bass Publishers, 1990.

7. K. E. Warner, T. M. Wickizer, R. A. Wolfe, J. E. Schildroth, and M. H. Samuelson. Economic Implications of the Workplace Health Promotion Programs: Review of the Literature. *Journal of Occupational Medicine*, 1988, 30(2), 106–112.

8. R. E. Herzlinger and D. Calkins. How Companies Tackle Health Care Costs: Part I. *Harvard Business Review*, 1985, 63(4), 68–81; Herzlinger and Calkins. How Companies Tackle Health Care Costs: Part II. *Harvard Business Review*, 1986, 64(1), 70–80.

9. J. L. Bly, R. C. Jones, and J. E. Richardson. Impact of Worksite Health Promotion on Health Care Costs and Utilization: Evaluation of Johnson and Johnson's Live for Life Program. *JAMA*, 1986, 256(23), 3235–3240; S. N. Blair, P. V. Piserchia, C. S. Wilbur, and J. H. Crowder. A Public Health Intervention Model for Worksite Health Promotion. *JAMA*, 1986, 255(7), 921–926.

10. E. E. Lawler, III, A. M. Mohrman, S. A. Mohrman, G. E. Ledford, Jr., and T. G. Cummings. *Doing Research That Is Useful for Theory and Practice*. San Francisco: Jossey-Bass Publishers, 1985; J. Brewer and A. Hunter, *Multimethod Research: A Synthesis of Styles*. Newbury Park, Calif.: Sage Publishing, 1989.

11. D. L. Barton. A Dual Methodology for Case Studies: Synergistic Use of a Longitudinal Single Site with Replicated Multiple Sites. *Organization Science*, 1990, 1, 248–266; K. M. Eisenhardt. Building Theories from Case Research. *Academy of Management Review*, 1989, 14, 532–550.

12. R. B. Dunham and F. J. Smith. *Organizational Surveys*. Glenview, Ill.: Scott, Foresman and Company, 1979; N. W. Schmitt and R. J. Klimoski. *Research Methods in Human Resources Management*. Cincinnati: South-Western Publishing, 1991.

13. M. E. Gordon, L. A. Slade, and N. S. Schmitt. The Science of the Sophomore Revisited: From Conjecture to Empiricism. *Academy of Management Review*, 1986, 11, 191–207; K. E. Weick. Laboratory Experimentation with Organizations: A Reappraisal. *Academy of Management Review*, 1977, 2, 123–127; personal interview by John Slocum with Jan Beatty, director of The Challenge, Chili's, Inc., January 1991, Dallas.

14. J. P. Campbell. Labs, Fields, and Straw Issues. In E. A. Locke (ed.). *Generalizing from Laboratory to Field Settings*. Lexington, Mass.: Lexington Books, 1986, 269–274.

15. D. W. Bowne, M. L. Russell, M. A. Morgan, S. Optenberg, and A. Clarke. Reduced Disability and Health Care Costs in an Industrial Fitness Program. *Journal of Occupational Medicine*, 1984, 26, 809–816.

16. W. H. Glick, G. P. Huber, C. C. Miller, D. H. Doty, and K. M. Sutcliffe. Studying Changes in Organizational Design and Effectiveness: Retrospective Event Histories and Periodic Assessments. *Organization Science*, 1990, 1, 293–312.

17. S. Sudman and N. M. Bradburn. *Asking Questions: A Practical Guide to Questionnaire Design*. San Francisco: Jossey-Bass Publishers, 1982.

18. J. Goodale. *The Fine Art of Interviewing*. Englewood Cliffs, N.J.: Prentice-Hall, 1982.

19. Dunham and Smith, *Organizational Surveys*.

20. B. A. Gutek, A. M. Konrad, and A. G. Cohen. Predicting Social-Sexual Behavior at Work: A Contact Hypothesis. *Academy of Management Journal*, 1990, 33, 560–577.

21. R. H. Doktor. Asian and American CEOs: A Comparative Study. *Organizational Dynamics*, Winter 1990, 46–57.

22. D. Lei and J. W. Slocum, Jr. Global Strategic Alliances: Payoffs and Pitfalls. *Organizational Dynamics*, Winter 1991, 44–62.

23. Adapted from R. H. Doctor, Asian and American CEOs: A Comparative Study. *Organizational Dynamics*, Winter 1990, 46–56; S. Moffat, Should You Work for the Japanese? *Fortune*, December 3, 1990, 107–120; R. M. Steers, Y. K. Shin, and G. R. Ungson, *The Chaebol: Korea's New Industrial Organization*. New York: Harper Business, 1989; and K. H. Chung and H. C. Lee, *Korean Managerial Dynamics*. Westport, Conn.: Praeger Publishers, 1989.

24. B. G. Glaser and A. L. Strauss. *Discovery of Grounded Theory: Strategies for Qualitative Research*. Chicago: Aldine, 1967.

25. J. Van Maanen and S. R. Barley. Cultural Organization: Fragments of a Theory. In P. Frost (ed.). *Organizational Culture*. Beverly Hills, Calif.: Sage Publications, 1985, 31–53; M. O. Patton, *Qualitative Evaluation and Research Methods*. Newbury Park, Calif.: Sage Publications, 1990.

26. J. M. Jermier, J. W. Slocum, Jr., L. W. Fry, and J. Gaines. Organizational Subcultures in a Soft Bureaucracy: Resistance behind the Myth and Facade of an Official Culture. *Organization Science*, 1991, 2, 170–194.

27. E. McCormick and D. Ilgen. *Industrial and Organizational Psychology*, 8th ed. Englewood Cliffs, N.J.: Prentice-Hall, Inc., 1985.

28. D. Schwab. Construct Validity in Organizational Behavior. In L. L. Cummings and B. M. Staw (eds.). *Research in Organizational Behavior*, Vol. 2. Greenwich, Conn.: JAI Press, 1980, 3–44.

29. Adapted from Why Shell Canada's Experiment in Change Flourishes While Others Fail. *World of Work Report*, February 1983, 11–13.

30. H. J. Chalykoff and T. A. Kochan. Computer-Aided Monitoring: Its Influence on Employee Job Satisfaction and Turnover. *Personnel Psychology*, 1989, 42, 807–834; J. R. Larson, Jr. and C. Callahan. Performance Monitoring: How It Affects Work Productivity. *Journal of Applied Psychology*, 1990, 75, 530–538.

31. *Publication Manual of the American Psychological Association*, 3rd ed. Washington, D.C.: American Psychological Association, 1983.

32. N. H. Snyder and K. E. Blair. Dealing with Employee Theft. *Business Horizons*, May–June 1989, 27–34; J. Greenberg. Employee Theft as a Reaction to Underpayment Inequity: The Hidden Cost of Pay Cuts. *Journal of Applied Psychology*, 1990, 75, 561–568.

33. J. P. Near and M. P. Miceli. Whistle-Blowers in Organizations: Dissidents or Reformers? In L. L. Cummings and B. M. Staw (eds.). *Research in Organizational Behavior*, Vol. 9. Greenwich, Conn.: JAI Press, 1987, 321–368.

34. *Ibid.*

35. *Ibid.*

36. Adapted from J. Finegan. Coping with Drugs, *INC.*, November 1990, 122 and 127.

37. Adapted from J. Hoerr. Sharpening Minds for a Competitive Edge. *Business Week*, December 17, 1990, 72–78.

PART II

INDIVIDUAL PROCESSES

CHAPTER 3

PERSONALITY AND ATTITUDES

LEARNING OBJECTIVES

When you have finished studying this chapter, you should be able to:

- Define personality and describe the basic sources of personality differences.
- Provide some examples of personality dimensions that influence individual behavior.
- Explain the concept of attitudes and describe their components.
- Describe the general relationship between attitudes and behavior.
- Define job satisfaction and explain why it is important.

OUTLINE

HUMAN BEHAVIOR IS A MYSTERY TO ME

Anna and David had been hired about the same time as management trainees at Allied Products. They were both assigned as team leaders on adjacent lines producing metal fasteners for wiring assemblies. For each, this was the second of three six-month assignments that rotated them among various first-line supervisory positions in order to provide hands-on management experience.

David and Anna had become good friends and frequently had lunch together to discuss their work. "One of the things that bugs me," David was saying, "is my inability to predict just how some of the members of my team are going to respond. For example, several weeks ago, I had to issue written reprimands to Kate and Terry for repeated tardiness. You name it—they've done it. They come in late in the mornings, they come back late from lunch, they stretch twenty-minute coffee breaks into thirty or forty minutes. I tried everything. I warned them repeatedly, I counseled them—they never seemed to take my concerns seriously. Finally, I decided to get their attention by issuing a formal written reprimand. I sent copies to the human resources department and informed Kate and Terry that the reprimands would become a part of their permanent personnel files."

"Now here's the part I find confusing," David continued. "Since the reprimand, Kate has become a model employee. She immediately apologized, saying she had no idea her behavior was creating such a problem, and vowed to do better. Terry's behavior, on the other hand, headed south. In addition, our relationship has deteriorated to the point where he will hardly speak to me. Frankly, I don't think he has much future at Allied, and I find this very distressing. Terry is a bit of a free spirit but still a fine person in many respects. I feel like a failure," David confessed. "My strategy to get their attention and change their behavior worked well with Kate but obviously elicited a very different response from Terry."

"I know what you mean," said Anna. "You may remember my mentioning the trouble I had during our performance review last quarter. I gave my two best-performing team members—Amy and Mary Pat—the highest raises Allied would allow. Amy was thrilled with hers, while Mary Pat seemed irritated that her raise was not higher. Now, her productivity is down this quarter from last. I just don't know," sighed Anna. "You try to be fair and treat everyone equally, but people just don't respond the same. I guess human behavior is pretty much a mystery to me."

When confronted with an identical situation, different people do not necessarily behave the same way, as we see in the Preview Case. Some two thousand years ago, the Greek philosopher Theophrastus asked, "Why is it that while all Greece lies under the same sky and all Greeks are educated alike, it has befallen us to have characters variously constituted?"[1] This question—Why are people different?—is as important for understanding human behavior today as it was in ancient Greece. Managers and employees must comprehend and appreciate individual differences in order to understand the behavior of people in complex social settings, such as organizations.[2] (Recall our discussion of the "organizational iceberg" in Chapter 1, as well as the description of the increasing diversity of the work force.)

The behavior of an employee always involves a complex interaction of the person and the situation. Events in the surrounding environment (including the presence and behavior of others) strongly influence the way people behave at any particular time; yet people always bring something of themselves to the situation. We often refer to this "something," which represents the unique qualities of the individual, as *personality*.

To fully understand an individual's behavior, we need to know many things about that person—past experiences, personality traits, attitudes, values, and so on. We also need information about the situation within which the individual is behaving. This part of the book is devoted to "individual processes" within organizations. We focus first on the individual in order to develop an understanding of organizational behavior. In general, the term **individual differences** refers to the fact that people differ in a variety of ways. In this chapter, we discuss some of these individual differences, specifically personality and attitudes.

PERSONALITY: AN INTRODUCTION

No single definition of personality is accepted by all authorities. A key idea is that personality represents personal characteristics that lead to consistent patterns of behavior. People seek to understand these behavioral patterns in interactions with others. In fact, most people engage in informal attempts to understand human behavior all of their lives. The study of personality represents a more formal, systematic attempt to do the same thing.[3] Certainly in organizations, managers and employees need to understand others' behaviors in a variety of situations.

A well-known personality theorist, Salvatore Maddi, has proposed the following definition of **personality:**

> Personality is a stable set of characteristics and tendencies that determine those commonalities and differences in the psychological behavior (thoughts, feelings, and actions) of people that have continuity in time and that may not be easily understood as the sole result of the social and biological pressures of the moment.[4]

This definition contains some important ideas. First, note that nothing in the definition suggests limiting the influence of personality to only certain behaviors, certain situations, or certain people. Personality theory is a **general theory of behavior**—an attempt to understand or describe the behavior of all people, all of the time.[5] In fact, some people would argue that to attempt to define the concept of personality is to attempt to explain the very essence of what it means to be human.

Second, the phrase "commonalities and differences" suggests an important aspect of human behavior. An often quoted adage states that every person is in certain respects

- like all other people;
- like some other people; and
- like no other person.

Theories of personality often make statements both about things that are common to all people and things that set people apart from each other. To understand the personality of an individual, then, is to understand what that individual has in common with others, as well as what makes that particular individual unique. For the manager, this means that each subordinate is unique and may or may not respond the same way as others to requests, praise, reprimands, pay raises, and so on, as was described in the Preview Case. This complexity is one of the things that makes managing and working with people so challenging.

Finally, Maddi's definition refers to personality as being "stable" and having "continuity in time." Most people intuitively recognize this stability. If a person's entire personality could change suddenly and dramatically, that individual's family and friends would be confronted with a stranger. While major changes do not normally occur suddenly, an individual's personality may change over time. Personality development occurs to a certain extent throughout life, although the greatest changes occur in early childhood.[6] Experience—being exposed to new people and situations—influences personality. People learn new ways of behaving and can vary their behavior from previously established patterns. For example, new employees are often influenced significantly by the demands of their work setting, and some aspects of their personalities may change over time as a result of the socializing influence of the organization.

SOURCES OF PERSONALITY DIFFERENCES

What determines an individual's personality? This question has no single answer because too many variables contribute to the development of each individual's personality. As shown in Figure 3.1, the sources of personality differences can be grouped into several major categories, such as heredity, culture, family, group membership, and life experiences. Examining these categories helps us to understand why individuals are different.

Heredity

A belief in a genetic basis for personality is deeply ingrained in many people's notions of personality. Expressions such as "She is just like her father" and "He gets those irritating qualities from your side of the family, dear," imply a genetic explanation for personality. Heredity determines physique, eye color, hair color, certain physiological characteristics of the muscle and nervous systems, and so on. However, the extent to which genetic factors influence personality is hotly debated. The **nature-nurture controversy** in personality theory concerns that very question. The extreme *nature* position argues that personality is largely inherited. The extreme *nurture* position is that personality attributes are not inherited but rather are determined by a person's experiences. We can summarize current thinking with regard to the nature-nurture debate as follows:

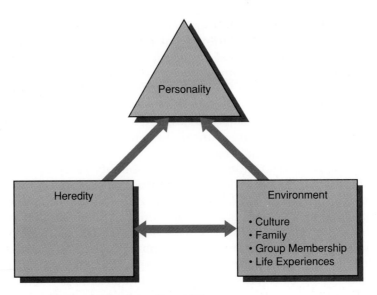

FIGURE 3.1   Sources of Personality Differences

- The degree to which personality is genetically or environmentally determined varies a great deal from one personality characteristic to another.
- To understand personality development, we must examine the interaction between heredity and environment, since each plays a part.
- Heredity sets limits on the range of development of characteristics; within this range, characteristics are determined by environmental forces.[7]

On balance, many experts have held that the environment plays a larger role in shaping personality than do inherited characteristics. However, recent research on the personalities of twins who have been raised apart indicates that genetic determinants are quite important and may play a larger role than many experts had believed. Some studies of twins have suggested that as much as 50 to 55 percent of personality traits may be inherited.[8]

Culture

In the most general sense, **culture** refers to the distinctive ways that different populations or societies of humans organize their lives. Anthropologists working in different cultures have clearly demonstrated the important role that culture plays in personality formation.[9] Individuals born into a particular culture are exposed to existing values and norms of acceptable and appropriate behavior. Culture defines how the different roles necessary to life in that society are to be performed. For example, U.S. culture rewards people for being independent and competitive; Japanese culture rewards individuals for being cooperative and group oriented.

While culture determines, in part, broad patterns of behavioral similarity among people, extreme differences in behavior can exist among individuals within a culture. For example, the Protestant work ethic (hard work is valued; an unwillingness to work is sinful) is usually associated with Western culture, but it is incorrect to assume that this value influences all individuals within this culture to the same degree. Thus, managers must recognize that culture has an impact on the development of employees' personalities, but they must not assume that all individuals respond to the influence of their culture equally or that cultures are homogeneous.

Family

The primary vehicle for socializing an individual into a particular culture is the person's immediate family. Both parents and siblings play important roles in personality development for most individuals. Members of the extended family—grandparents, aunts, uncles, cousins—can also influence personality formation. In particular, parents—or a single parent—influence their children's development in three important ways:

* Through their own behaviors, they present situations that bring out certain behaviors in children.
* They serve as role models with which children often strongly identify.
* They selectively reward and punish certain behaviors.[10]

In addition, the family's situation also is an important source of personality differences among people. Situational influences include the socioeconomic level of the family, family size, birth order, race, family religion, geographical location, parents' educational level, and so on. For example, a person raised in a poor family simply has different experiences and opportunities than does a person raised in a wealthy family. Being an only child is different in some important respects from being raised with several brothers and sisters.

Group Membership

The first group to which most individuals belong is the family. People also participate in a wide variety of groups during their lives, beginning with their childhood playmates and continuing through schoolmates, sports teams, social groups, and so on into adult work and social groups. The numerous roles and experiences people have as members of various groups represent another important source of personality differences. Although playmates and school groups early in life may have the strongest influences on personality formation, social and group experiences in later life continue to influence and shape personality. To fully understand a person's personality, we have to understand the groups—past and present—to which that person belongs.

Life Experiences

In addition to genetic, cultural, family, and group membership differences, each individual's life is unique in terms of specific events and experiences.

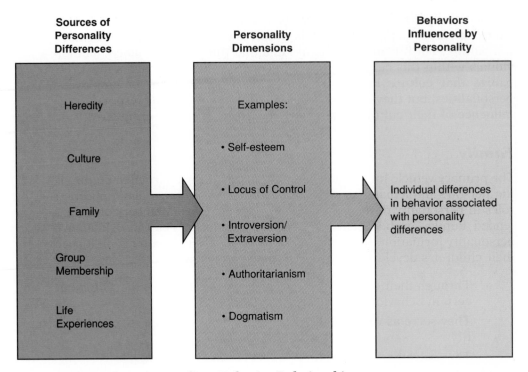

FIGURE 3.2   Personality—Behavior Relationships

These events and experiences can serve as important determinants of personality. For example, the development of self-esteem (a personality dimension to be discussed shortly) depends upon a series of experiences that include the opportunity to achieve goals and meet expectations, evidence of the ability to influence important others, and a clear sense of being valued by others. Thus, a complex series of events and interactions with other people unfolds to establish the level of self-esteem in the adult personality.

PERSONALITY AND BEHAVIOR

Does personality have any concrete, identifiable impact on individual behavior? Figure 3.2 presents the general answer to this question. A "yes" is also suggested by the following report of a study of Canadian managers.

IN PRACTICE

PERSONALITY CHARACTERISTICS OF CANADIAN IDEA CHAMPIONS

Jane Howell and Christopher Higgins of the University of Western Ontario were interested in understanding the unique individual qualities of employees that

---

TABLE 3.1   Some Personality Characteristics and Behaviors of Idea Champions

Personality Characteristics	Distinctive Behaviors
• Self-confident	• Expresses captivating vision
• Persistent	• Pursues unconventional action plans
• Energetic	• Develops others' potential
• Risk taking	• Gives recognition to others

Source: Adapted from J. M. Howell and C. A. Higgins, Champions of Change: Identifying, Understanding, and Supporting Champions of Technological Innovations. *Organizational Dynamics*, Summer 1990, 41.

---

might motivate them to actively promote new ideas in organizations. Such individuals are often called "idea champions" or "champions of change." Howell and Higgins interviewed 150 managers in twenty-five large Canadian firms. From these initial interviews, they selected twenty-five middle managers for in-depth study. The researchers described the common personality characteristics of these twenty-five managers as follows: "Extremely high self-confidence, persistence, energy, and risk taking are the hallmark personality characteristics of champions. Champions show extraordinary confidence in themselves and their mission. They are motivated by a passionate belief in, and enthusiasm about, the [idea] and what it can do for the company." Further, Howell and Higgins were able to link these personality characteristics to patterns of behavior exhibited by these managers. The personality characteristics and distinctive behaviors of these idea champions are summarized in Table 3.1.

Howell and Higgins described the approach taken by one idea champion: Andrew T., vice president of sales and marketing for a multinational automobile manufacturer, decided that a computerized network was essential for rapid communication among his geographically dispersed sales offices. Andrew worked hard to gain the support of key stakeholders. At every opportunity, he pushed for the innovation: at coffee breaks, in hallways, and at management meetings across the country. With self-confidence, persistence, and energy, Andrew built a groundswell of informal support for his vision before attempting to make a formal case to purchase the new computer network. When the formal request was made, the firm's executive committee readily approved it.[11]

———

Recall that personality accounts for consistency in people's behavior in various situations. Behavioral science research has isolated a number of personality dimensions, or traits, that can be linked convincingly to behavior.[12] This section describes several personality dimensions that are particularly important for understanding aspects of organizational behavior.[13] Additional personality traits that are important for understanding power and political behavior (such as Machiavellianism, need for power, and risk-seeking tendencies) will be discussed in Chapter 16.

Self-Esteem

Self-esteem is the evaluation an individual makes of himself or herself. People have opinions of their own behavior, abilities, appearance, and worth. These general assessments, or judgments, of their worthiness are affected somewhat by situations, success or failure, and the opinions of others. Nevertheless, they are stable enough to be widely regarded as a basic characteristic or dimension of the personality. As such, self-esteem affects behavior in organizations and other social settings in several important ways. For example, self-esteem is related to initial vocational choice. Individuals with high self-esteem will take more risks in job selection, may be more attracted to high-status occupations, and are more likely to choose unconventional or nontraditional jobs than individuals with low self-esteem. A study of college students engaged in the job search process reported that students with high self-esteem (1) received more favorable evaluations from organizational recruiters, (2) were more satisfied with their job search, (3) received more job offers, and (4) were more likely to accept a job before graduation than were students with low self-esteem.[14]

Self-esteem is related to a number of important social and work behaviors. For example, low self-esteem individuals are more easily influenced and high self-esteem individuals less easily influenced by the opinions of others in the work setting. Low self-esteem individuals will set lower goals for themselves; high self-esteem employees will tend to set higher goals. In a general sense, self-esteem is positively related to attempts to achieve or a willingness to expend effort to accomplish tasks.

Locus of Control

Locus of control refers to the extent to which individuals believe that they can control events affecting them. Individuals who have a high **internal locus of control** (internals) believe that the events in their lives are primarily (but not necessarily totally) the result of their own behavior and actions. Individuals who have a high **external locus of control** (externals), on the other hand, believe that the events in their lives are primarily determined by chance, fate, or other people.

Many differences between internals and externals are significant in explaining some aspects of behavior in organizational settings. There is some evidence that internals have better control over their own behavior, are more active politically and socially, and more actively seek information about their situations than do externals. Compared to externals, internals are more likely to try to influence or persuade others and are less likely to be influenced by others. Internals may be more achievement oriented than externals. Some evidence shows that externals, compared with internals, prefer a more structured, directive style of supervision. A recent study found that managers with a high internal locus of control adjusted more readily to international transfers than did managers with a high external locus of control.[15]

Much research remains to be done, but real differences in behavior have been demonstrated across a wide range of people and settings. Locus of control beliefs seem to represent a personality dimension of some importance for understanding human behavior in organizations and other settings. A questionnaire that you can use to measure your own locus of control beliefs is contained in the Management Cases and Exercises section at the end of this chapter.

Introversion/Extraversion

In everyday speech, the labels *introvert* and *extravert* describe a person's sociability: introverts are shy, retiring people, while extraverts are socially gregarious and outgoing. The terms have similar meanings when used to refer to a personality dimension. **Introversion** is a tendency of the mind to be directed inward and have a greater sensitivity to abstract ideas and personal feelings. **Extraversion** is an orientation of the mind toward other people, events, and objects.

The terms *introversion* and *extraversion* are often associated with the personality theory of Carl Gustav Jung, whose ideas are presented in Chapter 5. In addition, the research of Hans Eysenck has contributed much to the acceptance of introversion/extraversion as a personality dimension having important implications for social behavior. The work of Eysenck and others suggests that the extravert is best described as "sociable, lively, impulsive, seeking novelty and change, carefree, and emotionally expressive." The introvert, in contrast, is described behaviorally as "quiet, introspective, intellectual, well-ordered, emotionally unexpressive, and value oriented; prefers small groups of intimate friends; and plans well ahead."[16]

Most of us can probably think of individuals who tend to characterize the extremes of introversion and extraversion. Most people, however, are only moderately introverted or extraverted or even relatively balanced between the extremes. A wide distribution of introvert and extravert types occurs across educational levels, genders, and occupations. As might be expected, extraverts are well represented in managerial occupations. Research even suggests that some extraversion is important to managerial success. Since the manger's decisional role often involves identifying and solving problems with and through other individuals (see Chapter 1), a certain degree of extraversion may be essential. However, either extreme extraversion or extreme introversion can interfere with an individual's effectiveness in an organization.

One of the most striking implications of the introversion/extraversion personality dimension for organizational behavior involves task performance in different environments. Some evidence suggests that introverts perform better in an environment where there is little sensory stimulation, whereas extraverts perform better in an environment with greater sensory stimulation—more people, noise, change, and so on. Thus, the extreme introvert might work best alone in a quiet office, and the extreme extravert may well prefer a noisy office with many people and a high level of activity.

Recall our discussion of the sources of personality differences among people. Interestingly, many experts consider introversion/extraversion to be an example of a personality dimension with a relatively high genetically determined component.[17]

Authoritarianism and Dogmatism

The original research on **authoritarianism** was spurred by the events of World War II. It was designed to identify personalities susceptible to fascistic or antidemocratic appeals. Over time, however, the concept broadened. The authoritarian personality is now described as one that rigidly adheres to conventional values, readily obeys recognized authority, exhibits a negative view of mankind, is concerned with power and toughness, and opposes the use of subjective feelings.

Dogmatism is a closely related term that essentially refers to the rigidity of a person's beliefs. The highly dogmatic individual sees the world as a threatening place, often regards legitimate authority as absolute, and accepts or rejects other people on the basis of their agreement or disagreement with accepted authority or doctrine. In short, the high dogmatic (HD) individual is close-minded, and the low dogmatic (LD) person is open-minded.

There is some evidence that HDs depend more on authority figures in the organization and are more easily influenced by them than are LDs. In addition, the authoritarian personality probably is subservient to authority figures and may even prefer superiors who have a highly directive, structured leadership style. There also appears to be some relationship between the degree of dogmatism and interpersonal and group behavior. For example, HDs typically need more group structure than LDs to work effectively with others. This means that the performance of HDs on task forces, committee assignments, and so on may vary somewhat depending on how the group goes about doing its task. Some evidence also suggests that a high degree of dogmatism is related to a limited search for information in decision situations and, perhaps as a result, sometimes leads to poor managerial performance.

Organizational Implications

We have identified and discussed some personality dimensions that have important implications for organizational behavior. For example, a recent study showed that high self-esteem individuals placed more value on attaining performance goals than did employees having low self-esteem.[18] Notice that similar, *specific* relationships are identified for each personality dimension discussed in the preceding paragraphs. It would be wrong, however, for you to conclude from this discussion that managers or work groups should try to change or otherwise directly control employee personality. This is, of course, impossible and, even if it were possible, would be highly unethical. Rather, the challenge for managers and employees is to understand the crucial role played by personality in explaining some aspects of human behavior in work settings.[19] Knowledge of this important individual difference provides managers and students of organizational behavior with valuable insights and a framework that can be used to diagnose events and situations.

THE PERSON AND THE SITUATION

At this point in examining individual differences, it is important to again recognize that behavior always occurs within a particular situation or context. Although understanding individual differences, such as personality, is important, you must remember that behavior is always a complex interaction of the person and the situation. Sometimes the demands of the situation may be so overwhelming that individual differences among people seem relatively unimportant. For example, if a room catches on fire, everyone in it may flee, yet the observation that everyone behaved in the same way certainly says nothing about important differences among the individuals involved. In other cases, individual differences may explain larger amounts of behavior. For example, the Preview Case describes situations in which employees received the same directions and information from their team leader yet exhibited very different behaviors because of important individual differences among them. The relative importance of situational versus personal determinants of behavior is the subject of an ongoing debate in psychology. However, there is considerable evidence for both personality and situational determinants of behavior.[20] To understand behavior in complex social settings, such as organizations, there are advantages to taking an **interactionist perspective.** That is, we must examine both the person and the situation in which the person is behaving in order to fully understand and explain the individual's behavior. The interactionist perspective is increasingly important for understanding organizational behavior.[21] As a result, we take this perspective consistently throughout this book. You will discover that many of the topics covered—such as leadership, political behavior, power differences, stress, and resistance to change—examine both personal and situational causes for the organizational behavior discussed. These personal and situational causes *interact* to determine behavioral outcomes. The following In Practice indicates our society's fascination with the concept of personality, as well as the complex interplay among personality, behavior, and situations.

IN PRACTICE

PRESIDENTIAL PERSONALITIES

U.S. citizens have long been fascinated by the personal characteristics of their presidents. Conventional wisdom holds that having an attractive, forceful personality is of great importance in getting elected to public office in the United States, particularly at the highest levels. Psychologist David Winter has analyzed and profiled the U.S. presidents in psychological terms. Winter examined each president's first inaugural address in order to determine his underlying "motive imagery." Specifically, Winter analyzed these speeches for indications of three important motives that, as research shows, are strongly related to identifiable personal characteristics and behaviors. These underlying motives and the personal characteristics they are commonly associated with are:

- The *achievement motive*—a concern for excellence associated with moderate risk taking, using feedback, and entrepreneurial success;
- The *affiliation motive*—a concern for close relations with others associated with interpersonal warmth, self-disclosure, and good overall adaptation to life; and

---

TABLE 3.2 Psychological Profiles of Selected U.S. Presidents

| | | Motive Scores* | | |
President	*Date of Inaugural Address*	*Achievement*	*Affiliation*	*Power*
George Washington	1789	39	54	41
Thomas Jefferson	1801	49	51	51
Andrew Jackson	1829	43	47	45
Abraham Lincoln	1861	36	45	53
Theodore Roosevelt	1905	62	38	38
Woodrow Wilson	1913	66	49	53
Franklin Roosevelt	1933	53	44	61
Harry Truman	1949	56	65	78
John Kennedy	1961	50	85	77
Richard Nixon	1969	66	76	53
Jimmy Carter	1977	75	59	59
Ronald Reagan	1981	60	51	63

*Overall mean for *all* U.S. presidents = 50 with a standard deviation of 10.

Source: Adapted from D. G. Winter, Leader Appeal, Leader Performance, and the Motive Profiles of Leaders and Followers: A Study of American Presidents and Elections. *Journal of Personality and Social Psychology,* 1987, *52,* 198.

- The *power motive*—a concern for impact and prestige associated with getting formal social power and also impulsive actions, such as aggression, drinking, and taking extreme risks.

The psychological profiles of several presidents in terms of their motive scores are shown in Table 3.2.

Winter then compared these psychological profiles to motive imagery profiles of society as a whole during each president's term of office. In addition, he examined the relationship of each president's personal characteristics with his performance while in office and his leadership appeal. The performance assessment was based on a number of indicators, including Senate rejection of court and cabinet nominees, percentage of vetoes overridden, and consensus of "greatness" by historians. Leadership appeal was measured by such things as margin of victory in elections, whether the president was reelected, and so on.

Winter drew two major conclusions of interest from these comparisons. First, the president's leader appeal or "electability" is very much a function of his fit with society (the situation). That is, how well his motive profile matched those of U.S. citizens at the time. However, the president's performance while in office depended on his personal characteristics and was not related to a match between motive profiles of the president and society. Indeed, Winter concluded that the greatest U.S. presidents have often been those whose psychological profiles were least congruent with their followers in society.[22]

ATTITUDES: AN INTRODUCTION

Attitudes are relatively lasting feelings, beliefs, and behavior tendencies directed towards specific persons, groups, ideas, issues, or objects.[23] Attitudes represent another type of *individual difference* that affects behavior in organizations. An individual's attitudes are a result of the person's background and various life experiences. As with personality development, significant people in a person's life—parents, friends, members of social and work groups—strongly influence attitude formation.

We often think of attitudes as a simple concept, clearly related to individual behavior. In reality, attitudes and their effects on behavior can be extremely complex.[24] Some insight is offered by social psychologists, who often describe an attitude in terms of three components:

- An *affective* component, or the feelings, sentiments, moods, and emotions about some person, idea, event, or object.
- A *cognitive* component, or the beliefs, opinions, knowledge, or information held by the individual.
- A *behavioral* component, or the intention and predisposition to act.[25]

The components of an attitude do not exist or function separately. An attitude represents the *interplay* of a person's feelings, cognitions, and behavioral tendencies with regard to something—another person or group, an event, an idea, and so on. For example, suppose that an individual holds a very strong, negative attitude about the use of nuclear power. During a job interview with the representative of a large corporation, this person discovers that the company is a major supplier of nuclear power generation equipment. The person might feel a sudden intense dislike for the company's interviewer (the affective component). The person might form a negative opinion of the interviewer based on beliefs and opinions about the kinds of people who would work for such a company (the cognitive component). The individual might be tempted to make an unkind remark to the interviewer or suddenly terminate the interview (the behavioral component). The person's actual behavior will depend on a number of factors, including the strength of the attitude toward nuclear power.

ATTITUDES AND BEHAVIOR

To what extent do attitudes predict or cause behavior? For a long time, it was thought that individuals' behaviors were consistent with their attitudes. While there is little doubt that attitudes are related to behavior, it is now widely accepted that a simple, direct link between attitudes and behavior frequently does not exist. In the preceding example, the person being interviewed might have the negative feelings, opinions, and intentions described and yet choose not to behave negatively toward the interviewer because (1) the individual desperately needs a job; (2) the norms of courteous behavior are stronger than the person's desire to express a negative attitude; (3) the individual decides that the interviewer is an inappropriate target for the negative behavior; or (4) the individual acknowledges the possibility of incomplete information.

Considerable interest has been shown in measuring attitudes and then trying to predict subsequent behavior. It has been found that the prediction of behavior from attitudes can be improved if three principles are observed:

- General attitudes best predict general behaviors.
- Specific attitudes best predict specific behaviors.
- The less the time that elapses between attitude measurement and behavior, the more consistent will be the relationship between attitude and behavior.[26]

For example, attitudes toward conservation in general would not be as good a predictor of whether someone will join the Sierra Club as would specific attitudes toward the Sierra Club. General attitudes toward religion would not be good predictors of specific behavior, such as giving to a certain church-related charity or observing a specific religious holiday, but may accurately predict general religious behavior, such as the overall level of involvement in church activities. Attitudes are learned and can change over time. As a rule of thumb, the longer the time between the measurement of an attitude and some behavior, the less likely it is that some relationship between them will be observed. This third principle is now well-known to political pollsters (after some earlier embarrassments), and they are typically careful not to predict voting behavior too far in advance of an actual election. (Or they may be careful to add certain qualifiers to published polls, such as "If the election were held today. . . .")

A model of the attitude-behavior relationship has been developed by Ajzen and Fishbein.[27] In their **behavioral intentions model,** they suggested that behavior is more predictable (and understandable) if we focus on a person's specific *intentions* to behave in a certain way rather than solely on his or her attitudes toward that behavior. The model is depicted in Figure 3.3 and shows that intentions depend on both attitudes and norms regarding the behavior. **Norms** are rules of behavior, or proper ways of acting, which have been accepted as appropriate by members of a group or by society. Norms thus present "social pressures" to perform or not to perform the behavior in question. (We will more fully explore the concept of norms in Chapter 10.)

If both attitudes and norms are positive with regard to the behavior, the intention to behave in a certain way will be high. If attitudes and norms conflict, their relative strengths may determine the individual's intentions and subsequent behavior. The behavioral intentions model further suggests that both attitudes and norms are affected by the individual's beliefs regarding specific behaviors. In the case of attitudes, the important beliefs are concerned with the relationship between the behavior and its consequences (outcomes). (These beliefs, sometimes called *expectancies,* also play an im-

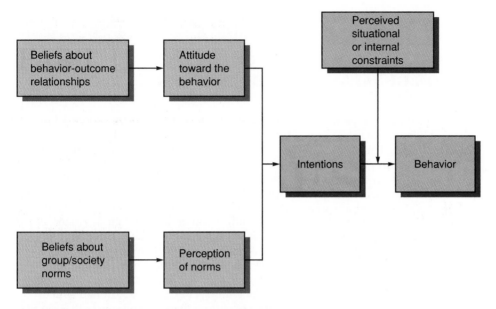

FIGURE 3.3 Behavioral Intentions Model

Source: Adapted from I. Ajzen and M. Fishbein, *Understanding Attitudes and Predicting Social Behavior.* Englewood Cliffs, N.J.: Prentice-Hall, 1980, 8.

portant role in our understanding of motivation; see Chapter 7.) Beliefs regarding norms reflect an individual's perceptions of how others expect that person to act. The behavioral intentions model seems to explain why the relationship between attitudes and behavior can sometimes be strong and at other times be weak. The behavioral intentions model has been revised to include another possible major explanation of social behavior— that is, real or perceived situational or internal obstacles or constraints that may prevent a person from performing an intended behavior.[28] For example, someone might fully intend to quickly and efficiently perform a work task and yet be prevented by a lack of skill from doing so. In addition, the perception or belief that the person lacks the necessary skills might prevent the individual from performing the task. (Note that this belief might have the same effect as the actual lack of skill.)

WORK ATTITUDES: JOB SATISFACTION

In organizational behavior, perhaps the attitude that is of greatest interest is the general attitude toward work or toward a job—often called job satisfaction.[29] In the most general sense, **job satisfaction** is "a pleasurable or positive emotional state resulting from the appraisal of one's job or job experiences."[30] This positive assessment or feeling seems to occur when work is in harmony with the individual's needs and values. (We will explore the kinds of needs that can be met in the work environment and the importance of these needs for understanding employee motivation and behavior in

◆ *ACROSS CULTURES*

A COMPARISON OF JAPANESE AND U.S. WORK ATTITUDES

Recently, data was gathered from 8,300 employees of 106 factories in the United States and Japan in an effort to investigate possible differences in labor productivity in the two countries. Among other things, the investigators suspected that some work attitudes might be different between Japanese and U.S. factory workers.

Interestingly, commitment to the company (one of the attitudes measured) seemed to be essentially the same for employees in the two countries. On the other hand, responses to survey questionnaires did reveal statistically significant differences in average job satisfaction scores between U.S. and Japanese factory workers. Contrary to some peoples' expectations, however, the U.S. employees reported *higher* satisfaction than did their Japanese counterparts. The average satisfaction scores obtained, as well as some of the questions used to measure job satisfaction in this study, are shown in Table 3.3.

The researchers were not very successful in linking these work attitudes to the underlying issues of motivation and productivity they were exploring. They did discover, however, that certain organizational practices designed to have positive effects on employee attitudes (such as job satisfaction) had the *same* positive effects in both Japanese and U.S. factories. For example, participation in quality circles, company-sponsored recreation opportunities, and training opportunities outside the firm had similar positive effects on work attitudes in both countries. After reading the section of this chapter concerned with the relationships between job satisfaction and performance, perhaps you can suggest a reason why we would want to be careful about predicting relative performance levels based on information concerning the job satisfaction of Japanese and U.S. employees.[31]

continues

some detail in Chapter 7.) Job satisfaction is of interest to managers and organizations in many countries around the world. The Across Cultures account in this chapter explores some interesting comparisons between the work attitudes of Japanese and U.S. workers.

Sources of Job Satisfaction

Job satisfaction is sometimes regarded as a single concept. That is, a person is satisfied with the job or not. However, it is best considered as a collection of related job attitudes that can be divided into a variety of job aspects. For example, a popular measure of job satisfaction—the Job Descriptive Index (JDI)—measures satisfaction in terms of five specific aspects of a person's job: pay, promotion, supervision, the work itself, and co-workers.[32] An employee can obviously be satisfied with some aspects of the job and, at the same time, dissatisfied with others.

The sources of job satisfaction and dissatisfaction vary from person to person. Sources thought to be important for many employees include the challenge of the job, the degree of interest that the work holds for the

TABLE 3.3   A Comparison of Job Satisfaction between U.S. and Japanese Employees

Job Satisfaction Question	Japan Mean	U.S. Mean
All in all, how satisfied would you say you are with your job? (0 = not at all, 4 = very)	2.12*	2.95
If a good friend of yours told you that he or she was interested in working at a job like yours at this company, what would you say? (0 = would advise against it, 1 = would have second thoughts, 2 = would recommend it)	.91	1.52
Knowing what you know now, if you had to decide all over again whether to take the job you now have, what would you decide? (0 = would not take job again, 1 = would have some second thoughts, 2 = would take job again)	.84	1.61
How much does your job measure up to the kind of job you wanted when you first took it? (0 = not what I wanted, 1 = somewhat, 2 = what I wanted)	.43	1.20

*The differences in average response to each question are statistically significant, which means that the differences between U.S. and Japanese responses are large enough that they do not appear to be chance results.

Source: Adapted from J. R. Lincoln, Employee Work Attitudes and Management Practice in the U.S. and Japan: Evidence from a Large Comparative Survey. *California Management Review,* Fall 1989, 91.

person, the extent of required physical activity, working conditions, rewards available from the organization (such as the level of pay), the nature of co-workers, and so on. Table 3.4 lists a number of work factors that research indicates are often related to levels of employee job satisfaction. Notice that an important implication of the relationships suggested by Table 3.4 is that job satisfaction should perhaps be considered primarily as an *outcome* of the individual's work experience. Thus, high levels of dissatisfaction might indicate to managers that problems exist with physical working conditions, the reward structure of the organization, role conflict or clarity, and so on.

Job Satisfaction and Job Behavior

Of particular interest to managers and organizations are the possible relationships between job satisfaction and various job behaviors and other outcomes at work. For example, a commonsense notion suggests that job satisfaction should lead directly to better performance on a task. ("A happy worker is a good worker.") Yet, numerous studies have shown that a simple, direct linkage between job attitudes and job performance often does not

TABLE 3.4 Effects of Various Work Factors on Job Satisfaction

Work Factors	Effects
Work itself	
Challenge	Mentally challenging work that the individual can successfully accomplish is satisfying.
Physical demands	Tiring work is dissatisfying.
Personal interest	Personally interesting work is satisfying.
Reward structure	Rewards that are equitable and that provide accurate feedback for performance are satisfying.
Working conditions	
Physical	Satisfaction depends on the match between working conditions and physical needs.
Goal attainment	Working conditions that promote goal attainment are satisfying.
Self	High self-esteem is conducive to job satisfaction.
Others in the organization	Individuals will be satisfied with supervisors, co-workers, or subordinates who help them attain rewards. Also, individuals will be more satisfied with colleagues who see things the same way they do.
Organization and management	Individuals will be satisfied with organizations that have policies and procedures designed to help them attain rewards. Individuals will be dissatisfied with conflicting roles and/or ambiguous roles imposed by the organization.
Fringe benefits	Benefits do not have a strong influence on job satisfaction for most workers.

Source: Adapted from F. J. Landy, *Psychology of Work Behavior,* 4th ed. Pacific Grove, Calif.: Brooks/Cole, 1989, 470.

exist.[33] The difficulty of relating attitudes to behavior is pertinent here. Earlier, we noted that general attitudes best predict general behaviors and specific attitudes are most strongly related to specific behaviors. These principles explain, at least in part, why expected relationships between job satisfaction and performance often do not exist.[34] Overall job satisfaction, as a collection of numerous attitudes toward various aspects of the job, represents a very general attitude. Performance of a specific task, such as preparing a particular monthly report, cannot necessarily be predicted on the basis of the general attitude.

Although job satisfaction does not lead directly to good performance, employee job satisfaction is very important for organizations for a number of valid reasons. One was suggested above. That is, since satisfaction represents an outcome of work experience, high levels of dissatisfaction can provide an important diagnostic tool for management in identifying aspects of the organization that need attention. In addition, job dissatisfaction has been linked convincingly to absenteeism, turnover, and physical and mental health problems.[35] For example, highly dissatisfied employees are more likely to be absent from work and are more likely to leave the job for other employment. With regard to job satisfaction as well as other attitudes, the greatest understanding of attitude-behavior relationships probably comes from examining *specific* attitudes related to a behavior along with other variables (such as norms) that influence a person's *intention* to behave in a certain way.[36]

INDIVIDUAL DIFFERENCES AND ETHICAL BEHAVIOR

Ethical behavior in business firms and other organizations is receiving increased attention during the 1990s.[37] Part of this attention focuses on the influence that individual differences might have on ethical behavior. For example, a recent study has suggested that locus of control and cognitive moral development are important in explaining some aspects of whether people will behave ethically or unethically.[38] **Cognitive moral development** refers to an individual's level of moral judgment. Individuals seem to pass through various stages of moral reasoning and judgment as they mature. With psychological maturity, an individual's judgments with regard to right and wrong become less dependent on outside influences (such as parents) and also less self-centered ("It's right because it's right for me."). At higher levels of cognitive moral development, individuals develop a deeper understanding of principles of justice, ethical behavior, balancing individual and social rights, and so on.

Research has demonstrated that individuals with high internal locus of control exhibit more ethical behavior when making organizational decisions than do individuals with high external locus of control. Further, individuals with higher levels of cognitive moral development are more likely to behave ethically than are others. Differences in cognitive moral development may be reflected in the differences in management ethics described in the following In Practice.

IN PRACTICE

THREE TYPES OF MANAGEMENT ETHICS

Archie Carroll, a management professor, has suggested that an important individual difference among managers is captured by the terms *immoral, amoral,* and *moral* management.

Immoral Management. Immoral management is represented by managerial behaviors devoid of any ethical principles. Its operating strategy is maximum exploitation of opportunities for corporate or personal gain to the extent that no other consideration matters. Any "corner will be cut" if doing so appears useful. Even legal standards are viewed as barriers to be overcome rather than as guides for appropriate behavior.

The Frigitemp Corporation provides an example of immoral management at the highest levels of the firm. According to testimony provided during federal investigations and criminal trials, corporate officials (including the chairman of the board of directors and the president) admitted making illegal payoffs of millions of dollars. In addition, corporate officers embezzled funds, exaggerated earnings in reports to shareholders, took kickbacks from suppliers, and even provided prostitutes for customers. Frigitemp eventually went bankrupt because of management's misconduct.

Moral Management. Moral management represents the opposite extreme from immoral management. That is, managerial behaviors are focused on and guided by ethical norms, professional standards of conduct, and compliance with applicable regulations and laws. It would be a mistake to interpret moral management as being uninterested in profits. Such is not the case; rather, the moral manager will not pursue profits outside the boundaries created by the law and sound ethical principles.

McCulloch Corporation, a manufacturer of chain saws, provides a good example of moral management. Chain saws can be dangerous to use, and studies have consistently shown large numbers of injuries from saws not equipped with chain brakes and other safety features. The Chain Saw Manufacturers Association fought hard against mandatory federal safety standards, preferring to rely on voluntary standards even in the face of evidence that voluntary standards were not high enough and were not working. During this time, McCulloch consistently practiced and supported higher safety standards. (For example, chain brakes have been standard on McCulloch saws since 1975.) McCulloch made numerous attempts to persuade the Chain Saw Manufacturers Association to adopt higher standards when research results indicated that they could greatly reduce injuries. When McCulloch failed to persuade the association to support these higher standards, it withdrew from the association.

Amoral Management. Amoral management is characterized by managerial behaviors that are indifferent to ethical considerations, as though different standards of conduct apply to business than to other aspects of life. Amoral managers seem to lack awareness of ethical or moral issues and engage in behaviors with no thought for the impact that decisions and actions might have on others.

An example of amoral management is provided by Nestle's decision to market infant formula in underdeveloped, Third World countries. Nestle received a lot of negative publicity for this marketing strategy, and investigations were launched in several countries around the world. These investigations seemed to indicate that Nestle apparently gave no thought to the possible disastrous health consequences of selling the formula in areas of illiteracy and poverty where there was high likelihood that it would be mixed with impure, disease-ridden water.[39]

A story is often told about Calvin Coolidge, the U.S. president who was famous for being a "man of few words." One Sunday, President Coolidge had attended church without his wife. Later in the day, Mrs. Coolidge inquired as to the subject of the minister's sermon. "Sin," replied Coolidge. "What did he say about it?" his wife persisted. "He was against it," answered Coolidge. This story illustrates part of the problem of dealing with a topic such as ethics or ethical behavior in organizations. It's not enough just to be against unethical behavior. Managers and employees need a framework to understand ethical behavior and diagnose ethical problems in the work setting. In this book, we are going to explore ethical issues with regard to a number of areas in organizational behavior, such as organizational culture (Chapter 15), decision making (Chapter 19), and organizational change (Chapter 22).

Of course, as we discussed earlier, an organization cannot directly manage personality dimensions, such as locus of control, or cognitive individual differences, such as cognitive moral development. Still, managers and organizations can take steps to instill moral management by fostering ethical attitudes in their work force. Some suggestions for doing this are:

- Identify ethical attitudes crucial for the firm's operation. For example, a security firm might stress honesty, while a drug manufacturer may identify responsibility as most important to ensure product quality. After identifying important ethical attitudes, training programs can focus on developing these ethical attitudes among employees.

- Select employees with desired attitudes. The firm might develop and use standard interview questions that assess an applicant's ethical values.

- Incorporate ethics in the job evaluation process. Criteria that individuals are evaluated on will have an important influence on work-related attitudes that they develop. Organizations should make ethical concerns part of the job description and evaluation.

- Establish a work culture that reinforces ethical attitudes. Managers and organizations can take many actions to influence organizational culture. This culture, in turn, has a major influence on ethical behavior in the organization.[40] (We will explore the concept of organizational culture, including its relationship to ethical behavior, in great detail in Chapter 15.)

Citicorp provides a good example of an organization that has made significant attempts to develop ethical attitudes among its employees. Citicorp is a huge, multinational financial services corporation with some eighty-eight thousand employees in ninety-one countries. Its concerns about ethical behavior resulted in the development and use of an ethics game or exercise entitled "The Work Ethic—An Exercise in Integrity." The game is used in training programs, staff meetings, and department retreats, as well as to orient new employees. The goals of the game are to help employees recognize ethical dilemmas in decision making, to teach employees how Citicorp will respond to misconduct, and to develop increased understanding of its rules and policies regarding ethical behavior. Citicorp does not require that the game be used, but it has proved so popular that the firm estimates that almost forty thousand of its employees around the world have played it.[41] The ethics game is not the only ethics training that Citicorp uses, but it is an excellent example of how an organization might attempt to develop ethical attitudes among managers and employees.

SUMMARY

Personality represents a person's characteristics and traits that account for consistent patterns of behavior in various situations. Each individual is in some ways like other people and in some ways unique. An individual's personality is the product both of inherited traits or tendencies and experiences. These experiences occur within the framework of the individual's biological, physical, and social environment—all of which are modified by the culture, family, and other groups to which the person belongs. A number of specific personality dimensions, such as self-esteem, locus of control, and introversion/extraversion, have important implications for behavior in organizations. The study of personality and the understanding of interactions between the person and the situation are increasingly important for comprehending organizational behavior.

Attitudes are patterns of feelings, beliefs, and behavior tendencies directed toward specific persons, groups, ideas, issues, or objects. Attitudes have affective, cognitive, and behavioral components. The relationship between attitudes and behavior is not always clear, although important relationships exist. The attitude-behavior relationship may become clearer if we can examine the individual's intentions to behave in a certain way as well as understand the specific attitudes and norms that might be related to the behavior. Job satisfaction—the general collection of attitudes an individual holds toward the job—is among the attitudes that are of greatest interest for organizational behavior.

Some individual differences, such as locus of control and cognitive moral development, are related to ethical behavior. Organizations can take constructive steps to foster ethical attitudes among managers and employees.

Key Words and Concepts

Attitudes
Authoritarianism
Behavioral intentions model
Cognitive moral development
Culture
Dogmatism
External locus of control
Extraversion
General theory of behavior
Individual differences

Interactionist perspective
Internal locus of control
Introversion
Job satisfaction
Locus of control
Nature-nurture controversy
Norms
Personality
Self-esteem

Discussion Questions

1. Describe the concept of personality and give some examples of how personality might affect employee behaviors at work.

2. Discuss the basic categories of factors that influence personality development.

3. Describe the opposing positions in the nature-nurture controversy over personality formation. What influences on personality formation seem most important to you? Why?

4. Identify and explain some personality dimensions that are important for understanding organizational behavior.

5. Which of the personality dimensions discussed in the chapter seems most important for managerial behavior? Why?

6. Discuss the interactionist perspective with regard to the relationships among personality, situations, and behavior. *p.85*

7. What is an attitude? Describe the basic components of attitudes.

8. Explain why the behavioral intentions model can be used to understand how attitude-behavior relationships can sometimes appear to be weak and other times appear to be strong. *p. 88-89* *p.90-93 table p.90 3.4*

9. What is the meaning of job satisfaction? Why is it important?

10. Compare and contrast moral management, immoral management, and amoral management. Give an example of each.

11. Suggest some specific actions that organizations might take to encourage ethical behavior by managers and employees.

◆ MANAGEMENT CASES AND EXERCISES

MEASURING LOCUS OF CONTROL

The questionnaire below is designed to measure locus of control beliefs. Researchers using this questionnaire in a recent study of college students found a mean of 51.8 for men and 52.2 for women, with a standard deviation of 6 for each. The higher your score on this questionnaire, the more you tend to believe that you are generally responsible for what happens to you; in other words, higher scores are associated with internal locus of control. Low scores are associated with external locus of control. Scoring low indicates that you tend to believe that forces beyond your control, such as powerful other people, fate, or chance, are responsible for what happens to you.[42]

For each of these ten questions, indicate the extent to which you agree or disagree using the following scale:

1 = strongly disagree
2 = disagree
3 = slightly disagree
4 = neither disagree nor agree

5 = slightly agree
6 = agree
7 = strongly agree

_____ 1. When I get what I want, it's usually because I worked hard for it.
_____ 2. When I make plans, I am almost certain to make them work.
_____ 3. I prefer games involving some luck over games requiring pure skill.
_____ 4. I can learn almost anything if I set my mind to it.
_____ 5 My major accomplishments are entirely due to my hard work and ability.
_____ 6. I usually don't set goals, because I have a hard time following through on them.
_____ 7. Competition discourages excellence.
_____ 8. Often people get ahead just by being lucky.

_____ 9. On any sort of exam or competition, I like to know how well I do relative to everyone else.

_____ 10. It's pointless to keep working on something that's too difficult for me.

To determine your score, reverse the values you selected for questions 3, 6, 7, 8 and 10 (1 = 7, 2 = 6, 3 = 5, 4 = 4, 5 = 3, 6 = 2, 7 = 1). For example, if you strongly disagreed with the statement in question 3, you would have given it a value of "1." Change this value to a "7." Reverse the scores in a similar manner for questions 6, 7, 8, and 10. Now add the point values from all ten questions together.

Your score:_____

DO YOU LIKE YOUR JOB?

Linda Herring gazed at her coffee and pie. After a hectic day, she was trying to unwind in a coffee shop frequented by business people. She looked up to notice an old college friend coming through the door. It had been almost two years since she had seen Anne Youngblood when they were in the same organizational behavior class.

"Anne!" Linda waved to catch her attention. "Have a seat. I haven't seen you in ages. I didn't know you were in town."

"I've been at Griffin Insurance as a management trainee for the past eighteen months," replied Anne. "How about you?"

"I'm with Albanese and Hitt, an advertising agency. I've been with them for almost a year," said Linda.

"What's it like?" asked Anne. "I hear they're a pretty high-pressure outfit."

"I don't know where you get your information," Linda responded, "but you're right. The pay is really good, but they get their pound of flesh from us every day. The people I work with are very sharp, but they're real competitive. I think Albanese and Hitt has an unwritten policy. They like to pit all the new people against each other, and the 'winner' gets promoted. People who don't get promoted don't seem to last very long. They either look elsewhere or get asked to look elsewhere, if you know what I mean."

A sympathetic look crossed Anne's face. "I have my own hassles at Griffin, but they're different. My salary is pretty low, but I think I'm close to a promotion. I'd better be. When I started, they said we'd be moving up after nine months of training. Those nine months became twelve, then fifteen. I've been there eighteen months now, and nobody in my group has moved up yet. We've had two resignations in the positions above mine, so they'll be moving two of us up soon. I hope I'm one of them. Their policy is to bring you along slowly. There's a lot of legal stuff to learn. I've picked up a lot, but I'm getting anxious to use it. My boss is terrific. Right when I feel really frustrated, she takes me aside and says I'm doing great. She shows me the corporate staffing projections and says she'll recommend me highly for an opening. I guess I'm just too impatient."

Linda stared back at her coffee. "My boss is a dunce, but he's a slick dunce. He surrounds himself with people that make him look good. They do all the work; he gets all the credit. I've learned more from my peers than I have from him. I don't understand how someone like that survives in Albanese and Hitt. You'd think by now they'd be on to him. He must be a better actor than I give him credit for."

"You like what you do?" asked Anne.

"Yeah, it's interesting stuff," answered Linda. "A lot more complicated than what we learned in college. I wish more of our professors had discussed company politics. I wish I knew something about how to make my boss look good, because that's what I need to do."

They both fell silent for a while. Finally, Anne said, "Say, a Broadway touring company is in town on Friday to perform *Evita*. I've got an extra ticket. Would you like to go with me?"

"I'd like to, Anne," said Linda, "but Richard has really been on my case lately about bringing a lot of work home. I promised him we'd take in a show Friday night. Maybe we can get together later, okay?"

"Sure," Anne replied, "right after we both get promoted."

They both laughed, and Anne reached for her coat.[43]

QUESTIONS

1. How would you assess the satisfaction with specific aspects of their jobs of both Linda Herring and Anne Youngblood?

2. Which person feels the more *overall* satisfaction with her job and why?

3. Do the two women seem to attach different degrees of importance to the various aspects of their jobs? If so, which aspects seem most important for whom?

References

1. Quoted in Eysenck, H. J. *Personality, Genetics, and Behavior.* New York: Prager, 1982, 1.
2. For an excellent review supporting this point, see Weiss, H. M., and Adler, S. Personality and Organizational Behavior. In B. M. Staw and L. L. Cummings (eds.), *Research in Organizational Behavior,* vol. 6. Greenwich, Conn.: JAI Press, 1984, 1–50.
3. Engler, B. *Personality Theories,* 3d ed. Boston: Houghton Mifflin, 1991; Liebert, R. M., and Spiegler, M. D. *Personality: Strategies and Issues,* 6th ed. Pacific Grove, Calif.: Brooks/Cole, 1990; Schultz, D. *Theories of Personality,* 4th ed. Pacific Grove, Calif.: Brooks/Cole, 1990.
4. Maddi, S. R. *Personality Theories: A Comparative Analysis,* 4th ed. Homewood, Ill.: Dorsey, 1980, 10.
5. Hall, C. S., and Lindzey, G. *Theories of Personality,* 3d ed. New York: Wiley, 1978, 17–19.
6. Collins, W. A., and Gunnar, M. R. Social and Personality Development. *Annual Review of Psychology,* 1990, *41,* 387–416.
7. Pervin, L. A. *Current Controversies and Issues in Personality,* 2d ed. New York: Wiley, 1984, 36–38.
8. Brody, N. *Personality: In Search of Individuality.* San Diego, Calif.: Academic Press, 1988, 68–101; Holden, C. The Genetics of Personality. *Science,* August 7, 1987, 598–601.
9. Buss, D. M. Evolutionary Personality Psychology. *Annual Review of Psychology,* 1991, *42,* 459–491; Hettma, P. J. (ed.). *Personality and Environment: Assessment of Human Adaptation.* New York: Wiley, 1989; Low, B. S. Cross-cultural Patterns in the Training of Children: An Evolutionary Perspective. *Journal of Comparative Psychology,* 1989, *103,* 311–319.
10. Pervin, L. A. *Personality: Theory and Research,* 4th ed. New York: Wiley, 1984, 10.
11. Based on Howell, J. M., and Higgins, C. A. Champions of Change: Identifying, Understanding, and Supporting Champions of Technological Innovations. *Organizational Dynamics,* Summer 1990, 40–55.
12. Digman, J. M. Personality Structure: Emergence of the Five-Factor Model. *Annual Review of Psychology,* 1990, *41,* 417–440; Liebert and Spiegler, *Personality: Strategies and Issues,* 218–221.
13. Descriptions of the following personality dimensions are based on Blass, T. (ed.). *Personality Variables in Social Behavior.* Hillsdale, N.J.: Lawrence Erlbaum Associates, 1977; Engler, *Personality Theories;* Jackson, D. N., and Paunonen, S. V. Personality Structure and Assessment. *Annual Review of Psychology,* 1980, *31,* 503–551; Lefcourt, H. M. *Locus of Control: Current Trends in Theory and Research,* 2d ed. Hillsdale, N.J.: Lawrence Erlbaum Associates, 1982; Liebert and Spiegler, *Personality: Strategies and Issues;* Schultz, *Theories of Personality.*
14. Ellis, R. A., and Taylor, M. S. Role of Self-Esteem within the Job Search Process. *Journal of Applied Psychology,* 1983, *68,* 632–640.
15. Black, J. S. Locus of Control, Social Support, Stress, and Adjustment in International Transfer. *Asia Pacific Journal of Management,* April 1990, 1–30.
16. Morris, L. W. *Extraversion and Introversion: An Interactional Perspective.* New York: Hemisphere, 1979, 8.
17. Engler, *Personality Theories,* 329–334; Eysenck, *Personality, Genetics, and Behavior,* 161–197.
18. Hollenbeck, J. R., and Brief, A. P. The Effects of Individual Differences and Goal Origins on Goal Setting and Performance. *Organizational Behavior and Human Decision Processes,* 1987, *40,* 392–414.
19. See, for example, George, J. M. Personality, Affect, and Behavior in Groups. *Journal of Applied Psychology,* 1990, *75,* 107–116; Locke, E. A., and Latham, G. P. *A Theory of Goal Setting & Task Performance.* Englewood Cliffs, N.J.: Prentice Hall, 1990, 213–218; Pierce, J. L., Gardner, D. G., Cummings, L .L., and Dunham, R. B. Organization-Based Self-esteem: Construct Definition, Measurement, and Validation. *Academy of Management Journal,* 1989, *32,* 622–648.
20. Carson, R. C. Personality. *Annual Review of Psychology,* 1989, *40,* 227–248; Pervin, L A. Personality: Current Controversies, Issues, and Directions. *Annual Review of Psychology,* 1985, *36,* 83–114.

21. See, for example, Greenberger, D. B., and Strasser, S. The Role of Situational and Dispositional Factors in the Enhancement of Personal Control in Organizations. In L. L. Cummings and B. M. Staw (eds.), *Research in Organizational Behavior*, vol. 13. Greenwich, Conn.: JAI Press, 1991, 111–145; Mitchell, T. R., and James, L. R. (eds.), Theory Development Forum—Situational versus Dispositional Factors: Competing Explanations of Behavior. *Academy of Management Review*, 1989, *14*, 330–407; Woodman, R. W., and Schoenfeldt, L. F. Individual Differences in Creativity: An Interactionist Perspective. In J. A. Glover, R. R. Ronning, and C. R. Reynolds (eds.), *Handbook of Creativity*. New York: Plenum, 1989, 77–91.

22. Based on Winter, D. G. Leader Appeal, Leader Performance and the Motive Profiles of Leaders and Followers: A Study of American Presidents and Elections. *Journal of Personality and Social Psychology*, 1987, *52*, 196–202. A description of this study can also be found in Presidents: Men of the Hour Don't Stand the Test of Time. *Psychology Today*, May 1987, 13.

23. Olson, J. M., and Zanna, M. P. Attitudes and Beliefs. In R. M. Baron, W. G. Graziano, and C. Stangor (eds.), *Social Psychology*. Fort Worth, Texas: Holt, Rinehart, and Winston, 1991, 196.

24. Chaiken, S., and Stangor, C. Attitudes and Attitude Change. *Annual Review of Psychology*, 1987, *38*, 575–630; Cooper, J., and Croyle, R. T. Attitudes and Attitude Change. *Annual Review of Psychology*, 1984, *35*, 395–426; Tesser, A., and Shaffer, D. R. Attitudes and Attitude Change. *Annual Review of Psychology*, 1990, *41*, 479–523.

25. See, for example, Baron, R. A., and Byrne, D. *Social Psychology: Understanding Human Interaction*, 5th ed. Boston: Allyn and Bacon, 1987, 116; Breckler, S. J. Empirical Validation of Affect, Behavior, and Cognition as Distinct Components of Attitude. *Journal of Personality and Social Psychology*, 1984, *47*, 1191–1205; Olson and Zanna. Attitudes and Beliefs, 199–212.

26. Penrod, S. *Social Psychology*. Englewood Cliffs, N.J.: Prentice-Hall, 1983, 345–347.

27. Ajzen, I., and Fishbein, M. *Understanding Attitudes and Predicting Social Behavior*. Englewood Cliffs, N.J.: Prentice-Hall, 1980.

28. Ajzen, I. From Intentions to Actions: A Theory of Planned Behavior. In J. Kuhl and J. Beckmann (eds.), *Action-Control: From Cognition to Behavior*. Heidelberg: Springer, 1985, 11–39.

29. O'Reilly, C. R. Organizational Behavior. *Annual Review of Psychology*, 1991, *42*, 427–458.

30. Locke, E. A. Nature and Causes of Job Satisfaction. In M. D. Dunnette (ed.), *Handbook of Industrial and Organizational Psychology*. Chicago: Rand McNally, 1976, 1300.

31. Based on Lincoln, J. R. Employee Work Attitudes and Management Practice in the U.S. and Japan: Evidence from a Large Comparative Survey. *California Management Review*, Fall 1989, 89–106.

32. Smith, P. C., Kendall, L. M., and Hulin, C. L. *The Measurement of Satisfaction in Work and Retirement*. Chicago: Rand McNally, 1969.

33. Iaffaldano, M. T., and Muchinsky, P. M. Job Satisfaction and Job Performance: A Meta-Analysis. *Psychological Bulletin*, 1985, *97*, 251–273.

34. Fisher, C. D. On the Dubious Wisdom of Expecting Job Satisfaction to Correlate with Performance. *Academy of Management Review*, 1980, *5*, 607–612.

35. Muchinsky, P. M. *Psychology Applied to Work*, 3d ed. Pacific Grove, Calif.: Brooks/Cole, 1990, 327–337; Saal, F. E., and Knight, P. A. *Industrial/Organizational Psychology: Science and Practice*. Pacific Grove, Calif.: Brooks/Cole, 1988, 312–322; Schneider, B. Organizational Behavior. *Annual Review of Psychology*, 1985, *36*, 573–611.

36. Ajzen, I. Attitude Structure and Behavior. In A. R. Prathanis, S. J. Breckler, and A. G. Greenwald (eds.), *Attitude Structure and Function*. Hillsdale, N.J.: Erlbaum, 1989, 241–274; Tesser and Shaffer, Attitudes and Attitude Change, 489–491.

37. See, for example, Richardson, John E. (ed.). *Business Ethics 90/91*. Guilford, Conn.: Dushkin Publishing Group, 1990.

38. Trevino, L. K., and Youngblood, S. A. Bad Apples in Bad Barrels: A Causal Analysis of Ethical Decision Making Behavior. *Journal of Applied Psychology*, 1990, *75*, 378–385.

39. Based on Carroll, A. B. In Search of the Moral Manager. *Business Horizons*, March/April 1987, 2–6.

40. Goddard, R. W. Are You an Ethical Manager? *Personnel Journal*, March 1988, 38–47.

41. Trevino, L. K. A Cultural Perspective on Changing and Developing Organizational Ethics. In W. A. Pasmore and R. W. Woodman (eds.), *Research in Organizational Change and Development*, vol. 4. Greenwich, Conn.: JAI Press, 1990, 195–230.

42. Adapted from Burger, J. M. *Personality: Theory and Research*. Belmont, Calif.: Wadsworth, 1986, 400–401.

43. Adapted from Muchinsky, *Psychology Applied to Work*, 339–340.

CHAPTER 4

PERCEPTION AND ATTRIBUTION

LEARNING OBJECTIVES

When you have finished studying this chapter, you should be able to:

- Define perception and describe the major elements in the perceptual process.
- Explain the concepts of perceptual selection and organization.
- Describe the factors that determine how one person perceives another.
- Identify five kinds of perceptual errors.
- Explain the process of attribution and how attributions influence behavior.
- Describe important attributions that people make in the work setting.

OUTLINE

THE HIGH COST OF MISPERCEPTIONS

Sometimes perception can literally be a matter of life or death. Each year in the United States, there are approximately eight thousand collisions between automobiles and trains at railroad crossings. Safety engineers and transportation experts have long been puzzled about the high number of these accidents. Many railroad crossings have warning signals and gates, locomotive engineers typically sound their train's horn when approaching railroad crossings, and a huge, moving train would seem to be a very conspicuous object—one highly likely to be noticed.

What accounts for these accidents? Is it stupidity, or do they reflect people's willingness to take foolish chances? Researchers eventually determined that a common error in motion perception plays a key role in many car-train accidents. To most observers, the size of a moving object and its apparent speed are inversely related. That is, if you are observing two objects of different sizes that are moving at the same speed, the larger one will appear to be moving more slowly. You can verify this phenomenon for yourself at an airport. Most commercial jets land at approximately the same speed. You may notice, however, that jumbo jets (such as DC-10s or 747s) appear to land much more slowly. This is an illusion caused by their larger size. This same type of perceptual error appears to be a factor in many car-train collisions. The large size of the train that makes it easy to see also, unfortunately, causes its speed to be seriously underestimated. Motorists frequently misjudge the speed of an approaching train and may attempt to cross in front of it, believing they have time to do so.[1]

The Preview Case illustrates the importance of perceptions in understanding the world (and also just how wrong these perceptions can sometimes be). People behave on the basis of what they perceive reality to be, not necessarily on the basis of what it really *is*. As people receive information from the world about them, they assemble and incorporate it into an experience that makes sense to them. No two people will necessarily perceive any situation in exactly the same way. In a very real sense, each individual lives in his or her own perceptual world. Recognition of the difference between the perceptual world of employees and managers and the reality of the organization is important in understanding organizational behavior. In this chapter, we continue to explore *individual differences*. Here, we focus on the important processes of *perception* and *attribution*.

THE PERCEPTUAL PROCESS

Perception is the selection and organization of environmental stimuli to provide meaningful experiences for the perceiver. It represents the psychological process whereby people take information from the environment and make sense of their world.[2] Perception includes an awareness of the world—

events, people, objects, situations, and so on—and involves searching for, obtaining, and processing information about that world.[3]

The key words in the definition of perception are *selection* and *organization*. Perceptions of any situation may differ from person to person, both in terms of what they selectively perceive and how those things perceived will be organized and interpreted. Figure 4.1 summarizes the basic elements in the perceptual process from the initial observation to the final response.

We observe stimuli from the environment through the five senses: taste, smell, hearing, sight, and touch. We selectively pay attention to some as-

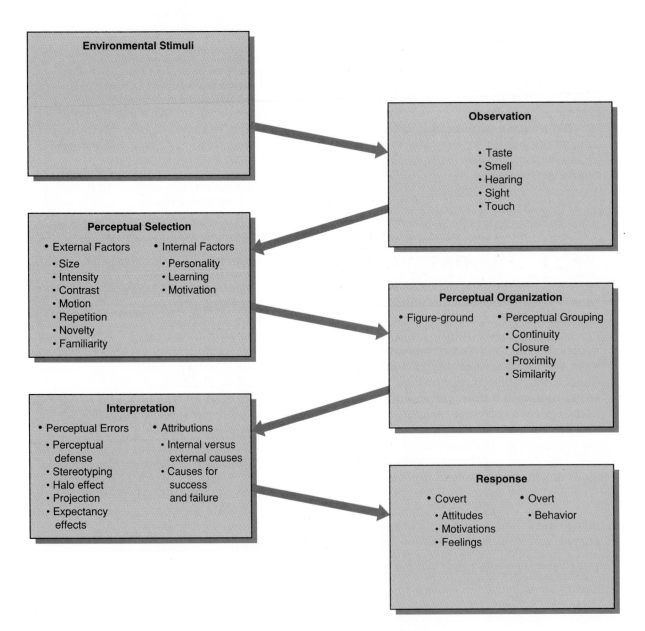

FIGURE 4.1   Basic Elements in the Perceptual Process

pects of our environment and selectively ignore other aspects at any given time. For example, we may listen expectantly for a friend's footsteps in the hall but ignore the sounds of people upstairs. In an office, we ignore the bell announcing the arrival of the elevator, but we jump at the sound of the coffee cart's bell. A selection process involving both external and internal factors filters sensory perceptions to determine which will receive the most attention.

We then organize the stimuli selected into meaningful patterns. How we interpret what we perceive also varies considerably. A wave of the hand could be interpreted as a friendly gesture or as a threat, depending on the circumstances and our state of mind.

A person's interpretation of sensory stimuli will lead to a response, either overt (actions) or covert (motivation, attitudes, and feelings) or both. Each person selects and organizes sensory stimuli differently and thus has different interpretations and responses. As does personality, perceptual differences help to explain why people behave differently in the same situation. People often perceive the same things in different ways, and their behavioral responses depend, in part, on these perceptions. We will explore the external and internal factors that influence perception, the ways that people organize perceptions, the process of *person perception*, and various errors in the perceptual process.

PERCEPTUAL SELECTION

The phone is ringing, your roommate is watching television, a dog is barking outside, your PC is making a strange noise, and you smell coffee brewing. Which of these stimuli will you ignore, and which will you pay attention to?

Perceptual selection is the process by which people filter out most stimuli so that they can deal with the more important ones. Perceptual selection depends on a number of factors, some of which are in the external environment and some of which are internal to the perceiver.

External Factors

The external factors of perception are characteristics that influence whether the stimuli will be noticed. Some examples of these external factors may be stated as *principles* of perception:

- *Size.* The larger the size of an external factor, the more likely it is to be perceived.

- *Intensity.* The more intense an external factor, the more likely it is to be perceived (bright lights, loud noises, and the like). In addition, even the language in a memo from a boss to an employee can reflect the intensity principle. A memo that reads "Please stop by my office at your convenience" will not fill you with the sense of urgency that you would get from a memo that reads "Report to my office *immediately!*"

- *Contrast.* External factors that stand out against the background or that are not what people expect are the most likely to be perceived. In addition, the contrast of objects with others or with their background may influence *how* they are perceived. Figure 4.2 illustrates this aspect of the contrast principle. Which of the solid center circles is larger? The one on the right appears to be larger, but it is not: the two circles are the same size. The solid circle on the right appears larger because its background—its frame of reference—is composed of much smaller circles. The solid circle on the left appears smaller because it is seen in contrast to larger surrounding circles.

- *Motion.* A moving factor is more likely to be perceived than a stationary factor. Soldiers in combat learn this principle very quickly. In the Preview Case, we saw an example of how size and motion may be related in the perceptual process.

- *Repetition.* A repeated factor is more likely to be perceived than a single factor. Marketing managers use this principle in trying to get the attention of prospective customers. An advertisement may repeat key ideas, and the advertisement itself may be presented many times for greater effectiveness.

- *Novelty* and *familiarity.* Either a familiar or a novel factor in the environment can attract attention, depending on circumstances. People quickly notice an elephant walking along a city street. (Both novelty and size increase the probability of perception.) You are most likely to perceive the face of a close friend among a group of people walking toward you.

A combination of these or other similar factors may be operating at any time to affect perception. They, in combination with certain internal factors of the person doing the perceiving, determine whether any particular stimulus is more or less likely to be noticed.

Internal Factors

The internal factors of perception are aspects of the perceiver that influence perceptual selection. Some of the more important internal factors include personality (Chapter 3), learning (Chapter 6), and motivation (Chapter 7).

The internal factors of perception, particularly learning, are important in developing perceptual sets. A **perceptual set** is an expectation of a per-

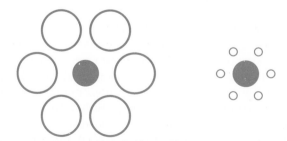

FIGURE 4.2   Contrast Principle of Perception

FIGURE 4.3   Test of Perceptual Set

ception based on past experience with the same or similar stimuli. What do you see in Figure 4.3? If you see an attractive, elegantly dressed woman, your perception concurs with the majority of first-time viewers. However, you may agree with a sizable minority and see an ugly, old woman. Which woman you see depends on your perceptual set. The powerful role that personality, learning, and motivation play in perception manifests itself in many ways, as we see in the following In Practice.

IN PRACTICE

SELECTIVE PERCEPTION OF MANAGERS

An experiment concerning the impact of internal factors on perception was conducted with twenty-three executives enrolled in a company-sponsored training program. Six of these executives were in sales, five in production, four in accounting, and eight in other functional areas of the company. Researchers gave the participants in the training program a ten-thousand-word case history dealing with another company's organization and activities. The assignment was to examine the case history and to determine the most important problem facing the firm. Five of the six sales executives felt that the major company problem was in the sales area. Four of the five production people said the problem was related to production. Three of the four accounting people who worked closely with sales stated that sales was the most important problem. The researchers concluded that, although the case history called for looking at the problem from a companywide rather than a departmental perspective, most of the executives perceived the problem in terms of their own backgrounds.[4] This research has long been considered a classic example of the problem with the selective perception of managers. Its results are not the end of the story, however.

Recently, a similar but more rigorous study was performed with 121 managers attending a graduate program at a large university. As in the earlier study, participants read a case history and were asked to (1) identify problems facing the firm and (2) indicate additional information that might be needed. Results both partially supported and partially refuted the earlier study. The managers tended to frame the issues in terms of their own backgrounds. (For example, accounting and finance managers sought out more accounting and financial information than did managers with other backgrounds.) On the other hand, the managers in this study demonstrated an ability to recognize problems in areas other than their own and sought information from these other areas of expertise as well. Current research thus suggests that we should avoid overly simplistic assumptions about the abilities of people to process information and make decisions. Internal factors clearly influence and even bias which information managers and employees might be most attentive to. At the same time, people can, through education and experience, learn to overcome perceptual sets.[5]

Personality Personality has an interesting relationship to perception. Personality is shaped, in part, by perceptions; in turn, personality affects what and how people perceive. In Chapter 3, we discussed a number of personality dimensions. Any of them, along with numerous other traits, could influence the perceptual process. Under many circumstances, personality appears to strongly affect how an individual perceives other people—the process of "person perception," which we will discuss shortly. A specific example of the relationship between personality and perception is provided by an aspect of the personality called **field dependence/independence.** A field-dependent person tends to pay more attention to external environmental cues, whereas a field-independent person relies mostly on bodily sensations. For example, in a test where a subject has to decide whether an object is vertically upright, a field-dependent individual will rely on cues from the environment, such as the corners of rooms, doors, and so on. The field-independent individual will rely mostly on bodily cues, such as the pull of gravity, to make the same judgment. A field-dependent person will take longer to find hidden figures embedded in complex geometrical designs than will the field-independent person. The field-dependent person is influenced more by the background or surrounding design than is the field-independent person.

Interestingly, this personality difference has some implications for organizational behavior. For example, in comparison to a field-dependent employee, the field-independent employee interacts more independently with others in the organization. That is, the field-independent employee relies less on cues from others (such as a team leader or supervisor) with regard to appropriate interpersonal behavior. In addition, the field-independent employee seems to be more aware of important differences in others' roles, status, and needs.[6]

Learning Perception is strongly influenced by past experiences and what was learned from those experiences. For example, imagine a real estate appraiser, an architect, and a lawyer from Trammell Crow Company all approaching a tall office building. These three individuals may notice distinctly different things about the building. The appraiser may first perceive the general condition of the building and of the surrounding area, factors that would influence the building's price and salability. The architect may first notice the architectural style and the construction materials used in the building. The lawyer may perceive that the size and placement of advertising on the building violates a zoning regulation. Each employee pays attention to different aspects of the same general stimulus because of his or her own background and training. That is why Trammell Crow, Prudential, Equitable, and other organizations might assign a team of employees to evaluate the value of commercial real estate.

Many of life's experiences are determined by the culture into which a person is born, and cultural differences can influence the perceptual process. This chapter's Across Cultures illustrates differences in the perception of time across different cultures.

Motivation Motivation also plays an important role in determining what a person perceives. A person's most urgent needs and desires at any particular time can influence what he or she perceives.

> Everyone has had the following maddening experience. While taking a shower, you faintly hear what sounds like the telephone ringing. Do you get out of the shower, dripping wet, to answer it? Or do you conclude that it is only your imagination?
>
> Your behavior in this situation may depend on factors other than the loudness of the ringing. If you are expecting an important call, you are likely to scurry out of the shower. If you are not expecting a call, you are more likely to attribute the ringing sound to shower noises. Your decision, then, has been influenced by your expectations and motivations.[7]

This example illustrates a significant aspect of perception—the interpretation of sensory information is influenced by internal or nonsensory factors. Similarly, an employee whose firm has just announced the pending layoff of five thousand workers is more sensitive to help-wanted advertisements than an employee at another firm whose job is not threatened.

In general, people perceive things that promise to help satisfy their needs and that they have found rewarding in the past. They tend to ignore mildly disturbing things (a barking dog) but will perceive very dangerous ones (the house being on fire). An important aspect of the relationship between motivation and perception is summarized by the **pollyanna principle,** which states that pleasant stimuli are processed more efficiently and accurately than less pleasant ones.[8] For example, an employee who has received both positive and negative feedback during a performance appraisal session with her boss, may find it easier (and more pleasant) to remember clearly the positive statements that were made.

PERCEPTUAL ORGANIZATION

Perceptual organization is the process by which people group environmental stimuli into recognizable patterns. In the perceptual process, once selection has occurred, organization takes over. The stimuli selected for

TIME PERCEPTION

There is value in understanding and appreciating the sense of time in other cultures. For the traveler or the person attempting to live in another culture, adjusting to a different perception of time may be quite difficult. For example, an investigation of "culture shock" among U.S. Peace Corps volunteers revealed that two of the three greatest sources of adjustment difficulties were related to perceptions of time: the "general pace of life" and the "punctuality of the people."

Researchers have attempted to measure the general pace at which people live their lives in various cultures. One study has compared the pace of life in six countries: England, Japan, Indonesia, Italy, Taiwan, and the United States. In each country, researchers collected data from the largest city and one medium-size city. They took three measures of the pace or tempo of life:

- The accuracy of bank clocks. Fifteen clocks were checked in each downtown area and compared to a verifiable correct time.
- The speed at which pedistrians walk. In each city, one hundred pedestrians, walking alone, were timed for how long they took to walk one hundred feet.

- The length of time needed to purchase a stamp. In each city, researchers measured the amount of time taken to respond to a written request to purchase a commonly used denomination of stamp.

The results of this study are shown in Figure 4.4. Japanese cities rated the highest on all three measures. They had the most accurate bank clocks, the fastest pedestrians, and the quickest postal clerks. U.S. cities were second in two of the three categories. Indonesian cities had the least accurate clocks and the slowest pedestrians. Italian cities had the slowest postal clerks.

From this and related studies, researchers have concluded that a city and a culture have a "pace of life" that influences people's behaviors. This pace of life is different in different cultures and can be important in understanding the perceptions of time in these cultures. Adjusting to a new pace of life is one of the challenges facing employees and managers of multinational corporations when they are transferred from their home country to a foreign assignment.[9]

continues

attention are now seen as a whole. For example, all of us have a mental picture of an object with the following properties: wood, four legs, a seat, a back, and armrests. This is our image of a chair. When we see an object that has all these properties, we recognize it as a chair. We have organized the incoming information into a meaningful whole.

There is still a great deal to learn about how the human mind assembles, organizes, and categorizes information. However, certain factors in perceptual organization, such as the *figure-ground principle* and *perceptual grouping,* are considered to be important by many authorities.[10]

Figure-Ground Principle

The **figure-ground principle** states that people tend to perceive the factor they are most attentive to as standing out against a background. Figure 4.5 illustrates what can happen when there is no clear figure-ground pattern.

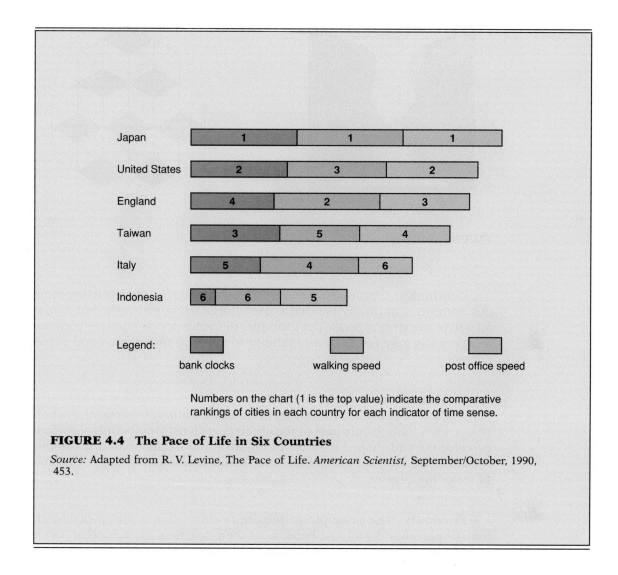

FIGURE 4.4   The Pace of Life in Six Countries

Source: Adapted from R. V. Levine, The Pace of Life. *American Scientist,* September/October, 1990, 453.

These illusions are called *reversible figure-ground patterns.* In Figure 4.5(a), do you see a wine glass on a dark background or facing silhouettes on a white background? Do you see six or seven blocks in Figure 4.5(b)? Turning the page upside down may help you to see seven blocks. Seeing both sets of blocks without turning the page upside down is difficult, because once we are locked into one way of organizing what we see, we often find it very hard to change that view. Life would be very difficult if we were constantly confronted with such figure-ground ambiguity. Often, however, the figure-ground principle is an important aid in understanding the world.

Perceptual Grouping

Perceptual grouping is the tendency to form individual stimuli into a meaningful pattern by such means as continuity, closure, proximity, or similarity.

(a)

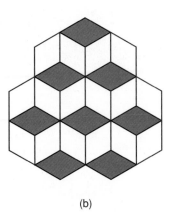
(b)

FIGURE 4.5   Reversible Figure-Ground Patterns

Continuity   Continuity is the tendency to perceive objects as continuous patterns. Continuity is often a useful organizing principle, but it may also have negative aspects. For example, the tendency to perceive continuous patterns may result in an inability to perceive uniqueness and detect change.

Closure   Closure is the tendency to complete an object so that it is perceived as a constant, overall form. It is the ability to perceive a whole object, even though only part of the object is evident. Most people somehow perceive the odd-shaped inkblots in Figure 4.6 as a dalmatian dog walking toward a tree. Someone who had never seen a dalmatian would not be able to make the closure.

Proximity   The principle of proximity states that a group of objects may be perceived as related because of their nearness to each other. Often employees working together in a department are perceived as a team or unit because of their physical proximity. Suppose that four people on the third floor of a large office building quit their jobs. Even if they did so for completely unrelated reasons, the human resources department may perceive it as a problem on the third floor and examine morale, pay, and working conditions there in an attempt to determine what is wrong.

Similarity   The principle of similarity states that the more alike objects are, the greater is the tendency to perceive them as a common group. Similarity is very important in most team sports, thus the use of uniforms. In football, for example, the quarterback must be able to spot an open receiver without a moment's hesitation. Many organizations, especially those in buildings with open floor plans, color code the partitions and other accessories of each department to visually define separate functions and responsibilities. An organization might require visitors to its plant to wear yellow

FIGURE 4.6 An Example of Closure

Source: Reproduced by permission from R. Sekuler and R. Blake, *Perception,* 2d ed. New York: McGraw-Hill, 1990, 129.

hard hats while employees wear white hard hats. Employees can then easily identify people who are unfamiliar with everyday precautions and routines when they are in the work area.

These principles and, in general, the ways that individuals organize their perceptions to make sense of the world are not something that managers and organizations can safely ignore. The following account explores the impact that office design can have on perceptions.

IN PRACTICE

INFLUENCES OF OFFICE DESIGN ON PERCEPTION

Office design—the layout and arrangement of an individual's office, its furnishings, and other physical objects in it—can influence the perceptions of customers, suppliers, prospective employees, and other visitors. In addition, employees may be affected in various ways by the design of their office. Many managers seem unaware of the relationships between office design and employee perceptions, attitudes, and behaviors.

Both office layout and office decor can influence perceptions of the workplace. Office layout—in terms of who is located next to whom—influences perceptions of which individuals and functions the organization values most. For example, offices arranged by "rank," where the highest-level managers occupy the top floors, the most desirable office space, and so on, convey the message that the organization places a high value on status. By contrast, when Union Carbide moved into new corporate headquarters, all managers were assigned offices of identical size to emphasize for both employees and visitors the importance placed on equality. Even the arrangement of furniture in an office may influence perceptions of the firm. For example, one study showed that visitors to a reception area had very different impressions of the organization depending on whether the chairs were placed directly opposite one another or at right angles to one another. Organizations where chairs were placed opposite one another were perceived as more "rigid," "tense," and "deliberate" than were organizations using the right-angle layout for visitor seating. Further, executives visiting the firms where seating was at right angles perceived these organizations as "warmer," "friendlier," and more "comfortable." Importantly, the executive visitors strongly preferred to do business with the "warmer and friendlier" firms.

Office decor may influence perceptions as well. For example, a study found that professors who had posters on the wall and plants in their office were perceived by students as being more friendly than professors who did not display these objects. In organizations, such items as flags, corporate logos, and pictures of company officers are perceived as indicators of a highly structured organization where employees have limited autonomy. An organization that displays certificates of achievement, plaques, and trophies is likely to be perceived as one that values and rewards good performance. Studies of the work setting have consistently shown that flowers and plants increase perceptions of warmth and friendliness. Artwork, on the other hand, is likely to be tricky. Having art on the walls is generally perceived positively, but the content of some pictures might have the opposite effect. For example, one firm that was having trouble recruiting women discovered that pictures of men on horseback displayed prominently throughout the building were perceived by prospective women employees as being cold, hostile, and indicative of a generally unfriendly environment.[11]

PERSON PERCEPTION

Of particular interest in organizational behavior is the process of *person* or *social* perception.[12] **Person perception** is the process by which individuals attribute characteristics or traits to other people. The process of person perception is closely related to the *attribution* process, which we will discuss later in this chapter.

The person perception process is the same as the general process of perception shown in Figure 4.1. That is, the process follows the same sequence of observation, selection, organization, interpretation, and response. However, the element being perceived in the environment is another human being. Although perceptions of situations, events, objects, and so on are important, individual differences in perceptions of others are critical for understanding behavior in complex social settings. For example, suppose that you are introduced to a new employee. In order to get acquainted and to make her feel at home, you invite her to lunch. During lunch, she begins to tell you her life history and spends a great deal of time describing her many accomplishments. Because her conversation is completely concerned with herself (she asks you no questions about yourself), you may form the impression that she is very self-centered. Later, you may come to see other aspects of her personality, but your perceptions may always be strongly affected by this first impression, which is called a **primacy effect.** The following In Practice describes an attempt to determine how individuals form their impressions of other people.

FORMING IMPRESSIONS OF OTHERS

A recent research study investigated how students formed impressions of their classmates over a seven-week period. On a weekly basis, each student in the study provided a written description of every other student in the class. These descriptions were then coded into categories. The results were that 65 percent of the descriptions were based on personality or trait terms (for example, ''honest'' or ''friendly''); 23 percent were behavioral descriptions (such as ''leans back in his chair'' or ''talks a lot''); 6 percent were physical characteristics (attractiveness, gender, age, height, and so on); and some 3 percent were statements about demographic characteristics (for example, family, social, or financial status).

Interestingly, over time, these people became less and less likely to use behaviors to describe another and more likely to rely on personality and trait descriptions. This suggests that eventually individuals' impressions come to rely less on specific details of the other's behavior and more on judgments about underlying personality (what the person is ''really like''). However, despite these shifts in perceptions, the results of this research suggested that primacy effects were strong. That is, impressions first formed among these students continued to account for much of the information used to describe others over the entire seven weeks of the study.[13]

The factors influencing person perception are, in a general sense, the same as those that influence perceptual selection. That is, both external and internal factors affect person perception. However, it is particularly useful to categorize factors that influence how a person perceives another as:

- characteristics of the person being perceived;
- characteristics of the perceiver; and
- the situation or context within which the perception takes place.

Characteristics of the Person Perceived

In perceiving someone else, we process a variety of cues about the person: facial expressions, general appearance, skin color, posture, age, gender, voice quality, personality traits, behaviors, and so on. Some cues may contain important information about the person, but many do not. People seem to have **implicit personality theories** about which physical characteristics, personality traits, and specific behaviors are related to others.[14] These implicit personality theories may affect how individuals view, treat, and remember others. At best, the way that people group characteristics and traits helps them to organize their perceptions to better understand their world. At worst, implicit personality theories lead to perceptual errors, such as stereotyping (to be discussed shortly).

Characteristics of the Perceiver

Listening to an employee describe the personality of a co-worker may tell us as much about the employee's personality as it does about the personality of the person being described. Does this surprise you? Recall that perception is influenced by factors internal to the perceiver, including personality, learning, and motivation—and internal factors are particularly important in person perception. How we perceive another person is, in part, determined by our own personality traits, values, attitudes, current mood, past experiences, and so on. For example, accurately perceiving the personality of an individual raised in another culture is often difficult.[15] One reason is that we interpret our perceptions of that person's traits and behavior in light of our own cultural experiences, attitudes, and values. Often these factors are not adequate for making accurate judgments about the personality and behavior of persons from a different culture as is shown in the following In Practice.

IN PRACTICE

INTERCULTURAL PERCEPTIONS OF CHINESE AND AMERICAN BUSINESS ASSOCIATES

Individuals from different cultures often do not perceive the same events or people in the same way. Many of these differences in perception stem from cultural differences in accepted patterns of behavior. For example, some interesting differences in managerial behavior among Chinese and American managers can contribute to misperceptions and miscommunications. In particular, two aspects of managerial behavior—decision making and negotiating—seem markedly different between Chinese and American managers.

For the Chinese manager, decision making is usually a "collectivist" or group process pointed toward building consensus for a decision. American managers rely more on individual decision making. When American managers use a participative approach, it is more likely to be a "majority rule" outcome than true consensus building. A second major difference in managerial behavior exists in the approach to completing a business deal or contract. Chinese managers place great importance on working relationships. They typically prefer to build relationships first and then do business. American managers are more action oriented and typically want to close deals quickly.

Concern about these fundamental differences in managerial behaviors prompted a group of researchers to examine how (1) Chinese managers perceived their American business associates and (2) American managers perceived their

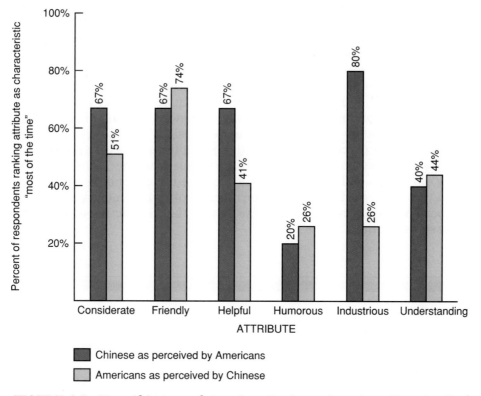

FIGURE 4.7   How Chinese and American Business Associates Perceive Each Other

Source: Adapted from K. F. White, V. Luk, and M. Patel, Personal Attributes of American and Chinese Business Associates: A Study of Intercultural Perceptions. Paper presented at the Southwest Federation of Administrative Disciplines, San Antonio, Texas, March 6, 1988.

Chinese business associates. All of the managers in the study worked for import/export firms in Hong Kong and Houston.

Both Chinese and American managers were asked to evaluate their foreign business associates on a variety of personal characteristics. Some of these responses are summarized in Figure 4.7. The most positive traits of American managers as perceived by their Chinese associates were "friendly" and "considerate." The Chinese managers' most outstanding attribute as perceived by Americans was "industrious." The Chinese also received high marks for "considerate," "friendly," and "helpful."

It is interesting but not entirely surprising that both sets of managers gave their lowest ratings to "humorous." Humor is closely tied to culture and language and is among the more difficult and subtle traits for individuals to accurately perceive across cultures.[16]

The Situation

The situation or setting also influences how one person perceives another. While aspects of the situation may always influence person perception to a certain extent, the situation may be particularly important in understanding first impressions or primacy effects. For example, if you meet someone for the first time and he is with another person that you respect and admire, your assessment of him may be positively influenced. On the other hand, if he is accompanied by a person you intensely dislike, you may form a negative impression. Of course, these initial perceptions (whether positive or negative) may change over time as you interact with the individual in a variety of settings and come to a more accurate understanding of the person. Nevertheless, the first information received often continues to color our later perceptions of individuals, as we saw in the In Practice on forming impressions of others.

PERCEPTUAL ERRORS

The perceptual process can result in errors in judgment or understanding in a number of ways. We will explore accuracy of judgment in person perception. In addition, we will discuss five of the most common types of perceptual errors: perceptual defense, stereotyping, the halo effect, projection, and expectancy effects.[17]

Accuracy of Judgment in Person Perception

How accurate are people in their perceptions of others? This is an important question in organizational behavior. For example, misjudging the characteristics, abilities, or behaviors of an employee during a performance appraisal review could result in an inaccurate assessment of the employee's current and future contributions to the firm. Another organizational example of the importance of accurate person perception comes from the employment interview. Authorities have long been concerned about the judgmental and perceptual errors that could be made by interviewers forced to make employment decisions based on information gathered from a face-to-face interview. The more common interview errors include:

- *Similarity error.* Interviewers are positively predisposed toward job candidates who are similar to them (for example, in background, interests, or hobbies) and negatively biased against job candidates most unlike them.

- *Contrast error.* Interviewers have a tendency to compare job candidates to other candidates interviewed at the same time, rather than to some absolute standard. For example, an average candidate might be rated too highly if she were preceded by several mediocre candidates; a candidate might be scored too low if preceded by an outstanding applicant.

- *Overweighting of negative information.* Interviewers tend to overreact to negative information as though looking for an excuse to disqualify a job candidate.

- *First-impression error.* The primacy effect previously discussed may play a role in the job interview as some interviewers tend to form impressions quickly that are resistant to change.[18]

There are no easy answers to the general problems of accuracy in person perception. It is a crucial issue in understanding behavior that has received a great deal of research attention.[19] We do know that accuracy in person perception represents another important *individual difference.* That is, some people are quite accurate in judging and assessing others, and some people seem extremely inept in doing so. We also know that people can learn to make more accurate judgments in person perception. For example, our perceptions of others will be more accurate if we can avoid (1) generalizing from a single trait to a whole constellation of traits; (2) assuming that a single behavior will show itself in all situations; and (3) placing too much reliance on physical appearance. In addition, since person perception is influenced by characteristics of the perceiver and the situation, accuracy in person perception can be improved when the perceiver understands these potential biases as well. Unfortunately, the errors that individuals make in person perception (and in other aspects of the perceptual process) are so common that names have been given to some of them. We now turn our attention to these perceptual errors.

Perceptual Defense

Perceptual defense is the tendency for people to protect themselves against ideas, objects, or situations that are threatening. A well-known folk song suggests that people hear what they want to hear and disregard the rest. Once established, our way of viewing the world may become very resistant to change. The discussion of perceptual selection mentioned that people perceive things that are supportive and satisfying and tend to ignore disturbing things. Avoiding unpleasant stimuli often is more than escapism; it may be a sensible defensive device. People can become psychologically deaf or blind to disturbing parts of their environment. For example, an employee who really enjoys his work, likes most of his colleagues, and is satisfied with his pay, might simply ignore some aspect of his work experience that is negative (such as an irritating co-worker).

Stereotyping

Stereotyping is the tendency to assign attributes to someone solely on the basis of a category in which that person has been placed. We expect someone identified as a doctor, president of a company, or minister to have certain positive attributes, even if we have met some who did not. A person categorized as a dropout, ex-convict, or alcoholic is automatically perceived negatively. Even identifying an employee by such broad categories as African-American, "older worker," or female, which should not bring to mind any attributes beyond the obvious physical characteristics, can lead to misperceptions. The perceiver may dwell on certain characteristics expected of all persons in the assigned category and fail to recognize the characteristics that distinguish the person as an individual. The following In Practice suggests some of the problems that stereotyping can create for a young professional woman.

IN PRACTICE

THE "CORPORATE DAUGHTER" STEREOTYPE

From the "mommy track" to the "glass ceiling," women have a number of gender-related barriers to overcome in their attempts to attain important managerial positions in organizations. The "corporate daughter" stereotype is yet another problem. Jeanne Westervelt Rice describes the corporate daughter syndrome as follows.

"I spent most of my twenties as a 'corporate daughter.' And I'm not alone. It seems the stigma of being 'fathered' to death in today's corporate culture frustrates many young professional women. Unlike sexual harassment cases, charges cannot be filed against men who patronize young professional women in a fatherly manner. And unlike the usual harassers, people who treat you like a daughter are, after all, just trying to be nice.

"But the consequences can be stifling. Without intent, 'fatherly' executives can jeopardize your stature within the corporation and inhibit your personal and professional growth. You'll never be asked to play hardball while doting executives are doing their best to protect you from the harsh business world.

"I once attended a meeting with five senior executives. I participated, offered thoughts, contributed ideas, and asked questions. I felt good. I felt productive. But within moments, my confidence was shattered. As I turned to walk out the door, I overheard one executive exclaim to the others: 'Isn't she just so cute? I'd love to fix her up with my son!'

"Cute? I wasn't trying to be cute. In fact, I was trying to be anything but cute. Cute is not professional. Cute is not taken seriously. But then, any woman would be hard-pressed to bring legal action against any man who, in all sincerity, just meant to be nice. (Yes, Your Honor, I swear he called me cute. And, even worse he has treated me almost like a daughter.)"[20]

Halo Effect

The **halo effect** is the process by which the perceiver evaluates all dimensions of another person based solely on one impression, either favorable or unfavorable. A *halo* blinds the perceiver to other attributes that should be evaluated in attaining a complete, accurate impression of the other person. The halo effect often plays a major role in employee performance rating. A manager may single out one trait and use it as the basis for judgment of all other performance measures. For example, an excellent attendance record may produce judgments of high productivity, quality work, and industriousness—whether they are accurate or not.

Projection

Projection is the tendency for people to see their own traits in other people. That is, they project their own feelings, tendencies, or motives into their judgment of others. This may be especially true for undesirable traits that perceivers possess but fail to recognize in themselves. For example, an employee frightened by rumors of impending organizational changes may not only judge others to be more frightened than they are but may also assess various policy decisions as more threatening than they really are. People whose personality traits include stinginess, obstinancy, and disorderliness tend to rate others higher on these traits than do people who do not have these personality traits.

Expectancy Effects

Expectancy effects in the perceptual process are the extent to which prior expectations bias how events, objects, and people are actually perceived. Sometimes the extent to which people perceive what they expect to perceive is amazing, as in the following dialogue from Shakespeare's *Hamlet*:

> *Polonius:*   My lord, the Queen would speak with you, and presently.
> *Hamlet:*   Do you see yonder cloud that's almost in the shape of a camel?
> *Polonius:*   By th' mass, and 'tis like a camel indeed.
> *Hamlet:*   Methinks it is like a weasel.
> *Polonius:*   It is back'd like a weasel.
> *Hamlet:*   Or like a whale?
> *Polonius:*   Very like a whale. (Act III, scene ii)

Of course, Shakespeare was making a joke about an individual (Polonius) who would seemingly agree to anything in an attempt to curry favor with the Prince of Denmark (Hamlet). Faced with an ambiguous stimulus, however, (in this case, a cloud), many individuals could be led to expect to see a particular object, and this expectation would color their perceptions.

Expectancy effects can also bias perceptions even in less ambiguous situations. For example, your perceptions of a committee to which you have been assigned recently may be positive if you were told by your boss that the committee's work is important and that it will be staffed by talented people from several departments. However, your perceptions may be negative if you were told that the committee exists solely for "political reasons" and contains some real deadwood from other departments. You might also perceive identical behavior by other members of the committee very differently under each set of expectations. Earlier, we noted that past experiences and learning are very important to the perceptual process. As a result, people often approach situations expecting certain things to happen or other people to have certain attributes. These expectations may strongly influence their perceptions of reality.

Another aspect of expectancy effects is the **self-fulfilling prophecy.** That is, expecting certain things to happen shapes the behavior of the perceiver in such a way that the expected is more likely to happen.[21] For example, a team leader who has been led to believe that a new employee has very high potential might do two things: (1) he might assess the employee's performance as being better than it really is (an expectancy effect) and (2) he might behave toward the new employee in such a fashion (for example, by providing encouragement or additional training) that the new employee's performance is, in fact, very good (a self-fulfilling prophecy).

ATTRIBUTIONS: PERCEIVING THE CAUSES OF BEHAVIOR

In the most general sense, the **attribution process** refers to the ways in which people come to understand the causes of others' (and their own) behavior.[22] Attributions play an important role in the process of person perception. The attributions we make about the causes of another's behavior may affect the judgments we make concerning fundamental characteristics or traits of that individual (what he or she is "really like").

The attributions that employees and managers make concerning the causes of behavior are important in understanding behavior in organizations. For example, managers who attribute poor performance directly to the subordinates involved will tend to behave much more punitively than will managers who attribute poor performance to circumstances beyond the control of the subordinates.[23] A manager who believes an employee failed to perform a task correctly because she lacked proper training might be very understanding and try to provide the employee with better instructions or training in the future. The same manager might be quite angry if she believes a subordinate made mistakes simply because the subordinate did not try very hard. The relationship between attributions and behavior will become clearer as we examine the attribution process.

The Attribution Process

Basically, people make attributions in an attempt to understand the behavior of other people and to make better sense of their environment. Individuals do not, of course, *consciously* make attributions in all circumstances (although it is possible that they *unconsciously* do so much of the time). However, under certain circumstances, people are very likely to make causal attributions consciously. For example, causal attributions are common when:

- The perceiver has been asked an explicit question about another's behavior. (Why did Angelita do that?)

- An unexpected event occurs. (I've never seen him behave that way. I wonder what's going on?)

- The perceiver depends on another person for a desired outcome. (I wonder why my boss made that comment about my expense account?)

- The perceiver experiences feelings of failure or loss of control. (I can't believe I failed my midterm exam!)

A basic model of the attribution process is shown in Figure 4.8. People infer "causes" to behaviors they observe in others, and these interpretations often largely determine their reactions to those behaviors. The perceived causes of behavior are a result of several *antecedents:* (1) the amount of information the perceiver has about the people and the situation and how that information is organized by the perceiver; (2) the perceiver's beliefs (implicit personality theories, what other people might do in a similar situation, and so on); and (3) the motivation of the perceiver (for example, the importance to the perceiver of making an accurate assessment). Recall our discussion of the internal factors influencing perception—learning, personality, and motivation. In the attribution process, we can see another example of the influence of these internal factors. The information and beliefs of the perceiver depend on previous experience and are influenced by the perceiver's personality.

Based on information, beliefs, and motives, the perceiver often distinguishes between internal and external causes of behavior; that is, whether people did something because of a real desire or because of the pressure of circumstances. The assigned cause of the behavior—whether internal or external—helps the perceiver to attach meaning to the event and is important for understanding the subsequent *consequences* for the perceiver. Among the consequences of this attribution process are the subsequent behavior of the perceiver in response to the behavior of others, the impact on feelings or emotions (how the perceiver now feels about events, people, and circumstances), and the effects on the perceiver's expectations of future events or behavior.

Internal Versus External Causes of Behavior

Imagine the following scene in a busy department. Stu, the office manager, and Mike, a section head for accounts receivable, are arguing loudly in Stu's

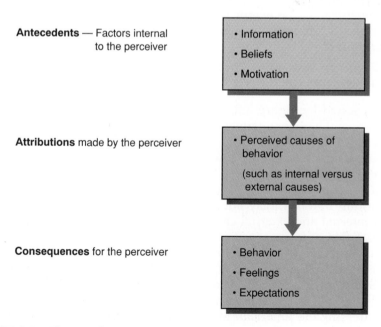

FIGURE 4.8   The Attribution Process

private office. Even though they were careful to close the door before start-ing their discussion, their voices have gotten louder until everyone else in the office has stopped working and is staring in discomfort and embarrass-ment at the closed door. After several minutes, Mike jerks open the door, yells a final, unflattering remark at Stu, slams the door, and stomps out of the department.

Anyone observing this scene is likely to wonder about what is going on and make certain attributions about why Mike behaved the way that he did. Attributions regarding Mike's behavior could focus on internal causes: Mike gets mad easily because he has a bad temper; Mike behaved this way be-cause he is immature and does not handle pressure well; or Mike is not getting his work done and thus was called on the carpet by Stu. On the other hand, some observers might make external attributions: Mike behaved this way because Stu provoked him or Mike and Stu's behavior is caused by unreasonable work goals imposed on the department by the organization. Of course, many individuals may perceive more than a single cause for a complex social interaction such as this. Also, as should be clear by now, different members of the department are likely to make different interpre-tations of the events they have just witnessed.

A central question in the attribution process concerns *how* perceivers determine whether the behavior of another person stems from internal causes (such as personality traits, emotions, motives, or ability) or external causes (other people, the situation, or chance). A widely accepted model proposed by Harold Kelley attempts to explain how people determine why others behave as they do.[24] This model, depicted in Figure 4.9, states that in making attributions, people focus on three major factors:

- *Consensus*—the extent to which others, faced with the same situa-tion, behave in a manner similar to the person perceived.
- *Consistency*—the extent to which the person perceived behaves in the same manner on other occasions when faced with the same situation.
- *Distinctiveness*—the extent to which the person perceived acts in the same manner in different situations.[25]

As suggested by Figure 4.9, under conditions of high consensus, high consistency, and high distinctiveness, the perceiver will tend to attribute the behavior of the person perceived to external causes. However, when con-sensus and distinctiveness are low, the perceiver will tend to attribute the behavior of the person to internal causes. Of course, other combinations of high and low consensus, consistency, and distinctiveness are possible. Some combinations, however, may not provide the perceiver with a clear choice between internal and external causes. Note that consistency is high under both attribution outcomes in Figure 4.9. When consistency is low, the per-ceiver may attribute the behavior to either or both internal and external causes. For example, imagine that a candidate running for president of the United States gives a speech in favor of price supports for tobacco while campaigning in North Carolina and in favor of removing those supports when addressing the American Medical Association. In this case, either or both internal and external attributions might be made—the audience

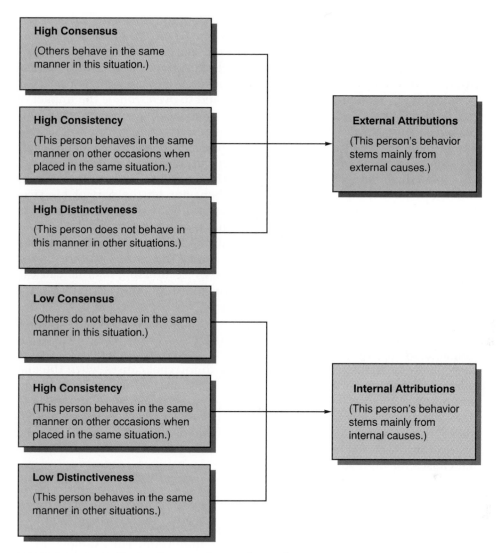

FIGURE 4.9 Kelley's Theory of Causal Attributions

Source: Adapted from R. A. Baron, and D. Byrne, *Social Psychology: Understanding Human Interaction,* 5th ed. Boston: Allyn and Bacon, 1987, 53.

"causes" the politician to change his speech or a character flaw "causes" the politician to tell these people what he thinks they want to hear.

In the example of the argument between Stu and Mike, observers would be likely to attribute causation to Mike if others typically did not have similar arguments with Stu (low consensus) and Mike often has similar arguments with others in a variety of work situations (low distinctiveness). On the other hand, if other individuals frequently have run-ins with Stu (high consensus) and Mike seldom has arguments in other situations with his fellow employees (high distinctiveness), then observers may attribute Mike's behavior to external causes (in this case, Stu). You may want to reread this paragraph while examining each portion of Figure 4.9 to make sure that you understand the differences leading to either external or internal attributions of behavior.

With regard to internal versus external causes of behavior, it is well worth noting that observers often make what is known as the **fundamental attribution error.** This error is the tendency to *underestimate* the impact of situational or external causes of behavior and to *overestimate* the impact of personal or internal causes of behavior when seeking to understand why people behave the way they do.[26] In organizations, employees often tend to assign blame for political behavior (Chapter 16), conflict (Chapter 14), or resistance to change (Chapter 21) to the individuals involved and do not recognize the effects of the dynamics of the situation. For example, a CEO might attribute a high level of political behavior on the part of his vice-presidents to aspects of their personalities and fail to recognize that competition for scarce resources is causing much of the political behavior.

Interestingly, there may be some cultural differences in the fundamental attribution error. For example, in North America, this error would be as just described (underestimating external causes, overestimating internal causes). In India, however, evidence indicates that the more common attribution error is to *overestimate* situational or external causes for the observed behavior.[27]

The fundamental attribution error is not the only bias that can influence judgments concerning internal versus external causes of behavior. For example, a recent study of 188 supervisors found that these individuals were more likely to attribute high performance to internal causes when the employee was a valued or high-status member of their work group. Employees who were less valued or perceived to be of lower status were less likely to have effective performance attributed to internal causes. Similarly, supervisors were more likely to attribute ineffective performance to internal causes for low-status employees and less likely to attribute failure to internal causes for high-status employees.[28]

Attributions of Success and Failure

In terms of task performance, the attributions that employees and managers make regarding success or failure are very important. For example, managers may make decisions about rewards and punishments depending on their perceptions of *why* subordinates have succeeded or failed in performing some task. In general, individuals often attribute their own (and others') success or failure to four causal factors: *ability, effort, task difficulty,* and *luck.* For example:

- I succeeded (or failed) because I had the skills to do the job (or because I did not have the skills to do the job). Such statements are *ability* attributions.
- I succeeded (or failed) because I worked hard (or because I did not work hard). Such statements are *effort* attributions.
- I succeeded (or failed) because it was easy (or because it was too hard). Such statements are attributions about *task difficulty.*
- I succeeded (or failed) because I was lucky (or unlucky). Such statements are attributions about *luck* or the circumstances surrounding the task.[29]

Causal attributions of ability and effort are internal, and causal attributions of task difficulty and luck are external. These attributions about success or failure are influenced by differences in self-esteem and locus of control—personality dimensions discussed in Chapter 3.

The organizational importance of these success and failure attributions is demonstrated by research in hospitals that examined the feedback provided to nurses by their managers.[30] When managers perceived that poor performance was due to a lack of effort, their feedback messages were more likely to be punitive or negative in tone. These attributions affected the specific content of feedback as well. For example, when managers inferred that poor performance was due to a lack of ability, message content focused on *instructions* for doing the job better; when poor performance was thought to be due to a lack of effort, message content tended to stress *orders* to be followed. Thus, managers in this study made attributions about the reasons for performance failures by the nursing staff, and these attributions influenced their communications behavior, as suggested by the model of the attribution process shown in Figure 4.8.

You will probably not be surprised to learn that people have a strong tendency to attribute their success with a task to internal factors (ability or effort) and to attribute their failures to external factors (task difficulty or luck).[31] This tendency is known as a **self-serving bias.** The tendency of employees to accept responsibility for good performance but to deny responsibility for poor performance can present a major challenge for managers and supervisors during performance appraisals.[32] A self-serving bias can also create problems in other ways. For example, it can prevent an individual from accurately assessing his or her own performance and abilities or make it more difficult for a group of managers to determine why some course of action they selected has failed. As a related issue, the general tendency to blame others for one's personal failures is a problem often associated with difficulties with effective performance and in establishing satisfying interpersonal relationships at work and in other social settings.[33]

SUMMARY

Perception is the psychological process whereby people select information from the environment and organize it to make sense of their world. Two major components of the perceptual process are selection and organization. People use perceptual selection to filter out less important information in order to focus on more important environmental cues. Both external factors in the environment and factors internal to the perceiver influence perceptual selection. Perceptual organization represents the process by which people assemble, organize, and categorize information from the environment. This organization process groups environmental stimuli into recognizable patterns (wholes), which allows the person to interpret what is perceived.

How people perceive each other is particularly important for understanding organizational behavior. Person perception is a function of the characteristics of the person perceived, the characteristics of the perceiver, and the situation within which the perception takes place. Unfortunately, the perceptual process can result in errors of judgment or understanding in a number of ways, such as denying the reality of disturbing information or assigning attributes to someone solely on the basis of some category or group they belong to. Fortunately, through training and experience, individuals can learn to judge or perceive others with greater accuracy.

Attribution deals with the perceived causes of behavior. People infer causes for the behavior of others, and their perceptions of why behavior is occurring have an important influence on their own subsequent behavioral responses and feelings. Whether behavior is internally caused by the "true" nature of the person or is externally caused by circumstances is an important attribution that people make about the behavior of others. Individuals also make attributions concerning task success and failure, which have important implications for behavior in organizations.

Key Words and Concepts

Attribution process
Expectancy effects
Field dependence/independence
Figure-ground principle
Fundamental attribution error
Halo effect
Implicit personality theories
Perception
Perceptual defense
Perceptual grouping

Perceptual organization
Perceptual selection
Perceptual set
Person perception
Pollyanna principle
Primacy effect
Projection
Self-fulfilling prophecy
Self-serving bias
Stereotyping

Discussion Questions

1. Explain perceptual selection and perceptual organization.

2. Identify the factors that determine the probability that some stimulus will be perceived.

3. Give an example from your own experience of when people seemed to interpret the same situation differently. Why did they do this?

4. Describe the key factors in person perception.

5. Identify and explain the most common perceptual errors.

6. From your own experience, which of the perceptual errors discussed seems most likely to occur? Give an example of a situation in which this error was made.

7. What perceptual errors by managers could create special problems in their evaluation of subordinates' job performance? In their evaluation of a job applicant?

8. Describe how a person determines whether someone else's behavior represents what he or she is truly like or simply reflects the circumstances of the situation.

9.   Explain the fundamental attribution error. Provide an example, either from your own experience or something you have read, of when an observer seemed to make the fundamental attribution error.

10. From your own experience, give an example of attributions made following either success or failure on some task.

◆ *MANAGEMENT CASES AND EXERCISES*

WOMEN AS MANAGERS

Gender-role stereotypes can limit the opportunity for women to advance to managerial positions in many firms. There is some evidence that these stereotypes are slowly changing. Nevertheless, the attitudes toward women as managers held by many individuals can present a difficult barrier to career opportunities for women.

Because specific attitudes and stereotypes can be pervasive and powerful influences on behavior, it is important to consider their role in the treatment—by both men and other women—of women in managerial positions. Attitudes about

the managerial abilities of women may affect how a manager or executive judges a woman's performance in a managerial role. In addition, such attitudes may influence the granting or withholding of developmental opportunities.

The questionnaire below is designed to help you explore your attitudes toward women as managers. Notice that each set of three statements asks you to select the one with which you *most* agree or which is most characteristic of you. From the two remaining statements, you then select the one with which you *least* agree.

Instructions: From each *set* (of three) statements below, select the one statement with which you *most agree* and place an M (for "most agree") in the blank to the right of that statement. For each *set*, also select the one statement with which you *least agree* and place an L (for "least agree") in the blank to the right of that statement. Note that one statement in each set will not be chosen at all.

1. A. Men are more concerned with the cars they drive than with the clothes their wives wear.   _____
    B. Any man worth his salt should not be blamed for putting his career above his family.   _____
    C. A person's job is the best single indicator of the sort of person he is.   _____

2. A. Parental authority and responsibility for discipline of the children should be divided equally between the husband and the wife.   _____
    B. It is less desirable for women to have jobs that require responsibility than for men.   _____
    C. Men should not continue to show courtesies to women, such as holding doors open for them and helping them with their coats.   _____

3. A. It is acceptable for women to assume leadership roles as often as men.   _____
    B. In a demanding situation, a female manager would be no more likely to break down than would a male manager.   _____
    C. There are some professions and types of businesses that are more suitable for men than for women.   _____

4. A. Recognition for a job well done is less important to women than it is to men.
    B. A woman should demand money for household and personal expenses as a right rather than a gift.
    C. Women are temperamentally fit for leadership positions. _____

5. A. Women tend to allow their emotions to influence their managerial behavior more than men. _____
    B. The husband and the wife should be equal partners in planning the family budget. _____
    C. If both husband and wife agree that sexual fidelity is not important, there is no reason why both should not have extramarital affairs. _____

6. A. A man's first responsibility is to his wife, not to his mother. _____
    B. A man who is able and willing to work hard has a good chance of succeeding in whatever he wants to do. _____
    C. Only after a man has achieved what he wants from life should he concern himself with the injustices in the world. _____

7. A. A wife should make every effort to minimize irritations and inconveniences for the male head of the household. _____
    B. Women can cope with stressful situations as effectively as men can. _____
    C. Women should be encouraged not to become sexually intimate with anyone, even their fiancés, before marriage. _____

8. A. The "obey" clause in the marriage service is insulting to women. _____
    B. Divorced men should help to support their children but should not be required to pay alimony if their former wives are capable of working. _____
    C. Women have the capacity to acquire the necessary skills to be successful managers. _____

9. A. Women can be aggressive in business situations that demand it. _____
    B. Women have an obligation to be faithful to their husbands. _____
    C. It is childish for a woman to assert herself by retaining her maiden name after marriage. _____

10. A. Men should continue to show courtesies to women, such as holding doors open for them or helping them with their coats. _____
    B. In job appointments and promotions, females should be given equal consideration with males. _____
    C. It is all right for a wife to have an occasional, casual, extramarital affair. _____

11. A. The satisfaction of her husband's sexual desires is a fundamental obligation of every wife. _____
    B. Most women should not want the kind of support that men traditionally have given them. _____
    C. Women possess the dominance to be successful leaders. _____

12. A. Most women need and want the kind of protection and support that men traditionally have given them. _____
    B. Women are capable of separating their emotions from their ideas. _____
    C. A husband has no obligation to inform his wife of his financial plans. _____

Score your responses by using the form and following the instructions on the next page. Your total score indicates your feelings about women managers. The higher your score, the more prone you are to hold negative gender-role stereotypes about women in management. Possible total scores range from 10 to 70; a "neutral" score (one that indicates neither positive nor negative attitudes about women as managers) is in the range of 30 to 40.[34]

Instructions:

1. Record your response for the indicated items in the spaces provided.
2. On the basis of the information provided below, determine the points for each item and enter these points in the space provided to the right. For example, if in item 3, you chose alternative A as the one with which you *most* agree and alternative B as the one with which you *least* agree, you should receive three points for item 3. Note that items 1 and 6 are "buffer items" and are *not* scored.
3. When you have scored all ten scorable items, add the points and record the total at the bottom of this page in the space provided. This is your total score.

Your Response	Item No.	Points per Item Response*						Points
		1	3		5		7	
	1	Not Scored						
M ____ L ____	2	C(M) B(L)	A(M) B(L)	C(M) A(L)	A(M) C(L)	B(M) A(L)	B(M) C(L)	
M ____ L ____	3	A(M) C(L)	A(M) B(L)	B(M) C(L)	C(M) B(L)	B(M) A(L)	C(M) A(L)	
M ____ L ____	4	C(M) B(L)	C(M) A(L)	A(M) B(L)	B(M) A(L)	A(M) C(L)	B(M) C(L)	
M ____ L ____	5	C(M) A(L)	C(M) B(L)	B(M) A(L)	A(M) B(L)	B(M) C(L)	A(M) C(L)	
	6	Not Scored						
M ____ L ____	7	B(M) A(L)	B(M) C(L)	C(M) A(L)	A(M) C(L)	C(M) B(L)	A(M) B(L)	
M ____ L ____	8	C(M) B(L)	C(M) A(L)	A(M) B(L)	B(M) A(L)	A(M) C(L)	B(M) C(L)	
M ____ L ____	9	A(M) B(L)	A(M) C(L)	C(M) B(L)	B(M) C(L)	C(M) A(L)	B(M) A(L)	
M ____ L ____	10	B(M) A(L)	B(M) C(L)	C(M) A(L)	A(M) C(L)	C(M) B(L)	A(M) B(L)	
M ____ L ____	11	C(M) A(L)	C(M) B(L)	B(M) A(L)	A(M) B(L)	B(M) C(L)	A(M) C(L)	
M ____ L ____	12	B(M) A(L)	B(M) C(L)	C(M) A(L)	A(M) C(L)	C(M) B(L)	A(M) B(L)	

Total ____

*M indicates item chosen as "most"; L indicates item chosen as "least."

THE INTERNSHIP

"Well, Ken, it's been a pleasure, and if I can ever do anything for you, feel free to give me a call." These words were spoken by Don Ahearn, industrial relations manager at ARC Corporation, to Ken Barrett, student intern, as they shook hands on the final day of Ken's internship project. As he drove away from ARC's plant in Boston, Ken could not help thinking about Mr. Ahearn's parting remark. Although the internship may have been a pleasure for Mr. Ahearn, Ken thought the most enjoyable part about it was getting it over with.

It all began in September. As a junior at Babson College in Wellesley, Massachusetts, Ken had enrolled in "Problems in Organizational Behavior," a course coordinated by Dr. Ned Berry. It was a field placement course, in which Dr. Berry placed students in a management internship position for the semester, and they would report back to him weekly with progress reports. For a final grade in the course, the students had to submit (1) a report of their particular project, counting 30 percent, (2) an organizational setting analysis of the impact of physical facilities on employee attitudes and behavior in each student's host organization, counting 40 percent, (3) an oral presentation to class members at the end of the semester, counting 15 percent, and (4) a grade submitted by the host organization, counting 15 percent. Dr. Berry produced a list of participating organizations and a brief description of the projects required at each. ARC Corporation listed its project as "research concerning the implementation of an automated personnel system." Since Ken was majoring in management and considering personnel management as a career choice, he requested placement at ARC. He received the placement, wrote a letter of introduction to Mr. Don Ahearn, and scheduled an appointment to meet with Mr. Ahearn one week later.

In that following week, Dr. Berry kept his students busy. Since each student was now placed in a host organization and was scheduled to meet with his or her contact person at the organization within two weeks, Dr. Berry used class periods to prepare the students for the internship experience. Through discussion and role-playing, Dr. Berry stressed the importance of setting project parameters at the initial interview. He felt it would benefit both the host company and the student to know exactly what to expect from each other, in terms of time spent with the company, work space provided, expense reimbursement, support systems such as use of copy machines and secretarial service, and, most important, what specific project outcomes were expected from the student by the end of the semester. He also stressed the fact that each student was on his or her own in setting the project parameters. Dr. Berry was available as an advisor, but each student was responsible for seeing his or her own project through.

Ken was anxious to begin work on his project, but he did have one concern which he discussed with Dr. Berry. Although he had a good understanding of the BASIC computer programming language, he was not an expert in computer programming in any way. He hoped that his project did not involve actual computer programming. Although Dr. Berry had only spoken with Mr. Ahearn over the phone and, like Ken, had only sketchy details about the project, he felt sure from his conversation with Mr. Ahearn that the project was primarily a research project and that Ken would not be involved in computer programming. Ken was relieved and looked forward to his appointment at ARC the following week.

The next Monday morning, Ken found ARC located in an old manufacturing facility in an industrial section of Boston. He met Mr. Ahearn in his basement office and began the interview by asking for a more detailed description of the project. Mr. Ahearn looked puzzled and replied, "Oh Ken, there is no project." He went on to explain that he had an idea of automating the personnel department to cut down on time he spent meeting the heavy reporting demands of the Office of Federal Contract Compliance and similar government agencies. He wanted Ken to do some research on automated personnel systems. Ken thought this was fine but pressed Mr. Ahearn for more details on what he wanted the automated personnel system to do, whether or not he would integrate payroll functions into the system, and how much he wanted to pay for the system.

Throughout the next hour, Mr. Ahearn remained vague and did not really address Ken's questions. Consequently, the entire time was spent attempting to define the project, and Ken had little time to discuss other parameters. He did mention that a requirement of the internship was to conduct an organizational setting analysis, which would require him to distribute a questionnaire to thirty or so ARC employees. Mr. Ahearn said that was fine but asked to see the questionnaire before it was distributed. At the end of the hour, Ken left disappointed. He had had no time to discuss parameters and still had only a vague idea of what he was to do. Since Mr. Ahearn would be out of town, Ken's next appointment with him was set for three weeks later.

During this first meeting, however, Ken did learn some things about ARC. It processed sheet aluminum for construction and was a division of a large Fortune 500 diversified communications firm. ARC employed roughly 700 people, 450 of which were hourly production workers. Personnel records were currently maintained on a Kardex file system. Although Mr. Ahearn made passing mention of a computer already used by ARC in payroll, Ken did not see it, and Ahearn did not seem interested in talking much about it.

Not sure where to begin and knowing nothing about automated personnel systems, Ken decided to begin in the college library. He found some articles dealing indirectly with automated data processing in the personnel setting; there seemed little written on the subject. After this research, he called four computer firms to gather information and to try to arrange interviews. All four of the computer firms assured Ken that there was no such thing as an automated personnel system. However, they did state that a distributed processor could certainly be tailored to personnel operations.

At this point in each conversation, two problems developed. First, when the sales representatives asked Ken for details on the applications of the system, he was unable to give them, as he did not know them himself. Second, the computer firms were generally not very enthusiastic about spending much time speaking with a college student "doing research," as this would probably not lead to a sale. To complicate matters, Mr. Ahearn had asked Ken not to use the name ARC Corporation in any of his inquiries, for reasons Mr. Ahearn did not disclose. Only one computer firm, Sonex Equipment, offered to speak with Ken in person but only if he would bring a letter of introduction from "whatever firm you're doing work for." Although disheartened, Ken called Mr. Ahearn and obtained the letter. He then spent two hours with the sales representative at Sonex and left with a great deal of information on a distributed processor priced at twenty-four thousand dollars.

At his next appointment with Mr. Ahearn, Ken planned to present the information he had received at Sonex and get Mr. Ahearn's reaction to it. However, when he appeared for his appointment, Mr. Ahearn led Ken into a vacant office, brought in a large box, and placed it on the desk. He then told him, "There's a computer in the box. Why don't you set it up and play around with it for a while, so you'll know what we already have available." He explained that not much had been done with the computer since ARC purchased it, although he had purchased a prerecorded blackjack program and had played it at home a few times with his kids. Before opening the box, Ken explained about his interview with Sonex and handed Mr. Ahearn the sales material he had received. Mr. Ahearn said, "Oh," placed the sales material on the desk, and went back to his office. Ken was disappointed that Mr. Ahearn did not take the time to look at the material, but he proceeded to open the box on the desk. He did not know that Ahearn already had a computer.

The contents of the box turned out to be a small personal computer, consisting of a CRT display, a keyboard, and a cassette tape recorder used for data storage. Included was a beginner's instruction manual for programming the computer in BASIC. Ken recalled seeing such systems advertised for about six hundred dollars.

Since Mr. Ahearn did not seem interested in discussing his research at Sonex, Ken set the computer up and "played around with it" for about two hours. When he went to find Mr. Ahearn around noon, which was his scheduled time to leave, Mr. Ahearn had already left the building for lunch. Ken left a note with Mr. Ahearn's secretary that read:

> Mr. Ahearn: I will be back next week at this same time. If that's not a good time for you, give me a call at home at 555-1234. Also, I will bring a copy of my organizational setting analysis questionnaire for you to look at. If you like it, maybe you could give me that plant tour you promised, and we could distribute the questionnaire to twenty or so people. Sincerely, Ken.

In the following week, Ken wrote his questionnaire and first presented it to Dr. Berry, who remarked, "It is one of the better surveys I've seen." With that, Ken brought his questionnaire to ARC the following week. Since Mr. Ahearn had meetings scheduled all day, he only had a moment to speak to Ken and put the questionnaire in his "in" basket. They had a short conversation about ARC's personal computer, and Mr. Ahearn asked Ken, "Do you think we could put an automated personnel system on it?" Ken explained briefly some of the limitations of the BASIC language, but since Mr. Ahearn was on his way to a meeting, there was not much time to talk. Ken spent the next several hours looking through the computer manual, then left. His next appointment with Mr. Ahearn was two weeks later.

During those next two weeks, Ken did some thinking about the project. He felt he had accomplished nothing, and the semester was half over. Since he sensed that ARC was really not interested in a large computer system but more interested in the personal computer, he thought he should change the direction of the project to center on the personal computer. He was beginning to feel that the outside research work was only "busy work," so he decided to present Mr. Ahearn with an alternative project. He would suggest that he discontinue the outside research and concentrate on writing a simulation program for the personal computer. Although he did not think the personal computer was appropriate for such heavy commercial applications, Mr. Ahearn did, and Ken thought the best way to illustrate the computer's limitations might be to make it work and demonstrate how much time was involved in the process. He would offer the simulation program alternative to Mr. Ahearn at their next meeting. He also resolved to get Mr. Ahearn's approval on the organizational setting analysis questionnaire, so he could get started on that.

When Ken visited ARC for his next appointment, Mr. Ahearn's secretary informed him that Mr. Ahearn had left on a business trip two days ago and had left no message. She suggested that he give Mr. Ahearn a call the following Friday to schedule another appointment.

When he called on Friday, neither he nor Mr. Ahearn mentioned the business trip, but they did set up another appointment. Ken also took the opportunity to ask Mr. Ahearn if he had looked over the questionnaire. Mr. Ahearn said yes, so Ken asked him what he thought of it. Mr. Ahearn replied, "I find it unacceptable." Ken pressed for elaboration, but Mr. Ahearn was vague, replying, "You know we have three unions here, and the situation is volatile. I can't have you asking my people some of these questions." This surprised Ken, because although he did know that Mr. Ahearn dealt with three unions, he also remembered Mr. Ahearn bragging about how great relations were with all three unions. He told Mr. Ahearn that they would need to discuss it at their next meeting, and Mr. Ahearn agreed. In the interim, he reviewed his questionnaire to try and determine which questions might be objectionable to ARC. He could pinpoint none. He hoped that Ahearn did not object to more than five or six of the thirty-one questions, as the questionnaire worked best when taken as a whole. Dropping or modifying more than a few questions would render the questionnaire far less useful.

At the next meeting, Ken was shocked to find that Mr. Ahearn objected to sixteen of the thirty-one questions and did not like any of the remaining questions either. In a mocking tone of voice, Mr. Ahearn read some of the questions back to Ken and asked what they were suppose to measure. Although Ken attempted to explain, he could see he was getting nowhere. He then told Mr. Ahearn that the organizational setting analysis was required of all interns and that if he could not distribute a questionnaire, he would have to conduct interviews. They both agreed that interviews were too time-consuming, but Mr. Ahearn still did not want to distribute a questionnaire, and Ken still could not get a clear reason why. Mr. Ahearn remarked that ARC had conducted an extensive attitude survey two years ago and offered to get the results for Ken, saying, "Maybe you can look at those results and do something with them." At a loss for what to do next, Ken agreed to look at the results. Mr. Ahearn said he would leave the results with his secretary so Ken could pick them up on the following Friday. They spent the remaining time discussing the simulation program, about which Mr. Ahearn was very enthusiastic.

When Ken went to ARC the following Friday to pick up the results, Ahearn's secretary said that Mr. Ahearn had left nothing with her and had left several days ago on business.

Not knowing what to do next, Ken turned to Dr. Berry. During their weekly meetings, he had kept Dr. Berry informed of the problems he had been having at ARC, and the professor had suggested possible solutions. However, at this point, Dr. Berry offered him the option of doing some outside research work in lieu of the organizational setting analysis. Dr. Berry said, "This is bound to prove more valuable than continued fighting over the questionnaire." Since his classmates were still required to do the analysis, this again felt a little like defeat, but Ken gladly agreed.

When Ken finally did obtain the results of the ARC study, they turned out to be the text of a speech the company president had made to the workers, summarizing some of the firm's problems. Ken was glad he had taken Dr. Berry's option, as the speech provided no information for analyzing the organizational setting.

Over the next several weeks, Ken worked on his computer simulation program. Since he was not an expert programmer, the program took about twenty-two hours to write, test, and enter on the ARC personal computer. The finished program was roughly four hundred steps long and held a sample of twenty employee files. He was pleased because he felt the program ran well and really did simulate what could be (and could not be) done with the personal computer. He scheduled an appointment with Mr. Ahearn to show him the program. Since Mr. Ahearn had been busy at meetings during Ken's last few appointments, he had not seen much of what the student had been doing. Mr. Ahearn informed Ken that he had invited his boss, the personnel manager, to see the presentation with him.

In addition to the simulation program, Ken prepared a six-page report on what qualities he felt ARC should look for in a computer for the personnel department. Since he knew that Mr. Ahearn and his department did not know much about computers, he thought an informational report of this type would be most helpful. Based on the criteria set forth in the report, he concluded with a recommendation that the small personal computer not be used in the personnel department. Since he felt that Mr. Ahearn really did want to use the existing computer, he hesitated before making this recommendation, but

based on the criteria set up in his report, his only choice was to recommend that the existing system not be used.

The presentation with Mr. Ahearn and the personnel manager went well, although it consisted only of Ken letting both men run through the simulation program and answering a few questions about it. Neither asked to see his report or recommendations, so he did not push those forward. At the end of the demonstration, the personnel manager remarked, "That's an excellent program, Ken. It looks like you put a lot of work into it." Mr. Ahearn agreed, then shook hands with Ken and made the remark appearing at the beginning of the case. Ken handed him the report and simulation tape, and his internship was over.

One week later, Dr. Berry received the grade determined for Ken by ARC: a B minus. Ken was disappointed and wondered what he had done wrong and what exactly he had learned from the whole experience.[35]

QUESTIONS

1. Make a list of the possible differences in the way the internship was perceived by Ken and by Mr. Ahearn.

2. To what things might Ken attribute Mr. Ahearn's behavior?

3. To what things would you expect Ken to attribute his "failure"?

4. What were the major problems faced by Ken during his internship project? Why did these problems arise?

5. If you were given this internship, what would you have done to improve the situation?

References

1. Adapted from Sekuler, R., and Blake, R. *Perception*, 2d ed. New York: McGraw-Hill, 1990, 263.
2. Banks, W. P., and Krajicek, D. Perception. *Annual Review of Psychology*, 1991, *42*, 305–331; Sekuler and Blake, *Perception*.
3. Simon, H. A. Invariants of Human Behavior. *Annual Review of Psychology*, 1990, *41*, 1–19.
4. Dearborn, D., and Simon, H. A. Selective Perception: A Note on the Departmental Identifications of Executives. *Sociometry*, 1958, *21*, 140–144.
5. Walsh, J. P. Selectivity and Selective Perception: An Investigation of Managers' Belief Structure and Information Processing. *Academy of Management Journal*, 1988, *31*, 873–896.
6. McBurney, D. H., and Collings, V. B. *Introduction to Sensation/Perception*, 2d ed. Englewood Cliffs, N.J.: Prentice-Hall, 1984, 327–345.
7. Adapted from Sekuler and Blake, *Perception*, 16.
8. Matlin, M. W. *Perception*. Boston: Allyn and Bacon, 1983, 287–307.

9.   Based on Levine, R. V. The Pace of Life. *American Scientist,* September/October, 1990, 450–459; Levine, R. V., and Wolff, E. Social Time: The Heartbeat of Culture. *Psychology Today,* March 1985, 28–35.

10. Aslin, R. N., and Smith, L. B. Perceptual Development. *Annual Review of Psychology,* 1988, *39,* 435–473; Banks and Krajicek, Perception; Cutting, J. C. Perception and Information. *Annual Review of Psychology,* 1987, *38,* 61–90; Galambos, J. A., Abelson, R. P., and Black, J. B. (eds.). *Knowledge Structures.* Hillsdale, N.J.: Lawrence Erlbaum, 1986.

11. Based on Ornstein, S. The Hidden Influences of Office Design. *Academy of Management Executive,* 1989, *3,* 144–147; Ornstein, S. Impression Management through Office Design. In R. A. Giacalone and T. Rosenfeld (eds.), *Impression Management in the Organization.* Hillsdale, N.J.: Lawrence Erlbaum, 1989, 411–426.

12. Ilgen, D. R., and Klein, H. J. Organizational Behavior. *Annual Review of Psychology,* 1989, *40,* 332.

13. Based on Baron, R. M., Graziano, W. G., and Stangor, C. Social Perception and Social Cognition. In R. M. Baron, W. G. Graziano, and C. Stangor (eds.), *Social Psychology.* Fort Worth: Holt, Rinehart, and Winston, 1991, 113; Park, B. A Method for Studying the Development of Impressions of Real People. *Journal of Personality and Social Psychology,* 1986, *51,* 907–917.

14. Baron, Graziano, and Stangor. Social Perception and Social Cognition, 122–123.

15. See, for example, Zebrowitz-McArthur, L. Person Perception in Cross-Cultural Perspective. In M. H. Bond (ed.), *The Cross-Cultural Challenge to Social Psychology.* Newbury Park, Calif.: Sage, 1988, 245–265.

16. Based on White, K. F., Luk, V., and Patel, M. Personal Attributes of American and Chinese Business Associates: A Study of Intercultural Perceptions. Paper presented at the Southwest Federation of Academic Disciplines annual meeting, San Antonio, Texas, March 6, 1988.

17. Descriptions of these and other perceptual errors can be found in Brigham, J. C. *Social Psychology.* Boston: Little, Brown, 1986, 38–41; Cook, M. (ed.), *Issues in Person Perception.* London: Methuen, 1984; Higgins, E. T., and Bargh, J. A. Social Cognition and Social Perception. *Annual Review of Psychology,* 1987, *38,* 369–425.

18. Fisher, C. D., Schoenfeldt, L. F., and Shaw, J. B. *Human Resource Management.* Boston: Houghton Mifflin, 1990, 269–270.

19. See, for example, Cook, *Issues in Person Perception;* DePaulo, B. M., Kenny, D. A., Hoover, C. W., Webb, W., and Oliver, P. V. Accuracy of Person Perception: Do People Know What Kinds of Impressions They Convey? *Journal of Personality and Social Psychology,* 1987, *52,* 303–315; Kruglanski, A. W. The Psychology of Being Right: The Problem of Accuracy in Social Perception and Cognition. *Psychological Bulletin,* 1989, *106,* 395–409.

20. Rice, J. W. When Fatherly Concern Is Not Welcome. *The Wall Street Journal,* February 25, 1991, A10.

21. Baron, Graziano, and Stangor, Social Perception and Social Cognition, 129; Miller, D. T., and Turnbull, W. Expectancies and Interpersonal Processes. *Annual Review of Psychology,* 1986, *37,* 233–256.

22. Baron, R. A., and Byrne, D. *Social Psychology: Understanding Human Interaction,* 6th ed. Boston: Allyn and Bacon, 1991, 55–83; Jaspars, J., Fincham, F. D., and Hewstone, M. *Attribution Theory and Research: Conceptual, Developmental and Social Dimensions.* London: Academic Press, 1983.

23. Martinko, M. J., and Gardner, W. L. The Leader-/Member Attribution Process. *Academy of Management Review,* 1987, *12,* 235–249.

24. Kelley, H. H. The Process of Causal Attribution. *American Psychologist,* 1973, *28,* 107–128.

25. Good explanations of Kelley's model may be found in Baron and Byrne, *Social Psychology,* 57–64; Brigham, *Social Psychology,* 49–53.

26. Baron, Graziano, and Stangor, Social Perception and Social Cognition, 144–148; Harvey, J. H., and Weary, G. Current Issues in Attribution Theory and Research. *Annual Review of Psychology,* 1984, *35,* 431–432.

27. Miller, J. G. Culture and the Development of Everyday Causal Explanation. *Journal of Personality and Social Psychology,* 1984, *46,* 961–978.

28. Heneman, R. L., Greenberger, D. B., and Anonyus, C. Attributions and Exchanges: The Effects of Interpersonal Factors on the Diagnosis of Employee Performance. *Academy of Management Journal,* 1989, *32,* 466–476.

29. Babladelis, G. *The Study of Personality.* New York: Holt, Rinehart and Winston, 1984, 76.

30. Kim, Y. Y., and Miller, K. I. The Effects of Attributions and Feedback Goals on the Generation of Supervisory Feedback Message Strategies. *Management Communication Quarterly,* 1990, *4,* 6–29.

31. Olson, J. M., and Ross, M. Attribution: Past, Present, and Future. In J. H. Harvey and G. Wells (eds.), *Attribution: Basic Issues and Applications.* New York: Academic Press, 1988, 282–311.

32. Sims, H. P., and Gioia, D. A. Performance Failure: Executive Response to Self-Serving Bias. *Business Horizons,* January–February, 1984, 64–71.

33. Tennen, H., and Affleck, G. Blaming Others for Threatening Events. *Psychological Bulletin,* 1990, *108,* 209–232.

34. Adapted from Yost, E. B., and Herbert, T. T. Attitudes toward Women as Managers. In L. D. Goodstein and J. W. Pfeiffer (eds.), *The 1985 Annual: Developing Human Resources.* San Diego, Calif.: University Associates, 1985, 117–127. Reprinted with permission.

35. Case prepared by Professors Neal Thornberry and Joseph Weintraub of Babson College with the help of student Carl Brooks based on his experiences as a student intern and reprinted with permission. Copyright © 1981.

CHAPTER 5

INDIVIDUAL PROBLEM-SOLVING STYLES

LEARNING OBJECTIVES

When you have finished studying this chapter, you should be able to:

* Describe the four stages of the problem-solving model.
* State two methods that individuals use to gather data.
* State two methods that individuals use to evaluate information.
* Identify your own problem-solving style.
* List the strengths and weaknesses of four individual problem-solving styles.

OUTLINE

138

BILL GATES, MICROSOFT

Microsoft was started by Bill Gates in 1975 when he was just nineteen years old and had dropped out of Harvard University. Now with some 5,200 employees and over $1 billion in sales, it offers a broad range of products in the personal computer software business. How has he done it?

One key is his ability to spread himself around. He and his employees break down technological improvements into concise business goals that can be assigned to small groups of programmers and marketers. Microsoft has a dozen of these groups, some of which employ as few as thirty people. Each group is in charge of a particular type of software. Each knows exactly how its software stacks up against its competitors by every conceivable measure, from the technical sophistication of a program to the amount of labor that went into building it. These groups are small enough to permit Gates to chat with key members around a coffee table. If a group does not outperform its competitors, it hears about it from Gates, either personally or through the company's electronic mail (E-mail). Gates tries to personally respond to each message he gets on his E-mail the same day he receives it.

Although he freely delegates, his capacity for business and technical details enables him to understand intimately both the forest and the trees. At meetings with his managers, he is just as likely to check the math in hand-outs and overhead slides for errors as he is to critique fuzzy marketing strategies. He also loves to join Microsoft programmers in the brainstorming sessions that give birth to new products. According to Gates, it is very important to him and to those who work with him for Microsoft to feel like a small company. In small companies, everybody "hangs in there" together.

Microsoft works its employees long and hard. Many routinely put in seventy-five-hour weeks. But turnover is low—about 8 to 10 percent. Gates keeps people by telling them of his vision—to be the dominant manufacturer of disk operating systems—and by having their stock options related to the overall performance of the organization. Programmers can earn just as much as managers, and when an employee gets promoted, Gates has a big celebration for the person.

Just like other organizations, Microsoft has problems. First, the company has a tendency to introduce a mediocre product the first time out. It may get it right eventually, but Gates is sometimes too willing to compromise on design aspects just to get the business going. Therefore, some of its marketing research tends to be too elementary. Second, Gates is a thinker who likes new ideas. One of his employees once said, "Microsoft makes the world's best plumbing, but we never think about the toilet seat."[1]

A question often asked is: "What factors contribute to being a successful manager?" From reading about Microsoft, you might say that Bill Gates has employees who are talented, have good interpersonal skills, the right experience, lots of energy, and are sometimes just plain lucky. While each of these factors can obviously contribute to a manager's job success, hidden factors also often underlie the success of many managers and employees. These factors have to do with perceptions, attributions, personality, and attitudes. Yet because they are hidden or covert (see Figure 1.1), they are hard for others to see. All these factors contribute to a **problem-solving style** that reflects the way a person visualizes and thinks about situations. Thus, problem-solving style involves perceptions and ways of thinking.

INDIVIDUAL PROBLEM-SOLVING PROCESSES

Most people have various problem-solving abilities. They use these abilities to attain high levels of skill in such activities as playing chess, analyzing stocks, conducting business deals, and learning languages. These skills are not easily learned, sometimes requiring years of experience and thousands of hours of practice. Nevertheless, people compress years of experience and learning into split-second decision making.

The same problem-solving processes that underlie the greatest mental accomplishments also create some problems. For instance, individuals tend to believe that important events occur more frequently than they do and everything is a crisis. People also tend to be overconfident and make complex decisions when they have little information. Finally, people are not very good at assessing the interrelationships of factors affecting a decision. That is, people often view factors one at a time and do not look at whether all the factors fit together to form a coherent picture. Unless complex relationships are very clear, many people tend to rely on prior experiences and perceive things that are not there.[2]

In making day-to-day decisions, individuals rely on a general problem-solving process. A basic model of this process is shown in Figure 5.1. It shows how people process information and make decisions.

Starting at the left in Figure 5.1, the decision maker responds to two major sources of stimuli: (1) internal (such as job requirements and communications with employees); and (2) external (such as customers, governmental bodies, and suppliers). The decision maker's frame of reference includes such factors as personal needs, personality characteristics, past experiences, and attitudes.[3] Perceptual filtering, or information bias, relates to the person's attitude structure (see Chapter 3), which may range from being too rigid to flexible. Recall that in Chapter 3, we described a person having a rigid attitude as a dogmatic person. Such a person holds fast to attitudes and beliefs, even in the face of facts to the contrary. On the other hand, a person having a flexible attitude is less likely to ignore new information or ways of doing activities.

The amount of information that an individual can process also affects that person's ability to make a decision. **Cognitive complexity** measures a person's ability to process information.[4] People with low cognitive complexity filter out much of the information in the environment because they do not want to be overwhelmed by it. If they are overwhelmed, they become frustrated with their inability to make sense of what is happening in their

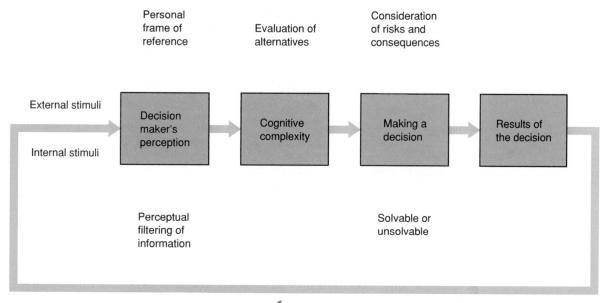

FIGURE 5.1 Individual Problem-Solving Process

Source: Adapted from A. J. Rowe and R. O. Mason, *Managing with Style: A Guide to Understanding, Assessing, and Improving Decision Making.* San Francisco: Jossey-Bass, 1987, 61.

environment. On the other hand, Bill Gates and other people with high cognitive complexity process a lot of divergent information, evaluate numerous alternative possibilities, and process this information quickly. An individual's self-image, values, and personality all affect the processing of information.

If the individual has the cognitive complexity to process the information, then he or she must be able to interpret it. **Problem interpretation** refers to the process of giving meaning and definition to those problems that have been recognized by the individual. Perceptions, the filtering out of new information, and defensiveness all may contribute to ineffective problem interpretation. There is no simple, one-to-one relationship between availability of data, the person's ability to process it, and how the data are processed in the problem interpretation stage.

In recent years, Japanese products have gained increasing popularity in the United States because many customers believe that these products, such as cameras, cars, and VCRs, among others, are more reliable. To determine the reasons for these differences, a researcher asked first-line managers working for Japanese and U.S. organizations to rate the importance of various manufacturing objectives within their firm.[5] Not only were Japanese managers much more likely to rate quality problems higher, but they also believed that the quality problems were much more serious than did their U.S. counterparts. Japanese managers emphasized quality as their primary manufacturing objective, policies were formulated and communicated focusing on that objective, and workers displayed a strong commitment to the quality goal. In the United States, quality received far less emphasis by managers than meeting production schedules, and its importance was not communicated to employees by these first-line managers. Therefore, when a Japanese manager received feedback on quality, even the smallest defect was interpreted as a problem and received attention. In the United States, many quality problems simply were not interpreted as significant enough to warrant a first-line manager's attention. Today, with the emphasis on quality, many U.S. organizations are reinterpreting their quality data and taking actions to drastically improve their quality. Tennant Company, described in Chapter 6, is a good example of how one organization successfully tackled the quality problem and won.

Although individuals often decide to work on problems that offer them opportunities for success, deciding which problems to tackle is not easy. How people define and rank problems is heavily influenced by the risks and consequences involved, including their judgment of the problem's solvability. Many individuals run a quick feasibility check on the problem to see if it is solvable. Only if they judge it solvable will they invest further energy to understand its causes and implications. Thus, individuals tend not to think very much about a problem unless they sense that it is solvable. Managers must also weigh the risks and consequences of not making a decision. For example, Jim Stevens, a manager at Dart Transportation, told the authors, "I could spend my time making rules to guide the decisions of my subordinates. But the real problem is for me to decide what my boss wants. Once I can discover this, the consequences and risks of choosing one alternative over another become clearer. Unfortunately, my boss seldom tells me."

Because of the uncertainty in many management and business issues, managers face having to make a lot of decisions based on their judgment and experience.[6] These decisions lead to an outcome: inaction or action. Customers, suppliers, governmental representatives, and others give managers feedback about the success of the decision.

PSYCHOLOGICAL FUNCTIONS IN PROBLEM SOLVING

Psychologist Carl Gustav Jung defined four psychological functions that are involved in information gathering and evaluation: sensation, intuitive, thinking, and feeling.[7] A primary orientation in terms of these factors dominates an individual's behavior. However, a person may also have a secondary orientation for fine-tuning his or her basic approach to perceiving and making judgments about the world. According to Jung, individuals gather information either by sensation or intuition—but not by both simultaneously. These two functions represent the orientation extremes in gathering information. **Sensing** means that you would rather work with known facts than look for possibilities. **Intuitive** means that you would rather look for possibilities than work with facts. Similarly, the thinking and feeling functions represent the orientation extremes in evaluating information.

Thinking means that you base your judgments more on impersonal analysis and logic than on personal values. **Feeling** means that you base your judgments more on personal values than on impersonal analysis.

Before reading any farther, you should complete the questionnaire in Table 5.1. Because this questionnaire has been validated with many students, your scores may be reasonably accurate and usually remain relatively constant for some time. We help you to interpret your scores in the remainder of this chapter. According to Jung, only one of the four functions is dominant in an individual. The dominant function is normally backed up by one (and only one) of the functions from the other set of paired opposites. For example, the thinking function may be supported by the sensation function, or vice versa. The sensation-thinking combination characterizes most of the people in today's Western industrialized societies. As a result, intuition and feeling are the functions most likely to be disregarded, undeveloped, or repressed. However, Jung also believed that individuals tend to move toward a balance, or integration, of the four psychological functions.

Let's first consider each of the four psychological functions as a dominant type. We will then consider the two information-gathering orientations (sensation and intuition) in combination with the two information-evaluating orientations (thinking and feeling) as they relate to managerial styles.

Sensation versus Intuition in Gathering Information

Individuals perceive or gather information differently, according to whether sensation or intuition dominates. Table 5.2 describes behavioral patterns and general characteristics of people with sensation- and intuition-type information-gathering styles. Over 56 percent of U.S. managers report a preference for gathering information through sensation, while 44 percent indicate a preference for intuition.[8] However, people may not belong to one clearly defined group or the other; the classification merely provides a good starting point for understanding ourselves and the expectations others have of us.

Sensation-Type Person   The **sensation-type person** wants, trusts, and remembers facts and would rather work with facts than look for possibilities and relationships.[9] Such a person believes in experience and relies on the past in approaching current problems. When interviewing someone for a job, a sensation-type manager wants to know the details of the applicant's past experience. The applicant's experience provides this type of manager with a basis for a sound decision. The sensation-type person uses such words as *actual, down-to-earth, realistic, practical,* and *utility* when making a presentation to others. In terms of a problem-solving style, the sensation-type person tends to:

- dislike new problems, unless there are standard ways to solve them;
- enjoy using skills already acquired more than learning new ones;
- work steadily, with a realistic idea of how long a task will take;
- work through a task or problem to a conclusion;
- be impatient when details get complicated; and
- distrust creative inspirations.

Please indicate the response that usually describes *your* concerns and behaviors. There are no *right* or *wrong* answers to the questions. For each question, indicate which of the two alternative statements is most characteristic of you. Some statements may seem to be equally characteristic or uncharacteristic of you. While we anticipated this, try to choose the statement that is *relatively more* characteristic of what you do or feel in your everyday life. You will be working with pairs of statements and will have 5 points to distribute among the statements. Points may be divided between each A and B statement in any of the following combination pairs:

- If A is completely characteristic of you and B is completely uncharacteristic, write a "5" on your answer sheet under A and "0" under B, thus:

A	B
5	0

- If A is considerably more characteristic of you and B is somewhat characteristic, write a "4" on your answer sheet under A and a "1" under B, thus:

A	B
4	1

- If A is only slightly more characteristic of you than B, write a "3" on your answer sheet under A, and a "2" under B, thus:

A	B
3	2

- Each of the above three combinations may be used in reverse order. For example, should you feel that B is slightly more characteristic of you than A, write a "2" on your answer sheet under A and a "3" under B, thus: (And so on, for A = 1, B = 4, or A = 0, B = 5.)

A	B
2	3

Be sure that the numbers you assign to each pair sum to 5 points. Relate each question in the index to your own behavior. *Remember, there is no right or wrong answer.* Attempts to give a "correct" response merely distort the meaning of your answers and render the inventory's results valueless.

Questions		**Score**
1. Are you more	(a) pragmatic	A B
	(b) idealistic	
2. Are you more impressed by	(a) standards	A B
	(b) sentiments	
3. Are you more interested in that which	(a) convinces you by facts	A B
	(b) emotionally moves you	
4. It is worse to be	(a) impractical	A B
	(b) having a boring routine	
5. Are you more attracted to	(a) a person with good common sense	A B
	(b) a creative person	
6. In judging others, are you more swayed by	(a) the rules	A B
	(b) the situation	
7. Are you more interested in	(a) what has happened	A B
	(b) what can happen	
8. Do you more often have	(a) presence of mind	A B
	(b) warm emotions	
9. Are you more frequently	(a) a realistic sort of person	A B
	(b) an imaginative sort of person	

TABLE 5.1 *continued*

Questions		Score
10. Are you more	(a) faithful (b) logical	A B
11. Are you more	(a) action-oriented (b) creation-oriented	A B
12. Which guides you more	(a) your brain (b) your heart	A B
13. Do you take pride in your	(a) realistic outlook (b) imaginative ability	A B
14. Which is more of a personal compliment	(a) you are consistent in your reasoning (b) you are considerate of others	A B
15. Are you more drawn to	(a) basics (b) implications	A B
16. It is better to be	(a) fair (b) sentimental	A B
17. Would you rather spend time with	(a) realistic people (b) imaginative people	A B
18. Would you describe yourself as	(a) hard (b) soft	A B
19. Would your friends say that you are	(a) someone who is filled with new ideas (b) someone who is a realist	A B
20. It is better to be called a person who shows	(a) feelings (b) reasonable consistency	A B

Answer Form

Please enter the numbers for your response to each question in the appropriate columns.

	Column				Column	
	I	*II*			*III*	*IV*
Questions	*A*	*B*		**Questions**	*A*	*B*
1	___	___		2	___	___
3	___	___		4	___	___
5	___	___		6	___	___
7	___	___		8	___	___
9	___	___		10	___	___
11	___	___		12	___	___
13	___	___		14	___	___
15	___	___		16	___	___
17	___	___		18	___	___
19	___	___		20	___	___
Total	☐	☐			☐	☐
Score	S	N			T	F

TABLE 5.1 *continued*

Directions for Scoring

1.   Add down each column to obtain a total for score "A" and write it in the total box. Do the same for "B."

2.   Compare the totals for columns I and II. If your highest point total is for "A," circle the letter **S**. "**S**" refers to sensation. If your highest point total is for "B," circle the letter **N**. "**N**" refers to intuitive. If your total scores for A and B are equal, circle the letter **S**.

3.   Compare the totals for columns III and IV. If your highest point total is for "A," circle the letter **T**. "**T**" refers to thinking. If your highest point total is for "B," circle the letter **F**. "**F**" refers to feeling. If your total scores for A and B are equal, circle the letter **T**.

Source: This questionnaire is based on the earlier works by D. Kiersay and M. Bates, *Please Understand Me.* Del Mar, Calif.: Prometheus Nemesis Book Company, 1987; W. H. Agor, *Intuitive Management: Integrating Left and Right Brain Management Skills.* Englewood Cliffs, N.J.: Prentice-Hall, 1984; and S. Hirsh and J. M. Kummerow, *Lifetypes.* New York: Warner Books, 1989.

The sensation-type person dislikes dealing with unstructured problems because they contain considerable uncertainty. These usually require the individual to exercise judgment in deciding what to do and how to do it. Such a person may experience great anxiety in making decisions in hazy areas because their consequences are not clear-cut. The sensation-type per-

---

TABLE 5.2   Comparisons of Sensation and Intuitive Types of People

Characteristic	Sensation Type	Intuitive Type
Focus	Details, practical, action, getting things done quickly.	Patterns, innovation, ideas, long-range planning.
Time Orientation	Present, live life as it is.	Future achievement, change, re-arrange.
Work Environment	Pay attention to detail, patient with details and do not make factual errors, not risk takers.	Look at the "big picture," patient with complexity, risk takers.
Strengths	Pragmatic, results-oriented, objective, competitive.	Original, imaginative, creative, idealistic.
Possible Weaknesses	Impatient when projects get delayed, decide issues too quickly, lack long-range perspective, can oversimplify a complex task.	Lack follow-through, impractical, make errors of facts, take people's contributions for granted.

Source: Adapted from B. Roach, "Organizational Decision Makers: Different Types for Different Levels," *Journal of Psychological Type,* 1986, *12,* 16–24; T. Moore, "Personality Tests Are Back," *Fortune,* March 30, 1987, 74–82; U. C. V. Haley and S. A. Stumpf, "Cognitive Traits in Strategic Decision-Making: Linking Theories of Personalities and Cognitions," *Journal of Management Studies,* 1989, *26,* 477–496.

son is mentally oriented to physical reality, external facts, and concrete experiences. This person is not inclined toward personal reflection or introspection.

Sensation-type people emphasize action, urgency, and bottom-line results. Through an assertive, quick-paced, and "let's do it now" approach to life and work, they learn by doing, not by imagining or thinking.

Intuitive-Type Person An **intuitive-type person** looks first at ideas and possibilities rather than facts. Such a person likes to solve new problems, dislikes repetitive work, may jump to conclusions, becomes impatient with routine details, and dislikes taking time to be precise.[10]

An intuitive-type individual would probably dislike and may perform poorly the routine and structured job that the sensation-type individual enjoys and often performs well. Intuitive-type people are better at coming up with ideas than implementing them. The intuitive-type person tends to perceive the organization as a whole—as it is and as it might change—and lives in anticipation. When conducting a job interview, the intuitive-type manager is not likely to emphasize the details of what the applicant has done in the past. This type of manager is much more interested in the applicant's imagination, the applicant's ability to understand the organization's growth possibilities, and how the applicant would creatively go about solving a messy problem.

The intuitive-type person's speaking and writing are filled with metaphors and imagery. Such a person often uses such words as *possible, fascinating, ingenious,* and *imaginative* to describe people and events—and often daydreams and fantasizes. The sensation-type person may describe the intuitive-type person as someone who has his or her head in the clouds. If the intuitive-type person's head is in the clouds, he or she may be subject to greater errors of fact than the sensation-type person.[11] A person once described an intuitive manager as one "who can see around corners." In terms of a problem-solving style, the intuitive-type person tends to:

- keep the total picture or overall problem continually in mind as problem-solving proceeds;
- show a tendency, willingness, and openness to continually redefine the problem;
- rely on hunches and nonverbal cues;
- almost simultaneously consider a variety of alternatives and options and quickly discard those judged unworkable; and
- jump around or back and forth among the usual sequence of steps in the problem-solving process and may even suddenly want to reassess whether the "true" problem has even been identified.

Unlike the sensation-type person, the intuitive-type person feels suffocated by stable conditions and seeks to create new possibilities. Such a person is often a venture capitalist, politician, entrepreneur, or stockbroker. This type of person often starts and promotes new enterprises, services, concepts, and other innovations in both the public and private sectors. They skip from one activity to the next, perhaps completing none. Jung described the intuitive-type person as one who plants a field and then is off to something new before the crop is even beginning to break ground. Instead of staying around to see the vision come to fruition, the individual is off looking for new fields to plow.

Intuitive-type people are imaginative, creative, and futuristic. They enjoy playing mind-testing games, such as Rubik's Cube, chess, and bridge. Technical details often slip past them. They become impatient with people who do not see the immediate value of their ideas. Although they may appear to be daydreaming, they are probably forming ideas and reflecting on experiences in relation to these ideas.

Feeling versus Thinking in Evaluating Information

Information evaluation involves making a judgment based on the information gathered. Jung believed that people rely on two basic psychological functions when making a judgment: thinking and feeling. Some people are more comfortable with making impersonal, objective judgments and are uncomfortable with making personal, subjective judgments. Other people are more comfortable with subjective judgments and less comfortable with objective judgments. However, both ways of making judgments are necessary and useful. Table 5.3 summarizes the characteristics typically associated with these functions. About 64 percent of the U.S. population uses thinking when evaluating information, while the other 36 percent emphasizes feeling.[12]

TABLE 5.3 Comparisons of Thinking and Feeling Types of People

Characteristic	Thinking Type	Feeling Type
Focus	Logic of situation, truth, organization principles.	Human values and needs, harmony, feelings, emotions.
Time Orientation	Past, present, future.	Past.
Work Environment	Businesslike, impersonal, treat others fairly, well organized.	Naturally friendly, personal, harmony, care and concern for others.
Strengths	Good at putting things in logical order, tend to be firm and tough-minded, rational, objective, predict logical results of decisions.	Enjoy pleasing people, sympathetic, loyal, draw out feelings in others, take interest in person behind the job or idea.
Possible Weaknesses	Overly analytical, unemotional, too serious, rigid, verbose.	Sentimental, postpone unpleasant tasks, avoid conflict.

Source: Adapted from B. Roach, "Organizational Decision Makers: Different Types for Different Levels," *Journal of Psychological Type*, 1986, *12*, 16–24; T. Moore, "Personality Tests Are Back," *Fortune*, March 30, 1987, 74–82; U. C. V. Haley and S. A. Stumpf, "Cognitive Traits in Strategic Decision-Making: Linking Theories of Personalities and Cognitions," *Journal of Management Studies*, 1989, *26*, 477–496.

Feeling-Type Person A **feeling-type person** is aware of other people and their feelings, likes harmony, needs occasional praise, dislikes telling people unpleasant news, is sympathetic, and relates well to most people.[13] Feeling-type people base their decisions on how those will affect the emotional well-being of others. They look to moral values for their guidance. Feeling-type individuals would probably conform highly to norms and accommodate themselves to other people. Such people strive to make decisions that win approval from others (peers, subordinates, and superiors). In terms of a problem-solving style, the feeling-type person tends to:

- enjoy pleasing people, even in ways that others consider unimportant;
- dislike dealing with problems that require telling other people something unpleasant;
- be responsive and sympathetic to other people's problems;
- emphasize the human aspects in dealing with organizational problems and view the causes of inefficiency and ineffectiveness as interpersonal and other human problems.

Feeling-type people emphasize emotional and personal factors in decision making. They usually avoid problems that are likely to result in disagreements. When avoidance or smoothing over of differences is not possible, they often change their positions to those that are more acceptable to others. Establishing and maintaining friendly relations may be more important to them than achievement, effectiveness, and decision making. Feeling-type managers may have a difficult time suspending or discharging subordinates for poor performance, even when the need to do so is widely recognized by others, including the employees' peers.

In other words, feeling-type people are emotional and spontaneous, and known for their love of people. Whether buying a car or choosing a friend, they base their decisions on feelings, and they often are self-indulgent. They choose words that reflect a personal tone, such as *subjective, values, intimacy,* and *extenuating circumstances*. The ready use of such words makes the feeling-type person good at persuasion or negotiating.

Thinking-Type Person At the other extreme, the **thinking-type person** prefers impersonal principles and is not comfortable unless there is a logical or analytical basis for a decision. Such a person is generally unemotional and uninterested in other people's feelings. The activities and decisions of this type of individual are usually controlled by intellectual processes based on external data and generally accepted ideas and values; problems and their solutions are fitted into standardized formulas.[14] When making decisions, the person may lose sight of all personal considerations, even his or her own welfare. For the sake of some principle, a thinking-type person may neglect health, finances, family, or other interests that people would normally regard as important.

Thinking-type people are organized and structured, and they doggedly pursue facts. They seldom leap to conclusions but prefer to consider the options carefully before deciding. They are conservative, both in dress and risk taking. They are the Oliver Wendell Holmeses of the world in their painstaking research and accuracy. On the negative side, thinking-type people can get bogged down in analyzing situations over and over again. At worst, they can be perceived by others to be rigid, blunt, aloof, and too impersonal. In terms of a problem-solving style, a thinking-type person is likely to:

* make a plan and look for a method to solve a problem;
* be extremely conscious of and concerned with the approach to a problem;
* define carefully the specific constraints in a problem;
* proceed by increasingly refining an analysis; and
* search for and obtain additional information in a very orderly manner.

There is considerable similarity among the thinking-type person's problem-solving style, the major elements in the scientific method, and what U.S. society characterizes as rational problem solving. Moreover, educational institutions emphasize development of the thinking function. Obviously, this characteristic is important in an advanced industrialized society, but the assumed superiority of the thinking over the feeling function has been overemphasized.

To this point in the discussion, we have focused on each of the four dominant psychological functions used by people to gather and evaluate information. Think back to the Preview Case for a moment. Based on the information presented in it, what would you say is the dominant combination of psychological functions exhibited by Bill Gates? If you answered that under normal conditions, he exhibits many of the characteristics of an intuitive-thinking manager, you would agree with our assessment.

INDIVIDUAL PROBLEM-SOLVING STYLES

Figure 5.2 shows a model of individual problem solving based on the four psychological functions.[15] The vertical axis represents the thinking-feeling continuum, and the horizontal axis represents the sensation-intuition continuum. Although most of us gather and evaluate information both ways in our daily lives, we usually prefer one way of gathering information and one way of evaluating information. Go back to the questionnaire in Table 5.1, look at your results, and then find yourself on the grid in Figure 5.2. According to your scores, are you primarily an ST, NT, NF, or SF? Or do your scores suggest that you are balanced among the four psychological functions?

Much can be learned about a person's problem-solving style from his or her brief written description of an ideal organization. Take ten minutes and write such a description. Then compare it with the highlights culled from

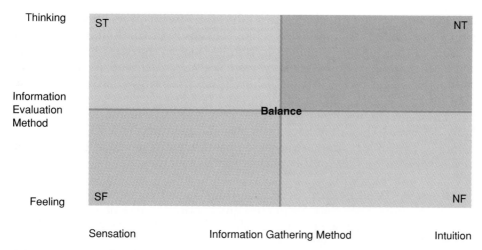

FIGURE 5.2   Individual Problem-Solving Styles Model

those of thousands of managers, as presented in the following sections, to identify your own problem-solving style.

Sensation-Thinkers

Sensation-thinkers want to establish order, control, and certainty.[16] They place importance on knowing the details and specifics of a situation before making any decision. They may oversimplify and quantify messy or novel decisions to give them order and meaning. They seldom make errors of fact. They can absorb, remember, manipulate, and manage many details, objects, or facts. Qualitative (subjective) information tends to be downplayed since it disrupts the order and structure of factual data. They like to clarify, settle, and conclude problems and situations. These people may reject novel or innovative solutions because usually there is little "hard" data to support these solutions. They are not risk takers. Their preference for analytic precision means that they do not follow hunches. ST people persevere, work steadily, and have realistic ideas of how long tasks will take to complete. As managers, they are tough-minded individuals who can get others to do their jobs.

ST managers give an organization stability and run their department or organization by facts. They are on time for meetings and expect others to be on schedule. When in charge of a meeting, they have a well-laid out agenda and are briefed to the last detail. They like to establish clear-cut organizational goals and use the organization's hierarchy to implement them.

An organization that does not have some ST managers may not be run as efficiently and effectively as those organizations that have these type of managers. Plant use may be inefficient. Control over materials and organizational procedures will probably be lax. An organization without any ST managers may find itself in a constant state of change without a base of sound, accepted policy and regulations from which to work.

Dealing with Others Sensation-thinkers want others to get to the point fast and stick to it. They enjoy dealing with data and want facts presented in a highly organized fashion by logical thinkers. When dealing with other people, however, they may become frustrated by not always being able to get facts. This may show itself, for example, in an insistence that others follow formal procedures and policies.

These people withhold rewards unless they believe the rewards to be fully deserved. They may have difficulty giving symbolic rewards, such as honors and trophies, and are more comfortable giving verbal or monetary rewards based on measurable performance objectives.

Possible Weaknesses Sensation-thinkers get impatient with project delays. At times, they may decide too quickly on a course of action and not notice complications or new situations that need attention. Since they excel in preserving the organization's procedures and rules, they may also preserve less valuable ones to maintain stability. These responses may not be desirable when rapid change is necessary.

These people often overlook interpersonal events, such as complimenting people, in favor of getting the job done. Their relationships with others are often tense. They tend to blame others when things do not go their way. They are concerned about the possibility of negative consequences. They may repeatedly analyze situations and thus expend a great deal of energy worrying about dealing with situations that never occur. They believe that everyone can contribute to the company if only they work hard and long enough.

Occupations Thirty-seven percent of U.S. managers are sensation-thinkers. Sensation-thinkers are interested in occupations that deal with the physical and impersonal side of the organization. These individuals may be attracted to jobs in fields such as accounting, production, quality control, computer programming, scheduling, copy editing, drafting, engineering, statistics, stock-brokerage, and finance. Their idea of organizational effectiveness tends to focus on objective indicators, such as sales per full-time salesperson, inventory cost per dollar of sales, scrap loss per unit produced, rate of return on invested capital, profits, value of production per labor hour, and cost of goods sold. Most organizations, as well as the advanced industrialized societies and their educational systems, place considerable emphasis on developing and using the problem-solving style characteristics of sensation-thinkers.

Marshall Hahn has been called the United States' toughest papermaker. He is the chairman of Georgia-Pacific Company and illustrates many of the characteristics of a sensation-thinker.

IN PRACTICE

MARSHALL HAHN, GEORGIA-PACIFIC COMPANY

Since Marshall Hahn took the company over in 1982, sales at Georgia-Pacific have more than doubled and profits have risen greatly. This has enabled Hahn to buy competitors, such as Great Northern, pay off debt, and lead Georgia-Pacific to the top in the distribution of building supplies. Says one competitor, "He's got steel in his spine. He works like the dickens and requires all employees to do the same."

Before assuming his present job, Hahn was president of Virginia Polytechnic Institute, a twenty thousand-student college in Blacksburg, Virginia. When Institute students were protesting the Vietnam War in the 1970s, they barricaded themselves inside a campus building. Hahn called the police and ordered them to rip off the doors and take the protesters to jail. When the protesters were released from jail, he had them expelled from school. Says a friend, "Marshall told those crazy kids what the rules were, and they wouldn't stop. So, he got the law in and had them severely punished."

Hahn joined Georgia-Pacific in 1975 to head up its chemical divisions and by 1983 was named CEO. In 1983, top management saw the Southeast as a vast and undervalued source of timber. Early in 1985, bad economic times arrived in the housing industry. With housing starts plunging, the organization's debt started to climb. The former CEO had not adopted a plan to deal with this situation.

Hahn immediately formulated a detailed game plan. He restructured the company, eliminating layers of middle managers that separated him from the managers at each of the company's saw mills. Now, each mill manager reports directly to him and is accountable for profits and losses. According to one manager, "That's good but also frightening. If you're producing, fine. If you're having problems, Hahn will fire you without taking the smile off his face." Hahn calls it a disciplined, friendly approach. He requires managers to compete against each other for resources. Those managers who run their saw mills efficiently get more funds for their operations and extra compensation. He demands that his managers work as hard as he does. Hahn gives them impossible budgets and production schedules. He hired a business strategist from a competitor and told him to get more rigorous in Georgia-Pacific's planning. Hahn and this person are now busy installing analytical tools for all managers to use in their decision making. Hahn is also taking the whole company apart to better understand it.

Georgia-Pacific's sales staff are expected to produce results, even if it means ruthlessly cutting prices. The basic philosophy is: "Make the product as inexpensively as you can, ram it into the marketplace as expensively as customers will buy it, and keep your mills going. God forbid that any sales manager shuts down a mill."[17]

Intuitive-Thinkers

An effective manager who is an **intuitive-thinker** (NT) is the architect of progress and ideas. Such people are interested in the principles on which the organization was built and seek answers to why events occur.[18] Their ability to see across departmental lines enables NT managers to make sense of the events that occur in the organization. They focus on possibilities but analyze them impersonally. For example, when they move into an organization, they are likely to analyze immediately the power base and determine how tasks really get done. The intuitive-thinker is intellectually ingenious and is an excellent innovator in technical and administrative matters. NT individuals favor long-term, open-ended projects.

An organization that does not have some NTs in its management will undergo minimal change, and sooner or later, organizational profits will decline. If NT managers perceive that the organization's goal is stability, they drift off to other jobs or form quiet pockets of passive resistance. They are inclined to ignore rules simply out of sheer boredom. They set goals that are innovative and let the organization create new products or services.

They may prefer to work with other NTs, but they also need to work with those who can persuade, conciliate, and negotiate cooperation. As managers, they should be supported by a staff that can carry out the details of projects and ideas. They value an administrative assistant who can read over contracts, keep track of details, check records, proofread, call attention to fine details, and patiently perform the same tasks repeatedly.

Dealing with Others   Intuitive-thinkers typically track the thought processes and ideas of others quite easily—and enjoy doing so. They respond well to others' new ideas, and they also champion their own causes. They enjoy solving new problems or a colleague's problem. They will be stimulated rather than feel put upon by having to solve it. They have the courage of their convictions, even if others believe that they are wrong.

Employees know where these managers stand but only if they ask. NT managers believe that their positions are quite obvious and therefore to state them would be redundant. Such managers answer questions about their opinions frankly. They admire reason, logic, and intelligence in others and do not feel a need to minimize the contributions of others.

In an organization, NT managers are labeled as the "architects of ideas." These managers easily focus on desired results and goals. They are comfortable in organizations that focus on long-term results, rather than on procedures and rules.

They must consciously try to remember social rituals that others find important. Although they may be most appreciative of others' ideas and contributions, they may fail to express this to other people. They are most likely to respond to praise that involves recognition of accomplishments and will value recognition of the influence their work has had on others.

Possible Weaknesses   When involved in the creative process, intuitive-thinkers have enormous drive. Once a program is designed, however, they are more than willing to let someone else implement it. Because they focus on principles and abstract thinking, they tend to discount arguments based on data. NTs tend to operate with little specific data and rely on their intuitive abilities to identify common patterns running through data. At times, they may not be aware of others' feelings and may not consider employees (subordinates or superiors) to be valuable unless they believe them to be intellectually competent.

They may have trouble with interpersonal relations because they believe that everyone should be as competent, adequate, and professional as possible. Thus, NTs expect a great deal of themselves and others—often more than they or anyone else can deliver. They need to remind themselves that people have both strengths and weaknesses. They often feel restless and unfulfilled, tending to raise standards for themselves and others and often being intolerant of mistakes and reflection after a decision has been made.

Occupations   Positions that deal with new possibilities and nonroutine tasks attract NTs. Twenty-six percent of U.S. managers have this problem-solving style. They are entrepreneurs and teachers in such fields as economics, business, philosophy, and the physical sciences. They are also in systems design and analysis, architectural design, law, mathematics, and engineering design. They probably determine organizational effectiveness by such variables as rate of new product development, market share, cost of capital, growth in earnings and long-run profits, new market development, and degree of action on and response to environmental changes.

John Reed, chairman and CEO of Citicorp, displays many of the behaviors of an NT. It is because of his leadership that Citicorp has become the largest bank in the United States, with more than $230 billion in deposits. More than 35 million people have Citicorp credit cards.

IN PRACTICE

JOHN S. REED, CITICORP

John Reed has been described by others as totally undisciplined, idealistic, willing to take risks, and one who has the ability to see the future. If you entered his office on Park Avenue in New York City, you would find no phone, no computer, only books. There are history books on Latin America, books on politics and on art. The serenity of the library suggests a management-by-meditation. His game plan to enter the consumer banking market was thought up while he was vacationing in Jamaica. His "notes from the beach" memo in 1976 started out with this quote: "In the beginning, give me your tired, your poor, your huddled masses, and I'll build a business." This memo outlined the foundation for Citicorp to enter the consumer market, but in a way unlike other banks had done. His strategy was to establish banking centers all over the globe. Citicorp would do this through automated teller machines (ATMs), the credit card, and mortgage loans. These services would all be linked together with sophisticated management information system technologies. Citicorp now has eight hundred branches over all Europe, several in the Far East, and more than ninety-two thousand employees.

In many ways, this has been a big experiment. Reed's management style is that of an entrepreneur: try things; if they don't work, bag them. But try new things. Citicorp has been described by other bankers as a loosely structured corporation ruled by kind of a chaotic creativity. Huge risks are taken and rewarded. Reed controls by logic. Details are best left to others. For example, in May 1987, when the bank announced it would lose $2.6 billion that quarter so that it could build up $3 billion in reserves against Third World loans, Reed was asked why he had chosen $3 billion. He grinned, licked his finger, and held it up to the wind. He said that after reams of computer analyses and conferences with top Washington bankers, that was his best answer.

His staff is constantly challenged to do things differently. He states, "The challenge is, how do you cause an organization to be smart?" Almost any worthwhile idea is tested. Sometimes millions of dollars are wasted before Reed can convince people that the idea might eventually pay off. For example, Citicorp was the first bank to install ATMs. Most bankers thought that he was crazy. But Reed saw it as a low-cost way of reaching millions of people. In 1978 and 1979, Citicorp lost more than $125 million when people did not pay their credit card bills and interest rates rose. He canceled all bonuses for everybody at the bank, largely because of his mistake. Managers and their spouses attacked him for his mistake. In 1990, however, Citicorp earned more than $842 million, more than half of the bank's profits, from its credit card operation.

To help Citicorp hedge its bets against a declining commercial U.S. real estate market, he has cut staff and once again cut the bank's dividends and bonuses. Citicorp has also sold off some unprofitable ventures. Reed is trying to convince people in Washington to let major banks around the world swap existing portions of business and let corporations, such as IBM, American Airlines, and others, make equity investments in banks.[19]

Sensation-Feelers

An effective manager who is a **sensation-feeler** (SF) places importance on interpersonal relations and on dealing with concrete problems in a methodical fashion. These managers negotiate with ease and are natural troubleshooters or diplomats. They are good at putting out fires and unsnarling interpersonal problems that arise among employees—and doing it quickly. They have the talent for getting people to cooperate with them and with each other on the basis of expediency. They have an attitude of sureness and "damn the torpedoes, full speed ahead" that causes others to have total confidence in their decisions and directions. If sensation-feelers experience self-doubt, they do not share it with those around them. They can analyze their day-to-day work systems, see how they are working, spot breakdowns and errors, and determine the types of corrections needed.[20]

As managers, SFs understand the organization better than any other type of manager because they astutely observe the details of how it is run. They are probably best at getting others to cooperate in planning and decision making. They excel in producing written documents. Since they can spot trouble in an organization while it is still minor, thus preventing small problems from becoming larger ones, operations run smoothly. Subordinates working for such managers say that things seem to happen effortlessly, without wasted time and motion. These managers do not fight the current system; they use the means available to solve problems, rather than to try to change the reality of the system.

They can spur action in a management team. Group activities are sure to happen with SF managers around. Productivity is apt to be high, and SF managers will be aware of employee comfort and working conditions. They are not likely to allow bad working conditions to exist without attempting to do something about them.

Sensation-feelers typically do not judge their co-workers and accept their behaviors at face value, rather than seek underlying motives and meanings. To motivate subordinates, SF managers reward them only when they have completed a task. They prefer symbolic rewards, such as plaques, lapel pins, and company newspaper stories.

Dealing with Others Sensation-feelers usually respond to others' ideas only if those ideas are concrete. They are predictable in working with colleagues, who find them easy to get along with. They consult with others before making decisions and try to reach consensus and acceptance of the decision. The possibility of their own failure or that of others does not threaten SFs, who take calculated risks and encourage others to do the same. They can change their position easily, as facts change and new situations arise. They do not worry about what might have been; they deal with what is.

Possible Weaknesses Sensation-feelers may be reluctant to accept radical new theories and may become impatient with abstract ideas. SF managers often seem more interested in promoting group discussions than actually solving the problem, especially if it is an abstract problem. The SF managers' need for acceptance by others may prompt them to promote others' ideas instead of their own. They are very adaptable until the point of breaking the system's rules and procedures. They live primarily for the moment and may experience difficulty in honoring commitments and decisions made in the past when they do not expect support for doing so from their group.

Occupations Sensation-feelers are usually interested in jobs that require personal contact with others in the organization or with customers. Seventeen percent of U.S. managers are sensation-feelers. These managers excel at selling, direct supervision, counseling, negotiating, teaching, interviewing, human resources functions, and many types of service work. They enjoy talking with other people. For them, organizational effectiveness is determined by employee loyalty, attitudes, grievances, turnover, and absenteeism.

The Across Cultures in this chapter illustrates how Koo Cha-Kyung, chairman of Lucky-Goldstar, uses this style of problem-solving to operate a Korean chaebol. A **chaebol** is a business group consisting of large diversified companies that produce a wide variety of product lines and is owned or managed by a family.[21] Lucky-Goldstar consists of twenty-nine companies, has more than ninety thousand employees, and ranks in the top thirty organizations in the world in terms of sales.

To understand Koo Cha-Kyung's problem-solving style, you must understand traditional Korean values. Korean values can be traced to Confucius, a civil servant who lived in China around 500 B.C. There are four important Korean values that affect decisions. First, the family is most important. It defines who people are and where they belong in society. The family looks after its own. Lucky-Goldstar is the employees' family. Second, social order must be arranged according to strict seniority. The young should show respect to the old and the old assume responsibility for the well-being and future of the young. Third, trust must be established and maintained in both good and bad times. Trust is the key to all human relationships. Fourth, absolute loyalty is to be maintained. The president of the company is to be respected and his decisions followed without question.[22]

Now that we have some understanding of several core Korean values, let's read how they affect Cha-Kyung's management of Lucky-Goldstar.

KOO CHA-KYUNG, LUCKY-GOLDSTAR

Most strategic decisions at Lucky-Goldstar are made by family members. While there are few family members, they hold important positions in all of Lucky-Goldstar's twenty-nine companies. Lucky-Goldstar is a very conservative organization that has avoided risky ventures and stresses group harmony in all businesses. In fact, the company motto, "inhawa," means group harmony. Most of Lucky-Goldstar's new products are logical extensions of existing businesses. Considerable emphasis is placed on the sustainability of the group and its companies in all decisions. Managers at the twenty-nine different companies are free to run their companies as they see fit. However, the principle of *nunch'i* governs many decisions. *Nunch'i* means the ability to look in someone's eyes. Through this process, employees make decisions that reflect how their manager would expect them to decide.

Cha-Kyung meets weekly with his senior managers, asks them a series of questions concerning their businesses, and settles pressing issues on the spot. Cha-Kyung expects his managers to assume personal responsibility for the development of their subordinates, and he expects subordinates to show respect for and obedience to their manager. For example, it is not uncommon for a manager to take his subordinates out drinking one night a week to discuss both business and personal matters. This helps foster group harmony. Moreover, a manager is expected to take an active interest in his subordinate's personal and family life by attending birthday parties, weddings, funerals, and the like. Conflict or problems at home may affect work performance and, thus, must be effectively resolved by the manager.

The pay system also reflects both Korean values and Cha-Kyung's managerial style. Lucky-Goldstar pays employees a fixed monthly amount that is based on a formula estimate of all the employee's expenses. This simplifies having to calculate each benefit for each employee on a monthly basis. Bonuses amounting to about four to six months' salary are paid. Even if the company is not making a good profit, bonuses are paid in order to maintain group harmony within the organization. The bonus is based on one's level in the hierarchy. Managers at Lucky-Goldstar believe that it is simply not possible to have different bonus levels for employees at the same level. It would disturb group harmony. Bonuses are usually paid out four times a year to coincide with major Korean holidays.

Promotions at Lucky-Goldstar are based on seniority. Following the Confucian philosophy, it is easier to make decisions based on seniority than to rely on imprecise personnel evaluations. Seniority preserves group harmony by having older employees supervise younger ones.

When layoffs are necessary, Lucky-Goldstar encourages older workers to leave and provides extra financial incentives for them to do so. The company assumes that with Korea's extended family system, the incomes of all family members are pooled and the laid-off employees can be cared for by their families.[23]

These values and the sensation-feeling problem-solving style combine to affect the managerial practices employed at Lucky-Goldstar.

Intuitive Feeler

Effective managers who are **intuitive-feelers** (NF) rely on personal charisma and commitment to the people they lead. These managers are organizational "cheerleaders."[24] They usually use language well and, through it, communicate their caring and enthusiasm for customers, suppliers, employees, and others. They easily see abstract possibilities for their organizations and particularly for the people in democratically run organizations. They excel at loosely structured decisions that enable them and others to participate in the decision-making process. NFs enjoy creative problem solving and often reject traditional methods and standard operating procedures in favor of novel solutions. They are patient with complicated situations and can wait for the right time to move forward on an idea; they are like chemical catalysts. Reasoning by analogies may help NFs communicate their new ideas to others. Intuition-feelers make excellent top managers, especially if they must represent and promote the organization to customers, employees, and government agencies.

The employees of an organization that does not have NF managers may find the environment cold, sterile, joyless, and dull. Such managers focus on developing individuals within the organization. They are deeply committed to the career progress of subordinates and strive to enhance subordinates' personal growth. When NFs are in leadership roles, their focus may be primarily on developing the potential of employees, with the development of the organization being secondary. They look for and react to the best in others and give them feedback and coaching.

They head an organization well if they are given a free rein to manage, but they may rebel if they believe the system has placed too many constraints on them. To motivate others, NF managers give many psychological rewards. If they receive sufficient praise, they are excellent managers; if not sufficiently praised, they can become ineffective, discouraged, and uninvolved—and they will look outside the organization for rewards.

Dealing with Others   Intuitive-feelers relate well to others, who often view them as the most popular people. They hunger for personal contact and go out of their way to find it. They are sociable, adventurous, and risk-taking and enjoy being where people are gathered. They frequently consult and maintain close personal contact with their bosses. They find their organization a source of social satisfaction, as well as a place to work.

Possible Weaknesses   Intuitive-feelers may find themselves making decisions on the basis of their personal likes and dislikes, rather than on the basis of performance measures. Powered by enthusiasm, they work in great bursts of energy, but they require frequent rest periods to recharge their energy levels. They need the approval of both subordinates and superiors and at times may find themselves to be the champion of two opposing groups. They understand the emotions of others so well that they are vulnerable to them and want to "please all the people all the time," which inevitably gets them into difficult situations, especially when in managerial jobs.

They are likely to feel pressured because their belief systems make it necessary for every person, especially significant others, to love and admire them. This belief may cause NFs to spend too much time seeking approval and to constantly check with others until they show approval. Under these conditions, such individuals may become so responsive to the demands of others that they lose sight of their own values, beliefs, and goals.

Occupations Intuitive-feelers, like SFs, usually prefer occupations that deal with the human side of the organization but without so many of the close, personal contacts that SFs prefer. Intuitive-feelers deal comfortably with individuals and groups alike, either directly or indirectly. They excel at public relations work and shine as spokespersons for their organization because they work well with all types of people, can sell the organization to others, and help employees feel good about themselves and the organization. These individuals often do well in such occupations as public relations, politics, advertising, human resource management, some types of sales, art, and teaching. They believe that organizational effectiveness is reflected in consumer satisfaction, social responsibility, ability to identify problems or new opportunities, quality of life, and community satisfaction with the organization.

The problem-solving style of Mary Kay Ash, founder of Mary Kay Cosmetics, demonstrates many of the behaviors of an intuitive feeler. Ash's approach to managing her employees is shared by nineteen percent of U.S. managers. Her focus is on looking for ways to enhance employees' job satisfaction and to develop managers with leadership skills to meet both employee and corporate goals.

IN PRACTICE

MARY KAY ASH, MARY KAY COSMETICS

After spending more than twenty-five years working for direct sales in other organizations, Mary Kay Ash started her own company in 1963. Mary Kay Cosmetics sells skin care products directly to women through more than fifty thousand beauty consultants. Sales take place at an event at someone's home. No smoking or liquor is allowed at these events. Top beauty consultants can earn more than $250,000 annually.

Ash's organization is governed by six rules:

1.   Follow the golden rule—do unto others as you would have them do unto you—in dealing with employees and customers. If you help them get what they want, they will help you get what you want.
2.   The people are more important than the plan. Make them feel important, praise them, listen to them, and let them contribute. In return, you will get their best efforts and their support. Managers get their best ideas from their employees.
3.   Managers must lead by getting their hands dirty.
4.   Managers have a responsibility to their employees. They must instill in their employees a sense of pride and pleasure in the work and try to provide a low-stress environment in which people can do their best. All employees are called by their first names, regardless of title.
5.   There are no "little people" in the organization. Everyone is important to the organization's success. All new employees meet personally with Mary Kay Ash during their first month of employment. Promotions should come from within the organization.

6.   Beauty consultants are the lifeblood of this organization. They should be rewarded and respected for their efforts. Mary Kay Ash personally answers all their letters and sends inscribed birthday cards to each.

Beauty consultants who follow these guiding rules can earn diamonds, minks, and the company's trademark—a Cadillac in "Mary Kay Pink." These incentives are passed out during the organization's annual sales convention. Held in the Dallas Convention Center once a year for about eight thousand beauty consultants, this multimillion-dollar, three-day event has been described as part Miss America pageant, part sorority meeting, and part old-time revival meeting. Company songs are sung, testimonials are spoken, and trophies are passed out "just for being wonderful." Promotions to sales director are awarded in an elaborate ceremony. Ash personally announces promotions and asks the beauty consultant to repeat the "Mary Kay oath." The top beauty consultant for the year is crowned and given expensive gifts (such as a mink coat, a Cadillac, or diamonds) by Ash that symbolize this person as a leader and motivator.[25]

MANAGERIAL IMPLICATIONS

We have all experienced situations where teamwork was great. Effective teamwork calls for the recognition and use of certain valuable differences among members of the team. Effective teams do not necessarily have members who agree all of the time, nor do ineffective teams have members who disagree constantly. A good team needs a division of labor, mutual respect, communication, openness, appreciation of differences, and action. It is not unusual for a team to be composed of individuals who have different problem-solving styles. The effective manager of a team, therefore, must understand how each person's problem-solving style affects other members of the team and, ultimately, the team's effectiveness.

Many organizations have used an understanding of problem-solving styles to improve their team's effectiveness, including IBM, Citicorp, Exxon, General Electric, Apple, and LTV.[26] These organizations help their managers better understand how they come across to others who see things differently. This increases their effectiveness by understanding how different problem-solving styles could effectively contribute to the group's teamwork. For example, at LTV, a team was headed by an intuitive-thinking manager. Staff meetings frequently became sessions of far-ranging and undisciplined discussions of ideas, theories, and possibilities. The manager would gloss over the facts and instead focus on examination of possible solutions. The sensation-thinkers on the staff felt rather lost and constantly tried to bring the group back to "reality." They frequently complained about the lack of focus and tended to be absent from meetings. The manager thought of these people as stick-in-the-muds. When a consultant pointed out these differences, the manager agreed to spend more time on sticking to tasks on the agenda. He agreed that more down-to-earth discussions would make more productive use of his staff members' ideas. Once the sensation-thinking staff members were satisfied with the problem's definition and the resultant goals, the group's effectiveness and morale increased.

If individual differences are respected and appreciated, teamwork is often more effective when members who have different problem-solving styles are combined into one group. Brooklyn Union Gas Company puts intuitive-thinkers (NT) with sensation-feelers (SF) to work on the same team. It looks like a bad fit. The NT is an architect of ideas, whereas the SF is a persuader. But as it works out, the SF essentially can sell the NT's ideas to others. While the NT might be all consumed with the idea, the SF anchors the NT by focusing on the processes by which others can become committed to the NT's ideas. Similarly, combining NF and ST problem solvers might create an effective team. The intuitive-feeler (NF) is a person who takes on management crusades, such as environmental issues, having a drug-free workplace, and the like. NFs question others about the meaning of life and what significant things the organization is doing to further mankind. The sensation-thinker (ST) is likely to think of specific ways that these idealistic notions can be put into place in the organization. The NF thinks about long-range problems and solutions, while the ST thinks about short-range problems and the implementation of solutions.

Ideally, tasks should dictate which type of problem-solving person might be best suited to carry them out. If the task is structured and has numerous facts and details, sensation-thinker people might be better suited for it than intuitive-feeler persons. Sensation-thinkers like to organize facts and set rules that will guide their decision making. They are more interested in the here and now than in future possibilities. They are happy in performing tasks that demand factual accuracy. The intuitive-feeler may challenge such a straightforward analysis just to challenge the group to see various alternatives. If, on the other hand, the problem focuses on improving group harmony, the intuitive-feeler might be better suited to lead the group. Since intuitive-feeling managers place a high value on people, they tend to focus on ways to improve communications and gaining members' loyalty to their group. They will try to help people see others' viewpoints in a nonthreatening manner.

Excellence in management is not simply managing the bottom line. It also includes managing production, growth, and competitiveness; employee recruitment, retention, and motivation; social responsibility; and many other aspects of organizational life. Problem-solving style plays an important part in helping managers address these issues.

SUMMARY

The discussion of individual problem-solving styles focused on why and how individuals differ in gathering and evaluating information from the environment. This chapter, along with the preceding two chapters on personality, attitudes, perception, and attribution, suggests ways of understanding how we affect others, view ourselves and others, and learn to appreciate and build on differences between ourselves and others. Individuals gather data from the environment either by intuition or their senses. Sensing people gather specific factual data from their environment, whereas intuitive people gather global or more abstract data. After gathering data, people make decisions on the basis of thinking or feeling. Thinking people solve a problem by breaking it into logical parts, whereas feeling people use their instinct when making a decision.

The discussion of problem-solving styles concentrated on four distinct styles. Sensation-thinkers (STs) gather facts and numbers from their environment and then apply logic to solve problems. Intuitive-thinkers (NTs) use abstract principles and logic to solve problems. Intuitive-feelers (NFs) use intuition to gather data and then apply personal values when making a decision. Sensation-feelers (SFs) gather specific facts and figures from their environment and they rely on personal values when making a decision. However, many people exhibit characteristics of each style at various times and in different situations. People also tend to move toward a balance and integration of the four psychological functions. Although one problem-solving style is not necessarily better than another, the requirements of certain positions or roles in organizations may naturally favor one style over the others.

Key Words and Concepts

Chaebol	Problem interpretation
Cognitive complexity	Problem-solving style
Feeling	Sensing
Feeling-type person	Sensation-feeler (SF)
Intuition	Sensation-thinker (ST)
Intuitive-feeler(NF)	Sensation-type person
Intuitive thinker (NT)	Thinking
Intuitive-type person	Thinking-type person

Discussion Questions

1. Using the problem-solving model shown in Figure 5.1, describe how you chose the course(s) you are taking.

2. What is the likely influence of your problem-solving style on your selection of a job? Why do some people want to match the demands of the job with their preferred problem-solving style?

3. If an organization has managers representing all four problem-solving styles, why may building a consensus be difficult?

4. The following stories were written by senior managers while attending an executive development program. Identify the problem-solving style of each and the reasons for your choice.

   Story 1 The organization I would like to work for would need to be highly attentive to the personal needs of the employees. Also, I would need to produce a good product—one that society thinks is important. The organization should have a fine service department to service the product it sells. To keep moving forward, the company would need to be innovative and able to stay in front of the competition. These factors all lead to a more profitable organization.

Story 2 Organizations that have the greatest success in reaching established goals and objectives are those that have a staff of people who know what they are doing. Ideally, the organization would have a unique product, be a medium size (less than a thousand employees), have formal lines of communication, and produce a return on investment of at least 12 percent on operating assets. The organization would be located in a single facility in the Sun Belt. The unique product line would have limited competition, and the competition would have relatively similar quality standards.

The organization would consist of a chief executive officer with a staff of officers of marketing, finance, operations, human resources, and accounting. The structure below these officers would allow a hands-on management style that would capitalize on the ideas of all personnel.

Story 3 Characteristics: (1) one product, (2) a highly centralized location, and (3) a small staff of professionals.

My organization operates through the efforts of several groups. Each group is loosely organized to achieve its goals and objectives and has professional personnel with the various skills required to produce our product. Each group has an adviser or consultant who functions to help the group in its task. He or she does not function as the group leader but knows all aspects of the job.

The groups set their own goals, choose their own leaders, and discipline and reward their members. Their production rates and quality are closely monitored and reported to the leaders. To some extent, the group is rewarded for high profitability. Leaders are elected by the group and change from time to time.

Story 4 My ideal organization would consist of people who are all dedicated to achieving the goals of the organization and who are willing to do so in a friendly, cooperative way. To be effective, all the people must have a servant attitude toward one another (that is, they must think not of their own interests first but of the interests of others). An attitude of humility would prevail, and the needs of others would be met before our own.

I think of the New Testament church in its beginnings as an ideal organization. There was a structure, but it permitted everyone to share everything so no one was in need. As the organization grew and prospered, so did the people. People's needs come before the organization.

5.   Should organizations attempt to select people for positions on the basis of their problem-solving styles? What would be the benefits? The dangers?

JEFFREY JORDAN, PEPSI-COLA

Jeffrey Jordan is only twenty-seven years old, but he is already the production/warehouse manager for Pepsi-Cola South in Houston, Texas. Prior to this assignment, he served as a liaison between Pepsi-Cola's bottling plants in the southern division and corporate headquarters in Somers, New York. His department produced more than seven million cases of soda last year. He oversees a budget of nearly $40 million and wears several managerial hats. As a production manager, he heads the production of two-liter, sixteen-liter, and twenty-ounce bottles. And as warehouse manager, he is responsible for supplying nine warehouses in southern Texas. He also oversees the warehouse's inventory.

His office is filled with books and trade publications on the soda industry. He likes manufacturing because "you're responsible for making something tangible." One of his major tasks was the supervision of a half a million dollar automation project. Last year, the plant's soda production line changed from manual to computer operation. He had to decide what products to produce, how much, and when to produce them while the line was down. He also had to coordinate the inventory with other warehouses to make sure that they did not run out of soda while the line was being automated. When three

lines were out of commission for three weeks, the other four kept going. He had to adjust schedules and switch some employees to lines that were still in operation.

He also had to dispel fears of workers who were intimidated by the new computerized line. He took teams of fifteen employees to several automated Pepsi plants to give them a chance to see how the automated lines actually ran.

Jordan seeks to maintain a balance between his business and personal life. He teaches an economics class once a week at Houston's predominantly black high school. He tries to tell his students what it is like to be a black manager in a white organization.[27]

QUESTIONS:

1. What's Jordan's problem-solving style? What are the requirements of his job? Is there a fit between these?

2. Assume you are Tom McLoughlin, manager of manufacturing services for Pepsi-Cola, Jordan's immediate supervisor. What kinds of managerial job assignments might you recommend that Jordan be assigned to if he aspires to become a general manager? Why did you choose those?

PHIL FITZGERALD, ALPHAGRAPHICS

Phil Fitzgerald has worked at Alphagraphics, a small printing shop in Bellefonte, Pennsylvania, that employs forty people, for the past ten years. Until last year, he was an administrative assistant in the production department. His job duties included scheduling production and maintenance, processing employees' payroll cards, managing inventory levels, and assisting the production manager in other tasks. He generally did what was assigned to him. In May, the production manager left the company. Rather than fill this position, the president decided to reassign the responsibilities between Fitzgerald and San-

dra Cardinal, a person from the quality control department. Since that time, the following problems have surfaced in the Production Department between Fitzgerald and Cardinal.

1. Fitzgerald believes that Cardinal is not assertive enough with production employees. One of her responsibilities is scheduling employees for overtime. This requires that she get information from all employees and assign employees to overtime based on their departmental seniority. Cardinal usually waits until the last minute to ask employees

to work overtime. Most of the production employees have families. She believes that they want to spend more time with them and not work overtime. This causes problems for the supervisor because she cannot schedule her work in advance.

2. Fitzgerald wants Cardinal to help run the department on a day-to-day basis and help keep track of what activities need to be done for that day. She does not want to do this.

3. Cardinal waits to be told what to do by Fitzgerald, rather than initiate activity herself. She says that she will do what is wanted but that Fitzgerald is so wrapped up in the day-to-day activities of running the department, he rarely spends time with her.

4. Cardinal has told the manager in the Human Resources Department that she feels unappreciated and unwanted. She has not told Fitzgerald of her feelings.

QUESTIONS

1. Using your knowledge of problem-solving styles, explain the problems that Fitzgerald and Cardinal are having.

2. What recommendations would you give to both Fitzgerald and Cardinal to resolve these problems?

3. What is your problem-solving style? How has your style affected your recommendations to Fitzgerald and Cardinal?

References

1. Adapted from Schlender, B. How Bill Gates Keeps the Magic Going. *Fortune,* June 18, 1990, 82–89; McMullen, J. Microsoft in the Age of Networks, *Datamation,* May 1, 1990, 36–39; Microsoft: What Comes after Seven Fat Years?, *Economist,* March 24, 1990, 72–73.

2. Ruble, T. L., and Cosier, R. A. Effects of Cognitive Style and Decision Making on Performance. *Organizational Behavior and Human Decision Processes,* 1990, *46,* 283–295; Ferguson, J., and Fletcher, C. Personality Type and Cognitive Style. *Psychological Reports,* 1987, *60,* 959–964.

3. Rowe, A. J., and Mason, R. O. *Managing with Style: A Guide to Understanding, Assessing, and Improving Decision Making.* San Francisco Jossey-Bass, 1987; Hunt, R. G., Krystofiak, F. J., Meindl, J. R., and Yousry, A. M. Cognitive Style and Decision Making. *Organizational Behavior and Human Decision Processes,* 1989, *44,* 436–453. Vassallo, H. G., and Lanasa, T. M. The Effects of Cognitive Style on the Design of Expert Systems. *Review of Business,* Winter 1990/1991, 37–43.

4. Haley, U. C. V., and Stumpf, S. A. Cognitive Trails in Strategic Decision-Making: Linking Theories of Personalities and Cognitions. *Journal of Management Studies,* 1989, *26,* 477–496; Henderson, J. C., and Nutt, P. C. The Influence of Decision Style on Decision-Making Behavior. *Management Science,* 1980, *26,* 371–386.

5. Garvin, D. A. Quality Problems, Policies, and Attitudes in United States and Japan: An Exploratory Study. *Academy of Management Journal,* 1986, *29,* 653–673.

6. Dutton, J. E., and Duncan, R. B. The Creation of Momentum for Change through Strategic Issue Diagnosis. *Strategic Management Journal,* 1987, *8,* 279–295.

7. Jung, C. G. *Psychological Types.* London: Routledge and Kegan Paul, 1923. For an expansion of Jung's ideas, see Keirsay, D., and Bates, M. *Please Understand Me.* Del Mar, Calif.: Prometheus Nemesis Book Company, 1984.

8. Roach, B. Organizational Decision-Makers: Different Types for Different Levels. *Journal of Psychological Type,* 1986, *12,* 16–24; Craig, D. L., Craig, C. H., and Sleight, C. C. Type Preferences of Decision-Makers: Corporate and Clinical. *Journal of Psychological Type,* 1988, *16,* 33–37.

9. Hellriegel, D., and Slocum, J. W., Jr. Preferred Organizational Designs and Problem-Solving Styles: Interesting Companions. *Human Systems Management,* 1980, *1,* 151–158.

10. Hoy, F., and Vaught, B. C. The Relationship between Problem-Solving Styles and Problem-Solving Skills among Entrepreneurs. *Research in Psychological Type,* 1981, *4,* 38–45.

11. Schweiger, D. M., and Jago, A. G. Problem-Solving Styles and Participative Decision Making. *Psychological Reports,* 1982, *50,* 1311–1316; Cosier, R. A. The Role of Intuition in Managerial Decisions. *International Journal of Management,* 1985, *2(2),* 81–86.

12. McCaulley, M. H. The Selection Ratio Type Table: A Research Strategy for Comparing Type Distributions. *Journal of Psychological Type,* 1985, *10,* 46–56.

13. Kilmann, R. H., and Herden, R. P. Toward a Systematic Methodology for Evaluating the Impact of Interventions on Organizational Effectiveness. *Academy of Management Review*, 1976, *1*, 87–98; Hoy, F., and Hellriegel, D. The Kilmann and Herden Model of Organizational Effectiveness Criteria for Small Business Managers. *Academy of Management Journal*, 1982, *25*, 308–322.

14. Hirsh, S. H. *Using the Myers-Briggs Type Indicator in Organizations.* Palo Alto, Calif.: Consulting Psychologists Press, 1985.

15. Hellriegel, D., and Slocum, J. W., Jr. Managerial Problem-Solving Styles. *Business Horizons*, December 1975, 29–37.

16. Campbell, D. P., and Van Velsor, E. *The Use of Personality Measures in the Leadership Development Program.* Greensboro, N.C.: Center for Creative Leadership, 1985.

17. Adapted from Calonius, E. America's Toughest Papermaker. *Fortune*, February 26, 1990, 80–83; Schultz, J. Mergers and Acquisitions: How GP Won the Battle of the Paper Giants. *Institutional Investor*, May 1990, 159 ff; Deutschman, A. No Paper Tiger: T. M. Hahn's Bid for Great Northern. *Fortune*, December 4, 1989, 173.

18. Mitroff, I. I., and Kilmann, R. H. Stories Managers Tell: A New Tool for Organizational Problem-Solving. *Management Review*, 1975, *64*(7), 18–28.

19. Loomis, C. J. Citicorp's World of Troubles, *Fortune*, January 14, 1991, 90–99; Andrews, S. Deconstructing the Mind of America's Most Powerful Businessman: What Citi's John Reed Sees That Other Bankers Don't. *Manhattan, Inc.*, May 1990, 61–69. Reed, J. S. *From the Beach.* New York: Citicorp, March 9, 1976.

20. Bayne, R. A New Direction for the Myers-Briggs Type Indicator. *Personnel Management*, March 1990, 48–51; Nutt, P. C. Influence of Decision Styles on Use of Decision Models. *Technological Forecasting and Social Change*, 1979, *14*, 77–93; McCaulley, M. H. *The Myers-Briggs Type Indicator and Leadership.* Paper presented at Conference on Psychological Measures and Leadership. Center for Creative Leadership and The Psychological Corporation, October 1988, San Antonio, Texas.

21. Lei, D., Slocum, J. W., Jr., and Slater, R. W. Global Strategy and Reward Systems: The Key Roles of Management and Corporate Culture, *Organizational Dynamics*, Autumn 1990, 27–43.

22. Steers, R. M., Shin, Y. K. and Ungson, G. R. *The Chaebol.* Philadelphia: Ballinger, 1989.

23. Adapted from Shin, Y. K., Steers, R. M., Ungson, G. R., and Nam, S. Work Environment and Management Practice in Korean Corporations. *International Human Resource Management Review*, 1990, *1*, 95–108; Steers, R. M., Shin, Y. K., and Ungson, G. R. *The Chaebol.* Philadelphia: Ballinger, 1989; Chung, K. H., and Lee, H. C. *Korean Managerial Dynamics.* Westport, Conn.: Praeger Publishers, 1989.

24. Myers, I. *Differing Gifts.* Palo Alto, Calif.: Consulting Psychologist Press, 1980; Hirsh, S., and Kummerow, J. M. *Lifetypes.* New York: Warner Books, 1989.

25. Adapted from Ash, M. K. *Mary Kay on People Management.* New York: Warner Books, 1984; Levering, R., Moskowitz, M., and Katz, M. *The 100 Best Companies to Work for in America.* Reading, Mass.: Addison-Wesley Publishing Company, 1984, 199–202; McMurran, K. Mary Kay Ash, *People*, July 29, 1985, 57–61; Biggart, N. W. *Charismatic Capitalism: Direct Selling Organizations in America.* Chicago: University of Chicago Press, 1989.

26. For illustrations of organizations that have used the Myers-Briggs instrument to improve their understanding of employee behaviors, see Kummerow, J. M., and McAllister, L. W. Team-Building with the Myers-Briggs Type Indicator: Case Studies. *Journal of Psychological Type*, 1988, *15*, 26–32; Rice, G. H., Jr., and Lindecamp, D. P. Personality Types and Business Success of Small Retailers. *Journal of Occupational Psychology*, 1989, *62*, 177–182; Gaster, W., Tobacyk, J., and Dawson, L. Jungian Type in Retail Store Managers. *Journal of Psychological Type*, 1984, *7*, 19–24; Martin, D. C., and Bartol, K. M. Holland's Vocational Preference Inventory and the Myers-Briggs Type Indicator as Predictors of Vocational Choice Among Master's of Business Administration. *Journal of Vocational Behavior*, 1986, *29*, 51–65; and Roach, B. *Strategy Styles and Management Types: A Resource Book for Organizational and Management Consultants.* Stanford, Calif.: Balestrand Press, 1989.

27. Adapted from Gite, L. Taking Charge. *Black Enterprise*, August 1989, 44–50.

CHAPTER 6

LEARNING AND REINFORCEMENT

LEARNING OBJECTIVES

When you have finished studying this chapter, you should be able to:

- Discuss the differences among classical, operant, and social learning.
- Describe the contingencies of reinforcement.
- List the methods used to increase desired behaviors and reduce undesired behaviors.
- Describe the procedures and principles of behavioral modification.
- State two limitations of behavioral modification.

OUTLINE

DRIVER BEHAVIORS AT UPS

For United Parcel Service (UPS), the slogan "the tightest ship in the shipping business" is a holy grail. With more than sixty-two thousand drivers and a fleet of planes that has made it the tenth largest U.S. airline, UPS is the biggest and most profitable organization in the shipping business. How does UPS do it?

At 8:45 each morning, all UPS drivers begin their routes in freshly washed trucks. Packages are arranged by sorters from midnight until 7:00 A.M. Sorters are expected to sort 1,124 packages per hour and make no more than one mistake per 2,500 packages. Employees then load each truck just so. Drivers must be able to see the packaging labels quickly and easily. Drivers start at sixteen dollars per hour and can earn more with overtime. Every route is timed down to the traffic lights. Drivers are trained to perform their tasks over and over again without much wasted effort. Drivers hold their clipboard under their right arm and a package under their left. Keys, teeth up, are on the middle finger of a driver's right hand. They are allowed only one look at the package to fix the address in their mind. They trot to a house at three feet a second. Drivers are trained to knock first and then search for the doorbell. The driver takes the customer's money face up and puts it in sequential order. Paperwork for that customer is completed on the way back to the truck, where a driver's left foot always hits the step first. During an average day, a driver will make 145 stops to deliver 246 packages and pick up 70 others.

UPS relies on extensive written records and has installed a computer system to keep accurate records. Operating costs and production runs are constantly compared to its largest competitors, Federal Express and the U.S. Postal Service. Daily worksheets specifying performance objectives and work output are kept on every employee and department. Employees' daily quotas and achievements are then accumulated on a weekly and monthly basis.[1]

UPS efficiency is based on specific principles drawn from an area of psychology called learning theory. The **learning theory** approach stresses the assessment of behavior in objective, measurable (countable) terms. Behavior must be publicly observable, which deemphasizes unobservable, inner, cognitive behavior. In this chapter, we explore the development, maintenance, and change of employee work behaviors, using principles derived from learning theory.

Desirable work behaviors contribute to achieving organizational goals; conversely, undesirable work behaviors hinder achieving these goals. Labeling behavior as "desirable" or "undesirable" is entirely subjective and depends on the value system of the person making the assessment. For example, a secretary who returns late from a coffee break exhibits undesirable behavior from the manager's viewpoint, desirable behavior from the viewpoint of friends with whom the worker chats during the break, and desirable behavior from the worker's own viewpoint because of the satisfaction of social needs.

The work setting and organizational norms are the bases for determining whether a behavior is desirable or undesirable. The more a behavior deviates from organizational norms, the more undesirable it is. At UPS, undesirable behavior includes anything that results in poor quality and causes packages not to arrive to customers on time. Norms vary considerably from one organization to another. For example, a research and development laboratory may encourage scientists to question top management's directives because professional judgment is crucial to the organization's final output. A military organization, however, would consider such questioning as insubordination and justification for severely sanctioning the questioner.

Effective managers do not try to change employees' personalities or basic beliefs. Rather, they identify observable employee behaviors and the environmental conditions that affect these behaviors. They then attempt to control external events in order to influence employee behavior. As we discussed in Chapters 3 through 5, an individual's personality, attitudes, and problem-solving style influence the manner in which he or she behaves. Because they often have a difficult time uncovering these characteristics in employees, managers usually have to focus on those behaviors that they can observe.

TYPES OF LEARNING

Learning is a relatively permanent change in the frequency of occurrence of a specific individual behavior.[2] In an organization, a manager wants employees to learn productive work behaviors. To a great extent, learning new work behaviors depends on environmental factors. The manager's goal, then, is to provide learning experiences in an environment that will promote employee behaviors desired by the organization. In the work setting, learning can take place in one of three ways: classical conditioning, operant conditioning, and social learning. Of these three types of learning, operant conditioning and social learning are most important in terms of understanding organizational behavior.

Classical Conditioning

Classical conditioning is the process by which individuals learn reflex behavior. A **reflex** is an involuntary or automatic response that is not under an individual's conscious control. Examples of reflexive behavior are shown in Table 6.1. In classical conditioning, an unconditioned stimulus (environmental event) brings out a reflexive response. Sometimes a neutral environmental event, called a conditioned stimulus, can be paired with the unconditioned stimulus that brings out the reflex. Eventually, the conditioned stimulus alone brings out the reflexive behavior. In classical conditioning, environmental events that precede a reflexive response control it.

The name most frequently associated with classical conditioning is Ivan Pavlov, the Russian physiologist whose experiments with dogs led to the early formulations of classical conditioning theory.[3] In Pavlov's famous experiment, the sound of a metronome (the conditioning stimulus) was paired with food (the unconditioned stimulus). The dogs eventually exhibited a

TABLE 6.1	Examples of Reflexive Behavior		
		Stimulus (S)	**Response (R)**
The Individual	•	is stuck by a pin and	flinches.
	•	is shocked by an electric current and	jumps or screams.
	•	has something in his or her eye and	blinks.
	•	hits an elbow on the corner of a desk and	flexes arm.

salivation response (the reflex response) to the sound of the metronome alone. The classical conditioning process is shown in Figure 6.1.

The distinction between reflexive and nonreflexive behaviors has become somewhat blurred. Some behaviors formerly thought to be exclusively reflex responses can be under the individual's control. For example, biofeedback techniques can effectively change heart rate, blood pressure, muscle tension, and galvanic skin response—responses once considered to be exclusively reflexive.

From the managerial viewpoint, classical conditioning is usually not considered applicable to the work setting. Desired employee behaviors usually do not include reflexive responses that can be changed by using classical conditioning techniques. Instead, managers are interested in the voluntary behaviors of employees and how they can be changed.

Operant Conditioning

The person most closely linked with this type of learning is B. F. Skinner.[4] He coined the term **operant conditioning** to refer to a process by which individuals learn voluntary behavior. Voluntary behaviors are operants because they operate, or have some influence, on the environment. Learning occurs because of the consequences that follow the behavior. Many employee work behaviors in organizations are operant behaviors. In fact, most behaviors in everyday life (such as talking, walking, reading, or working) are

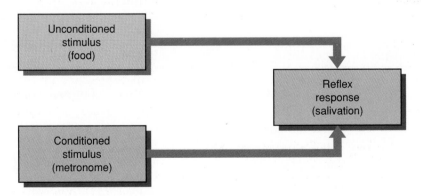

FIGURE 6.1 Classical Conditioning

forms of operant behavior. Table 6.2 shows some examples of operant behaviors and consequences.

Managers are interested in operant behaviors because they can influence, or manage, such behaviors by their results. For example, the frequency of an employee behavior can be increased or decreased by changing the results of that behavior. The critical aspect of operant conditioning is what happens as a consequence of the behavior. The strength and frequency of operantly conditioned behaviors are determined mainly by consequences. Thus, managers must understand the effects of different kinds of consequences on the task behaviors of employees. At UPS, one consequence of a driver wasting thirty seconds on each stop is to work one hour and ten minutes more that day to deliver all packages.

Social Learning

Albert Bandura and others have extended and expanded the work of Skinner by demonstrating that people can learn new behavior by watching others in a social situation and then imitating their behavior. This type of learning is called social learning.[5] **Social learning** refers to those behaviors we learn from observing others and imitating their behavior. People first watch others who act as models and then develop a mental picture of the behavior and its results. They then try out the behavior; if the results are positive, they then repeat the behavior; if an unpleasant result occurs, they do not repeat the behavior. Learning occurs when the person tries the behavior and experiences a favorable result.

Social learning integrates modeling, symbolism, and self-control, as shown in Figure 6.2. People imitate parents, friends, teachers, heros, and others because they can identify with them. The symbolic process allows us to set guidelines for our behavior. If a golfer observes Nancy Lopez or Jack Nicklaus swinging a golf club with good results, this observation creates an image in the mind that the person retains. These images or mental road maps help the person engage in the proper swing next time he or she tries to hit the golf ball. We also attempt self-control by not engaging in behaviors that we have seen have unpleasant consequences for people who do engage in them. Many people, for example, have exercised self-control and stopped smoking because of its link to various forms of cancer. They have seen or read how smoking has affected the health of others.

TABLE 6.2   Examples of Operant Behaviors and Their Consequences

	Behaviors	Consequences
The Individual	• works and	is paid.
	• is late to work and	is docked pay.
	• enters a restaurant and	eats.
	• enters a football stadium and	watches a football game.
	• enters a grocery store and	buys food.

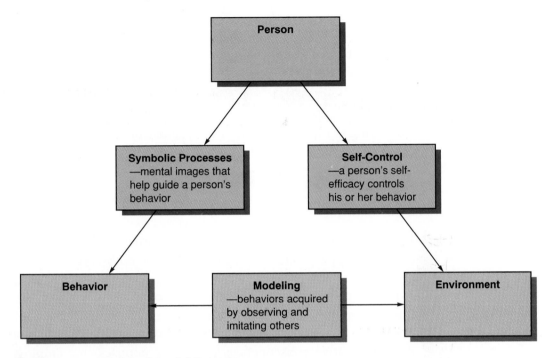

FIGURE 6.2   A Model of Social Learning

Source: Adapted from R. Kreitner and F. Luthans. A Social Learning Approach to Behavioral Management: Radical Behaviorists 'Mellowing Out.' *Organizational Dynamics,* Autumn 1984, 55.

A central part of social learning theory is the concept of self-efficacy. **Self-efficacy** refers to the belief that one can perform adequately in a situation.[6] Employees with high self-efficacy believe that (1) they have the ability needed, (2) they are capable of the effort required to achieve the goal, and (3) no outside events will prevent them from obtaining a desired level of performance. If workers have low self-efficacy, they believe that no matter how hard they try, something will happen to prevent them from reaching their desired level of performance. Self-efficacy influences our choice of tasks and how long we will try to reach our goals. For example, if you are a novice golfer and have only taken a few lessons, you might shoot a good round. Under such circumstances, most of us would probably attribute our score to "beginner's luck" and not to our abilities. On the other hand, after many lessons and hours of practice, if low self-efficacy persons still cannot break one-hundred, they may conclude that the demands are too great to spend any more time on this task. It may be because of the lack of time and not their lack of ability that they are not successful. High self-efficacy individuals will try even harder to reach their performance goals. This might include taking more lessons, watching videotapes of their swing, and practicing even harder.

A manager's expectations about a subordinate's behavior can affect a person's self-efficacy. If a manager holds high expectations for the person and gives the person the proper training to succeed, the person's self-efficacy is likely to increase. If a manager holds low expectations for the subordinate, the subordinate performs poorly, and the manager gives little constructive advice, then the poor behavior might persist because the employee is likely to form an impression that he or she cannot achieve the task.

When people believe that they are not capable of doing the required work, their motivation to perform the task will be low. **Learned helplessness** occurs when the motivation to perform the task is so low that the worker just simply gives up. Employees suffering from learned helplessness simply stop trying to find out what they are capable of doing. Many workers who are unemployed for extended periods of time suffer from learned helplessness.

Applications of social learning theory for improving behavior in organizations are just starting to emerge.[7] Researchers have suggested the managers do the following things:

- Identify the behaviors that will lead to improved performance.
- Select the appropriate model for employees to observe.
- Make sure that employees are capable of meeting the technical skill requirements of the required new behaviors.
- Structure a positive learning situation to increase the likelihood that employees will learn the new behaviors and act in the proper manner.
- Provide positive consequences (praise or bonuses) for employees who engage in proper modeling behaviors.
- Develop management practices that maintain these newly learned behaviors.

In the next section, we return to the operant conditioning theory that behavior is influenced by its consequences. It is the most widely used theory of learning and has organizational implications for designing effective reward systems. To fully understand this theory, we need to review its basic elements.

CONTINGENCIES OF REINFORCEMENT

A **contingency of reinforcement** is the relationship between a behavior and the preceding and following environmental events that influence that behavior. A contingency of reinforcement consists of an antecedent, a behavior, and a consequence.[8]

An **antecedent** precedes and is a stimulus to a behavior. The probability that a particular behavior will occur can be increased by presenting or withdrawing a particular antecedent. At UPS, each driver prepares a "to do" list. This routes the driver's deliveries for the day. The drivers are simply organizing their tasks and trying to focus their attention on specific behaviors. The "to do" list is an antecedent that the drivers use to influence their behavior.

A **consequence** is the result of a behavior. A consequence of a behavior can be either positive or negative in terms of goal or task accomplishment.

The manager's response to the employee is contingent on the consequence of the behavior (and sometimes on the behavior itself, regardless of consequence).

Figure 6.3 shows an example of a contingency of reinforcement. First, the employee and manager jointly set a goal (say, selling one hundred thousand dollars worth of equipment next month). Next, the employee performs tasks to achieve this goal (such as calling on four new customers a week, having regular lunches with current buyers, and attending a two-day executive training program on new methods of selling). If the employee reaches the sales goal, the manager praises the employee—an action contingent on achievement of the goal. If the employee does not reach the goal, the manager does not say anything or reprimands the employee.

To further understand the contingency of reinforcement concept, we have to identify the major types of contingency. First, an event can be presented (applied) or withdrawn (removed), contingent on employee behavior. The event also may be positive or aversive. **Positive events** are desired, or pleasing, to the employee. **Aversive events** are undesired, or displeasing, to the employee. Figure 6.4 shows how these events can be combined to produce four major types of contingencies of reinforcement. It also shows whether a particular type of contingency increases or decreases the future frequency of the employee behavior. Figure 6.4 is the basis for the following discussion of contingencies of reinforcement. Note that reinforcement, whether positive or negative, *always* increases the frequency of the employee behavior. Omission and punishment *always* decrease the frequency of the employee behavior.

Positive Reinforcement

Reinforcement is a behavioral contingency that increases the frequency of a particular behavior that it follows. **Positive reinforcement** presents a

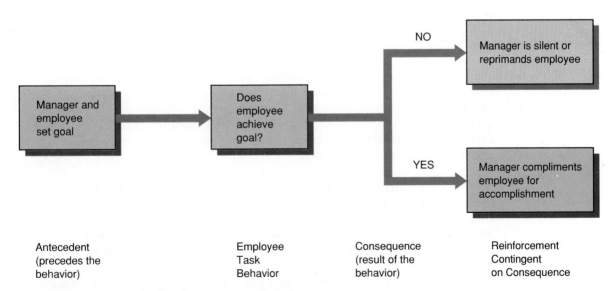

| Antecedent (precedes the behavior) | Employee Task Behavior | Consequence (result of the behavior) | Reinforcement Contingent on Consequence |

FIGURE 6.3 Example of Contingent Reinforcement

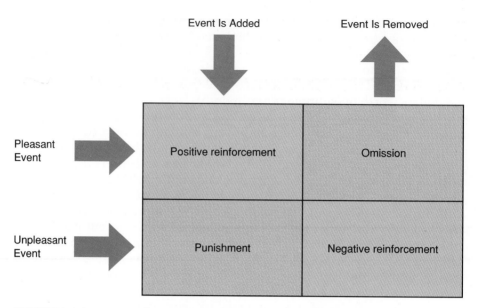

FIGURE 6.4   Types of Contingencies of Reinforcement

pleasant consequence for occurrence of a desired behavior. That is, a manager provides a positive reward contingent on an employee's behavior that the manager views as desirable or leading toward achievement of the organization's goals.[9]

Reinforcement versus Reward   The terms *reinforcement* and *reward* are often confused in everyday usage. A **reward** is an event that a person finds desirable or pleasing. Thus, whether a reward acts as a reinforcer is subjective to the individual. For example, the manager who singles out and praises an employee before his or her co-workers for finding an error in the group's report believed that the desired behavior was being reinforced. Later, however, the manager learned that the employee was given the silent treatment by co-workers and that the employee has stopped looking for errors. To qualify as a reinforcer, a reward must increase the frequency of the behavior it follows. Recall that at UPS, drivers can earn more money if they work overtime scheduled by management. The extra money can be regarded as a positive reinforcer for a particular individual only if the frequency of desired behavior (in this case, high performance) increases. A reward does not act as a reinforcer if the frequency of the behavior decreases or remains unchanged.

Primary and Secondary Reinforcers   A **primary reinforcer** is an event for which the individual does not have to learn the value of the reinforcer. Food, shelter, and water are primary reinforcers for most people. However, primary reinforcers do not always reinforce. For example, food may not be a reinforcer to someone who has just completed a five-course meal.

Most behavior in organizations is influenced by **secondary reinforcers.** A secondary reinforcer is an event that once had neutral value but has taken

◆ *ACROSS CULTURES*

WORKING ON THE ASSEMBLY LINE AT SAMSUNG

Samsung manufactures microwave ovens in Suwon, South Korea. More than half of its assemblers are single women. The company has a reputation of being good to its workers. All employees work eleven hours a day, twenty-seven days a month. This averages out to about sixty-eight hours per week. A few years ago, the basic wage was just over $350 a month—a little more than $1.20 per hour. In addition, medical services and lunches are free, and breakfasts and dinners can be bought for fifteen cents. Employees receive ten days off for vacation, five in the summer and five in the winter. If they wish, they can spend this time at company-run resorts on the seacoast. The employees also receive gifts several times a year: clothes, shoes, hiking bags, tape re-

corders. Housing is provided free in company-sponsored dormitories. There are fifteen dormitories in the Suwon complex, each of which houses 420 women, six to a room. If employees want to live outside the dormitory in an apartment, Samsung loans them money for rent. They repay Samsung, with interest, from each paycheck.

Women who live in the dorm get up at 6:00 A.M. and have breakfast by 7:00 A.M. They are at their work stations by 8:00 A.M. Jang Mee Hur is one of Samsung's employees who works on the assembly line. If you own a GE Spacemaker microwave, chances are that she has worked on it. She attaches twelve hundred oven doors per shift. After work, single women must be back in the dormitories by 9:30 P.M., even on the three Sundays off they receive each month.[10]

on some value (positive or negative) for an individual because of past experience. Money is an obvious example of a secondary reinforcer. Although it cannot directly satisfy a basic human need, money has value because an individual can use it to purchase both necessities and nonessentials.

Often organizations provide employees with both primary and secondary reinforcers. When General Electric (GE) sold its microwave oven division to Samsung, a Korean organization, Samsung needed to design a world-class electronics organization to mass-produce these microwaves. By reading this chapter's Across Cultures, you should be able to understand how Samsung uses both primary and secondary reinforcers to motivate its employees.

Principles of Positive Reinforcement   Several factors can influence the intensity of positive reinforcement.[11] These factors can be thought of loosely as principles because they help to explain optimum reinforcement conditions.

The **principle of contingent reinforcement** states that the reinforcer must be administered only if the desired behavior is performed. According to this principle, a reinforcer loses effectiveness if it is administered when the desired behavior has not been performed.

The **principle of immediate reinforcement** states that the reinforcer will have more effect if it is administered immediately after the desired behavior has occurred. The more time that elapses, the less effective the

---

TABLE 6.3   Rewards Used by Organizations

Material Rewards	Supplemental Benefits	Status Symbols
• Pay	• Company automobiles	• Corner offices
• Pay raises	• Health insurance plans	• Offices with windows
• Stock options	• Pension contributions	• Carpeting
• Profit sharing	• Vacation and sick leave	• Drapes
• Deferred compensation	• Recreation facilities	• Paintings
• Bonuses/Bonus plans	• Child care support	• Watches
• Incentive plans	• Club privileges	• Rings
• Expense accounts	• Parental leave	

Social/ Interpersonal Rewards	Rewards from the Task	Self- Administered Rewards
• Praise	• Sense of achievement	• Self-congratulation
• Developmental feedback	• Jobs with more responsibility	• Self-recognition
• Smiles, pats on the back, and other nonverbal signals	• Job autonomy/ self-direction	• Self-praise
• Requests for suggestions	• Performing important tasks	• Self-development through expanded knowledge/skills
• Invitations to coffee or lunch		• Greater sense of self-worth
• Wall plaques		

---

reinforcer will be. Thus, the reinforcer should be delivered as soon as practical following completion of the desired behavior.

The **principle of reinforcement size** states that the larger the amount of reinforcer delivered after the desired behavior, the more effect the reinforcer will have on the rate of the desired behavior. The amount, or size, of the reinforcer is relative. A reinforcer that might be large to one person may be small to another person. Thus, the size of the reinforcer must be determined in relation both to the behavior and the individual.

The **principle of reinforcement deprivation** states that the more a person is deprived of the reinforcer, the greater effect it will have on the future occurrence of the desired behavior. However, if an employee recently has had enough of a reinforcer and is satiated, the reinforcer will have less effect.

Organizational Rewards

What types of rewards do organizations commonly use? Material rewards—salary, bonuses, fringe benefits, and so on—are obvious. However, most organizations offer a wide range of rewards, many of which are not immediately apparent. They include verbal approval, assignment to desired tasks, improved working conditions, and extra time off. At Sharp, a Japanese electronics manufacturer, top performers are rewarded by being assigned to a "gold badge" project team that reports directly to the company president. The privilege instills pride and gets other employees scrambling for new ideas and products in the hope that they, too, will make the team. In addition, self-administered rewards are important. Self-congratulation for accomplishing a particularly difficult assignment can be an important personal reinforcer. Table 6.3 contains an extensive list of potential organizational rewards. Remember, however, these rewards will act as reinforcers only if the individual receiving the reward finds it desirable or pleasing.

The following In Practice shows how Victor Kiam, president of Remington Products, turned around this organization by using a variety of organizational rewards to reinforce desired employee behaviors. When he bought the organization from Sperry Corporation in 1979, its sales lagged behind Norelco. Now, some eleven years later, it has become a leader in the electric razor industry. Let's read how Kiam achieved this turnaround.

IN PRACTICE

TURNAROUND AT REMINGTON PRODUCTS

Victor Kiam had to convince employees that Remington Products could succeed and that they needed to work hard to help the organization succeed. Unfortunately, he had to lay off seventy employees almost immediately after buying the organization from Sperry Corporation to save it from bankruptcy.

He then established incentives to reward individual performance; one-third of an employee's salary, for example, consists of incentive payments for reaching performance targets. There is also a profit-sharing plan that ties an employee's performance to that of the entire organization. Some managers can earn a bonus based on the profits earned by their division.

Kiam also believes in equity on the job. There are no organization perks, such as cars or special dining rooms, for managers. He holds monthly meetings on the shop floor, where he reviews the organization's performance with all employees who care to attend the meeting. Employees call him by his first name, and he knows many of them by their first names. It is during these meetings that he takes time to recognize employees and praise people for their performance during the past month.

Remington also holds regular coffee sessions with employees to generate new ideas or solutions to problems. These meetings bring together workers from different divisions and levels of the organization. Employees are encouraged to speak up and not worry about offending some top manager. At one meeting, a woman on the assembly line suggested a new product—the preoperative surgical shaver—that soon after became a product for the organization. She was rewarded with a free trip anywhere in the world.

When people make mistakes, Kiam tells them so. He wants employees to put their mistakes behind them and try again. He encourages employees to take risks and make decisions on their own.[12]

Where Kiam at Remington has used positive reinforcement, behavior change has been dramatic and sustained. Positive reinforcement was used selectively in areas where work could be measured and quantifiable standards set (if they did not already exist) and in areas where observation showed that the existing level of performance was far below standard. Many other organizations—Du Pont, Tandem, ITT, Procter & Gamble, Florida Power and Light, and Emory Air Freight—have used positive reinforcement programs with similar results.[13]

Negative Reinforcement

In **negative reinforcement** (see Figure 6.4), an unpleasant event is presented before the employee behavior and is then removed when the behavior occurs. This procedure increases the likelihood that the desired behavior will occur. Negative reinforcement is sometimes confused with punishment because both use unpleasant events to influence behavior. Negative reinforcement is used to *increase* the frequency of a desired behavior. Omission and punishment are used to *decrease* the frequency of an undesired behavior.

Managers frequently use negative reinforcement when an employee has not done something that is desired. For example, air-traffic controllers want the capability to activate a blinking light and a loud buzzer in the cockpits when airplanes come too close together. The air-traffic controllers would not shut these off until the planes moved farther apart. This type of procedure is called escape learning because the pilots begin to move their planes away from each other in order to escape the light and buzzer. In **escape learning,** an unpleasant event occurs until an employee performs a behavior, or escape response, to terminate it.

Avoidance is closely related to escape. In **avoidance learning,** a person prevents an unpleasant event from occurring by completing the proper behavior before the unpleasant event is presented. After several encounters with a computer because you cannot program it properly, you will learn the programming language to avoid the computer's error messages. Escape and avoidance are both types of negative reinforcement that result in an increase in the desired behavior and removal of unpleasant events.

Omission

Omission means all reinforcing events are stopped. Whereas reinforcement increases the frequency of a desirable behavior, omission decreases the frequency and eventually extinguishes an undesirable behavior (see Figure 6.4). Managers remove reinforcers to diminish undesirable employee behaviors. Omission reduces the occurrence of employee behaviors that do not lead to achievement of organizational goals. The omission procedure consists of three steps:

1. Identifying the behavior to be reduced or eliminated.
2. Identifying the reinforcer that maintains the behavior.
3. Stopping the reinforcer.

Omission is a useful technique for reducing behaviors that are undesirable or that disrupt normal work flow. For example, a group reinforces the disruptive behavior of a member by laughing at the behavior. When the group stops laughing (the reinforcer), the disruptive behavior will diminish and eventually stop.

Omission can also be regarded as a failure to reinforce a behavior positively. In this regard, the omission of behaviors can be quite accidental. If managers fail to reinforce desirable behaviors, they may be using omission without recognizing it. As a result, the frequency of desirable behaviors may inadvertently decrease.

Omission may effectively decrease undesirable employee behavior, but it does not automatically replace the undesirable behavior with desirable behavior. Often when omission is stopped, the undesirable behavior is likely to return if alternative behaviors have not been developed to replace the behavior. Therefore, when omission is used, it should be combined with other methods of reinforcement to develop the desired behaviors.

Punishment

Punishment (see Figure 6.4) is an unpleasant event that follows a behavior and decreases its frequency. As in positive reinforcement, a punishment contingency may include a specific antecedent that cues the employee that a consequence (punisher) will follow a specific behavior. Whereas a positive reinforcement contingency encourages the frequency of a desired behavior, a punishment contingency decreases the frequency of an undesired behavior.

To qualify as a punisher, an event must decrease the undesirable behavior. Just because an event is thought of as unpleasant, it is not necessarily a punisher. The event must actually reduce or stop the undesired behavior before it can be defined as a punisher.

Organizations typically use several types of unpleasant events to punish individuals. Material consequences for failure to perform adequately, for example, include a cut in pay, a disciplinary layoff without pay, a demotion, or a transfer to a dead-end job. The final punishment is the firing of an employee for failure to perform. In general, unpleasant material events are not used widely in organizations except in cases of serious behavior problems.

Interpersonal punishers are used extensively on a day-to-day basis. Examples include a manager's oral reprimand of an employee for unacceptable behavior or nonverbal punishers, such as frowns, grunts, and aggressive body language. Certain tasks themselves can be unpleasant. The fatigue that follows hard physical labor can be considered a punisher, as can harsh or dirty working conditions. However, care must be exercised in labeling a punisher. In some fields or to some employees, harsh or dirty working conditions could be considered as just something that goes with the job.

The principles of positive reinforcement discussed earlier have equivalents in punishment. For maximum effectiveness, a punisher should be directly linked to the undesirable behavior (principle of contingent punishment); the punisher should be administered immediately (principle of immediate punishment); and in general, the greater the size of the punisher, the stronger the effect will be on the undesirable behavior (principle of punishment size).

Negative Effects An argument against the use of punishment is the chance of its negative effects, especially over long periods of time or through sustained periods of punishment. Even though punishment may stop an undesirable employee behavior, the potential negative consequences may be greater than the original undesirable behavior. Figure 6.5 illustrates some potential negative effects of punishment.

Punishment may cause undesirable emotional reactions. For example, a worker who has been reprimanded for staying on break too long may react with anger toward the manager and the organization. This may lead to

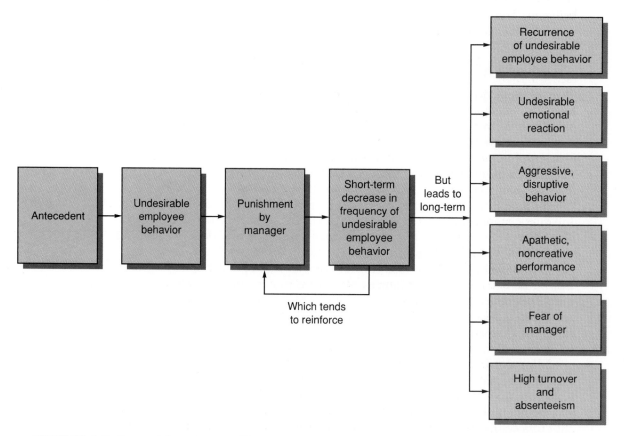

FIGURE 6.5 Potential Negative Effects of Punishment

behavior detrimental to the organization. Sabotage, for example, typically is a result of a punishment-oriented behavioral management system.

Punishment frequently leads only to short-term suppression of the undesirable behavior, rather than to its elimination. Continuous suppression of an undesirable behavior over a long time usually requires continued punishment. Another problem is that control of the undesirable behavior becomes contingent on the manager's presence. When the manager is not present, the undesirable employee behavior is likely to recur.

In addition, the punished individual may try to avoid or escape the situation. From an organizational viewpoint, this reaction may be undesirable if an employee avoids a particular task that is necessary for normal operations. High absenteeism is a form of avoidance that is likely to occur in situations where punishment is used frequently. Voluntary termination is the employee's final form of escape. Organizations that depend on punishment are likely to have high rates of employee turnover. While some turnover is desirable, excessive rates are undesirable because of increased recruitment and training costs and because useful, adequately performing employees are more likely to leave.

Punishment suppresses employee initiative and flexibility. Reacting to punishment, many an employee has said, "I'm going to do just what I'm told and nothing more." Such an attitude is undesirable because organizations depend on the personal initiative and creativity that individual employees bring to their jobs. Overusing punishment produces apathetic employees, who are not an asset to an organization. Sustained punishment can also lead to negative employee self-esteem. Low self-esteem, in turn, undermines the employee's self-confidence, which is necessary for performing most jobs (see Chapter 3).

Punishment produces a conditioned fear by the employees who work for the manager. That is, the employee develops a general fear of the punishment-oriented manager. The manager becomes an environmental cue that indicates to the employee the probability of an aversive event. This is an obvious problem, especially if many day-to-day situations require normal and positive interaction between employee and manager. Responses to fear, such as "hiding" or reluctance to communicate with a manager, may well hinder employee performance.

Many managers rely on punishment because it often produces fast results in the short run.[14] In essence, the manager is reinforced for using punishment because the approach does produce an immediate change in an employee's behavior. However, the manager may overlook punishment's long-term detrimental negative effects, which can be cumulative. A few incidents of punishment may not produce negative effects. Its long-term, sustained use by the manager, however, most often results in negative outcomes for the organization.

Effective Use of Punishment   Positive reinforcement is more effective than punishment over the long run. Effectively used, however, punishment does have an appropriate place in management.

The most common form of punishment in organizations is the oral reprimand. It is intended to diminish or stop an undesirable employee behavior. An old rule of thumb is "Praise in public; punish in private." Private punishment establishes a different type of contingency of reinforcement than public punishment. In general, a private reprimand can be constructive and instructive in nature. A public reprimand is likely to have negative effects.

Punishment should be connected as immediately, directly, and obviously as possible to the undesirable behavior. An unnecessarily long interval between the behavior and the punishment makes the punishment less effective. Oral reprimands should never be given about behavior in general and especially never about a so-called bad attitude. An effective reprimand pinpoints and specifically describes the undesirable behavior to be avoided in the future. It focuses on the target behavior and avoids threatening the employee's self-image. The effective reprimand punishes specific undesirable behavior, not the person.

Punishment (by definition) trains a person in what not to do, not in what to do. Therefore, a manager must specify an alternative behavior to the employee. When the employee performs the desired alternative behavior, it is then essential for the manager to reinforce that behavior positively.

Finally, managers should strike an appropriate balance between the use of pleasant and unpleasant events. It is not the absolute number of unpleasant events that is important but the ratio of positive to unpleasant events. When a manager uses positive reinforcement frequently, an occasional deserved punishment can be quite effective. However, if a manager never uses positive reinforcement, relying entirely on punishment, the long-run negative effects are likely to counteract any short-term benefits. Positive management procedures should dominate in any well-run organization.

In the 1970s, Richard Grote started a new form of discipline at Frito-Lay. He began searching for a better management technique after a disgruntled worker wrote a vulgar message on a corn chip and it was discovered by a consumer. Grote gave the employee a day off with pay and called it "positive discipline." Grote noticed that it had a positive effect on morale and cut down the number of terminations. Since then companies such as AT&T, General Electric, and Union Carbide, among others, have used positive discipline to change negative behaviors of employees. The following account shows how Tampa Electric Company has used this form of punishment to achieve positive results.

IN PRACTICE

POSITIVE DISCIPLINE AT TAMPA ELECTRIC

When Tampa Electric Company first told Dean Broome about "positive discipline," he laughed at the idea of dealing with problem employees by giving them a paid day off. It did not sound like punishment to Broome, a station manager for the company. Nevertheless, Broome was having a problem with a lazy mechanic, so he told him, "Take a day off and decide if you want your job." That got the mechanic's attention, and he turned around his behavior.

On the face of it, positive discipline sounds like a contradiction in terms. Positive disciplinary systems at Tampa Electric work like this. Employees who come in late, do a sloppy job, or are rude to other employees first get an oral "reminder" rather than a formal reprimand. Next comes the written reminder, then a paid day off. Tampa Electric employees call the day off a "decision-making leave day."

After a day on the beach, the golf course, or wherever, employees must agree in writing that they will be on their best behavior for the next year. The paid day off is a one-shot chance to reform. If employees do not change their behavior, they are fired. The process is documented, so employees often have little legal recourse.

In the eight years since Tampa Electric started using positive discipline, more employees have improved their job performance than have left the company. According to Broome, "Before, we punished employees and treated them worse and worse and expected them to act better. I don't ever recall suspending someone who came back ready to change."[15]

Using Contingencies of Reinforcement

Figure 6.6 demonstrates the use of contingencies of reinforcement (positive and negative reinforcement, omission, and punishment). Remember, for a positive reinforcer to cause a desired behavior to be repeated, it must have value for the employee. If the employee is consistently on time, the manager positively reinforces this behavior by complimenting the employee. On the other hand, if the employee has been reprimanded in the past for coming to work late and then reports to work on time, the manager uses negative reinforcement and refrains from saying anything to embarrass the em-

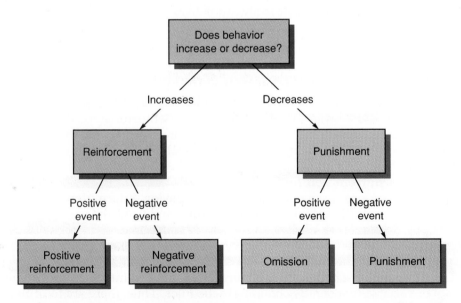

FIGURE 6.6 Responses to Behavior: Reinforcement, Omission, and Punishment

ployee. The manager hopes that the employee will learn to avoid unpleasant comments by coming to work on time.

If the employee continues to come to work late, the manager can use either omission or punishment to try to stop this undesirable behavior. The manager who chooses omission does not praise the tardy employee but simply ignores the employee. The manager who chooses punishment may reprimand, fine, or suspend the employee—and ultimately fire the employee if the behavior persists.

The following guidelines are recommended for using contingencies of reinforcement in the work setting:

- Do not reward all employees the same.
- Remember that failure to respond to behavior has reinforcing consequences; superiors are bound to shape the behavior of subordinates by their use or nonuse of rewards. Carefully examine the consequences of nonactions as well as actions.
- Let employees know which behaviors get reinforced.
- Let employees know what they are doing wrong.
- Do not punish employees in front of others.
- Make the response equal to the behavior by not cheating workers out of their just rewards.[16]

SCHEDULES OF REINFORCEMENT

Schedules of reinforcement determine when reinforcers are applied. Deliberately or not, reinforcement is always delivered according to some schedule.[17]

Continuous and Intermittent Reinforcement

In **continuous reinforcement,** the behavior is reinforced each time it occurs, the simplest schedule of reinforcement. Unfortunately, the manager seldom has the opportunity to deliver a reinforcer every time the employee demonstrates a desired behavior. Therefore, behavior is typically reinforced intermittently.

In **intermittent reinforcement,** a reinforcer is delivered after some, but not every, occurrence of the desired behavior. Intermittent reinforcement can be subdivided into interval and ratio and fixed and variable schedules. An **interval schedule** means that reinforcers are delivered after a certain amount of time has passed. A **ratio schedule** means that reinforcers are delivered after a certain number of behaviors have been performed. These two major schedules can be further subdivided into fixed (not changing) or variable (constantly changing) schedules. Thus, there are four major types of intermittent schedules: fixed interval, variable interval, fixed ratio, and variable ratio.

Fixed Interval Schedule

In a **fixed interval schedule,** a constant amount of time must pass before a reinforcer is provided. The first desired behavior to occur after the interval has elapsed is reinforced. For example, in a fixed interval, one-hour schedule, the first desired behavior that occurs after an hour has elapsed is reinforced.

Administering rewards according to this type of schedule tends to produce an uneven pattern of responses. Prior to the reinforcement, the behavior is frequent and energetic. Immediately following the reinforcement, the behavior becomes less frequent and energetic. Why? Because the individual rather quickly figures out that another reward will not immediately follow the last one. A common example of administering rewards on a fixed interval schedule is the payment of employees on a weekly, biweekly, or monthly basis. That is, monetary reinforcement comes regularly at the end of a specific period of time. Such time intervals, unfortunately, are generally too long to be an effective form of reinforcement for newly acquired work-related behavior.

Variable Interval Schedule

In a **variable interval schedule,** the amount of time between reinforcers varies. For example, Jeff Weekly, an operations manager at Greyhound, makes it a point to walk through the bus maintenance repair area on the average of once a day. However, he varies the times, going perhaps twice on Monday, once on Tuesday, not on Wednesday, not on Thursday, and twice on Friday. During these walks, he reinforces any desirable behavior he observes.

Fixed Ratio Schedule

In a **fixed ratio schedule,** the desired behavior must occur a certain number of times before it is reinforced. The exact number of behaviors is specified. Administering rewards under a fixed ratio schedule tends to produce a high response rate characterized by steady behavior. The employee soon determines that reinforcement is based on the number of responses and performs the responses as quickly as possible to receive the reward. The individual piece-rate system used in many manufacturing plants is an example of such a schedule. Production workers are paid on the basis of how many acceptable pieces they produce (number of responses). Other things being equal, the employee's performance should be steady. In reality, other things are never equal, and a piece-rate system may not lead to the desired behavior.

Let's read how Du Pont Company uses a fixed ratio schedule to motivate its employees. You will also read why some employees are skeptical about such plans.

IN PRACTICE

INCENTIVE PLAN AT DU PONT

Du Pont Company established an incentive plan that covers its twenty thousand employees in its fiber division. Under the plan, employees will receive smaller pay raises over the next five years than other Du Pont employees until their salaries are 6 percent lower than other Du Pont employees. Over the same five-year period, the company will phase in incentives that could result in incentive pay for fiber division workers that exceeds other divisions. Thus, the fiber division employees will have a lower fixed-wage base but an incentive pay system that could result in substantial dollar increases.

If the fiber division's profits are equal to or exceed 80 percent of the division's profit goal, employees will receive a bonus of 3 to 18 percent, depending on the size of the profits. If annual profits fall below 80 percent of the division's profit goal, there will be no bonus and workers will only receive their base salary.

Du Pont's managers believe that under this program, employees could improve their performance by as much as 150 percent and receive big bonuses. Under this plan, employees are encouraged to find solutions to their own problems and set their own schedules. At one plant, vacation time is taken by the hour. During slack times when three of the four members of each team can do the work, the other person takes off to attend to personal business. Some employees, however, believe that management might make decisions, such as writing off assets, in order to reduce the division's profits and, therefore, the size of their bonus. They are also worried that since the fiber division faces stiff competition from major chemical companies in Eastern Europe and the Far East, Du Pont may lower its own price to compete. The effect would be to cut down profits unless sales would rise to offset a potential loss of revenues.[18]

Variable Ratio Schedule

In a **variable ratio schedule,** a certain number of desired behaviors must occur before the reinforcer is delivered, but the number of behaviors varies around some average. Managers frequently use variable ratio schedules with nonmaterial reinforcers. Praise and recognition, for example, are often given on a variable ratio schedule. Managers do not reinforce every behavior. The number of behaviors that occur before they give verbal approval varies from one time to the next.

Comparison of Intermittent Reinforcement Schedules

Table 6.4 summarizes the four types of intermittent reinforcement schedules. Which is superior? Although the data are inconclusive, it appears that the ratio reward schedules—fixed or variable— lead to better performance than either of the two interval schedules. Ratio schedules are more closely related to the occurrence of desired behaviors than interval schedules, which are based on the passage of time.

BEHAVIORAL MODIFICATION

Behavioral modification refers to procedures and principles that are based on operant conditioning. Figure 6.7 depicts the procedures and principles of behavioral modification.[19]

	TABLE 6.4 Comparison of Schedules of Reinforcement		
Schedule	**Form of Reward and Example**	**Influence on Performance**	**Effects on Behavior**
Fixed interval	Reward on fixed time basis; Weekly or monthly paycheck	Leads to average and irregular performance	Fast extinction of behavior
Fixed ratio	Reward tied to specific number of responses; Piece-rate pay system	Leads quickly to very high and stable performance	Moderately fast extinction of behavior
Variable interval	Reward given at varying periods of time; Unannounced inspections or appraisals and rewards given at random times each month	Leads to moderately high and stable performance	Slow extinction of behavior
Variable ratio	Reward given for some behaviors; Sales bonus tied to selling X accounts but X constantly changing around some mean	Leads to very high performance	Very slow extinction of behavior

Pinpointing Relevant Behaviors

Not all employee behaviors are desirable or undesirable from a managerial viewpoint. Many behaviors are neutral; they neither add to nor detract from the achievement of organizational goals. Thus, the first and most important step in applying behavioral modification principles is to identify the behaviors that have a major impact on an employee's overall performance. The manager will concentrate on them, trying to increase desirable behaviors and decrease undesirable behaviors. Pinpointing relevant behaviors consists of three activities:

1.   Observing the behaviors.
2.   Measuring the behaviors. - *Checklist*
3.   Describing the situation in which the behaviors occur.

Training is often necessary to enable managers to pinpoint behaviors. Frequently, the untrained manager confuses employee attitudes, feelings, and values with behaviors.

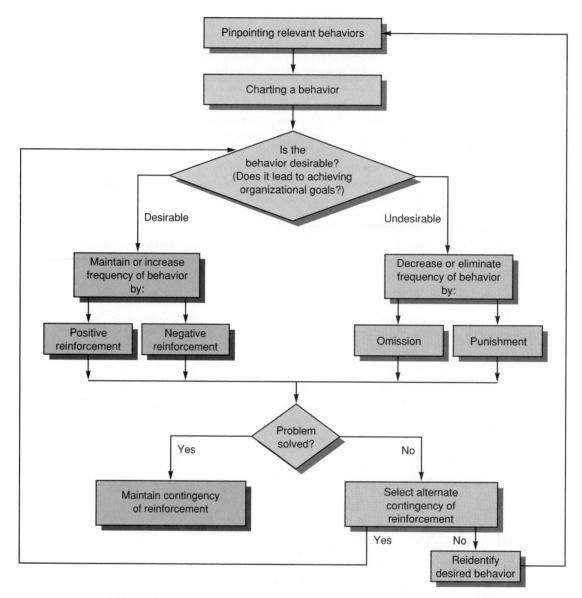

FIGURE 6.7   **Behavioral Modification Procedures and Principles**

Charting Behavior

One of the ways to keep track of employee behaviors is by **charting,** or measuring, them over time. Figure 6.8 shows an example of an employee behavior chart. The horizontal axis reflects time in months. The vertical axis represents employee behavior for past-due projects. Each bar on the chart represents the measurement of the employee's behavior during a one-month period.

Typically, an employee behavior chart is divided into at least two periods. The first is the baseline period, during which behavior is measured before any attempt is made to change it. In Figure 6.8, the baseline period covers June through September. Usually, observations during the baseline period are made without the employee's knowledge by the manager to get an accurate measurement.

The second major period is the intervention period. During this period, the employee's behavior is measured after one or more contingencies of reinforcement—positive reinforcement, negative reinforcement, omission, or punishment—is used. During the intervention period (October through March in Figure 6.8), the employee might be shown the chart, which is a type of feedback. Sometimes this feedback in itself is enough to cause a change in behavior. However, a reward or penalty frequently accompanies feedback and itself may have some effect on the behavior.

Charting has two overall objectives. First, observations during the baseline period show the frequency of certain behaviors. Sometimes, charting a behavior reveals that the behavior is not as much of a problem as was originally thought. Second, by charting through the intervention period, the manager can determine whether the intervention strategy is actually working. Charting then becomes an evaluation method. Sometimes a chart reveals no change in behavior, which means that the intervention was not successful.

Choosing a Contingency of Reinforcement

After a behavior has been identified and charted for a baseline period, the manager selects a contingency of reinforcement aimed at changing the behavior (See Figure 6.8). For desirable behaviors, the manager will use techniques to increase or maintain it. Positive reinforcement, obviously, is the first alternative to consider. The manager must make a judgment about which type of reward will have the desired effect on the employee's behavior. The other alternative is to apply negative reinforcement.

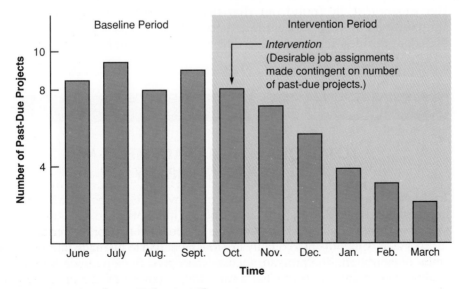

FIGURE 6.8   Employee Behavior Chart

However, if the behavior is undesirable, the manager's goal will be to decrease or stop it. Either punishment or omission would be appropriate. The manager might also choose to use a combination of reinforcement contingencies to extinguish undesirable behaviors while reinforcing (increasing) other, desirable behaviors.

Problem Solved?

Experience gives the effective manager a valuable tool in choosing contingencies of reinforcement to modify employee behaviors. The ability to generalize from similar past situations or from similar incidents with the same employee is essential. If the manager has indeed been successful in affecting the target behavior, the contingency of reinforcement must be maintained for lasting results.

Of course, there is no guarantee that a chosen contingency of reinforcement will be effective. Every manager encounters situations where the first intervention tactic fails. The manager then should either try a different contingency of reinforcement or reidentify the desired behavior (See Figure 6.8). In either case, the manager must again consider the various steps of the procedure. In addition, the procedure can be simplified by an evaluation of the previous effort. The manager may conclude that a different form of positive reinforcement is needed and use it in an attempt to increase the desired behavior. The manager might also try a different type of reinforcement contingency—for instance, a change from positive to negative reinforcement. Or the manager might try a combination of reinforcement contingencies.

Tennant Company has used these principles to evaluate its Total Quality Management Program. Tennant is the world's largest manufacturer of industrial cleaning equipment. In 1979, the company received notices from its customers that its machines had been leaking hydraulic oil. Oddly enough, these complaints were from Japanese customers. When the president called U.S. customers, he found out that their machines also leaked, but they simply wiped up the mess without a complaint. It was at that time that the president decided Tennant would develop a reputation for quality products.

IN PRACTICE

TOTAL QUALITY MANAGEMENT AT TENNANT COMPANY

To develop a quality program, Tennant Company sent its director of manufacturing to attend Philip Crosby's Quality College in Winter Park, Florida. He was trained in Crosby's quality approach, where he learned that for the program to be successful, a commitment to quality improvement had to be made throughout the entire organization. The program focuses managers' thinking toward producing quality products and services. That meant stripping down the manufacturing process to find and eliminate problems, identifying customers (other departments within the company as well as those outside) and satisfying their needs, eliminating waste, making products with zero defects, and having employees inform management of problems that prevented them from performing error-free work.

Upon returning to Tennant, the manufacturing director helped the company establish quality benchmarks. The company found that rework was eating up 15 percent of the assembly space and that 20 percent of Tennant's best mechanics were working overtime to get faulty machines ready for shipment. The company also found that it averaged one leak for every seventy-five hydraulic joints assembled.

The Crosby program was installed and specific goals were set. For example, one goal was that there should be no more than one leak for every twenty-eight hundred joints. Second, ten rework mechanics were transferred to the assembly line to catch mistakes on the line instead of when the machines were ready to be shipped to customers. Third, all parts from suppliers were to be inspected for defects. Defective parts were returned to the supplier. Fourth, a dozen small groups of employees were formed to get employees involved in all aspects of the company. Some of these groups tackled issues on giving positive feedback, exploring opportunities for advancement, creating a wellness program, providing supervisory and management training, controlling inventory, and even establishing a stop-smoking group. These groups all made presentations to management.

What are the results? The inventory group's recommendations alone have saved the company more than one hundred thousand dollars a year. Tennant started to insist that its suppliers now start quality-improvement programs of their own. There is no space reserved for rework since all rework is now done on the assembly line. Only one mechanic is now available for any rework that needs to be done.

Employees receive 30 percent of first-year savings generated by an accepted suggestion. Although some of these are small, ranging anywhere from ten to fifty dollars, Tennant recently saved more than $1.7 million. Lastly, Tennant's market share has increased. Japanese companies are not cutting into its market share because Tennant's quality is now second to none.[20]

Limitations of Behavioral Modification

There are two general limitations to the use of behavioral modification procedures and principles: individual differences and group norms.[21] We will state each limitation and briefly describe ways in which the effective manager can overcome them.

Individual Differences   Behavioral modification often ignores individual differences in needs, values, abilities, and desires. When Tennant and Remington set up their positive reinforcement systems, managers assumed that all employees valued prizes and that all employees had the ability to perform their tasks. However, what is reinforcing to one person may not be to another.

Effective managers can account for these individual differences in two ways. First, they can try to select and hire employees who value the rewards offered by the organization. Proper employee selection can lead to hiring those employees whose needs most closely match the reinforcers provided by the organization. While this is not easy to do, it can be an effective way for managers to take individual differences into account.

Second, managers can allow employees to participate in determining their rewards. Thus, if the present contingencies of reinforcement are ineffective, the manager can ask employees what they would do to correct the situation. This method allows employees to have a greater voice in designing their work environment and should lead to greater employee involvement. However, if this method is used simply to exploit employees, they will look for ways to get around it.

Group Norms When workers feel that management is trying to exploit them, group norms emerge that aim to control the degree of cooperation with management. This control typically takes the form of restricting output. When this situation exists, the implementation of a program (particularly one that relies on praise and other nonmaterial rewards) is likely to meet with stiff resistance from the work group. Group members feel there is little reason to cooperate with management since this behavior may likely lead to pressure to increase productivity, without a corresponding increase in pay.

The power of group norms can reduce the effectiveness of most reward systems. When employees and managers have a history of distrust, the principles covered in this chapter probably will not help. It is first necessary to build an atmosphere of trust between employees and managers. Once that has been done, these principles have a better chance of working.

Ethics of Behavior Modification

Behavioral modification has stirred some controversy in organizations. The criticisms center around a person's freedom and dignity. According to proponents of behavioral modification, the way to manage people effectively is to establish control systems that shape their behaviors. Recognizing that behaviors are shaped by their consequences, managers should administer rewards in ways that promote desirable behaviors from the organization point of view and not worry too much about the individuals' freedom to choose which behaviors to engage in to satisfy their own desires and wants. Others argue that there is an ethical question of whether someone should decide what is good or beneficial for other people and have enough power to manipulate them into doing it. These managers question what manipulation does to a person's sense of self-worth. Promising employees a reward for doing a task they already enjoy doing can lead them to see the reward as the motivation for performing the task, thus undermining their enjoyment of the task. A person may think, "If I have to be bribed or forced into doing this, then I must not enjoy doing the task for its own sake." In essence, is it better for an individual to enjoy a task than for managers to manipulate employees into doing a task? Furthermore, in the place of widespread use of punishment, would not the use of positive reinforcers be more humanitarian?

Managers have some other problems to consider as well. Employees may engage in only those behaviors that can be measured and ignore those that their manager is not measuring. For example, managers may reward the quantity of work produced and overlook its quality. Or they may rely on measuring tardiness or absenteeism of employees, both of which can easily be measured, rather than evaluate the quality of their employees' work, which often is more difficult to measure. Under such conditions, the quality of the employees' work may suffer, but they show up on time for work. Second, many managers feel societal pressures to reinforce behaviors that they really do not desire themselves. This emphasis may lead employees to engage in behaviors, such as recycling campaigns or carpooling, even though such behaviors may interfere with employees' effectiveness.

SUMMARY

Classical conditioning began with the work of Pavlov, who studied reflex behaviors. A metronome (conditioning stimulus) was rung at the same time food was placed in the dog's mouth (unconditioned stimulus). Soon, the sound of the metronome alone evoked salivation.

Operant conditioning learning focuses on the effects of reinforcement on desirable and undesirable behaviors. Changes in behavior result from the consequences of previous behavior. People tend to repeat a behavior that leads to a pleasant result and not to repeat a behavior that leads to an unpleasant result. In short, when a behavior is reinforced, it is repeated; when it is punished or not reinforced, it is not repeated.

Social learning theory focuses on people learning new behaviors by observing others and then modeling their own behavior after that person. A central part of the theory is a person's self-efficacy. A person's self-efficacy influences how a person performs in a situation, how long the person persists in doing a task, and how much effort the person will expend during an activity.

There are two types of reinforcement: (1) positive reinforcement, which increases a desirable behavior because the person is provided with a pleasurable outcome after the behavior has occurred; and (2) negative reinforcement, which also maintains the desirable behavior by presenting an unpleasant event before the behavior occurs and stopping the event when the behavior occurs. Both positive and negative reinforcement increase the frequency of a desirable behavior. Conversely, omission and punishment reduce the frequency of an undesirable behavior. Omission involves stopping everything that reinforces the behavior. A punisher is an unpleasant event that follows the behavior and reduces the probability that the behavior will be repeated.

There are four schedules of reinforcement. The fixed interval schedule gives rewards on a fixed time basis (for example, a weekly or monthly paycheck). In the variable interval schedule, the reward is given around some average time during a specific period of time (for example, the plant manager walking through the plant on the average of five times every week). The fixed ratio schedule ties rewards to certain outputs (for example, a piece-rate system). In the variable ratio schedule, the reward is given around some mean, but the number of behaviors varies (as does a slot machine).

The procedures that managers can use in applying the principles of behavior modification include pinpointing behaviors, charting these behaviors, and choosing a contingency of reinforcement to obtain desirable behaviors and stop undesirable behaviors.

Key Words and Concepts

Antecedent
Aversive events
Avoidance learning
Behavioral modification
Charting
Classical conditioning
Consequence
Contingency of reinforcement
Continuous reinforcement
Omission
Operant conditioning
Positive events
Positive reinforcement
Primary reinforcer
Principle of contingent reinforcement
Principle of immediate reinforcement
Principle of reinforcement deprivation

Escape learning
Fixed interval schedule
Fixed ratio schedule
Intermittent reinforcement
Interval schedule
Learned helplessness
Learning
Learning theory
Negative reinforcement
Principle of reinforcement size
Punishment
Ratio schedule
Reflex
Reinforcement
Reward
Secondary reinforcer
Self-efficacy
Social learning
Variable interval schedule
Variable ratio schedule

Discussion Questions

1. How can managers apply the principles of learning to improve the performance of employees?
2. What ethical considerations should be considered before using a behavioral modification program at work?
3. How can managers use punishment effectively?
4. How did Victor Kiam, president of Remington Products, apply the guidelines for using contingencies of reinforcement to turn around this organization?
5. Which are the most effective reinforcement schedules for maintaining desirable behaviors over the long run?
6. Identify the types of reinforcement used by managers in the Tennant Company? Why were these effective?
7. Describe the basic differences between classical conditioning, social learning, and operant conditioning theories. Which type is most important for managers? Why?

8. What are some pitfalls in Du Pont's incentive program? How can these be overcome?

9. Visit either a local health club or diet center and ask for an interview with the manager. What kinds of rewards do they give their members who achieve targeted goals? Do they use punishment?

10. Is it likely that U.S. managers can use the same types of reinforcers that Samsung's managers use? If so, what are some roadblocks that must be overcome?

11. How can a manager use social learning theory to improve the performance of employees?

◆ MANAGEMENT CASES AND EXERCISES

STONEBRIAR COUNTRY CLUB

Stonebriar Country Club has an exercise program. People who join this program are scheduled to meet with one of two fitness leaders for a general assessment of their physical fitness. This includes a comprehensive physical examination by their own doctor and the person's statement as to his or her desired goals. After these evaluations, the leaders determine the fitness-related activities that people can do, those that they can develop, and the activities that are slowing down the development of each person's fitness.

The fitness leader also discusses the overall goal of the program. It is based on a point system that relates directly to cardiovascular fitness. For example, jogging two miles in twenty minutes is worth six points. Walking on the tread mill at 3.7 miles per hour on an incline of eight degrees for twenty minutes is worth five points. For general fitness, a person should achieve thirty points per week.

With the overall goal of thirty points, the fitness leaders set specific week-by-week goals for members during the first three months. The short-range goals are always measurable and objective. For example, a member's goal might be to get ten points the first week, walk a mile a day for two weeks, and attend two fitness classes. When members reach a goal, a reward is given, such as a tote bag, sweatshirt, T-shirt, or jogging suit. There are numerous other rewards for specific behaviors, such as getting one's name on the lost-pounds list.

To ensure that members know how many points they have earned, members log in on the computer after they have done an activity. The computer keeps track of the number of points earned and provides a sense of immediate feedback. The computer also displays a member's total points earned for the month. Each month, the members are mailed a printout with their total points. The two fitness leaders also receive copies of each member's report. If a member has not been logging in points, he or she receives a cartoon card from the activity leader saying that the member was missed. If the member still does not log any points, the fitness leader calls the member to see if there are any physical reasons why the member is not logging points. If there are no physical reasons, the fitness leader tries to counsel the member into returning to the program.

QUESTIONS:

1. What types of reinforcers are used at Stonebriar Country Club?

2. What schedule of reinforcement is used with its members?

PETER GIFFEN

Prince International is a large, multinational consumer products company with operations in some forty countries. In Canada, it manufactures a full line of products in several plants, the largest and oldest of which is in Kitchener, Ontario.

A large warehouse operation is crucial to the efficiency of the Kitchener plant. As products come off the manufacturing and packaging lines in the north part of the plant, they are sent by conveyor belt across the main road to the south warehouse. This is a nonstop, two-shift operation. If warehouse employees get behind, the whole system becomes clogged and finished products stack up in the manufacturing plant.

Twenty-eight, single, and with seven years' service with the company, Peter Giffen works in the south warehouse. His duties usually involve putting finished products on pallets and stacking them, sometimes using hand dollies, sometimes a forklift.

Peter still lives at home with his mother and father—that is, when he sleeps at home. It's widely known that Peter likes a good time. This socializing costs a fair amount, and Peter complains loudly and often about how broke he always is. He must spend quite a lot of money since his living expenses at home are low and his father is still working and bringing in a good wage. Peter also has additional income from part-time jobs, refereeing men's softball games in the summer and women's basketball games in the winter. He participates in sports a lot himself—"pick-up" hockey games in the winter and bowling in the summer. He seems to enjoy the socializing afterwards at least as much as the sport itself.

Peter has a history of sporadic absences from work, extending over several years. He seems to go through periods when he misses a lot of time, usually in several episodes. During the last three years, he had missed:

1989   12 days--5 episodes
1990   9 days--7 episodes
1991   10 days--8 episodes

In addition, he has been late for work on numerous occasions, once or twice disrupting warehouse operations.

Although his current manager, Joy Legrange, does not think that excessive drinking or socializing are the reason for his absences, she is not sure what is. She does know that it keeps him out late at night—he often boasts about how late he was out and what a great time he had when he shows up for work the following day.

Peter has been absent several times following pick-up hockey games. He claims that playing hockey has aggravated an old back condition. When she examined his personnel file, Joy noticed that two years before, Peter had been sent to see the plant doctor about his back, following his return to work from a sports-related absence. The only notation from the doctor was that his examination revealed no reason why Peter could not continue to work.

Joy was the fourth supervisor that Peter had worked for over the last three years. Others had made comments about his attendance in the file. Each had allowed a record of absences to build up and had then confronted him about it. In all of these sessions, Peter had agreed that his attendance could be improved, while claiming that all his absences were genuinely related to illness or injuries. After each of these "counseling" sessions, his attendance had improved markedly.

Between the periods of absenteeism, Peter was a good worker—not great, just good. He did his job without complaint but never really went "the extra mile." As she looked over the file, Joy recognized his three previous supervisors. Two were "hands-off" types of managers, letting their employees do their job with a minimum of supervision. The other was a real "hands-on" type, always keeping tabs on how things were going, coaching and helping his crew, and criticizing them when they did not do the job right. He was tough but well liked by most people in the plant. It seemed to Joy that Peter's absenteeism tended to be higher when he was with this "hands-on" supervisor's crew and less when he was left alone to do his job his own way.

At 8:00 A.M., Monday, January 7, Peter was not at work, which left the warehouse crew shorthanded. As she dug out his file, it looked to Joy that Giffen was in the midst of another period of absences—he had already missed three days earlier in December. She was thinking about what action to take when he showed up for work again.[22]

QUESTIONS

1.   What contingencies of reinforcement have Peter's supervisors used to motivate him? Have these been effective?

2. Using the procedures and principles of behavior modification, what should Joy do?

3. How can Joy use social learning to change Peter's behavior?

━━━━━

References

1. Adapted from Vogel, T., and Hawkins, C. Can UPS Deliver Goods in the New World? *Business Week,* June 4, 1990, 80-82; Labich, K. Big Changes at Big Brown. *Fortune,* January 18, 1988, 56-64.

2. Akin, G. Varieties of Managerial Learning. *Organizational Dynamics,* Autumn 1987, 36-48.

3. Rescorla, R. A. Pavlovian Analysis of Goal-Directed Behavior. *American Psychologist,* 1987, *42,* 119-129.

4. Skinner, B. F. *About Behaviorism.* New York: Knopf, 1974.

5. For excellent overviews, see Wood, R., and Bandura, A. Social Cognitive Theory of Organizational Management. *Academy of Management Review,* 1989, *13,* 361-384; Bandura, A. *Social Learning Theory.* Englewood Cliffs, N.J.: Prentice-Hall, 1977; Kreitner, R., and Luthans, F. A Social Learning Approach to Behavioral Management: Radical Behaviorists 'Mellowing Out.' *Organizational Dynamics,* Autumn 1984, 47-65.

6. Gist, M. E. Self-Efficacy: Implications in Organizational Behavior and Human Resource Management. *Academy of Management Review,* 1987, *12,* 472-485; Bandura, A. Self-Efficacy Mechanism in Human Agency. *American Psychologist,* 1982, *37,* 122-147. .

7. Zalesny, J. D., and Ford, J. K. Extending the Social Information Processing Perspective: New Links to Attitudes, Behaviors and Perceptions. *Organizational Behavior and Human Decision Processes,* 1990, *47,* 205-246; Gist, M. E., Schwoerer, C., and Rosen, B. Effects of Alternative Training Methods of Self-Efficacy and Performance in Computer Software Training. *Journal of Applied Psychology,* 1989, *74,* 884-891; Sutton, D. D., and Woodman, R. W. Pygmalion Goes to Work: The Effects of Supervisor Expectations in a Retail Setting. *Journal of Applied Psychology,* 1989, *74,* 943-950. Gist, M. E. The Influence of Training Method on Self-Efficacy and Idea Generation among Managers. *Personnel Psychology,* 1989, *42,* 787-805.

8. Luthans, F., and Kreitner, R. *Organizational Behavior Modification and Beyond.* Glenview, Ill.: Scott, Foresman, 1985.

9. Miller, L. *Principles of Everyday Behavior Analysis.* Monterey, Calif.: Brooks/Cole, 1975.

10. Adapted from I. C. Magaziner and M. Patinkin. Fast Heat: How Korea Won the Microwave War. *Harvard Business Review,* January-February 1989, 83-92; R. M. Steers, Y. K. Shin, and G. R. Ungson, *The Chaebol.* Philadelphia: Ballinger Division, 1989, 109-111.

11. These principles are based on Thorndike's law of effect and can be found in Thorndike, E. L. *Educational Psychology: The Psychology of Learning.* vol. 2. New York: Columbia Teachers College, 1913.

12. Adapted from Much, M. Would You Buy a Shaver from This Man? *Industry Week,* August 24, 1987, 37-38; Fahey, A. Kiam Gets Some Help. *Advertising Age,* November 13, 1989, 90; Kiam, V. K. Growth Strategies at Remington. *Journal of Business Strategy,* January-February 1989, 22-26.

13. For an excellent overview, see O'Hara, K., Johnson, C. M., and Beehr, T. A. Organizational Behavior in Management in the Private Sector: A Review of Empirical Research and Recommendations for Further Investigation. *Academy of Management Review,* 1985, *10,* 848-864.

14. Klass, B. S., and Wheeler, H. N. Managerial Decision Making about Employee Discipline: A Policy-Capturing Approach. *Personnel Psychology,* 1990, *43,* 117-134.

15. Adapted from Brown, L. Punishing Workers with a Day Off. *Business Week,* June 16, 1986, 80.

16. Hamner, W. C., and Hamner, E. Behavior Modification on the Bottom Line. *Organizational Dynamics,* Winter 1976, 2-21.

17. Bandura, A. *Principles of Behavior Modification.* New York: Holt, Rinehart and Winston, 1969.

18. Adapted from Hays, L. All Eyes on DuPont's Incentive-Pay Plan. *Wall Street Journal,* December 5, 1988, B1; Dumaine, B. Creating a New Company Culture. *Fortune,* January 15, 1990, 127-131.

19. Luthans, F., and Schweizer, J. How Behavior Modification Techniques Can Improve Total Organizational Performance. *Management Review,* September 1979, 43-50.

20. Adapted from Oberle, J. Quality Gurus: The Men and Their Message. *Training,* January 1990, 47-59; Oberle, J. Employee Involvement at Tennant. *Training,* May 1990, 73-80.

21. Komaki, J. L., Desselles, M. L., and Bowman, E. D. Definitely Not a Breeze: Extending an Operant Model of Effective Supervision to Teams.

Journal of Applied Psychology, 1989, *74,* 522-529; Locke, E. A. The Myths of Behavior Mod in Organizations. *Academy of Management Review,* 1977, *2,* 543-553.

22. Adapted from Gandz, J., and Rush, J. Peter Giffen. Unpublished case, University of Western Ontario, School of Business Administration, London, Ontario, Canada, 1984. Used with permission.

CHAPTER 7

WORK MOTIVATION

LEARNING OBJECTIVES

When you have finished studying this chapter, you should be able to:

- Define motivation and describe the process of motivation.
- Explain and apply four content theories of motivation: needs hierarchy theory, ERG theory, achievement motivation theory, and motivator-hygiene theory.
- Describe and apply two process theories of motivation: expectancy theory and equity theory.
- State the organizational implications for each of the motivation theories.

OUTLINE

CHOOSING THE RIGHT MOTIVATION SYSTEM AT SOLAR PRESS

The managers of Solar Press, based in Naperville, Illinois, have found that choosing the right motivation system is more of an art than a science. As a direct-mail printing and packaging organization, the company has grown from 20 employees in 1970 to more than 375 today, with sales over $37 million.

When the business was small, John Hudetz, the founder, handed out bonus checks, usually for twenty to sixty dollars, to all employees. No one knew how the amount was calculated, but no one complained. Soon the employees took that amount for granted. Hudetz knew all employees by their first names and often passed out the checks while walking around and chatting with employees.

But during the early 1980s, when sales passed the $2 million mark, new people had to be hired. Hudetz decided to get employees more focused on production. The company needed a motivation plan that was linked to performance. Working with a computer spreadsheet, the management team came up with a bonus plan for employees working in the shipping room. Employees were assigned to specific machines in small groups of five people. The more the team produced for the month, the bigger the bonus for each member. The system had an immediate effect. Packaging machines ran faster than ever before as employees strived for bigger paychecks. In many cases, production doubled. Soon, similar motivational systems were installed throughout the organization.

It was not long before problems arose. Because the pressure and rewards for performance were so great, employees neglected maintenance, so machines broke down more often than before. With the focus on speed, quality suffered. Lots of jobs had to be reworked before they left the plant. When employees did find better ways of doing a task, they did not share them with co-workers for fear of reducing their own pay. By the end of 1986, the system was out of hand and management pulled the plug on the program. Performance levels immediately dropped off.

During the following year, management studied what happened and agreed that internal competition among employees hurt the plan. At the end of 1987, another plan was installed. This plan rewarded everyone for profitability according to a clear-cut formula. If the company met its profit goals, 25 percent of any additional profits went into a bonus pool. Employees received a statement at the end of each . quarter showing the amount in their bonus pool. The decision to tie bonuses to companywide results has done two things. First, when the company did not make a profit, such as in the last six months of 1988, employees did not get a bonus check. A memo from management detailed what happened and asked employees for suggestions to make sure that it did not happen again. Second, the system ties all of the employees to common goals and has stopped conflict among teams. People share information with others so that all employees can earn a bonus based on firm profitability.[1]

The cycle of trial and error used by managers at Solar Press occurs over and over again in many organizations. Employees focus on their own jobs and neglect the organization's broader goals. The founder often has a good idea and knows all employees on a first-name basis. But as the business grows, the challenge is to figure out how to stimulate higher performance and keep people focused on providing customers with quality products or services. This is the role of motivation.

Motivation represents the forces acting on or within a person that cause the person to behave in a specific, goal-directed manner. The specific work motives of employees affect their productivity. One job of management is to effectively channel employee motivation toward achieving organizational goals. Alain Gomez, chairman and CEO of Thomson, a high-technology French industrial corporation, says that his greatest challenge is to attract, manage, and develop a worldwide work force. With Thomson's RCA and GE brands competing for the high end of the United States television market, Gomez must set up motivational systems that will result in improved cost-effectiveness, while maintaining high-quality workmanship. Permitting employees to participate in incentive programs in its Marion, Indiana, plant has led to improved productivity. Providing housing and safe working conditions has improved the productivity of employees in Thomson's new low-cost TV manufacturing plant in Bangkok, Thailand.[2]

Surprisingly, many employees are not sure which behaviors their managers value. At the same time, unsure of what workers want from their jobs, managers are often surprised by low worker productivity. A recent study revealed that growth in U.S. output per worker lagged behind that of many other countries. One reason for this decline might be the average number of hours worked by U.S. managers versus those in other nations. For example, managers in Korea work an annual average of 2,833 hours, or 53.8 hours per week, compared to 2,168 annual hours in Japan, 1,895 in the United States, and 1,625 in Germany. Similarly, although entitled to more, the average manager in Korea takes 4.5 days vacation per year, compared to 9.6 in Japan, 19.5 in the United States, and 30.2 in Germany.[3] The growth in U.S. productivity recently has ranked near the bottom among industrialized countries. In fact, the United States now ranks poorly among the top thirteen industrialized nations. While manufacturing has managed a slight productivity gain in recent years—following painful downsizing, concessions in union agreements, and closing or modernization of obsolete plants—U.S. managers still need to develop new ways to motivate their "human capital." This conclusion implies that there is a need to understand more clearly what motivates employees.

While people might not agree about what motivates workers, they do agree that the organizational and work settings must allow three activities to occur:

- People must be attracted not only to join the organization but also to remain in it.
- People must perform the task for which they were hired.
- People must go beyond routine performance and become creative and innovative in their work.

Thus, for an organization to be effective, it must tackle the motivational problems involved in stimulating people's desires to be members of the organization and to be productive workers.

BASIC MOTIVATIONAL PROCESSES

A key motivational principle states that people's performance is based on their level of ability and motivation. This principle is often expressed by the following formula:

$$\text{Performance} = f(\text{ability} \times \text{motivation}).$$

According to this principle, no task can be performed successfully unless the person who is to carry it out has the ability to do so. **Ability** is the person's talent for performing goal-related tasks. This talent might include intellectual competencies, such as verbal and spatial skills, and manual competencies, such as physical strength and dexterity.

Regardless of how intelligent, skilled, or dexterous a person may be, ability alone is not enough to attain a high level of performance. The person must also desire to achieve that performance level. When individuals discuss motivation, they are concerned with (1) what drives behavior, (2) what direction behavior takes, and (3) how to maintain this behavior.

Core Phases

The motivational process begins with identifying a person's needs. This is shown as phase 1 in Figure 7.1. **Needs** are deficiencies that a person experiences at a particular time. These deficiencies may be psychological (such as the need for recognition), physiological (such as the need for water, air, or food), or social (such as the need for friendship). Needs are viewed as energizers. Thus, when need deficiencies are present, the individual is likely to exert effort (phase 2). Need deficiencies create tensions within the individual, who finds them uncomfortable and wants to reduce or eliminate them.

Motivation is goal directed (phase 3). A **goal** is a specific result the individual wants to achieve.[4] An employee's goals may be viewed as forces that attract the individual. Moreover, accomplishing desirable goals can

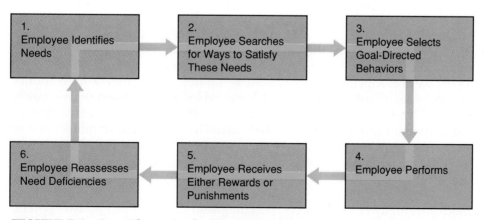

FIGURE 7.1   Core Phases in the Motivation Process

significantly reduce need deficiencies. Some employees have a strong desire for advancement—and an expectation that working long hours will lead to a promotion. Such needs, desires, and expectations create tensions within these employees, making them uncomfortable. Believing that some specific behaviors can overcome this feeling, these employees act. They direct their behaviors toward the goal of reducing this state of tension. Initiation of behaviors sets up cues that feed information back to them on the impact of their behavior. For example, employees who seek to advance may try to work on major problems facing their organization in hopes of gaining more visibility with senior managers and influence in attaining the organization's goals (phase 4). If they receive promotions and raises, the company is sending signals (feedback) to them that their need for advancement and their behaviors are appropriate (phase 5). Once the employees receive either rewards or punishments, they reassess their needs (phase 6).

Complications in the Process

This general model of the motivational process is simple and straightforward. In the real world, of course, the process is not so clear-cut. The first complication is that motives can only be inferred; they cannot be seen. Pat Finnell, plant manager at AC Rochester in Wichita Falls, Texas, notices two employees in the quality control department inspecting spark plugs. She knows that both employees are responsible for the same type of work, have similar abilities, and have been with the organization for about five years. One employee is able to spot quality problems more easily and faster than the other. Since she knows that both employees have similar abilities and training, the difference in their output strongly suggests that they have different motivations. Finnell would have to investigate further to determine what specifically motivates each quality control employee.

A second complication centers on the dynamic nature of needs. At any one time, everyone has many needs, desires, and expectations. Not only do these factors change, but they may also conflict with each other. Employees who put in many extra hours at work to fulfill their needs for accomplishment may find that these extra work hours conflict directly with needs for affiliation and their desire to be with their families.

A third complication is the considerable differences in the way people select certain motives over others and in the energy with which people pursue these motives. Just as organizations differ in the products they manufacture or the services they offer, people differ in terms of what motivates them. Recall in the Preview Case that the employees at Solar Press in the 1970s were not primarily interested in money. John Hudetz used money simply to say thanks for a job well done. When Solar decided to use money as a motivator, remember what happened? Productivity increased, but so did competition among people. Decreases in quality and maintenance of equipment quickly followed. Hudetz soon learned that Solar employees worked for money. They did not value helping their co-workers earn more money.

There is no shortage of motivation theories and tactics that attempt to motivate employees.[5] However, we can group the theories into two general categories: content and process theories.

CONTENT THEORIES OF MOTIVATION

Content theories try to explain the factors within a person that energize, direct, and stop behavior. These theories focus on specific factors that motivate people. For example, an attractive salary, good working conditions, and friendly co-workers are important factors to most people. Hunger (the need for food) or a desire for a steady job (the need for job security) are also factors that arouse people and may cause them to set specific goals (earning money to buy food or working in a financially stable industry). Four widely recognized content theories of motivation are Maslow's needs hierarchy, Alderfer's ERG theory, McClelland's achievement motivation theory, and Herzberg's two-factor theory.

Needs Hierarchy Theory

The most widely recognized theory of motivation is the **needs hierarchy theory.** Abraham H. Maslow suggested that people have a complex set of exceptionally strong needs, which can be arranged in a hierarchy.[6] Underlying this hierarchy are the following basic assumptions:

- A satisfied need does not motivate. However, when one need is satisfied, another need emerges to take its place, so people are always striving to satisfy some need.
- The needs network for most people is very complex, with several needs affecting the behavior of each person at any one time.
- Lower-level needs must be satisfied, in general, before higher-level needs are activated sufficiently to drive behavior.
- There are more ways to satisfy higher-level needs than lower-level needs.

This theory states that a person has five needs: physiological, security, affiliation, esteem, and self-actualization. Figure 7.2 shows these five needs categories, arranged in Maslow's hierarchy.

Physiological Needs   The needs for food, water, air, and shelter are all **physiological needs** and are the lowest level in Maslow's hierarchy. People concentrate on satisfying these needs before turning to higher-order needs. Managers and others should understand that, to the extent that employees are motivated by physiological needs, their concerns do not center on the work they are doing. They will accept any job that serves to meet their needs. Individuals who focus on physiological needs in trying to motivate subordinates assume that people work primarily for money and are primarily concerned with comfort, avoidance of fatigue, and the like.

Security Needs   The needs for safety, stability, and absence of pain, threat, or illness are all **security needs.** Like physiological needs, unsatisfied security needs cause people to be preoccupied with satisfying them.

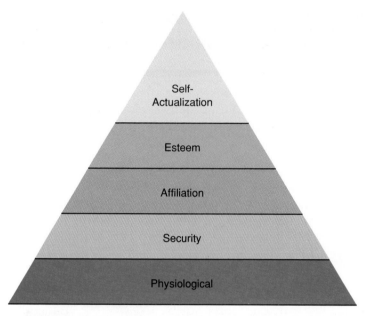

FIGURE 7.2   Maslow's Hierarchy of Needs

People who are motivated primarily by security needs value their jobs mainly as a defense against the loss of basic need satisfactions. Managers who feel that security needs are most important focus on them by emphasizing rules, job security, and fringe benefits. Managers who think subordinates are primarily interested in security may not encourage innovation by them and will not reward risk taking. The employees, in turn, will strictly follow rules.

Affiliation Needs   The needs for friendship, love, and a feeling of belonging are all **affiliation needs.** When physiological and security needs have been satisfied, affiliation needs emerge and motivate people. Managers must realize that when affiliation needs are the primary source of motivation, people value their work as an opportunity for finding and establishing warm and friendly interpersonal relationships. Managers and team leaders who believe that employees are striving primarily to satisfy these needs are likely to act in supportive and permissive ways. They emphasize employee acceptance by co-workers, extracurricular activities (such as organized sports programs and company picnics), and team-based norms.

Esteem Needs   Personal feelings of achievement and self-worth and recognition or respect from others meet **esteem needs.** People with esteem needs want others to accept them for what they are and to perceive them as competent and able. Managers who focus on esteem needs try to motivate employees with public rewards and recognition for services. These managers may use lapel pins, articles in the company paper, achievement lists on the bulletin board, and the like to promote their employees' pride in their work.

Self-Actualization Needs Self-fulfillment is the meeting of **self-actualization needs.** People who strive for self-actualization experience acceptance of themselves and others and increased problem-solving ability. The exercise entitled "Are you Self-Actualized?" at the end of this chapter lets you determine your level of self-actualization. Managers who emphasize self-actualization may involve employees in designing jobs, make special assignments that capitalize on employees' unique skills, or give employee teams leeway in planning and implementing work procedures.

Organizational Implications   Maslow's needs hierarchy theory specifically states the goals that people value. It also suggests the types of behaviors that will help fulfill various needs.

This theory provides less complete information about the origin of needs. The theory, however, implies that higher-level needs are potentially present in most people. Moreover, these higher-level needs will motivate most people if the situation does not block their emergence.

Maslow's work has received much attention from managers, as well as psychologists.[7] Research has found that top managers are more able to satisfy their esteem and self-actualization needs than are lower-level managers; top managers have more challenging jobs and opportunities for self-actualization. Employees who work on teams have been able to satisfy their higher-level needs by making decisions that affect their team and company. For example, at LTV's Camden, Arkansas, plant, employees are trained to perform multiple tasks, including hiring, training, and firing team members who fail to meet performance standards. As team members learn new tasks, they start satisfying their higher-level needs. Employees who have little or no control over their work (such as assembly line workers) may not even experience higher-level needs in relation to their jobs. Studies have also shown that the fulfillment of needs differs according to the job a person performs, a person's age or race, and the size of the company.

ERG Theory

Clay Alderfer agrees with Maslow that individuals have a hierarchy of needs. Instead of the five categories of needs suggested by Maslow, however, Alderfer's **ERG theory** holds that the individual has three sets of basic needs: existence, relatedness, and growth.[8] Alderfer describes them as follows:

- **Existence needs,** or material needs, are satisfied by food, air, water, pay, fringe benefits, and working conditions.
- **Relatedness needs** are met by establishing and maintaining interpersonal relationships with co-workers, superiors, subordinates, friends, and family.
- **Growth needs** are expressed by an individual's attempt to find opportunities for unique personal development by making creative or productive contributions at work.

The arrangement of these categories of needs is similar to Maslow's. Existence needs are similar to Maslow's physiological and safety needs;

relatedness needs are similar to Maslow's affiliation needs; and growth needs are similar to Maslow's esteem and self-actualization needs.

The two theories differ, however, in their views of how people may satisfy the different sets of needs. Maslow states that unfilled needs are motivators and that the next higher-level need is not activated until the preceding lower-level need is satisfied. Thus, a person progresses up the needs hierarchy as each set of lower-level needs is satisfied. In contrast, ERG theory suggests that in addition to this *fulfillment-progression process,* a *frustration-regression process* is at work. That is, if a person is continually frustrated in attempts to satisfy growth needs, relatedness needs will re-emerge as a major motivating force. The individual will return to satisfying this lower-level need instead of attempting to satisfy growth needs, and frustration will lead to regression. Figure 7.3 illustrates these relationships. The solid line indicates a direct relationship between the sets of needs, desires, and needs satisfaction. The dotted line represents what happens when a set of needs is frustrated. For example, if a person's growth needs are frustrated, the importance of relatedness needs increases. The same behavior that had led to the frustration of growth needs now becomes the means for the person to satisfy relatedness needs. The frustration-regression process assumes that existence, relatedness, and growth needs vary along a continuum of concreteness, with existence being the most concrete and growth being the least concrete. Alderfer further assumes that when the lesser concrete needs are not met, more concrete need fulfillment is sought. (Note that the direction of the dotted lines in Figure 7.3 is downward from needs frustration to needs importance.)

Organizational Implications   The ERG theory states that individuals are motivated to engage in behavior to satisfy one of the three sets of needs.

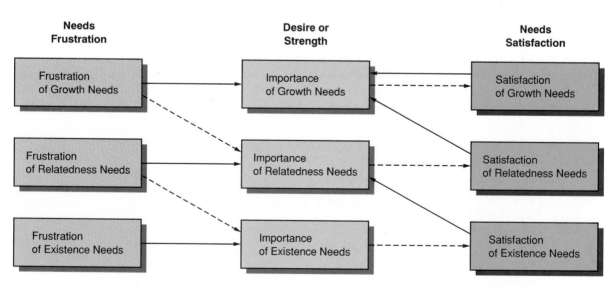

FIGURE 7.3   Graphic Representation of Alderfer's ERG Theory
Source: F. J. Landy, *Psychology of Work Behavior,* 3d ed. Homewood, Ill.: Dorsey, 1985, 324.

Thus, Alderfer's ERG theory provides an important insight for team leaders. If a team leader sees that a subordinate's growth needs are blocked—perhaps because the job does not permit satisfaction of these needs or there are no resources to satisfy them—the team leader should try to redirect the employee's behavior toward satisfying relatedness or existence needs.[9]

Very few research studies have tested the ERG theory of motivation. Several studies do support the three sets of needs in the ERG theory, rather than the five categories of needs in Maslow's hierarchy. Some people question the theory's universality, however, finding that it does not help them understand what motivates employees in their organization.[10]

We believe that Maslow's need and Alderfer's ERG theories both offer a useful way of thinking about employee motivation. The fact that there is disagreement over the exact number of categories of needs should be noted, but both theories agree that satisfying needs is an important part of motivating employees.

Managers in global organizations find that needs models of motivation help them understand the motivations of their employees. To further explore how these models work, this chapter's Across Cultures focuses on a specific example. The microwave oven, invented in the United States over forty years ago, recently became the best-selling major appliance in the world. Yet, if you buy a microwave oven in the United States today, chances are that it was built in South Korea by Samsung. This company makes more than eighty thousand ovens a week. How Samsung succeeded in motivating its employees illustrates the effective application of understanding their needs.

Achievement Motivation Theory

David McClelland has proposed a theory of motivation that he believes is rooted in culture.[11] He states that we all have three particularly important needs: for achievement, affiliation, and power. When a need is strong in a person, its effect will be to motivate the person to engage in behaviors to satisfy the need. His research has focused mainly on ways that managers can develop subordinates' desire to achieve. McClelland has studied achievement motivation extensively, especially with regard to entrepreneurship. **Achievement motivation theory** states that people are motivated according to the strength of their desire either to perform in terms of a standard of excellence or to succeed in competitive situations. McClelland indicates that almost all people feel they have an "achievement motive," however, probably only 10 percent of the U.S. population is strongly motivated to achieve. The amount of achievement motivation that people have depends on their childhood, their personal and occupational experiences, and the type of organization for which they work.

According to McClelland's theory, motives are "stored" in the preconscious mind just below the level of full awareness. They lie between the conscious and the unconscious, in the area of daydreams, where people talk to themselves without quite being aware of it. A basic premise of the theory is that the pattern of these daydreams can be tested, and people can be taught to change their motivation by changing these daydreams.

◆ *ACROSS CULTURES*

MOTIVATING EMPLOYEES IN SOUTH KOREA

 At Samsung's Suwon micro-wave oven complex, more than half of the assemblers are women. Most are employed for four or five years, arriving with high-school educations and leaving when they get married. Jo Yon Hwang and Jang Mee Hur are in their early twenties. Both wanted to work at Samsung because of its reputation for being good to its workers. Samsung typically accepts only one-third of those who apply for jobs.

Upon their arrival at Suwon, new employees are given blue uniforms and two weeks of training. Then they are put to work on the microwave line for eleven hours a day, twenty-seven days a month, just like everyone else. The two women say this is why they feel so committed to the company—their bosses work the same schedule. Last year, their basic wage was just over $375 a month, a little over $1.25 an hour. Annual salary increases are small, and promotions to managerial positions are very rare. Medical services are free, as is lunch. Dinner and breakfast, offered in company dining rooms, cost 15 cents each. Workers receive ten days off for vacation, five in the summer and five in the winter. If they wish, they can spend their time at company-run resorts. Four times a year, they receive gifts from the company, such as clothes, shoes, hiking bags, and tape recorders.

Like most company employees, Hwang lives for free in a company-run dormitory. There are fifteen dormitories for women, each housing 420 women, six to a room. Hur lives outside of the complex in an apartment. Samsung loaned her two-thousand dollars-for the deposit on the apartment. Hur pays Samsung 10 percent interest on the loan. When she leaves Samsung, she will give back the deposit to Samsung.

Both women get up at 6:00 A.M. and have breakfast by 7:00. Hwang walks to her factory; Hur comes by company bus. At the day's end, Hwang has to be back in the dorm by 9:30 P.M., even on the three Sundays a month she is off.

Hwang is convinced that no workers pay as close attention to products as her friends at Samsung. She checks her own work at least once even after an inspector has checked it. Her task is to attach serial numbers and name-brand labels to microwave ovens. If you own a GE Spacemaker, chances are that Hwang attached the label, since she puts on twelve hundred labels a day. Hur attaches twelve hundred microwave doors each day. Both claim that quality is very important to them and that they do their best to produce a perfect product every time. Doing it perfectly is a way of teaching themselves excellence. As Hwang explains, "I put my spirit and soul into this product."

Like most other assembly line workers, they would love higher wages, but they see themselves as helping their fellow Koreans afford a better life. Higher wages might mean fewer workers. Many workers still remember a Korea of dirt roads, few cars, and many slums. Performing their jobs well gives Hur and Hwang a feeling of helping the whole nation.[12]

Measurement of Achievement Motivation   McClelland measures the strength of a person's achievement motivation by using the **Thematic Apperception Test (TAT).** The TAT uses unstructured pictures that may arouse many kinds of reactions in the person being tested. Examples include an ink blot that a person can perceive as many different objects or a picture that can generate a variety of stories. There are no right or wrong answers, and the person is not given a limited set of alternatives from which to choose. A major objective of the TAT is to obtain the individual's own perception of the world. It is called a projective method because it emphasizes individual perceptions of stimuli, the meaning each individual gives to them, and how each individual organizes them. (The process of perception was discussed in Chapter 4).

One projective test involves looking at the picture in Figure 7.4 for ten to fifteen seconds and then writing a short story about it that answers these questions:

What is going on in this picture?

What is the woman thinking?

What has led up to this situation?

Write your own story about the picture. Then compare it with the following story written by a manager exhibiting strong achievement motivation, whom McClelland would describe as a high achiever.

The individual is an executive officer of a large corporation who wants to get a contract for her company. She knows that the competition will be tough, because all the big firms are bidding on this contract. She is taking a moment to think how happy she will be if her company is awarded the large contract. It will mean stability for the company and probably a large raise for her. She is satis-

FIGURE 7.4   Sample picture used in a projective test.

fied because she has just thought of a way to manufacture a critical part that will enable her company to bring in a low bid and complete the job with time to spare.

Characteristics of High Achievers   Self-motivated high achievers have three major characteristics.[13] First, they like to set their own goals. Seldom content to drift aimlessly and let life happen to them, they nearly always are trying to accomplish something. They are quite selective about the goals to which they commit themselves. For this reason, they are unlikely to automatically accept the goals that other people—including their superiors—select for them. They tend to seek advice or help only from experts who can provide needed knowledge or skills. High achievers prefer to be as fully responsible for attaining their goals as possible. If they win, they want the credit; if they lose, they accept the blame. For example, assume that you are given a choice between rolling dice with one chance in three of winning or working on a problem with one chance in three of solving the problem in the time allotted. Which would you choose? A high achiever would choose to work on the problem, even though rolling the dice is obviously less work and the odds of winning are the same. High achievers prefer to work at a problem rather than leave the outcome to chance or to other people.

Second, high achievers avoid selecting extremely difficult goals. They prefer moderate goals that are neither so easy that attaining them provides no satisfaction nor so difficult that attaining them is more a matter of luck than ability. They gauge what is possible and then select as difficult a goal as they think they can attain—the hardest practical challenge. The game of ringtoss illustrates this point. Most carnivals have ringtoss games that require participants to throw rings over a peg from some minimum distance but specify no maximum distance. Imagine the same game but with people allowed to stand at any distance they wish from the peg. Some will throw more or less randomly, standing close and then far away. Those with high achievement motivation will seem to calculate carefully where they should stand to have the greatest chance of winning a prize and still feel challenged. These individuals seem to stand at a distance that is not so close as to make the task ridiculously easy and not so far away as to make it impossible. They set a distance that is moderately far away but from which they can potentially ring a peg. Thus, they set challenges for themselves and enjoy tasks that will make them stretch themselves.

Third, high achievers prefer tasks that provide immediate feedback. Because of the goal's importance to them, they like to know how well they are doing. This is one reason why the high achiever often enters a professional career, a career in sales, or entrepreneurial activities. Golf would appeal to most high achievers: golfers can compare their scores to par for the course or to their own previous performance on the course; performance is related to both feedback (score) and goal (par).

Monetary Incentives   Money has a complex effect on high achievers. High achievers usually highly value their services and place a high price tag on them. High achievers are self-confident because they are aware of their abilities and limitations and thus are confident when they choose to do a particular job. They are unlikely to remain very long in an organization that does not pay them well if they are high performers. It is questionable whether an incentive plan actually increases their performance, since they normally work at peak efficiency anyway. They value money as a strong symbol of their achievement and adequacy, but money may create dissatisfaction if they feel that it inadequately reflects their contribution.

When achievement motivation is operating, good job performance may become very attractive to people. Achievement motivation, however, does not operate when high achievers are performing routine or boring tasks or when there is no competition. June Lavelle has tackled a challenging job for the past ten years. She has used her drive for achievement to overcome more business problems than most business people ever face. Let's read how she accomplished this.

IN PRACTICE

JUNE LAVELLE, A STREET-SMART HIGH-ACHIEVER

June Lavelle had never even purchased a car before she bought an old warehouse in Chicago in 1980 for $320,000. The building was located in one of the city's worst neighborhoods. It was so bad that the alarm system got ripped off one night without a sound. The vehicles parked on surrounding streets consisted mainly of burned-out wrecks.

Lavelle's idea was to offer, at deeply discounted prices, entrepreneurs a space to start new businesses. As president of the Industrial Council of Northwest Chicago (a job that no one else wanted for $12,000 a year), she obtained a $1.7 million federal grant to start her project. When she arrived at the building, she had to get the roof repaired, get rid of rats and pigeons, and build spaces for tenants. Within a few months, she had run up a $165,000 heating bill at Peoples Gas, Light and Coke Company. With no money, she could not pay the bill. She went to the power company and negotiated an installment plan to pay the bill off. What had she to lose? She thought she had a 60 percent chance that the utility would approve her plan. If it did not, the property would simply stay at its present form and generate no future income for the electric company.

She convinced high-priced consultants to work with her clients and charge them on the basis of whether their advice improved their profitability; if it did not, the consultants did not get paid. Through her business connections, she sought funding for many of the small businesses in her warehouse. To date, none has defaulted on a loan.

Working eighty or more hours per week, Lavelle keeps most information in her head, not in a computer. She knows what tenants need what money; who owes what; who is making a profit; who is about to go under; who needs more space; and whose key employee got mugged on the way home last night.

Her accomplishments? Forty-two healthy start-ups have moved out into bigger spaces. Of the 143 companies that have started in the warehouse since 1980, only 16 percent have failed. Of the 77 companies that are presently using space, about 30 of these are minority-owned. A total of 1,171 jobs have been created, and many of these have been filled by people from the neighborhood. She has been offered some "pretty hefty salaries" to join large corporations, but she has turned each one down, reasoning that she just does not have the motivation to work for them.[14]

Organizational Implications   Most of the research supporting the achievement motivation theory has been conducted by McClelland and his associates at McBer and Company. Based on this research, they recommend the following:

- Arrange tasks so that employees receive periodic feedback on their performance. Feedback will enable employees to modify their performance.
- Provide good role models of achievement. Employees should be encouraged to have heroes to copy.
- Modify employee self-images. High-achievement individuals accept themselves and seek job challenges and responsibilities.
- Control employee imaginations. Employees should think about setting realistic goals and the ways that they can attain them.

One of the major problems with the achievement motivation theory is also its greatest strength.[15] The TAT method is valuable because it allows the researcher to tap the preconscious motives of people. This method has some advantages over questionnaires, but the interpretation of a story is more of an art than a science. As a result, the method's reliability is open to question. The permanency of the theory's three needs has also been questioned, and further research is needed.

Motivator-Hygiene Theory

The **motivator-hygiene theory** is one of the most controversial theories of motivation, probably because of two unique features. First, the theory stresses that some job factors lead to satisfaction, whereas others can prevent dissatisfaction but not be sources of satisfaction. Second, it states that job satisfaction and dissatisfaction do not exist on a single continuum.

Frederick Herzberg and his associates examined the relationship between job satisfaction and productivity in a group of accountants and engineers. Through the use of semistructured interviews, they accumulated data on various factors that these employees said had an effect on their feelings about their jobs. Two different sets of factors emerged: motivators and hygienes.[16]

Motivator and Hygiene Factors   The first set of factors, **motivator factors,** includes the work itself, recognition, advancement, and responsibility. These factors are associated with an individual's positive feelings about the job and are related to the content of the job itself. These positive feelings, in turn, are associated with the individual's experiences of achievement, recognition, and responsibility. They are predicated on lasting rather than temporary achievement in the work setting.

The second set of factors, **hygiene factors,** includes company policy and administration, technical supervision, salary, working conditions, and interpersonal relations. These factors are associated with an individual's negative feelings about the job and are related to the context or environment in which the job is performed. That is, these are **extrinsic factors,** or factors external to the job. In contrast, motivators are **intrinsic factors,** or internal factors directly related to the job.

Viewed somewhat differently, extrinsic outcomes are largely determined by the organization (for example, salary, policies and rules, and fringe benefits). They serve as rewards for high performance only if the organization recognizes high performance. On the other hand, intrinsic outcomes (for example, a feeling of accomplishment after successful task performance) are largely internal to the individual. The organization's policies have only an indirect impact on them. Thus, by defining exceptional performance, an organization may be able to influence individuals to feel that they have performed their tasks exceptionally well.

One of the important themes of our book is managing diversity in the work force. As U.S. organizations continue to expand overseas and foreign organizations establish manufacturing sites in Canada, Mexico, and the United States, managers must be aware of cultural differences and how these can affect the motivation of employees. Herzberg believes that despite cultural differences, hygienes and motivators affect workers similarly around the world.[17] The data in Figure 7.5 support his viewpoint. It shows that for U.S. workers, about 80 percent of the factors that lead to job satisfaction can be traced to motivators. And for workers in other countries, motivators can account for 60 to 90 percent of the reason for their job satisfactions. Hygiene factors account for most of the reasons why workers

FIGURE 7.5   Hygienes and Motivators in Different Countries

Motivators	Satisfying Job Events	Dissatisfying Job Events
United States	80 percent	20 percent
Japan	82 percent	40 percent
Finland	90 percent	18 percent
Hungary	78 percent	30 percent
Italy	60 percent	35 percent
Hygienes		
United States	20 percent	75 percent
Japan	10 percent	65 percent
Finland	10 percent	80 percent
Hungary	22 percent	78 percent
Italy	30 percent	70 percent

Source: Adapted from N. J. Alder and J. L. Graham, Cross-Cultural Interaction: The International Comparison Fallacy. *Journal of International Business Studies,* Fall 1989, 515-537; F. Herzberg, Workers Needs: The Same around the World. *Industry Week,* September 21, 1987, 29-32.

are dissatisfied with their jobs. In Finland, 80 percent of the workers indicated that hygiene factors contribute mainly to job dissatisfaction, whereas only 10 percent said hygiene factors contribute to their job satisfaction.

This theory also states that satisfaction and dissatisfaction do not form a single continuum but are on a separate and distinct continua, as indicated in Figure 7.6. A person can be satisfied and dissatisfied at the same time. According to this theory, hygiene factors, such as working conditions and salary, cannot increase or decrease job satisfaction; they can only affect the amount of job dissatisfaction.

Organizational Implications The research designed to test the motivator-hygiene theory has not provided clear-cut evidence that either supports or rejects it. One aspect of the theory that appeals to managers is the use of common terms to explain how to motivate people. There is no need to translate psychological terms into everyday language. Therefore, among business people, it has become a very popular theory. In Chapter 17, we describe how the principles of this theory can be applied to designing jobs that give individuals an opportunity to satisfy their needs for esteem and self-actualization.

Despite its attractive features, several criticisms have been leveled at motivator-hygiene theory.[18] One major criticism is that Herzberg used a method-bound procedure; that is, the method he used to measure the factors determined the results. He asked two key questions: "Can you describe, in detail, when you felt exceptionally good about your job?" and "Can you describe, in detail, when you felt exceptionally bad about your job?" In response to such questions, people tend to give socially desirable answers, that is, answers they think the researcher wants to hear or that sound "reasonable." Also, people tend to attribute good results from their job to their own efforts and to attribute reasons for poor performance to others (recall our discussion of the self-serving bias attribution in Chapter 4).

A second major criticism of the motivator-hygiene theory questions whether satisfaction and dissatisfaction really are two separate dimensions, as Figure 7.6 indicates. Research results are mixed. Some researchers have found factors that can contribute to both satisfaction and dissatisfaction,

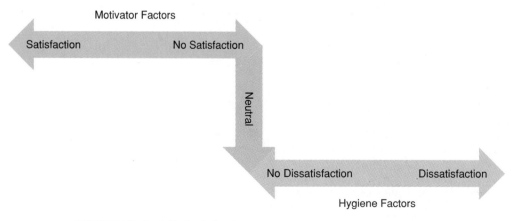

FIGURE 7.6 Job Satisfaction Continua

whereas others have found that motivator factors can contribute to dissatisfaction and hygiene factors can contribute to satisfaction. For example, in Hungary, employees reported that while hygiene factors were related to many dissatisfying features of their jobs, some hygiene factors were also related to satisfying events (see Figure 7.5). These findings raise serious questions about Herzberg's theory. They have not, however, disproved the concept that satisfaction and dissatisfaction are two different continua.

Some evidence—although not strong—links such experiences as increasing job responsibility, challenge, and advancement opportunities to high performance. Unfortunately, researchers have paid little attention to constructing a theory that explains why certain job factors affect performance positively or negatively. Similarly, few attempts using content theories have been made to explain why certain outcomes are attractive to employees or why people choose one type of behavior over another to obtain a desired outcome.[19]

Comparisons among Content Theories

The four content theories emphasize the basic motivational concepts of needs, achievement motivation, and hygiene-motivators. Figure 7.7 highlights the relationships among these four theories. The needs hierarchy theory served as the basis for the ERG theory. Therefore, there are some important similarities between the two: self-actualization and esteem needs make up growth needs; affiliation needs are similar to relatedness needs; and security and physiological needs are the building blocks of existence needs in ERG theory. A major difference between these two theories is that the hierarchy-of-needs theory offers a static needs system based on

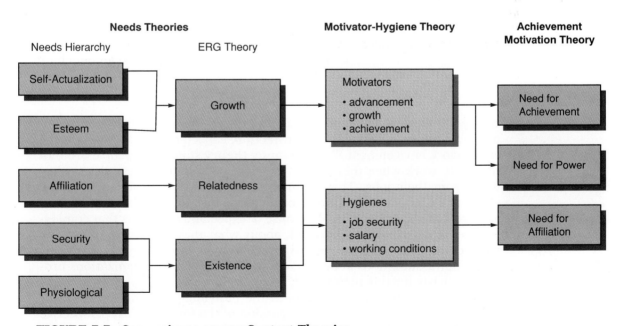

FIGURE 7.7   Comparisons among Content Theories

fulfillment-progression, whereas the ERG theory presents a flexible three-needs classification system based on frustration-regression.

The motivator-hygiene theory draws on both of the needs theories. That is, if hygiene factors are present, security and physiological needs (needs hierarchy) are likely to be met. Similarly, if hygiene factors are present, relatedness and existence needs (ERG theory) are not likely to be frustrated. Motivator factors focus on the job itself and the opportunity for the person to satisfy his or her own higher-order needs, or growth needs (ERG theory).

Achievement motivation theory does not recognize lower-order needs. The need for affiliation can be satisfied if a person meets hygiene factors on the job. If the job itself is challenging and provides an opportunity for a person to make meaningful decisions, it is motivating. These conditions go a long way toward satisfying the need for achievement.

The content theories provide team leaders with an understanding of the particular work-related factors that start the motivational process. These theories, however, promote little understanding of why people choose a particular behavior to accomplish task-related goals. This aspect of choice is the major focus of process theories of motivation.

PROCESS THEORIES OF MOTIVATION

Process theories try to describe and analyze how personal factors (internal to the person) interact and influence each other to produce certain kinds of behavior. An example would be that individuals exert more effort to obtain rewards that satisfy important needs than to obtain rewards that do not. The four best-known process theories of motivation are expectancy, reinforcement, equity, and goal setting. In this section, we cover the expectancy and equity theories of motivation. In Chapter 6, we discussed reinforcement theory, and in Chapter 8, we present the goal-setting theory.

Expectancy Theory

Expectancy theory differs widely from the content theories we have just covered. Instead of focusing on factors in the work environment that contribute to job dissatisfaction or satisfaction, expectancy theory looks at the entire work environment.[20] **Expectancy theory** states that people are motivated to work when they expect they will be able to achieve things they want from their jobs. These things might include satisfaction of safety needs, the excitement of doing a challenging task, or the ability to set and achieve difficult goals. A basic premise of expectancy theory is that employees are rational people who think about what they have to do to get rewarded and how much the reward means to them *before* they perform their jobs. Four assumptions about the causes of behavior in organizations provide the basis for this theory.[21]

First, a combination of forces in the individual and the environment determines behavior (recall our discussion of the interactionist perspective from Chapter 3). Neither the individual nor the environment alone determines behavior. As the account of employees working on Samsung's micro-wave assembly line illustrated, people join organizations with expectations about their jobs that are based on their needs, motivations, and past experiences. These factors all influence how people respond to an organization. But these factors can and do change over time, as we found out in our Preview Case. At Solar Press, once employees got rewarded for speed, they ignored quality and their co-workers. The change in environment (reward system) and their desire for money jointly combined to affect their behavior.

Second, individuals decide their own behaviors in organizations. Many constraints are placed on individual behavior (for example, through rules, technology, and work-group norms). Most individuals make two kinds of conscious decisions: (1) decisions about coming to work, staying with the same organization, and joining other organizations (membership decisions); and (2) decisions about how much to produce, how hard to work, and the quality of workmanship (job-performance decisions).

Third, different individuals have different needs and goals. Employees want different rewards from their work (for example, job security, promotion, good pay, and challenge). Not all employees want the same things from their jobs. What did June Lavelle want from her job as president of the Industrial Council? How does that compare with what Hwang and Hur wanted from their jobs at Samsung?

Fourth, individuals decide among alternatives based on their perceptions of whether a given behavior will lead to a desired outcome. Individuals do the things that they perceive will lead to desirable rewards and avoid doing the things that they perceive will lead to undesirable outcomes.

In general, the expectancy theory holds that individuals have their own needs and ideas about what they desire from their work (rewards). They act on these needs and ideas when making decisions about what organization to join and how hard to work. The theory also holds that individuals are not inherently motivated or unmotivated, that motivation depends on the situation facing individuals and how it fits their needs.

To understand expectancy theory, we must define the important variables of the theory and explain how they operate. The five most important variables of the theory are: first-level and second-level outcomes, expectancy, valence, and instrumentality.

First-Level and Second-Level Outcomes The results of behaviors associated with doing the job itself are called **first-level outcomes.** They include such outcomes as productivity, absenteeism, turnover, and quality of work. **Second-level outcomes** are those rewards (either positive or negative) that first-level outcomes are likely to produce, such as a pay increase, promotion, acceptance by co-workers, and job security.

Expectancy The belief that a particular level of effort will be followed by a particular level of performance is called **expectancy.** It can vary from the belief that there is absolutely no relationship between effort and performance to the certainty that a given level of effort will result in a corresponding level of performance. Expectancy has a value ranging from 0, indicating no chance that a first-level outcome will occur after the behavior, to plus 1, indicating certainty that a particular first-level outcome will follow a behavior. For example, if you believe that you have no chance of getting a good grade on the next exam by studying this chapter, your expectancy value would be 0. With this expectancy, you might not study this chapter.

Instrumentality The relationship between first-level outcomes and second-level outcomes is called **instrumentality.** It can have values ranging from minus 1 to plus 1. A minus 1 indicates that attainment of a second-level outcome is inversely related to the achievement of a first-level outcome. For example, if one of your desired second-level outcomes is to pass this course but you receive a failing grade, it would be impossible for you to achieve your second-level outcome. A plus 1 indicates that the first-level outcome is positively related to the second-level outcome. For example, if you received an A on all your exams, the probability that you would achieve your desired second-level outcome (passing this course) is approaching plus 1. If there is no relationship between your performance on a test and either passing or failing this course, your instrumentality would approach 0.

Valence An individual's preference for a particular second-level outcome is called **valence.** For example, in recent negotiations, United Auto Workers members who work for General Motors preferred a small wage increase and guaranteed jobs over a large wage increase with no job security. An outcome is positive when it is preferred and negative when it is not preferred or is to be avoided. An outcome has a valence of zero when the individual is indifferent about receiving it.

In brief, expectancy theory holds that work motivation is determined by individual beliefs regarding effort-performance relationships and the desirability of various work outcomes associated with different performance levels. Simply put, you can remember the important features by the saying:

People exert	to	task	and	work-related
	$\rightarrow$		$\rightarrow$	
work effort	achieve	performance	receive	outcomes.

General Model Using these five key variables, we can build a general expectancy theory of motivation, as shown in Figure 7.8. Motivation is the force that causes individuals to spend effort. Effort alone is not enough, however. Unless an individual believes that his or her effort will lead to some desired performance level (first-level outcome), that person will not make much of an effort. Effort-performance relationship is based on a perception of how difficult it will be to achieve a particular behavior (say, getting an A in this course) and the probability of achieving that behavior. For example, you may have a high expectancy that if you attend class, study the book, take good notes, and prepare for exams, you could achieve an A in this class. On the other hand, if you believe that even if you attend class, study the book, take good notes, and prepare for exams, your chances of getting an A are only 20 percent, the probability of your expending effort on these activities to achieve an A is much less.

The level of performance is important in obtaining desired second-level outcomes. In Figure 7.8, there are four desirable outcomes: passing the

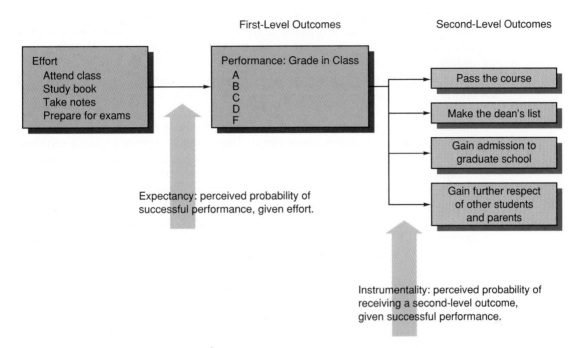

FIGURE 7.8   General Model of Expectancy Theory

course, making the dean's list, gaining admission to graduate school, and gaining further respect from other students and parents. In general, if you feel that a particular level of performance (A, B, C, D, or F) will lead to these desired outcomes, you are more likely to try to perform at that level. If you really desire these four second-level outcomes and you can achieve them only if you get an A in this course, the instrumentality between receiving an A and these four outcomes will be plus 1. On the other hand, if you believe that getting an A in this course means that you will lose some friends and that these friends are most important to you, the instrumentality between an A and this outcome will be negative. That is, the higher the grade, the more your friends will ignore you. Given this condition, you might choose not to get an A in this course.

Research Findings   Researchers are still working on ways to test this model, which has presented some problems.[22] First, the theory tries to predict choice or the amount of effort an individual will expend on one or more tasks. However, there is little agreement about what is choice or effort among different individuals. So, this important variable is difficult to measure accurately. Second, expectancy theory does not specify which second-level outcomes are important to a particular individual in a given situation. Although researchers are expected to address this issue, comparison of the limited results to date is often difficult because each study is unique. Take another look at the second-level outcomes in Figure 7.8. Would you choose them? What others might you choose? Finally, the theory contains an implicit assumption that motivation is a conscious choice process. That is, the individual consciously calculates the pain or pleasure that he or she expects to attain or avoid when making a choice. Expectancy theory says nothing about unconscious motivation or personality characteristics. We know that people often do not make conscious choices about which outcomes to seek. Can you recall going through this process concerning your grade while taking this course?

Organizational Implications Although there are still problems with expectancy theory, it has some direct implications for motivating employees. These implications can be grouped into six suggestions for action.[23]

First, managers should try to determine the outcomes that each employee values. They can do so by (1) using a questionnaire; (2) observing employee reactions to different rewards; and (3) asking employees about the kinds of rewards they want from their jobs. However, managers must understand that employees can and do change their minds about desired outcomes. We read about this at Solar Press. The effective manager correctly diagnoses these changes and does not assume that desired outcomes will remain stable over time.

Second, managers should determine the kinds of desired performance. They must define good performance, adequate, and poor performance in terms that are observable and measurable. Employees need to understand what is expected of them. For example, Joyce Haggard, safety manager at Dart Transportation, developed criteria for good truck driving. These criteria, used to measure a driver's performance over a six-month period, included: (1) having no chargeable accidents (damages of more than $750); (2) having no moving violations; (3) being less than fifteen minutes late for all pickups and deliveries; (4) driving more than 40,000 miles per six months; (5) averaging at least 5.6 miles per gallon of fuel; and (6) maintaining tire cost at or below 2.8 cents per mile.

Third, managers should make sure that desired levels of performance set for employees can be attained. If employees feel that the level of performance necessary to get a reward is higher than they can reasonably achieve, their motivation to perform will be low. For example, if the trucking company cannot get enough freight to guarantee its drivers forty thousand miles in six months, that desired level of performance is too high.

Fourth, managers should directly link the specific performance they desire to the outcomes desired by employees. Recall that in Chapter 6 we discussed how operant conditioning principles can be applied to improve performance. If an employee has achieved the desired level of performance for a promotion, the employee should be promoted as soon as possible. If a high level of motivation is to be created and maintained, it is extremely important for employees to see clearly the reward process at work in a timely manner. Concrete acts must accompany statements of intent in linking performance to rewards.

We should not forget that it is an individual's perceptions—not reality—that determines motivation. It does not matter, for example, whether we feel that employees' pay is related to their performance. Employees will be motivated to perform by pay raises only if they see the relationship. Too often, managers misunderstand the behavior of employees because they tend to rely on their own perceptions of the situation and forget that the employees' perceptions may be different.

Fifth, managers should analyze the situation for conflicts. Having set up positive expectancies for employees, managers must look at the entire situation to see whether other factors conflict with the desired behaviors (for example, the informal work group or the organization's formal reward system). Motivation will be high only when employees see many rewards and few negative outcomes associated with good performance.

And sixth, managers should make sure that changes in outcomes or rewards are large enough to motivate significant behavior. Trivial rewards may result in minimal efforts, if any, to improve performance. Rewards must be large enough to motivate individuals to make the effort required to significantly change performance.

Let's read how managers at the Hyatt Regency Hotel in Chicago used these six principles to motivate their employees. When you have finished reading this In Practice, you should be able to identify these principles.

IN PRACTICE

HYATT REGENCY HOTEL MOTIVATIONAL PROGRAMS

John Allegritti remembers the day when he decided to quit. After two years of working on the switchboard and as an assistant in housekeeping at the Hyatt Regency Hotel, he hated the repetition of his work. Since Allegritti was a high-performing employee, Don DePorter, a senior manager, was anxious to retain him. DePorter assigned Allegritti to head a project to reduce waste at the two-thousand-room hotel. Allegritti did so well that the hotel corporation let him develop and run a new waste-consulting company called ReCycleCo Inc. Besides several large Hyatt hotels, ReCycleCo now has twenty-four clients in eight states.

Figuring out ways to keep employees motivated has become a way of life at the Hyatt Hotel chain. In the 1960s, it took as little as three years for a high-performing management trainee to become a hotel manager. Now, aspiring employees must wait eight years or longer to run even a small hotel. This is because Hyatt is not opening as many new hotels as it once did and it has done a better job of retaining high performers. More than 60 percent of Hyatt's managers started their careers as trainees.

To keep employees like Allegritti, Hyatt holds monthly worker "rap sessions" at its hotels. Employees are urged to make suggestions. Hyatt is helping employees start their own businesses. In the past three years, employees' suggestions have prompted Hyatt to spin off six new ventures, such as party catering, retirement apartment complexes, and sporting-equipment rental shops. And like Allegritti, employees who help develop the ideas are usually allowed to run the new ventures. Hyatt sets up the ventures as separate companies and lends its staff to help support the new companies. For example, James Jones's idea was to have Hyatt provide entertainment and catering at professional sporting events. His venture, Regency Productions by Hyatt, managed the corporate hospitality tents for the 1991 Super Bowl, as well as the 1991 U.S. Open golf tournament. According to Jones, "It's the most challenging time of my life but also the most rewarding, exciting, and phenomenal growth period of my life."[24]

Equity Theory

Feelings of unfairness were among the most frequently reported sources of job dissatisfaction found by Herzberg and his associates. Some researchers have made this desire for fairness, justice, or equity a central focus of their theories. Assume that you just received a 5-percent raise. Will this raise lead to higher performance, lower performance, or no change in your performance? Are you satisfied with this increase? Would your satisfaction with this pay increase vary with the consumer price index, with what you expected to get, or with what others in the organization performing the same job and at the same performance level received?

Equity theory focuses on an individual's feelings of how fairly he or she is treated in comparison with others.[25] The theory has two major assumptions. First, individuals evaluate their interpersonal relationships just as they would evaluate the buying or selling of a home, shares of stock, or a car. The theory views interpersonal relationships as exchange processes in which individuals make contributions and expect certain results.

Second, individuals do not operate in a vacuum. Instead, individuals compare their situations with those of others to determine the equity of their own situations. The extent to which people view an exchange favorably is influenced by what happens to them compared to what happens to the others involved. These others may include co-workers, relatives, neighbors, and so on.

General Equity Model Equity theory is based on the comparison of two variables: inputs and outcomes. **Inputs** represent what an individual contributes to an exchange; **outcomes** are what an individual receives from the exchange. Some typical inputs and outcomes are shown in Table 7.1. The items in the two lists are not paired and do not represent specific exchanges.

TABLE 7.1   Typical Inputs and Outcomes in an Organizational Setting

Inputs	Outcomes
Age	Challenging job assignments
Attendance	Fringe benefits
Communication skills	Job perquisites (parking space or
Interpersonal skills	office location)
Job effort (long hours)	Job security
Level of education	Monotony
Past experience	Promotion
Performance	Recognition
Personal appearance	Responsibility
Seniority	Salary
Social status	Seniority benefits
Technical skills	Status symbols
Training	Working conditions

According to equity theory, individuals assign weights to various inputs and outcomes according to their perceptions of the situation. Since most situations involve multiple inputs and outcomes, the weighting process is not precise. However, people generally can distinguish between important and less important inputs and outcomes. After they arrive at a ratio of inputs and outcomes for themselves, they compare it with their perceived ratios of inputs and outcomes of relevant others in the same or a similar situation. These relevant others become the objects of comparison for individuals in determining whether they feel equitably treated.

Equity exists whenever the ratio of a person's outcomes to inputs equals the ratio of outcomes to inputs for similar others. For example, an individual may feel properly paid in terms of what he or she puts into a job compared to what other workers are getting for their inputs. **Inequity** exists when the ratios of outcomes to inputs are not equal. For example, let's say that a person who works harder than co-workers, completes all tasks on time while others do not, and puts in longer hours than others receives the same pay raise as the others. What happens? The employee believes that his or her inputs are greater than those of co-workers and therefore should merit a greater pay raise. Inequity can also occur when people are overpaid. In this case, the overpaid employees might be motivated by guilt or social pressure to work harder to reduce the imbalance between their inputs and outcomes in comparison to their co-workers.

Consequences of Inequity Inequity causes tension within an individual—and among individuals. Since tension is not pleasurable, a person is motivated to reduce it to a tolerable level. In order to reduce a perceived inequity and the corresponding level of tension, a person can choose among the following types of action.[26] This tension-reduction process is shown in Figure 7.9.

> People can change their inputs either upward or downward to what might be an equitable level. For example, underpaid people can reduce the quantity of their production, work shorter hours, be absent more frequently, and so on. Figure 7.10 shows these relationships graphically.
>
> People can change their outcomes to restore equity. Many union organizers try to attract nonmembers by pledging to improve working conditions, hours, and pay without an increase in employee effort (input).
>
> People can distort their own inputs and outcomes. As opposed to actually changing inputs or outcomes, people can mentally distort

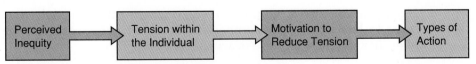

FIGURE 7.9   Motivational Process of Inequity

Source: Adapted from Richard M. Steers, *Introduction to Organizational Behavior,* 3d ed., 167. Copyright © 1988 by Scott, Foresman and Company. Reprinted by permission.

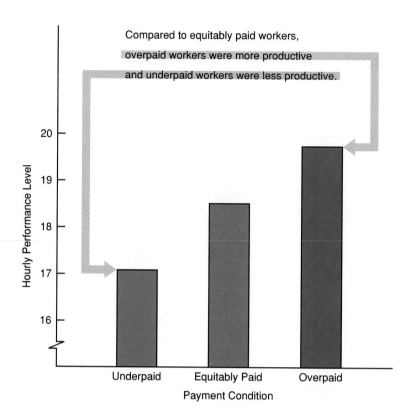

FIGURE 7.10 Performance Levels for Underpaid and Overpaid Workers

them to achieve the same results. For example, people who feel inequitably treated can distort how hard they work ("This job is a piece of cake") or attempt to increase the importance of the job to the organization ("This is really an important job!"). By mentally distorting the input-outcome ratio, people achieve a more favorable balance.

- People can leave the organization or request a transfer to another department. In doing so, they hope to find a more favorable balance.

- People can shift to a new reference group to reduce the source of the inequity. The star high school athlete who does not get a scholarship to a Big Ten university might decide that a smaller school has more advantages, thereby justifying his or her need to look at smaller schools when making a selection.

- People can distort the inputs or outcomes of others. People may come to believe that the comparison group actually works harder than they do and therefore deserves greater rewards.

Keeping these six actions in mind, let's read about Nordstrom Stores' payment policy. After reading about these four situations, you should be able to predict what each employee did.

PAYING THE PRICE AT NORDSTROM STORES

A single parent who returned to the job market at forty, Patty Bemis joined Nordstrom Stores in 1981. Since that time, she has been one of her department's top sellers. She won a companywide sales contest and received, she recalls, "a pair of PJs—whoopie-doo!" She has logged many unpaid hours, delivering cosmetics to customers and unpacking hundreds of boxes of makeup. She recalls that "working off the clock was just standard." "Working off the clock" was the manager's way of saying that there was nonselling work to do. Some of that work even involved taking out the trash. **What did Bemis do?**

Lori Lucas came to one of the mandatory Saturday morning department meetings at Nordstrom's and saw a sign saying, "Do Not Punch the Clock." She assumed that the clock was broken or that the timecards were lost. She and several other clerks just marked down their time manually and handed the paper to their manager. The manager simply erased the hours and accused the clerks of not being "team players." Like other sales clerks, she had daily quotas of thank-you letters to write and monthly customer-service books to generate—photo albums that were supposed to be filled with pictures of grateful customers. These tasks were not to be done on company time and were supposed to take only a few hours. On many occasions, Lori would be doing her letters until 3:00 A.M. If a salesperson complained, the manager would schedule them with bad hours, sales per hour would fall, and next thing they knew, they would be fired. **What did Lucas do?**

Every pay period, Nordstrom's posts a chart of employee sales. It ranks employees by sales per hour. Those who fall below a certain sales target are fired. For example, management set a long list of goals for sales clerks in the menswear department and attached the following memo, "In the next sixty days, if any of these areas are not met to our expectations, you will be fired." One salesperson, Jeffrey Hamilton, was always at the top and was on his way to receive the "Pacesetter Award"—a prestigious title given to top sales clerks. **How did Hamilton do it?**

Doris Quiros, a salesperson in the women's sportswear department, says that working at Nordstrom's makes her feel the best that she can be. She is encouraged to use her head, not follow rules, and be her own boss.[27] **What did Quiros do?**

━━━━━━

Let's see how you did at predicting each sales clerk's behavior. Patty Bemis quit her job. She could not take the grueling hours and constant pressure. Lori Lucas and others found friends and relatives to write fake letters for them to reach their goal. After working twenty-two days without a day off, however, she demanded a lunch break. On her lunch break, she applied for and got a new job. She remembers thinking, "I'm making less than twenty thousand dollars a year and killing myself. Why?" Jeffrey Hamilton, the top salesperson, was accused by fellow workers of stealing their sales and was eventually fired. Doris Quiros continued to be a top performer at Nordstrom's. She did not mind writing thank-you notes at home.

In the first two instances, the employees believed that their inputs (long hours) exceeded their outcomes (pay). In an attempt to restore equity, they changed their inputs to maintain a balance between their inputs and outcomes. Both Bemis and Lucas compared their inputs to working conditions at other similar retail stores and found major differences. Since they could not adjust their inputs while working at Nordstrom Stores, they quit. Hamilton, the salesperson who stole sales from his co-workers, was also attempting to restore equity by adjusting his inputs. By overstating his sales (outcomes), he was compensating for long hours (inputs). Finally, Quiros believed that her inputs and outcomes were in balance. No change in her behavior was needed. Equity theory would predict that as long as Quiros maintains a balance between inputs and outcomes, her performance would remain high.

Equity Theory Findings   Most of the research on equity theory focuses on pay or other compensation issues. A review of the studies, however, reveals some shortcomings.[28] First, the comparison person or group is always specified. The typical research procedure is to ask a person to compare themselves to some specific person. If the situation changes, would the individual choose a different comparison person or group? Do people also change comparison persons at various times during their careers?

Second, the research focuses mainly on short-term comparisons. Are the factors (pay, working hours, and so on) that a person considers to be inputs or outcomes likely to remain the same over time? Longitudinal research, which examines what happens if inequity exists over an extended period of time, is needed. Do perceptions of inequity increase, decrease, or stabilize? Answers to these types of questions would help us to understand better the dynamic character of equity and inequity.

Third, equity theory does not specify the type of action (from among the six possible types) that a person would choose to reduce inequity in a given situation. That is, is one strategy used primarily when pay is involved, another when absenteeism or turnover is involved, and yet another when productivity is involved? How did you do at predicting the behaviors of Nordstrom's employees?

Organizational Implications   Despite these limitations, equity theory is widely used by managers and compensation specialists to set pay scales for jobs in most organizations.[29] Equity theory makes two primary recommendations. First, employees should be treated fairly. When individuals believe that they are not being treated fairly, they will try to correct the situation and reduce tension by means of one or more of the six types of actions just discussed. A sizable inequity increases the probability that individuals will choose more than one type of action to reduce it. For example, individuals may partially withdraw from the organization by being absent more often, arriving at work late, and not completing assignments on time. The organization, on the other hand, may try to reduce their inputs by assigning these people to monotonous jobs, taking away some perquisites, and giving them only small pay increases.

Second, people make decisions concerning equity only after they compare their inputs and outcomes with those of comparable employees. These others may be employees of the same organization or employees of other organizations. The latter presents a major problem for managers, who cannot control what other organizations pay their employees. For example, the vice-president for human resources at a large corporation hired a recent business school graduate for $28,500, the maximum the company could pay for the job. The new employee thought that this salary was very good until she compared it to the $31,000 that fellow graduates were getting at other firms. She felt that she was being underpaid in comparison with her former classmates, causing an inequity problem for her (and the company).

The idea that fairness in organizations is determined by more than just money has received a great deal of attention from managers. Organizational fairness is influenced by how rules and procedures are used and how much employees are consulted in decisions that affect them. The perceived fairness of rules and procedures is referred to as **procedural justice**.[30] Employees are motivated to attain fairness in *how* decisions are made, as well as *what* those decisions are. Research has shown that pay raises, for example, are greatly affected by employees' perceptions about the fairness of the raises. If in the minds of the employees the pay raises were administered fairly, the employees were more satisfied with their increases than if the procedures used to make these increases were judged to be unfair. The perceived fairness of the procedures used to allocate pay raises is a better predicator of pay satisfaction than the absolute amount of pay received. Employees' assessments of procedural justice have also been related to their trust in management, intention to leave the organization, evaluation of their supervisor, and job satisfaction. Consider some of the relatively small day-to-day issues in an organization that are affected by procedural justice: decisions about who will cover the phones during lunch while others are away from their desks, the choice of the site of the company picnic, or who gets the latest software for their personal computer.

Procedural justice has also been found to affect the attitudes of those workers who survive a layoff. When workers are laid off, survivors (those who remain on the job) are often in good positions to judge the fairness of the layoff in terms of how the layoffs were made. When the layoffs are handled fairly, survivors feel more committed to their organization than when they believe that the laid-off workers were not fairly treated.

Let's think about your behavior in this class. If you receive a high grade, you may think that it is fair because it benefits you. You may think of yourself as a good student, and good students deserve high grades. What if you receive a low grade? Thinking of yourself as a good student, you might not like the grade. But you will accept the grade if you believe that the instructor graded the test in a fair manner. You might think your grade was unfair if the instructor's "pets" all received the high grades.

Comparisons among Process Theories

The expectancy and equity theories emphasize different aspects of motivation. Expectancy theory assumes employees are rational and evaluate how much the reward means to them before they perform their jobs. How well employees perform their jobs will depend, in part, on what they believe is expected of them. Once their team leader or manager communicates these expectations, then employees assign probabilities that their efforts will lead to desired first-level outcomes (performance, quality, absenteeism, and so on). These outcomes are linked to valued rewards (for example, high pay or job security) they desire from their jobs. It is the manager's job to make the desired rewards attainable to employees by clearly linking rewards and performance. Allowing employees to choose among rewards, such as improved insurance, child-care and elder-care facilities for family members, and additional vacation days, is important because all employees do not value the same rewards. **Cafeteria-style benefit plans**—reward systems that permit employees to select their fringe benefits from a menu of alternatives—are becoming very popular in organizations. In many organizations, fringe benefits represent 35 percent of payroll costs. So, letting employees choose those that they find rewarding and linking these to their performance is important for organizations.[31]

In contrast to expectancy theory, where employees make internal judgments of the value of rewards, equity theory assumes that what is equitable is determined by employees comparing themselves to similar others. According to equity theory, people are motivated to escape inequitable situations and are attracted to remain on the job and perform at high levels in equitable situations. Because equity theory deals with perceptions of fairness among employees, it is reasonable to expect that they react to inequitable situations in different ways.

Both theories emphasize the future role of rewards and an individual's decision-making processes. These theories suggest that managers concerned about improving employee performance should actively create proper work environments, match employees to jobs, and establish clear performance-reward systems. Motivation for high performance will not exist unless managers recognize such performance when it occurs and reward it quickly.

SUMMARY

A motivational model was presented indicating that individuals behave in certain ways to satisfy their needs. The reasons why individuals behave in certain ways were the focus of this chapter.

To understand these reasons, we examined two major classes of theories of motivation: content and process. Content theories focus on the factors within the person that drive, sustain, or stop behavior. They attempt to determine the specific needs that motivate people. The theories of motivation of Maslow, Alderfer, McClelland, and Herzberg were examined as content theories. Process theories provide a description and analysis of how behavior is driven, sustained, or stopped. Expectancy and equity theories of motivation were examined as process theories.

Maslow assumes that people have five needs: physiological, security, affiliation, esteem, and self-actualization. Once a need is satisfied, it no longer serves to motivate a person. Alderfer agrees with Maslow that needs motivate people but claims that people have only three needs: existence, relatedness, and growth. If a person's growth need cannot be satisfied, then the person focuses on his or her relatedness needs to find satisfaction. McClelland believes that people have three needs (achievement, affiliation, and power) that are rooted in the culture of a society. We focused on the role of the achievement need and indicated the characteristics associated with high achievers. The final content theory discussed was that of Herzberg. He claimed that there are two types of factors that affect a person's motivation: hygienes and motivators. Hygiene factors, such as working conditions, can only prevent job dissatisfaction; they cannot lead to job satisfaction. Motivators, such as job challenge, can only lead to job satisfaction and cannot lead to job dissatisfaction.

Our first process theory was expectancy theory. Expectancy theory holds that individuals have their own ideas about what they desire from work. They make decisions about what activities they choose to do only after they believe that these activities will satisfy these needs. The critical components of this theory were first- and second-level outcomes, expectancy, instrumentality, and valence. Unless the individual believes that his or her effort will lead (expectancy) to some desired level of performance (first-level outcome) and that this level of performance will lead (instrumentality) to desired rewards (second-level outcomes and valences), the person will not be motivated to extend any effort. Equity theory focuses on the individual's feelings of how fairly he or she was treated in comparison to similar others. To make this judgment, an individual compares his or her inputs (experience, age) and outcomes (salary) to those of similar others. If equity exists, the person is not motivated to behave. If inequity exists, the person can engage in any one of six behaviors to reduce this situation.

Key Words and Concepts

Ability	Inputs
Achievement motivation theory	Instrumentality
Affiliation needs	Intrinsic factors
Cafeteria-style benefit plans	Motivation
Content theories	Motivator-Hygiene theory
Equity	Motivator factors
Equity theory	Needs
ERG theory	Needs hierarchy theory
Esteem needs	Outcomes
Existence needs	Physiological needs
Expectancy	Procedural justice
Expectancy theory	Process theories
Extrinsic factors	Relatedness needs
First-level outcomes	Second-level outcomes
Goal	Security needs
Growth needs	Self-actualization needs
Hygiene factors	Thematic Apperception Test (TAT)
Inequity	Valence

Discussion Questions

1. Think about the worst job you have had. What motivation approach was used in that organization? Now think about the best job you have had. What motivation approach was used in that organization?

2. How would expectancy theory explain the behaviors of the four sales clerks at Nordstrom's?

3. Using equity theory, explain what happened to Solar Press when the new incentive system was installed.

4. What motivational lessons can be learned from Samsung's motivational approach with its assembly line workers in South Korea?

5. How could a manager apply ERG theory to motivate employees on the job?

6. How can cafeteria-style benefits plans motivate employees?

7. What is the value of motivator-hygiene theory?

8. If high achievers are better performers, why do organizations not simply hire high achievers?

9. Discuss the organizational implications for overpayment and underpayment.

10. Evaluate the statement: "A satisfied worker is a productive worker." Under what conditions is the statement false? True?

◆ MANAGEMENT CASES AND EXERCISES

ARE YOU SELF-ACTUALIZED?

Maslow's need of self-actualization is often difficult to define. In his writings, Maslow described the self-actualized person as one who is in the process of developing to his or her full stature. The following self-actualizing characteristics questionnaire is based on Maslow's descriptions of the self-actualizing person. It is designed for two purposes: (1) to teach you what the concept of self-actualization means, and (2) to provide you with some feedback on your own self-appraisal.

The questionnaire contains thirty-five items, five derived from each of Maslow's seven characteristics of self-actualizing persons.[32] We would like you to decide to what degree each question is accurate or true for you using the following scale:

- N Not at all, definitely untrue for me
- O Occasionally this is true for me—at least 25 percent of the time
- F Frequently this is an accurate description of me—about 50 percent of the time
- M Most of the time this would be descriptive of me
- H Highly characteristic, definitely true for me

Questions

1.	I meet the needs of other people.	N	O	F	M	H
2.	My perception of people and situations is accurate.	N	O	F	M	H
3.	My daily life is full of surprises.	N	O	F	M	H
4.	I avoid doing what I believe is wrong.	N	O	F	M	H
5.	I strive to keep my life simple and natural.	N	O	F	M	H
6.	Every day is different for me.	N	O	F	M	H
7.	I delight in learning new things.	N	O	F	M	H
8.	Nothing is routine for me.	N	O	F	M	H
9.	I think clearly.	N	O	F	M	H
10.	I believe the end never justifies the means.	N	O	F	M	H
11.	I can tolerate chaos and disorder.	N	O	F	M	H
12.	Working toward a goal is more enjoyable than attaining it.	N	O	F	M	H
13.	I experience no pressure to conform to social norms.	N	O	F	M	H
14.	The meaning of my life is clear to me.	N	O	F	M	H
15.	I enjoy discussing philosophical issues.	N	O	F	M	H
16.	I know the difference between what I want and what I need.	N	O	F	M	H
17.	My life has a definite purpose.	N	O	F	M	H
18.	My major satisfactions come from within.	N	O	F	M	H
19.	I can let go of my own interests.	N	O	F	M	H
20.	Art, music, and beautiful things strengthen and enrich me.	N	O	F	M	H
21.	I see the positive side of things.	N	O	F	M	H
22.	I can make myself at home anywhere.	N	O	F	M	H
23.	I am my own person.	N	O	F	M	H
24.	Achievement is less important to me than contentment.	N	O	F	M	H
25.	I am rarely self-conscious.	N	O	F	M	H
26.	I can let things happen without planning.	N	O	F	M	H
27.	I do original work.	N	O	F	M	H
28.	I am an uninhibited person.	N	O	F	M	H
29.	I have definite moral standards.	N	O	F	M	H
30.	I learn something new every day.	N	O	F	M	H
31.	I am excited by experimentation and risk taking.	N	O	F	M	H
32.	My actions are based on my choices, not needs.	N	O	F	M	H
33.	I rarely censor my thoughts.	N	O	F	M	H
34.	I am never bored.	N	O	F	M	H
35.	Determining what is real and what is phony is easy for me.	N	O	F	M	H

Score Sheet

Instructions: Transfer your letter responses from the questionnaire to each of the seven scales below and write in the value for each response:

N = −2
O = −1
F =   0
M = +1
H = +2

Sum the values of the items in each scale for a score.

Scale

1. Efficient Reality Perception

Items

2	9	11	16	35
letter				
value				

Score _____

2. Spontaneity, Simplicity, Naturalness

Items

5	8	24	26	33
letter				
value				

Score _____

3. Problem Centeredness

Items

1	15	17	19	25
letter				
value				

Score _____

4. Autonomy and Independence of Culture and Environments

Items

13	18	22	23	32
letter				
value				

Score _____

5. Freshness of Appreciation

Items

6	20	21	30	34
letter				
value				

Score _____

6. Ethical Standards

Items

4	10	12	14	29
letter				
value				

Score _____

7. Creativeness

Items

3	7	27	28	31
letter				
value				

Score _____

PROFILE SHEET

Directions: Enter your total score for each scale in the box provided, and then chart each score at the appropriate point on the graph. The more positive your score, the more the category description fits you.

Scale	**Score**
1. Efficient Reality Perception Perceiving the real world accurately; making correct discriminations between the real and the spurious; capacity to deal with facts rather than opinions and wishes; appreciation of the unknown as a source for new learning; willingness to let go of the familiar; lack of obsessiveness.	

2. Spontaneity, Simplicity, Naturalness
   Motivated by choice rather than need; in
   touch with inner feelings and an ability to
   communicate those feelings effectively to
   others; an ethical code that is individualized rather than conventional; interest in
   personal growth and development; appreciation of the simple and unpretentious.

3. Problem Centeredness
   Ability to focus on problems outside the
   self; task oriented; lack of self-
   consciousness; ability to attend to the
   needs of others; lack of obsessive introspection; concern with basic questions and
   philosophical issues.

4. Autonomy and Independence of Culture
   and Environments
   Independent of material things or others'
   opinions; self-motivated; disregard of social rewards or prestige; stability in the
   face of frustrations and adversity; maintaining an inner serenity.

5. Freshness of Appreciation
   Capacity for wonder and awe; richness of
   inner experience; perceiving familiar
   things as fresh and new; lack of boredom
   or jadedness; focus on the positive aspects
   of experience; "original mind"; responsive
   to beauty.

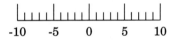

6. Ethical Standards
   Strong ethical sense, definite moral standards; clear notion of right and wrong;
   seeking to do right and avoiding wrongdoing; fixed on ends rather than means.

7. Creativeness
   Creativity in everyday life, rather than in
   artistic endeavors; ability to perceive the
   true and the real more so than others; creativity that is childlike and playful; having
   fewer inhibitions or restrictions.

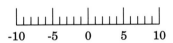

A MOTIVATION CHALLENGE AT BOB HOLIDAY REAL ESTATE COMPANY

Ever since Carlos de la Cruz and his wife, Rosa, bought out Bob Holiday Real Estate Company from its owners, Susan Howard's sales have been in a slump. Susan had been a leading salesper-son for the past twenty years, often enjoying a bonus check twice as large as her salary. She had been proud of this extra money and used it to put her children through college. It has helped her live comfortably as a single parent. In the three months since Carlos and Rosa took over,

Susan's sales have fallen off sharply. Her enthusiasm and commitment to her customers has declined, even though the same bonus system is in effect. In fact, she had not collected her bonus check since the company's ownership changed. Rosa had tried to meet with her informally several times, but Susan was always in too great a hurry.

Rosa did learn from other salespersons that Susan resented working for owners who are younger than she and not native-born Americans. Susan ranted and raved during last week's meeting about how Carlos was trying to squeeze salespeople to sell more in a down market. She told him privately that she was "selling real estate in Texas before he was old enough to know what real estate was," and it was her problem if she did not earn her bonus checks, not his.

Carlos was shocked by Susan's outrage and very concerned about her resentment and hostility toward him. As rumors flew around the office, Carlos learned from other salespersons that Susan was really a company person, even though her current sales figures did not reflect her dedication to the new owners. He also learned that she was receiving sales tips from Don Otto, her former boss, who was now with a competitor. Carlos had chosen not to retain Don when he bought the company because Don's administrative talents were not up to the new standards he demanded.

After attending a breakfast meeting on motivation, Carlos tried to "motivate" higher sales from Susan by adding a new section of luxury homes to her territory. These new homes sold for half a million dollars and up. If Susan listed and sold a home, she would earn a 5-percent real estate commission, and his company would earn 1 percent. He also moved her into a larger, more plush office located near the front door where she could easily see new clients entering the office. He hoped that these changes would arouse new energy in her. Unfortunately, none of these changes seemed to work. Finally, he asked her if she wanted to quit. It seemed that nothing he did worked.

QUESTIONS:

1.   What motivational tactics did Carlos try to use to motivate Susan? Why did these not seem to work?

2.   If you were Carlos, what would you have done?

MOTIVATING WORKERS AT JOHNSONVILLE FOODS

When Ralph Strayer became president of Johnsonville Foods in 1980, the company was in good financial shape. Johnsonville was selling its sausages in Wisconsin, Michigan, and Minnesota and growing by a rate of about 20 percent a year. Customers bought its product because of its quality. However, Strayer noticed that employees did not seem to care about their own performance. People made dumb mistakes, such as mislabeling products, adding the wrong seasonings, or failing to mix the sausages properly. Another employee ruined a big batch of fresh sausage by spraying it with water while cleaning the area. Generally, people did what they were told for eight hours, then went home.

To get employees more motivated and committed to the company, he and his senior managers decided to permit employees to make decisions. They assigned quality to employees. Top management stopped tasting the sausage, and the people who made sausage started tasting it. They started to become committed to making high-quality sausage. They even asked for information about costs and customers' reactions to various types of sausages. Another group of employees developed a new vacuum-sealed plastic package that prevented air leaks. This group gathered data, identified problems, worked with suppliers and with other workers, and even visited retail stores to find out how to make a better package. The team took responsibility for measuring quality and then used those measurements to improve production processes. Now employees started to complain about fellow workers whose performance was slipshod or indifferent. In fact, they complained to senior management to either train them or fire them. Instead of firing them, the team designed ways to coach them so that they could improve their performance.

Strayer, his top managers, and a group of workers also designed a new pay system called "company performance share." Under this pay system, a fixed percentage of pretax profits is divided every six months among all employees. Individual shares are based on the employee's performance appraisal, an appraisal designed and administered by employees from various departments. Some of the items on which employees are evaluated are their contribution to their group, communication, willingness to work on a team, attendance, and safety.

Finally, teams of employees are responsible for selecting, training, and evaluating, and, when necessary, firing, fellow employees. They make decisions about schedules, budgets, quality measurements, and capital improvement. These teams have taken over many of the jobs supervisors normally perform in manufacturing plants.

Strayer attributes his success to six guidelines:

1. People want to be great. If they aren't, it's because management won't let them.
2. Performance begins with individual expectations. Motivate people by telling them what you expect, and you influence how people perform.

3. Expectations are driven by goals and pay systems.
4. The actions by supervisors and other managers greatly affect an employee's expectations.
5. Each employee is capable of learning a whole variety of new tasks on the job.
6. The organization's results reflect me and my performance. My job is to create conditions under which an individual's superb performance serves both the individual and the company.[33]

QUESTIONS:

1. How do Strayer's motivational policies satisfy Maslow's needs?

2. Explain the success of the policies using expectancy theory.

3. Would you like to work at Johnsonville Foods? Why?

4. Did Strayer emphasize hygiene or motivator factors in the program?

References

1. Adapted from Posner, B. Z. If at First You Don't Succeed. *INC.*, May 1989, 132-134.
2. Annual Report, 1989. Thomson. Paris, France.
3. Shin, Y. K., Steers, R. M., Ungson, G. R., and Nam, S. Work Environment and Management Practice in Korean Corporations. *International Human Resource Management Review*, 1990, *1*, 95-108; Lee, S.M., Yoo, S., and Lee, T.M. Korean chaebols: Corporate Values and Strategies. *Organizational Dynamics*, Spring 1991, 36–50.
4. Locke, E. A., and Latham, G. P. *A Theory of Goal Setting and Task Performance*. Englewood Cliffs, N.J.: Prentice Hall, 1990, 6-8.
5. Steers, R. M., and Porter, L. W. (eds.). *Motivation and Work Behavior*, 5th ed. New York: McGraw-Hill, 1989; Kanfer, R. L. Motivation Theory and Industrial/Organizational Psychology. In M. D. Dunnette (ed.), *Handbook of Industrial and Organizational Psychology*, 2d ed. Palo Alto, Calif.: Consulting Psychologists Press, 1990, 75-170.
6. Maslow, A. H. *Motivation and Personality*. New York: Harper and Row, 1970.
7. For a review, see Pinder, C. C. *Work Motivation*. Glenview, Ill.: Scott, Foresman, 1984.

8. Alderfer, C. P. *Existence, Relatedness and Growth: Human Needs in Organizational Settings*. New York: The Free Press, 1972.
9. Wanous, J. P., and Zwany, A. A Cross-Sectional Test of the Need Hierarchy Theory. *Organizational Behavior and Human Performance*, 1977, *18*, 78-97.
10. Alderfer, C. P., and Guzzo, R. A. Life Expectancies and Adults' Enduring Strength of Desires in Organizations. *Administrative Science Quaraterly*, 1979, *24*, 347-361; also see Landy, F. J., and Becker, W. S. Motivation Theory Reconsidered. In L. L. Cummings and B. M. Staw (eds.), *Research in Organizational Behavior*, vol. 9. Greenwich, Conn.: JAI Press, 1987, 1-38.
11. McClelland, D. C. *Motivational Trends in Society*. Morristown, N.J.: General Learning Press, 1971.
12. Adapted from Magaziner, I. C., and Patinkin, M. Fast Heat: How Korea Won the Microwave War. *Harvard Business Review*, January-February 1989, 83-93; Steers, R. M., Shin, Y. K., and Ungson, G. R. *The Chaebol*. New York: Ballinger, 1989, 109-110.
13. McClelland, D. C., and Burnham, D. Power Is the Great Motivator. *Harvard Business Review*,

March-April 1976. 100-111; McClelland, D. C., and Boyatzis, R. E. Leadership Motive Pattern and Long-term Success in Management. *Journal of Applied Psychology*, 1982, *67*, 744-751.

14. Adapted from Mamis, R. A. Mother of Invention. *INC.*, October 1989, 119-127.

15. Machungiva, P. D., and Schmitt, N. Work Motivation in a Developing Country. *Journal of Applied Psychology*, 1983, *58*, 31-42; Stahl, M. J. *Managerial and Technical Motivation: Assessing Needs for Achievement, Power and Affiliation*. New York: Praeger, 1986; Winter, D. G. The Power Motive in Women and Men. *Journal of Personality and Social Psychology*, 1988, *54*, 510-519.

16. Herzberg, F. I., Mausner, B., and Snyderman, B. B. *The Motivation to Work*. New York: John Wiley and Sons, 1959.

17. Herzberg, F. I. Worker's Needs: The Same around the World. *Industry Week*, September 21, 1987, 29-32.

18. Evans, M. G. Organizational Behavior: The Central Role of Motivation. *Journal of Management*, 1986, *12*, 203-222; Kanfer, R. L. Motivation Theory and Industrial/Organizational Psychology. In D. M. Dunnette (ed.), *Handbook of Industrial and Organizational Psychology*, 2d ed. Palo Alto, Calif.: Consulting Psychologist Press, 1990, 75-170.

19. Klein, J. I. Feasibility Theory: A Resource-Munificence Model of Work Motivation and Behavior. *Academy of Management Review*, 1990, *15*, 646-665.

20. Vroom, V. H. *Work and Motivation*. New York: John Wiley and Sons, 1964.

21. Miller, L. E., and Grush, J. E. Improving Predictions in Expectancy Theory Research: Effects of Personality, Expectancies, and Norms. *Academy of Management Journal*, 1988, *31*, 107-122; Kernan, M. C., and Lord, R. G. Effects of Valences, Expectancies and Goal-Performance Discrepancies in Single and Multiple Goal Environments. *Journal of Applied Psychology*, 1990, *75*, 194-203.

22. Harrell, A., and Stahl, M. J. Additive Information Processing and the Relationship between Expectancy of Success and Motivational Force. *Academy of Management Journal*, 1986, *29*, 424-433.

23. Larson, U. R. Supervisor's Performance Feedback to Subordinates: The Effect of Performance Valence and Outcome Dependence. *Organizational Behavior and Human Decision Processes*, 1986, *37*, 391-409.

24. Adapted from Ellis, J. E. Feeling Stuck at Hyatt? Create a New Business. *Business Week*, December 10, 1990, 195.

25. Adams, J. S. Toward an Understanding of Inequity. *Journal of Abnormal and Social Psychology*, 1963, *67*, 422-436. Also see Huseman, R. C., Hatfield, J. D., and Miles, E. A. A New Perspective on Equity Theory: The Equity Sensitivity Construct. *Academy of Management Review*, 1987, *12*, 222-234.

26. Greenberg, J. Equity and Workplace Status: A Field Experiment. *Journal of Applied Psychology*, 1988, *73*, 606-613; Martin, J. E., and Peterson, M. W. Two-Tier Wage Structures: Implications for Equity Theory. *Academy of Management Journal*, 1987, *30*, 297-315; Griffeth, R. W., Vecchio, R. P., and Logan, J. W., Jr. Equity Theory and Interpersonal Attraction. *Journal of Applied Psychology*, 1990, *74*, 394-401.

27. Adapted from Faludi, S. C. At Nordstrom Stores, Service Comes First—but at a Big Price. *Wall Street Journal*, February 20, 1990, A1 and A12; Schwadel, F. Nordstrom to Post First Decline in Annual Profit. *Wall Street Journal*, February 20, 1990, A12.

28. Hesterly, W. S., Liebeskind, J., and Zenger, T. R. Organizational Economics: An Impending Revolution in Organization Theory. *Academy of Management Review*, 1990, *15*, 402-420; Cosier, R. A., and Dalton, D. R. Equity Theory and Time: A Reformulation. *Academy of Management Review*, 1983, *8*, 311-319.

29. Greenberg, J. Cognitive Reevaluation of Outcomes in Response to Underpayment Inequity. *Academy of Management Journal*, 1989, *32*, 174-184; Denis, A. S., and Summers, T. P. In Search of Adam's Other: Reexamination of Referents Used in the Evaluation of Pay. *Human Relations*, 1990, *43*, 497-512.

30. Folger, R., and Greenberg, J. Procedural Justice: An Interpretive Analysis of Personnel Systems. In K. M. Rowland and G. R. Ferris (eds.), *Research in Personnel and Human Resource Management*, vol. 3. Greenwich, Conn.: JAI Press, 1985, 141-183; Greenberg, J. Looking Fair versus Being Fair: Managing Impressions of Organizational Justice. In L. L. Cummings and B. M. Staw (eds.), *Research in Organizational Behavior*, vol. 12. Greenwich, Conn.: JAI Press, 1990, 111-158; Greenberg, J. Organizational Justice: Yesterday, Today, and Tomorrow. *Journal of Management*, 1990, *16*, 399-432.

31. Schuler, R. S., and Huber, V. L. *Personnel and Human Resource Management*, 4th ed. St. Paul: West Publishing Company, 1990, 348-349.

32. Adapted from Banet, A. G., Jr. Inventory of Self-Actualizing Characteristics. In J. W. Pfeiffer and J. H. Jones (eds.), *The 1976 Annual Handbook for Group Facilitators*. LaJolla, Calif.: University Associates, 1976, 67-77.

33. Adapted from Strayer, R. How I Learned to Let My Workers Lead. *Harvard Business Review*, November-December 1990, 66-69; 72-76; 80-83.

CHAPTER 8

GOAL SETTING AND PERFORMANCE ENHANCEMENT

LEARNING OBJECTIVES

After you have finished studying this chapter, you should be able to:

* Explain the role of customers, suppliers, and others in the goal-setting process.
* List the key factors in individual goal setting and performance and describe their relationships.
* Discuss how management by objectives (MBO) can be applied as a management philosophy and system.
* Describe how performance can be enhanced through an appropriately designed and implemented performance appraisal process.
* Explain three contemporary reward systems for enhancing performance.

OUTLINE

THE RACE IS ON

The numbers are nearly incredible. General Electric used to take three weeks after an order to deliver a custom-made industrial circuit breaker box. Now it takes three days. AT&T used to need two years to design a new phone. Now it can do the job in one. Motorola used to turn out electronic pagers three weeks after the factory got the order. Now it takes two hours.

Speed is catching on fast. A recent survey of fifty major U.S. companies by Kaiser Associates, a Vienna, Virginia, consulting firm, found that practically all put *time-based strategy*, as the new approach is called, at the top of their priority lists. Why? Because speed kills the competition.

Quickly developing, making, and distributing products or services brings important competitive benefits. Market share grows because customers like getting their orders *now*. Inventories of finished goods shrink because they are not necessary to ensure quick delivery. The fastest manufacturers can make and ship an order the day it is received. For this and other reasons, costs decrease. Many employees enjoy their jobs more because they are working for a more responsive, successful organization. Speeding up operations often requires managers to give employees more flexibility and responsibility.

Consider the system of performance goals at General Electric's circuit breaker factory in Salisbury, North Carolina. On the factory wall, a giant electronic sign hung twenty-five feet off the ground tells workers in flashing red letters how long it is taking them to make each circuit breaker box, how many boxes they have to make that day, and how many they have made so far. The sign lets employees pace themselves and make their own scheduling decisions. Says Dottie Barringer, a high achiever who has worked at the plant for the past thirteen years: "I like to be my own boss. I don't like to be told what to do. I know if I can't get it done in eight hours, I can do it in ten without getting permission for overtime. We're behind right now. No one has to tell us we have to work Saturday."

The plant, which used to have a two-month backlog of orders, now works with a two-day backlog. Productivity has increased 20 percent over the past year. Manufacturing costs have dropped 30 percent, or $5.5 million a year, and return on investment is running at over 20 percent. As noted in the opening of this preview case, the speed of delivery has shrunk from three weeks to three days for a higher-quality product with more features. GE is gaining share in a flat market. Says William Sheeran, GE general manager: "We had to speed up or die."[1]

The establishment of challenging goals that take into account both time and quality is no longer optional to survive in the global competitive markets of the 1990s. It must happen! As noted at the beginning of the Preview Case, AT&T used to take two years to design a new telephone. But, says John Hanley, an AT&T vice-president of product development, "We came to the realization that if you get to market sooner with new technology, you can charge a premium until the others follow." AT&T began developing a new cordless phone for the home called the 4200 in early 1988. Rather than trying to save 10 percent in time here and 5 percent there, Hanley's goal was to reduce the development cycle by 50 percent. He says: "It made us change the way we did everything."[2]

The common elements that cut across the achievements noted in the Preview Case are setting goals and developing feedback and reward systems that guide individuals and teams toward those goals. In this chapter, we first outline the role played by customers, suppliers, and other stakeholders and how they affect goal setting. Second, we present an individual-based model of goal setting and performance. In this section, we note how this model provides the foundation for our discussion of management by objectives as a management philosophy and system that attempts to integrate goal setting into organizational life. The third section demonstrates how performance and the achievement of goals are likely to be enhanced through a well-designed performance appraisal process. The last section returns to the topic of reward systems, which was also considered in Chapters 6 and 7. Here, we review three of the newer reward systems being used by organizations.

INTRODUCTION TO GOAL SETTING

Goal setting is a process intended to increase efficiency and effectiveness by specifying the desired outcomes toward which individuals, departments, teams, and organizations should work. **Goals** are the future outcomes (results) that individuals, groups, and organizations desire and strive to achieve.[3] An example of one individual goal is: "I am planning to graduate with a 2.5 grade-point average by the end of the spring semester, 1995."

Purposes of Goal Setting

Even though goal setting is no easy task, the purposes served by establishing goals generally make the effort worthwhile. Setting goals often increases the efficiency and effectiveness of individuals, groups, and organizations. The following are among the more important purposes of goals:

- Goals guide and direct behavior. They increase role clarity by focusing effort and attention in specific directions, thereby reducing uncertainty in day-to-day decision making.
- Goals provide challenges and standards against which individual, departmental, team, or organizational performance can be assessed.
- Goals serve as a source of legitimacy. They justify various activities and the use of resources to pursue them.
- Goals define the rationale for the organization's structure. They determine, in part, communication patterns, authority relationships, power relationships, and division of labor. Goals thus serve an organizing function.
- Goals reflect what the goal setters consider important and thus provide a framework for planning and control activities.[4]

Role of Stakeholders

Goals and goal setting are often the object of disagreement and conflict, as we will discuss in Chapter 14. Because diverse groups have a stake in organizational decisions, managers are faced with the continuing need to develop, modify, and discard goals. **Stakeholders** are groups having potential or real power to influence the organization's decisions, such as choice of goals, and actions. Stakeholders commonly include customers/clients, employees, suppliers, shareholders, government agencies, unions, public interest groups, and lenders, among others.

Table 8.1 contains several categories of organizational goals of particular interest to six stakeholder groups. Some of these categories may be incompatible with each other. Creating a unified and logical system of goal setting for an organization is very difficult in the following situations:

- Each stakeholder group has substantial power in relation to the organization.
- Each stakeholder group pushes to maximize its own interests and perceives the interests of some or all other groups as incompatible with its own.
- The stakeholders keep changing what they expect (want) from the organization.

TABLE 8.1 Typical Stakeholders and Their General Goals for an Organization

Customers/Clients	**Shareholders**
Price always competitive	Growth in dividend payments
Emphasis on quality	Growth in share price
Satisfaction guaranteed	Growth in net asset value
Employees	**Government**
Good compensation and job security	Being an efficient user of energy and natural resources
Sense of meaning or purpose in the job	Adhering to the country's laws
Opportunities for personal development	Payment of taxes
Lenders	**Suppliers**
Liquidity of the organization	Timely payment of debts
Maintenance of assets that serve as security on loans	Adequate liquidity
Improvements in productivity to lower break even point	Repeat customer

Source: Adapted from A. L. Mendelow. Setting Corporate Goals and Measuring Organizational Effectiveness: A Practical Approach. *Long Range Planning*, February 1983, 75–76.

- The management team itself is divided into competing groups within the organization.[5]

Taken together, these situations present a worst-case scenario. Fortunately, managers and other employees are not usually confronted with such a diversity and incompatibility of demands in setting goals. Table 8-1 illustrates the goals that various stakeholders may have for a typical organization. Notice that some of these goals, if pushed to extremes, may be incompatible and will require managers to use keen negotiation skills to balance or resolve the resulting conflicts.

On a day-to-day basis, the most important stakeholders for any organization are its customers or clients. Their goals need to be reflected in the goals of the organization as a whole, as well as in the goals of individual employees and groups within the organization. This perspective was certainly reflected in the goal-setting process at General Electric's circuit breaker factory and the goal of reducing the time of the development cycle by 50 percent for the 4200 model telephone at AT&T.

Customer Service Quality Goals

How might an employee, team, or entire organization set goals related to customer service quality? Two critical factors need to be recognized in answering this question. The first factor is that customers or clients are the sole judge of service quality. Customers assess service by comparing the service they perceive with the service they desire. An organization can achieve a strong reputation for quality service only when it consistently meets customer service expectations or goals. The second factor is how easy it is for managers and other employees to forget the first factor.[6]

Customer service goals are categorized below into five overall dimensions. Following each definition there is a sample comment from a dissatisfied customer indicating an unmet goal.

- *Reliability*—the ability to perform the promised service dependably and accurately. Truck leasing customer: "Too often they take care of your problems too fast. They fix your truck, and two days later you have to take it back for the same problem. They could be a little more attentive and fix the problem permanently."
- *Tangibles*—the appearance of physical facilities, equipment, personnel, and communication materials. Hotel customer: "They get you real pumped up with the beautiful ad. When you go in, you expect bells and whistles to go off. Usually, they don't."
- *Responsiveness*—the willingness to help customers and to provide prompt service. Business equipment repair customer: "You put in a service call and wait. No one calls back; there is no communication."
- *Assurance*—the knowledge and courtesy of employees and their ability to convey trust and confidence. Computer software customer: "I quote stuff from their software instruction manuals to their own people, and they don't even know what it means."
- *Empathy*—the provision of caring, individualized attention to customers or clients. Airline customer: "They'll out-and-out lie to you

about how delayed a flight will be so that you don't try to get a flight on another airline."[7]

As demonstrated in the following In Practice, the setting and achievement of service goals is an evolving process.

IN PRACTICE

SERVICE GOALS AT AMERICAN EXPRESS

American Express (Am Ex) began its white-collar quality work program in the late 1970s with a pilot project in Phoenix, where 6,800 employees process 18 million charge slips a month for cardholders in the Western states. Even before the program began, Am Ex tracked errors and timeliness. It soon realized, however, that most of these measures focused on internal processes, such as how fast or accurately a department did its work.

In 1978, the company created new indices to measure quality through the eyes of its customers. This cast a new light on the business. Am Ex previously had measured how quickly the credit department processed a new card application. Customers did not get a response until the request had been through at least four other departments. The new system measured how long customers waited for all steps to be finished.

The Phoenix experiment led to one of the most sophisticated office-quality measurement systems in the country, called a service tracking report (STR). The STR looks at more than one hundred tasks, from how quickly phones are answered to the accuracy of monthly statements. It has become a tool for constant quality improvement at Am Ex's five U.S. customer service centers. Using monthly reviews of the numbers, officials in New York periodically nudge up goals to produce higher quality in hundreds of functions. In the past ten years, Am Ex has cut processing time for new applications by half, from twenty-two to eleven days. Since 1980, such improvements—coupled with computerization—have more than doubled the revenue per employee throughout Am Ex's travel division, which includes credit cards. In 1990, the figure reached $191,000 per employee.

In the tradition of McDonald's Hamburger University, Am Ex now has a Quality University in Phoenix. It offers courses for line employees and their managers, such as "How to Treat the Customer 101." Heroic moments in quality—such as the Boston employee who arose in the middle of the night to deliver a card to a stranded customer at Logan Airport—are illustrated in a series of "Great Performers" booklets distributed to all forty-five thousand Travel Related Services division employees worldwide.[8]

GOAL SETTING AND PERFORMANCE

In this section, we focus on key elements of goal setting and performance. We hold in the background the types of issues and factors that can complicate organizational goal setting. In addition, we will discuss the setting of goals when employees work relatively independently and when they are highly interdependent with others in performing their tasks.

Locke and Latham Goals Model

Ed Locke and Gary Latham, two well-known scholars, developed a sophisticated model of individual goal setting and performance. A simplified version of their model is shown in Figure 8.1.[9] It shows the key variables and the general relationships that can lead to high individual performance. Some of the concepts included in their model have been discussed in previous chapters.

Challenge   The model starts with the challenges provided for the individual employee or manager. For the individual, *goal setting* is the process of developing, negotiating, and formalizing targets that he or she is responsible for accomplishing.[10] Employees with unclear goals or no goals are more prone to work slowly, perform poorly, lack interest, and accomplish less than employees whose goals are clear and challenging. In addition, employees with clearly defined goals appear to be more energetic, challenged, and productive. They get things done on time and then move on to other activities (and goals).

Goals can be implicit or explicit, vague or clearly defined, and self-imposed or externally imposed. Whatever their form, goals serve to structure the individual's time and effort. Two key attributes of goals are particularly important for individual goal setting:

- **Goal difficulty**
  Goals should be challenging. If they are too easy to attain, the individual may procrastinate or approach the goal lackadaisically. The individual may not accept a goal if it is too difficult and thus not try to meet it.

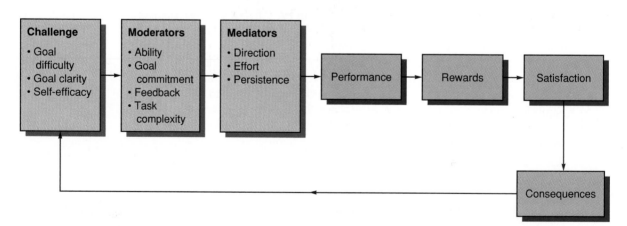

FIGURE 8.1   Simplified Locke and Latham Goals Model

Source: Adapted from E. A. Locke and G. P. Latham. *A Theory of Goal Setting and Task Performance.* Englewood Cliffs, N.J.: Prentice-Hall, 1990, 253.

- **Goal clarity**

   Goals must be clear and specific if they are to be useful for directing effort. The individual thus will know what he or she is expected to accomplish—and not have to guess.

Clear and challenging goals lead to higher performance than do vague or general goals.[11] Bloomingdale's store in Manhattan has set an annual goal of half a million dollars for each salesperson in its shoe department. It has found it is better to set a salesperson's goal at a specific amount to be sold than to set a goal of "trying to increase sales" or "doing your best." Goals that are difficult—but not impossible—will lead to higher performance than will easy goals. Unrealistically high goals that cannot be reached may not be accepted or may lead to high performance only in the short run. Individuals eventually get discouraged and stop trying, as predicted by expectancy theory (see Chapter 7).[12] Goal setting can be used to effectively enhance creativity when a creativity goal is assigned to individuals. In order to be creative, individuals need to have their attention and effort focused on either a do-your-best or a difficult creativity goal.[13]

With clear and challenging goals, employee efforts are more likely to be focused on job-related tasks, high levels of performance, and goal achievement. Table 8.2 provides a summary of the key links between goal setting and individual performance.

A third key factor that influences the establishment of challenging goals is self-efficacy. As discussed in Chapter 6, *self-efficacy* is the individual's strength of belief that he or she can perform at a certain level in a situation. It may be assessed by having individuals rate their confidence in attaining different performance levels. As you might predict, individuals who set high goals have higher self-efficacy than those who set lower goals.[14]

The following In Practice demonstrates how goal difficulty, goal clarity, and high self-efficacy came together at Velcro when a major customer threatened to drop Velcro's product line unless quality improved. The voice is that of K. Theodor Krantz, the president of Velcro USA.

TABLE 8.2 Common Impacts of Goal Setting on Performance

When Goals Are	Performance Will Tend to Be
Specific and clear	Higher
Vague	Lower
Difficult and challenging	Higher
Set participatively	Higher
Accepted by employees	Higher
Rejected by employees	Lower
Accompanied by positive incentives	Higher

IN PRACTICE

VELCRO MEETS THE QUALITY CHALLENGE

The phone call came out of the blue one morning in August 1985. It was from our Detroit sales manager, who told me that General Motors (GM) was dropping us from its highest supplier quality rating to the next to lowest level, four (on a one-to-five scale). We had ninety days to set up and start a program of total quality control at our plant in Manchester, New Hampshire, or face the loss of not only an important customer but also our most promising growth market.

To get an idea of what we had to do, we needed to talk to GM quality control people. So five Velcro managers flew to Detroit and met for a couple of hours with GM people. They told us that our products—which included tape for binding fabric to a car's roof—were not bad but needed improvement. While we were meeting their delivery schedules, they said our progress was unacceptable: we were *inspecting* quality into the product, we were not *manufacturing* quality into the product.

GM was dissatisfied with the fact that it was throwing away 5 percent to 8 percent of the tape, depending on the product. It wanted quality maintained up and down the line to prevent such waste. We flew back east, feeling thoroughly beat. It was no consolation to realize that all three U.S. auto producers were feeling great pressure to upgrade their quality, cut costs, and reduce the number of suppliers. We were not alone in getting the heat.

We had to get all five hundred Manchester employees through a quality course, we had to work up a fairly exhaustive quality manual, and we had to start the basics of a statistical process control program in the plant. Velcro managers and employees accepted these challenging goals to meet these threats.

It was a long time before Velcro got quality instilled throughout the organization. But it has happened, as these figures on waste reduction as a percentage of total manufacturing expenses show:

1987, 50 percent reduction from 1986
1988, 45 percent reduction from 1987

We got our house in relatively good order and soon were back in GM's good graces. We expected to move up to a two rating, but by that time, GM had changed its supplier quality program to Targets of Excellence. Even as our quality improved, the goals against which we are measured were moving higher as well.

In the search for quality, there's no such thing as good enough; there's never a finish line. Moreover, the finish line sometimes seems farther away than ever. Now Velcro is a customer-driven company where quality is in the eye of the customer. Whether a production run is acceptable is something the customer ultimately decides.[15]

Moderators   Four of the factors that moderate the strength of the relationship between goals and performance are shown in Figure 8.1. We start with *ability* because it puts limits on the individual's capacity to respond to a challenge. The relation of goal difficulty to performance is curvilinear. That is, performance levels off after the limits of a person's ability have been reached.

Goal commitment, the second factor, refers to the individual's attachment to or determination to reach a goal, regardless of where the goal came from. It can apply to any goal, whether it was set by the individual, established jointly with others, or assigned by a superior. Many factors have been found to affect the degree of goal commitment. The effect of participation on goal commitment is an intricate one.[16] In general, our view is that positive goal commitment is more likely if employees participate in setting goals. Participation often leads to a sense of ownership. If employees do not expect or want to be involved in goal setting, the importance of participation on goal commitment is reduced. Even when it is necessary to assign goals without the participation of the employees who must implement them, more focused efforts and better performance will result than if no goals were set.

The expected rewards for achieving goals play an important role in the degree of goal commitment.[17] The greater the extent to which employees believe that positive rewards (merit pay raises, bonuses, promotions, opportunities to perform interesting tasks, and the like) are contingent on achieving goals, the greater the goal commitment. These notions are very similar to the ideas contained in the expectancy theory of motivation in Chapter 7. Similarly, if employees expect to be punished for not achieving goals, the probability of goal commitment is also higher.[18] Recall that in Chapter 6, we discussed why punishment and the fear of punishment as primary means of guiding behavior may create a number of problems.

Employees compare expected rewards against rewards actually realized. This comparison is based on the individual's perceptions. If the realized and expected rewards are in agreement and positive, the reward system is likely to continue to support goal commitment. If employees think that the realized rewards are much less than the expected rewards, they may experience a sense of inequity. As noted in Chapter 7, if inequity exists, employees eventually develop a lower level of goal commitment. Another factor affecting goal commitment is the strength of peer pressure, which is considered in Chapter 10.[19]

Feedback makes goal setting and individual responses to goal achievement (performance) a dynamic process.[20] It provides information to an employee and others about the outcomes and degree of goal achievement by the employee.[21] Feedback enables the individual to compare the expected rewards against realized rewards. This, in turn, can influence changes in the degree of goal commitment.

Task complexity is the last moderator we consider as an influence on the strength of relationship between goals and performance. On simple tasks (for example, stuffing envelopes), the effort encouraged by challenging goals leads directly to task performance. In more complex tasks (for example, studying to achieve a high grade), effort does not lead directly to effective performance. One must also decide where and how to allocate effort.[22] We consider a variety of issues associated with simple and complex jobs in Chapter 17, which discusses job design.

Mediators Let's assume the individual has challenging goals and the moderating factors support the achievement of these goals. Let's quickly consider how three mediators—shown as direction, effort, and persistence in Figure 8.1—affect performance. *Direction of attention* means that goals focus behaviors on those activities expected to result in goal achievement and at the same time steer people away from activities irrelevant to the goals. The *effort* mechanism depends substantially on the difficulty of the goal. The greater the goal challenge, the greater the effort expended assuming that goal commitment is persistent. Finally, the *persistence* mechanism means that goals (assuming goal commitment) will affect people's willingness to work at the task over an extended period of time until the results are achieved.

Performance Task performance is likely to be high when: (1) challenging goals are present, (2) the moderators (e.g., ability, goal commitment, feedback, and task complexity) are present, and (3) the mediator mechanisms (direction of attention, effort, and persistence) are operating. Three basic types of quantitative outcome measures can be used to assess performance. They are: units of production or quality (amount produced, number of errors); dollars (profits, costs, income, sales); and time (job attendance, lateness in meeting deadlines).

When quantitative outcome goals and measures are unavailable or inappropriate, qualitative goals and indicators may be used. Consider the case of ethics training. The ultimate qualitative goals of ethics training are presumably to avoid unethical behavior, adverse publicity, and lawsuits and to gain a strategic advantage. The more specific qualitative goals of ethics training may include the following:

- To develop the ability to recognize the ethical components of decisions.
- To legitimize the consideration of ethics as part of decision making.
- To avoid variability in decision making caused by a lack of awareness of rules or norms.
- To avoid ambivalence in decision making caused by an organizational reward system that appears to reward unethical behavior.
- To provide decision-making frameworks for analyzing ethical choices and to help employees to apply such frameworks.[23]

Rewards The concept of rewards was discussed at length in Chapters 6 and 7. In brief, once high performance has been shown, rewards can become important inducements to continue to perform. Of course, rewards can be external (bonuses, paid vacations, and so on) or internal. Internal, self-administered rewards that can occur following high performance include a sense of achievement based on attaining a certain level of excellence, pride in accomplishment, and feelings of success and efficacy.

This chapter's Across Cultures suggests both similarities and differences among employees, supervisors, and managers with respect to the work goals that they value. It is based on a sample of over eight thousand employees from Belgium, Great Britain, West Germany, Israel, Japan, the Netherlands, and the United States.

◆ *ACROSS CULTURES*

WORK GOALS IN SEVEN COUNTRIES

Employees from seven countries were asked to rank eleven work goals. Each work goal was considered separately to determine its relative importance. The most important work goal, by a wide margin, was that of "interesting work." Employees in four countries (Belgium, Great Britain, Israel, and the United States) ranked this goal as the most important aspect of their work lives; those in the remaining three countries (Japan, the Netherlands, and West Germany) ranked it second or third. A similar pattern among countries was generally revealed regardless of the type of work or educational level of the employees. The goals of "good pay" and "good interpersonal relations" followed in order. The mean rank for "good pay" ranged from a high of 7.80 out of a highest rating of 11 in Britain to a low of 6.27 in the Netherlands. The range for "good interpersonal relations" was from a high of 7.19 in the Netherlands to a low of 6.08 in the United States. Next in respective order came the three work goals of "good job security," "a good match between you and your job," and "a lot of autonomy." These showed large differences between countries, the mean ranks by country ranging from 4.69 to 7.83.

The dominant place of "interesting work" in the lives of workers receives further testimony in an analysis by organizational level. With only minor exceptions, this goal was ranked first—the most important work goal—at every organizational level in all participating countries. A similar trend characterizes the work goal of "good pay," although managers ranked this item as having only moderate importance. Apparently managers who enjoy higher pay probably perceive this work goal to be less important than do their subordinates and, consequently, rank it lower. Two work goals that were of particular importance to managers but of consistently less importance to respondents at the lower organizational levels were "work autonomy" and "match between job requirements and one's abilities."

Another highly rated work goal was "good interpersonal relations," which ranked second among managers, third among employees, and fourth among supervisors. In the Netherlands, this item was ranked first overall among employees and second among managers. Israeli respondents ranked this goal second at all organizational levels. The United States deviated from the rest of the countries in regard to this item, which received only seventh place in the national sample.

The major findings emerging from this study on work goals in seven countries have some practical implications. The emphasis that workers place on interesting work points to an intrinsic orientation. Thus, having the opportunity to be employed in a work setting that assists a person to satisfy his or her needs for esteem or to attain self-actualization is important in all of the countries in this study. Moreover, when work is interesting and challenging, people are inspired to perform more than is needed to satisfy basic job requirements. They exert additional effort in order to experience a sense of fulfilling their potential and accomplishing worthwhile ends.[24]

Satisfaction   The experience of job satisfaction is a function of many factors. In this model, the primary focus is on the degree of satisfaction with having reached one's goals. Of course, as Locke and Latham state:

> High goals may lead to less-experienced satisfaction than low goals, since they are attained, by definition, less frequently. Satisfaction with performance is positively associated with the number of successes experienced. Thus some

compromise on goal difficulty may be necessary in order to maximize both satisfaction and performance. However, there are sources of satisfaction associated with simply trying for hard goals, such as the satisfaction of complying with a respected authority figure, the satisfaction of responding to a challenge, the satisfaction of making some progress toward the goals, and the belief that future benefits may accrue in terms of skill development.[25]

Consequences   Individuals who are both satisfied with and thus committed to the organization should be more likely to stay with the organization and to accept the challenges that it presents to them. Turnover and absenteeism rates for these individuals are low. This link brings us back full circle to the beginning of the Locke and Latham goals model (see Figure 8.1).

What might be the consequences if things go badly and the individual experiences dissatisfaction rather than satisfaction? Individual responses fall into at least six possible categories: (1) job avoidance (quitting); (2) work avoidance; (3) psychological defenses (e.g., drug abuse); (4) constructive protest (e.g., complaining); (5) defiance (refusing to do what is asked); and (6) aggression (theft, assault). Of course, quitting is the most common outcome of severe dissatisfaction.[26]

Organizational Significance   The Locke and Latham goals model has important implications for the management of employees. First, it provides an excellent framework to assist the manager in diagnosing the potential problems with low- or average-performance employees. Several diagnostic questions might be: (1) How were the goals set?; (2) Are the goals challenging?; (3) What is affecting goal commitment?; and (4) Does the employee know when he or she has done a good job? Second, it provides concrete advice to the manager on how to create a high-performance work environment. Third, it portrays the *system* of relationships and *interplay* among key factors—such as goal difficulty, goal commitment, feedback, rewards, and others—to achieve high performance.

Individual-Focused Management by Objectives

Management by objectives (MBO) is a philosophy and system of management that serves as both a planning aid and way of work life. A widely used management approach, it reflects a positive philosophy about people and a participative management style. Hewlett-Packard and Procter & Gamble are among the organizations that use MBO successfully.

Management by objectives involves managers and their subordinates in jointly setting goals for work performance and personal development, evaluating progress toward these goals, and integrating individual, departmental, team, and organizational goals. Employee success in attaining the goals is evaluated over time.

While many people have contributed to the development of MBO, Peter Drucker coined the term *management by objectives* in about 1950.[27] A variety of forms of MBO are used. We discuss two models of MBO: one that emphasizes the individual and a second that focuses on the work team and interdependent groups. Goals and goal setting are central to both of these two models.

The **individual-focused MBO model** contains four basic components, each of which consists of a number of dimensions. As Figure 8.2 shows, these components are goal setting, subordinate participation, implementation, and performance appraisal and feedback. The arrows indicate that a strong interrelationship exists among the components and that all should operate simultaneously to make the MBO process effective.

Goal setting Subordinates and superiors define and focus on job goals rather than rules, activities, and procedures. For our discussion, we use *goals* synonymously with *objectives, outputs, results, ends,* or *performance standards.*[28] The goal-setting process includes identifying specific areas of job responsibility, developing performance standards in each area, and, possibly, formulating a work plan for achieving the desired results. Table 8.3 provides a hypothetical example of selected task-related areas of responsibility for a salesperson and a specific goal for each area.[29]

Particular job responsibilities usually change less dramatically and less frequently over time than does the specific goal associated with each responsibility area. In Table 8.3, the salesperson will continually be responsible for sales volume, but specific levels in sales volume can vary dramatically because of general economic conditions, changed market acceptance, more or fewer opportunities in a sales territory, and so on.

A variety of prescriptions have been offered to managers on how to set goals with subordinates. Here is one example:

- *State what must be done.* If you are setting goals with a subordinate, you may find a job description helpful. It should list the tasks to be performed, the outcomes expected, the other jobs with which this one coordinates, necessary equipment, supervisory duties, and so on. Critical job requirements, on which job success depends, can further clarify the job description.

- *Specify how performance will be measured.* Often you can use time, money, or physical units. Sometimes, though, success is more sub-

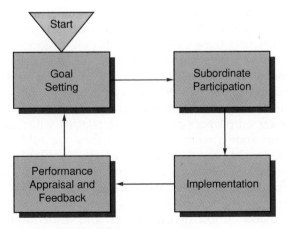

FIGURE 8.2 Individual-Focused MBO Model

TABLE 8.3 Hypothetical Responsibilities and Goals for a Salesperson

Responsibility	Specific Goal
Sales volume	Increase sales volume by 8 percent.
Gross margin on goods sold	Keep average gross margin on goods sold at 40 percent.
Number of calls per day	Increase to seven the average number of calls per day.
Order/call ratio	Increase order/call ratio to 20 percent.
Average order size	Increase average order size to three hundred dollars.
New accounts	Generate twenty-four new accounts.

---

jective and hard to measure quantitatively. Managers can still define performance by specifying behaviors or actions that they know will lead to success.

- *Specify the performance standard.* A readily accepted approach is to start goal setting by letting previous performance set the standard. Most employees consider their average previous performance, or that of their group, to be a fair goal. Performance in some jobs, though, cannot be measured so precisely. The job may be unique or so new that no previous performance measures are available. If so, goal setting becomes a matter of judgment, in which a manager should involve his or her subordinates.

- *Set deadlines to reach goals.* Some goals lend themselves to daily or weekly accomplishment. Others can be accomplished only monthly, quarterly, or annually.

- *Rank goals in order of importance.* Manager and subordinate must agree on goal priority to avoid misunderstandings.

- *Rate goals as to difficulty and importance.* Managers may need to be precise when they deal with multiple goals, as in the case of an employee's job description or a departmental goal.[30]

Participation A moderate to high level of participation by subordinates in the goal-setting process is claimed to be the most effective with MBO. Before subordinates can effectively participate, they must have sufficient leeway in their jobs, or an increase in discretion must be planned. Discretion enables employees to plan and control what they do and how they do it, rather than merely doing what they are told. Management by objectives requires that subordinates plan and control their own tasks. Thus, managers should redesign highly routine and programmed jobs before applying the MBO approach to them.

Implementation Implementation of the individual-focused MBO model requires translating the outcomes from the goal-setting process into actions that ultimately will lead to the attainment of the desired goals. The implementation phase is often accompanied by action planning, which indicates how goals are to be achieved. During implementation, superiors must give greater latitude and choice to subordinates, perhaps by discontinuing the day-to-day oversight of their activities. Superiors must be available to coach and counsel subordinates to help them reach their goals. They must play a more helping or facilitating role and less of a judgmental role. Superiors should hold periodic meetings during the year with subordinates to review progress, discuss any assistance needed, and make any necessary changes in goals, which should be modified as needed. This approach prevents employees from perceiving MBO as a rigid system and encourages them to address major new problems or changes as they occur.[31]

Performance Appraisal and Feedback   Performance appraisal under MBO involves (1) *identifying* measurement factors or goals against which to evaluate performance; (2) *measuring* performance against such goals; (3) *reviewing* performance levels attained by individuals; and (4) *developing* improved future performance.[32] Subordinates develop a clear understanding of their progress through performance appraisal and feedback. Feedback is a key element of MBO because it identifies the extent to which employees have attained their goals. The knowledge of results is essential to improved job performance and personal development in the form of new skills, attitudes, and motivation.

Management by objectives encourages self-evaluation of performance. Subordinates who know their own goals and the measures of results should gain substantial insight into their own performance and the possible need to modify their behaviors. For example, two goals for the salesperson in Table 8.3 were increasing sales volume by 8 percent and maintaining the average gross margin on goods sold at 40 percent. So long as the salesperson receives feedback in these areas, understanding of outcomes in relation to these goals is possible. The procedures of performance appraisal under MBO will be presented in a later section as one of four methods of appraisal.

Organizational Significance   Critics have attacked the individual-focused MBO model, particularly with respect to ways that organizations apply it. These criticisms relate mainly to how managers actually use the process, rather than to how it is supposed to be used. Some of these criticisms are:

- Too much emphasis is placed on reward-punishment psychology (that is, people are rewarded for accomplishing goals and punished for not doing so).
- An excessive amount of paperwork and red tape develops—the very things that MBO is supposed to reduce.
- The process is really controlled and imposed from the top, allowing little opportunity for real employee participation.
- The process turns into a zero-sum (win-lose) game between superior and subordinate.
- Aspects of jobs that can be quantitatively rather than qualitatively measured receive the most emphasis.

- Too much emphasis on individual goals and performance drives out recognition of the need for collaborative teamwork and group goals. Individuals may optimize their own goals to the detriment of overall goals.[33]

Team-Focused Management by Objectives

The **team-focused MBO model** is fundamentally consistent with the key elements of the individual-focused MBO model. The team-focused goal-setting process includes entire work groups. The team-focused model attempts to overcome two major deficiencies in the individual-focused MBO model. First, the team model clearly recognizes the interdependencies between jobs, especially at the managerial level. Second, it encourages integration of goals among the individuals who must work together, rather than placing the entire responsibility for coordination on a common superior.[34]

As with the individual-focused MBO model, the degree of participation and influence of work groups in setting goals can vary widely in the team-focused MBO model. One process for implementing the team-focused MBO model can be summarized as follows:

- In team meetings, top executives develop overall organization goals to be achieved within a certain time period, primarily on the basis of consensus.

- Departmental or team goals to facilitate the attainment of overall organizational goals are again developed in team or group sessions, primarily through consensus.

- Individuals develop their own goals within this framework. A major difference from the individual-focused MBO model in this phase is that in the team-focused model, team members may discuss one another's goals, suggest changes, and openly discuss the interdependent nature of their responsibilities.

- While performance reviews take place between superiors and subordinates, matters of concern to the team are discussed in regularly scheduled team meetings.[35]

The team-focused MBO model probably has the greatest potential for success only under certain conditions. First, a real need for cooperation among individuals must exist. Second, top management must cooperate and offer assistance instead of engaging in political power struggles. Third, the participants must have some degree of skill in group processes and interpersonal relations.

The following In Practice is based on the results of a two-year field study of 360 new-product managers in 52 high-technology companies. It reports on several of the key characteristics of innovative product teams. As you will see, the team-focused MBO model is often used to achieve high-performance innovation teams.

IN PRACTICE

TEAM MBO FOR INNOVATION

Project goals and their importance must be clear to all personnel involved with an innovation-oriented activity. Senior management can help develop a "priority image" and communicate the basic project's scope and guidelines. Management must convey why it wants this innovation and what it will be used for (goal clarity). While operationally the project might have to be fined-tuned to the changing environment, the "top-down goal and mission" should remain stable. Managers and team leaders at lower organization levels need this stability to develop challenging goals with their people. It is an important prerequisite for establishing benchmarks and gaining innovative performance. Moreover, establishing and communicating clear and stable goals helps to build an image of high visibility, value, priority, and interesting work for project team members. It is a pervasive process that fosters a climate of active participation at all levels. It helps to attract and hold quality people, unifies the team, and minimizes dysfunctional conflict.

Comprehensive project development planning early in the project life cycle will have a favorable impact on the work environment and team effectiveness. Because tasks must be integrated across functional lines, proper planning requires the participation of the entire team, including support departments, subcontractors, and management. One of the side benefits of proper project planning is the involvement of personnel at all organizational levels. Managers should drive such an involvement, at least with their key personnel, and especially during the project definition phases.

Managers should try to accommodate the professional interests and desires of their personnel whenever possible. Innovative performance seems to increase with the individual's perception of professionally interesting and stimulating work. It leads to increased involvement, better communications, lower conflict, and higher commitment.[36]

ENHANCING PERFORMANCE THROUGH APPRAISAL

In the first two parts of this chapter and in Chapters 6 and 7, we emphasized that challenging goals are crucial to any motivational plan. Also, rewards must be valued by employees, and their distribution must be equitable. All things being equal, high-performing employees should receive more rewards than lower-performing ones. Whether this actually happens or not depends upon the organization's performance evaluation system. **Performance evaluation** is a process of assessing each employee's performance and potential for future development.

Developing effective performance evaluation systems requires two things. First, there must be a performance evaluation system to permit the assignment of the strengths and weaknesses of each employee. While these systems are by their nature somewhat subjective and susceptible to perceptual errors (see Chapter 4), they do determine the extrinsic rewards that employees receive. Second, there must be an understanding of the rewards that motivate employees. For example, some employees want a pay-for-performance system, while others prefer a system that allocates rewards based on seniority. Two major areas that bear directly on enhancing performance are discussed in the next two sections: (1) the performance appraisal process and (2) alternative reward systems for helping to guide employee behavior.

Performance Appraisal Process

Performance appraisal is the systematic process of evaluating each employee's job-related achievements, strengths, and weaknesses, as well as determining ways to improve performance. This process is essential if the organization is to reward fairly the efforts of good performers and to know when to dismiss inadequate performers. Few organizations have been able to develop and implement effective performance appraisal systems. As a result, performance appraisal continues to be one of the most important challenges facing managers and other employees.

What are some of the characteristics of a good performance appraisal system? In general, it is one that is designed to help employees reach their potential and increase their effectiveness.[37] A good system can accomplish this overall goal in three specific ways:

- By providing clear feedback on how well employees are doing. With clear, accurate performance feedback, they can decide how to improve performance and what is adequate and acceptable behavior. Thus, managers should not keep performance appraisals secret but should share them with employees.

- By providing a means for employee growth and development by examining potential as well as actual work behavior. Effective managers realize that it is their responsibility to see that both the individual and the organization benefit from improved performance.

- By helping managers make short- and long-range decisions. For example, some administrative decisions include who is to receive a pay increase, promotion, transfer, or demotion. If such rewards are based on performance, employees will continue to engage in behaviors beneficial to the organization.

A good example of an effective system is that used by Brooklyn Union Gas Company. There are three major parts to its performance appraisal system. First, each employee and manager develops a list of five or six key job responsibilities that they then use to identify specific performance goals. In order for this process to work effectively, supervisors must have good communication and goal-setting skills. Second, a two-day training program, designed by the company's human resource department, covers the critical skills that managers need to know. Finally, to keep goals up to date and specific, performance appraisals are held every six months.[38]

Uses of Performance Appraisals   Performance appraisals are invaluable aids to making many human resource management decisions, as Brooklyn Union Gas has discovered. A particularly important use is helping managers distinguish between good and poor performers. Performance appraisal information can be used in three important ways.

First, most organizations try to motivate employees by basing pay, bonuses, and other financial rewards on performance. **Merit pay plans** are designed to compensate people according to their job performance. In many managerial jobs, merit pay plans are used because there are limited hard data on which to judge a manager's performance. That is, managers do not sell life insurance policies, write computer programs, and the like. Managers lead, plan, control, and coordinate the efforts and activities of those people who actually perform those activities. A major problem with both merit pay plans and performance bonuses is how to accurately measure an employee's performance, a topic that we discuss in the next few pages of this chapter.

Second, performance appraisal information helps managers decide on *personnel movement*. Who should receive a promotion? Who should be transferred, demoted, or dismissed? Like many other major organizations, the McDonnell Douglas Corporation started a job rotation program to develop future general managers. Based on their performance appraisals, highly rated managers are offered a three-year rotation outside of their division and functional area. After completing the program, they should have a breadth of experiences that will enable them to perform the duties of general managers.

Lastly, by identifying areas of poor performance, the manager can suggest training or other programs to improve certain skills or behaviors. Training programs range from classes to teach specific activities, such as how to operate a piece of equipment, to developing proficiency in managing subordinates.

Problems in Appraisal

According to most people who have given or received a performance appraisal, a major problem is the subjective nature of the process. We will briefly describe four of the typical problems in the appraisal process.[39]

The first problem relates to characteristics of the rater. These have a subtle and often indirect influence on performance appraisals. Younger and less experienced raters, who may have received low evaluations themselves, tend to evaluate others more strictly than older, more experienced managers. The personality traits of the rater also affect the process. More accurate performance appraisals are given by individuals who have high self-esteem, low anxiety, good social skills, and emotional stability than individuals with the opposite personal attributes.

A second common (and often intentional) rating error is leniency. **Leniency** occurs when an individual wishes to avoid conflict and rates others in a group higher than they should be. This is particularly likely when there are no organizational norms against high ratings and when rewards are not tied to performance appraisals. When rewards *are* tied to appraisals, there is a natural limit to the number of extraordinarily high ratings the organization can afford or a manager can give. Other reasons for leniency might be to give employees a morale boost, to make the rater look good, or to create a good record for the group.

A third typical problem is the *halo effect* (see Chapter 4), which occurs when the rater's knowledge of an individual's performance on one dimension colors the rating on all other dimensions. In some cases, the halo effect does not reflect an error in judgment. An employee may actually perform at the same level across all dimensions. However, most people do some things better than others, and thus their ratings should differ from one performance dimension to another.

Finally, the problem of **central tendency** occurs when the rater judges all employees to be average, even when their performance varies. Raters with many subordinates and little opportunity to observe behavior are likely to play it safe and rate most of them in the middle of the scale, rather than high or low.

Methods of Appraisal

These problems show how difficult it is for raters to evaluate performance objectively. Most attempts to solve these problems focus on devising new methods of doing appraisals. As a result, many different types of rating-scale formats and evaluation techniques exist.[40] We will focus on four general types of methods: ranking, graphic, behaviorally anchored, and goals-based ratings.

Ranking Ratings To compare employees doing the same or similar work, **ranking methods** are used. In simple ranking, the rater merely lists employees from best to worst. A variation of this method, alternation ranking, requires the rater to select the best employee, then the worst, the second best, the second worst, and so on.

Ranking methods are easy to use. They are also effective in combating leniency, because the rater cannot give everyone a high evaluation. Rankings are particularly useful in making defensible promotion decisions or in reducing the size of the work force. The manager has only to select from the top down on the ranking list until all promotion vacancies are filled—or, conversely, from the bottom up until all necessary reductions are made.

Ranking methods also have disadvantages that limit their usefulness for certain performance appraisal purposes. Since rankings tend to be based on overall performance, they are not very useful for providing specific feedback. To know that you are ranked fourth out of ten people, for example, does not tell you what you need to do to become the top-ranked employee or even the second. Furthermore, rankings indicate that one person is performing better than another but not by how much or in what ways. Thus, this method is of limited usefulness in making pay decisions. To determine equitable pay raises, managers need to know something about the degree of difference among those evaluated. Another problem with ranking is that raters must be familiar with the performance of all employees being ranked. This usually limits the number of employees that can be evaluated using ranking methods.

Graphic Ratings In a performance appraisal using **graphic ratings,** the individual is evaluated on a series of performance dimensions, usually through the use of a five- or seven-point scale. Graphic ratings are the most widely used forms of performance evaluation. A typical rating scale may be 1 to 5, with 1 representing poor performance and 5 representing outstanding performance. Figure 8.3 illustrates four common rating scales to evaluate a salesperson's sales volume. The more clearly and specifically the scales and the performance dimensions are defined, the better. According to goal setting theory, it is always a good idea to state precisely what is meant by each dimension of performance, such as quantity.

FIGURE 8.3 Samples of Graphic Rating Scale Formats

A. Quantity   High ___|_____|_____|_____|_____|___ Low
B. Quantity   High ___|_____|_____|_____|_____|___ Low
                      5   4   3   2   1
C. Quantity   High ___|_____|_____|_____|_____|___ Low
                      5   4   3   2   1
              Well above Above   Average Below   Well below
               average   average   average   average

D.	Job Dimension	1	2	3	4	5	6	7	8	9	10	11	12	13	14	15	16	17	18	19	20
	Quantity	Always low				Enough to get by				Average				Sometimes superior				Always outstanding		

E. Quantity of Work is the amount of work an individual does in a workday.

Does not meet minimum requirements	Does just enough to get by	Volume of work is satisfactory	Industrious: does more than is required	Superior work production record

F. Quantity In rating work quantity, give careful consideration to such items as amount of work produced in terms of the specific job, employee's application to the job, effect of employee on the general flow of work, and skill in handling special assignments. For *supervisors,* work quantity also includes skill in getting work out. Poor. 1–6; Average. 7–18; Good. 19–25

Score   18

Source: Adapted from R. S. Schuler and V. L. Huber, *Personnel and Human Resource Management,* 4th ed. St. Paul, West, 1990, 203.

Behaviorally Anchored Ratings   To more clearly define various aspects of an employee's job, some organizations are using **behaviorally anchored rating scales (BARS).** These indicate whether the employee has performed certain job behaviors and how frequently. The BARS approach relies on the use of critical incidents to construct the rating scale. A critical incident is an activity by an employee that is thought to be important to performance.

In constructing a BARS scale, subordinates and their managers jointly define the six to eight important activities in the subordinate's job. Each activity is based on observable behaviors and is meaningful to the employee being rated. By being involved in the development of a BARS, subordinates can have input into what activities are really important in determining their job performance. Once these activities have been defined, they are then used as anchors to discriminate between high, moderate, and low performance.

Table 8.4 shows a BARS for measuring one activity of a nurse's clinical knowledge. The anchors on the scale (points ranging from 0 to 10) are statements reflecting the range of activities. If a nurse receives a seven on this activity, he or she is provided an example of the specific performance incident used by the immediate supervisor to make such a rating.

The advantages of BARS include: (1) they are based on job-related activities; (2) items are clearly stated; (3) subordinates and superiors jointly develop the dimensions and incidents used to evaluate performance; and (4) they permit accurate feedback on specific behaviors that employees can use to improve their performance.

The disadvantages of BARS include: (1) they are costly to construct; (2) they require significant training time for subordinates and superiors to use well; and (3) they are not that much better in improving rating errors than graphic scales.

Goals-Based Ratings   Compared to the three ratings methods reviewed so far, the rating process is more complicated under MBO or other types of goals-based systems. Factors other than the individual's own behavior, such as product quality, may create gaps between the stated goals and the outcomes. Moreover, portions of some jobs may not lend themselves to the development of quantitative goals for measuring performance. As we noted earlier, subjective performance evaluation can vary from person to person. Thus, the problem of determining whether a goal was achieved may exist even before questions of why it was or was not attained can be answered.

Five important characteristics of effective performance appraisals under goals-based ratings are:

- High levels of subordinate participation in the performance appraisal process result in employees being satisfied with both the appraisal process and the manager who conducted it.
- Employee acceptance of the appraisal and satisfaction with the manager increases to the extent that the manager is supportive of the employee.

TABLE 8.4   A BARS Performance Dimension for a Nurse

Clinical Knowledge

Nurse possesses the required clinical knowledge and exercises good judgment in fulfilling his or her job duties in a competent fashion.

My observations of this nurse's job knowledge and judgment include:

Nurse demonstrates the knowledge and judgment needed to provide quality nursing care for patients with unusual conditions.	— 10 If asked to follow the order for 300 units of insulin, this nurse would question the physician and report to the nursing director regarding physician's response.
	— 9 This nurse questions the doctor if she thinks a new prescription would counteract other medication.
	— 8 If patient has difficulty swallowing medication, this nurse would be expected to crush pills and mix them with appropriate food or beverage to insure that the patient received prescribed drugs.
	— 7 This nurse checks trays to make sure that diabetic patients do not receive inappropriate food.
	— 6 If this nurse were short of time, she would chart critical patients first, before making routine entries.
Nurse demonstrates the knowledge and judgment needed to perform the basic nursing care assignments required for most patients.	— 5 If several call lights came on at the same time, this nurse could be expected to answer some of them herself.
	— 4 This nurse encourages patients to dress themselves when they are physically able to do so.
	— 3 This nurse places unused medication back in containers.
	— 2 This nurse would place medication on the patient's table and leave the room without checking to see whether the patient took medication.
Nurse does not demonstrate the knowledge and judgment needed to carry out the basic nursing responsibilities of her job.	— 1 If asked to give an IM injection, this nurse would forget the alcohol swab.
	— 0 This nurse would forget to check whether blood had been drawn for electrolytes when a patient has been on diuretics for 3 months.

Source: John E. Sheridan, School of Health Related Professions, University of Alabama-Birmingham, June, 1991.

- Discussing problems that may be hampering the subordinate's current job performance and working toward solutions have a positive effect on productivity.

- The number of criticisms in an appraisal interview is positively related to the number of defensive reactions shown by the employee. Those areas of job performance that are most criticized are least likely to show an improvement. There appears to be a chain reaction between criticisms made by the manager and defensive reactions shown by the subordinate, with little or no change in the subordinate's behavior.

- The more the subordinates are allowed to voice opinions during the appraisal, the more satisfied they will feel with the appraisal.[41]

Although MBO and other goals-based ratings do not prescribe a passive role for superiors in the performance review and feedback process, they require superiors to play more of a helping and mutual problem-solving role than a judgmental role. Some managers have interpreted this element, and thus the whole MBO process, as managerially weak. This criticism is not valid; managers can discipline, demote, and dismiss individuals under the goals-based system. In fact, the rationale for any such action should be readily apparent under the goals-based ratings. It is often easier for a superior to confront a subordinate under a goals-based system since the subordinate probably participated in setting the goals he or she is responsible for achieving.

Organizational Significance   Regardless of the method used, effective and accurate performance appraisal is difficult to achieve. Virtually all the problems, individual differences, and biases associated with human judgments and interactions that we have discussed in previous chapters (see, especially, Chapter 4) find their way into the performance appraisal process. Although these problems and biases probably cannot be eliminated, they can be substantially reduced by following the guidelines we have presented.

ENHANCING PERFORMANCE THROUGH REWARD SYSTEMS

The typical list of rewards to employees in organizations has been discussed in Chapters 6 and 7. Fringe benefits, opportunities to engage in demanding assignments, and the achievement of challenging goals are viewed as rewards by many employees. In this section, three of the newer reward systems that organizations use to motivate employees are discussed. These contemporary reward systems include flexible benefit plans, banking time off, and skill-based pay.[42] The strengths and weaknesses of each of the three systems are summarized in Table 8.5. Another contemporary reward system, gain-sharing, is discussed in Chapter 11.

TABLE 8.5 Comparison of Three Contemporary Reward Systems		
Contemporary Reward System	**Strengths**	**Weaknesses**
Flexible Benefit Plans	Plans tailored to fit employee needs.	Administration of plans can become costly and complex.
Banking Time Off	Is contingent on an employee's performance.	Requires that an organization let its high performers have more time off.
Skill-Based Pay	Employee must learn and use new skill before being paid more.	Training costs to improve employee skills are high. Labor costs increase as employees master more skills.

Source: E. E. Lawler, III, *Strategic Pay.* San Francisco: Jossey-Bass, 1990.

Flexible Benefit Plans

A **flexible benefit plan** allows employees to choose what benefits they want, rather than having management choose for them. According to Towers Perrin, a global compensation consulting firm, a corporation's benefit plan costs about 40 percent of its total employee cash compensation package. This represents a huge cost to organizations, considering that only 7 percent or less is set aside for merit pay increases in most organizations. In a flexible benefit plan, employees decide how they would like to receive the benefit amount. They tailor the benefit package according to their needs. It is assumed that employees can make important and intelligent decisions about their benefits. A few employees take all of their benefits in cash; others choose additional life insurance, child or elder care, dental insurance, or retirement plans. Extensive benefits options, for example, may be highly attractive to an employee with a family and a spouse at home, while most benefits might be only minimally attractive to a young, single employee. Older employees value retirement plans more than younger ones, and they are willing to put more money into retirement. Employees with elderly parents may desire financial assistance in providing care for them. At Traveler's Insurance Company, for example, employees can choose benefits of up to five thousand dollars a year for the care of dependent elderly parents.

Flexible benefits plans are now offered by more than 30 percent of the Fortune 1,000 corporations. Why have these become so popular? Flexible benefit plans offer three distinct advantages. First, they allow employees to make important decisions about their personal finances. Second, the organization does not have to assume a paternalistic role of knowing what is best for each employee. Employees can choose what gives them the greatest personal benefit. Many traditional benefit plans were targeted for employees who have families and are in the middle of their working careers. Although there are many of these individuals, they are dwindling as more and more families have two wage earners, divorce has increased, and women have entered the work force in greater numbers (see Chapter 20). Third, it highlights the economic value of many benefits to employees. Most employees have little idea of the cost of such benefits because their organization is willing to buy the benefits for them even though they might not want them.

The following In Practice illustrates how John Hancock, a Boston-based financial services firm, implemented a benefits program that attempts to balance work and family demands. Hancock recognized that the life-styles and needs of its employees had been changing. The increase in dual wage earner families and working parents presented Hancock with some interesting opportunities to creatively use its benefits plan. The program was designed to fill a gap between traditional child care arrangements and Hancock's employees' needs.

IN PRACTICE

KIDS-TO-GO

Called Kids-to-Go, the John Hancock program is designed for children ages six to thirteen and only operates on Martin Luther King and Columbus Day holidays, during school vacation weeks in February and April, and for one week in June between the end of school and the start of community day programs. It was started as a result of an employee attitude survey that showed that family care needs was the single most important employee need.

Employees may drop their children off as early as 7:30 A.M. at work. During the morning, the children are divided into age groups for prearranged field trips. For example, some children might go to the Brookline Puppet Theater, others might take a cruise of the Boston Harbor, and still others might spend a day at the beach.

Employees pay twenty dollars per day for each child. To help defray the costs, the company holds drawings for a limited number of ten-dollar-a-day scholarships. There is one staff member for every eight children.

What have been the results? Of John Hancocks's 6,200 employees, approximately two-thirds are women. About 20 percent have school-age children, and another 15 percent have at least one preschool-age child. To date, 115 families have participated in the program. For those employees, absenteeism has decreased and morale and performance have increased.[43]

There are a few problems associated with flexible benefits plans. First, because of the different choices among employees, record keeping becomes more complicated. Sophisticated computer systems are essential to keep straight the details of employees' records. Second, it is difficult for organizations to accurately predict the number of employees that might choose each benefit. This may affect the firm's group rates for life and medical insurance, since these are based on the number of employees covered by the plan.

Banking Time Off

Time off from work with pay is attractive to some people. Typically, vacation schedules and their length are based on the number of years the employee has worked for the organization. An extension of such a system is basing time off on performance. That is, employees can bank time off credit contingent on their performance. At Tandem Computers, high-performing employees earn extra vacation time and can bank this time for one year. If the employees do not use their vacation time, they can roll the credit over to a savings investment plan. In setting up such programs, organizations should be aware of some potential problems. What if the employee wants to use his or her banked time during a busy time for the organization? The employee's absence may have a negative effect on productivity. How long can an employee retain his or her banked time?

Skill-Based Pay

Paying people according to their value in the labor market makes a great deal of sense.[44] After all, it is the employees who develop multiple skills that are valuable assets for the organization. However, with **skill-based pay,** the employee's compensation depends on the number and level of job-related skills the employee has learned. About 40 percent of the large U.S. organizations, such as TRW, Honeywell, and Westinghouse, use it for their blue-collar employees somewhere in their operations.

Skill-based pay is easiest to describe in the case of a production team in a manufacturing plant. Typically, it is relatively easy for management to identify all of the skills needed to perform the tasks and pinpoint what skills employees need to learn. Employees' pay is based on their skill ability. Each skill is given a financial value, say fifty cents an hour. Often, the size of the pay raise is the same regardless of the content of the job learned. Once the employee learns the skill, his or her pay increases. This approach fits particularly well with employees who set high but attainable goals and who want to manage themselves and participate in a number of decisions that affect their performance. The Shell Canada chemical plant in Sarnia, Ontario, permits individuals to learn all of the jobs in the plant. Individuals reach top pay only when they have accomplished this level of competency, which typically can take eight or more years. At Digital Equipment Company, some employees are rewarded for economic skills and knowledge of the business and corporation.

The most obvious advantage of skill-based pay in a production situation is flexibility. When employees can perform multiple tasks, managers gain tremendous flexibility in utilizing their work force. Largely as a result of the Tylenol poisoning tragedy, Johnson & Johnson decided to completely redo its packaging of Tylenol to add greater safety. Because of the firm's skill-based pay system, employees understood the technology involved and were able to quickly introduce the new packaging changes. Johnson & Johnson also found out that skill-based pay can increase productivity, while decreasing supervisory costs. Employees are more motivated to gain and use their skills because they are equitably rewarded by their organization for learning.

There are some disadvantages to skill-based pay. The most obvious disadvantage has to do with the high pay rates that it tends to produce. The very nature of the plan encourages individuals to become more valuable to the organization and as a result, to be paid more. Skill-based pay systems are designed to increase the opportunity to learn multiple skills. This requires a large investment in training and lost production time as employees try to learn new skills. Thus, the organization sometimes has inexperienced and overpaid employees doing the work. A worse-case scenario for the organization is that many employees know how to do every job, but at any one point in time, all jobs are being done by employees who do not know how to perform them at a high level of proficiency. Finally, employees can be frustrated when no openings are available in job areas for which they have learned these new skills. Most skill-based programs require employees to regularly perform skills in order to be paid for them.

SUMMARY

Goal setting is a process intended to increase efficiency and effectiveness by specifying the desired outcomes toward which individuals, departments, teams, and organizations should work. Goal setting does not take place in a vacuum. Stakeholders—such as customers, shareholders, and employees—influence the selection of goals by organizations and their employees. On a day-to-day basis, customers or clients are probably the key driving force in the selection of goals that are most crucial to organizational and employee performance.

The Locke and Latham goals model was reviewed because of its soundness in helping to explain the critical factors and their relationships to individual goal setting and performance. The model starts with the challenges provided for the individual. This sense of challenge is explained in terms of goal difficulty, goal clarity, and self-efficacy. The strength of the relationship between challenging goals and performance is influenced by four moderating factors. Then, three mediators—direction of attention, effort, and persistence—were identified as facilitators of goal attainment. Linkages from performance to rewards to satisfaction to consequences were also reviewed.

Management by objectives (MBO) was presented as both a philosophy and a management system. Two models of MBO were discussed: the individual-focused MBO model and the team-focused MBO model. A set of specific prescriptions for use by a manager in setting goals with a subordinate was presented.

Performance appraisal was presented as a crucial component in the process of enhancing performance. The varied uses of performance appraisal were noted—to motivate employees by linking rewards to performance, to help decide on personnel movements (promotions, demotions, transfers), and to identify training needs. There are many problems in achieving accurate appraisals. Four of the general methods of appraisal that attempt to deal with some of these problems were reviewed: ranking ratings, graphic ratings, behaviorally anchored ratings, and goals-based ratings.

We concluded the chapter with a discussion of three contemporary reward systems designed to enhance performance. The features, advantages, and disadvantages of flexible benefit plans, banking time off plans, and skill-based plans were explored.

Key Words and Concepts

Behaviorally anchored rating scales (BARS)
Central tendency
Flexible benefit plan
Goal clarity
Goal commitment
Goal difficulty
Goal setting
Goals
Graphic ratings
Individual-focused MBO model

Leniency
Management by Objectives (MBO)
Merit pay plans
Performance appraisal
Performance evaluation
Ranking methods
Skill-based pay
Stakeholders
Team-focused MBO model

Discussion Questions

1. Identify the key stakeholders of the academic department in which you are enrolled. Suggest two probable high-priority goals of each stakeholder with respect to this department.

2. What goals has the academic department set in response to the goals of these stakeholders, as identified in question 1?

3. Think of an organization for which you currently work or have worked. How would you evaluate this organization and its employees in terms of the five service quality goals stated in the chapter?

4. List your five most important personal goals. Evaluate each of these goals on its goal difficulty and goal clarity. What implications, if any, are there for you from this assessment?

5. Think of a current or previous job. Evaluate your level of goal commitment. What factors do you think influenced your self-assessed level of goal commitment?

6. Why is performance appraisal necessary for most employees?

7. Have you ever "suffered" from one or more of the typical problems in the appraisal process? Explain.

8. What are the similarities and differences between merit pay and skill-based pay?

9. Which of the three contemporary reward systems is most appealing to you? Why?

◆ *MANAGEMENT CASES AND EXERCISES*

JOB GOALS QUESTIONNAIRE

Instructions: The following statements refer to a job you currently hold or have held. Read each statement and then select a response from the scale below that best describes your view. You may want to use a separate sheet of paper to record your responses.

Scale: Almost Never   1   2   3   4   5   Almost Always

_____ 1.   I understand exactly what I am supposed to do on my job.

_____ 2.   I have specific, clear goals to aim for on my job.

_____ 3.   The goals I have on this job are challenging.

_____ 4.   I understand how my performance is measured on this job.

_____ 5.   I have deadlines for accomplishing my goals on this job.

_____ 6.   If I have more than one goal to accomplish, I know which ones are most important and which are least important.

_____ 7.   My goals require my full effort.

_____ 8.   My superior tells me the reasons for giving me the goals I have.

_____ 9.   My superior is supportive with respect to encouraging me to reach my goals.

_____ 10. My superior lets me participate in the setting of my goals.

_____ 11. My superior lets me have some say in deciding how I will go about implementing my goals.

_____ 12. If I reach my goals, I know that my superior will be pleased.

_____ 13. I get credit and recognition when I attain my goals.

_____ 14. Trying for goals makes my job more fun than it would be without goals.

_____ 15. I feel proud when I get feedback indicating that I have reached my goals.

_____ 16. The other people I work with encourage me to attain my goals.

_____ 17. I sometimes compete with my co-workers to see who can do the best job in reaching their goals.

_____ 18. If I reach my goals, my job security will be improved.

_____ 19. If I reach my goals, my chances for a pay raise are increased.

_____ 20. If I reach my goals, my chances for a promotion are increased.[45]

Scoring and Interpretation Add the points shown for items 1 through 20. Scores of 70 to 100 may indicate a high-performing, highly satisfying work situation. Your goals are challenging and you are committed to them. When you achieve your goals, you are rewarded for your accomplishments. Scores of 51 to 69 may suggest a highly varied work situation with motivating and satisfying attributes on some dimensions and just the opposite on others. Scores of 20 to 50 may suggest a low-performing, dissatisfying work situation.

ALLIANCE FOR CHILD RESCUE

The Alliance for Child Rescue (ACR) is a non-profit organization that works in war-torn countries to help children who are homeless or orphaned. While ACR is over forty years old, its most dramatic growth has been in the past ten years. It now has workers in sixteen countries and operates on a sparse $5 million budget. ACR's major goal is to provide shelter and food for children affected by war until a permanent home can be found for them.

John Workman John Workman is a member of the national board of directors for ACR. As one of twenty such board members, he is responsible for helping set policy, approving budgets, and soliciting funds. Workman was appointed when the executive director of ACR actively solicited the president of Workman's company for a major gift. Once the gift was secured, ACR asked the president to be on the board. The president in turn asked Workman, a rising young vice-president, to serve in his place on ACR's board. The president told Workman when he asked him to serve that such service is imperative for company executives, not just as a public relations gesture to the nonprofit sector but also as a form of community service.

John Workman was at first reluctant to take on one more extracurricular task. He felt such work further detracted from his time with his family. As a young man clearly on the rise with the company, Workman seems to project an image of having unbounded energy. He was sure that was why the president asked him to serve. Workman is a Vietnam veteran who saw first-hand what war could do to children. He did not want to relive some of those experiences. After discussing the president's request with his wife and family, Workman was inclined to say no. However, during his meeting with the president, it became clear his service was expected. He agreed to take on the task.

Workman was most pleasantly surprised when his initial fears about service on the ACR were not realized. He found himself impressed with the work of ACR. He admired how the organization operates on a small budget and with a small staff. Most of the support comes from wealthy individuals (with a small but growing amount coming from the corporate world) whose contributions are secured by the executive director of ACR making personal calls.

Workman was also impressed by the ACR staff members, most of whom work in the field. They seemed well trained and dedicated. At semiannual ACR board meetings, these field workers often reported on their efforts in warring countries. Once some of the children helped by ACR were able to meet with the board. Workman was impressed with ACR's success stories.

Needs of the Organization In the three years that Workman has served on ACR's board, he and other board members have realized that the budget needed to be increased substantially. In response to this need and at the direction of the board, the executive director of ACR hired a fund-raising consultant, Bob Opman. Opman did a complete study of the finances of ACR and the potential for the organization to raise more money. His recommendation, circulated in a detailed report to all board members prior to the upcoming meeting, was that ACR attempt to make its name better known to the public.

Opman's proposal was an elaborate public relations campaign that would be built around an "ACR telethon" over a holiday weekend. He said openly in the report that the telethon would not be expected to bring in vast amounts of money from the general public. But it would make ACR better known to the public. This would, in turn, create a more favorable climate for soliciting corporate gifts and foundation support. He demonstrated rather convincingly that the telethon would at least break even financially and could even raise an extra hundred thousand dollars. But, he said, the real benefit will be the increased public awareness of ACR which, he projected, will open doors to more and larger corporate gifts. Projections on the budget indicate the donations could double over the next three years.

An integral part of the telethon would be a documentary film about Maria, a little girl in a Latin American country where the fighting during a revolution had destroyed her home. The consultant found the story of Maria in the ACR files. She had written a simple but moving letter thanking the "Americans" for helping her survive.

At the board meeting of ACR, Opman outlined in detail his plans for the documentary, which would be called "Maria Finds Her Home." The film would be simply done, with a narrator telling Maria's story while the audience saw pictures of a little girl in her bombed-out home, wandering the streets, and at an orphanage. He recommended the film have an emotional and happy ending in which the audience would see ACR workers reunite Maria with her family. The film could be used in other fund-raising events as well. Opman has designed much of the public relations campaign around this film.

Board Debate After his presentation, several board members seriously questioned the climax of the film as being unrepresentative of the work ACR does. They argued in one way or another that most children helped by ACR are orphans. Maria's story simply was not typical. Others wondered if Maria was not now too old to be shown as the little girl in the film. Others questioned showing the film as a documentary since clearly the scenes would need to be recreated. Others suggested ACR bring Maria to the United States so that she could be interviewed on the telethon live.

After several minutes of questioning, Opman slowly began to reveal that the film would use an actress to play Maria. He said the real Maria was too grown up to be used as a little girl in the film. He also said she had been badly burned in the attack on her village by military patrols. Her appearance was not the "right type" for the kind of film ACR needed. Under further questioning, he revealed that Maria had never actually been reunited with her parents, although a search was continuing under ACR guidance.

Some board members clearly opposed the use of the actress in a documentary. Others raised questions about the whole project. They said ACR does most of its work with orphans. The proposed documentary would misrepresent the work of ACR.

Others sided with Opman, who explained that the "dramatization" of "real life" stories was common in television. They said such strategies were used all the time in fund-raising. They seemed especially excited about the prospect of generating high visibility for ACR from the Maria story. They argued that helping children is the issue. They also said that since the search was continuing for Maria's family, the situation was ambiguous enough to allow ACR to present the message Opman proposed. Finally, they argued that Opman's plan seemed to be sufficiently well worked out to generate the much needed resources. They pointed to the success Opman had raising funds for other nonprofit organizations.

Workman sensed that the vote to approve the project would be very close. He also sensed that Opman is not willing to negotiate much in his recommendations.[46]

QUESTIONS

1. Identify all of the key stakeholders in this case. What are the stated and implicit goals of each stakeholder group and the Alliance for Child Rescue?

2. How would you characterize John Workman's role in the Alliance for Child Rescue in terms of goal difficulty and goal clarity? Explain.

3. Is goal commitment of the board members a problem in this case? Explain.

4. What are the ethical issues in this case?

5. Should John Workman vote to approve the telethon with the "Maria Finds Her Home" documentary? Why?

References

1. Adapted from Dumaine, B. How Managers Can Succeed through Speed. *Fortune*, February 13, 1989, 54–59; Sherman, S. P. The Mind of Jack Welch. *Fortune*, March 27, 1989, 39–50.

2. Keller, J. J., and Maremont, M. Bob Allen Is Turning AT&T into a Live Wire. *Business Week*, November 6, 1989, 140–152.

3. Richards, M. D. *Setting Strategic Goals and Objectives*, 2d ed. St. Paul: West, 1986.

4. Locke, E. A., and Latham, G. P. *Goal Setting: A Motivational Technique That Works*. Englewood Cliffs, N.J.: Prentice-Hall, 1984.

5. Hill, C. W., and Jones, G. R. *Strategic Management: An Integrated Approach*, 2d ed. Boston: Houghton Mifflin, 1992.

6. Berry, L. L., Zeithaml, V. A., and Parasuraman, A. Five Imperatives for Improving Service Quality. *Sloan Management Review*, Summer 1990, 29–38.

7. Adapted from Parasuraman, A., Berry, L. L., and Zeithaml, V. A. Understanding Customer Expectations of Service. *Sloan Management Review*, Spring 1991, 39–48.

8. Adapted from Bernstein, A. Quality Is Becoming Job One in the Office Too. *Business Week*, April 29,

1991; Newport, J. P., Jr. American Express: Service That Sells. *Fortune*, November 29, 1989, 80–90.

9. Locke, E. A., and Latham, G. P. *A Theory of Goal Setting and Task Performance*. Englewood Cliffs, N.J.: Prentice-Hall, 1990.

10. Tubbs, M. E., and Ekeberg, S. E. The Role of Intentions in Work Motivation: Implications for Goal Setting Theory and Research. *Academy of Management Review*, 1991, *16*, 180–199.

11. Wright, P. M. Operationalization of Goal Difficulty as a Moderator of the Goal Difficulty-Performance Relationship. *Journal of Applied Psychology*, 1990, *75*, 227–234.

12. Kernan, M. C., and Lord, R. G. Effects of Valence, Expectancies, and Goal-Performance Discrepancies in Single and Multiple Goal Environments. *Journal of Applied Psychology*, 1990, *75*, 194–203.

13. Shalley, C. E. Effects of Productivity Goals, Creativity Goals, and Personal Discretion on Individual Creativity. *Journal of Applied Psychology*, 1991, *76*, 179–185.

14. Earley, P. C., and Lituchy, T. R. Delineating Goal and Efficacy Effects: A Test of Three Models. *Journal of Applied Psychology*, 1991, *76*, 81–92.

15. Adapted from Krantz, K. T. How Velcro Got Hooked on Quality. *Harvard Business Review*, September-October 1989, 34–40; Schaffer, R. H. Demand Better Results—And Get Them. *Harvard Business Review*, March-April 1991, 142–149.

16. Leana, C. R., Locke, E. A., and Schweiger, D. M. Fact and Fiction in Analyzing Research on Participative Decision Making: A Critique of Cotton, Vollrath, Froggatt, Lengnick-Hall, and Jennings. *Academy of Management Review*, 1990, *15*, 137–146; Cotton, J. L., Vollrath, D. A., Lengnick-Hall, M. L., and Froggatt, K. L. Fact: The Form of Participation Does Matter—A Rebuttal to Leana, Locke, and Schweiger. *Academy of Management Review*, 1990, *15*, 147–153.

17. Wright, P. M. Goals as Mediators of the Relationship between Monetary Incentives and Performance: A Review and NPI Theory Examination. *Human Resource Management Review*, 1991, *1*, 1–22.

18. Arvey, R. D., and Ivancevich, J. M. Punishment in Organizations: A Review, Propositions, and Research Suggestions. *Academy of Management Review*, 1980, *5*, 123–132.

19. Sauers, D. A., and Bass, K. Sustaining the Positive Effects of Goal Setting: The Positive Influence of Peer Competition. *ARER*, 1990, *21*(4), 30–40.

20. Earley, P. C., Northcraft, G. B., Lee, C., and Lituchy, T. R. Impact of Process and Outcome Feedback on the Relation of Goal Setting to Task Performance. *Academy of Management Journal*, 1990, *33*, 87–105.

21. Podsakoff, P. M., and Farh, Jing-Lih. Effects of Feedback Sign and Credibility on Goal Setting and Task Performance. *Organizational Behavior and Human Decision Processes*, 1989, *44*, 45–67.

22. Chesney, A. A., and Locke, E. A. Relationship among Goal Difficulty, Business Strategies, and Performance on a Complex Management Simulation Task. *Academy of Management Journal*, 1991, *34*, 400–424; Wood, R. E., and Locke, E. A. Goal Setting and Strategy Effects on Complex Tasks. In B. M. Staw and L. L. Cummings (eds.),*Research in Organizational Behavior*, vol. 12. Greenwich, Conn.: JAI Press, 1990, 73–109.

23. Harrington, S. J. What Corporate America Is Teaching about Ethics. *Academy of Management Executive*, February 1991, 21–30; Wolford, T. E. Breaking the Mold. *Hispanic*, June 1991, 18–24.

24. Adapted from Harpaz, I. The Importance of Work Goals: An International Perspective. *Journal of International Business Studies*, First Quarter 1990, 75–93.

25. Locke and Latham. *A Theory of Goal Setting and Task Performance*, 262.

26. Ibid, 265–266.

27. Greenwood, R. G. Management by Objectives: As Developed by Peter Drucker, Assisted by Harold Smidy. *Academy of Management Review*, 1981, *6*, 225–230.

28. Boardman, S. L., and Melnick, G. Keeping Productivity Ratings Timely. *Personnel Journal*, March 1990, 50–51.

29. Evaluating the Sales Force: Measuring Sales Efforts and Results. *Small Business Report*, June 1987, 44–48.

30. Locke, E. A., and Latham, G. P. *Goal Setting: A Motivational Technique That Works!* Englewood Cliffs, N.J.: Prentice-Hall, 1984, 27–40.

31. Weihrich, H. *Management Excellence: Productivity through MBO*. New York: McGraw-Hill, 1985.

32. Latham, G. P. *Increasing Productivity through Performance Appraisal*. Reading, Mass.: Addison-Wesley, 1992.

33. Rondrasuk, J. N., Flager, K., Morrow, D., and Thompson, R. The Effect of Management by Objectives on Organization Results. *Group and Organization Studies*, 1984, *9*, 531–539; Pringle, C. D., and Longenecker, J. G. The Ethics of MBO. *Academy of Management Review*, 1982, 7, 305–312.

34. Schrader, A. W., and Seward, G. T. MBO Makes Dollar Sense. *Personnel Journal*, July 1989, 32–37.

35. Wellins, R. S., Byham, W. C., and Wilson, J. M. *Empowered Teams: Creating Self-Directed Work Groups That Improve Quality, Productivity, and Participation*. San Francisco: Jossey-Bass, 1991; French, W. L., and Holloman, C. R. Management by Objectives: The Team Approach. *California Management Review*, 1975, *16*, 13–22.

36. Adapted from Thamhain, H. J. Managing Technologically Innovative Team Efforts toward New Product Success. *Journal of Product Innovation Management*, 1990, 7, 5–18; Thamhain, H. J., and Kamm, J. B. Drivers of Innovation. Paper presented at the 1988 annual meeting of the Academy of Management. Anaheim, Calif. August 1988.

37. Hodgetts, R. M., and Kroeck, G. *Personnel and Human Resource Management.* New York: Harcourt Brace Jovanovich, 1992; McDonald, T. The Effects of Dimension Content on Observation and Ratings of Job Performance. *Organizational Behavior and Human Decision Processes,* 1991, *48,* 252–271.

38. Conversation with Harry Sutherland, Brooklyn Union Gas Company, June 1991.

39. Schuler, R. S. *Managing Human Resources,* 4th ed. St. Paul: West, 1992; Wayne, S. J., and Kacmar, K. M. The Effects of Impression Management on the Performance Appraisal Process. *Organizational Behavior and Human Decision Processes,* 1991, *48,* 70–88.

40. De Vries, D. L., Morrison, A. M., Shullman, S. L., and Gerlach, M. L. *Performance Appraisal on the Line.* Greensboro, N.C.: Center for Creative Leadership, 1986.

41. Sashkin, M. *Assessing Performance Appraisal.* San Diego: University Associates, 1981; Campbell, D. J., and Lee, C. Self-Appraisal in Performance Evaluation: Development versus Evaluation. *Academy of Management Review.* 1988, *13,* 302–314.

42. Lawler, E. E. III. *Strategic Pay: Aligning Organizational Strategies and Pay Systems.* San Francisco: Jossey-Bass, 1990; Weber, C. L., and Rynes, S. L.

Effects of Compensation Strategy on Job Pay Decisions. *Academy of Management Journal,* 1991, *34,* 86–109.

43. Adapted from Santora, J. E. Kids-to-Go. *Personnel Journal,* March 1991, 66–70.

44. Heneman, R. *Merit Pay.* Reading, Mass.: Addison-Wesley, 1992.

45. Adapted from Locke and Latham. *Goal Setting: A Motivational Technique That Works,* 173–175; Locke and Latham. *A Theory of Goal Setting and Task Performance,* 355–358.

46. Smitter, R. Alliance for Child Rescue. In L. L. Goulet (ed.), *Annual Advances in Business Cases, 1989.* South Bend, Ind. Midwest Society for Case Research, 1990, 35–37. This case was prepared by Roger Smitter of North Central College in Naperville, Illinois, as a basis for class discussion, rather than to illustrate either effective or ineffective handling of an administrative situation. The names of the organizations, individuals, locations, and/or financial information have been disguised to preserve the organization's desire for anonymity. Presented and accepted by the referred Midwest Society for Case Research. All rights reserved to the author. Copyrighted © by Roger Smitter. Used with permission.

CHAPTER 9

WORK STRESS

LEARNING OBJECTIVES

When you have finished studying this chapter, you should be able to:

- Explain the concepts of stress and stressors.
- Describe the general nature of the body's response to stressors.
- Diagnose the sources of stress in organizations.
- Describe the effects of stress on health.
- Explain the relationship between stress and job performance.
- Understand the nature and causes of job burnout.
- Identify some methods that individuals and organizations can use to cope with stress.

OUTLINE

STRESS TAKES ITS TOLL

Robert Hearsch lived a nightmare that never seemed to end. Hearsch, a supervisor for Hughes Aircraft, was successful and well regarded by his co-workers. When General Motors took over the company, however, his career took a nosedive. After the company was reorganized, Hearsch was demoted and put in charge of purchasing pencils and pens. When he took over this purchasing operation, he found it in considerable disarray. Morale was low, orders were backlogged, records were incomplete and often missing. Hearsch spent a significant portion of each work day appeasing angry secretaries and trying to get the needed supplies of pencils and pens flowing again to the right offices. Possibly because hard work had always paid off in the past, Hearsch gamely soldiered on. He arrived early, worked through breaks, and left late.

Despite his best efforts, things only got worse. His diligent attempts to straighten out his operations were ignored while every small mistake seemed to be recorded in his personnel file. His boss repeatedly hinted that Hearsch's position might be eliminated if enough progress was not made. Some attempts to harass Hearsch were petty: Once when things did not seem to be going well enough in the judgment of his manager, Hearsch was intentionally left off the guest list for a department office party.

The stress created by this work situation eventually took its toll. Hearsch suffered a minor nervous breakdown and lost twenty pounds. His marriage broke up. Hearsch filed a workers' compensation claim that blamed his emotional and health problems on Hughes Aircraft. Eventually, he settled with the company for $20,000. Robert Hearsch described the money as small consolation: "I lost my wife, my house, and my career."[1]

Most people have a "bad day" from time to time and experience the resulting stress. The Preview Case illustrates the unfortunate consequences when the "bad days" go on and on without letup. Sometimes stress can have positive effects; at other times, it can be harmful. Having enough stress to work at peak efficiency can create satisfaction, bring a sense of well-being and accomplishment, and earn the rewards associated with career success. On the other hand, excessive stress at work can result in a loss of efficiency, failure to perform well, and adverse effects on mental and physical health. People need a balance in their personal and work lives in order to cope with stress. Unfortunately, recognizing the appropriate balance and achieving it are not easy to do.

Managers and employees need to understand the effects of work stress, the relationship between stress and performance, and the sources of stress within an organization. Everyone should appreciate the relationships between stress and health. In this chapter, we examine the nature of stress, the sources of stress at work, and the effects of stress. People can handle varying amounts of stress effectively, and we explore some of these individual differences. Finally, we will examine ways that employees and organizations can cope with stress.

NATURE OF STRESS

Stress is a consequence of or a general response to an action or situation that places special physical or psychological demands, or both, on a person. Stress involves the interaction of a person and that person's environment. The physical or psychological demands from the environment that cause stress are called **stressors.** Stressors can take a variety of forms. However, all stressors have one thing in common: they create stress or the potential for stress when an individual perceives them as representing a demand that may exceed his or her ability to respond.

Fight-or-Flight Response

Suppose you come home late one night after an extremely exhausting day at work or school. You are so tired that you have been hardly able to stay awake during the drive home. As you open your front door, you suddenly see flashlights inside and you hear hushed voices. Immediately and spontaneously, you become wide awake. A complex biochemical process has been set off in your body, and the following kinds of reactions occur: Photochemical changes take place in your retinas so that your eyes adjust to the darkness more quickly than they would have under normal circumstances; your hearing becomes momentarily more acute; your breathing and heart rates alter; blood rushes from the extremities to your chest cavity so that your vital organs will have all the blood necessary to operate at peak capacity; your brain wave activity goes up as extra supplies of blood rush to your head to allow your brain to function maximally; your muscles ready themselves for action.[2]

These biochemical and bodily changes represent a natural response to an environmental stressor: the **fight-or-flight response.**[3] An animal attacked by a predator in the wild has basically two choices: to fight or to flee. The animal's bodily responses to the stressor (the predator) increase its chances of survival. Similarly, our cave-dwelling ancestors benefited from this biological response mechanism. People gathering food away from their cave would have experienced a great deal of stress upon meeting a saber-toothed tiger. In dealing with the tiger, they could have run away or stayed and fought. The biochemical changes in their body prepared them for either alternative and contributed to the probability of their survival.[4]

The human nervous system still responds the same way to environmental stressors as it did for our ancestors. While this has survival value in a true emergency, for most people, the "tigers" are imaginary, rather than real. In most work situations, for example, a fight-or-flight response is no longer appropriate. If an employee receives an unpleasant work assignment from a manager, it is not appropriate for the employee to physically assault the manager or to storm angrily out of the office. Instead, the employee is expected to calmly accept the assignment and do the best job possible. This may be especially difficult when an assignment is perceived as a threat, or stressor, and the body is prepared to act accordingly.

Medical science has discovered that the human body has a standard response to demands placed on it—whether psychological or physical. Medical researcher Hans Selye first used the term *stress* to describe the body's biological response mechanisms. Selye considered stress to be the nonspecific response of the human body to any demand made on it.[5] The body has only a limited capacity to respond to stressors. The workplace makes a variety of demands on people, and too much stress over too long a period of time will exhaust their ability to cope with environmental stressors.

The Stress Experience

IN PRACTICE

THE NAVY PILOT

The story is told of a Harvard University undergraduate who had to drop out of college due to serious psychological problems. Eventually, this individual enlisted in the U.S. Navy and became a jet pilot. He was based on an aircraft carrier much of the time, a variety of flying that is often considered the most dangerous by military pilots. Despite this danger, the Navy pilot served with distinction for a number of years and felt psychologically well during this time. When he finally retired from the Navy, he again enrolled in Harvard. As before, the individual experienced psychological difficulties, which became so severe this time that he required hospitalization.[6]

This story dramatically illustrates individual differences in stress reactions. Situations that cause stress in one individual may not in another. Many individuals (probably most) would find flying a plane from an aircraft carrier to be extremely stressful, while being a student would be relatively less so. Yet, for this Navy pilot, exactly the opposite was the case.

Whether an individual experiences stress at work or in other situations is determined by a number of factors. Four major factors are identified in Figure 9.1: (1) the person's perception of the situation; (2) the person's past experiences; (3) the presence or absence of social support; and (4) individual differences with regard to stress reactions.

Perception   In Chapter 4, we defined perception as a key psychological process whereby a person selects and organizes environmental information into a concept of reality. Employee perceptions of a situation can influence how (or whether) they experience stress. For example, two managers had their job duties substantially changed—a situation likely to be stressful for many people. The first manager saw the new duties as an opportunity to learn new skills and thought that the change was a vote of confidence from higher management in her ability to be flexible and take on new challenges. The second manager perceived the same situation to be extremely threatening and concluded that higher management was unhappy with his performance in his original job.

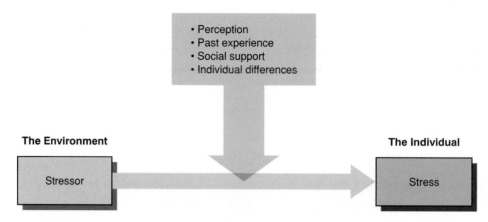

FIGURE 9.1   The Relationship between Stressors and Stress.

Past Experience   A person may experience a situation as more or less stressful, depending on how familiar the person is with the situation and what prior experience he or she has had with the particular stressors involved. Past practice or training may allow some employees in an organization to deal calmly and competently with stressors that would greatly intimidate less-experienced employees. The relationship between experience and stress is based on reinforcement (see Chapter 6). Positive reinforcement or success in a similar situation previously can reduce the level of stress that a person experiences in the present situation; punishment or past failure under similar conditions can increase stress in the present situation.

Social Support   The presence or absence of other people influences how individuals in work settings experience stress, as well as their behavior in response to stressors.[7] The presence of co-workers may increase an individual's confidence, allowing that person to cope more effectively with stress. For example, working alongside a person who performs confidently and competently in a stressful situation may help an employee behave in a similar manner. Alternatively, the presence of fellow workers may irritate people or make them anxious, reducing their capability to cope with stress.

Individual Differences   Personality characteristics may explain some of the differences in the ways that employees experience and respond to stress.[8] Individual differences in needs, values, attitudes, and abilities also influence how employees experience work stress. Simply stated, people are different. What one person considers a major source of stress, another may hardly notice. We discuss relationships between personality and stress later in this chapter.

SOURCES OF STRESS

Individuals commonly experience stress both from their personal and work lives. It is important to understand both of these sources of stress and their possible interaction. A greater understanding of the effects of stress on employee performance and well-being is achieved by taking into account the combined effects of job stress and personal life stress.[9] For a manager to consider either in isolation gives an incomplete picture of the stress that an employee may be experiencing.

Work Stressors

IN PRACTICE

STRESS ON THE JOB

A 1990 survey of New Jersey firms found that 25 percent of their employees suffered from stress-induced ailments. A similar, 1989 nationwide survey of human resource managers and medical directors of 201 corporations produced an identical number: 25 percent of employees suffered from anxiety or stress-related disorders. In California, mental stress claims in worker's compensation cases rose 700 percent between 1980 and 1990.

Too few organizations realize just how much stress their employees are under. Stress seems to be a major by-product of companies asking more and more of employees in their attempts to remain competitive. Organizations are restructuring and downsizing. Organizational charts in some North American companies are becoming as flat as pancakes. Streamlining the bureaucracy is designed to provide better customer service, faster product development, and higher profits. But the restructuring can add to employee stress. Managers and employees may have more ambiguous roles and fuzzier lines of authority. A greater emphasis on teamwork brings its own stress as employees accustomed to acting on orders are suddenly expected to participate in goal setting and decision making.

At a Citibank unit where major layoffs were announced, two employees took their own lives. Downsizing is not only stressful for the employees let go but can create stress for those left behind as well. More work is sometimes piled on those who have kept their jobs. Leaner organizations may mean heavier work loads with reduced chances for promotion and advancement. Employees may begin to worry about where their careers are going. One manager described the stress of a leaner organization this way: "Employees become more visible, and there aren't enough layers to protect average performers."

In addition to the stress from restructuring and downsizing, evidence indicates that the sources of job stress are numerous and growing. Some examples help to understand the job stress experienced by employees. A former manager at Food Lion, a supermarket chain, says: "I lived, ate, breathed, and slept Food Lion. I put in more and more time—a hundred hours a week. But no matter how many hours I worked or what I did, I could never satisfy the bosses." Karen Richards, a thirty-seven-year-old vice-president who supervises bond trading at First Eastern Bank, has to sell twice as many municipal bonds as she did five years ago to make the same profit. Her schedule is so full that there is little time for stress coping activities, such as exercise. A United Airlines flight reservationist suffered a nervous breakdown when a supervisor threatened to fire her because she took too much time to go to the bathroom. Reportedly, some reservation clerks at United were permitted only twelve minutes of "bathroom break" time during each seven-and-a-half hour shift.

Rapid shifts in corporate strategy can create stress. Bob Swain, founder of an outplacement firm in New York City, tells the story of one manager who was given a priority goal of market share. Next, the focus was on improved profit margins, then new accounts, then cost cutting. Although the manager received top evaluations for efforts in each of these areas, he quit in disgust. The demands seemed to keep coming, and eventually, he could not bring himself to inspire his subordinates to head off in yet another new direction.

The increase in stress in the workplace can sort of sneak up on employees. A former executive at Banker's Trust says, "Nobody ever stood on top of their desk and yelled, 'Work harder.' But somebody would call an occasional 8 A.M. meeting. Then this became the 'regular' 8 A.M. meeting. Then there would be the occasional 7 A.M. meeting. Then we started dinner meetings. The work day just kept expanding."

Many authorities—consultants, time-management experts, business school professors—say that they have never seen companies put as much pressure on managers and employees to work long and hard as they do today. While not all stress is bad, it does not pay to create a sullen, dispirited work force. Organizations must walk a fine line between motivating employees to give their best efforts and turning them into nervous wrecks.[10]

As we see in this In Practice, work stressors can take a variety of forms. A number of studies have been made in organizations to identify specific stressors and their effects. For example, a survey identified the following issues as major sources of stress. (The percentage of employees naming each stressor is shown in parenthesis.)

- "Not doing the kind of work I want to" (34 percent).
- "Coping with current job" (30 percent).
- "Working too hard" (28 percent).
- "Colleagues at work" (21 percent).
- "A difficult boss" (18 percent).[11]

A survey of 794 top managers of independent oil and gas producing firms revealed that 88 percent considered their work to be moderately to very stressful. The most frequently mentioned stressors were deadlines and work load ("I have too little time to do the job," "multiple decisions that must be made quickly," and "too many deadlines and insufficient data"); people problems ("the failure of people to perform" and "dumb employees"); dry wells ("having to report dry holes to investors"); and self-induced stress ("I do it to myself" and "me").[12]

Managers in many countries around the world perceive similar stressors in their work. In a worldwide comparative study of work stress, researchers gathered information from 1,065 managers in ten countries on five continents: Brazil, Great Britain, Egypt, Germany, Japan, Nigeria, Singapore, South Africa, Sweden, and the United States. Time pressures and deadlines were the most frequently cited source of work stress, being mentioned as a stressor by 55 percent of all respondents. This was closely followed by work overload, mentioned by almost 52 percent of the managers in the study. Other frequently identified stressors included inadequately trained subordinates, long working hours, attending meetings, and conflicts between work and family and social relationships.[13]

These and similar studies have identified many stressors that seem common to both managers and employees in a variety of organizations. In addition, studies have indicated that certain jobs inherently generate more stress than others. The American Stress Institute and the National Institute on Workers Compensation have identified the jobs shown in Table 9.1 as being the most stressful.[14]

Managers and employees need a usable framework for thinking about and diagnosing sources of work stress. Figure 9.2 identifies six major sources of work stress. As previously discussed, factors internal to the person influence the ways in which individuals experience these stressors in a given situation.

Workload   For many people, having too much work to do and not enough time or resources to do it can be stressful. **Role overload** exists when demands exceed the capacity of a manager or employee to meet all of them adequately. Many stressful jobs can be described as being in a condition of role overload. Notice that all three surveys described previously (including the one conducted internationally) listed work overload or "working too hard" as a major source of stress. Interestingly, having too little

---

TABLE 9.1   Examples of Stressful Jobs

High stress jobs due to danger, extreme pressure, or having responsibility without control.

- Air traffic controller
- Customer service or complaint department worker
- Inner-city high school teacher
- Journalist
- Medical intern
- Miner
- Police officer
- Secretary
- Stockbroker
- Waitress

High stress jobs due to high "occupational risk" of depression serious enough to require therapy.

- Air traffic controller
- Artistic performer
- Clergyman
- Computer programmer
- Dentist
- Government worker
- Lawyer
- Middle manager
- Physician
- Police officer
- Politician
- Teacher
- Therapist

Source: Based on A. Miller, Stress on the Job. *Newsweek,* April 25, 1988, 40-45; R. Sandroff, Is Your Job Driving You Crazy? *Psychology Today,* July/August 1989, 41-45.

work to do can also create stress. If you have ever been in a job situation where so little was demanded of you that the work day seemed to stretch out forever, you can understand why many people find an "underload" situation stressful. In addition to work overload or underload situations, the nature of the work itself has a great deal to do with the experience of stress, as suggested by Table 9.1.

Job conditions   Another important set of job stressors is related to poor working conditions. Temperature extremes, loud noise, too much or too little lighting, radiation, and air pollution are just a few examples of the working conditions that can cause stress for employees. Studies have indicated that job performance deteriorates, sometimes markedly, when environmental stressors (such as bad lighting, noise, or unpleasant temperatures) are present. Further, the effects of these environmental stressors are cumulative across time, and they interact with other sources of stress. Organizations need to be aware that noisy conditions, bad lighting, and long hours all add up to increase stress and decrease performance.[15]

Role Conflict and Ambiguity   Whenever differing expectations or demands are placed on a person's role at work, there is **role conflict.** (We will discuss role conflict in detail in Chapter 14.) **Role ambiguity** describes the situation in which there is uncertainty about job duties and responsibilities. Role conflict and role ambiguity are particularly important sources of much

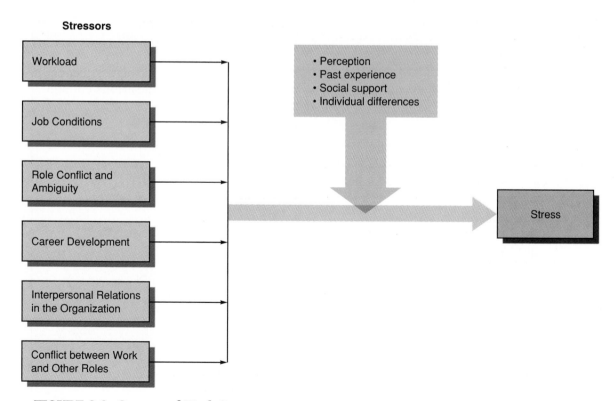

Stressors

- Perception
- Past experience
- Social support
- Individual differences

Workload

Job Conditions

Role Conflict and Ambiguity

Career Development

Interpersonal Relations in the Organization

Conflict between Work and Other Roles

Stress

FIGURE 9.2   Sources of Work Stress

job-related stress.[16] While many employees might suffer from role conflict and ambiguity, conflicting expectations and uncertainty are particularly common in the managerial role. Having responsibility for the behavior of others and a lack of opportunity to participate in important decisions affecting the job are other aspects of employees' roles that may be stressful.

Career Development   Major stressors related to career planning and development involve job security, promotions, transfers, and developmental opportunities. (We will explore career planning and development in Chapter 20). As with too much or too little work, an employee can feel stress by underpromotion (failure to advance as rapidly as desired) or overpromotion (promotion to a job that exceeds the individual's capabilities). As we saw in the In Practice description of job stress, the current wave of reorganizations and downsizing may seriously threaten careers. When jobs, departments, work teams, or entire organizations are restructured, employees may have a number of career-related concerns: Can I perform competently in the new situation? Can I advance? Is my new job secure? Typically, employees find these concerns stressful.[17]

Interpersonal Relations in the Organization   Groups have a tremendous impact on the behavior of people in organizations. (We will explore these dynamics in Chapters 10 and 11.) Individuals must have good working relationships with peers, subordinates, and superiors. Relationships and interactions with others are a crucial part of organizational life and a potential source of stress. For example, a study of clerical employees indicated that intrusions by others—interruptions from noisy co-workers, ringing telephones, and people walking into and around their work stations—were important sources of stress.[18] A high level of political behavior or "office politics" may create stress for some managers and employees (see Chapter 16). Good interpersonal relationships help achieve many personal and organizational goals; poor interpersonal relationships cause stress. As we discussed earlier, relationships with co-workers may influence how employees will react to stressors in other categories as well. In other words, interpersonal relationships can be both a source of stress as well as provide the social support that affects how employees react to other stressors (see Figures 9.1 and 9.2).

Conflict between Work and Other Roles   A person plays many roles in life, only one of which is typically associated with work (although some individuals may hold more than one job at a time). These roles may present conflicting demands that serve as a source of stress. Furthermore, work typically meets only some of an employee's goals and needs. Other personal goals and needs may conflict with career goals, which presents an additional source of stress. For example, a manager's personal needs to spend time with the family may conflict with the extra hours the person must work to advance his or her career. The conflict between family and work roles is not unique to managers and employees in North America. This chapter's Across Cultures account describes the work-family dilemma one French manager faced.

♦ *ACROSS CULTURES*

EXPATRIATE MANAGER'S FAMILY PROBLEMS

 Guy Martin is a manager in the international division of the French consumer appliances manufacturer Ridoux SA. His return flight from Marseilles had been delayed twice and finally landed more than four hours late at London's Heathrow Airport. It was 1 A.M. when Marie, Guy's wife, heard the key click in the front door lock. The guests at their daughter's birthday party had departed, their children had gone to bed, and she had spent the last hour alone cleaning up the mess.

Guy did not immediately notice Marie's unhappiness because he was returning with exciting news, an offer from Ridoux's CEO Pierre Moreau to run the company's new acquisition in Australia. "Guess what? Moreau has offered me Australia," Guy exclaimed, dropping his suitcase near the door and rushing over to kiss his wife briskly on both cheeks. "It's a great assignment, and he wants my answer tomorrow."

Marie didn't budge, and her face turned to granite. "*Incroyable!* Two years in a row you miss Louise's birthday party, and all you can talk about is uprooting us again and go-ing to Australia?" she snapped. "What's happened to that promise of setting priorities, Guy? I'm not only talking about Louise's two birthday parties, I'm talking about all the postponed dinners, all the times you're away . . . . Fifteen years of moving around like gypsies from Germany to Switzerland to Britain and now Australia. Enough is enough. After all, you're forty-three years old, and there comes a time to settle down, put down roots, and place your family before your career. Why can't we stay here in Britain, or you get a job at headquarters?"

Guy tried to calm her down by pointing out that his British replacement had already been chosen. He also expressed concern about the value of his overseas experience if he was assigned to corporate headquarters. "They wouldn't know what to do with me," he said. "I'd probably be given a nice title and end up shuffling papers, serving out my time to retirement. Is that what you want me to do?"

"No, but I don't want to go to Australia either, and that's final," Marie said. "Do what you have to do, but don't make us the victims," she practically shouted as she stalked off to bed.[19]

Life Stressors

The distinction between work and nonwork stressors is not always clear. For example, as both Figure 9.2 and the Across Cultures account show, one possible source of stressors lies in potential conflicts between work and family demands. Much of the stress felt by managers and employees may stem from stressors in their personal lives, or **life stressors.** Work stress and life stress are often related. High stress in one area can reduce a person's ability to cope with stress in the other.

Just as in the work setting, there is great variety in the possible life stressors that people must cope with. In addition, there are important individual differences in dealing with life stressors. Events that cause stress for one person may be unimportant for another. An observation, however, that seems to apply to almost everyone is that much of the stress in personal life seems to be caused by major changes, such as divorce, marriage, the death of a family member, and so on. As discussed previously, the human body has a limited capacity to respond to stressors. Too much change too quickly can exhaust the ability of the body to respond with negative consequences for physical and mental health (to be discussed shortly).

Patients in stress-related counseling are often asked to calculate their susceptibility to health changes by examining the major events and changes in their lives over the past year. For example, Table 9.2 contains some stressful events typically faced by college students. These events are rated on a 100-point scale where 1 indicates the least stressful event and 100 the most stressful. In Table 9.2, events labeled "high levels of stress" are given between 71 and 100 points, depending on the specific circumstances in the life of the college student being evaluated. "Moderate levels of stress" are scored from 31 to 70 points, and "low levels of stress" are assigned scores from 1 to 30. If a college student faces events during the course of a year that total 150 points or more, then he or she has a 50-50 chance of getting ill as a result of this excessive stress.[20]

Recall that Selye's medical science definition emphasized that stress is the body's general response to any demand made on it. Note that the list of stressful events in Table 9.2 contains both unpleasant events, such as failing

---

TABLE 9.2   Stressful Events for College Students

Events Having High Levels of Stress
- Death of parent
- Death of spouse
- Divorce
- Flunking out
- Unwed pregnancy

Events Having Moderate Levels of Stress
- Academic probation
- Change of major
- Death of close friend
- Failing important course
- Finding a new love interest
- Loss of financial aid
- Major injury or illness
- Parents' divorce
- Serious arguments with romantic partner

Events Having Relatively Low Levels of Stress
- Change in eating habits
- Change in sleeping habits
- Change in social activities
- Conflict with instructor
- Lower grades than expected
- Outstanding achievement

Source: Adapted from R. A. Baron and D. Byrne, *Social Psychology: Understanding Human Interaction*, 6th ed. Boston: Allyn and Bacon, 1991, 573.

a course, and events normally considered pleasant, such as finding a new love interest. Thus, it is important to note that life stressors are not limited to negative occurrences in one's personal life but also may include positive experiences. For example, vacations and holidays can actually be quite stressful for many people. In addition, viewing life events as having only negative effects is incorrect. People often can cope with unpleasant events and, to a certain extent, need the stimulation of pleasurable events, such as significant accomplishments, vacations, gaining a new family member, and so on.

EFFECTS OF STRESS

Work stress has both positive and negative effects, but research on work stress has tended to focus on its negative effects. This focus seems well-directed. The Research Triangle Institute estimated the cost to the U.S. economy from stress-related disorders as $187 billion in 1990.[21] This loss includes lost productivity, job errors, and medical costs.

The effects of work stress occur in three major areas: physiological, emotional, and behavioral. Examples of the effects of excessive stress in these three areas are as follows:

- **Physiological effects of stress** include increased blood pressure, increased heart rate, sweating, hot and cold spells, breathing difficulties, muscular tension, and increased gastrointestinal disorders.
- **Emotional effects of stress** include anger; anxiety; depression; lowered self-esteem; poorer intellectual functioning, including an inability to concentrate and make decisions; nervousness; irritability; resentment of supervision; and job dissatisfaction.
- **Behavioral effects of stress** include decreased performance, absenteeism, higher accident rates, higher turnover rates, higher alcohol and other drug abuses, impulsive behavior, and difficulties in communication.

These effects have important implications for organizational behavior. We will examine some of the implications of work stress for the health and performance of managers and employees. We will also explore the phenomenon of *job burnout.*

Health and Stress

Considerable evidence links stress to coronary heart disease. Other major health problems commonly associated with stress include such physical ailments as back pain, headaches, and stomach and intestinal problems, as well as a variety of mental problems. Medical researchers have recently discovered possible links between stress and cancer. Although it is difficult to determine the precise role stress plays in health in all individual cases, it is becoming increasingly clear that a great many illnesses are stress-related.[22]

Stress-related illnesses place a considerable burden on people and organizations. The costs to individuals are sometimes more obvious than the costs to organizations. It is possible, however, to identify at least some of the organizational costs associated with stress-related disease. First, costs to employers include not only increased premiums for health insurance but also lost work days from serious illnesses, such as heart disease, and less-serious illnesses, such as stress-related headaches. Current estimates are that each employee who suffers from a stress-related illness loses an average of sixteen days of work a year. Second, over three-fourths of all industrial accidents are caused by an inability to cope with emotional problems worsened by stress. Third, legal problems for employers are growing. For example, the number of stress-related worker's compensation claims is growing at a tremendous rate. Experts predict that if the current growth rate continues, stress-related worker's compensation claims will outnumber *all* other claims during the 1990s.[23]

Performance and Stress

Nowhere are both the positive and negative aspects of stress more apparent than in the relationship between stress and performance. Figure 9.3 shows the performance-stress relationship. The vertical axis represents the level of performance. The horizontal axis represents the amount of stress experienced. At low levels of stress, employees may not be sufficiently alert, challenged, or involved to perform at their best. As the curve in Figure 9.3 indicates, increasing a low amount of stress can improve performance—up to a point. An optimum level of stress probably exists for most tasks. Past this point, performance begins to deteriorate. At excessive levels of stress, employees are too agitated, aroused, or threatened to perform at their best. Investigations of the performance-stress relationship in work settings have frequently demonstrated the curvilinear relationship shown in Figure 9.3.[24] The following account provides an example of the relationship between performance and stress.

IN PRACTICE

"JUST ENOUGH BUT NOT TOO MUCH"

Laura was puzzled. During the past several months, she had presented three major reports to the executive committee of the board of directors. The first had been a catastrophe. She had been so nervous that she could actually remember little that had gone on. She did know, however, that she had somehow gotten through her formal presentation—which seemed to go okay—before disaster really struck. It came in the form of a series of questions, each more confusing than the last. The board members eventually took pity on her and suddenly stopped the questioning, thanked her for her good efforts on the report, and turned their attention to other matters. Later, Elizabeth—her boss and the firm's president—had helped Laura analyze her performance. They had determined that, with one or two exceptions, Laura actually was well acquainted with the answers to the questions asked. What had seemed to happen, they decided, was that she was far too agitated to think clearly and, indeed, was so upset that she even had trouble in focusing on what was being asked. Several times she had to ask for questions to be repeated. Elizabeth's advice had been preparation and practice. "You have got to make stress work for you—but you can't be so stressed out that you can't think straight."

Laura did not fully understand the implications of Elizabeth's last comment, but she carefully prepared for her next presentation to the board. Like a highly trained athlete before the big game, she was actually looking forward to the presentation. Although certainly "keyed up" when the time came, she made a superb presentation full of energy and enthusiasm and fielded the board members' questions with confidence. Board members were effusive in their praise (and probably a little relieved, since the first experience had gone so badly).

Now Laura had just come from her third presentation to the board. Even though well prepared, today she had been "flat." She had not really been at all nervous; indeed, she had been working on another project right up until the time she went into the boardroom for her presentation. While things certainly went better than the first time, she knew without being told that her performance had not measured up to the peak performance of last time. "What's going on?" Laura wondered. With Elizabeth's help, she again attempted to diagnose her performance. After some discussion, they finally decided that, while Laura had felt too much stress during her first presentation, the last time she had, ironically, probably not felt enough.

Managers often want to know the optimum stress points for both themselves and their subordinates. This information, however, is difficult to obtain. For example, an employee may be absent from work frequently because of boredom (too little stress) or because of overwork (excessive stress). Also, the curve shown in Figure 9.3 changes with the situation; that is, the curve varies for different people and different tasks. Too little stress for one employee may be just right for another on a particular task. The optimum amount of stress for a specific individual for one task may be too much or too little for that person's effective performance of other tasks.

As a practical matter, managers often need to be more concerned about the "excessive stress" side of the curve in Figure 9.3 than with how to add to employee stress. Certainly, motivating individuals to perform better is always a critical issue (see Chapter 7). However, studies of the performance-stress relationship in organizations often find a strong negative correlation between the amount of stress in a group, work team, or department and its overall performance.[25] That is, the greater the stress that employees are experiencing, the lower will be their productivity. This negative relationship indicates that these work settings are operating on the right-hand side (excessive stress) of Figure 9.3. Managers and employees in these settings need to find effective ways to reduce the number and magnitude of stressors.

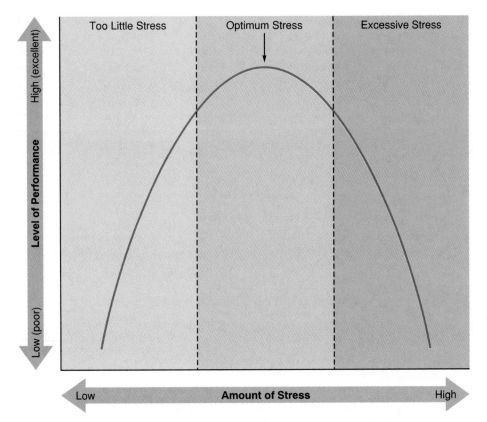

FIGURE 9.3   Typical Relationship between Performance and Stress

Job Burnout

Job burnout refers to the adverse effects of working conditions where stressors seem unavoidable and sources of job satisfaction and relief from stress seem unavailable. The burnout phenomenon typically contains three components:

- A state of *emotional exhaustion;*
- *depersonalization* of individuals dealt with in the work setting; and
- *feelings of low personal accomplishment.*[26]

In this context, **depersonalization** refers to treating people like objects. For example, a nurse might refer to the "broken knee" in room 107, rather than using the patient's name.

Most job-burnout research has focused on the human services sector of the economy—sometimes called the "helping professions." Generally, burnout is thought to be most prevalent in occupations characterized by continuous direct contact with people in need of aid. The professionals who may be most vulnerable to job burnout include social workers, nurses, physicians, police officers, air traffic controllers, teachers, and lawyers.[27] (Notice that this list contains many of the same high-stress occupations

listed in Table 9.1) However, burnout may occur among any individuals—
including managers, shop owners, and professionals—who must deal extensively with other people as part of their job or who constantly face stressors with little relief. The following account suggests some of the conditions
under which a manager or employee might experience job burnout.

IN PRACTICE

BURNOUT!

Wilfred Jennings had been under tremendous pressure for months. Jennings, a
systems manager for a London-based multinational corporation, was responsible
for managing a team transferring all customer accounts to a computer data base.
The data base being established would be available for access by the company's
subsidiaries worldwide.

Jennings had a reputation for being a workaholic, often being the first in the
office in the morning and the last one out at night. Normally relishing a
challenge, Jennings nevertheless became filled with doubts as the deadline for
start-up of the new system approached. His project was falling behind schedule, and thoughts of failure caused him to drive his team and himself even
harder than usual.

His boss sensed the project was behind schedule and urged Jennings to "work
smarter, not harder." But Jennings really did not know how to respond to that
suggestion. Somewhat reluctant to delegate crucial decisions even in the best of
times, Jennings now did even less delegating. He began to assume more responsibility for routine tasks previously left to subordinates, taking work home at night
and on weekends. Jennings was growing increasingly resentful of the extra work
load and felt that he was having to correct too many mistakes by his staff. Jennings
started to feel that he was the only one who cared about the success of the project.
He became extremely critical of his subordinates and soon became isolated from
his team.

Jennings's wife and children began to suffer from his angry outbursts at home
over even the most trivial things. He no longer had time to help his children with
their schoolwork or to help with normal household duties. Jennings began to feel
physically exhausted and to experience frequent headaches. He had trouble
sleeping, lost his appetite, and complained of feeling inadequate.

Finally, Jennings found it almost impossible to get out of bed in the morning.
He could concentrate on nothing except his problems at work. Eventually, he had
trouble even concentrating on work and began to procrastinate on important
decisions. This behavior caused further delays in the project.

At this point, Jennings was overwhelmed by guilt for the way he was treating
his family and a sense of impending doom at work based on fear that the project
was going to fail. His wife finally succeeded in talking him into making an appointment with the family physician. The doctor's diagnosis was that Jennings
suffered from the classic symptoms of job burnout. Unless there was a radical
change in his life-style—both at home and at work—he was heading for a major
nervous breakdown.[28]

Individuals who experience job burnout seem to have some common characteristics. Three characteristics in particular are associated with a high probability of burnout:

- Burnout candidates experience a great deal of stress as a result of job-related stressors.
- Burnout candidates tend to be idealistic and self-motivating achievers.
- Burnout candidates often seek unattainable goals.[29]

The burnout syndrome represents a combination of certain individual characteristics and the job situation. Individuals who suffer from burnout often have unrealistic expectations concerning their work and their ability to accomplish desired goals, given the nature of the situation in which they find themselves. Unrelieved stressful working conditions, coupled with unrealistic expectations or ambitions of the individual, can lead to a state of complete physical, mental, and emotional exhaustion. Under conditions of burnout, the individual can no longer cope with the demands of the job, and the willingness to try drops dramatically.

The costs of job burnout, both to the employees suffering from this syndrome and to their organizations, can be high. Managers and employees need to be aware of the characteristic symptoms of burnout, as well as the stressors that can contribute to this outcome. Table 9.3 contains examples of some of the physical, emotional, and behavioral symptoms of job burnout. Strategies for coping with stress, which we will examine in the last section of this chapter, are often useful in reducing causes and symptoms of job burnout.

TABLE 9.3   Symptoms of Job Burnout

Physiological Symptoms
- A noticeable decline in physical appearance
- Chronic fatigue
- Frequent infections, especially respiratory infections
- Health complaints, such as headaches, backaches, or stomach problems
- Signs of depression, such as a change in weight or eating habits

Emotional Symptoms
- Appearance of boredom or apathy
- Cynicism and resentfulness
- Depressed appearance, such as a sad expression or slumped posture
- Expressions of anxiety, frustration, and hopelessness

Behavioral Symptoms
- Absenteeism and tardiness
- Abuse of drugs, alcohol, or caffeine; increased smoking
- Excessive exercise to the point of injury
- Hostile behavior; easily irritated
- Reduced productivity; inability to concentrate or complete a task
- Withdrawal; listlessness

Source: Adapted from H. F. Stallworth, Realistic Goals Help Avoid Burnout. *HR Magazine,* June 1990, 171.

TABLE 9.4 A Self-Assessment of Type A Personality

Choose from the following responses to answer the questions below:

A. Almost always true   C. Seldom true
B. Usually true   D. Never true

Answer each question according to what is generally true for you:

_____ **1.** I do not like to wait for other people to complete their work before I can proceed with my own.

_____ **2.** I hate to wait in most lines.

_____ **3.** People tell me that I tend to get irritated too easily.

_____ **4.** Whenever possible, I try to make activities competitive.

_____ **5.** I have a tendency to rush into work that needs to be done before knowing the procedure I will use to complete the job.

_____ **6.** Even when I go on vacation, I usually take some work along.

_____ **7.** When I make a mistake, it is usually due to the fact that I have rushed into the job before completely planning it through.

_____ **8.** I feel guilty for taking time off from work.

_____ **9.** People tell me I have a bad temper when it comes to competitive situations.

_____ **10.** I tend to lose my temper when I am under a lot of pressure at work.

_____ **11.** Whenever possible, I will attempt to complete two or more tasks at once.

_____ **12.** I tend to race against the clock.

_____ **13.** I have no patience for lateness.

_____ **14.** I catch myself rushing when there is no need.

continues

PERSONALITY AND STRESS

Personality influences (1) how individuals are likely to perceive situations and stressors, and (2) how they will react to these environmental stressors. A study of coping behaviors following a flood in Harrisburg, Pennsylvania, illustrates the ways in which personality influences perceptions of and reactions to stressors. Information gathered from ninety owner-managers of small businesses in Harrisburg indicated that locus of control (a personality dimension described in Chapter 3) was highly related to the experience of stress and the choice of coping behaviors.[30] Owner-managers with a high external locus of control experienced greater stress during the flood and displayed more emotional coping behaviors after the flood. Examples of their responses included hostility and withdrawal (such as quitting the busi-

TABLE 9.4 *continued*

Score your responses according to the following key:

- *An intense sense of time urgency* is a tendency to race against the clock, even when there is little reason to. The person feels a need to hurry for hurry's sake alone, and this tendency has appropriately been called "hurry sickness." Time urgency is measured by items 1, 2, 8, 12, 13, and 14. Every A or B answer to these six questions scores one point. Your Score = ☐

- *Inappropriate aggression and hostility* reveals itself in a person who is excessively competitive and who cannot do anything for fun. This inappropriately aggressive behavior easily evolves into frequent displays of hostility, usually at the slightest provocation or frustration. Competitiveness and hostility is measured by items 3, 4, 9, and 10. Every A or B answer scores one point. Your Score = ☐

- *Polyphasic behavior* refers to the tendency to undertake two or more tasks simultaneously at inappropriate times. It usually results in wasted time due to an inability to complete the tasks. This behavior is measured by items 6 and 11. Every A or B answer scores one point. Your Score = ☐

- *Goal directedness without proper planning* refers to the tendency of an individual to rush into work without really knowing how to accomplish the desired result. This usually results in incomplete work or work with many errors, which in turn leads to wasted time, energy, and money. Lack of planning is measured by items 5 and 7. Every A or B response scores one point. Your Score = ☐

TOTAL SCORE = _____

If your score is 5 or greater, you may possess some basic components of the Type A personality.

Source: Reproduced with permission of the Robert J. Brady Co., Bowie, Maryland, 20715, from its copyrighted work *The Stress Mess Solution: The Causes and Cures of Stress on the Job*, by G. S. Everly, and D. A. Girdano, 1980, 55.

ness or moving from the area). Owner-managers with a high internal locus of control experienced less stress in the same situation. In addition, they used more task-oriented coping behaviors, such as problem solving and acquiring the resources to maintain operations.

Many personality dimensions or traits can be related to stress including self-esteem, tolerance for ambiguity, introversion/extraversion, and dogmatism. A personality trait may affect the probability that a situation or event will be perceived as a stressor. For example, an individual with low self-esteem may be more likely to experience stress in demanding work situations than a person with high self-esteem. This may be because the high self-esteem individual typically has more confidence in his or her ability to meet job demands. We will explore some aspects of personality that seem to be related to the ways in which individuals experience stress.

Before reading further, however, respond to the statements in Table 9.4. This self-assessment exercise is related to the discussion that follows.

Type A Personality

People with a **Type A personality** are involved in a never-ending struggle to achieve more and more in less and less time. Characteristics of this personality type include:

- A chronic sense of urgency about time;
- an extremely competitive, almost hostile orientation;
- an aversion to idleness; and
- an impatience with barriers to task accomplishment.

Two medical researchers first identified the Type A personality when they noticed a recurrent personality pattern in their patients who suffered from premature heart disease.[31] In addition to the above characteristics, extreme Type A individuals often speak rapidly, are preoccupied with themselves, are dissatisfied with life, and tend to evaluate the worthwhileness of activities in terms of numbers.

The questionnaire in Table 9.4 measures four sets of behaviors and tendencies associated with the Type A personality: (1) time urgency, (2) competitiveness and hostility, (3) polyphasic behavior (trying to do too many things at once), and (4) a lack of planning. Medical researchers have discovered that these behaviors or tendencies often relate to life and work stress. They tend to cause stress or to make stressful situations worse than they otherwise might be.

Evidence links Type A behavior with a vulnerability to heart attacks. Conventional wisdom among medical researchers was that Type A individuals were two to three times more likely to develop heart disease than were Type B individuals. (The **Type B personality** is considered to be the polar opposite of the Type A. The Type B individual is easygoing and relaxed, unconcerned about time pressures, and less likely to overreact to situations in hostile or agressive ways.) Recent research, however, has suggested that the Type A personality description is too broad in terms of predicting coronary heart disease. Rather, research indicates that only certain aspects of the Type A personality—particularly anger, hostility, and aggression—have a strong relationship to stress reactions and heart disease.[32]

The Hardy Personality

There has been a great deal of recent interest in identifying aspects of the personality that might buffer or protect individuals from, in particular, the negative health consequences of stress. A collection of personality traits that seem to reduce the effects of stress is known as the *hardy personality*. As a personality type, **hardiness** is defined as "a cluster of characteristics that includes feeling a sense of commitment, responding to each difficulty as representing a challenge and an opportunity, and perceiving that one has control over one's own life."[33] Hardiness includes the following behaviors and tendencies:

- A sense of positive involvement with others in social situations;
- tendency to attribute one's own behavior to internal causes (Recall our discussion of attribution in Chapter 4.); and

- tendency to perceive or welcome major changes in life with interest, curiosity, and optimism.[34] (Recall our earlier discussion of change as a major life stressor.)

A number of studies have suggested that a high degree of hardiness reduces the negative effects of stressful events.[35] Hardiness seems to reduce stress by altering how stressors are perceived. Earlier, we discussed the important role played by individual differences in the experience of stress. The concept of the hardy personality provides a useful way to understand the role of individual differences in terms of stress reactions to environmental stressors. When an individual has high levels of hardiness, fewer events are perceived as stressful; low hardiness individuals tend to perceive more events as stressful.

A person with high levels of hardiness is not overwhelmed by challenging or difficult situations. Rather, faced with a stressor, the high-hardiness individual copes or responds constructively by trying to find a solution—to control or influence events. The result of this behavioral response is typically a reduction in stress reactions, lower blood pressure, and reduced probability of illness.

STRESS MANAGEMENT

Articles in newspapers and popular magazines often suggest various ways of coping with stress, such as therapy, exercise, time management, proper diet, adequate sleep, meditation and relaxation, and recreational activity. The frequency with which these articles appear demonstrates the prevalence of stress in our society. In addition, organizational programs to help employees cope with stress have become increasingly popular as the tremendous toll taken by stress has become more widely known. We will explore some methods that can be used by individuals and organizations to manage stress and reduce its harmful effects.

Individual Stress Coping Methods

Stress management by individuals includes activities and behaviors designed to (1) eliminate or control the sources of stress and/or (2) make the individual more resistant to stress or better able to cope with stress. For example, one set of suggestions is based on insight developed from the concept of *hardiness*, which we discussed earlier. While individuals cannot consciously alter their basic personality, they can purposefully adopt attitudes and behaviors that parallel the attributes and behavioral patterns exhibited by high-hardiness individuals. Some suggestions, based on research on the hardy personality, include:

- Maintain a positive attitude.
- Stick with a decision.
- Think of setbacks as challenges, instead of disasters.

- Exercise, eat a balanced diet, and take care of yourself.
- Always take the time to have fun.
- Learn a relaxation technique to lower your physiological arousal on demand.[36]

A recent in-depth study of six very successful top executives revealed similar behavioral patterns among the executives in their use of stress coping methods.[37] First, each of these individuals worked very hard at balancing work and family concerns. While work was central to their lives, it was not their sole focus. Each executive also made effective use of leisure time in reducing stress. In addition, the executives were skilled with time management techniques. An important component of effective time use was identifying priority goals and careful planning to attain these objectives. Having a good sense of which goals were most crucial and developing constructive plans to pursue them was a major strategy of stress reduction for these executives. Finally, each of the executives cited the important role of social support in coping with stress. These people did not operate as loners; rather, they received emotional support and important information from a diverse network of family, friends, co-workers, and industry colleagues. Additionally, these executives worked hard at maintaining an equitable, reciprocal exchange in these relationships. That is, the executives both received support from others and served as a source of social support *for* others in their network.

Organizational Stress Coping Methods

Stress management by organizations is designed to reduce harmful effects of stress in three ways, as shown in Figure 9.4: (1) identify and then modify or eliminate work stressors, (2) help employees modify their perceptions and understandings of work stress, and (3) help employees to cope more effectively with the consequences of stress.[38]

Programs of stress management that fit into the first category of Figure 9.4 (attempts to eliminate or modify work stressors) often include one or more of the following:

- Improvements in the physical work environment;
- Job redesign (see Chapter 17);
- Structural reorganization (see Chapter 18);
- Management by objectives or other goal-setting programs (see Chapter 8);
- Greater levels of employee participation, particularly in planning changes that affect them (see Chapter 22); and
- Workshops dealing with role clarity and role analysis (see Chapter 14).

Programs that promote role clarity and role analysis can be particularly useful in removing or reducing role ambiguity and role conflict—two major sources of stress. When diagnosing stressors in the workplace, managers should be particularly aware of the large amount of research showing that

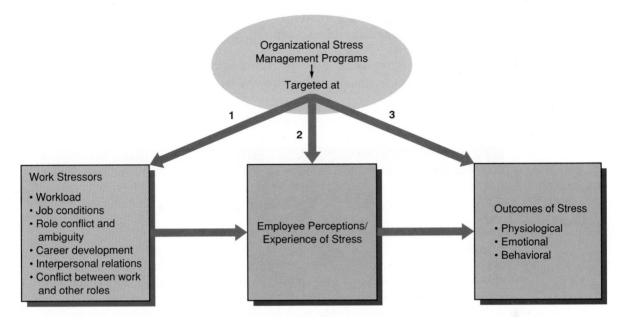

FIGURE 9.4   Targets of Organizational Stress Management Programs

Source: Adapted from J. M. Ivancevich, M. T. Matteson, S. M. Freedman, and J. S. Phillips, Worksite Stress Management Interventions. *American Psychologist,* 1990, *45,* 253.

stress is heightened by uncertainty and perceived lack of control.[39] Thus, involvement of employees in organizational change efforts, work redesign that reduces uncertainty and increases control of the work pace, and improved clarity and understanding of roles should all serve to reduce employee stress.

Programs of stress management targeted at the second and third categories shown in Figure 9.4 might include one or more of the following:

- Behavior modification (see Chapter 6);
- Career counseling (see Chapter 20);
- Workshops on time management;
- Workshops on job burnout to help employees understand its nature and symptoms;
- Training in relaxation techniques; and
- Physical fitness or "wellness" programs.

Dividing stress management programs into these categories is not intended to suggest that these are necessarily separated in practice. In addition, programs that appear in the two lists above obviously might overlap in terms of their impact on the three target areas shown in Figure 9.4. For example, a workshop dealing with role problems might clarify roles and thus reduce the magnitude of this potential stressor. At the same time, through greater knowledge and insight into roles and role problems, employees might be able to cope more effectively with this source of stress. Similarly, career counseling might reduce career concerns as a source of stress while improving the ability of employees to cope with remaining career problems.

Wellness programs are currently extremely popular. In general, **wellness programs** are activities that organizations engage in to promote good health habits or to identify and correct health problems.[40] Estimates are that over fifty thousand U.S. firms provide some type of company-sponsored health promotion program. The following account describes the wellness program at AT&T.

IN PRACTICE

AT&T'S WELLNESS PROGRAM

AT&T's Total Life Concept (TLC) program began in 1983 at several test sites. Some twenty-four hundred employees took part in the first wellness program, which began with ambitious goals and an agenda designed to improve stress coping skills, fitness, and health among AT&T's employees. One year after the start of this program, AT&T found substantial improvements in health and morale. Program participants reduced their cholesterol levels by 10 percent on average, and 78 percent of the employees who wanted to lower their blood pressure had managed at least a 10 percent decrease. Over 80 percent of employees who joined smoking-cessation courses quit smoking; after one year, 50 percent were still nonsmokers. The current director of TLC says, "People's attitudes changed. We sent a message to employees that said, 'We care about your health and well-being.' They got the message."

Currently, eighty thousand AT&T employees are enrolled in TLC. The first step in joining the program is free blood-pressure and cholesterol tests. Employees can then choose among various courses designed to address concerns over blood pressure, cholesterol, nutrition, stress, cancer, and the like. Some courses are free, while others might have small costs, depending on the facilities and resources required. People typically need encouragement after they have started an exercise program or have quit smoking, so "graduates" of the courses get together in support groups to help each other make the life-style changes last.

The TLC motto is "A healthy workplace makes good business sense," and AT&T managers seem to take this slogan seriously. AT&T is currently spending around fifty dollars for each employee in the program. With eighty thousand participating, this amounts to about $4 million annually.[41]

There are three major types of wellness programs.[42] First, there are programs that operate at the level of awareness or information. These programs may or may not directly improve health; rather, they are designed to inform employees about the consequences of unhealthy behavior. For example, Sara Lee provides female employees with a series of workshops on prenatal care, nutrition, and strategies for preventing disease. Johnson & Johnson has lunch-hour seminars on stress coping techniques. Often these programs are used to generate interest in more active programs of exercise and life-style changes.

A second type of wellness program involves the employees in ongoing efforts to modify life-styles. Such efforts might involve physical fitness programs (such as jogging or walking), smoking-cessation programs, weight control programs, and the like. For example, L. L. Bean has a running club for employees plus programs that provide lessons in ballroom dancing and cross-country skiing. Bonne Bell encourages employees to ride bikes to work and has arranged for its employees to purchase bikes at cost. Bonne Bell also provides an extensive series of exercise programs for employees and has built tennis and volleyball courts, a running track, and shower and locker facilities. Employees can use all of these facilities for free and even get an extra thirty minutes for lunch if they want to exercise. The firm sells running suits and shoes at discount prices and currently offers a $250 bonus for employees who exercise at least four days a week.

A third variety of wellness program has as its goal the creation of an environment that will help employees to maintain the healthy life-style developed in the other programs. The In Practice description of AT&T provides an example of this when employees formed support groups to help each other maintain their healthy life-style changes. The exercise facilities provided free of charge to employees by Bonne Bell are another example. At Safeway, employees built their own fitness center on company grounds. The firm now provides a full-time fitness director to oversee the exercise programs and activities.

Wellness programs can provide substantial benefits to both individuals and organizations. Safeway estimates that its wellness program has almost completely eliminated workplace accidents and reduced tardiness and absenteeism by more than 60 percent. The In Practice described some of the dramatic health benefits at AT&T in terms of reduced blood pressure and cholesterol levels of participating employees. Similar positive health consequences have been reported at many companies. At Johnson & Johnson locations that used the wellness program, hospital costs during the first five years increased by only one-third as much as they did at company locations without the program. Absenteeism was reduced 18 percent by Johnson & Johnson's wellness program. In addition to showing a substantial improvement in employee morale, an evaluation of Honeywell's wellness program indicated the increase in the cost of their health-care services is averaging only 4 percent a year. (Nationwide, health-care costs are currently increasing at an average of 14 percent a year.)[43]

SUMMARY

Stress is a consequence of or a response to a situation that places either physical or psychological demands, or stressors, on a person. The body's general biological response to stressors prepares the individual to fight or flee, behavior generally inappropriate in work settings. Many factors determine how employees experience work stress, including their perception of the situation, past experiences, the presence or absence of other employees, and a variety of individual differences.

Stressors at work stem from many sources. The general categories discussed included (1) work load, (2) job conditions, (3) role conflict and ambiguity, (4) career development, (5) interpersonal relations, and (6) conflict between work and other roles. In addition, major changes or other events in an individual's personal life may also be a source of stress.

Stress affects people physiologically, emotionally, and behaviorally. Researchers have linked stress to several major health problems, particularly coronary heart disease. An inverted U-shaped relationship exists between stress and performance. An optimum level of stress probably exists for any given task, and less or more stress than the optimum level leads to reduced performance. Job burnout is a major result of unrelieved job-related stress.

Several personality dimensions can be related to stress. Individuals having a Type A personality are prone to stress and have an increased chance of heart disease. Some specific dimensions of the Type A personality, such as hostility, are particularly important in terms of stress-related illness. On the other hand, the collection of personality traits known as hardiness seems to reduce the effects of stress.

Stress is a crucial issue for individuals and organizations. Fortunately, various techniques and programs can help manage stress in the work environment. Wellness programs are particularly promising in this regard.

Key Words and Concepts

Behavioral effects of stress	Role conflict
Depersonalization	Role overload
Emotional effects of stress	Stress
Fight-or-flight response	Stress management
Hardiness	Stressors
Job burnout	Type A personality
Life stressors	Type B personality
Physiological effects of stress	Wellness programs
Role ambiguity	

Discussion Questions

1. Why is stress an important issue for individuals and organizations?

2. Explain the role of individual differences in the experience of stress.

3. Describe some of the stressors in a job you have held. Which were the more difficult ones to deal with?

4. Give an example of a time when the fight-or-flight response seemed particularly inappropriate for your own behavior.

5. Identify the possible health consequences of excessive stress.

6. Describe the general relationship between performance and stress.

7. Discuss the conditions and circumstances leading to job burnout.

8. Design a stress management program for an organization. Justify the various components of your suggested program.

9.   What strategies or techniques do you use to cope with stress in your personal life? In your work (either a job or school)?

◆   *MANAGEMENT CASES AND EXERCISES*

MEASURING YOUR JOB'S STRESS LEVEL

Thinking of a job you currently hold, or one you used to have, respond to the following questions. Assign each question a number according to how often you felt that way or had the described experience. Use the following scale for your answers:

1 = Never, 2 = Sometimes, 3 = Frequently, 4 = Almost always

Your Score

1.   The working conditions are hard physically. _____
2.   The work is dangerous or hazardous. _____
3.   The workplace is uncomfortable or depressing. _____
4.   I find that office politics interfere with my work. _____
5.   I don't have the information I need for my work. _____
6.   There is a competitive, backbiting atmosphere at work. _____
7.   What is expected of me is not clear. _____
8.   I am asked to do conflicting things. _____
9.   I feel overloaded at work. _____
10.   I have ethical problems with my job duties. _____
11.   I am not able to advance as I would like in this job. _____
12.   Relationships among co-workers are poor and full of conflict. _____
13.   I am not clear where I stand; I'm uncertain if my contributions are valued. _____
14.   I do not participate in decisions that affect my job. _____

TOTAL SCORE _____

Add your responses to get a total score. The maximum possible score is 56. Scores from 34 to 41 indicate a job that is moderately stressful. Scores of 42 or above indicate a job with considerable stress.[44]

THE STRESS OF SHIFT WORK

Marilyn Baker sat at her kitchen table and leafed through the entertainment section of the local paper, gratefully sipping her second cup of coffee. An Academy Award-winning movie was playing in town, and she hoped it would stay for several weeks so that she and her husband, Carl, could fit it into their hectic schedules. Carl had recently changed jobs and was now working for St. Regis Aluminum, a manufacturer of light-weight metal products. St. Regis worked shifts, and Carl was about to start a two-week stint on the night shift (midnight to 8 A.M.). Neither Carl nor Marilyn had had previous experience with shift work, and the switch from more normal working hours was proving to be difficult.

Carl worked cycles that included two weeks of day shift (8 A.M. to 4 P.M.), two weeks of swing shift (4 P.M. to midnight), and two weeks of night shift. Then, the whole cycle began again. It was necessary to plan their family life around Carl's changing schedule, but Marilyn could not seem to get the hang of it. Little things that would have been minor irritants before now seemed to become major problems. For example, the boy next door was taking trumpet lessons and practiced after school. When Carl needed to sleep in the afternoon, the noise of the trumpet often woke him. Marilyn and Carl had already had two arguments about whether to call the boy's mother to request that he practice at another time.

Marilyn was an excellent cook and particularly enjoyed preparing foods that her family liked. Yesterday, there had been a sale of beef roasts, one of Carl's favorite foods. However, with Carl starting the night shift, Marilyn decided to freeze the roast and wait for a time that the whole family could enjoy it. Even though Carl could set down to a "full" meal after coming off the night shift, that time was not very appealing to the rest of the family. So, Marilyn was learning that "special" meals were pretty much restricted to the times when Carl worked the day shift.

Shift work was also proving awkward for their social life. Marilyn and Carl were members of a poker club that played twice a month on Friday nights. Couples in the club usually met at 8 P.M. and played for four or five hours. When Carl was on the swing shift, there was no way they could play. When he worked the night shift, they could only stay for part of the evening, as Carl would have to leave in time to get ready for work. Only when Carl was on the day shift could they participate fully. So, now they were playing with their club only once or twice every two months. Their friends had gotten another couple to substitute for them, but Marilyn and Carl were afraid they might have to drop out of the club since the substitute couple was playing more frequently than they were.

Marilyn had started to feel a bit sorry for herself. Still, she admitted to herself that this shift work must be more stressful to Carl than it is to her. She remembered that Carl was working the swing shift on the weekend when the Custom Boat and Trailer Show came to town. Carl had been looking forward to seeing the new bass boats for weeks but only got to visit the show for about an hour before leaving for work. Weekends seemed particularly hard on Carl. On Saturdays and Sundays, just when he found something he liked to do, it often was time to go to work.

Their ten-year-old son, Tom, wandered into the kitchen holding a Little League schedule in his hand. "Mom," Tom said, "the regional tournament is in three weeks. Will you and Dad be able to see my games?" Marilyn got up to look at Carl's work schedule, which was taped to the refrigerator door. "Dad will be working the swing shift that week, but I can come. I'll work some extra hours and can trade days off with some of my work team. So, I'll be able to take off enough to see all of your games," Marilyn said. Tom loved to have his mother at his baseball games, but still his face fell. "Dad sure doesn't see many of my games any more," he said, as he slowly walked from the kitchen.[45]

QUESTIONS

1. Identify the stressors that exist in this situation. Which do you think are the most important sources of stress?

2. Can you predict other possible disruptions in the Baker's family life that might stem from shift work?

3. Suggest some things that St. Regis Aluminum might do to reduce stress for shift workers.

4. Suggest some stress coping strategies that could be used by Marilyn and Carl.

References

1. Based on a description provided in Miller, A. Stress on the Job. *Newsweek*, April 25, 1988, 40–45.

2. Yates, J. E. *Managing Stress: A Businessperson's Guide.* New York: AMACOM, 1979, 20.

3. Contrada, R., Baum, A. S., Glass, D., and Friend, R. The Social Psychology of Health. In R. M. Baron, W. G. Graziano, and C. Stangor (eds.), *Social Psychology*. Fort Worth: Holt, Rinehart and Winston, 1991, 620–624.

4. This example is based on Matteson, M. T., and Ivancevich, J. M. *Controlling Work Stress: Effective Human Resource and Management Strategies*. San Francisco: Jossey-Bass, 1987, 12–14.

5. Selye, H. The Stress Concept and Some of Its Implications. In V. Hamilton and D. M. Warburton (eds.), *Human Stress and Cognition*. New York: Wiley, 1979, 12; Selye, H. *The Stress of Life*, rev. ed. New York: McGraw-Hill, 1976, 1.

6. This story is attributed to Henry Murray as described by Pervin, L. A. Persons, Situations, Interactions: The History of a Controversy and a Discussion of Theoretical Models. *Academy of Management Review*, 1989, *14*, 350–360.

7. See, for example, Cummins, R. C. Job Stress and the Buffering Effect of Supervisory Support. *Group & Organization Studies*, 1990, *15*, 92-104; Ganster, D. C., Fusilier, M. R., and Mayes, B. T. Role of Social Support in the Experience of Stress at Work. *Journal of Applied Psychology*, 1986, *71*, 102–110.

8. Contrada, Baum, Glass, and Friend, The Social Psychology of Health, 626-627; Frew, D. R., and Bruning, N. S. Perceived Organizational Characteristics and Personality Measures as Predictors of Stress/Strain in the Work Place. *Journal of Management*, 1987, *13*, 633–646.

9. Bhagat, R. S., McQuaid, S. J., Lindholm, H., and Segovis, J. Total Life Stress: A Multimethod Validation of the Construct and Its Effects on Organizationally Valued Outcomes and Withdrawal Behaviors. *Journal of Applied Psychology*, 1985, *70*, 202–214; Lewis, S. N. C., and Cooper, C. L. Stress in Two-Earner Couples and Stage in the Life Cycle. *Journal of Occupational Psychology*, 1987, *60*, 289–303.

10. Based on Hymowitz, C. When Firms Slash Middle Management, Those Spared Often Bear A Heavy Load. *Wall Street Journal*, April 5, 1990, B1, B5; Kiechel, W. Overscheduled, and Not Loving It. *Fortune*, April 8, 1991, 105–107; O'Boyle, T. F. Fear and Stress in the Office Take Toll. *Wall Street Journal*, November 6, 1990, B1, B3; O'Reilly, B. Is Your Company Asking Too Much? *Fortune*, March 12, 1990, 38–46; Stewart, T. A. Do You Push Your People Too Hard? *Fortune*, October 22, 1990, 121–128.

11. McCarthy, M. J. Stressed Employees Look for Relief in Workers' Compensation Claims. *Wall Street Journal*, April 7, 1988, 31.

12. Youngblood, S. A., Lyon, L., Allen, J., Boyd, J., Molleston, J., Senia, S., and Woodman, R. W. *A Survey of Senior Executives of United States Independent Oil and Gas Producing Firms*. Technical report prepared for Korn/Ferry International, April 1982.

13. Cooper, C. L., and Arbose, J. Executive Stress Goes Global. *International Management*, May 1984, 42–48.

14. Miller, Stress on the Job, 43.

15. Nykodym, N., and George, K. Stress Busting on the Job. *Personnel*, July 1989, 56–59; Shostak, A. B. *Blue-Collar Stress*. Reading, Mass.: Addison-Wesley, 1980, 19–28.

16. See, for example, Leigh, J. H., Lucas, G. H., and Woodman, R. W. Effects of Perceived Organizational Factors on Role Stress-Job Attitude Relationships. *Journal of Management*, 1988, *14*, 41–58; Newton, T. J. and Keenan, A. Role Stress Reexamined: An Investigation of Role Stress Predictors. *Organizational Behavior and Human Decision Processes*, 1987, *40*, 346–368.

17. Isabella, L. A. Downsizing: Survivors' Assessments. *Business Horizons*, May/June 1989, 35–41.

18. Sutton, R. I., and Rafaeli, A. Characteristics of Work Stations as Potential Occupational Stressors. *Academy of Management Journal*, 1987, *30*, 260–276.

19. Adapted from Arbose J. Expatriate Manager's Family Problems Raise a Touchy Corporate Issue. *International Management*, June 1987, 14.

20. Baron, R. A., and Byrne, D. *Social Psychology: Understanding Human Interaction*, 6th ed. Boston: Allyn and Bacon, 1991, 571–573.

21. Stewart, Do You Push Your People Too Hard?, 121.

22. Cohen, S., and Williamson, G. M. Stress and Infectious Disease in Humans. *Psychological Bulletin*, 1991, *109*, 5–24; Maes, S., Spielberger, C. D., Defares, P. B., and Sarason, I. G., (eds.). *Topics in Health Psychology*. Chichester, England: Wiley, 1988; Quick, J. C., and Quick, J. D. *Organizational Stress and Preventive Management*. New York: McGraw-Hill, 1984.

23. Allen, D. S. Less Stress, Less Litigation. *Personnel*, January 1990, 32–35; Hollis, D., and Goodson, J. Stress: The Legal and Organizational Implications. *Employee Responsibilities and Rights Journal*, 1989, *2*, 255–262.

24. Joure, S. A., Leon, J. S., Simpson, D. B., Holley, C. H., and Frye, R. L. Stress: The Pressure Cooker of Work. *Personnel Administrator*, March 1989, 92–95.

25. See, for example, Greer, C. R., and Castro, M. A. D. The Relationship between Perceived Unit Effectiveness and Occupational Stress: The Case of Purchasing Agents. *Journal of Applied Behavioral Science*, 1986, *22*, 159–175; Motowidlo, S. J., Packard, J. S., and Manning, M. R. Occupational Stress: Its Causes and Consequences for Job Performance. *Journal of Applied Psychology*, 1986, *71*, 618–629.

26. Jackson, S. E., Schwab, R. L., and Schuler, R. S. Toward an Understanding of the Burnout Phenomenon. *Journal of Applied Psychology*, 1986, *71*, 630–640; Lee, R. T., and Ashforth, B. E. On the Meaning of Maslach's Three Dimensions of Burnout. *Journal of Applied Psychology*, 1990, *75*, 743–747.

27. See, for example, Burke, R. J. Burnout in Police Work. *Group & Organization Studies*, 1987, *12*, 174–188; Russell, D. W., Altmaier, E., and Van Velzen, D. Job-Related Stress, Social Support, and Burnout among Classroom Teachers. *Journal of Applied Psychology*, 1987, *72*, 269–274.

28. Adapted from Arbose, J. Dilemma and Decision. *International Management*, July 1990, 58.

29. Niehouse, O. I. Controlling Burnout: A Leadership Guide for Managers. *Business Horizons*, July-August 1984, 81–82.

30. Anderson, C. R., Hellriegel, D., and Slocum, J. W., Jr. Managerial Response to Environmentally Induced Stress. *Academy of Management Journal*, 1977, *20*, 260–272.

31. Friedman, M., and Rosenman, R. *Type A Behavior and Your Heart*. New York: Knopf, 1974.

32. Eysenck, H. J. Health's Character. *Psychology Today*, December 1988, 28–35; Friedman, H. S., and Booth-Kewley, S. Personality, Type A Behavior and Coronary Heart Disease: The Role of Emotional Expression. *Journal of Personality and Social Psychology*, 1987, *53*, 783–792; Ganster, D. C., Schaubroeck, J., Sime, W. E., and Mayes, B. T. The Nomological Validity of the Type A Personality among Employed Adults. *Journal of Applied Psychology*, 1991, *76*, 143–168.

33. Baron and Byrne, *Social Psychology*, 606.

34. Contrada, Baum, Glass, and Friend, The Social Psychology of Health, 626–627.

35. Baron and Byrne, *Social Psychology*, 574–575; Contrada, R. J. Type A Behavior, Personality Hadiness, and Cardiovascular Responses to Stress. *Journal of Personality and Social Psychology*, 1989, *57*, 895–903; Roth, D.L., Wiebe, D.J. Fillingham, R.B., and Shay, K.A. Life Events, Fitness, Hardiness, and Health: A Simultaneous Analysis of Proposed Stress-Resistance Effects. *Journal of Personality and Social Psychology*, 1989, *57*, 136–142.

36. Bernstein, A. J., and Rozen, S. C. Dinosaur Brains and Managing Stress. *Nation's Business*, November 1989, 46–47.

37. Nelson, D. L., Quick, J. C., and Quick, J. D. Corporate Warfare: Preventing Combat Stress and Battle Fatigue. *Organizational Dynamics*, Summer 1989, 65–79.

38. Ivancevich, J. M., Matteson, M. T., Freedman, S. M., and Phillips, J. S. Worksite Stress Management Interventions. *American Psychologist*, 1990, *45*, 252–261.

39. Beehr, T. A., and Bhagat, R. S. *Human Stress and Cognition in Organizations: An Integrated Perspective*. New York: Wiley, 1985; Lee, C., Ashford, S. J., and Bobko, P. Interactive Effects of Type A Behavior and Perceived Control on Worker Performance, Job Satisfaction, and Somatic Complaints. *Academy of Management Journal*, 1990, *33*, 870–881; Tetrick, L. E., and LaRocco, J. M. Understanding Prediction and Control as Moderators of the Relationships between Perceived Stress, Satisfaction, and Psychological Well-Being. *Journal of Applied Psychology*, 1987, *72*, 538–543.

40. Gebhardt, D. L., and Crump, C. E. Employee Fitness and Wellness Programs in the Workplace. *American Psychologist*, 1990, *45*, 262–272.

41. Adapted from Roberts, M., and Harris, T. J. Wellness at Work. *Psychology Today*, May 1989, 55.

42. Gebhardt and Crump, Employee Fitness and Wellness Programs in the Workplace.

43. Company examples in this section are drawn from Roberts and Harris, Wellness at Work, 54–58.

44. Adapted from Modic, S. J. Surviving Burnout: The Malady of Our Age. *Industry Week*, February 20, 1989, 30.

45. Adapted from Muchinsky, P. M. *Psychology Applied to Work*, 3d ed. Pacific Grove, Calif.: Brooks/Cole, 1990, 556–557.

PART III

INTERPERSONAL AND GROUP PROCESSES

CHAPTER 10

DYNAMICS WITHIN GROUPS

LEARNING OBJECTIVES

When you have finished studying this chapter, you should be able to:

- Explain the tensions between group interests and individual interests.
- State the different types of groups and teams found in organizations.
- Describe the five-stages model and the punctuated equilibrium model of group development.
- Discuss seven of the major factors that can influence group behaviors and effectiveness.
- Identify and explain the six phases of effective group decision making.
- Diagnose why groups and teams may be ineffective and inefficient.
- Explain how group or team creativity can be stimulated through the nominal group technique and electronic brainstorming.

OUTLINE

310

BOEING'S TEAM DESIGN SYSTEM

There is a new way of doing things at the world's dominant aerospace company. The new 777 passenger jet may yet embody the changes Boeing has been attempting to make over the past decade. Boeing's senior managers have taken steps to assure cooperation becomes the rule, rather than the exception, in the '90s. Since the early 1980s, Boeing has pursued a grab bag of initiatives designed to replace the company's ponderous, military-style hierarchy with responsive, Japanese-style participatory management. The results have been mixed.

Expectations are running high that the 777's painstakingly laid-out team design system will do for Boeing what similar changes have done for Procter & Gamble, General Motors, Pratt & Whitney, and Champion International. These companies, and a host of others large and small, have begun replacing autocratic, turf-minded supervisors with self-regulating, cross-discipline work teams. Boeing itself has used work teams at factories in Auburn and Spokane, Washington,

and Corinth, Texas, on smaller military, computer, and space programs and in a variety of pilot projects. But until the 777 passenger jet came along, the company had avoided what is known as "organizational redevelopment" on a wide scale.

The 777 trailblazing organizational plan revolves around an intense collaboration between designers, production experts, customer-support personnel, and finance specialists. Grouped into small teams of eight or ten, they have been assigned to refine and integrate all aspects of the aircraft program. The idea is to have each team consider the aircraft as a whole and to empower each team to act quickly on ideas, free from chain-of-command second-guessing.

Computer modeling, used partially to develop the 767 and 757 jets in the late '70s, is a crucial tool. The teams have the capability, via a computer screen, to design and match up parts for the entire aircraft, minimizing the need for expensive mock-ups to see if parts fit and alterations work.[1]

Boeing is just one of many organizations that are increasingly using teams and other types of groups to make decisions, perform tasks, and accomplish goals. This chapter focuses on the factors and processes that determine whether formal groups are efficient and effective—like the self-regulating, cross-discipline work teams at Boeing—or inefficient and ineffective. There are no simple prescriptions for creating and maintaining effective *formal* groups (those specifically created by management) or *informal* groups (those that form out of the day-to-day interactions of individuals.[2]

In this chapter, we focus on ways to *diagnose* formal and informal groups and—based on the diagnosis—ways to increase their efficiency and effectiveness. We emphasize (1) the relations between individuals and groups; (2) seven major factors that affect group behaviors and effectiveness; and (3) effective group decision-making processes. As might be expected, many of the other components of decision making discussed in this book, such as leadership and interpersonal communication, contribute to the skills needed for effective management of and participation in groups.

A **group** is those persons with shared goals who communicate with one another often over a span of time and are few enough so that each person may communicate with all the others face to face, not secondhand through other people.[3] Three conditions must be met for a group to exist. First, the members are able to see and hear each other. Second, each member engages in personal communication with every other member. Third, the individuals see themselves as members of the group with shared goals.

INDIVIDUAL-GROUP RELATIONS

In a number of countries, people strongly believe in the importance and centrality of the individual. For example, in the United States and Canada, educational, governmental, and business institutions frequently proclaim that their reason for existence ultimately relates to enhancing the goals of the individual.

Individualism versus Collectivism

The cultural belief in *individualism* creates uneasiness and ambivalence over the influence that groups should have in organizational decision making and other actions. The cultural belief in *collectivism* in such countries as China and Japan seems to have the opposite effect within organizations. The use of groups is a natural extension of their cultural values. Their ambivalence and uneasiness revolves around the relative influence and assertiveness of the individual in groups. Thus, we might characterize the basic difference between individualism and collectivism in certain cultures as the tension between "fitting into the group" and "standing out within the group." Even in societies that value individualism, the actual impact of groups on individuals is substantial.[4]

Group versus Individual Interests

The potential for the group and individual members to have incompatible interests clearly exists. But these interests need not always conflict and in fact are often compatible.[5] The following observations reflect these potential conflicting and common interests:

- Groups do exist, and all employees need to take them into account.
- Groups mobilize powerful forces that produce important effects for individuals.
- Groups may produce both good and bad results.
- Groups can be managed to increase the benefits from them.[6]

The potential for conflicting group and individual interests is suggested by the free-rider concept. A **free rider** refers to a group member who obtains benefits from membership but does not bear a proportional share of the responsibility for generating the benefit.[7] Students sometimes experience the free rider problem when an instructor assigns a group project for which all of the members receive the same (group) grade. Let's assume that there are seven students in the group and that one member makes little or no contribution. This noncontributing member obtains the benefit of the group grade but does not bear a proportional share of the demands in earning the group grade.

When group members fear that one or more other members may free ride, a phenomenon known as the **sucker effect** may occur: one or more individuals in the group decide to withhold effort in the belief that others (the free riders) are planning to withhold effort. The sucker role is repulsive to many group members for three reasons. First, the free riding of others violates an equity standard: members don't want others receiving the same levels of rewards for less input or effort. Second, it violates a standard of social responsibility: everyone should do their fair share. Third, the free riding of others may violate a standard of reciprocity or exchange.[8] A group is doomed to ineffectiveness with both free riders and other members acting on the basis of the sucker effect.

GROUP TYPES AND DEVELOPMENT

In this section, we describe several types of groups that are commonly found in organizations and the development sequences that have been observed for many groups. Individuals usually belong to many types of groups, and there are numerous ways of classifying groups, depending on a person's perspective. For example, a person concerned with the degree of difficulty in gaining membership or becoming accepted as a group member might develop a classification scheme that separates groups according to whether they are *open* or *closed* to new members.

Friendship and Task Groups

A person evaluating groups in an organization according to the primary purpose they serve might find useful the classification of friendship group and task group. A **friendship group** informally evolves to serve the primary purpose of meeting its members' personal needs of security, esteem, and belonging. A **task group** is formally created by management to accomplish organizationally defined goals. The small teams of eight to ten specialists that have been formed at Boeing to develop and integrate all aspects of the 777 passenger airline program are examples of task groups. In this chapter, we focus on task groups, sometimes referred to as work groups or teams. Of course, a single group in an organization may serve both friendship and task purposes.

Interdependence in Task Groups

Task groups can be further classified on the basis of the interdependencies between group members in accomplishing some task or goal. The three basic types of task groups so identified are counteracting, coacting, and interacting.[9]

A **counteracting group** exists when members interact to resolve some type of conflict, usually through negotiation and compromise. A labor-management negotiating group illustrates a counteracting group. The representatives from management and the union usually believe that at least some of their goals conflict.

When group members perform their jobs relatively independently in the short run, a **coacting group** exists. *Relatively* and *in the short run* indicate that without interdependence over time, there would be no task group. For example, faculty members in an academic department may independently teach their courses from day to day, but they act interdependently when considering course changes or new course offerings.

An **interacting group** exists when a group cannot accomplish its goal(s) until all members have completed their share of the task or jobs. For example, the assembly team of a large luggage manufacturer consists of about ten people who perform the separate jobs required to assemble a complete piece of luggage. If one job is not undertaken, the goal—the finished suitcase—cannot be completed. Common forms of interacting groups include committees, task forces, project teams, boards, advisory councils, work crews, review panels, and the like. The idea of working in groups is no longer limited to managers and other professionals. An increasing portion of the work force is being called upon to work in a *team environment*.[10]

Types of Interacting Teams

A team environment often involves the use of one or more of the following types of interacting teams:

Problem-solving teams may consist of five to twenty-one employees, often volunteer hourly and salaried employees, drawn from different areas of a department. They may meet one to two hours a week, or as needed, to discuss ways of improving quality, productivity (efficiency), and the work environment. In some organizations, these teams are called *quality circles* (see Chapter 22). The authority of problem-solving teams to implement their ideas may range from none to limited. These teams can improve quality and reduce costs. However, they do not fundamentally reorganize work or change the role of managers. For example, teams of workers at the Philadelphia Zoo meet to suggest ways to draw more visitors.[11]

Special-purpose teams may consist of five to thirty employees, often from various departments and sometimes two organizational levels, with such tasks as designing and introducing work reforms and new technology, meeting with customers and suppliers to improve inputs or outputs, linking separate functions (marketing, finance, manufacturing, human resources) to increase product or service innovations, and establishing better links between tactical and strategic decisions and plans. These teams usually operate with a much greater degree of empowerment than problem-solving teams. They emerged during the early-to-middle 1980s and are spreading rapidly, including into unionized companies. For example, Oryx Energy Company, a Texas-based oil and gas exploration and production firm, formed twenty-six teams to come up with solutions to its poor effectiveness and low efficiency. One team worked on the destructive competition between Oryx exploration and production divisions, which had fought over new projects and capital. Today, a team with members from both units meets when needed to share information on projects and work through mutual problems.[12]

Self-managing teams normally consist of five to fifteen employees who work together on a daily basis to produce an entire good (or major identifiable component) or service. These teams typically perform a variety of managerial tasks, including work and vacation scheduling; rotation of job tasks and assignments among members; ordering materials; deciding on team leadership, which can rotate among members; setting of some team goals; and the like. Each member often learns all of the jobs and tasks that have to be performed by the team. The impacts of self-managing teams are usually enormous. They have raised productivity 30 percent or more and substantially raised quality. They fundamentally change how work is organized and empower the team members to control how they perform their jobs. One or more managerial levels are typically eliminated with the introduction of these teams, thereby creating a flatter organization. Self-managed teams began to spread rapidly in the late 1980s and appear to be the wave of the future. For example, at Volvo in Kalmar, Sweden, teams of fifteen to twenty employees assemble and install components in an unfinished automobile chassis conveyed by motorized carriers. The teams elect their own leaders and divide their tasks, but they do have production goals set by higher management to meet.[13]

Coalitions

A **coalition** is a set of individuals (or organizations) who band together to pursue a specific goal. Four key features of a coalition include: (1) it is deliberately created by the members; (2) it operates independently of the formal organization structure; (3) it is formed to achieve a specific and mutual goal(s); and (4) it requires united action by the coalition members.[14] A coalition could be as simple as ten students banding together to try to reverse a decision to deny tenure to their favorite instructor. A more complex coalition is the Organization of Petroleum Exporting Countries (OPEC). It attempts to persuade member countries to limit the supply of oil as a means of raising prices and, thus, total revenues for member countries.

Five-Stage Developmental Sequence

Some groups appear to go through a five-stage developmental sequence: forming, storming, norming, performing, and adjourning.[15] The types of task-oriented behaviors and relations-oriented (social) behaviors often observed in groups differ from stage to stage. Figure 10.1 shows the five stages on the horizontal axis, starting with the forming stage and ending with the adjourning stage. The vertical axis indicates the level of group maturity, starting with an immature state during which the group is inefficient and ineffective. Figure 10.1 also indicates that a group can fail (disband) during each stage or when moving from one stage to another. Pinpointing the developmental stage of a group at any specific time is difficult. Nevertheless, managers and members of teams must understand the developmental stages of groups because each stage can influence effectiveness. Let's con-

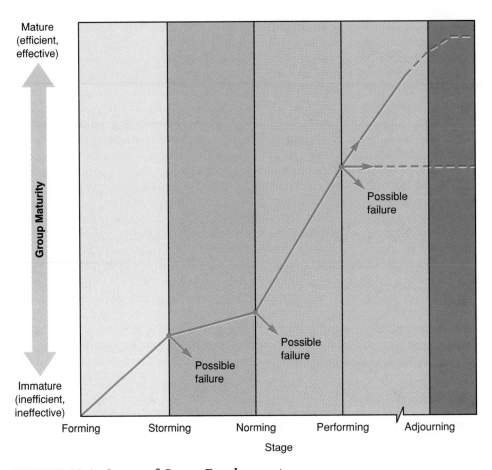

FIGURE 10.1   Stages of Group Development

Source: Adapted from B. W. Tuckman, and M. A. C. Jensen, Stages of Small-Group Development Revisited. *Group & Organization Studies,* 1977, 2, 419–442.

sider the task-oriented and relations-oriented behaviors we might find in each of these stages. As we do so, you need to realize that groups may not evolve in the straightforward manner shown in Figure 10.1. For example, time pressures from a higher authority could speed up or change the evolution of a team or other type of formal group.[16]

Forming   In the forming stage, members focus their efforts on defining goals and developing procedures for performing their task. Relations-oriented behaviors deal with member feelings and the tendency of most members to depend too much on one or two other members. Group development in this stage involves getting acquainted and understanding leadership and other member roles. In this stage, individual members might: (1) keep feelings to themselves until they know the situation; (2) act more secure than they actually feel; (3) experience confusion and uncertainty about what is expected of them; (4) be nice and polite, or at least certainly not hostile; and (5) try to size up the personal benefits relative to the personal costs of being involved in the group or team.[17]

Storming   Things get serious in the storming stage. Conflicts emerge over task behaviors, relative priorities of goals, who is to be responsible for what, and the task-related guidance and direction of the leader. Relations-oriented behaviors are a mixture of expressions of hostility and strong feelings. Competition over the leadership role and conflict over goals are dominant themes at this stage. Some members may withdraw or try to isolate themselves from the emotional tension generated. The key is to manage conflict during this stage, not to suppress it or withdraw from it. The group cannot effectively evolve into the third stage if the leader and members go to either extreme. Suppressing conflict will likely create bitterness and resentment, which will last long after members attempt to express their differences and emotions. Withdrawal can cause the group to fail more quickly.

Norming   Task-oriented behaviors in the norming stage evolve into a sharing of information, acceptance of different opinions, and positive attempts to reach mutually agreeable, or compromise, decisions on the group's goals. This is also the stage during which the group sets the rules by which it will operate. Relations-oriented behaviors focus on empathy, concern, and positive expressions of feelings leading to a group cohesion. Cooperation within the group is a dominant theme. A sense of shared responsibility for the group develops. We cover the specific impacts of norms—positive and negative—on group behaviors and effectiveness later in this chapter.

Performing   During the performing stage, the group shows how effectively and efficiently it can perform its task. The roles of individual members are accepted and understood. The members usually understand when they should work independently and when they should help each other. The two dashed lines in Figure 10.1 suggest that groups differ after the performing stage. Some groups continue to learn and develop from their experiences and new inputs. These groups will improve their efficiency and effectiveness. Other groups—especially those that developed norms not fully supportive of efficiency and effectiveness—may perform only at the level needed for their survival. A minimally adequate level of performance may be caused by excessive self-oriented behaviors by group members, the development of norms that inhibit task effectiveness and efficiency, poor group leadership, or other factors.[18]

Adjourning   The adjourning stage involves the termination of task behaviors and disengagement from relations-oriented behaviors. Some groups, such as a project team created to investigate and report on a specific problem within six months, have a well-defined point of adjournment. Other groups, such as the executive committee at Chrysler Corporation, may go on indefinitely. "Adjourning" for this type of group is more subtle and takes place when one or more key members—say, Lee Iacocca, CEO—leave the organization. The new CEO may then change the executive committee's membership.

Punctuated Equilibrium Developmental Process

The five-stage developmental sequence—forming, storming, norming, performing, and adjourning—does not apply to all groups. Some groups, particularly project teams, appear to develop through what has been called a *punctuated equilibrium process*.[19] In this process, project teams have been found to establish a framework of behavioral patterns and assumptions at their first meeting. The project team may stay with that framework through the first half of its life. The team may show little progress during this time. The members do not appear to know how to use the information they are generating until they revise the initial framework. At the calendar midpoint of the project, the team may break out of its inertia (little is getting accomplished) and experience a major transition. This transition may involve the dropping of old patterns, developing new ways to reach its goals, and even redefining (with higher management) the goals. The revised plans that come out of this transition period are not likely to be altered for the remaining life of the team.

During its final meetings, a project team is likely to exhibit the following characteristics: (1) editing and preparing materials for external use, (2) sharply increased attention to outside requirements and expectations, and (3) increased expressions by members of their positive and/or negative feelings about each other and their accomplishments. In the *punctuated equilibrium process*, the context (or environment) of the project team is especially important. Contextual influences include the goals established for the project team (easy versus difficult, short-term versus long-term, minor importance versus major importance, etc.), the degree of decision-making authority and resources granted to the project team, and so on. A contextual influence may be something as simple as a memo to the team members from the president who formed the team that states (in part): "It is imperative that your recommendations for dealing with the rights of smokers and nonsmokers in the workplace be submitted to me within two months. I know this is a complicated and emotional issue."

The developmental sequences of groups—regardless of the framework used to describe and explain them—are not easy to traverse. Failure can occur at any point in the sequence, as explicitly noted in Figure 10.1. In this and other chapters, we indicate ways in which both group members and leaders can progress through all the stages of group development. In the next section, we review the primary factors that affect group behaviors and effectiveness. These factors also further explain why there can be so much diversity between groups and within a specific group over time.

GROUP BEHAVIORS AND EFFECTIVENESS

Figure 10.2 identifies seven factors that often influence group behaviors and effectiveness. These factors, as you might expect, are interdependent. All of them need to be *diagnosed* independently and in relation to each other to gain a richer understanding of the group's behaviors and its degree of effectiveness or ineffectiveness. For example, the context of the group, such as support or threat from higher management, is likely to influence the group's goals and norms.

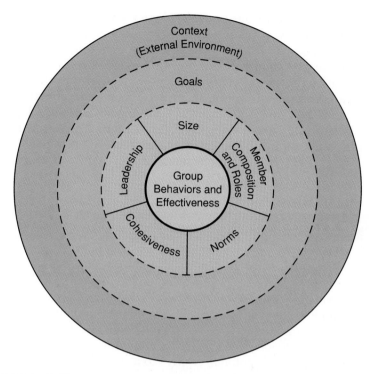

FIGURE 10.2 Influences on Group Behaviors and Effectiveness

Context

The context (external environment) can influence each of the six other factors shown in Figure 10.2, as well as directly affect the behaviors and effectiveness of a group. The group's **context** encompasses the conditions and factors outside the group that it cannot directly control. You might think of them as *givens* for group members. The group's context might include technology, physical working conditions, management practices, formal rules, higher managerial leadership, and organizational rewards and punishments.[20]

New information technology has become an increasingly important contextual force, creating changes for individuals, groups, and organizations. **Information technology** refers to the many means of assembling and electronically storing, transmitting, processing, and retrieving words, numbers, images, and sounds, as well as to the electronic means for controlling machines of all kinds—from everyday appliances to automated factories.[21] Information technology is not just computers and computer software but also communications (including telephone, video, and radio) and office equipment (such as word processors, copiers, and facsimile machines). Let's assume that management wants to introduce a technological change, such as automatically controlled machines, and turns the problem over to a problem-solving team. Through its actions, the team influences how this external technological force is introduced and assimilated into the organization. Hence, the team can influence and interact with the external environment, rather than always reacting to the external environment.

Computer-based information technologies are beginning to have a significant impact on how team and group members network with each other. These technologies are part of a concept known as **groupware:** an approach to using specialized computer aids, communication tools, and designated physical facilities that enable teams and groups to work faster, share more information, communicate more accurately, and more effectively achieve their goals.[22] The basic groupware building blocks are the telephone, the computer (with software), and the conference room. The following In Practice provides one example of how groupware has created a new context for the process of quality improvement teams at Ford Motor Company.

IN PRACTICE

FORD'S TOTAL QUALITY GROUPWARE

Ford Motor Company has developed its own groupware program to support the creation and modification of a set of quality techniques for problem identification, problem prevention, and market or vehicle planning. This groupware development effort is part of a general move by Ford into the area of "quality function deployment," the name the automaker gives to a system for translating customer demands into products.

At Ford, a team of eight to twelve people meets repeatedly in a room with a PC, a PC projection system, and perhaps an overhead projector operated by a "scribe." The participants come from varied backgrounds, such as planning, styling, marketing, product development, purchasing, manufacturing, assembly, and engineering. Specific product quality attributes are discussed and agreed upon. A graphic summary display of the quality attributes is continuously developed, discussed, and revised by the team.

A typical quality function deployment process at Ford will take three to twelve months to complete. The completed set of quality attributes includes an excellent graphic summary of the many variables considered by the team. The electronic groupware assists the team in developing the quality attributes and linking them together. More important, modifications can be made, and the overall diagram (which can become quite complex) can be redrawn quickly by the software program. Ford claims it has shorter product development cycles, fewer problems during production, and better fulfillment of consumer needs through use of the quality function deployment process. The company is now considering the possibility of making the software commercially available, or at least available to its suppliers.[23]

Throughout this chapter, we present other examples of how *context* can influence group behavior and effectiveness.

Goals

In Chapter 8, we reviewed many aspects of goals. Throughout the book, we return again and again to the concept that goals influence the effectiveness and efficiency of individuals, groups, and organizations, each of which has multiple goals. Obviously, individual and organizational goals are likely to influence the types of group goals and actual group behaviors in pursuit of these goals. **Group goals** are the end states desired for the group or team as a whole, not just those desired by each individual member.[24]

Both compatible and conflicting goals may exist within and between individuals, groups, and organizations. For example, teams typically have both relations-oriented goals and task-oriented goals. Effective teams have both types of goals, spending two-thirds or more of their time on task-oriented issues and roughly one-third or less on relations-oriented issues. The pursuit of only one or the other over the long run can reduce effectiveness and efficiency, increase conflicts, and result in dissolution of the team or group.[25] The influence of goals on group behaviors and effectiveness becomes even more complex when the possible compatibilities and conflicts among individual member goals, group goals, and organizational goals are considered. Tensions created by these complex influences and their resolution are illustrated in the following In Practice.

IN PRACTICE

TEXAS INSTRUMENTS' SELF-DIRECTED WORK TEAM

Texas Instruments's (TI) Denison, Texas, facility is piloting one of several management redesign efforts underway at the firm. Beginning in October 1988, a *self-directed work team* was formed with the electronic assemblers working on the HARM (High-Speed Antiradiation Missile) program. A *work design team* was then formed from a subset of HARM electronics assemblers and selected support personnel. The work design team attended training in work redesign taught by Michael Donovan.

As the work design team began the process of changing the existing technical system, the importance of "buy in" was learned. A barrier emerged between design team members and those assemblers not on the design team. This barrier, which was apparently caused by a lack of communication and shared goals, threatened the success of the self-directed work team pilot program. At this point, higher management felt the only solution was to put all electronic assemblers on the design team. This cumbersome solution could probably have been avoided had higher management placed more initial emphasis on timely and complete communication between work design team members and nondesign team members. Communication and shared goals at all levels are critical when implementing self-directed work teams.

Since this shaky start, the self-directed work team pilot has made strides towards becoming fully self-directed. The pilot team is responsible for filling open positions on the assembly line. It has hired from both internal and external sources. It is also responsible for the production control aspects of its project, including daily line balancing and schedules adjustments to meet customer requirements. In addition, the pilot team members approve and correct their own payroll as well as carry out many other administrative duties usually reserved for supervisors.

With the team empowered to run its project, each team member's effectiveness and self-esteem has been improved. Barbara Johnson, a HARM team member, said: "We've got a chance to make decisions now. We're excited about it. There's no way we would go back to the old way."[26]

Size

Effective group size can range from two members to a normal upper limit of sixteen members. Twelve members is probably the biggest size that enables each member to easily react and interact with every other member.[27] Table 10.1 lists some of the possible effects of group size. It shows nine dimensions of groups in three categories (leadership, members, and group process). The likely effects of group size on each of these dimensions varies from low to moderate to high. A range—"low to high," "moderate to high," and so on—suggests changes that may occur as the number of group members increases within the group size brackets (such as two to seven members). As shown in Table 10.1, members of groups of seven or less interact differently than do members in groups of thirteen to sixteen. A sixteen-member board of directors will operate differently from a board of seven members. Large boards of directors often form subgroups of five to seven members to consider specific decisions in greater depth than is possible in a meeting of the entire board.

As with all factors that can influence groups, the effects identified in Table 10.1 need to be qualified.[28] For example, adequate time and sufficient member commitment to the group's task and goals might lead to less pronounced effects for a group of eight or more members than in a hurried and less-committed group of the same size. If the group's primary task and goal were to tap the expertise of the members and to arrive at decisions based primarily on expertise rather than judgment, a larger group would not necessarily reflect the effects identified in Table 10.1.

Member Composition and Roles

Similarities or differences among individual members and the roles they prefer to assume in the group influence group behavior and effectiveness.

Problem-Solving Styles In Chapter 5, we discussed different individual problem-solving styles. Recall that we classified individuals by their preference in obtaining information from the outside world (either by sensation or intuition) and by the two basic ways of reaching a decision (either by thinking or feeling). Combining the two information-input approaches and the two decision-making approaches resulted in a model containing four basic types of problem-solving styles: sensation thinker, sensation feeler, intuitive thinker, and intuitive feeler.

The particular combination of member styles in a problem-solving group can affect its process and decisions.[29] For example, a team with three strong sensation thinkers and three intuitive feelers, all of whom are extraverts, is likely to generate more conflict and divergence of opinion than a

TABLE 10.1 Some Possible Effects of Size on Groups			
	Group Size		
Category/Dimension	*2–7* *Members*	*8–12* *Members*	*13–16* *Members*
● Leadership			
1. Demands on leader	Low	Moderate	High
2. Differences between leaders and members	Low	Low to moderate	Moderate to high
3. Direction by leader	Low	Low to moderate	Moderate to high
● Members			
4. Tolerance of direction from leader	Low to high	Moderate to high	High
5. Domination of group interaction by a few members	Low	Moderate to high	High
6. Inhibition in participation by ordinary members	Low	Moderate	High
● Group Process			
7. Formalization of rules and procedures	Low	Low to moderate	Moderate to high
8. Time required for reaching judgment decisions	Low to moderate	Moderate	Moderate to high
9. Tendency for subgroups to form within group	Low	Moderate to high	High

team consisting of members who all use the same problem-solving style. Although divergence of viewpoint may be highly desirable, it can also lead to conflict, which, if escalated, may render the team ineffective.

Managers can rarely alter the problem-solving styles of team members. Thus, they may find it more useful to try to influence the behavioral roles in the group or team. These roles can be classified as task-oriented, relations-oriented, and self-oriented.[30]

Task-Oriented Role The **task-oriented role** of members facilitates and coordinates decision-making tasks. This role can be divided into the following subroles:

- *Initiators* offer new ideas or modified ways of considering group problems or goals as well as suggest solutions to group difficulties, including new group procedures or a new group organization.
- *Information seekers* try to clarify suggestions and to obtain authoritative information and pertinent facts.
- *Information givers* offer facts or generalizations that are authoritative or relate experiences that are pertinent to the group problem.
- *Coordinators* clarify relationships among ideas and suggestions, pull ideas and suggestions together, and coordinate members' activities.

- *Evaluators* assess the group's functioning; they may evaluate or question the practicality, logic, facts, or suggestions of other members.

Relations-Oriented Role The **relations-oriented role** of members builds group-centered tasks, sentiments, and viewpoints. This role can be divided into the following subroles:

- *Encouragers* praise, agree with, and accept the ideas of others; they indicate warmth and solidarity toward other members.
- *Harmonizers* mediate intragroup conflicts and relieve tension.
- *Gatekeepers* encourage participation of others by saying such things as "Let's hear from Sue," "Why not limit the length of contributions so all can react to the problem?" and "Bill, do you agree?"
- *Standard setters* express standards for the group to achieve or apply in evaluating the quality of group processes, raise questions about group goals, and assess group movement in light of these goals.
- *Followers* go along passively and serve as friendly members.
- *Group observers* tend to stay out of the group process and give feedback on the group as if they were detached evaluators.

Self-Oriented Role The **self-oriented role** focuses only on members' individual needs, possibly at the expense of the group. This role can be divided into the following subroles:

- *Blockers* are negative, stubborn, and unreasoningly resistant; for example, they may try to repeatedly bring back an issue that the group considered carefully and intentionally rejected.
- *Recognition seekers* try to call attention to themselves; they may boast, report on personal achievements, and, in unusual ways, struggle to avoid being placed in an inferior position.
- *Dominators* try to assert authority by manipulating the group or certain individuals in the group; they may use flattery or assertion of their superior status or right to attention; and they may interrupt contributions of others.
- *Avoiders* maintain distance from others; these passive resisters try to remain insulated from interaction.

Effective problem-solving groups and teams are often composed of members who play both task-oriented and relations-oriented roles. Obviously, each individual member often performs two or more subroles. A particularly adept individual who can perform certain subroles valued by the group probably has relatively high *status*—the relative rank of an individual in the group. A group dominated by individuals who are primarily performing self-oriented subroles is likely to be ineffective.

Table 10.2 provides a questionnaire for evaluating your task-oriented, relations-oriented, and self-oriented behaviors as a group member. The scale enables you to see how often you perform each role. In sum, group

TABLE 10.2 Questionnaire for Evaluating Your Behaviors as a Group Member				
	Never	Seldom	Often	Always
Task-oriented behaviors: In a group, I . . .				
1. initiate ideas or actions.	1	2	3	4
2. facilitate the introduction of facts and information.	1	2	3	4
3. clarify issues.	1	2	3	4
4. evaluate.	1	2	3	4
5. summarize and pull together various ideas.	1	2	3	4
6. keep the group working on the task.	1	2	3	4
7. ask to see if the group is near a decision (determine consensus).	1	2	3	4
8. request further information.	1	2	3	4
Relations-oriented behaviors: In a group, I . . .				
9. support and encourage others.	1	2	3	4
10. reduce tensions.	1	2	3	4
11. harmonize (keep the peace).	1	2	3	4
12. compromise (find common ground).	1	2	3	4
13. encourage participation.	1	2	3	4
Self-oriented behaviors: In a group, I . . .				
14. express hostility.	1	2	3	4
15. seek recognition.	1	2	3	4
16. avoid involvement.	1	2	3	4
17. dominate the group.	1	2	3	4
18. nitpick.	1	2	3	4

composition and member roles greatly influence group or team behavior. Either too much or too little of certain member behaviors or roles can adversely affect group effectiveness and efficiency.[31] Scores of 24 to 32 on task-oriented behaviors, 15 to 20 on relations-oriented behaviors, and 5 to 10 on self-oriented behaviors would suggest an effective functioning group.

Work Force Diversity The growing diversity of the work force adds complexity—beyond differences in problem-solving styles and behavioral roles of individuals in groups—to understanding group behavior and processes. As we discussed in Chapter 1, the composition of the work force—and thus, teams and groups in organizations—is undergoing rapid change in terms of age, gender, and racial composition. Team and group effectiveness will be hampered to the extent that the majority-group team members have false stereotypes about the minority-group members—whether the *minority* is defined by age, gender, or race.[32] We will discuss the challenge of managing cultural diversity within organizations in Chapter 15. As suggested in the following In Practice, teams may even be used to manage diversity.

IN PRACTICE

TEAMING UP FOR DIVERSITY

Many companies rely on teams, boards, and committees to address the wide-ranging issue of work force diversity.

Digital started the concept of core groups, where employees from different backgrounds join together to form small teams that, in an ongoing way, try to work through issues of diversity and stereotypes. Digital also has teams within departments started up by members of the core groups.

Corning, Inc., which started its diversity program in 1986, has established two teams led by management committee members to focus on female and black employees. "Since both environmental and behavioral changes are necessary to remove gender and racial constraints, these quality improvement teams have very broad charters," according to Corning's Dawn M. Cross, corporate director of cultural diversity at Corning, New York. These include identifying gender and race issues; finding remedial actions; recommending funding for and guiding the development, and monitoring the implementation of diversity programs; and measuring results.

"A part of our operating philosophy is to include people with firsthand knowledge about an issue in defining the solution to that issue," Cross said. "Each team's membership consists of a diagonal slice of the organization to ensure representation by race, gender and positions."[33]

Norms

Norms are the rules and patterns of behavior that are accepted and expected by members of a group.[34] In general, norms define the kind of behaviors that group members believe are necessary to help the group reach its goals. Individuals may join groups in which many of the norms have already been established.

Norms versus Organizational Rules Norms differ from organizational rules. Managers may write and distribute organizational rules to employees in the form of manuals and memorandums, but these rules are sometimes unacceptable to and widely ignored by employees. However, norms are unwritten, and group members must accept them and behave in ways consistent with them before they can be said to exist. Some type of power or influence system must back up a norm. If a member consistently and excessively violates group norms, the other members sanction the individual in some way. Sanctions can range from physical abuse to threats to ostracism to positive inducements (rewards) for compliance. Members who consistently meet group norms receive praise, recognition, and acceptance.

Members may be only vaguely aware of some of the norms that operate in their group. These unconscious group norms should be brought to the level of conscious awareness for at least two reasons. First, awareness increases the potential for individual and group freedom and maturity. Second, norms can positively or negatively influence the effectiveness of individuals, groups, and organizations.[35] For example, group norms of minimizing and correcting defects are likely to reinforce the formal quality standards of the organization.

Relation to Group Goals A natural correspondence generally exists between group goals and group norms. That is, groups often adopt norms to help them attain their goals.[36] Moreover, some organizational development efforts are aimed at helping group members evaluate whether group norms are consistent, neutral, or conflicting in relation to group and organizational goals. (We discuss organizational development programs in Chapters 21 and 22). For example, a team may claim that one of its goals is to improve its own efficiency to meet organizational efficiency goals. Close inspection of the members' behavior might actually reveal norms counterproductive to this expressed goal, that is, norms that specify not to produce too much and not to make too many changes.

Even if team members are aware of norms like these, they may rationalize them as being necessary in order to achieve their effectiveness goal. Members may claim that producing more than the norm will "burn them out" or reduce product or service quality and result in lower long-term effectiveness. If group goals include such things as minimizing managerial influence and increasing the opportunity for social interaction among members, norms restricting employee output could be perceived as desirable by the members. Take the case of Ginny in the following account. She is socializing a new packer by telling him that packing eighty pieces is the production goal for ensuring a "fair day's work for a fair day's pay."

IN PRACTICE

EIGHTY PIECES IS FAIR

For eighteen years, Ginny has been doing about the same thing: packing expandrium fittings for shipment. She is so well practiced that she can do the job perfectly without paying the slightest attention. This, of course, leaves her free to socialize and observe the life of the company around her. Today, Ginny is breaking in a new packer.

"No, not that way, Look, Jim, if you hold it that way, well, then you have to twist your arm when you pack this corner, see. This way it's easier."

"But that's the way Mr. Wolf [the methods engineer] said we had to do it."

"Sure he did, Jim. But he's never had to do it eight hours a day like me. You just pay attention to what I say."

"But what if he comes around and says I should pack the other way?"

"Oh, that's easy. When he's here, you do it his way. Anyway, after a couple of weeks, you won't see him again. Slow down. You'll wear yourself out. No one's going to expect you to do eighty pieces for a week anyway."

"But Mr. Wolf said ninety."

"Sure he did. Let him do it. Look, here's how to pace yourself. It's the way I was taught, and it works. You know the 'Battle Hymn of the Republic'?" Ginny hums a few bars. "Well, you just work to that, hum it to yourself, use the way I showed you, and you'll be doing eighty next week."

"But what if they make me do ninety?"

"They can't. You know, you start making mistakes when you go that fast. No, eighty is right. I always say, a fair day's work for a fair day's pay."[37]

This account illustrates several things about groups in organizations. First, group norms and goals may differ from the standards or goals higher management sets for employees. Second, co-workers may have as much, if not more, influence than higher management in pressuring employees to follow certain norms and goals. Third, employees are concerned with both task-oriented and relations-oriented behaviors. In their efforts to change task-oriented behaviors, managers must consider their possible impact on relations-oriented behaviors. The failure to do so is likely to lead to group or team resistance.

Conditions for Norm Enforcement   Groups do not establish norms for every conceivable situation. They generally form and enforce norms with respect to behaviors that they believe to be particularly important. Group norms are most likely to be enforced if they:

- Aid in group survival and the provision of benefits. For instance, a group might develop a norm not to discuss individual salaries with members of other groups in the organization to avoid calling attention to pay inequities in its favor.

- Simplify or make predictable the behavior expected of group members. When colleagues go out for lunch together, there can be some awkwardness about how to split the bill at the end of the meal. A group may develop a norm that results in some highly predictable way of behaving: split the bill evenly, take turns picking up the tab, or individually pay for what each ordered.

- Help the group to avoid embarrassing interpersonal problems. Groups might develop norms about not discussing romantic involvements (so that differences in moral values do not become too obvious) or about not getting together socially in members' homes (so that differences in taste or income do not become too obvious).

- Express the central values or goals of the group and clarify what is distinctive about the group's identity. When employees of an advertising agency label the wearing of unstylish clothes as deviant behavior, they say: "We think of ourselves, personally and professionally, as trendsetters, and being fashionably dressed conveys that to our clients and our public."[38]

Conformity to Norms   Many popular writers criticize large organizations for maintaining and encouraging conformity to norms with such phrases as "It is best to keep opinions to yourself and play it safe" and "The most important thing is to appear to work hard, regardless of the results." Unfortunately, we do not have much data on the extent to which conformity to these types of norms actually exists in organizations.

The pressures to adhere to norms may result in conformity. There are two basic types of conformity: compliance and personal acceptance.[39] **Compliance conformity** occurs when a person's behavior becomes or remains similar to the group's desired behavior because of real or imagined group pressure. Many types of conformity in organizations and task groups result from compliance, even though the individuals do not necessarily believe personally in the desirability or appropriateness of the norms.

People may comply without personal acceptance for a variety of reasons. They may feel that the appearance of a united front is necessary for success in accomplishing the group's goals. On a more personal level, a person may comply in order to be liked and accepted by others. Meeting this need may apply especially to members of lower status in relation to those of higher status, such as a subordinate and a superior. Finally, someone may comply because the costs of conformity are much less than the costs of nonconformity, which could threaten the personal relationships in the group.

The second type of conformity is based on positive personal support of the group's norms. In **personal acceptance conformity,** the individual's behavior and attitudes or beliefs are consistent with the group's norms and goals. This type of conformity is, by definition, much stronger than compliance conformity. In brief, the person is a true believer in the group's goals and norms.

All of this helps to explain why some members of highly conforming groups may easily change their behavior (compliance type of conformity), whereas others may oppose changes and find them highly stressful (personal acceptance type of conformity). Without norms and reasonable conformity to them, groups would be chaotic, and few tasks could be accomplished. At the other extreme, excessive and mechanistic conformity threatens the important place claimed for the individual in certain societies, as well as the ability of groups to deal with change, uncertainty, and complex problems.

Cohesiveness

Cohesiveness is the strength of the members' desire to remain in the group and their commitment to it. It is influenced by the degree of compatibility between group goals and individual members' goals. A group whose members have a strong desire to remain in the group and personally accept its goals would be considered highly cohesive in relation to a group whose members do not.

No one-to-one relationship exists between cohesiveness and conformity, but low cohesiveness is usually associated with low conformity. However, high cohesiveness does *not* exist only in the presence of high conformity. For example, mature groups may have high member commitment and desire to stick together while simultaneously respecting and encouraging individual differences in behavior and thought. This situation is more likely when cohesion is based on a common commitment to task group goals. Moreover, in confronting complex problems, members of a cohesive group may not only tolerate but actually encourage and support moderate to high nonconformity.[40]

Relation to Groupthink   When decision-making groups are both conforming and cohesive, a phenomenon called groupthink might take place. **Groupthink** is an agreement-at-any-cost mentality that results in ineffective group decision making and poor decisions. Irving L. Janis, who coined the term *groupthink,* focused his research on high-level governmental policy groups faced with difficult problems in a complex and dynamic environment. Of course, group decision making is quite common in all types of organizations, so the possibility of groupthink exists in private-sector organizations as well as those in the public sector.

Figure 10.3 summarizes the initial conditions that are likely to lead to groupthink, its characteristics, and the types of defective decision making that will result from it. Groupthink is identified by the following characteristics:

- An *illusion of invulnerability* is shared by most or all group members, which creates excessive optimism and encourages taking extreme risks. "No one can stop us now" or "The other group has a bunch of jerks" are statements made by members suffering from an illusion of invulnerability.

- *Collective rationalization* discounts warnings that might lead group members to reconsider their assumptions before committing them-

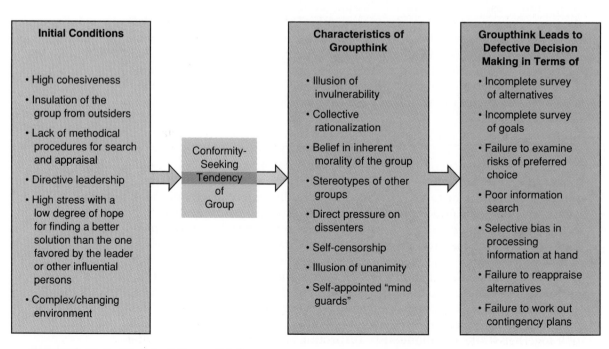

FIGURE 10.3   Model of Groupthink

selves to major policy decisions. For example, "We are confident that only a small segment of auto buyers are willing to buy Japanese-made autos." This type of statement was made by North American auto executives in the early 1970s.

- An unquestioned belief in the *group's inherent morality* leads members to ignore the ethical or moral consequences of their decisions.

- *Stereotyped views* of rivals and enemies (other groups) picture them as too evil to warrant genuine attempts to negotiate or too weak or stupid to counter whatever attempts are made to defeat their purposes.

- *Direct pressure* is exerted on any member who expresses strong arguments against any of the group's illusions, stereotypes, or commitments, making clear that such dissent is contrary to what is expected of all loyal members. The leader might say: "What's the matter? Aren't you a member of the team anymore?"

- *Self-censorship* of deviations from the apparent group consensus reflects the inclination of members to minimize the importance of their doubts and not present counterarguments. A member might think: "If everyone feels that way, my feelings must be wrong."

- A shared *illusion of unanimity* results, in part, from self-censorship and is reinforced by the false assumption that silence implies consent.

- The emergence of *self-appointed "mind-guard"* members serves to protect the group from adverse information that might shatter the shared complacency about the effectiveness and morality of their decisions.[41]

Groupthink is not inevitable, and several steps can be taken to decrease it. For example, a leader should try to remain neutral and encourage criticism and new ideas. Small subgroups or outside consultants can be used to introduce different viewpoints. People holding alternative views could be encouraged to present them.[42] We have more to say about increasing the effectiveness of decision-making groups later in this chapter.

Impact on efficiency The degree of group cohesion is important because it can affect both group effectiveness and efficiency. **Efficiency** is the relationship between the inputs consumed (labor hours and costs, raw materials, money, machines, and the like) and the outputs created (quantity and quality of goods and services). We might more appropriately think of cohesion and efficiency as potentially interdependent, particularly for teams having highly task-related goals. If the team is successful in reaching its goals, the positive feedback of its attainments may heighten member commitment. For example, a winning basketball team is more likely to be cohesive than one with a poor record, everything else being equal. Conversely, a cohesive basketball team may be more likely to win games.

On the other hand, low cohesiveness may interfere with a team's ability to obtain its goals. The reason is that members are not as likely to communicate and cooperate to the extent necessary to reach the goals. High cohesiveness in teams may actually be associated with low efficiency if team goals are contrary to organizational goals. Therefore, the relationships between cohesion and efficiency or effectiveness cannot be anticipated or understood unless the group's goals and norms are also known.[43]

Leadership

Studies of small groups in organizations have emphasized the importance of emergent, or informal, leadership in accomplishing goals. An **informal leader** is an individual who emerges over time with relatively high influence in the group. The leader's influence is usually based on a unique ability to help the group reach its goals.

Multiple Leaders   We often think of group leadership in terms of a single individual. However, since a group often has both relations-oriented and task-oriented goals, it may also have two leaders. One may provide leadership with respect to relations-oriented goals, and the other may provide leadership with respect to task-oriented goals. Achieving these two types of goals may require different personal characteristics and skills, creating a set of demands that one person may have difficulty satisfying.[44]

Informal leaders of task groups are not likely to emerge unless the formal leader ignores task-related responsibilities or lacks the necessary skills to carry them out.[45] In contrast, relations-oriented leaders of task groups are much more likely to emerge informally.

Effective Group Leaders   Virtually all the other factors affecting group behaviors and effectiveness (such as size, member composition and roles, norms, goals, and the context) are influenced greatly by an effective group leader. For example, the effective group leader often assumes a key role in the relations between the group and external groups or individuals. Also, the leader probably influences the selection of new group members. Even when the group participates in the selection process, the group leader commonly screens potential members, thereby limiting the number and range of alternatives. We have only touched on the behaviors and qualities of effective group leaders, which we discuss further in Chapter 12.

Based on the seven group factors reviewed thus far (see Figure 10.2), it is clear that the establishment of effective groups or teams is no easy task. The challenge is even greater when a group or team consists of members from different cultures and with different native tongues, which is illustrated in this chapter's Across Cultures.

EFFECTIVE GROUP DECISION MAKING

Groups face different types of tasks and experience varying degrees of member interdependency for different problems over a period of time. Both individual and group decision making can be expected in effective groups and teams. In the chapter on leadership (Chapter 12), we discuss the criteria leaders can use for deciding when to rely on (1) individual decision making,

◆ *ACROSS CULTURES*

PAN-EUROPEAN TEAMWORK

The group of managing and marketing directors from nine national subsidiaries of a large international company had gathered in a European capital city for a three-day meeting with a dual purpose. Their primary task was to draw up a pan-European marketing strategy to exploit the European Community (EC) single market. The meeting was also seen as an opportunity for the executives to learn about working within a multicultural team and to recognize how it differed from their teamwork back home. I [Robert J. Brown, director (Europe) of Moran, Stahl and Boyer, specialists in intercultural management] was one of two consultants assigned to facilitate the process and crystalize the learning.

As with many multicultural groups, the first difficulties emerged over language. The meeting was conducted in English, but not all the participants were equally fluent or confident about expressing themselves [in that language]. Not surprisingly, native English speakers dominated the early discussions, until I asked others for their ideas. This intervention, however, only exposed another cultural trait that impeded progress. Impatient with the time it took others to formulate their views, British and U.S. participants frequently interrupted the long periods of silent contemplation with even more suggestions of their own. To construct coherent arguments in a nonnative language takes time and requires concentration.

The use of only one language was the most obvious barrier to multicultural [teamwork].

As the first working session progressed, however, the comments made and ideas proposed revealed how unconscious cultural biases and corporate myths dominated the participants' thinking. French executives argued for their proposal since it was manifestly the most logical. No, said the Germans, their approach should be endorsed because it was technically superior and had a proven track record. No one gave serious consideration to the Danish proposal. The ideas produced by the Italians were seen as elegant and intriguing but impractical.

The team members made liberal use of preconceived stereotypes about the nations (cultures) they did not know. Or where they had some experience, they generalized by using one past incident to predict the behavior of the nationality (culture). [As in] groupthink, where all members of a team hone in on one powerfully argued but possibly flawed idea, this multicultural team was taking refuge in simplistic stereotypes and overgeneralizations. To address this obstacle to effective teamwork, time was taken to learn about the characteristic behavior of the nations present. Each national group had to act as informants on their own culture and heard how their cultural behavior influenced the perceptions and attitudes of others.

Many significant messages and difficult observations were delivered in jest and mimicry throughout the remainder of the three-day meeting. But all the participants acknowledged the pain of learning and the importance of more accurate perceptions in putting together a draft marketing strategy.[46]

(2) group decision making, or (3) various combinations of the two. In brief, excessive costs are incurred with the inappropriate use of either individual or group decision-making approaches. The inappropriate use of group decision making wastes organizational resources because the participants' time could have been used more effectively on other tasks, creates boredom, and results in a feeling that time is being wasted and thus reduces motiva-

TABLE 10.3   Continuum of Team Decisions

Decision Type	Degree of Team Autonomy
Team can influence its qualitative goals.	9 (Very high)
Team can influence its quantitative goals.	8
Team decides on additional tasks to undertake.	7
Team decides when it will work.	6
Team decides which methods to use.	5
Team decides on recruitment of new members.	4
Team decides on internal leadership.	3
Team members individually decide how each will perform his or her own job.	2
Team members have almost no influence on decisions about group functions.	1 (Very low)

tion. On the other hand, the inappropriate use of individual decision making can result in poor coordination, lower quality and less creativity in decision making, and more errors.[47]

Continuum of Team Decisions

As a team or group deals with decisions of increasing importance, it gains more autonomy. Table 10.3 shows examples of the types of decisions a team might make and the corresponding levels of team autonomy. Moreover, these types of decisions are cumulative. That is, a team that can decide questions of recruitment for its membership will usually be able to influence the team's internal leadership and methods used to carry out its task.

Group Decision-Making Model

Once the decision has been made that a high degree of group or team participation is appropriate and that the group or team should consider matters of important content, how should a manager proceed in order to obtain effective group decision making? A six-phase model for group decision making is shown in Table 10.4.[48] We expand on that summary in the following paragraphs. This model assumes the group or team has achieved the *performing stage* of group development (See Figure 10.1).

Phase I: Problem Definition   Group members often assume that they know what the problem is in a situation, but they may be wrong and look at only a symptom or a part of the problem. In Phase I, the group should fully explore, clarify, and define the problem. Even when the problem has been correctly identified, the group often needs to collect more detailed information to define it more sharply. Thus, a key part of problem definition is the generation and collection of information. Finally, problem definition re-

TABLE 10.4 Summary of Group Decision-Making Model	

	Phase	Activities
I.	Problem definition	Explaining the problem situation; generating information; clarifying and defining the problem
II.	Problem solution generation	Brainstorming solution alternatives; reviewing, revising, elaborating, and recombining solution ideas
III.	Ideas to actions	Evaluating alternatives; examining probable effects and comparing them with desired outcomes; revising ideas; developing a list of final action alternatives and selecting one for trial
IV.	Solution action planning	Preparing a list of action steps, with the names of people who will be responsible for each step; developing a coordination plan
V.	Solution evaluation planning	Reviewing desired outcomes and developing measures of effectiveness; creating a monitoring plan for gathering evaluation data as the solution is put into action; developing contingency plans; assigning responsibilities
VI.	Evaluation of the product and the process	Assembling evaluation data to determine the effects of actions and the effectiveness of the group's problem-solving process

Source: Reprinted by permission from W. C. Morris, and M. Sashkin, *Organizational Behavior in Action.* St. Paul: West, 1976, 3. Copyright © 1976 by West Publishing Company. All rights reserved.

quires that the group identify or recognize the goals that it is trying to achieve by solving the problem. When group members are clear about goals—which in itself can be a major problem area—they can better determine whether the problem really exists and, if it does, the relative priority that should be assigned to solving the problem.

Phase II: Problem Solution Generation Many groups tend to be more solution-oriented than problem-oriented. They often tend to choose the first or one of the first solutions suggested. Phase II prolongs the idea-generating process and discourages premature decisions. An eventual solution can be much better if many ideas and alternative solutions are considered. The more ideas generated, the more likely the group is to come up with a greater number of *good* ideas.

Phase III: Ideas to Actions In Phase III, the group evaluates ideas and comes up with a solution. Even though an idea may not work alone, it may provide a useful part of the solution. Thus, the group should take time to combine the good parts of various ideas. It then can carefully evaluate each alternative. Rather than weeding out poor alternatives (and making those who suggested them feel defensive), the group should select the best ones and concentrate on them until everyone can agree on a solution.

Phase IV: Solution Action Planning   Now that there is a solution to test, careful planning of actions to put it into operation is needed to make it work smoothly. In Phase IV, the group anticipates implementation problems, makes plans to involve those whose support will be needed, and assigns and accepts action responsibilities. Only if the group determines who is to do what and when can the agreed-on solution get a fair test.

Phase V: Solution Evaluation Planning   Unfortunately, most groups stop at Phase IV, losing the chance to learn from experience. Even if a solution is a tremendous success, a group benefits from knowing exactly what made the solution work well, so that it can be repeated when appropriate. If a solution is a total disaster, group members may feel like hiding the fact that they had anything to do with it. A group that knows exactly what went wrong can avoid making the same mistakes in the future. In real life, solutions generally work moderately well; most are neither great successes nor great failures. By keeping track of exactly what is happening, a group can make minor improvements or adjustments that will help significantly in other group problem-solving efforts. Diagnosis should not be based on guesswork or trial and error but on hard, accurate information about the effects of actions. Phase V offers the greatest potential for group learning in problem solving. In order to take advantage of this opportunity, a group must determine what kind of evaluation information is needed, who will obtain it, and when it must be collected.

Phase VI: Evaluation of the Product and the Process   When enough information has been collected to evaluate how well the solution worked, it is time for another group evaluation meeting. In Phase VI, the group can see the outcomes and whether the problem was solved. If the problem or some part of it remains, the group can recycle it by looking at the information, perhaps even redefining the problem, and coming up with new ideas or trying a previously rejected alternative. Phase VI also involves a review and evaluation of how well the group members worked together. As we suggested in the discussion of group development stages, open and constructive evaluation of the product and process usually occurs in mature groups.

Assessment   Group decision making *rarely* proceeds so neatly or systematically as suggested in the descriptions of these six phases.[49] Problem-solving groups often jump around or skip phases. However, this group decision-making model, if followed as closely as possible, should improve the effectiveness of decision making in most groups. The group decision-making model assumes that *members have expertise* and that a norm of *full participation* among members underpins the group process. The group decision-making model (Table 10.4) has been proposed for improving the effectiveness of *interacting task groups*, especially in countries like the United States and Canada.

Interacting task groups—even if operating properly—are generally more effective in phase III (ideas to actions) through phase VI (evaluation of the product and the process) than in Phases I and II. Phase I (problem definition) and II (problem solution generation) benefit from processes different from the usual face-to-face interactions. A variety of processes and procedures have been developed for improving the effectiveness of decision-making groups in addition to those suggested by the group decision-making model.[50] For example, in the last section of this chapter, we consider two aids especially designed to improve group effectiveness in Phases I and II. First, we present an account of team decision making at Compaq Computer. It reflects the practice of many of the ideas we have suggested for effective group decision making. This following In Practice is based primarily on the views of Rod Canion, the CEO and president as well as one of the founders of Compaq.

IN PRACTICE

TEAM DECISION MAKING AT COMPAQ

Compaq stresses discipline, balance, continuity, and consensus. That's the way to survive in an industry that changes as fast as ours does. There are lots of values behind these characteristics, but perhaps the most important is teamwork. That means treating other people with respect and expecting to be treated with respect. Our entire orientation toward customers and technology—and the process that brings the two together—depends on discipline and balance. Our management process is designed to meet customers' needs, use the latest technology, and—most important—get to market quickly.

Our management process is based on the concept of consensus management. The real benefit of the process is not that you get the answer but all the things you go through to get the answer. You get a lot of facts, you get a lot of people thinking, and the result is that everybody owns the decision when you get through. Originally, we used consensus management at the top to address the really tough, critical, long-term decisions. But as people participated in the process, they could see how to use it at all levels. Today it permeates the company all the way down to the manufacturing floor. When something isn't working right, the teams get together and try to figure it out.

The normal way a company works is that a team comes to the boss at the end of the process and presents its results. So if the boss has something to contribute, he or she says, "No, we really want to do it this way." Since it's the boss, he or she usually prevails. But a lot of bad things happen right there. The people feel that he's changing the decision just because he wants to or because he can. Also, the boss doesn't have all the information they do, so his critique may not even be correct.

At Compaq, the consensus process does not assume that because I'm the boss, I have the final answer. It's built around a team, and any time there's a team of people, you expect everybody to contribute in one way or another. If I'm going to contribute an idea, experience, or knowledge, the best time for me to do it is early in the process rather than at the very end. That way people don't think of it as getting my stamp of approval; they think of it as getting my contribution.

A part of the consensus process is not just coming up with the best decision that the group can make today. It's being willing to recognize when you really don't have enough information to make the right decision. So you say, "Time out, let's go get more information." And you keep doing that until you have enough information to make what the group believes is the right decision.

Another part is keeping an open mind so that people feel that it's OK to ask questions and test assumptions. In many company cultures, if you question people, they think that you're trying to shoot them down. The result is that people won't speak up. They may speak up if it's important but not if it's just a little deal. But then a lot of those little deals add up and they can end up getting you off the right track.[51]

STIMULATING GROUP CREATIVITY

The two approaches presented in this section for stimulating group creativity are the nominal group technique and electronic brainstorming.

Nominal Group Technique

The **nominal group technique (NGT)** is a structured process designed to stimulate creative group decision making where agreement is lacking or the members have incomplete knowledge concerning the nature of the problem. This technique has a special purpose: to make individual judgments essential inputs in arriving at a group decision. That is, situations are created where group members must pool their judgments in order to solve the problem and determine a satisfactory course of action. The following account illustrates what can happen when a group inadequately addresses phases I and II.

IN PRACTICE

ABSENTEEISM TASK FORCE

Robert was chairperson of a task force charged with producing fresh ideas about how to deal with a continuing absenteeism problem in one of the company's plants. He gazed dismally at the clutter left from the task force meeting just completed. It had been, he decided, an absolute disaster. As often happened, Roy had dominated much of the discussion. The meeting had ended with only a few ideas or solutions to the problem even being considered by the group. Those solutions seemed to reflect the personal opinion of Roy, rather than the thinking of the entire task force. Robert did not want to be unfair to Roy. He had to admit that Roy was a talented person who often had exciting plans and ideas—if only Robert could just get him to shut up long enough to get input from others in the group.

Gail, for instance, had tried at least twice to get the group to consider some of her ideas, but she had been shouted down on both occasions because some members seemed to think that her proposals were not feasible. "Come to think of it," Robert mused, "we were particularly critical today concerning the 'feasibility' of suggested solutions." Almost invariably, every new suggestion was greeted with a list of reasons why it would not work, could not be done, violated this or that accepted "way of doing things," and so on. "What now?" Robert wondered, "How will I get this task force off and running?"[52]

Some of the fault for the lack of progress by this task force lies with Robert. He (and his group) have committed a classical mistake in group decision making: failing to separate the idea-generating phase from the task of evaluating ideas and making a decision to implement some particular proposal. Additionally, Robert has perhaps been guilty of attempting to conduct a meeting in which both idea generation and critical evaluation are needed as though it were a "routine" meeting in which goals and techniques for achieving those goals were clear to all participants. The nominal group technique is a form of group decision making particularly well suited for situations such as this one.[53]

As a group decision-making process, NGT is most useful for (1) identifying the critical variables in a specific situation; (2) identifying key elements of a plan designed to implement a particular solution to some problem; or (3) establishing priorities with regard to problem to be addressed, goals to be attained, and so on. In all of these circumstances, aggregating individual judgments into group decisions often seems beneficial. But NGT is not particularly well suited for routine group meetings that focus primarily on task coordination or information exchange. Nor is it appropriate for the negotiating or bargaining that takes place in counteracting groups (such as a union and management bargaining committee, if each has conflicting goals).

The process of decision making using NGT consists of four distinct steps.[54] A number of useful ideas for modifying or tailoring these steps to specific group conditions have been suggested.[55]

Step 1: Generating Ideas   The first step in the process is to have group or team members generate key ideas. Each participant writes down separately his or her ideas in response to a statement of the problem, a *stimulus question*, or some other central focus of the task group. A question could be something as simple as: "What problems do you think we should consider over the next year?" followed by "Take five minutes to write some of your own ideas on the piece of paper in front of you." The generation of ideas or solutions privately by individuals while in a group setting is advantageous. This procedure avoids direct pressures resulting from status differences or competition among members to be heard. Yet it retains some of the peer and creative tension in the individual generated by the presence of others. This step and the subsequent steps provide time for thinking and reflection and avoid premature choosing among ideas.

Step 2: Recording Ideas The second step is to record, in round-robin fashion, the ideas generated in step 1 on a flip chart or other device visible to all members of the group or team. This is done by asking for, and writing down, one idea from each group member in turn. A variation is to have members submit their ideas anonymously on index cards. The process continues until the group members are satisfied that the list reflects all the ideas individually generated. This round-robin process emphasizes the equal opportunity for participation by all members and serves to avoid losing ideas considered significant by individuals. The public listing depersonalizes ideas and makes potential conflict less threatening. Group members are often impressed and pleased with the list of ideas presented, which provides momentum and enthusiasm for continuing the process.

Step 3: Clarifying Ideas During step 3, each idea on the list is discussed in turn. The purpose of this discussion is to clarify the meaning of each idea and to allow group or team members to express agreement or disagreement with any item. The intent of this phase is to present the logic and thinking behind the ideas and to reduce misunderstanding. It is *not* to win arguments concerning the relative merits of the ideas. The differences of opinion will not be resolved at this step, but rather by the voting procedure in step 4.

Step 4: Voting on Ideas A nominal group will often list at least twelve and perhaps as many as thirty ideas. There are several ways to proceed at this point. Perhaps the most common voting procedure is to have the group or team members individually select a specific number (say, five) of the ideas they believe are most important. Each person writes these five ideas on individual index cards. The group members are then asked to rank their five items in order from most to least important. The index cards are collected and the votes tabulated to produce the priority list for the meeting. An alternative to this single vote is to feed back the results of a first vote, allow time for group discussion of the results, and then to vote again. Feedback and discussion seem to result in a final decision that more closely reflects the true preferences of the group.[56]

Regardless of format, the voting procedure determines the outcome of the nominal group meeting: a group decision that incorporates the individual judgments of the participants. The procedure is designed to document the group or team decision and to provide a sense of accomplishment and closure.

Conditions for Effectiveness The potential advantages of the NGT over usual interacting group methods include greater emphasis and attention to idea generation, increased attention to each idea, and greater likelihood of balanced participation and presentation by each group member. Nominal groups may not be superior to interacting groups "when the task of problem identification is performed by persons who are both (1) aware of the existing problems and (2) willing to communicate them."[57] The nominal group technique may be most effective when there are certain blockages or problems in a group, such as a few dominating members.

Electronic Brainstorming

Brainstorming is a group process, usually done with five to twelve people, in which individuals state as many ideas as possible during a twenty- to sixty-minute period. The key guidelines for a brainstorming group include: (1) the wilder the ideas the better; (2) do not be critical of any ideas; and (3) hitchhike on or combine previously stated ideas. The suspension of judgment of ideas and the group setting was thought to generate many more and better ideas than with the same number of individuals working alone.[58] Research into the effectiveness of the brainstorming technique has not substantiated this claim. In fact, the nominal group technique (NGT) has proven to be much more effective than brainstorming as an aid for generating ideas.[59] Why might this be so?

In face-to-face brainstorming groups, people may be prevented from producing an idea and immediately producing another idea because someone else is talking. As a result, group members may get bogged down waiting for other people to finish talking. To brainstorm effectively is to think of an idea, express it, and get on with thinking of and expressing more new ideas. Electronic brainstorming may help do just that.

Electronic brainstorming is the use of computer technology to facilitate the entry and automatic dissemination of ideas in real time to all members of a group, each of whom may be stimulated to generate other ideas. GroupSystems has a software tool called *Electronic Brainstorming*. With this system, each group member has a computer terminal connected to all other terminals. The brainstorming software allows individuals to enter their ideas as they occur to them. Every time an individual enters an idea, a random set of the groups' ideas is presented on the individual's screen. The individual can continue to see new random sets of ideas at will by pressing the appropriate key.[60]

Preliminary research on electronic brainstorming is encouraging. It has been found that interacting electronic groups produce significantly more nonredundant ideas than nonelectronic groups.[61] We see considerable potential for electronic brainstorming, especially since it removes a major barrier of traditional brainstorming groups in organizations where the members can see and hear whose ideas were whose. Electronic brainstorming permits anonymity and, thus, lets members contribute more freely to idea generation. There is no need to fear "sounding like a fool" to fellow employees or supervisors in the spontaneous generation of ideas.[62]

SUMMARY

Groups are pervasive in organizations and life. With the cultural belief in individualism, there is an uneasiness over the influence and role of groups in our work and personal lives. The tensions between group and individual interests are illustrated by the free rider and sucker-effect concepts.

Groups are classified in numerous ways, depending on the classifier's perspective. In an organizational setting, useful classifications according to the group's primary purpose include friendship and task groups. Task groups, in turn, may be counteracting, coacting, or interacting. We discussed three types of interacting teams: problem-solving teams, special-purpose teams, and self-managing teams.

There are a variety of ways of understanding the developmental sequences of groups. We reviewed two of them. First, there is the five-stage developmental sequence of forming, storming, norming, performing, and adjourning. Second, there is the punctuated equilibrium process, which has been found to be representative of many project teams.

Seven major factors that affect group behaviors and effectiveness were reviewed: context, goals, size, member composition and roles, norms, cohesiveness, and leadership. Group member behavioral roles may be task-oriented, relations-oriented or self-oriented. Norms differ from rules in important ways and can be positive or negative in relation to organizational goals and effectiveness. In groups, the pressures to adhere to norms may result in conformity—either compliance conformity or personal acceptance conformity. Another factor affecting groups, cohesiveness, is related to conformity, groupthink, and efficiency. Finally, a group can operate with both formal and informal leaders.

The study of group decision-making concepts and techniques—in particular, the group decision-making model, the nominal group technique, and electronic brainstorming—can help both group members and leaders become more effective. Several themes were addressed in the discussion of group decision making: use of group decision making versus individual decision making; relationship between group processes and the relative autonomy of teams or groups; factors that should be considered in group decision making; emphasis on certain phases of group problem solving to increase the effectiveness of interacting task groups; and the nominal group technique and electronic brainstorming.

Key Words and Concepts

Brainstorming
Coacting group
Coalition
Cohesiveness
Compliance conformity
Context
Counteracting group
Efficiency
Electronic brainstorming
Free rider
Friendship group
Group
Group goals
Groupthink
Groupware

Informal leader
Information technology
Interacting group
Nominal group technique (NGT)
Norms
Personal acceptance conformity
Problem-solving teams
Relations-oriented role
Self-managing teams
Self-oriented role
Special-purpose teams
Sucker effect
Task group
Task-oriented role

Discussion Questions

1. Identify an important group of four to sixteen members that you belong to or have belonged to. Was there any evidence of the free rider or sucker-effect concepts in this group? Explain why you think the behaviors associated with these concepts were or were not present.

2. For the group identified in 1 above, at what stage of development is this group in terms of the five-stage developmental sequence (see Figure 10.1) and the punctuated equilibrium developmental process?

3. How would you assess the effects of size on that group? Did group size affect it in the ways shown in Table 10.1?

4. To what extent did that group operate as a self-managing team? How would you characterize the decision-making activities of this group in terms of the continuum of team decisions shown in Table 10.3?

5. What was the context of this group in terms of technology, organizational rules, higher managerial leadership, and organizational rewards and punishments? In what ways did the context appear to affect the group's behaviors and effectiveness?

6. What were the formal and informal goals of this group? Were the informal group goals consistent and supportive of the formal group goals? Explain.

7. Identify another group of which you are currently or have been a member. How would you describe this group as a whole in terms of task-oriented behaviors, relations-oriented behaviors, and self-oriented behaviors? Which of the behaviors seemed to contribute most to the group's effectiveness or ineffectiveness?

8. Identify three prevalent norms in a task group of which you have been a member. Did you or other group members conform to these norms on the basis of compliance or personal acceptance? Explain.

9. What are the similarities and differences between cohesiveness, conformity, and groupthink?

10. The group decision-making model (see Table 10.4) is a prescription for the step-by-step sequence by which groups should proceed. In what ways can any three of the seven factors identified in Figure 10.2 help to work for or against the implementation of any two of the phases of this model?

11. What are the similarities and differences between the nominal group technique (NGT) and electronic brainstorming?

◆ *MANAGEMENT CASES AND EXERCISES*

TEAM EFFECTIVENESS INVENTORY[63]

Instructions: Think of a group or team in which you are currently or have been a member. Please respond on the basis of your degree of agreement or disagreement with each statement. Use the following scale: strongly disagree (SD), disagree (D), undecided/neutral (U), agree (A), strongly agree (SA).

Statements	SD	D	U	A	SA
Task Performance					
1. We plan ahead for problems that might arise.	1	2	3	4	5
2. We are an effective problem-solving team.	1	2	3	4	5
3. We achieve high performance goals.	1	2	3	4	5
Influence					
4. Team members are willing to listen to and understand each other.	1	2	3	4	5
5. Members are active in influencing the future of the team.	1	2	3	4	5
6. Members are willing to disagree and make suggestions to each other.	1	2	3	4	5
Satisfaction					
7. I enjoy working with my team members.	1	2	3	4	5
8. I am able to make good use of my skills and abilities on this team.	1	2	3	4	5
9. Considering everything, it is a pleasure to be a member of this team.	1	2	3	4	5
Member Relations					
10. I trust the members of my team.	1	2	3	4	5
11. There is no free riding by members.	1	2	3	4	5
12. We are a cooperative and cohesive group.	1	2	3	4	5
Creativity					
13. Divergent ideas are encouraged.	1	2	3	4	5

14. Our norms encourage change and the exploration of new ideas.

| 1 | 2 | 3 | 4 | 5 |

15. The creative talents of member are drawn on to improve the quality and quantity of the team's outputs.

| 1 | 2 | 3 | 4 | 5 |

Interpretation: Add the point values for each scale: Task Performance = _____ ; Influence = _____ ; Satisfaction = _____ ; Member Relations = _____ ; and Creativity = _____ . Point values of 12 to 15 suggest the team is effective on that dimension, whereas point values of 3 to 8 suggest ineffectiveness. Point values of 9 to 11 suggest uncertainty and ambiguity on that dimension. Total point values for items 1 through 15 of 60 to 75 suggest a highly effective team, whereas a total score of 15 through 30 suggests a team that is probably ineffective.

ARTISAN INDUSTRIES MANAGEMENT TEAM

Part I: In mid-October, twenty-nine-year-old Bill Meister, president of Artisan Industries, had to meet with his management team to consider increasing prices. A year before, he had taken over the failing $9-million-a-year wooden gift manufacturing company from his father. It had been a hectic year, but he had arrested the slide to bankruptcy. However, much work was still needed in almost every area of the company.

The people in his office for the 11:00 meeting are described in the following paragraphs.

Bob was the thirty-year-old vice-president of finance. He had three years with the company, coming from the staff of a Big Eight accounting firm. He headed accounting and the office staff in general.

Cal was thirty-five years old and had been with the company eight years. Although he had a bachelor's degree in accounting, he had held many jobs in the company. Now he was installing a small computer system and reported to Bob.

Edith was Bill's forty-year-old sister and manager of the routine sales activity as it interfaced with the home office. The sales force was made up of independent sales representatives. Only clerical people reported to Edith. She had no college training.

Bill called the meeting to order in the presence of a management consultant who happened to be visiting to discuss other plans for improvement.

BILL: OK, we've been discussing the need for a price increase for some time now. Bob recommends increasing prices 16 percent right away. I'd like to get all of your thoughts on this. Bob?

BOB: My analysis of profit statements to date indicates that a 16 percent increase is necessary right now if we are to have any profit this year. My best estimate is that we're losing money on every order we take. We haven't raised prices in over a year and have no choice but to do so now.

CAL: I agree. What's the sense in taking orders on which we lose money?

BOB: Exactly. If we raise prices across the board immediately, we can have a profit of about three hundred thousand dollars at year end.

CAL: It would've been better to have increased prices with our price list last May or June, rather than doing it on each order here in the middle of our sales season, but we really have no choice now.

BOB: There's just no way we can put it off.

BILL (pausing, looking around the room): So, you all recommend a price increase at this time?

CAL AND BOB: Yes.

BOB: We can't wait to increase prices as new orders are written in the field or through a new price list. Right now, we already have enough of a backlog of orders accepted at the old prices and orders awaiting our acknowledgement to fill the plant until the season ends in six to eight weeks. We must only accept orders at the new prices.

CAL: If we acknowledge all the orders we have now, like that thirty-page one Edith has for $221,000, then the price change won't even be felt this year.

BOB: No, we should not acknowledge any orders at the old prices. I would hold the orders and send each customer a printed letter telling them of the price increase and asking them to reconfirm their orders with an enclosed mailer if they still want them.

CAL: Orders already acknowledged would keep the plant busy until they responded.

BILL: So, is this the best thing to do?

BOB: We're in business to make money; we'd be crazy not to raise prices!

BILL: Edith, you look unhappy. What do you think?

EDITH (shrugging): I don't know.

BOB (visibly impatient): We're losing money on every order.

EDITH: I'm just worried about trying to raise prices right in the middle of the season.

CAL: Well, if we wait, we might as well forget it.

BOB: Just what would you suggest we do, Edith?

EDITH: I don't know. (Pause.) This order (picking up the thirty-page order) took the salesman a month to work up with the customer. There are over 175 items on it, and the items must be redistributed to the customer's nine retail outlets in time for Christmas. I'm worried about it.

BOB: It's worthless to us as it is.

CAL: Look, in our letter, we can mention the inflation and that this is our first increase in a long while. Most customers will understand this. We've got to try. It's worth the risk, isn't it, Edith?
(Edith shrugs.)

BILL: What do you suggest, Edith?

EDITH: I don't know. We need the increase, but it bothers me.

BOB: Business is made of tough decisions; managers are paid to make 'em.
(All become quiet, look around the room, and finally look at Bill.)

QUESTIONS FOR PART I

1. Explain what happened at this meeting: What was each person's role? What was each person doing and trying to do? Diagram the interactions. Was it a good meeting? Why?

2. What is the decision going to be? Give all the specifics of the decision.

3. What do you think of the decision? Can you think of ways to improve upon it?

4. What would you do if you were there?

PART II: Consultant (calmly): I think Edith has raised a good point. We *are* considering making a big move right in the middle of our busy season. It will cause problems. If we can't avoid the increase, then what can we do to avoid or minimize the problems?

BOB (hostile and obviously disgusted): It would be ridiculous to put off the price increase.

CONSULTANT (calmly): That may be true, but is it being done in the best way? There are always alternatives to consider. I don't think we are doing a good job of problem solving here. (Pause.) Even with the basic idea of an increase, it can be done poorly or done well. There is room for more thought. How can it be done with the least penalty? (All are quiet as consultant looks around the team, waiting for anyone to add comments. Hearing none, she continues.) For example, by the time we mail them a letter and they think about it and mail it back, two or three weeks may pass. The price increase wouldn't take effect until the season is almost over. How can we get the increase making us money right away? And though we are bound to lose some orders, what can we do to minimize these? (She pauses to allow comments).

EDITH: Yes, that's what I meant.

CONSULTANT: On this order, for example (picking up the $221,000 order), we could call them right now and explain the situation and possibly be shipping at the higher prices this afternoon.

BOB (with no hostility and with apparent positive attitude): OK. I will call them as soon as we leave here.

CAL: We have a pile of orders awaiting acknowledgement. . . .

BOB: Right, we can get some help and pick out the bigger orders and start calling them this afternoon.

CONSULTANT: How about involving the sales force?

EDITH: Yes, the salespeople know the customers best. We should call them to contact the customer. They got the order and know the customer's needs. But we will have to convince the salespeople of the necessity for the increase. I can start getting in touch with them by phone right away.

BOB: OK, we can handle the bigger orders personally by phone and use the letter on the small ones.

CONSULTANT: What do you think about making them act to keep the order? Why not make it so no action keeps the order. Tell them that we are saving their place in our shipping schedule and will go ahead and ship if they don't contact us in five to seven days. Is it best to put the control in their hands?

EDITH: That bothered me. Increasing the price is serious, and we need to handle it carefully if it's to work. I think most people will go ahead and accept the merchandise.

BOB: Edith and I can get together this afternoon on the letter. (All become silent again.)

BILL: OK, can you all get started after lunch? Let's meet in the morning to see how it's going.[64]

QUESTIONS FOR PART II

1. What do you think of the decision now? Is it improved? Why might you call the first decision "suboptimal"?

2. Would the team have made the new decision without help? Why?

3. It can be said that initially, the team was not involved in problem solving. Why?

4. What did the consultant see that had to be done with the team? How could she do it? Did the consultant want to make the decisions herself? Could Bill have taken this role?

5. What does this incident say about the management team and the work environment at Artisan? What should and could be done about it?

6. What does this case illustrate about group problem solving? About communication?

References

1. Adapted from Acohido, B. Boeing Workforce Tries New Direction. *Dallas Morning News*, May 5, 1991, 8H; Jones-Yang, D. How Boeing Does It. *Business Week*, July 9, 1990, 46–50.

2. Worchel, S., Wood, W., and Simpson, J. A. (eds.). *Group Process and Productivity*. Newbury Park, Calif.: Sage, 1991; Smith, K. K., and Berg. D. N. *Paradoxes of Group Life*. San Francisco: Jossey-Bass, 1987.

3. Homans, G. C. *The Human Group*. New York: Harcourt, Brace and World, 1959, 2. Also see Miller, J. Living Systems: The Group. *Behavioral Science*, 1971, *16*, 302–398.

4. Hofstede, G., Neuijen, B., Ohayv, D. D., and Sanders, G. Measuring Organizational Cultures: A Qualitative and Quantitative Study across Twenty Cases. *Administrative Science Quarterly*, 1990, *35*, 286–316.

5. Mitchell, T. R., and Scott, W. G. America's Problems and Needed Reforms: Confronting the Ethic of Personal Advantage. *Academy of Management Executive*, vol. 4, August 1990, 23–35.

6. Zander, A. *The Purpose of Groups and Organizations*. San Francisco: Jossey-Bass, 1985.

7. Albanese, R., and Van Fleet, D. D. Rational Behavior in Groups: The Free-Riding Tendency. *Academy of Management Review*, 1985, *10*, 244–255.

8. Schnake, M. E. Equity in Effort: The "Sucker Effect" in Co-Acting Groups. *Journal of Management*, 1991, *17*, 41–55.

9. Fiedler, F. E. *A Theory of Leadership Effectiveness*. New York: McGraw-Hill, 1967.

10. Hirchhorn, L. *Managing in the New Team Environment*. Reading, Mass.: Addison-Wesley, 1991.

11. Hoer, J. The Payoff from Teamwork. *Business Week*, July 10, 1989, 56–62.

12. Mack, T. Energizing a Bureaucracy. *Forbes*, September 17, 1990, 16–80.

13. Sundstrom, E., DeMeuse, K P., and Futrell, D. Work Teams: Applications and Effectiveness. *American Psychologist*, 1990, *45*, 120–133.

14. Stevenson, W. B., Pearce, J. L., and Porter, L. W. The Concept of "Coalition" in Organization The-

ory and Research. *Academy of Management Review,* 1985, *10,* 256–268.

15. Tuckman, B. W. Development Sequence in Small Groups. *Psychological Bulletin,* 1965, *63,* 384–399; Tuckman, B. W., and Jensen, M. A. C. Stages of Small Group Development Revisited. *Group and Organization Studies,* 1977, *2,* 419–427; Obert, S. L. Developmental Patterns of Organizational Task Groups: A Preliminary Study. *Human Relations,* 1983, *36,* 37–52.

16. Kormanski, C. A Situational Leadership Approach to Groups Using the Tuckman Model of Group Development. In L. D. Goodstein and J. W. Pfeiffer (eds.), *The 1985 Annual: Developing Human Resources.* San Diego: University Associates, 1985, 217–226; Gersick, C. J. Time and Transition in Work Teams: Toward a New Model of Group Development. *Academy of Management Journal,* 1988, *31,* 9–41.

17. Napier, R. W., and Gershenfeld, M. K. *Groups: Theory and Experience,* 3d ed. Boston: Houghton Mifflin, 1985, 459–460.

18. Staw, B. M. *Psychological Dimensions of Organizational Behavior.* New York: Macmillan, 1991.

19. Gersick, C. J. G. Time and Transition in Work Teams: Toward a New Model of Group Development. *Academy of Management Journal,* 1988, *31,* 9–41; Gersick, C. J. G. Revolutionary Change Theories: A Multilevel Exploration of the Punctuated Equilibrium Paradigm. *Academy of Management Review,* 1991, *16,* 10–36.

20. Davis, T. R. The Influence of the Physical Environment in Offices. *Academy of Management Review,* 1984, *9,* 171–183; Fry, L. W., and Slocum, J. W., Jr. Technology, Structure, and Workgroup Effectiveness: A Test of a Contingency Model. *Academy of Management Journal,* 1984, *27,* 211–246.

21. Gerstein, M. S. *The Technology Connection.* Reading, Mass.: Addison-Wesley, 1987, 5.

22. Johansen, R. *Groupware: Computer Support for Business Teams.* New York: Free Press, 1988.

23. Adapted from Johansen, R. et al. *Leading Business Teams: How Teams Can Use Technology and Group Process Tools to Enhance Performance.* Reading, Mass.: Addison-Wesley, 1991, 67–70.

24. Mackie, D. M., and Goethals, G. R. Individual and Group Goals. In C. Hendrick (ed.). *Group Processes.* Newbury Park, Calif.: Sage, 1987, 144–166.

25. Sneizek, J. A., May, D. R., and Sawyer, J. E. Social Uncertainty and Interdependence: A Study of Resource Allocation Decisions in Groups. *Organizational Behavior and Human Decision Processes,* 1990, *46,* 155–180.

26. Adapted from White, A. F. SDWT Pilot at TI Denison: Communication Is Key. In M. Beyerlein (ed.), *Self-Managed Work Teams Newsletter.* Denton, Texas: University of North Texas, February 1991, 4.

27. Berelson, B., and Steiner, G. A. *Human Behavior: An Inventory of Scientific Findings.* New York: Harcourt, Brace and World, 1964, 356–360.

28. Stoneman, K. G., and Dickinson, A. M. Individual Performance as a Function of Group Contingencies and Group Size. *Journal of Organizational Behavior Management,* 1989, *10,* 131–150; Hare, A. P. Group Size. *American Behavioral Scientist,* 1981, *24,* 695–708.

29. Driskill, J. E., Hogan, R., and Salas, E. Personality and Group Performance. In C. Hendrick (ed.), *Group Processes and Intergroup Relations.* Newbury Park, Calif.: Sage, 1987, 91–112.

30. Hoffman, L. R. Applying Experimental Research on Group Problem Solving to Organizations. *Journal of Applied Behavioral Science,* 1979, *15,* 375–391.

31. Bales, R. F. *Personality and Interpersonal Behavior.* New York: Holt, Rinehart, and Winston, 1970; Lustig, M. W. Bales' Interpersonal Rating Forms: Reliability and Dimensionality. *Small Group Behavior,* 1987, *18,* 99–107.

32. Falkenberg, L. Improving the Accuracy of Stereotypes within the Workplace. *Journal of Management,* 1990, *16,* 107–118; Gutek, B. A., Cohen A. G., and Konrad, A. M. Predicting Social-Sexual Behavior at Work: A Contact Hypothesis. *Academy of Management Journal,* 1990, *33,* 560–577.

33. Adapted from Overman, S. Managing the Diverse Workforce. *HR Magazine,* April 1991, 32–36; Alexander, K. L. Both Racism and Sexism Block the Path to Management for Minority Women. *Wall Street Journal,* July 25, 1990, B1, B4.

34. Bettenhausen, K. L., and Murnighan, J. K. The Development of an Intragroup Norm and the Effects of Interpersonal and Structural Changes. *Administrative Science Quarterly,* 1991, *36,* 20–35.

35. Harvey, J. B. *The Abilene Paradox and Other Mediations on Management.* Lexington, Mass.: D. C. Heath, 1988; Pearce, J. L., and Peters, R. H. A Contradictory Norms View of Employer-Employee Exchange. *Journal of Management,* 1985, *11,* 19–30.

36. Roethlisberger, F. J., and Dickson, W. J. *Management and the Worker: Technical versus Social Organization in an Industrial Plant.* Cambridge: Harvard University Press, 1939.

37. Reprinted and adapted with permission from Ritti, R. Richard, and Funhouser, G. Ray. *The Ropes to Skip and the Ropes to Know.* Columbus, Ohio: Grid Publishing, 1977, 188–189.

38. Feldman, D. C. The Development and Enforcement of Group Norms. *Academy of Management Review,* 1984, *9,* 47–53. Also see Spich, R. S., and Keleman, R. S. Explicit Norm Structuring Process: A Strategy for Increasing Task-Group Effectiveness. *Group and Organization Studies,* 1985, *10,* 37–59.

39. Kiesler, C. A., and Kiesler, S. B. *Conformity.* Reading, Mass.: Addison-Wesley, 1969; Kahn, W. A. Psychological Conditions of Personal Engagement and Disengagement at Work. *Academy of Management Journal,* 1990, *33,* 692–724.

40. Galem, S., and Moscovici, S. Toward a Theory of Collective Phenomena: Consensus and Attitude Changes in Groups. *European Journal of Social*

Psychology, 1991, *21,* 49–74; Cosier, R. A., and Schwenk, C. R. Agreement and Thinking Alike: Ingredients for Poor Decisions. *Academy of Management Executive,* February 1990, 69–74.

41. Janis, I. L. *Victims of Groupthink: A Psychological Study of Foreign Policy Decisions and Fiascos.* Boston: Houghton Mifflin, 1972; Janis, I. L. *Groupthink,* 2d ed. Boston: Houghton Mifflin, 1982. For a study that questions the relation between groupthink and high cohesiveness, see Leana, C. R. A Partial Test of Janis' Groupthink Model: Effects of Group Cohesiveness and Leader Behavior on Defective Decision Making. *Journal of Management,* 1985, *11,* 5–17; Posner-Weber, C. Update on Groupthink. *Small Group Behavior,* 1987, *18,* 118–125.

42. Whyte, G. Groupthink Reconsidered. *Academy of Management Review,* 1989, *14,* 40–56; Hogg, M. A., Turner, J. C., and Davidson, B. Polarized Norms and Social Frames of Reference: A Test of the Self-Categorization Theory of Group Polarization. *Basic and Applied Social Psychology,* 1990, *11,* 77–100.

43. Schaffer, R. H. Demand Better Results—and Get Them. *Harvard Business Review,* March-April 1991, 142–149; Keller, R. T. Predictors of the Performance of Project Groups in R&D Organizations. *Academy of Management Journal,* 1986, *29,* 715–726.

44. Bales, R. F. *Interaction Process Analysis.* Reading, Mass.: Addison-Wesley, 1950; Stayer, R. How I Learned to Let My Workers Lead. *Harvard Business Review,* November-December 1990, 66–69, 72, 74, 76, 80, 82, 83.

45. Larson, C. E., and Lafasto, F. M. J. *Teamwork: What Must Go Wrong/What Can Go Wrong.* Newbury Park, Calif.: Sage, 1989.

46. Adapted from Brown, R. J. Pan-European Teamwork. *International Management.* August 1990, 61. Used with permission.

47. Kinlaw, D. C. *Developing Superior Work Teams: Building Quality and the Competitive Edge.* Lexington, Mass.: Lexington Books, 1991; Cook, R. A., and Kernagan, J. A. Estimating the Difference between Group versus Individual Performance on Problem-Solving Tasks. *Group and Organization Studies,* 1987, *12,* 319–342.

48. Morris, W. C., and Sashkin, M. *Organization Behavior in Action: Skill Building Experiences.* St. Paul: West, 1976.

49. Trist, E., and Murray, H. (Eds.) *The Social Engagement of Social Science: A Tavistock Anthology,* vol. I. Philadelphia, PA: University of Pennsylvania Press, 1990.

50. Cummings, L. L., and Staw, B. M. (Eds.). *Leadership, Participation, and Group Behavior.* Greenwich, Conn.: JAI Press, 1990; Brightman, H. J. *Group Problem Solving: An Improved Managerial Approach.* Atlanta: University of Georgia College of Business Administration, 1988.

51. Adapted from Webber, A. M. Consensus, Continuity, and Common Sense: An Interview with Compaq's Rod Canion. *Harvard Business Review,* July-August 1990, 115–123.

52. Adapted from Woodman, R. W. Use of the Nominal Group Technique for Idea Generation and Decision Making. *Texas Business Executive,* Sprig 1981, 50. Also see Peters, T. Get Innovative or Get Dead. *California Management Review,* Winter 1991, 9–23.

53. Major portions of this discussion for the nominal group technique are excepted from Woodman, R. W. Use of the Nominal Group Technique for Idea Generation and Decision Making. *Texas Business Executive,* Spring 1981, 50–53.

54. Delbecq, A. L., Van de Ven, A. H., and Gustafson, D. H. *Group Techniques for Program Planning: A Guide to Nominal and Delphi Processes.* Glenview, Ill.: Scott, Foresman, 1975.

55. Fox, W. M. *Effective Group Problem Solving.* San Francisco: Jossey-Bass, 1987; Bartunek, J. M., and Murninghan, J. K. The Nominal Group Technique: Expanding the Basic Procedure and Underlying Assumptions. *Group and Organization Studies,* 1984, *9,* 417–432; Burton, G. E. The "Clustering Effect": An Idea-Generation Phenomenon during Nominal Grouping. *Small Group Behavior,* 1987, *18,* 224–238.

56. Huber, G. P., and Delbecq, A. L. Guidelines for Combining the Judgments of Individual Group Members in Decision Conferences. *Academy of Management Journal,* 1972, *15,* 161–174.

57. Green, T. B. An Empirical Analysis of Nominal and Interacting Groups. *Academy of Management Journal,* 1975, *18,* 63–73.

58. Osborn, A. F. *Applied Imagination* (rev. ed.). New York: Scribner, 1957.

59. Diehl, M., and Strobe, W. Productivity Loss in Brainstorming Groups: Toward the Solution of the Riddle. *Journal of Personality and Social Psychology,* 1987, *53,* 497–509.

60. Gallupe, R. B., Bastianutti, L. M., and Cooper, W. H. Unblocking Brainstorms. *Journal of Applied Psychology,* 1991, *76,* 137–142.

61. *Ibid.*

62. Jessup, L M., Connolly, T., and Gelegher, J. The Effects of Anonymity on GDSS Group Process with an Idea-Generating Task. *MIS Quarterly,* September 1990, 313–321.

63. Developed from Kaplan, I. T. Measuring Work Group Effectiveness: A Comparison of Three Instruments. *Management Communication Quarterly,* 1989, *2,* 424–448; Friedlander, F. Performance and Interactional Dimensions of Organizational Work Groups. *Journal of Applied Psychology,* 1966, *50,* 257–265; Wilson Learning Corporation, *Team Interaction Profile Is Valid and Reliable.* Eden Prairie, Minn.: Wilson Learning Corporation, 1988; Honeywell, Inc. *Job Reaction Questionnaire User's Guide.* Minneapolis: Honeywell, Inc., 1985.

64. Prepared by and adapted with permission from F. C. Barnes, associate professor, University of North Carolina at Charlotte (presented at Southern Case Research Association).

CHAPTER 11

DYNAMICS BETWEEN GROUPS

LEARNING OBJECTIVES

When you have finished studying this chapter, you should be able to:

- Describe the impact of intergroup relations on organizational effectiveness.
- Explain how each of six major factors can affect intergroup behaviors and effectiveness.
- Diagnose the causes of cooperative versus competitive relations between two or more groups.
- Explain how winning or losing in intergroup competition can affect the dynamics within a group.
- Describe seven approaches that can be used to create effective intergroup dynamics.

OUTLINE

MANAGING WORK FORCE DIVERSITY AT BARDEN

Radical changes in work force demographics mean that organizations need to develop knowledge and an understanding of how to manage a diverse work force that includes larger percentages of African-Americans, Hispanics, Asians, and women. Organizations are also finding it necessary to design programs to manage the diversity of groups with different language skills. This is illustrated in the views of Donald Brush, vice-president and general manager of Barden, a precision ball bearing manufacturer in Danbury, Connecticut.

A couple of years ago, Barden had an opportunity to significantly increase its business. In order to achieve its goals, Barden needed to increase the hourly work force by about 125 employees (over and above normal turnover, retirements, etc.) in one year. The human resources department tested the waters, recognizing that unemployment in the Danbury labor market had reached an unprecedented low of about 2.5 percent. The answer that came back was a qualified yes. That is, Barden could find these workers by using imagination (e.g., bounties to employees for successful referrals and imaginative publicity, such as an open house) and by recruiting people whose English was very poor. By recruiting these individuals, Barden was able to achieve its goal in about six months' time—twice as fast as its original target. The firm already had some experience with such workers. In recent years, it had realized that Portuguese immigrants, for example, became very reliable, long-term employees, so Barden had used a buddy system to help these employees learn their jobs and to acquire a modest "Barden" vocabulary.

During this latest recruiting push, Barden found a significant pool of bright potential employees who spoke little or no English. The buddy system, however, was wholly inadequate to deal with this veritable United Nations, since these people were from such countries as Cambodia, Laos, Colombia, Brazil, the Dominican Republic, Guatemala, Chile, Lebanon, Pakistan, Thailand, and Yemen.

To begin to be qualified Barden employees, newcomers must master the basic "Barden" vocabulary and be able to read standard operating procedures as well as material safety data sheets. They also must master basic shop mathematics, measurement processes, and blueprint reading. This is a tall order for the immigrants, even though many had received good educations in their home countries.

The human resources department investigated how Barden might teach these people enough English to become productive employees. The upshot was that Barden retained Berlitz for language training. A special, intensive course was developed in cooperation with the human resources department's training unit. Barden has educated many groups of eight members each. All students are on the payroll; they meet with a Berlitz instructor for four hours a day for fifteen consecutive work days during working hours. The effect has been electric. The confidence level of the students has soared as they have tried out their new language ability. Supervisors are impressed. And the word has gotten out in the community with positive results.[1]

$\mathbf{T}$he Preview Case demonstrates how the increasing diversity of individuals coming into organizations creates new requirements for collaboration between groups within the organization. This program is working effectively because of support and collaboration among the following groups at Barden: the top management team, the human resources department (especially the training unit), the production supervisors as a group, and the different groups of employees receiving the training. These groups were motivated to work together because their goals were compatible and mutually reinforcing: (1) to respond to the opportunity for new business, management had to increase the work force by 125 employees in a very tight labor market; and (2) the new and diverse employee groups needed English language skills to achieve better economic and employment opportunities. Of course, this Preview Case also illustrates how factors in the external environment—in this instance, scarcity of labor in the Danbury area—can trigger changes within the organization.

The ability to diagnose and understand intergroup relations is important to most employees because (1) groups often must work with and through other groups to accomplish their goals;(2) other groups within the organization often create problems and demands on one's own group; and (3) the quality of the dynamics between groups can affect the degree of organizational effectiveness.

In this chapter, we discuss the dynamics between groups of various sizes. The meaning of *group* in this chapter goes beyond our Chapter 10 definition of groups, which involved face-to-face relations. In this chapter, a group may refer to: (1) the many types of groups identified in Chapter 10, (2) a department (such as the human resources department at Barden), (3) a formal classification of employees (such as the supervisors at Barden), and (4) various other classifications that may be formed on the basis of common attributes or goals (race, gender, religion, occupation, educational background, language skills, and so on).[2] Groups need not always be a part of the formal organizational structure. In considering intergroup dynamics, the concept of coalition is especially useful. In Chapter 10, we defined a *coalition* as a set of individuals or groups that band together to pursue a specific goal. Coalitions can form on the basis of the various attributes noted above or a specific issue.

We begin this chapter by presenting six basic factors that often influence intergroup dynamics. Then we discuss seven approaches that independently— or in combination with the other approaches—can be used to create effective intergroup dynamics. Although we consider some aspects of intergroup conflict in this chapter, we deal much more extensively with it in Chapter 14.

KEY INFLUENCES ON INTERGROUP DYNAMICS AND EFFECTIVENESS

Six key factors may influence the behaviors and effectiveness in intergroup relations. Figure 11.1 identifies these factors as: uncertainty, goals, substitutability, task relations, resource sharing, and attitudinal sets. The potential influence of all six factors and their interactions should be diagnosed to obtain a complete understanding of intergroup dynamics. As suggested in

Figure 11.1, the degree of uncertainty and the nature of group goals are fundamental to a diagnosis of any set of intergroup relations. These should be assessed to properly interpret the influence of the other four factors.

Uncertainty

In its most basic sense, **uncertainty** is the inability to predict something accurately.[3] Individuals and groups in organizations are often concerned with three types of perceived uncertainty: state, effect, and response.

- **State uncertainty** means that an individual, group, or organization does not understand how factors of its environment might change. Uncertainty about whether a labor union will call a strike, whether top management will sell the division for which you work, and whether competitors will react in a certain way if deregulation takes place are examples of state uncertainty.

- **Effect uncertainty** is the inability to predict the impact of a future state of the environment on the individual, group, or organization. Effect uncertainty is a lack of understanding of cause-effect relationships. For example, let's assume there was little uncertainty that the union will strike or top management will sell the division for which you work. There could still be uncertainty as to the *effect* (impact) of such a strike or sale of the division on your work team.

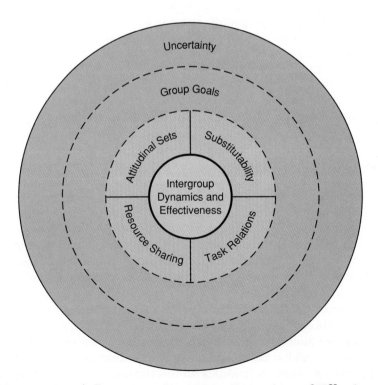

FIGURE 11.1   Key-Influences on Intergroup Dynamics and Effectiveness

- **Response uncertainty** is a lack of knowledge of alternatives and/or the inability to predict the likely consequences of alternatives.[4] Top management may experience response uncertainty over how to deal with a strike by the union. Or, when the Southland Corporation (which operates 7-Eleven stores) cut its management and staff employees, many of them experienced response uncertainty about their career alternatives.

One way of managing these types of uncertainty involves assigning particular groups or individuals to deal with them. Thus, individuals or groups may absorb particular types of uncertainty for others in the organization. **Uncertainty absorption** occurs when one group makes particular decisions for another group or sets the decision-making premises for another group.[5] In the Preview Case, the Barden human resources department absorbed *state uncertainty* for higher management as to whether it would be possible to recruit 125 employees in the local labor market as well as *response uncertainty* in terms of how to achieve the goal of 125 new employees.

Effects on Group Power   Uncertainty and uncertainty absorption often have an important impact on the relative power of groups. Power has three major dimensions: weight, domain, and scope.[6] The *weight* of a group's power is the degree to which it can affect the behavior of another group. The *domain* of a group's power is the number of other groups it can affect. The *scope* of a group's power is the range of behaviors or decisions that the group can determine for another group. An accounting department has a heavy weight with respect to expense account procedures. Its domain in expense account matters is relatively encompassing, affecting virtually all members of the organization. Finally, the scope of behaviors affected in marketing, for example, by these procedures is probably small, relative to marketing's important behaviors and goals. We discuss the sources of power in organizations—as well as the relationships of individual and group power to decision making, information, and resources—in Chapter 16.

Relation to Technical Expertise   The technical expertise of one group relative to others strongly influences the process of uncertainty absorption.[7] The human resources department in the Preview Case absorbed technical uncertainties for the top management group and the supervisory group with respect to (1) how to determine if potential employees would be available from the Danbury labor market and (2) how to train the diverse employees recruited to make them productive. The impact of technical expertise on uncertainty absorption and the amount of power it gives one group relative to others is normally limited to specific areas of knowledge and skills.

Significance to Organizations   Uncertainty absorption by groups is important for three reasons. First, uncertainty absorption requires top managers to decide which groups will have the authority to make decisions that affect others. Second, uncertainty absorption influences the relative power of various groups—and individuals within those groups—in organizations. These power differences can be an important factor in understanding conflicts and other intergroup problems. Third, uncertainty absorption requires top managers to make sure that the uncertainties being absorbed by groups are consistent with their knowledge and expertise.

The following In Practice describes how wrenching environmental changes created uncertainties within and between groups in a production plant in the Netherlands.

THREATS TO THE STATUS QUO AT TKB

TKB is a sixty-year-old chemical production plant in the Netherlands. Many of its employees are old-timers. Stories about the past abound. Workers tell about how heavy the jobs used to be when loading and unloading was done by hand. They tell about heat and physical risk. TKB used to be seen as a rich employer. For several decades, the demand for its products exceeded the supply and money was made very easily. Products were not sold but distributed. Customers had to be nice and polite in order to be served. TKB's management style used to be paternalistic. The old general manager made his daily morning walk through the plant, shaking hands with everyone he met. This, people say, was the start of a tradition that still exists today of shaking hands with one's co-workers in the morning.

The working atmosphere was good-natured with a lot of freedom left to employees and work groups. The plant has been pictured as a club, a village, a family. Twenty-fifth and fortieth anniversaries are given lots of attention; the plant's holiday season parties are famous. These celebrations are rituals with a long history that people still value. In TKB's culture, or, as people express it, in "the TKB way," unwritten rules for social behavior are very important. One does not live in order to work, one works in order to live. What one does counts less than how one does it. One has to fit into the informal network, and this holds for all organizational levels. "Fitting in" means avoiding conflicts and direct confrontations, covering other people's mistakes, and exhibiting loyalty, friendliness, modesty, and good-natured cooperation.

This picture, however, has recently been disturbed by outside influences. First, market conditions changed. TKB found itself in an unfamiliar competitive situation with other European suppliers. Costs had to be cut and manpower reduced. In the TKB tradition, this problem was resolved, without layoffs, through early retirements. However, the old-timers who had to retire early were shocked that the company did not need them anymore. Second, TKB has been severely attacked by environmentalists because of its pollution, a criticism that has received growing support in political circles. It is not impossible that the licenses necessary for TKB's operation will one day be withdrawn. TKB's management has tried to counter this problem with an active lobbying effort with the authorities, with a press campaign, and through organizing public visits to the company, but its success is by no means certain.

Inside TKB, these threats are downplayed. People are reluctant to imagine that one day there may be no more TKB. "Our management has always found a solution. There will be a solution now." But the anxieties and uncertainties are barely below the surface. In the meantime, attempts are being made to increase TKB's competitiveness through quality improvement and product diversification. These also imply the introduction of new people from the outside. These new trends, however, clash with TKB's traditional culture, including the warm and personal relationships within and between groups.[8]

Group Goals

Group goals can have a powerful effect on intergroup dynamics. Like individuals, groups use goals to reveal their preferences.[9] An ideal state exists in an organization when each group views its goals, the goals of the entire organization, and the goals of other groups as compatible and mutually reinforcing. This is a win-win situation. Each group can attain its goals if the other groups achieve theirs. The Preview Case clearly demonstrated a win-win situation for the many groups involved with recruiting, training, and orienting the new, diverse groups of employees. In this situation, we usually find free-flowing communication, cooperation, mutual concern, respect for each other's problems, and rapid problem solving between groups. However, employees and groups do not always perceive goals to be compatible and mutually reinforcing.

Goal Conflict   When one group's goals are viewed by one or more other groups as preventing them from attaining most or all of their goals, **goal conflict** occurs. Widespread goal incompatibility, that is, a win-lose situation, is unlikely to occur within an organization. A win-lose situation does exist, however, when one group attains its goals at the direct expense of another group. On occasion, confrontation between a union and management takes on the characteristics of an extreme win-lose situation, particularly during bitter strikes. This situation may include expressions of hostility, some physical violence and property damage, unwillingness of the parties to listen to one another or to compromise, and the like. One example of goal conflict was the strike that took place between Eastern Airlines and its unions. Their lengthy intergroup conflicts are considered to be one of the major factors that led to the failure and dissolution of Eastern Airlines in 1991.[10]

Mixed Goal Conflict   Goal conflict between groups is more often *mixed* than a total win-lose situation. Mixed goal conflict often serves as a basis for creating coalitions in organizations.[11] Let's consider briefly an example of a coalition's potential power. Several years ago, an executive of one of the divisions of Dresser Industries, a supplier of tools and equipment for oil and gas drilling, issued a memorandum to the eight thousand employees in his division forbidding women to wear slacks at work. At that time, the division had centralized computer operations. In response to that memo, twenty-eight women who operated the centralized computer system walked off the job. The entire division needed daily information and reports from the computer center. Only the women knew how to operate it. This small coalition of women—who were not members of a union—discovered that they had real power. The executive reversed his order within forty-eight hours, and the women immediately returned to work and resumed performing their jobs effectively.

Intergroup Competition Structured competition between groups represents an example of goal conflict. It is most obvious when the groups are highly interdependent. When Penn State and Pittsburgh, Ohio State and Michigan, or Texas A&M and the University of Texas, meet on the football field each year, each wants to win (goal conflict) and each game requires two teams that are interdependent. Outcomes are predictable when competing groups are interdependent and must interact. The following questions and answers highlight these outcomes.

- *What happens within each competing group?* Each group becomes more cohesive and gets greater loyalty from its members; members close ranks and bury many of their personal differences. Each group increases its task-oriented behaviors. Leadership becomes more structured and directive, and the group members become more willing to accept this type of leadership. Finally, each group demands more loyalty and conformity so that it can present a united front to the other group(s).

- *What happens between the competing groups?* Each group may begin to see the other as the enemy. Distortion of perceptions takes place. Members view their own group in positive terms and the other group in negative terms. Each group soon forms stereotypes and makes negative attributions of the other(s); for example, "they are dirty players." Each group feels and expresses increasing hostility toward the other. Communication between the groups declines. When the groups do "communicate," they tend to emphasize and listen only to their own concerns and to discount the statements of the other group(s).

- *What happens to the winner?* The winning group often becomes more cohesive and tends to release the tension created by the competition in a victory celebration. Over time, the winner may become complacent ("fat and happy") and feel little need to change.

- *What happens to the loser?* The loser(s) may deny or distort the reality of losing. In sports, statements like the following are common: "The referees were biased," "It was an unlucky day," or "They had a home court advantage." When the losing group accepts the loss, conflicts within the group may surface, fights may break out, and members blame others for their loss. The result is more tension and less intragroup cooperation than in the winning group. Over time, the losing group may reevaluate its behaviors and stereotypes about others. This could lead to reorganization, new leadership, and other changes.[12]

Substitutability

Substitutability is the degree to which one group can obtain the services or goods provided by another group from alternative sources. If alternative services or goods are readily available, the power of the provider group is weaker than if no alternatives existed.[13] For example, at the University of Washington, the department of management in the School of Business has neither the authority nor the ability to select an alternative provider to the university's fiscal department to handle expense account matters.

Limits on Substitutability In order to utilize resources fully, organizations frequently have rules requiring that departments use the services provided by other departments within the organization. For example, if the department of management at the University of Washington wants a new brochure printed, it is required to go through the university's printing department unless special permission is received for an exception. The university might enforce this rule even if the department of management could get an outside firm to do the job faster and cheaper. From an organizational standpoint, the increased costs to the department of management might be less significant than the low utilization of labor and equipment in the university's printing department. However, an increasing number of organizations have shown a willingness to eliminate entire departments or work groups and subcontract out the work they perform. Subcontracting hits service groups, such as custodial, food, printing, maintenance, and information processing groups, as well as production groups that manufacture component parts.[14]

Significance to Organizations Everything else being equal, the lower the substitutability of a group's goods or services, the greater is its power within the organization.[15] Groups that provide vital, nonsubstitutable services sometimes find that groups to which they provide these services try to (1) win them over through the provision of extra rewards or (2) eliminate the service group or its management by complaining to top management. Some computer department managers, for example, have been dismissed because the amount of their control over vital information threatened higher management. Computer departments provide vital and nonsubstitutable services. Thus even a perceived attempt to exercise too much power and control by a computer processing manager can create a backlash from others.

Types of Task Relations

As illustrated in Figure 11.2, there are three basic types of possible intergroup task relations: independent, interdependent, and dependent.

Independent Task Relations In **independent task relations,** none to few interactions are needed between two groups or those that do occur take place at the discretion of the two groups. This type of task relation between groups is based on a view of organizations as loosely coupled systems.[16] **Loose coupling** occurs when groups affect each other occasionally (rather than constantly), negligibly (rather than significantly), and indirectly (rather than directly).[17] The creation of self-managing teams, as described in the previous chapter, represents a means of decreasing the coupling between work groups.

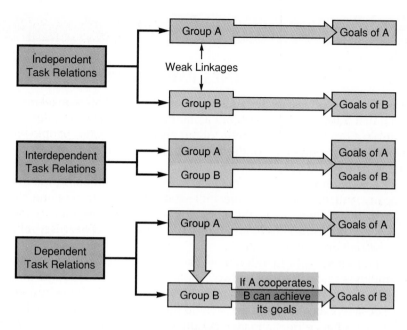

FIGURE 11.2   Three Types of Task Relations between Groups

Some large organizations maintain internal consulting groups that contract, on mutually agreeable terms, to work with various departments. Corning Glass's organizational development group operates principally in this way. If a department at Corning wants to improve its problem-solving effectiveness in committee meetings, for example, it can call in a representative from the organizational development group to diagnose the problems and assist the group in changing its processes. Once groups start working together, their relations are interdependent for the duration of the project. If both groups have the freedom to withdraw from the relationship at any time, they probably perceive a relatively independent task relationship. Neither group has much power relative to the other.

Interdependent Task Relations   In **interdependent task relations,** collaboration, integration, and mutual decision making are necessary and desirable between groups for them to achieve their own goals.[18] For effective interdependent task relations to exist, no single group or individual within a group should dictate or unilaterally determine the outcome of all interactions.[19]

The Coosa Pines paper mill, located in Coosa Pines, Alabama, is owned by the Kimberly-Clark Corporation. In 1988, the choice became clear to Kimberly-Clark chief executive Darwin Smith that many changes would have to occur at the mill to increase its productivity or it would need to be sold. The road to a new beginning for this mill required collaboration and mutual decision making among many groups. The following In Practice highlights these.

IN PRACTICE

COOSA PINES PAPER MILL

Darwin Smith, the CEO of Kimberly-Clark Corporation, and his management team concluded that $200 million worth of capital improvements were needed in the forty-year old Coosa Pines paper mill. About eighteen hundred people work for the mill. Another twenty-five hundred not directly employed by Kimberly-Clark harvest and haul wood used by the mill.

Smith decided it would be pointless to spend $200 million on the mill until the company and its workers at the mill would commit to working together. Instead of fighting each other, the company and its unions had to join in a common battle against domestic and foreign competition. Otherwise, selling the mill was the only logical alternative.

Smith prepared a special video tape just for the mill's workers. In the video, he told employees he had received five unsolicited inquiries about the possibility of selling the Coosa mill in the previous four months. He shared the business plan with the Coosa workers, saying Coosa would devote more output to quality paper and reduce its reliance on standard newsprint. He said that in the future, if the workers accepted the team approach, they would determine their own working arrangements. Pay would be based on skill and not seniority. Kimberly-Clark would provide continual training for all employees who wanted it.

Smith's talk kicked off a nearly six-month-long scramble to convince the thirteen hundred union workers at Coosa that committing to teamwork was the best alternative. "One of the toughest jobs we had was convincing workers that Smith was serious about selling the mill," says mill manager Jack Lavallet. The negotiations with the six unions went on for over five months. The unions wanted to protect employees' job security and the seniority system in determining pay and work assignments. The company wanted more flexibility in making assignments, allowing employees to do work outside their main trades, and cutting some jobs. Lavallet said the target was to cut about 250 union and management jobs, 160 of which would come about through early retirement incentives and the rest through normal turnover.

Five and one-half months after Smith made his tape for Coosa employees, a memorandum of agreement was reached between the mill and its union locals—pipefitters, machinists, electrical workers, and paperworkers. The unions agreed to accept the work-rule changes and the early retirement program. Kimberly-Clark agreed to spend the $200 million over the next five years modernizing the facility. The agreement, in the form of a contract extension between Kimberly-Clark and the unions, also stipulated that no workers would be laid off or suffer wage reductions as a result of the team approach. In fact, two bonuses of five hundred dollars each and small wage increases are called for over the three-year contract extension.[20]

Dependent Task Relations, In **dependent task relations,** one group has the ability and power to determine the behaviors and outputs of other groups.[21] Dependent task relations often occur when (1) one group absorbs uncertainty for one or more other groups; (2) the services that one group provides for one or more other groups are not readily substitutable; or (3) one or more groups depend on another group for needed resources. A dramatic example of dependent task relations occurs between an organization's top-management planning and budget committee and its operating departments. Resource allocations and possibly even the survival of departments may depend on the decisions of the budget committee.

When individuals are dependent on the actions of another individual or group, they may unite by forming a coalition or respond by joining an organization that represents their interests. One goal of such a coalition is to reduce the dependency of the individual members on the unilateral actions of those who are perceived as having more power.[22] Some employees form or join unions to reduce their dependency on the actions of management. They believe that "in unity, there is strength," that is, less dependency.

Significance to Organizations The diagnosis of intergroup task relations is essential to long-term effectiveness. First, the achievement of important organizational goals—such as productivity, innovation, and profitability—is often influenced by the nature and degree of task relations between groups and individuals. Second, some degree of interdependent task relations between groups—such as quality control and production—is needed and must be managed. Third, a wide range—not a single set—of task relations exists between lateral or vertical groups within organizations.[23]

Resource Sharing

Resource sharing refers to the degree to which two or more groups must obtain needed goods or services from a common group and the degree to which these goods or services are adequate to meet the needs of all the groups.[24] Consider the effects of resource sharing by groups involved with a document processing department, as described in the following account.

IN PRACTICE

THE DOCUMENT PROCESSING DEPARTMENT

Three departments, which lack the skills and resources to perform the work themselves, use the same document processing department to prepare most letters, memorandums, reports, and documents. When the document processing department was set up, it had adequate resources (operators, word processors, paper, reproduction equipment, and so on) to meet the demands of the three departments. The sharing of the document processing department initially caused few, if any, problems among the three departments.

Each department gradually expanded its work load and number of employees, but the document processing department's resources remained constant. This was a deliberate strategy by higher management to save money. The document processing department was staffed to meet peak demand and consequently was underutilized much of the time. Higher management felt that better planning and more realistic deadlines for the document processing department would result in much higher output with no additional personnel. This belief was reinforced by previous complaints from several operators who said they had to work frantically one day and were bored by inactivity the next.

The three user departments responded by pressuring the document processing department to treat every job as urgent. Next, each department established priorities for its own materials. However, this did not solve the problem. Finally, representatives of the three departments and the document processing department met and worked out a set of mutually acceptable priorities.

Significance to Organizations The need for two or more groups to share a common pool of resources can result in competition or cooperation between them.[25] In the situation involving the document processing department, the groups initially cooperated, then competed, and eventually cooperated again when they faced their problems. Management should encourage collaborative problem solving among groups that share a pool of scarce resources and should help set priorities to minimize unnecessary competition and destructive conflicts. As illustrated in the document processing department account, management also is in a unique position to influence the attitudinal sets that groups have toward each other when they experience difficulties in sharing resources and/or working together.

Attitudinal Sets

Attitudinal sets are the thoughts and feelings that members of two or more groups have toward each other. These thoughts and feelings are the positive or negative predispositions the groups have about one another.[26] The sets of attitudes that the members of the group hold toward another group and its members can be both a cause and a result of intergroup behaviors and effectiveness. The intergroup dynamics might begin with the groups trusting and cooperating with each other. These attitudes often influence the goals, uncertainty, substitutability, task relations, and resource sharing. If two groups trust each other, each tends to consider the other group's point of view more, avoid blaming the other when problems occur, and check with each other before making decisions that jointly impact them. If intergroup dynamics begin with attitudes of distrust, competitiveness, secrecy, and closed communication, the opposite tendencies can be expected.

The attitudinal sets of groups can also be a consequence of the other factors in intergroup dynamics. What if top management evaluates the performance of its internal auditing department solely on the basis of its ability to find errors and report them to higher management? The audited departments are likely to develop attitudes of distrust, competitiveness, and closed communication toward the auditing department. Of course, these attitudes are more likely to prevail if management uses the reports from auditing primarily to punish the audited departments, rather than to help them improve operations. In this situation, the audited departments may appear to be cooperative and open in their communications with the auditing department when in fact they are not.[27]

The possibility of gender differences among managers provides an interesting example of attitudinal sets. The following In Practice provides a summary of the research evidence on the question of possible differences between female and male managers.

IN PRACTICE

DO FEMALE AND MALE MANAGERS DIFFER?

Three distinct attitudinal sets have emerged in response to the question: Do female and male managers differ?

- *No differences.* Women who pursue the nontraditional career of manager reject the feminine stereotype and have needs, values, and leadership styles similar to those of men who pursue managerial careers.
- *Stereotypical differences.* Female and male managers differ in ways predicted by stereotypes. This is a result of early socialization experiences that reinforce masculinity in males and femininity in females.
- *Nonstereotypical differences.* Female and male managers differ in ways opposite of the stereotypes. This is because female managers have to be exceptional to compensate for early socialization experiences that are different from those of men.

Before you read further, select which of three attitudinal sets best represents your personal attitudes.

What does the research evidence show? There are no consistent gender differences in task-oriented behavior, people-oriented behavior, effectiveness ratings of actual managers, and subordinates' responses to actual managers. Stereotypical differences in some types of managerial behavior and in some ratings of managers in laboratory studies favor male managers, such as more decisive and better planners. On the other hand, when differences in motivational profiles for managerial roles are controlled, the slight stereotypical differences are eliminated. The results regarding gender differences in commitment are inconclusive. Moreover, when gender differences are found, they are not as extensive as other types of differences. On balance, the research evidence supports the *no differences* view of gender differences in management. Gary Powell, author of *Women and Men in Management*, comments:"Managers are a self-selecting population. Those who choose managerial careers, like firefighters, have a lot in common. The best embody stereotypes of both genders."

Therefore, organizations should not assume that male and female managers differ in personal qualities. They also should make sure that their policies, practices, and programs minimize the creation of gender differences in managers' experiences on the job. There is little reason to believe that either women or men make superior managers or that women and men are different types of managers.

Instead, there are likely to be excellent, average, and poor male and female managers. Success in today's highly competitive marketplace calls for organizations to make the best use of the talent available to them. To do this, they need to identify, develop, encourage, and promote the most effective managers, regardless of gender.[28]

Cooperation versus Competition The attitudinal sets that groups hold about each other often become *stereotypes*; that is, standardized short-cut evaluations that reflect present or past perceptions of relations between groups or specific individuals within the groups (see Chapter 3).[29] A number of attitudinal and behavioral consequences have been identified for groups that stereotype their relationships as basically cooperative or competitive.[30] Recall that earlier in this chapter, we discussed some of these outcomes for competing groups that win and lose.

Figure 11.3 provides a brief questionnaire for diagnosing the attitudinal sets and behavioral relations between two groups. The relationships range from extremely cooperative to competitive. In extremely competitive relationships, groups tend to be distrustful, emphasize self-interests, communicate only when required to do so, and resist influence or control from each other. On the other hand, a highly cooperative relationship tends to be characterized by trust, emphasis on mutual interests, easy and frequent communication, and acceptance of mutual influence or control. However, intergroup dynamics are rarely focused at one extreme or the other of all the dimensions shown in Figure 11.3. Intergroup problem solving and effectiveness tend to be greater when relations are cooperative, rather than competitive.

Significance to Organizations Attitudinal sets—whether cooperative or competitive—can significantly affect the ability and willingness of groups to work together to achieve organizational goals. If groups are *interdependent*, competitive attitudinal sets probably will reduce goal accomplishment. The reason is that these groups must expend considerable time and energy trying to "get one up" on the other. In the next section, we focus on ways to maintain or create effective relations between interdependent groups. First, we direct your attention to the following Across Cultures on negotiating challenges created by culturally based attitudinal differences between U.S. and Korean managers. This Across Cultures draws from an in-depth study of eighteen cooperative ventures formed between U.S. and Korean organizations. It also reveals the importance of bridging differences for effective intergroup communications and decision making.[31]

CREATING EFFECTIVE INTERGROUP DYNAMICS

There are seven major approaches for managing intergroup dynamics within organizations: superordinate group goals and rewards, information

Instructions: For each of the dimensions shown below, place a check mark in the response category that best represents your view of the relationships between the two groups. The middle response category, which shows a "3", should be used only if the relationships are "neutral" or you are undecided.

	Cooperative	1	2	3	4	5	**Competitive**
1.	Trust	1	2	3	4	5	Distrust
2.	Flexibility	1	2	3	4	5	Rigidity
3.	Openness and authenticity	1	2	3	4	5	Secrecy and deceptiveness
4.	Mutual interests and goals	1	2	3	4	5	Self-interest and goals
5.	Friendliness or neutrality	1	2	3	4	5	Aggressiveness or enemy status
6.	Listening to each other	1	2	3	4	5	Listening to selves
7.	Accepting mutual control	1	2	3	4	5	Resisting control of each other
8.	Collaboration and compromise	1	2	3	4	5	Force and avoidance

Scoring: For items 1 through 8, sum the point values shown in each category checked. Total scores of 8 to 16 would suggest conditions of cooperation between the two groups. Total scores of 32 to 40 would suggest intergroup conditions of competition and conflict.

FIGURE 11.3   Questionnaire for Diagnosing Attitudinal Sets and Behavioral Relations between Two Groups

technologies, organizational hierarchy, plans, linking roles, task forces, and integrating roles and groups. The conflict resolution and negotiation processes related to effectively managing intergroup relations are presented in Chapter 14.

The seven approaches are shown in Figure 11.4. The vertical axis shows the *additional resources* required to use each method. Additional resources include the extra time people spend in meetings, the increase in paper flow and memos between groups, the extra employees who must be hired, and the like. The horizontal axis shows the *complexity* of each method. The plus (+) signs between methods suggest the probable use of the previously identified method or methods along with the new method. With the exception of

◆ *ACROSS CULTURES*

DIFFERENCES IN ATTITUDINAL SETS BETWEEN U.S. AND KOREAN MANAGERS

In comparing their experiences in Korea with those in Japan and China, many of the U.S. executives felt that their Korean counterparts were illogical. Some complained that they did not understand why Koreans could become adamant over trivial matters while glossing over the major ones. Others cited instances in which decisions to embark on a major project were made solely because another Korean competitor was doing so—not because the situation had been objectively analyzed.

One U.S. executive said, "Many is the time . . . I have been accused of being *logical*. That is considered to be sinful in some cases. . . . They say, 'Well . . . that is just the logical point of view. You have to understand that in Asia, things do not work according to logic.'"

The Koreans acknowledged that Western reasoning alone may not be adequate to persuade a Korean to adopt a particular course of action. Personal considerations can be equally important, if not more so. The Koreans may often respond to *kibun*. *Kibun* is the "personal feeling, the attitude, the mood, the mental state . . . which is an extremely important factor in ego fulfillment."

U.S. and Korean executives appear to differ widely in their attitudes toward the worth of a written contract. The typical U.S. view is that a contract defines the rights and responsibilities of the parties involved and that

there can be no deviation from it because it is considered a legal document binding on both parties. The Koreans, on the other hand, like their Japanese and Chinese counterparts, believe that contracts are living documents that can change as conditions evolve. Many U.S. managers complained that a written contract does not mean much in the Korean context. According to one U.S. executive, "A lot of people have said that the signing of a contract in Korea is only the beginning of the negotiations and that as circumstances change, the Koreans feel that the contract should also change." This can prove very frustrating for U.S. managers.

It's easy to see why the U.S. firm that seeks to enter Korea for short-term gains may be disappointed. As with Japanese and Chinese counterparts, the Korean partner expects the foreign investor to have a long-term commitment to remaining in the country. One Korean partner compared the joint-venturing process to that of child rearing: "It has to be long-term. . . . It is like raising your children. You don't give up on raising children when they are only three or four years old. It is a continual process, and you must really look forward to the time when the child becomes a succesful, wholesome person. Companies are the same—there are going to be ups and downs. There are going to be difficult times, but this is all part of the learning process."[32]

superordinate group goals and rewards and information technologies, these approaches tend to be related to each other in a hierarchy of complexity. For example, if the use of linking roles is appropriate in integrating two or more groups, some uses of hierarchy and plans have probably already been implemented.

Superordinate Group Goals and Rewards

Superordinate group goals are those common ends that might be pursued by two or more groups that cannot be achieved without cooperation from

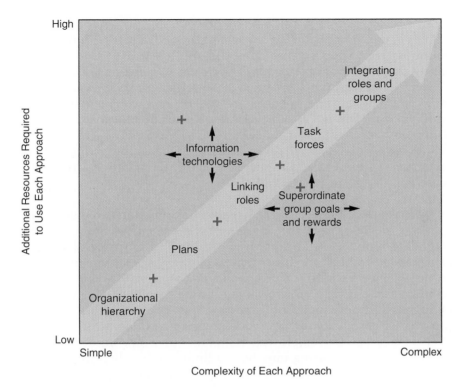

FIGURE 11.4   Seven Approaches for Creating Effective Intergroup Dynamics

all groups.[33] These goals do not replace or eliminate the other group goals. Superordinate group goals can be qualitative or quantitative. An example of a qualitative goal would be: "Marketing and production need to pull together for the good of the company." An example of a quantitative goal would be: "Marketing and production need to work together if we are to reach company goals of launching the new X line within nine months and achieving sales of five thousand units per month within fifteen months. The company's survival is at stake."

Superordinate group goals are likely to have a more powerful effect on the willingness of groups to cooperate if accompanied by superordinate group rewards.[34] **Superordinate group rewards** are those benefits received by the members of the groups that are partially determined through the results of their joint efforts.

Wide Range of Use   As suggested by the multidirectional arrows in Figure 11.4, superordinate group goals and rewards cover a wide range in terms of complexity and the resources required to use them. A company president might state: "During this past year, we needed extensive cooperation among all our departments and divisions in order to achieve our company goal of a 12 percent increase in profits. I would like to express my appreciation to all of you for pulling together—even when we had to deal with several sticky issues involving some departments and divisions. Through everyone's efforts, we did it. I am pleased to report that profits are up 16 percent."

Based on Figure 11.4, this statement would fall at the *simple* end of the complexity continuum and the *low* end of the additional resources required continuum. But suppose that he added the following: "Under our profit sharing program, I am pleased to report that 90 percent of our employees will receive bonuses ranging from 8 to 16 percent of their salaries. As all of you should know, these bonuses are based on a weighted system of (1) individual merit rating, (2) achievement of departmental goals, and (3) overall company profitability." These additional comments suggest that the superordinate group goals and rewards are probably at the *complex* end of the complexity continuum and at the *high* end of the additional resources required continuum in Figure 11.4.

Gain-sharing Plans   Through **gain-sharing plans,** regular cash bonuses are provided from the division of the benefits of improved productivity, cost reductions, or improved quality.[35] Many gain-sharing plans also include methods for involving employees in decision making. They are not "quick fixes" to major management problems but do provide methods for creating superordinate group goals and rewards. Gain-sharing plans differ from profit-sharing plans. **Profit-sharing plans** award employees a proportion of *total* company profits. In contrast, gain-sharing plans usually reward employees for plant, division, or department improvements. Profit sharing may have a limited effect because the individual employee in a large company may feel powerless to influence the firm's profitability to any noticeable degree. Moreover, company profits are affected by many external factors (such as competitors' actions, inflation, and government policies) that are well beyond the employee's control or influence.[36]

The Scanlon plan represents the first use of gain-sharing. The **Scanlon plan** basically consists of a management philosophy and a system of rewards and labor-management practices. The philosophy includes building a g   ployee-management partnership (which could include a union), creating greater employee participation, and sharing the benefits from improvements with employees. The system of rewards and procedures includes a suggestion system, elected committees of employees, and a bonus formula based on productivity gains. The bonus formula is based on a relationship of labor costs to the sales value of products. According to one commonly used Scanlon formula, the base ratio equals sales (minus returned goods plus changes in inventory) divided by payroll (wages, salaries, and employee benefits). The base ratio is used to compare actual costs to expected costs. If actual costs are less than expected costs, the difference goes into a bonus pool.[37] Establishing a network of committees that involves almost everyone in productivity improvement is necessary for a Scanlon plan to be successful because everyone can win. In addition, the organization must also be able to measure the difference between plant output and total payroll costs so that plantwide bonuses can be objectively determined. Let's consider the experience of one plant that was about to close and then was saved through the effective implementation of a Scanlon plan. The employees won by saving their jobs, and their company won by restoring the plant's economic competitiveness, as the following In Practice highlights.

IN PRACTICE

SAVING A PLANT THROUGH THE SCANLON PLAN

The plant manufactured abrasive cut-off wheels for cutting steel and other metals and employed 140 production workers. Its production standards had been the source of considerable tension between management and the union. Four wildcat strikes and several work slowdowns began to cause financial difficulties. After contract negotiations failed, top management announced plans to close the plant for economic reasons.

As a result of the decision to close the plant, the state government and the union's district director became involved. An agreement was negotiated whereby the plant could remain open. Prior to the decision to close, the Scanlon plan had been considered but rejected by top management. Plant managers were now able to convince top management that the Scanlon plan offered a real alternative to closing. The union also offered its full cooperation to improve productivity and to end negotiated production standards. In return, management agreed not to lay off any employees as a result of suggestions from the Scanlon committees.

Productivity rose abruptly following introduction of the Scanlon plan. For the first three years of the plan, employee bonuses averaged about 4 percent, 4.5 percent, and 9 percent. Twenty percent of the union employees were laid off in the six months prior to the start of the plan. Following the plan's introduction, employment stabilized. In following years, the Scanlon plan continued to be successful, and ten years after its installation, it remained active.[38]

Information Technologies

As introduced in Chapter 10, a variety of information technologies are available to assist group members with their processes of interaction and decision making. Figure 11.4 also suggests that information technologies can vary greatly in terms of their degree of complexity and the resources required for their use. You will recall that we defined *groupware* in Chapter 10 as an approach to using specialized computer aids, communication, tools, and designated facilities that enable teams and groups to work faster, share more information, communicate more accurately, and more effectively achieve their goals. In this section, we note the use of several information technologies that aid interpersonal relations within and between groups.

> *Teleconferencing* allows for meetings to be conducted where participants (from the same or different groups) in one room can view and interact with those in another room that may be thousands of miles away. This technology has been useful in helping groups that are located at considerable distances from one another yet are interdependent in their task relations to solve problems and communicate on a timely basis. It can help the groups to avoid the formation of negative and competitive attitudinal sets toward one another. AT&T, Bank of America, and Texas A&M University are among the increas-

ing number of organizations that use teleconferencing to help their groups work together more frequently and conveniently, even though they may be separated by hundreds or even thousands of miles.

- *Facsimile (FAX)* machines scan a sheet of paper electronically and convert the light and dark areas to electrical signals that can then be sent over telephone lines. At the other end, a similar machine reverses the process and produces the original image instantly on a sheet of paper. This technology is proving to be very helpful to individuals and groups that must share documents and receive feedback on a timely basis regarding the contents of these documents. The groups or individuals can be linked in a matter of minutes worldwide. Less than ten years ago, a one-way linkage required one to two days via express mail.

- *Electronic mail (E-mail)* allows users to pass written messages from one person or group to another through their terminal or personal computer. The terminals or personal computers are connected through networking.

- *Integrated systems* refers to the linking of various information systems through telephone lines and computer networks. The idea is to achieve closer links among design, production, and service activities in an organization, as well as extending integration to include direct information exchanges with customers and suppliers.[39]

Organizational Hierarchy

Organizational hierarchy is an approach for obtaining integration or coordination between two or more groups through a common superior. The use of hierarchy to integrate groups or specific individuals within groups rests on the assumption that people at upper levels in an organization have more power than those at lower levels. As shown in Figure 11-4, organizational hierarchy is probably the simplest method and involves the least *additional* cost for achieving integration.

Organizational hierarchy exists for many purposes other than creating effective intergroup relations. However, its use to resolve intergroup integration problems may be especially appropriate when there are few integration requirements and only minor differences between the groups. Of course, the use of hierarchy does not necessarily prevent employees in the groups from sitting down with their common superior and working through the issues together.

Plans

Plans and planning processes can be used to help achieve effective intergroup relations. In its broadest sense, **planning** is the process of setting forth the organization's: (1) destination (vision and goals); (2) strategies for getting there; (3) desired achievements at specific times; (4) anticipated obstacles; and (5) the approaches for dealing with these obstacles.[40]

Following accepted or agreed on plans, groups can act and make day-to-day decisions without constantly communicating with each other. Sticking to the plans enables the groups to be integrated and interdependent in seeking to achieve their goals. For example, construction crews in England and France started working on different sections of the tunnel under the English Channel. Because the engineers prepared precise plans, each construction crew made accurate decisions based on the plans. The crews met where they were supposed to meet under the English Channel.

Linking Roles

Linking roles are performed by people in specialized positions who facilitate communication and problem solving between two or more interdependent groups. The creation of such a role is important when the exclusive use of organizational hierarchy, plans, or both becomes too slow or time-consuming. For example, if minor issues were continually referred up the hierarchy, the superior might become overloaded, increasing the response time. However, someone in a linking role could solve these minor problems and reduce the common superior's workload. A linking role may involve nothing more than handling and tracking the flow of paperwork between groups and following up on issues as required.

Boundary-Spanning Roles   People performing specialized linking roles can also tie groups to other groups or organizations. These **boundary-spanning roles** are often essential in facilitating the information flow and decision making.[41] For example, a safety manager might fill a boundary-spanning role between the organization and the U.S. Occupational Safety and Health Administration (OSHA) with respect to work-related safety and health issues. Boundary-spanning roles may also involve representing the group or organization to outside groups. For example, boundary spanners in the collective bargaining process include negotiators representing management on one side and those representing a union on the other. Also, a corporate spokesperson is often used to deal with the media in responding to questions related to a crisis or disaster.[42]

Research on teams has found four basic types of boundary-spanning roles and activities:

- *Ambassador* activity refers to obtaining the personnel, funding, equipment, and legitimacy from higher management or other groups. This activity appears to be somewhat political: identifying threat and opposition in top levels of the organization and other groups and working to build support from them.

- *Task coordinator* activity represents specific efforts to coordinate and synchronize with other groups, typically those involved with a specific product or project.

- *Scout* activity represents a more general scanning aimed at obtaining competitive, market, and technical ideas.

- *Guard* activity represents a means of decreasing, rather than meeting, dependence through the control of information flow out of the group.[43]

All of these forms of boundary-spanning activity may be necessary to the team's success. Moreover, these roles may be performed by more than one person, not just the team leader.

Task Forces

Task forces are special groups that consist of one or more representatives from each of the groups working on specific problems of mutual concern. Task forces are usually formed to work on temporary issues or problems and disbanded when the issues or problems are resolved.[44] Some members of a task force may be engaged full-time and others part-time. The members often link the task force with their group. Members usually can provide information and ideas regarding common problems, serve as transmitters of ideas and information between the task force and their groups, and help assess the impact of task force decisions on their group. For example, at Ford Motor Company, a task force named "Team Taurus" was formed to design the Taurus and Sable automobiles. Once the Taurus and Sable models were designed and in full production, the team was disbanded. Its members returned to their regular units on a full-time basis.

Task forces can develop on a formal or informal basis. An informal task force can simply involve several people who get together to consider a mutual problem. Higher management creates and recognizes a formal task force, usually in writing, by stating the problem area and goals it is to deal with and by assigning employees to the task force.

Integrating Roles and Groups

Integrating roles are performed by employees who are permanently assigned to help two or more groups work together. An integrating role is performed by one person, whereas in an integrating group, several employees are formally assigned the task of integrating two or more groups. There are many positions and groups that often have integrating responsibilities (in addition to those previously discussed). They include product managers, program coordinators, project managers, group vice-presidents, plant productivity committees, annual meetings of corporate and division general managers, boards of directors, union leaders, union-management committees, chief information officers, chief technology officers, and human resource managers.

One role of the integrating person or group is usually to help resolve conflicting goals and problems that develop between groups. These issues often surface, for example, between production and marketing departments and between union and management. Intergroup issues could include disagreements over major capital investment priorities, production schedules, cost estimates, quality standards, human resource problems, and the like.[45] The decision to use one person or a specialized group to achieve integration usually depends on the situation. An integrating group is more costly to use than an integrating person. Organizations tend to use integrating groups when (1) intergroup differences are large; (2) the need for integration increases because of interdependent task relations; and (3) the need to deal with nonroutine problems between the groups increases.

The following In Practice reveals how one organization used a variety of approaches to create effective intergroup and intragroup dynamics to meet its need for increased productivity.

IN PRACTICE

HOPE CREEK GENERATING STATION

When the organizations involved in the construction of Hope Creek Generating Station, a nuclear power plant located in southern New Jersey, found themselves placed under tight budget and schedule constraints, the only way that they could complete the project was through increased productivity. The question was: "How?" The primary owner, Public Service Electric & Gas Company (PSE&G), decided to implement a program designed to boost productivity by tapping the creativity of a vast and diverse workforce. This meant a new way of managing construction. To foster an atmosphere in which ideas and feelings moved both up and down the chain of command required that everybody involved had to work as cooperating teams, not as individuals.

The Hope Creek project was an enormous undertaking. The total cost of the project was estimated at over $3.5 billion. Almost eight thousand people were employed in the effort. Of this number, thirty-five hundred were union craftsmen, another two thousand were salaried contractor employees, fifteen hundred were subcontractors (e.g., General Electric), and PSE&G added another five hundred. The union craftsmen were drawn from fourteen different unions. Over twenty subcontractors, large and small, performed about 25 percent of the work. The primary contractor's "nonmanual" staff included more than four hundred field engineers, seventy quality control engineers, and a planning and scheduling staff of more than thirty.

Because employee participation was the cornerstone of Hope Creek's program, all decisions concerning the program were made by committee. A steering committee, which included representatives from all major groups, held executive powers for the program. A special subcommittee developed a name for the program: PRIDE (for People Respecting Integrity, Dedication, Excellence). A logo was designed that eventually found its way onto all stationery, hard hats, flag poles, and posters.

A broad outline was developed dictating the size and scope of the program. The components of the PRIDE Program were:

- *Steering committee*—a representative group drawn from management, salaried, and union ranks; the steering committee authorized or approved PRIDE activities and provided ongoing evaluation of the program.
- *Suggestion program*—a representative committee reviewed all suggestions and made awards determinations.
- *Quality circles*—created from a large pool of volunteers, these were formed and dissolved on an ad hoc basis.
- *Recognition program*—administered by a committee; employees could nominate other employees for recognition for conspicuous service on or off the job.

- *Surveys*—both a comprehensive annual and spot surveys of employee opinions were used.
- *Hotline*—employees used this anonymously to verify rumors.
- *Events and recreation*—these included project open houses, fishing, golf, softball, football, and tennis tournaments.

Teams were formed to improve parking facilities, to provide better employee facilities, and to provide for improved litter disposal. Other teams addressed issues relating directly to the work at hand, such as cable pulling, heating, ventilation, and air conditioning installation, and so forth.

The most important factor in maintaining the viability of all of these programs was prompt response by management. It was essential that program facilitators had constant access to senior management and that management responded quickly and openly to ideas brought forth through the program.[46]

SUMMARY

This chapter demonstrated the importance of intergroup dynamics to organizational effectiveness. We reviewed how each of six major factors can affect intergroup behaviors and effectiveness, including uncertainty, group goals, substitutability, task relations, resource sharing, and attitudinal sets.

When the goals of two or more groups are perceived as being incompatible, conflict and poor coordination may occur. When one group absorbs uncertainty for other groups, its power usually increases. When substitutability of the services or goods of a group is not permitted, the group's power is often greater than it otherwise would be. When task relations between two or more groups are highly interdependent, extensive collaboration, coordination, and mutual decision making is required. When groups have to share resources, the likelihood of conflict is greater than when sharing is not needed. Groups need to establish priorities and ground rules for sharing the common resource. When the attitudinal sets that groups hold toward each other are characterized by trust, flexibility, openness, mutuality of interests, and friendliness, high levels of intergroup cooperation often result. Intergroup competition and conflict go hand in hand with opposing attitudinal sets.

Seven approaches for creating effective intergroup dynamics were discussed. Each approach can be used independently or in relation to one or more of the others. The approaches include superordinate group goals and rewards, information technologies, organization hierarchy, plans, linking roles, task forces, and integrating roles and groups.

Managers should view the dynamics of intergroup interaction as a set of contingencies. That is, only after careful diagnosis can we draw conclusions about the best approach or combination of approaches for creating effective intergroup dynamics. Managers may pay too little or too much attention to intergroup relations. Too little attention can result in poor integration, duplication of effort, and destructive conflict. Too much attention can result in unnecessary paperwork and meetings, an excessive expenditure of resources on achieving integration, and a lack of sense of accomplishment by the groups.

Key Words and Concepts

Attitudinal sets
Boundary-spanning roles
Dependent task relations
Effect uncertainty
Gainsharing plans
Goal conflict
Independent task relations
Integrating roles
Interdependent task relations
Linking roles
Loose coupling
Organizational hierarchy

Planning
Profit sharing plans
Resource sharing
Response uncertainty
Scanlon plan
State uncertainty
Substitutability
Superordinate group goals
Superordinate group rewards
Task forces
Uncertainty
Uncertainty absorption

Discussion Questions

1. Identify a group of which you are a member and another group which is of importance to your group. How may this *other group* create state uncertainty, effect uncertainty, and response uncertainty for your group?

2. With respect to the *other group* identified above, how does it impact on the weight, domain, and scope of your group's power?

3. Focus on the relationships between the student government and the administration of your college or university. Give one example of the following between each of these groups: mutual goals, goal conflict, and mixed goal conflict.

4. How does the concept of substitutability apply to the following units on a college campus: dormitories, food services, copy center, and book store? What policies or practices does your college pursue to put limits on substitutability for these services? Are they effective?

5. In what ways can a human resources department absorb uncertainty for other departments in an organization?

6. What are the types of task relations that probably exist between a purchasing department and a production department? Between purchasing and the human resources department? Between purchasing and the top management team? What factors probably influence the differences in these profiles of task relations?

7. Do you think the concept of resource sharing is becoming a smaller or larger problem in organizations? Why?

8. Give examples of how attitudinal sets impact on the relationships between any two groups that are highly interdependent. Use the

diagnostic questionnaire shown in Figure 11-3 to develop the profile of the attitudinal sets between these two groups.

9.   What aspects of intergroup relationships are likely to be aided by new information technologies? Why?

10. Based on your experiences in organizations, have the methods they used for integrating groups worked well or poorly? Illustrate and explain your conclusion.

◆ MANAGEMENT CASES AND EXERCISES

MADISON ELECTRONICS COMPANY

The Madison Electronics Company (MEC) is a nonunionized manufacturer of electrical components for a number of major U.S. firms. The standards for the components vary with the customer but usually must conform to rather close tolerances. Historically, MEC competed successfully with its larger competitors. However, in the mid-1980s, MEC started being underbid by many of its competitors. A consulting team was hired to evaluate the production and pricing policies of MEC.

The consultants interviewed managers, researched the practices of competing firms, and reached the conclusion that MEC was not as efficient as its competitors. The consultants made what all managers and most employees agree were minor changes in jobs and work flow to lower unit costs and to increase efficiency. One major change was the introduction of a piece-rate incentive system. Time and motion studies were used to establish rates for the various jobs throughout the company. While there was initial resistance to using such a system, most employees have discovered that they can exceed the base rate and thus earn more than their base pay. Management's goal of lowering per unit costs has been achieved, and worker output increased faster than increases in wages. Most em-

ployees are happy because their earning ability has increased with the new incentive system.

One department that has been unable to meet the established rate is the trimming department. The department trims the various parts prior to their being assembled and sold to the customers. The parts are sent directly to trimming from the casting department. The trimmers insert the part into a shearing machine, which trims away burrs and other irregular formations on the parts. After trimming, the parts are sent to milling, where they are smoothed and prepared for assembly and shipped to the intended customer. The work flow is shown in Figure 11.5. If the part does not fit into the shearing equipment, it is rejected and returned to the casting department for possible reworking.

The standard rate set for the trimmer is five hundred units per hour, or four thousand units per day. When the casting machines are properly adjusted, this rate can be attained by a trained employee. However, if the trimmer rejects a part because it does not fit the shearing machine, it is not counted as a unit completed and does not count toward the rate set for the operator. As the dies in the casting department become worn, it becomes increasingly difficult for trimming employees to achieve their established rates of pro-

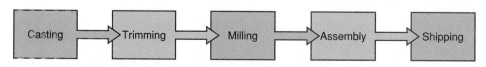

FIGURE 11.5 Work Flow of Cast Components

duction. This creates special problems since once the parts are trimmed, employees in the assembly and shipping operations are able to achieve their rates and earn their bonus. Trimmers are quite dissatisfied with the existing system, and turnover for the department is excessive.

The manager of the trimming department has asked the casting manager numerous times to replace the dies before they become so worn. The casting manager is reluctant to replace the dies sooner than is absolutely necessary because this increases the downtime for casting employees and keeps them from achieving their established rates. Doing "extra" maintenance on the dies increases overhead costs, which the casting manager wants to avoid.

Management has been very reluctant to change the established piece-rate system. The standard reply has been that the system was developed by specially trained time and motion experts and that they knew what they were doing.

QUESTIONS

1. What are the major problems facing the managers of MEC? Explain.

2. How would you advise the managers in this case to resolve the problems identified above?

3. What do you think of the piece-rate compensation system? Why?

4. Evaluate the boundary-spanning roles of the managers of the casting and trimming departments in solving the problems identified?

RUSHTON MINING COMPANY

The president of Rushton Mining Company and the president of the United Mine Workers of America signed a letter of agreement to collaborate on a quality-of-work-life experiment at Rushton Coal Mine in Pennsylvania. The experiment was designed by a team of researchers to improve employee skills, safety, and job satisfaction while simultaneously raising the level of performance and earnings.

After five months of deliberations by representatives of management and the union, the firm posted job bids requesting volunteers for an autonomous ("independent") work group. These miners would have direct responsibility for the production of an entire section of the mine. The supervisors of the section would abandon their traditional roles as "pushers" and develop new roles as advisors, consultants, trainers, and planners to the miners.

The autonomous work group employed an entire twenty-seven-person section, composed of three shifts and three supervisors. The group met with the research team two days a week for six weeks in an above-ground classroom, where they received training in safety laws, good mining practices, job safety analysis, and group problem solving. On the remaining three days, the miners mined coal in their new underground section and learned to work toward a common goal—safely maximizing production of the section, rather than the shift. To encourage job switching and shared responsibility for the work, all twenty-seven miners received the same rate of pay as the highest-skilled job classification on that section. This resulted in an increase to the top rate of fifty dollars a day for fifteen of the miners.

Following the orientation period, the group met in the classroom with the research team at six-week intervals to discuss productivity, absenteeism, costs, and health and safety matters. During this time, they developed several means for resolving intragroup conflict and enhancing intershift coordination. These included a joint committee comprised of one person from each shift, two local union leaders, one supervisor, the mine's safety director, a training director, and two members of management. Foremen meetings, higher-level management meetings, and underground visits by the research team occurred several times a week.

SEEDS OF CONFLICT

While intragroup coordination improved, intersection hostility grew. At first, the other miners found the activities of the autonomous group and its association with the university research teams amusing, and they humorously used such terms as "automatic miner" and "superminer" when the members of the autonomous section entered the waiting room before boarding the cars that would take them down into the mine. In time, however, the good-natured banter changed to silent hostility and eventually to open opposition as other miners grew jealous of the privileged status of the autonomous section of the mine. Subsequent interviews with the miners in the other sections suggested that they felt deprived because the research team gave them no information and little attention. Not only did the autonomous group work under generally favorable physical conditions, but it also received special training and, when requested, special tools and equipment. It had its own university researcher who spent an entire shift several times a week interviewing and observing the group's miners, sharing their danger and fatigue, and helping with training, development, and conflict resolution. The group had the privilege of spending one day every six weeks out of the mine in a conference with top management and union officials. In addition, several of the miners attended quality-of-work-life conferences at the company's expense, enjoying rides to and from the airport in the mine president's helicopter and receiving honoraria for their presentations. Moreover, the president treated the autonomous section to a steak-and-lobster dinner at the conclusion of its training period.

A few of the members of the autonomous section aggravated this already difficult situation by behaving in a haughty, arrogant manner toward other miners who questioned their preferential treatment. For example, when one of the miners from another section complained of a "hard-nosed" boss who "works your tail off," the autonomous worker replied that he could tell his boss "where to get off." Another worker bragged that he had "retired" when he went into the autonomous section and planned to start bringing a sleeping bag with him into the mine so he could be more comfortable during his shift. Some evidence exists, however, that many of the autonomous workers felt hurt by the criticism of their peers.

GROWTH AND SPREAD OF CONFLICT

About ten months after the experiment began, the mine opened a new section. The members from the original autonomous section, many of whom had never attended a union meeting before, had become enthusiastic supporters of "our way of working." They strongly influenced a favorable union vote that permitted the new section to be organized along autonomous lines.

When the company opened the new section, management and the researchers anticipated that experienced members would bid from other positions all over the mine to fill the vacancies. This, however, did not occur. Because of a reluctance to leave established patterns of working, a resentment toward being kept uninformed, and rising hostility toward the project, the veteran miners refused to place bids for jobs in the new section. New miners who had been hired to fill the anticipated vacancies in other parts of the mine and who still wore the yellow hat of the inexperienced and uncertified miner got positions in the new autonomous section. The section consisted mostly of miners with less than one year's experience. Nevertheless, they drew the same or higher pay as miners with at least forty years of experience.

Although the section rapidly became one of the highest producers, it initially had the lowest production rate in the mine. This appeared to stem from the inexperience of the miners and from the fact that they had to work with used equipment that continually broke down. Frequently, mechanics from other parts of the mine had to help the young, inexperienced mechanics from the new section repair their equipment. The combination of high pay, inexperience, and perceived low production of the new section increased the hostility and resentment the other miners felt towards the experiment.

As the weeks progressed, other miners became increasingly nasty in their comments. They accused autonomous miners of "riding the gravy train" and being spoon-fed. They called them "parasites" who were carried by the rest of the miners. Rumors began to spread throughout the mine with increasing frequency and intensity. Some of the most widely circulated ones held that autonomous groups constituted a communist plot since everybody received the same top rate and that the company was being subsidized by the government and was "making out" at the expense of the miners.

An extremely damaging rumor defined the quality-of-work-life project as a management plot in collusion with "pinko" college people to "bust the union." This rumor seemed especially credible since the company president had strongly resisted the unionization attempts led by "Jock" Yablonski of the United Mine Workers of America ten years earlier. Many of the older miners who had been involved in the organizing effort felt greatly concerned that the project's committees, joint decision making, and universally high pay rate could cause a weaning away of the younger miners from the traditional values of the United Mine Workers and possibly result in an independent or company union. The rumors and innuendoes continued. Five months after the formation of the new section, the union membership voted to terminate the experiment unless all miners were given a chance to work at the top rate of pay.

CONSEQUENCES OF CONFLICT

During the next two months, the research team interviewed and observed the miners in other sections so that the team could perform the analysis required for a proposal for mine-wide autonomous working. In addition, the researchers made great efforts to explain the principles of autonomous working to all the miners and to refute the rumors that sprang up in the darkness and gloom of the underground environment. What appeared to be ridiculous speculation outside in the bright sunlight somehow seemed believable hundreds of feet underground. This process ended in a request by the local union for written proposals that would

specify how the rest of the mine would become autonomous. The research team submitted proposals to the union members, who voted on them at a special election. The miners rejected the proposals by a vote of 79 to 75. The experiment was ended.

QUESTIONS

1. What are the identifiable groups that played a part in this experiment and the eventual outcomes?

2. What appeared to be the goals and interests of each of these groups with respect to the quality-of-work-life experiment?

3. How did this quality-of-work-life experiment seem to impact the factors of uncertainty absorption, substitutability, and task relations within the autonomous independent work groups and between the other groups at Rushton?

4. Why did the attitudinal sets between the groups deteriorate?

5. What actions might have been taken from the very beginning of the experiment to increase the probability of approval rather than rejection of the mine-wide autonomous group proposal? Your answer should indicate possible actions by each of the key groups.

References

1. Adapted from Schuler, R.S., and Walker, J.W. Human Resources Strategy: Focusing on Issues and Actions. *Organizational Dynamics*, Summer 1990, 4-19.
2. Fisher, R.J. *The Social Psychology of Intergroup and International Conflict Resolution*. New York: Springer-Verlag, 1990.
3. Milliken, F.J. Three Types of Perceived Uncertainty about the Environment: State, Effect, and Response Uncertainty: *Academy of Management Review*, 1987, *12*, 133-143.
4. Ibid., 133-143. Also see Lang, J.R., and Lockhart, D.E. Increasing Environmental Uncertainty and Changes in Board Linkage Patterns. *Academy of Management Journal*, 1990, *33*, 106-128.
5. Thompson, J.D. *Organizations in Action*. New York: McGraw-Hill, 1967.
6. Kaplan, D. Power in Perspective. In R.L. Kahn and K.E. Boulding (eds.), *Power and Conflict in Organizations*. London: Tavistock, 1964, 11-32.
7. Goodman, P.S., and Sproull, L.S., and Associates. *Technology and Organizations*. San Francisco: Jossey-Bass, 1990.
8. Adapted from Hofstede, G., Neuijen, B., Ohayv, D.D., and Sanders, G. Measuring Organizational Cultures: A Qualitative and Quantitative Study across Twenty Cases. *Administrative Science Quarterly*, 1990, *35*, 286-315.
9. Locke, E.A., and Latham, G.P. *A Theory of Goal Setting and Task Performance*. Englewood Cliffs, N.J.: Prentice-Hall, 1990.
10. DeGeorge, G., and Payne, S. The Law of the Jungle Takes to the Skies. *Business Week*, February 4, 1991, 49.
11. Boeker, W. The Development and Institutionalization of Subunit Power in Organizations. *Administrative Science Quarterly*, 1989, *34*, 388-410.
12. Schein, E.H. *Organizational Psychology*. Englewood Cliffs, N.J.: Prentice-Hall, 1980, 172-176;

Tjosvold, D. *The Conflict-Positive Organization: Stimulate Diversity and Create Unity*. Reading, Mass.: Addison-Wesley, 1991.

13. Lackman, R. Power from What? A Reexamination of Its Relationships with Structural Conditions. *Administrative Science Quarterly*, 1989, *34*, 231-251.

14. McMillan, J. Managing Suppliers: Incentive Systems in Japanese and U.S. Industry. *California Management Review*, Summer 1990, 38-55.

15. Hickson, D.J., Hinnings, C.R., Lee, C.A., Schneck, R.E., and Pennings, J.M. Strategic Contingencies Theory of Organizational Power. *Administrative Science Quarterly*, 1971, *16*, 216-229.

16. Orton, J.D., and Weick, K.E. Loosely Coupled Systems: A Reconceptualization. *Academy of Management Review*, 1990, *15*, 203-223.

17. Weick, K.E. Management of Organizational Change among Loosely Coupled Elements. In P.S. Goodman and Associates (eds.), *Change in Organizations*. San Francisco: Jossey-Bass, 1982, 375-408 (380).

18. Victor, B., and Blackburn, R.S. Interdependence: An Alternative Conceptualization. *Academy of Management Review*, 1987, *12*, 486-498.

19. McCann, J.E., and Ferry, D.I. An Approach for Assessing and Managing Interunit Interdependence. *Academy of Management Review*, 1979, *4*, 113-119.

20. Adapted from Jacobson, G. A Teamwork Ultimatum Puts Kimberly-Clark's Mill Back on the Map. *Management Review*, July 1989, 28-31.

21. Salancik, G.R. An Index of Influence in Dependency Networks. *Administrative Science Quarterly*, 1986, *31*, 194-211.

22. Cook, K.S., and Gillmore, M.R. Power, Dependence, and Coalition. In E.J. Lawler (ed.), *Advances in Group Processes*. Greenwich, Conn.: JAI Press, 1984, 27-58; Sniezek, J.A., May, D.R., and Sawyer, J.E. Social Uncertainty and Interdependence: A Study of Resource Allocation Decisions in Groups. *Organizational Behavior and Human Decision Processes*, 1990, *46*, 155-180.

23. Cordery, J.L., Mueller, W.S., and Smith, L.M. Attitudinal and Behavioral Effects of Autonomous Group Working: A Longitudinal Field Study. *Academy of Management Journal*, 1991, *34*, 464-476.

24. Walker, G., and Poppo, L. Profit Centers, Single-Source Suppliers, and Transaction Costs. *Administrative Science Quarterly*, 1991, *36*, 66-87.

25. Taylor, D.M., and Moghaddam, F.M. *Theories of Intergroup Relations*. New York: Praeger, 1987.

26. Simon, B., and Pettigrew, T.F. Social Identity and Perceived Group Homogeneity: Evidence for the Ingroup Homogeneity Effect. *European Journal of Social Psychology*, 1990, *20*, 269-286.

27. Cobb, A.T. Political Diagnosis: Applications in Organization Development. *Academy of Management Review*, 1986, *11*, 482-496.

28. Adapted from Powell, G.N. One More Time: Do Female and Male Managers Differ? *Academy of Management Executive*, August 1990, 68-75; Fierman, J. Do Women Manage Differently? *Fortune*, December 17, 1990, 115-118; Powell, G.N. *Women and Men in Management*. Newbury Park, Calif.: Sage, 1988.

29. Sherif, M., and Sherif, C. *Groups in Harmony and Tension: An Integration of Studies on Intergroup Relations*. New York: Octagon, 1966, 231; Smith, K.K. Social Comparison Processes and Dynamic Conservatism in Intergroup Relations. In L.L. Cummings and B.M. Staw (eds.), *Research in Organizational Behavior*. Greenwich, Conn.: JAI Press, 1983, 199-233.

30. Blake, R.R., and Morton, J.S. *Solving Costly Organizational Conflicts*. San Francisco: Jossey-Bass, 1984; Likert, R., and Likert, J.G. *New Ways of Managing Conflict*. New York: McGraw-Hill, 1976.

31. Gudykunst, W.B. *Bridging Differences: Effective Intergroup Communication*. Newbury Park, Calif.: Sage, 1991.

32. Adapted from Tung, R.L. Handshakes across the Sea: Cross-Cultural Negotiating for Business Success. *Organizational Dynamics*, Winter 1991, 30-40; Jang, Song-Hyon, Managing Joint Venture Partnership in Korea. Paper presented at the Korean-American Business Institute Annual Seminar on Doing Business in Korea. Seoul, Korea, May 3-4, 1988.

33. Sherif, M. Superordinate Goals in the Reduction of Intergroup Conflict. *American Journal of Sociology*, 1958, *68*, 349-358.

34. Kramer, R.M. Intergroup Relations and Organizational Dilemmas: The Role of Categorization Processes. In B.M. Staw and L.G. Cummings (eds.), *Research in Organizational Behavior*, vol. 13. Greenwich, Conn.: JAI Press, 1991, 191-228.

35. Graham-Moore, B., and Ross, T.L. *Gainsharing: Plans for Improving Performance*. Washington, D.C.: Bureau of National Affairs, 1990.

36. Pierce, J.L., and Furo, C.A. Employee Ownership: Implications for Management. *Organizational Dynamics*, Winter 1990, 32-43; Lawler, E.E., III. *Strategic Pay: Aligning Organizational Strategies and Pay Systems*. San Francisco: Jossey-Bass, 1990.

37. Schuster, M.H. The Scanlon Plan: A Longitudinal Analysis. *Journal of Applied Behavioral Science*, 1984, *20*, 23-38.

38. Adapted from Schuster, M.H. *Union-Management Cooperation*. Kalamazoo, Mich.: W.E. Upjohn Institute, 1984, 140-144. Used with permission.

39. Fulk, J. (ed.). *Organizations and Communication Technology*. Newbury Park, Calif.: Sage, 1990; Eden, C., and Radford, J. *Tackling Strategic Problems: The Role of Group Decision Support*. Newbury Park, Calif.: Sage, 1990.

40. David, F.R. *Strategic Management*, 3d. ed. New York: MacMillan, 1991.

41. Schwab, R.C., Ungson, G.R., and Brown, W.B. Redefining the Boundary-Spanning-Environment Relationship. *Journal of Management*, 1985, *11*, 75-86.

42. Troester, R. The Corporate Spokesperson in External Organization Communication. *Management Communication Quarterly*, 1991, *4*, 528-540.

43. Ancona, D.G., and Caldwell, D. Beyond Boundary-Spanning: Managing External Dependence in Product Development Teams. *Journal of High Technology Management Research*, 1990, *1*, 121-135.

44. McIsaac, C.M., and Aschauer, M.A. Proposal Writing at Atherton Jordon, Inc. *Management Communication Quarterly*, 1990, *3*, 527-560.

45. Tsui. A.S. A Multiple-Constituency Model of Effectiveness: An Empirical Examination at the Human Resource Subunit Level. *Administrative Science Quarterly*, 1990, *35*, 458-483.

46. Adapted from McCune, W.B. Internal Communications and Participatory Management: An Experiment in Team Building. *Public Relations Quarterly*, Fall 1989, 14-18.

47. Thomas, J.G. Madison Electronics Company. In S.L. Willey (ed.), *Annual Advances in Business Cases: 1988*. Ames, Iowa: Midwest Society for Case Research, 1988, 289-290. This case was prepared by Professor Joe G. Thomas, Middle Tennessee State University, as a basis for class discussion, rather than to illustrate either effective or ineffective handling of an administrative situation. Presented to the Midwest Society for Case Research Workshop, 1988. All rights reserved to the author. Copyright @ 1988 by Joe Thomas. Used with permission.

48. Adapted from Blumberg, M., and Pringle, C.D. How Control Groups Can Cause Loss of Control in Action Research: The Case of Rushton Coal Mine. *Journal of Applied Behavioral Science*, 1983, *19*, 409-425; Blumberg, M. Job Switching in Autonomous Work Groups: An Exploratory Study in a Pennsylvania Coal Mine. *Academy of Management Journal*, 1980, *23*, 287-306; Blumberg, M., and Alber, A. The Human Element: Its Impact on the Productivity of Advanced Batch Manufacturing Systems. *Journal of Manufacturing Systems*, 1982, *1*, 43-52; Goodman, P.S. *Assessing Organizational Change: The Rushton Quality of Work Life Experiment*. New York: John Wiley, 1979.

CHAPTER 12:

LEADERSHIP

LEARNING OBJECTIVES

When you have finished studying this chapter, you should be able to:

- Identify the differences between leaders and managers.
- List the skills and sources of power that leaders can use to influence subordinates.
- Describe the traits approach to leadership.
- Define the two behavioral leadership dimensions found by the Ohio State University leadership studies.
- Describe Fiedler's contingency model.
- Explain the leadership and contingency variables in both Hersey and Blanchard's situational leadership model and House's path-goal model.
- Discuss the situational variables in the Vroom-Jago model.
- Describe the attributional and charismatic theories of leadership.

OUTLINE

RICHARD NICOLOSI AT PROCTER & GAMBLE

In the 1970s, Procter & Gamble's (P & G) paper products division began to lose market share to its competitors. By 1984, its products, such as Pampers and Bounty Paper Towels, had lost more than 23 percent of their market. That year, Richard Nicolosi was put in charge of the division. What he found was a bureaucratic organization with strong centralized controls and little direction.

To turn the division around, he immediately began to stress the need to become more creative and market-driven, instead of being a low-cost producer. This new direction stressed the need for teamwork and for employees to perform multiple leadership roles. He delegated decision-making authority to teams to manage their major brands. He met with the advertising agency and got to know key creative people. He asked the marketing manager of diapers to report directly to him, eliminating a layer of middle management, and talked directly to employees working on new product-development projects.

In June 1985, several thousand employees from the paper products division met in Cincinnati. Nicolosi told them that each one of them was a leader. The message was that innovations came from employees dealing with new products and not simply market researchers. In the spring of 1986, a few of the division's secretaries developed a Secretaries Network. This network established committees on training, on rewards and recognition, and on the "Secretary of the Future." Echoing the feelings of many employees, one secretary said, "I don't see why we, too, can't contribute to the division's new direction."

By the end of 1988, revenues at the division were up by 40 percent over a four-year period and profits were up 66 percent.[1]

Nicolosi is an effective leader. If we examine how he steered the rebirth of this division, two important behaviors stand out. First, he developed an agenda for himself and the division that included a new vision of what the division could and should be. It was a vision of a competitive and profitable firm that produced high-quality, innovative products. Second, he gained cooperation from employees by motivating them to buy into this vision. He worked hard to delegate decision making to teams of employees who could make decisions. Employees now had a sense of belonging, recognition, and self-esteem, along with a feeling of control over their lives and the ability to live up to their own ideals. These feelings elicited a powerful motivational response from all team members. Nicolosi maintained these feelings by regularly involving employees in deciding how to achieve the division's goals. He rewarded success that gave the employees a sense of accomplishment and made them feel like they were a part of a team. Because he did those things, employees' work became intrinsically motivating.[2]

Leadership is the process whereby one person influences other members toward a goal.[3] **Leaders** are people who do the right thing to accomplish their team's visions. Nicolosi exercised leadership because he was able to guide, steer, and influence employees in accomplishing his new vision for that division.

Not all employees or managers exercise leadership. Many employees are good *managers* but not *leaders*. A **manager** is a person who directs the work of employees and is responsible for results. An effective manager brings a degree of order and consistency to his or her staff. Leadership, by contrast, is about coping with change.[4] Let's explore these differences more closely.

Managers manage complexity through *planning* and *budgeting*—setting goals, establishing steps to achieve those goals, and then allocating resources to achieve those goals. By contrast, leading starts with setting a *direction* or *vision* of what the future might look like and then developing strategies for producing changes needed to achieve that direction. According to William McCowan, chairman and CEO of MCI Communications, vision is the art of seeing beyond the present to seeing the possible. In uncertain times, employees look to leaders for vision. Like yeast, it is a leavening agent, and it stimulates the organization to grow and change. In its earliest days, MCI's vision of leadership in the global communications industry kept the company on course. This vision helped MCI beat the competition and enabled employees to take risks and to be innovative entrepreneurs.

Effective managers achieve their goals by *organizing* and *staffing*—creating an organizational structure and sets of jobs for accomplishing the plan's requirements, staffing the jobs with qualified employees, communicating the goals to those employees, and devising systems to monitor the employees' progress toward achieving those goals. Leaders try to *align* employees who share their vision. They create teams who understand and share their vision.

Finally, managers ensure that employees reach goals by *controlling* their behaviors. That is, they monitor results in great detail by means of reports and meetings, and they note deviations from the goal. Effective leadership requires *motivating* and *inspiring* teams of employees. It taps their needs, values, and emotions. That is what Nicolosi did at P & G to successfully motivate employees to overcome the obstacles that the division faced when he took over.

In sum, while some managers are leaders, others are not. Figure 12.1 shows this. Each role—manager and leader—requires different behaviors.

The difference between leaders and managers can be illustrated by considering Harold Geneen, former CEO at ITT.[5] Geneen managed the corporation in a highly disciplined manner. He required managers to continuously produce detailed plans and budgets aimed at achieving the financial objectives he set. Powerful economic incentives and control systems to get employees to accomplish those plans and budgets were needed. This management style was remarkably successful in the 1960s. During that time, ITT bought more than one hundred different companies and then made them more profitable by managing each more efficiently. The problem with this style of management was that few employees at ITT were able to be effective when the environment became unpredictable in the 1970s. In an unpredictable environment, financial planning becomes more difficult. Geneen's ever more elaborate control systems to monitor his employees discouraged innovation. Under Geneen's chairmanship, emphasizing very disciplined management, ITT's financial performance declined steadily from 1975 to 1985. Geneen was a manger, not a leader. He did not project a vision of

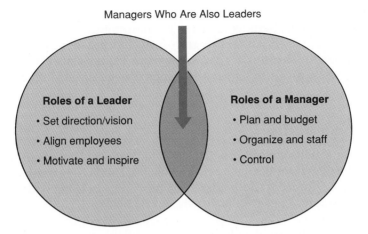

FIGURE 12.1 Roles of Leaders and Managers

success, nor did he help others find meaning in their work. In short, he did not exercise visionary leadership.

THE LEADERSHIP PROCESS

Leadership has always been, and probably always will be, important to organizations. Recently, the need for managerial leadership and the difficulty of providing it has grown considerably because of the increasing complexity of our world. Hundreds of firms and dozens of industries have been restructured to remain competitive. The banking industry provides a good example. Since federal deregulation, the local bank's competition is not just the bank down the street. It is also Sears, Merrill Lynch, American Express, foreign banks, and General Electric. The airline, insurance, automobile, health care, and other industries face new competitive pressures every day.

Leader-Subordinate Relationships

Leadership is considered valuable by subordinates, but leaders become an integral part of an organization, group, or team only after proving their value to subordinates. People in leadership positions also gain economic and psychological rewards. People at the top of many organizations are paid up to eighty-five times as much as the lowest-paid employees.[6] (Notwithstanding the possibility that some people may not be worth that much more than others, someone thinks so.) However, people seek leadership even when there are no economic rewards. The captain of a collegiate basketball team, a union steward, and the chairperson of a civic or church committee do not hold paid positions, but they usually exercise leadership. Leadership rewards people with power over others; with this power, people believe that they can influence to some extent the well-being of others and can affect their own destinies.

Leaders receive their authority from subordinates because the subordinates have accepted them as leaders. To maintain a leadership position, a person must enable the others to gain satisfactions that are otherwise beyond their reach. In return, they satisfy the leader's need for power and prominence and give the leader the support necessary to reach organizational goals.

Leadership Skills

If we look at the leadership practices of Nicolosi and McCowan, we can see that both leaders have been successful. The methods they use to reach their goals are quite different. Both share several common skills with many other successful leaders. These skills are shown in Figure 12.2.[7]

Creating a Vision Leaders have the skill to pull employees toward them by creating a new vision. People want to be part of an organization that has a vision larger than reality. When a leader can share his or her vision with others and get them committed to it, this vision "grabs" others. Both Nicolosi of P & G and McCowan of MCI are excellent visionary leaders. Employees become so caught up in what they are doing that they absorb and commit themselves to the goals and values of these leaders. The visions that leaders convey instill confidence in others, a confidence that leads them to believe that they can succeed.

Meaning through Communication Successful leaders have the skill to communicate effectively with organizational members. Such leaders can relate a compelling vision of a desired state of affairs—the kind of vision that induces enthusiasm and commitment in others. In Nicolosi's case, this communication often takes the form of intense meetings with all employees. In this case, communication creates meaning for others.

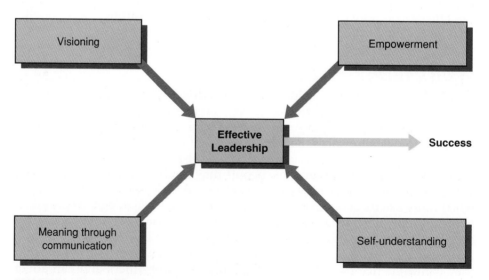

FIGURE 12.2 Effective Leadership Skills

Empowerment   The skill of sharing power with employees is **empowerment.** It means that the leader allows organizational members to share in developing goals and strategies—and the satisfactions derived from reaching those goals. An example of this is when the secretaries of P & G formed their Secretaries Network so they could contribute to the division's new vision. Effective leaders usually are not dictators, like Geneen was at ITT—at least not over the long run. Effective leaders are powerful but sensitive to the needs of employees. They tap the motivations and capabilities in others to pursue shared goals. The behaviors associated with empowerment include taking delight in an employee's development, realizing that visions are achieved by teams and not by single employees, and helping employees reach their personal goals. John Bryan of Sara Lee, J. Carter Fox of Chesapeake, and Reuben Mark of Colgate all believe that empowerment is important because it permits employees to share the leader's goals. In effect, the leader clones himself or herself by empowering other employees. Responsible employees will not make decisions that are inconsistent with their goals, especially ones that they helped shape. Since many of its employees are scattered throughout the world, Colgate sends around quarterly videotapes that explain the firm's position on a variety of issues, such as its policies on South Africa and the rights of women. Such tactics help employees distant from headquarters to share Colgate's goals.

Self-Understanding   Effective leaders have the skill to recognize their strengths and weaknesses. They tend to hire employees who can compensate for their self-perceived weaknesses. They are eager to receive feedback on their performance. Effective leaders continually take an inventory of themselves: "What am I really good at?" "What are my strengths?" "What do I lack?" "What do I need to work on?"

These leadership skills can be learned. In many organizations, such as Texas Instruments, General Foods, and Johnson & Johnson, potential leaders get the types of job experience early in their careers that help them develop these skills. The following account describes how Johnson & Johnson develops leadership skills in its employees.

IN PRACTICE

DEVELOPING LEADERS AT JOHNSON & JOHNSON

The largest U.S. pharmaceutical company, Johnson & Johnson, is broken up into 165 units worldwide, some with only a few dozen employees, some with as many as 5,000. Each of these units has considerable freedom to make decisions affecting its own operations. The unit presidents in the United States have full responsibility for their unit's research and development, manufacturing, sales, and marketing. Headquarters in New Brunswick, New Jersey, sets corporate policy on financial and administrative matters but otherwise leaves the presidents, many in their late thirties and early forties, on their own. According to Irwin Holzman, vice-president for organization planning and development, "We believe in keeping the units small and recruiting the best people we can find, giving them as much responsibility as early as we can, moving them up rapidly, and keeping track of them." At Johnson & Johnson, leaders watch for employees who have high energy levels, flexibility, judgment, maturity, and most of all, success at selling ideas and products to other unit members.

Carl Spalding was thirty-eight when Johnson & Johnson sent him to South Africa as director of its consumer products unit. Not only did he have to run the business, but he had to hire, train, and promote black employees and even build housing for them, sometimes in conflict with apartheid laws. After three years, he was transferred back to the United States and was picked to run Johnson & Johnson's dental care unit, which merged the company's consumer and professional dental businesses into one.[8]

Sources of a Leader's Power

To influence others, a person must appeal to one or more of their needs (see Chapter 7). If a robber is pointing a gun at a bank teller and is ready to fire it, chances are that the teller will do what the robber asks. History proves, however, that in many situations, people refuse to obey an order even when faced with death. Thus, effective leadership depends as much on acceptance of direction by the follower as on the leader giving it.

Power and influence are central to a leader's job. In Chapter 16, we discuss the sources of a manager's power. Therefore, here we consider only briefly the sources of a leader's power.[9]

Legitimate Power Employees may do something because the leader has the right to request them to do it and they have an obligation to comply. This **legitimate power** comes from the leader's position in the organization. Employees at ITT followed Geneen's orders because he was the CEO.

Reward Power Employees may do something to get rewards that the leader controls (such as promotions, pay raises, and better assignments). Thus, **reward power** comes from the leader's ability to provide something desired by team members in return for their desired behaviors. By buying into McCowan's vision for MCI, MCI has grown to be a major competitor in the telecommunications industry.

Coercive Power Employees may do something to avoid punishments that the leader controls (such as demotions, reprimands, no pay raises, and termination). Unfortunately, **coercive power** does not encourage desired behavior. In Chapter 6, we described how team members whom managers reprimand for poor workmanship may suddenly slow production, stop working altogether, be absent more often, and take other negative actions.

Referent Power Employees may do something because they admire the leader, want to be like the leader, and want to receive the leader's approval. **Referent power** is usually associated with individuals who have admired personal characteristics, such as charisma, integrity, and courage.

Expert Power   Employees may do something because they believe that the leader has special knowledge and expertise and knows what is needed to accomplish the task. **Expert power** has a narrow scope: employees are influenced by a leader only within that leader's area of expertise.

Effective Use of Power   Figure 12.3 divides these sources of power into the personal and the organizational. Legitimate, reward, and coercive powers are organizational, and company rules prescribe them. Part of the leader's job is to use them wisely to motivate members. A team probably will not achieve exceptional levels of performance if its leader relies solely on organizational power. Thus, reliance on referent and expert power—personal power—can lead to higher job satisfaction and less absenteeism or turnover. However, a leader must use all five sources of power at times, depending on the situation, to obtain both follower satisfaction and productivity.[10]

The bases of power are changing within organizations because of changing technology, ability of employees to use information to make decisions, and the flattening of the management hierarchy. In *The New Realities*, Peter Drucker says that leaders must empower employees to get results.[11] One leader who has practiced this is Ralph Strayer, CEO of Johnsonville Foods, a specialty foods and sausage maker in Sheboygan, Wisconsin. Said Stayer, "Flattening pyramids doesn't work if you don't transfer the power, too. Before, I didn't have power because I had people wandering around not giving a damn. Real power is getting people committed. It comes from giving it to others who are in a better position to do things than you are. The only control a leader can possibly have comes when people are controlling themselves."[12]

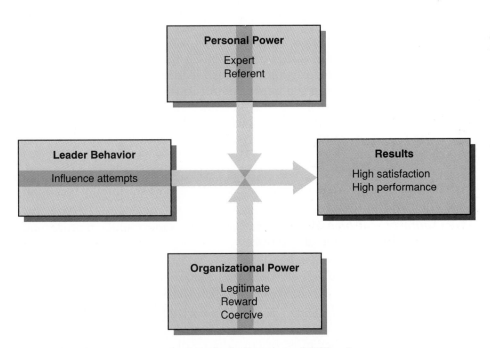

FIGURE 12.3   Sources of a Leader's Power and Effectiveness

LEADERSHIP APPROACHES

Many people believe that they have the intuitive ability to identify outstanding leaders. Often they believe that people with pleasing personalities will be highly successful leaders and recommend as leaders those who have personal charm.

Although some people have the intuitive ability to select individuals who become good leaders, most of us do not. There are different ways to assess leadership effectiveness and potential. In the remainder of this chapter, we present and examine five general approaches to assessing leadership: traits, behavioral, contingency, and two of the latest approaches—attributional and charismatic.

Traits Model

The **traits model** is based on observed characteristics of many leaders—both successful and unsuccessful. The resulting lists of traits are then compared to those of potential leaders to predict their success or failure. There is support for the notion that effective leaders have interests and abilities and, perhaps, even personality traits that are different from those of less effective leaders. Most researchers, however, believe that the traits approach is inadequate for successfully predicting leadership performance for at least three reasons.[13]

First, although more than one hundred personality traits of successful leaders have been identified, no consistent patterns have been found.[14] The trait stereotypes of successful leaders in charge of salespeople include optimism, enthusiasm, and dominance. Successful production leaders are usually progressive, introverted, cooperative, and genuinely respectful of employees. These descriptions are simply stereotypes. Many successful leaders of salespeople and production employees do not have all, or even some, of these characteristics. In fact, the list of personality traits never ends, and researchers often disagree over which traits are the most important for an effective leader. Furthermore, two leaders with significantly different traits have been found to be successful in the same situation.

Despite these difficulties, the evidence does suggest that four traits are shared by most (but not all) successful leaders. These traits, which are more likely to be found in middle-level and top leaders than in team leaders or first-line supervisors, are:

- *Intelligence.* Leaders tend to have somewhat higher intelligence than their subordinates.
- *Maturity and breadth.* Leaders tend to be emotionally mature and have a broad range of interests.
- *Inner motivation and achievement drive.* Leaders want to accomplish things; when they achieve one goal, they seek another. They do not depend primarily on employees for their motivation to achieve goals.
- *Employee-centered.* Leaders are able to work effectively with employees in a variety of situations. They respect others and realize that, to accomplish tasks, they must be considerate of others' needs and values.

The second criticism of the traits model relates physical characteristics such as height, weight, appearance, physique, energy, and health to effective leadership. However, most of these factors also correlate with many situational factors that can significantly affect a leader's effectiveness. For example, military or law enforcement people must be a certain minimum height and weight in order to perform certain tasks effectively. While these characteristics may help an individual to rise to a leadership position in such organizations, neither height nor weight correlates highly with performance. In educational or business organizations, on the other hand, height and weight play no role in performance and thus are not requirements for a leadership position.

The final criticism of the traits model is that leadership itself is complex. A relationship between personality and a person's interest in particular types of jobs could well exist and a study relating personality and effectiveness not reflect it. For example, one study found that high earners (a measure of success) in small firms were more aspiring, tended to have interests similar to those of human resources employees, were more open-minded, and described themselves as more considerate than low earners. In small firms, it should be noted, a leader usually performs numerous jobs. Those leaders who like performing multiple jobs may seek out small firms that permit them to do so.

Behavioral Models

Because of the failure of the traits model to accurately predict successful leadership, researchers shifted their emphasis from trying to identify leaders' traits to studying leaders' behavior. That is, what leaders actually *do* and *how* they do it. Behavioral models suggest that effective leaders assist individuals, teams, and groups in achieving their goals in two ways: (1) by having task-centered relations with members that focus attention on the quality and quantity of work accomplished; and (2) by being considerate and supportive of members' attempts to achieve personal goals (such as work satisfaction, promotions, and recognition), settling disputes, keeping people happy, providing encouragement, and giving positive reinforcement.

Ohio State University Leadership Studies   The greatest number of studies of leader behavior have come from the **Ohio State University leadership studies** program, which began in the late 1940s under the direction of Ralph Stogdill.[15] That research was aimed at identifying those leader behaviors that are important for attaining team and organizational goals. These efforts resulted in the identification of two dimensions of leader behavior: consideration and initiating structure.

Consideration is the extent to which leaders are likely to have job relationships characterized by mutual trust, two-way communication, respect for employees' ideas, and consideration for their feelings. Leaders with this style emphasize the needs of the employee. They typically find time to listen to members, are willing to make changes, look out for the personal welfare of employees, and are friendly and approachable. A high degree of consideration indicates psychological closeness between a leader and his or her employees; a low degree shows greater psychological distance and a more impersonal leader.

Initiating structure is the extent to which leaders are likely to define and structure their roles and those of employees toward accomplishing the organization's goals. Leaders with this style emphasize direction of group activities through planning, communicating information, scheduling, assigning tasks, emphasizing deadlines, and giving directions. They maintain definite standards of performance and ask subordinates to follow standard rules. In short, leaders with a high degree of initiating structure concern themselves with accomplishing tasks by giving directions and expecting them to be followed.

Research indicates that a leader who emphasizes consideration generally fosters employee satisfaction, group harmony, and cohesion. Studies also suggest that a leader who emphasizes initiating structure generally improves productivity, at least in the short run. However, leaders that rank high on initiating structure and low on consideration generally have large numbers of grievances, absenteeism, and high turnover rates among employees. We might rank Harold Geneen high on initiating structure and low on consideration. We might rank Richard Nicolosi high on initiating structure and high on consideration.

The Ohio State University researchers made an assumption that leader behavior is related not only to indirect measures of performance, such as absenteeism, grievances, and turnover, but also to direct measures of performance, such as the number of units produced. Later studies by others have failed to show a significant relationship between leadership behavior and group performance.[16] This failure indicates that individual productivity is influenced by other factors, including (1) the employee's social status within the group; (2) the technology used; (3) employee expectations of a certain style of leadership; and (4) employee psychological rewards from working with a particular type of leader.

When Consideration Is Effective The most positive effects of leader consideration on members' productivity and job satisfaction occur when (1) the task is routine and denies employees any job satisfaction; (2) employees are predisposed toward participative leadership; (3) team members must learn something new; (4) employees feel that their involvement in the decision-making process is legitimate and affects their job performance; and (5) few status differences exist between leader and subordinate.[17]

When Initiating Structure Is Effective The most positive effects of leader initiating structure on members' productivity and job satisfaction occur when (1) a high degree of pressure for output is imposed by someone other than the leader; (2) the task satisfies employees; (3) employees depend on the leader for information and direction on how to complete the task; (4) employees are psychologically predisposed toward being told what to do and how to do it; and (5) more than twelve employees report to the leader.

This chapter's Across Cultures illustrates some of the leadership problems U.S. leaders face in Eastern European countries. We caution you not to generalize GE's results to other organizations but hope that it helps you to understand the difficulty in providing leadership to employees in other

GE IN HUNGARY: LET THERE BE LIGHT

 At a turn-of-the-century light bulb plant in Tungsram, near Budapest, Hungary, a group of leaders from General Electric is tackling one of GE's toughest management experiments of the 1990s—turning a sluggish state-owned factory into a profit-making capitalist venture.

Even the most basic business terms are mysterious to employees. David Gadra, an expert in information systems, discussed the importance of keeping close track of inventory and receivables in order to measure their effect on profits. "What profit means?" asked one Hungarian engineer. No sooner did he answer that question than another employee asked, "Why profit?"

George Varga, GE's general manager at its plant, says that managing in Eastern Europe is very difficult. At Tungsram, labor accounts for one-quarter of the cost of making a light bulb, compared with one-half in the United States. Raw materials make up most of the rest of the expenses. Therefore, controlling costs of raw materials is very important.

Product development is also crucial. Tungsram derives more than 50 percent of its sales from the glass tungsten light bulb first manufactured in 1906. These bulbs are of high quality, but they are cheap. The market growth of these bulbs in Eastern European countries is slow. GE is losing ground to new growth products, such as compact fluorescent bulbs for home and office use, high-pressure sodium lamps for street lighting, and miniature lights that sparkle.

Since the state operated the plant for more than fifty years, there are additional problems. Office equipment is old. Clerks still enter billing and inventory information by pencil into large accounting ledgers. For example, when GE checked warehouses in France and Germany, it found $3 million worth of six-watt car headlights. Unfortunately, these have not been used by automobile manufacturers since the 1970s. Numerous rules keep bureaucracy very high and add staff to the plant's payroll. For example, since checking accounts rarely exist for employees, a staff of 150 employees is needed to manually stuff 17,000 pay envelopes with cash every month.

Wages are so low that it often does not make sense to replace employees with equipment. On the average, an employee at Tungsram makes $3,000 a year, compared with more than $30,000 at its competitors in the United States and Western Europe.

To help lower costs without cutting employees, GE is bringing in more than thirty manufacturing experts to help improve the efficiency of the assembly line. For example, one production line turns out three million outdoor spotlights a year. But between poor equipment and unskilled employees, a half-million of these are broken. The floor is covered with glass and discarded bulbs.[18]

countries. After reading this account, what style of leadership do you think will work best with these employees?

Major Weaknesses of the Model The major weakness of the Ohio State University research was the limited attention it gave to the effects of the situation on leadership style. It paid attention to relationships between leader and members but gave virtually no attention to the situation in which the relationships occurred. The importance of the situation is considered by the contingency, or situational, models of leadership.

CONTINGENCY MODELS OF LEADERSHIP

Research into the leadership process before the mid-1960s showed no consistent relationship between leadership style and measures of performance, group processes, and job satisfaction. Although many researchers concluded that the situation in which a leader functions plays a significant role in determining the leader's effectiveness, they did little to identify the key situational variables.

Contingency leadership theorists, in contrast, direct their research toward discovering the variables that permit certain leadership characteristics and behaviors to be effective in a given situation. For example, contingency theorists would suggest that a college administrator and a drill sergeant need substantially different characteristics and behaviors because they face entirely different situations.

Four contingency variables are frequently suggested as influences on a leader's behavior: (1) a leader's personal characteristics; (2) employees' personal characteristics; (3) the group's characteristics; and (4) the structure of the group, department, or organization.[19] As suggested in Figure 12.4, these four contingency variables interact to influence a leader's style of behavior. The leadership process is very complex, and simple prescriptions (such as "democratic leaders have more satisfied employees than autocratic leaders") just do not work.

In this section, we present and discuss four specific contingency models of leadership: Fiedler's contingency model, Hersey and Blanchard's situational leadership model, House's path-goal model, and the Vroom-Jago model. Each at least partially explains how some of the contingency variables affect the leadership process.

Fiedler's Contingency Model

Fred Fiedler and his associates developed the first contingency model of the leadership process.[20] **Fiedler's contingency model** specifies that a perfor-

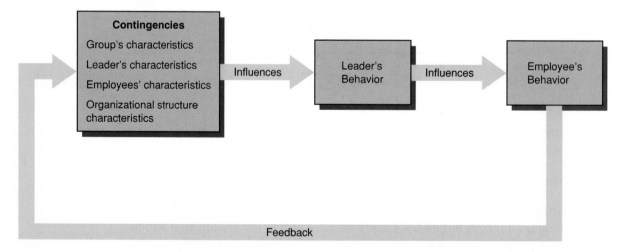

FIGURE 12.4 Key Contingency Variables That Affect Leader Behavior

mance is contingent upon both the leader's motivational system and the degree to which the leader controls and influences the situation. The model's three contingency variables—group atmosphere, task structure, and the leader's position power—are shown in Figure 12.5. In combination, the three contingency variables create eight situations as shown in Figure 12.6.

Group Atmosphere Group atmosphere refers to a leader's acceptance by the team. The leader who is accepted by and inspires loyalty in employees needs few signs of rank to get them to commit themselves to a task. When leader and employees get along well together, there is less friction. In groups that reject the leader, the leader's basic problem is to keep from being undercut or having the task sabotaged.

Task Structure The extent to which a task performed by employees is routine or nonroutine is the degree of **task structure.** A routine task is likely to have clearly defined goals, to consist of only a few steps or procedures, to be verifiable, and to have a correct solution. At the other extreme is the task that is completely nonroutine. In this situation, the leader may no more know how to perform the task than the employees do. Such a task is likely to have unclear goals and multiple paths to accomplishment; the task cannot be done by the "numbers."

Jean-Marie Descarpentries runs Franco-British CMB Packaging. He describes the task as unstructured and himself as an orchestra leader. He runs each of his ninety-four organizations as separate businesses, but in the end, they all must work together to achieve the organization's goals. Instead of tight budgets, he and his staff set financial targets that are designed to stretch all employees, including themselves. He uses these primarily to get employees to dream the impossible. Because each business has its own sets of problems and opportunities, he evaluates them mainly on how well they do this year versus last year and how they stack up against industry leaders. Descarpentries calls it "management by pride." As a leader, his job is offering consulting advice, not orders.[21]

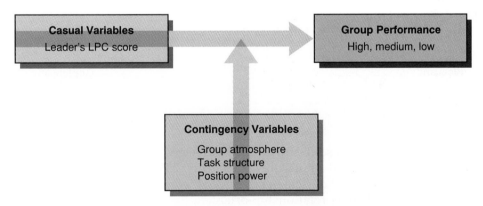

FIGURE 12.5 Major Variables in Fiedler's Contingency Model

Source: G. A. Yukl, *Leadership in Organizations,* 196. Copyright © 1989 by Prentice-Hall, Inc., Englewood Cliffs, N.J. Adapted with permission.

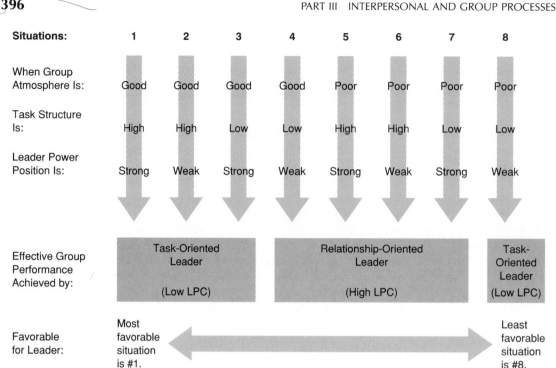

Memorize

Situations:	1	2	3	4	5	6	7	8
When Group Atmosphere Is:	Good	Good	Good	Good	Poor	Poor	Poor	Poor
Task Structure Is:	High	High	Low	Low	High	High	Low	Low
Leader Power Position Is:	Strong	Weak	Strong	Weak	Strong	Weak	Strong	Weak

Effective Group Performance Achieved by:

Task-Oriented Leader (Low LPC) — Relationship-Oriented Leader (High LPC) — Task-Oriented Leader (Low LPC)

Favorable for Leader:

Most favorable situation is #1. ⟷ Least favorable situation is #8.

FIGURE 12.6 Continuum of the Three Basic Leadership Variables

Position Power Position power is the extent to which a leader has reward, coercive, and legitimate power. In most business organizations, leaders have high position power, including the authority to hire, discipline, and fire employees. In most voluntary organizations, committees, and social organizations, leaders tend to have low position power.

Leadership Style Fiedler developed the **least preferred co-worker (LPC)** scale to measure leadership style. Scores are obtained by asking employees to first think about all the people with whom they have worked and then to identify the individual with whom they have worked least well. The person then rates this least preferred co-worker on a set of eighteen scales, two of which are as follows:

Pleasant	—	—	—	—	—	—	—	—	Unpleasant
	8	7	6	5	4	3	2	1	
Friendly	—	—	—	—	—	—	—	—	Unfriendly
	8	7	6	5	4	3	2	1	

Low-LPC leaders describe their least preferred co-worker in negative terms and are classified as task-oriented. *High-LPC* leaders give a more positive description of their least preferred co-worker, are sensitive to others, and are classified as relationship-oriented.

How Well Does It Work? Fiedler's answer to how well it works is: it all depends. What it all depends on is the situational factors—leader-member relations, task structure, and leader power. Fiedler suggests that whether low-LPC or high-LPC leaders are more effective depends on the degree to which the situation is favorable to the leader. That is, the degree to which the situation provides the leader with control over others.

Figure 12.6 represents the basic contingency model. It shows the average results of the studies conducted by Fiedler and his associates. Task-motivated (low-LPC) leaders performed more effectively than high-LPC leaders in the most favorable situations (1, 2, and 3) and in the least favorable situation (8). Low-LPC leaders are motivated basically by task accomplishments. In the most favorable situation—when their group supports them, their power position is high, and the task is structured (situation 1)—leaders will strive to develop pleasant work relations in directing group members. They realize that conditions are very good and that successful task performance is highly likely. As a result, they can turn their attention to improving their relations with team members and often adopt a "hands off" style. Employees value such treatment, and satisfaction and performance remains high. In the least favorable situation (8)—when the task is unstructured, they lack group support, and their position power is low—these leaders will devote their energies to achieving organizational goals by telling employees what to do.

Figure 12.6 also shows situations in which high-LPC leaders will probably perform more effectively than low-LPC leaders. High-LPC leaders get the best performance under conditions that are moderately favorable (situations 4 through 7). Situations 4 and 5 describe cases in which (1) the group has a structured task but dislikes the leader, who must demonstrate concern for the emotions of employees; or (2) the group likes the leader but has an unstructured task, and the leader must depend on the willingness and creativity of group members to accomplish the goals. As a result, high-LPC leaders may shift their attention to task performance. Shelly Pierce, a project leader at Texas Instruments, is a high-LPC leader who provides guidance to her team members when they start a new task. Once they have learned how to proceed and their task becomes more structured, she delegates decision-making authority to them and supports them.

There are several problems with Fiedler's contingency model.[22] In particular, critics have questioned the use of LPC, arguing that better measures of leader behaviors are needed. They call LPC a one-dimensional concept; that is, it implies that if individuals are highly motivated toward task accomplishment, they are unconcerned with relations among employees and vice versa. In addition, critics say that Fiedler's model does not consider that leaders can influence both the task structure and group atmosphere because of their knowledge of the situation. That is, the task can be changed by the leader and therefore is not a dependent variable in the model. The nature of the employee's task can be determined, at least in part, by the leader's style.

Organizational Implications   In spite of these criticisms, Fiedler's contingency model has three important organizational implications.[23] First, both relationship-motivated and task-motivated leaders perform well in certain situations but not in others. Outstanding leaders at one level who get promoted to another level may fail at the higher level because their leadership style does not match the demands of the situation.

Second, leaders' performance depends both on their motivational bases and the situation. Therefore, an organization can affect leadership by changing the reward system for the manager or by modifying the situation itself. For example, how might GE structure the situation at its Tungsram light bulb plant to increase the odds of George Varga's effectiveness?

Third, leaders themselves can do something about their situations. Table 12.1 presents some of Fiedler's suggestions for changing particular contingency variables. He is suggesting that leaders can be taught how to become better leaders. **Leader match** is a self-teaching process utilizing a programmed learning text that instructs the individual about how to match his or her LPC level with the situation. This match could be achieved by

---

TABLE 12.1   Leadership Actions to Change Contingency Variables

Modifying Group Atmosphere

1. Spend more—or less—informal time with your employees (lunch, leisure activities, etc.).
2. Request particular people to work in your team.
3. Volunteer to direct difficult or troublesome employees.
4. Suggest or effect transfers of particular employees into or out of your department.
5. Raise morale by obtaining positive outcomes for team members (e.g., special bonuses, time off, attractive jobs).

Modifying Task Structure

If you wish to work with less structured tasks, you can:

1. Ask your superior, whenever possible, to give you the new or unusual problems and let you figure out how to get them done.
2. Bring the problems and tasks to your team members and invite them to work with you on the planning and decision-making phases of the tasks.

If you wish to work with more highly structured tasks, you can:

1. Ask your superior to give you, whenever possible, the tasks that are more structured or to give you more detailed instructions.
2. Break the job down into smaller subtasks that can be more highly structured.

Modifying Position Power

To raise your position power, you can:

1. Show others "who's boss" by exercising fully the powers that the organization provides.
2. Make sure that information to others gets channeled through you.

To lower your position power, you can:

1. Call on team members to participate in planning and decision-making functions.
2. Delegate decision making to others.

Source: Developed from F. E. Fiedler and J. E. Garcia, *New Approaches to Effective Leadership.* New York: John Wiley & Sons, 1987, 49–93.

changing the situation to mesh with the leader's LPC style or moving to a new position in the organization.

Hersey and Blanchard's Situational Leadership Model

Hersey and Blanchard's situational leadership model is based on the amount of relationship (supportive) and task (directive) behavior that a leader provides in a situation.[24] The amount of either relationship or task behavior is based on the readiness of the follower.

Task behavior is the extent to which a leader spells out to followers what to do, where to do it, and how to do it. Leaders who use task behavior structure, control, and closely supervise the behaviors of their followers. *Relationship behavior* is the extent to which a leader listens, provides support and encouragement, and involves followers in the decision-making process. *Follower readiness* is defined as subordinates' ability and willingness to perform the task. Followers have various degrees of readiness, as shown in Figure 12.7. In R1, the followers are either unable or unwilling to perform the task, whereas in R4, they are very able, willing, and confident that they can achieve the task. R2 is a situation where followers are unable but willing or confident to perform a task. In follower readiness level R3, subordinates are able to do the task, but are either unwilling or not totally confident about their abilities to perform the task. According to situational leadership, as the readiness level of individuals increases from R1 to R4, a leader should change his or her style to increase subordinates' commitment, competence, and performance.

Style of Leader and Readiness of Followers Figure 12.7 shows the model linking task and relationship leader behaviors and follower readiness. The appropriate style of leadership is shown by the curve running through the four leadership quadrants.

A *telling style* provides clear and specific instruction. Since subordinates are either unable or unwilling to perform the task, specific direction and close supervision is needed. That is, the leader tells subordinates what to do and where to perform various tasks.

A *selling style* is effective when the subordinates are willing but somewhat unable to carry out their task. The selling style provides both task and relationship leader behaviors. Since subordinates still are unable to perform the task, but are eager to do the task, a selling style is most effective. This style encourages two-way communication between the leader and subordinates and helps subordinates build confidence in their ability to perform the task.

A *participating style* works best when the subordinates are able but not fully confident of their ability to perform the task. This moderate level of follower readiness requires the leader to maintain two-way communication and to encourage and support the skills the followers have developed.

When followers are very able, willing, and confident to perform their tasks, a delegating style of leader behavior is most appropriate. A *delegating style* provides little task or relationship behaviors because subordinates are permitted to run the show. They decide how and when to do things.

The following In Practice focuses on leadership practices at Chaparral Steel, a Midlothian, Texas, steel company. It is one of the most efficient steel mills in the world. The leaders of this organization practice a delegating

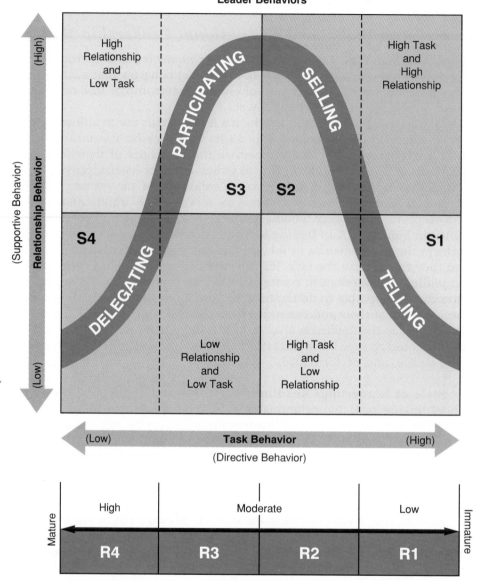

FIGURE 12.7   Hersey and Blanchard's Situational Leadership Model

Source: Paul Hersey and Kenneth H. Blanchard, *Management of Organizational Behavior: Utilizing Human Resources,* 5th ed. Englewood Cliffs, N.J.: Prentice-Hall, 1988. Used by permission from Ronald Campbell, President, Leadership Studies, Escondido, CA. September, 1991.

style of leadership. After reading this In Practice, you should know why the delegating style works so effectively at Chaparral.

IN PRACTICE

CHAPARRAL STEEL

During a recent tour, a visiting manager asked a Chaparral Steel manager, "How do you schedule coffee breaks in the plant?" "The workers decide when they want a cup of coffee" was the reply. "Yes, but who tells them when it's okay to leave the machines?" the visitor asked. The Chaparral manager just shrugged his shoulders.

All new employees take a course entitled "The Chaparral Process." This course tells them what happens to a piece of steel as it moves through the mill. It also covers accounting, finance, marketing, and sales. Once trained, they understand how their job relates to the welfare of the entire organization. Financial statements are posted monthly in the mill, including a chart that tracks profits.

Several years ago, a team leader and several employees went to Asia, Europe, and South America to evaluate new steel mills. After the team returned, they discussed the advantages and disadvantages of various mills with other employees and top management. When the choices were narrowed down to a few, they took off again to evaluate the final ones before making a recommendation to buy.

Top management and the team chose a new mill. The team ordered it and even oversaw its installation. While other companies may spend more than two years studying and finally installing a machine, Chaparral employees did the entire project in one year.[25]

Organizational Implications   The Hersey and Blanchard situational leadership model has generated a lot of interest.[26] The idea that people should be flexible in choosing a leadership style is appealing to many leaders. The readiness level of the employees must constantly be checked in order for the leader to determine what combination of task and relationship behaviors would be most appropriate. An inexperienced employee (low readiness) may perform at as high a level as an experienced employee if directed and closely supervised by a manager. If the style is appropriate, it should also help employees increase their level of readiness. Thus, as a leader develops a team and helps them learn to manage themselves, there is a need to change the leadership style to fit the situation.

There are some drawbacks to this model.[27] First, can leaders actually choose a leadership style when faced with different situations? The answer to this question has important implications for management selection, placement, and promotion. At Chaparral, a recommendation might be to promote a person only if he or she has a flexible leadership style. Some people can read situations better and adapt their style more effectively than others. While leaders at Chaparral Steel have adapted effectively, what are the costs of training leaders to be flexible? Do these costs exceed the benefits? Second, the model ignores many other factors, such as personality traits and the power base of the leader, which could influence a leader choosing a style. Third, a work group or team may be composed of employees with differing levels of readiness. Under this condition, what is the best common style? Large groups may make a generalized leadership choice almost impossible. Finally, the model does not distinguish between types of tasks (routine versus nonroutine, simple versus complex).

House's Path-Goal Model

Puzzled by the contradictory research findings on leadership, Robert J. House developed a model based on the expectancy theory of motivation (see Chapter 7). **House's path-goal model of leadership** suggests that in order to be effective, a leader must select a style most appropriate to the particular situation.[28]

The model states essentially that a leader should try to enhance employees' satisfaction with their jobs and increase their performance level. A leader can make job satisfaction easier to obtain and increase employees' satisfaction by clarifying the nature of the task, reducing roadblocks to successful task completion, and increasing the opportunities for them to obtain job satisfactions. The model states further that employees will be motivated when the leader performs these functions. Employees are satisfied with their jobs to the extent that performance leads to rewards they value highly. House's general model is shown graphically in Figure 12.8.

Leader Behaviors   The model identifies four distinct types of leader behavior:

- **Supportive leadership,** which includes considering the needs of employees, displaying concern for their welfare, and creating a friendly climate in the work group. This behavior is similar to the Ohio State University consideration style.

- **Directive leadership,** which involves letting members know what they are expected to do, giving them specific guidance, asking them to follow rules and regulations, scheduling and coordinating their work, and setting standards of performance for them. This behavior is similar to the initiating structure style previously discussed.

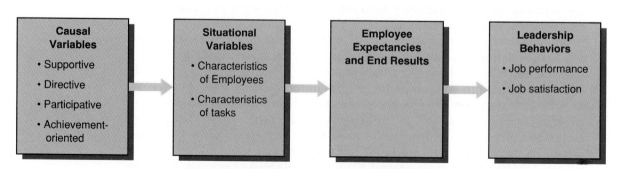

FIGURE 12.8   The Path-Goal Leadership Model

- **Participative leadership,** which includes consulting with others and evaluating their opinions and suggestions when making decisions.
- **Achievement-oriented leadership,** which entails setting challenging goals, seeking improvements in performance, emphasizing excellence in performance, and showing confidence that members will achieve high standards of performance.

Contingency Variables: Employees Needs and Tasks   House's model has two contingency variables: *employees needs* and *task characteristics*. The personal characteristics of employees determine how they will react to a leader's behavior. Employees with strong needs for acceptance and affiliation may find their needs satisfied with a supportive leader. On the other hand, employees with strong needs for autonomy, responsibility, and self-actualization will probably be motivated more by participative and achievement-oriented leaders than by supportive leaders.

A routine task has the following characteristics: (1) it does not call for use of a variety of skills; (2) it represents bits and pieces of a job, rather than the whole job; (3) it requires few decisions regarding scheduling and methods to be used; and (4) it provides little information about how well it has been performed. A nonroutine task has the opposite characteristics. Figure 12.9 illustrates the application of supportive and directive leadership styles to routine and nonroutine tasks.

Effects of Different Leadership Styles   When employees have a task that is tedious, boring, or routine, a leader can make performance of the task more pleasant by considering and supporting the employees' needs. For example, employees taking parking tolls at airports all day long derive little self-esteem or self-actualization from performing these highly structured and routine tasks. They would probably perceive a directive leadership style as excessive and unnecessary. A leader with a supportive style, however, could increase employee satisfaction with the work by asking the employee about his or her personal life and preferred working hours.

On the other hand, a more directive leadership style is appropriate for highly unstructured, complex, and nonroutine tasks. Directive leaders can help employees cope with task uncertainty and clarify the paths to high job satisfaction and performance. For example, this style would be appropriate for George Varga when he took over at GE's Tungsram plant in Budapest, because employees did not know what to do. Employees would not perceive this style to be excessive when they are given guidance and direction on how to improve the manufacturing process. Rather, directive leadership helps employees gain a sense of job satisfaction when they properly complete their tasks.

Participative leadership involves sharing information, power, and influence between managers and employees. When the task is clear and employees' egos are not involved in the work, participative leadership will likely contribute to satisfaction and performance only for highly independent employees. For ambiguous, ego-involving tasks, participative leadership will have positive effects on performance and job satisfaction regardless of an employee's needs for self-esteem or achievement.

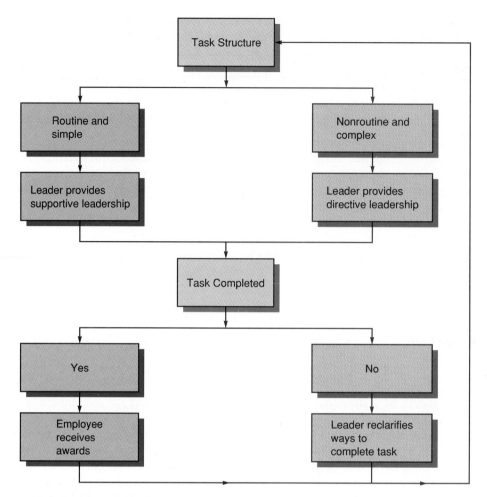

FIGURE 12.9 Some Relationships between Leadership Styles and Task Characteristics

Achievement-oriented leaders set challenging goals, expect employees to perform at their highest level, and show a high degree of confidence that employees will assume responsibility for accomplishing these challenging tasks. This type of leadership can lead employees to strive for high standards and build confidence in meeting challenging goals, especially among employees who are working on unstructured tasks. The In Practice on Chaparral Steel illustrates how an achievement-oriented team leader can get great results from employees.

Organizational Implications Research findings show that employees who perform highly routine or tedious tasks report higher job satisfaction when their leader uses a supportive (as opposed to directive) leadership style.[29] On the other hand, employees who perform unstructured tasks are more productive and satisfied when their leader uses a more directive style.

Achievement-oriented leadership has little effect on members' performance and job satisfaction when they are performing routine and repetitive tasks. Unless employees have some discretion over the what, when, and how of performing a task, the achievement-oriented leader can have little impact on employees' performance and satisfaction. Participative leadership increases employees' efforts if they are performing an unstructured task. When they participate in decision making about tasks, goals, plans, and procedures, employees learn more about the tasks and feel that they have a better chance of successfully completing them. If employees have a highly structured task and a clear understanding of the job, however, participative leadership has little effect on performance.

We can gain some insight into how this model works by looking at how Richard Miller at Wang turned around this organization. We have identified the different styles of leadership he used, depending on the circumstances, in the following In Practice.

IN PRACTICE

A TURNAROUND LEADER AT WANG LABS

Richard Miller is a leader with impressive credentials. He had learned valuable leadership lessons from his jobs at Penn Central and GE's consumer electronics division. When he got a call to become CEO at Wang in the summer of 1989, one of the first things he had to do was to figure out a way to stop Wang from losing any more money. Not knowing much about the business, he put together a team of employees to help him (participative leadership). This team consisted of employees from all parts of the organization. Among their duties, he asked them to find assets that could be sold to help Wang balance its books (directive leadership).

After forty days, the team turned up computer leases, small businesses, and real estate in Scotland that could be sold for $800 million. He and his team members made sure that they did not sell off anything that could someday fit into Wang's strategy of offering customers information in any form, data, image, or voice.

While that team was doing its tasks, Miller was busy trying to empower other employees. He called in one employee and gave him a big assignment: analyze Wang's computer pricing worldwide (achievement leadership). In just three weeks, the employee surveyed pricing for the organization and its competitors on six continents. He not only found where the problems were but also suggested how to fix them. For example, customers complained about Wang's service. The employee suggested to Miller that with some of the large computers that Wang sells, it should give away a fax machine and the number for a fax machine installed on Miller's desk. If a customer had a complaint about service, they could fax the CEO directly. Miller praised the employee because he took initiative, acted fast, and came up with creative solutions. According to Miller: "That's leadership."[30]

Vroom-Jago Leadership Model

Victor Vroom and Arthur Jago developed a leadership model that focuses on the role played by leaders in making decisions.[31] The **Vroom-Jago leader-**

ship model indicates that various degrees of participative decision making are appropriate in different situations. These researchers assume that the leader can choose a leadership style along a continuum ranging from highly autocratic to high participative, as shown in Table 12.2.

Vroom and Jago use shorthand notation *AI* to refer to instances in which the leader makes the decision alone without further information collection; *AII* is similar but permits the leader to request certain specific information from others. ("A" stands for "autocratic"; the roman numerals refer to degrees of autocratic processes.) The notation *CI* means "consultation" on a one-to-one basis with relevant parties; *CII* means consultation in a group setting. The notation *GII* represents group decision making with consensus as the goal.

Decision Effectiveness **Decision effectiveness** (D_{eff}) depends on decision quality, acceptance, and timeliness. The extent to which a method of handling a situation produces *decision quality* is represented by D_{qual}. The degree to which employee commitment is generated by a process is termed *decision acceptance* (D_{accept}). Employees are more likely to implement a decision that is consistent with their values and preferences than one that they view as harmful to them (such as a layoff, demotion, or cut in pay). The

---

TABLE 12.2 Decision Styles for Leading a Group

Leading a Group

AI You solve the problem or make the decision yourself, using information available to you at that time.

AII You obtain any necessary information from employees, then decide on the solution to the problem yourself. The role played by your employees in making the decision is clearly one of providing specific information that you request, rather than generating or evaluating solutions.

CI You share the problem with relevant team members individually, getting their ideas and suggestions without bringing them together as a group. Then you make the decision. This decision may or may not reflect their influence.

CII You share the problem with your employees in a group meeting. In this meeting, you obtain their ideas and suggestions. Then you make the decision, which may or may not reflect their influence.

GII You share the problem with your subordinates as a group. Together, you generate and evaluate alternatives and attempt to reach a consensus on a solution. Your role is much like that of chairperson, coordinating the discussion, keeping it focused on the problem, and making sure that the critical issues are discussed. You do not try to influence the group to adopt "your" solution, and you are willing to accept and implement any solution that has the support of the entire group.

Source: V. H. Vroom and P. W. Yetton, *Leadership and Decision Making.* Pittsburgh: University of Pittsburgh Press, 1973, 13.

term D_{tp} stands for "decision time penalty." This means that decisions must be made in a timely manner. Leaders make most decisions when time is of the essence. For example, air traffic controllers, emergency rescue squads, and individuals responsible for nuclear energy plants may have limited time to get inputs from others before making a decision. The time penalty term takes on a value of zero when there are no severe time pressures on the leader to make a quick decision. The model of decision effectiveness is represented by the following equation:

$$\mathbf{D_{eff} = D_{qual} + D_{accept} - D_{tp}}$$

Decision effectiveness criteria should be used only if the leader has ample time to make a decision and team members' development is not important. If time is not available or development is important, another criterion is needed. It is called overall effectiveness (O_{eff}). **Overall effectiveness** is not only influenced by decision effectiveness but also by time and the need for employees' development. The following equation expresses overall effectiveness:

$$\mathbf{O_{eff} = D_{eff} - Cost + Development}$$

Negative effects on what Vroom and Jago call "human captial" occur because participative and consultative leadership processes use time and energy—which can be translated into costs—even if there are no severe time constraints. Recall from Chapter 1 that many employees spend almost 70 percent of their time in meetings. Time always has a value, although its precise cost varies with the reasons for the meeting. For example, while managers are in a meeting, which other tasks are not being completed? Some of the benefits from employees participating in a meeting include being members of a team, strengthening their commitment to the organization's goals, and contributing to the development of their leadership skills (mainly self-understanding and communication). The cost of holding a meeting must be compared with the cost of not holding a meeting. Costs, therefore, represent the value of time lost through the use of participative decision making.

If participation has negative effects on "human capital," it can also have some positive effects, as we read about with Richard Miller of Wang and at Chaparral Steel. Participative leader behaviors help develop the technical and managerial talents of employees, help build teamwork, and help build loyalty and commitment to organizational goals and objectives.

Decision Tree   The Vroom-Jago model considers the trade-offs among four criteria by which a leader's decision-making behavior can be evaluated: decision quality, employee commitment, time, and employee development. Figure 12.10 shows a decision tree representing the Vroom-Jago model. Note the eight problem attributes or situational variables that can be used to describe differences among decision-making situations.

At the end of each branch of the decision tree, the letters and roman numerals correspond to those used to identify leadership styles in Table 12.2. That is, AI represents a leadership style in which you solve the problem yourself, using the information available to you at that time, and so on for

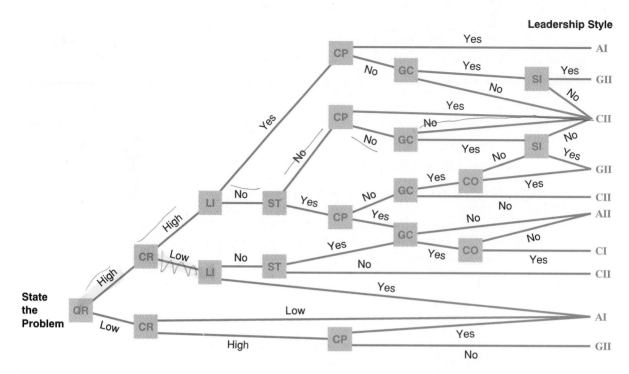

Problem Attributes

QR	Quality requirement:	How important is the technical quality of this decision?
CR	Commitment requirement:	How important is subordinate commitment to the decision?
LI	Leader's information:	Do you have sufficient information to make a high-quality decision?
ST	Problem structure:	Is the problem well structured?
CP	Commitment probability:	If you were to make the decision by yourself, is it reasonably certain that your subordinate(s) would be commited to the decision?
GC	Goal congruence:	Do subordinates share the organizational goals to be attained in solving this problem?
CO	Subordinate conflict:	Is conflict among subordinates over preferred solutions likely?
SI	Subordinate information:	Do subordinates have sufficient information to make a high-quality decision?

FIGURE 12.10   Vroom-Jago Decision Tree

Source: Reprinted from V. H. Vroom and A. G. Jago, *The New Leadership.* Englewood Cliffs, N.J.: Prentice-Hall, 1988, 184.

the various leadership styles. Leader style and problem attributes are combined through a series of complex equations that are beyond the scope of our presentation. The decision tree, however, represents the solution of those equations.

The following In Practice sets the stage for helping you understand how the Vroom-Jago model works. It focuses on a manager who wants to save meeting time and minimize subordinate development. Following this account, we ask you to choose a leadership style and "walk you through" the decision-tree solution.

MARIA VALDIVIESO

Maria Valdivieso is project manager in a telecommunications company in Dallas, Texas. Her company has been under pressure from MCI, AT&T, Sprint, and others to reduce its costs and increase its efficiency. Several months ago, the manufacturing manager requested funds for new fiber optic equipment. Maria gave her permission to buy and install it. Much to Maria's surprise, productivity has not increased, but employee turnover has.

Maria believes that nothing is wrong with the machines and that they were installed properly. Other companies in Dallas have similar machines and have not reported declines in productivity. Representatives of the company that built the machines in Ohio have checked their installation and told Maria that the machines were properly installed and should operate "just fine."

Maria suspects that changes in the ways people are now required to work might be a problem. However, this view is not widely shared by the manufacturing manager or her first-line supervisors. They indicate that production has declined because of poor training, lack of adequate financial incentives to increase production, and low morale. Clearly, these issues affect the operation of the entire plant and are ones over which Maria and others might disagree.

The vice-president of operations has just called Maria into her office. She is displeased with the production figures for the last three months and expresses her concern that Maria "get to the bottom of this problem quickly." Both the quality and quantity of work have fallen off since these new machines were installed. She indicates to Maria that the problem is "yours to solve" but that she would appreciate knowing of "your plans" within the next week or so.

Maria shares the vice-president's concern about the decline in productivity and knows that the manufacturing manager and her first-line supervisors are also upset. Her problem is to decide what to do to correct the situation.[32]

If you were Maria Valdivieso—and using the decision tree in Figure 12.10—what leadership style should you choose? Start with State the Problem on the left-hand side of Figure 12.10. The first box to the right is *QR* (quality requirement). You must make a decision about whether the importance of quality requirements is high or low. After you make that decision, go to the next box, or *CR* (commitment required). Once again you must make a decision about the importance of having employees committed to the final decision. After you have made that decision, you face another decision and then another. As you make each decision, follow the proper line to the next box. Eventually, at the far right-hand side of Figure 12.10, you will arrive at the best style of leadership for use, given your previous eight decisions. To determine the style of leadership, follow our logic.

Analysis		Answers
QR	Quality requirement: How important is the technical quality of the decision?	Highly Important
CR	Commitment requirement: How important is employee commitment to the decision?	Highly Important
LI	Leader's information: Do you have sufficient information to make a high-quality decision?	Probably Not
ST	Problem Structure: Is the problem well structured?	No
CP	Commitment probability: If you were to make the decision by yourself, is it reasonably certain that your team members would be committed to the decision?	Probably Not
GC	Goal congruence: Do employees share the organizational goals to be attained in solving this problem?	Yes
CO	Subordinate conflict: Is conflict among employees over preferred solutions likely?	Yes
SI	Subordinate information: Do employees have sufficient information to make a high-quality decision?	Yes

Factors not considered by Maria:

| TC | Time constraints: Are time constraints important? | |
| MD | Motivation development: Do you want to develop your employees' skills? | |

Answer:

Most leaders choose GII style of leadership. What did you choose?

Organizational Implications This model is so new that we cannot yet properly evaluate it. Certainly, it is consistent with the earlier work on leadership and with our knowledge of effective teams.[33] The Vroom-Jago model represents a significant conceptual breakthrough. If valid in practice, it will further encourage the training of future leaders in diagnosis. If leaders can diagnose situations correctly, choosing the best leadership style for those situations becomes easier. These choices, in turn, will enable them to make high-quality, timely decisions. If the situation requires delegation, the leader must learn how to establish the desired goals and set limitations—then let employees determine how best to achieve the goals within those limitations. If the situation calls for the leader alone to make the decision, the leader should be aware of potential positive and negative consequences.

Comparing the Four Contingency Models

Choosing the most appropriate leadership style can be difficult. A strongly stated preference for democratic, participative decision making in organizations prevails in the business community today. Evidence from Japanese management experience shows that this leadership style can result in productive, healthy organizations. Participative management, however, is not appropriate for all situations, as contingency theorists note. Table 12.3 shows the differences in leader behaviors, situational variables, and outcomes for the four contingency models that we have discussed.

Leadership Differences   Fiedler's model is based on the LPC style of a leader (high or low LPC) and the degree to which the situation is favorable for the leader. The leadership style of a leader is considered to be relatively rigid, and Fiedler recommends that the leader choose a situation that matches his or her leadership style. Hersey and Blanchard use the same two leadership dimensions that Fiedler identified: task and relationship behaviors. They went one step further by considering each as either high or low and then combining them into four specific leadership styles: directive, supportive, participating, and delegating. House's path-goal model states that leaders should try to improve the job satisfaction and performance of employees by removing roadblocks that stand in their way. The leader can choose a supportive, participative, directive, or achievement-oriented leadership style. Vroom and Jago believe that leaders can choose from among a variety of leadership styles, ranging from highly autocratic to highly consultative. The leader's role in choosing a style is to: (1) improve the quality and acceptance of the decision; (2) increase the probability that employees will accept and implement the decision on a timely basis; and (3) develop

---

TABLE 12.3   Comparing the Four Contingency Leadership Models

Model	Leader Behaviors	Contingency Variables	Leader Effectiveness Criteria
Fiedler	Task-oriented: Low LPC Relationship-oriented: High LPC	Group atmosphere Task structure Leader position power	Performance
Hersey and Blanchard	Task and Relationship	Readiness level of team members	Performance and job satisfaction
House's Path-Goal	Supportive Directive Participative Achievement-oriented	Employee characteristics Task characteristics	Employee job satisfaction Job performance
Vroom-Jago	Continuum of autocratic to participative	Eight problem attributes	Employee development Time Decision effectiveness Overall effectiveness

effective leadership skills in employees. Thus, each of the four contingency models identifies different styles of leadership and views the leader's ability to choose among styles differently.

Contingency Variables   All four models emphasize somewhat different contingency variables. Fiedler's model suggests that the way the variables (group atmosphere, task structure, and leader position power) are arranged in a situation determines whether and to what extent the situation is favorable or unfavorable to the leader. As the combination of the three contingency variables changes, so do the leadership requirements.

Hersey and Blanchard's contingency variable is the readiness of the employee. If the employee has a low level readiness, he or she is unable or unwilling to take on responsibility or to do something on his or her own. If an employee's readiness level is high, he or she is both willing and knows what to do, can work independently from the leader, and always meet deadlines.

House's model uses the contingency variables of task structure and the employees' characteristics. Employees who believe that rewards are based on their own efforts generally feel more satisfied with a participative style of leadership. If the task is unstructured, a directive style of leadership will lead to higher job satisfaction and performance than a participative style.

Vroom and Jago's model identifies eight different contingencies for the leader to consider in deciding whether a more autocratic or a more participative style would be more effective in a particular situation. Subordinate participation in the decisions that a leader encounters increases quality, generates commitment, and develops employee leadership skills—but increases the time required for the leader to make a decision.

Leadership Effectiveness   All four models use somewhat different criteria for evaluating leadership effectiveness. Fiedler emphasizes performance; Hersey and Blanchard and House use both employee job satisfaction and performance; and Vroom and Jago emphasize decision effectiveness and overall effectiveness. If a decision must be made with a group, the Vroom and Jago model may best assist leaders in choosing the most appropriate leadership style. On the other hand, if improving individual performance is most important, perhaps either Fiedler's, Hersey and Blanchard's, or House's model may be more useful.

EMERGING PERSPECTIVES ON LEADERSHIP

The four contingency theories of leadership you have just studied have not answered all our questions about leadership. All four theories tried to describe which leadership style is the most effective in a particular situation. But as you read, there are no consistent answers among the four. Further, there are some unanswered questions. For example, what impact do leaders' perceptions of their employees have on their choice of leadership style? What about a leader's charisma? In this final section of this chapter, we will focus on two theories—attributional and transformational leadership theories—that attempt to answer these questions.

Attributional Theory of Leadership

In Chapter 4, we discussed attribution theory in relation to perception. Attribution theory, as you may remember, deals with people trying to make sense out of cause-effect relationships. When something happens, they want to attribute it to something. The **attribution theory of leadership** suggests that a leader's judgment about his or her employees is influenced by the leader's attribution of the causes of the employees' performance.[34] The leader's attributions, as much as employees' behaviors, determine how the leader responds to their performance. That is, a leader obtains information about employees and their behaviors through daily observations of their work. Based on this information, the leader makes an attribution of the cause of each employee's behaviors and selects actions to deal with these behaviors.

Leaders' Attributional Processes As part of diagnosing the situation, leaders must determine whether personal or situational factors cause an employee's behavior. As illustrated in Chapter 4, attributions are based upon the leader's ability to process information based on three dimensions of behavior: *distinctiveness* (Did the behavior occur on this task only?), *consensus* (Is this level of performance usual for other employees?), and *consistency* (Is this level of performance usual for this employee?). The answers to these three questions identify for the leader either external (situational) or internal (personal) causes for the employee's performance.

This attribution is critical to leader-employee relations. An employee whose successes or failures are attributed to personal skills will have different interpersonal relations with the leader than a subordinate whose successes or failures are attributed to environmental factors over which the employee has little control, such as a downturn in the general economy. Leaders attempt to change an employee's behavior *only* when an internal attribution is made. For example, if Gabrielle Steffen, an operations scheduler at Mobil Oil Corporation, believes that her subordinate's poor performance is caused by the situation, then she is more likely to provide resources, redesign his job, or change the situation in some way. If she believes that his poor performance is attributable to personal reasons, she will more likely try to motivate him (see Chapter 7) to improve his behavior, offer him training to improve his skills, or reprimand him. Figure 12.11 illustrates the attribution model of leadership.

Employees' Attributional Processes Employees, too, attribute certain causes to their leader's behavior. Employees tend to view their leader as having an effect on their performance, whether the leader does or not, and develop either positive or negative attitudes about their leader. Employees want to believe that their leader can influence their performance. Past performance of employees has been found to influence their rating of their leader's effectiveness. When employees are successful, they tend to rate their leader as successful. When a team is unsuccessful, employees will try

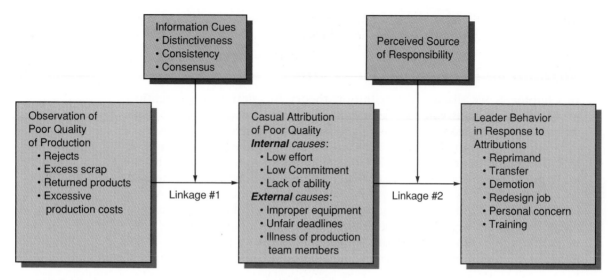

FIGURE 12.11 An Attributional Leadership Model

Source: Adapted from Terence R. Mitchell and Robert E. Wood. An Empirical Test of an Attributional Model of Leader's Responses to Poor Performance. In *Academy of Management Proceedings,* ed. Richard C. Huseman. Starksville, MS: Academy of Management, 1979, p. 94.

to distance themselves from their leader. Employees perceive their leader as ineffective and attribute their team's or their personal performance problems to the leader's actions, rather than their own. (Recall our discussion of *self-serving bias* in Chapter 4.) In sports teams, it is often the manager who gets fired and not the players. In organizations, it is the CEO who gets fired. The firing of the manager symbolizes top management's or the stockholders' conviction that steps must be taken to improve effectiveness.

Organizational Implications Managers tend to be biased toward making internal attributions about poor performance, and this leads to greater use of punitive actions directed at employees. As we read about in Chapters 6 and 7, punitive actions are usually resented by employees who do not feel responsible for the problem. Once the leader attributes performance problems to employees, they are likely to get less support, coaching, and resources from the leader. Yet when these employees make mistakes or have performance difficulties, the leader is likely to blame these employees rather than recognizing situational causes or his or her own contribution to the problem. Therefore, leaders need to learn to be more careful, fair, and systematic about evaluating employee performance. They need to become more aware of the many options available for dealing with different causes of performance problems and the importance of selecting an appropriate one.

Charismatic Leadership Theory

Charismatic leadership theory is an extension of attribution theory. **Charismatic leaders** concern themselves with developing a common vision of what could be, discovering or creating opportunities, and increasing employees' desire to control their own behaviors.[35] Charismatic leaders use dominance, self-confidence, a need for influence, and a conviction of moral righteousness to increase their charisma and consequently their leadership effectiveness. Many of these behaviors were shown in Figure 12.2 (See page 386).

Using their charismatic ability to inspire others, these leaders are often called transformational leaders. **Transformational leaders** rely on their referent and personal sources of power to arouse intense feelings and heighten the motivations of their employees.[36] A transformational leader influences employees by engaging in three types of behaviors. First, the

---

TABLE 12.4 Behaviors of Charismatic and Noncharismatic Leaders

	Noncharismatic Leader	Charismatic Leader
Future goal	Goal not too discrepant from status quo	Idealized vision that is highly discrepant from status quo
Likableness	Shared perspective makes him or her likable	Shared perspective and idealized vision makes him or her a likable and honorable hero worthy of identification and imitation
Trustworthiness	Disinterested advocacy in persuasion attempts	Disinterested advocacy by incurring great personal risk and cost
Expertise	Expert in using available means to achieve goals within the framework of the existing order	Expert in using unconventional means to transcend the existing order
Behavior	Conventional, conforming to existing norms	Unconventional
Articulation	Weak articulation of goals and motivation to lead	Strong articulation of future vision and motivation to lead
Power base	Position power and personal power (based on reward, expertise, and liking for a friend who is a similar other)	Personal power (based on expertise, respect, and admiration for a unique hero)
Leader-employee relationship	Egalitarian, consensus seeking, or directive Nudges or orders people to share his or her views	Elitist, entrepreneurial, and exemplary Transforms people to share the radical changes advocated; possibility of uncovering specific personal attributes that make for good leadership in various situations

Source: Adapted from J. A. Conger and R. N. Kanungo. Toward a Behavioral Theory of Charismatic Leadership, *Academy of Management Review*, 1985, *12*, 637–647.

leader helps employees recognize the need for revitalizing the organization by developing their need for change. For example, at Chaparral Steel, leaders encourage teams of employees to look at how other organizations make steel. By visiting other steel companies, its employees recognize that Chaparral's status quo would not enable it to be competitive. Second, the transformational leader creates a new vision and motivates employees to gain their commitment, such as Nicolosi achieved at Procter & Gamble. Third, transformational leaders institutionalize the change by replacing old technical and political networks with new ones. Miller at Wang did this when he formed a task force that took employees from various departments (something not done before) to outline ways that Wang could cut costs.

Who are some transformational leaders? Lee Iacocca transformed Chrysler; Steve Jobs transformed Apple Computer; Mary Kaye Ash transformed Mary Kay cosmetics; Wayne Huizenga transformed Blockbuster Video. These types of leaders almost have magical appeal to employees. Through their charismatic appeal, these transformational leaders are able to change the organization, its environment, and members' motivations. Table 12.4 compares the key behaviors that differentiate charismatic and noncharismatic leaders.

Let's read, in his own words, how Lee Iacocca used his transformational leadership abilities and his charismatic skills to turn around Chrysler. You should be able to identify some of his charismatic behaviors with those listed in Table 12.4.

IN PRACTICE

LEE IACOCCA

If I had to sum up in one word the qualities that make a good manager, I'd say that it all comes down to decisiveness. You can use the fanciest computers in the world and you can gather all the charts and numbers, but in the end, you have to bring all your information together, set up a timetable, and act.

And I don't mean act rashly. In the press, I'm sometimes described as a flamboyant leader and a hip-shooter, a kind of fly-by-the-seat-of-the-pants operator. I may occasionally give that impression, but if that image were really true, I could never have been successful in business.

Actually, my management style has always been pretty conservative. Whenever I've taken risks, it's been after satisfying myself that the research and the market studies supported my instincts. I may act on my intuition—but only if my hunches are supported by the facts.

Too many managers let themselves get weighed down in their decision-making, especially those with too much education. I once said to Philip Caldwell, who became the top man at Ford after I left, "The trouble with you, Phil, is that you went to Harvard, where they taught you not to take any action until you've got all the facts. You've got 95 percent of them, but it's going to take you another six months to get that last 5 percent. And by the time you do, your facts will be out of date because the market has moved on you. That's what life is about—timing."

A good business leader can't operate that way. It's perfectly natural to want all the facts and to hold out for the research that guarantees a particular program will work. After all, if you're about to spend $300 million on a new product, you want to be absolutely sure you're on the right track.

That's fine in theory, but real life just doesn't work that way. Obviously, you're responsible for gathering as many relevant facts and projections as you possibly can. But at some point, you've got to take that leap of faith. First, because even the right decision is wrong if it's made too late. Second, because in most cases, there's no such thing as certainty. There are times when even the best manager is like the little boy with the big dog waiting to see where the dog wants to go so he can take him there.

In corporate life, you have to encourage all your people to make a contribution to the common good and to come up with better ways of doing things. You don't have to accept every single suggestion, but if you don't get back to the guy and say, "Hey, that idea was terrific," and pat him on the back, he'll never give you another one. That kind of communication lets people know they really count.

You have to be able to listen well if you're going to motivate the people who work for you. Right there, that's the difference between a mediocre company and a great company. The most fulfilling thing for me as a manager is to watch someone the system has labeled as just average or mediocre really come into his own, all because someone has listened to his problems and helped solve them.

It's important to talk to people in their own language. If you do it well, they'll say, "God, he said exactly what I was thinking." And when they begin to respect you, they'll follow you to the death. The reason they're following you is not because you're providing some mysterious leadership. It's because you're following them.[37]

As you can learn from reading about Lee Iacocca, transformational leaders consider themselves as change agents; are courageous risk takers; believe in team members and try to empower others; and can dream and share this dream with others. Transformational leaders build confidence among their team members by helping them increase their competence and giving them freedom to take initiative.

Organizational Implications Transformational leaders using their charismatic leadership skills may be most appropriate when the organization is newly formed or when its survival is threatened. The ill-structured problems faced by such organizations call for leaders with vision, confidence, and determination. These leaders will have to influence others to assert themselves, to join enthusiastically in team efforts, and arouse their feelings about what they are attempting to do.

Transformational leadership is not a universal cure-all for organizations. For example, Steve Jobs achieved unwavering loyalty and commitment from his employees during the late 1970s and early 1980s. He created a vision for them by which personal computers would dramatically change the way people lived. However, once the need for this vision was fulfilled, Jobs became a liability for Apple. He was unable to listen to what experts in the PC industry were saying about Apple, became uncomfortable when employees challenged his views, and began to hold an unjustifiable belief in his "rightness" about issues. Because of these problems, he was replaced by a less charismatic leader, John Sculley.

Exxon and other organizations have found that transformational leadership and its philosophy can become an integral part of their operating style. That is, organizations in the '90s must support and have an understanding and appreciation for those employees who are willing to make unpopular decisions, who know when to reject traditional ways of doing something, and who can accept reasonable risks. There must be a "right to fail" that is nurtured and embedded in the organization's culture.[38]

SUMMARY

Leadership is a process of creating a vision for others and having the power to translate the vision into reality and sustain it. The ways in which leaders attempt to influence others depend in part on the power available to them and their skill. Leaders can draw on five sources of power—legitimate, reward, coercive, referent, and expert—to influence subordinates. Visioning, empowerment, meaning through communication, and self-understanding are skills that help leaders become more effective.

Three basic approaches to leadership are: traits, behavioral, and contingency. The traits approach emphasizes the personal qualities of leaders and attributes success to certain abilities, skills, and personality characteristics. However, this approach fails to determine why certain people succeed and others fail at leadership.

The behavioral approach emphasizes leaders' actions instead of their personal traits. We focused on two leader behaviors—initiating structure and consideration—and how they affect the performance of employees. However, most research indicates a need to analyze also the situation in which the leader operates.

The contingency approach emphasizes the importance of the situation. The contingency models of Fiedler, Hersey and Blanchard, House, and Vroom and Jago were presented and evaluated. Fiedler focuses on the effective diagnosis of the situation in which the leader will operate. Thus, he emphasizes understanding the nature of the situation and then matching the correct leadership style to that situation. According to this model, three contingency variables need to be diagnosed: group atmosphere, task structure, and the leader's position power. All leaders have a motivational system (LPC) that indicates the combinations of situations in which their styles probably will be effective.

Hersey and Blanchard state that leaders should choose a style that matches the readiness level of their employees. If employees are not ready to perform the task, then a directive leadership style will be more effective than a relationship one. As the readiness level of the employees increases, a leader should change his or her style to being more participative, as opposed to telling.

House suggests that leadership behavior is contingent on the characteristics of subordinates and the nature of the task. The leader's goal is to reduce the roadblocks that hinder employees in reaching their goals. For a routine task, a leader who is more considerate of employees will more likely have satisfied and productive employees than a leader who is not as considerate.

Vroom and Jago base their model on an analysis of how a leader's style affects decision effectiveness and overall effectiveness. Vroom and Jago propose five leadership styles that managers can use. Their set of rules can help a manager to determine the leadership style to avoid in a given situation because decision effectiveness and overall effectiveness might be low.

The attributional leadership model suggests that a leader's judgment about his or her subordinates is influenced by the leader's attribution of the causes of the employees' behaviors. These causes may either be external or internal. Effective leaders identify the correct cause and then act accordingly.

Charismatic leadership theory focuses on transformational leaders. A transformational leader is one who uses his or her charismatic skill to excite, arouse, and inspire employees to put forth extra effort to achieve goals. These leaders have a clear vision, can communicate this vision to others, and pay attention to the developmental needs of their subordinates.

Key Words and Concepts

Achievement-oriented leadership

Attribution theory of leadership

Charismatic leaders

Coaching

Coercive power

Consideration

Decision effectiveness

Delegating style

Directive behavior

Directive leadership

Directive style

Empowerment

Expert power

Fiedler's contingency model

Follower readiness

Group atmosphere

Hersey and Blanchard's situational leadership model

House's path-goal leadership model

Initiating structure

Leader

Leader match

Leadership

Least-preferred co-worker (LPC)

Legitimate power

Manager

Ohio State University leadership studies

Overall effectiveness

Participative leadership

Position power

Referent power

Reward power

Selling Style

Supporting

Supportive behavior

Supportive leadership

Task structure

Traits model

Transformational leaders

Vroom-Jago leadership model

Discussion Questions

1. What are some of the conditions under which a leader does not make a difference?

2. When someone was once asked what it took to be an effective leader, the response was: "Great team members!" What are your thoughts on this question?

3. Choose a theory of leadership and analyze your own leadership style. Under what conditions was it effective? Ineffective?

4. Suppose that a leader's style does not seem to match the situation that faces the leader. Can a leader's style be changed to produce a better match? What would Fiedler's theory say?

5. Are transformational leaders really different from other leaders? If so, in what ways?

6. Under what conditions would a leader get higher performance by making the decisions autocratically, rather than in a consultative manner?

7. According to David Glass of Wal-Mart Stores, "At Wal-Mart, our philosophy is that the best ideas come from associates—employees—on the firing line." What style of leadership works most effectively in promoting this philosophy?

8. Richard Mahoney at Monsanto describes himself as demanding. He seldom forgives mistakes and expects employees to hit their performance targets on time without excuses. What is his leadership style?

9. What are some major differences between the four contingency models? Why do these exist?

10. Assume that you are a student in a class and have been assigned to do a team project with five other classmates. How might the Vroom-Jago leadership model help you choose a leadership style?

◆ *MANAGEMENT CASES AND EXERCISES*

ARE YOU A TRANSFORMATIONAL LEADER?

Intructions: The following statements refer to the possible ways in which you might behave toward others when you are in a leadership role. Please read each statement carefully and decide to what extent it applies to you. Then put a check on the appropriate number.

To a Very Great Extent	1
To a Considerable extent	2
To a Moderate Extent	3
To a Slight Extent	4
To Little or No Extent	5

You. . . .

1. pay close attention to what others say when they are talking.	5	4	3	2	1
2. communicate clearly.	5	4	3	2	1
3. are trustworthy.	5	4	3	2	1
4. care about other people.	5	4	3	2	1
5. do not put excessive energy into avoiding failure.	5	4	3	2	1
6. make the work of others more meaningful.	5	4	3	2	1
7. seem to focus on the key issues in a situation.	5	4	3	2	1
8. get across your meaning effectively, often in unusual ways.	5	4	3	2	1
9. can be relied on to follow through on commitments.	5	4	3	2	1
10. have a great deal of self-respect.	5	4	3	2	1
11. enjoy taking carefully calculated risks.	5	4	3	2	1
12. help others feel more competent in what they do.	5	4	3	2	1
13. have a clear set of priorities.	5	4	3	2	1
14. are in touch with how others feel.	5	4	3	2	1
15. rarely change once you have taken a clear position.	5	4	3	2	1
16. focus on strengths, of yourself and of others.	5	4	3	2	1
17. seem most alive when deeply involved in some project.	5	4	3	2	1
18. show others that they are all part of the same group.	5	4	3	2	1
19. get others to focus on the issues you see as important.	5	4	3	2	1
20. communicate feelings as well as ideas.	5	4	3	2	1
21. let others know where you stand.	5	4	3	2	1
22. seem to know just how you "fit" into a group.	5	4	3	2	1
23. learn from mistakes, do not treat errors as disasters, but as learning.	5	4	3	2	1
24. are fun to be around.	5	4	3	2	1

Interpretation

The questionnaire measures each of the six basic behavior leader patterns, as well as a set of emotional responses. Your score can range from four to twenty. Each question is stated as a measure of the extent to which you engage in the behavior—or elicit the feelings. The higher your score, the more you demonstrate transformational leader behaviors.

Index 1: **Management of Attention** (1, 7, 13, 19). Your score _____. You pay especially close attention to people with whom you were communicating. You are also "focused in" on the key issues under discussion and help others to see clearly these key points. They have clear ideas about the relative importance or priorities of different issues under discussion.

Index 2: **Management of Meaning** (2, 8, 14, 20). Your score _____. This set of items center on your communication skills, specifically your ability to get the meaning of a message across, even if this means devising some quite innovative approach.

Index 3: **Management of Trust** (3, 9, 15, 21). Your score _____. The key factor is your perceived trustworthiness as shown by your willingness to follow through on promises, avoidance of "flip-flop" shifts in position, and willingness to take clear positions.

Index 4: **Management of Self** (4, 10, 16, 22). Your score _____. This index concerns your general attitudes toward yourself and others; that is, your overall concern for others and their feelings, as well as for "taking care of" feelings about yourself in a positive sense (e.g., self-regard).

Index 5: **Management of Risk** (5, 11, 17, 23). Your score _____. Effective transformational leaders are deeply involved in what they do and do not spend excessive amounts of time or energy on plans to "protect" themselves against failure (a "CYA" approach). These leaders are willing to take risks, not on a hit-or-miss basis, but after careful estimation of the odds of success or failure.

Index 6: **Management of Feelings** (6, 12, 18, 24) Your score _____. Transformational leaders seem to consistently generate a set of feelings in others. Others feel that their work becomes more meaningful and that they are the "masters" of their own behavior, that is, they feel competent. They feel a sense of community, a "we-ness" with their colleagues and co-workers.[39]

HOW BOB HAAS MAKES IT WORK AT LEVI STRAUSS

Levi Strauss, led by Robert Haas, the founder's great-great-grand-nephew, has increased its sales by 31 percent (to more than $3.6 billion) and profits by more than 50 percent since 1985. The spectacular results have come about because Levi Strauss changed the way it did business. First, Levi poured tens of millions of dollars into new-product development, marketing, and computer technology. Second, Haas has focused the organization on basic product lines, downsized the organization by laying off more than four thousand managers, and trimmed the number of products by two-thirds. Third, a new computer system helped streamline manufacturing and distribution by linking Levi directly to retailers and fabric suppliers. This new system enables customers to order and pay electronically for new inventory. Links with suppliers let Levi fine-tune the amounts and kinds of fabrics it orders to meet consumer demand. The goal of the system is to electronically monitor the manufacture of a pair of jeans. When the customer buys jeans in some store, that sale is communicated directly to a plant. If the plant's inventory level for that style of jeans is low, an order to manufacture them is automatically placed. Lastly, Levi started to pay attention to what its customers wanted. In just four years, Docker's, a line of casual clothing aimed at the less slim, over twenty-five market, has become a half-billion-dollar a year success.

Haas paid attention to the global market. As markets open and geographic barriers have become increasingly blurred, Levi took advantage of these changes. In Japan, a jeans revolution is going on. Even women are now wearing jeans. Until recently, few people would have ever imagined this happening in Japan. In addition to selling overseas, Levi is manufacturing overseas as well. Most Dockers, for example, are made in the Caribbean basin. The reason: Dockers require twice the amount of labor that 501 jeans do. The greater the labor, the more the emphasis is to manufacture outside of the United States.

To raise productivity as well as help keep morale high, Levi is trying a gain-sharing program. At its jeans factory in Blue Ridge, Georgia, employees and plant management set productivity improvement goals and agreed to split the savings with employees. Last year, each employee earned an extra $450. Before the gain-sharing program, this was Levi's second-best plant. Now, it is the best. At another one of its jeans plants in El Paso, Texas, employees work in teams. Each team of four employees sews buttons on 4,037 pairs of button-fly jeans a day. According to Peter Thigpen, vice-president of manufacturing, all managers at Levi are trying to make work for employees more meaningful. Managers are urged to speak openly to employees, reward them for quality work, and give them more power to make decisions in areas that directly affect them.

The following "Aspirations Statement" reflects what Levi Strauss values:

> We all want a company that our people are proud of and committed to, where all employees have an opportunity to contribute, learn, grow, and advance based on merit, not politics or background. We want our people to feel respected, treated fairly, listened to, and involved. Above all, we want satisfaction from accomplishments and friendships, balanced personal and professional lives, and to have fun in our endeavors.

> When we describe the kind of Levi Strauss & Co. we want in the future, what we are talking about is building on the foundation we have inherited: affirming the best of our company's traditions, closing gaps that may exist between principles and practices, and updating some of our values to reflect contemporary circumstances. What type of leadership is necessary to make our Aspirations a Reality?

> *New Behaviors:* Leadership that exemplifies directness, openness to influence, commitment to the success of others, willingness to acknowledge our own contributions to problems, personal accountability, teamwork, and trust. Not only must we model these behaviors but we must coach others to adopt them.

> *Diversity:* Leadership that values a diverse work force (age, sex, ethnic group, etc.) at all levels of the organization, diversity in experience, and diversity in perspectives. We have committed to taking full advantage of the rich backgrounds and abilities of all our people and to promoting a greater diversity in positions of influence. Differing points of view will be sought; diversity will be valued and honesty rewarded, not suppressed.

> *Recognition:* Leadership that provides greater recognition—both financial and psychic—for individuals and teams that contribute to our success. Recognition must be given to all who contribute: those who create and innovate and also those who continually support the day-to-day business requirements.

> *Ethical Management Practices:* Leadership that epitomizes the stated standards of ethical behavior. We must provide clarity about our expectations and must enforce these standards through the corporation.

423

Communications: Leadership that is clear about company, unit, and individual goals and performance. People must know what is expected of them and receive timely, honest feedback on their performance and career aspirations.

Empowerment: Leadership that increases the authority and responsibility of those closest to our products and customers. By actively pushing responsibility, trust, and recognition into the organization, we can harness and release the capabilities of all our people.[40]

QUESTIONS:

1. What leadership skills has Haas shown?
2. Why can employees work without a boss? What leadership style will work most effectively with those employees?
3. What are some problems of leading people who live in foreign countries? How does Levi's "Aspirations Statement" help leaders do this easier?

References

1. Kotter, J. P. What Leaders Really Do. *Harvard Business Review,* May–June 1990, 110. Also see Kotter, J. P. *The Leadership Factor,* New York: Free Press, 1988.
2. Motowildo, S. Leadership and Leadership Processes. In M. D. Dunnette (ed.). *Handbook of Industrial/Organizational Psychology,* 2d ed. Palo Alto, Calif.: Consulting Psychologists Press, in press.
3. Yukl, G. A. *Leadership in Organizations,* 2d ed. Englewood Cliffs, N.J.: Prentice Hall, 1989, 2–3.
4. Conger, J. A. Inspiring Others: The Language of Leadership. *Academy of Management Executive,* 1991, *5,* 31–45.
5. Geneen, H. S., and Moscow, A. *Managing.* Garden City, N.Y.: Doubleday, 1984.
6. Fierman, J. The People Who Set the CEO's Pay. *Fortune,* March 12, 1990, 58, 62, 69; Crystal, G. S. The Great CEO Pay Sweepstakes. *Fortune,* June 18, 1990, 949–102. Byrne, J. A., Symonds, W. C., and Siler, J. F. CEO Disease. *Business Week,* April 1, 1991, 52–58.
7. Bennis, W., and Nanus, B. *Leaders: The Strategies for Taking Charge.* New York: Harper and Row, 1985.
8. Adapted from Labich, K. The Innovators. *Fortune,* June 6, 1988, and Main, J. Wanted: Leaders Who Can Make a Difference. *Fortune,* September 28, 1987, 92–102.
9. French, J. R. P. and Raven, B. H. The Bases of Social Power. In D. Cartwright and A. Zander (eds.). *Group Dynamics: Research and Theory,* 2d ed. New York: Harper and Row, 1960, 607–623; Schriesheim, C. A., Hinkin, T. R., and Podsakoff, P. M. Can Ipsative and Single-Item Measures Produce Erroneous Results in Field Studies of French and Raven's (1959) Five Bases of Power? *Journal of Applied Psychology,* 1991, *76,* 106–114.
10. Kanter, R. M. Power Failure in Management Circuits. *Harvard Business Review,* July–August 1979, 67; Lachman, R. Power from What? A Re-examination of Its Relationships with Structural Conditions. *Administrative Science Quarterly,* 1989, *34,* 131–151; Hinkin, T. R., and Schriesheim, C. A. Relationship between Subordinate Perceptions of Supervisory Influence Tactics and Attributed Bases of Power. *Human Relations,* 1990, *43,* 221–238; Stewart, T. A. New Ways to Exercise Power. *Fortune,* November 6, 1989, 52–58, 62–64; Yukl, G. A., and Falbe, C. M. Influence Tactics and Objectives in Upward, Downward, and Lateral Influence Attempts. *Journal of Applied Psychology,* 1990, *75,* 132–140.
11. Drucker, P. F. *The New Realities: In Government, in Politics, in Economics and Business, in Society and World View.* New York: Harper and Row, 1989.
12. Stayer, R. How I Learned to Let My Workers Lead. *Harvard Business Review,* November–December 1990, 66–69, 72–76, 80–83; Also see Byrne, J. A., Symonds, Wm. C., and Siler, J. F., CEO Disease: Egotism Can Breed Corporate Disaster—and the Malady Is Spreading. *Business Week,* April 1, 1991, 52–60.
13. Bass, B. M. *Handbook of Leadership: A Survey of Theory and Research.* New York: Free Press, 1981.
14. Yukl. *Leadership in Organizations,* 173–202.
15. Stogdill, R. M. *Handbook of Leadership: A Survey of the Literature.* New York: Free Press, 1974.
16. Schriesheim, C. A., and Kerr, S. Theories and Measures of Leadership: A Critical Appraisal. In J. G. Hunt and L. L Larson (eds.). *Leadership: The Cutting Edge.* Carbondale, Ill.: Southern Illinois University Press, 1977, 9–45.
17. Kerr, S., Schriesheim, C. A., Murphy, C., and Stogdill, R. M. Toward a Contingency Theory of Leadership Based on Consideration and Initiating Structure. *Organizational Behavior and Human Performance,* 1974, *12,* 68–82.
18. Adapted from Tully, S. GE in Hungary: Let There Be Light. *Fortune,* October 22, 1990, 137–142.
19. Zaleznik, A. The Leadership Gap. *Academy of Management Executive,* 1990, *4,* 7–22.

20. Fiedler, F. E. *A Theory of Leadership*, New York: McGraw-Hill, 1967.

21. Adapted from Chang, G. Let the Manager Do His Thing—or Replace Him. *Fortune*, March 26, 1990, 42; Tully, S. The CEO Who Sees Beyond Budgets. *Fortune*, June 4, 1990, 186.

22. Peters, L. H., Hartke, D. D., and Pohlmann, J. T. Fiedler's Contingency Theory of Leadership: An Application of the Meta-Analysis Procedures of Schmidt and Hunter. *Psychological Bulletin*, 1985, 97, 224–285.

23. Fiedler, F. E., and Chemers, M. M. *Leadership and Effective Management*. Glenview, Ill.: Scott, Foresman, 1974.

24. Hersey, P., and Blanchard, K. H. *Management of Organizational Behavior*, 5th ed. Englewood Cliffs, N.J.: Prentice Hall, 1988.

25. Adapted from Dumaine, B. Who Needs a Boss? *Fortune*, May 7, 1990, 52–58.

26. Graeff, C. L. The Situational Leadership Theory: A Critical View. *Academy of Management Review*, 1983, 8, 285–291.

27. Blank, W., Weitzel, J. R., and Green, S. G. A Test of Situational Leadership. *Personnel Psychology*, 1990, 43, 579–598.

28. House, R. J., and Mitchell, T. R. Path-Goal Theory of Leadership. *Journal of Contemporary Business*, Autumn 1974, 81–98.

29. Yukl, G. A. Managerial Leadership: A Review of Theory and Research. *Journal of Management*, 1989, 15, 251–290; Keller, R. T. A Test of the Path-Goal Theory of Leadership with Need for Clarity as a Moderator. *Journal of Applied Psychology*, 1989, 74, 208–212.

30. Adapted from McWilliams, G. G. Wang's Turn-around Specialist Prepares for Surgery. *Business Week*, December 11, 1989, 108–109; Dumaine, B. The New Turnaround Champs. *Fortune*, July 16, 1990, 36, 38–44.

31. Vroom, V. H., and Jago, A. G. *The New Leadership*, Englewood Cliffs, N.J.: Prentice Hall, 1988.

32. Adapted from ibid., 43.

33. Field, R. H. G., and House, R. J. A Test of the Vroom-Yetton Model Using Manager and Subordinate Reports. *Journal of Applied Psychology*, 1990, 75, 362–366.

34. McElroy, J. C. A Typology of Attribution Leadership Research. *Academy of Management Review*, 1982, 7, 413–417; Meindl, J. R., and Ehrlich, S. B. The Romance of Leadership and the Evaluation of Organizational Performance. *Academy of Management Journal*, 1987, 30, 91–109; Puffer, S. M., and Weintrop, J. B. Corporate Performance and CEO Turnover: A Comparison of Performance Indicators. *Administrative Science Quarterly*, 1991 36, 1–19.

35. Howell, J. M. Two Faces of Charisma: Socialized and Personalized Leadership in Organizations. In J. A. Conger and R. N. Kanungo (eds.). *Charismatic Leadership: The Elusive Factor in Organizational Effectiveness*. San Francisco: Jossey-Bass, 1988, 213–236; Conger J. A., and Kanungo, R. N. Behavioral Dimensions of Charismatic Leadership. In Conger and Kanungo, *Charismatic Leadership*, 79–97.

36. Bass, B. M. From Transactional to Transformational Leadership: Learning to Share the Vision. *Organizational Dynamics*, Winter 1990, 19–31; Kouzes, J. M., and Posner, B. Z. *The Leadership Challenge: How to Get Extraordinary Things Done in Organizations*. San Francisco: Jossey-Bass, 1987; Tichy, N., and Devanna, M. *Transformational Leadership*. New York: John Wiley & Sons, 1986; Conger, J. A. Inspiring Others: The Language of Leadership. *Academy of Management Executive*, 1991, 5, 31–45; Meindl, J. R. On Leadership: An Alternative to the Conventional Wisdom. In B. M. Staw and L. L. Cummings (eds.). *Research in Organizational Behavior*, vol, 12. Greenwich, Conn.: JAI Press, 1990, 159–204.

37. Adapted from Iacocca, L., and Novak, Wm. *Iacocca: An Autobiography*. New York: Doubleday Books, 1984; Iacocca, L., and Kleinfield, S. *Talking Straight*. New York: Bantam Books, 1988; Taylor, A., III. Can Iacocca Fix Chrysler—Again? *Fortune*, April 8, 1991, 51–54.

38. Bass, B. M., and Avolio, B. J. The Implications of Transactional and Transformational Leadership for Individual, Team, and Organizational Development. In W. A. Pasmore and R. W. Woodman (eds.). *Research in Organizational Change and Development*, vol. 4. Greenwich, Conn.: JAI Press, 1990, 231–272.

39. Modified from Sashkin, M., and Morris, W. C. *Experiencing Management*. Reading, Mass.: Addison–Wesley, 1987, 132–134; for additional measures of leadership, see Clark, K. E., and Clark, M. B. *Measures of Leadership*. Greensboro, N.C.: Center for Creative Leadership, 1990.

40. Adapted from Schlender, B. R. How Levi Strauss Did an LBO Right. *Fortune*, May 7, 1990, 105–107; Howard, R. Values Make the Company: An Interview with Robert Haas. *Harvard Business Review*, September–October 1990, 132–144.

CHAPTER 13

INTERPERSONAL COMMUNICATION

LEARNING OBJECTIVES

When you have finished studying this chapter, you should be able to:

- Explain the elements of the interpersonal communication process and their relationships to one another.
- Discuss how interpersonal communications can vary across cultures.
- Describe the degree of richness of various media in sending and transmitting messages.
- Evaluate the effects and implications of different types of communication networks.
- Describe the changing role of information technologies in the communication process.
- Explain the importance of communication openness.
- Improve your effectiveness in giving feedback, engaging in self-disclosure, and listening to others.
- Give examples of five types of nonverbal communication.

OUTLINE

Preview Case: Phil and Sue

Basic Communication Process
Sender and Receiver
Transmitters and Receptors
Messages, Channels, and Noise
Meaning, Encoding, Decoding, and Feedback
Across Cultures: Communication Process in High-versus Low-Context Cultures

Interpersonal Communication Networks
Types of Networks
Effects of Different Networks
Organizational Implications
Role of Information Technologies
In Practice: "Communicaholic" Manager

Communication Openness
Openness Continuum
Situational Risk Factors

In Practice: Communicating Commitment
Giving Feedback
Appropriate Self-Disclosure
Active Listening
Implications for Ethical Behavior

Nonverbal Communication
Types of Nonverbal Cues
In Practice: The Silent Language Across Cultures
Status and Nonverbal Cues
Gender Differences and Nonverbal Cues

Management Cases and Exercises
Interpersonal Communication Survey
Jane Brady and Mr. Sato

PHIL AND SUE

Phil is walking past the vending machines, a place where social and work-related communications often take place. Suddenly, Sue, the vice-president of operations, appears. She is obviously late for an important Monday morning meeting. As Sue breezes by Phil, she says, "How about the report for production planning? Don't they want it soon?" Before Phil can respond, other than to say "okay," Sue enters an office off of the corridor and shuts the door. Phil heard the words Sue uttered. She was informing him that production planning needed the report soon.

Phil decides to get in touch with production planning to find out when they want it. Phil has a leisurely conversation over coffee with the manager and two other members of the production planning department. It is agreed that the report will be submitted by the end of the week.

On Wednesday, Phil receives an early morning call from Sue:

SUE: "Phil, where the heck is my copy of that report for production planning? I needed it yesterday."

PHIL: "But I spoke with production planning, and they said it would be okay to have it to them on Friday. I was going to begin working on it tomorrow morning."

SUE: "That's not good enough, Phil. I told you to get it done on Tuesday."

PHIL (biting his tongue): "I'll get on it immediately and should have it to you later this afternoon"[1]

When the short conversation between Phil and Sue ended, both parties moved on in the belief that they were in "harmony" with each other. In fact, the two had engaged in **bypassing,** which refers to an *apparent* agreement and understanding between two or more individuals and ultimately leads to erroneous expectations by each person about the near-term behavior of the other person.[2] Bypassing occurs because: (1) individuals assume that *meanings* are simply in the words spoken, rather than in the intended thoughts and feelings of people; (2) individuals think they can communicate the same way and with the same degree of success in high-pressure (stress) situations as well as low-pressure situations; and (3) individuals treat communication as easier to accomplish than it is.

For those who think communicating is simple, consider the usage of two common words: *soon* and *immediately*. Thirty-one managers in a public accounting firm were asked to indicate the maximum amount of time attached to each of these words. The results for *immediately* (with number of respondents shown in parentheses) were: right now (3), one hour (7), two to six hours (4), end of the day (6), twenty-four hours (3), one and a half to three days (2), end of the week (2), and one week (4). The results for *soon* were: twenty-four hours (2), one and a half to three days (3), one week (10), two to three weeks (4), two to six months (5), and one year (7).[3]

The problem of bypassing as demonstrated between Phil and Sue, as well as the different meanings assigned to simple words like *immediately* and *soon,* is only one of the many challenges involved in achieving effective interpersonal communication. Most often, people think of the active part of interpersonal communication as only the words, emotions, gestures, and other cues provided by the sender to the receiver. However, even the most eloquent speaker is doomed to failure if the receiver does not actively listen. Thus, our definition of **interpersonal communication** is the transmission and reception of ideas, facts, opinions, attitudes, and feelings—through one or more information media—that produce a response.[4] Through active listening, the messages intended by the sender are more likely to be accurately understood and interpreted by the receiver.[5] In Chapter 1, we described the central role of face-to-face communication in the daily work of managers and other employees. In this chapter, we develop the process, types, and patterns of verbal, nonverbal, and other forms of communication used by employees in their work roles.

BASIC COMMUNICATION PROCESS

Accurate interpersonal communication takes place only if the ideas, facts, opinions, attitudes, feelings, or meanings that the sender intended to transmit are the same as those understood and interpreted by the receiver. As we discussed in earlier chapters, both internal and external factors often lead individuals to inaccurate perceptions and poor interpersonal communication. Management and labor representatives may well disagree with each other while negotiating a new contract. But so long as opposing viewpoints are being transmitted, received, and understood with the intended meaning, accurate interpersonal communication is taking place.

Sender and Receiver

Interpersonal communication obviously requires two or more people. Figure 13.1 presents a model of the communication process involving only two people. Since interpersonal communication often includes a number of exchanges between people, the labeling of one person as the *sender* and the other as the *receiver* is arbitrary. These roles shift back and forth, depending on where the people are in the process at any given time. When the *receiver* responds to the *sender,* he or she becomes the *sender* and the initiating *sender* becomes the *receiver.*

Consider the comment of a supervisor of security services about dealing with a vice-president of operations:

> I wanted an assistant so that I could have some help in managing my department and would not have to handle the petty problems of my employees. I (sender) tried to convince my boss (receiver) that I was overworked since my staff has almost doubled and I was having a lot of people problems. I failed because I was just trying to make it easier on myself and wanted an assistant to do the job that I was supposed to be doing. I was also asking to increase the payroll of the company with no plans to increase revenue or profits. After my

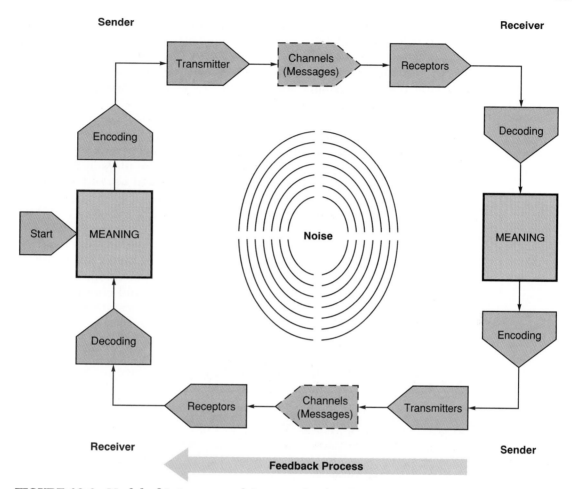

FIGURE 13.1 Model of Interpersonal Communication Process

boss (sender) turned me (receiver) down, I pouted for a few weeks and later learned that my boss thought I was immature. I then decided to forget about past disappointments and only worry about the future.[6]

As suggested by this commentary, the goals of the sender and receiver substantially influence the communication process. For example, the sender may have certain goals for communicating, such as adding to or changing the ideas, opinions, attitudes, or behavior of the receiver or changing the relationship with the receiver.[7] If the receiver does not agree with these goals, the probability of distortion and misunderstanding can be quite high. The fewer the differences in goals, attitudes, and values, the greater the probability that accurate communication will occur.

Transmitters and Receptors

Transmitters (used by the sender) and **receptors** (used by the receiver) refer to the means (media) available for sending and receiving messages. In interpersonal communication, they usually involve one or more of the senses: seeing, hearing, touching, smelling, and tasting. Thus, transmission can take place through both verbal and nonverbal means. Once transmission begins, the communication process moves beyond the complete control of the sender. A message that has been transmitted cannot be brought back. How many times have you thought to yourself, "I wish I hadn't said that"?

A variety of communication media is available for transmitting or receiving messages, as suggested in Figure 13.2. They vary substantially in terms of **media richness,** which is a medium's capacity for carrying multiple cues and providing rapid feedback. The richness of each medium is based on the blend of four criteria: (1) the rapidity and use of feedback so that errors can be corrected and/or intended meanings confirmed, (2) the tailoring of messages to the individual circumstances of the receiver, (3) the ability to convey multiple cues simultaneously, and (4) language variety (for example verbal language versus numbers).[8] Communications that require a long time to digest or that cannot overcome different biases are therefore low in richness. **Data** are simply the output of communication. Words spoken face-to-face, telephone calls, letters and memos, and computer printouts represent various forms of data. They become information when they reinforce or change the understanding of receivers with respect to *their* ideas, facts, opinions, attitudes, feelings, or meanings.[9]

As shown in Figure 13.2, face-to-face interpersonal communication is considered to be the richest medium. Why? Face-to-face interaction provides immediate feedback so that receivers can check the accuracy of their understanding and make corrections if needed. The face-to-face medium also allows the sender and receiver to simultaneously observe body lan-

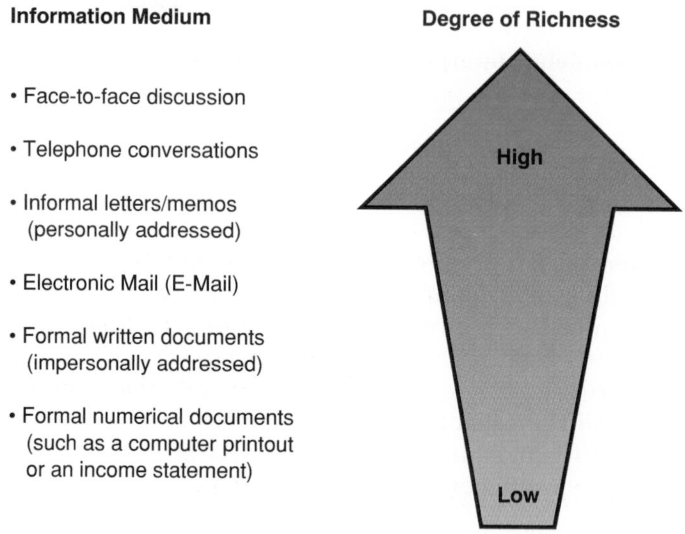

Information Medium

- Face-to-face discussion

- Telephone conversations

- Informal letters/memos
  (personally addressed)

- Electronic Mail (E-Mail)

- Formal written documents
  (impersonally addressed)

- Formal numerical documents
  (such as a computer printout
  or an income statement)

Degree of Richness

High

Low

FIGURE 13.2   Continuum of Media Richness for Sending and Receiving Messages

Source: Adapted from R. H. Lengel, "Managerial Information Processing and Communication-Media Source Selection Behavior." Unpublished Ph.D. dissertation, Texas A&M University, 1983.

guage, tone of voice, and facial expression. These observations may communicate more than the spoken words. Finally, face-to-face interaction enables the sender and receiver to more quickly identify and use language that is natural and more personal. Because of these characteristics, we almost always find that solving the important and tough problems—especially those involving uncertainty and ambiguity—requires face-to-face interpersonal communication.[10]

Messages, Channels, and Noise

Messages include the transmitted data and the coded symbols that are intended to give particular meanings to the data. The sender hopes that messages are interpreted as meant. To understand the difference between the original meaning and the received message, think about an occasion when you tried to convey your inner thoughts and feelings of love, rage, or fear to another person. Did you find it difficult or impossible to transmit your true "inner meaning"? The greater the difference between the interpreted meaning and the original message, the poorer will be the interpersonal communication. Words and nonverbal symbols have no meaning in and of themselves. Their meaning is created by the sender *and* the receiver and, to a certain extent, the situation or context.[11]

Recall Sue's comment to Phil in the Preview Case: "How about the report for production planning? Don't they want it soon?" She could have been employing one of several meanings in the message sent to Phil.

Directing: "You should get the report to me now. That's an order."

Suggesting: "I suggest that we consider getting the report out now."

Requesting: "Can you do the report for me now? Let me know if you can't."

Informing: "A report is needed soon by production planning."

Questioning: "Does production planning want the report soon?"[12]

Phil provided feedback to Sue with the word *okay,* which implied to her that the intended meaning was the interpreted meaning.

Channels are the means by which messages travel from sender to receiver. For example, a conversation may be carried by the air in a face-to-face conversation or by a telephone line. **Noise** is any interference with the intended message in the channel. A radio playing loud music while someone is trying to talk to someone else is an example of noise. Noise can be overcome by repeating the message or increasing the intensity (for example, the volume) of the message.

Meaning, Encoding, Decoding, and Feedback

As Figure 13.1 indicates, the sender's message is transmitted through channels to the receiver's receptors, or senses. The received messages are changed from their symbolic form (such as spoken words) to a form that has meaning. **Meanings,** as noted previously, represent a person's ideas, facts, values, attitudes, and feelings.

Encoding is the translation of meanings into messages that can be sent. Vocabulary and knowledge play an important role in the sender's ability to encode. Some professionals have difficulty communicating with the general public because they tend to encode meanings in a form that can be understood only by other professionals in the same field. For example, legal contracts that directly affect consumers often have been written on the assumption that only lawyers will encode and decode them. Consumer groups have pressed to have such contracts written in language that everyone can understand— a reaction to legal terminology that can be understood only by lawyers. As a result, many banks, credit card firms, and other organizations have changed the language in their contracts so that their customers can understand them.

Decoding is the translation of received messages into interpreted meanings. Using a shared language, people can decode many messages so that the meanings received are reasonably close to the meanings transmitted. Decoding accurately becomes an even greater challenge in communicating across cultures. Below, we share several comments made by Japanese and Japanese-Americans who have worked closely with North Americans:

- "Sometimes Americans don't understand that we are smiling and laughing not because we like what they are doing but because they are making us nervous."
- "Americans ought to watch us more carefully as we are not as verbal as they are. We don't like to say no for instance, but when we suck air in through our teeth and grab the back of our necks, we mean no."
- "Americans just don't understand the process of establishing relationships with the Japanese; the investment of time and expense seems like too much for them. They just aren't comfortable with the expectations, and they are not used to creating lasting, permanent business relationships. They think once the deal is done, it's over. They need to learn how to nurture relations: pay attention, follow up, make return visits—not only when something goes wrong."[13]

The accuracy of interpersonal communication is evaluated in relation to the *ideal state*. In this state, the sender's intended meanings and the receiver's interpretation of them are the same. The transmission of factual information of a nonthreatening nature most easily approximates the ideal state. For example, sharing the recipe for a cake will generally result in easier and more accurate interpersonal communication than will communication between a manager and a subordinate during a performance evaluation session.[14]

Feedback is the receiver's response to the message. Feedback lets the sender know whether the message was received as intended. Through feedback, interpersonal communication becomes a dynamic, two-way process, rather than just an event.

Fundamental cultural and language differences between individuals from various countries certainly heighten interpersonal communication problems. This chapter's Across Cultures account highlights the attributes of interpersonal communications in *low-context* cultures that emphasize

◆ ACROSS CULTURES

COMMUNICATION PROCESS IN HIGH VERSUS LOW-CONTEXT CULTURES

 In this account, Robert Moran, professor of international studies and director of the program of cross-cultural communications at the American Graduate School of International Management, Arizona, shares some of his personal experiences in and insights on the interpersonal communication process in high-context versus low-context cultures.

Moran recounts: "On a recent business trip to Europe, I asked a German executive out to dinner. 'Yes,' he responded, 'I will go to dinner with you. What time shall we meet?' Several days later in France, I made the same request of a French businessman. 'Thank you,' he replied. While it was clear from what the German said that he would dine with me, I was unsure whether or not the Frenchman had indicated he would join me for dinner that night. What was not in doubt was that while the German was using 'low-context communication,' the Frenchman was transmitting on a 'high-context' frequency.

"Individuals who want to communicate on the wavelength of people from such high-context cultures as those in France, Japan, Saudi Arabia, South Korea, China, and Spain have first to be aware that their approach must be indirect and less dependent on the spoken word. In fact, individuals from these countries rely more on what is unsaid when receiving and sending messages. They tend to skirt around issues, and the information they provide often lacks crucial detail. Body language, pauses, long periods of silence, physical proximity, trusting relationships, and empathy are all part of the cultural rituals that people from high-context cultures use to exchange ideas. Nonverbal communication in business situations is considered so important in France, for example, that some universities and schools regularly offer seminars on body language.

"In contrast, people from low-context cultures, such as those in Germany, Sweden, the United States, Canada, and Great Britain, rely extensively on direct verbal communication to send and receive accurate messages. Unlike high-context communicators, they put great store on being candid, 'spelling it out,' and 'laying your cards on the table.' Germany is a prime example of a low-context culture. Asked to do something or reach a decision, Germans feel the need to put it in the right context. They have relatively more compartmentalized information that is brought together through low-context communication. This is reflected in their organizations, where the average German worker and manager need procedures and explicit directions to function effectively. They become uncomfortable when high-context communicators do not provide them with enough information.

"Low-context communicators can best overcome their difficulties in understanding high-context messages by attuning their listening skills. This is easier said than done, because most have been through education systems that develop reading, writing, and articulation at the expense of listening skills. While students who have problems with reading, writing, and speaking receive assistance to develop their competence, listening remains the most used but least taught communication skill."[15]

direct communications (such as German, Swiss, Scandinavian, North American, and English) versus *high-context* cultures that emphasize indirect communications (such as Chinese, Korean, Japanese, Vietnamese, Arab, French, and Spanish).

INTERPERSONAL COMMUNICATION NETWORKS

An **interpersonal communication network** is defined as those individuals who are linked by patterned communication flows to a specific individual.[16] This concept focuses on communication **relationships** among individuals, rather than on the individuals themselves. Networks involve the flow of oral, written, and nonverbal signals (data) between two or more individuals. Networks emphasize the pattern of signal flow (for example, flow between network members A and B or between member A and all other network members simultaneously), rather than whether the signal sent was received as intended by the sender. Of course, communication networks can influence the likelihood of a match between the intended messages sent and the messages actually received and interpreted.

Types of Networks

The model of the interpersonal communication process shown previously in Figure 13.1 is based on the involvement of only two people. Obviously, communication often takes place among many individuals and larger groups. For example, a manager must link up with a variety of people within and outside the organization. A manager's communication networks extend both laterally and vertically. *Vertical networks* include the manager's immediate superior and subordinates as well as the superior's superiors and the subordinates' subordinates. *Lateral networks* include people at the same level (peers) and at different levels (lateral superiors and lateral subordinates). *External networks* for managers often include customers, suppliers, regulatory agencies, pressure groups, and professional associations. As you can readily see, an employee's communication network can become quite involved.[17]

Group size limits the possible communication networks within a group. In principle, as the size of a group increases arithmetically, the number of possible communication interrelationships increases exponentially. Accordingly, communication networks are much more varied and complex in a twelve-person group than in a three-person group. While every member (theoretically) may be able to communicate with all other group members, the direction and number of communication channels in an organization are often somewhat limited. In committee meetings, for example, varying levels of formality influence who may speak, what may be discussed, and in what order. The relative status or ranking of group members also may differ. Members having higher status will probably dominate the communication network more than those with lower status. Even when an open network is encouraged, the members may actually use a more limited network arrangement.

To provide a sense of the potential and powerful effects of communication networks, we will consider a single group—which could be a work team or informal social group—of five members. This will reduce the complicating effects of different numbers of members in groups. There are about sixty possible communication networks for a five-person group. However, we will concentrate on the five basic communication networks for a group of this size: the *star* (sometimes called the *wheel*), the *Y,* the *chain,* the *circle,* and the *all-channel network.* These five networks, presented in Figure 13.3, illustrate the possible major differences in a five-person group. Each line between each pair of names represents a two-way communication channel. The degree of restriction on members in the use of communication channels differentiates the networks. The star network is the most restricted: All communication must flow between Jane and each of the other members. At the other extreme, the all-channel network is the least restricted and most open. Each member communicates with all other members simultaneously.

Effects of Different Networks

The importance of communication networks lies in the potential effects of different networks on such variables as predicting group leaders, effectiveness, efficiency, and member satisfaction.[18] Table 13.1 provides a rough

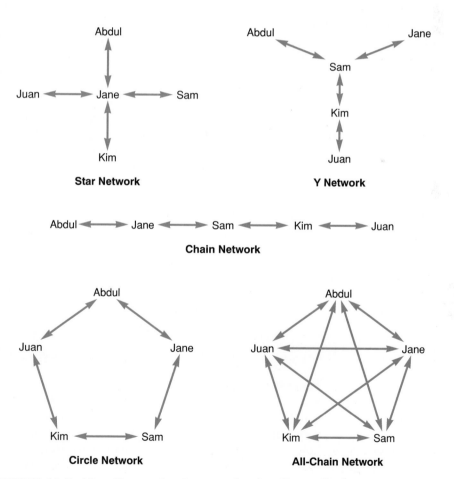

FIGURE 13.3   Five Alternative Communication Networks for a Five-Person Group

synthesis and comparison of the communication networks in terms of four assessment criteria. The first criterion, *degree of centralization,* is the extent to which some group members have access to more communication channels than other members. The star network is the most centralized, because all communication flows from and to only one member. The all-channel network is the least centralized, because any member can communicate with any or all other members at the same time.

The criterion of *leadership predictability* is the ability to anticipate which group member is likely to emerge as the group leader. In Figure 13.3, the following individuals are likely to emerge as leaders: Jane in the star network; Sam in the Y network; and possibly Sam in the chain network. In each of these three networks, the anticipated leaders should possess greater amounts of information and greater control over the dissemination of information and suggestions than the other group members.

The third and fourth assessment criteria in Table 13.1 measure the *average satisfaction* of the group members as a whole within each network and the *range in satisfaction* between group members. A number of interesting relationships exist between these two criteria. In the star network, the average member satisfaction in the group is likely to be the lowest compared with the other networks, but the range in individual member satisfaction is likely to be the highest relative to the other networks. Jane would find the star network highly satisfying, because she is the center of attention and has considerable influence over the group. However, the other members are highly dependent on Jane and may well play a relatively marginal role compared with hers in the decision process. Accordingly, the average satisfaction of the group as a whole is likely to be relatively low. In contrast, the all-channel network creates the potential for greater participation by all members in terms of their interest and ability to contribute to the group. Thus, while the average group satisfaction may be relatively high, the range between the satisfaction scores of individual members will probably be smaller than for the other networks.

Organizational Implications

There are no simple organizational implications for applying the knowledge of communication networks under all conditions. Knowing the types of communication networks used is especially important in understanding

---

TABLE 13.1   Effects of Five Communication Networks

| | **Types of Communications Networks** | | | | |
	Star	*Y*	*Chain*	*Circle*	*All-Channel*
Degree of Centralization	Very high	High	Moderate	Low	Very low
Leadership Predictability	Very high	High	Moderate	Low	Very low
Average Group Satisfaction	Low	Low	Moderate	Moderate	High
Range in Individual Member Satisfaction	High	High	Moderate	Low	Very low

power and control relationships among employees in organizations.[19] For example, powerful individuals may limit access to information by others as one way of maintaining or increasing their power. (Information as a source of power is discussed in Chapter 16.) Also, problems basically can be differentiated as simple or complex. Simple problems, such as scheduling overtime work, make few demands on the members in terms of (1) collecting, categorizing, and evaluating information; (2) generating goals to be achieved; (3) developing and evaluating alternatives; and (4) coping with interpersonal problems associated with the tasks at hand. In contrast, complex problems, such as deciding whether to build a new plant, are characterized by a high degree of one or more of these types of demands. Simple networks (such as superior to subordinate) are often effective for solving simple problems. All-channel or open networks (as in a work team) are often more effective for solving complex problems.

Another qualifying factor in problem solving is the degree of member interdependence required to accomplish the group's tasks. With problems requiring little member interdependence, communication may be effectively handled through one of the more centralized networks (such as superior to subordinate). For example, in swimming, track, or golf, the coach is usually the central person in task coordination and communication. Team members can perform most of their tasks with minimal transactions with other team members. With a high degree of member interdependence—as in basketball, ice hockey, and soccer—all-channel networks are much more effective than a simple, centralized network. A complex communication network is required—both between coach and players and among players as they perform their roles.

Networks also have several implications for day-to-day communication processes in organizations. First, no single network is likely to prove effective in all situations for a work team or group having a variety of tasks and goals. The apparently efficient and low-cost simple method of a superior instructing subordinates is likely to be ineffective if used exclusively. Dissatisfaction may become so great that individuals will leave the group or lose their motivation to contribute. Second, groups that face complex problems requiring high member interdependence may deal with them ineffectively because of inadequate sharing of information, consideration of alternatives, and so on. Third, a group must consider trade-offs or opportunity costs. A work team committed to the exclusive use of the all-channel network may deal inefficiently with simple problems and tasks that require little member interdependence. In such cases, members may also become bored and dissatisfied with team processes. They simply come to feel that their time is being wasted. Another trade-off with the all-channel network is its implied labor costs. That is, more time must be spent on processing a problem in group meetings with the all-channel network. A group should use the type of network that is most appropriate to its tasks and problems.[20]

Role of Information Technologies

Within the past decade, an increasing range of information technologies became available to support and extend interpersonal communication networks. These information technologies are sometimes substituting for the face-to-face communication commonly used to achieve networking in organizations. In this section, we discuss a few of the technologies that are making it easier for people at work to communicate with one another. We start with an account of how Peter Kelley uses several of these information technologies.

IN PRACTICE

THE "COMMUNICAHOLIC" MANAGER

Peter Kelley is the first to admit that he's a "communicaholic." He has a car phone, of course, as befits the vice-president for operations of Metro Mobile, which provides cellular telephone service to three different areas of the United States. In the morning, during his one-and-a-half-hour drive to Manhattan from New Jersey, his general managers typically report in to him. In the afternoon, as the phone messages pile up on his desk, Peter stuffs the ones from the West Coast into his shirt pocket, then makes the calls on the commute home. Peter is so far gone a "communicaholic" that, he reports, "when I get into a car without a phone, I feel very frustrated."

Partly to avoid such frustration, he carries a small portable phone, weighing less than two pounds, in a special, easy-access compartment of his briefcase. "Typically, it's on as soon as I leave the office, when I get in the cab to go to LaGuardia," he says. While federal regulations prohibit its use in flight, it comes in handy on trips, even if only in his hotel room, where it sits by his bed in its recharging stand, freeing him from the hotel switchboard.

Sometimes, though, mere talk is not enough; you need to see the paperwork. For these occasions, the mobile phone company executive keeps a portable facsimile machine that can churn out the pages either in the trunk of his car or at home. Does all this connectedness make Peter a better manager? He certainly thinks so. "It's not just the convenience," he says, "'but also the security of knowing that your office or home can get in touch with you in emergencies."[21]

Electronic mail (E-mail) is a computer-based system that enables participating individuals to exchange and store messages through their computers. In sophisticated E-mail systems, the user may get a digest of all the incoming mail, with headings noting the name of the sender, the time and date it was sent, and what it is about. The recipient can choose which full messages to call up. In addition to transmitting messages between employees down the hall or overseas, E-mail technology has advanced to the *open network*. This permits computer-to-computer exchanges of purchase orders, invoices, electronic payment of bills, and so on.[22]

E-mail reduces barriers of *time* and *distance* in the creation of communication networks. It also cuts down on the game of "phone tag," in which individuals trade numerous phone calls before catching up with each other. The U.S. Forest Service has placed about nine hundred ranger stations on a nationwide E-mail system. The rangers can exchange messages over their computers to order supplies, relay news of a spreading fire, and so on. The bulk of the rangers' communications that had taken place by telephone or the Postal Service now occurs through each ranger's personal computer.[23]

Voice mail is a computer-based messaging system accessed by telephone. People can use it as they would an answering machine to receive recorded messages or as they would memoranda to transmit recorded messages to others. Although more expensive to operate than an E-mail system, voice mail is a richer information medium (see Figure 13-2 for continuum of media richness). Recent research suggests that voice mail may be an excellent medium for sending short, simple, and noncontroversial messages over moderate or great distances.[24]

Telecommuting refers to the practice of working at home while linked to the office or plant through some type of computer or terminal. It may also include those who work out of a customer's office or communicate with the office or plant via a laptop computer or mobile phone. Of course, telecommuting may incorporate E-mail, voice mail, and other information technologies. Successful telecommuting jobs usually involve some combination of the following characteristics:

- Tasks that can be accomplished or transmitted through computer terminals;
- High daily or weekly use of the telephone;
- Routine information handling;
- Tasks that can be performed independently of others and, if necessary, be integrated into the whole later; and/or
- Project-oriented job tasks with well-defined milestones of accomplishment at specific times.

A few of the occupations most often found amenable to telecommuting include salesperson, real estate agent, computer systems analyst, data entry clerk, consultant writer, security broker, and copy editor. It is estimated that 3 million to 4 million U.S. employees have already formed telecommuting arrangements with their employers, and the number is growing. Among the more well-known companies with successful programs for some of their employees are IBM, Xerox, American Express, Du Pont, Pacific Bell, J.C. Penney, and Apple Computer.[25]

The advantages of the new information technologies are fairly obvious. They have made it easier, quicker, and less expensive for people to communicate with one another. However, some problems need to be guarded against. First, these technologies have not been effective for relationship building or complex group problem solving where face-to-face discussion (the richest medium) continues to be crucial. Second, these technologies can break down the boundaries between work time and nonwork time that are especially useful in managing work stress (see Chapter 9). Thus, these technologies, if not managed carefully, can evolve into a continuous invasion of privacy by enabling managers and other workers to easily contact the employee at any time and place. Third, hyperconnectedness may erode the delegation of authority (empowerment of subordinates) by creating too much and too frequent communications between superiors and subordinates. That is, superiors may start to oversupervise the work of subordinates because it is too easy to get feedback from them. Fourth, these technologies open the possibility of wasting time on increased volumes of meaningless data (junk) with the consequence of unnecessary work overload. Of course, we do not want to suggest that these problems with information technologies are inevitable. Awareness is the first step to avoidance.[26]

COMMUNICATION OPENNESS

The model of the interpersonal communication process (Figure 13-1), effective interpersonal communication networks (Table 13-1), and the expanded means of interpersonal communication through new information technologies are all based on a fundamental assumption: there will be *openness in communication*. In this section, we present a continuum of communication openness, forces that work for and against such openness, and how movement toward greater openness can be achieved by effective feedback, listening, and self-disclosure.

Openness Continuum

Figure 13.4 suggests that communication openness may be viewed as a continuum ranging from closed, guarded, and defensive to open, candid, and nondefensive.[27] At the extreme left side of the continuum, every message (regardless of the medium of transmission) by the sender is weighed, analyzed, and scrutinized. Communication occurs on the direct level and the meta-communication (hidden) level. **Meta-communication** refers to

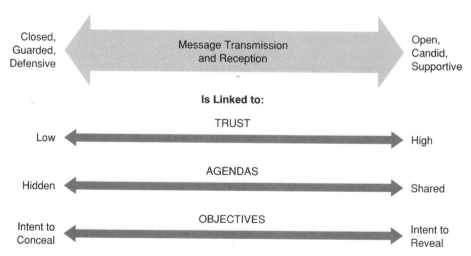

FIGURE 13.4   The Communication Openness Continuum

Source: Adapted from L. Sussman, "Managers: On the Defensive." *Business Horizons,* January-February 1991, 83. Copyright 1991 by the Foundation for the School of Business at Indiana University. Used with permission.

the assumptions, inferences, and interpretations made by the parties that form the basis of overt messages. In closed communications, the real agendas and "messages" are *consciously* and *purposely* hidden. Thus, *game playing* is rampant. Meta-communications of a hidden nature focus on such inferences as: (1) "what I think you think about what I said"; (2) "what I think you really mean"; (3) "what I really mean but hope you don't realize that I mean"; (4) "what you're saying but what I think you really mean"; and (5) "what I think you're trying to tell me but aren't directly telling me because. . .(you're afraid of hurting my feelings, you think being totally open could hurt your chances of promotion, etc.)."

At the right side of the continuum, the communications are totally open, candid, and supportive. The words and nonverbal cues sent convey the intended message that is authentic and chosen without hidden agenda. Communications are designed to *reveal* intent, not *conceal* it. In brief, the individuals express what they mean and mean what they convey. Breakdowns in communications at this end of the continuum are primarily due to honest errors in the communication process itself (such as the different meanings that are assigned to words like *soon* or *immediately*).

Communication openness is a matter of degree rather than absolutes. The nature of language, linguistics, and different interpersonal relationships (co-worker to co-worker, subordinate to superior, friend to friend, spouse to spouse, etc.) create the situational forces that allow for degrees of shading, coloring, amplification, and deflection in the use of words and nonverbal cues as symbols of meaning.

Situational Risk Factors

Our position is that the degree of openness must be considered in relation to the situational risk factors associated with such openness. (These factors are addressed at length in Chapter 16 on power and political behavior, Chapter 15 on organizational cultures, and Chapter 14 on conflict and negotiation.) Thus, we just note three of them here. First, perhaps the most significant factor affecting trust and risk taking in interpersonal communication is history. Has the other party violated your or others' trust in the past? Has the other party provided cues (verbal or nonverbal) soliciting or reinforcing your attempts to be open and candid? Or has the other party provided cues to the contrary? Has history created a level of such comfort that both parties can focus on direct communication, rather than meta-communication?[28]

Second, if the encounter is likely to be adversarial (such as union and management wage negotiations) and the other party is committed to damaging or weakening your position or gaining at your expense, then engaging in guarded communication is rational. Prior to the Persian Gulf War, U.S. and allied commanders engaged in public communications to make the Iraqi generals and others believe that the major offensive would come from the sea and through the southeast (coastline) portion of Kuwait. This deception was by design and worked. Conversely, if the encounter is likely to be friendly and the other party is trying to please you, strengthen your position, or enhance your esteem, then guarded communication can be seen as irrational.

Third, when we communicate with someone of higher status and power, we communicate with someone who has control over our fate. This person may appraise our performance, judge our promotability, and determine our merit increases. Our tendency to project the most favorable image possible, to encode negative messages in euphemisms and qualifiers, is understandable and rational, especially if past encounters reinforced the use of hidden over honest disclosures.[29] Consider the comment by a top manager of a Fortune 500 company:

> Listen, I've attended enough seminars and read enough self-help books to know that relationships ought to be based on honesty, mutual support, and open communications. But I've also managed long enough in this company and other companies to know that honesty can hurt both parties and the organization. The principle isn't always worth the cost of hurt feelings and ruined relationships.[30]

The following statement provides an interesting summary of the research findings on closed (defensive) versus open (supportive) interpersonal communications:[31]

> When people feel defensive, they want to *strike* out; when they feel understood, they want to *reach* out. When people feel defensive, they want to do something *to* the other person; when they feel understood, they want to do something *for* the other person and for people in general.

The need for effective feedback, listening, and self-disclosure in achieving open communications is demonstrated in the following account on communicating commitment. Meta-communication is clearly in evidence in the exchanges among senior representatives from the sales, design, production, and marketing departments. This In Practice demonstrates the various ways of communicating commitment.

IN PRACTICE

COMMUNICATING COMMITMENT

Production: "Why can't we hold this meeting off-site for a change? You never get people's undivided attention when it's in-house, and it takes twice as long as it needs to." *Sales:* "Sounds good. Marketing, will you book a room at the Sheraton?" *Marketing:* I'll do my best. Will you see that your people know?" *Sales:* "As soon as I can get to it. Design, will you get all the samples over there?" *Design:* I'll try. Production, could you tell the out-of-town people not to book the Hilton? It's across town." *Production:* "I'll look into it." *Sales:* "Great. That takes care of that."

We have now moved our meeting to a hotel and arranged for all the salespeople to attend, all the samples to be brought, and all the out-of-town attendees to be notified, right? Want to bet? The first way of communicating commitment is to make vague statements like "I'll do my best" or "As soon as I can get to it." What happens if " as soon as I can get to it" is two minutes before the meeting?

An acceptance, the second way of communicating commitment, is a straight-forward agreement to the conditions of the request: *Marketing:* "Production, will you have one sample from each product line at the meeting Wednesday?" *Production:* "Yes." Nothing is ambiguous, and action occurs.

A decline also moves events; you now know you need to explore other alternatives. Counteroffers are a form of declination. *Marketing:* "Production, will you have one sample from each product line at the meeting Wednesday?" *Production:* "No, I can't do that. I can have one sample from each line in category one and a few other samples from the other lines." Here, Production has declined Marketing's request and is counteroffering an alternative solution, the third way of communicating commitment. Note that no action will occur until Marketing responds to Production's counteroffer: *Marketing:* "That's fine."

Contrast that response with another counteroffering scenario:

Marketing: "I really would like to see more than that." *Design:* "It's never been necessary in the past." *Production:* "You're really asking me to put pressure on our Far East operations, and you know how tough things have been over there lately." *Sales:* "I think if we saw complete sketches, that would serve our purposes just as well." *Production:* "Excellent idea. Marketing, why don't you bring your sketches?" *Marketing:* "Most of the sketches will be there anyway." *Sales:* "Hey, how were those sketches?" *Marketing:* "Oh, we're not going to go through that again, are we? I thought this was resolved last month." *Production:* "Actually, it's a very complex issue. . . ." And off we go. Whether there will be samples, sketches, or some combination thereof at the meeting is anybody's guess. Marketing never received a committed response to its counteroffer, with the result that whatever action does occur will occur by accident, not by design.

The fourth committed response is a promise-to-promise:

Sales: "Marketing, can you book a conference room at the Sheraton for this meeting?" *Marketing:* "I don't know. If one is available, I'll book it, and I'll let you know whether that happened by 10 A.M. tomorrow." A promise-to-promise says, in essence, "You can count on this action by this time." It sets up future action and forwards events by placing clear-cut parameters around the expected future action. The fifth type of committed response is a contingent promise, which says: "I promise to give you X at a specified point in the future provided Y happens":

Sales: "Marketing, will you distribute copies of the marketing research reports on Monday to prepare for the line reviews?" *Marketing:* "I promise you will have a set of the reports on Monday—provided I receive them from all the brand managers by Friday at noon. I'll let you know by 3 P.M. on Friday whether that happened."[32]

Giving Feedback

Giving feedback is the degree to which we share our thoughts and feelings about others with them. Feedback can involve very personal feelings or more abstract thoughts, such as reactions to others' ideas or proposals. The emotional impact of feedback varies according to how personally it is focused. When attempting to achieve a high degree of communication openness (see Figure 13.4), feedback should be *supportive* (reinforcing ongoing behavior) or *corrective* (indicating that a change in behavior is appropriate). The following are principles of effective feedback under open communications:

- Feedback ideally should be based on a foundation of trust between sender and receiver. If the organization's culture is characterized by extreme personal competitiveness, emphasis on the use of power to punish and control, and rigid superior-subordinate relationships, it will lack the level of trust necessary for effective feedback, thereby contributing to closed communications.

- Feedback should be specific rather than general, with clear and, preferably, recent examples. Saying "You are a dominating person" is not as useful as saying "Just now when we were deciding the issue, you did not listen to what others said. I felt I had to accept your argument or face attack from you."

- Feedback should be given at a time when the receiver appears to be ready to accept it. Thus, when a person is angry, upset, or defensive is probably not the time to bring up other, new issues.

- Feedback should be checked with the receiver to determine whether it seems valid. The sender can ask the receiver to rephrase and re-state the feedback to see whether it matches what the sender intended.

- Feedback should include those things the receiver may be capable of doing something about.

- Feedback should not include more than the receiver can handle at any particular time. For example, the receiver may become threatened and defensive if the feedback includes everything the receiver does that annoys the sender.[33]

Personal feedback helps people to look at their behavior by revealing to them the feelings aroused in others or by enabling them to see themselves as others do. Someone who is given and accepts accurate feedback does not necessarily change in the direction implied by the feedback. Individual change is not always that easy.[34]

Various types of interpersonal feedback are used by employees in organizations.[35] Although this is true for all employees, it is especially so for managers and other professionals who maintain a wide-ranging interpersonal communication network. Table 13.2 provides a questionnaire that can be used by employees to diagnose interpersonal feedback practices within their organization. The scoring system goes from 1 point (disagree strongly) to 5 points (agree strongly) for each statement. Thus, the greater the frequency of "agree" and "strongly agree" responses to the fifteen feedback practices, the greater the degree of open communications within the organization.

The first four items in Table 13.2 concern corrective feedback from superiors and co-workers. Corrective feedback is not necessarily bad for the person who is receiving it. Its effectiveness is largely determined by how the feedback is given. The second section in Table 13.2 concerns the degree to which positive feedback is given by individuals at higher organizational levels (items 5 through 8). Positive feedback reinforces and rewards certain behaviors so that they will be repeated in the future. The third section (items 9 through 12) concerns the degree to which positive feedback is given by individuals who are *not* in a hierarchical authority relationship with the

---

TABLE 13.2 **Diagnosis of Feedback Practices**

Read each of the following statements and record your perceptions about the feedback practices you experienced in a previous job. Respond on the continuum that ranges from disagree strongly to agree strongly.

	(1) Disagree Strongly	(2) Disagree	(3) Neutral	(4) Agree	(5) Agree Strongly
Corrective Feedback					
1. Your manager lets you know when you make a mistake.	____	____	____	____	____
2. You receive a formal report of poor performance.	____	____	____	____	____
3. Co-workers tell you that you have done something wrong.	____	____	____	____	____
4. You are told when you should be doing something else.	____	____	____	____	____
Positive Feedback from Higher Authority					
5. You receive thanks after completed jobs.	____	____	____	____	____
6. Your manager tells you when you are doing a good job.	____	____	____	____	____
7. You have a regular performance review with your manager.	____	____	____	____	____
8. The manager treats you as a mature adult.					
Positive Feedback from Nonhierarchical Others					
9. Co-workers congratulate you for how much you accomplish.	____	____	____	____	____
10. Co-workers compliment you for the quality of your work.	____	____	____	____	____
11. You know more people are using the company's product or service because of your efforts.	____	____	____	____	____
12. Co-workers like you very much.					
Internal Feedback					
13. You know when you have met your goals.	____	____	____	____	____
14. You can see the results of finding better ways of doing the job.	____	____	____	____	____
15. You know how much you can do without making a mistake.	____	____	____	____	____

person doing the diagnosis. Thus, the first three sections all concern the degree to which positive or negative feedback is received from sources external to the individual. By contrast, the fourth section (items 13 through 15) focuses on internal feedback, or the degree to which individuals observe and assess themselves.

This diagnostic questionnaire clearly shows that several forms of feedback are available to individuals in organizations. A lack of compatibility among these forms of feedback for a number of employees may indicate serious problems in an organization's networks of interpersonal communication.

Feedback practices of employees with customers are also vital to an organization's effectiveness. Consider one customer feedback practice: the apology. "I get a lot of people saying, 'If that doctor had just said he was sorry, I wouldn't be here suing him,' " says Robert Sullivan, a New York City attorney specializing in personal injury lawsuits. Although Sullivan acknowledges that an apology could come back to haunt someone in legal action—as in "He felt so guilty he even said he was sorry"—he believes it is worth the risk. "I think 'I'm sorry' goes a long way, and I recommend it," he says.[36]

"Often when you're mistreated as a consumer, it's not just your pocketbook that hurts, it's your pride," says Cleo Manuel of the National Consumers League. "A lot of people call us for sympathy, so we do a lot of apologizing for companies we have no control over. Half the time when we say 'I'm sorry this happened,' there's this weight lifted off their shoulders." Manuel's telephone service was recently cut off by mistake. Apologies? The telephone company "not only didn't say they were sorry for the inconvenience, they said I was lucky they didn't make me pay an extra deposit," Manuel says.[37]

Appropriate Self-Disclosure

Self-disclosure is any information that individuals consciously communicate (verbally or nonverbally) about themselves to others. People also often unconsciously disclose much about themselves by what they say and how they present themselves to others.[38] The ability to express oneself to one or a few significant other individuals is often basic for the individual's personal growth and development. The relationship between self-disclosure and an individual's effectiveness in an organization appears to be curvilinear. Nondisclosing individuals may repress their real feelings because revealing their feelings is threatening. Total-disclosure individuals, who expose a great deal about themselves to anyone they meet, may actually be unable to communicate with others because they are too preoccupied with themselves. A healthy openness between superior and subordinate, co-workers, or employee and customer can facilitate discussion and sharing of work-related problems.[39]

The ties among personality and self-disclosure have been expressed as follows:

> Healthy personality is manifested by a model of what we call authenticity, or more simply, honesty. Less healthy personalities, people who function less than fully, who suffer recurrent breakdowns or chronic impasses, may usually be found to be liars.

They say things they do not mean. Their disclosures have been chosen more for cosmetic value than for truth. The consequence of a lifetime of lying about oneself to others, of saying and doing things for their sound and appearance, is that ultimately the person loses contact with his real self. The authentic being manifested by healthier personalities takes the form of unself-conscious disclosure of self in words, decisions, and actions.[40]

Organizational level often complicates self-disclosure in interpersonal communication. Individuals are likely to dampen self-disclosure to those with higher formal power because of their ability to allocate rewards (such as pay raises or promotions) or punishments (such as demotions or dismissal). Even when a subordinate is able and willing to engage in "appropriate" forms of self-disclosure at work, a perception of the superior's trustworthiness in not using the revealed information to punish, intimidate, or ridicule is likely to influence the amount and form of self-disclosure.[41]

Active Listening

Active listening is necessary to encourage maximum levels of feedback and openness. **Listening** is a process that integrates physical, emotional, and intellectual inputs in a search for meaning and understanding.[42] Listening is effective when the receiver understands the sender's message as intended.

As much as 40 percent of an eight-hour work day of many employees is devoted to listening. Tests of listening comprehension, however, suggest that people often listen at only 25 percent efficiency.[43] Listening skills influence the quality of peer, superior-subordinate, and employee-customer relationships. Conversely, such relationships affect a person's ability or willingness to listen.[44] For example, employees who dislike their superior may find it extremely difficult to listen attentively to the superior's comments during performance review sessions. The following guidelines are suggested for increasing listening skills:

- Have a reason or purpose for listening. Good listeners tend to search for value and meaning in what is being said, even if they are not predisposed to be interested in the particular issue or topic. Poor listeners tend to rationalize any or all inattention on the basis of a lack of initial interest.

- Suspend judgment, at least initially. Good listening requires concentrating on the sender's whole message, rather than forming evaluations on the basis of the first few ideas presented.

- Resist distractions, such as noises, sights, and other people, and focus on the sender.

- Pause before responding to the sender.

- When the message is emotional or unclear, rephrase in your own words the content and feeling of what the sender seems to be saying.

- Seek the sender's important themes by listening for the overall content and feeling of the message.

- Use the time differential between the rate of thought (400 to 500) words per minute) and the rate of speech (100 to 150 words per minute) to reflect on content and search for meaning.[45]

Most of these guidelines for improving listening ability are interrelated. That is, we cannot practice one without improving the others. Unfortunately, like the guidelines for improving feedback, the listening-skills guidelines are much easier to understand than to develop and practice. To the extent that these communication skills are practiced, there will be a greater degree of open communications within the organization.

Implications for Ethical Behavior

Recall from Figure 13-4 that open communication includes the following attributes: (1) supportive and candid message transmission and reception, (2) a high level of direct communication with the explicit sharing of agendas, (3) the revealing of true intentions with little or no concealment, and (4) trusting relationships. In this communication environment, the probability of unethical behavior is likely to be minimized. Just the opposite is likely to be the case under highly closed communications, where we find (1) guarded and defensive message transmission and reception, (2) little direct communication with presence of many hidden agendas, (3) little desire to reveal intentions and much effort to conceal them, and (4) little trust among the parties. In this communication climate, there is likely to be the need for many externally imposed monitors (people checking on people) and detailed rules and procedures to *enforce* a minimal level of ethical behavior. In brief, it is our view that the prevailing *process* of interpersonal communication can work *against* (closed communication) or *for* (open communication) ethical behaviors.[46]

NONVERBAL COMMUNICATION

With the exception of our discussion of information technologies, we have focused up to this point in the chapter on verbal, face-to-face interaction. The other major form of face-to-face interaction—nonverbal communication—is more subtle.

Nonverbal communication includes nonlanguage human responses (such as body motions and personal physical attributes) and environmental characteristics (such as a large or small office). Nonverbal cues may contain many hidden messages and can influence the process and outcome of face-to-face communication. Even a person who is silent or inactive in the presence of others may be sending a message, which may or may not be the intended message (for example, boredom, fear, anger, or depression).[47]

Types of Nonverbal Cues

Table 13.3 outlines the basic types of nonverbal cues and illustrates the numerous ways people can and do communicate without saying or writing a word. Nonverbal communication is closely related to verbal communication in that neither is adequate by itself for effective interpersonal communication. Verbal and nonverbal cues can be related in the following ways:

TABLE 13.3 Nonverbal Cues	
Basic Type	**Explanation and Examples**
Body motion	Gestures, facial expressions, eye behavior, touching, and any other movement of the limbs and body.
Personal physical characteristics	Body shape, physique, posture, body or breath odors, height, weight, hair color, and skin color.
Paralanguage	Voice qualities, volume, speech rate, pitch, nonfluencies (saying "ah," "um," or "uh"), laughing, yawning, and so on.
Use of space	Ways people use and perceive space, including seating arrangements, conversational distance, and the "territorial" tendency of humans to stake out a personal space.
Physical environment	Building and room design, furniture and other objects, interior decorating, cleanliness, lighting, and noise.
Time	Being late or early, keeping others waiting, cultural differences in time perception, and the relationship between time and status.

- By repeating, as when verbal directions to some location are accompanied by pointing.

- By contradicting, as in the case of the person who says, "What, me nervous?" while fidgeting and perspiring anxiously before taking a test. This is a good example of how the nonverbal message might be more believable when verbal and nonverbal signals disagree.

- By substituting nonverbal for verbal cues, as when a manager returns to the office with a harried expression that says, "I've had a horrible meeting with my boss," without a word being spoken.

- By complementing the verbal cue through nonverbal "underlining," as when a manager pounds the table, places a hand on the shoulder of a co-worker, or uses a tone of voice indicating the importance attached to the message.[48]

In the following account, we note some of the ways that nonverbal cues, the *silent language,* varies across cultures.

IN PRACTICE

THE SILENT LANGUAGE ACROSS CULTURES

Verbal communications are often accompanied by nonverbal actions in which the hands play a crucial role. The snag with many hand gestures is that their meanings vary according to where you are. In the United States and many other countries, for example, the rounded, pinched-thumb and index-finger "A-OK" gesture is easily recognized as meaning "fine," "perfect," or simply "okay." In Japan, the traditional meaning of the gesture is "money." In Portugal and some other countries, this gesture has an offensive or obscene meaning.

To signify stupidity, the French, Germans, and Italians generally simply tap their own heads. Germans slapping their forehead with an open hand are saying the nonverbal equivalent of "You are crazy." Like North Americans, French, and Italians, Germans also make spiral motions at the head with the forefinger to indicate a loony idea. By contrast, when a Briton or Spaniard taps the forehead, this is widely recognized as an expression of self-praise. Although the gesture has a trace of self-mockery, it acknowledges one's own cleverness and is equivalent to saying, "What a brain!" If a Dutch person raises an index finger while tapping the forehead, it means the person is clever. But if the index finger points sideways, it means the other person is an idiot. Germans often raise their eyebrows in recognition of a clever idea. The same expression in Britain is a sign of skepticism.

The French have some of the most expressive hand gestures. To symbolize exquisiteness, a French person pinches the fingertips, raises them to the lips, and softly tosses a kiss into the air with the chin held high. On the other hand, if a French person rubs the base of the nose with the forefinger, it's a warning that "something smells bad," "be cautious," "we can't trust these people." Very similar is the Italian gesture of tapping the side of the nose with the forefinger. Its meaning: "Take care. There is danger ahead. They are getting crafty." In the Netherlands, this gesture means "I'm drunk" or "you're drunk." In England, a forefinger tap on the side of the nose means conspiracy or secrecy. The wagging finger has a multitude of interpretations. In the United States, Italy, and Finland, it might signify mild disapproval or a threat or merely emphasize the spoken word. In Central Europe, especially southern Germany and Austria, the same gesture is a sign of having burned one's finger metaphorically. In the Netherlands and France, the wagging finger merely means a refusal. A reprimand is shown by shaking an index finger next to the head.[49]

This limited list of meanings given in this In Practice to fairly standard gestures shows how easy it is, even for seasoned global travelers, to unintentionally offend those from another culture. A conscious effort to anticipate the reactions of others by observing their body language can help avoid misunderstandings.

Nonverbal cues have been linked to a wide variety of concepts and issues. We briefly consider two: (1) status, in terms of the relative ranking of individuals and groups, and (2) gender differences.

Status and Nonverbal Cues

Three main principles relate organizational status and nonverbal cues:

- Employees of higher status will have better offices than employees of lower status. In organizations, executive offices tend to be more spacious, located on the top floors of the building, and have finer carpets and furniture than those of first-line managers. The most senior offices will be at the corners so they have windows on two sides.

- The offices of higher-status employees are better protected than those of lower-status employees. Consider how much more difficult it would be for you to arrange to visit the governor of your state than for the governor to arrange to visit you. Top executive areas are typically least accessible and are often sealed off from intruders by several doors and assistants. Even lower-level managers and many staff personnel are "protected" by having an office with a door and a secretary who answers the telephone.

- The higher the employee's status, the easier that employee finds it to invade the territory of lower-status employees. A superior typically feels free to walk right in on subordinates, whereas subordinates are more careful to ask permission or make an appointment before visiting a superior.[50]

Gender Differences and Nonverbal Cues

Physical differences between men and women contribute to differences in their nonverbal behavior. However, they are miniscule compared to differences based on cultural influences. In addition to communicating gender, body language communicates status and power: many signs of dominance and submission are exchanged through nonverbal communication. Some nonverbal behaviors are associated with the subordinate position for either gender. But many of these same behaviors have been associated with women, regardless of status.[51] In this section, we describe a few of these nonverbal patterns, especially as they differ by gender.[52] These patterns reflect generalities and certainly do not apply to all men and women. Moreover, we know that in some segments of United States and Canadian societies, these patterns are changing.[53]

Use of Space Women's bodily behavior is often restrained and restricted. Their femininity is gauged, in fact, by how little space they take up. Masculinity is judged by men's expansiveness and the strength of their gestures. Men control greater territory and personal space, a property associated with dominance and high status in both human beings and animals. Studies have found that people tend to approach women more closely than men, to seat themselves closer to women, and to cut across women's paths in hallways, and so on more than men's.

Eye Contact Eye contact may be greatly influenced by gender. In personal interactions, women look more at the other person than men do—and they maintain more woman-to-woman eye contact. In fact, research consistently demonstrates that women are more skilled than men in accurately decoding nonverbal cues.[54] People tend to maintain more eye contact with those from whom they want approval. Women are stared at and reciprocate by not looking back more than men. Women are routinely stared at by men in public. Our language even has specific words, such as *ogling* and *leering*, for this practice.

Touching Touching may be another gesture of dominance. Cuddling in response to touch may be a corresponding gesture of submission. Just as the manager can put a hand on the worker, the master on the servant, and the teacher on the student, so men more frequently put their hands on women, despite folklore to the contrary.

There is another side to touching, which is much better understood: touching symbolizes friendship and intimacy. The power aspect of touching does not rule out its intimacy aspect. A particular touch may have both components and more, but it is the *pattern* of touching between two individuals that tells us the most about their relationship. When touching is reciprocal—that is, when both parties have equal touching privileges—we have information about the intimacy of the relationship. Much touching indicates closeness, and little touching indicates distance. When one party is free to touch the other but not vice versa, we have information about status or power. The person with greater touching privileges probably has higher status or more power.

Breaking the Mold Many women have been reversing these nonverbal interaction patterns. Women now feel freer to stop smiling when they are unhappy, stop lowering their eyes, stop getting out of men's way on the street, and stop letting themselves be interrupted. They can stare people in the eye, address someone by first name if that person addresses them by their first name, and touch when they feel it is appropriate. Men need to become more aware of what they are signifying nonverbally. Men can restrain their invasions of personal space through staring, touching (if not by mutual consent), and interrupting.[55]

SUMMARY

Communication—particularly direct interpersonal communication—is the lifeblood of organizations. When individuals engage in effective interpersonal communication, they increase their own sense of well-being and become more effective. The essential variables in the communication process include: senders, receivers, transmitters, receptors, messages, channels, noise, meaning, encoding, decoding, and feedback. All are interrelated.

Interpersonal communication involving face-to-face discussion is the medium with the highest degree of information richness. An information-rich medium is especially important for performing complex tasks and resolving social-emotional issues that involve considerable uncertainty and ambiguity. Important issues usually contain significant amounts of uncertainty, ambiguity, and people-related (especially social and emotional) problems.

The interpersonal communication process may be repeated dozens of times each day by individuals through their many communication networks. Individuals' communication networks operate vertically and laterally. These networks can range from closed and centralized to open and decentralized. Electronic mail (E-mail), voice mail, and telecommuting are only a few of the information technologies available to support and extend interpersonal communication networks.

We presented a continuum of communication openness from closed (defensive and guarded) to open (candid and supportive). Situational risk factors, such as past history of the parties, are important for creating the conditions for relatively closed or open communications. The skills and abilities for increasing openness were presented in the discussions of feedback, appropriate self-disclosure, and active listening. Several implications of the degree of communication openness for ethical behavior were noted.

Nonverbal cues play a powerful role in interpersonal communication. The six basic types of nonverbal cues are closely related to verbal communication. For example, formal organizational status is often tied to nonverbal cues. The potential for status and gender differences in the use of nonverbal cues was explored.

Key Words and Concepts

Bypassing	Meanings
Channels	Media richness
Data	Messages
Decoding	Meta-communication
Electronic mail (E-mail)	Noise
Encoding	Nonverbal communication
Feedback	Receptors
Interpersonal communication	Self-disclosure
Interpersonal communication	Telecommuting
network	Transmitters
Listening	Voice mail

Discussion Questions

1. What is the difference between encoding and decoding?

2. Give two examples of how interpersonal classroom communications are likely to vary in a high-context versus a low-context culture.

3. Is there one best communication network? Explain.

4. What types of issues are less likely to be effectively communicated through E-mail than face-to-face discussion? Explain.

5. Think of an organization or group of which you are a member. How would you assess this organization or group in terms of the continuum of communication openness (see Figure 13-4)?

6. What types of problems and limitations prevent meaningful self-disclosure between superiors and subordinates?

7. What similarities and differences are there in this chapter's recommendations for improving feedback skills versus listening skills?

8. Describe the various nonverbal forms of communication used by someone you have worked for or by one of your teachers. Were the nonverbal cues consistent or inconsistent with this person's verbal expressions? Explain.

MANAGEMENT CASES AND EXERCISES

INTERPERSONAL COMMUNICATIONS SURVEY[56]

This survey is designed to assess your understanding of and behavior in your interpersonal communications practices. There are no right or wrong responses. Rather, the requested response is simply the one that comes closest to representing your practices.

For each item on the survey, you are requested to indicate which of the alternative reactions would be more characteristic of the way *you* would handle the situation described. Some alternatives may be equally characteristic of you or equally uncharacteristic. Although this is a possibility, please choose the alternative that is *relatively* more characteristic of you. For each item, you will have five points that you may *distribute* in any of the following combinations, where 5 = most characteristic and 0 = least characteristic:

	A	B
1.	5	0
2.	4	1
3.	3	2
4.	2	3
5.	1	4
6.	0	5

Thus, there are six possible combinations for responding to the pair of alternatives presented to you with each survey item. *Be sure the numbers you assign to each pair sum to 5.*

To the extent possible, please relate each situation in the survey to your own personal experience. As used throughout this survey, the words *he, him,* and *his* include both the masculine and feminine genders unless specifically stated.

1. If a friend of mine had a personality conflict with a mutual acquaintance of ours with whom it was important for him to get along, I would:

    _____ A. Tell my friend that I felt he was partially responsible for any problems with this other person and try to let him know how the person was being affected by him.

    _____ B. Not get involved because I would not be able to continue to get along with both of them once I had entered into the conflict.

2. If one of my friends and I had a heated argument in the past and I realized that he was ill at ease around me from that time on, I would:

    _____ A. Avoid making things worse by discussing his behavior and just let the whole thing drop.

    _____ B. Bring up his behavior and ask him how he felt the argument had affected our relationship.

3. If a friend began to avoid me and act in an aloof and withdrawn manner, I would:

    _____ A. Tell him about his behavior and suggest he tell me what was on his mind.

    _____ B. Follow his lead and keep our contacts brief and aloof since that seems to be what he wants.

4. If two of my friends and I were talking and one of my friends slipped and brought up a personal problem of mine that involved the other friend, and of which he was not yet aware, I would:

    _____ A. Change the subject and signal my friend to do the same.

    _____ B. Fill my uninformed friend in on what the other friend was talking about and suggest that we go into it later.

5. If a friend were to tell me that, in his opinion, I was doing things that made me less effective than I might be in social situations, I would:

    _____ A. Ask him to spell out or describe what he has observed and suggest changes I might make.

    _____ B. Resent the criticism and let him know why I behave the way I do.

6. If one of my friends aspired to an office in our student organization for which I felt he was unqualified and if he had been tentatively assigned to that position by the president of the student society, I would:

_____ A. Not mention my misgivings to either my friend or the president and let them handle it in their own way.

_____ B. Tell my friend and the president of my misgivings and then leave the final decision up to them.

7. If I felt that one of my friends was being unfair to me and his other friends, but none of them had mentioned anything about it, I would:

_____ A. Ask several of those people how they perceived the situation to see if they felt he was being unfair.

_____ B. Not ask the others how they perceived our friend but wait for them to bring it up to me.

8. If I were preoccupied with some personal matters and a friend told me that I had become irritated with him and others and that I was jumping on him for unimportant things, I would:

_____ A. Tell him I was preoccupied and would probably be on edge a while and would prefer not to be bothered.

_____ B. Listen to his complaints but not try to explain my actions to him.

9. If I had heard some friends discussing an ugly rumor about a friend of mine that I knew could hurt him and he asked me what I knew about it, if anything, I would:

_____ A. Say I didn't know anything about it and tell him no one would believe a rumor like that anyway.

_____ B. Tell him exactly what I had heard, when I had heard it, and from whom I had heard it.

10. If a friend pointed out the fact that I had a personality conflict with another friend with whom it was important for me to get along, I would:

_____ A. Consider his comments out of line and tell him I didn't want to discuss the matter any further.

_____ B. Talk about it openly with him to find out how my behavior was being affected by this.

11. If my relationship with a friend has been damaged by repeated arguments on an issue of importance to us both, I would:

_____ A. Be cautious in my conversations with him so the issue would not come up again to worsen our relationship.

_____ B. Point to the problems the controversy was causing in our relationship and suggest that we discuss it until we get it resolved.

12. If in a personal discussion with a friend about his problems and behavior, he suddenly suggested we discuss my problems and behavior as well as his own, I would:

_____ A. Try to keep the discussion away from me by suggesting that other, closer friends often talked to me about such matters.

_____ B. Welcome the opportunity to hear what he felt about me and encourage his comments.

13. If a friend of mine began to tell me about his hostile feelings about another friend who he felt was being unkind to others (and I wholeheartedly agreed), I would:

_____ A. Listen and also express my own feelings to him so he would know where I stood.

_____ B. Listen but not express my own negative views and opinions because he might repeat what I said to him in confidence.

14. If I thought an ugly rumor was being spread about me and suspected that one of my friends had quite likely heard it, I would:

_____ A. Avoid mentioning the issue and leave it to him to tell me about it if he wanted to.

_____ B. Risk putting him on the spot by asking him directly what he knew about the whole thing.

15. If I had observed a friend in social situations and thought that he was doing a number of things that hurt his relationships, I would:

_____ A. Risk being seen as a busybody and tell him what I had observed and my reactions to it.

_____ B. Keep my opinions to myself, rather than be seen as interfering in things that are none of my business.

16. If two friends and I were talking and one of them inadvertently mentioned a personal problem that involved me but of which I knew nothing, I would:

_____ A. Press them for information about the problem and their opinions about it.

_____ B. Leave it up to my friends to tell me or not tell me, letting them change the subject if they wished.

17. If a friend seemed to be preoccupied and began to jump on me for seemingly unimportant things and to become irritated with me and others without real cause, I would:

_____ A. Treat him with kid gloves for a while on the assumption that he was having some temporary personal problems that were none of my business.

_____ B. Try to talk to him about it and point out to him how his behavior was affecting people.

18. If I had begun to dislike certain habits of a friend to the point that it was interfering with my enjoying his company, I would:

_____ A. Say nothing to him directly but let him know my feelings by ignoring him whenever his annoying habits were obvious.

_____ B. Get my feelings out in the open and clear the air so that we could continue our friendship comfortably and enjoyably.

19. In discussing social behavior with one of my more sensitive friends, I would:

_____ A. Avoid mentioning his flaws and weaknesses so as not to hurt his feelings.

_____ B. Focus on his flaws and weaknesses so he could improve his interpersonal skills.

20. If I knew I might be assigned to an important position in our group and my friends' attitudes toward me had become rather negative, I would:

_____ A. Discuss my shortcomings with my friends so I could see where to improve.

_____ B. Try to figure out my own shortcomings by myself so I could improve.

Scoring Key In the Interpersonal Communication Survey, there are ten questions that deal with your receptivity to feedback and ten that are concerned with your willingness to self-disclose. Transfer your scores from each item to this scoring key. Add the scores in each column. Now, transfer these scores to Figure 13-15 by drawing a vertical line through the feedback score and a horizontal line through the self-disclosure line.

Receptivity to Feedback	**Willingness to Self-Disclose**
2.B _____	1.A _____
3.A _____	4.B _____
5.A _____	6.B _____
7.A _____	9.B _____
8.B _____	11.B _____
10.B _____	13.A _____
12.B _____	15.A _____
14.B _____	17.B _____
16.A _____	18.B _____
20.A _____	19.B _____
Total: _____	Total: _____

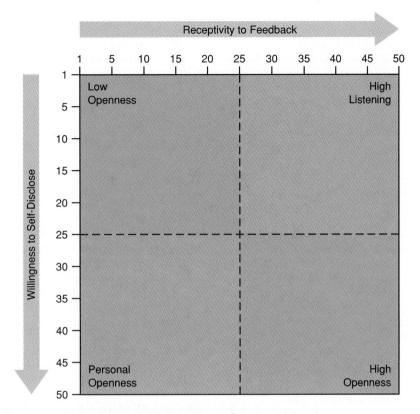

FIGURE 13.5 Personal Openness in Interpersonal Communications

As suggested through Figure 13.5, higher scores on *receptivity to feedback* and *willingness to self-disclose* indicate a greater willingness to engage in personal openness in interpersonal communications. Of course, we need to be mindful of the situational factors that may influence our natural personal predispositions to be relatively more open or closed in interpersonal communications.

JANE BRADY AND MR. SATO

When Jane Brady arrived at the plant one morning, her new boss, Mr. Sato, looked worried. He had only recently arrived in the United States on his first tour of duty outside of Japan. However, his English was good, and his superiors were confident that he could handle the job.

"Why so glum, Mr. Sato?" asked Ms. Brady as she seated herself across from him in his office for their morning conference. "Last night, I received a telex from Tokyo," he replied. "Here, take a look."

She reached across the desk and took the paper. The message was short and assertive, just like all the others she had seen in her two years working for Kumitomo America, a firm organized to supply the Japanese parent company with printing machinery for its giant publishing business in Japan.

> You must not let inventory build up. You must monitor carrying costs and keep them under control. Ship any job lots of more than twenty-five units to us at once.

As she read the letter, she nodded. "This is no problem, Sato-san. I can get right on it." "How many lots do we have to ship? I want to get them out of here right away."

Ms. Brady consulted a printout in the manila file folder she had with her. "No problem. We've only got three lots. I'll start the paperwork and get everything moving today. They'll be on the ship in Portland within two weeks."

Mr. Sato smiled weakly. He liked Americans, but he had been told that they were generally not as trustworthy as Japanese. It was not that they were bad people. It was just that they saw everything as a deal or an arrangement—you do this for me and I'll do this for you. They didn't do things simply because they were sincere. Ms. Brady, however, seemed different. She always did the job, and he did not have to spell everything out for her. All he needed to do was give her a general goal and she took care of the rest. He relaxed, turning his attention to the important trip to New York he would soon undertake.

Six weeks later, Ms. Brady was at the other end of the plant when the summons came. She hurried to Mr. Sato's office. He sat behind his desk, his face was red. She knew something was wrong. "I thought you were a good person, Ms. Brady," he said sadly. "This is very bad." He handed her a telex.

> Why didn't you do what we told you? Your quarterly inventory report indicates you are carrying forty lots that you were supposed to ship to Japan. You must not violate our instructions.

Ms. Brady could not believe what she was reading. "Sir, I shipped every lot more than twenty-five. Those were my orders and I carried them out." Mr. Sato grabbed the telex out of her hand. "What about this? This doesn't lie," he shouted. "I checked this morning. We have forty lots of more than twenty-five units each."

"That's not so. We don't."

"We do!"

"No, we don't!"

They stared at each other. Finally, Ms. Brady said softly, "Please, let's go and look." Mr. Sato got up silently, and Ms. Brady followed him out of the office. In the warehouse, they began with the first lot. Both of them counted. There were twenty-five units in the lot.

"Ms. Brady, why didn't you ship this lot as you were told to do?"

Her eyes widened. She felt herself losing control. Before answering, she breathed deeply. "Tokyo's instructions referred to lots of more than twenty-five. Is that correct?"

"Yes, exactly."

"Well, this lot only has twenty-five. In fact, many of the lots are like this one. They have twenty-five units."

"But you should have shipped them," he said, his voice tightening. "You should ship anything that's twenty-five, twenty-six, twenty-seven, and so forth."

"What? Since when does 'more than twenty-five' include twenty-five?"

His face became twisted in a look of withering scorn. "More than twenty-five always includes twenty-five. It's simple enough. Once again, your American education system has let you down."

"How dare you! Why don't you take the trouble to learn English if you are going to work in this country?" They glared at each other. Mr. Sato sighed, "I think we need to have a long talk, Ms. Brady." She nodded.[57]

QUESTIONS

1. What examples of bypassing are evident in this case?

2. How would you evaluate the listening skills of Ms. Brady and Mr. Sato?

3. How would you evaluate the feedback skills of Ms. Brady and Mr. Sato?

References

1. Adapted from Sullivan, J., Kameda, N., and Nobu, T. Bypassing in Managerial Communications. *Business Horizons*, January–February 1991, 71–80.
2. Ibid., 73.
3. Ibid., 76.
4. Krone, K. J., Jablin, F. M., and Putnam, L. L. Communication Theory and Organizational Communication: Multiple Perspectives. In F. M. Jablin, L. L. Putnam, K. H. Roberts, and L. W. Porter (eds.), *Handbook of Organizational Communication.* Newbury Park, Calif.: Sage, 1987, 18–40.
5. Axley, S. R. Managerial and Organizational Communication in Terms of the Conduit Metaphor. *Academy of Management Review*, 1984, 9, 428–437.

6. Adapted from Keys, J. B., and Case, T. L. How to Become an Influential Manager. *Academy of Management Executive*, November 1990, 38–51.

7. Huseman, R. C., Lahiff, J. M., and Penrose, J. M. *Business Communications: Strategies and Skills*, 3d ed. New York: Dryden, 1988.

8. Russ, G. S., Daft, R. L., and Lengel, R. H. Media Selection and Managerial Characteristics in Organizational Communications. *Management Communication Quarterly*, 1990, *4*, 151–175.

9. Saunders, C., and Jones, J. W. Temporal Sequences in Information Acquisition for Decision Making: A Focus on Source and Medium. *Academy of Management Review*, 1990, *15*, 29–46.

10. Trevino, L. K., Lengel, R. H., Bodensteiner, W., Gerloff, E. A., and Kanoff-Muir, N. The Richness Imperative and Cognitive Style: The Role of Individual Differences in Media Choice Behavior. *Management Communication Quarterly*, 1990, *4*, 176–197.

11. Downs, C. W. *Communication Audits in Organizations*. Glenview, Ill.: Scott, Foresman, 1988.

12. Sullivan, Kameda, and Nobu. Bypassing in Managerial Communication, 72.

13. Barnum, C. F. Mirror on the Wall: Who's the Wisest One of All? *International Executive*, July-August 1989, 39–41.

14. Rasmussen, R. V. A Communication Model Based on the Conduit Metaphor. *Management Communication Quarterly*, 1991, *4*, 363–374.

15. Adapted from Moran, R. "Watch My Lips." *International Management*, September 1990, 77. Used with permission.

16. Monge, P. R., and Eisenberg, E. M. Emergent Communication Networks. In F. M. Jablin, L. L. Putnam, K. H. Roberts, and L. W. Porter (eds.), *Handbook of Organizational Communication*. Newbury Park, Calif.: Sage, 1987, 304–342.

17. Bonacich, P., Communication Dilemmas in Social Networks: An Experimental Study. *American Sociological Review*, 1990, *55*, 448–459.

18. Toshio, Y., Gilmore, M. R., and Cook, K. S. Network Connections and the Distribution of Power in Exchange Networks. *American Journal of Sociology*, 1988, *93*, 833–851.

19. Clampitt, R. G. *Communicating for Managerial Effectiveness*. Newbury Park, Calif,: Sage, 1991.

20. Eisenberg, E. M., and Witten, M. G. Reconsidering Openness in Organization Communication. *Academy of Management Review*, 1987, *12*, 418–426; Beck, C. E., and Beck, E. A. The Manager's Open Door and the Communication Climate. *Business Horizons*, January-February 1986, 15–19.

21. Adapted from Kiechel, W. III. Hold for the Communicaholic Manager. *Fortune*, January 2, 1989, 107–108.

22. Seghers, F. Electronic Mail: Neither Rain nor Sleet nor Software. *Business Week*, February 20, 1989, 36; Komasky, S. H. A Profile of Users of Electronic Mail in a University. *Management Communication Quarterly*, 1991, *4*, 310–340.

23. Reitman, V. Business Plugs in to Electronic Mail. *Houston Chronicle*, September 3, 1990, 2B.

24. Reinsch, N. L. Jr., and Beswick, R. W. Voice Mail versus Conventional Channels: A Cost Minimization Analysis of Individuals' Preferences. *Academy of Management Journal*, 1990, *33*, 801–816.

25. Goodrich, J. N. Telecommuting in America. *Business Horizons*, July-August 1990, 31–37; Metzger, R. O., and Von Glinow, M. A. Off-Site Workers: At Home and Abroad. *California Management Review*, Spring 1988, 101–111.

26. Lederer, A. L., and Nath, R. Making Strategic Information Systems Happen. *Academy of Management Executive*, August 1990, 76–83.

27. This section draws heavily from Sussman, L. Managers: On the Defensive. *Business Horizons*, January-February 1991, 81–87.

28. Ibid., 84.

29. Ibid., 85.

30. Ibid., 82.

31. Gordon, R. D. The Difference between Feeling Defensive and Feeling Understood. *Journal of Business Communication*, Winter 1988, 53–64.

32. Adapted from Massimilian, R. D., The New Language Barrier: Closer to Home than You Think. *Business Horizons*, July-August 1990, 52–57.

33. Karp, K. The Lost Art of Feedback, in J. W. Pfeiffer (ed.), *The 1987 Annual: Developing Human Resources*. San Diego: University Associates, 1987, 237–245; Albrecht, T. L., and Adelman, M. B. *Communicating Social Support*. Newbury Park, Calif.: Sage, 1987.

34. Brett, J. M., Feldman, D. C., and Weingart, L. R. Feedback-Seeking Behavior of New Hires and Job Changers. *Journal of Management*, 1990, *16*, 737–749; Downs, T. M. Predictors of Communication Satisfaction during Performance Appraisal Interviews. *Management Communication Quarterly*, 1990, *3*, 334–354.

35. Baskin, O. W., and Aronoff, C. E. *Interpersonal Communication in Organizations*. Santa Monica, Calif.: Goodyear, 1980.

36. Crossen, C. Simple Apology for Poor Service Is in Sorry State. *Wall Street Journal*, November 29, 1990, B1, B6.

37. Ibid.; Kiechkel, W. III. How to Escape the Echo Chamber. *Fortune*, June 18, 1990, 129–130.

38. McCroskey, J. C., and Daly, J. A. (eds.). *Personality and Interpersonal Communication*. Newbury Park, Calif.: Sage, 1987; Cozby, P. C. Self-Disclosure: A Literature Review, *Psychological Bulletin*, 1973, *79*, 73–91.

39. Notarantonio, E. M., and Cohen, J. L. The Effects of Open and Dominant Communication Styles on Perceptions of the Sales Interaction. *Journal of Business Communication*, 1990, *27*, 171–184.

40. Jourard, S. M. *Disclosing Man to Himself*. New York: Van Nostrand Reinhold, 1968, 46–47. Also see Markus, H., and Nurius, P. Possible Selves. *American Psychologist*, 1986, *41*, 954–969.

41. Penley, L. E., Alexander, E. R., Jernigan, I. E., and Henwood, C. I. Communication Abilities of Managers: The Relationship to Performance. *Journal of Management*, 1991, *17*, 57–76; Sinetar, M. Building Trust into Corporate Relationships. *Organizational Dynamics*, Winter 1988, 73–79.

42. Chartier, M. R. Five Components Contributing to Effective Interpersonal Communications. In J. W. Pfeiffer and J. E. Jones (eds.), *1974 Annual Handbook for Group Facilitators*. La Jolla, Calif.: University Associates, 1974, 125–128.

43. Hamlin, S. *How to Talk So People Listen*. New York: Harper & Row, 1988.

44. Gurevitch, Z. D. The Power of Not Understanding: The Meeting of Conflicting Identities. *Journal of Applied Behavioral Science*, 1989, *25*, 161–173.

45. Brownell, J. *Building Active Listening Skills*. Englewood Cliffs, N.J.: Prentice-Hall, 1986; Kurtz, T. Dynamic Listening: Unlocking Your Communication Potential. *Supervisory Management*, September 1990, 7.

46. Pettit, J. D. Jr., Vaught, B., and Pulley, K. J. The Role of Communication in Organizations: Ethical Considerations. *Journal of Business Communication*, 1990, *27*, 233–249.

47. Wieman, J. M., and Harrison, R. P. (eds.). *Nonverbal Interaction*. Newbury Park, Calif.: Sage, 1983.

48. Harper, R. G., Wiens, A. N., and Matarzzo, J. D. *Nonverbal Communication: The State of the Art*. New York: Wiley, 1978.

49. Adapted from Moran, R. Watch Your Body Language. *International Management*, May 1990, 84; Harris, P. R., and Moran, R. T. *Managing Cultural Differences*, 2d ed. Houston: Gulf, 1987.

50. Goldhaber, G. M. *Organizational Communication*. Dubuque, Ia.: Wm.C. Brown, 1979, 152–187.

51. McCaskey, M. B. The Hidden Messages Managers Send. *Harvard Business Review*, November-December 1979, 135–148; Stablein, R., and Nord, W. Practical and Emancipatory Interests in Organizational Symbolism: A Review and Evaluation. *Journal of Management*, 1985, *11*, 13–28.

52. Henley, N., and Thorne, B. Womanspeak and Manspeak: Sex Differences and Sexism in Communication, Verbal and Nonverbal. In A. G. Sargent (ed.), *Beyond Sex Roles*. St. Paul: West Publishing, 1977, 201–218; Kohn, A. Girl Talk, Guy Talk. *Psychology Today*, February 1988, 65–66; Thayer, S. Close Encounters. *Psychology Today*, March 1988, 31–36.

53. Grant, J. Women as Managers: What They Can Offer to Organizations. *Organizational Dynamics*, Winter 1988, 56–63; Powell, G. N. *Women and Men in Management*. Newbury Park, Calif.: Sage, 1988; Steckler, N. A., and Rosenthal, R. Sex Differences in Nonverbal and Verbal Communication with Bosses, Peers, and Subordinates. *Journal of Applied Psychology*, 1985, *70*, 157–163

54. Graham, G. H., Unruh, J., and Jennings, P. The Impact of Nonverbal Communication in Organizations: A Survey of Perceptions. *Journal of Business Communication*, 1991, *28*, 45–60.

55. Fierman, J. Do Women Manage Differently? *Fortune*, December 17, 1990, 115–117.

56. Source: Douglas Roberts, formerly manager of training, LTV Missiles and Electronics Group, Grand Prairie, Texas.

57. Adapted from Sullivan, J., Kameda, N., and Nobu, T. "Bypassing in Managerial Communication: *Business Horizons*, January-February 1991, 71–80. Copyright 1991 by the Foundation for the School of Business at Indiana University. Used with permission.

CHAPTER 14

CONFLICT AND NEGOTIATION

LEARNING OBJECTIVES

When you have finished studying this chapter, you should be able to:

- Define the basic forms of conflict within organizations.
- Describe the negative, positive, and balanced views of conflict.
- Explain the major levels of conflict within organizations.
- Identify five interpersonal conflict-handling styles and state the conditions under which each may be effective.
- Explain the basics of negotiations.
- Describe the unilateral and interactive negotiation strategies as well as conditions under which each may be effective.
- Describe five structural methods for managing conflicts.

OUTLINE

LEARNING TO NEGOTIATE

Marjory Williams is founder and chief executive officer of SHE Inc./Laura Caspari Ltd., an affiliated women's clothing retail chain. She shares below how her views on negotiating and conflict management changed with experience:

"The art of negotiation has not come naturally to me. It's taken a while to realize that the process is easier when tempered with patience—by no means my long suit. And the truth is, I started out backwards. I prepared for each round by focusing on my goals and alternatives first and then on the people I was negotiating with. My reasoning went something like this: Who has ever won the Olympics without knowing where the finish line is? Who has ever won a chess tournament without assessing alternative moves and outcomes?

"This strategy doesn't always work, as I found out around twelve years ago, during my first job as a buyer for a large department store. I'd been working there only a short time when my boss laid out my assignment: 'Marjory, the department is overstocked, and the markdowns are way too high. One of the major problems is "such-and-such" vendor. On this New York City trip, go tell him the inventory levels are too high, the goods aren't moving, we need to send back 25 percent of our inventory, and we need eight thousand dollars to help cover our markdowns.'

"No sooner had I shaken hands with the vendor in his Manhattan showroom than I told him precisely that. It was my first experience with the 'boom-zero' effect. He was insulted and angry. Who was I, a newcomer to the business, to say his products weren't good? And who was I to make demands of him? By ignoring his needs, not to mention his feelings, I scored a fat zero. Still, I couldn't go back to Minneapolis empty-handed. Over the next three or four weeks, we arrived at a compromise. However, it was clear to me that I had achieved an acceptable solution only by the sheer force of the store's buying power and by my will and determination. By guts, not skill. By force, not finesse. I had won financial concessions, but I had not built a strong business relationship. I'm in a business where positive ongoing relations with vendors are important. More important than the financial results that I brought out of that experience was an awareness that we ignore the feelings of the other side at our own risk. Determination and goal setting may complement people skills, but they are not good substitutes.

"Some people think of negotiating as a game. That is certainly the way I first looked at it, with my Olympics-and-chess mind-set. On the surface, this analogy has a lot of appeal. The idea is that each person is out to pursue his or her own good and to win. While all this is partially true, I believe that negotiating is *not* a game. It's a business relationship in action. Nothing can kill a negotiation more quickly and more completely than a 'me against you' attitude. While the 'gotcha' approach may work in a single transaction, it's hardly likely to produce a successful, ongoing business relationship. Over time, both partners have to win. Otherwise, the loser will drop out.

"The thing that strikes me about great negotiators is that they are outstanding problem solvers. And they are persuasive. Now, when working with these experts, I focus strongly on my own goals, so that I am not swept into a situation that is bad for my company. I remember times when I let my guard down too much, and the reason I can remember those times so easily is that I'm still living with the results."[1]

Managing conflict is a common activity in the world of organizations. For our purposes, **conflict** refers to any situation in which there are incompatible goals, thoughts, or emotions within or between individuals or groups that lead to opposition. And, as Williams' comments reveal, attitudes and conflict styles play an important role in determining whether such conflict will lead to destructive or mutually beneficial outcomes.

Effective conflict management involves more than specific techniques. The ability to understand and correctly diagnose conflict is the first step in managing it.[2] We direct considerable attention toward understanding conflict and then how to manage it within organizations. **Conflict management** consists of diagnostic processes, interpersonal styles, negotiating strategies, and structural interventions that are designed to avoid unnecessary conflicts, reduce or resolve excessive conflicts, or even increase insufficient conflict. In the Preview Case, Marjory Williams emphasized the importance of *perceptions* to the management of conflict. As a new buyer, she defined her goals as getting a vendor to acknowledge that his products were to blame for an overstock. She also defined the *means* of resolving the problem as convincing the vendor to take back 25 percent of the inventory and contribute eight thousand dollars for marked-down goods. The vendor was insulted and angry. Why? His goals had been totally ignored. The conditions for destructive conflict were firmly in place. Another important lesson Williams learned about conflict management was the necessity of protecting herself against exploitation by those who take a "me against you" approach to conflict situations.

In this chapter, we examine conflict and negotiations from a variety of viewpoints. First, we consider three views of conflict and the levels and sources of conflict that can occur within organizations. Second, we discuss five interpersonal styles in conflict management and the conditions under which each style may be appropriate. Third, we review various negotiating strategies, including a model that will help you to decide when each strategy may be appropriate. In the last section, we discuss various structural methods that may be used to reduce or resolve conflicts within organizations.

INTRODUCTION TO CONFLICT

The essence of conflict is disagreement or incompatibility and comes in several basic forms, including:

- **Goal conflict,** in which desired end states or preferred outcomes appear to be incompatible. In the Preview Case, Williams shared how she started out her career with the view that all negotiating situations represent extreme goal conflicts.

- **Cognitive conflict,** in which ideas or thoughts are perceived as incompatible. Williams' story of how she thought she could resolve the overstocking situation through the Manhattan vendor created cognitive conflict. He had other thoughts on her proposed solution of his taking back 25 percent of the inventory and rebating eight thousand dollars to help cover the markdowns.

- **Affective conflict,** in which feelings or emotions are incompatible; that is, people literally become angry with one another. The vendor became insulted and angry at Williams for her unilateral approach to the situation and the implication that his products were not good enough.

- **Procedural conflict,** in which the parties differ on the process to use for resolving a conflict. The vendor's anger toward Williams arose, in part, out of the lack of a procedure for working through the conflict. Williams noted: "Over the next three or four weeks, we arrived at a compromise. However, it was clear to me that I had achieved an acceptable solution only by the sheer force of the store's buying power and by my will and determination." Union-management negotiations often contain procedural conflicts prior to the start of the actual negotiations. The parties may have procedural conflicts over *who* will be involved in the negotiations, *where* they will take place, and *when* sessions will be held (and how long they will be). Different interpretations about how a grievance system is to operate provides another example of procedural conflict.

Views of Conflict

The four basic forms of conflict need not necessarily lead to ineffectiveness. In fact, there are three views of conflict: positive, negative, and balanced.

Positive View Conflict in organizations can be a positive force. The creation and/or resolution of conflict often leads to constructive problem solving. The need to resolve conflict can cause people to search for ways of changing how they do things. The conflict-resolution process is often a stimulus for positive change within an organization. The search for ways to resolve conflict may not only lead to innovation and change, but it may make change more acceptable.[3] This view was demonstrated in a recent study of managers. The positive effects they noted generally fell into three major categories: beneficial effects on productivity ("our work productivity went up"; "we produced quality products on time"), relationship outcomes ("sensitivity to others was increased"; "better communication methods were developed"), and constructive organizational change ("we adopted more effective controls"; "better job descriptions and expectations were drawn up").[4]

The intentional introduction of conflict into the decision-making process can be beneficial. For example, in group decision making, a problem may arise when a cohesive groups' desire for agreement interferes with its consideration of alternative solutions. As discussed in Chapter 10, a group may encounter the problem of *groupthink,* which it can reduce if the introduction of conflict takes the form of one or more dissenting opinions.

Finally, people may come to quite different conclusions about what is fair and ethical in specific situations. A positive view of conflict encourages people to work out their differences, participate in developing an ethical and fair organization, and deal directly with injustices.[5]

Negative View Conflict can also have serious negative effects and divert efforts from goal attainment. Instead of directing organizational resources primarily toward reaching desired goals, the conflict may deplete resources, especially time and money. Conflict can also negatively affect the psychological well-being of employees. Conflicting thoughts, ideas, and beliefs, if severe, can result in resentment, tension, and anxiety. These feelings appear to result from the threat that conflict poses to important personal goals and beliefs. Over an extended period of time, conflict may make the establishment of supportive and trusting relationships difficult.[6]

Finally, deep conflicts and competition where cooperation between employees is required appear to negatively affect results.[7] Pressure for results tends to emphasize immediate and measurable goals—such as product quantity—at the expense of longer range and more important goals—such as product quality. When high product quality is a primary organizational goal, conflict based on competition is often ill-advised.

Balanced View Most effective individuals have a balanced view of conflict. They recognize that conflict may sometimes be highly desirable and at other times destructive. These individuals know that while they can reduce conflict, they will have to resolve and properly manage that which remains.

Figure 14.1 illustrates the balanced view of conflict. The vertical axis represents the consequences of conflict, ranging from negative outcomes (loss of skilled employees, sabotage, low quality of work, and personal stress) to positive outcomes (creative alternatives, increased motivation and commitment, high quality of work, and personal satisfaction).[8] The horizontal axis indicates the intensity of conflict experienced between individuals or *within* oneself, ranging from low to high. The horizontal dashed line approximates the division between positive and negative outcomes. The curve in Figure 14.1 represents the general relationship between conflict outcomes and conflict intensity. As indicated, people and organizations can suffer from too little or too much conflict.

There are four major levels of conflict within organizations: *intrapersonal* (within an individual), *interpersonal* (between individuals), *intragroup* (within a group), and *intergroup* (between groups). Conflict can also occur at an *interorganizational* level (between organizations), which we note only briefly in this chapter. These levels of conflicts are often interrelated. For example, an employee struggling with whether he or she wants to stay with the current career path may, as a result, act aggressively or hostilely toward fellow workers, thus triggering interpersonal conflicts.

Intrapersonal Conflict

Intrapersonal conflict occurs within an individual and often involves some form of goal or cognitive conflict. Goal conflict occurs when a person's behavior will result in outcomes that are mutually exclusive or have incompatible elements (both positive and negative outcomes). A college graduate may have to decide whether to take a job in business or in government (mutually exclusive outcomes). Moreover, certain jobs in business pay more but offer less security (incompatible elements) than do certain jobs in government. There are three basic types of intrapersonal goal conflict:

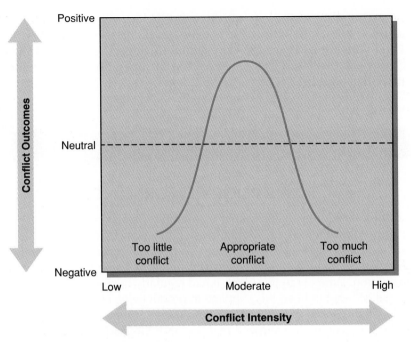

Figure 14.1   Balanced View of Conflict

Source: Adapted from L. D. Brown, *Managing Conflict at Organizational Interfaces.* Reading, Mass.: Addison-Wesley, 1983, 8. Adapted and used with permission.

- **Approach-approach conflict,** in which an individual must choose among two or more alternatives that have positive outcomes (such as a choice between two jobs that appear to be equally attractive).
- **Avoidance-avoidance conflict,** in which an individual must choose among two or more alternatives that have negative outcomes (such as a threatened demotion or increased out-of-town traveling).
- **Approach-avoidance conflict,** in which an individual must decide whether to do something that has both positive and negative outcomes, (such as accepting an offer of a good job in a bad location).

Day-to-day decisions frequently involve the resolution of intrapersonal goal conflict and approach-avoidance conflict. The intensity of intrapersonal conflict generally increases under one or more of the following conditions: (1) there are several realistic alternative courses of action for coping with the conflict; (2) the positive and negative consequences of the alternative courses of action are perceived as roughly equal; or (3) the source of conflict is perceived as important to the decision maker.

Intrapersonal conflict may also be a consequence of **cognitive dissonance,** which occurs when individuals recognize inconsistencies in their thoughts, attitudes, values, and/or behaviors.[9] The existence of substantial and recognized inconsistencies is usually stressful and uncomfortable. Sufficient discomfort usually motivates a person to reduce the inconsistency (dissonance) and achieve balance. In brief, balance can be achieved by (1) changing thoughts, attitudes, values, and/or behaviors or (2) obtaining more information about the issue that is causing the dissonance.

The following In Practice is presented through the eyes of Tom's superior. It is clear that Tom was experiencing intrapersonal conflict, including cognitive dissonance.

IN PRACTICE

TOM'S POOR PERFORMANCE

Tom is the manager of one of our five assembly plants and reports to me. He's been in the job for five years. I had managed the plant before him and supported his promotion. He had always struck me as a personable guy and I liked him. . .he was honest and loyal. After one year, Tom's plant became the poorest performer in my division. When I ran this plant, it had regularly been number one or two out of the five. When I noticed this slippage in productivity, I began to question Tom. In the beginning, he made promises to turn things around. He told me how some things he was working on showed real promise. He sold me. I believed.

Initially, when my boss would question Tom's performance, I would make excuses for him. Soon, it became clear that my ability to manage Tom was being questioned. I began to cut his annual salary raises. He said he understood, but still nothing changed. Finally, about a year ago, I decided I had to take some action. I talked and he listened. I told him how I had grappled with the problem and had tried to avoid it; how I felt he and I had to begin addressing what was happening. You know what? He agreed.

He told me how lousy he felt that he was unable to get his plant moving; how he hated to come to plant manager meetings, especially when performance issues were talked about; how he had begun to seriously doubt his career choice. We met again and talked some more. At that time, I asked him to develop a plan that would improve his performance over the next two years. We agreed that this would be a good way to test his potential as a plant manager and to provide evidence of whether he should continue on his present career track or look for an assignment more suited to his ability. One year has gone by since the plan was developed. So far, the results are not too encouraging. I have serious doubts that he will improve. But two things are different now. First, we are talking openly about what's happening, and second, I am convinced that he will be much more receptive to a job change. In the meantime, my boss is very pleased with my approach to managing Tom.[10]

Both goal conflict and cognitive conflict exist for many important personal decisions. Some authorities suggest that the greater the goal conflict before the decision, the greater will be the cognitive dissonance following the decision. Individuals experience dissonance because they know that the alternative accepted has negative (avoidance) elements and the alternative rejected has positive (approach) elements. The more difficulty individuals have in arriving at the original decision, the greater is their need to justify the decision afterward. Some cognitive dissonance is inevitable in life. Otherwise, the inner world and the external world as an individual interprets it would be in perfect harmony.

Interpersonal Conflict

Interpersonal conflict involves two or more individuals who perceive themselves as being in opposition to each other over preferred outcomes (goals) and/or attitudes, values, or behaviors. Many interpersonal and intrapersonal conflicts are based on some type of role conflict or role ambiguity.

Role Conflict   A **role** is the cluster of tasks that others expect a person to perform in doing a job. Figure 14.2 presents a model of a *role episode*. A role episode begins before a message is sent. Role senders have expectations, perceptions, and evaluations of the focal person's behaviors, which in turn influence the actual role messages that the senders transmit. The focal person's perceptions of these messages and pressures may then lead to role conflict. Accordingly, **role conflict** occurs when a focal person perceives incompatible messages and pressures from the role senders. Finally, the focal person responds with coping behaviors that serve as inputs to the role senders' experiences.

A **role set** is the group of role senders that directly affect the focal person. A role set might include the employee's manager, fellow team members, close friends, immediate family members, important clients or customers served, and the like. Four types of role conflict may occur as a result of incompatible messages and pressures from the role set:

- **Intrasender role conflict,** in which different messages and pressures from a single member of the role set are incompatible.

- **Intersender role conflict,** in which messages and pressures from one role sender oppose messages and pressures from one or more other senders.

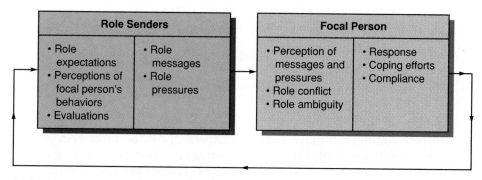

FIGURE 14.2   Role Episode Model

Source: Based on R. L. Kahn, et al. *Organizational Stress: Studies in Role Conflict and Ambiguity.* New York: John Wiley, 1964, 26.

- **Interrole conflict,** in which role pressures associated with membership in one group are incompatible with pressures stemming from membership in other groups.

- **Person-role conflict,** in which role requirements are incompatible with the focal person's own attitudes, values, or notions of acceptable behavior.[11]

The following In Practice clearly demonstrates the person-role conflicts a number of individuals experience over work versus leisure activities.[12]

IN PRACTICE

HILTON TIME VALUES SURVEY

A Hilton Time Values Survey of 1,010 adults shows Americans are losing their race against the clock—by an average of seven hours a week. A finding of the Hilton study was that the average American has 19 hours of free time each week to spend on leisure activities but wants 26 hours. The 27 percent shortfall is called "missed" time. "The amount of 'missing' time is about equal for women, men, single and married respondents," said John P. Robinson, director of the Americans' Use of Time project at the University of Maryland.

Robinson, who interpreted the survey findings for Hilton Hotels & Resorts, reports that among full-time workers, the gap between ideal and actual free time rose to 33 percent: They had only 17.6 free hours a week but wanted 26.3. Employed women had only 12 hours for leisure each week, the least amount of free time; on the average, they wanted 20.1 hours a week.

And almost half of U.S. workers say they would give up a day's pay for an extra day off each week.

"We are at a point in history where the value of time is reaching parity with the value of money," said Robinson, who has studied time, attitudes, and social trends for twenty-five years.

Other study findings were:

- 21 percent say they "don't have time for fun anymore."
- 38 percent cut back on sleep to "make" more time.
- 20 percent called in sick at least once in the last year to take time to relax.
- 29 percent constantly feel stressed.[13]

Role Ambiguity In addition to experiencing one or more of the four types of role conflict, an individual may experience discomfort because of role ambiguity. **Role ambiguity** is the person's perception of a lack of clear, consistent information about the required job tasks. Like role conflict, severe role ambiguity often causes stress and subsequent coping behaviors. These behaviors may include (1) aggressive action and hostile communication; (2) withdrawal; and (3) approaching the role sender or senders to attempt joint problem solving. Research findings are not clear-cut on the relationships among role conflict, role ambiguity, and outcomes, such as stress reactions, aggression, hostility, and withdrawal behavior (turnover and absenteeism).[14] However, stress is a common reaction to severe role conflict and role ambiguity. In Chapter 9, we examined the sources of work stress and ways for dealing with this stress.

Intragroup Conflict

Intragroup conflict refers to clashes among some or all of the group's members, which often affect the group's processes and effectiveness.[15] Family-run businesses can be especially prone to severe intragroup and other types of conflicts. These conflicts are most evident when an owner-founder approaches retirement, retires, or dies. The following account dramatizes some of the many types of conflict found in family-run businesses.

IN PRACTICE

FAMILY FEUD AT U-HAUL

A man or woman who builds a business for a living does not think often about dying. It usually takes a near-fatal illness or the death of a close friend to shake the founder into admitting that to everything has a season. Even so, getting down to particulars is tough. Peter Davis, who runs the family business program at the Wharton School, comments: "The founder feels that anything given up to the children is another nail in the coffin."

Certainly, you could not blame Leonard S. Shoen for seeing it that way. The seventy-four-year-old Shoen, who started U-Haul International, the Phoenix-based car and truck rental business, began transferring stock to his children while they were still young. Trouble was, the Shoen kids kept coming—eight sons (one of them adopted) and five daughters from three different mothers. Never expecting to father a rugby team, Shoen parceled out the shares as the kids arrived and ultimately gave away 95 percent of the company.

U-Haul grew into Amerco, with revenues of about $1 billion. In 1986, two of Shoen's sons, Edward and Mark, seized control. The senior Shoen found himself voted out of the business. Soon after, his eldest son, Sam, who had been running the company, quit. The family has since split into two camps. Edward and Mark are running the show, while Leonard and Sam are suing to regain control of the company.

The battle has gotten violent, with stockholders' meetings turning into slug-fests. In the most outlandish incident so far, Michael Shoen was reportedly beaten up by Edward and Mark. A photograph of Michael, complete with bruises, was splashed across the business section of the *Arizona Republic* newspaper. Says the dad: "I created a monster."[16]

Intergroup Conflict

Intergroup conflict refers to opposition and clashes between two or more groups. Intergroup conflict often occurs in union-management relations.

Such conflicts are sometimes highly intense, drawn out, and costly to the groups involved. Under extreme conditions of competition and conflict (as discussed in Chapter 11), the groups develop attitudes and relationships toward each other that are characterized by distrust, rigidity, a focus only on self-interests, a failure to listen, and the like. We will review three special types of intergroup conflicts within organizations.

Vertical Conflict   *Vertical conflict* refers to clashes between levels in an organization. Such conflict often occurs when superiors attempt to control subordinates too tightly and the subordinates resist.[17] Subordinates may resist because they believe that the controls infringe too much on the discretion needed to do their jobs. Vertical conflicts can also arise because of inadequate communication, goal conflicts, or a lack of consensus concerning perceptions of information and values (cognitive conflict).

Horizontal Conflict   *Horizontal conflict* refers to clashes between groups of employees at the same hierarchical level in an organization. Horizontal conflict occurs when each department strives only for its own goals, disregarding the effects on other departments. These goals may be incompatible across departments, causing goal conflict. Contrasting attitudes of employees in different departments may also lead to conflict.

Line-Staff Conflict   *Line-staff conflict* often involves clashes over authority relationships. Most organizations have staff departments to assist the line departments. Line managers normally are responsible for some process that creates a part or all of the firm's goods or services. Staff managers often serve an advisory or control function that requires specialized technical knowledge. Line managers may feel that staff managers are imposing on their areas of legitimate authority. Staff personnel may specify the methods and partially control the resources used by line managers.[18] For example, in many manufacturing organizations, staff engineers specify how each product is to be made and what materials are to be used. At the same time, line managers are held responsible for the output. Line managers may experience conflict when they perceive that the engineers are directing production tasks. Line managers often believe that staff managers reduce their authority over workers while their responsibility for the output remains unchanged; that is, their perceived authority is less than their perceived responsibility because of staff involvement.

INTERPERSONAL STYLES IN CONFLICT MANAGEMENT

Individuals attempt to manage interpersonal conflict in a variety of ways.[19] Figure 14.3 provides a basic model for understanding and comparing five interpersonal conflict-handling styles. They are identified by their locations in two dimensions: *concern for self* and *concern for others*. The desire to

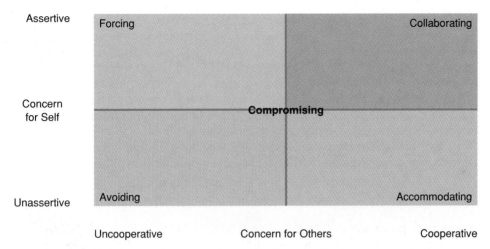

FIGURE 14.3 Interpersonal Conflict-Handling Styles

Source: Adapted with permission from K. W. Thomas, Conflict and Conflict Management. In M. D. Dunnette (ed.) *Handbook of Industrial and Organizational Psychology.* Chicago: Rand McNally, 1976, 900.

satisfy your own concerns depends on the extent to which you are *assertive* or *unassertive* in pursuing personal goals. Your desire to satisfy the concerns of others depends on the extent to which you are *cooperative* or *uncooperative*. The five interpersonal conflict-handling styles thus represent different combinations of assertiveness and cooperativeness. Although an individual may have a natural tendency toward one or two of the styles, there is nothing to preclude an individual from using all of the styles as the context and parties change.[20] The styles one uses in working through a conflict with a good friend may be quite different than those employed with a stranger after a minor auto accident.

Avoiding Style

The **avoiding style** involves behavior that is unassertive and uncooperative. People use this style to stay out of conflicts, ignore disagreements, or remain neutral. This approach might reflect a decision to let the conflict work itself out, or it might reflect an aversion to tension and frustration. Ignoring important issues often frustrates others. The consistent use of this interpersonal conflict-handling style usually results in unfavorable evaluations by others.[21] Some statements that reflect an avoiding style are:

- "If there are rules that apply, I cite those, and if there aren't, I leave the other person free to make his or her own decision."
- "I usually don't take positions that will create controversy."
- "I shy away from topics that are sources of disputes with my friends."
- "That's okay. It wasn't important anyway. Let's leave well enough alone."

When unresolved conflicts affect goal accomplishment, the avoiding style will lead to negative results for the organization. Under certain circumstances, this style may be desirable. These are when: (1) the issue is minor or only of passing importance and thus not worth the individual's time or energy to confront the conflict; (2) there is not enough information available to the individual to effectively deal with the conflict at that time; (3) the individual's power is so low relative to the other person's that there is little chance of causing change (such as disagreement with a major new strategy approved by top management); and (4) other individuals can more effectively resolve the conflict.

The following In Practice presents a creative use of the avoiding style with superiors and suggests constructive actions to resolve ethical problems.

IN PRACTICE

POSITIVE AVOIDANCE TO RESOLVE ETHICAL ISSUES

How can one avoid direct confrontation with a more powerful individual but expose the unethical behavior of that individual? Two strategies for doing so are illustrated below.

Quietly blowing the whistle to a responsible higher-level manager.

When Evelyn Grant was first hired by the company where she is now a human resource manager, her job included administering a battery of psychological tests that, in part, determined which employees were promoted to supervisory positions. Grant explained:

> There have been cases where people will do something wrong because they think they have no choice. Their boss tells them to do it, and so they do it, knowing it's wrong. They don't realize there are ways around the boss. . . .When I went over his [the chief psychologist's] data and analysis, I found errors in assumptions as well as actual errors of computation. . . .I had two choices: I could do nothing, or I could report my findings to my supervisor. If I did nothing, the only persons probably hurt were the ones who "failed" the test. To report my findings, on the other hand, could hurt several people, possibly myself.

She quietly spoke to her boss, who quietly arranged for a meeting to discuss the errors with the chief psychologist. When the chief psychologist did not show up for the meeting, the test battery was dropped.

Quietly refraining from implementing an unethical order or policy.

Frank Ladwig was a top salesman and branch manager with a large computer company for more than forty years. At times, he had trouble balancing his responsibilities. For instance, he was trained to sell solutions to customer problems, yet he had order and revenue quotas that sometimes made it difficult for him to concentrate on solving problems. He was responsible for signing and keeping important customers with annual revenues of between $250,000 and $500,000 and for aggressively and conscientiously representing new products that had required large research and development investments. He was required to sell the full line of products and services, and sometimes he had sales quotas for products that he believed were not a good match for the customer or appeared to perform marginally.

Ladwig would quietly not sell those products, concentrating instead on the products he believed in. He would explain the characteristics of the questionable products to his knowledgeable customers and get their reactions, rather than making an all-out sales effort. When he was asked by his sales manager why a certain product was not moving, he explained what the customers objected to and why.[22]

Forcing Style

The **forcing style** is behavior that is assertive and uncooperative. It reflects a win-lose approach to interpersonal conflict. Those who use this style try to achieve their own goals without concern for others. The forcing style often involves aspects of coercive power and dominance.[23] The forcing person feels that one side must win and, by necessity, one side must lose. This style can sometimes help a person to achieve individual goals. However, like avoidance, forcing tends to result in unfavorable evaluations by others. Recall the Preview Case and Marjory Williams's description of her initial use of the forcing style with the vendor. She noted that the "me against you" attitude (the forcing style) does not go very far in business, especially where the parties need to have a long-term relationship. Some statements that reflect a forcing style are:

- "I like to put it plainly: Like it or not, what I say goes, and maybe when others have had the experience I have, they will remember this and think better of it."
- "I convince the other person of the logic and benefits of my position."
- "I insist that my position be accepted during a disagreement."
- "I usually hold on to my solution to a problem after the controversy starts."

Forcing-prone individuals assume that conflicts involve win-lose situations. When dealing with conflicts between subordinates or departments, forcing-style managers may threaten or actually use demotion, dismissal, negative performance evaluations, or other punishments to gain compliance. When conflicts occur between peers, an employee using the forcing style might try to get his or her own way by appealing to the manager. This represents an attempt to use the manager to force the decision on the opposing individual.

Overreliance on forcing by a manager lessens the employee's work motivation because his or her interests have not been considered. Relevant information and other possible alternatives are usually ignored. However, there are some situations in which the forcing style may be necessary, such as when (1) emergencies require quick action, (2) unpopular courses of action must be taken for long-term organizational effectiveness and survival (such as cost-cutting and dismissal of employees for unsatisfactory performance, and (3) the person needs to take action for self-protection and to stop others from taking advantage of him or her.

Accommodating Style

The **accommodating style** represents behavior that is cooperative but not assertive. Accommodations may represent an unselfish act, a long-term strategy to encourage cooperation by others, or a submission to the wishes of others. Accommodators are usually favorably evaluated by others but also are perceived as weak and submissive. Some statements that reflect an accommodating style are:

- "Conflict is best managed through the suspension of my personal goals to maintain good relationships with those whom I value."
- "If it makes other people happy, I am all for it."
- "I like to smooth over disagreements by making them appear less important."
- "I ease conflict by suggesting our differences are trivial and then show good will by blending my ideas into those of the other person."

When using the accommodating style, individuals may act as though the conflict will go away in time and appeal for cooperation. These individuals try to reduce tensions and stress by reassurance and support. This style shows concern about the emotional aspects of conflict but little interest in working on its substantive issues. The accommodating style simply encourages individuals to cover up or gloss over their feelings. Therefore, it is generally ineffective if used as a dominant style.[24] However, the accommodating style may be effective on a short-term basis when: (1) the individuals are in a potentially explosive emotional conflict situation, and smoothing is used to defuse it; (2) keeping harmony and avoiding disruption are especially important in the short run; and (3) the conflicts are based primarily on the personalities of the individuals and cannot be easily resolved.

Collaborating Style

The **collaborating style** is behavior that is strongly cooperative and assertive. It reflects a win-win approach to interpersonal conflict. The collaborating style represents a desire to maximize joint outcomes. People who use this style tend to have the following characteristics: (1) they see conflict as natural, helpful, and even leading to a more creative solution if handled properly; (2) they show trust and candor with others; and (3) they recognize that when conflict is resolved to the satisfaction of all, commitment to the solution is likely.

People who use the collaborating style are often seen as dynamic individuals and evaluated favorably. In addition to her comments in the Preview Case, Marjory Williams states: "Aside from the 007s of the world, I've found that most business people respond favorably to looking for mutually beneficial solutions. 'Mutually beneficial' means not only that they have to benefit from the deal but also that they have to *perceive* that they are benefiting." Some statements that reflect this style are:

- "I first try to overcome any distrust that might exist between us. Then I try to get at the feelings we both have about the topics. I stress that nothing we decide is cast in stone and suggest that we find a position we can both give a trial run."
- "I tell the other person my ideas, actively seek out the other person's ideas, and search for a mutually beneficial solution."

- "I like to suggest new solutions that build on a variety of viewpoints that may have been expressed."
- "I try to dig into an issue to find a solution good for all of us."

With this style, conflicts are recognized openly and evaluated by all concerned. Sharing, examining, and assessing the reasons for the conflict should lead to development of an alternative that effectively resolves the conflict and is fully acceptable to all parties.[25] **Collaboration** is most practical when there is: (1) sufficient *required interdependence* so that it makes sense to expend the extra time and energy needed with collaboration to work through individual differences; (2) sufficient *parity in power* among individuals so that they feel free to interact candidly, regardless of their formal superior/subordinate status; (3) the potential for *mutual benefits,* especially over the long run, for resolving the dispute through a win-win process; and (4) sufficient *organizational support* for taking the time and energy to resolve disputes through collaboration. The norms, rewards, and punishments of the organization—especially as set by top management—provide the framework for encouraging or discouraging the use of collaboration.[26]

Compromising Style

The **compromising style** represents behavior that is at an intermediate level in terms of cooperation and assertiveness. This style is based on give and take and typically involves a series of concessions. Compromise is commonly used and widely accepted as a means of resolving conflict. Some statements that reflect the compromising style are:

- "I want to know how and what others feel. When the timing is right, I explain how I feel and try to show them where they are wrong. Of course, it's often necessary to settle on some middle ground."
- "After failing in getting my way, I usually find it necessary to seek a fair combination of gains and losses for both of us."
- "I give in to others if they are willing to meet me halfway."
- "As the old saying goes, a half a loaf is better than nothing. Let's split the difference."

Those who compromise with others tend to be evaluated favorably. Various explanations are suggested for the favorable evaluation of the compromising style, including: (1) it may be seen primarily as a cooperative "holding back"; (2) it may reflect a pragmatic way for dealing with conflicts; and (3) it may help maintain good relations in the future.

In one study, individuals with a preference for the compromising style felt that it did provide a solution ("not coming up with a solution is weak") and that it required strength to accept that the other person's ideas are also important. Implicit in these two ideas seems to be the notion that insisting on your own viewpoint can be self-indulgent, since it fails to recognize the ideas of others. However, those individuals with a strong preference for the forcing style saw the main benefit of compromising as a quick way to deal with the conflict. Most of the individuals thought that the initially positive reactions to a compromise are soon replaced by doubts about the fairness of the outcome, the equality of each party's concessions, and the other party's motives and honesty.[27] These findings suggest that the compromising style is most effective as a backup style to the collaborating style.

If used too early in conflict situations, the compromising style may create several problems. First, managers may be encouraging compromise on the stated issues, rather than on the real ones. The first issues raised in a conflict are often not the real ones. Again, premature compromise often prevents full diagnosis or exploration of the real issues at conflict. For example, students telling professors that their courses are really tough and challenging may be trying to negotiate an easier grading system. Second, it is easier to accept an initial position presented than to search for alternatives that are more acceptable to all of the parties. Third, compromise may be inappropriate to all or part of the situation. There may be a better way of resolving the conflict.

Compared to the collaborating style, the compromising style tends not to maximize joint satisfaction. Rather, compromise achieves moderate, but only partial, satisfaction for each party. This style is likely to be appropriate when: (1) agreement enables each party to be better off or at least not worse off than if no agreement were reached; (2) it simply is not possible to achieve a total win-win agreement; and (3) conflicting goals or opposing interests block agreement on one party's proposal.

Significance to Organizations

A number of studies have been conducted on the use of different interpersonal conflict-handling styles. Collaboration tends to be characteristic of (1) more successful rather than less successful individuals and (2) high-performing rather than medium- and low-performing organizations. In addition, studies have shown that people tend to perceive collaboration in terms of the constructive use of conflict. Finally, the use of collaboration seems to result in positive feelings in others, as well as favorable self-evaluations of performance and abilities.

In contrast to collaboration, forcing and avoiding often have negative effects. Forcing and avoiding tend to be associated with a less constructive use of conflict, negative feelings from others, and unfavorable self-evaluations of performance and abilities. The effects of accommodation and compromise appear to be mixed. In one study, the use of accommodation seemed to result in positive feelings from others. But these individuals did not form favorable evaluations of the performance and abilities of those using the accommodating style. The use of the compromising style is generally followed by positive feelings from others.[28]

NEGOTIATIONS IN CONFLICT MANAGEMENT

Negotiation is a process in which two or more parties, having both common and conflicting goals, state and discuss proposals concerning specific terms of a possible agreement. Negotiation normally includes a combination of compromise, collaboration, and possibly some forcing on particular issues that are vital to one or more of the parties.

Concepts and Issues in Negotiations

There are at least four basic types of negotiations: distributive negotiations, integrative negotiations, attitudinal structuring, and intraorganizational negotiations.[29]

Distributive Negotiations   Traditional win-lose, fixed-pie situations—where one party's gain is another party's loss—reflect **distributive negotiations.** Distributive negotiations often occur over economic issues. The interaction patterns may include guarded communications, limited expressions of trust, use of threats, and disguised statements and demands. In short, the parties are engaged in intense conflict. Eastern Airlines and the unions representing its employees were engaged in distributive negotiations over wages, hours of work, benefits, and work rules prior to the airline's failure in 1991.

Integrative Negotiations   Joint problem solving to achieve solutions by which both parties can gain is the focus of **integrative negotiations.** The parties identify mutual problems, identify and assess alternatives, openly express preferences, and jointly reach a mutually acceptable solution. Rarely perceived as equally acceptable, the choice is simply advantageous to both sides. The parties are strongly motivated to solve problems, exhibit flexibility and trust, and explore new ideas. There was little evidence of integrative negotiations between Eastern Airlines management and the union leadership. Each tended to blame the other for all of the customer and financial problems facing the airline. Shortly before Eastern failed, a new chief executive officer was hired who tried to turn the airline around and emphasized greater collaboration with the unions, but it was too late.

Attitudinal Structuring   Throughout the negotiations, the parties exhibit a relationship pattern (such as hostility/friendliness and competitiveness/cooperativeness) that influences their interactions. **Attitudinal structuring** is the process by which the parties seek to establish desired attitudes and relationships. Hostile and competitive attitudes prevailed between the union leaders and the top managers of Eastern Airlines.

Intraorganizational Negotiations.   When two or more groups negotiate through representatives, the representatives may reach agreement, but it may still be necessary to obtain the agreement of their respective constituencies. In **intraorganizational negotiations,** the key players on each side seek to build a consensus for agreement within their side. The aim is to resolve intragroup conflict.

Negotiations between individuals or organizations can be quite complex. Negotiations between parties from different cultures and legal and political systems can be especially difficult. The following Across Cultures account provides a glimpse of the complexity of negotiating between individuals from different countries—in this instance, between the French and the Americans.

♦ *ACROSS CULTURES*

NEGOTIATING WITH THE FRENCH

The French are friendly, humorous, and sardonic. Unlike most Americans, they show no need to be liked. They are more likely to be interested in a person who disagrees with them than one who agrees. The French are very hard to impress and are impatient with those who try too hard to do so. The French frequently gain recognition and develop their identity by thinking and acting against others. They base many of their behaviors on inner feelings, preferences, and expectations.

Decision making is more centralized in French companies than in U.S. firms; reaching and applying decisions thus take more time. Status consciousness runs very high with the French. Most of the U.S. negotiators interviewed found that the French insisted that the French negotiator have the same organizational status as his or her U.S. counterpart. Thus, the U.S. negotiator may want to determine the French negotiator's title and adjust his or her own title accordingly.

The French, partly because they live in a society with relatively little social mobility, are used to conflict. They are aware that some situations are irreconcilable and that people must live with these. They even respect others who carry conflict off with style

and get results. The French are also less concerned than Americans about negative reactions from those with whom they are in conflict.

The French are extremely difficult to negotiate with. Often, they will not accept facts, no matter how convincing they may be. Although they may consider themselves to be experts at negotiating, at times they tend to be inadequately prepared. They are quite secretive about their position during negotiations. It is difficult to obtain data from them, even in support for their position. Emotionalism and theatrics are rather common tactics employed by the French. The U.S. negotiator should not panic in such a situation; the passage of time will bring the situation to a manageable level. When asked "How do you deal with an excitable Frenchman?", one experienced negotiator responded, "Don't get excited with him. Stop the meeting for a cooling-off period. Don't play their game. They are masters at it. Their apparent emotionalism may be real or a game or a tactic!"

The French seem to enjoy negotiating for its own sake. When they are in this mood—sometimes for several days—little real progress is made. Sooner or later, though, they tire of the game and want to reach closure.[30]

SBS Model   These concepts of negotiations and the various interpersonal styles in conflict management served as a starting point for Grant Savage (S), John Blair (B), and Rich Sorenson (S) in the development of their model of negotiations. This SBS model is one of the few that systematically integrates the individual's (or group's) priorities with the other party's (or group's) priorities under different negotiating contexts (situations).[31]

A basic assumption of the SBS model is that any one approach to negotiation will not work in all situations. The model suggests that the best negotiation strategy depends on desired *substantive* and *relationship* outcomes. A crucial context for any negotiation is the individual's current and desired relationship outcome (feelings and attitudes) with the other party. To secure the best possible substantive outcome (issues and goals at stake), individuals may overlook the impact of the negotiation on their relationships. This oversight can hurt an individual's relationship with the other party, thus limiting his or her ability to obtain desired substantive outcomes now or in the future.[32]

Each interaction with another negotiator constitutes an episode that is influenced by current relationships and affects future relationships. Intertwined with concerns about relationships are concerns about substantive outcomes. At times, negotiators may be motivated to establish or maintain positive relationships and willingly "share the pie" through mutually beneficial collaboration. Other negotiations involve substantive outcomes that can benefit one negotiator only at the expense of the other (a fixed pie). These cases may motivate negotiators to discount the relationship and claim as much of the pie as possible.

Many negotiations, however, are not win-win or win-lose situations but combinations of both. Such mixed-motive situations in which both collaboration and competition may occur are particularly difficult for individuals to handle. The relationship that exists prior to the negotiation, the relationship that unfolds during negotiations, and the desired relationship often will influence whether either negotiator will be motivated to share the pie, grab it, give it away, or re-create it.[33]

The SBS model is developed in more detail in the next four sections. First, we present four unilateral negotiating strategies based on the interpersonal styles of conflict management. Second, five interactive negotiation strategies are described that take into account the other party's substantive and relationship priorities. Next, we place the four unilateral strategies and five interactive strategies into a decision tree framework. It guides the individual through a series of questions to which he or she answers yes or no. The answers to the questions will lead the individual to the one or two negotiation strategies suggested for use in that situation. Finally, we present the negotiating tactics proposed by the SBS model in each of four negotiation phases.

Unilateral Negotiation Strategies

Before selecting a negotiation strategy in the SBS model, the individual should consider his or her interests and, for managers, the interests of the organization. These interests will shape the answers to two basic questions: (1) Is the substantive outcome (goals and issues at stake) very important to the individual? and (2) Is the relationship outcome (feelings and attitudes between the parties) very important to the individual?[34]

Four unilateral strategies emerge from the answers: *trusting collaboration, firm competition, open subordination,* and *active avoidance.* They are called unilateral strategies because individuals consider only their own interests or the interests of their organization, ignoring for the time being the interests of the other party.

Trusting Collaboration (C1) If both relationship and substantive outcomes are important, the individual should consider trusting collaboration. The focus of this strategy is openness on the part of both parties. By encouraging cooperation as positions are asserted, the individual should be able to achieve important relationship and substantive outcomes. The individual seeks a win-win outcome both to achieve substantive goals and to maintain a positive relationship. Trusting collaboration is generally easiest to use and most effective when the individual and the other party are interdependent and mutually supportive. These circumstances normally create a trusting relationship in which negotiators reciprocally disclose their goals and needs. In this climate, an effective problem-solving process and a win-win settlement typically result.[35]

Open Subordination (S1)   If individuals are more concerned with establishing a positive relationship with another party than with obtaining substantive outcomes, they should be openly subordinate (accommodating). The individual has little to lose by yielding to the substantive interests of the other party. Open subordination can be a key way to dampen hostilities, increase support, and foster more interdependent relationships.

Firm Competition (P1)   If substantive interests are important but the relationship is not, the individual should consider firmly competing. This situation often occurs when an individual has little trust in the other party or the relationship is not good to begin with. In this situation, the individual may want to exert his or her power to gain substantive outcomes. To follow this strategy, he or she may also become highly aggressive, bluff, threaten the other party, or otherwise misrepresent his or her intentions. Such tactics hide the individual's actual goals and needs, preventing the other party from using that knowledge to negotiate his or her own substantive outcomes. When following a firmly competitive strategy, the individual seeks a win-lose substantive outcome and is willing to accept a neutral or even a bad relationship.

Active Avoidance (A1)   Individuals should consider actively avoiding negotiation if neither the relationship nor the substantive outcomes are important to them or the organization. Refusing to negotiate is the most direct and active form of avoidance. Individuals can tell the other party they are not interested in or willing to negotiate. Such an action, however, will usually have a negative impact on the relationship with the other party. Moreover, individuals must determine which issues are a waste of time to negotiate.

The SBS model assumes that these strategies are likely to be successful only in a limited set of situations. In the next section, various modifications are added that make these strategies applicable to a wider set of negotiation situations for employees and managers.

Interactive Negotiation Strategies

Before using the unilateral strategies, the SBS model suggests that the individual should examine the negotiation from the other party's perspective as well. The choice of a negotiation strategy should be based not only on the interests of the individual or organization but also on the interests of the other party. The individual should anticipate the other party's substantive and relationship priorities, assessing how the negotiation is likely to progress when the parties meet. This step is crucial because the unilateral strategies could lead to problems if the other party's priorities differ. For example, when using either trusting collaboration or open subordination, the individual is open to exploitation if the other party is concerned only about substantive outcomes. When anticipating the other party's substantive and relationship priorities, individuals should consider the kinds of actions the other party might take. Are those actions likely to be supportive or hostile? Will they represent short-term reactions or long-term approaches to the substantive issues under negotiation? Are those actions likely to change the party's degree of dependence on, or interdependence with, the individual or the organization? The answers will depend on (1) the history of the individual's relations with the other party and (2) the influence of key individuals and groups on the individual and the other party.[36]

Principled Collaboration (C2) The C1 (trusting collaboration) strategy assumes that the other party will reciprocate whenever the individual discloses information. However, if the individual negotiates openly and the other party is not open or is competitive, the individual could be victimized. Under such circumstances, the individual should use the modified collaborative strategy of principled collaboration. Rather than relying on only trust and reciprocity, the individual persuades the other party to conduct negotiations based on a set of mutually agreed-upon principles that will benefit each negotiator. For example, the parties may agree to share certain documents prior to the start of negotiations.

Focused Subordination (S2) The openly subordinative strategy (S1) assumes that the substantive outcome is of little importance to the individual or organization. Sometimes, however, an individual has both substantive and relationship interests, but the other party has little stake in either interest. By discovering and then acquiescing to those key needs that are of interest only to the other party, individuals can still gain some substantive outcomes for themselves or the organization while assuring a relatively positive relationship outcome. Here, individuals both create substantive outcomes for the other party and achieve substantive outcomes for themselves or their organization.

Soft Competition (P2) Under some circumstances, the directness of the firmly competitive strategy (P1) may need to be softened according to the SBS model. For example, even though the individual may place little importance on the relationship outcome, this relationship may be very important to the other party. If the other party is powerful and potentially threatening, the individual would be wise to use a competitive strategy that maintains the relationship. Here, the individual would avoid highly aggressive tactics.

Passive Avoidance (A2) If the individual does not consider either the relationship or the substantive outcome important but the other party views the negotiation as important for a relationship outcome, the individual probably should delegate the negotiation. By passively avoiding the negotiation, the individual allows someone else to explore possible outcomes and keep the relationship from becoming hostile. Delegating ensures that possible opportunities are not ignored while freeing the individual from what appears to be a low-priority negotiation.

Responsive Avoidance (A3) By contrast, if the individual considers neither the relationship nor the substantive outcome important and the other party considers the substantive outcome important and the relationship unimportant, the individual should regulate the issue. Direct interaction with the other party is not necessary. The individual can be responsive but still avoid negotiating by either applying standard operating procedures or developing new policies that address the other party's concern. This strategy is most likely to be feasible only for those in managerial or other types of leadership roles.

Framework of Negotiation Strategies

The framework of negotiation strategies in Figure 14.4 connects unilateral and interactive negotiation strategies. In many instances, the interactive strategies are modifications of the unilateral strategies. The SBS model bases the decision to modify or replace a unilateral strategy almost exclusively on the individual's and the other party's differing outcome priorities. Three core outcome conditions influence the choice of interactive strategies.

Outcome Condition One The individual may value the relationship, but the other party may not. For example, an individual who assumes that trust and cooperation will result in a fair outcome may be taken advantage of by another party who is concerned with only substantive outcomes. Thus, the framework of the negotiation strategies (see Figure 14.4) suggests either principled collaboration or soft competition for such cases to ensure that the other party does not take advantage of the individual. On the other hand, the individual may simply want to create a long-term relationship with someone who currently is interested in neither substantive nor relationship outcomes. In such a case, the individual should choose to subordinate in a focused fashion—rather than to trustingly collaborate—to establish a relationship with the other party.

Outcome Condition Two The individual may not value the relationship, but the other party may. Given only their own substantive priorities, individuals would firmly compete or actively avoid negotiation under these circumstances. However, if the other party is interested in the relationship, the individual may not have to compete firmly to obtain desired substantive outcomes. The individual may collaborate or softly compete and still gain substantive goals without alienating the other party (see Figure 14.4). Such strategies may also foster a long-term relationship with substantive dividends for the individual.

Similarly, in situations where neither substantive nor relationship outcomes are important to the individual but the relationship is important to the other party, the individual may choose an interactive strategy other than avoidance. The other party is in a position to choose a subordinative strategy and may offer substantive incentives to the individual. If the individual

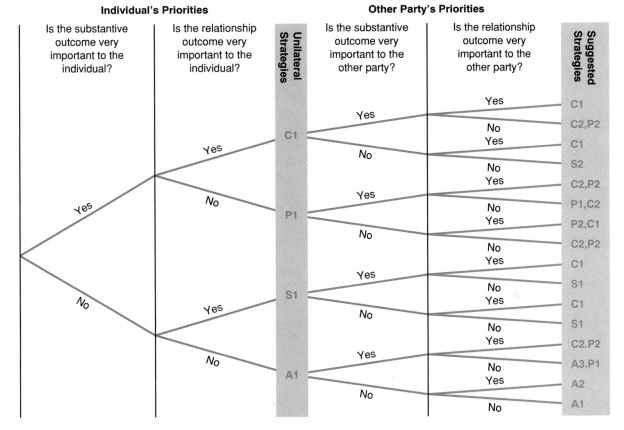

Strategies

C1: Trusting Collaboration
C2: Principled Collaboration
P1: Firm Competition
P2: Soft Competition
S1: Open Subordination
S2: Focused Subordination
A1: Active Avoidance (refuse to negotiate)
A2: Passive Avoidance (delegate negotiation)
A3: Responsive Avoidance (apply regulations)

FIGURE 14.4   Framework of Negotiation Strategies

Source: Adapted from G. T. Savage, J. D. Blair, and R. L. Sorenson, Consider Both Relationships and Substance When Negotiating Strategically. *Academy of Management Executive,* February 1989, 42. Used with permission.

chooses principled collaboration or soft competition, he or she may gain some positive substantive outcomes.

Outcome Condition Three   Both parties may value the relationship, but the individual may not value substantive outcomes. In such a case, whether or not the other party is interested in substantive outcomes, the individual may chose a trustingly collaborative strategy to maintain positive ties with the other party.[37]

Tactics within Negotiation Phases

The last major component in the SBS model focuses on the tactics during the various negotiation phases. The SBS model views tactics in two ways: (1) as clusters of specific actions associated with the implementation of one negotiating strategy or another and (2) as actions that derive their impact from the particular phase of the negotiation in which they are used. Table 14.1 combines these two perspectives to provide descriptions of competitive, collaborative, and subordinative tactics across various phases of negotiation. Most negotiations go through four phases: (1) the search for an arena and agenda formulation, (2) the stating of demands and offers, (3) a narrowing of differences, and (4) final bargaining. Not every negotiation will involve all of these phases. Thus, a specific phase may be skipped or never attained.[38]

Table 14.1 should help individuals recognize (1) how using certain tactics during various phases of a negotiation is essential to implementing their negotiation strategy and (2) how the tactics of the other party reflect a particular strategic intent. An unanticipated negotiating strategy implemented by the other party may indicate that the individual inaccurately assessed the negotiation context or under- or overestimated the strength of the other party's priorities. Thus, once the individual recognizes the other party's actual strategy, he or she should reassess the negotiation, repeating the process discussed in previous sections to check the appropriateness of his or her strategies.

The SBS model is unique in that it shows, step by step, how negotiation strategies should address both parties' substantive and relationship priorities. Further, it encourages individuals to view negotiation as a continuous and often confusing process. It requires individuals to anticipate and monitor the other party's actions. The other party's tactics will inform individuals as to whether their assumptions about the other party's priorities and strategy are correct. Based on this assessment, individuals can modify their negotiation strategies as needed during current or future episodes.[39]

The competitive strategies and tactics reviewed create the potential for the parties to engage in lying during the negotiation process. Lying is not likely to be much of a problem with the collaborative or subordinative strategies and tactics. The following In Practice is intended to increase your awareness of potential legal issues as well as broader ethical issues of lying in the negotiation process.

IN PRACTICE

LYING IN NEGOTIATIONS

U.S. law disclaims any general duty of good faith in the negotiation of commercial agreements. As the U.S. Court of Appeals for the Seventh Circuit recently stated:

> In a business transaction both sides presumably try to get the best deal. That is the essence of bargaining and the free market . . . [N]o legal rule bounds the run of

TABLE 14.1 Competitive, Collaborative, and Subordinative Tactics within Negotiation Phases

Negotiation Phases	Competitive Tactics	Collaborative Tactics	Subordinative Tactics
I. The Search for an Arena and Agenda Formulation	Seek to conduct negotiations on your home ground Demand discussion of your agenda items; curtail discussions of the other party's items Ignore or discount the other party's demands and requests	Seek to conduct negotiations on neutral ground Elicit the other party's agenda items and assert your items; incorporate both Consider the other party's demands and requests	Seek to conduct negotiations on the other party's ground Elicit the other party's agenda items and subvert your items Concede to the other party's demands and requests
II. The Stating of Demands and Offers	Insist the other party make initial offers or demands on all items Respond with very low offers or very high demands Commit to each item; exaggerate your position and discredit the other party's	Alternate initial offers and demands on items with the other party Respond with moderate offers or moderate demands Indicate reasons for your commitment to item outcomes; probe the other party's reasons	Make initial offers or demands on all items of the other party Make high offers or low demands Accept the other party's commitments to items; explain your commitments
III. Narrowing of Differences	Demand that the other party make concessions; back up your demand with threats Delete, add, or yield only on your low-interest items Magnify the degree of your concessions; downplay the other party's	Seek an equitable exchange of concessions with the other party Delete, add, or yield items if mutual interests converge Honestly assess your and the other party's concessions	Concede to the other party's demands Delete, add, or yield to any item of the other party Acknowledge the other party's concessions; downplay your concessions
IV. Final Bargaining	Seek large concessions from the other party Concede only minimally on your high-interest items Use concessions on your low-interest items as bargaining chips	Seek an equitable exchange of concessions from the other party Seek mutually beneficial outcomes when conceding or accepting concessions on items	Yield to the other party's relevant preferences by accepting low offers and making low demands

Source: Adapted from G. T. Savage, J. D. Blair, and R. L. Sorenson, Consider Both Relationships and Substance When Negotiating Strategically. *Academy of Management Executive,* February 1989, 45. Used with permission.

business interest. So one cannot characterize self-interest as bad faith. No particular demand in negotiations could be termed dishonest, even if it seemed outrageous to the other party. The proper recourse is to walk away from the bargaining table, not sue for "bad faith" in negotiations.

This general rule assumes, however, that no one has committed fraud. Fraud law reaches deep into the complexities of negotiation behavior. Of course, there are no legal problems with lying about how much you might be willing to pay or which of several issues in a negotiation you value more highly. Demands and reservation (bottom line) prices are not, as a matter of law, material to a deal.

Legal fraud can come in many forms. We consider just the case of the commercial tenant who entered into negotiations to renew a lease on a warehouse and railroad yard. The warehouse was vital to the tenant's continued business relationship with its main client, the Scott Paper Company. Scott used the warehouse as a regional product distribution facility. At a meeting during contract renewal negotiations, the landlord assured all parties, including Scott, that the tenant's lease would be renewed for a three-year term.

Unbeknownst to the tenant, the landlord was secretly negotiating to sell the property to the Boeing Company at the same time it was negotiating the lease renewal. The sale went through, and the landlord notified the tenant that it would have to vacate within twenty days. As a result, the tenant lost the Scott Paper contract and incurred extraordinary relocation expenses. The court found that the landlord's promise regarding the lease renewal was fraudulent, essentially made to string the tenant along in case the sale did not go through. It awarded damages for the tenant's lost profits from the Scott Paper contract and required the defendant to pay the tenant's extra moving expenses.

Business negotiation law is infused with the norms of ethical business conduct. Indeed, the leading legal treatise writers on fraud candidly admit that "a new standard of business ethics" has resulted in complete shifts of legal doctrine in the past fifty years. Unethical bargaining practices are, as often as not, illegal or become so after they are brought to light. The law simply expands to include them, definitions notwithstanding.

In commenting on Michael Milken's guilty plea to securities law violations, financier H. Ross Perot gave this advice to young businesspeople: "Don't govern your life by what's legal or illegal, govern it by what's right or wrong." It turns out this is good legal as well as business advice, at least insofar as negotiation is concerned. In negotiation, people who rely on the letter of legal rules as a strategy for plotting unethical conduct are very likely to get into deep trouble. But people who rely on a cultivated sense of right and wrong to guide them in legal matters are likely to do well.[40]

Third-Party Facilitator

Most negotiation occurs directly between the involved parties. When the parties are likely to get locked into win-lose conflict, a third-party facilitator, acting as a *neutral* party, may be able to assist them in resolving their differences.[41]

Skills and Functions   Taking on the role of a third-party facilitator is much easier than acting effectively in that role. Effective third-party facilitators need particular skills. First, they must be able to diagnose the conflict. Second, they must be skilled in breaking deadlocks and facilitating discussions at the right time. Finally, they must show mutual acceptance and have the personal capacity to provide emotional support and reassurance. Thus, the third-party facilitator's style must instill confidence and acceptance by the parties in conflict. Key functions of this role are to:

- *Ensure mutual motivation.* Each party should have incentives for resolving the conflict.

- *Achieve a balance in situational power.* If the situational power of the parties is not equal, it may be difficult to establish trust and maintain open lines of communication.

- *Coordinate confrontation efforts.* One party's positive moves must be coordinated with the other party's readiness to do likewise. A failure to coordinate positive initiatives and readiness to respond can undermine future efforts to work out differences.

- *Promote openness in dialogue.* The third party can help to establish norms of openness, provide reassurance and support, and decrease the risks associated with openness.

- *Maintain an optimum level of tension.* If the threat and tension are too low, the incentive for change or finding a solution is minimal. However, if the threat and tension are too high, the parties may be unable to process information and see creative alternatives. They may begin to polarize and take rigid positions.[42]

Intergroup Confrontation Technique   A third-party facilitator usually tries to assist negotiations without setting down a specific set of procedures for the parties to follow. Occasionally, however, a structured approach is useful to ensure that the parties concentrate on the appropriate issues and direct their efforts toward resolving them. One example of such an approach is the intergroup confrontation technique.[43] One procedure for such a confrontation includes the following steps:

- Each group meets in a separate room and develops two lists. On one list, they indicate how they perceive themselves as a group, particularly in their relationship with the other group. On the second list, they indicate how they view the other group.

- The two groups come together and share perceptions. The third-party facilitator helps them to clarify their views and, it is hoped, better understand themselves and the other group.

- The groups return to their separate rooms to look deeper into the issues, diagnose the current problem, and determine what each group contributes to the conflict.

- The groups meet together again to share their new insights. The third-party facilitator urges them to identify common issues and plan the next stages for seeking solutions.

Like most methods of negotiation and conflict management, the intergroup confrontation technique does not guarantee successful conflict resolution. Instead, it provides a process for the parties in conflict to explore and work through their differences. A skillful third-party facilitator uses the technique to move the parties toward a resolution.

STRUCTURAL METHODS IN CONFLICT MANAGEMENT

The structural approach to conflict management is used to prevent, resolve, or reduce conflicts. The methods used in this approach often physically separate the parties. This tends to minimize the direct expression of conflict. Organizations commonly use five structural methods in managing conflict: dominance through position, decoupling, buffering with inventory, buffering with a linking pin, and buffering with an integrating department. These methods overlap with several of the methods presented in Chapter 11 for managing the dynamics between groups.

Dominance through Position

Managers may attempt to resolve employee conflict by simply issuing a directive specifying the course of action subordinates are expected to follow. For example, two vice-presidents in the same firm are working on the organization's strategy. One vice-president advocates a strategy of growth based on decentralized decision making. The other vice-president desires a growth strategy that requires authority to be concentrated at the top levels of the organization. The president may exercise positional authority to select the centralized over the decentralized approach or some combination of the two.

Managers can use positional authority to settle conflicts within or between departments. Within a department, the manager may issue a directive to resolve the conflict. Between departments, a higher-level manager with responsibility for the departments involved may issue a directive to resolve the conflict. Of course, as you saw in the Preview Case, dominance through position can also increase the conflict. Positional authority does not always effectively resolve interdepartmental conflict. It is unrealistic to expect a vice-president to resolve all of the conflict issues that arise among lower-level departments. Furthermore, the dominance method does little to prevent conflict from recurring because it applies primarily to resolving conflict after the fact.

Decoupling

An organization's design can directly reduce interdependence among departments. This is achieved by providing departments with independent resources and inventories to *decouple* them and thus reduce the likelihood of interdepartmental conflict. Of course, independence may result in duplication of efforts and equipment and thus increase costs.

Buffering with Inventory

Completely decoupling departments, or making them totally independent, may be too costly. Thus, an organization may want to buffer the work flow between departments with inventory. If department A produces a product that serves as an input to department B, inventory can prevent department B from being severely affected by a temporary shutdown or slowdown in department A. Thus, the likelihood that employees in department B will become upset with department A declines.

Linking Pin

An organization can incorporate linking pins into its structure when poor interdepartmental integration and unnecessary conflict exist. A **linking pin** is an individual assigned to help integrate two departments that have overlapping tasks. This person is expected to understand the operations of both departments and coordinate their overlapping tasks. The linking pin must keep information flowing between the departments. In order to do this, the person must be perceived as someone who can be trusted by both departments, not as someone with loyalty to either department. The linking pin must often remind both departments of their commitments and loyalties to the overall organization and its goals. Such reminders reduce the tendency of the departments to focus on their own subgoals and lose sight of the bigger picture in conflict situations. The linking pin must also discourage each department from taking unilateral action on those issues that may affect—directly or indirectly—the other department. An effective linking pin must be a strong advocate and user of the collaborating and compromising conflict management styles.

Integrating Department

An integrating department typically has formal authority to issue orders affecting tasks that interdependent departments must carry out in an integrated manner. Thus, an integrating department generally has much more formal authority than does a linking pin to direct departmental activities and resolve conflicts. For example, a manufacturing firm may have a customer services department that integrates activities of the sales department and production department. Among other tasks, the customer services department attempts to resolve conflicts concerning delivery times and shipping instructions to key customers.

SUMMARY

Conflict is inevitable in organizational life, but it need not have destructive consequences for the organization. Depending on how the conflict is managed, the negative effects may be minimized, and positive effects may result from the conflict. Effective conflict management is based, in part, on a solid understanding of the different ways conflict emerges and can be resolved. Conflict occurs at four different levels within organizations: intrapersonal, interpersonal, intragroup, and intergroup.

A model for understanding and comparing five interpersonal conflict-handling styles was presented. These styles include the avoiding style, the forcing style, the accommodating style, the collaborating style, and the compromising style. The circumstances for the use of each style were noted. An individual may have a preference for one or two of the styles but is likely to use all of them over time when dealing with various conflict situations.

The basic concepts and issues that span a variety of negotiating situations include distributive negotiations, integrative negotiations, attitudinal structuring, and intraorganizational negotiations. These basics and the interpersonal conflict-handling styles are incorporated into the SBS (Savage, Blair, and Sorenson) model of negotiations.

The SBS model asserts that the best negotiation strategy depends on the desired substantive and relationship outcomes. Four unilateral strategies and five interactive negotiation strategies were reviewed. A framework was presented to assist the individual in deciding when each strategy or combination of negotiation strategies is most likely to be effective. The competitive, collaborative, and subordinative tactics that are likely to be found in each of four negotiation phases were noted. When the parties cannot resolve a conflict, the skills and functions of a third-party facilitator may be employed to break the stalemate.

Finally, five structural methods for managing conflict—dominance through position, decoupling, buffering with inventory, linking pin, and integrating departments—can be used in some conflict situations.

Key Words and Concepts

Accommodating style
Affective conflict
Approach-approach conflict
Approach-avoidance conflict
Attitudinal structuring
Avoidance-avoidance conflict
Avoiding style
Cognitive conflict
Cognitive dissonance
Collaboration
Collaborating style
Compromising style
Conflict
Conflict management
Distributive negotiations
Forcing style
Goal conflict

Integrative negotiations
Intergroup conflict
Interpersonal conflict
Interrole conflict
Intersender role conflict
Intragroup conflict
Intraorganizational negotiations
Intrapersonal conflict
Intrasender role conflict
Linking pin
Negotiation
Person-role conflict
Procedural conflict
Role
Role ambiguity
Role conflict
Role set

Discussion Questions

1. What is your personal view of conflict—positive, negative, or balanced? Cite two incidents from your personal experience that illustrate your view.

2. How might goal conflict, cognitive conflict, and affective conflict all come into play in a conflict situation? Illustrate how all of them came into play in a personal conflict situation.

3. Give personal examples of your experience with approach-approach conflict, avoidance-avoidance conflict, and approach-avoidance conflict.

4. What are the similarities and differences among intrasender role conflict, intersender role conflict, and person-role conflict?

5. In which of your roles do you experience the most role ambiguity? Explain.

6. What are the five interpersonal conflict-handling styles? Give examples of situations in which each style would be appropriate.

7. Why isn't the collaborative conflict-handling style used in all conflict situations?

8. What difficulties might an individual encounter in trying to apply the SBS model of negotiations?

9. How can the SBS model of negotiations contribute to your personal skills?

10. What do the following structural methods of conflict management have in common: dominance through position, decoupling, and buffering with inventory? How do they differ?

◆ *MANAGEMENT CASES AND EXERCISES*

VERBAL AGGRESSIVENESS SCALE

This survey is concerned with how we try to get people to comply with our wishes. Indicate how often each statement is true for you personally when you try to influence other persons. Use the following scale.

$$1 = \text{almost never true for you}$$
$$2 = \text{rarely true for you}$$
$$3 = \text{occasionally true for you}$$
$$4 = \text{often true for you}$$
$$5 = \text{almost always true for you}$$

_____ 1. I am extremely careful to avoid attacking individuals' intelligence when I attack their ideas.

_____ 2. When individuals are very stubborn, I use insults to soften the stubbornness.

_____ 3. I try very hard to avoid having other people feel bad about themselves when I try to influence them.

_____ **4.**   When people refuse without good reason to do a task I know is important, I tell them they are unreasonable.

_____ **5.**   When others do things I regard as stupid, I try to be extremely gentle with them.

_____ **6.**   If individuals I am trying to influence really deserve it, I attack their character.

_____ **7.**   When people behave in ways that are in very poor taste, I insult them in order to shock them into proper behavior.

_____ **8.**   I try to make people feel good about themselves even when their ideas are stupid.

_____ **9.**   When people simply will not budge on a matter of great importance, I lose my temper and say rather strong things to them.

_____ **10.**   When people criticize my shortcomings, I take it in good humor and do not try to get back at them.

_____ **11.**   When individuals insult me, I get a lot of pleasure out of really telling them off.

_____ **12.**   When I dislike individuals greatly, I try not to show it in what I say or how I say it.

_____ **13.**   I like poking fun at people who do things that are very stupid in order to stimulate their intelligence.

_____ **14.**   When I attack a person's ideas, I try not to damage his or her self-concepts.

_____ **15.**   When I try to influence people, I make a great effort not to offend them.

_____ **16.**   When people do things that are mean and cruel, I attack their character in order to help correct their behavior.

_____ **17.**   I refuse to participate in arguments when they involve personal attacks.

_____ **18.**   When nothing seems to work in trying to influence others, I yell and scream in order to get some movement from them.

_____ **19.**   When I am not able to refute others' positions, I try to make them feel defensive in order to weaken their positions.

_____ **20.**   When an argument shifts to personal attacks, I try very hard to change the subject.[44]

Scoring: 1. Add the point values shown for items 2, 4, 6, 7, 9, 11, 13, 16, 18, 19.

Subtotal = _____

2. Reverse the point values shown for items 1, 3, 5, 8, 10, 12, 14, 15, 17, 20.
(That is, 5 = 1, 4 = 2, 3 = 3, 2 = 4, 1 = 5).

Subtotal = _____

Total (add the two subtotals) = _____

Interpretation: Verbal aggression is the tendency to attack the self-concepts of individuals instead of, or in addition to, their positions on topics of communication.[45] Scores of 70 to 100 may suggest a tendency to use verbally aggressive communications while engaged in negotiations. This communication tendency is most associated with the forcing and compromise conflict-handling styles. Scores of 20 to 50 may suggest a tendency to use supportive personal communications while engaged in negotiations. This communication tendency is most associated with the collaborative and accommodating conflict-handling styles. Scores of 51 to 69 may suggest a lack of any strong personal predisposition with respect to verbal aggressiveness while engaged in negotiations.

———

THE AUDIT

Sue was puzzled as to what course of action to take. She had recently started her job with a na-

tional accounting firm and she was already confronted with a problem that could affect her future with the firm. On an audit, she encountered a client who had been treating payments to a large number, but by no means a majority, of its workers as payments to independent contractors. This practice saves the client the payroll taxes that would otherwise be due on the payments if the workers were classified as employees. In Sue's judgment, this was improper as well as illegal and should have been noted in the audit. She raised the issue with John, the senior accountant to whom she reported. He thought it was a possible problem but did not seem willing to do anything about it. He encouraged her to talk to the partner in charge if she did not feel satisfied.

She thought about the problem for a considerable time before approaching the partner in charge. The ongoing professional education classes she had received from her employer emphasized the ethical responsibilities that she had as a certified public accountant and the fact that her firm endorsed adherence to high ethical standards. This finally swayed her to pursue the issue with the partner in charge of the audit. The visit was most unsatisfactory. Paul, the partner, virtually confirmed her initial reaction that the practice was wrong, but he said that many other companies in the industry follow such a practice. He went on to say that if an issue was made of it, Sue would lose the account, and he was not about to take such action. She came away from the meeting with the distinct feeling that should she choose to pursue the issue, she would create an enemy.

Sue still felt disturbed and decided to discuss the problem with some of her co-workers. She approached Bill and Mike, both of whom had been working for the firm a couple of years. They were familiar with the problem since they had encountered it when doing the audit the previous year. They expressed considerable concern that if she went over the head of the partner in charge of the audit, they could be in big trouble since they had failed to question the practice during the previous audit. They said that they realized it was probably wrong but they went ahead because it had been ignored in previous years and they knew their supervisor wanted them to ignore it again. They did not want to cause problems. They encouraged her to be a "team player" and drop the issue.

Sue considered her dilemma. She could go over the head of the partner in charge of the audit and take her chances. She realized that even if she was vindicated, she would probably have to change jobs. Certainly, her co-workers would not appreciate her actions. Another course of action was to do nothing. She thought the people in her firm would be the happiest with that alternative and it would probably help her career in the company. The only problem was she would still have to deal with her conscience. She knew she had to decide soon.[46]

QUESTIONS

1. Is there evidence of goal conflict, cognitive conflict, and affective conflict in this case? Explain.

2. What types of role conflict is Sue probably experiencing?

3. How would you diagnose this situation through the use of the concepts of approach-approach conflict, avoidance-avoidance conflict, and approach-avoidance conflict?

4. State the role ambiguities being experienced by Sue.

5. What should Sue do? Why?

References

1. Adapted from M. Williams, "How I Learned to Stop Worrying and Love Negotiating," *Inc;* September 1987, 132. Reprinted with permission, *Inc.* magazine, September 1987. Copyright @ 1987 by Inc. Publishing Company, 38 Commercial Wharf, Boston, Mass. 02110.

2. Tjosvold, D. *The Conflict-Positive Organization: Stimulate Diversity and Create Unity.* Reading, Mass.: Addison-Wesley, 1991.

3. Cosier, R. A., and Dalton, D. R. Positive Effects of Conflict: A Field Experiment. *International Journal of Conflict Management,* 1990, *1,* 81–92.

4. Baron, R. A. Positive Effects of Conflict: A Cognitive Perspective. *Employee Responsibilities and Rights Journal,* 1991, *4,* 25–35.

5. Tjosvold, D. Rights and Responsibilities of Dissent: Cooperative Conflict. *Employee Responsibilities and Rights Journal,* 1991, *4,* 13–23.

6. Baron, R. A., and Richardson, D. R. *Human Aggression,* 2d ed. New York: Plenum Press, 1991.

7. Kohn, A. *No Contest: The Case against Competition.* Boston: Houghton Mifflin, 1986.

8. Kolb, D. M., and Silbey, S. S. Enhancing the Capacity of Organizations to Deal with Disputes. *Negotiation Journal,* October 1990, 297–304.

9. Festinger, L. *A Theory of Cognitive Dissonance.* Evanston, Ill.: Row, Peterson, 1967.

10. Adapted from Veiga, J. F. Face Your Problem Subordinates Now! *Academy of Management Executive,* May 1988, 145–152.

11. Netemeyer, R. G., Johnston, M. W., and Burton, S. Analysis of Role Conflict and Role Ambiguity in a Structural Equations Framework. *Journal of Applied Psychology,* 1990, *75,* 148–157; Kahn, R. L., et al. *Organizational Stress: Studies in Role Conflict and Role Ambiguity.* New York: John Wiley, 1964.

12. Also see Duxbury, L. E., and Higgins, C. A. Gender Differences in Work-Family Conflict. *Journal of Applied Psychology,* 1991, *76,* 60–74.

13. Adapted from Klelman, C. America's Workers Want More Leisure Time. *Bryan-College Station Eagle,* June 2, 1991, 4C.

14. Jackson, S. E., and Schuler, R. S. A Meta-Analysis and Conceptual Critique of Research on Role Ambiguity and Role Conflict in Work Settings. *Organizational Behavior and Human Decision Processes,* 1985, *36,* 16–78.

15. Kabanoff, B. Equity, Equality, Power, and Conflict. *Academy of Management Review,* 1991, *16,* 416–441; Wall, V. D., Jr., and Nolan, L. L. Small Group Conflict: A Look at Equity, Satisfaction, and Styles of Conflict Management. *Small Group Behavior,* 1987, *18,* 188–211.

16. Adapted from Pare, T. P. Passing on the Family Business. *Fortune,* May 7, 1990, 81–85; Gupta, U., and Robichaux, M. At Family Firms, Reins Tangle Easily. *Wall Street Journal,* August 9, 1989, 81.

17. Pondy, L. R. Organizational Conflict: Concept and Models. *Administrative Science Quarterly,* 1967, *12,* 296–320.

18. Hall, R. H. *Organizations: Structures, Process, and Outcomes,* 5th ed. Englewood Cliffs, N.J.: Prentice-Hall, 1991, 113–118.

19. Womack, D. F. Assessing the Thomas-Kilman Conflict Mode Survey. *Management Communication Quarterly,* 1988, *1,* 321–349; Thomas, K. W. The Conflict Handling Modes; Toward More Precise Theory. *Management Communication Quarterly,* 1988, *1,* 430–436.

20. King, W. C., and Miles, E. W. What We Know—and Don't Know—about Measuring Conflict: An Examination of the ROCI-II and the OCCI Conflict Instruments. *Management Communication Quarterly,* 1990, *4,* 222–243.

21. Baron, R. A., Fortin, S. P., Frei, R. L., Hauver, L. A., and Shack, M. L. Reducing Organizational Conflict: The Role of Socially Induced Positive Affect. *International Journal of Conflict Management,* 1990, *1,* 133–152.

22. Adapted from Nielson, R. P. Changing Unethical Organizational Behavior. *Academy of Management Executive,* May 1989, 123–130.

23. DeWine, S., Nicotera, A. M., and Parry, D. Argumentativeness and Aggressiveness: The Flip Side of Gentle Persuasion. *Management Communication Quarterly,* 1991, *4,* 386–411.

24. Lee, Chang-Won. Relative Status of Employees and Styles of Handling Interpersonal Conflict: An Experimental Study with Korean Managers. *International Journal of Conflict Management,* 1990, *1,* 327–340.

25. Hirschorn, L. *Managing in the New Team Environment.* Reading, Mass.: Addison-Wesley, 1991.

26. Blake, R. R., and Mouton, J. S. *Solving Costly Organizational Conflicts.* San Francisco: Jossey-Bass, 1984.

27. Kabanoff, B. Why is Compromise So Favorably Viewed? In F. Hoy (ed.), *Academy of Management Best Paper Proceedings.* Mississippi State, Miss.: Academy of Management, 1987, 280–284.

28. M. A. Rahim (ed.). *Managing Conflict: An Interdisciplinary Approach.* New York: Praeger, 1988.

29. Walton, R. E., and McKersie, R. B. *A Behavioral Theory of Labor Negotiations.* New York: McGraw-Hill, 1965; Cooke, W. N. *Labor-Management Cooperation: New Partnerships or Going in Circles?.* Kalamazoo, Mich.: W. E. Upjohn Institute, 1990.

30. Adapted from Burt, D. N. The Nuances of Negotiating Overseas. *Journal of Purchasing and Materials Management,* Winter 1989, 56–62; Schmidt, K. D. *Doing Business in France.* Menlo Park, Calif.: SRI International, 1987; Griffin, T. J., and Daggatt, W. R. *The Global Negotiator: Building Strong Business Relationships Anywhere in the World.* New York: Harper Business, 1990.

31. The presentation of the Savage (S), Blair (B), and Sorenson (S) SBS model of negotiations is based on Savage, G. T., Blair, J. D., and Sorenson, R. L. Consider Both Relationships and Substance When Negotiating Strategically. *Academy of Management Executive,* February 1989, 37–47. Used with permission. Also see Blair, J. D., Savage, G. T., and Whitehead, C. J. A Strategic Approach for Negotiating with Hospital Stakeholders. *Health Care Management Review,* 1989, *14*(1), 13–23; Blair, J. D., and Fottler, M. D. *Challenges in Health Care Management.* San Francisco: Jossey-Bass, 1990, 172–217.

32. Kremenyuk, V. A. (ed.). *International Negotiation: Analysis, Approaches, Issues.* San Francisco: Jossey-Bass, 1991.

33. Neale, M. A., and Northcraft, G. B. Behavioral Negotiation Theory: A Framework for Conceptualizing Dyadic Bargaining. In B. M. Staw (ed.), *Research in Organizational Behavior,* vol. 13. Greenwich, Conn.: JAI Press, 1991, 147–190.

34. Thompson, L., and Hastie, R. Social Perception in Negotiation. *Organizational Behavior and Human Decision Processes*, 1990, *47*, 98–123.

35. Nielson, R. P. Generic Win-Win Negotiating Solutions. *Long Range Planning*, 1989, *22*(5), 137–143.

36. Yukl, G., and Falbe, C. M. Influence Tactics and Objectives in Upward, Downward, and Lateral Influence Attempts. *Journal of Applied Psychology*, 1990, *75*, 132–140.

37. Neale, M. A., and Bazerman, M. H. *Cognition and Rationality in Negotiation*. New York: Free Press, 1991.

38. Pendergast, W. R. Managing the Negotiation Agenda. *Negotiation Journal*, April 1990, 135–145.

39. Savage, G. T., Nix, T. W., Whitehead, C. J., and Blair, J. D. Strategies for Assessing and Managing Stakeholders. *Academy of Management Executive*, May 1991, 61–75.

40. Adapted from Shell, G. R. When Is It Legal to Lie in Negotiations? *Sloan Management Review*, Spring 1991, 93–101.

41. Honeyman, C. On Evaluating Mediators. *Negotiation Journal*, January 1990, 23–36; Stratek, S. Grievance Mediation: Does It Really Work?. *Negotiation Journal*, July 1990, 269–280.

42. Rowe, M. P. Helping People Help Themselves: An ADR Option for Interpersonal Conflict. *Negotiation Journal*, July 1990, 239–248; Conlon, D. E., and Fasolo, P. M. Influence of Speed of Third-Party Intervention and Outcome on Negotiator and Constituent Fairness Judgments. *Academy of Management Journal*, 1990, *33*, 833–846.

43. Blake, R. R., Shepard, H. A., and Mouton, J. S. *Managing Intergroup Conflict in Industry*. Houston: Gulf, 1964; Fisher, R. J. Third-Party Consultation as a Method of Intergroup Conflict Resolution. *Journal of Conflict Resolution*, 1983, *27*, 301–334.

44. DeWine, Nicotera, and Parry. Argumentativeness and Aggressiveness: The Flip Side of Gentle Persuasion. Scale used with permission of the authors.

45. Infante, D. A. Aggressiveness. In J. C. McCrosky and J. A. Daly (eds.), *Personality and Interpersonal Communication*. Newbury Park, Calif.: Sage, 1987, 157–191.

46. Kilpatrick, J., Gantt, G., and Johnson, G. The Audit. In R. A. Cook (ed.), *Annual Advances in Business Cases 1990*. South Bend, Ind.: Midwest Society for Case Research, 1990, 67–68. This case was prepared by John Kilpatrick, Gamewell Gantt, and George Johnson of Idaho State University as a basis for class discussion, rather than to illustrate either effective or ineffective handling of an administrative situation. Presented to the Midwest Society for Case Research Workshop, 1990. All rights reserved to the authors. Copyright @ 1990 by John Kilpatrick, Gamewell Gantt, and George Johnson. Used with permission.

PART IV

ORGANIZATIONAL PROCESSES

CHAPTER 15

ORGANIZATIONAL CULTURE

LEARNING OBJECTIVES

When you have finished studying this chapter, you should be able to:

* Explain the concept of organizational culture.
* Describe how organizational cultures are developed, maintained, and changed.
* Understand the possible relationships between organizational culture and performance.
* Discuss the implications of organizational culture for ethical behavior in organizations.
* Explain the importance of effectively managing cultural diversity.
* Describe the process of organizational socialization and explain its relationship to organizational culture.

OUTLINE

500

BASEBALL TEAM, CLUB, ACADEMY, OR FORTRESS

According to Professor Jeffrey Sonnenfeld of Emory University, the labels of *baseball team, club, academy,* and *fortress* describe the most common types of organizational cultures in the business world. Each of these cultures has distinctive characteristics.

Baseball Team. Organizations with a baseball team culture attract entrepreneurs, innovators, and risk takers. Employees are paid for what they produce. Top performers can receive large salaries or other financial rewards and considerable autonomy. However, risks are high in the baseball team culture, and long-term security is virtually nonexistent. High performers tend to see themselves as free agents, much like professional athletes. Job hopping is common, with employees readily leaving one firm for greater rewards or freedom at another. Baseball team cultures are common in advertising agencies, biotechnology firms, consulting firms, investment banks, law firms, and software developers, such as Microsoft and Lotus.

Club. Age and experience are valued in the club culture. Organizations with a club culture reward seniority and provide stable, secure employment. The club culture also rewards loyalty, commitment, and "fitting in." Managers typically perform a number of jobs in different functions during a slow, steady progression up the corporate hierarchy; quick upward mobility is very unusual. Employees often start young and may spend thirty-five to forty years with the same firm. For example, at United Parcel Service (UPS), the CEO and his entire top management team began their UPS careers as clerks, delivery drivers, or management trainees. Other club cultures include Delta Airlines, most commercial banks, many utilities (such as the Bell companies), government agencies, and the U.S. military.

Academy. Organizations with an academy culture also tend to hire recruits early—particularly directly from college—as do those with club cultures. However, academy cultures place much greater emphasis on training employees to become expert in a particular function. Someone hired as a marketing representative would be unlikely to serve a stint in manufacturing, for example. The academy culture stresses continuity of service, functional expertise, and institutional wisdom. While there is some opportunity for "fast trackers," the academy culture is more likely to appeal to the steady climber who enjoys developing a thorough mastery of the job. Academy cultures exist at Coca-Cola, IBM, Proctor & Gamble and many other consumer product firms, the Big Three U.S. automakers, pharmaceutical companies, and many electronic and office products companies.

Fortress. The fortress culture is preoccupied with survival. Organizations with a fortress culture can promise little in the way of job security and have great difficulty in rewarding employees for good performance. Typically, they may be in the process of downsizing or restructuring, causing the dismissal of many employees. While a fortress culture might appeal to individuals who relish the challenge of turning a company around, it will not appeal to those who desire a sense of belonging, opportunities for professional growth, or secure future income. Some fortress organizations were previously baseball teams, clubs, or academies that have fallen on hard times. Others are firms in businesses that are characterized by periodic cycles of boom or bust. Currently, the ranks of fortress companies include some forest products firms, hotels, oil and gas companies, publishers, large retailers, the remnants of the savings and loan industry, and textile firms.[1]

The Preview Case offers some insight into several types of organizational culture. Many organizations, of course, cannot be categorized neatly as either baseball teams, clubs, academies, or fortresses. Some firms might be a blend of these types; others may be in transition between types. For example, Sonnenfeld suggests that Apple Computer started with a baseball team culture but has matured into an academy.

Other authorities, of course, suggest other labels or categories of cultural types. One observation, however, that many experts on organizational culture would agree with is that the effectiveness and success of an organization are not determined solely by the abilities and motivations of employees and managers. Nor is effectiveness measured solely by how well groups of people can work together, although both individual and group processes are crucial for organizational success.

> The organization itself has an invisible quality—a certain style, a character, a way of doing things—that may be more powerful than the dictates of any one person or any formal system. To understand the soul of the organization requires that we travel below the charts, rule books, machines, and buildings into the underground world of corporate cultures.[2]

The cultural types mentioned in the Preview Case are offered as a way of introducing the concept of culture and understanding some important distinctions among organizations. We must be careful, however, not to oversimplify the concept of culture. Indeed, two organizations might be in essentially the same business, be located in the same geographic area, have similar forms of organization structure, and yet, somehow, be very different as places to work. What makes organizations different? How do they get that way? The concept of organizational culture provides a useful way to answer such questions.

In this chapter, we introduce a part of the book devoted to "organizational processes." Up to this point, we focused first on individual behavior and then on interpersonal and group behavior. We now shift our attention to the organization as a whole. In this chapter, we examine the concept of organizational culture and how cultures are formed, maintained, and changed. We also explore some possible relationships between organizational culture and performance; the relationship between organizational culture and ethical behavior; the challenge of managing a culturally diverse work force; and, finally, how organizations socialize individuals into their particular culture.

CHARACTERISTICS AND DYNAMICS OF ORGANIZATIONAL CULTURE

The culture of an organization represents a complex pattern of beliefs and expectations shared by its members. More specifically, **organizational culture** is defined as shared philosophies, ideologies, values, beliefs, assumptions, expectations, attitudes, and norms.[3] It includes the following components:

- *Observed behavioral regularities* when people interact, such as organizational rituals and ceremonies and the language commonly used.

- The *norms* that are shared by working groups throughout the organization, such as "a fair day's work for a fair day's pay."

- The *dominant values* held by an organization, such as "product quality" or "price leadership."

- The *philosophy* that guides an organization's policy toward employees and customers.

- The *rules* of the game for getting along in the organization or the "ropes" that a newcomer must learn in order to become an accepted member.

- The *feeling* or *climate* that is conveyed in an organization by the physical layout and the way in which members of the organization interact with customers or other outsiders.[4]

None of these components individually represents the culture of the organization. Taken together, however, they reflect and give meaning to the concept of organizational culture.

Organizational culture exists on several levels.[5] As indicated by Figure 15.1, the most superficial level of culture consists of symbols. **Cultural symbols** are words (jargon or slang), gestures, and pictures or other physical objects that carry a particular meaning within a culture. Some expressions used at McDonald's Corporation provide an example of corporate jargon. McDonald's employees take training classes at Hamburger University; loyal employees are said to have "ketchup in their veins."

At the next level are **cultural heroes,** persons (alive or dead, real or imaginary) who possess characteristics highly valued by the culture and thus serve as role models for the culture. For example, at the University of Virginia, which was founded by Thomas Jefferson, administrators reportedly still ask, "What would Mr. Jefferson do?" when faced with a challenging decision.

Organizational rites and ceremonies are organized, planned activities or rituals that have important cultural meaning.[6] These will be discussed in more detail shortly. Finally, the deepest level, or the core, of culture is **cultural values.** These shared values represent collective beliefs, assumptions, and feelings about what things are good, normal, rational, valuable, and so on.

As indicated by the definition of culture, the listing of its components, and Figure 15.1, organizational culture has aspects that are subjective (such as shared values, assumptions, and expectations) and objective (such as pictures of heroes, observed behaviors, and organizational rituals). This culture—the ways of thinking, talking, and acting—is shared to a greater or lesser extent by all members of the organization and is transmitted by senior employees to new ones.[7] We now examine how organizational cultures are developed, how they are sustained over time, and how they might be changed.

Developing Organizational Culture

How does an organizational culture develop? Edgar Schein suggests that organizational culture forms in response to two major sets of problems that

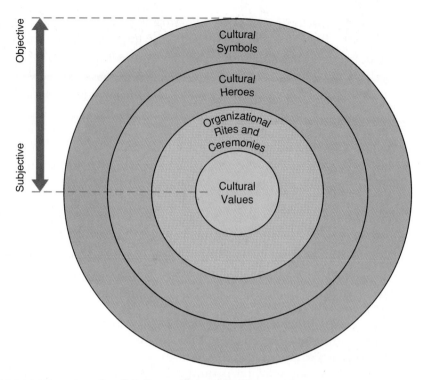

FIGURE 15.1   Levels of Culture: From Shallow to Deep

Source: Adapted from G. Hofstede, B. Neuijen, D. D. Ohayv, and G. Sanders, Measuring Organizational Cultures: A Qualitative and Quantitative Study across Twenty Cases. *Administrative Science Quarterly,* 1990, *35,* 291.

confront every organization: (1) problems of external adaptation and survival and (2) problems of internal integration.[8] Examples of these problems are listed in Table 15.1.

Problems of **external adaptation and survival** have to do with how the organization will find a niche in and cope with its constantly changing external environment. Problems of **internal integration** are concerned with establishing and maintaining effective working relationships among the members of the organization. An organizational culture emerges when members share knowledge and assumptions as they discover or develop ways of coping with these problems.

At least two additional influences on the origins of organizational culture are worth noting. First, early in the development of a new company, the firm's founder—such as Ed Land at Polaroid or Ken Smith at Federal Express—may largely determine the organization's culture. Later in the life of the organization, its culture will reflect a complex mixture of the assumptions, values, and ideas of the founder and the subsequent learning and experiences of other organizational members. Second, the national culture, customs, and societal norms of the country within which the firm operates also shape organizational culture. In other words, the culture of the larger society influences the culture of organizations operating within it.[9]

TABLE 15.1 Problems that Influence the Formation of Organizational Culture

---

Problems of External Adaptation and Survival

- *Mission and strategy.* Determining the organization's primary mission and main tasks; selecting strategies to use in pursuing this mission.
- *Goals.* Setting specific goals; achieving agreement on goals.
- *Means.* Determining the methods to use in achieving the goals; getting agreement on methods to be used; deciding what the organizational structure, division of labor, reward system, authority system, and so on will be.
- *Measurement.* Establishing criteria to use to measure how well individuals and groups are fulfilling their goals; determining the appropriate information and control systems.
- *Correction.* Identifying the actions needed if individuals and groups do not achieve goals.

Problems of Internal Integration

- *Common language and conceptual categories.* Identifying methods of communication; defining the meaning of the jargon and concepts to be used.
- *Group boundaries and criteria for inclusion and exclusion.* Establishing criteria for membership in the organization and its groups.
- *Power and status.* Addressing the issue of rules for acquiring, maintaining, or losing power; determining and distributing status.
- *Intimacy, friendship, and love.* Setting rules for social relationships and for handling relationships between the sexes; determining the level of openness and intimacy appropriate in the work setting.
- *Rewards and punishments.* Identifying desirable and undesirable behaviors.

Source: Adapted from E. H. Schein, Organizational Culture. *American Psychologist*, 1990, *45*, 113.

The dominant values of a national culture can be reflected in the constraints imposed on organizations by the environment within which it must operate. For example, the form of government may have a dramatic impact on how an organization does business in a country. In addition, the members of the organization have been raised in a particular society and thus bring the dominant values of the society into the firm. For example, individuals learn values, such as freedom of speech or a respect for individual privacy, from their society. The presence or absence of these and other values within the larger society has implications for organizational behavior. Finally, increased global operations have forced an awareness that differences in national culture may seriously affect organizational effectiveness. Multinational corporations, such as IBM, Ford, and GE, are discovering that organizational structures and cultures that might be effective in one part of the world may be very ineffective in another.[10] For these

◆ *ACROSS CULTURES*

EFFECTS OF NATIONAL CULTURAL VALUES ON ORGANIZATIONS

 Geert Hofstede, a Dutch social scientist, has developed a framework consisting of several cultural dimensions that can be used to compare national cultural values. Recently, Hofstede's cultural dimensions have been used to examine the potential impacts of national culture on organizations. Two of these cultural dimensions—power distance and uncertainty avoidance—will be examined here.

Power distance refers to the extent to which a society encourages unequal distributions of power among people. In low power distance societies, more interaction takes place among people from different social classes, and individuals can more easily move up in social status. Examples of low power distance societies would include Austria, Sweden, and the United States. India, Mexico, and the Philippines are considered to be examples of high power distance countries. In these societies, typically, the distance between individuals of high and low status is considerable, and advancement into the upper classes is often difficult. Table 15.2 shows some differences between organizations in low and high power distance cultures.

The organizational characteristics shown in Table 15.2 can lead to important differ-

---

TABLE 15.2   Some Effects of the Power Distance Dimension on Organizations

Power Distance Dimension	
Low (Austria, Denmark, Israel, Sweden, United States)	*High* (Brazil, Hong Kong, India, Mexico, Philippines)
• Less centralization	• Greater centralization
• Fewer levels in organizational hierarchy	• More levels in organizational hierarchy
• Fewer supervisory personnel	• More supervisory personnel
• Smaller wage differentials	• Large wage differentials
• White-collar jobs and blue-collar jobs are equally valued	• White-collar jobs are valued more than blue-collar jobs

Source: Adapted from E. F. Jackofsky, J. W. Slocum, Jr., and S. J. McQuaid, Cultural Values and the CEO: Alluring Companions? *Academy of Management Executive,* 1988, 2, 40.

continues

---

and other reasons, organizational researchers and managers have recently become interested in exploring the linkages between national and organizational cultures. This chapter's Across Cultures account illustrates the impact of a society's culture on the organizational culture of firms operating in that society.

continued

ences in organizational culture as well. For example, managers and employees are more highly interdependent in low power distance societies and may prefer a Theory Y style of management (see Chapter 1). In high power distance societies, a more autocratic, Theory X style of managing people may be expected and even preferred. Theory X versus Theory Y assumptions and values can contribute to very different organizational cultures.

Uncertainty avoidance refers to the extent to which individuals in a society feel threatened by ambiguous and unstable situations and try to avoid them. In a high uncertainty avoidance culture, organizations will tend to have more written rules and procedures, will impose more structure on employee activities, and will reward managers for risk avoidance. The opposite tendencies characterize organizations in a national culture where un-

certainty avoidance is low, as indicated by Table 15.3.

One implication for global corporations is that an organizational culture that fits one society might not be readily transferrable to other societies. For example, one study examined the Hong Kong subsidiary of Hewlett-Packard in relation to its fit with Hong Kong's cultural values. The Hewlett-Packard subsidiary's organizational culture was viewed as low power distance and low uncertainty avoidance—identical to the parent firm's culture in the United States. Hong Kong's culture, on the other hand, was viewed as high power distance and low uncertainty avoidance. The study's authors predicted that Hewlett-Packard's corporate culture may not be fully accepted by its Hong Kong employees.[11]

TABLE 15.3 Some Effects of the Uncertainty Avoidance Dimension on Organizations

Uncertainty Avoidance Dimension

Low *(Denmark, Great Britain, Hong Kong, Sweden, United States)*	*High* *(France, Greece, Japan, Peru, Portugal)*
• Less task structure • Fewer written rules • More generalists • Greater willingness to take risks • Less ritualistic behavior	• Greater task structure • More written rules • More specialists • Less willingness to take risks • More ritualistic behavior

Source: Adapted from E. F. Jackofsky, J. W. Slocum, Jr., and S. J. McQuaid, Cultural Values and the CEO: Alluring Companions? *Academy of Management Executive,* 1988, *2,* 41.

Maintaining Organizational Culture

The ways in which an organization functions and is managed may have both intended and unintended effects on maintaining or changing organizational culture. In Figure 15.2, a basic method of maintaining an organization's culture is shown: the organization attempts to hire individuals who, in some

FIGURE 15.2   Methods of Maintaining Organizational Culture

sense, *fit* the organizational culture. (Later in the chapter, we discuss the socialization of new employees into the organization's culture.) In addition, cultures are maintained by the removal of employees who consistently or markedly deviate from accepted behaviors and activities.

Specific methods for maintaining organizational culture, however, are a great deal more complicated than just hiring and firing the right people (which in itself really is not all that simple). The most powerful reinforcers of the organization's culture are: (1) what managers pay attention to, measure, and control; (2) the ways managers (particularly top managers) react to critical incidents and organizational crises; (3) managerial role modeling, teaching, and coaching; (4) criteria for allocating rewards and status; (5) criteria for recruitment, selection, promotion, and removal from the organization; and (6) organizational rites, ceremonies, and stories.[12]

What Managers Pay Attention to, Measure, and Control   One of the more powerful methods of maintaining organizational culture involves the processes and behaviors that the managers pay attention to, that is, the things that get noticed and commented on. Dealing with things systematically sends strong signals to employees about what is important and expected of them. For example, a large toy manufacturer installed a management-by-objectives (MBO) performance appraisal system (see Chapter 8 for a description of MBO). After a few years, top management discovered that the MBO program was working well in one part of the corporation but not another. An investigation revealed that in the part of the organization where MBO was working well, senior management was enthusiastic and committed. These managers perceived real benefits from the program and conveyed these beliefs to others. In the part of the organization where MBO was failing, senior management viewed MBO as just another bureaucratic exercise. Subordinates quickly learned to complete the paperwork but ignore the purpose of the MBO system. The firm's top management concluded that MBO would work only when employees believe that managers care about the results and pay attention to them.[13]

Reactions to Critical Incidents and Organizational Crises   When an organization faces a crisis, the handling of that crisis by managers and employees reveals a great deal about the culture. The manner in which the crisis is dealt with can either reinforce the existing culture or bring out new values and norms that change the culture in some manner. For example, an organization facing a dramatic reduction in demand for its product might react by laying off or firing employees. Or it might reduce employee hours or rates of pay with no reduction in the work force. The alternative chosen indicates the value placed on human resources and can serve to reinforce and maintain the current culture—or indicate a major cultural change. This situation occurred at Hewlett-Packard during an early point in its history. Hewlett-Packard responded to reduced demand for its products by choosing to reduce hours. Hewlett-Packard went to a schedule of working nine days out of every two weeks—a 10 percent reduction in work schedule with a corresponding cut in pay—rather than fire or lay off any employees. The firm thus sent a clear message to its employees about the value it placed on human resources. This response has become deeply ingrained in the corporation's folklore and, in turn, now serves to reinforce this aspect of its culture.

Role Modeling, Teaching, and Coaching   Aspects of the organization's culture are communicated to employees by the way managers fulfill their roles. In addition, managers may specifically incorporate important cultural messages into training programs and day-to-day coaching on the job. For example, training films shown to new employees might emphasize customer service. Also, managers might strive to demonstrate good customer or client service practices in their interactions with customers. The repeated emphasis placed on good customer relations in both training and day-to-day behavior in turn would help to create and maintain a customer-oriented culture throughout the organization.

Criteria for Allocation of Rewards and Status   Employees also learn about their organization's culture through its reward system. The rewards and punishments attached to various behaviors convey to employees the priorities and values of both individual managers and the organization. Similarly, the organization's status system maintains certain aspects of its culture. The distribution of *perks,* such as a corner office on an upper floor, carpeting, a private secretary, or a private parking space, helps to demonstrate which roles and behaviors are most valued by the organization. It is important to note that organizations may be quite ineffective in using rewards and status symbols in any consistent way. If this happens, an organization is missing an important opportunity to influence its culture since there is evidence that the reward practices of an organization and its culture may be strongly linked.[14] In fact, some authorities think that the most effective method for influencing organizational culture may be through the reward system.

Criteria for Recruitment, Selection, Promotion, and Removal   As Figure 15.2 suggests, one of the fundamental ways that organizations maintain a culture is through the recruitment process. In addition, basic aspects

TABLE 15.4   Organizational Rites and Ceremonies

Type	Example	Possible Consequences
Rites of passage	Basic training, U.S. Army	Facilitate transition into new roles; minimize differences in way roles are carried out
Rites of degradation	Firing a manager	Reduce power and identity; reaffirm proper behavior
Rites of enhancement	Mary Kay Cosmetics Company seminars	Enhance power and identity; emphasize value of proper behavior
Rites of integration	Office party	Encourage common feelings that bind members together

Source: Adapted from J. M. Beyer and H. M. Trice, How an Organization's Rites Reveal Its Culture. *Organizational Dynamics,* Spring 1987, 11.

of a culture are demonstrated and reinforced by the criteria used to determine who is assigned to specific jobs or positions, who gets raises and promotions and why, who is removed from the organization by firing or early retirement, and so on. Criteria used in these human resource decisions tend to become known throughout the organization and can serve to maintain or change an existing culture.

Organizational Rites, Ceremonies, and Stories   Certain managerial or employee activities can become organizational rituals that are interpreted as part of the organizational culture. Organizational rites and ceremonies that can be used to sustain organizational culture include rites of passage, degradation, enhancement, and integration. Table 15.4 contains examples of each of these four types of rites and identifies some of their desirable consequences.

A ceremony used at Mary Kay Cosmetics Company provides a good example of rites of enhancement. During elaborate awards ceremonies, gold and diamond pins, fur stoles, and the use of pink Cadillacs are presented to saleswomen who achieve their sales quotas. The ceremonies are held in a setting reminiscent of a Miss America pageant with all the participants dressed in glamorous evening clothes. The setting is typically a large auditorium with a stage in front of a large, cheering audience.[15] This ceremony is clearly intended to increase the identity and status of high-performing employees and emphasize the rewards for proper behavior.

Many of the underlying beliefs and values of an organization's culture are expressed as legends and stories that become part of the organizational folklore.[16] These stories and legends are a way of transmitting the existing culture from senior employees to new ones and serve to emphasize important aspects of that culture. Some stories may persist for a long time and become a source of resistance to cultural change, as seen in the following In Practice.

IN PRACTICE

THE LEGEND OF SAM

A Fortune 500 manufacturer had a factory with a history of hostile labor-management relations, low productivity, and poor quality. The company hired a consultant who started out by talking with the employees in the plant. They eagerly told him about the plant manager, a three-hundred-pound gorilla named Sam with a disposition that made King Kong look like Bonzo the chimp.

Once, Sam examined a transmission, did not like the work he saw, picked up a sledgehammer, and smashed the transmission to pieces. Another story told of employees who would throw up upon being summoned to Sam's office. On another occasion, Sam reportedly drove his car onto the floor of the factory, got up on the roof of the car, and started screaming at the workers. One employee was so outraged by this behavior that he poured a line of gasoline to the car and lit it.

The stunned consultant made an appointment to see the plant manager. When the consultant walked into the manager's office, he saw a slim, pleasant-looking man behind the desk who introduced himself as Paul. "Where's Sam?" asked the consultant. Paul, looking puzzled, replied, "Sam has been dead for nine years."[17]

Changing Organizational Culture

The same basic methods used to maintain an organization's culture can serve to change it. Culture might be changed, for example, by (1) changing what managers pay attention to, (2) changing how crisis situations are handled, (3) changing criteria for recruiting new members, (4) changing criteria for promotion within the organization, (5) changing criteria for allocating rewards, (6) changing organizational rites and ceremonies, and so on. For example, an organizational culture that tends to punish risk taking and innovation and reward risk avoidance might be deliberately altered through changes in the reward system. Employees could be encouraged to set riskier and more innovative goals for themselves in coaching and goal-setting sessions. In performance appraisal sessions and through merit raises, individuals could be rewarded for attempting more challenging tasks, even if they failed sometimes, than for attaining safe goals that required no innovative behavior, and so on.

Changing organizational culture can be a tricky business. At least two perspectives suggest caution when attempting cultural change. First, while recognizing that many organizations need to change deeply ingrained habits that are ineffective, well-known management expert Peter Drucker questions whether the deep, core values of organizational culture are amenable to change.[18] In his view, it is more meaningful to restrict managerial focus and efforts to changing ineffective behaviors and procedures than to attempt changes in organizational culture. Further, Drucker argues that changing behavior will work only if it can be based on the existing culture.

A second perspective that suggests caution in cultural change considers the difficulties in accurately assessing organizational culture. For example, in a study of the culture of an adult rehabilitation center, employees were asked to identify the culture of their organization using the following categories:

- *The tough-guy, macho culture.* A world of individualists who take high risks and get quick feedback on whether their actions were right or wrong.

- *The work hard/play hard culture.* Fun and action are the rule here, and employees take few risks, all with quick feedback; the culture encourages them to succeed by maintaining a high level of relatively low-risk activity.

- *The bet-your-company culture.* A world of big-stakes decisions, where years pass before employees know whether decisions have paid off; high-risk, slow-feedback environment.

- *The process culture.* A world of little or no feedback, where employees find it hard to measure what they do; instead, they concentrate on how it is done. When the processes get out of control, this is called bureaucracy.[19]

Forty percent of the employees in this rehabilitation center described their culture as a work hard/play hard culture; 30 percent described the culture as a bet-your-company culture; 20 percent said the culture was best described as tough-guy macho; and 10 percent described the organizational culture as process-oriented and bureaucratic.[20] Faced with such differences in perceptions, researchers and managers may be hard pressed to identify *the* culture of an organization. The reality is that many large, complex organizations may have more than one culture. General Electric, for example, has distinctly different cultures in different units of the corporation. Sometimes these multiple cultures are called **subcultures.**

Despite these cautionary concerns, many authorities are convinced that changing organizational cultures is both feasible and, in the case of failing organizations, sometimes essential.[21] Key ideas for successful cultural change include:

- Understand the old culture first; a new culture cannot be developed unless managers and employees understand where they are starting from.

- Provide support for those employees who have ideas for a better culture and are willing to act on their vision.

- Find the most effective subculture in the organization and use it as an example from which employees can learn.

- Don't attack culture head on. Find ways to help employees do their jobs more effectively; a better culture will result.

- The vision of a new culture serves as a guiding principle for change; it will *not* work miracles.

- Significant organization-wide improvement in terms of cultural change takes five to ten years.

- Live the new culture—actions speak louder than words.[22]

We cover planned organizational change extensively in Chapters 21 and 22. Many of the specific techniques and methods for changing organizational behaviors presented in those chapters can also be used to change organizational culture. Indeed, any comprehensive program of organizational change is, in some sense, an attempt to change the culture of the organization. The following In Practice provides some interesting comparisons between cultural change at AT&T and the dramatic changes occurring in the Soviet Union.

IN PRACTICE

THE CHANGING CULTURES OF MA BELL AND MOTHER RUSSIA

There are some fascinating parallels between the cultural changes occurring at AT&T following the divestiture of its Bell operating companies and the changes occurring in the Soviet Union in the wake of *perestroika*. Both AT&T and organizations in the Soviet Union have been changing from cultures of maternalism to cultures of accountability. A **maternalism culture** is protective of individual security and does not emphasize individual accountability. Maternalistic cultures tend to exist in environments where there are few competitors. An **accountability culture** holds individuals accountable for their behavior and performance. Accountability cultures tend to exist in markets where there are many competitors.

Prior to *perestroika,* most major Soviet industries were subject to central planning. The government typically set production targets, product mixes, prices that an organization must pay for raw materials, and so on. Although an estimated 10 percent of enterprises were operated at a loss, bankruptcy was not permitted, nor could organizations discharge excess employees. The measure of organizational performance or effectiveness was meeting production goals set by the government. Soviet managers had little autonomy, and no incentive to produce more (or better) products than the planned goals called for.

The court-ordered divestiture and reorganization of AT&T, which occurred in January 1984, is one of the most significant such events in U.S. business history. This reorganization triggered one of the most dramatic cultural changes on record. Literally, AT&T's old culture became obsolete—an impediment to what the company needed to do to survive. Prior to the divestiture, AT&T was a highly centralized, rigidly structured monopoly. A large corporate staff provided detailed central planning for the entire organization. In terms of the cultural types described in the Preview Case, the old AT&T was a strong example of a club culture with an emphasis on lifetime careers, loyalty, and conformity. As a regulated monopoly, AT&T was guaranteed a reasonable profit and protected from competition. Lower- and middle-level managers had little autonomy and were evaluated by how well they carried out centrally directed procedures. Table 15.5 contains examples of some similarities between the external environment and organizational cultures of Soviet organizations and AT&T prior to the changes.

Both Soviet organizations and AT&T faced similar changes in the external environment that necessitated corresponding changes in organizational culture.

**TABLE 15.5   Common Characteristics of the Old External Environment
and Organizational Cultures of Soviet Organizations and AT&T**

Characteristics of the External Environment

- Monopoly—no competition
- Government regulation and control
- Low uncertainty
- Guaranteed profit/organizational survival

Characteristics of the Organizational Culture

- Centralized control of policies—planning, production, etc.
- Rewards not tied to performance
- No incentive to perform above standard
- Strong club culture—emphasis on loyalty, "fitting in"; high job security

Source: Adapted from J. B. Shaw, C. D. Fisher, and W. A. Randolph, From Maternalism to Accountability: The Changing Cultures of Ma Bell and Mother Russia. *Academy of Management Executive*, 1991, *5*(1), 9.

Table 15.6 summarizes some of the current similarities in the environment and cultures of these organizations.

Changes in Soviet organizations are being implemented in stages and certainly have not always gone smoothly. However, the goal seems to be to create more autonomous, self-managing enterprises. Organizations will no longer be subsidized and will need to learn to buy and sell in the marketplace. AT&T, as well as the independent Bell operating companies, faces a new world of external competition. Individual managers now have responsibility for strategic planning

---

**TABLE 15.6   Common Characteristics of the New External Environment
and Organizational Cultures of Soviet Organizations and AT&T**

Characteristics of the External Environment

- More competitive
- Less government control
- Increased uncertainty
- Profits or organizational survival not guaranteed

Characteristics of the Organizational Culture

- Greater decentralization
- Rewards tied to performance
- Emphasis on individual responsibility and accountability
- Uncertainty about roles and responsibilities

Source: Adapted from J. B. Shaw, C. D. Fisher, and W. A. Randolph, From Maternalism to Accountability: The Changing Cultures of Ma Bell and Mother Russia. *Academy of Management Executive*, 1991, *5*(1), 11.

and decision making. One overriding imperative now that AT&T no longer has a monopoly position is that AT&T has had to learn how to *sell*. Soviet organizations and AT&T are moving toward a culture of accountability in order to compete and survive.[23]

PERFORMANCE AND ORGANIZATIONAL CULTURE

The underlying assumption of an emphasis on cultural change, as illustrated by the preceding In Practice, is that there is some relationship between the type of culture possessed by an organization and its performance or effectiveness. The rationale, thus, for attempting cultural change is to create a more effective organization.

Indeed, the common theme of a number of recent popular books is that strong, well-developed cultures are an important characteristic of organizations with a record of high performance.[24] Conventional wisdom suggests that strong cultures are likely to be associated with good performance for two reasons.[25] First, a strong culture often provides for a better fit between strategy and culture. This fit is considered essential for successfully implementing corporate strategy. Second, a strong culture leads to increased commitment by employees. In this view, culture is crucial for developing the dedication to perform well that often is characteristic of successful organizations.

Despite this conventional wisdom, however, there is mixed evidence regarding the existence of a strong culture-performance relationship. A study of this issue in thirty-four companies reported finding a strong relationship between organizational culture and performance. Specifically, firms with participative cultures and well-organized workplaces had better performance records than those firms without these characteristics.[26] On the other hand, a comparison of the cultures of 334 institutions of higher education revealed no differences in organizational effectiveness between those with strong cultures versus those with weak cultures.[27] However, this study did uncover relationships between the *type* of culture possessed by these institutions and their effectiveness. Also, studies have shown that the relationship between many cultural attributes (featured in the popular press as being important for performance) and high performance has not been consistent over time.[28] Given what is known about culture-performance relationships, a contingency approach seems to be a good one for managers and organizations to take. Future investigations of this issue are unlikely to discover a "best" culture that fits all organizations, all people, all national values, and so on.

High degrees of participative management and an emphasis on teamwork are often cited as characteristics of successful organizational cultures. In **participative management,** managers share decision-making, goal-setting, and problem-solving activities with employees. However, high levels of participation do not fit all settings and tasks; to change an organization from a more traditional management approach to greater collaboration with employees may be extremely difficult.

A type of organizational culture designed to foster high performance with high levels of employee involvement is called a **high performance-high commitment work culture.** Five characteristics define the high performance-high commitment culture: delegation, teamwork across boundaries, empowerment, integration of people and technology, and a shared sense of purpose.[29] The *delegation* characteristic means that employees having the most relevant information or the most appropriate work skills are given responsibility for actions and decisions. *Teamwork across boundaries* means that employees are not focused primarily on their own function or department. Rather, all employees are focused on servicing the product and the customer for the product. *Empowerment* means that everyone is expected to accept responsibility for getting his or her job done as well as helping others accomplish their work—no one in the organization is free to say: "It's not my job." *Integrating people and technology* refers to an objective of allowing employees to control the technology, rather than be controlled by it. Finally, a *shared sense of purpose* means that employees share a vision of the organization's purpose and the methods for accomplishing this purpose. This shared vision provides the basis for the organization's culture. High performance-high commitment work cultures or systems will be examined in greater detail in Chapter 22.

We can summarize the performance-related effects of organizational culture with four key ideas.[30] First, knowing the culture of an organization allows employees to understand the firm's history and current approach. This knowledge provides guidance about expected behaviors in the future. Second, organizational culture can serve to establish commitment to corporate philosophy and values. This provides organizational members with shared feelings of working toward common goals. Third, organizational culture, through its norms, serves as a control mechanism to channel employee behaviors toward desired and away from undesired behaviors. Finally, certain kinds of organizational cultures may be related to greater effectiveness and productivity than others.

Another potential effect of organizational culture can be found in its relationship to ethical behavior by managers and employees. Possible culture-ethical behavior relationships will be explored next.

ETHICAL BEHAVIOR AND ORGANIZATIONAL CULTURE

Ethical problems in organizations continue to greatly concern managers and employees. The potential impact that organizational culture can have on ethical behavior is only now beginning to be explored.[31] It does seem, however, that organizational culture affects ethical behavior in several ways.

The ethics component of organizational culture is composed of a complex interplay of formal and informal systems that can support either ethical or unethical organizational behavior. The formal systems include leadership, structure, policies, reward systems, orientation and training programs, and decision-making processes. Informal systems include norms, heroes, rituals, language, myths, sagas, and stories.[32]

In a very real sense, ethical business practices stem from ethical organizational cultures. For example, a culture emphasizing ethical norms provides support for behaving in an ethical manner. Thus, when the Tylenol disaster struck, Johnson & Johnson employees knew what to do. In addition, top management plays a key role in fostering ethical behavior. Moreover, all authority figures—managers and other professionals—in the organization can encourage or discourage ethical behavior. The presence or absence of ethical behavior in managerial actions is both influenced by the prevailing culture and, in turn, helps to partially determine the culture in terms of ethical issues. The organizational culture may promote responsibility for the consequences of actions taken, thereby increasing the probability that individuals will behave in an ethical manner. Alternatively, the culture may diffuse responsibility for the consequences of unethical behavior, thereby making such behavior more likely.

Acts of personal and professional courage may be required to behave ethically. One such act is described in the following In Practice.

IN PRACTICE

BLOWING THE WHISTLE AT BEECH-NUT

In August 1981, Jerome LiCari sent a memo that would significantly affect the fortunes of Beech-Nut Nutrition Corporation, a subsidiary of Nestlé, the giant Swiss food company. LiCari's memo helped to bring about one of the most serious admissions ever of criminal wrongdoing by a major corporation. The experience at Beech-Nut provides an example of how even the most reputable of companies can suffer an ethical breakdown through poor judgment.

LiCari was director of research and development (R&D) for Beech-Nut, the second largest baby food producer in the United States. For some time, he had been worried that the apple concentrate Beech-Nut was buying for its apple juice products was adulterated—that is, it was a blend of synthetic ingredients—rather than being "100 percent fruit juice," as Beech-Nut advertised. After some investigation, LiCari became convinced that the apple concentrate was, in fact, adulterated and so informed senior executives in a memorandum and a series of meetings. When his superiors took no action, LiCari resigned.

As reported in *Business Week:*

> The "smoking gun" memo, as prosecutors later termed it, was key evidence in a federal grand jury investigation that led to a 470-count indictment of Beech-Nut and its two top executives in November 1986. In November 1987, Beech-Nut pleaded guilty to 215 felony counts and admitted to willful violations of the food and drug laws by selling adulterated apple products from 1981 to 1983.

The admission by Beech-Nut that it sold millions of jars of phony apple juice shocked many company employees, as well as industry executives and consumers. Since 1891, purity, high quality, and natural ingredients had served as the foundation of its corporate culture and had been a consistent marketing theme. What had caused Beech-Nut to stray from its heritage and reputation?

The answer to this question is complex. Underlying the company's ethical failure were strong financial pressures. Beech-Nut was losing money, and the use of the cheap, adulterated concentrate saved millions of dollars. The involved Beech-Nut employees seemed to use two arguments to justify their actions: (1) they believed that many other companies were selling fake juice, and (2) they were convinced that their adulterated juice was perfectly safe to consume. In addition, some employees took refuge in the fact that no conclusive test existed to determine natural from artificial ingredients. With regard to this latter point, however, Beech-Nut seems to have shifted the burden of proof around. Other juice makers have been known to cut off suppliers if the supplier cannot demonstrate that its product is genuine. At Beech-Nut, senior management apparently told R&D that *they* would have to prove that an inexpensive supplier's product was adulterated before the company would switch to another supplier. Beech-Nut compounded its problems when government investigations began by stonewalling, rather than cooperating, apparently in order to gain time to unload a $3.5 million inventory of adulterated apple juice products. Thus, while at first Beech-Nut appeared to have been the innocent victim of unscrupulous suppliers, the company, by its later actions, changed a civil matter into criminal charges.

An internal Beech-Nut document described the director of R&D as "colored by naivete and impractical ideals." After these events had transpired, LiCari was asked if he was naive. "I guess I was," he replied, "I thought apple juice should be made from apples."[33]

An important concept linking organizational culture to ethical behavior is principled organizational dissent. **Principled organizational dissent** is the effort by individuals in the organization to protest the status quo because of their objection, on ethical grounds, to some practice or policy.[34] Some cultures might permit, or even encourage, principled organizational dissent; other cultures might punish such behavior.

An employee might use a number of strategies in an attempt to change unethical behavior. These include:

- Secretly or publicly blowing the whistle within the organization.
- Secretly or publicly blowing the whistle outside the organization.
- Secretly or publicly threatening an offender or a responsible manager with blowing the whistle.
- Quietly or publicly refusing to implement an unethical order or policy.

An example of publicly blowing the whistle inside the organization occurred when John Young, the chief of the National Aeronautic and Space Administration's (NASA) astronaut office, wrote a twelve-page internal memorandum following the Challenger explosion that killed seven astronauts. The memo was sent to ninety-seven key individuals within NASA and detailed a large number of safety problems that endangered crews of the space shut-tles. This communication was instrumental in broadening safety investiga-tions conducted throughout NASA.

An example of secretly blowing the whistle outside the organization occurred when William Schwartzkopf of Commonwealth Electric Company anonymously sent a letter to the Justice Department that identified in-stances of bid rigging among the largest U.S. electrical contractors. These contractors paid more than $20 million in fines as a result of investigations into these illegal bidding practices.[35] Of course, these types of whistle-blowing activities are not without their risks.[36] There are the obvious risks to the individuals engaging in these forms of principled organizational dissent—dismissal, demotion, and so on. There is also the possibility that the whistle-blower could be wrong about individual or organizational ac-tions. Thus, employees or organizations might be harmed unnecessarily by misguided attempts to stop unethical behavior.

Much remains to be learned with regard to creating organizational cul-tures that encourage ethical behavior. As a beginning, the following sugges-tions are made:

- Be realistic in setting values and goals regarding employment rela-tionships. Do not promise what the organization cannot deliver.

- Encourage input from throughout the organization regarding ap-propriate values and practices for implementing the culture. Choose values that represent the views of employees as well as managers.

- Do not automatically opt for a "strong" culture. Explore methods to provide for diversity and dissent, such as grievance or complaint mechanisms or other internal review procedures.

- Provide training programs for managers and supervisors on adopt-ing and implementing the organization's values. These programs should explain the underlying ethical and legal principles and present the practical aspects of carrying out procedural guidelines.[37]

An effective organizational culture should encourage ethical behavior and discourage unethical behavior. Admittedly, ethical behavior may "cost" the organization. An example might be the loss of sales when a global firm refuses to pay a bribe to secure business in a particular country. Certainly, individuals might gain by behaving unethically (partic-ularly if they do not get caught). In a similar fashion, an organization might seem to gain from unethical actions. For example, a purchasing agent for a large corporation might be bribed to purchase all needed office supplies from a particular supplier. However, such gains are often short-term. The Beech-Nut experience provides a clear example of this outcome. In the long run, an organization cannot successfully operate if its prevailing culture and values are not congruent with those of society. This is just as true as the observation that, in the long run, an organiza-tion cannot survive unless it provides goods and services that society wants and needs. Thus, an organizational culture that promotes ethical behavior is not only more compatible with prevailing cultural values but also, in fact, makes good business sense.[38]

MANAGING CULTURAL DIVERSITY

Organizations are becoming increasingly diverse in terms of gender, race, ethnicity, and nationality.[39] More than half of the U.S. work force consists of women, minorities, and immigrants. Only approximately 15 percent of the increase in the U.S. work force during the remainder of this century will be white males.[40] The growing diversity of employees at many organizations can bring substantial benefits, such as more successful marketing strategies for different types of customers, improved decision making, and perhaps greater creativity and innovation. But there are costs and concerns as well, including communication difficulties, higher levels of organizational conflict, and the potential for higher turnover. Effectively managing cultural diversity promises to be a significant challenge for organizations during the 1990s and beyond. Consider the following In Practice example.

IN PRACTICE

CORPORATE CULTURE VERSUS ETHNIC CULTURE

Lakeview Enterprises has twenty thousand employees worldwide. Keisha Gibson started as a word processor for Lakeview and has performed well, receiving two promotions. Currently, she is the secretary for Alan Hirsh, who is director of benefit programs in the human resources department.

Gibson and Hirsh have a good working relationship. Hirsh describes Gibson as conscientious and highly skilled. Gibson describes Hirsh as a good boss who provides the right amount of responsibility, feedback, and recognition.

Gibson is an African-American. She frequently wears attractive African-style prints, jewelry, and headwraps. Gibson is proud of her heritage and expresses it through her style of clothing. Hirsh, who is white, considers himself a proponent of equal employment opportunity and affirmative action.

A problem arose when Gibson requested Hirsh's recommendation to participate in a vacation substitute program for secretaries of the firm's top executives. Understandably, Gibson wants this visibility to senior management and knows this could put her in line for promotion to the highest paying secretarial positions. Hirsh's dilemma arises because he knows the executive floor is a bastion of conservatism, particularly with regard to dress. With *no* exceptions, secretaries and executives observe unwritten rules or norms with regard to their attire—dark suits and white shirts for the men, business suits or dresses for the women.

If Gibson, despite her skills and potential for advancement, fails to find acceptance on the executive floor, will it be because she is an African-American or because she expresses this ethnic identity through her manner of dress? On the other hand, if everyone else is required to conform to this dress code, why should Gibson be an exception? How should Hirsh manage this potential clash between corporate and ethnic cultures?[41]

There are no easy answers to the challenges raised by a culturally diverse work force. Successful organizations have to work hard at acculturation processes. **Acculturation** refers to methods by which cultural differences between a dominant culture and minority or subcultures are resolved and managed.[42]

A good example of managing cultural diversity can be found at Proctor & Gamble (P&G).[43] P&G formed a Corporate Diversity Strategy Task Force to clarify the concept of diversity, define its importance for the company, and identify strategies for successfully managing a culturally diverse work force. The task force was composed of men and women from all parts of the company. They quickly realized that learning to manage diversity would require a long-term process of organizational change. P&G offers voluntary programs on diversity training that have gradually expanded their focus from gender and race awareness to include self-realization for individuals working in a culturally diverse environment. The company conducts periodic surveys to identify problems facing employees and continually monitors all programs and activities to ensure they meet the needs of all members of a culturally diverse work force. Similar programs exist at Avon, Corning, Digital, and Xerox, among other companies.

Individual managers, such as Alan Hirsh in the preceding In Practice, cannot necessarily wait for their organization to come to their rescue with a corporate program every time they are faced with conflict between cultures. Guidelines for managing cultural diversity include:

- Don't avoid the issue of diversity. Bring it out in the open and talk about it.
- Explore how all employees come to the workplace with a unique combination of background influences. Start with yourself and your own background.
- Be an intercultural ambassador by making tact and respect the rule for discussions of ethnic, cultural, racial or gender differences.
- Don't tolerate racist or sexist behaviors. Stay within equal employment opportunity (EEO) guidelines.
- Help employees balance personal and professional needs.
- Explain the unwritten rules of the organization to employees.
- Refer employees to co-workers so they get a well-rounded perception.[44]

ORGANIZATIONAL SOCIALIZATION

Organizational socialization is the systematic process by which organizations bring new employees into their culture. In the general meaning of the term, *socialization* is the process by which older members of a society transmit to younger members the social skills and knowledge needed to effectively perform the roles of that society. Organizational socialization has a similar meaning: the transmission of culture from senior to new employees, providing the social knowledge and skills needed to successfully perform organizational roles and jobs. Socialization provides the means by which individuals learn the ropes upon joining an organization. As such, organizational socialization includes learning work group, department, and organizational values, rules, procedures, and norms; developing social and working relationships; and developing skills and knowledge needed to perform the new job. Interestingly, the stages an employee goes through during socialization resemble, in many respects, the stages in group development discussed in Chapter 10.[45] We will further discuss the socialization of new employees joining an organization in Chapter 20.

Process of Socialization

An example of an organizational socialization process is shown in Figure 15.3. This diagram is not intended to depict the socialization process of all organizations. However, Richard Pascale argues that many firms with strong cultures—such as IBM, P&G, AT&T, and Delta Airlines—frequently follow these seven steps for socializing new employees:

- *Step One.* Entry-level candidates are carefully selected. Trained recruiters use standardized procedures and seek specific traits that tie to success in the business.

- *Step Two.* Humility-inducing experiences in the first months on the job cause employees to question their prior behavior, beliefs, and values. For example, this might be accomplished by giving a new employee more work to do than can reasonably be done. The self-questioning promotes openness toward accepting the organization's norms and values.

- *Step Three.* In-the-trenches training leads to mastery of one of the core disciplines of the business. Promotion is tied to a proven track record.

- *Step Four.* Careful attention is given to measuring operational results and rewarding individual performance. Reward systems are comprehensive and consistent and focus on those aspects of the organization that are tied to success and corporate culture.

- *Step Five.* Adherence to the organization's values is emphasized. The identification with common values allows employees to justify personal sacrifices caused by their membership in the organization.

- *Step Six.* Reinforcing folklore provides legends and interpretations of important events in the organization's history that validate its culture and goals. Folklore reinforces a code of conduct for "how we do things around here."

- *Step Seven.* Consistent role models and consistent traits are associated with those recognized as on the fast track to promotion and success.[46]

Outcomes of Socialization

All organizations and groups socialize new members in some way, but the process can vary greatly in terms of how explicit, comprehensive, and lengthy it is. Generally, rapid socialization is advantageous. For the individual, it quickly reduces the uncertainty and anxiety surrounding the new job. For the organization, rapid socialization helps the new employee to perform

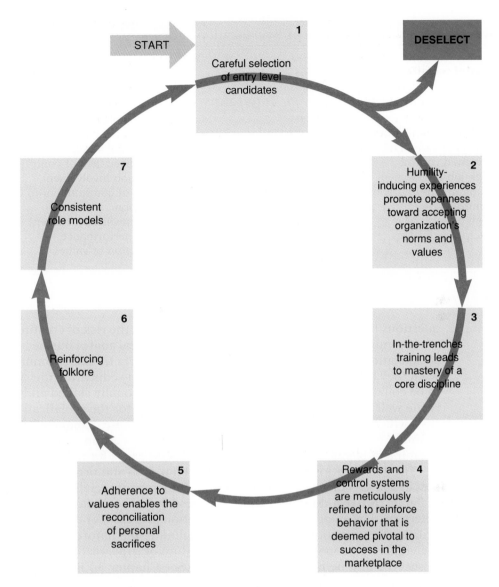

FIGURE 15.3   The Process of Organizational Socialization

Source: Adapted from R. T. Pascale, The Paradox of "Corporate Culture": Reconciling Ourselves to Socialization. *California Management Review,* Winter 1985, 38.

at an acceptable level more quickly. Organizations with strong cultures may
be particularly skillful at socializing individuals. If the culture is effective,
the socialization process will contribute to organizational success. However, if the culture needs changing, a strong socialization process reduces
the prospects for making the needed changes.

Some additional dilemmas are created by strong socialization. For example, business schools are concerned with issues surrounding the socialization of their students.[47] How strong should their socialization be? Does
the business school want students to think alike, at least in terms of a
certain level of logic and intelligent analysis? To have the same appropriate
values and sense of professionalism? In some sense, the answer to these

---

TABLE 15.7   Possible Outcomes of Socialization Process

Successful socialization is reflected in	Unsuccessful socialization is reflected in
• Job satisfaction	• Job dissatisfaction
• Role clarity	• Role ambiguity and conflict
• High work motivation	• Low work motivation
• Understanding of culture, perceived control	• Misunderstanding, tension, perceived lack of control
• High job involvement	• Low job involvement
• Commitment to organization	• Lack of commitment to organization
• Tenure	• Absenteeism, turnover
• High performance	• Low performance
• Internalized values	• Rejection of values

---

questions has to be yes. Yet, oversocialization runs the risk of creating rigid, narrow-minded corporate men and women. The ideal goal of business school socialization, then, is perhaps to develop independent thinkers committed to what they believe to be right, while at the same time educating the students to be collaborative team players who are interpersonally skilled and able to relate well to others. These goals pose a challenge for the socialization process, which, in order to be effective, must balance these demands. While the example here has been the business school, to a certain extent the same dilemma of balance in the socialization process exists for all organizations.

The socialization process may affect employee and organizational success in a variety of ways.[48] Some possible outcomes of socialization are listed in Table 15.7. We do not intend to suggest that these outcomes are solely determined by an organization's socialization process. For example, job satisfaction is a function of many things, including the nature of the task, the individual's personality and needs, the nature of supervision, opportunities to succeed and be rewarded, and so on. (See Chapter 3.) Rather, the point here is that successful socialization may contribute to job satisfaction, whereas unsuccessful socialization may contribute to dissatisfaction.

SUMMARY

Organizational culture is the pattern of beliefs and expectations shared by organizational members. Culture includes behavioral norms, shared values, company philosophy, the "rules of the game" for getting along and getting things done, and ways of interacting with outsiders, such as customers. Aspects of organizational culture are manifested by cultural symbols, heroes, rites, and values.

One explanation for the development of any particular organizational culture is that it is a response to problems of external adaptation and survival and of internal integration. The formation of an organization's culture is also influenced by the culture of the larger society within which the firm must function.

The primary methods for both maintaining and changing organizational culture include (1) what managers pay attention to, measure, and control; (2) the ways managers and employees react to crises; (3) role modeling, teaching, and coaching; (4) criteria for allocating rewards; (5) criteria for recruitment to, selection and promotion within, and removal from the organization; and (6) organizational rites, ceremonies, and stories.

Organizational culture can affect employee behaviors and commitment to the organization. There is also some evidence that culture may be related to effective organizational performance, although there is no evidence that there exists a "best" organizational culture that fits all organizations, all employees, or all societies. In addition, organizational culture can affect ethical behavior by managers and employees of the firm. Managing cultural diversity is predicted to be one of the major managerial challenges of the 1990s.

Organizational socialization is the process by which new members are brought into the organization's culture. At firms having a strong culture, the socialization process is well developed and the focus of careful attention. All organizations socialize new members, but depending on how this is done, the effects could be either positive or negative in terms of job performance, satisfaction, and commitment to the organization.

Key Words and Concepts

Accountability culture	Maternalism culture
Acculturation	Organizational culture
Cultural heroes	Organizational rites and
Cultural symbols	ceremonies
Cultural values	Organizational socialization
External adaptation and survival	Participative management
High performance-high commitment work culture	Principled organizational dissent
Internal integration	Subcultures

Discussion Questions

1. Define the concept of organizational culture and provide some examples of how culture is typically manifested or revealed.

2. Identify the major influences on the formation of organizational culture.

3. Describe an organizational culture with which you are familiar. Explain how, in your opinion, the organization developed its culture.

4. List and describe the primary methods for maintaining and changing organizational cultures.

5. Discuss some constraints or limitations on cultural change.

6. Describe the methods used to maintain the culture of an organization with which you are familiar.

7. Explain the relationship between organizational culture and performance.

8. Suggest ways that an organization might use culture to increase the probability of ethical behavior and/or decrease the probability of unethical behavior by its members.

9. Discuss the issue of managing cultural diversity. Suggest ways that organizations and managers might deal with this challenge.

10. Describe the process of organizational socialization. Identify some key issues in organizational socialization.

◆ MANAGEMENT CASES AND EXERCISES

ASSESSING ETHICAL CULTURE

Think of a job you currently hold or used to have. Indicate whether you agree or disagree with the following statements about your organization. Use the scale below and write the number of your response into the space next to each question.

Completely False 1	Mostly False 2	Somewhat False 3	Somewhat True 4	Mostly True 5	Completely True 6

_____ 1. In this organization, employees are expected to follow their own personal and moral beliefs.

_____ 2. Employees are expected to do anything to further the organization's interests.

_____ 3. In this organization, employees look out for each other's welfare.

_____ 4. It is very important to strictly follow the rules and procedures of this organization.

_____ 5. In this organization, the major consideration is whether a decision violates any law or ethical codes.

_____ 6. In this organization, employees protect their own interests above other considerations.

_____ 7. An important consideration is what is best for everyone in the organization.

_____ 8. The most efficient way is always the right way in this organization.

_____ 9. In this organization, employees are always expected to do what is right for the customer and the public.

Your score

Scoring: Add questions 1, 3, 5, 7, and 9 together: _____
Reverse the scores on questions 2, 4, 6
and 8 (1 = 6, 2 = 5, 3 = 4, 4 = 3, 5 = 2, 6 = 1).
Add these scores: _____
Total: _____

Scores could range from 9 to 54 on this questionnaire. Scores of 36 and above indicate an organizational culture that tends to support or encourage ethical behavior. Scores of 28 to 35 indicate a culture that may be somewhat ambivalent with regard to ethical issues. Scores of 27 or below indicate a culture that tends to increase the probability that individuals will behave in an unethical manner.[49]

CULTURAL CHANGE AT AT&T'S GENERAL BUSINESS SYSTEMS

In recent years, AT&T has been trying to shift its strategy and culture from a service-oriented utility to a market-driven communications business. This change is largely in response to rapidly growing opportunities in the communications/information industry and followed the divestiture of its Bell operating companies. After this court-mandated reorganization, AT&T Information Systems was created as an unregulated equipment-marketing unit of AT&T. Information Systems was organized into two parts: General Business Systems, headed by newly appointed Vice-President William Buehler, which sells smaller systems at high volume, and National Business Systems, run by Robert Casale, which markets large accounts.

In attempting to create a new market-oriented corporate culture at General Business Systems, Buehler drew heavily from Tom Peters and Robert Waterman's bestseller *In Search of Excellence*. He developed and gave to his sales force a sheet of marching orders titled "What We Aspire to Be." It contained verbatim phrases from the book, such as: "customer is king"; "reward results, not process"; "staff supports the line"; and "keep it simple." This list was the only guide given the work force; there were no detailed plans or directives. Buehler stated: "I wanted the team to know from the start that this was an entrepreneurial venture, and they were to abide by these points in a way that worked best for them."

Also from the start, Buehler was highly visible. He was a charismatic leader who loved the limelight and constantly dominated meetings and conversations with his market-oriented, performance-driven message. Putting aside his family life and hobbies, Buehler began working sixteen-hour days. He traveled to all twenty-seven branches to meet his people. For many, this was the first time they had seen an AT&T vice-president. During these visits, Buehler often had lunch (for example, hoagie sandwiches) with the lowest-level staff, a radical departure from AT&T standards.

Buehler instituted a number of organizational changes to support the new culture. He reduced AT&T's endless memos and meetings and often ignored the firm's strict chain of command. He also discarded planning manuals, threw out employee tests, and put salespeople on the highest commission plan in AT&T's history. Buehler posted individual sales monthly in a prominent place in each sales office. Then, each month, he got rid of those who could not meet his tough quotas. In the first year, about one-third of the salespeople quit, were transferred, or were fired.

In moving General Business Systems to the new culture, Buehler demanded strict obedience from his team. When managers disagreed with his decisions, he often told them to support the decisions as if they were their own. He bluntly stated: "If I found one of my managers trying to sabotage any decision I made, I'd cut his neck off."

Buehler's salespeople had trouble at first picking up the new culture and achieving results. Few sales were made in the first quarter, while the more traditional National Business Systems was meeting its quota. Equally troublesome was the reception Buehler's group was getting from the rest of AT&T. He recalled: "Employees in different parts of the country enjoyed seeing us fail." About the same time, Buehler's boss and major supporter, Archie McGuill, left the company. McGuill, a former IBM executive, had been brought in to reshape AT&T's business marketing. Like Buehler, he was the antithesis of the traditional Bell manager. He was combative and performance-driven, and he encouraged his managers to be entrepreneurs. Insiders suggested that McGuill had left AT&T rather than take a lesser job because higher-ups found him difficult to control.

Shortly after McGuill's departure, General Business Systems caught "Buehler fever" and started bringing in the sales. Salespeople were exceeding quotas, and managers were growing accustomed to the new, free-wheeling culture. They began putting demands on Buehler to speed things up. He responded by guaranteeing faster delivery of equipment, streamlining the sales contract, and speeding up approval of customer designs and bids. One account executive put it: "Decisions that would have taken two years in the Bell System were made in days by Bill Buehler." The results were impressive, and the Buehler group soon out-performed its traditionally run rival, National Business Systems.

But twelve months after starting the new culture in General Business Systems, Buehler was removed from his job and transferred to an obscure planning position. This weakened the culture. Said one account executive, "We're all upset and worried that we'll lose our new culture."

There was a difference of opinion at AT&T about why Buehler lost his job. Charles Marshall, chairman of AT&T Information Systems, explained the move as a means of having small-system sales report up the same channels as the large-systems unit. To others, however, Buehler was removed because he was too threatening to the traditional AT&T culture. Despite his success, he was viewed more as a maverick than as a visionary.[50]

QUESTIONS

1. List the major issues and ideas from this chapter that appear, in one form or another, in this case.

2. Describe the old culture of General Business Systems.

3. Describe the new culture of General Business Systems.

4. Buehler seems to have "won the battle but lost the war." Suggest how this outcome might have been avoided.

References

1. Adapted from Thompson, G. Fitting the Company Culture. In T. Lee (ed.), *Managing Your Career*. New York: Dow Jones & Company, 1990, 16.
2. Kilmann, R. H. Corporate Culture. *Psychology Today*, April 1985, 63.
3. Gordon, G. G. Industry Determinants of Organizational Culture. *Academy of Management Review*, 1991, *16*, 396–415; Kilmann, R. H., Saxton, M. J., and Serpa, R. Introduction: Five Key Issues in Understanding and Changing Culture. In R. H. Kilmann et al., *Gaining Control of the Corporate Culture*. San Francisco: Jossey-Bass, 1985, 5.
4. Schein, E. H. *Organizational Culture and Leadership*. San Francisco: Jossey-Bass, 1985, 6.
5. This perspective as well as descriptions of the following key words are based on Hofstede, G., Neuijen, B., Ohayv, D. D., and Sanders, G. Measuring Organizational Cultures: A Qualitative and Quantitative Study across Twenty Cases. *Administrative Science Quarterly*, 1990, *35*, 286–316. See also Rentsch, J. R. Climate and Culture: Interaction and Qualitative Differences in Organizational Meanings. *Journal of Applied Psychology*, 1990, *75*, 668–681.
6. Trice, H. M., and Beyer, J. M. Using Six Organizational Rites to Change Culture. In Kilmann et al., *Gaining Control of the Corporate Culture*, 372.
7. Duncan, W. J. Organizational Culture: "Getting a Fix" on an Elusive Concept. *Academy of Management Executive*, 1989, *3*, 229–236.
8. Schein, E. H. How Culture Forms, Develops, and Changes. In Kilmann et al., *Gaining Control of the Corporate Culture*, 17–43; Schein, *Organizational Culture and Leadership*; Schein, E. H. Organizational Culture. *American Psychologist*, 1990, *45*, 109–119.

9. DeFrank, R. S., Matteson, M. T., Schweiger, D. M., and Ivancevich, J. M. The Impact of Culture on the Management Practices of American and Japanese CEOs. *Organizational Dynamics*, Spring 1985, 62–76; Doktor, R. H. Asian and American CEOs: A Comparative Study. *Organizational Dynamics*, Winter 1990, 46–56.
10. Evans, P. A. L. Organizational Development in the Transnational Enterprize. In R. W. Woodman and W. A. Pasmore (eds.), *Research in Organizational Change and Development*, vol. 3. Greenwich, Conn.: JAI Press, 1989, 1–38; Gray, B. Building Interorganizational Alliances: Planned Change in a Global Environment. In W. A. Pasmore and R. W. Woodman (eds.), *Research in Organizational Change and Development*, vol. 4. Greenwich, Conn.: JAI Press, 1990, 101–140.
11. Based on Kirkbride, P. S., and Chaw, S. W. The Cross-Cultural Transfer of Organizational Cultures: Two Case Studies of Corporate Mission Statements. *Asia Pacific Journal of Management*, 1987, *5*, 55–66; Jackofsky, E. F., Slocum, J. W., Jr., and McQuaid, S. J. Cultural Values and the CEO: Alluring Companions? *Academy of Management Executive*, 1988, *2*, 39–49.
12. The description of these methods is based on Schein, *Organizational Culture and Leadership*, 223–243; Schein, Organizational Culture.
13. O'Reilly, C. R. Corporations, Culture, and Commitment: Motivation and Social Control in Organizations. *California Management Review*, Summer 1989, 9–25.
14. See, for example, Kerr, J., and Slocum, J. W., Jr. Managing Corporate Culture through Reward Systems. *Academy of Management Executive*, 1987, *1*, 99–108; Sethia, N. K., and Von Glinow,

M. A. Arriving at Four Cultures by Managing the Reward System. In Kilmann et al., *Gaining Control of the Corporate Culture*, 400–420.

15. Beyer, J. M., and Trice, H. M. How an Organization's Rites Reveal Its Culture. *Organizational Dynamics*, Spring 1987, 15.

16. Boje, D. M. The Storytelling Organization: A Study of Story Performance in an Office-Supply Firm. *Administrative Science Quarterly*, 1991, *36*, 106–126.

17. Dumaine, B. Creating a New Company Culture. *Fortune*, January 15, 1990, 127–131.

18. Drucker, P. F. Don't Change Corporate Culture—Use It! *Wall Street Journal*, March 28, 1991, A14. See also Fitzgerald, T. H. Can Change in Organizational Culture Really Be Managed? *Organizational Dynamics*, Autumn 1988, 5–15.

19. Deal, T. E., and Kennedy, A. A. *Corporate Cultures: The Rites and Rituals of Corporate Life*. Reading, Mass.: Addison-Wesley, 1982, 107–108.

20. Duncan, Organizational Culture: "Getting A Fix" on an Elusive Concept.

21. See, for example, Bate, P. Using the Culture Concept in an Organization Development Setting. *Journal of Applied Behavioral Science*, 1990, *26*, 83–106; Woodman, R. W. Organizational Change and Development: New Arenas for Inquiry and Action. *Journal of Management*, 1989, *15*, 205–228.

22. Dumaine, Creating a New Company Culture, 128.

23. Based on Shaw, J. B., Fisher, C. D., and Randolph, W. A. From Maternalism to Accountability: The Changing Cultures of Ma Bell and Mother Russia. *Academy of Management Executive*, 1991, *5*(1), 1–19.

24. See, for example, Deal and Kennedy, *Corporate Cultures: The Rites and Rituals of Corporate Life*; Peters, T. J., and Austin, N. *A Passion for Excellence*. New York: Random House, 1985; Peters, T. J., and Waterman, R. H. *In Search of Excellence*. New York: Harper & Row, 1982.

25. O'Reilly, Corporations, Culture, and Commitment: Motivation and Social Control in Organizations.

26. Denison, D. R. Bringing Corporate Culture to the Bottom Line. *Organizational Dynamics*, Autumn 1984, 5–22.

27. Cameron, K. S., and Freeman, S. J. Cultural Congruence, Strength, and Type: Relationships to Effectiveness. In R. W. Woodman and W. A. Pasmore (eds.), *Research in Organizational Change and Development*, vol. 5. Greenwich, Conn.: JAI Press, 1991, 23–58.

28. Hitt, M. A., and Ireland, R. D. Peters and Waterman Revisited: The Unended Quest for Excellence. *Academy of Management Executive*, 1987, *1*, 91–98.

29. Sherwood, J. J. Creating Work Cultures with Competitive Advantage. *Organizational Dynamics*, Winter 1988, 5–27.

30. Martin, J., and Siehl, C. Organizational Culture and Counterculture: An Uneasy Symbiosis. *Organizational Dynamics*, Autumn 1983, 52–64.

31. See, for example, Murphy, P. E. Creating Ethical Corporate Structures. *Sloan Management Review*, Winter 1989, 81–87; Reilly, B. J., and Myroslaw, J. K. Ethical Business and the Ethical Person. *Business Horizons*, November-December, 1990, 23–27; Trevino, L. Ethical Decision Making in Organizations: A Person-Situation Interactionist Model. *Academy of Management Review*, 1986, *11*, 601–617.

32. Trevino, L. K. A Cultural Perspective on Changing and Developing Organizational Ethics. In W. A. Pasmore and R. W. Woodman (eds.), *Research in Organizational Change and Development*, vol. 4. Greenwich, Conn.: JAI Press, 1990, 195.

33. Adapted from Welles, C. What Led Beech-Nut Down the Road to Disgrace. *Business Week*, February 22, 1988, 124–128.

34. Graham, J. W. Principled Organizational Dissent: A Theoretical Essay. In B. M. Staw and L. L. Cummings (eds.), *Research in Organizational Behavior*, vol. 8. Greenwich, Conn.: JAI Press, 1986, 2.

35. Intervention strategies and examples are based on Nielsen, R. P. Changing Unethical Organizational Behavior. *Academy of Management Executive*, 1989, *3*, 123–130.

36. Miceli, M. P., and Near, J. P. The Incidence of Wrongdoing, Whistle-Blowing, and Retaliation: Results of a Naturally Occurring Field Experiment. *Employee Responsibilities and Rights Journal*, 1989, *2*, 91–108; Near, J. P., and Miceli, M. P. Whistle-Blowers in Organizations: Dissidents or Reformers? In L. L. Cummings and B. M. Staw (eds.), *Research in Organizational Behavior*, vol. 9. Greenwich, Conn.: JAI Press, 1987, 321–368.

37. Drake, B. H., and Drake, E. Ethical and Legal Aspects of Managing Corporate Cultures. *California Management Review*, Winter 1988, 120–121.

38. Bhide, A., and Stevenson, H. H. Why Be Honest If Honesty Doesn't Pay? *Harvard Business Review*, September-October 1990, 121–129.

39. Cox, T. The Multicultural Organization. *Academy of Management Executive*, 1991, *5*(2), 34–47.

40. Thomas, R. R. From Affirmative Action to Affirming Dignity. *Harvard Business Review*, March-April 1990, 107–117.

41. Adapted from Goldstein, J., and Leopold, M. Corporate Culture versus Ethnic Culture. *Personnel Journal*, November 1990, 83.

42. Cox, The Multicultural Organization, 35.

43. Thomas, From Affirmative Action to Affirming Dignity, 113.

44. Goldstein and Leopold, Corporate Culture versus Ethnic Culture, 83–92.

45. Baum, H. S. *Organizational Membership*. Albany: State University of New York Press, 1990, 59–74; Hall, D. T. Careers and Socialization. *Journal of Management*, 1987, *13*, 302.

46. Pascale, R. The Paradox of "Corporate Culture": Reconciling Ourselves to Socialization. *California Management Review,* Winter 1985, 29–33.

47. See, for example, Leavitt, H. J. Socializing Our MBAs: Total Immersion? Managed Culture? Brainwashing? *Selections,* Winter 1991, 1–13.

48. Allen, N. J., and Meyer, J. P. Organizational Socialization Tactics: A Longitudinal Analysis of Links to Newcomer's Commitment and Role Orientation. *Academy of Management Journal,* 1990, *33,* 847–858; Jones, G. R. Socialization Tactics, Self-Efficacy, and Newcomers' Adjustments to Organizations. *Academy of Management Journal,*
1986, *29,* 262–279; Van Maanen, J., and Schein, E. H. Toward a Theory of Organizational Socialization. In B. M. Staw (ed.), *Research in Organizational Behavior,* vol. 1. Greenwich, Conn.: JAI Press, 1979, 209–264; Wanous, J. P. *Organizational Entry.* Reading, Mass.: Addison-Wesley, 1980.

49. Adapted from Cullen, J. B., Victor, B., and Stephens, C. An Ethical Weather Report: Assessing the Organization's Ethical Climate. *Organizational Dynamics,* Autumn 1989, 56.

50. Cummings, T. G., and Huse, E. F. *Organization Development and Change,* 4th ed. St. Paul: West, 1989, 430–431. Reprinted with permission.

CHAPTER 16

POWER AND POLITICAL BEHAVIOR

LEARNING OBJECTIVES

When you have finished studying this chapter, you should be able to:

- Explain the concepts of organizational power and organizational politics.
- Identify five interpersonal sources of power.
- Describe four major categories of structural and situational sources of power.
- Discuss effective and ineffective uses of power.
- Diagnose the personal and situational factors that contribute to the occurrence of political behavior.
- Explain why political behavior is not necessarily undesirable.
- Identify some personality dimensions that are related to political behavior.

OUTLINE

CEOS REPORT A SHIFT IN POWER

U.S. CEOs see major changes occurring in who has power in their organizations and how that power is used. According to results from a survey of 216 top executives of the largest corporations, formerly powerful headquarters staffs have been reduced in size, and their power has shrunk. Louis Pepper, CEO of Washington Mutual Savings Bank in Seattle, states: "The headquarters staff, at one point, were running the entire show. That power has been diminished to allow more of management to become involved." The corporate hierarchy has been flattened and layers of management reduced as well. One result has been to push decision making lower in the organization. Consequently, the majority of CEOs surveyed report that middle management's power has increased.

In comparing the balance of power between their organization and their customers, these CEOs say that customer power is growing. In response, Square D, an electrical equipment manufacturer, has reorganized to give employees who deal with customers greater autonomy and power, says Jerry Stead, CEO. In addition, CEOs must listen more to their board of directors, which increasingly contain more outside representatives. The majority of these CEOs report that their boards are more powerful than they were five years ago.

The CEOs agree that consensus building characterizes their management style. Compared to the traditional, more autocratic or "imperial" CEO, 74 percent of these CEOs describe themselves as more participatory, more consensus-oriented, and relying more on communication skills than on "command and control." Harry Todd, CEO of Rohr Industries, says, "No more one-man band. We're all group-oriented." This theme was echoed by Vincent Sarni of PPG Industries, who describes the new style of successful CEOs as team-oriented and participatory. In this view, CEOs should set a strategic direction, get employees to agree, give them resources and authority, and leave them alone.

Indeed, these powerful corporate heads agree that personality and leadership skills are the most important sources of power in the organization today. The exercise of control has become less important than the exercise of leadership. Reuben Mark, CEO of Colgate-Palmolive, sums up the new power-sharing philosophy: "The more [power] you have, the less you should use. You consolidate and build power by empowering others." In terms of power, these CEOs argue that staff is down, tyranny is out, and the customer and middle manager are king.[1]

In this chapter, we focus on power and political behavior in organizations. People often are uncomfortable discussing the concepts of power and organizational politics. Both terms carry emotional, often negative, implications. We argue that this should not be the case; these labels are simply descriptive terms that apply to certain aspects of the behavior of people in organizations. Managers and employees need to understand power and political behavior in order to fully understand organizational behavior.

Certainly, political behavior can be unproductive for the organization, and people can use power in unfair or harmful ways. Managers must try to avoid these outcomes, but they cannot change reality by refusing to accept the existence of power differences or political behavior. We will discuss the nature of power, the sources of power in organizations, and the effective and ineffective uses of power. We will also explore political behavior in organizations and some relationships between personality and political behavior.

THE NATURE OF POWER

Power is the capacity to influence the behavior of others.[2] We can use the term *power* in referring to individuals, groups, organizations, and countries. For example, a certain group or department within an organization might be labeled as powerful, which suggests that it has the ability to influence the behavior of individuals in other groups or departments. This influence may affect resource allocations, goal setting, hiring decisions, or many other outcomes and behaviors in the organization.

People continually attempt to influence the behavior of others in the normal course of everyday living. For example, people quite naturally attempt to *reinforce* the pleasing or satisfying behaviors of family members and friends. Likewise—and often without conscious awareness—people fail to reinforce or even attempt to *punish* undesirable behaviors. The behavior of people at work is no different.

Power is a *social* term; that is, an individual has power in relation to other people, a group has power in relation to other groups, and so on. The concept of power characterizes interactions among people—more than one person must be involved for the concept to apply. Further, power is never absolute or unchanging. It is a dynamic relationship that changes as situations and individuals change. For example, a manager may have a strong influence on the behavior of one subordinate and, at the same time, have only marginal influence with another. Managers may be very powerful with respect to their own subordinates but unable to influence the behavior of employees in other departments. In addition, relationships change with time. Last month's successful influence attempt may fail tomorrow, even though the same people are involved in both situations. Therefore, understanding power relationships requires specifying the situation and individuals involved.

The terms *power* and *authority*, while closely related, do not mean exactly the same thing. **Authority** is power legitimated through (1) being formally granted by the organization and (2) being accepted by employees as being right and proper.[3] The most obvious organizational example is the superior-subordinate relationship. An organization has a formal authority structure with individuals, groups, departments, and so on being charged with responsibility for certain activities and functions. When individuals join an organization, they generally recognize the authority structure as legitimate; that is, employees accept the manager's right to set policy and give orders and directives. So long as these orders are reasonable and related to the job, employees generally obey them. Authority is narrower in scope than power and applies to fewer behaviors in an organization.

In addition to perceived authority, there are many other possible reasons for the ability of an individual or group to influence the behavior of other people in an organization. In general, power sources in an organization can be categorized as (1) interpersonal and (2) structural and situational, as shown in Figure 16.1. We can identify both of these categories of power in the Across Cultures description of Japanese CEOs.

INTERPERSONAL SOURCES OF POWER

Many studies of power in organizations have focused on interpersonal relationships between manager and subordinates or leader and followers.[4] French and Raven identified five interpersonal sources of power: reward power, coercive power, legitimate power, expert power, and referent power.[5] We introduced you to these concepts in Chapter 12, discussing them in the context of a leader's ability to influence the behavior of followers. Here, we explore these sources of power in a broader organizational context.

Reward Power

Reward power is an individual's ability to influence others' behavior by rewarding their desirable behavior. For example, to the extent that subordinates value rewards that the manager can give—praise, promotions, money, time off, and so on—they may comply with requests and orders. A manager who controls the allocation of merit pay raises in a department has reward power over the employees in that department. Employees may comply with some influence attempts by others because they expect to be rewarded for compliance.

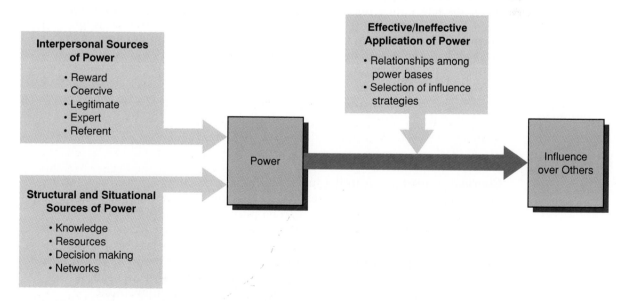

FIGURE 16.1   Sources of Power in Organizations

POWER AND THE JAPANESE CEO

 Japanese CEOs have sometimes been portrayed as powerless. This observation is based on a misunderstanding of the bottom-up decision-making processes common in large Japanese organizations. The assumption is that the complex proposal (*ringi*) system relegates the Japanese CEO to a role of rubber stamping decisions collectively agreed to at lower levels of the organization.

Contrary to this view, many observers think that Japanese CEOs wield forceful influence over their organizations. This influence is derived both from the personal power of the CEO and his position in the firm, as indicated by Figure 16.2.

It is the responsibility of a Japanese CEO to preside over the top management team (whose members are called *torishimariyaku*). This group of *torishimariyaku* are the environmental scanners, the strategy formulators, and the policy implementers of the organization. CEOs are thus at the center of the most powerful group in the organization. Often, they personally control both the frequency and agenda of top-management team meetings, as well as the selection of new *torishimariyaku*. In addition, most large Japanese firms are members of industrial groups characterized by complex overlapping ownership and a strong sense of community.

These industrial groups have "president's clubs" that serve as a decision-making body for each group. Many of the most important contacts in the industrial group thus occur at the CEO level. The Japanese CEO serves as the primary link between the individual firm and the industrial group and is in a powerful position in terms of access to external resources and influence. The position power of the Japanese CEO is solidified by organizational and societal norms that emphasize and reinforce hierarchical relationships, respect for authority, and so on.

The personal power of Japanese CEOs resides in the expert and charismatic influence developed through the human resources management practices of Japanese organizations. Through slow promotion practices, extensive job rotation (which broadens knowledge), and intensive on-the-job training, Japanese managers acquire considerable expertise as they advance through the company. Those receiving promotions are widely viewed as legitimate recipients of greater authority. A second source of personal power is the CEO's social network (*jimmyaku*). This far-reaching network, too, is a product of Japanese human resources practices. For example, the policy of job rotation gives interpersonally skillful managers an opportunity to establish broad networks of acquaintances both inside and outside of the organization.[6]

continued

Coercive Power

Coercive power is an individual's ability to influence others' behavior by means of punishment for undesirable behavior. For example, subordinates may comply because they expect to be punished for failure to respond favorably to managerial influence attempts. Punishment may take the form of reprimands, undesirable work assignments, closer supervision, tighter enforcement of work rules, suspension without pay, and the like. The ultimate punishment, from the organization's perspective, is firing the employee—which organizations euphemistically prefer to call "outplacement."

Recall from Chapter 6, however, that punishment can have undesirable side effects. The employee who receives an official reprimand for shoddy

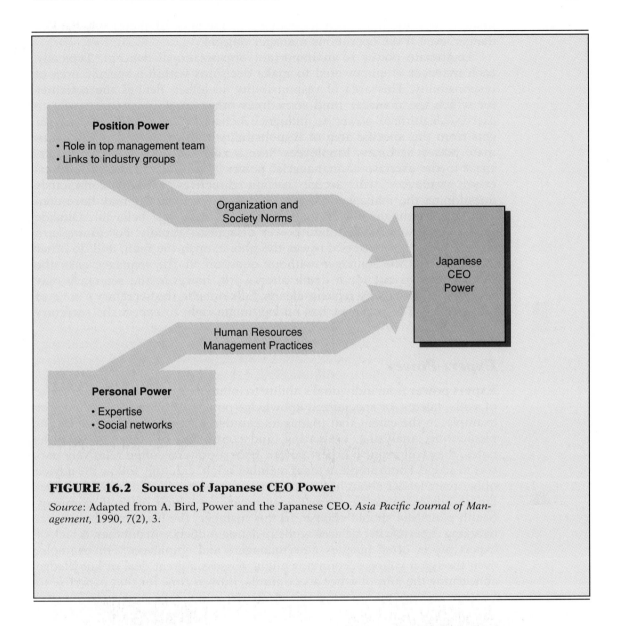

FIGURE 16.2   Sources of Japanese CEO Power

Source: Adapted from A. Bird, Power and the Japanese CEO. *Asia Pacific Journal of Management*, 1990, 7(2), 3.

work, for example, may find ways (other than the obvious one the organization wants) to avoid the punishment, such as by refusing to perform the task, falsifying performance reports, or being absent frequently.

Legitimate Power

Legitimate power most frequently refers to a manager's ability to influence subordinates' behavior because of the manager's position in the organizational hierarchy. Subordinates may respond to managerial influence attempts because they acknowledge the manager's legitimate right to prescribe certain behaviors. Sometimes nonmanagerial employees might possess legitimate power. For example, a safety inspector might have legitimate power to shut down a production operation if there is imminent danger, even if the operations manager objects.

Legitimate power is an important organizational concept. Typically, each manager is empowered to make decisions within a specific area of responsibility. This area of responsibility, in effect, defines the activities for which the manager (and sometimes other employees) can expect to exercise legitimate power to influence behavior. The farther a manager gets from this specific area of responsibility, the weaker his or her legitimate power becomes. Employees have a **zone of indifference** with respect to the exercise of managerial power.[7] Within the zone of indifference, employees will accept certain directives without consciously questioning the manager's power, and thus, the manager may have considerable legitimate power to influence subordinates' behavior. Outside this zone, however, legitimate power disappears rapidly. For example, a secretary will type letters, answer the phone, open the mail, and do other like tasks for the manager without question. If the manager asks the secretary to go out for a drink after work, however, the secretary may refuse. The manager's request clearly falls outside the secretary's zone of indifference. The manager has no legitimate right to expect the secretary to comply.

Expert Power

Expert power is an individual's ability to influence others' behavior because of skills, talents, or specialized knowledge possessed by the individual. For example, to the extent that managers can demonstrate competence in implementing, analyzing, evaluating, and controlling the tasks of subordinates, they will acquire expert power. Expert power is often relatively narrow in scope. For example, a team member might carefully follow the advice of her team leader about how to program a numerically controlled lathe yet ignore advice from the team leader regarding which of three company health plans she should choose. In this instance, the team member is recognizing expertise in one area while resisting influence in another. A lack of expert power often plagues new managers and employees. For example, even though a young accountant might possess a great deal of knowledge concerning the jobs of other accountants, it takes time for that expertise to become known and accepted.

Referent Power

Referent power is an individual's ability to influence others' behavior as a result of being liked or admired. For example, subordinates' identification with a manager often forms the basis for referent power. This identification may include the desire of the subordinates to emulate the manager. A young manager may copy the leadership style of an older, admired, and more experienced manager. The older manager thus has some ability—some referent power—to influence the behavior of the younger manager. Referent power usually is associated with individuals who possess admired personality characteristics, charisma, or a good reputation. Thus, it is often associated with political leaders, movie stars, sports figures, or other well-known individuals (hence their use in advertising to influence buying behavior). However, managers and employees can also have considerable referent power because of the strength of their personalities.

Relationships among Interpersonal Sources of Power

Managers and other employees possess varying amounts of these interpersonal sources of power. As implied by Figure 16.1, these power sources do not operate independently. A study conducted in two paper mills provides an example of how these power sources are related.[8] One of the mills dropped an incentive pay plan based on performance in favor of a pay plan based strictly on seniority. Compared with the second plant, which retained the incentive system, subordinates' perceptions of the use of various sources of power by supervisors changed noticeably in the first plant. Discontinuing the incentive plan lowered the perceived reward power of supervisors, as might be expected, but other results were more complex. Perceptions of supervisors' use of punishment increased (attributable perhaps to less control over rewards), and the perceived use of referent and legitimate power decreased. Expert power appeared to be unaffected. These findings suggest that the interpersonal sources of power that influence behavior are complex and interrelated.

In general, the way in which managers and other employees use one type of power can either enhance or limit the effectiveness of power from another source. For example, managers who administer rewards to subordinates also tend to be well-liked and seem to have greater referent power than managers who do not give out rewards. On the other hand, the use of coercive power can reduce referent power. The explanation seems to be that the threatened or actual use of punishment reduces liking or admiration, leading to a reduction in referent power. Further, employees often view managers who possess knowledge valuable to them as having greater legitimate power in addition to expert power.

These five sources of interpersonal power can be divided into two broad categories: organizational and personal. Reward power, coercive power, and legitimate power have organizational bases; that is, top managers can give to or take away from lower-level managers or other key employees the right to administer rewards and punishments. The organization can change employees' legitimate power by changing their positions in the formal authority hierarchy or by changing job descriptions, rules, and procedures. Referent power and expert power, however, depend much more on personal characteristics—personalities, leadership styles, and knowledge brought to the job. In the long run, the organization may influence expert power by, for example, making additional training available. However, the individuals determine how they use that training—the extent to which the new knowledge is applied. In summary, some sources of interpersonal power to influence employee behavior are under the direct control of the organization, and other sources depend more on the personal characteristics of the individual. In the survey described in the Preview Case, CEOs reported that these personal sources of power (expert and referent power) were more important than the organizational sources (legitimate, reward, and coercive power).

STRUCTURAL AND SITUATIONAL SOURCES OF POWER

Much of the attention directed toward power in organizations has tended to focus on hierarchical relationships, that is, the power of managers over subordinates. This power is important, but it is not the only dimension of power. Another perspective is that power is determined, in part, by many aspects of the situation, including the design of the organization, the type of departmental structure, the opportunity to influence, access to powerful individuals and critical resources, the nature of the position an individual holds, and so on.[9] For example, the power associated with a particular position or job is affected by its visibility to upper management and its importance or relevance with respect to the organization's goals or priorities. Table 16.1 contains some examples of position characteristics that determine relative power within the organization. Note that whereas the legitimate power previously discussed applies primarily to managerial positions, the characteristics described in Table 16.1 are relevant for both managerial and nonmanagerial positions.

In general, structural and situational sources of power are created by the division of labor and departmentalization, which naturally result in unequal access to information, resources, decision making, and other individuals and groups. Any of an almost infinite variety of specific situational factors could become a source of power in an organization. We will discuss

TABLE 16.1 Position Characteristics Associated with Power

Characteristic	Definition	Example
Centrality	Relationship among positions in a communication network	More-central positions will have greater power.
Criticality	Relationship among tasks performed in a work-flow process	Positions responsible for the most critical tasks will have more power.
Flexibility	Amount of discretion in decision making, work assignments, and so on	More-autonomous positions will have more power.
Visibility	Degree to which task performance is seen by higher management in the organization	More-visible positions will have more power.
Relevance	Relationship between tasks and high-priority organizational goals	Positions most closely related to important goals will have more power.

Source: Adapted from D. A. Whetten and K. S. Cameron, *Developing Managerial Skills.* Glenview, Ill.: Scott, Foresman, 1984, 259.

several major categories of these factors, including knowledge as power, resources as power, decision making as power, and networks as power.

Knowledge as Power

Organizations are information processors that must use knowledge to produce goods and services. The concept of **knowledge as power** means that individuals, groups, or departments that possess knowledge crucial to attaining the organization's goals have power. People and groups in a position to control information about current operations, develop information about alternatives, or acquire knowledge about future events and plans have enormous power to influence the behavior of others. This explains why certain staff and support activities—a data processing center, for example—sometimes seem to have influence disproportionate to their relationship to the organization's major goals and activities.

The increased use of personal computers and computerized work stations is having a dramatic impact on access to and use of information—and thus on power relationships—in many organizations. Information is more widely available to many employees. Greater access to information tends to flatten the hierarchy and make it more difficult to hoard information previously controlled by a centralized authority.

Knowledge is extremely important in most organizations. Recently, the argument has been advanced that *intellectual capital* is corporate America's most valuable asset. **Intellectual capital** represents the knowledge, know-how, and skill that exists in the organization. This intellectual capital can provide an organization with a competitive edge in the marketplace. For example, Dr. P. Roy Vagelos, the CEO of Merck & Company, states: "A low-value product can be made by anyone anywhere. When you have knowledge no one else has access to—that's dynamite." In the annual *Fortune* Magazine poll, Merck was voted the most admired U.S. company five years in a row and has invented more new medicines than any other U.S. pharmaceutical company.[10]

If managers or other professionals seriously lack the ability to use knowledge competently, they may have little effective power. In other words, organizational power from other sources can be destroyed or wasted if managers or employees do not understand the importance and correct use of information.

Resources as Power

Organizations need a variety of resources to survive, including human resources, money, equipment, materials, supplies, customers, and so on. The importance of specific resources to a firm's success and the difficulty of obtaining them vary. The concept of **resources as power** suggests that departments, groups, or individuals who can provide critical or difficult-to-obtain resources acquire power in the organization. Which resources are the most important depends on the situation, the organization's goals, the economic climate, and the goods or services being produced. The old saying that "he who has the gold makes the rules" sums up the idea that resources are power.

Decision Making as Power

Decisions in organizations often are made sequentially, with many individuals or groups participating (see Chapter 19). This decision-making process creates additional power differences among groups or individuals. The concept of **decision making as power** means that individuals or groups acquire power to the extent that they can affect some part of the decision-making process. They might influence the goals being developed, premises being used in making a decision (for example, estimates of resource availability), alternatives being considered, outcomes being projected, and so on. For example, a task force charged with studying a problem and making recommendations for action may have a great deal of power. Even if the task force is not going to make the final decision, it may control the consideration of possible solutions. A powerful machine politician in New York City is reputed to have said, "I don't care who does the electing, as long as I have the power to do the nominating."

The ability to influence the decision-making process is a subtle and often overlooked source of power. Decision-making power does not necessarily reside with the final decision maker in an organization or in society. For example, Southern California Edison uses a technique known as *scenario planning* to develop strategic plans for the future of the electric utility.[11] Scenario planners might look ahead ten years and develop a dozen possible versions of the future—another Middle East oil crisis, heightened environmental concerns, an economic boom in southern California, a major recession, and so on. Each scenario has implications for needed electricity generation capacity, funds for investment, human resources, and the like. Most observers would agree that the individuals and departments involved in scenario planning at Edison wield considerable influence, regardless of whether they make the final decisions regarding resource allocations.

Networks as Power

The existence of structural and situational power depends not only on access to information, resources, and decision making but also on the ability to get cooperation in carrying out tasks. Managers and departments need connecting links with other individuals and departments in the organization in order to be effective, as suggested by Figure 16.3. Traditional superior-subordinate relationships (shown vertically in Figure 16.3) are important aspects of power. In addition, the horizontal linkages provided by networks and coalitions are a major factor in understanding power differences. The concept of **networks as power** implies that various affiliations and coalitions, both inside and outside the organization, represent sources of power. For example, power is provided by the following connecting links, each of which relates to factors already discussed:

- *Information links.* To be effective, managers and employees must be "in the know" in both the formal and informal sense (knowledge is power).
- *Supply links.* Influence outward, over others and the environment, means that managers or other key professionals can bring in what

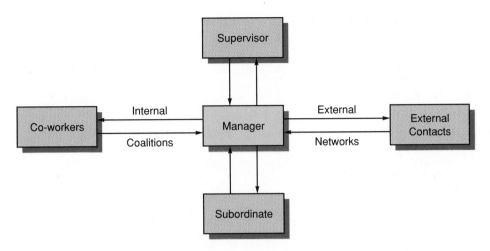

FIGURE 16.3 **Work Relationships and Power**

Source: Adapted from B. R. Ragins and F. Sundstrom, Gender and Power in Organizations: A Longitudinal Perspective. *Psychological Bulletin,* 1989, *105,* 65.

their own organizational domain needs, such as materials, money, resources to distribute as rewards, and perhaps even prestige (resources are power).

Support links. In a formal sense, a manager's job must allow for decision-making discretion—the exercise of judgment. Managers must know that they can make decisions and assume innovative, risk-taking activities without each decision or action having to go through a stifling, multilayered approval process. In an informal sense, managers and other professionals need the backing of other important figures in the organization, whose tacit approval becomes another resource they bring to their own work unit (participation in decision making is power and an important indicator of support links).[12]

The notion of networks as power is captured by the following In Practice description of a purchasing department threatened with the loss of its role in the organization.

IN PRACTICE

THE PURCHASING DEPARTMENT

At a small electronics firm in the Southwest, the purchase of components and raw materials had been centralized and delegated to a purchasing department. This department had developed procedures to select vendors and evaluate their quality, as well as to ensure that price and quality control standards were met. The manufacturing operation within the firm used the purchasing department to obtain necessary supplies. Over time, conflict developed between the two departments. Manufacturing was most concerned about having enough materials of high enough quality on a timely basis. It was much less concerned with the cost of the materials and whether or not the suppliers had favorable or unfavorable credit terms. Manufacturing was particularly unconcerned with the bureaucratic niceties of the procurement process, the filling out of requisitions, obtaining bids, evaluating vendors, and placing of orders. Finally, manufacturing went to the president of the company and argued that it should be allowed to purchase directly. This would fulfill its requirements more satisfactorily and also permit the corporation to save money by eliminating the purchasing department.

Having gone through the process of establishing relationships with certain vendors for various supply requirements, the purchasing department had developed close and at times personal ties with these vendors. The vendors could not be sure that if the purchasing process were changed, they would still be able to generate the same volume of business. In addition, they had grown accustomed to the procedures and people in purchasing. To change procedures and develop a new set of relationships would be time-consuming and uncertain. Thus, an external network composed of those currently selling to the firm was there to be mobilized against the change manufacturing was seeking.

The purchasing personnel informed the current vendors about what was going on within the firm. Purchasing implied that if manufacturing took over the ordering, the same business relationships likely would not be maintained. The various vendors then wrote to the president of the firm, noting that the procedures and practices followed by the purchasing department in this firm and by similar departments in other firms enabled the vendors to plan production rates, quality standards, and specifications for their product. If the electronics firm were to use another purchasing process, it was possible that order delivery, product reliability, and willingness to work with the firm might be harmed. Input quality and delivery were important factors in controlling manufacturing costs and in ensuring product quality. Thus, rather than risk offending these necessary and powerful suppliers for the sole reason of satisfying a single department within the firm, the president maintained the present organizational arrangements. The future of purchasing was secure, and the department had more power than before when dealing with manufacturing.[13]

The Power of Lower-Level Employees

Although we commonly think of power as something that managers have, lower-level employees may wield considerable power as well.[14] For example, some sources of interpersonal power—expert power, in particular— may allow subordinates to influence their managers. While lower-level employees may have some interpersonal power, their ability to influence others' behavior more likely stems from structural or situational sources.

Figure 16.4 suggests that the power of lower-level employees is a result of their positions in the organization. When in certain positions, they may be able to control access to information or resources, as well as important aspects of the decision-making process. In addition, networks or affiliations with powerful individuals or groups may be a source of their power. Further, the expertise of employees and the amount of effort expended also

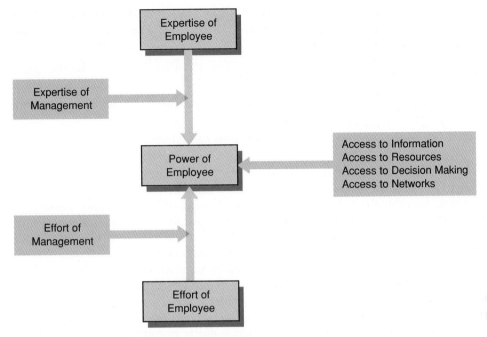

FIGURE 16.4   Model of Lower-Level Employee Power

influence the extent of their power. As Figure 16.4 illustrates, whether expertise and effort increase employees' power depends, in part, on their superior's expertise and effort. For example, if an employee's manager has little knowledge about a certain task and the employee has considerable knowledge, the relative power of the employee increases. Employees also can acquire power by expending effort in areas where management puts little effort.

INFLUENCE STRATEGIES: THE EFFECTIVE USE OF POWER

When managers or employees face a situation in which they wish to influence the behavior of others, they must decide which of various strategies may be effective. There is considerable interest in identifying effective influence strategies and understanding the situations where each might be used.[15] For example, managers from firms in England, Australia, and the United States were surveyed to measure the ways in which they try to influence their superiors and their subordinates. The study examined the following seven influence strategies:

- *Assertiveness*—the use of a direct and forceful approach.
- *Bargaining*—the use of negotiation through the exchange of benefits or favors.

- *Coalition*—the mobilization of other people in the organization.
- *Friendliness*—the use of impression management and flattery and the creation of goodwill.
- *Higher authority*—gaining the support of higher levels in the organization to back up requests.
- *Reason*—the use of facts and data to support the development of a logical argument.
- *Sanctions*—the use of rewards and punishments.[16]

In all three countries, the frequency with which managers used the various influence strategies was virtually identical. These results are presented in Table 16.2. When seeking to influence their superiors, managers reported that they relied most often on reason, followed by coalitions, and then by friendliness. Going over the "boss's head" or resorting to higher authority was used least often to influence superiors.

The rank order of preferred strategies was somewhat different when influencing subordinates. Once again managers reported that the most frequently used strategy was reason. Interestingly, however, the second most popular strategy was assertiveness. This is not surprising—managers can logically be more aggressive when seeking compliance from subordinates than when seeking to influence their superiors. The study also identified some additional variables that affected the selection of influence strategies. The power sources that the manager has available, the goals the manager was trying to attain, and the manager's expectation of the target person's willingness to comply all entered into the selection of an influence strategy.[17]

TABLE 16.2   Relative Popularity of Influence Strategies

	When Managers Influenced Superiors*	When Managers Influenced Subordinates
Most Popular	Reason	Reason
	Coalition	Assertiveness
	Friendliness	Friendliness
to	Bargaining	Coalition
	Assertiveness	Bargaining
	Higher Authority	Higher Authority
Least Popular		Sanctions

*The strategy of sanctions is omitted in the scale that measures upward influence.

Source: D. Kipnis, S. M. Schmidt, C. Swaffin-Smith, and I. Wilkinson, Patterns of Managerial Influence: Shotgun Managers, Tacticians, and Bystanders. *Organizational Dynamics*, Winter 1984, 62.

In addition to selecting the correct influence strategy, effective influence in organizations often depends on an exchange process. The **exchange process** in power relationships is based on the "law of reciprocity"—the almost universal belief that people should be paid back for what they do.[18] For example, imagine the situation where an employee was asked by her boss to work through the weekend on an important project. The employee does so but receives no recognition, no extra time off, no extra pay—not even a "thank you." The employee later discovers that her boss took sole credit for the project, which was quite successful. This employee, and most observers, would agree that an important aspect of a good working relationship has been violated in this instance. The expectation of reciprocal exchange occurs repeatedly in organizations. In part, because people expect to be "paid back," influence becomes possible in many situations. The exchange process is particularly important in relationships, such as networks of peers or colleagues, where formal authority to compel compliance is absent. Power in the exchange process stems from the ability to offer something that others need. The metaphor of "currencies" provides a useful way to understand how the process of exchange is used to influence behavior. Many types of "currencies" are traded in organizations. Table 16.3 provides some interesting examples. Notice the similarities between these "currencies" and the sources of power previously discussed.

TABLE 16.3   Organizational Currencies Traded in the Exchange Process

Currencies	Examples
Resources	Lending or giving money, budget increases, personnel, space
Assistance	Helping with existing projects or undertaking unwanted tasks
Cooperation	Giving task support, providing quicker response time, approving a project, or aiding implementation
Information	Providing organizational or technical knowledge
Advancement	Giving a task or assignment that can aid in promotion
Recognition	Acknowledging effort, accomplishment, or abilities
Network/contacts	Providing opportunities for linking with others
Personal support	Giving personal and emotional backing

Source: Adapted from A. R. Cohen and D. L. Bradford, Influence without Authority: The Use of Alliances, Reciprocity, and Exchanges to Accomplish Work. *Organizational Dynamics*, Winter 1989, 11.

Having the *capacity* to influence (power) the behavior of others and effectively using this capacity are not the same thing. Managers who believe that they can effectively influence the behavior of others by acquiring enough power to simply order other people around are generally unsuccessful. In addition, there is considerable evidence that the ineffective use of power has many negative implications, both for the individual and the organization. For example, one study examined the consequences of over-reliance on assertiveness and persistence as an influence strategy. Managers who were very assertive and persistent with others—characterized by a refusal to take no for an answer, reliance on repeated reminders, frequent use of face-to-face confrontations, and the like—suffered a number of negative consequences. Compared to other managers studied, these aggressive managers (1) received the lowest performance evaluations, (2) earned less money, and (3) experienced the highest levels of job tension and stress.[19] The following In Practice provides another example of negative consequences from overreliance on a single influence strategy.

IN PRACTICE

INGRATIATION: THE OVERUSE OF WINING AND DINING

John Brucker, human resources director at a medium-size company, often cultivated support for new programs by taking people out to fancy restaurants for an evening of fine food and wine. He genuinely derived pleasure from entertaining, but at the same time, he created subtle obligations. One time, a new program he wanted to introduce required the agreement of William Adams, head of engineering. Adams, a long-time employee, considered Brucker's proposal as an unnecessary frill, mainly because he did not see any real benefits to the organization. Brucker responded to Adams's negative comments as he always did in such cases—by becoming more friendly and insisting that they get together for dinner. After several of these invitations, Adams became furious. Insulted by what he considered to be Brucker's attempts to buy him off, he fought even harder to kill the proposal. Not only did the program die, but Brucker lost all possibility of influencing Adams in the future. Adams saw Brucker's attempts at socializing as a sleazy and crude way of trying to soften him up. For his part, Brucker was totally puzzled by Adams's attitudes and behavior and assumed that he was against all progress. He never realized that Adams had a deep sense of integrity and a real commitment to the good of the organization. Thus, Brucker lost his opportunity to sell a program that, ironically, Adams would have found valuable, had it been implemented.[20]

The effective use of power is a difficult challenge for managers, employees, and organizations. The goal of the effective use of power is to influence the behavior of others in ways that are consistent with the needs of the organization and the needs of its members. If the use of power is not carefully managed, powerful individuals may exploit those with less power in the organization and confuse their self-interests with the legitimate interests of the organization. Managers and employees who are effective often have the following five characteristics.[21]

First, they understand the interpersonal as well as the situational and structural sources of power and the most effective methods of influencing people using these different sources. For example, professionals, such as research and development scientists, engineers, lawyers, or professors, tend to be more readily influenced by expertise than by other interpersonal sources of power. Effective managers and employees often recognize the structural and situational problems that exist in a power relationship and modify their own behavior to fit the actual situation. As a result, they tend to develop and use a wide variety of power sources and influence strategies. Some unsuccessful managers rely too much on one or a few power bases or influence strategies, as we saw in the preceding In Practice.

Second, effective managers and employees understand the nature of the exchange process underlying many successful influence attempts. They recognize that, over time, unless reciprocal exchanges are roughly equivalent and fair, hard feelings will result and the ability to influence others will be reduced.

Third, effective managers and employees understand what is and what is not legitimate behavior in acquiring and using power. The misuse or lack of understanding of a source of power can destroy its effectiveness. For example, individuals erode expert power if they attempt to draw on expertise in an area in which they do not have the required knowledge. Individuals may lose referent power by behaving in ways that are inconsistent with characteristics or traits that are attractive to others.

Fourth, effective managers and employees tend to seek positions that allow the development and use of power. In other words, they choose jobs in the mainstream of critical issues and concerns of an organization. These jobs provide opportunities for and, indeed, demand influencing the behavior of others. Successful performance in these positions, in turn, allows the managers or other employees to acquire power.

Finally, effective managers temper their use of power with maturity and self-control. They recognize that their actions influence the behaviors and lives of others. While they are not necessarily reluctant or afraid to use their power—recognizing that influencing the behavior of employees is a legitimate and necessary part of the manager's role—they nevertheless apply power carefully, in principled and fair ways that are consistent with organizational needs and goals.

Based on the above characteristics and previously described research, here are five practical suggestions for establishing influence in an organization:

- Develop a reputation as a knowledgeable person or an expert.
- Balance the time spent in each crucial work relationship according to the needs of the work, rather than out of habit or personal preferences.
- Develop a network of resource persons who can be called on for assistance.

- Choose the correct combination of influence strategies for the goals and for the target to be influenced.
- Implement influence strategies with sensitivity and flexibility, using adequate levels of communication.[22]

POLITICAL BEHAVIOR

Political behavior of individuals and groups consists of their attempts to influence the behavior of others and the course of events in the organization in order to protect their self-interests, meet their own needs, and advance their own goals. Described in this way, almost all behavior may be regarded as political. Labeling behavior as political, however, usually implies a judgment that individuals or groups are gaining something at the expense of other employees, groups, or the organization. People are often self-centered when labeling actions as political behavior. For example, employees may perceive their own behavior as defending legitimate rights or interests yet call a similar behavior by others as "playing politics."

Organizational Politics

Organizational politics involves actions by individuals or groups to acquire, develop, and use power and other resources in order to obtain preferred outcomes when there is uncertainty or disagreement about choices.[23] When people share power and differ about what must be done, many decisions and actions quite naturally will be the result of a political process. In the following In Practice, we can see the political process at work in the selection of a new CEO at Booz, Allen & Hamilton.

IN PRACTICE

PICKING A SUCCESSOR AT BOOZ, ALLEN, & HAMILTON, INC.

Booz, Allen, & Hamilton, Inc., the large New York-based management consulting firm, had a policy that top managers should step aside when they reached fifty-five years of age. Managers did not necessarily need to leave the firm or retire at fifty-five, but they were expected to return to consulting work and pass executive responsibility into younger, supposedly more energetic hands. Consequently, when he turned fifty-four, James Farley, head of Booz, Allen, proposed a plan for selecting his successor. Rather than simply handpicking a qualified successor, which, as chief executive, he might have done, Farley proposed a "winner-take-all" race among the top partners of the firm. Farley established a selection committee of fifteen partners, which he would chair. His intention was to stay out of the process and allow the committee to select his successor in a democratic fashion. The selection committee would develop a list of desirable criteria for the top job, interview prospective candidates, and gather other information about them. Farley announced that anyone interested should step forward; seven of the firm's best and brightest declared their candidacy, and the race was on.

By all accounts, it was a disaster. The intent of Farley's plan may have been to reduce organizational politics and to increase the probability that his successor would be the best person for the job. However, Farley's approach seems to have had the opposite of its intended effects. The selection process went on for ten months and was very disruptive of normal operations. Gossip was heavy, and work slowed. The open political contest pitted candidates against each other in many of the worst possible ways. One former partner was quoted as saying, "To say the process created bad feelings does not capture the essence."

The selection process at Booz, Allen is widely regarded as having resulted in producing the candidate who was least offensive to the largest number of people. The new CEO has not received high marks for subsequent performance. He immediately reorganized the company in a manner that created enormous ill-will and a large number of resignations. Booz, Allen, & Hamilton has continued to lose market share to rival consulting firms, such as McKinsey & Company.[24]

Factors that increase the probability of political behavior include disagreements over goals, unclear goals, different ideas about the organization and its problems, different information about the situation, the need to allocate scarce resources, and so on. After all, if everyone knew what was best for the organization and its employees, if resources were infinite, and if people agreed completely on goals and how to achieve them, perhaps political behavior in organizations would not occur. However, outcomes are never certain, resources are never infinite, and people must make difficult choices among competing goals and methods to attain them. Thus, political behavior will occur as employees and groups attempt to obtain their preferred outcomes. Managers should not try to prevent the inevitable—organizational politics—but rather should try to ensure that these activities do not have negative consequences for the organization.

Unfortunately, the negative labels that people commonly attach to political behavior and organizational politics can block their understanding of this crucial aspect of organizational behavior. People tend to assume that political behavior does not result in the best organizational decisions or outcomes and that somehow, by advocating their own position, individuals or groups produce inferior actions or decisions. However, political behavior is not always detrimental to an organization. For example, a study involving ninety managers in thirty organizations indicated that these managers were able to identify beneficial, as well as harmful, effects of political behavior. Beneficial effects included career advancement, recognition and status for individuals looking after their legitimate interests, and achievement of organizational goals—getting the job done—as a result of the normal political process in the organization. Harmful effects included demotions and loss of jobs for "losers" in the political process, as well as a misuse of resources and creation of an ineffective organizational culture.[25] The effect on culture may be among the most undesirable consequences of a high level of political behavior. For example, there is some evidence that organizational politics arouses anxieties that cause employees to withdraw emotionally from the organization.[26] This withdrawal, in turn, makes it very difficult to create the type of organizational culture characterized by high performance and high commitment that was described in Chapter 15.

Political behavior, then, can meet appropriate and legitimate individual and organizational needs, or it can result in negative outcomes. In any event, managers and employees must understand political behavior because it will occur. It is not possible to eliminate all political behavior—only to manage it.[27]

Occurrence of Political Behavior

Employees are often concerned about office politics. Like power, politics is a subject more often discussed than understood. People commonly agree on the existence of organizational politics. Typically, they also believe that an ideal work setting would be free from political behavior. However, this is an unattainable and probably undesirable goal. On the other hand, excessive political behavior can be detrimental to individuals, groups, and organizations. Thus, managers and employees should understand and be able to diagnose both the reasons for political behavior and where political behavior is most likely to occur in the organization.

One perspective on political behavior suggests that managers and employees are more likely to observe political behavior when (1) decision-making procedures and performance measures are highly uncertain and complex and (2) competition among individuals and groups for scarce resources is strong. Conversely, in simpler environments where decision processes are clear and competitive behavior is less, high levels of political behavior are unlikely.[28] These ideas are illustrated by Figure 16.5. Using this figure, we would have predicted that the search for James Farley's successor at Booz, Allen, & Hamilton would result in a high level of political behavior.

In one research study, 428 managers were asked to rank organizational decisions from the most to the least political.[29] They ranked decisions related to interdepartmental coordination, promotions and transfers, and delegation of authority first, second, and third, respectively. Decisions in these areas usually lack established rules and procedures and rely on subjective or ambiguous criteria. Areas the managers ranked as least political are characterized by established policies, precedents, and more objective criteria. Examples of less politically sensitive areas were human resource policies (such as vacation schedules and benefit plans), hiring, and disciplinary penalties.

A study of 123 managers in the industrial uniform industry found that these managers awarded higher merit pay raises to employees when they were more dependent on the employee's expertise. Further, perceived political connections within the organization of subordinates also had an impact on the managers' pay decisions.[30] In a similar vein, the following In Practice account describes political behavior surrounding the performance appraisal process.

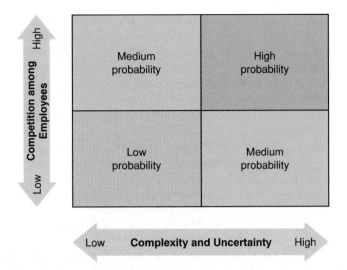

FIGURE 16.5   Probability of Political Behavior in Organizations

Source: Adapted from D. R. Beeman and T. W. Sharkey, The Use and Abuse of Corporate Politics. *Business Horizons*, March-April 1987, 27.

IN PRACTICE

THE POLITICS OF EMPLOYEE APPRAISAL

There is really no getting around the fact that whenever I evaluate one of my people, I stop and think about the impact—the ramifications of my decisions on my relationship with the guy and his future here. I'd be stupid not to. Call it being politically minded, or using managerial discretion, or fine-tuning the guy's ratings, but in the end, I've got to live with him, and I'm not going to rate a guy without thinking about the fallout. There are a lot of games played in the rating process, and whether we (managers) admit it or not, we are all guilty of playing them at our discretion.

The above statement comes from one of sixty executives that participated in in-depth interviews concerning their performance appraisal processes. These sixty executives—from seven large corporations—had performance appraisal experience in a total of 197 different companies. An analysis of over one hundred hours of tape-recorded interviews resulted in the following conclusions:

- Political considerations were nearly always part of the performance evaluation process.
- Politics played a role in the performance appraisal process because (1) executives took into consideration the daily interpersonal dynamics between them and their subordinates; (2) the formal appraisal process results in a permanent written document; and (3) the formal appraisal can have considerable impact on the subordinate's career and advancement.

In addition, these executives believed there was usually a justifiable reason for generating appraisal ratings that were less than accurate. Overall, they felt it was within their managerial discretion to do so. Thus, the findings suggest that the formal appraisal process is indeed a political process and that few ratings are determined without some political consideration.

Perhaps the most interesting finding from the study (because it debunks a popular belief) is that accuracy is *not* the primary concern of these practicing executives when appraising subordinates. Their main concern is how best to use the appraisal process to motivate and reward subordinates. Hence, managerial discretion and effectiveness, not accuracy, are the real goals. Managers made it clear that they would not allow excessively accurate ratings to cause problems for themselves and that they attempted to use the appraisal process to their own advantage.[31]

Decisions in some areas can be made less political by adopting such strategies as increasing the resources available (thus reducing conflict over scarce resources) or by making the decisions seem less important than they really are. However, strategies to reduce the political behavior associated with organizational decisions may have some unintended consequences, which translate into real costs for the firm. Table 16.4 shows examples of strategies used to avoid organizational politics and the potential costs associated with each strategy.

TABLE 16.4   Strategies for Avoiding the Use of Political Behavior in Decision Making and Their Possible Costs

Strategy	Costs
Slack or excess resources, including additional administrative positions	Inventory, excess capacity, extra personnel and salary
Strong culture—similarity in beliefs, values, and goals produced through recruitment, socialization, use of rewards and punishments	Fewer points of view, less diverse information represented in decision making, potentially lower-quality decisions
Make decisions appear less important	Decision avoided; critical analysis not done; important information not uncovered
Reduce system complexity and uncertainty	Creation of rigid rules and procedures; reduction of capacity for change

Source: Adapted from J. Pfeffer, *Power in Organizations.* Marshfield, Mass.: Pitman, 1981, 93.

Another interesting issue concerns the specific kinds of behaviors that organizational members consider political. A sample of chief executive officers, high-level staff managers, and supervisors was asked to describe the most commonly used organizational political tactics. Their responses indicated that attacking or blaming others when things go wrong, withholding or restricting access to information, and engaging in image building or "impression management" were behaviors that they most readily perceived as political.[32]

POLITICAL BEHAVIOR AND PERSONALITY

So far, we have stressed the situational and structural determinants of political behavior. However, just as power has personal as well as situational sources, some individuals appear more likely to engage in political behavior than others. Several personal traits are related to a willingness to engage in political behavior (and in some cases, a willingness to use power). We will discuss four of these: the need for power, Machiavellianism, locus of control, and risk-seeking propensity.[33]

Need for Power

The **need for power** is a motive, or basic desire, to influence and lead others and to be in control of one's environment. As a result, individuals with a high need for power are more likely to engage in political behavior in organizations. Successful managers often have high needs for power.[34] The desire to have an impact, to control events, and to influence others is frequently associated with effective managerial behaviors, equitable treatment of subordinates, and, hence, higher morale.

Some aspects of strong power needs may not be particularly useful for effective management. The need for power may take two different forms: personal power and institutional power. Managers who emphasize personal power strive for dominance over others; they create loyalty to themselves, rather than to the organization. When this type of manager leaves the organization, the work group may fall apart. On the other hand, managers who emphasize institutional power demonstrate a more socially acceptable need for power. They create a good climate or culture for effective work, and their subordinates develop an understanding of and loyalty to the organization. Interestingly, some research has indicated that female managers often demonstrate higher needs for institutional power and lesser needs for personal power than their male counterparts.[35] In any event, not all characteristics of a need for power contribute to effective management, but better managers frequently have strong desires to influence behavior and to play leadership roles.

Machiavellianism

Niccolò Machiavelli was a sixteenth-century Italian philosopher and statesman whose best-known writings include a set of suggestions for obtaining and holding governmental power. Over the centuries, Machiavelli has come to be associated with the use of deceit and opportunism in interpersonal relations. Thus, *Machiavellians* are people who view and manipulate others for their own purposes.

It is possible to measure **Machiavellianism** as a personal trait or style of behavior toward others. It is characterized by (1) the use of guile and deceit in interpersonal relationships; (2) a cynical view of the nature of other people; and (3) a lack of concern with conventional morality.[36] For example, a person who scores high on a test to measure Machiavellianism would probably agree with the following statements:

- The best way to handle people is to tell them what they want to hear.
- Anyone who completely trusts anyone else is asking for trouble.
- Never tell anyone the real reason you did something unless it is useful to do so.
- It is wise to flatter important people.

Machiavellians are likely to be effective manipulators of other people. They often effectively influence others, particularly in face-to-face contacts, and tend to initiate and control social interactions. As a result, Machiavellianism can be associated with a tendency to engage in political behavior. For example, a study that examined the relationship between a propensity to engage in political behavior in organizations and a variety of individual differences reported that Machiavellianism was the strongest correlate of political behavior among the variables investigated.[37] The study concluded that Machiavellianism may be a good predictor of political behavior in many organizational situations.

Locus of Control

As described in Chapter 3, **locus of control** refers to the extent to which individuals believe that they can control events that affect them. Individuals with a high internal locus of control believe that events result primarily from their own behavior. Those with a high external locus of control believe that powerful others, fate, or chance primarily determine events. Internals tend to exhibit more political behaviors than externals and are more likely to attempt to influence other people. Further, they are more likely to assume that their efforts will be successful. The study of relationships among political behavior and individual differences referred to in the preceding section also supported the notion that the propensity to engage in political behavior is stronger for individuals who have a high internal locus of control than for those who have a high external locus of control.

Risk-Seeking Propensity

Individuals differ (sometimes markedly) in their willingness to take risks, or their **risk-seeking propensity.** Some people are risk avoiders, and others can be described as risk seekers. Some studies have identified negative outcomes (such as demotions, lower performance ratings, and loss of influence) for individuals and groups that engage or appear to engage in political behavior in organizations.[38] Thus, engaging in political activity would not seem to be risk free; to advocate a position and to seek support for it is to risk being perceived as opposing some other position. In many situations, risk seekers are more willing to engage in political behavior, whereas risk avoiders tend to avoid such behavior because of its possible consequences.

SUMMARY

Power is the capacity to influence the behavior of others. Sources of power stem from interpersonal, structural, and situational factors in an organization. Interpersonal power sources can be categorized as reward power, coercive power, legitimate power, expert power, and referent power. Situational or structural power differences stem from unequal access to information, resources, decision making, and networks with others. Lower-level employees, in spite of their location in the organizational hierarchy, can have considerable power to influence events and behavior. Individuals who are effective in influencing others' behavior usually understand clearly the sources of power, as well as the appropriate and fair uses of power. Such individuals also usually understand the important role that the exchange process plays in the ability to influence the behavior of others.

Organizational politics involves the use of power and other resources by individuals or groups to obtain their own preferred outcomes. Political behavior is inevitable, owing to naturally occurring disagreements and uncertainty about choices and actions. Political behavior can have both positive and negative consequences; it may or may not result in optimal decisions, and there are some real costs associated with avoiding political behavior.

Certain personality traits predispose some people to political behavior. Specifically, the probability that individuals will engage in political influence attempts increases if they have (1) a high need for power, (2) a Machiavellian interpersonal style, (3) a high internal locus of control, and (4) a preference for risk taking.

Key Words and Concepts

Authority	Need for power
Coercive power	Networks as power
Decision making as power	Organizational politics
Exchange process	Political behavior
Expert power	Power
Intellectual capital	Referent power
Knowledge as power	Resources as power
Legitimate power	Reward power
Locus of control	Risk-seeking propensity
Machiavellianism	Zone of indifference

Discussion Questions

1. Define power and identify some of the primary sources of power in organizations.

2. Describe a situation when you had the power to influence the behavior of others. Explain the source or sources of your power.

3. Describe a situation when someone else had the power to influence your behavior. Explain the source or sources of their power.

4. Provide some suggestions for the effective use of power.

5. Explain the nature of the exchange process in power relationships. Provide some examples of "currencies" that might be exchanged in an organization.

6. Based on your own experiences, give examples of both the effective and ineffective use of power. Explain why each outcome occurred.

7. Define political behavior and describe some factors that can contribute to the occurrence of organizational politics.

8. Based on your own experience, describe a situation when political behavior seemed to be high, and explain why this was occurring.

◆ MANAGEMENT CASES AND EXERCISES

INFLUENCE IN GROUPS: HOW MUCH POWER DO YOU HAVE?

Think of a group of which you are a member. This could be a work group or team, a committee, a group project at your school, or the like. Respond to the statements below using the following scale.

Strongly Disagree	Disagree	Slightly Disagree	Neither Agree nor Disagree	Slightly Agree	Agree	Strongly Agree
1	2	3	4	5	6	7

_____ **1.** I am one of the more vocal members of the group.

_____ **2.** People in the group listen to what I have to say.

_____ **3.** I often volunteer to lead the group.

_____ **4.** I am able to influence group decisions.

_____ **5.** I often find myself on "center stage" in group activities or discussions.

_____ **6.** Members of the group seek me out for advice.

_____ **7.** I take the initiative in the group and often am one of the first to speak out on important issues.

_____ **8.** I receive recognition in the group for my ideas and contributions.

_____ **9.** I would rather lead the group than be a participant.

_____ **10.** My opinion is held in high regard by group members.

_____ **11.** I volunteer my thoughts and ideas without hesitation.

_____ **12.** My ideas are often implemented.

_____ **13.** I ask questions in meetings just to have something to say.

_____ **14.** Group members often ask for my opinions and input.

_____ **15.** I often play the role of scribe, secretary, or note taker during meetings.

_____ **16.**   Group members usually consult me about important matters before they make a decision.

_____ **17.**   I clown around with other group members.

_____ **18.**   I have noticed that group members often look at me, even when not talking directly to me.

_____ **19.**   I jump right into whatever conflict the group members are dealing with.

_____ **20.**   I am very influential in the group.

Scoring:	Visibility		Influence	
	Item	Your Score	Item	Your Score
	1.	_____	2.	_____
	3.	_____	4.	_____
	5.	_____	6.	_____
	7.	_____	8.	_____
	9.	_____	10.	_____
	11.	_____	12.	_____
	13.	_____	14.	_____
	15.	_____	16.	_____
	17.	_____	18.	_____
	19.	_____	20.	_____
	Total	_____	Total	_____

Using the scores from the above calculations, mark your position on the Visibility/Influence matrix in Figure 16.6. The combinations of visibility and influence shown in Figure 16.6 are described as follows:

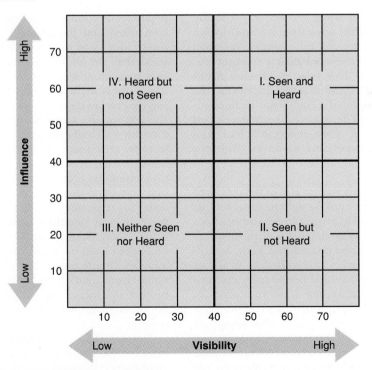

FIGURE 16.6   Visibility/Influence Matrix

Source: Adapted from W. B. Reddy and G. Williams, The Visibility/Credibility Inventory: Measuring Power and Influence. In J. W. Pfeiffer (ed.), _The 1988 Annual: Developing Human Resources._ San Diego: University Associates, 124.

1. *High visibility/high influence.* Group members in quadrant I exhibit behaviors that bring high visibility, as well as allow them to exert influence on others. In large organizations, these people may be the upwardly mobile or "fast trackers."

2. *High visibility/low influence.* Group members in quadrant II are highly visible but have little real influence. This could be due to their personal characteristics but may also indicate that formal power resides elsewhere in the organization.

3. *Low visibility/low influence.* Group members in quadrant III, for whatever reason, are neither seen nor heard. Individuals who find themselves in this category may have difficulty advancing in the organization.

4. *Low visibility/high influence.* Group members in quadrant IV are "behind the scenes" influencers. These individuals are often opinion leaders and "sages" who wield influence but are content to stay out of the limelight.[39]

THE NASA MOONLANDER MONITOR: A CASE STUDY IN ORGANIZATIONAL POLITICS

As a young engineer, Chuck House played a key role at Hewlett-Packard (H-P) in developing new applications for oscilloscope technology. H-P's technology eventually was used in NASA's moon missions, although this happy ending was not without its political battles.

The story began when the Federal Aviation Administration (FAA) advertised its need for an improved airport control tower monitor. Hewlett-Packard developed such a monitor but lost out when the FAA selected another firm's design. However, House was convinced that the H-P design represented a significant technological breakthrough. The model his team developed was smaller, faster, more energy efficient, and brighter than conventional monitors. Unfortunately, the model did not seem to have a niche in the marketplace.

House set out to convince H-P of the merits of his team's monitor, even though the firm had lost the FAA contract. He proved to be a master political gamesman who violated a number of organizational rules and procedures. First, he collected his own market research data in direct violation of organizational boundaries, circumventing the marketing department. During an unauthorized trip, he visited forty computer manufacturers to demonstrate the prototype model to these potential customers. Not only did this arouse the ire of the marketing department, but it violated a security rule against showing prototypes to customers. However, based on marketing information gathered during the trip,

House was able to convince senior management to continue development of the monitor, at least temporarily.

The next obstacle to continuation of the project came during an annual review of progress by senior management. The marketing department conducted a telephone survey that concluded that the total projected demand for the product was thirty-two monitors. House argued that the marketing data was flawed and that marketing was resistant to the project because of his incursion into its territory, Further, the marketing department failed to understand the appropriate strategy for marketing the new monitor and had called only upon current oscilloscope customers. House's position was that new products required new customers. In addition, since the product was difficult to describe, only in-person demonstrations could sell it. Despite this reasoning, the marketing department's projection of potential demand was accepted, rather than House's projection. (House's data had again been obtained through organizationally illegitimate means.) As if the political resistance from marketing were not enough, the project also lacked the support of the chief corporate engineer, who favored an alternate technology.

Not surprisingly, the senior management annual review concluded that there was insufficient market demand and a lack of technological support from others in the organization for this product. The project was to be canceled. David

Packard, one of the two founders of H-P, even said: "When I come back next year, I don't want to see that project in the lab!"

At this point, House's political skills were put to their greatest test. House chose to interpret Packard's statement to mean that the project should be out of the lab in one year and in production, rather than that the project should be scrapped. With covert support from his boss, House and his group hid the development cost of the new monitor under other items in the budget. They then raced to complete the project within a year's time (easily only one-half of the normal time such development might be expected to take). The marketing department mounted continual opposition to the project, but House countered by convincing interested potential customers to personally intervene with senior management and express interest in the monitor.

Fortunately for House and the project, he and his team made the deadline. When Packard returned for the next annual review, the monitor was in the marketplace. Packard was said to be both angered and amused by this obvious reinterpretation of his order. However, perhaps because he was himself something of a maverick,

Packard now chose to support the monitor. Rather than being punished, House and his development team were given the green light to continue to seek additional applications. The eventual uses for this oscilloscope monitor included the NASA moon mission, the medical monitor used in the first artificial heart transplant, and a large-screen oscilloscope that was part of a television special effects system that won an Emmy award. These important innovations could easily have fallen victim to opposing political forces in Hewlett-Packard.[40]

QUESTIONS

1. List and explain the sources of power that Chuck House used.

2. Identify and explain the factors that increased political behavior in Hewlett-Packard during this time.

3. Do you think Chuck House used power effectively or ineffectively? Defend your answer.

4. Suggest some strategies that House might have employed to reduce the political resistance to this innovation.

References

1. Based on Stewart, T. A. CEOs See Clout Shifting. *Fortune*, November 6, 1989, 66; Stewart, T. A. New Ways to Exercise Power. *Fortune*, November 6, 1989, 52–64.

2. Keys, B., and Case, T. How to Become an Influential Manager. *Academy of Management Executive*, 1990, 4(4), 38–51; Ragins, B. R., and Sundstrom, E. Gender and Power in Organizations: A Longitudinal Perspective. *Psychological Bulletin*, 1989, *105*, 51–88.

3. Biggart, N. W., and Hamilton, G. G. The Power of Obedience. *Administrative Science Quarterly*, 1984, *29*, 540–549; Hamilton, G. G., and Biggart, N. W. Why People Obey: Theoretical Observations on Power and Obedience in Complex Organizations. *Sociological Perspectives*, 1985, *28*, 3–28; Pfeffer, J. *Power in Organizations*. Marshfield, Mass.: Pitman, 1981, 4–6.

4. Hollander, E. P., and Offerman, L. R. Power and Leadership in Organizations. *American Psychologist*, 1990, *45*, 179–189.

5. French, J. R. P., and Raven, B. The Bases of Social Power. In D. Cartwright (ed.), *Studies in Social*

Power. Ann Arbor: University of Michigan Institute for Social Research, 1959, 150–167. See also Hinkin, T. R., and Schriesheim, C. A. Development and Application of New Scales to Measure the French and Raven (1959) Bases of Social Power. *Journal of Applied Psychology*, 1989, *74*, 561–567; Podsakoff, P. M., and Schrieshiem, C. A. Field Studies of French and Raven's Bases of Power: Critique, Reanalysis, and Suggestions for Future Research. *Psychological Bulletin*, 1985, *97*, 387–411; Yukl, G., and Falbe, C. M. Importance of Different Power Sources in Downward and Lateral Relations. *Journal of Applied Psychology*, 1991, *76*, 416–423.

6. Based on Bird, A. Power and the Japanese CEO. *Asia Pacific Journal of Management*, 1990, 7(2), 1–20.

7. Barnard, C. I. *The Functions of the Executive*. Cambridge: Harvard University Press, 1938. For additional perspectives on this issue, see Zelditch, M., and Walker, H. A. Legitimacy and the Stability of Authority. In S. B. Bacharach and E. J. Lawler (eds.), *Advances in Group Processes*, vol. 1. Greenwich, Conn.: JAI Press, 1984, 1–25.

8. Greene, C. N., and Podsakoff, P. M. Effects of Withdrawal of a Performance-Contingent Reward on Supervisory Influence and Power. *Academy of Management Journal*, 1981, *24*, 527–542.

9. Allen, R. W., and Porter, L. W. *Organizational Influence Processes*. Glenview, Ill.: Scott, Foresman, 1983; Bacharach, S. B., and Lawler, E. J. *Power and Politics in Organizations*. San Francisco: Jossey-Bass, 1982, 33–38; Krackhardt, D. Assessing the Political Landscape: Structure, Cognition, and Power in Organizations. *Administrative Science Quarterly*, 1990, *35*, 342–369; Lackman, R. Power from What? A Reexamination of Its Relationships with Structural Conditions. *Administrative Science Quarterly*, 1989, *34*, 231–251. Pfeffer, *Power in Organizations*, 101–122.

10. Stewart, T. A. Brainpower. *Fortune*, June 3, 1991, 44–60.

11. Henkoff, R. How to Plan for 1995. *Fortune*, December 31, 1990, 70–81.

12. Kanter, R. M. Power Failure in Management Circuits. *Harvard Business Review*, July-August 1979, 66.

13. Pfeffer, *Power in Organizations*, 158–159. Copyright © 1981 by Jeffrey Pfeffer. Reprinted with permission of Ballinger Publishing Company.

14. See, for example, Blackburn, R. S. Lower Participant Power: Toward a Conceptual Integration. *Academy of Management Review*, 1981, *6*, 127–131; Mechanic, D. Sources of Power of Lower Participants in Complex Organizations. *Administrative Science Quarterly*, 1962, *7*, 349–364; Porter, L. W., Allen, R. W., and Angle, L. L. The Politics of Upward Influence in Organizations. In L. L. Cummings and B. M. Staw (eds.), *Research in Organizational Behavior*, vol. 3. Greenwich, Conn.: JAI Press, 1981, 109–149.

15. See, for example, Schriesheim, C. R., and Hinkin, T. R. Influence Tactics Used by Subordinates: A Theoretical and Empirical Analysis and Refinement of the Kipnis, Schmidt, and Wilkinson Subscales. *Journal of Applied Psychology*, 1990, *75*, 246–257; Yukl, G., and Falbe, C. M. Influence Tactics and Objectives in Upward, Downward, and Lateral Influence Attempts. *Journal of Applied Psychology*, 1990, *75*, 132–140.

16. Kipnis, D., Schmidt, S. M., Swaffin-Smith, C., and Wilkinson, I. Patterns of Managerial Influence: Shotgun Managers, Tacticians, and Bystanders. *Organizational Dynamics*, Winter 1984, 60–61.

17. Kipnis, Schmidt, Swaffin-Smith, and Wilkinson, Patterns of Managerial Influence, 58–67.

18. Cohen, A. R., and Bradford, D. L. Influence without Authority: The Use of Alliances, Reciprocity, and Exchange to Accomplish Work. *Organizational Dynamics*, Winter 1989, 5–17.

19. Schmidt, S. M., and Kipnis, D. The Perils of Persistence. *Psychology Today*, November 1987, 32–34.

20. Cohen and Bradford, Influence without Authority, 14–15.

21. These characteristics of managerial effectiveness are based, in part, on Kotter, J. P. Power, Dependence, and Effective Management. *Harvard Business Review*, April 1977, 125–136; Kotter, J. P. *Power and Influence*. New York: Free Press, 1985.

22. Keys and Case, How to Become an Influential Manager, 43.

23. Baum, H. S. *Organizational Membership*. Albany: State University of New York Press, 1990, 212; Pfeffer, *Power in Organizations*, 7.

24. Based on Machan, D. Gladiators' Ball. *Forbes*, December 26, 1988, 130–134.

25. Madison, D. L., Allen, R. W., Porter, L. W., Renwick, P. A., and Mayes, B. T. Organizational Politics: An Exploration of Managers' Perceptions. *Human Relations*, 1980, *33*, 79–100.

26. Baum, H. S. Organizational Politics against Organizational Culture: A Psychoanalytic Perspective. *Human Resource Management*, Summer 1989, 191–206.

27. Carnall, C. A. *Managing Change in Organizations*. New York: Prentice-Hall, 1990, 123–137; Kumar, K., and Thibodeaux, M. S. Organizational Politics and Planned Organization Change. *Group & Organization Studies*, 1990, *15*, 357–365.

28. Beemon, D. R., and Sharkey, T. W. The Use and Abuse of Corporate Politics. *Business Horizons*, March-April 1987, 26–30.

29. Gandz, J., and Murray, V. V. The Experience of Workplace Politics. *Academy of Management Journal*, 1980, *23*, 237–251.

30. Bartol, K. M., and Martin, D. C. When Politics Pays: Factors Influencing Managerial Compensation Decisions. *Personnel Psychology*, 1990, *43*, 599–614.

31. Excerpted with permission from Longenecker, C. O., Sims, H. P., and Gioia, D. A. Behind the Mask: The Politics of Employee Appraisal. *Academy of Management Executive*, 1987, *1*, 183–193.

32. Allen, R. W., Madison, D. L., Porter, L. W., Renwick, P. A., and Mayes, B. T. Organizational Politics: Tactics and Characteristics of Its Actors. *California Management Review*, 1979, *22*(1), 77–83.

33. The sections on these personality differences are based, in part, on House, R. J. Power and Personality in Complex Organizations. In B. M. Staw and L. L. Cummings (eds.), *Research in Organizational Behavior*, vol. 10. Greenwich, Conn.: JAI Press, 1988, 305–357; Porter, et al., The Politics of Upward Influence in Organizations, 120–122; Ragins and Sundstrom, Gender and Power in Organizations, 70–72.

34. House, R. J., and Singh, J. V. Organizational Behavior: Some New Directions for I/O Psychology. *Annual Review of Psychology*, 1987, *38*, 672–678; McClelland, D. C. *Human Motivation*. Glenview, Ill.: Scott, Foresman, 1985; McClelland, D. C., and Boyatzis, R. E. Leadership Motive Pattern

and Long-Term Success in Management. *Journal of Applied Psychology*, 1982, *67*, 737–743.

35. Ragins and Sundstrom, Gender and Power in Organizations, 70; Chusmir, L. H., and Parker, B. Gender Differences in Personalized and Socialized Power among Managerial Women and Men. Paper presented at the annual meeting of the Academy of Management, Boston, 1984.

36. Christie, R., and Geis, F. L. *Studies in Machiavellianism*. New York: Academic Press, 1970.

37. Woodman, R. W., Wayne, S. J., and Rubinstein, D. Personality Correlates of a Propensity to Engage in Political Behavior in Organizations. *Proceedings of the Southwest Academy of Management*, 1985, 131–135. See also Nelson, G., and Gilbertson, D. Organizational Machiavellianism: The Ruthlessness of Opportunism. *Proceedings of the Southwest Academy of Management*, 1991, 119–122.

38. See, for example, Madison, et al., Organizational Politics: An Exploration of Manager's Perceptions; Schilit, W. K., and Locke, E. A. A Study of Upward Influence in Organizations. *Administrative Science Quarterly*, 1982, *27*, 304–316.

39. Adapted from Reddy, W. B., and Williams, G. The Visibility/Credibility Inventory: Measuring Power and Influence. In J. W. Pfeiffer (ed.), *The 1988 Annual: Developing Human Resources*. San Diego: University Associates, 1988, 115–124.

40. Adapted from Frost, P. J., and Egri, C. P. The Political Process of Innovation. In L. L. Cummings and B. M. Staw (eds.), *Research in Organizational Behavior*, vol. 13. Greenwich, Conn.: JAI Press, 1991, 246–248.

CHAPTER 17

JOB DESIGN

LEARNING OBJECTIVES

After you have finished studying this chapter, you should be able to:

- Describe five approaches to job design and state the differences between them.
- Explain the linkages between technological factors and job design.
- Understand and diagnose the problems caused by poorly designed jobs.
- Describe the job characteristics enrichment model and explain how it may increase performance, motivation, and satisfaction.
- Explain how the sociotechnical systems model attempts to integrate the needs and goals of employees with those of the organization.

OUTLINE

INSURANCE APPLICATION PROCESSING AT MUTUAL BENEFIT LIFE

Mutual Benefit Life (MBL), the country's eighteenth largest life insurance carrier, has redesigned its processing of applications. MBL used to handle customers' applications with a long, multistep process that involved credit checking, quoting, rating, underwriting, and so on. An application would have to go through as many as thirty separate steps, spanning five departments and involving nineteen people. At the very best, MBL could process an application in twenty-four hours, but more typically, it took from five to twenty-five days—with most of the time spent passing information from one department to the next.

MBL's rigid process led to many complications. For instance, when a customer wanted to cash in an existing policy and purchase a new one, the old business department first had to authorize the treasury department to issue a check made payable to MBL. The check would then accompany the paperwork to the new business department.

The president of MBL, intent on improving customer service, decided that this had to stop and demanded a 60 percent improvement in productivity. It was clear that such an ambitious goal would require more than tinkering with the existing process. Strong measures were in order, and the management team assigned to the task looked to technology and job redesign as means of achieving them. The team realized that shared data bases and computer networks could make many different kinds of information available to a single person and could help people with limited experience make sound decisions. Applying these insights led to a new approach to the application-handling process, one with wide organizational implications and little resemblance to the old way of doing business.

MBL swept away existing job definitions and departmental boundaries and created a new position called a case manager. Case managers have total responsibility for an application from the time it is received to when a policy is issued. Unlike clerks, who performed a fixed task repeatedly under the watchful gaze of a supervisor, case managers work autonomously. No more handoffs of files and responsibility, no more shuffling of customer inquiries.

Case managers are able to perform all the tasks associated with an insurance application because they are supported by powerful PC-based workstations that run a system designed to assist decision making and connect to a range of automated systems on a mainframe. In particularly tough cases, the case manager calls for assistance from a senior underwriter or physician. But these specialists work only as consultants and advisers to the case manager, who never relinquishes control.

Empowering individuals to process entire applications had a tremendous impact on operations. MBL can now complete an application in as little as four hours, and average turnaround takes only two to five days. The company has eliminated one hundred field office positions. Case managers can handle more than twice the volume of new applications the company previously could process.[1]

New information technologies are affecting how many employees perform their jobs, as well as the types of tasks that make up their jobs. Mutual Benefit Life is only one of many organizations that has introduced radical changes in the design of jobs, the flow of work between jobs, and the use of information technologies to improve productivity and better customer service.

The information technology revolution appears to be affecting the design of jobs from retail sales to factory to office and from top managers to secretaries.[2] The introduction of personal computers as substitutes for electric typewriters, for example, has (1) expanded the skill of secretaries as they have learned how to use this new technology effectively; (2) eliminated or substantially reduced the amount of time spent on routine letter, memo, and document preparation; and (3) increased the productivity of secretaries in terms of both the quantity and quality of letters, memos, and documents produced. Along with the growing impact of new information technologies, social forces and attitudes must increasingly be taken into account in how jobs are designed. In Chapter 21, we will discuss the implications of information technology for organizational change.

This chapter is organized into four sections. First, we review the nature of and five approaches to job design. The second section presents a framework for diagnosing how job design is likely to vary according to different technological situations. The job characteristics enrichment model and sociotechnical systems model are covered in detail in the next two sections. These two approaches are usually the most effective in meeting the needs of employees and the organization. Of course, some aspects of job design have been woven into the topics of previous chapters. The importance of appropriately designed jobs was mentioned in Herzberg's model of work motivation discussed in Chapter 7. His motivator factors in the motivator-hygiene theory focus on the nature of the work itself. Chapter 8 noted the importance of designing jobs so that challenging goals can be established for individuals. Our discussion of dynamics within groups in Chapter 10 included many ideas relevant to job design. For example, the introduction of problem-solving teams, special-purpose teams, or self-managing teams into organizations serves to change and enlarge the tasks performed by employees in their jobs. In brief, this chapter is an extension and addition to job design concepts and issues presented in earlier chapters.

NATURE OF JOB DESIGN

Job design is the specification of tasks that are to be performed by employees, including the expected interpersonal relationships and task interdependencies with others. In effect, every time managers assign work, give instructions, or verify that a task is being done, job design occurs. Consciously or unconsciously, managers constantly change the tasks of their subordinates. Because both tasks and the best means for performing them change, managers need to know how to formally design and redesign jobs to make them as motivating and meaningful as possible. The ideal state occurs when jobs effectively use employees' competencies and skills and meet the needs of the organization to create higher-quality products and services more efficiently.[3] This ideal state is not always attainable, but substantial improvements in job design are usually possible. These improvements benefit the employee, the organization, and the consumer. Through improved design of production workers' jobs in automobile plants, for example, the quality of cars has improved. This directly benefits car owners and improves the firms' position in the market. In sum, we share the view of others that the needs and goals of employees and the organization both should be considered in the design or redesign of jobs.[4]

Impact and Complexity

Figure 17.1 shows five approaches to job design. These approaches are contrasted in terms of two dimensions: impact and complexity. *Impact* refers to the extent to which a job design approach is likely to be linked to factors beyond the immediate job—such as reward systems, performance appraisal methods, leadership practices of managers, organization structure, physical working conditions, and group composition and norms—as well as its likely effects on changes in productivity and quality. *Complexity* means the extent to which a job design approach is likely to require: (1) changes in many factors; (2) the involvement of individuals with diverse skills at various organizational levels; and (3) high levels of decision-making skills for successful implementation. The redesign of the system for processing insurance applications at Mutual Benefit Life, as described in the Preview Case, is high on both the *impact* and *complexity* dimensions shown in Figure 17.1.

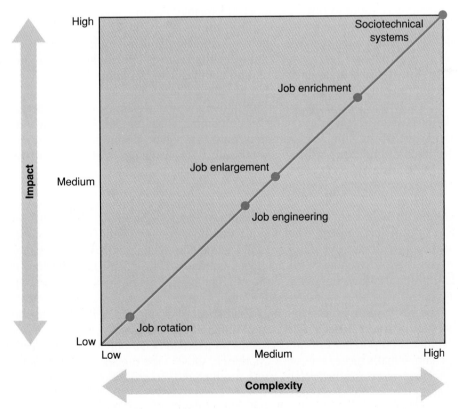

FIGURE 17.1 **Relative Impact and Complexity of Five Job Design Approaches**

Job Rotation

Job rotation involves moving employees from job to job, giving them an opportunity to perform a greater variety of tasks. Job rotation is low on both *impact* and *complexity* because its primary focus is on retaining the current types of jobs while moving employees among them. Most often, job rotation focuses on adding variety to reduce employee boredom. If all tasks are similar and routine, however, job rotation may not have much effect. For example, rotating automobile assembly line workers from bolting bumpers on cars to bolting on tire rims is not likely to reduce their boredom. Job rotation may be of benefit if (1) it is part of a larger redesign effort and/or (2) it is used as a training technique to improve the skills and flexible use of employees. The following In Practice describes how Lechmere, Inc., a retail store chain owned by the Dayton Hudson Corporation, experienced just such benefits when it opened an outlet in Sarasota, Florida.

IN PRACTICE

JOB ROTATION AT LECHMERE, INC.

Lechmere was about to open an outlet in Sarasota, Florida, and capable workers were in short supply. Like other retailers, the company customarily hires many entry-level part-timers, typically teenagers and homemakers plugging them into time slots as needed. This gives Lechmere the requisite flexibility in a business where store traffic ebbs and flows unpredictably across departments. With unemployment low, however, few people were available for hire in Sarasota.

So Lechmere picked the new store to test a way of dealing with the shortages of labor it faces around the country. The company offered the Sarasota workers raises based on the number of jobs they learn to perform. Cashiers are encouraged to sell records and tapes. Sporting goods salespersons were taught how to operate forklifts. In this way, Lechmere can quickly adjust to shifts in staffing needs simply by redeploying existing workers.

Kathleen Horan, hired to do customer service at Lechmere, studied on her own time to learn how to sell home health products, work the cash register, and fill in at the switchboard. She has learned how to sell in the sporting goods, housewares, and photo departments. "I feel like I'm in charge of my own destiny," she says. Her co-worker Brad Davis has learned seven jobs, qualifying him for $2.50 an hour above base pay. "I love it," he says. "It's a chance to work with everybody."

The pay incentives, along with the prospect of a more varied and interesting work day, proved valuable lures in recruiting. The Sarasota store now has a work force that is 60 percent full-timers versus an average of 30 percent for the rest of the chain. What's more, says Paul Chaddock, senior vice-president for personnel, the Sarasota store is substantially more productive than the others. Lechmere has extended the idea to other stores.[5]

Job Engineering

Late in the nineteenth century, Frederick W. Taylor established the foundation for modern industrial engineering. It is concerned with product design, process design, tool design, plant layout, work measurement, and operator methods. **Job engineering** focuses on the tasks to be performed, methods to be used, work flow between employees, layout of the workplace, performance standards, and interdependencies between people and machines. These job-design factors are often examined by means of time-and-motion studies. These studies determine the time required to do each task and the movements needed to perform it efficiently.

Specialization of labor and efficiency are the cornerstones of job engineering. High levels of specialization are intended to (1) allow workers to rapidly learn a task; (2) permit short work cycles so performance can be almost automatic, with little or no mental effort; (3) make hiring easier, since lower-skilled people can be easily trained and paid relatively low wages; and (4) reduce the need for supervision, owing to simplified jobs and standardization.

Many managers and industrial engineers now recognize that traditional job engineering can also create boring jobs. Yet it remains an important job-design approach because its immediate cost savings can be easily measured. In addition, this approach is concerned with appropriate levels of automation—tending to look for ways to replace human beings with machines to perform the most physically demanding and routine tasks.[6] The following account demonstrates the coupling of traditional job engineering principles with computer-based information technology.

IN PRACTICE

THE CHECKROBOT GROCERY CHECKOUT

The latest innovation at the supermarket will let customers become do-it-yourselfers at the checkout lane—and not only for bagging. They will be able to run packaged products over a scanner and weigh their own produce before going to a central cashier. But do not try to slip an extra can of peas or bunch of bananas past the computer. A security system in the CheckRobot, Inc., lanes reverses the conveyer if any unscanned, unweighed, or switched product is placed on it. And a gentle electronic voice says, "Please set the last item aside and continue scanning."

Scott M. Sloan, vice-president of marketing for CheckRobot, says the benefits of the system and a new cooperative marketing agreement with IBM should make it popular. "It's rare that you'll find a piece of equipment in the food industry that will address the retailer's greatest concern—labor shortage—as well as address the single greatest concern of shoppers—and that's speed of checkout," Sloan says. The systems, on the market for about a year, are already installed in eleven supermarkets, including locations in Ontario, Canada; New Jersey; Virginia; Florida; and Wisconsin.

Stores can still provide baggers and decide how many cash registers they want to use. To get the financial benefit from the machines, it is recommended that each cashier handle at least three lines, Sloan says.

A computer screen and two rows of buttons face the shopper bringing groceries to the line. Prices of scanned products appear on the screen, while anything that needs to be weighed is put on the scanner surface, which is also a scale. Buttons have pictures of different kinds of produce, such as grapes. Put the grapes on the scale and hit the button, and the price is recorded. For more detailed lists, a button might say "Fruit Screen," and a checkerboard of several varieties appear on the screen. A touch of the right square registers the weight and price. All of this is done with or without a computer voice stating the price and with recorded video of a person to give some messages—including "Help is on the way" for those who touch the "Help" square on the screen. A receipt at the end of the line is taken to the cashier for payment.[7]

Job Enlargement

Job enlargement expands the number of different tasks performed by the employee. For example, one automobile assembly line worker's job was enlarged from installing just one taillight to installing both taillights and the trunk. An auto mechanic switched from only changing oil to changing oil, greasing, and changing transmission fluid. Job enlargement attempts to add similar tasks to the job so that it will have more variety and be more interesting. As suggested in Figure 17.1, job enlargement is viewed as an extension of job engineering but more responsive to the higher-level needs of employees by providing more variety in their jobs.

Although this approach often has positive effects, employees may resist it. Some employees view job enlargement as just adding more routine, boring tasks to their already boring job. Other employees may view it as eliminating the advantage of being able to perform their job almost automatically. These employees may value their opportunity to daydream about a big date that night or a vacation next month. Others may simply prefer to spend their time socializing with nearby workers. If an enlarged job requires more careful attention and concentration, some employees may find it interesting, whereas others may view it negatively. The importance of individual differences should not be underestimated in attempting to anticipate or understand the reactions of employees to redesigned jobs.

Job Enrichment

Job enrichment adds tasks to employees' jobs by allowing them to assume more responsibility and accountability for planning, organizing, controlling, and evaluating their own work.[8] The job-enrichment approach originated in the 1940s at International Business Machines (IBM). In the 1950s, the number of companies interested in job enrichment grew slowly. Successful and widely publicized experiments at AT&T, Texas Instruments (TI), and Imperial Chemicals led to an increasing awareness of and interest in job enrichment in the 1960s.[9] Herzberg's two-factor theory of motivation—introduced in the 1950s—was one of the first models to emphasize job enrichment as a way for increasing employee work motivation and job satisfaction (see Chapter 7).[10]

The techniques used for enriching jobs are often specific to the job being redesigned. We will discuss these techniques in the section on the job characteristics enrichment model.

Sociotechnical Systems

The sociotechnical systems approach considers every organization to be made up of people (the social system) using tools, techniques, and knowledge (the technical system) to produce goods or services valued by customers (who are part of the organization's external environment). The social and technical systems need to be designed with respect to one another and to the demands of groups in the external environment. To a large extent, this determines how effective the organization will be. Although every organization is a sociotechnical system, every organization is not designed using the principles and techniques that have come to be a part of this approach.[11]

The fundamental goal is to find the best *possible* match among the technology available, the people involved, and the organization's needs.[12] The sociotechnical system recognizes the interdependence of tasks, which become the basis for forming natural work groups. After these work groups have been formed, the specific tasks to be performed by each member of a work group are considered.[13]

This approach has been applied most successfully—as has the job-enrichment approach—in industrialized societies. This chapter's Across Cultures account describes one of the most extreme interpretations and applications of the sociotechnical systems approach to job design.

JOB DESIGN AND TECHNOLOGY

The design and development of **technology** consists of the application of science to invent a technique and machines to accomplish the transformation of objects (materials, information, people) in support of certain goals.[15] Drawing from this definition, the **technical system** of an organization consists of the tools, techniques, methods, procedures, and knowledge used by employees to acquire inputs, transform inputs into outputs, and provide outputs or services to clients or customers.[16] Various approaches can be used to relate job design to technology.[17] Our job design-technology discussion relates work-flow uncertainty, task uncertainty, and task interdependence to job design.[18]

Work-Flow and Task Uncertainty

Work-flow uncertainty is the degree of knowledge that an employee has about when inputs will be received and required for processing. When there is little work-flow uncertainty, an employee may have little discretion (autonomy) to decide which, when, or where tasks will be performed. **Task uncertainty** is the degree of knowledge that an employee has about how to perform the job when it needs to be done. When there is little task uncer-

NORWAY'S SOCIOTECHNICAL SYSTEMS APPROACH

Nowhere are ideas about sociotechnical systems (STS) design of work taken more seriously than in Norway. At least three important public (governmental) policies affecting Norwegian industrial democracy during the past twenty-five years have roots in STS theory and concepts. In 1977, Norway passed a unique law affecting the work environment. The law's provisions relevant to job design came directly from STS criteria. Specifically, the law seeks to outlaw alienating and dehumanizing labor by improving the social and psychological working conditions, or the quality of working life (QWL). The law also mandates company QWL councils. These are charged with studying, planning, and carrying out QWL improvements. One of the important objectives is self-study and self-managed change at the worker level. This makes participation a means of empowering workers to study, change, and control their own workplaces.

In 1982, the Norwegian Trade Union Confederation (LO) signed a national agreement with the Norwegian Employers Association (NAF) to increase union-supported worker participation in management decision making, particularly in decisions affecting labor-management company development programs. The LO-NAF company development fund—approximately seven hundred thousand dollars per year—supports participatory planning and employee-controlled work design or redesign efforts. Although by 1985, the program had barely gone beyond its formative stage, more than 150 companies had already become involved in it. Its aim clearly is to support "do-it-yourself," employee-managed change; the LO-NAF funds cannot go to consultants.

The third and most recent example of Norwegian public policy built on STS ideas is an official government inquiry by a special commission addressing democratization of industry. This commission emphasizes direct forms of participation in the workplace and has recommended that further democratization be a national industrial development strategy. Such democratization promotes direct participation that should increase workers' involvement and learning and promote more effective use of human resources. According to the commission, workers having more influence in the decisions directly affecting them will benefit a variety of stakeholders. Such empowering participation enhances both industrial democracy and industrial development.

These are not the only public policies aimed at promoting democracy in working life. Other Norwegian legislation has placed workers on company boards, and Norway has an unusually cooperative and comprehensive system of trade-union representation. Nearly everyone in Norway seems to belong to a trade union, professional association, or other bargaining unit. The three policies discussed emphasize increasing workers' direct control over their own workplaces—that is, the development of autonomy-based work organizations. This approach stems from such sociotechnical system ideas as autonomous ways of organizing tasks, cooperative labor–management change processes, and humanistic-democratic values.[14]

tainty, an employee has relatively complete knowledge about how to go about producing the desired results. In contrast, with high task uncertainty, there are few (if any) prespecified ways for dealing with some or many of the job's tasks. This condition means that experience, judgment, intuition, and problem-solving ability are usually required by the employee.

Figure 17.2 shows the possible combinations of work-flow uncertainty and task uncertainty. Each of the four cells contains examples of jobs that generally fall into each category. We must be careful not to stereotype particular jobs (high school teacher, bartender, assembly line worker, manager), thinking of them only in terms of a single position on the grid. Through job redesign, jobs are often modified, and their task uncertainty and work-flow uncertainty can change. Managerial jobs—including some top-management jobs—could range from the extreme upper right corner in cell three to closer to the center of the grid. Another important point is that some jobs do not clearly fit into a single cell. For example, an auditor's job in a public accounting firm might generally be plotted somewhere in the middle of the grid.

Job enrichment programs generally increase task uncertainty and/or work-flow uncertainty. However, the assembly line job shown in cell one of Figure 17.2 could be enriched but still be generally classified as a cell-one type of job. This framework also suggests how jobs could become too enriched. Some people who occupy cell-three types of jobs could experience stress from too much uncertainty (see Chapter 9).

Task Interdependence

Task interdependence is the degree to which decision making and cooperation between two or more employees is necessary for them to perform their jobs. For example, erecting the structural steel framework of a high-rise building involves a high degree of task interdependence among the crane operator, ground crew, and assembly crew in moving and joining the steel girders. (Recall the discussion of independent, interdependent, and dependent task relations in Chapter 10.)

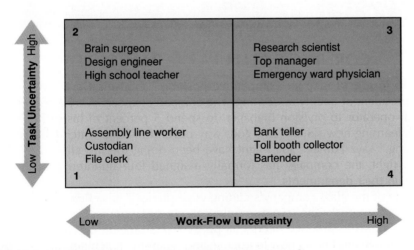

FIGURE 17.2   Job Design and Technology Framework

Source: Adapted from J. W. Slocum, Jr., and H. P. Sims, Jr. Typology for Integrating Technology, Organization and Job Design *Human Relations*, 1980. *33:* 196: G. I. Susman. *Autonomy at Work A Sociotechnical Analysis of Participative Management.* New York: Praeger, 1980, 132.

There are basically three types of interdependent task relations: pooled, sequential, and reciprocal.[19] **Pooled interdependence** occurs when each employee is not required to interact with other individuals to complete the task(s). The tasks involved in mailing a brochure on an academic department's graduate program to five hundred selected individuals and institutions is an example of pooled interdependence. Clerical staff members might work independently in typing address labels, putting the labels on envelopes, inserting brochures into the envelopes, sealing the envelopes, and putting the envelopes in the mail. Mailing five hundred brochures represents the pooled output.

Sequential interdependence occurs when one employee must complete certain tasks before other employees can perform their tasks. In other words, the outputs from some employees become the inputs for other employees. The sequence of interdependencies can be a long chain in some mass-production technologies. The traditional automobile assembly line is an excellent example of sequential interdependence.

Reciprocal interdependence occurs when outputs from one individual (or group) become the inputs for others and vice versa. Reciprocal interdependencies are common in everyday life. A few examples include: (1) a family; (2) a basketball team; (3) a surgical team; (4) a decision-making group; and (5) a class project assigned to a small group of students. Reciprocal interdependence usually requires a high degree of collaboration, communication, and group decision making. The capacity of employees to cope with task uncertainty, work-flow uncertainty, and reciprocal interdependence can be substantially increased through various types of training and on-the-job learning.[20] This is demonstrated in the following In Practice.

IN PRACTICE

CORNING'S CELLULAR CERAMICS PLANT

"We're in a mad race for competitive position," explains David Luther, senior vice-president of quality at Corning. The company expects every employee, from forklift operator to division manager, to spend 5 percent of his or her working hours learning new skills. "This goes way beyond the old 'watch Joe' method of teaching," says Luther. "Joe might have been doing the job all wrong." To get things right, the company has formally assigned four hundred people to train others in their departments.

One of the glass company's cutting-edge plants is its cellular ceramics plant in Erwin, New York. The seventy employees, most of whom never went to college, work in teams to produce filters that purify molten metal. Everyone on the four production teams knows how to operate and repair the machines, load the ovens, pack and ship the filters, order parts, and control for quality. These tasks used to be assigned one to a person.

The more you learn, the more you earn at Corning's ceramics plant. The varied production tasks every team member performs are broken down into four levels of difficulty. Progressing through each level brings a raise—up to $2.25 extra an hour for those who reach the top. Fail to complete the second level after two years and you are fired.

Talking with the ceramic associates, as Corning calls them, makes it plain that morale has improved along with wages. So has quality. Plant manager Corbin Plymale says the reorganization has saved "tens of thousands of dollars," twice as much as the investment in training. In five years, Corning has cut the cost of each filter by 60 percent. Even more noteworthy: Corning had to toss out ninety-five hundred of every million filters in 1986. By 1991, there were only five rejects per million.[21]

In designing new jobs or redesigning existing jobs, managers often must consider and make changes in task uncertainty, work-flow uncertainty, and/or task interdependence. For example, *increasing* pooled interdependence *decreases* the amount of required coordination between jobs. That is, less coordination between jobs means less sequential and/or work-flow uncertainty for the individuals involved.

JOB CHARACTERISTICS ENRICHMENT MODEL

Richard Hackman and Greg Oldham developed the job characteristics enrichment model.[22] It has become one of the most popular approaches to job enrichment. The model is shown in graphic form in Figure 17.3.

Basic Framework

The **job characteristics enrichment model** focuses on increasing the amount of skill variety, task identity, task significance, autonomy, and job feedback in a job. These five core job characteristics are identified in Figure 17.3. The model suggests that the levels of these job characteristics can affect three critical psychological states. These psychological states, in turn, may create a number of positive personal and work-related outcomes.

Recall from Chapter 7 that employees may experience positive feelings toward their jobs to the extent that they (1) receive feedback (knowledge of results) about task performance; (2) experience personal responsibility for tasks; and (3) feel a sense of meaningfulness about the tasks performed. If all three psychological states are present, a self-perpetuating cycle of positive work motivation based on self-generated rewards is activated and maximum task-based motivation can occur. A job without meaningfulness, responsibility, or feedback is incomplete and does not strongly motivate an employee to perform the job. Because of our in-depth coverage of motivation in Chapter 7, we will discuss further only the job characteristics and individual differences components of the model here.

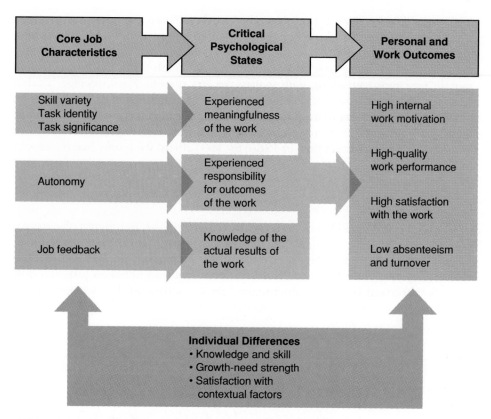

FIGURE 17.3   Job Characteristics Enrichment Model

Source: J. R. Hackman and G. R. Oldham, *Work Redesign* Copyright © 1980. Addison-Wesley Publishing Co., Inc., Reading, Massachusetts (Adapted from Fig. 4.6 on p. 90). Reprinted with permission.

Job Characteristics

The five job characteristics that are the key to job enrichment efforts are:

- **Skill variety**—the degree to which a job requires a range of personal competencies and abilities to carry out the work.

- **Task identity**—the degree to which a job requires completion of a whole and identifiable piece of work, that is, doing a task from beginning to end with a visible outcome.

- **Task significance**—the degree to which the job is perceived by the employee as having a substantial impact on the lives of other people, whether those people are within or outside of the organization.

- **Autonomy**—the degree to which the job provides freedom, independence, and discretion to the employee in scheduling tasks and in determining procedures to be used in carrying out the tasks.

- **Job feedback**—the degree to which carrying out the job-related tasks provides the individual with direct and clear information about the effectiveness of his or her performance.[23]

Skill variety, task identity, and task significance may be especially powerful in influencing the experienced meaningfulness of work. Autonomy usually fosters increased feelings and attitudes of personal responsibility for work outcomes. Job feedback gives the employee the knowledge of results directly from performing the job. This is feedback from the work itself, not from a superior's performance appraisal.

The job of surgeon can be used to illustrate these points. That job seems to rate high on all core job characteristics. It provides a constant opportunity for using highly varied skills, abilities, and talents in diagnosing and treating illnesses. Task identity is high because the surgeon normally diagnoses a problem, performs the operation, and monitors the patient's recovery period. Task significance is also very high—much of the surgeon's work can mean life or death to the patient. Autonomy is quite high because the surgeon is often the final authority on the procedures and techniques used. However, the growing prevalence and threat of malpractice suits may have lowered the surgeon's sense of autonomy recently. Finally, the surgeon receives excellent feedback from the job, knowing in many cases almost immediately whether an operation is successful.

Individual Differences

According to Hackman and Oldham, three major individual differences (see Figure 17.3) are likely to influence the way in which employees respond to enriched jobs: (1) knowledge and skill; (2) strength of growth needs; and (3) satisfaction with contextual factors.[24] These differences can affect the relationship between job characteristics and personal/work outcomes in several important ways and should be considered in designing jobs or planning the redesign of jobs.

Knowledge and Skill   Employees with the knowledge and skill needed to perform an enriched job well are likely to experience positive feelings about the tasks they perform. Employees who are not competent to perform an enriched job effectively may experience frustration, stress, and job dissatisfaction. These feelings and attitudes may be especially intense for employees who desire to do a good job but realize that they are performing poorly. Thus, diagnosing the knowledge and skills of employees whose jobs are to be enriched is important. A training and development program may be needed with an enrichment program to help the person learn the new skills needed by the job.

Growth-Need Strength   The degree to which an individual desires the opportunity for self-direction, learning, and personal accomplishment at work is **growth-need strength.** This concept is essentially the same as Alderfer's growth needs and Maslow's esteem needs and self-actualization needs (see Chapter 7). Individuals who have high growth needs tend to respond favorably to job enrichment programs. They derive greater satisfaction from work, are more highly motivated internally, are absent less, and produce better quality work when their jobs are enriched.[25] Some evidence suggests that individuals who have low growth needs are indifferent to having their jobs enriched. Their sense of satisfaction with work and internal work motivation do not appear to change after job enrichment. Research has not shown job enrichment to be negatively related to satisfaction or performance for individuals with low growth needs. Except in unusual cases, employees' responses to enriched jobs range from indifferent to highly positive.[26]

Satisfaction with Contextual Factors The degree to which employees are satisfied with contextual factors at work may affect their willingness or ability to respond positively to enriched jobs. Recall the presentation of Herzberg's two-factor theory in Chapter 7. Some contextual factors are hygiene factors in the two-factor model. These factors include company policy and administration, technical supervision, salary, interpersonal relations, and work conditions (lighting, heat, safety hazards, and the like). Employees who are extremely dissatisfied with their superiors, salary level, and safety measures are less likely to respond favorably to enriched jobs than are employees who are satisfied with these conditions. Other contextual factors—such as employee satisfaction with the organization's culture, power and political processes, and work-group norms—can all play a part in affecting employees' responses to their jobs.[27]

Job Diagnosis

A variety of useful methods can be used to diagnose jobs, determine whether job-design problems exist, and estimate the potential for job-enrichment success.[28] We limit our consideration to two of these methods: the structural clues method and the survey method.

Structural Clues Method The structural clues method involves checking for contextual factors that are often associated with deficiencies in job design.[29] Analysis of five specific structural factors often gives important clues regarding job-design problems and possible employee acceptance of job enrichment:

- *Inspectors or checkers.* When inspectors or checkers, rather than the employees themselves, examine work, autonomy is usually much lower. Feedback is less direct since it does not come from the job itself.

- *Troubleshooters.* The existence of troubleshooters usually means that the exciting and challenging parts of a job have been taken away from the employees. Thus, they have less sense of responsibility for work outcomes. Task identity, autonomy, and feedback are usually poor.

- *Communications and customer relations departments.* These departments usually cut the link between employees who do the job and customers or clients. Thus, such departments often dilute feedback and task identity.

- *Labor pools.* Pools of word processors, computer programmers, and other employees are appealing because they seem to increase efficiency and the ability to meet fluctuations in workloads. However, such pools may destroy workers' feelings of ownership and task identity.

- *Narrow span of control.* A manager who has only a few subordinates (say, five to seven) is more likely to become involved in details of their day-to-day tasks than a manager who has a wider span of control. Centralization of decision making and overcontrol may result from too narrow a span of control and seriously affect autonomy.

Survey Method   Several types of questionnaires are available for use in diagnosing jobs relatively easily and systematically.[30] One of these is the **job diagnostic survey** (JDS). It was constructed by Hackman and Oldham to measure the job dimensions in their model (see Figure 17.3) and the likely outcomes of job redesign.[31]

The five questions in Table 17.1 are taken from a revised version of the JDS. They measure perceived autonomy (item 1), task identity (item 2), skill variety (item 3), task significance (item 4), and feedback from the job (item 5). The complete revised JDS uses several questions to measure each job characteristic.

You can develop your own job profile by answering the questions in Table 17.1. By using your score of 1 to 7 for each job dimension, you can calculate an overall measure of job enrichment called the **motivating potential score (MPS).** The MPS is calculated as follows:

$$\text{MPS} = \frac{\text{Skill variety} + \text{Task identity} + \text{Task significance}}{3} \times \text{Autonomy} \times \text{Feedback}.$$

The MPS formula sums the scores for skill variety, task identity, and task significance and divides the total by three. The combination of these three job characteristics is given the same weight as autonomy and feedback. Why? The job characteristics enrichment model (see Figure 17.3) requires that both experienced responsibility and knowledge of results be present for high internal job motivation. This outcome can be achieved only if reasonable degrees of autonomy and job feedback are present.

Techniques of Implementation

Five techniques may be used to implement a job-enrichment program. Of course, all five techniques need not be used in every job-enrichment effort nor are these techniques mutually exclusive. The two major techniques are vertical loading and the formation of natural work groups. The other three techniques—establishment of client relationships, employee ownership of the product, and employee receipt of direct feedback—are often used within one of the two major techniques.

Vertical Loading   Delegating to employees responsibilities that were formerly reserved for management or staff specialists is called **vertical loading.** The elements of vertical loading include:

TABLE 17.1   Selected Questions from the Revised Job Diagnostic Survey

The following section provides a series of statements that may or may not describe some aspect of your job. Please indicate how much each characteristic is present in your job by choosing the "best" number on the scale.

1. How much *autonomy* is there in your job? That is, to what extent does your job permit you to decide *on your own* how to go about doing the work?

   1   2   3   4   5   6   7

   Very little   Moderate autonomy   Very much

2. What extent does your job involve doing a *"whole" and identifiable piece of work?* That is, is the job a complete piece of work that has an obvious beginning and end? Or is it only a small *part* of the overall piece of work, which is finished by other people or by automatic machines?

   1   2   3   4   5   6   7

   My job is only part of   My job is a moderate-sized   My job involves doing a
   the work.   "chunk" of the overall   whole piece of work
                                 piece of work.   from start to finish.

3. How much *variety* is there in your job? That is, to what extent does the job require you to do many different things at work, using a variety of your skills and talents?

   1   2   3   4   5   6   7

   Very little   Moderate variety   Very much

4. In general, how *significant or important* is your job? That is, are the results of your work likely to significantly affect the lives or well-being of other people?

   1   2   3   4   5   6   7

   Not very significant   Moderately significant   Highly significant

5. To what extent does *doing the job itself* provide you with information about your work performance? That is, does the actual *work itself* provide clues about how well you are doing—aside from any" feedback" co workers or managers may provide?

   1   2   3   4   5   6   7

   Very little   Moderately   Very much

Source: Used with permission of Jacqueline R. Idaszak. Also see J. R. Idaszak, and F. A. Drasgow, Revision of the Job Diagnostic Survey: Elimination of a Measurement Artifact. *Journal of Applied Psychology*, 1987, 72, 69–74; J. R. Idaszak, W. P. Bottom, and F. A. Drasgow, A Test of the Measurement Equivalence of the Revised Job Diagnostic Survey: Past Problems and Current Solutions. Department of Psychology, University of Illinois, Urbana–Champaign, 1988.

- Employees can be given leeway in setting schedules, determining work methods, and deciding when and how to check on the quality of the work produced.

- Employees can make their own decisions about when to start and stop work, when to take breaks, and how to assign priorities.

- Employees can be encouraged to seek solutions to problems on their own, consulting with other organization members as necessary, rather than calling immediately for the manager when problems arise.

Many employees can schedule their own work. The manager may set deadlines or goals, but within these guidelines, employees may be allowed some freedom to set their own schedule and pace. **Flextime** allows employees, within certain limits, to vary their arrival and departure times to suit their individual needs and desires. Flextime helps self-scheduling of work. With the new capabilities of information technology—such as computer hookups between home and office—an increasing number of jobs can be performed primarily in the employee's residence. This development, known as *telecommuting*, was discussed in Chapter 13.

Natural Work Groups   The formation of natural work groups combines individual jobs into a formally recognized unit (such as a section, group, or department). The criteria for this grouping is logical and meaningful to the employee. The following are among the possible criteria for forming natural work groups.

- *Geographical.* Salespersons might be given a particular section of the city, state, or country as their territory.
- *Type of business.* Insurance claims adjusters might be assigned to business groups, such as utilities, manufacturers, or retailers.
- *Organizational.* Word-processing operators might be given work that originates in a particular department.
- *Alphabetical or numerical.* File clerks could be made responsible for materials in specified alphabetical groups (A to D, E to H, and so on); library-shelf readers might check books in a certain range of the library's cataloging system.
- *Customer groups.* Employees of a public utility might be assigned to serve particular residential or commercial accounts.

Client Relationships   One of the most important concepts of job-enrichment is putting employees in touch with the users of their output. The establishment of client relationships is often a natural outcome if natural work groups are formed. Employees too often wind up working directly for their superiors, rather than the customer or client. For example, in word-processing centers, certain operators can be assigned to specific clients or groups of clients, such as salespeople or engineers. When problems arise, the operator can work directly with the client to resolve them.

Tektronix, a manufacturer of electronic equipment, has pioneered direct communication between customers and shop-floor employees. Into the shipping carton of every oscilloscope it sells, the company inserts a postcard listing the names of the workers who built the scope, along with an "800" number to a phone on the shop floor. Every day, the factory gets several calls from customers. The six people working in the repair area who answer them have all received telephone training. Customers call for various reasons: questions about the use of their oscilloscopes, complaints about quality performance, requests for information about other Tektronix products, and so on. Workers and managers meet daily to discuss these calls; if necessary, further conversations with the customer are held following the meetings. In some cases, workers will call customers six months after delivery to find out how well their products are performing.[32]

Ownership of Product   Employees who assemble entire television sets or washing machines or type entire reports identify more with the finished products than do employees who only perform part of the same job. Allowing employees to build an entire product or complete an entire task cycle helps to create a sense of pride and achievement. Assigning people as much responsibility as possible for a certain geographical area may also create the feeling of ownership. The Indiana Bell Company found substantial improvements in employee performance and satisfaction when it assigned telephone directory compilers to their own city or part of the city.[33]

Direct Feedback   The job-enrichment approach stresses feedback to the employee directly from performance of the task.[34] Reports or computer outputs may be routed directly to employees, instead of just to their manager. A common technique is to let people check their own work so that they can catch most of their own errors before others do. This technique also increases employee autonomy. Direct communication with others may also improve the timeliness and accuracy of feedback, eliminating distortions and delays.

Job Characteristics and Technology

We will now merge the earlier discussion of the job design and technology framework (see Figure 17.2) with that of the job characteristics enrichment model (see Figure 17.3). In order to change one or more of the five job characteristics, it is usually necessary to make objective changes in one or more of the three technological dimensions. Let's consider a job-redesign situation where management decides to use a combination of vertical loading and the formation of natural work groups.

Vertical loading increases the amount of task uncertainty and work-flow uncertainty that must be handled by employees in redesigned jobs. Moreover, some of the changes caused by vertical loading tend to increase pooled interdependence and decrease sequential and reciprocal interdependence. For example, reducing the need to constantly check with a quality-control specialist for approval before proceeding with other tasks lessens sequential interdependence among groups. Each group may become a self-managed team.

Forming natural work groups has the most direct impact on task interdependence. All the criteria for forming natural work groups tend to increase pooled interdependence and decrease sequential and reciprocal interdependence.

Figure 17.4 shows the technological changes that will probably accompany a job-redesign program involving vertical loading and the formation of natural work groups. These changes, in turn, can be expected to lead to changes in job characteristics. Research clearly points to the close and intricate links between technological dimensions and job-design characteristics.[35]

The following account presents a summary of a study on the long-term effects of work redesign for bank tellers. It demonstrates several linkages between the introduction of new information technology and job enrichment.

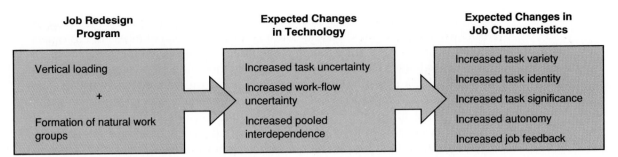

**FIGURE 17.4   Expected Job-Characteristic and Technological Links in a Job-
Redesign Program**

Source: Adapted from J. W. Slocum, Jr., and H. P. Sims, Jr. A Typology for Integrating Technology. Organization and Job Design. *Human Relations*, 1980, *33*, 205.

IN PRACTICE

BANK TELLERS: THE MERGING OF JOB REDESIGN AND TECHNOLOGY

The research was conducted at the thirty-eight member banks of a large Southwestern bank holding corporation over four years. The member banks were located in seven metropolitan areas. The respondents included 526 bank tellers, 85 percent of whom were women. Their average employment with the bank corporation was slightly less than four years.

The bank's management decided to implement an on-line computer network to speed up tasks the tellers had performed manually and to enrich the tellers' job. The purpose of the job redesign program was to make the job more professional and intrinsically rewarding. The automated information network was supposed to decrease errors and increase the speed at which changes in customer accounts were posted. Several changes were targeted to increase responsibility, authority, and accountability. First, tellers would have a wider range of activities than before. Previously, they cashed checks and accepted deposits and loan payments, referring commercial and travelers check customers to special tellers. Under the new system, each teller was trained in all functions and could carry out all of these for a customer. Under the old system, tellers held documents on deposits and withdrawals in a tray until the documents were collected and taken to another work room, where bookkeeping employees posted them. Under the new system, each teller had an on-line computer terminal. Deposits, payments, and withdrawals were posted immediately and verified later by bookkeeping. Tellers also received more autonomy over routine decisions. Previously, they needed a supervisor's signature for immediate crediting of all deposits and for withdrawals of greater than one hundred dollars. After the job changes, tellers could post local checks immediately and perform withdrawals as long as the information system indicated there were adequate funds in a customer's account. Several other similar decisions were formally delegated to the tellers.

Feedback was also enhanced. Under the old system, errors were not reported back to the tellers until the end of the day or, in some cases, the next morning. The automated system allowed bookkeeping to transmit error messages as soon as errors were discovered. The system also recorded the total numbers of customers and transactions each teller handled each day and displayed these figures at all times on the teller's monitor. Thus tellers could monitor their own work pace at all times. Finally, a closer link between tellers and customers was established. The receipt for each transaction was changed to include a special message at the bottom giving the name of the teller who had performed the transaction and inviting the customer to contact the teller first in the event of an error or question. The teller could then handle the question or inquiry alone or refer it to someone more appropriate if he or she could not take care of it.

An interesting pattern of results emerged. First, the job redesign program significantly increased employee perceptions of their core job characteristics (see Figure 17.3) in the predicted and desired directions. Moreover, these changed perceptions remained at their new level for the duration of the study. Second, satisfaction and commitment increased quickly but then diminished back to their initial levels. Finally, although performance did not increase initially, it did improve significantly over the study period.[36]

Social Information Processing

The job characteristics enrichment model assumes that employees can respond reasonably, accurately, and objectively about the characteristics of their jobs. However, their perceptions of job characteristics may be influenced by **social information,** which refers to comments, observations, and similar cues provided by people whose view of the job an employee considers important. It may be provided by people directly associated with the job, such as co-workers, managers, and customers. Social information also may be provided by people not employed by the organization, such as family members and friends. Some aspects of a job are not likely to be influenced by cues from others (a hot work environment will be hot despite what anyone tells a worker). However, most of an employee's perceptions of job characteristics are subject to influence from information provided by others with whom the employee has contact.[37]

Based on this perspective, the **social information processing model** states:

- The individual's social environment may provide cues as to which dimensions might be used to characterize the work environment.

- The social environment may provide information concerning how the individual should weigh the various dimensions—whether autonomy is more or less important than skill variety or whether pay is more or less important than social usefulness or worth.

- The social context provides cues concerning how others have come to evaluate the work environment on each of the selected dimensions.

- It is possible that the social context provides direct evaluation of the work setting along positive or negative dimensions, leaving it to the individual to construct a rationale to make sense of the generally shared affective reactions.[38]

The potential impact of the social information processing model can be illustrated with a simple example. Two employees performing the same tasks with the same job characteristics under different managers might respond differently to the objective characteristics of their jobs on the job diagnostic survey (JDS). The differences in perceived social information cues might account for some of the variation in the employees' responses on the JDS. For example, one manager may praise subordinates a great deal, while another manager may criticize subordinates repeatedly. The social information processing model suggests that receiving praise or criticism could affect how employees respond to the JDS.

An integrated perspective may be more accurate than one or the other points of view. The integrative perspective suggests that (1) job characteristics and social information (cues) combine to affect employees' reactions to their jobs and (2) introducing changes in the work environment can produce those reactions.[39]

The intricate and varied ways that social information in the workplace can affect the perceptions of job characteristics is beyond the scope of our discussion here.[40] To reduce possible distortions caused by social information influences, the employees' manager and possibly a trained job analyst should also rate the characteristics of jobs that are being considered for redesign.

SOCIOTECHNICAL SYSTEMS MODEL

The important role of technology in job design and redesign has always been recognized in the sociotechnical systems model. Moreover, the **sociotechnical systems model**—unlike the job characteristics enrichment model—emphasizes grouping jobs into work teams in which there is a high degree of reciprocal and/or sequential interdependence among jobs that cannot be reduced.[41] The use of pooled interdependence therefore tends to occur between work groups rather than between individual jobs (as is the case with the job characteristics enrichment model). In addition, the model focuses on vertical job loading to the cluster of jobs within the group as a whole, rather than to each individual job.

The sociotechnical systems model deliberately designs work roles to integrate people with technology and to optimize relationships between the technological and social systems.[42] When applied to manufacturing, changes in technology are often difficult and costly to make in an existing plant. Thus, the sociotechnical systems model usually works best in designing jobs for an entirely new plant. Numerous organizations in Western Europe and North America have implemented sociotechnical systems projects, including General Foods, GM, Weyerhauser, TRW, Rushton Mining, Volvo, and the Tennessee Valley Authority.[43] We suggest that you reread the Across Cultures feature on Norway's sociotechnical systems approach that appeared earlier in the chapter. Although many significant successes with this model have been reported, there are certainly exceptions.[44]

Figure 17.5 presents the sociotechnical systems model. It consists of three major parts: the social system, the technological system, and moderators.

Social System

The social system includes those aspects of the "human side" of the organization that can influence how individuals and groups perform tasks, as well as their attitudes toward work and the organization. The social system factors listed in Figure 17.5 were addressed in previous chapters. (Chapters 10, 12, and 15, in particular, presented the main elements and processes of the work-related social system). For example, if employees characterize their organization as one marked by distrust, back-stabbing, and infighting, creating self-managing work groups is likely to be very difficult until some degree of trust and cooperation is established.

Technological System

Task uncertainty, work-flow uncertainty, and task interdependence need to be diagnosed. These three technological dimensions are likely to vary with the type of production process being used or planned. The type of production process (assembly line or small unit) is an important technological characteristic, and different production processes require different approaches to job design. In a process-technology operation, such as an oil refinery, most of the work is automated. A relatively few number of workers spend much of their time monitoring dials and performing maintenance tasks. By contrast, in small-unit technologies, such as plumbing, television repair, sales, and investment brokering, relatively larger amounts of labor are applied in achieving the outputs.

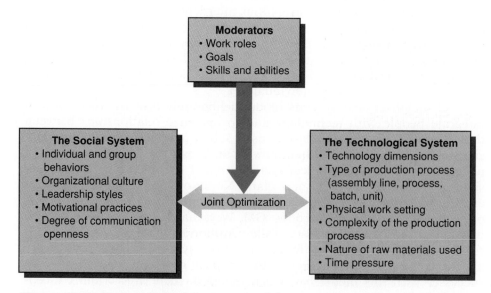

Figure 17.5 Sociotechnical Systems Model

Another technological characteristic is the physical work setting (amount of light, temperature, noise, pollution, geographical isolation, and orderliness). For example, if it is too hot or noisy, employees may have a more difficult time performing tasks that require intense thought and concentration than if these characteristics are not present.

Complexity of the production process is also an important technological characteristic. A person might easily learn how to build an entire toaster, but one person probably could not learn to build a major system of a complex jet aircraft. In general, the more complex the production process, the greater are the degrees of task and work-flow uncertainty and the requirements for reciprocal task interdependence.

Other important technological characteristics are the nature of raw materials used in production and the time pressure inherent in the production process. For example, newspapers are published on a tight and rigid time schedule. Bottlenecks must be dealt with quickly, and workers must speed up their pace if production falls behind schedule by even a few minutes.

Moderators

Work roles act as moderators in the sociotechnical systems model. They establish a set of expected behaviors for each employee; they help to define the relationships between the people who perform tasks and the technological requirements of those tasks; and they help to stabilize work relationships and provide the glue that binds the sociotechnical system together.

Goals also moderate the relationship between the social and technological systems. For example, autonomous work teams at LTV's Camden, Arkansas, plant may have a goal of producing a certain number of subassemblies per day. So long as this goal is compatible with technical-system goals, the work team can perform somewhat autonomously. It can structure the work any way it wants to, so long as it meets its output goal.

A final moderator includes the skills and abilities of the employees. Use of the sociotechnical systems model is more likely to be effective in a plant with a highly skilled and educated work force than in a plant where skills and educational levels are quite low. If the needed skills are not available, changing the production process and simplifying jobs may be necessary.

Key Principles

The degree to which an organization operates according to the principles of sociotechnical systems design can be assessed in terms of the following six areas:

- *Innovativeness*—the extent to which organizational leaders and members maintain a futuristic versus historical orientation; their propensity for risk taking; rewards for innovation.

- *Human resource development*—the extent to which the talents, knowledge, skills, and abilities of organizational members are developed and tapped; work design; supervisory roles; organizational structure; work-flow structure.

- *Environmental agility*—the extent to which the organization maintains awareness of the environment and responds appropriately to it; customer importance; proactivity versus reactivity; structural flexibility; technical flexibility; product/service flexibility.

- *Cooperation*—the extent to which individuals and departments work together to accomplish common goals; teamwork; mutual support; shared values; common rewards.

- *Commitment/energy*—the extent to which employees are dedicated to accomplishing organizational goals and are prepared to expend energy in doing so; reward systems; information availability.

- *Joint optimization*—the extent to which the organization is designed to use both its social and technical resources effectively; the appropriateness of technology; the extent to which technology is designed to support teamwork, flexibility, and changes in organizational structure.[45]

Organizational Significance

It should now be apparent that the factors to be diagnosed in designing jobs can be quite complex.[46] Perhaps the most basic issue is the management philosophy and values that define the organization's culture. Managers interested in improving both the quality of work life and organizational effectiveness would find the job-enrichment or sociotechnical models appropriate. Managers interested only in production and efficiency would concentrate on the job-engineering, job-enlargement, or job-rotation approaches.

Technology is a major variable in job design. Some jobs cannot be enriched without redesigning the whole operation. When changing a job is impossible, other techniques (such as flextime) may soften the effects of a boring job.[47] Moreover, new information technologies, especially those involving robots in manufacturing, are being used increasingly to eliminate routine jobs and thus the need to redesign them.[48] Perhaps the best strategy is to understand fully the various methods of designing jobs and to use the method or combination of methods that best fits the organization or department.[49]

SUMMARY

Job design is a continuous task in organizations. Ideally, jobs will be both efficient and satisfying to employees. There are five major approaches to job design: job rotation, job engineering, job enlargement, job enrichment, and the sociotechnical system. These approaches vary significantly in terms of their relative impact on the organization and complexity of implementation. Job engineering includes traditional industrial engineering techniques that simplify a job in order to make it more efficient. Job enlargement and job rotation seek to make boring jobs more interesting by adding variety.

Job enrichment seeks to make jobs more meaningful and challenging. The job characteristics enrichment model focuses on modifying five job characteristics: task variety, task identify, task significance, autonomy, and job feedback. Technological dimensions that affect these job characteristics must usually be changed. The three technological dimensions involved are: task uncertainty, work-flow uncertainty, and task interdependence (pooled, sequential, and reciprocal). The techniques for implementing the job enrichment approach include vertical loading, formation of natural work groups, establishment of client relationships, employee ownership of the product, and employee receipt of direct feedback. Employees in properly designed jobs are more likely to be satisfied and perform better. Individual differences are important in redesigning jobs because some people may not want enriched jobs or may not want to work in groups. Also, some organizational or technological situations may not permit job enrichment.

The sociotechnical systems model of job design attempts to integrate the organization's technological and social systems. Three moderators—work roles, goals, and skills and abilities—serve to influence the joint optimization of the social system and the technological system. Relative to the other approaches to job design, it is the most complex and offers the greatest potential impact on the organization as a whole. The principles of this model address six key areas: innovativeness, human resource development, environmental agility, cooperation, commitment/energy, and joint optimization.

Job design decisions, like other decisions, contain many contingencies that must be diagnosed. Perhaps the best way to understand and balance these contingencies is by having a thorough knowledge of the various job-design approaches that can be applied.

Key Words and Concepts

Autonomy
Flextime
Growth-need strength
Job characteristics enrichment
  model
Job design
Job diagnostic survey
Job engineering
Job enlargement
Job enrichment
Job feedback
Job rotation
Motivating potential score (MPS)
Pooled interdependence
Reciprocal interdependence

Sequential interdependence
Skill variety
Social information
Social information processing
  model
Sociotechnical systems model
Task identity
Task interdependence
Task significance
Task uncertainty
Technical system
Technology
Vertical loading
Work-flow uncertainty

Discussion Questions

1.   Why should job design be an important area of concern for organizations during the 1990s?

2. What are the similarities and differences between job rotation and job enlargement?

3. How do the assumptions of job engineering differ from those of job enrichment?

4. Think about your role as a student as though it were a job. Analyze your student job in terms of task uncertainty, work-flow uncertainty, and task interdependence. Can this analysis vary by specific course and instructor? Explain.

5. Why do technological dimensions often need to be changed as a first step in changing job characteristics?

6. How would you compare each of the job characteristics in your instructor's job with those in your job as a student? What are the similarities and differences?

7. What clues might you look for in determining whether the manager's job of a local sporting shoe store needs to be redesigned?

8. Why might some managers and employees welcome the sociotechnical systems approach to job design and others oppose it?

◆ MANAGEMENT CASES AND EXERCISES

JOB CHARACTERISTICS INVENTORY

Directions: Listed below are a number of statements that could be used to describe a job. Please indicate the extent to which you agree or disagree with each statement as a description of a job you currently hold or have held. Write the appropriate number next to the statement. Try to be as objective as you can in deciding your answer to the statement.

−2	−1	0	1	2
Strongly disagree	Disagree	Uncertain	Agree	Strongly agree

This job . . .

_____ 1. . . . provides much variety.

_____ 2. . . . permits me to be left on my own to do my work.

_____ 3. . . . is arranged so that I often have the opportunity to see jobs or projects through to completion.

_____ 4. . . . provides feedback on how well I am doing as I am working.

_____ 5. . . . is relatively significant in my organization.

_____ 6. . . . gives me considerable opportunity for independence and freedom in how I do the work.

_____ 7. . . . provides different responsibilities.

_____ 8. . . . enables me to find out how well I am doing.

_____ 9. . . . is important in the broader scheme of things.

_____ 10. . . . provides an opportunity for independent thought and action.

_____ 11. . . . provides me with considerable variety at work.

_____ 12. . . . is arranged so that I have the opportunity to complete the work that I start.

_____ **13.**   . . . provides me with the feeling that I know whether I am performing well or poorly.

_____ **14.**   . . . is arranged so that I have the chance to do a job from the beginning to the end (i.e., a chance to do the whole job).

_____ **15.**   . . . is one where a lot of other people can be affected by how well the work gets done.[50]

Scoring: For each of the five scales, compute a score by summing the answers to the designated questions.

Scores

Skill variety: Sum the points for items: 1 + 7 + 11 + =   _____

Task identity: Sum the points for items: 3 + 12 + 14 + =   _____

Task significance: Sum the points for items: 5 + 9 + 15 + =   _____

Autonomy: Sum the points for items: 2 + 6 + 10 + =   _____

Job feedback: Sum the points for items: 4 + 8 + 13 + =   _____

Total Score   _____

Interpretation: A score of +3 to 6 on a scale is likely to positively contribute to one or more possible critical psychological states (see Figure 17.3). A score of −6 to 0 on a scale is likely to contribute to one or more negative critical psychological states. A total score of +15 to 30 suggests the core job characteristics are contributing to overall positive critical psychological states that, in turn, have led to desirable personal and work outcomes. A total score of −30 to 0 would suggest just the opposite.

AMERICAN STEEL AND WIRE COMPANY

Since its inception in 1986, American Steel and Wire Company (AS&W) has operated under the philosophy that people are its number-one resource and that quality and customer advantage come from the efforts of hard-working, dedicated "entrepreneurial" employees. This strategy enabled AS&W to become a profitable, high-quality producer of rod and wire products in just eleven months. Today, the company continues to thrive. Its success is even more impressive considering that 75 percent of its current work force never worked in a steel mill prior to being employed by AS&W.

AS&W was the dream of Thomas N. Tyrrell, the former vice-president of marketing for Raritan River Steel. Tyrrell believed that buyers of rod and wire wanted products that would fill their needs rather than having to adapt their needs to the products made available by the mills. Tyrrell convinced executives of Chicago West Pullman Corporation to purchase three USX Corporation plants in a $40 million deal that included state loans and private investments. The three plants were the Cuyahoga (a shut-down unionized facility), the tube-launched, optically tracked and wire-guided (TOW) (a salaried, nonunion plant), and the Joliet (a unionized facility). The Cuyahoga plant was started up again from scratch, the TOW plant remained salaried, and the collective bargaining agreement was renegotiated at Joliet (the wage package was reduced by over 40 percent, job classes were cut from 33 to 3, and employment dropped from 145 to 113). In all three plants, the overriding philosophy was "people are our number-one resource."

This philosophy is based on the premise that if you treat employees with respect and as equals, the work attitude improves dramatically. This attitude pervades both communication and actions. Colored hats, a symbol of hierarchy and authority in most steel plants, are passe. Implementation of this philosophy embraces employee involvement, that is, employees have the right to have input into any decision that affects their work lives.

Tyrrell, president of the new company, felt that all employees should have a financial stake in the company as an incentive to both follow their own money and keep a keen watch on shareholders' equity. He also believed that this investment would increase involvement in keeping the plant clean and eliminating plant theft. To accomplish this, he requested that the parent company set aside a piece of the company for employees. Additionally, every person hired at AS&W is required to purchase one hundred dollars worth of stock as a condition of employment. This has been a major commitment for AS&W employees, since many of them were unemployed prior to joining the company. Today, employees own approximately 18 percent of the company and participate in quarterly shareholders' meetings. The company also has a profit-sharing plan covering all employees. Bonuses have been paid out every quarter since the first month of profitability.

To further increase employee involvement, production and maintenance workers are responsible for hiring new personnel. At each plant, employees are grouped into hiring teams. Each team takes the responsibility for interviewing and selecting applicants. Once someone is hired, there is no probationary period. It is the consensus of management and employees that if employees are interviewed and selected properly, there is no reason for probation.

Involving employees carries through to concern for customer relations. The AS&W philosophy is to consider the customer's interest in every decision. To accomplish this, customer value teams, consisting of seven employees each, meet biweekly to discuss problems or suggestions for improvement and methods of resolution. Team membership is voluntary. Only one shift manager can participate on a team; he or she cannot chair the group. Problems that cannot be decided by a customer value team are sent to the chairs' committee, which meets monthly and is composed of the chairs of the various customer value teams. This group's responsibility is twofold: (1) to discuss problems broader than the sphere of responsibility of the individual customer value teams and (2) to discuss unresolved problems submitted by the individual teams. The chairs' committee does not resolve the problems submitted to it. Instead, it defines and dissects the problems and passes them back down to the appropriate team for reevaluation.

The corporate steering committee, which meets quarterly, is the final committee level. It includes the president, the vice-presidents for human resources, marketing, operations, and finance, and the chairs of the customer value teams. In addition to reporting responsibilities in the areas of financial and marketing perspectives and operational results from a productivity-and-yield standpoint, the steering committee discusses customer value team activities. Any unresolved problems from the chairs' committee are also discussed. But rather than resolving them, the steering committee evaluates the problems and sends them back with suggestions.

The customer value teams were asked to deal with the issue of a salaried work force. It was management's desire to have a fully salaried work force to emphasize equity among all organizational levels. Senior workers were skeptical of the idea, fearing that younger workers would take advantage of the situation. After a thorough examination, though, everyone ultimately agreed with the idea. With the salaried work force, overtime is paid when employees work more than forty hours per week; however, like management, no one is penalized when a sick day is taken. Prior to implementation, the salaried work force absenteeism rate was 1.2 percent annually; under the new program it is less than 1 percent. Absenteeism rates in the steel-related products industry average about 5 percent annually.

In addition to being salaried, all AS&W employees are on a common benefit program. There is no difference based on management status. While salary and benefits are competitive, the decision was more difficult for much of management, who were accustomed to a more substantial, differentiated benefit plan. In keeping with the philosophy of equality within the organization, the decision seemed the only logical choice for the company's long-term success.

Paying attention to the details has been a key to AS&W's success. For employees, this includes making their families an integral part of AS&W. On one occasion, a paint party was held for employees and their families. In the rod mill, five-foot-long gray steel hooks carry two thousand-pound rod coils through the mill. The paint party gave employees and their families the opportunity to be creative and paint each of the hooks with some slogan that was especially important to them. The purpose was simple: to make the families feel they were a part of the company. On another occasion, a beautification day was held; employees and their families planted shrubbery and cleaned up the grounds. Children of employees can participate in a birthday card design competition. The winning card is sent to all employees' homes on their birthdays.

Performance appraisal, which is tied to the profit-sharing program, is also seen as a means to allow employees to reach their performance potential. Employees are taught to do self-appraisals and establish individual goals and objectives. Each employee is reviewed by his or her supervisor twice a year; approximately half of the evaluation is a self-appraisal. The importance of performance appraisal is highlighted by the fact that a focus team has been established to continually review and improve the program.

Productivity and quality are two important measures of competitiveness in the steel industry. Operating with 22 percent fewer people than industry averages (75 percent of whom had never worked in a steel mill), AS&W achieved an average productivity rate of 484 tons per turn mill utilization at its Cuyahoga plant. When this plant was under United States Steel (USX), with a very senior work force, the numbers were only slightly better—about 500 tons per turn, during its best times. It should be noted that the USX plant was considered a quality rod mill. The problems that led to the shutdown of the mill stemmed from, among other things, poor management-employee relations.

As one might guess, given the company's mission, that quality has been an area of primary concentration at AS&W—and one in which it has excelled. Quality is often measured in terms of yield (tons in and tons out). At the Cuyahoga plant (the only plant that has completely implemented the AS&W philosophy), the yield rate has been at 94 percent, about 1 percent better than the industry average. A clearer indication of performance is shown in a study conducted by National Standard Company of Stillwater, Oklahoma, a major customer of AS&W. National Standard found AS&W had a rod-to-size deficiency ration of one in

373,800 pounds, compared to a one in 39.4 pound average ratio for its other suppliers. In breakage per million feet of steel, AS&W's ratio was one in 743,000, compared to an average of one to 58.5 for the others in the study.

Rejection rate by customers is another indication of AS&W's quality performance. Although industry average figures were not available, a study conducted by another major customer indicated that AS&W had rejection rates far lower than its U.S. competitors and comparable to one Japanese firm.

According to Tyrrell, one key to AS&W's success is that its people never get comfortable. The fact that AS&W is presently planning for how it will fit in the U.S. market five and ten years from now is evidence of this. Tyrrell believes the number-one key to success is "having the ability to reinvest to make a profit and keep yourself ahead of the changes being made by your competition. The mill that can produce a competitive, quality product and keep its wages and costs in line is the mill that will succeed."[51]

QUESTIONS

1. What concepts and processes from the job characteristics enrichment model seem to be practiced at AS&W? Identify specific descriptive statements in the case and link them to the concepts and processes in the job characteristics enrichment model.

2. What concepts and processes from the sociotechnical systems model of job design seem to be practiced at AS&W? Identify specific descriptive statements in the case and link them to the concepts and processes in the sociotechnical systems model.

3. What features of the system at AS&W do you think should be applied to other organizations? Why?

4. What features of the system at AS&W do you think would meet with opposition at some other organizations? Why?

References

1. Adapted from Hammer, M. Reengineering Work: Don't Automate, Obliterate. *Harvard Business Review*, July-August 1990, 104–112.

2. Keen, P. G. *Shaping the Future: Business Design through Information Technology*. Boston: Harvard Business School Press, 1991.

3. Juran, J. M. *Juran's New Quality Road Map: Planning, Setting, and Reaching Quality Goals.* New York: Free Press, 1991.

4. Griffin, R. W. *Task Design: An Integrative Approach.* Glenview, Ill.: Scott, Foresman, 1982.

5. Adapted from Alster, N. What Flexible Workers Can Do. *Fortune,* February 13, 1989, 60–62.

6. Davis, R. V. Information Technology and White-Collar Productivity. *Academy of Management Executive,* February 1991, 55–67.

7. Adapted from System Gets a Jump on Eliminating Checkers. *Bryan-College Station Eagle,* May 13, 1990, C1.

8. Macy, B. A., Peterson, M. F., and Norton, L. W. A Test of Participation Theory in Work Redesign Field Setting: Degree of Participation and Comparison Site Contrasts. *Human Relations,* 1989, *42,* 1095–1165.

9. Herzberg, F., Mausner, B., and Snyderman, B. *The Motivation to Work.* New York: Wiley, 1959.

10. Myers, M. S. *Every Employee a Manager.* New York: McGraw-Hill, 1970.

11. Pasmore, W. A. *Designing Effective Organizations: The Sociotechnical Systems Perspective.* New York: John Wiley & Sons, 1988.

12. Susman, G. I. *Autonomy at Work: A Sociotechnical Analysis of Participative Management.* New York: Praeger, 1976.

13. Cummings, T. G. A Concluding Note: Future Directions of Sociotechnical Theory and Research. *Journal of Applied Behavioral Science,* 1986, *22,* 355–360.

14. Reprinted with permission from NTL Institute, "Sociotechnical Systems Ideas as Public Policy in Norway: Empowering Participation through Worker-Managed Changed," by Max Elden, *Journal of Applied Behavioral Science,* 1986, *22*(3) 239–255. Copyright 1986.

15. Davis, L. E. Job Design: Overview and Future Directions. *Journal of Contemporary Business,* 1977, *6*(2), 85–102.

16. Pasmore, W. A. *Designing Effective Organizations: The Sociotechnical Systems Perspective.* New York: John Wiley & Sons, 1988, 51–68.

17. Kelley, M. R. New Process Technology; Job Design and Work Organization: A Contingency Model. *American Sociological Review,* 1990, *55,* 191–208; Wall, T. D., Corbett, J. M., Clegg, C. W., Jackson, P. R., and Martin, R. Advanced Manufacturing Technology and Work Design: Toward a Theoretical Framework. *Journal of Organizational Behavior,* 1990, *11,* 201–219.

18. Slocum, J. W., Jr., and Sims, H. P., Jr. A Typology for Integrating Technology, Organization, and Job Design. *Human Relations,* 1980, 33, 193–212; Wall, T. D., Corbett, J. M., Martin, R., Clegg, C. W., and Jackson, P. R. Advanced Manufacturing Technology, Work Design, and Performance: A Change Study. *Journal of Applied Psychology,* 1990, *75,* 691–697; Bowen, D. E., Siehl, C., and

Schneider, B. A Framework for Analyzing Customer Service Orientations in Manufacturing. *Academy of Management Review,* 1989, *14,* 75–95.

19. Larson, R., and Bowen, D. E. Organization and Customer: Managing Design and Coordination of Services. *Academy of Management Review,* 1989, *14,* 213–223; Thompson, J. D. *Organizations in Action,* New York: McGraw-Hill, 1967.

20. Senge, P. M. *The Fifth Discipline: The Art and Practice of the Learning Organization.* New York, Doubleday, 1990.

21. Adapted from Fierman, J. Shaking the Blue-Collar Blues. *Fortune,* April 22, 1991, 209–218; Hoerr, J. Sharpening Minds for a Competitive Edge. *Business Week,* December 17, 1990, 72–78.

22. Hackman, J. R., and Oldham, G. R. *Work Redesign.* Reading, Mass.: Addison-Wesley, 1980.

23. Hackman and Oldham, *Work Redesign,* 77–80. Also see Staw, B. M., and Boettger, R. D. Task Revision: A Neglected Form of Work Performance. *Academy of Management Journal,* 1990, *33,* 534–559.

24. Hackman and Oldham, *Work Redesign,* 82–88. Also see Gardner, D. G. Activation Theory and Task Design: An Empirical Test of Several Predictions. *Journal of Applied Psychology,* 1986, *71,* 411–418.

25. Graen, G. B., Scandura, T. A., and Graen, M. R. A Field Experimental Test of the Moderating Effects of Growth-Need Strength on Productivity. *Journal of Applied Psychology,* 1986, *71,* 484–491; Glick, W. H., Jenkins, G. D., Jr., and Gupta, N. Method versus Substance: How Strong Are Underlying Relationships between Job Characteristics and Attitudinal Outcomes? *Academy of Management Journal,* 1986, *29,* 441–464.

26. Campion, M. A., and McClelland, C. L. Interdisciplinary Examination of the Costs and Benefits of Enlarged Jobs: A Job Design Quasi-Experiment. *Journal of Applied Psychology,* 1991, *76,* 186–198; Zaccaro, S. J., and Stone, E. F. Incremental Validity of an Empirically Based Measure of Job Characteristics. *Journal of Applied Psychology,* 1988, *73,* 245–252.

27. Perlman, S. L. Employees Redesign Their Jobs. *Personnel Journal,* November 1990, 37–40; Oldham, G. R., Kulik, C. T., Stepina, L. P., and Ambrose, M. L. Relations between Situational Factors and the Comparative Referents Used by Employees. *Academy of Management Journal,* 1986, *29,* 599–608.

28. Schuler, R. S. *Managing Human Resources,* 4th ed. St. Paul: West, 1992.

29. Whitsett, D. A. Where Are Your Enriched Jobs? *Harvard Business Review,* January-February 1975, 74–80.

30. Campion, M. A., and Thayer, P. W. Development and Field Evaluation of an Interdisciplinary Measure of Job Design. *Journal of Applied Psychology,* 1985, *70,* 29–43; Aldag, R. J., Barr, S. H., and

Brief, A. P. Measurement of Perceived Task Characteristics. *Psychological Bulletin*, 1981, *90*, 415–431.

31. Hackman, J. R., and Oldham, G. R. Development of the Job Diagnostic Survey. *Journal of Applied Psychology*, 1975, *60*, 159–170.

32. Chase, R. B., and Garvin, D. A. The Service Factory. *Harvard Business Review*, July-August 1989, 61–69.

33. Ford, R. N. Job Enrichment Lessons from AT&T. *Harvard Business Review*, January-February 1973, 96–106.

34. Ryan, K. D., and Oesrteich, D. K. *Driving Fear Out of the Workplace: How to Overcome the Invisible Barriers to Quality, Productivity and Innovation*. San Francisco: Jossey-Bass, 1991; Herold, D. M., and Parsons, C. K. Assessing the Feedback Environment in Work Organizations: Development of the Job Feedback Survey. *Journal of Applied Psychology*, 1985, *70*, 290–305.

35. Fulk, J., and Steinfield, C. (Eds.) *Organizations and Communication Technology*. Newbury Park, Calif: Sage, 1990.

36. Adapted from Griffin, R. W. Effects of Work Redesign on Employee Perceptions, Attitudes and Behaviors: A Long-Term Investigation. *Academy of Management Journal*, 1991, *34*, 425–435.

37. Thomas, J. G., and Griffin, R. W. The Power of Social Information in the Workplace. *Organizational Dynamics*, Winter 1989, 63–75.

38. Pfeffer, J. Management As Symbolic Action: The Creation and Maintenance of Organizational Paradigms. In L. L. Cummings and B. M. Staw (eds.), *Research in Organizational Behavior*, vol. 3. Greenwich, Conn.: JAI Press, 1981, 1–32. Also see Sandelands, L. E. Perceptual Organization in Task Performance. *Organizational Behavior and Human Decision Processes*, 1987, *40*, 287–306.

39. Griffin, R. W., Bateman, T. S., Wayne, S. J., and Head, T. C. Objective and Social Factors as Determinants of Task Perceptions and Responses: An Integrated Perspective and Empirical Investigation. *Academy of Management Journal*, 1987, *30*, 501–523; Ornstein, S. The Hidden Influences of Office Design. *Academy of Management Executive*, May 1989, 144–147; Head, T. C., Griffin, R. W.,

Bateman, T. S., Lohman, L., and Yates, V. L. The Priming Effect in Task Design Research. *Journal of Management*, 1988, *14*, 31–39.

40. Kulik, C. T. The Effects of Job Categorization on Judgments of the Motivating Potential of Jobs. *Administrative Science Quarterly*, 1989, *34*, 68–90.

41. Cherns, A. Principles of Sociotechnical Design Revisited. *Human Relations*, 1987, *40*, 153–162; Pava, C. Redesigning Sociotechnical Systems Design: Concepts and Methods for the 1990s. *Journal of Applied Behavioral Science*, 1986, *22*, 201–221.

42. Gattiker, U.E. *Technology Management in Organizations*. Newbury Park, Calif: Sage, 1990.

43. Dumaine, B. Who Needs a Boss? *Fortune*, May 7, 1990, 52–60.

44. Wall, T. D., Kemp, N. J., Jackson, P. R., and Clegg, C. W. Outcomes of Autonomous Workgroups: A Long-Term Field Experiment. *Academy of Management Journal*, 1986, *29*, 280–304.

45. Pasmore, W. A. *Designing Effective Organizations: The Sociotechnical Systems Perspective*. New York: John Wiley, 1988, 157–186; Argyris, C. Teaching Smart People How to Learn. *Harvard Business Review*, May-June, 1991, 99–109.

46. Cunningham, J. B., and Eberle, T. A Guide to Job Enrichment and Redesign. *Personnel*, February 1990, 56–61.

47. Deutschman, A. Pioneers of the New Balance. *Fortune*, May 21, 1991, 60–68.

48. Turnage, J. J. The Challenge of New Workplace Technology for Psychology. *American Psychologist*, February 1990, 171–178.

49. Lawler, E. E., III,. The New Plant Revolution Revisited. *Organizational Dynamics*, Autumn 1990, 5–14; Griffin, R. W. *Task Design: An Integrative-Approach*. Glenview, Ill.: Scott, Foresman, 1982.

50. Adapted from Sims, H. P., Jr., Szilagyi, A. D., and Keller, R. T. The Measurement of Job Characteristics. *Academy of Management Journal*, 1976, *19*, 195–212.

51. Adapted from Oswald, S., Scott, C., and Warner, W. Strategic Management of Human Resources: The American Steel and Wire Company. *Business Horizons*, May-June 1991, 77–82.

CHAPTER 18

ORGANIZATION DESIGN

LEARNING OBJECTIVES

When you have finished studying this chapter, you should be able to:

- Explain the influence of environmental forces, strategic choices, and technological factors on the design of organizations.
- Evaluate the extent to which an organization is organic or mechanistic.
- Diagnose interdepartmental relations through the use of three key variables.
- Identify the bases of departmentalization and circumstances under which each may be effective.
- Describe the multidivisional structure and multinational corporation as complex organization designs.
- Describe the network organization and explain how it overcomes the limitations of other designs.
- Discuss the influence of organization design on employee and organizational effectiveness.

OUTLINE

◆ *PREVIEW CASE*

RESTRUCTURING AT BECTON DICKINSON

Becton Dickinson (BD) found itself worrying about the competition, despite a history of fast growth and annual revenues of around $2 billion. The maker of high-tech diagnostic systems, such as blood analyzers, started exploring ways to encourage competitive success through its organization design. BD still maintains traditional functions within divisions such as marketing, sales, engineering, and manufacturing. However, BD modified its design to encourage employees to take the initiative. They form teams to innovate and go after business in new ways. Explains CEO Raymond Gilmartin: "We're creating a hierarchy of ideas. You say, 'This is the right thing to do here,' not 'We're going to do this because I'm boss.' "

Instead of directing strategy from the top, Gilmartin lays out a very broad vision—develop proprietary ideas and beat the competition to market with them—and then lets the fifteen company divisions develop their own business strategies. The division heads structure their businesses to meet their needs. Says Chuck Baer, head of the company's consumer products divisions: "We reorganized ourselves by the way we work. We organized cross-functional teams that include not only our own people but also vendors, suppliers, and people from other divisions. We set the strategy and the team carries it out."

This is harder than it sounds and less than completely democratic. In 1990, BD developed a new instrument called the Bactec 860, designed to process blood samples. A team leader was assigned and immediately put together a project team of engineers, marketers, manufacturers, and suppliers. Although the team eventually launched the Bactec 860 some 25 percent faster than its previous best effort, Gilmartin was not satisfied.

There was still too much time-wasting debate between marketing and engineering over product specifications, he found. Marketing argued that Bactec 860 needed more features to please the customer. Engineering said that the features would take too long to design and be too costly. Further debate led to the core of the problem. The team leader reported to the head of engineering and did not have sufficient authority to resolve the conflict between the two sides. Today, the company makes sure all of its team leaders have direct access to a division head. This gives them the authority to settle disputes between different functions.[1]

Organization design is the process of diagnosing and selecting the structure and formal system of communication, division of labor, coordination, control, authority, and responsibility necessary to achieve the organization's

597

goals. In the Preview Case, we see how concerns about increased competitive pressures triggered a reevaluation of BD's organization design. The firm's division of labor is illustrated by the traditional functions of marketing, sales, engineering, and manufacturing. The authority and responsibility concepts are portrayed in the empowerment of divisions to reorganize according to the way they work. This is accompanied by the use of teams to improve communication and coordination in the implementation of new projects, such as Bactec 860. The ambiguities over authority relations were dealt with through organization design.

Organization design requires a decision-making process that takes account of environmental forces, technological factors, and strategic choices.[2] Specifically, organization design should meet three needs:

- Ease the flow of information and decision making in order to better manage the demands of customers and other stakeholders critical to organizational success.

- Clarify the authority and responsibility in jobs and departments so the potential benefits from the division of labor and effective job design can be realized.

- Create the desired levels of integration (coordination) between departments (for example, between manufacturing and marketing).

Many previous chapters have discussed aspects of organization design. One cornerstone to organization design is the design of individual jobs, which was our focus in Chapter 17. A second cornerstone is the formation and use of groups—such as problem-solving teams, special-purpose teams, and self-managing teams—which was the focus of Chapter 10. A third cornerstone is the design of intergroup relations—including a consideration of such influences as group goals, substitutability, types of task relations, and resource sharing—which was the focus of Chapter 11. In Chapter 11, organization design mechanisms for managing intergroup relations included organization hierarchy, linking roles, task forces, and integrating roles and groups. The last cornerstone is organizational culture, the focus of Chapter 15. Organizational culture sets forth the shared philosophies, values, assumptions, and norms of the organization. Organization design decisions, such as changes in the delegation of authority or the effective use of teams, are likely to be influenced by the prevailing organizational culture.

In this chapter, we extend your understanding of organization design. First, we note how environmental forces, strategic choices, and technological factors can influence the design of an organization. Second, a broad framework is presented for diagnosing the extent to which organizations can be characterized as mechanistic or organic. Third, three key factors—differentiation, integration, and uncertainty—in the design of interdepartmental relations are discussed. The various bases of departmentalization are reviewed, including the advantages and disadvantages of each. The multidivisional structure and multinational corporation are presented as complex designs in which multiple bases of departmentalization are used. Finally, an emerging organization design—the network organization—is presented as one intended to overcome the limitations of these other forms in the face of complex and changing environments.

THREE FACTORS IN DESIGN

Organization design decisions—such as greater decentralization and changes in responsibility and authority—may solve one set of problems but can create others. Every organization design has some problems. The key is to select an organization design that minimizes the problems.

Three important factors—environmental forces, strategic choices, and technological factors—affect how managers make design decisions. Table 18.1 identifies several variables for each factor.[3]

Environmental Forces

The environmental forces managers and other employees need to assess are: (1) the *characteristics* of the present and possible future environments and (2) the *demands* of those environments on the need to process information, cope with uncertainties, and achieve desired levels of differentiation (division of labor) and integration (coordination).

Task Environment and Structure The **task environment** includes the external stakeholders and forces with which the organization has direct contact.[4] Table 18.2 shows the primary types of stakeholders within the task environment of most for-profit organizations. It illustrates a simple functional structure in which separate departments specialize in dealing with each major stakeholder in the task environment. For example, the marketing department normally has more direct contact with customers than any of the other departments. The top executive team, especially the chief executive officer, is likely to have direct decision-making involvement with many of the stakeholders. This is because the top executive team, including the board of directors, is usually responsible for the following: (1) setting the major strategies and policies to be followed by the departments in contacts with stakeholders; (2) approving the organization's strategic plan,

---

TABLE 18.1 Important Factors in Organization Design Decisions

Factors	Sample Variables
Environmental forces	Degree of complexity
	Degree of dynamism
Strategic choices	Top management's philosophy
	Types of customers
	Geographic areas served
Technological factors	Work-flow uncertainty
	Task uncertainty
	Task interdependence

TABLE 18.2	Functional Form of Organization and the Task Environment
Organizational Department	**Primary Links to External Stakeholders**
Marketing	Customers, competitors
Manufacturing	Suppliers, customers, regulatory agencies
Purchasing	Suppliers
Human resources	Potential employees, unions, health and life insurance companies, regulatory agencies
Research and development	New scientific knowledge and technology
Legal services	Shareholders, regulatory agencies, courts
Finance and accounting	Creditors and debtors, regulatory agencies

which is to be followed by each functional department; (3) monitoring and evaluating the organization's effectiveness as a whole, as well as that of key departments; and (4) monitoring changes in environment and making the key decisions based on their diagnosis, such as to approve major new plant construction, set dividend policy, approve acquisition of a supplier, and the like.[5]

Environmental Characteristics After the relevant stakeholders and forces in the task environment have been defined, managers need to assess their characteristics and relative importance to the organization.[6] Environmental characteristics vary in terms of two major dimensions: complexity and dynamism.

The **complexity dimension** relates to whether the factors considered are few in number and similar to each other (homogeneous) or many in number and different from each other (heterogeneous). Employees in a planning department typically face a heterogeneous environment because they must consider virtually all the stakeholders shown in Table 18.2. At the other extreme, employees in a custodial department face a homogeneous environment. Rating an environment as homogeneous or heterogeneous depends both on the number of factors and the number of subenvironments involved. Five factors in one subenvironment, such as the customer subenvironment, would not be as complex as five factors in three subenvironments, such as customers, suppliers, and competitors.

The **dynamism dimension** relates to whether the factors in the environment remain basically the same (are stable) or change (are unstable). In the Preview Case, it was apparent that Becton Dickinson saw the competitive environment changing and decided to modify its organization design to make it more responsive to these changes.

Types of Task Environments Figure 18.1 classifies task environments in terms of complexity and dynamism. The four "pure" types of task environments are: homogeneous-stable, heterogeneous-stable, homogeneous-unstable, and heterogeneous-unstable. We can locate the environment of an organization or one of its departments anywhere on this grid.

The *homogeneous-stable environment* (box 1, Figure 18.1) represents the easiest management situation. The task environment holds few surprises, and the manager's role is to make sure that employees consistently follow well-established routines and procedures. Managers and other employees need relatively less skill, formal training, and job experience to operate successfully in this environment than in the others.

The *heterogeneous-stable environment* (box 2, Figure 18.1) poses some risks for managers and other employees. Under conditions of risk, the environment and the alternatives are fairly well understood. Employees can assign probabilities to the effects of various alternatives. The environment is relatively stable, but organization members may need considerable training and experience to understand and manage it. For example, the registrar's office of a college or university must communicate with academic departments, current and prospective students, the central administration, and

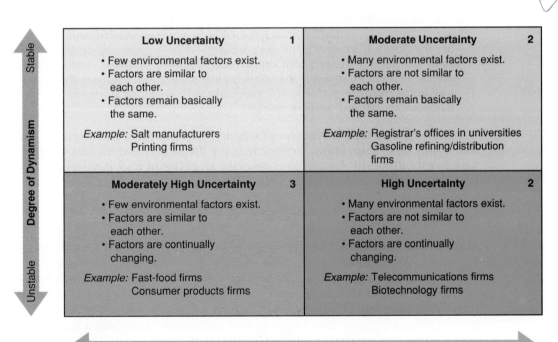

FIGURE 18.1 Basic Types of Task Environments

Source: Adapted from A. Rasheed and J. E. Prescott, Dimensions of Organizational Task Environments: Revisited. Paper presented at 1987 Academy of Management meeting, New Orleans, 1987: R. Duncan, What Is the Right Organization Structure? Decision Tree Analysis Provides the Answer. *Organizational Dynamics,* Winter 1979, 60–64.

governmental education agencies. The nature of these communications does not change frequently, and they are usually guided by extensive rules and procedures.

The *homogeneous-unstable environment* (box 3, Figure 18.1) requires managers, employees, and organization designs to be flexible. A number of changes take place, but they can be handled with a reasonable level of skill and motivation. Computer-based information systems often help keep track of the changes. McDonald's, for example, frequently offers new menu items, but all must be relatively easy to make.

The *heterogeneous-unstable environment* (box 4, Figure 18.1) represents the most difficult organization situation because the environment contains numerous uncertainties. Of all task environments, this one requires the most managerial and employee sophistication, insight, and problem-solving ability. Decision-making techniques can aid managers and others, but they are no substitute for human judgment. Mangers cannot solve the problems confronting them by merely using standardized rules and procedures. As discussed in the Preview Case, Becton Dickinson operates in a heterogeneous-unstable environment. The organization design changes were made to encourage employees to take the initiative and form teams to innovate and go after business in new ways.

The problems and opportunities confronting most complex organizations have become more numerous and diverse.[7] One authority commented:

> The new managerial calculus suggests that only 20 percent of business factors are, in any sense, controllable and that 80 percent are noncontrollable. What is beyond business' control is its environment—that "buzzing, blooming confusion" (to many managers and employees) of global, national, and business events. This environment is the source of the shocks and surprises that batter traditional business performance and make mincemeat of strategies that are inadequately attuned to these changes.[8]

Each type of task environment requires unique ways of designing and managing an organization, department, or division. Later in this chapter, we identify different designs and describe the type of task environment in which each is most likely to be effective.

Strategic Choices

Many of top management's strategic choices can affect organization design decisions.[9] We highlight only three of them here. First, top management's values and philosophy play a role in the strategic choice between a centralized and decentralized design and control system. A philosophy of centralization requires more levels in the hierarchy with more resources devoted to monitoring and controlling lower-level departments than does a decentralized design. For example, quality control, human resources, and auditing departments may be given relatively large budgets and considerable authority if top management's philosophy is centralization.

A second strategic choice involves top management's decisions about the types of customers they want to serve. A firm that tries to sell to industrial, commercial, and residential customers often needs a different organization design than a firm that only tries to sell to industrial customers.

Firms that sell multiple lines of goods or services, such as ITT, Gulf & Western, and Procter & Gamble, group together the resources needed to manufacture and market each product line.

A third strategic choice in organization design is top management's strategy of where to market and produce goods and services. For example, Allstate Insurance has a strategy to market insurance only in North America. Ford Motor Company, Kentucky Fried Chicken, and Sony are organizations that have defined the world as their market. They usually need to create much more complex organization designs than do firms that only manufacture and market in a particular country or region of the world.

These few examples of how strategic choices can affect organization design illustrate a key point: Organization designs are often created and modified as a result of strategic choices.[10] The following In Practice demonstrates the close interplay between environmental forces and strategic choices on organization design.

IN PRACTICE

CCL INDUSTRIES OF CANADA

A year before the signing of the free trade agreement between the United States and Canada, CCL Industries, Inc., of Willowdale, Ontario, saw the writing on the wall. It opted for drastic redesign. This involved the sale of Continental Can, a division that comprised more than half of its business. This division had been established to serve a protected Canadian market with aluminum cans. It had enjoyed a 50 percent market share in Canada but only 3 percent share in all of North America. With the import duty scheduled to be removed from cans, Continental Can's status threatened to shrink from whale to minnow.

A frightening glimpse of the future came in 1987 during a can war among the major manufacturers in the United States. Prices fell, making the difference between Canadian and U.S. can suppliers apparent. Continental Can's customers were all multinationals, such as Coca-Cola Ltd. and Pepsi-Cola Canada Ltd. It came under more and more pressure to match U.S. pricing or lose this business to U.S. can companies. The average duty on cans was about 10 percent. But U.S. prices were already 15 percent to 20 percent lower than Continental's because of the much higher production volumes. Continental was too small a customer to have much influence on the prices it paid for aluminum to such giants as Alcan. Wayne McLeod, CEO of CCL, says, "We were the ham in the sandwich, caught between big customers and big suppliers, all of which could dictate price. We had no leeway for profitability."

Fearing the situation would only worsen with free trade, McLeod assembled a committee of senior managers to look at options for the future. CCL was uncomfortable with anything but dominant market position. The committee recommended that CCL sell its biggest holding, Continental Can, to one of the U.S. can giants. The dollars from the sale were used to buy and build North American market dominance in CCL's other packaging niches. Says McLeod: "Impending free trade showed us that we had to restructure the company with the view to being the major player in each business. The only piece that didn't fit this scenario happened to be our major business."

The businesses CCL decided to keep were the parts already positioned on both sides of the border—the custom manufacture of personal care products, pressure sensitive labels, and aluminum aerosol cans. In November 1989, CCL sold Continental Can to one of the world's largest can manufacturers, Crown Cork & Seal Company, Inc., of Philadelphia, for $390 million.

Then the acquisitions began. To consolidate its positions in custom manufacturing, CCL went straight after the largest player in the United States, Hi-Port Industries, Inc., of Houston. This acquisition gave CCL dominance of the North American market in custom-manufactured antiperspirant aerosols, liquids, and sticks. CCL, already the largest pressure-sensitive label manufacturer in North America, continued to build with the purchase of Janus Label Corporation of Sacramento, California. This resulted in a total of six U.S. and two Canadian plants. In the aerosol-can business, CCL was already the dominant North American producer, with Ontario-based Advanced Monobloc. Next was Europe. McLeod and his management team pursued an acquisition strategy to gain a foothold in the European market. They have already purchased two of the leading aerosol companies in the United Kingdom and are looking at other firms on the Continent.[11]

Technological Factors

We discussed in Chapter 17 the ways by which work-flow uncertainty, task uncertainty, and task interdependence affect job design. These three technological factors also influence organization design, particularly in terms of the creation of departments, the delegation of authority and responsibility, and the need for formal integrating mechanisms among them.

Work-Flow and Task Uncertainty   From an organization design perspective, *work-flow uncertainty* is the degree of knowledge in a department about when inputs will be received for processing. When work-flow uncertainty is low, a department has little discretion to decide which, when, or where tasks will be performed. *Task uncertainty* is the degree of well-defined knowledge in a department with respect to performing the tasks assigned to it.[12] When task uncertainty is low, members of the department generally know how to produce the desired outcomes. Where there is high task uncertainty, there are few (if any) prespecified ways for dealing with the tasks assigned to the department. In this case, key members of the department usually have to apply experience, judgment, and intuition—and jointly define and solve problems—in order to achieve the desired goals.

Parallel to the discussion of job design and technology in Chapter 17 (see, especially, Figure 17.3), we first consider the effects of work-flow uncertainty and task uncertainty on organization design and then discuss the effects of task interdependence on organization design.[13] Figure 18.2 shows possible linkages between work-flow uncertainty and task uncertainty. Both can range from low to high, again giving us four combinations.

Examples of departments that often are characteristic of each combination are listed in each cell in Figure 18.2. Remember, a department can fit

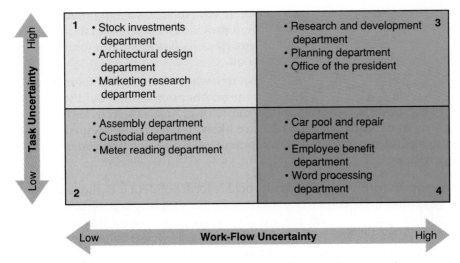

FIGURE 18.2   Technology and Organization Design Framework

Source: Adapted from J. W. Slocum, Jr., and H. P. Sims, Jr. Topology for Integrating Technology, Organization, and Job Design. *Human Relations,* 1980, *33:* 196; G. I. Susman, *Autonomy at Work: A Sociotechnical Analysis of Participative Management.* New York: Praeger, 1980, 132.

into more than one of these cells. Through organization redesign, most departments can be modified and the task uncertainty and work-flow uncertainty changed. The office of the president and the planning department are generally characterized by high task uncertainty and high work-flow uncertainty. However, some of the specific tasks that they perform could be classified anywhere on the matrix. Another important point is that some departments do not fit clearly into a single cell. For example, the auditing department in a public accounting firm might generally be placed somewhere in the middle of Figure 18.2. One of the implications of the framework in Figure 18.2 is that departments may be formed on the basis of similarities in technological characteristics. This is most often done by creating functional departments, such as those shown.

Task Interdependence   We identified three major types of task interdependence in Chapter 17: pooled, sequential, and reciprocal. From an organization design perspective, we can characterize these types of interdependence as follows:

- *Pooled interdependence* occurs when each department is relatively autonomous and makes an identifiable contribution to the organization. For example, the many sales and services offices of State Farm Insurance do not engage in day-to-day decision making, coordination, and communication with each other. The local offices are interdependent with regional offices that coordinate and set policies for the local sales and services offices. The performance of each local office is readily identifiable.

- *Sequential interdependence* occurs when one department must complete certain tasks before one or more other departments can perform their tasks. For example, at Whirlpool's washing machine factory, the fabrication department provides its outputs to the assembly department, which, in turn, provides its outputs to the painting and finishing department, and so on.

- *Reciprocal interdependence* occurs when the outputs from one department become the inputs for another department and vice versa. For example, the planning, marketing, and research and development departments at AT&T are likely to have many reciprocal interdependencies in the development of new telecommunication services.

As shown in Figure 18.3, reciprocal interdependence is the most complex type, and pooled interdependence is the simplest type. Greater interdependence generally requires greater integration of departments. Placing reciprocally interdependent departments under a common superior often improves integration and minimizes information-processing costs. For example, at Brooklyn Union Gas Company, the marketing research, advertising, and sales departments report to the vice-president of marketing. Employees in these departments must communicate and coordinate more with each other than with employees in the maintenance department.

In Chapter 17, we discussed how new information technologies are changing the jobs of many employees. These information technologies also

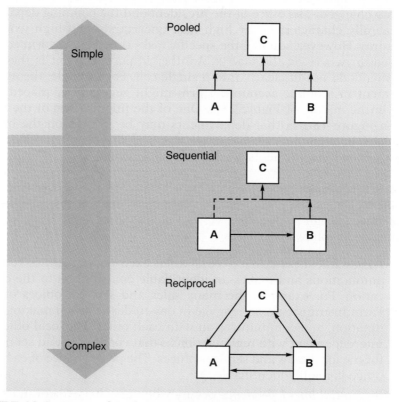

FIGURE 18.3   Types of Task Interdependence in Organization Design

have an impact on the design of organizations and the flows of information through them.[14] For example, the following In Practice reveals how the Digital Equipment Corporation is using computer-based information technologies to improve its ability to manage numerous task interdependencies.

IN PRACTICE

EASYNET NETWORK

Easynet is Digital Equipment Corporation's (DEC) twenty-seven thousand-computer, twenty six-nation central nervous system. Directly accessible to most of DEC's 120,000 employees, the network "has changed the corporation," says Robert E. McCauley, who runs the unique system. Most companies' networks restrict communications more or less along rigid organizational lines. Not so with DEC's; a programmer in Australia can send a message directly to CEO Kenneth H. Olsen. Because the information network is so flexible, DEC can simply extend it as the company grows, without having to change it. All this fits DEC's culture. "Computer systems reflect the organizations that build them," says Thomas W. Malone, an office-automation theorist at The Massachusetts Institute of Technology's Sloan School of Management. He adds, "DEC's management style is one of a great deal of lateral networking."

Easynet helps DEC in other ways. Product development is fast, despite extensive management reviews. Engineers use the network to win support for proposed projects and then to share design work. Marketing, sales, engineering, and manufacturing staffs all can get details of an intended product. Over Easynet, teams made up of engineers in several different countries can exchange memos, circuit diagrams, and even software.

Formed in 1984 from several existing networks, Easynet has also helped slash operating costs. A central computer takes a customer's order from a branch office, bills the buyer, and relays orders to DEC's factories for the appropriate components. The parts are sent directly to the customer site and assembled there. The result: a 50 percent reduction in inventory since 1984. Average manufacturing time has been halved to one hundred and twenty days from chip production to finished system. And the network helps engineers speed last-minute changes to the factory floor.

Product catalogs stored on the network let DEC salespeople prepare proposals in one day that used to take ten. DEC has extended Easynet to suppliers to speed order and payment processing.[15]

MECHANISTIC VERSUS ORGANIC SYSTEMS

A **mechanistic system** is characterized by extensive use of formal rules and regulations, centralization of decision making, narrowly defined job responsibilities, and rigid hierarchy of authority. In contrast, an **organic system** is characterized by low-to-moderate use of formal rules and regulations, decentralized and shared decision making, broadly defined job responsibilities, and a flexible authority structure with fewer levels in the hierarchy.[16] Organizations using a routine technology (low task and work-flow uncertainty) and operating in homogeneous-stable environments may effectively use the mechanistic system. In contrast, organizations using nonroutine technology (high task and work-flow uncertainty) and operating in heterogeneous-unstable environments may effectively use an organic system.

A mechanistic system is a bureaucracy. Max Weber, a German sociologist and economist in the early 1900s, defined a **bureaucracy** as an organization having the following characteristics:

- The organization operates according to a body of rules, or laws, that are intended to tightly control the behavior of employees.

- All employees must follow impersonal rules and procedures in making decisions.

- Each employee's job has a specified arena of expertise, with strictly defined obligations, authority, and powers to compel obedience.

- The organization follows the principle of hierarchy; that is, each lower position is under the control and direction of a higher one.

- Candidates for jobs are selected on the basis of "technical" qualifications. They are appointed, not elected.

- The organization has a career ladder. Promotion is by seniority or achievement. Promotion depends on the judgment of superiors.[17]

The word *bureaucracy* often conjures up thoughts of rigidity, incompetence, red tape, inefficiency, and ridiculous rules. In principle, the basic characteristics of bureaucracy may make it a reasonable and attractive way to organize in certain situations.[18] Thus, any discussion of a bureaucratic organization (mechanistic system) must distinguish between the way it should ideally function and the way some large-scale organizations actually operate.[19]

The degrees to which an organization emphasizes a mechanistic or an organic system can vary substantially. As shown in Figure 18.4, the same is also true of the departments or divisions within a single organization. Department B in Figure 18.4 represents a relatively mechanistic system across all of the selected dimensions. Department A, which is more varied in its emphasis on each dimension, represents an organic system. Department B could be the assembly line operation for VCRs at Samsung, whereas department A could be Samsung's research and development department.

The organic system emphasizes employee competence, rather than the employee's formal position in the hierarchy, as a basis for influence in decision making. This system has a less rigid hierarchy and permits employees greater flexibility for dealing with uncertainties in technology and their task environment.[20] In the following paragraphs, we briefly describe each of the dimensions identified in Figure 18.4.

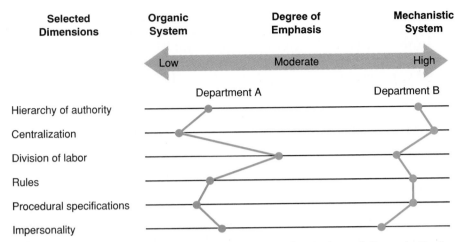

FIGURE 18.4   Possible Characteristics of Mechanistic and Organic Systems

Hierarchy of Authority

Hierarchy of authority represents the extent to which an organization structures decision making and defines the formal power allocated to each position. Higher-level departments or positions assign or approve goals and budgets for lower-level departments or positions.

The hierarchy-of-authority dimension is sometimes confused with centralization. **Centralization** is a relative concept: It is present when all major, and oftentimes many minor, decisions are made only at the top levels of the organization.[21] Centralization is common in mechanistic systems, whereas decentralization and shared decision making among levels are common in an organic system.[22]

Division of Labor

Division of labor refers to the various ways of dividing up tasks and labor to achieve goals.[23] Adam Smith, the father of the capitalistic economic system, recognized the importance of this concept in organization design in his book *An Inquiry into the Nature and Cause of the Wealth of Nations*, published in 1776. Smith noted that the wealth of a nation could be increased if organizations used a high degree of division of labor. In general, the greater the division of labor in an organization, the greater would be the efficiency of the organization.[24]

The mechanistic system typically follows Smith's views. As we noted in Chapter 17, a continued increase in the division of labor may eventually become counterproductive. Employees who perform only very routine and simple jobs that require few skills may become bored and frustrated with their work. The results may be low quality and productivity, high turnover, and high absenteeism. In addition, the managerial costs (many reports, more managers, and more controls to administer) of integrating highly specialized departments are usually high. In contrast, the organic system tends to reduce these costs by delegating decision making to lower-level employees in the organization. Delegation also encourages employees to develop a deeper sense of responsibility for achieving their tasks and linking them to the needs of the entire organization. The organic system takes advantage of the benefits from the division of labor. But it is much more sensitive to recognizing when further increases in the division of labor may become counterproductive.

Rules and Procedures

Rules are formal, written statements specifying acceptable and unacceptable behaviors and decisions by organization members. One of the paradoxes of rules that attempt to reduce individual autonomy is that someone must still decide which rules apply to specific situations. Rules are an integral part of both mechanistic and organic systems. In a mechanistic system, the tendency is to create uniform rules to handle tasks and decisions *whenever possible.* In an organic system, the tendency is to create rules *only when necessary* (such as safety rules to protect life and property). Managers and employees also tend to question the need for new rules, as well as existing rules, in organic systems. In mechanistic systems, they tend to accept the need for extensive rules and to formulate new rules in response to new situations.

Procedures are the preset sequences of steps that managers and employees must follow in performing tasks and dealing with problems. Procedures often consist of a number of rules to be used in a particular sequence. In order to obtain reimbursement for travel expenses in most organizations, employees must follow a well-defined set of procedures. Procedures are essentially made up of rules. Thus, they have many of the same positive and negative features that characterize rules and are most often embraced in a mechanistic system. Managers in organic systems are usually alert to how rules and procedures can make the organization too rigid and thus lower employee motivation, innovation, and creativity.

Impersonality

Impersonality is the extent to which organizations treat their employees, as well as outsiders, without regard to individual characteristics. Managers in a mechanistic system are likely to place greater emphasis on impersonal factors, such as college degrees, certificates earned, test scores, training programs completed, length of service, and the like, when making hiring, salary, and promotion decisions. Although these factors may be considered by managers in an organic system, they are more likely to emphasize actual achievements and the judgments from several individuals than strictly following rules. At Merck, a leading pharmaceutical company that operates as an organic system, a college graduate applying for a job typically goes through an extensive interview process. This process involves several managers and many (if not all) of the employees with whom the applicant would work. It is not unusual for someone to be "interviewed" casually and informally by a group of employees. The person responsible for filing the open position solicits the opinions and reactions from these employees before making a decision. In some instances, the manager may even call the employees and other managers who participated in the interview process together to discuss the candidate(s).

The following In Practice notes how lateral integrating mechanisms and the process of participation typical of an organic system can be carried to extremes. Hewlett-Packard ended up—albeit unintentionally—becoming partly a mechanistic system.

IN PRACTICE

HEWLETT-PACKARD REORGANIZES

It is amazing that Bob Frankenberg ever got anything done at all. Until 1990, the Hewlett-Packard general manager dealt with no fewer than thirty-eight in-house committees. They decided everything from what features to include in a new software program to what city would be best for staging a product launch. Just coming up with a name for the company's New Wave Computing software took nearly one hundred people on nine committees seven months. "There was a lot of decision overhead," says John A. Young, H-P's chief executive officer.

Could this be the same company whose "H-P Way" encouraged innovation by abolishing rigid chains of command, doing away with fancy executive offices, and putting managers and employees on a first-name basis? By the late 1980s, an unwieldy web of committees, originally designed to foster communication between H-P's diverse operating groups, had pushed up costs and slowed down product development. The company's entrenched culture, which was built around the "H-P Way" philosophy of equality and mutual respect, promoted consensus. But, critics say, the culture placed too much emphasis on rapport among managers and others and failed to penalize those who missed opportunities.

The cure was the company's most drastic reorganization in ten years. Young announced it in October 1990. Young wiped out H-P's committee structure and flattened the organization. To cut costs, H-P had already launched an early retirement program. Young's reorganization divided the computer business into two main groups. One handles personal computers, printers, and other products sold through dealers. The second group oversees sales of workstations and minicomputers to big customers.

In place of the single corporate sales force established in the mid-1980s, each of the two computer units now has its own sales and marketing team. "The results are incredible," says Frankenberg, who now deals with three committees instead of thirty-eight. "We are doing more business and getting product out quicker with fewer people."[25]

INTERDEPARTMENTAL RELATIONS

An essential part of organization design is to determine the desired relationships among departments. Much of the presentation in Chapter 11 regarding the dynamics between groups is useful for understanding interdepartmental relations. Interdepartmental relations are primarily affected by three variables: (1) the degree of differentiation between departments; (2) the degree of required integration between departments; and (3) the degree of uncertainty (including task, work-flow, and environmental) confronting each department. As Figure 18.5 shows, each of these variables can range from low to high. The diagnosis of these variables and their impact on operations is a necessary step in designing an effective organization.

Differentiation

Differentiation is the degree to which departments differ in structure (low to high), members' orientation to a time horizon (short to long), managers' orientation to other people (permissive to authoritarian), and members' views of the task environment (certain to uncertain).[26]

Production departments often have a high degree of formal structure. There are many rules and procedures, tight supervisory control, and frequent and specific reviews of individual and departmental performance (mechanistic system). Research departments and planning departments often are just the opposite (organic system). Research and planning personnel tend to prefer open and close relationships with one another. Production personnel may prefer more directive and structured relationships with co-workers. Production personnel tend to have short time horizons (hours and days) and think about immediate problems. Research and planning employees tend to think months and even years into the future. In general, the greater the differences between departments, the more problems managers have in getting them to work together (such as marketing with production).[27]

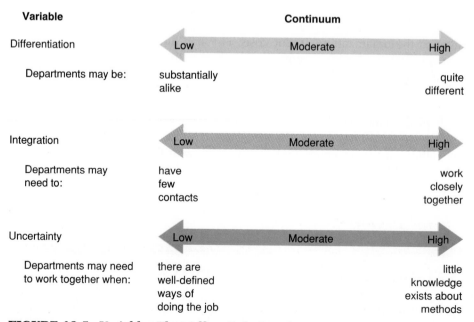

FIGURE 18.5   Variables That Affect Relations between Departments

Integration

Integration is the degree of collaboration and mutual understanding required among departments to achieve their goals. The division of labor and task interdependencies create the need for integration. This need is greatest between departments that are reciprocally interdependent and least when they are in a pooled interdependent relationship.

Managers must be careful not to establish too much or too little integration among departments. Too little integration will probably lead to lower-quality decisions and the misuse of resources, because each department can "do its own thing." The costs associated with too much integration are likely to far exceed any possible benefits.[28] Moreover, with excessive integration, departments often get in the way of each other, rather than help each other perform their tasks and achieve their goals. This became a problem at Hewlett-Packard, as described in the previous In Practice.

Four organization design mechanisms were presented in Chapter 11 for achieving integration among groups (departments): hierarchy, linking roles, task forces, and integrating roles and groups (departments). The effective use of one or more of these mechanisms can minimize the likelihood of too little or too much integration.

Uncertainty

Uncertainty is the gap between what is known and what needs to be known to make sound decisions and perform tasks effectively. The following factors should be evaluated in determining the degree of uncertainty that confronts departments:

- The extent to which there is a clearly defined body of knowledge or guidelines available to departmental employees in the performance of their tasks.

- The frequency with which departments can be expected to face independent or mutual problems that they do not know how to solve and that they must take time to think through before taking any action.

- The amount of actual thinking time that departments must spend before trying to implement solutions to independent or mutual problems.

- The probability that departments can be reasonably sure of the results of their independent and mutual efforts.[29]

Organizational Significance

The combinations of the three variables have several significant implications for organization design and management. First, the easiest situation to manage occurs when there is low uncertainty, low differentiation, and low required integration. In this situation, departments are practically independent of each other. The produce and canned/boxed goods departments in a supermarket provide an example.

Second, increases in the degrees of uncertainty, differentiation, and integration require increases in the expenditure of resources, the number of formal coordinating mechanisms, and the use of certain behavioral processes to obtain integration. Extensive collaboration took place between manufacturing, marketing, planning, design, and engineering departments at the Ford Motor Company in the creation of the Ford Taurus-Mercury Sable models.

Third, the most difficult interdepartmental situation to manage is likely to occur under conditions of high uncertainty, high differentiation, and high required integration. Organizations must spend considerable resources and use a wide variety of formal integration mechanisms and behavioral processes to manage interdepartmental relations under this set of conditions. Consider the case of Procter & Gamble. Its introduction of calcium-enriched Citrus Hill orange juice involved unusually close coordination between three diverse divisions: health-care, beverage, and laundry and detergents. In the course of developing drugs to treat bone disease, researchers in the health-care division had become aware of rapidly worsening calcium deficiencies among U.S. adults. One obvious remedy was to put calcium into the orange juice marketed by Procter & Gamble's food and beverage division. The problem was how to make the mixture palatable. The answer came from a third division, laundry and detergents, which had long before learned how to suspend calcium particles in liquid soap products.[30]

FUNCTIONAL DEPARTMENTALIZATION

Functional departmentalization creates positions and units on the basis of specialized activities, such as engineering, marketing, and manufacturing. Early writers on organization design spent considerable time and effort developing concepts and principles for effective functional designs.

Departments of a typical manufacturing firm with a single product line are often grouped by function, such as engineering, manufacturing, shipping, sales, and finance. Tasks also are usually divided functionally by the *processes* used, such as stamping, plating, assembly, painting, and inspection (sequential interdependence). Figure 18.6 shows how an organization might incorporate both managerial functions and processes in its departmentalization. An organization design can reflect one, two, or even several types of functional classifications. Regardless of the functional division of labor, a common theme of the writers on functional design was the desirability of standardizing and routinizing repetitive tasks whenever possible. Management can then concentrate on exceptions to eliminate any gaps or overlaps.

Line and Staff Functions

Line functions are those jobs that directly affect the principal work flow in an organization. In a manufacturing firm, for instance, all production activities—such as engineering, stamping, plating, assembly, painting, in-

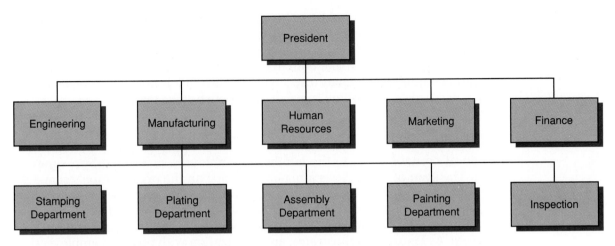

FIGURE 18.6   **Departmentalization by Managerial Function and Process**

spection, and shipping—are considered to be line functions. **Staff functions** are support jobs that provide service and advice to line departments. These usually include the human resource, legal, and finance departments. Figure 18.7 illustrates the traditional distinction between line and staff functions in an organization. For some activities, staff units may be given authority to ensure compliance with laws, regulations, and policies.[31]

Chain of Command

In addition to distinguishing line from staff functions, early writers on organization design stressed two basic ideas about the chain of command. First, in a **scalar chain of command,** authority and responsibility are arranged hierarchically. They flow in a clear, unbroken vertical line from the highest executive to the lowest employee. Clarity is at the heart of the scalar chain. Second, these writers emphasized **unity of command,** which states

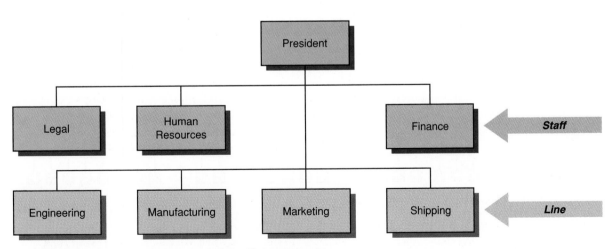

FIGURE 18.7   **Typical Line and Staff Organization**

that no subordinate should receive orders from more than one superior. Modern organizations do not always follow the unity of command throughout their structures. In general, a high level of overlapping lines of authority and responsibility can make both managing and working difficult. Without unity of command, who may direct whom to do what is not clear, and people must persuade or negotiate more to accomplish their tasks.

Span of Control

Span of control refers to the number of employees supervised by a superior. The span of control has a major influence on the organization's shape and structure. When span of control is broad, relatively few levels exist between the top and bottom of the organization. Conversely, when the span of control is narrow, more levels are required for the same number of employees. As Figure 18.8 illustrates, an organization with nineteen employees requires four levels with a narrow span and three levels with a broader span.

The span of control should vary with the nature of the tasks being performed. Thus, there is no one proper span of control. A manager of a relatively simple and repetitive operation might effectively manage twenty to thirty employees, such as in a McDonald's restaurant. At higher organizational levels, however, it may be effective for only five to seven subordinates to report to a general manager.

Organizational Significance

A functional design has both advantages and disadvantages. On the positive side, it permits clear assignment and identification of responsibilities. Employees easily understand this design. People doing similar work and facing similar problems work together, increasing the opportunities for interaction and mutual support.

A disadvantage is that the functional design encourages a limited point of view that focuses on a narrow set of tasks and may lose sight of the organization as a whole. Integration involving functional departments often becomes difficult as the organization increases the number of geographic areas served and the range of goods or services provided.

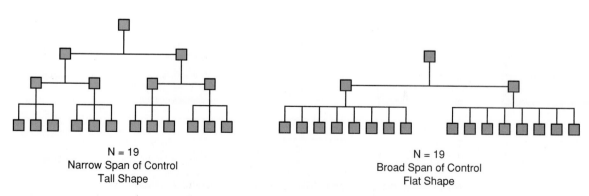

N = 19
Narrow Span of Control
Tall Shape

N = 19
Broad Span of Control
Flat Shape

FIGURE 18.8   Span of Control and Organization Shape

The functional design is likely to be effective when the organization has a narrow product line and does not have to respond to the pressures of serving different geographic areas or types of customers. The addition of specialized staff departments to the functional design may enable an organization to deal effectively with somewhat more complex and changing environments. Staff departments provide the line departments with the expert advice they need to make decisions about complex problems. The addition of integrating mechanisms, such as linking roles and task forces, may also permit the continued use of the basic functional design in heterogeneous-unstable environments.

PRODUCT DEPARTMENTALIZATION

As differentiation in an organization increases, product departmentalization is often more effective than the functional design. **Product departmentalization** is a design with relatively self-contained units, each capable of developing, producing, and marketing its own goods or services. This design increases the use of and emphasis on pooled interdependence between departments within the organization.

Typical Evolution

Organizations that produce multiple goods or services, such as Procter & Gamble, Heinz, PepsiCo, and General Foods, usually benefit from using product departmentalization. It reduces the complexity that would otherwise face managers and others in the more typical functional design. In the functional design, the marketing vice-president may have to be concerned with all the goods or services sold by the organization. When sales of different goods or services reach a certain point, the resulting complexity can be effectively reduced by creating multiple marketing vice-president positions, one vice-president for each product line. Moreover, the product design becomes an attractive alternative to a functional design when the competitive environment for each product line is different.

Organizations with a product design usually began with a functional design. Growth, complexity, and an increasing rate of environmental change created management problems that the functional design alone cannot effectively deal with. When changing to a product design, however, these companies usually do not altogether discard functional departments. Instead, the product design may incorporate functional departments within each product division.

Multidivisional Structure

A complex variation of the product design is the multidivisional structure, sometimes referred to as the "M-Form." The **multidivisional structure** organizes tasks into divisions on the basis of the product or geographic markets in which their goods or services are sold. Divisional managers are primarily responsible for the day-to-day operating decisions within their units. Top corporate-level managers have no day-to-day operating responsibilities. They concentrate on strategic issues, such as allocating resources to the various divisions, assessing new businesses to acquire and divisions to sell off, and communicating with shareholders and others. The corporation's top managers are often supported by elaborate accounting and control systems, as well as a large staff.[32] Of course, as illustrated in the Preview Case on Becton Dickinson, the divisions may be delegated the authority to develop their own strategic plans.

Sony USA primarily uses a multidivisional product design to manufacture and market its goods and services. Some of its divisions include: Sony Magnetic Products Group of America (video- and audiotape), Sony Engineering and Manufacturing Corporation of America (television and video and audio hardware), Materials Research Corporation (semiconductors), Columbia Pictures (entertainment), Digital Audio Disc Corporation (compact discs), SVS (video distribution), and Sony Music Entertainment (formerly CBS Records).[33] Of course, within each division at Sony USA, the functional bases of departmentalization are used.

Organizational Significance

Departmentalization by product lines eases problems of integration by focusing individual expertise and knowledge in specific goods or services. For example, the sales efforts of a marketing department may not be particularly effective if that department has to deal with nuclear power, solar energy, and laser-beam products. Each of these product lines is best handled by a department or division thoroughly familiar with each product and set of customers.

One potential disadvantage of the product (or multidivisional) design is that a firm must have a large number of managerial personnel to serve all of the product lines. Another disadvantage is the higher costs that result from the necessary duplication of various functions.

Adoption of the product (or multidivisional) design often reduces the environmental complexity facing any one department, division, or manager. The manager of a product group needs to focus only on the environment for one product line, rather than on those for multiple products. As with functional design, an organization with a product or multidivisional design can further deal with heterogeneous-unstable environments through the addition of integrating mechanisms, such as linking roles, task forces, and integrating roles and groups.

OTHER BASES OF DEPARTMENTALIZATION

Place Departmentalization

Place departmentalization involves the establishment of organization units according to geographic areas. Many of the tasks in a geographic territory are placed under one manager, rather than grouping functions under different managers or all tasks in one central office. Major companies, such as American Airlines, Federal Express, and Allstate, use the place design to establish regional and district offices. Similarly, many governmental agencies—the Internal Revenue Service (IRS) the Federal Reserve Board, the courts, and the Postal Service—use place departmentalization in providing their services. Many multinational firms use the place design to address cultural and legal differences in various countries, as well as the lack of uniformity between customers in different geographic markets. For example, Kendall Healthcare Products Company established a German subsidiary to manufacturer and market a wide line of products developed in the United States. A broad range of the parent company's products are locally manufactured for German consumption. Localized manufacturing has historically made sense, given that health-care product standards have varied considerably from country to country. Moreover, the German heath-care system has been a major consumer of Kendall's products.[34]

Ameritech is a major information company with revenues of over $10 billion and seventy-six thousand employees.[35] Figure 18.9 shows how it uses both place departmentalization and product departmentalization.

The following Across Cultures reviews a variety of global thrusts by Ameritech, including the formation of Ameritech International. It shows

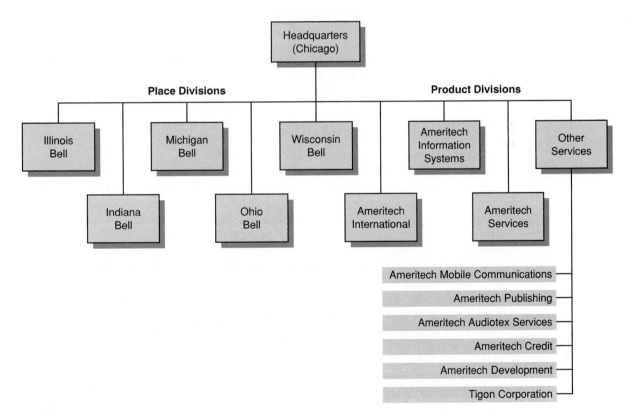

FIGURE 18.9 Place and Product Divisions at Ameritech

Source: Ameritech. *Ameritech 1990 Annual Report.* Chicago, 1991.

how a variety of design mechanisms have been used to implement new strategic choices, which, in turn, were made because of the globalization of the telecommunications industry.

Organizational Significance Place design has several potential advantages. If each department or division is in direct contact with customers or other stakeholders, it can adapt more readily to their demands. For manufacturing, this might mean locating near raw materials or suppliers and/or in the primary market area for finished products. Potential gains would include lower costs for materials, lower freight rates, and perhaps lower labor costs. For marketing, locating near customers might mean lower costs or better service. Salespeople could spend more time selling and less time traveling. Being closer to the customer could help the salesperson pinpoint the marketing tactic most likely to succeed in that particular region.[37] In the case of Ameritech, each of the five Bell companies are organized, in part, by state jurisdiction because of the important regulatory roles played by each state agency.

As we have indicated throughout this discussion, every form of organization and basis of departmentalization has potential disadvantages. Organizing by location clearly increases problems of control and coordination. If regional units become significantly different from one another, top management will have difficulty achieving integration. Further, regional and district managers will want some control over their own internal activities, such as purchasing and personnel. Also, employees may emphasize their own unit's goals and needs more than those of the whole organization. To help ensure uniformity and coordination, organizations such as the IRS, Southland (7-Eleven stores), Steak and Ale, Searle Optical, and Hilton Hotels make extensive use of rules that apply in all locations.

Matrix Departmentalization

Matrix departmentalization is an organization design based on multiple support systems and authority relationships in which some employees report to two superiors rather than one.[38] Figure 18.10 illustrates this key feature. Matrix departmentalization usually involves a combination of both functional and product designs through the use of dual authority, information, and reporting relationships and systems. Every matrix contains three unique sets of role relationships: (1) the top manager, who heads up and balances the dual chains of command; (2) the managers of functional and product departments, who share subordinates; and (3) the managers (or specialists) who report to both a functional manager and a product manager.[39] In an organization that has major operations throughout the world, matrix managers could be designated for each of the firm's major geographical areas, such as Europe, South America, North America, Pacific Rim, and the Middle East.[40]

Aerospace companies were the first to use the matrix design. Today, organizations in many industries (chemical, banking, insurance, packaged goods, electronics, and computer) and fields (hospitals, government agencies, and professional organizations) have adopted various adaptations of the matrix design.

AMERITECH GOES GLOBAL

The year 1990 saw the formation of Ameritech International under President Andres Bande, a native of Chile. This division explores appropriate international opportunities for Ameritech. It enables the company to better serve domestic customers requiring service overseas and to assist overseas firms with operations in the Great Lakes region.

Ameritech has entered into a number of international joint account-management agreements with foreign communications companies. It opened three international offices in 1991. During 1990, Ameritech and Paris-based France Telecom, the national telecommunications company of France, agreed to work together to bring customers the full benefits of new communications technologies and services. "Ameritech and France Telecom are recognized leaders in the application of one of these new technologies: integrated services digital network, known as ISDN," says Bande. "This technology enables businesses to link their locations and customers at the desktop through voice, data, and video. It will become increasingly important with the growing European market and the rising costs of transatlantic travel."

During 1990, Ameritech began a three-year agreement with ItalCable S.P.A., the Italian international communications carrier, to promote each others' services, share resources, and cooperate in a variety of possible projects. These are the fifth and sixth partnering agreements reached by Ameritech. Others involve PTT Telecom BV in the Netherlands, Copenhagen Telephone Company in Denmark, Nippon Telegraph and Telephone Corporation in Japan, and Telefonica in Spain. To further gain advantage internationally, Ameritech Publishing acquired a German industrial yellow-pages publisher, "Wer liefert was?" of Hamburg, in 1990. The firm—whose name translates as "Who Supplies What?"—is the leader in the German market, publishing German and Austrian editions and planning an edition in Switzerland.

The boldest global step by Ameritech was the acquisition of Telecom Corporation of New Zealand, with Bell Atlantic and two New Zealand firms, for $2.5 billion in 1990. The investment of Ameritech and Bell Atlantic in Telecom is being managed by New Zealand–based subsidiaries of the two companies. Thomas C. Burns, former president of C&P Telephone of West Virginia, is chairman and managing director of the subsidiaries. Burns serves on the new, nine-member board of directors of Telecom, along with Kirk A. Collamer, Ameritech's former manager of financial reporting who was appointed chief financial officer, secretary and treasurer of the subsidiaries.

Unlike Ameritech, Telecom is not restricted from manufacturing equipment or providing long-distance services. In fact, Telecom operates an international telephone service that has direct links to 37 countries by submarine cable and satellite networks and indirect links to another 150 countries. "In many ways, New Zealand is a harbinger of the future," says Bob Barnett, president of the Ameritech Bell Group. A politically stable member of the British Commonwealth, the country is moving toward a services-based and communications-intensive economy. New Zealand has a stable currency, declining inflation, and close access to the expanding Pacific Rim countries. The New Zealand government selected the consortium's bid for Telecom as part of its ongoing program of privatizing state-owned enterprises.[36]

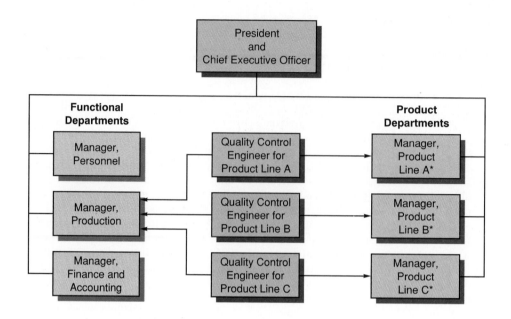

FIGURE 18.10 Partial Illustration of Basic Matrix Structure

*These product managers also have full responsibility for the marketing activities associated with their own product lines.

Typical Evolution   The matrix design typically evolves in stages. The first stage may be the use of a temporary task force. Composed of representatives from different departments or divisions of the organization, the task force is created to study a problem and make recommendations. Team members retain their usual departmental affiliations (an engineer continues to report to the head of engineering and a marketing representative to the head of marketing). But these temporary team members are also accountable to the leader of the task force.

The second stage usually involves the creation of permanent teams or committees organized to address specific needs or problems. Again, representatives from the various functional and product departments make up the team or committee, each representing the view of the home department.

The third stage may occur when a project manager is appointed and held accountable for integrating the team's activities and inputs for its final output. Project managers must often negotiate or "buy" the human resources necessary to carry out the tasks from the managers of functional departments. With the appointment of project managers, an organization is well on the way to a matrix design and faces all the difficulties and benefits of multiple-authority relationships.

The simple, straightforward, single chain of command is replaced by new multiple-authority relationships. This is the most distinguishing characteristic of the matrix design. While the traditional hierarchical design rests on formal reward or position power, the matrix design demands negotiation by peers with a high tolerance of ambiguous power relationships.[41] Managing these power relationships is one of the most troublesome aspects of the matrix design.

Organizational Significance The matrix design may be appropriate under the following conditions: (1) when it is absolutely essential for managers and others to be highly responsive to both functional or product line (or geographic area) concerns; (2) when organizations face heterogeneous-unstable task environments that generate very high information-processing requirements; and (3) when organizations must deal with limited financial resources, human resources, or both.[42] It makes specialized, functional knowledge available to all projects. Also, it uses people flexibly, since departments maintain reservoirs of specialists.

The matrix design demands substantial managerial resources while participants learn how to operate in the new organization. Learning may require two to three years because deep changes in attitude are required. The employees may be used to unity of command, a clear authority structure, and top-down orders. The matrix design changes all this. Special training programs are often needed to implement the new design. In order to work properly, a matrix design must maintain a continuing tension between multiple orientations (such as functional specialty and product line). This, in turn, requires effective interpersonal skills in communication, conflict resolution, and negotiation.[43]

Multinational Corporation

The **multinational corporation** is a very complex design that attempts to maintain three-way organizational perspectives and capabilities among products, functions, and geographic areas. Satisfying the need for the three-way consideration of issues is especially difficult because the multinational organization has operating units that are divided by distance and time, and managers who are separated by culture and language.[44] A "perfect" balance, if such were ever possible, between these perspectives would require a three-way matrix design. Most multinational corporations focus on the relative emphasis that should be given between place departmentalization (divisions) and product departmentalization (divisions). Figure 18.11 suggests the various combinations that might be selected. The likely effects of choosing a design based primarily on place (geographic area) or product line are shown in the figure as well. For example, the strong delegation of authority and control will give the country or region managers the ability to be responsive and adaptive to local needs and forces. In contrast, product line managers with worldwide authority and control may focus on achieving global efficiencies (integration) in production and universal (standard) products.

The growing presence and importance of global competitors, global customers, market demand for global products, information technologies, and efficient factories that manufacture for customers throughout the world all point to more global integration in many industries.[45] Thus, worldwide product divisions in firms facing such forces are likely to dominate in decisions relative to the geographically based divisions. However, pressures from national governments and local markets can also be strong. Multina-

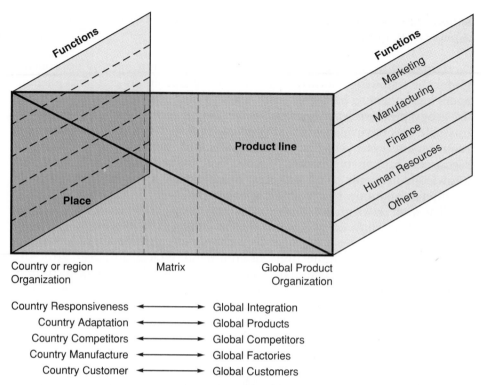

FIGURE 18.11   Basic Design Options for Multinational Corporations

Adapted from J. R. Galbraith, and R. K. Kazanjian, *Strategy Implementation: Structure Systems and Process,* 2d ed. St. Paul: West, 1986, 159.

tional corporations must participate in all key countries with a full product line. These product lines may not be open to companies without negotiating through the host government. Also, independent worldwide product divisions are not effective at opening up new territories. A geography-based division can establish relations with host governments, invest in distribution channels, develop brand recognition, and build an infrastructure that no single product line could afford. Thus, forces still remain that call for country or regional (Europe, North America, Latin America, Pacific Rim) organization.[46]

General Motors is a multinational corporation. It has product, place (geographic area), and functional divisions. A few of the product divisions include Hughes Aircraft Company, Saturn Corporation, Truck and Bus Group, and General Motors Acceptance Corporation. Several of the place divisions are: Asia and Pacific Operations; Chevrolet, Pontiac, GM of Canada Group; and Latin American Operations. Three of the functional divisions are Quality and Reliability Staff, Public Affairs and Marketing Group, and Legal Staff.

The following In Practice reveals some of the tensions inherent in deciding the tilt or balance between country (place), region of the world (place), and product designs for an international organization. Refer again to Figure 18.11 before reading this In Practice.

IN PRACTICE

PHARMEX: DIFFERENTIATION VERSUS UNIFORMITY

The international division of a U.S.-based, multinational pharmaceutical company that we will call "Pharmex" found that the patent on its mainstay product had expired, exposing the firm to severe price competition. The international division's economic environment was closing in on it, forcing management to question whether its organization structure was still cost-effective. Against this background, the division's president commissioned a study of Pharmex's international organization design.

The international division was managed by a U.S. headquarters unit of about 250 employees. Reporting to this divisional headquarters were three regional headquarters, each of which directed the business of subsidiaries located in twelve countries within its geographical area. The European region, by far the largest in terms of sales, was managed by a headquarters unit in France of about 150 people. The Latin American region had headquarters in Brazil, with about 30 employees. The Asian region, headquartered in Singapore, had about 20 employees. The Japanese subsidiary reported to the Asian headquarters, but its size and unique characteristics made it virtually a region unto itself.

In countries where Pharmex conducted its own business and did not operate through distributors, a wholly owned Pharmex subsidiary distributed and, in some cases, manufactured Pharmex products. Every subsidiary reported to the appropriate regional headquarters. Thus, for example, Pharmex Argentina reported to the Latin American regional headquarters in Brazil, which in turn reported to Pharmex's international division headquarters in the United States.

The debate centered on two basic questions: (1) Could significant savings be realized by reducing the staffs of regional and/or divisional headquarters units without seriously affecting efficiency? and (2) In the long run, would it be better to control subsidiary operations directly from U.S. divisional headquarters or to replace the international division by upgrading each region to divisional status with its own staff? Each group had its favorite definition of what every other group's role ought to be. Typically, a group felt that the other groups should have a more limited role than it had itself. Many alternatives were considered.

The alternative selected was to change the primary mission of the regions. The old mission was clearly a part of the problem. That is, costly controls were needed because subsidiary staffs were weak, but these controls also made it unnecessary for the subsidiaries to strengthen their staffs. The mission-changing option was more responsive to the division's problems than were any of the other options.

Pharmex created two small regional headquarters to replace the previous three. Their placement was determined by marketing considerations, not according to geography. One regional headquarters, which served developing countries whose primary needs were pediatric and anti-infective products, was based in California. The other regional headquarters was for developed countries that required products to serve the medical needs of aging populations. It was based in Europe. Japan continued to be, in effect, a region unto itself, and this subsidiary now reported directly to the international division.

Each region has a finance manager, a manufacturing manager, a human resources manager, and a marketing manager. The chief function of these managers is to advise and assist the subsidiaries. These few managers, along with tax specialists and secretaries, constitute the only layer that was placed between the country subsidiaries and headquarters. In effect, Pharmex chose a modified version of the centralizing option, but only after implementing the mission-changing option. This option has been effective.[47]

NETWORK ORGANIZATION

All of the organizational designs reviewed so far have been found lacking in enabling complex organizations to cope both effectively and efficiently with turbulent global environments and technologies.[48] The **network organization** is a design for managing complex relationships between people and departments or divisions, both within and external to the organization. This is achieved through a variety of lateral communication channels and decision-making, goal-setting, and mutual control processes. A key concern in all of the other organization designs was how to allocate authority and control among positions and departments or divisions. The network organization, while not ignoring these issues, focuses on how to mutually share authority, responsibility, and control among people and units that must cooperate and communicate frequently to achieve common goals.[49] The many different networks in a network organization are designed to change as the tasks to be performed and the goals to be achieved change.[50]

Key Characteristics

The network organization is sometimes called a spiderweb or cluster organization. It is a mosaic of mutually interdependent lateral mechanisms and processes. This mosaic cannot be captured through the use of typical organization charts that usually show vertical authority and reporting relationships. A number of the lateral processes and mechanisms of network organizations have been discussed in previous chapters. The earlier In Practice on Digital Equipment Corporation's Easynet Network notes some of the information technologies commonly found in this organization design. A network organization exists only when most of the following factors operate in support of one anther:

- *Distinctive competence*—innovative and adaptive by combining resources in novel ways.
- *Responsibility*—shared among the individuals or departments that must collaborate to perform their tasks. Organizational design mechanisms include extensive use of problem-solving teams, special-purpose teams, and self-managing teams.
- *Goal setting*—the formulation of common goals that are linked to satisfying the needs of one or more important external stakeholders,

such as customers/clients, suppliers, shareholders, lenders, and governments.

- *Communication*—All-channel networks are used both internally (between the relevant employees or departments) and externally (between the organization and relevant stakeholders). The focus is on lateral networks, rather than vertical networks. Access to information necessary to make decisions is widely shared and distributed. Open communications is the norm.

- *Information technologies*—Many diverse information technologies are employed to assist employees in networking internally (with others in the organization who may be at a great distance) or externally (with customers, suppliers, regulatory agencies, and so on). Typical information technologies include electronic mail (E-mail), voice mail, mobile phones, fax, telecommuting, teleconferencing, local and wide-area computer networks, decision support systems, and so on.

- *Attitudinal sets*—Interdependent employees are primarily cooperative rather competitive. They exhibit mutually reinforcing behaviors and attitudes of high trust, listening to each other, collaborating and compromising styles of conflict management, acceptance of mutual control, and flexibility in relationships.

- *Organizational culture*—The organization's culture focuses on both problems of external adaptation and of internal integration. This culture has a bias against the mechanistic management system and the many organization levels that often accompany it.

- *Balanced goals*—Individuals and departments do not see themselves as isolated islands with only their own goals. They also see themselves in relation to other individuals and departments with a concern for superordinate goals and rewards. Network forms of exchange evolve over time, based on the history of earlier transactions. The basic assumption of network relationships is that each person or unit is dependent on resources controlled by the other and that there are mutual gains to be had by the pooling of resources through the search for win-win solutions.[51]

Ericsson, with world headquarters in Stockholm, Sweden, is a leader in telecommunications with seventy thousand employees and activities in one hundred countries. Its six business (product) areas have global responsibilities for developing and delivering their systems and products. These areas include public telecommunications, radio communications, business communications, cable and network construction, components (such as fiber optical components and power supply equipment), and defense systems. In 1990, Ericsson reorganized to strengthen the local (geographically based) companies.

Local companies can be engaged in sales, product development, and manufacturing. These local companies work with and through one or more of the six business area divisions. The intent of this reorganization is to network Ericsson more closely to customers. Moreover, as suggested in the following statement, it is intended that Ericsson's units will continue to network with each other:

Ericsson's new organization does not impose boundaries between Business Areas, and between Business Areas and local companies. It is a market-driven organization that meets the requirements of the 1990's for greater flexibility and speed. The ultimate objective of the reorganization is to enable Ericsson to continue to set the pace in telecommunications in the future, consolidating and strengthening its presence in the world market.[52]

The following In Practice suggests some of the ways Ericsson operates as a network organization.

IN PRACTICE

ERICSSON'S GLOBAL NETWORKING

In the 1920s, Ericsson began to build a substantial worldwide network of operations sensitive and responsive to local national environments. It had a strong home market base and a parent company with technological, manufacturing, and marketing capability to support its network of companies. Keeping the balance between and among those units has required constant adjustment of organizational responsibilities and relationships, as most recently suggested by the 1990 reorganization.

Ericsson has maintained a flexible arrangement among its operating units. This has allowed the firm to develop entrepreneurial and innovative subsidiary companies that work within a corporate framework. Creative product and functional groups at headquarters help in this process.

Compared to some companies where relationships among national companies are competitive and where headquarters-subsidiary communications are often adversarial, the attitudinal sets in Ericsson are cooperative and collaborative. The maintenance of such attitudes is important since it allows the company's diverse units to work together in a way that maximizes the potential of their overall operations.

Ericsson management feels strongly that its most effective integrating device is strong central control over key elements of its strategic operation. Ericsson has not had strong or sophisticated administrative systems. But its operating systems have long been designed to provide strong worldwide coordination. Knowing that local changes would be necessary, the company designed its digital switch as a modular system with very clear specifications. National units could custom-tailor elements of the design to meet local needs without compromising the integrity of the total system design. Similarly, Ericsson's global computer-aided design and manufacturing system allows the parent company to delegate responsibility for component production and even design features to subordinates without fear of losing the ability to control and coordinate the entire manufacturing system.

In addition to strong systems, divisional cooperation requires good interpersonal relations. Ericsson has developed these with a long-standing policy of transferring large numbers of people back and forth between headquarters and divisions. Ericsson sends a team of fifty or one hundred engineers and managers from one division to another for a year or two. Ericsson's is a balanced two-way flow with people coming to the parent not only to learn but also to bring their expertise. Ericsson's multidirectional process involves all nationalities.

Ericsson is very conscious of the need to develop skills and capture ideas wherever they operate in the world. At the same time, local managers see themselves as part of the worldwide Ericsson group, rather than as independent autonomous units. Constant transfers and working on joint teams over the years have helped broaden many managers' perspectives from local to global. The local units' systemwide mandates for products have confirmed their identity with the company's global operations. This ability of headquarters and subsidiary managers to view the issues from each other's perspective distinguishes the company that can think globally yet act locally.[53]

External Networking

The network organization is particularly good at creating alliances with other organizations to achieve its goals.[54] Consider the following few examples of how firms network externally through the use of different types of strategic alliances:

- In the pharmaceutical industry, Merck, Eli, Lilly, Fujisawa, and Bayer often cross-license their newest drugs to one another, not only to support industrywide innovation but also to amortize the high fixed costs of research and development and distribution.

- Corning Incorporated uses its twenty-three joint ventures with such foreign partners as Siemens of West Germany, Samsung of South Korea, Asahi Chemical of Japan, and CIBA-GEIGY of Switzerland, to penetrate and thrive in a growing number of related high-technology markets.

- Airbus Industrie, the European consortium backed by four governments to produce commercial aircraft, is slowly but steadily gaining market share and experience in competing in this highly lucrative but risky industry.[55]

Network organizations treat their alliances as forms of flexible partnerships.[56] For example, the flexibility with which Corning approaches its partnerships—letting the form be determined by the goals and letting the ventures evolve in form over time—is one factor in its success. But even more important is the time and effort expended by Corning executives to create the conditions for long-lasting, mutually beneficial relationships.

Network organizations create successful partnerships by having "six I's" in place—importance, investment, interdependence, integration, information, and institutionalization. The relationship is *important*, and therefore, it gets adequate resources, management attention, and sponsorship. There is an agreement for longer-term *investment*, which tends to help equalize benefits over time. The partners are *interdependent*, which helps keep power balanced. The organizations are *integrated*, so that the appropriate points of contact and communication are managed. Each is *informed* about the plans and directions of the other. Finally, the partnership is *institutionalized*—bolstered by a framework of supporting mechanisms, from legal requirements to social ties to shared values, all of which make trust possible.[57]

SUMMARY

The design of organizations is a complex process. It is heavily influenced by the combination of three key contingencies: environmental forces, technological factors, and strategic choices. The task environment(s) confronting an organization as a whole and its various departments can vary greatly. This variability can be assessed in terms of complexity (homogeneous to heterogeneous) and dynamism (stable to unstable).

Strategic choices—such as top-management's philosophy and decisions about the range of markets and types of customers to be served—have a direct impact on organization design. If top management believes in tight, centralized control of day-to-day decisions, it is more likely to use a mechanistic system than an organic system.

As in job design, technological considerations play a role in organization design. The potential impact of three technological variables—workflow uncertainty, task uncertainty, and task interdependence (pooled, sequential, and reciprocal)—on organization design can be considerable.

The characteristics and conditions favoring the use of mechanistic and organic systems were discussed. Different departments or divisions of the same organization may be mechanistic or organic. In an organization with a functional design, it is quite possible for a production department to operate under a mechanistic system, while the research and development department operates with a relatively organic system.

Organization design is also affected by interdepartmental relationships, which, in turn, are strongly influenced by three variables: differentiation, integration, and uncertainty. Diagnosis of these variables is an important aspect of organization design.

Four bases of departmentalization were reviewed—functional, product, place, and matrix. The conditions under which each may be appropriate were noted. For example, an organization or its departments with a homogeneous-stable environment generally can effectively use basic functional departmentalization. The top executive integrates the functional areas. If a firm has a single product line and the environment is heterogeneous-unstable, the functional approach may continue to be effective if it is supplemented with staff services and integrating mechanisms, such as task forces, formal planning activities, linking roles, integrating groups, and the like.

The multidivisional structure and multinational corporation were presented as complex organization designs for firms providing a range of goods or services to geographically dispersed markets. The network organization attempts to overcome disadvantages inherent in the other designs. It provides lateral mechanisms and processes to manage complex sequential or reciprocal interdependencies between people and units, which are often located at great distances from each other.

Key Words and Concepts

Bureaucracy	Complexity dimension
Centralization	Differentiation

Division of labor
Dynamism dimension
Functional departmentalization
Hierarchy of authority
Impersonality
Integration
Line functions
Matrix departmentalization
Mechanistic system
Multidivisional structure
Multinational corporation
Network organization

Organic system
Organization design
Place departmentalization
Procedures
Product departmentalization
Rules
Scalar chain of command
Span of control
Staff functions
Task environment
Uncertainty
Unity of command

Discussion Questions

1. What are two similarities between the functional and product bases of departmentalization?

2. What are two differences between the functional and product bases of departmentalization?

3. Why do information technologies affect the design of organizations?

4. What basis of departmentalization is used by the college in which you are enrolled?

5. What alternative basis of departmentalization could be used for designing the college in which you are enrolled? What might be the advantages and disadvantages of this alternative structure?

6. Describe the mechanistic or organic characteristics of an organization of which you are a member.

7. Give three examples of organizational rules that you have encountered that seemed to be either helpful or counterproductive from the standpoint of organizational effectiveness.

8. How might top managers' values and beliefs influence the diagnosis of the task environment and organization design decisions?

9. What difficulties are associated with the matrix design? Would you like to work in a matrix structure? Why?

10. What forces work for and against the establishment of a network organization?

◆ MANAGEMENT CASES AND EXERCISES

INVENTORY OF EFFECTIVE ORGANIZATION DESIGN

Directions: Listed below are a number of statements describing an effective organization design. Please indicate the extent to which you agree or disagree with each statement as a description of an organization you currently or have worked for. Write the appropriate number next to the statement.

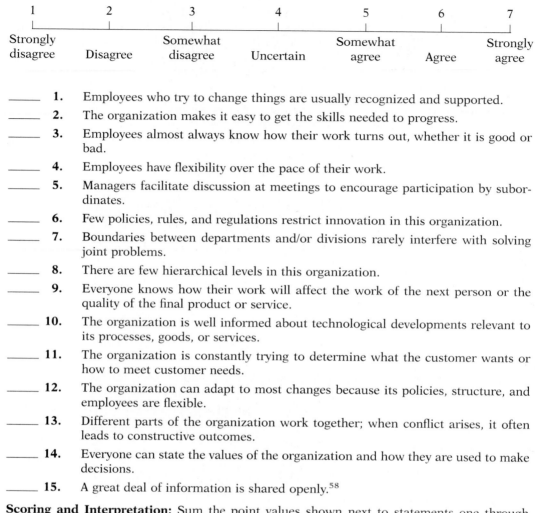

1	2	3	4	5	6	7
Strongly disagree	Disagree	Somewhat disagree	Uncertain	Somewhat agree	Agree	Strongly agree

_____ 1. Employees who try to change things are usually recognized and supported.

_____ 2. The organization makes it easy to get the skills needed to progress.

_____ 3. Employees almost always know how their work turns out, whether it is good or bad.

_____ 4. Employees have flexibility over the pace of their work.

_____ 5. Managers facilitate discussion at meetings to encourage participation by subordinates.

_____ 6. Few policies, rules, and regulations restrict innovation in this organization.

_____ 7. Boundaries between departments and/or divisions rarely interfere with solving joint problems.

_____ 8. There are few hierarchical levels in this organization.

_____ 9. Everyone knows how their work will affect the work of the next person or the quality of the final product or service.

_____ 10. The organization is well informed about technological developments relevant to its processes, goods, or services.

_____ 11. The organization is constantly trying to determine what the customer wants or how to meet customer needs.

_____ 12. The organization can adapt to most changes because its policies, structure, and employees are flexible.

_____ 13. Different parts of the organization work together; when conflict arises, it often leads to constructive outcomes.

_____ 14. Everyone can state the values of the organization and how they are used to make decisions.

_____ 15. A great deal of information is shared openly.[58]

Scoring and Interpretation: Sum the point values shown next to statements one through fifteen. A score of 75 to 105 suggests a very effective organization design. A score of 70 to 89 suggests a mediocre design that probably varies greatly in terms of how specific aspects of the organization work for or against effectiveness. Scores of 50 to 69 suggest there is a great deal of ambiguity about the organization and how it operates. Scores of 15 to 49 probably suggest the design is contributing to serious problems.

PITKIN STEEL: A PROBLEM OF ORGANIZATIONAL STRUCTURE

The Pitkin Steel company was founded in 1976 by Steve Mitchell and Joe Dove. They shared a common belief that there was a growth opportunity in supplying steel pipe and tubing to companies capitalizing on the energy boom in the western portion of the United States. An increasing demand for energy had led to intensive oil and gas explorations, and the demands for pipe and tubing were outstripping supply.

Primarily, Pitkin bought raw steel pipe and tubing from a major steel producer in the United States and reprocessed the raw product to meet customer demands for threading, copping, forming, and coating. The work was accomplished in a production facility adjacent to its corporate office in a large western city. An additional production facility was constructed in 1985 in another large western city approximately six hundred miles away. This second facility incorporated state-of-the-art technology and, therefore, provided greater productivity. Orders for the company's products were obtained by a field sales representative working out of a small office in Houston, Texas, or through telephone contact initiated by staff at the two plant facilities.

During the fall of 1980, Joe Dove sold his 51 percent share of the business to an investment group from Chicago. The group chose Steve Mitchell to continue to operate as president of the organization. He had approximately fifteen years of experience as a line manager for a Fortune 500 steel firm. In addition, he had an undergraduate degree in history and taught at the high school level for two years before deciding that teaching did not stimulate him. His subordinates acknowledged that he was a gifted humanist with a keen and perceptive mind. According to them, Mitchell thoroughly enjoyed the challenges of sales and was respected for his integrity and personable approach in relating to others. As far as he was concerned, Pitkin was one big happy family. Because of this attitude, the company continued to be managed with no formally established lines of reporting relationships other than to acknowledge that Mitchell was the president and whoever was best qualified to do a specific job in the company would take it on. For eight years, from 1980 to 1988, it seemed as though Mitchell's management approach was good for the organization. Year after year, the company did well. Everyone in the company appeared to be content, operating independently with very little or no guidance from management.

During the first quarter of 1989, Pitkin experienced its first quarterly loss and signs of employee discontent. While it was not expected, it was viewed with only mild concern. Mitchell talked with his key personnel individually, as was his custom when problems arose, and urged them to work harder. He often got on the phone himself to initiate or close a sale with a customer. In addition to his contact with the customers either by phone or in person, Mitchell welcomed every opportunity to become directly involved in Pitkin's day-to-day operations. As the months progressed, the anticipated upswing in

sales and employee morale failed to materialize. Mitchell was concerned and continued to tell all to work harder and consider what steps might be taken to help the company become more positive in its working environment.

Mitchell wanted to chat with Mike Childs about his upcoming meeting with the board of directors. After an hour or so of rehashing old concerns without a fresh approach, Childs suggested it was time that the company did a more formal appraisal of its operation. Childs knew that certain principles were essential to a business's success and that Pitkin had never really engaged in a structured approach to its operation. Consequently, Childs suggested that he contact one of his old professors and that he, Mitchell, and a few other key members of the organization spend a couple of days in retreat for a serious discussion of the organization.

As a preliminary step to the meeting, Childs met with Dr. Austin Foster, who brought with him Dr. Ron High. Childs had prepared an organizational chart of Pitkin Steel as he saw it. He apologized for not having a formal one to present. Childs acknowledged that none had ever been constructed or communicated to the employees of the company. After all, the company was small and everyone should know what his or her responsibilities were, so why bother adding "formality"? Childs proceeded to present an overview of the personnel.

The key players in the company, including Mitchell, were relatively young. But each had several years' experience in the industry and generally worked well together. Each did his or her own job separately, and if a problem arose, each would solve it. Ted Davis, the forty-year-old Vice-president of Production, had a engineering degree. He was a long-time friend of Mitchell and concentrated on the operations side of the business. He was not considered a team player by the other key managers. He wielded a great deal of influence with Mitchell and could block decisions that others had made. Davis always met the bottom line, did not procrastinate, was a no-nonsense manger, operated as a loner, and was viewed as a strong administrator. He was somewhat oblivious to the importance of interpersonal skills.

Mike Childs, thirty-five, was the marketing manager. He had a master's degree in business administration and had worked for the company ten years marketing the standard pipe products. He was also close to Mitchell and was extremely supportive. Because of his loyalty and tendency to be a good listener, he was the primary sounding board for Mitchell on most matters. He frequently had sound ideas on problems concerning operational matters but usually fell short of aggressively selling his suggestions.

Cathy Nichols, the forty-five-year-old sales manager, had been in the industry twenty-three years and joined Pitkin at its founding. She was a high school graduate, knew a lot about standard pipe, and had been successfully selling it during her tenure with the company.

Mark Jones, twenty-seven and a high school graduate, managed the sales of steel tubing and had been invited to join the company seven years ago after working sales for a competitor. The last of the group was Sherry Dove, twenty-five, daughter of Joe Dove, who worked out of the Houston, Texas, office. She had been calling on customers in the Southwest area for the past five years. She attended college for one year.

Those scheduled to attend the mountain retreat were Dove, Childs, Jones, Mitchell, and Nichols. The primary rationale for this selection was that each person had a marketing background and worked well together. Childs informed the professors that Mitchell was fully behind the meeting and would purposely absent himself from the first day's discussion to allow for free exchange of ideas and would like to be briefed the next day on what had been decided. Mitchell agreed to totally support the team's recommendations and would spend the second day with them formulating and implementing those recommendations for the board of directors meeting.

The session opened with a general airing of what each participant considered to be significant problems for Pitkin. Several things became immediately apparent to the consultants:

1) Each participant had a personal sense of where he or she fit into the organization and what his or her unit was expected to achieve. However, there was disagreement as to whether Pitkin was a manufacturer, wholesaler, distributor, or sales organization.

2) There was little understanding of one another's area of responsibility, how each person's activities affected the others, and what each one's area of responsibility should be. In addition, their individual strengths, weaknesses, likes and dislikes with respect to current or future positions were unknown.

3) There was a consensus of opinion that Mitchell was a personable, concerned, benevolent, hard-working, and knowledgeable person. But his organizational skills were poor, and he did not utilize them as valuable resources in the decision-making process. He was more prone toward being a worker than a corporate leader.

4) Each person considered himself or herself qualified in either production or sales but not as a manager well versed in management concepts.

5) Since the inception of this organization, there was never any written, formalized system of tasks, authority, or reporting relationships.[59]

QUESTIONS

1. What are the strengths and weaknesses of the Pitkin Steel Company?

2. How do you think the Pitkin Steel Company should be designed?

3. What concepts from this chapter support your recommendations?

References

1. Adapted from Dumaine, B. The Bureaucracy Busters. *Fortune*, June 17, 1991, 36–50.
2. Daft, R. L. *Organization Theory and Design*, 4th ed. St. Paul: West, 1992.
3. Hall, R. H. *Organizations: Structures, Processes, and Outcomes*, 5th ed. Englewood Cliffs, N.J.: Prentice-Hall, 1991.
4. Duncan, R. B. Characteristics of Organizational Environments and Perceived Environmental Uncertainty. *Administrative Science Quarterly*, 1972, *17*, 314. Also see Wholey, D. R., and Brittain, J. Characterizing Environmental Variation. *Academy of Management Journal*, 1989, *32*, 867–882.
5. Pearce J. A. II, and Robinson, R. B. Jr. *Strategic Management: Formulation Implementation and Control.* Homewood, Ill.: Irwin, 1991.
6. Milliken, F. J. Perceiving and Interpreting Environmental Change: An Examination of College Administrators' Interpretation of Changing Demographics. *Academy of Management Journal*, 1990,

33, 42–63; Milliken, F. J. Three Types of Perceived Uncertainty about the Environment: State, Effect, and Response Uncertainty. *Academy of Management Review*, 1987, *12*, 133–143.

7. Hitt, M. A., Hoskisson, R. E., and Harrison, J. S. Strategic Competitiveness in the 1990s: Challenges and Opportunities for U.S. Executives. *Academy of Management Executive*, May 1991, 7–22.

8. Wilson, I. Evaluating the Environment: Social and Political Factors. In W. D. Guth (ed.), *Handbook of Business Strategy*, Boston: Warren, Gorham and Lamont, 1985, 3–2.

9. Mintzberg, H. The Effective Organization: Forces and Forms. *Sloan Management Review*, Winter 1991, 54–67.

10. Hoskisson, R. E., and Turk, T. A. Corporate Restructuring: Governance and Control Limits of the Internal Capital Market. *Academy of Management Review*, 1990, *15*, 459–477.

11. Adapted from Litchfield, R. The '90s Way to Tackle the Recession. *Canadian Business*, November 1990, 80–88.

12. Fry, L. W., and Slocum, J. W., Jr. Technology; Structure, and Workgroup Effectiveness: A Test of a Contingency Model. *Academy of Management Journal*, 184, *17*, 221–246; Barley, S. R. The Alignment of Technology and Structure through Roles and Networks. *Administrative Science Quarterly*, 1990, *35*, 61–103.

13. Miller, C. C., Glick, W. H., Wang, Yau-De, and Huber, G. P. Understanding Technology-Structure Relationships: Theory Development and Meta-Analytic Theory Testing. *Academy of Management Journal*, 1991, *34*, 370–399.

14. Davenport, T. H., and Short, J. E. The New Industrial Engineering: Information Technology and Business Process Redesign. *Sloan Management Review*, Summer 1990, 11–27.

15. Adapted from Helm, L. How the Leader in Networking Practices What It Preaches. *Business Week*, May 16, 1988, 88–96; Leonard-Barton, D. The Case for Integrative Innovation: An Expert System at Digital. *Sloan Management Review*, Fall 1987, 7–19; Rifkin, G., and Harrar, G. *The Ultimate Entrepreneur: The Story of Ken Olsen and Digital Equipment Corporation*. New York: St. Martin's Press, 1990.

16. Burns, T., and Stalker, G. M. *The Management of Innovation*. London: Social Science Paperbacks, 1961, 96–125.

17. Adapted from Weber, M. *The Theory of Social and Economic Organization* (trans., T. Parsons). New York: Oxford University Press, 1947, 329–334.

18. Rogers, R. E. *Max Weber's Ideal Type Theory*. New York: Philosophical Library, 1969; Weiss, R. M. Weber on Bureaucracy: Management Consultant or Political Theorist? *Academy of Management Review*, 1983, *8*, 242–248.

19. Benveniste, G. *Professionalizing the Organization: Reducing Bureaucracy to Enhance Effectiveness.*

San Francisco: Jossey-Bass, 1987; Sjoberg, G., Vaughan, T. R., and Williams, N. *Bureaucracy as a Moral Maze. Journal of Applied Behavioral Science*, 1984, *20*, 441–453.

20. Carroll, H. O. Perestroika in the American Corporation. *Organizational Dynamics*, Spring 1990, 4–21.

21. Carter, N. M., and Cullen, J. B. A Comparison of Centralization/Decentralization of Decision Making Concepts and Measures. *Journal of Management*, 1984, *10*, 259–268.

22. Bushardt, S. C., Duhon, D. L., and Fowler, A. R. Jr. Management Delegation Myths and the Paradox of Task Assignment. *Business Horizons*, March-April 1991, 37–43.

23. Bedeian, A. G., and Zammuto, R. F. *Organizations: Theory and Design*. Hinsdale, Ill: Dryden, 1991.

24. Smith, A. *An Inquiry into the Nature and Causes of the Wealth of Nations* (1776). New York: Modern Library, reprint, 1937, 48.

25. Adapted from Buell, B., and Hof, R. D. Hewlett-Packard Rethinks Itself. *Business Week*, April 1, 1991, 76–81; Wiegner, K. K. Good-bye to the HP Way? *Forbes*, November 26, 1990, 36–37.

26. Lorsch, J. W., and Allen, S. A. III. *Managing Diversity and Interdependence: An Organizational Study of Multidivisional Firms*. Cambridge: Harvard University Graduate School of Business Administration, 1973. Also see Lawrence, P. R., and Lorsch, J. W. *Organization and Environment: Managing Differentiation and Integration*. Homewood, Ill.: Irwin, 1969.

27. Astley, W. G., and Zajac, E. J. Beyond Dyadic Exchange: Functional Interdepedence and Subunit Power. *Organization Studies*, 1990, *11*, 481–501.

28. Boschken, H. L. Strategy and Structure: Reconceiving the Relationship. *Journal of Management*, 1990, *16*, 135–150.

29. Lawrence, P. R. Organization and Environment Perspective: The Harvard Research Program. In A. H. Van de Ven and W. F. Joyce (eds.), *Perspectives on Organization Design and Behavior*. New York: Wiley, 1981, 311–337.

30. Adapted from Labich, K. The Innovators, *Fortune*, June 16, 1988, 51–64.

31. Rotschild, W. E. Staff Entrepreneurs? *Planning Review*, March-April 1987, 6–8.

32. Williamson, O. E. Comparative Economic Organization. The Analysis of Discrete Structural Alternatives. *Administrative Science Quarterly*, 1991, *36*, 269–296; Hill, C. W., and Hoskisson, R. E. Strategy and Structure in the Multiproduct Firm. *Academy of Management Review*, 1987, *12*, 331–341.

33. Rothman, A., and Grover, R. Media Colossus. *Business Week*, March 25, 1991, 64–74.

34. Morrison, A. J., Ricks, D. A., and Roth, K. Globalization versus Regionalization: Which Way for the Multinational? *Organizational Dynamics*, Winter 1991, 17–29.

35. Ameritech. *Ameritech 1990 Annual Report.* Chicago, 1991.

36. Adapted from *Ameritech 1990 Annual Report.*

37. Roenbloom, B. Motivating Your International Channel Partners. *Business Horizons,* March-April 1990, 53–57.

38. Davis, S. M., and Lawrence, P. R. *Matrix.* Reading, Mass.: Addison-Wesley, 1977; Hanna, D. P. *Designing Organizations for High Performance.* Reading, Mass.: Addison-Wesley, 1988.

39. Davis, S. M., and Lawrence, P. R. Problems of Matrix Organizations. *Harvard Business Review,* May-June 1978, 131–142.

40. Punnett, J., and Ricks, D. A. *International Business.* Boston: PWS-Kent, 1992.

41. Kolodny, H. F. Managing in a Matrix. *Business Horizons,* March-April 1981, 17–35.

42. Rosenzweig, P. M., and Singh, J. V. Organizational Environments and Multinational Enterprise. *Academy of Management Review,* 1991, *16,* 340–361.

43. Joyce, W. F. Matrix Organization: A Social Experiment. *Academy of Management Journal,* 1986, *29,* 536–561.

44. Bartlett, C. A., and Ghoshal, S. *Transnational Management: Text, Cases and Readings in Cross-Border Management.* Homewood, Ill: Irwin, 1992.

45. Porter, M. E. *The Competitive Advantage of Nations.* New York: Free Press, 1990.

46. Galbraith, J. R., and Kazanjian, R. K. *Strategy Implementation: Structure, Systems, and Process.* St. Paul: West, 1986.

47. Adapted from Gellerman, S. W. In Organizations, As in Architecture, Form Follows Function. *Organizational Dynamics,* Winter 1990, 57–68.

48. Pankratz, H. Strategic Alignment: Managing for Synergy. *Business Quarterly,* Winter 1991, 66–71.

49. Powell, W. W. Neither Market nor Hierarchy: Network Forms of Organization. in B. M. Staw and L. L. Cummings (eds.), *Research in Organizational Behavior,* vol. 12. Greenwich, Conn: JAI Press, 1990, 295–336; Fulk, J., and Boyd, B. Emerging Theories of Communication in Organizations. *Journal of Management,* 1991, *17,* 407–446.

50. McCann, J. E. Design Principles for an Innovating Company. *Academy of Management Executive,* May 1991, 76–93.

51. Mills, D. Q. *Rebirth of the Corporation.* New York: John Wiley, 1991; Keidel, R. W. Triangular Design: A New Organizational Geometry. *Academy of Management Executive,* November 1990, 21–37; White, R. E., and Poynter, T. A. Achieving Worldwide Advantage with the Horizontal Organization. *Business Quarterly,* Autumn 1989, 55–60; Rockart, J. F., and Short J. E. IT in the 1990s: Managing Organizational Interdependence. *Sloan Management Review,* Winter 1989, 7–17; Finholt, T., and Sproull, L. S. Electronic Groups at Work. *Organization Science,* 1990, *1,* 41–64; Barney, J. Firm Resources and Sustained Competitive Advantage. *Journal of Management,* 1991, *17,* 99–120.

52. Ericsson Media. *Ericsson 1990 Annual Report.* Stockholm, 1991, 16.

53. Adapted from Bartlett, C. A., and Ghoshal, S. Organizing for Worldwide Effectiveness: The Transnational Solution. *California Management Review,* Fall 1988, 54–74; *Ericsson 1990 Annual Report.*

54. Ghoshal, S., and Bartlett, C. A. The Multinational Corporation as an Interorganizational Network. *Academy of Management Review,* 1990, *15,* 603–625.

55. Lei, D., and Slocum, J. W. Jr. Global Strategic Alliances: Payoffs and Pitfalls. *Organizational Dynamics,* Winter 1991, 44–62. Also see Osborn, R. N., and Boughn, C. C. Forms of Interorganizational Governance for Multinational Alliances. *Academy of Management Journal,* 1990, *33,* 503–519.

56. Ricks, D. A., Toyne, B., and Martinez, Z. Recent Developments in International Management Research. *Journal of Management,* 1990, *16,* 219–253.

57. Kanter, R. M. Becoming PALs: Pooling, Allying, and Linking across Companies. *Academy of Management Executive,* August 1989, 183–193.

58. Adapted from Pasmore, W. A. *Designing Effective Organizations: The Sociotechnical Systems Perspective.* New York: John Wiley & Sons, 1988, 157–186.

59. Adapted from Knights, R. M., and Faurer, J. C. Pitkin Steel: A Problem of Organizational Structure. In R. A. Cook (ed.), *Annual Advances in Business Cases, 1990.* Southbend, Ind.: Midwest Society for Case Research, 1991, 522–525. This case was prepared by Dr. R. M. Knight and Dr. J. C. Faurer of Metropolitan State College as a basis for class discussion rather than to illustrate either effective or ineffective handling of administrative situation. Presented to the Midwest Society for Case Research Workshop, 1990. All rights reserved to the authors. Copyright © 1990 by Drs. Knights and Faurer. Used with permission.

CHAPTER 19

ORGANIZATIONAL DECISION MAKING

LEARNING OBJECTIVES

After you have finished studying this chapter, you should be able to:

- Discuss the core questions in ethical decision making.
- Outline three basic models of organizational decision making.
- Describe the phases of managerial decision making.
- Explain the human biases in information processing.
- Describe three methods for stimulating creativity in organizational decision making.

OUTLINE

ST. PAUL COMPANIES' CODE

The St. Paul Companies specializes in commercial and personal insurance and related products. The St. Paul Companies has an extensive corporate code, entitled *In Good Conscience*. All new employees are introduced to the code when they join the company. Management devotes two meetings a year to discussing the code's impact on day-to-day activities. The code offers specific guidance and examples for employees to follow. The statements below illustrate the kinds of issues contained in the code.

Insider information. For example, if you know that the company is about to announce a rise in quarterly profits or anything else that would affect the price of the company's stock, you cannot buy or sell the stock until the announcement has been made and published.

Gifts and entertainment. An inexpensive ballpoint pen or an appointment diary is a common gift and generally acceptable. But liquor, lavish entertainment, clothing, or travel should not be accepted.

Contact with legislators. If you are contacted by legislators on matters relating to the St. Paul companies, you should refer them to the governmental affairs or law department.

Employee-related issues. This section of the code is the most detailed and directly addresses the company's relationship to the individual. It spells out what employees can expect in terms of compensation (it should be based on job performance and administered fairly), advancement (promotion is from within, where possible), assistance (training, job experience, or counseling), and communications (there should be regular feedback; concerns can be expressed without fear of recrimination). It also states the St. Paul Companies' expectation of employees regarding speaking up (when you know something that could be a problem), avoiding certain actions (where the public's confidence could be weakened), and charting your career course.

The company also spells out employee privacy issues. The code outlines how work-related information for hiring and promotion is collected. Only information needed to make the particular decision is gathered, and it is collected directly from the applicant/employee where possible. The St. Paul Companies informs employees about what types of information are maintained. An individual's file is open for the employee to review at anytime.

The code covers other important personnel issues as well. It touches on equal opportunity by mentioning discrimination laws. The emphasis is on company recognition of past discrimination and its commitments to "make an affirmative effort to address this situation in all of its programs and practices." The code covers nepotism by stating that officers' and directors' relatives will not be hired. Other employees' relatives can be employed, so long as they are placed in different departments.[1]

Ethical decision making can be encouraged by providing clear guidelines for employees, communicating these guidelines on a regular basis, and—possibly most important—enforcing them. The St. Paul Companies's top management makes a serious effort to do these things. Employees may strongly disapprove of certain guidelines, but they are fully informed. The termination policy, for example, states that employment is voluntary and that individuals are free to resign at any time. The company, too, can terminate employees "at any time, with or without cause." Some people may consider that policy unfair, but the rules of the game are clear.[2]

Organizational decisions are influenced by ethical principles. Many of our previous chapters have illustrated this point by discussing one or more of the ethical issues relevant to the content of the chapter. Moreover, in previous chapters, we presented a number of recommendations for assessing and improving decision making. In Chapter 4, we discussed the powerful roles of perception and attribution in understanding our world and thereby influencing our decisions. In Chapter 5, we presented four major problem-solving styles based on how individuals may differ in gathering information and evaluating information. In Chapter 7, we described the process that should be followed in diagnosing problems of work motivation and the types of decisions that are likely to improve motivation and productivity. In Chapter 8, we discussed goal setting as a process for creating a sense of direction in day-to-day decision making and establishing priorities on decision issues. Of course, goal setting is, itself, one type of organizational decision making. In Chapter 10, we reviewed the six phases of group decision making that should lead to more effective decisions. As part of that discussion, we presented the nominal group technique as a specialized decision-making process for stimulating group creativity. In Chapter 12, we discussed the Vroom-Jago leadership decision model, which provides insight into leadership styles that typically result in high-quality decisions. And in Chapter 14, much of our discussion of conflict and negotiation focused on coping with decision situations when there is disagreement over goals, over how to achieve goals, or over the decision process to be used to resolve a conflict (e.g., procedural conflicts). In Chapter 16, we saw that access to the decision-making process provides a source of power for individuals and groups. Accordingly, this chapter serves to enrich and broaden our earlier discussions of organizational decision making.

In this chapter, we start with five core questions related to ethical decision making.[3] Second, we briefly outline the features of three major decision-making models. Third, we use some of the features of these three models in our presentation on the phases of managerial decision making. Finally, we review three aids designed to stimulate creativity in organizational decision making.

ETHICAL DECISION MAKING

Ethics deals with right and wrong in the actions and decisions of individuals and the communities (institutions) of which they are a part. Ethical issues in organizations are more pervasive and complex than generally recognized. In fact, ethical issues influence decisions employees make on a daily basis.[4] Many ethical issues involve factors that make the choice of "right and wrong" decisions muddy. Thus, many employees experience ethical dilemmas.[5] The major areas of these ethical dilemmas are suggested in Table 19.1. It shows a ranking of twenty-six ethical issues (areas) according to their importance. This table is based on a survey of the largest U.S. corporations. Data was provided by 711 companies. The participants in this study ranked the five most important ethical issues as relating to drug and

**TABLE 19.1   Major Ethical Issues Facing U.S. Industries:
In Rank Order of Importance**

Rank	Issue	Rank	Issue
1.	Drug and alcohol abuse	15.	False or misleading advertising
2.	Employee theft	16.	Giving excessive gifts and entertainment
3.	Conflicts of interest	17.	Kickbacks
4.	Quality control	18.	Insider trading
5.	Discrimination	19.	Relations with local communities
6.	Misuse of proprietary information	20.	Antitrust issues
7.	Abuse of expense accounts	21.	Bribery
8.	Plant closings and layoffs	22.	Political contributions and activities
9.	Misuse of company assets	23.	Improper relations with local government representatives
10.	Environmental pollution	24.	Improper relations with federal government representatives
11.	Misuse of others' information	25.	Inaccurate time charging to government
12.	Methods of gathering competitors' information	26.	Improper relations with foreign governments and their representatives
13.	Inaccuracy of books and records		
14.	Receiving excessive gifts and entertainment		

Source: Ethics Resource Center and Behavior Research Center. *Ethics Policies and Programs in American Business: Report of a Landmark Survey of U.S. Corporations.* Washington, D.C.: Ethics Resource Center, 1990, 17. Used with permission.

alcohol abuse, employee theft, conflicts of interest, quality control, and discrimination.[6]

Ethical decision making is extremely complex.[7] As with the presentation of ethical issues in previous chapters, our intent here is to help you internalize ethical reasoning. Checking decision possibilities against five basic questions is one approach for heightening your sensitivity to ethical issues.[8]

What Is the Ethical Intensity?

The ethical issues suggested in Table 19.1 are not of equal importance. **Ethical intensity** refers to the degree of importance given to an issue-related moral imperative. Accordingly, ethical intensity will vary substantially from issue to issue for decision makers.[9]

Ethical intensity is determined by the combined impact, as interpreted by the decision maker, of the following six components:

- The *magnitude of consequences* of the ethical issue, which is the total of the harm or benefits for individuals affected by the ethical act in question. For example:

  1. A decision that causes one thousand people to suffer a particular injury is of greater magnitude of consequence than a decision that causes ten people to suffer the same injury.

  2. A decision that causes the death of a human being is of greater magnitude of consequence than a decision that causes a person to suffer a minor injury.

- The *probability of effect* of the ethical decision, which is a joint result of the probability that the decision will be implemented and the decision will cause the harm or benefit predicted. For example:

  1. Producing a car that would be dangerous to occupants during routine driving maneuvers has greater probability of harm than producing a car that endangers occupants only when taking curves at a high speed.

  2. Selling a gun to a known armed robber has a greater probability of harm than selling a gun to a law-abiding citizen.

- The *social consensus* of the ethical issue, which is the degree of social agreement that a proposed decision is evil or good. For example:

  1. The evil involved in discriminating against minority-group job candidates has greater social consensus than the evil involved in refusing to act affirmatively on behalf of minority-group job candidates.

  2. The evil involved in bribing a customs official in the United States has greater social consensus than the evil involved in bribing a customs official in Saudi Arabia.

- A person will find it difficult to decide ethically if he or she does not know what good ethics prescribe in a situation; a high degree of social consensus reduces the likelihood of ambiguity.

- The *temporal immediacy* of the ethical issue, which is the length of time between the present and the start of consequences of the decision. A shorter length of time implies greater immediacy. For example:

  1. Releasing a drug that will cause 1 percent of the people who take it to have acute nervous reactions soon after they take it has greater temporal immediacy than releasing a drug that will cause 1 percent of those who take it to develop nervous disorders after thirty years.

  2. Reducing the retirement benefits of current retirees has greater temporal immediacy than reducing retirement benefits of employees who are currently between thirty and forty years of age.

- The *proximity* of the ethical issue, which is the feeling of nearness (social, cultural, psychological, or physical) that the decision maker has for victims or beneficiaries of the decision. For example:

  1. Layoffs in a person's work department have greater ethical proximity (physical and psychological) than do layoffs in a remote plant.

  2. For North Americans, the sale of dangerous pesticides in the North American markets has greater ethical proximity (social, cultural, and physical) than does the sale of such pesticides in Australia.

- The *concentration of effect* of the ethical decision, which is an inverse function of the number of people affected by a decision of given magnitude. For example:

  1. A change in a warranty policy denying coverage to ten people with claims of ten thousand dollars each has a more concentrated effect than a change denying coverage to ten thousand people with claims of ten dollars each.

  2. Cheating an individual or small group of individuals out of a thousand dollars has a more concentrated effect than cheating an institutional entity, such as General Motors or the Internal Revenue Service, out of the same sum.

These components of ethical intensity are all potential characteristics of the ethical issue itself. As a result, they are likely to have combined effects. Ethical intensity will increase if there is an increase in one or more of its components. Likewise, it will decrease if there is a decrease in one or more of its components, assuming all other components remain constant. Of course, individuals may differ in their ratings of ethical intensity simply because they value different principles of ethical decision making.

What Are the Decision Principles?

As suggested in Table 19.2, there is no agreed-upon set of decision principles for resolving ethical issues.[10] This table shows decision principles that have been advanced from business, philosophy, religion, and politics. We are not suggesting that all of these decision principles are necessarily good and desirable. They are presented in a sequence ranging from those that justify self-serving decisions to those that require a careful consideration of others' rights and costs. For example, the corporate code and related actions of St. Paul Companies presented in the Preview Case draws on the following principles stated in Table 19.2: organization ethic principle, utilitarian principle, disclosure principle, categorical imperative principle, and distributive justice principle.

Through laws, court rulings, and enforcement agencies, governments establish decision principles that organizations are expected to comply with in certain situations.[11] For example, Title VII of the 1964 U.S. Civil Rights Act forbids organizations from considering such personal characteristics as race, gender, religion, or national origin in decisions to recruit, hire, promote, or fire employees. This law is based on the ethical principle of distributive justice. The **distributive justice principle** means that treating individuals differently should not be based on arbitrarily defined characteristics.[12] This principle prescribes that: (1) employees who are similar in *relevant* respects should be treated similarly and (2) employees who differ in *relevant* respects should be treated differently in proportion to the differences between them. On this basis, the U.S. Equal Pay Act of 1963 holds that it is illegal to pay women and men different wages when the jobs in question require equal skill, effort, responsibility, and working conditions.

Violations of the distributive justice principle in employment practices for many cultures are not viewed with the same level of ethical intensity as in the United States and Canada. This chapter's Across Cultures suggests the differences between Japanese ethics in several areas of employment rela-

---

TABLE 19.2   Decision Principles Related to Ethical Behavior

1. *Hedonist principle*—do whatever one finds to be in one's own self-interest.
2. *Might-equals-right principle*—take what advantage one is strong enough to take without respect to ordinary social conventions and widespread practices or customs.
3. *Conventionalist principle*—bluff and take advantage of all legal opportunities and widespread practices or customs.
4. *Intuition principle*—go with one's "gut feeling" or what one understands to be right in a given situation.
5. *Organization ethic principle*—ask whether actions are consistent with organization goals and do what is good for the organization.
6. *Means-end principle*—ask whether some overall good justifies any moral transgression.
7. *Utilitarian principle*—determine whether the harm in an action is outweighed by the good.
8. *Professional ethic principle*—do only that which can be explained before a group of one's peers.
9. *Disclosure principle*—ask how it would feel to see the thinking and details of the decision disclosed to a wide audience.
10. *Distributive justice principle*—an individual's treatment should not be based on arbitrarily defined characteristics.
11. *Categorical imperative principle*—act in a way one believes is right and just for any other person in a similar situation.
12. *Golden rule principle*—look at the problem from the position of another party affected by the decision and try to determine what response the other person would expect as most virtuous.

Source: Adapted from P. V. Lewis, Ethical Decision-Making Guidelines: Executive/Student Perceptions. In L. H. Peters and K. A. Vaverek (eds). *Proceedings of the Annual Meeting of the Southwest Division of the Academy of Management.* Denton, Texas. Southwest Division of the Academy of Management, 1988, 44–48.

---

tions and U.S. laws that are based strongly on the distributive justice principle.

There is no one method or approach for ensuring that managers and other employees adhere to ethical principles and rules in their decision making. Building on our discussion of ethical behavior and organizational culture in Chapter 15, the following actions have been suggested for integrating ethical decision making into the day-to-day life of the organization:

- Ensure that a code of ethics is in place and followed.
- Ensure that a whistle-blowing and/or ethical concerns procedure is established.
- Involve employees in the identification of ethical problems to achieve a shared understanding and resolution of them, particularly through formal ethics training.
- Monitor departmental performance regarding ethical issues.

JAPANESE ETHICS AND DISTRIBUTIVE JUSTICE

Personal, corporate, and national interests in Japan are usually based on a type of extended enlightened self-interest. This pattern of ethical thought is consistent with several dominant aspects of Japanese culture. These include a sense of group membership, a sense of duty based upon personal relationships arising from Confucianism, and a sense of loyalty. These factors shape the nature of ethical decision making in Japan. In Japan, personal identity has traditionally been defined on the basis of group affiliation, most notably one's family and one's place of employment. The social norms emphasizing group affiliation grew out of the Japanese feudal system, which existed into the late 1800s, and the cooperative efforts necessary for the cultivation of rice. Accordingly, social norms play a major role in moral reasoning. The sense of group identification also produces a we-versus-them attitude. In its broadest form, this results in the Japanese sense of being unique among races and being in economic and cultural conflict with the rest of the world. Long-standing and successful efforts to restrict immigration of people from other countries is one consequence of this. So too is discrimination against minorities. These norms lead to sharp distinctions between those who are considered to be full-fledged members of the Japanese corporation and those who are not. This results in a two-tier employment system. Permanent employees are regarded as first-class citizens. Part-time and temporary workers (women are traditionally regarded as temporary workers) are treated as second-class citizens.

The group orientation also explains the reactions of Japanese males to women and minorities. Such people have traditionally been considered outside the corporate family. Thus, a whole new way of acting toward women and minorities is required for Japanese companies operating in the United States that do not want to run afoul of U.S. law and social norms. For Japanese managers who work in their company's U.S. operations, this is often difficult to do. It is surprising that there have not been far more discrimination suits against Japanese firms like the one at Sumitomo Bank. A pattern of restricted advancement opportunities resulted in a $2.6-million sex discrimination verdict against Sumitomo Bank's U.S. operations.

Other Japanese companies have faced similar problems. The United States operations of C. Itoh & Company, Inc., and Nikko Securities Company were charged with employment discrimination. Several years ago, Honda of America Manufacturing, Inc., in Marysville, Ohio, settled (for $6 million) a case that led the Equal Employment Opportunity Commission to investigate its hiring practices. Honda had been charged with racial and gender bias at the Ohio plant. This was partly the result of a rule that workers had to live within thirty miles of the plant even before applying for a job. The rule excluded, among others, residents of Columbus, Ohio, a city with a sizable African American population. In 1990, a Chicago federal court ruled that Quasar Company, a U.S. division of Japan's Matsushita Electric Corporation, discriminated against U.S. employees by reserving certain managerial positions for employees of Japanese national origin, evaluating and paying them on a different basis than that used for U.S. workers, and exempting all Japanese-origin managerial employees from a reduction in force. The verdict: $2.4 million to the employees.

Confucian ethics, in contrast, define morality in terms of duties in specific relationships, such as father-child, master-servant, and so on. In Confucian ethics, there is no generalized sense of charity. One has a certain duty to help people but only those with whom one has a relationship. This value of loyalty has survived to modern times. The feudal lord, however, has been replaced for many Japanese workers by the corporation, which provides all the necessities of life and guidelines for acceptable behavior. Loyalty to one's employer may take precedence over other duties, even to one's family and (in extreme cases) to following the law.[13]

- Integrate ethical decision making into the performance appraisal process.
- Publicize the organizational priorities and efforts related to ethical issues.[14]

Who Is Affected?

As suggested in our discussion of ethical intensity, ethical decision making generally requires an assessment of who will experience benefits or costs as a result of a particular decision. For major decisions, this assessment may include a variety of stakeholders—shareholders, customers, lenders, suppliers, employees, and government agencies, among others. The more specific you can be about individuals and groups that may experience benefits or costs from a particular decision, the more likely it is that ethical decisions will be made. Remember, ethics is about the *effects* of decisions on identifiable individuals and groups.

The ethical interpretation of the effects of decisions on identifiable individuals can change over time. Consider the **employment-at-will** concept. This common law concept assumes that parties to an employment agreement have equal bargaining power and, therefore, the right to fire is absolute and creates very little cost to either party. The employer presumably can easily find another employee, and the employee can as easily find another job. Historically, this doctrine was assumed to be valid unless (1) it is the result of an individual employment contract that specifies a fixed term, (2) it is contracted away by an employer (as in a labor union contract), or (3) it is legislated away (as in civil rights laws).[15]

Based on the distributive justice principle, the categorical imperative principle, and the golden rule principle (principles 10, 11, and 12 in Table 19.2), the employment-at-will doctrine has increasingly been successfully challenged on the basis of wrongful termination in courts. Before 1980, companies were free to fire most employees "at will." That is, they could be fired for any reason and without explanation. Employees rarely went to court to challenge a termination. The vast majority who did saw their suits dismissed. However, since 1980, the courts have been increasingly willing to rule for exceptions to at-will employment.[16]

Two management errors underlie a significant number of the terminations that wind up in court:

- Managers are unclear about their actual reasons for terminating someone. Their lack of clarity makes it difficult to judge whether the grounds are justifiable. Likewise, managers fail to understand the categories within which a termination can be responsibly justified and the special requirements for fair play.
- Managers are so concerned with finding good justifications to cover themselves in court that they have difficulty understanding what fairness means from the vantage point of the about-to-be terminated employee. They fail to balance the employee's need to be treated fairly with the company's needs for excellence and discipline. The courts are taking just such a balanced view.[17]

What Are the Benefits and Costs? 4

The answer to this question requires determining the interests and values of those affected. This is necessary to reasonably judge the benefits and costs they might experience as a result of a particular decision. When individuals or groups value something, they want that situation to continue or to occur in the future. **Values** are the relatively permanent and deeply held desires of individuals or groups. In one study, a group of business managers ranked a set of eighteen values most important in their lives. The top five values were self-respect, family security, freedom, accomplishment, and happiness. The bottom five values were pleasure, beauty, salvation, social recognition, and equality.[18] Managers need to guard against assuming that other individuals and groups share their priority of values. Conflicting values between stakeholders can lead to different interpretations of what are ethical responsibilities. Environmental groups, which probably have as one of their top values a world of beauty, often consider the managers of some organizations as both irresponsible and unethical in not showing adequate concern over air and water pollution, land use, and the like.

One common approach to the assessment of benefits and costs is utilitarianism. As noted by principle 7 in Table 19.2, **utilitarianism** emphasizes the provision of the greatest good for the greatest number in judging the ethics of decision making. An individual who is guided by utilitarianism considers the potential effect of alternative actions on those who will be affected and then selects the alternative benefiting the greatest number of people. The individual accepts the fact that this alternative may harm others. However, so long as potentially positive results outweigh potentially negative results, the individual considers the decision to be both good and ethical.[19] Some critics suggest utilitarianism has been carried to extremes in North America. These critics suggest that there is too much maximizing of personal advantage in the short run and too much discounting of the long-run costs of disregarding ethics, those living in poverty, and the environment. There are too many people acquiring wealth for the purpose of personal consumption and the means to get it are unimportant, according to these critics.[20]

Who Has Rights? 5

The notion of rights also is complex and has changed over time. One aspect of rights focuses on who is entitled to benefits or to participation in the decision to change the allocation of benefits and costs.[21] Union-management negotiations frequently involve conflicts and dilemmas over management's rights to hire, promote, fire, and reassign union employees. Slavery, racism, gender and age discrimination, and invasion of privacy have often been attacked by appeals to values based on concepts of fundamental rights.

As shown in Table 19.1, employee responsibilities and rights issues are numerous. They range in scope from (1) employee testing, privacy, and good faith dealing to (2) rights to serve public interest and self-responsibility and (3) plant closings, labor-management cooperation, and worker participation. Examples include issues of unfair and reverse discrimination, sexual harassment, employee rights to continued employment, employer rights to terminate the employment relationship "at will," employee and corporate free speech, due process considerations, acquired immune deficiency syndrome (AIDS), and a host of others. The issues are not only numerous but also highly varied in nature. According to some experts, the attention to workplace rights is the critical internal-to-the-organization issue facing management in the nineties.[22]

Privacy rights have become a major domain of ethical dilemmas in such issues as: (1) distribution and use of employee data from computer-based human resource information systems[23]; (2) increasing use of paper-and-pencil honesty tests as a result of polygraph testing being declared illegal in most situations[24]; (3) procedures and basis for AIDS testing and drug testing[25]; and (4) genetic testing. The ethical dilemmas in each of these areas revolve around the relative balance among the rights of the individual, the needs and rights of the employer, and the interests of the community at large.[26]

Genetic testing, although not as widespread as drug or AIDS testing, is expected to grow in frequency of use. **Genetic testing** refers to techniques used to determine the existence of inherited genetic changes that might cause a predisposition to certain illnesses.[27] The following In Practice suggests some of the ethical issues associated with genetic testing.

IN PRACTICE

ETHICS OF GENETIC TESTING

Serious privacy and confidentiality issues are raised by genetic testing. The tests can disclose not only a person's genetic makeup but also his or her medical history, use of drugs, diet, the presence of sexually transmitted disease, and probability of getting a disease. This information may or may not be job-related. Indeed, there may be serious disagreement about whether a particular piece of information is job-related or not.

The employers who know this information take on legal and ethical responsibilities. Disclosure of information to third parties, such as insurance companies, will undoubtedly result in lawsuits for invasion of privacy. To protect themselves from liability, employers must develop appropriate policies to safeguard employees' and applicants' privacy and ensure the confidentiality of test results. Legal liability for disseminating information to third parties is, however, only one aspect of the concern over accessibility of the information acquired through genetic testing. There also are concerns of whether and under what circumstances the person tested should be given access to the results. Access to such information would allow individuals to make informed decisions about their employment and health. Under many circumstances, this would not pose any particular medical or moral issues.

Let's assume that a test done on a twenty-year-old employee or applicant indicates that he or she has Huntington's disease. This is a fatal illness, but the symptoms do not generally appear until middle age. Under what circumstances should the test results be disclosed to the person tested? In the case of an employee, the Occupational Safety and Health Administration guarantees an individual access to his or her medical records. But company physicians retain some discretion over the disclosure of test results that indicate a terminal illness or psychiatric condition. This discretion burdens the employer with serious ethical questions. It is critical for management to carefully formulate a comprehensive policy that addresses a worker's right to know, including what information will be made available and under what circumstances. For disclosure of a life-threatening illness, management should consider what counseling and support services should be provided. In the case of a job applicant, these issues become even more difficult. Organizations should not undertake such testing until they have thought through completely the implications of the decision to do so.[28]

DECISION-MAKING MODELS

In this section, we briefly outline the major features of three decision-making models. Our goal is to demonstrate the significant variations in how decision making has been perceived and interpreted. All three models are useful for capturing the complexity and variety of decision-making situations found within organizations.[29]

Rational Model

The **rational model** holds that the outcomes of decision making are alternatives that have been intentionally chosen to bring maximum benefit(s) to the organization. The rational perspective requires a comprehensive problem definition, an exhaustive search for alternatives, and thorough data collection and analysis. Evaluation criteria are developed early on in the search process. Information exchange is unbiased and accurate. Individual preferences and organizational choices are a function of the best alternative for the entire organization.[30] In brief, the rational model of decision making assumes: (1) complete information concerning decision alternatives is available, (2) it is possible to rank these alternatives using objective criteria, and (3) the alternative selected will provide the maximum gain possible for the organization (or decision makers). This model implicitly assumes that ethical dilemmas do not exist in the decision-making process.

Bounded Rationality Model

The **bounded rationality model** emphasizes the limitations of the individual's rationality and thus provides a better picture of the day-to-day decision process often used by individuals. It partially explains why different individuals may make different decisions when they have exactly the same information. As suggested in Figure 19.1, the bounded rationality model reflects the individual's tendencies to: (1) select less than the best goal or alternative solution (that is, to "*satisfice*"); (2) engage in a limited search for alternative solutions; and (3) have inadequate information and control of

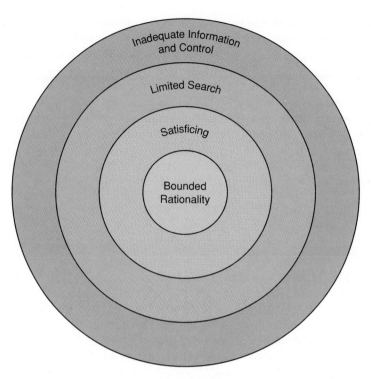

FIGURE 19.1   Model of Bounded Rationality

external and internal environmental forces influencing the outcomes of his or her decisions.[31] This model also recognizes the reality that complete information—concerning available alternatives or the outcome of some course of action—may be impossible to obtain, regardless of how much time or resources are used.

Satisficing   The practice of selecting an acceptable goal or alternative solution is called **satisficing.** In this case, *acceptable* might mean easier to identify and achieve, less controversial, or otherwise safer than the best available alternative. For example, profit goals are often quantified, such as a 12 percent rate of return on investment or a 6 percent increase in profits over the previous year. These goals may not be the maximum attainable. They may, in fact, represent little more than top management's view of reasonable goals, that is, challenging but not too difficult to achieve.[32]

In an interview almost thirty-five years after introducing the bounded rationality model, Herbert Simon described satisficing in these words for a management audience:

> Satisficing is intended to be used in contrast to the classical economist's idea that in making decisions in business or anywhere in real life, you somehow pick, or somebody gives you, a set of alternatives from which you select the best one—maximize. The satisficing idea is that first of all, you don't have the alternatives, you've got to go out and scratch for them—and that you might have shaky ways of evaluating them when you do find them. So you look for alter-

natives until you get one from which, in terms of your experience and in terms of what you have reason to expect, you will get a reasonable result.

But satisficing doesn't necessarily mean that managers have to be satisfied with what alternative pops up first in their minds or in their computers and let it go at that. The level of satisficing can be raised—by personal determination, setting higher individual or organizational standards, and by use of an increasing range of sophisticated management science and computer-based decision-making and problem-solving techniques.

As time goes on, you obtain more information about what's feasible and what you can aim at. Not only do you get more information, but in many, if not most, companies there are procedures for setting targets, including procedures for trying to raise individuals' aspiration levels [goals]. This is a major responsibility of top management.[33]

Limited Search   Individuals usually make a limited search for possible goals or alternative solutions to a problem. Individuals consider alternatives only until they find one that seems adequate. For example, in choosing the best job, college graduates cannot evaluate every available job in their field. They might hit retirement age before obtaining all the information needed for a decision.

Even the rational decision-making model recognizes that identifying and assessing proposed alternative solutions costs time, energy, and money. In the bounded rationality model, individuals stop searching for alternatives as soon as they discover an acceptable goal or solution.

Inadequate Information and Control   Individuals frequently have inadequate information about problems and face environmental forces that they cannot control. These conditions will influence the results of their decisions.[34] For example, management might decide to purchase automatic stamping machines to make disc brakes for automobiles. By reducing labor costs, the machines could pay for themselves within two years. But management might fail to anticipate either union resistance or declining automobile sales. In those cases, the machines could not be used effectively, and their pay-out time could more than double. In sum, the bounded rationality model provides meaningful insights into the limitations of how individuals often make decisions in organizations. It implicitly recognizes the potential for ethical dilemmas in decision making situations but provides no guidance on how to resolve them.

Political Model

According to the **political model,** organizational decisions reflect the desires of individuals to satisfy their own interests. Preferences are established early, usually on the basis of departmental goals, and seldom change as new information is acquired. Problem definitions, searches, data collection, and evaluation criteria are merely weapons used to tilt the decision outcome in someone's favor. Information exchange is biased toward the same end.

Decisions are a result of the distribution of power in the organization and the effectiveness of the tactics used by the various participants in the process.[35] In Chapter 16, we examined power and political behavior in detail. Dilemmas are not recognized in the model. However, this model draws from the following decision principles presented in Table 19.2: (1) *hedonistic principle*—do whatever one finds to be in one's own self-interest; (2) *market principle*—take selfish actions and be motivated by personal gains in business dealings; (3) *conventionalist principle*—bluff and take advantage of all legal opportunities and widespread practices or customs; and (4) *might-equals-right principle*—seize what advantages one is strong enough to take without respect to ordinary social conventions and laws.

PHASES OF MANAGERIAL DECISION MAKING

Managerial decision making begins with a recognition or awareness of problems and concludes with an assessment of the results of actions taken to solve those problems. Figure 19.2 provides a model of the phases of managerial decision making.[36] Although the phases are shown as proceeding in a logical order, managerial decision making is often quite disorderly and complex as it unfolds. In fact, it has been generally described as follows:

> Decisions are made and problems solved in fits and starts. The process is like a flowing stream, filled with debris, meandering through the terrain of managers and their organizations. There is no beginning or end.[37] Managers usually deal with the unexpected crises and petty little problems that require much more time than they're worth. . . . The manager may well go from a budget meeting involving millions to a discussion of what to do about a broken decorative water fountain.[38] Thus, managerial work is hectic and fragmented and requires the ability to shift continually from person to person, from one subject or problem to another.[39]

Problem Recognition

Managerial decision making rarely begins with a clean slate. Previous decisions and experiences and new information have a significant impact on whether there is any awareness or recognition of an existing problem. Moreover, the characteristics of individual managers also play an important role in problem recognition.[40] (See Chapter 5.)

With **structured problems,** the recognition stage is straightforward. For example, a marketing manager promises the delivery of an order within thirty days. After forty-five days, the customer calls and, in a state of irritation, states: "The order hasn't arrived. I need it pronto. What are you going to do?" The marketing manager is suddenly and forcefully made aware of a problem and the need to resolve it immediately.

With **unstructured problems,** problem recognition often is, itself, a problem.[41] The "problem" of problem recognition can result from unclear or inadequate information about developments and trends in the environment and organization. For example, Walt Disney, Hilton Hotels, and other organizations create marketing research departments to collect information about their customers to determine whether changing customer tastes and preferences are likely to create new problems.

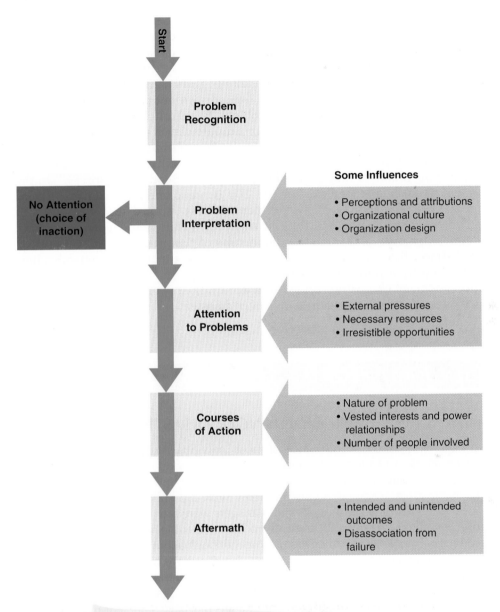

FIGURE 19.2 Phases of Managerial Decision Making

Source: Adapted from M. W. McCall, Jr., and R. E. Kaplan, *Whatever It Takes: The Realities of Managerial Decision Making,* 2d ed. Englewood Cliffs, N.J.: Prentice-Hall, 1990.

Let's return to the marketing manager who was called by an irate customer. This manager has been experiencing a 200 percent turnover in sales representatives. When asked about this level of turnover, the marketing manager replies: "That's the way it's always been, even before I became the marketing manager. I guess it's just part of the cost of doing business and the nomadic nature of sales reps. . . ." This response shows no awareness that a problem of high turnover might exist. Six months later, a new marketing manager is appointed. When reviewing the personnel files, she is astounded by the "major turnover problem, which must be corrected if we are ever to establish long-term and trusting relationships with our customers and eventually increase our sales to them."

The recognition of a problem usually triggers activities that may lead to a quick solution or may be part of a long, drawn-out process. It depends on the nature and complexity of the problem. For example, the new marketing manager may be confronted by a subordinate with a problem like this: "We are fifteen days late in the delivery of the West Publishing Company order. Should we ship it by our regular freight line, by air express, or what?" The marketing manager may immediately respond: "Send it air express." On the other hand, her recognition of the 200 percent annual turnover in sales personnel represents a major problem. It may require several months to (1) determine the reasons for the turnover, (2) implement a program to reduce turnover, and (3) assess the results of the program.

Major disasters or accidents often have long incubation periods characterized by a number of events signaling danger. These events often go unrecognized or misinterpreted and accumulate over time.[42] Consider the following In Practice on the *Challenger* disaster.

IN PRACTICE

THE *CHALLENGER* DISASTER

A nagging question in the minds of most individuals following the *Challenger* space shuttle explosion on January 28, 1986, is how on earth could NASA management officials have allowed the shuttle to take off, given what appears to have been clear-cut warnings about problems with the shuttle's solid-fuel booster rocket joints. Whatever pressure the managers were facing to launch the shuttle, did they not know enough technically to realize that the lives of the crew were in serious danger? If, in fact, they did not know enough about the technical apparatus of the shuttle, as good managers, should they not have been in constant contact with their trained professionals regarding the spacecraft's safety?

The findings of the presidential commission investigating the loss of the *Challenger* found that NASA management officials *did* have sufficient information to cancel the flight, although this information may not have reached all of the relevant managers. Furthermore, the information was made available to several key NASA managers by some engineering professionals as late as the evening before the flight. Allan J. McDonald, a senior engineer in charge of the solid-fuel booster rocket motor program at Morton Thiokol, Inc., NASA's principal contractor of booster rockets, argued strongly against the launch only hours before the *Challenger* was scheduled to lift off. In testimony before the presidential commission, McDonald and Roger Boisjoly, who had graphically demonstrated the erosion of the infamous O-rings in prior flights, testified about their objections. But their bosses had overruled them after presumably being pressured by NASA officials at the Marshall Space Flight Center. According to the testimony, McDonald stated that the engineers would not recommend a launch at temperatures below fifty-three degrees Fahrenheit. The commission also learned that engineers at another contractor, Rockwell International, had also warned about the adverse effects of cold weather on the shuttle's tiles.

On the morning of the launch, temperatures below ten degrees were recorded by NASA technicians on the booster rocket's exterior. Jerry Mason, former senior vice-president at Thiokol, testified how the decision to launch was reached by polling appropriate managers. When asked if company officials polled the engineers, Mason replied, "We only polled the management people."[43]

A variety of conditions can increase the likelihood of incorrect problem recognition and formulation. Seven of these conditions are:

- *Someone gives you a problem.* When you are asked to help solve a problem that someone else has defined, you are likely to take that problem as a "given" and work within the constraints of the problem statement. The more authority or power that the person wields, the more likely you are to be intimidated into accepting, without question, his or her statement of the problem.

- *A quick solution is desired.* If a decision is needed quickly, the amount of time spent in formulating or reformulating a problem is likely to be cut short. This was one of the conditions present in the *Challenger* launching.

- *A low-quality solution is acceptable.* People attach a lower priority for some problems than others. When this is the case, less time is likely to be spent formulating and solving the problem than if a high-quality solution were critical.

- *The problem seems familiar.* If a problem seems familiar to one that you have experienced recently, you are more likely to apply a ready-made solution than to question the "real" need(s). This can lead to a quick solution or a fix. For example, when a tire goes flat on your car, you immediately think of getting out the jack. If the jack does not work, the problem becomes how to fix the flat. The jack is a means to an end and not the end itself.

- *Emotions are high.* Stressful or emotional situations often lead to an abbreviated search for a satisfactory statement of the problem. This was one of the conditions present in the *Challenger* launching.

- *No prior experience in challenging problem definitions.* For most of us, questioning a problem statement requires training and practice. This habit is hard to get into (and easy to fall out of). If you are unaccustomed to challenging or reformulating a problem statement, you are unlikely to do so.

- *The problem is complex.* When a situation involves a lot of variables and the variables are hard to identify and/or measure, the problem is harder to formulate and solve.[44] This was another of the conditions present in the *Challenger* launching.

Problem Interpretation

The second phase in the decision making process requires an interpretation of the problem. A high turnover rate for sales representatives might be the result of looking for applicants in the wrong places, inadequate selection procedures, poor training, lack of supervision, a poor compensation system, or some combination of these. **Problem interpretation** refers to the process of giving meaning and definition to those problems that have been recognized.[45] Problem recognition does not ensure sufficient, if any, problem attention. Accordingly to Figure 19.2, one option for managers is to simply not give a recognized problem any attention—the choice of inaction. This choice may be a consequence of: (1) demands on the manager to deal with too many other high-priority problems, (2) a belief that the problem will go away with time, or (3) the judgment that an attempt to do something about the problem will only worsen the situation.

Preconceptions, the filtering out of new information, and defensiveness contribute to ineffective problem interpretation.[46] As suggested in Figure 19.2, some of the key influences on problem interpretation include perceptions and attributions (Chapter 4), organizational culture (Chapter 15), and organization design (Chapter 18). A common thread in these influences is the way information is processed and how it is used to interpret problems (Chapter 5).[47] There is no simple one-to-one relationship between the availability of "objective" information and how it is processed in the problem-interpretation phase.

A number of information processing biases can enter into decision making, particularly in this phase of the process. Five of these biases are noted as follows:

- **Availability bias**—if a person can easily recall specific instances of an event, he or she may overestimate how frequently such an event occurs (and vice versa). Individuals who have been in a serious automobile accident often overestimate the frequency of such accidents.

- **Selective perception bias**—what people expect to see influences what they do see. People seek information consistent with their own views. People downplay information that conflicts with their perceptions. An example might be parents who are unwilling to acknowledge that the reasons their child received a failing grade are poor performance and lack of effort, rather than poor instruction or instructor bias.

- **Concrete information bias**—vivid, direct experience dominates abstract information. A single personal experience can outweigh more valid statistical information. An initial bad work experience may lead the individual to conclude that managers cannot be trusted and are simply out to exploit their subordinates.

- **Law of small numbers bias**—small samples are deemed representative of the larger population (a few cases "prove the rule"), even when they are not. A number of Arab Americans experienced hostile comments and reactions by some non-Arabs after the invasion of Kuwait by Iraqi forces. Apparently, the individuals incorrectly attributed the unsavory characteristics of Saddam Hussein (sample of one) to Arab Americans in general.

- **Gambler's fallacy bias**—seeing an unexpected number of similar chance events leads to the belief that an event not seen will occur. For example, observing nine successive reds in roulette, the individual thinks the chances for a black on the next spin are greater than fifty-fifty.[48]

Specialization results in channeling information and problems to particular positions and departments. It can both aid and hinder problem recognition and interpretation. For example, when the marketing manager and her staff have been assigned goals to ensure customer satisfaction—such as "98 percent of all orders are to reach customers on the promised date of delivery"—and to take corrective action when the goals are not achieved, specialization probably aids problem recognition and interpretation. However, unless accompanied by integrating mechanisms, specialization may well lead to ineffective efforts and conflicts between specialties and departments. Managers have been known to conceal and distort information as a means of advancing their individual and departmental goals. There may also be a failure to recognize the importance of new information if it does not clearly fall within an existing specialty or the area of responsibility of one of the departments. Unfortunately, this tendency is most likely to occur in heterogeneous and unstable environments. This is the very environment in which effective problem recognition and problem interpretation becomes critical.[49]

The likelihood of managers learning to recognize and interpret problems effectively is strongly influenced by the characteristics of and processes within the organization's culture. **Organizational learning** is the process within an organization by which knowledge about action-outcome relationships and the effect of the environment on these relationships is developed. It requires a means through which an individual's knowledge can be shared, evaluated, and integrated with others in the organization.[50]

Attention to Problems

After problems have been recognized and interpreted, judgments need to be made as to which problems receive attention, how much, and in what order. Managers must be aware of the relative priorities they place on the problems they attend to. As suggested in Figure 19.2, the problems receiving the highest priority are likely to meet the following criteria:

- Attention to the problem is supported by strong *external pressure* (the executive vice-president insists on a report being completed within two weeks).
- Attention to the problem is supported by the *necessary resources* to take action (you are authorized to approve overtime pay and hire temporary workers to complete the report within two weeks).
- Attention to the problem represents an *irresistible opportunity* (the report deals with assessing an expansion in production capacity that could lead to a larger and more profitable firm, a promotion from production supervisor to production manager, or the potential of larger bonuses).

The key to understanding the demands of managerial decision making is straight forward. The volume and variety of recognized problems needing attention almost always exceed the manager's capacity for addressing and resolving all of them within the desired time frame. Pressures from the external environment can change the most carefully planned priorities for attending to recognized problems.[51] Let's return to the *Challenger* disaster presented in the previous In Practice. We now review some of the apparent external pressures and the sense of irresistible opportunities that helped to move the decision-making process to a launch decision.

CHALLENGER FLASHBACK

The *Challenger* tragedy was as much a failure of decision making as of technology. The normal procedures of NASA were circumvented. The objections of experts were either overruled or kept from key decision makers. The pressures on NASA were intense and varied. These included the desire to secure congressional funding through evidence of cost-effectiveness and productivity, the intense public interest in the heavily advertised "Teacher in Space" program, and the wish to demonstrate the capabilities of NASA technology. All of these created a powerful "pressure cooker" environment in which NASA decision makers stayed on a set of ideas and ignored negative information.

In the *Challenger* case, lift-off was clearly more desirable than delay. With a "go" decision, the flight schedule could be kept, the public would not be disappointed, and the shuttle program would achieve another major goal. Any interpretation of possible system failure would have suggested the need to spend more money, a conclusion NASA found distasteful in light of its commitment to cost-effectiveness and economy.

Since indecision and ambiguity are often stressful, any action may seem better than delay. This need for action often increases as a deadline draws near—exactly the condition that faced NASA officials with the *Challenger*. When the perceived costs of a bad decision or judgment seem high, a decision maker usually searches for alternatives and is normally sensitive to information about the flaws and pitfalls of a decision. With the *Challenger* mission, the fear seemed to be lost in a general atmosphere of enthusiasm. No one wanted to be pressed to recognize the possibility of an accident being much more likely than normal because of cold weather.

The main motivations of people involved in the *Challenger* decision varied depending on who they were. Top NASA managers were under great pressure to reach a decision; their desire for action encouraged reaching a decision to launch. Their concern for productivity and cost-effectiveness also made a positive decision more likely. By contrast, engineers at Morton Thiokol, the manufacturer of the solid-fuel rocket boosters, had less decision pressure, little concern about the decision's political and economic implications, and the greatest fear of disaster. They were the ones who objected to the launching. Top management at Thiokol had a different set of motivations. Highly dependent on NASA for a contract bringing in an estimated $400 million a year, Morton Thiokol's top managers could identify with NASA's concerns. Robert Lund, vice-president for engineering at Thiokol, testified how he initially opposed the launch. But he changed his position "after being told to take off his engineering hat and put on one representing management."[52]

Courses of Action

The development and evaluation of courses of action (alternatives) and the implementation of the selected alternative can range from a quick-action process to a convoluted-action process. A quick-action process is appropriate when (1) the nature of the problem is well structured (two subordinates fail to show up for work, creating a problem in meeting a deadline for the next day); (2) a single manager (or at most, two managers) is clearly recognized as having the authority and responsibility to resolve the problem (the manager authorizes overtime for some of the other employees to meet the deadline); and (3) the search for information about the problem and alternatives is quite limited (the manager might call the customer to determine whether to schedule overtime, bring in help from a temporary employment service, or check with other managers to see if any of them are less busy and could loan some workers). This quick-action process may well take place within a matter of minutes or take as long as several days.

At the other extreme, the convoluted-action process is drawn-out and mazelike. The *Challenger* situation prior to launch should have triggered a convoluted-action process within NASA and Morton Thiokol. It is usually necessary when:

- *The nature of the problem is unstructured.* NASA had never faced a launch situation at low temperatures. Research clearly indicated that the O-rings' effectiveness in directing the flow of gases was substantially reduced at low temperatures. Even at higher temperatures, there was evidence of problems with the O-rings.
- *A long period of time is required for problem solution.* NASA and Morton Thiokol officials recognized how a redesign of the O-rings could delay the planned shuttle schedule by as much as two years. This worked against adopting the needed convoluted-action process.
- *Many vested interests and power relationships are involved.* We indicated some of the vested interests and power relationships of various groups prior to launch in the *"Challenger* Flashback" account. After the disaster, even more vested interests and power relationships came into play: the Congress, the Office of the President, the astronauts, the courts (in assigning liability), and the U.S. Justice Department, among others.
- *Many people are involved in an extensive search for solutions.* Prior to the *Challenger* disaster, only a few engineers at Morton Thiokol were deeply involved in an extensive search to solve the O-ring problem. After the disaster, many groups and individuals were involved in the search for solutions to the O-ring problem and the broader problem of the flawed decision-making process at NASA and Morton Thiokol.

In either the convoluted- or quick-action processes, trade-offs, negotiation, conflict, and political processes are usually involved. (See, especially, Chapters 14 and 16.) The process leading up to the launch decision clearly suggests that these were present in the *Challenger* disaster. The worst trade-off was favoring the planned launch schedule over safety. Although managers continuously face a variety of problems, many can be addressed by the quick-action process. Far fewer require initiating the convoluted-action process. However, quick action may lead to poor decisions, when a more deliberate approach would have been more appropriate.[53]

Aftermath

During the **aftermath** of a decision, the results of the actions taken are evaluated. With structured problems, evaluation is usually rather simple. The costs and benefits associated with alternative actions can be easily calculated. Recall the example of the manager who scheduled overtime to meet a deadline when two workers failed to show up. If the overtime hours resulted in meeting the deadline, there is clear feedback of the decision leading to the intended result.

The selection of a course of action and its implementation to deal with an unstructured problem may involve many individuals, groups, and subjective judgments, as in the *Challenger* situation. The assessment of the course of action taken may require months or even years before the outcomes are known and their consequences can be determined.[54] At least eighteen months were required from the selection of the revised O-ring design to its use in a space shuttle launch. The long-term reliability of the redesign can only be determined under actual and repeated launch conditions. Unstructured problems usually require implementing a course of action in the face of risk and uncertainty.

Even the best managers make mistakes. The challenge is to learn from these mistakes. Most employees and managers guard their reputations as capable people and may go to extremes not to acknowledge their mistakes. Moreover, individuals and groups tend to overestimate the effectiveness of their judgment decisions.[55] In the aftermath of the *Challenger* disaster, most of the officials involved at NASA and Morton Thiokol denied making mistakes. They engaged in self-delusions that the disaster was primarily a result of a naturally high-risk program.

Sometimes the negative aftermath of a decision will result in an escalating commitment. **Escalating commitment** is a process of continuing or increasing the commitment of resources to a course of action, even though a substantial amount of feedback indicates that the action is wrong.[56] Consider the following reflections on the Vietnam War and the anticipation of the escalating commitment process.

At an early state of the U.S. involvement in the Vietnam War, George Ball, then Undersecretary of State, wrote the following statement in a memo to Lyndon Johnson: "The decision you face now is crucial. Once large numbers of U.S. troops are committed to direct combat, they will begin to take heavy casualties in a war they are ill-equipped to fight in a noncooperative if not downright hostile countryside. Once we suffer large casualties, we will have started a well-nigh irreversible process. Our involvement will be so great that we cannot—without national humiliation—stop short of achieving our complete objectives. Of the two possibilities I think humiliation would be more likely than the achievement of our objectives—even after we have paid terrible costs." (Memo dated July 1, 1965, from *Pentagon Papers,* 1971).[57]

One of the explanations for escalating commitment is that individuals feel responsible for negative consequences, which motivates them to justify previous decisions. In addition, individuals may become committed to a course of action simply because they believe consistency in action is a desirable form of behavior.[58] Our presentation in Chapter 4 on perception and attributions gives additional insights into the possible reasons for escalating commitment.

The following comments by two managers are instructive of the need to learn from the aftermath of a course of action, including those that turned out to be mistakes.

> Everybody knows you make mistakes, so why not admit it. I make it a point to admit the blunders. Once I admit it, I feel better about it. It doesn't bother me. It's really a painful thing to keep trying not to admit some things. You have to carry that around as a burden until you get it off your chest.[59]

> When one's decisions turn out all right, one should resist the temptation to spend very much time basking in the glory of those right decisions. They need to be reexamined on a continuous basis to be sure that the decision that was right yesterday continues to be right today.[60]

In our next section, we review several decision aids designed to stimulate organizational creativity for improved problem recognition, problem interpretation, and courses of action.

STIMULATING ORGANIZATIONAL CREATIVITY

Organizational creativity is the production of ideas that are novel and useful to the organization by an individual or group of individuals working together. This process may include the assistance of computer-based information technology. Innovation is built on novel and useful ideas. Accordingly, **organizational innovation** is the implementation of creative and useful ideas through unplanned or planned organizational change.[61] Chapters 21 and 22 are devoted to an in-depth discussion of planned organizational change.

Creativity helps managers and others to uncover problems, identify opportunities, and undertake novel courses of action to solve problems. We presented two approaches for stimulating creativity within organizations in Chapter 10, namely the nominal group technique and electronic brainstorming. Moreover, we have repeatedly addressed issues and processes for reducing barriers to creative and innovative thought and action. Some of these barriers include perceptual blocks, cultural blocks, and emotional blocks. Perceptual blocks include such factors as the failure to use all of the senses in observing, the failure to investigate the obvious, difficulty in seeing remote relationships, and the failure to distinguish between facets of cause-and-effect relationships. Cultural blocks include a desire to conform to established norms, overemphasis on competition or conflict avoidance and smoothing, the drive to be practical and narrowly economical above all things, and a belief that indulging in fantasy or other forms of open-ended exploration is a waste of time. Finally, emotional blocks include fear of making a mistake, fear and distrust of others, grabbing the first idea that comes along, and the like.[62]

NASA or Morton Thiokol officials did not exercise organizational creativity in confronting the O-ring problem. In fact, a seemingly endless series of memos reveal safety concerns from lower-level employees of both NASA and Morton Thiokol. If NASA officials had listened and acted on the early warning signals, in all likelihood they could have prevented the disaster. One of the most striking memos from an engineer within Morton Thiokol starts with the cry, "Help!" The memo goes on to say that if the shuttle continues to fly with the O-rings as they are designed, NASA is almost guaranteed a disaster. The managers ignored the bad news. Instead of deliberately designing monitoring systems to pick up danger signals, NASA designed, in effect, a management system that would intentionally tune out danger signals or downgrade their seriousness.[63]

Lateral Thinking Method

The **lateral thinking method** proposes a deliberate process for the generation of new ideas through a change in the individual's or group's typical logical pattern for processing and storing information. In contrast, **vertical thinking** is the logical step-by-step process where ideas are developed by proceeding on a continuous path from one bit of information to another. The major differences between lateral thinking and vertical thinking are presented in Table 19.3. The lateral thinking method was developed by Edward de Bono, a British physician and psychologist. The two processes are complimentary, not antagonistic. De Bono states:

> Lateral thinking is useful for generating ideas and approaches and vertical thinking is useful for developing them. Lateral thinking enhances the effectiveness of vertical thinking by offering it more to select from. Vertical thinking multiplies the effectiveness of lateral thinking by making good use of the ideas generated.
>
> Most of the time one might be using vertical thinking but when one needs to use lateral thinking, then no amount of excellence in vertical thinking will do instead.[64]

The lateral thinking method proposes a number of special techniques for (1) developing an awareness of current ideas and practices, (2) generating alternative ways for looking at a problem, and (3) assisting in the development of new ideas. We will consider four of the many lateral thinking techniques for assisting in the development of new ideas.[65]

Reversal   Using the reversal technique, new ideas can be suggested by examining the current problem and turning it completely around, inside

TABLE 19.3 Characteristics of Lateral versus Vertical Thinking

Lateral Thinking	Vertical Thinking
1. Tries to find new ways for looking at things; is concerned with change and movement.	1. Tries to find absolutes for judging relationships; is concerned with stability.
2. Avoids looking for what is "right" or "wrong." Tries to find what is different.	2. Seeks a yes or no justification for each step. Tries to find what is "right."
3. Analyzes ideas to determine how they might be used to generate new ideas.	3. Analyzes ideas to determine why they do not work and need to be rejected.
4. Attempts to introduce discontinuity by making "illogical" (free association) jumps from one step to another.	4. Seeks continuity by logically proceeding from one step to another.
5. Welcomes chance intrusions of information to use in generating new ideas; considers the irrelevant.	5. Selectively chooses what to consider for generating ideas; rejects any information not considered to be relevant.
6. Progresses by avoiding the obvious.	6. Progresses using established patterns; considers the obvious.

Source: Based on E. de Bono, *Lateral Thinking: Creativity Step by Step*. New York: Harper & Row, 1970; E. de Bono, *Six Thinking Hats*. Boston: Little, Brown, 1985.

out, or upside down. For ten years, IBM and Apple saw each other as major rivals in the very competitive PC markets. Their creative efforts were devoted to capturing customers from one another. In 1991, each revised its definition of the other. Subsequently, Apple and IBM formed a technology partnership. Apple will obtain the right to use an important IBM microprocessor. In exchange, IBM will gain access to Apple's proprietary software. By 1993, the venture could result in Apple and IBM workstations that could be easily linked—and even share applications software.[66] As with all lateral-thinking methods, it is not the correctness of the reversal that counts but how the perspective on the problem is changed.

Cross-fertilization The cross-fertilization technique involves asking experts from other fields how they would try to see the problem using methods from their areas. For it to be effective, the people listened to should be from fields entirely removed from the problem. An attempt can then be made to apply these methods to the problem.

Analogies An analogy is a statement about how objects, persons, or situations are similar to one another. Some examples of analogies are: this organization operates like a bee hive, or this organization operates like a fine Swiss watch. Analogies are used by translating the problem into an analogy, refining and developing the analogy, and then translating back to the problem to judge the suitability of the analogy. If an analogy is selected that is too similar to the problem, little will have been gained. Concrete and specific analogies should be selected over more abstract ones. Analogies should describe a specific, well-known issue or process in the organization. For a mechanistic organization that is ignoring increased environmental change, an analogy might be: The managers are like a flock of ostriches with their heads buried in the sand.

Random-Word Stimulation   A word is selected from a dictionary or specially prepared word list. A link is sought between the word and the problem. One option is to select a word using a table of random numbers to choose a page in a dictionary and then a position on a page. For most problems, however, less-than-random procedure is probably adequate. One important point in using this method is to try to stay with a word once it is selected. A premature judgment about a word's relevance could result in many useful ideas being overlooked.

We presented only a few of the techniques and ideas for stimulating lateral thinking. This approach has been formally introduced through training in such organizations as Unilever, General Electric, Shell, General Foods, and IBM. The lateral thinking method is consistent with a view of creative behavior as a complex person-situation interaction that is influenced by the past as well as current situation.[67]

Devil's Advocate Method

The **devil's advocate method** calls for a person or small task force to develop a systematic critique of a recommended course of action. The devil's advocate attempts to point out weaknesses in the assumptions underlying the proposal, internal inconsistencies in it, and problems that could lead to failure if it were followed. The devil's advocate acts like a good trial lawyer, by presenting arguments against the majority position as convincingly as possible.[68] The basic decision process with this method is presented in Figure 19.3.

It is a good idea to rotate people assigned to devil's advocate roles. This avoids any one person or task force being identified as the critic on all issues. The devil's advocate role may be advantageous for a person and the organization. Steve Huse, chairperson and CEO of Huse Food Group, states that the devil's advocate role is an opportunity for employees to demonstrate their presentation and debating skills. How well someone understands and researches issues is apparent when presenting a critique. The organization avoids costly mistakes by hearing viewpoints that identify pitfalls. In addition, the use of the devil's advocate approach may increase the probability of creative solutions to problems and reduce the probability of groupthink.[69] In Chapter 10, we discussed groupthink as one of the problems in decision making caused by excessive concensus and similarity of views in groups—a sure killer of organizational creativity.

The devil's advocacy method has been found to be quite effective in helping to surface and challenge assumptions in a proposed course of action.[70] This is a critical element in stimulating organizational creativity. Of

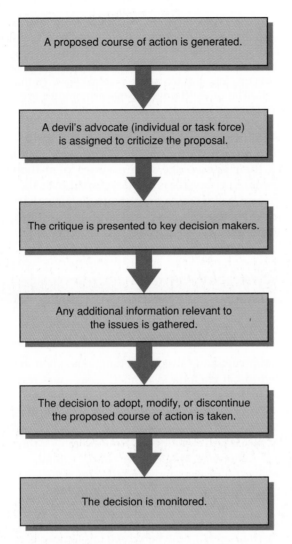

FIGURE 19.3   Decision Process with a Devil's Advocate

Source: Adapted from R. A. Cosier and C. R. Schrivenk, Agreement and Thinking Alike: Ingredients for Poor Decisions. *Academy of Management Executive,* February 1991, 71.

course, the devil's advocate method should not be overused. It is intended
for especially important and complex issues.

Artificial Intelligence

Artificial intelligence (AI) is an attempt to give computers and software
human-like capabilities, such as seeing, hearing, thinking, and learning. It is
beginning to affect managerial and professional jobs. **Expert systems** are a
subset of AI that attempt to achieve expert-level results in solving problems
through computer programs designed to imitate the behavior of an expert.[71]
It has been noted that:

Human experts can solve difficult problems, restructure knowledge, and determine relevance; and they know what they don't know. Expert systems mimic the first—the ability to solve problems—most successfully. Most systems also are able to explain themselves by backtracking through the steps used to arrive at a decision or conclusion, and a few expert systems have rudimentary learning capabilities as well. The other (human) expert attributes are not available in today's technology.[72]

Expert systems follow a set of rules to reach conclusions. To create an expert system, a computer programmer interviews experts in a particular field and translates their knowledge into a series of if-then rules. As the learning capabilities of expert systems are developed over the next ten years, they may contribute in novel ways to organizational creativity. As suggested in the following In Practice, expert systems are not limited to applications in high technology industries.

IN PRACTICE

HOW'S THE SOUP?

Aldo Cimino—the Campbell Soup Company's longtime expert in maintaining the complex cookers used to kill bacteria in canned soup—was nearing retirement. Management decided to preserve his many years of accumulated know-how in a computer program. The hope was that the program would enable workers to diagnose malfunctions and make repairs quickly, critical considerations in the soup-making process. As Cimino explained: "You have only a short period of time to correct the problem. Otherwise, you lose the soup." Cimino spent about seven months with Michael Smith, a computer scientist who reduced Cimino's knowledge to an if-then format for processing by an expert system.

"He would ask me 'What goes wrong with these things?' " Cimino recalled later. "And I would tell him. He'd say, 'Okay, let's take them one at a time,' so I would tell him step by step what I do when there are temperature problems or if the cooker doesn't run or whatever. I told him the solutions I would try for each problem." Finally, Smith put the problems and their solutions into the expert system and came up with a computer program. It has more than 150 rules of thumb to aid the operators of Campbell's cookers. If soup cans are bent when they come out of the cooker, for example, an operator can look for the reason by typing this problem in at a computer keyboard. The program displays a list of possible causes and suggested remedies on a console screen. After further dialogue with the program, the operator is able to pinpoint the problem and prepare a printout to give technicians instructions for repairs.

According to Cimino, this expert system can probably deal successfully with at least 95 percent of the problems likely to arise during normal sterilizer operations. But like its medical counterparts, the program will be stymied when presented with malfunctions that are not covered by its knowledge base. "There is always the oddball problem that will take somebody to analyze," Cimino observes. "In those cases, I used to talk to everybody who was even *near* the equipment. I doubt the computer system can take all of my job."[73]

Most of the applications of artificial intelligence to date, such as expert systems, stimulate organizational creativity indirectly. For example, expert systems require a surfacing of all assumptions and decision rules used by experts. This process has often triggered the recognition of better ways to accomplish particular goals. Also, expert systems can free up employees from routine tasks so that they have more time to focus on tasks requiring creativity.

SUMMARY

Managers and other employees sometimes experience ethical dilemmas when making decisions. Five basic questions should be asked to check ethical decision making: What is the ethical intensity? What are the decision principles? Who is affected? What are the benefits and costs? Who has rights?

Three models commonly used to describe decision making are the rational, bounded rationality, and political models. Each of these models captures some of the decision-making situations and processes experienced by managers. All three models are needed to cover the complexity and range of these situations and processes.

Managerial decision making is characterized as unending flows and crosscurrents of decisions. The phases of managerial decision making include problem recognition, problem interpretation, attention to problems, courses of action, and aftermath. These phases do not unfold for real-world managers in a neat and orderly sequence. Creativity is likely to be very important in addressing the most difficult type of decision: when there is ambiguity or disagreement over the goals to be sought and the best course of action to pursue.

Organizational creativity and innovation are crucial to the production of novel and useful ideas that can be implemented. Three approaches for stimulating organizational creativity were reviewed: lateral thinking method, devil's advocate method, and artificial intelligence.

Key Words and Concepts

Aftermath
Artificial Intelligence (AI)
Availability bias
Bounded rationality model
Concrete information bias
Devil's advocate method
Distributive justice principle
Employment at will
Escalating commitment
Ethical intensity
Ethics
Expert systems
Gambler's fallacy bias
Genetic testing
Lateral thinking method

Law of small numbers bias
Managerial decision making
Organizational creativity
Organizational innovation
Organizational learning
Political model
Problem interpretation
Rational model
Satisficing
Selective perception bias
Structured problems
Unstructured problems
Utilitarianism
Values
Vertical thinking

Discussion Questions

1. Think of an issue that created an ethical dilemma for you. How would you evaluate this dilemma in terms of each of the six components of ethical intensity?

2. Of the six components that go into ethical intensity, which two of them are likely to be most important in the majority of situations? Explain.

3. What are the similarities and differences between the distributive justice principle and utilitarianism?

4. Of the ethical principles stated in Table 19.2, rearrange them in a rank order from your most-preferred to least-preferred principle. What does this ranking tell you about how you are likely to interpret situations in terms of ethical dilemmas?

5. What are three ethical dilemmas that managers may experience when conducting performance appraisals?

6. At which managerial level—first-line, middle, and top—is a manager most likely to use each of the decision-making models (rational model, bounded rationality model, and political model)?

7. How is the decision-making process for managers likely to differ from that of nonmanagerial employees?

8. What are the most common problems in achieving effective problem recognition?

9. How might creativity help managers who experience difficulties in problem identification and interpretation?

10. What are three differences between the lateral thinking method and the devil's advocate method?

MANAGEMENT CASES AND EXERCISES

DECISION INCIDENTS

Listed below are ten short incidents. Please indicate the degree to which you find the decision in each incident to be acceptable or unacceptable. Write the appropriate number next to each statement. Use the following scale:

```
1            2            3            4            5            6            7
|_____|_____|_____|_____|_____|_____|
  Never                      Sometimes                  Always
acceptable                  acceptable                 acceptable
```

_____ 1. A company paid a $350,000 "consulting" fee to an official of a foreign country. In return, the official promised assistance in obtaining a contract that should produce a $10 million profit for the contracting company.

_____ 2. A company president found that a competitor had made an important scientific discovery that would sharply reduce the profits of his own company. He then hired a key employee of the competitor in an attempt to learn the details of the discovery.

_____ **3.** A highway building contractor did not like the uncertain bidding situation and cutthroat competition. He therefore reached an understanding with other major contractors to permit bidding that would provide a reasonable profit.

_____ **4.** A vice-president of marketing recognized that sending expensive Christmas gifts to purchasing agents might compromise their positions. However, he continued the policy since it was common practice and changing it might result in a loss of business.

_____ **5.** A corporate executive promoted a loyal friend and competent manager to the position of divisional vice-president instead of a better-qualified manager with whom he had no close ties.

_____ **6.** A comptroller selected a legal method of financial reporting that concealed some embarrassing financial facts that would otherwise have become public knowledge.

_____ **7.** An employer received applications for a supervisor's position from two equally qualified applicants but hired the male applicant because he thought that some employees might resent being supervised by a female.

_____ **8.** As part of the marketing strategy for a product, a firm changed its product's color and marketed it as "new and improved," even though its other characteristics were unchanged.

_____ **9.** A cigarette manufacturer launched a publicity campaign challenging new evidence from the surgeon general's office that cigarette smoking is harmful to the smoker's health.

_____ **10.** An owner of a small firm obtained a free copy of a copyrighted computer software program from a business friend, rather than spending five hundred dollars to get his own program from the software dealer.[74]

QUESTIONS

1. Based on the ethical principles shown in Table 19–2, what ethical principle did you use for responding to the degree of acceptability of the decision in each incident?

2. Which three incidents are probably characterized by the greatest degree of ethical intensity? Why?

3. Which three incidents are probably characterized by the lowest degree of ethical intensity? Why?

OLSON MEDICAL SYSTEMS

Olson Medical Systems (OMS) offers computer-based financial systems to hospitals and nursing homes throughout the United States. Founded ten years ago by T. G. Olson, a former health care administrator, OMS employs over forty analysts and programmers.

Once a month, the executive team of OMS meets to discuss plans, problems, and opportunities of the company. T. G. Olson calls and chairs the meetings. The other members include Frank Telsor (marketing), Karen Smith (operations), Terry Heath (systems development),

Damien O'Brien (finance/accounting), and Ali Hassan (systems analyst). At a recent meeting, "maintenance contracts" appeared on the agenda, producing the following discussion.

OLSON: Okay. Our last item is "maintenance contracts." O'Brien, this was your item.

O'BRIEN: Yes. I've been looking into the software maintenance contracts we have with some of our clients and I don't think we are getting a good return on investment. Based on my calculations, we would be better off selling enhanced versions of our Medicalc package every two years than offering maintenance contracts ... unless, of course, we increase the price of the maintenance agreement.

OLSON: How much would we have to increase the price?

O'BRIEN: Right now, we are breaking even.

OLSON: So, what are you proposing?

O'BRIEN: I think we should increase the annual fee for Medicalc by at least two hundred dollars.

TELSOR: If we do that, we're going to lose some business ... maybe not the people who are with us already but some potential clients.

OLSON: How many Medicalc users have maintenance contracts with us?

TELSOR: I don't know.

O'BRIEN: I think it's about 80 percent.

OLSON: What is the standard price, on a percentage basis, for maintenance packages?

TELSOR: It varies slightly with the price of the software, but it is related to the frequency of changes.

HEATH: Maybe we shouldn't be making so many changes. Last year, we made those changes to Schedule B and then Health and Social Services changed their minds. We could have been spending our time converting to the new IBM system.

SMITH: It didn't help that we lost Stan Freedson. He knew Medicalc inside and out.

OLSON: Yeah. Stan was good. Why don't we try to market the Medicalc maintenance agreement better? Does Health Data Systems or TMS make the kinds of changes we do and as frequently as we do? Let's let our clients know that our system is the most up-to-date in the market.

TELSOR: Sometimes I think they'd rather buy the enhanced version every two years.

O'BRIEN: There are two hospitals in the Southwest that purchased the maintenance agreement, went off it for a year, and then renewed. Why, I wonder?

TELSOR: One of them had a change of financial directors.

OLSON: Ali, we haven't heard from you yet. Any thoughts on how to keep the cost of maintenance down?

HASSAM: Not really. This sounds like a marketing problem to me ... how to sell the service contracts.

SMITH: I think we need more data. Maybe we should table this item until we know more about our clients' needs and so forth.

O'BRIEN: What, specifically, do we need to know?

OLSON: We need to know the projected changes in the schedules for the next couple of years and what it will cost to keep current.

SMITH: Excuse me, I have to leave. I have a meeting with Joe Bergmann at eleven.

O'BRIEN: Why don't we just raise the price $75 for new clients and see what happens? TMS raised theirs $150 last year.

OLSON: What do you think, Telsor?

TELSOR: Well, we can try it. We may lose some potential clients.

OLSON: Okay, let's try it.[75]

QUESTIONS

1. What problem statements were offered (explicitly or implicitly) during this meeting?

2. How are these statements related to each other (i.e., which statements are the means to solving other statements)?

3. What different purposes do problem statements serve (e.g., to keep people involved in the process, to avoid blame, etc.)? For what purposes were the statements offered in this case, in your opinion?

4. What other problem perspectives can you think of that might be useful to this team?

References

1. Adapted from Murphy, P. E. Creating Ethical Corporate Structures. *Sloan Management Review*, Winter 1988, 81–87.

2. *Ibid.*

3. Freeman, E. E. (ed.), *Business Ethics: The State of the Art*. New York: Oxford University Press, 1991.

4. Nash, L. L. *Good Intentions Aside: A Manager's Guide to Resolving Ethical Problems*. Boston: Harvard Business School Press, 1990.

5. Westin, A. F., and Aram, J. D. *Managerial Dilemmas*. Cambridge, Mass: Ballinger, 1988; Badaracco, J. L., and Ellsworth, R. P. *Integrity and Leadership: The Dilemmas and Prejudices*. Boston: Harvard Business School Press, 1989.

6. Ethics Resource Center and Behavior Research Center. *Ethics Policies and Programs in American Business: Report of a Landmark Survey of U.S. Corporations*. Washington, D.C.: Ethics Resource Center, 1990.

7. Weber, J. Managers' Moral Reasoning: Assessing Their Responses to Three Moral Dilemmas. *Human Relations*, 1990, *43*, 687–702; Trevino, L. K., and Youngblood, S. A. Bad Apples in Bad Barrels: A Causal Analysis of Ethical Decision-Making Behavior. *Journal of Applied Psychology*, 1990, *75*, 378–385.

8. Freeman, R. E., and Gilbert, D. R., Jr. *Corporate Strategy and the Search for Ethics*. Englewood Cliffs, N.J.: Prentice-Hall, 1988.

9. This section based on James, T. M. Ethical Decision Making by Individuals in Organizations: An Issue-Contingent Model, *Academy of Management Review*, 1991, *16*, 366–395. Also see Darley, J. M., and Shultz, T. R. Moral Rules: Their Content and Acquisition. In M. R. Rosenzweig and L. W. Porter (eds.), *Annual Review of Psychology*, vol 41. Palo Alto, Calif.: Annual Reviews, 1990, 525–556.

10. Brady, F. N. *Ethical Managing: Rules and Results*. New York: Macmillan, 1990; Behrman, J. N. *Essays on Ethics in Business and the Professions, 1988*. Englewood Cliffs, N.J.: Prentice-Hall, 1988.

11. Fisher, B. D. Positive Law as the Ethic of Our Time. *Business Horizons*, September–October 1990, 28–39.

12. Greenberg, J. Organizational Justice: Yesterday, Today, and Tomorrow. *Journal of Management*, 1990, *16*, 399–432.

13. Adapted from Wokutch, R. E. Corporate Social Responsibility Japanese Style. *Academy of Management Executive*, May 1990, 56–74; Payson, M. F., and Rosen, P. B. Playing by Fair Rules. *HR Magazine*, April 1991, 42–43.

14. Harrington, S. J. What Corporate America Is Teaching about Ethics. *Academy of Management Executive*, February 1991, 21–30; Weiss, A. Seven Reasons to Examine Workplace Ethics. *HR Magazine*, March 1991, 69–74.

15. Davis, E. G., and Hamilton, L. S. Challenges to Employment at Will: A Survey of the Natural Gas Transmission Industry. *Employee Responsibilities and Rights Journal*, 1989, *2*, 1989, 109–119.

16. Hilgert, R. L. Employers Protected by At-Will Statements. *HR Magazine*, March 1991, 57–60; Krueger, A. B. The Evolution of Unjust-Dismissal Legislation in the United States. *Industrial and Labor Relations Review*, 1991, *44*, 644–660.

17. Gilbert, S. A., and McDonough, J. J. Wrongful Termination and the Reasonable Manager: Balancing Fair Play and Effectiveness. *Sloan Management Review*, Summer 1990, 39–46.

18. Wartzman, R. Nature or Nurture?: Study Blames Ethical Lapses on Corporate Goals. *Wall Street Journal*, October 9, 1987, 21.

19. Ringleb, A. H., Meiners, R. E., and Edwards, F. E. *Managing in the Legal Environment*. St. Paul: West, 1990, 150–179.

20. Mitchell, T. R., and Scott, W. G. America's Problems and Needed Reforms: Confronting the Ethic of Personal Advantage. *Academy of Management Executive*, August 1990, 23–35.

21. Drake, B. H., and Drake, E. Ethical and Legal Aspects of Managing Corporate Cultures. *California Management Review*, Winter 1988, 107–123.

22. Osigweh, Y. C. Elements of an Employee Responsibilities and Rights Paradigm. *Journal of Management*, 1990, *16*, 835–850.

23. Taylor, G. S., and Spencer, B. A. Ethical Implications of Human Resource Information Systems. *Employee Responsibilities and Rights Journal*, 1990, *3*, 19–30.

24. Bergmann, T. J., Mundt, D. H. Jr., and Illgen, E. J. The Evolution of Honesty Tests and Means for Their Evaluation. *Employee Responsibilities and Rights Journal*, 1990, 215–223.

25. Stone, E. F., and Stone, D. L. Privacy in Organizations: Theoretical Issues, Research Findings and Protection Mechanisms. In G. R. Ferris and K. M. Rowland (eds.), *Research in Personnel and Human Resources Management*, vol. 8, Greenwich, Conn.: 1990, 349–411.

26. Overman, S. A Delicate Balance Protects Everyone's Rights. *HR Magazine*, November 1990, 36–39.

27. Hurd, S. N. Genetic Testing: Your Genes and Your Job. *Employee Responsibilities and Rights Journal*, 1990, *3*, 239–252.

28. Adapted from *ibid.*

29. Dean, J. W. Jr. Decision Processes in the Adoption of Advanced Technology. University Park, Pa.: Center for the Management of Technological and Organizational Change, Pennsylvania State University, May 1986.

30. Hogarth, R. M., and Reder, M. W. (eds.). *Rational Choice: The Contrasts between Economics and Psychology*. Chicago: University of Chicago Press, 1986.

31. Simon, H. A. *Reason in Human Affairs*. Stanford, Calif.: Stanford University Press, 1983; Simon, H. A. Making Management Decisions: The Role of Intuition and Emotion. *Academy of Management Executive*, 1987, *1*, 57–64; Martin, J. E., Kleindorfer, G. B., and Brashers, W. R. Jr. The Theory of Bounded Rationality and the Problem of Legitimation. *Journal for the Theory of Social Behavior*, 1987, *17*, 63–82.

32. Silver, W. S., and Mitchell, T. R. The Status Quo Tendency in Decision Making. *Organizational Dynamics*, Spring 1990, 34–46.

33. Roach, J. M. Simon Says: Decision Making Is a 'Satisficing' Experience. *Management Review*, January 1979, 8–9. Also see Simon, H. A. Bounded Rationality and Organizational Learning. *Organization Science*, 1991, *2*, 125–134.

34. Saunders, C., and Jones, J. W. Temporal Sequences in Informal Acquisition for Decision Making: A Focus on Source and Medium. *Academy of Management Review*, 1990, *15*, 29–46.

35. Pfeffer, J. *Power in Organizations*. Marshfield, Mass.: Pitman, 1981; Ferris, G. R., and Judge, T. A. Personnel/Human Resource Management: A Political Influence Perspective. *Journal of Management*, 1991, *17*, 447–488.

36. The perspective of this discussion was developed from McCall, M. W. Jr., and Kaplan, R. E. *Whatever It Takes: The Realities of Managerial Decision Making*. 2d ed. Englewood Cliffs, N.J.: Prentice-Hall, 1990.

37. McCall, M. W. Jr., and Kaplan, R. E. *Whatever It Takes: Decision Makers at Work*. Englewood Cliffs, N.J.: Prentice-Hall, 1985, XV.

38. Sayles, L. R. *Leadership: What Effective Managers Really Do . . . and How They Do It*. New York: McGraw-Hill, 1979, 15.

39. *Ibid.*, 17.

40. Rowe, A. J., and Mason, R. O. *Managing with Style: A Guide to Understanding, Assessing, and Improving Decision Making*. San Francisco: Jossey-Bass, 1987.

41. Cowan, D. A. Developing a Process Model of Problem Recognition. *Academy of Management Review*, 1986, *11*, 763–776; Cowan, D. A. Developing a Classification Structure of Organizational Problems: An Empirical Investigation. *Academy of Management Journal*, 1990, *33*, 366–390.

42. Vaughan, D. Autonomy, Interdependence, and Social Control: NASA and the Space Shuttle *Challenger*. *Administrative Science Quarterly*, 1990, *35*, 225–257.

43. Adapted from Raelin, J. A. The Professional as the Executive's Ethical Aide-de-Camp. *Academy of Management Executive*, August 1987, *1*, 177–182.

44. Adapted from Volkema, R. J. Factors Which Promote 'Solving the Wrong Problem.' Unpublished Statement. Fairfax, Va.: Institute for Advanced Study in the Integrative Sciences, George Mason University, 1988.

45. Janis, I. L., and Mann, L. *Decision Making: A Psychological Analysis of Conflict, Choice, and Commitment*. New York: Free Press, 1977, 81–106; Gilbert, D. T. How Mental Systems Believe. *American Psychologist*, 1991, *46*, 107–119.

46. Argyris, C. Bridging Economics and Psychology: The Case of the Economic Theory of the Firm. *American Psychologist*, 1987, *42*, 456–463; Carey, J. Getting Business to Think about the Unthinkable. *Business Week*, June 24, 1991, 104–107.

47. Isabella, L. A. Evolving Interpretations as a Change Unfolds: How Managers Construe Key Organizational Events. *Academy of Management Journal*, 1990, *33*, 7–41.

48. Kahneman, D. Judgment and Decision Making: A Personal View. *Psychological Science*, 1991, *2*, 142–145; Smith, J. F., and Kida, T. Heuristics and Biases: Expertise and Task Realism in Auditing. *Psychological Bulletin*, 1991, *109*, 472–489.

49. Starbuck, W. H., and Milliken, F. J. Executives' Perceptual Filters: What They Notice and How They Make Sense. In D. C. Hambrick (ed.), *The Executive Effect: Concepts and Methods for Studying Top Managers*. Greenwich, Conn.: JAI Press, 1988, 35–66.

50. Argyris, C. Teaching Smart People How to Learn. *Harvard Business Review*, May–June 1991, 99–109; Walsh, J. P., and Ungson, G. R. Organizational Memory. *Academy of Management Review*, 1991, *16*, 57–91.

51. Janis, I. L. *Crucial Decisions: Leadership in Policy Making and Crisis Management*. New York: Free Press, 1989.

52. Adapted from Kruglanski, A. W. Freeze-Think and the Challenger. *Psychology Today*, August 1986, 48–49; Mitroff, I. I., Shrivastava, P., and Udwadia, F. E. Effective Crisis Management. *Academy of Management Executive*, 1987, *1*, 283–292; Vaughan, D. Autonomy, Interdependence, and Social Control: NASA and the Space Shuttle *Challenger*. *Administrative Science Quarterly*, 1990, *35*, 225–257.

53. Beach, L. R. *Image Theory: Decision Making in Personal and Organizational Contexts*. Chichester, England: Wiley, 1990; Bazerman, M. H. *Judgment in Managerial Decision Making*. New York: Wiley, 1990.

54. Quinn, R. E. *Beyond Rational Management: Mastering the Paradoxes and Competing Demands of High Performance*, San Francisco: Jossey-Bass, 1988.

55. Neale, M. A., and Bazerman, M. H. *Cognition and Rationality in Negotiation*. New York: Free Press, 1991; Jagacinski, C. M. Personnel Decision Making: The Impact of Missing Information. *Journal of Applied Psychology*, 1991, *76*, 19–30.

56. Schwenk, C. R. Information, Cognitive Biases, and Commitment to a Course of Action. *Academy of Management Review*, 1986, *11*, 298–310.

57. Staw, B. M. The Escalation of Commitment: A Review and Analysis. *Academy of Management Review*, 1981, *6*, 577–587.

58. Staw, B. M., and Ross, J. Understanding Escalation Situations: Antecedents, Prototypes, and Solutions. In B. M. Staw and L. L. Cummings (eds.), *Research in Organizational Behavior*, vol. 9. Greenwich, Conn.: JAI Press, 1987; Bowen, M. G. The Escalation Phenomenon Reconsidered: Decision Dilemmas or Decision Errors? *Academy of Management Review*, 1987, *12*, 52–66.

59. McCall, M. W., and Kaplan, R. E. *Consequences, Issues and Observations*, Greensboro, N.C.: Center for Creative Leadership, February, 1985, 7.

60. McCall and Kaplan, 8. Also see McCall, M. W. Jr., Lombardo, M. M., and Morrison, A. M. *The Lesson of Experience*, Lexington, Mass.: Lexington Books, 1988.

61. Amabile, T. M. A Model of Creativity and Innovation in Organizations. In B. M. Staw and L. L. Cummings (eds.), *Research in Organizational Behavior*, vol. 10. Greenwich, Conn.: JAI Press, 1988, 123–167.

62. Martin, L. P. Inventory of Barriers to Creative Thought and Innovative Action. In J. W. Pfeffer (ed.), *The 1990 Annual: Developing Human Resources*. San Diego: University Associates, 1990, 131–141.

63. Mitroff, I. I., Shrivastava, P., and Udwaidia, F. Effective Crisis Management, *Academy of Management Executive*, November 1987, 286.

64. de Bono, E. *Lateral Thinking; Creativity Step by Step*, New York: Harper & Row, 1970, 50.

65. This discussion based on Van Gundy, A. B. *Techniques of Structured Problem Solving*. New York: Van Nostrand, 1981, 234–244; de Bono E. *Masterthinkers Handbook*. New York: International Center for Creative Thinking, 1985.

66. Hof, R. D., and Depke, D. A. An Alliance Made in PC Heaven. *Business Week*, June 24, 1991, 40–42.

67. Woodman, R. W., and Schoenfeldt, L. F. Individual Differences in Creativity: An Interactionist Perspective. In J. A. Glover, R. R. Ronning, and C. R. Reynolds (eds.), *Handbook of Creativity*. New York: Plenum Press, 1989, 77–91.

68. Schwenk, C. R. Devil's Advocacy and the Board: A Modest Proposal. *Business Horizons*, July–August 1990, 22–27.

69. Cosier, R. A., and Schwenk, C. R. Agreement and Thinking Alike: Ingredients for Poor Decisions. *Academy of Management Executive*, February 1990, 69–74.

70. Schwenk, C. R. Effects of Devil's Advocacy and Dialectical Inquiry on Decision Making: A Meta-Analysis. *Organizational Behavior and Human Decision Processes*, 1990, 47, 161–176.

71. Meyer, M. H., and Curley, K. F. Putting Expert Systems Technology to Work. *Sloan Management Review*, Winter 1991, 21–31.

72. Leonard-Barton, D., and Sviokla, J. J. Putting Expert Systems to Work. *Harvard Business Review*, March–April 1988, 93.

73. Adapted from Editors of Time-Life Books, *Artificial Intelligence: Understanding Computers*, Alexandria, Va.: Time-Life Books, 1986, 31–52.

74. Adapted from Longenecker, J. G. Jr., McKinney, J. A., and Moore, C. W. The Generation Gap in Business Ethics. *Business Horizons*, September–October 1989, 9–14.

75. Volkema, R. J. Problem Formulation at Olson Medical Systems. Used with permission. This case was developed under a grant from the National Institute for Dispute Resolution, 1988.

PART V

INDIVIDUAL AND ORGANIZATIONAL CHANGE

CHAPTER 20:

CAREER PLANNING AND DEVELOPMENT

LEARNING OBJECTIVES

When you have finished studying this chapter, you should be able to:

- Describe the socialization process.
- Define *career* and describe its components.
- State the factors that influence a person's choices of career and occupation.
- Describe the four career stages that most people go through.
- Identify the central activities and career concerns associated with each career stage.
- Discuss the factors that affect career planning.
- List the problems facing dual-career couples and employees who have been outplaced.

OUTLINE

ANGELA AZZARETTI

Angela Azzaretti, the daughter of Italian immigrants, graduated from the University of Illinois and took a job at Caterpillar's headquarters in Peoria, Illinois, during the summer of 1987. Angela was the first member of her family to graduate from college and work for a Fortune 500 company. Caterpillar trained her for a year in marketing and manufacturing before assigning Angela to her first job as a plant communicator in its heavy-duty engine plant in Mossville, Illinois. She wrote speeches for the division's top managers, published the plant's newsletter, and produced videotapes of company events that were viewed by employees and managers at monthly meetings.

She was successful at her job and was soon offered a promotion to join Caterpillar's headquarters staff. She turned it down. Then she was offered another promotion in another plant. Once again, she said no.

"Job satisfaction is the most important thing to me," says Angela. "In those other jobs, I would have less challenge and responsibility. The only benefit was more money. I know it sounds crazy, but I evaluated the situation and decided that I liked my current job better." When Angela asked other managers what they would have done, they said: "Ten or twenty years ago, it would have been a black mark to turn down those jobs. When a company asked you to go, you went."[1]

You might ask yourself whether, given Angela's situation, you would make the same decision. During the past couple of decades, a new breed of employees has come into the work force whose attitude toward life and work is vastly different from that of their parents. This new employee is not as motivated by traditional lures of money, titles, security, and ladder climbing. These employees insist on getting satisfaction from their jobs and are reluctant to make personal sacrifices just for the sake of the organization. Their attitude is that other interests—leisure, family, life-style, the pursuit of experience—are just as important as work. In Chapter 1, we highlighted the composition of this new work force and their needs and values. Instead of repeating ourselves, we ask you to please reread pages 6-10.

Most organizations have some type of program or procedure designed to recruit and orient new employees to their new jobs. While this process is complex, it essentially seeks the attainment of two major goals: (1) attracting employees to join the organization and (2) then orientating them to the practices, procedures, and culture of the organization. In the following section, we will explore these goals in more detail.

ORGANIZATIONAL SOCIALIZATION: THE PROCESS OF JOINING UP

Recall the jobs that you have held. What were your feelings during your first few weeks on each job? Often, this time was filled with frustrations. As a newcomer, you were faced with a new environment that was different in many respects from ones you had previously faced. All the people working with you were new and unfamiliar. At the same time, you may have had to establish a new residence in an unfamiliar town, which required finding a place to live, getting the phone and utilities turned on, establishing a new checking account, getting a driver's license, and so forth. Unless you found a job and city that was identical to the one you worked and lived in before, you had to learn new procedures, skills, and ways of relating to people.

Given the complexity of most jobs in organizations, it is important to "learn the ropes" fast. The ease and speed with which individuals learn their new job is important from both the individual's and the organization's point of view. For the individual, once personal concerns are settled, it means less frustration. For the organization, the individual will start turning his or her energies to the job, instead of worrying about other matters.

The process through which the individual learns about the new job and work environment is known as *organizational socialization*. In Chapter 15, we defined organizational socialization as the process by which organizations bring new employees into their organization and culture. At Caterpillar, Angela's formal socialization process lasted one year while she was moved from department to department, learning about the organization's practices and culture. In Arthur Andersen, a major accounting and consulting firm, the formal socialization process lasts ten weeks. All new employees are required to attend Andersen's school in Lake Charles, Illinois, to learn about the Andersen way of doing business.

In this section, we will focus on several of the key aspects of socialization. We'll describe the basic stages of socialization and consider various techniques used by organizations to help newcomers pass through this difficult period.

Major Stages in the Socialization Process

In one sense, socialization never ends. It begins well before the individual actually arrives at work and continues for long after his or her entry, as in the case of Angela Azzaretti. Recognizing this, it makes sense to discuss the socialization process in three distinct stages: getting in, breaking in, and settling in.[2] These stages are illustrated in Figure 20.1.

Getting In: Anticipatory Socialization Before individuals actually join an organization, they usually know quite a bit about it. In many cases, information is provided by friends, relatives, or employees already working for the organization. Other valuable sources of information may be newspaper articles, the organization's annual reports, and news items in professional journals highlighting the organization's practices. In essence, people socialize themselves prior to joining the organization in the hope that it may help them gain a job with the organization.[3] **Anticipatory socialization** is the process of accepting the beliefs and values of the group that individual aspires to become a member of before actually joining the organization. Anticipatory socialization can be seen among students in

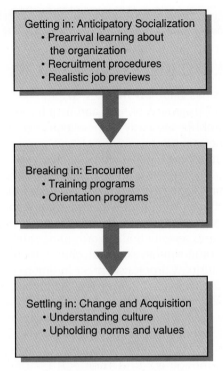

FIGURE 20.1 Stages in Employee Socialization

many professional schools (business, engineering, law and medicine) as they learn and practice the behaviors and values of the profession.[4] Such information, however, tends to bias the newcomer's perceptions about the organization, either correctly or incorrectly. PepsiCo has a fast-track development program for its bright newcomers. According to many employees, it is a make-or-break experience. The company demands a lot and the pressure is intense. Working seventy or more hours per week and moving around to various cities are common requirements. Since this information is widely known about PepsiCo's program, individuals who try to get into this program are often already well informed about the required behaviors and values.

To avoid the negative reactions of newcomers who discover that the organization is not what they were led to believe, many organizations conduct realistic job previews. A **realistic job preview** provides job applicants with an accurate description of the job they will perform and the department they will work in.[5] Growing evidence suggests that employees exposed to such previews report higher job satisfaction and have lower turnover than those who receive the standard, glowing—and often misleading—information about the job in question. The following In Practice highlights how Nissan uses realistic job previews at its Smyrna, Tennessee, plant to reduce absenteeism and turnover and improve performance.

IN PRACTICE

REALISTIC JOB PREVIEWS AT NISSAN

Bookkeeper Phyllis Baines has two minutes to grab fifty-five nuts, bolts, and washers, assemble them in groups of five, and attach them in order of size to a metal rack. But she fumbles nervously with several pieces and finishes the task seconds after her allotted time.

"I've got to get a little better at this, don't I?" She frets as she pulls the last of the fasteners out of a grimy plastic tray. Her tester, Harold Hicks, encourages her: "You're close. For the first night, you're probably doing a little better than normal."

It may appear that Baines (not her real name) is going through first-night jitters at an adult-school class in home repair. The thirty-one-year-old department store employee will be devoting seventy hours worth of her nights and weekends over the next few months doing similar exercises. She is trying to land a job at the Nissan Motor Manufacturing Corporation plant in Smyrna, Tennessee.

Baines and about 270 other job seekers are participating in Nissan's preemployment program. In exchange for a shot at highly paid assembly-line and other hourly jobs and Nissan's promise not to inform their employers, the moonlighters are working up to 360 hours—without pay—being tested and instructed in employment fundamentals by the Japanese automaker. "We hope the process makes it plain to people what the job is," says Thomas P. Groom, Nissan's manager of employment. "It's an indoctrination process," he says, as well as a screening tool.

Not all participants are fully satisfied with the program. A candidate who works as a machine adjuster at an envelope factory says that the lack of a job guarantee by Nissan "worries you, because you get your hopes up." And some candidates bemoan the lack of pay for their time. But many participants feel that the training and experience they receive outweigh any additional obstacles to getting hired. For one thing, they get a shot at some of the best-paying jobs in the state. If they do not get hired, they can take the skills they have learned elsewhere. Adds Judy McFarland, a press operator who went through the program in 1983: "It gave me a chance to see what Nissan expected of me without their having to make a commitment to me or me to them."[6]

Breaking In: The Encounter Stage.   The second major stage in organizational socialization begins when individuals actually assume their new job. During this stage, they perform several tasks. First, they must master the skills and roles—information, interpersonal, decisional—required by their new job. Second, they must become oriented to the practices, procedures, and culture of their new organization. **Orientation** is either a formal or an informal program that introduces new employees to their job responsibilities, their co-workers, and the company's policies. Effective orientation programs serve two purposes. First, they inform new employees about benefits, company policies, and procedures. Second, and more important, these programs fine-tune employee job-related and cultural expectations. Formal orientation programs reduce the time and effort required by managers to train new employees. In addition, if busy managers assign orientation to an assistant or a secretary, certain key points may be covered too lightly or skipped over.

PepsiCo has an effective orientation program that lasts several days. During this program, new employees learn that most successful employees have:

1. The ability to handle business complexities.
2. The ability to lead and manage people.
3. High drive and are results-oriented.

PepsiCo clearly communicates what each of these points mean and how new employees can learn these behaviors. PepsiCo believes that properly oriented employees can get up to speed quickly because they know which behaviors are valued and which are not.[7]

Settling In: Change and Acquisition. Sometime after the individual joins the organization, he or she attains full member status after he or she has learned the new attitudes and behaviors. In the *change and acquisition* stage, individuals develop self-images and behaviors that are consistent with the culture of the organization. Often, there is a ceremony, such as a dinner, lunch, or reception, during which they are formally recognized as a full member. Their titles are changed from trainee or apprentice to assistant manager or supervisor. At Brooklyn Union Gas Company, this ceremony occurs at a luncheon hosted by the president, during which employees receive their permanent identification number and are assigned a parking space in a covered garage. At the Fort Worth Museum of Science and History, there is no ceremony. Don Otto, its director, just sends a memo to all employees indicating that a change has taken place in a person's status. Otto and the person then go out to lunch.

Whatever form it takes, the settling-in phase of the socialization process marks important shifts for both individuals and organizations. Employees make permanent adjustments to their jobs, such as juggling child and/or elder care responsibilities. The organization now treats them as long-term members of the team, rather than as temporary employees.[8]

CAREERS: CHANGES THROUGHOUT LIFE

A **career** is a sequence of work-related positions occupied by a person during the course of a lifetime.[9] The popular view of a career is usually restricted to the idea of moving up the organizational ladder. However, a career also consists of attitudes and behaviors that are a part of ongoing work-related activities and experiences. Moreover, a person can remain in the same job, just as Angela Azzaretti did, acquiring and developing new skills, and have a successful career without ever getting promoted. Or people can build a career by moving among various jobs in different fields and organizations. Thus, our concept of career encompasses not only traditional work experiences but also the diversity of career alternatives, individual choices, and individual experiences.

Four assumptions serve to clarify the concept of career:

- The nature of career does not in itself imply success or failure or fast or slow advancement. Career success or failure is best determined by the individual, rather than by others, such as employers, parents, spouse, or friends.

- No absolute standards exist for evaluating a career. Career success or failure is related to the concept of self-actualization in the needs hierarchy (see Chapter 7). Individuals should evaluate their own career goals and progress in terms of what is personally meaningful and satisfying. The measurement of an individual's career success or failure is as unique as the person.

- A complete understanding of an individual's career requires examination of both its subjective and objective aspects. A career has subjective aspects: values, attitudes, personality, and motivations. These change over time. A career also has objective aspects: job choices, positions held, specific skills, and so on.

- A career is made up of work-related experiences, which include more than the work that is performed for pay. Volunteer work, work around the house, school work, or political activities are also important parts of many careers.[10]

- **Career development** requires an individual to make decisions and engage in activities to attain career goals.[11] The central idea in the career development process is time. The shape of a person's career over time is influenced by several factors. Let's consider one pair of factors—costs and benefits—within the context of job opportunities in an organization. When someone accepts a position, there are costs and benefits to both the individual and the organization. The individual gives time, talent, and effort in return for a salary. The organization gives up financial resources and gains human resources. In this arrangement, both parties either implicitly or explicitly attempt to match costs and benefits. In reality, these costs and benefits change in various ways over time, and both parties attempt to manage the fit continuously. When changes occur, the individual and/or the organization makes decisions. These decisions by either or both parties have a direct impact on the career-development process of the individual.

- Finally, career development processes also vary by culture.[12] That is, cultural norms in such countries as Japan, the Philippines, and India also influence the direction of a person's career. Evidence suggests that women are discriminated against as managers in various cultures. There are almost no Japanese female managers higher than clerical supervisors, especially in large, multinational corporations. As a society, Japan expects women to work until marriage, quit to raise children, and return, as needed, to low-level and part-time positions after the age of forty. Women from wealthy families in the Philippines can hold influential managerial positions because of family connections, but less than 3 percent of the working women hold administrative or managerial positions. In India, where women constitutionally are equal to men, the culture assigns them primarily to the role of homemaker.

Matching Organizational and Individual Needs

Effective career development requires a long-term fit between individual and organization. Recall that the individual's career is a process, or sequence, of work-related experiences. The organization has an important stake in this process, and its needs must be matched with the employee's needs and career goals. To the extent that the matching process is done well, both organization and employee benefit, as in the case of Angela at Caterpillar. The organization is more effective and productive, and the individual is more satisfied, happy, and successful.

Figure 20–2 highlights the organizational and individual issues inherent in career planning and development. It also shows some of the continuing matching processes needed to integrate organizational needs with individual needs and career goals.

Organizational Needs   A society's technology, cultural values, laws, and institutions determine the labor market and strongly influence the structure of occupations. The environment in which an organization must operate broadens or constrains the career opportunities that the organization can make available to its employees. An important organizational activity is identifying human resource needs and making plans for meeting them. How many people will be needed? When will they be needed? Where will they come from? What skills will they need to have? Organizations must continuously recruit, develop, transfer, and promote people to perform its functions. These planning and managing activities never stop unless the organization goes out of existence.

Individual Needs and Goals   Whereas an organization must meet its human resource and staffing needs if it is to be successful, the individual must develop a career plan in order to be successful.

A **career plan** is the individual's choice of occupation, organization, and career path. The career planning process will be discussed in more detail later in this chapter. If opportunities provided by the organization are not attractive career alternatives for individuals, the organization will be plagued by personnel problems, including those of recruiting and retaining qualified employees.[13]

The Matching Process   The central portion of Figure 20–2 shows ways that an organization can attempt to match its human resource needs with its employees' career stages.[14] The careers of most people seem to go through similar stages, with a beginning, a middle, and an end. People's needs, values, and goals change as they progress through these stages. The staffing needs of the organization also change over time. All of these changes—both individual and organizational—make matching organizational needs with individual needs and goals complex. Thus, organizations

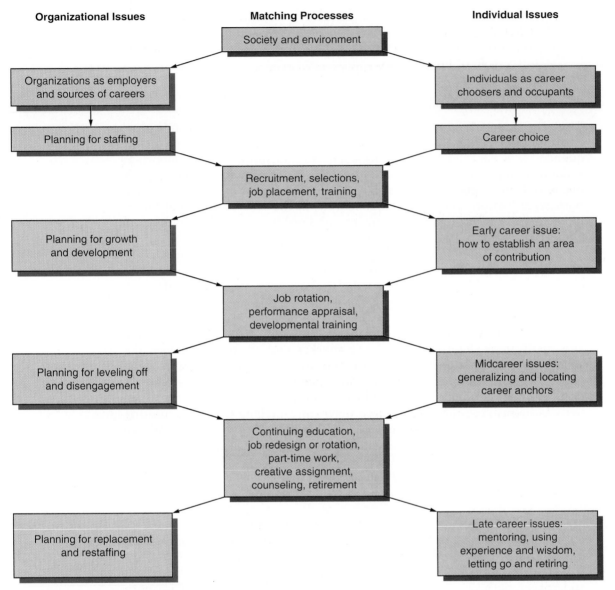

FIGURE 20.2 Matching Organizational and Individual Issues in Career Planning and Development

Source: Reprinted with permission from E. H. Schein, *Career Dynamics: Matching Individual and Organizational Needs*. Reading, Mass.: Addison-Wesley, Figure 1.2, p. 4. Copyright ©1978.

strive to translate their needs into opportunities that employees will consider attractive in terms of their own needs and career goals. The extent of this matching determines, in part, organizational effectiveness.[15]

Career Choices Why do people make the career decisions they do? Consider the dilemma faced by Len and Shilpa in the following In Practice and try to decide what you would do in a similar situation.

WHAT WOULD YOU DO?

Len and Shilpa were seniors majoring in business administration at a small mid-western university. On May 1, they were sitting in Shilpa's apartment discussing the decisions they faced. They had met during their junior year and had become engaged to be married. They faced different career and life-style options and were wrestling with the choices they had to make.

LEN'S BACKGROUND AND OPTIONS

Len had been raised in Cleveland. His father had a degree from Ohio State University and was an accountant with Arthur Andersen and Company. His mother had earned a degree in criminal justice from Kent State University and now worked part-time in Akron, Ohio. Len was the youngest of three boys. During the summers, he had worked at various manual labor jobs. Now he had the following job options:

- Burgundy Group, a small consulting firm in Lake Bluff, Illinois, had offered Len a job as a management trainee. He would be responsible for working with organizations in the Chicago area. Within a year or so, he would be responsible for developing computer-assisted software programs to consolidate and update financial records of Burgundy's clients.
- Telex Computer Products, Inc., a software development company in Tulsa, Oklahoma, had offered Len his choice of two positions: one in sales and the other in software development and systems engineering.
- Two accounting firms—Coopers and Lybrand and Arthur Andersen— had offered him jobs in their consulting divisions in Dallas, Texas. After several years of consulting experience in the United States, he would have the opportunity to transfer into their international divisions.
- Len was accepted into Northwestern's master's of business administration program. Len's parents indicated that they would help him financially if he chose to continue his education.

SHILPA'S BACKGROUND AND OPTIONS

Shilpa was born outside of Calcutta, India, and was raised with five brothers and a younger sister. Her parents came to the United States several years ago and settled in Brooklyn, New York. All are now U.S. citizens. Her mother is a computer programmer for Citicorp, and her father is a systems engineer for Brooklyn Union Gas Company. During the summers, Shilpa had worked in an oil and gas company in Manhattan as a secretary and had impressed her boss with her interpersonal and administrative skills.

- Shilpa could accept a position in the oil and gas company where she had worked during the summers. Her salary would be much higher than what she had made there before, and she knew everyone at the company. Her initial position would be as a trainee in the exploration department, with the promise of a quick move into a management position.

- Long Island University had offered her the job of assistant director of admissions. This position would require her to travel around New York state talking with high school seniors about educational opportunities at the college. She would also be in charge of two clerks who processed applications for admissions.

- Shilpa also had an offer from Salomon Brothers, Inc., a Wall Street firm, to work as a research analyst. This would require her to research industries and firms that brokers thought might be good prospects for their clients. This job offered the possibility of moving into a broker's job in two years. Her initial assignment would be in St. Louis, Missouri.

- Shilpa could also decide to stay at home and manage the household while Len worked. If they decided to have children, she would be there to raise them in a "traditional" household.[16]

Len and Shilpa, like all of us, have to make two initial career choices: (1) an occupation and (2) an organization. These choices have to be made along with other decisions, such as the kind of life-style they want to create in their marriage, where they want to live, whether they should rent an apartment or buy a house, and the like.

During the course of your career, you will have to make many such choices. These decisions are seldom irreversible. People like Len and Shilpa need not feel locked into these choices for life; instead, they can create or find other career opportunities. People's careers often involve working in many organizations, commuting long distances, or pursuing multiple occupations. Studies of college graduates indicate that five years after graduation, at least 50 percent have changed organizations at least once, and 20 percent have changed occupations.

Occupational Choice

Researchers and managers have long been fascinated by the possibility that individuals attracted to a specific occupation might have certain common characteristics or attributes. They also have studied whether certain sets of characteristics might be used to predict specific career choices and effective performance in those careers. While finer distinctions might be made, at least two general categories of personal characteristics seem to be related to career choices: personality and social background.

Personality: Vocational Behavior   John Holland advanced the most detailed theory relating personality to vocational behavior. He identified six basic personality types—**Holland's personality types**—each of which has a particular type of work environment with which it will be most congruent.[17] In a congruent situation, the basic orientation of the personality matches the demands and expectations needed for success in a particular work environment. Holland claims that these six classifications of personality types are good predictors of career aspiration and choice. For example, the enterprising personality type is likely to be attracted to an enterprising type of work environment, such as management. Empirical research supports the existence of a relationship between personality orientation and career choice. Some evidence also shows that a person is more likely to remain in a chosen occupation if it is congruent with his or her personality orientation.[18] When placed in incongruent environments, people will be less satisfied with the job, their job performance will be lower, and they will be more likely to quit.

Table 20.1 lists the six basic personality types in Holland's theory, along with some of their corresponding personality traits, interests, and representative occupations. The second column shows the problem-solving style (see Chapter 5) that seems to best fit each personality type. Note that no single problem-solving style appears to be typical of the enterprising personality type.

Occupational Interests   The right-hand column of Table 20.1 lists some of the occupational interests displayed by each of the six personality types. Since an occupation involves specific activities, people having the same occupation may share certain interests to a greater extent than do

---

TABLE 20.1   Holland's Personality Type Descriptions

Personality Type	Corresponding Problem-Solving Style	Personality Traits	Representative Occupations
Realistic	Sensation thinker (ST)	Stable, materialistic, persistent, practical	Architecture, trades (plumber, electrician), machinist, forest ranger
Investigative	Intuitive thinker (NT)	Analytical, critical, curious, intellectual, rational	Physicist, anthropologist, chemist, mathematician, biologist
Artistic	Intuitive feeler (NF)	Emotional, idealistic, imaginative, impulsive	Poet, novelist, musician, sculptor, playwright, composer, stage director
Social	Sensation feeler (SF)	Cooperative, friendly, sociable, understanding	Professor, psychologist, counselor, missionary, teacher
Enterprising	Sensation Thinker (ST) Intuitive Thinker (NT)	Adventurous, ambitious, energetic, optimistic, self-confident, talkative	Manager, salesperson, politician, lawyer, buyer
Conventional	Sensation thinker (ST)	Conscientious, obedient, orderly, self-controlled	Certified public accountant, statistician, bookkeeper, administrative assistant, postal clerk

Source: Adapted from J. V. Holland, *Making Vocational Choices: A Theory of Careers.* Englewood Cliffs, N.J.: Prentice-Hall, 1973, 111–117; A. A. Spokane, Review of Research on Person-Environment Congruence in Holland's Theory of Careers. *Journal of Vocational Behavior,* 1985, *26:* 306–343; T. Moore, Personality Tests Are Back. *Fortune,* March 30, 1987, 74–82.

people in general. Thus, an individual's interests can be compared to the profile of interests for samples of individuals in various occupations. This information can help an individual choose a vocation. There is considerable evidence that people tend to pursue careers that match their interests; there is some evidence that such interests play a part in career success or, at the least, in a person's remaining in a chosen occupation.

Personality: Self-Esteem   Another personality dimension related to occupational choice is a person's self-esteem. As defined in Chapter 3, *self-esteem* is an individual's evaluation of himself or herself. A person's self-esteem may strongly influence initial vocational choice. This choice may change over time as the value placed on an occupation and a career by others changes and as the person gains experience.

Social Background   The social background of the individual also influences career choice. **Social background** refers to early childhood experiences, the socioeconomic status of the family, the educational level and occupations of parents, and so on.[19] All these factors affect an individual's occupational goals and career choices by providing socialization experiences and setting practical constraints. For example, people may be more likely to consider a white-collar or professional career if one or both parents have such a career. The practical constraint of being unable to afford a college education may limit later occupational choices. Other, more subtle constraints include the socialization of girls to expect adult roles different from those of boys (for example, the roles of wife and mother). This early socialization may later influence the vocational choices made by many women.

Organizational Choice

Choosing an organization is the second major career decision that most people must make. A major factor in choosing a specific organization is the availability of opportunities for individuals at any given time. (What if Len and Shilpa had no job offers?)

Individuals use information about an organization to form opinions about working there. Anticipatory socialization is often a key to deciding on an occupational choice. Some typical questions that individuals have regarding an organization are shown in Table 20.2. Individuals tend to judge an organization by how well it fits their career goals and plans, and they tend to base their choice on perceptions of a fit between known organizational characteristics and their personal characteristics, values, and goals.

CAREER STAGES

A **career stage** in a person's life is a period of time characterized by distinctive and fairly predictable developmental tasks, concerns, needs, values, and activities. In this section, we examine career stages from two perspec-

> | **TABLE 20.2   Questions That You Should Ask When Assessing an Organization** |
> |---|
>
> 1. How large is the organization's industry and what are its prospects for growth?
> 2. What major changes are foreseen in the industry? How is the organization ready to respond?
> 3. What goods and services does it produce?
> 4. What are the organization's most important product developments?
> 5. Who are the organization's main competitors? How do they compete?
> 6. Where does the organization have other plants or divisions?
> 7. What jobs have its top managers held during their careers?
> 8. What do employees find most satisfying about working for the organization?
>
> *Source:* For the rest of an extensive list of such questions, see L. Dlabay, and J. W. Slocum, Jr., *How to Pack Your Career Parachute*. Reading, Mass.: Addison-Wesley Publishing Co., 1989.

tives: (1) career movement of an individual within a specific organization and (2) an individual's passage through career stages spanning his or her entire working life.

Career Movement within an Organization

Individuals most often think of career movement as advancement up some management or technical hierarchy with ever-increasing salary, status, and responsibilities. At J. C. Penney's, Dillard's, and Nordstrom's retail department stores, new college graduates with a business degree begin their employment as management trainees. They advance to assistant buyer or assistant merchandiser, buyer, assistant manager of an area (women's or men's apparel, jewelry, housewares) in a store, and finally store manager. Career moves in an organization actually are considerably more complex than this. Individuals really move in three directions in an organization: vertically, horizontally, and (more subtly) inclusively.[20] An understanding of the complexity of career moves in an organization can be extremely valuable in an individual's career planning and development.

Vertical Movement   A change up or down formal organizational levels is a **vertical career movement.** During a career in a particular organization, most people move vertically, typically receiving a series of raises and promotions. Of course, in this highly variable process, only a few individuals rise to the very top ranks of the organization, and some individuals reach their final hierarchical level early in their careers. Organizations differ dramatically in the number of hierarchical opportunities available: some may be quite flat in terms of steps to the top, and others may have many levels, or ranks.

Horizontal Movement The lateral change of individuals between functional or technical areas is a **horizontal career movement.** Horizontal movement relates to individuals' areas of knowledge, skills, and expertise. Common functional areas in businesses include production, marketing, finance, engineering, accounting, and human resources. Here, too, individual careers vary considerably: Some employees stay in the same functional or technical area for their entire careers, whereas others make frequent changes. The middle manager who is rotated among positions in production, marketing, and human resources is an example of horizontal movement. Organizations sometimes design this rotation to groom people for eventual promotion to the ranks of general management, where managers need the ability to see and understand overall operations. Anne Pol of Pitney Bowes thinks that lateral moves were critical to her moving up. Five years ago, after a career spent mostly in human resources, she left that senior position to run a plant that makes mailing machines. She considered herself a candidate for the company's highest jobs but knew she needed solid operating experience to have a reasonable shot. After running that plant for five years, she came back to the top human resources job and a position on Pitney Bowes's eleven-person corporate management committee.

Inclusion: Movement toward the Center Movement toward the inner circle, or core, of an organization is **inclusion career movement.** This type of movement occurs when a manager earns trust, develops greater understanding of the organization, gains greater responsibility, and is consulted on important matters more frequently. A relationship often exists between vertical and inclusion movement; yet a person often can make one move without the other. A person can become more "central" to the organization without being promoted to a higher rank by acquiring experience and the trust and confidence of a top manager and co-workers. Similarly, a person can move up in the hierarchy and yet still not be included in important core activities and decisions, as illustrated by the phrase "being kicked upstairs." Inclusion is the most subtle and confusing aspect of career moves within an organization. People may go through their entire careers completely unaware of their position in terms of inclusion or, perhaps, even be oblivious to the existence of inclusion.

The model illustrated in Figure 20.3 combines the three directions in which career moves can be made. Vertical movement is represented by a change up or down the cone. Horizontal movement is represented by a change around the circumference of the cone from one functional or technical area to another. Inclusion movement is a change from the outer surface of the cone toward the center.

Working-Life Career Stages

Individuals typically move through four distinct career stages during their working lives: establishment, advancement, maintenance, and withdrawal.[21] Figure 20.4 summarizes these stages and indicates the expected relative levels of performance as employees move through their careers. However, not all careers will be like those shown in Figure 20.4 because there will always be individual differences. For example, some people may

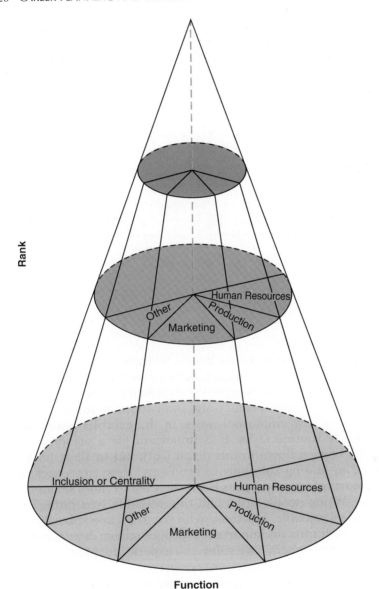

Rank

Human Resources

Production

Other

Marketing

Inclusion or Centrality

Human Resources

Production

Other

Marketing

Function

Figure 20.3 A Model of Career Movement in Organizations.

Source: Reprinted with permission from NTL Institute, "The Individual, the Organization, and the Career: A Conceptual Scheme" by Edgar H. Schein, p. 404, *The Journal of Applied Behavioral Science,* Vol. 7, No. 4, copyright 1971.

take longer than others in choosing careers; similarly, others may choose a different occupation later in life and thus have to learn new skills, which others learned earlier in their careers.

Establishment Career Stage When first joining an organization, a person is immediately faced with several challenges. First, the new employee must learn to perform at least some tasks competently and to decide which tasks are essential and which require less attention. At the same time,

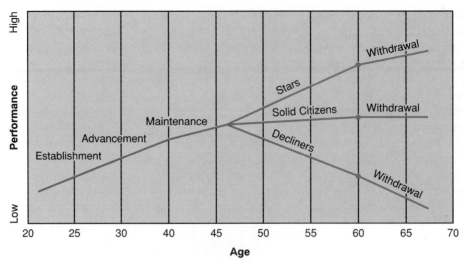

FIGURE 20.4 Working-Life Career Stages.

Source: Adapted from T. Hall, *Careers in Organizations.* Santa Monica, Calif.: Goodyear, 1976, 57.

the newcomer must also be socialized to learn how tasks get done, using both formal and informal channels of communication. Finally, the new employee must perform these tasks while being closely watched by one or more managers for competency and indications of future potential.[22]

Much of a new employee's work in the **establishment career stage** involves fairly routine tasks. It is important for a person not to become completely bogged down in this detail work but to show initiative and be innovative in finding solutions to problems. New employees are typically assigned parts of larger projects being directed by more senior employees or managers. Young people often find this situation frustrating. Such a reaction is understandable, but those who try to escape subordinate positions too quickly will miss an important aspect of career development: They will fail to learn what others have gained by experience. More important, if they undertake tasks for which they are not prepared, newcomers may be tagged as mediocre performers, a reputation that is hard to overcome. Effectively handling the subordinate-superior relationship and the types of tasks assigned may well be crucial in building an effective career.

Ideally, a newcomer will be assigned to a mentor who knows the organization, is successful, and has been trained to work with newly hired employees. A **mentor** is typically an older and more experienced employee who will sponsor and speak to others about the employee's accomplishments.[23] The mentor suggests what to do and what not to do and offers advice about organizational life not found in organizational charts and orientation brochures.

Mentors tend to be people with power and status in the organization. As a result, they are able to assist young employees without having their career be threatened when the younger employee makes a mistake.[24] How do mentors pick employees? First, a mentor is usually impressed with the person's performance. The mentor usually finds out about the person's performance through informal sources. Second, the mentor finds the person easy and pleasant to be around. This is because the mentor and the person may share similar attitudes, backgrounds, or leisure time activities. Third, in some organizations, such as British Petroleum, Heineken, or Honeywell, new employees are encouraged to approach would-be mentors and actively ask for help or attempt to initiate a relationship in other ways. Another tool for helping mentoring programs work is to integrate the results of such programs into a manager's performance appraisal. Amtrak, Coca-Cola, Merck, and Baxter Health Care, among others, all tie compensation to a manager's performance on mentoring. At Amtrak, manager promotion and compensation are tied to a review of career development and mentoring plans for at least ten female and minority employees. McDonald's "Black Career Development Program" provides mentoring opportunities for fast-track African-American managerial employees. Senior managers must advise employees on plans that they have for improving the company's response to increased workforce diversity.[25] Chapter 15 gave illustrations of how organizations are managing cultural diversity.

What do mentors want in return for helping the individual? First, they expect the individual to work hard and exert effort on assigned tasks. Second, they expect the individual to be a loyal supporter of the mentor's team within the organization and work the office politics to make sure that certain projects sponsored by the mentor go through smoothly. Third, mentors may gain recognition from others in their organization for helping to bring along young talent and can have their own performance enhanced by the success gained by the younger employee. Howard Johnson, a manager for J. C. Penney, believes that a mentor's protégés can enhance or limit a manager's performance. If the mentor has high-performing protégés, it means that he or she can pick good people and develop them. If few individuals choose a person for mentoring, it might signal others that this person cannot attract good people to work with him or her. Finally, the mentor may receive need satisfaction (especially self-esteem and self-actualization) from a sense of accomplishment in helping younger employees learn the ropes.

How important is it for you to have a mentor? Most successful managers have had one or more mentors in their careers. For women, having a mentor is much more important than it is for men. Many women are unable to climb the organization's ladder themselves because of the corporate culture, "old boys' networks," or other obstacles. To overcome some of these obstacles, Honeywell, Corning, Du Pont, and other organizations have started to formally team young women and minorities with more experienced executives. At Honeywell, for example, senior managers encourage and expect more informal contacts, such as picnics and bicycle rides instead of golf matches and poker games, between senior and junior managers. Tennis and swimming activities are part of organizational retreat activities. Coed managerial groups can be seen at Corning's favorite lunch spots or informal get-togethers after work. It is not that lunch, tennis, or swimming events per se are important, but women and minorities who were not included in them felt they were missing out on useful gossip. That could include news of someone being transferred or it could mean that an executive was interested in a new-product category. News like this is often at the bottom of one elusive element of success—the part that managers usually chalk up to being in the right place at the right time.

Of course, the potential gains from having a mentor are offset by risks. Employees who hitch their career to a mentor with little power or who has fallen out of power might find that their own career suffers setbacks. Indeed, they might find themselves without a job if a layoff occurs following the defeat of the mentor in a political power struggle. In addition, mentors are only human, so not all their advice will be helpful or even useful. Finally, there is always the danger that young employees will become so dependent upon their mentor that their own career development is slowed. They might be portrayed as not having self-reliance or independent judgment.[26]

The concerns of employees at this career stage are summarized in Table 20.3. This stage requires time for adjustment to the reality of the job, orientation to the organization, and establishment of a mentoring relationship with a supervisor. Completing routine jobs successfully can quickly lead to more challenging assignments. If new employees can pass through this stage successfully, they can usually reach their career goals more easily.

Table 20.4 shows the characteristics of successful employees at this career stage. Successful people want challenging work, describe themselves as successful, have established a mentoring relationship with a senior manager, are willing to job hop (if necessary) to gain personal goals, and understand the organization's reward system.

Advancement Career Stage The **advancement career stage** often involves new experiences: special assignments, transfers, promotions, offers from other organizations, and chances for visibility to higher management. Performance feedback becomes critical to feelings of success or failure. With greater self-confidence and knowledge of the organization, people are more likely to be concerned about promotion and advancement than about their ability to do the job. As they develop a track record, they begin to look ahead to having their own projects. Although they are not allowed to work alone, they are no longer closely supervised or given specific instructions for doing tasks.[27]

An important individual decision to be made at this stage concerns specialization. Specializing (such as in sales, tax accounting, or human resources) allows a person to become an expert in one area. The potential danger, though, is that of being pigeonholed. An alternative is to develop a set of specialized skills and apply them in a variety of areas. For example, a computer specialist (programmer or systems analyst) can apply those skills

---

TABLE 20.3   Concerns of Employees at the Establishment Stage—Ages 20–25

- Central Activities: Helping, learning, and following directions
- Primary Relationships: Being a subordinate and finding a mentor
- Needed from a Superior: Coaching, feedback, and visibility to senior management

---

TABLE 20.4   Characteristics of Successful Employees at the Establishment Stage

- Want to be promoted soon.
- Describe themselves as successful.
- Indicate that the job is not challenging.
- Have been tapped by a senior manager who is mentoring them.
- Have a considerate and supportive manager.
- Are eager and willing to move between organizations if this leads to greater job challenge, experience, and visibility to upper management.
- Understand how rewards (salaries, raises, promotions) are obtained in the organization.

Source: W. L. Cron and J. W. Slocum, Jr., The Influence of Career Stages on Salespeople's Job Attitudes, Work Perceptions, and Performance. *Journal of Marketing Research*, 1986, *23*, 119–130.

---

in marketing, accounting, human resources, manufacturing, and finance. The risk is that of becoming a jack of all trades and a master of none.

As they approach the age of thirty-five, many employees have developed skills that make them attractive to other organizations. Top managers recognize this and use golden handcuffs to retain valued employees. **Golden handcuffs** are the salary, perks (such as country club memberships, a plush office, and company car), and fringe benefits (such as deferred compensation plans and stock options) that organizations use to tie employees to them.[28] The independence once sought by the recent college graduate has now been replaced by a growing commitment to and dependence on the organization.

Peer relationships take on great importance at this stage. The individual relies less and less on a mentor for direction and advice and, instead, turns to the peer group. This provides an outlet for discussing inequalities, such as who did and did not get promoted and why, the size of pay increases and bonuses, and the like. The transition from relating to a mentor to relating to a peer group is not easy. Peer group members may exploit flaws in other group members when the opportunity arises. For example, if a person fails to receive an expected promotion, the individual will likely turn to the peer group for emotional support. The individual hopes that the peers will agree that the wrong person was promoted and offer advice to boost his or her self-esteem. However, some of them may secretly be glad that the person was not promoted because this opens opportunities for them to get promoted faster. Once someone has been passed over, the chances for being considered again decrease.[29]

During the advancement stage, a person's struggles to make decisions at work are often compounded by struggles to make important personal decisions. Work and personal decisions are often interrelated. Whether to take a promotion with its corresponding relocation, longer hours, more travel, and increased stress requires consideration of its effects on an individual's personal and family life. Whether to stay with an organization and become increasingly tied to it by golden handcuffs is yet another consideration. College graduates will change jobs an average of four times during their careers; many of those job changes will occur during the advancement stage.

The concerns of employees at this career stage are summarized in Table 20.5. As the potential for advancement is either realized or not, self-esteem and the probability of future advancement are determined.

Table 20.6 illustrates some of the characteristics of successful employees at this stage of their careers. Note that four characteristics of the establishment stage remain valid for successful employees at the advancement stage: they feel successful, state that the job is not challenging, have an open and supportive manager, and want to be promoted soon. The unique characteristics of successful managers at this stage are that they now have a different mentor and make few interorganizational moves. Because the manager and the former mentor might now be at similar organizational levels, a different mentor is often needed to maintain the manager's visibility to senior management, secure challenging job assignments, and the like.[30]

Maintenance Career Stage Moving into the **maintenance career stage** is often associated with a number of personal changes. Changes in physical appearance and stamina occur more rapidly after the age of forty: hair begins to turn gray, skin begins to wrinkle, and muscles begin to complain during tennis and racketball games. In addition to these types of changes, 35 percent of today's managers will probably experience a mid-life crisis. A **mid-life crisis** results in radical changes in a person's behavior and usually occurs between the ages of thirty-nine and forty-four.[31] A career that has not matched a person's dreams and expectations can lead to feelings of resentment, sadness, frustration, and severe personal problems. Someone experiencing such a crisis may quit a stable job and take a less secure one, become a middle-aged dropout, be unable to cope with family problems, or get divorced.

During this stage, a person may take one of three typical career paths: star, solid citizen, or decliner. The path taken will depend largely on the direction a career has taken during the first two stages. Those who have been picked by top managers as **stars** will continue to receive promotions, new job assignments, greater responsibility, and higher status. These people feel that they have almost made it. Special assignments and expanded mentoring roles are important to stars. Assignments may entail dealing with

---

TABLE 20.5 Concerns of Employees at the Advancement Stage—Ages 26–39

- Central activities: specialization, independent contributor, professional standing
- Primary relationship: peers
- Needed from superior: exposure, challenging work, sponsorship

TABLE 20.6 Characteristics of Successful Employees at the Advancement Stage

- Feel successful.
- State that their current job is not challenging.
- Have an open and supportive manager.
- Want to be promoted again, soon.
- Have another mentor.
- Report fewer interorganizational moves but more intraorganizational moves.

Source: W. L. Cron and J. W. Slocum, Jr., The Influence of Career Stages on Salespeople's Job Attitudes, Work Perceptions, and Performance. *Journal of Marketing Research,* 1986, *23,* 119–130.

others outside the organization, such as governmental agencies and large customers.

Many employees become **solid citizens.** They are reliable and do good work but, for one reason or another, have little chance for promotion. They may lack the technical skills needed to move to a higher level position, the desire for further promotion, the interpersonal skills needed to play the organization's political game, or they may be too valuable in their present positions for the organization to move them to other jobs. Managers having these characteristics constitute the largest group of managers in any large organization and accomplish most of its managerial work.

Regardless of the reason, these employees have reached a **career plateau,** a level at which the likelihood of future promotions is very low.[32] Plateauing does not ordinarily lead to poor performance. Nor is plateauing necessarily the result of poor performance. Rather, a plateau is reached in most cases simply because there are far more qualified people for higher-level positions than there are positions available.

Solid citizens face doing the same job for many years. They need to be patient, trying not to overreact to mistakes and helping newcomers learn from their mistakes. Many develop nonwork interests and become deeply involved in community and family activities.

Decliners have little chance for promotion. They are often given staff jobs that top managers have labeled dead-end positions. The performance of these employees is likely to decline to a point where it becomes marginal. They simply try not to make mistakes that will result in their getting fired. Decliners tend to have few relationships at work. Because they lack influence in the organization, their attempts at mentoring fail. They do not receive challenging assignments, and salary increases are minimal. By accepting positions out of the mainstream of decision making, they hope to hang on until retirement.

In summary, the maintenance stage is the time when most managers review their careers. The concerns of employees at this career stage are shown in Table 20.7. Stars continue to receive promotions and are assigned increasingly challenging and important tasks. Solid citizens are satisfied

TABLE 20.7   Concerns of Employees at the Maintenance Stage—Ages 40—60
• Central activities: training and directing others • Primary relationship: mentoring • Needed from superiors: autonomy, opportunity to develop others

with their careers, demonstrate loyalty to the organization, and can serve as mentors. Decliners are assigned duties that are out of the mainstream of the organization.

The characteristics of successful employees at the maintenance stage are shown in Table 20.8. Only two characteristics are shared with employees from the previous stages: feeling successful and indicating that the job lacks sufficient challenge. During the maintenance stage, successful employees are highly involved in their jobs, acknowledge that power and political games are a way of life, indicate that their boss exerts little pressure on them to produce, and have not experienced a mid-life crisis.

Withdrawal Career Stage.   The **withdrawal career stage** occurs for most people when they reach about sixty years of age.[33] Many employees who have been around an organization for a long time can bring together the resources and people to push new ideas to a successful conclusion, playing the role of maverick or internal entrepreneur. These roles are legitimate so long as they are performed successfully. A person's identity as a maverick or entrepreneur can often be established on the basis of a solid reputation in the company.

It is important for older employees to establish mentoring relationships with younger employees. Many will spend considerable time and energy on developing key people to replace themselves upon their retirement. They learn to think about the needs of the organization beyond the time of their involvement in it. Others will devote time to establishing relationships out-

TABLE 20.8   Characteristics of Successful Employees at the Maintenance Stage
• Feel successful. • Indicate that the job lacks challenge. • Are highly involved in the job. • Feel little pressure to produce from other managers. • Know how office power and politics work in the organization. • Have avoided a mid-life crisis. *Source:* W.L. Cron and J.W. Slocum, Jr., A Career Stages Approach to Managing Managers. *Journal of Consumer Marketing*, 1986, 3(4), 11—20.

side their organizations and representing their organizations in business, professional, and community affairs.

CAREER PLANNING ISSUES

Many of today's employees want more than money from their jobs. This new breed of employee includes women and minorities who are in the work force looking for the challenging careers they never had access to before. In a recent survey of some one hundred Fortune 500 companies, 86 percent indicated that they had started career planning programs for employees.[34] Career planning entails evaluating abilities and interests and considering alternative career development activities. The process results in decisions to enter a certain occupation, join a particular organization, accept or decline new job opportunities (relocations, promotions, or transfers), and ultimately leave an organization for another job or retirement.

Effects of Career Planning

A career planning program can help an organization meet its continuing staff requirements. In large organizations, a typical career planning program might include some or all the following activities:

- Career counseling by members of the human resources department.
- Workshops to help employees evaluate their skills, abilities, and interests and to formulate career development plans.
- Self-directed programs aimed at helping employees guide their own careers through self-assessment.
- Communication of job opportunities through job postings, videotapes, and publications.

Career planning has both positive and negative effects. In some organizations, managers are concerned that career planning will increase their work loads by requiring them to provide counseling and on-the-job development. Career planning may also lead to greater employee demand for career development resources. Participants in career planning programs rely on the company for training, education assistance (tuition reimbursement), and staff counseling. In addition, employees may request more information on job vacancies, pay practices, and career opportunities.

Finally, raised expectations may increase employee anxiety. Fundamental questions regarding individual strengths, weaknesses, and goals may be raised for the first time; group training sessions are rarely equipped to handle these issues. Unfulfilled expectations sometimes can lead to employee disappointment and reduce employee commitment. As a result, some employees may become less motivated to perform well, and others may seek work elsewhere.[35]

Despite these negative aspects, Humana Hospitals, Gulf Oil, IBM, GE, Xerox, the Internal Revenue Service and others have developed career planning programs to reduce turnover, enhance the quality of working life, and improve on-the-job performance. These organizations have found that it is in their best interests—and those of their employees—to stimulate realistic career aspirations. Moreover, these organizations have tried to dispel the "up-or-out" notion of career because many employees ultimately will be plateaued. Therefore, lateral career moves within specialized job areas can be attractive to many employees if career information focuses on personal development, work content, and job importance, rather than solely on promotability.

Career planning can also provide employees with information to enable them to make better career decisions. Rather than raising expectations with promises that probably will not be fulfilled, many companies candidly describe what their programs can and cannot do, as well as anticipated job opportunities. Let's now turn to three key career issues facing employees: dual-career couples, working women, and outplacement.

Dual-Career Couples

In approximately 60 percent of all U.S. couples, both people have careers outside the home.[36] By 1995, the U.S. Department of Labor predicts that 81 percent of all marriages will be dual career partnerships. **Dual careers** can cause stress for couples, as when one or both may travel or be asked to relocate. Stress is also created by the need to balance tight schedules, but the family may enjoy a better-than-average income.

In Thailand, Taiwan, South Korea and other fast-developing Asian countries, young professional dual-career couples together earn about $70,000 a year, nearly ten times the per capita income of the average person. Even with such income, most couples still live with their parents because they cannot afford housing in the major Asian cities. For example, a two-bedroom, 900-square-foot apartment within a one-hour commute of Taipei costs more than $230,000, while a similar one in Tokyo costs more than $825,000.[37]

The job selection process for dual-career couples tends to become increasingly complex, and the individuals' careers must become more integrated and better managed. Two of the major sources of concern for couples with dual careers are relocation and child care.

Relocation The increase in the number of dual-career couples has posed problems for companies when trying to relocate employees. In 1977, Merrill Lynch conducted a relocation survey and asked companies whether employees were resisting transfers because of working spouses. At that time, less than 20 percent indicated a concern. By 1981, that figure had increased to 26 percent, and Merrill Lynch estimates that by 1992, it will rise to more than 30 percent. Seventy percent of the companies surveyed believed that the spouse's job will play a larger role in future relocation decisions. To make the relocation decision easier, organizations typically provide job-finding assistance for the spouse. This service ranges from informational contacts with other employers in the area to elaborate outside

SO YOU WANT TO WORK FOR A FOREIGN CORPORATION

 For many Americans, the Japanese and Korean idea of loyalty and dedication to the organization often means subordinating family life to work. Managers essentially have little life outside the organization. Asian managers often continue important business matters over dinner. In Japan, for example, managers are expected to entertain associates at sake bars instead of going home after work. Isolated from the inner circle, especially if they cannot speak the local language, North American managers go home to their families after work, while their Asian colleagues socialize. On weekends, the Japanese executives play golf, discuss business, and informally hash out decisions. By Monday morning, most managers are aware of the decision, except the foreigners. This quickly relegates foreign managers to a second-class category.

North American managers enjoy greater upward mobility working for European organizations, such as Nestlé, British Petroleum, Siemens, and Hanson, than in working for Asian corporations. Both European and Asian organizations usually install top managers from the home country. But Europeans rely much more on North American middle and upper-middle managers and give them more authority than do Japanese organizations, such as Sony or Toyota. In Japanese subsidiaries, North American managers "hit the glass ceiling a lot sooner." Japanese executives sent out from the home office have the status of permanent employees who commit their entire careers to the company. These managers are rotated through assignments to help them learn the finer points of the job. Many Japanese corporations assume that foreign managers will jump ship as soon as a better offer comes along. Thus, they give them no job guarantees beyond what might be contained in their employment contract.

If North American managers do hold some top positions in Asian organizations, they tend to lack decision-making power. When these managers join Asian organizations, they bump into management philosophies, methods, and cultures that are alien to them. The Europeans generally share cultural and political traditions with the North Americans. For example, European, U.S., and Canadian organizations stress short-term results and favor managers over workers. The Asians, on the other hand, have developed a unique managerial style and worker relationship based on a tradition that emphasizes collective values over individualism. As a result, they invest for the long term and seek worker participation in shop-floor decisions.[38]

agency programs that offer much more formal assistance. These agencies generally guide spouses in the art of finding positions, including resumé preparation and review, specific job guidance and counseling, and actual employment search assistance.[39]

Taking a job in a foreign corporation and relocating to a different country present special difficulties, as this chapter's Across Cultures points out.

Child Care Child care has always been a problem for the working poor. Traditionally, they have relied on neighbors or extended families and, in the worst cases, have left their children alone at home or to roam the streets. However, two major events have transformed this problem into one for working women, including female managers.[40] First, the feminist movement of the 1960s encouraged homemakers to seek fulfillment in a career. Women now make up over 45 percent of the labor force, and they are expected to fill about 60 percent of the jobs between 1992 and the year 2000. Second, economic recessions and inflation struck in the 1970s. Between 1973 and 1991, the median inflation-adjusted income for families fell by more than 13 percent. Suddenly the middle-class dream of a house, car, and a college education for the children carried a dual-income price tag. So for most families, two paychecks are a necessity.

In 1991, more than 11 million preschoolers spent their days with someone other than their mothers. As U.S. women continue to enter the work force, the number will increase. By 2000, an estimated 80 percent of the women between the ages of twenty-five and forty-four will be working outside the home. Of those 80 percent, 90 percent will be mothers. This percentage represents a dramatic increase since the 1970s, when only 29 percent of working women were mothers.

Employers are aware that day-care worries can weigh heavily on mothers and fathers alike and can hurt productivity. As the competition for good workers heats up, many organizations will be forced to grapple with the problems working parents face or risk losing desirable employees.[41] IBM, among other organizations, offers employees a free child-care referral service and plans to spend over $22 million in the next few years to improve the quality of day care available in the towns and cities where most of its employees live. Johnson and Johnson has an on-site day care center at its headquarters in New Brunswick, New Jersey. Johnson and Johnson subsidizes part of its cost, but employees using the center still pay $110 to $130 a week, depending on the age of the child. American Bankers Insurance Group of Miami, like other smaller organizations, maintains a day-care center for employees' children between the ages of six weeks to five years. After that, the child can attend a company-run private school for an additional three years. The school takes care of the children from 8:00 A.M. to 6:15 P.M. and keeps its doors open during public school holidays and summer vacations. These companies believe that the centers have resulted in a 53 percent decline in absenteeism and tardiness and a 65 percent decrease in female-executive turnover.[42]

Working Women

It is rare today to find women at the top of the largest U.S. corporations. Less than 1 percent of the Fortune 1,000 companies have female corporate officers.[43] While an increasing number of women are employed, they are still underrepresented in powerful management positions in most of the world's largest corporations. Yet, in some corporations, such as Avon, CBS, Dayton-Hudson, IBM, and Corning, among others, women are making more progress. These corporations have tried to cut back on the travel, relocation, and long hours that can exclude many women with families. These firms also offer benefits, such as extended leaves, flex-time, and elder care assistance, that help women balance family issues that still fall most heavily on their shoulders.

Still, the top management jobs are mainly held by men. In an attempt to discover why this is so, the Center for Creative Leadership commissioned a three-year study to examine the role of top-level female managers in Fortune 100-size companies. In the following In Practice, we highlight the results of this insightful and in-depth analysis of managerial women, as well as those of other studies.

IN PRACTICE

PRESSURES ON EXECUTIVE WOMEN

Female executives face three different types of pressures. First, there is the pressure of the job itself. The demands on executives to satisfy irate customers, return numerous phone calls, and handle disgruntled subordinates seem endless. Executives must continuously address problems that seemingly have no answers but are only symptomatic of larger problems. They must use their extensive network of peers, superiors, and subordinates to gather information. Many things must be done quickly, and information is often limited. Second, a woman going into a high-level meeting sees few other women. She has few mentors. Thus, the pressure of being a minority and representing women as a group is great. In addition to being watched closely by other managers, "there is still the 'good ole boy' feeling in senior management." This protects men from managerial performance lapses because they are in the closed circle or "men's hut." Third, women are still expected to take major responsibility for maintaining a household, raising a family, and providing a caring and comforting environment at home. The role reversal—being tough, no-nonsense, and efficient in the office while being tender, playful, and caring at home—can be stressful.[44]

Major Success Factors Table 20.9 compares the success factors for female and male managers. For women, six factors are more important than for men. For women, getting help from a mentor is extremely important. The mentor provides all kinds of advice and general encouragement. Since there are few female manager role models, a mentor must spend more time grooming female than male managers. Mentors can help them become visible and get middle-management jobs with profit-and-loss responsibility. Having an outstanding track record, along with a mentor who helps justify a woman's success, is more important for women than it is for men. Successful female managers were described as always standing out in terms of completing assignments, being technically competent, having the ability to head off potential problems, and being highly professional.

Successful women also demonstrated their ability to handle the three pressures discussed earlier. These women were "willing to pay the price" and generally put family life on the back burner until they had established a career. Being mobile, never questioning a relocation, and being dedicated to the organization are more important for female executives than for men.

TABLE 20.9 Success Factors for Female and Male Managers		
	Percentage of Managers Who Agree on Importance of Factor	
Factor	Successful Women	Successful Men
● Help from above (mentor)	100%	55%
● Track record	89	75
● Desire to succeed	84	45
● Ability to manage subordinates	74	50
● Willingness to take career risks	74	15
● Ability to be tough, demanding, and decisive	68	20

Source: Adapted from A. M. Morrison, R. P. White, E. Van Velsor, and the Center for Creative Leadership. *Breaking the Glass Ceiling: Can Women Reach the Top of America's Largest Corporations?* Reading, Mass.: Addison-Wesley, 1987, 190; B. Hellwig, The Breakthrough Generation: 73 Women Ready to Run Corporate America. *Working Women,* April 1985, 99–148; A. M. Morrison and M. A. Von Glinow, Women and Minorities in Management. *American Psychologist,* 1990, *45,* 200–208.

The ability to manage subordinates, especially men, is critical. This ability includes hiring the right people and pulling in key people from other departments to get the job done.

Female managers also must take more career risks than men. Such risks include moving into an unfamiliar department, taking a promotion before being ready, or transferring to a lower-level job if that job gives a better shot at the top. Finally, female executives were frequently described by their subordinates as being tough, decisive, aggressive, and strong-willed. They spoke their minds.[45]

Outplacement

Called the dismantling of the Fortune 500 by many, between 1980 and 1991, more than 1 million managers lost their jobs. More and more companies are being forced to cut costs to stay competitive, and as a result, the number of attractive management positions has shrunk dramatically. Citicorp laid off 4,400 managers, and Digital Equipment laid off 3,450 more managers in 1991. The recession was partly to blame, but fierce global competition and heavy corporate debt loads have pressed organizations to cut back on the number of managers more than ever before. A survey by *Fortune* reported that 86 percent of the top one-thousand organizations significantly downsized in the past five years. By 1995, the managerial ranks of these corporations are expected to shrink even further.[46]

As in prior recessions, the managers most vulnerable to layoff are middle managers whose contribution to the bottom line is more difficult to measure. To handle this steady flow of managerial departures, outplacement agencies are being used by organizations. These firms have grown from a small business twenty years ago to an industry with over $500 million in annual revenues. **Outplacement firms** are organizations that assist laid-off managers in career planning and job hunting. Such assistance includes testing to uncover job preferences, extensive counseling, and the use of an office and support services. If nothing else, outplacement firms give these managers a place to go regularly to maintain some structure in their lives and some sense of involvement with others. Drake Beam Morin, the nation's largest outplacement firm, indicates that it now takes more than eight months for a manager to find a new position, two months longer than it took in 1989. Many managers experience going through stages of mourning, similar to what occurs following other tragic events in life. Thirty-year-old James Ohansian was funding manager for the securities trading department of a Dutch bank's New York City office when he lost his job because of downsizing. He says, "It came without warning at 10:00 A.M. on a Tuesday. We just waited to have exit interviews, cleared our desks, and left. I felt completely worthless."[47]

Outplacement counselors say people who bounce back the quickest are those who can express their anger and who immediately move on to the next phase of their life. Outplacement firms help by having people take a realistic look at themselves and their financial situation and assess their options. While large corporations typically give laid-off managers a severance check, they may also pick up the expenses of the outplacement firm, which range between 10 percent and 20 percent of the former manager's salary.

Nothing an outplacement firm gives a manager can do as much good as what the manager can do for himself or herself. Robert Humes, top manager with Squibb, has coped well with his outplacement because he never relied solely on his job to provide him with a sense of his self-esteem. He realized that when Squibb was acquired by Bristol-Myers in 1989, a Bristol manager would take over his responsibility. He knew he would be replaced as soon as the merger was completed. But after eighteen years of working for Squibb, he still found the layoff hard to take. His typical day begins with a visit to the office of an outplacement firm in Princeton, New Jersey. He makes a few calls and dictates a letter or two to a staff secretary. He has inquired about fifty jobs and pursued about six. He received an offer from one corporation that was located in Texas, but he did not want to move that far. Bob insists that he is flexible and open to jobs in organizations much smaller than Squibb and ones that probably cannot match his former six-figure salary. He maintains his active involvement in the Princeton chapter of the Red Cross because it enables him to keep up with business contacts and gives him a feeling of self-worth.[48]

Losing your job is an emotional blow, but it does not have to be a career disaster. Dan Weston, senior principal in King Chapman Broussard & Gallagher, a major outplacement agency, indicates that a manager can take several steps to make the period of unemployment shorter. These are:

- Stay calm. The worst mistake that managers make is to reach out frantically for the first job they can find. Get into the market with a plan, not emotions.

- Save your network of contacts and friends until you are ready to move. More than 70 percent of new managerial jobs come from networking.

- Be flexible. The more broadly a manager defines his or her skills, the greater are his or her options.

- Try to avoid emotional highs and lows. Searching for a new job is a roller coaster. Managers can ride it better if they keep their expectations for each new job prospect low and avoid disappointment after failed interviews.

- Do not pretend you were not fired. It does not carry the same stigma as it did five years ago, and interviewers will probably learn the truth anyway.

- Maintain a daily routine. Visit the outplacement firm regularly, eat well, exercise, and try to take time to relax.[49]

SUMMARY

In this chapter, we focused on gaining an understanding of how individuals decide on their career path. The first step in this path is to join an organization. Organizations try to socialize newcomers by putting them through a sequence of three activities: getting in, breaking in, and settling in. Individual and organizational factors affect the choice of a career, including the probability that a person will choose one in which he or she is likely to be successful. Individual factors that affect occupational choice include personality, vocational interests, self-esteem, and social background. Organizational factors include the type of industry, the nature of the organization, organizational culture, and the characteristics of the job. When there is a good match between the person and the organization, the employee is more likely to be satisfied with the job, be a high performer, and develop a solid commitment to the organization than where there is a poor match.

There are three distinct types of career movements within an organization: vertical, horizontal, and inclusion. Each presents an individual with a new series of challenges and career issues.

A person's working life can be broken into four career stages. Each of these stages presents certain problems that have to be resolved. In the establishment stage, the newcomer is a subordinate and will be expected to follow orders and perform routine tasks well. During this stage, the newcomer should find a mentor who will sponsor him or her in the organization.

After passing through the establishment stage, the individual moves into the advancement stage. The central activity at this stage involves specialization and making an independent contribution. Instead of relying solely on a mentor for sponsorship, the individual will likely turn to a peer group for encouragement and support.

As a person passes forty, he or she will probably enter the maintenance career stage. One of three paths can be followed during this stage: (1) those who are selected as stars will continue to receive assignments that involve greater levels of challenge, authority, and responsibility; (2) others become known as solid citizens who have little chance for further promotion because they have reached a career plateau but will continue to perform well; and (3) others become decliners because they let their performance slip, become indifferent, and will be bypassed and cut off from the mainstream of decision making.

In the withdrawal stage, the individual begins to think about retiring. Some play the maverick role and others the internal entrepreneurial role; still others spend time establishing relationships outside the organization. As managers proceed through the withdrawal stage, they begin to feel the loss of power and have to learn not to second-guess the decisions of subordinates.

Three important issues in career planning are (1) the impact of career choices on dual-career couples; (2) problems facing working women in their efforts to move up in organizations, and (3) outplacement.

Key Words and Concepts

Advancement career stage
Anticipatory socialization
Career
Career development
Career plan
Career plateau
Career stage
Decliners
Dual career
Establishment career stage
Golden handcuffs
Holland's personality types
Horizontal career movement

Inclusion career movement
Maintenance career stage
Mentor
Mid-life crisis
Orientation
Outplacement firms
Realistic job preview
Social background
Solid citizens
Stars
Vertical career movement
Withdrawal career stage

Discussion Questions

1. Think of the last job you held. What socialization activities did the organization practice? Were they successful?

2. Most successful employees report that they have had more than one mentor in their career. Do you think that having a mentor is important?

3. What are some factors that will probably influence your choice of occupation? Why did you choose those factors?

4. If promotions are coming more slowly and lateral moves are more •likely, how will these affect your career?

5. What are some problems for a manager who is managing employees at different career stages?

6. What are some of the personal and job-related frustrations for employees at the establishment career stage?

7. How would you motivate an employee who is a solid citizen differently than you would motivate a star?

8. What are some of the unique problems facing dual-career couples? How can organizations help them successfully cope with these problems?

9. Why are managerial success factors different for men and women?

10. What services do outplacement firms provide for employees?

◆ MANAGEMENT CASES AND EXERCISES

LIFE SUCCESS SCALE[50]

People have different ideas about what it means to be successful. Please rate each of the following ideas on life success by circling the number that best represents its importance to you.

	Always Important	Very Often Important	Fairly Often Important	Occasionally Important	Never Important
1. Getting others to do what I want	5	4	3	2	1
2. Having inner peace and contentment	5	4	3	2	1
3. Having a happy marriage	5	4	3	2	1
4. Having economic security	5	4	3	2	1
5. Being committed to my organization	5	4	3	2	1
6. Being able to give help, assistance, advice, and support to others	5	4	3	2	1
7. Having a job that pays more than peers earn	5	4	3	2	1
8. Being a good parent	5	4	3	2	1
9. Having good job benefits	5	4	3	2	1
10. Having a rewarding family life	5	4	3	2	1
11. Raising children to be independent adults	5	4	3	2	1
12. Having people work for me	5	4	3	2	1
13. Being accepted at work	5	4	3	2	1
14. Enjoying my nonwork activities	5	4	3	2	1
15. Making or doing things that are useful to society	5	4	3	2	1

16. Having high income and the resulting benefits	5	4	3	2	1
17. Having a sense of personal worth	5	4	3	2	1
18. Contributing to society	5	4	3	2	1
19. Having long-term job security	5	4	3	2	1
20. Having children	5	4	3	2	1
21. Getting good performance evaluations	5	4	3	2	1
22. Having opportunities for personal creativity	5	4	3	2	1
23. Being competent	5	4	3	2	1
24. Having public recognition	5	4	3	2	1
25. Having children who are successful emotionally and professionally	5	4	3	2	1
26. Having influence over others	5	4	3	2	1
27. Being happy with my private life	5	4	3	2	1
28. Earning regular salary increases	5	4	3	2	1
29. Having personal satisfaction	5	4	3	2	1
30. Improving the well-being of the work force	5	4	3	2	1
31. Having a stable marriage	5	4	3	2	1
32. Having the confidence of my bosses	5	4	3	2	1
33. Having the resources to help others	5	4	3	2	1
34. Being in a high-status occupation	5	4	3	2	1
35. Being able to make a difference in something	5	4	3	2	1
36. Having money to buy or do anything	5	4	3	2	1
37. Being satisfied with my job	5	4	3	2	1
38. Having self-respect	5	4	3	2	1
39. Helping others to achieve	5	4	3	2	1
40. Having personal happiness	5	4	3	2	1
41. Being able to provide quality education for my children	5	4	3	2	1
42. Making a contribution to society	5	4	3	2	1

SCORING THE LIFE SUCCESS

The STATUS/WEALTH SCORE is found by adding responses to items:

____	____	____	____	____	____	____	____	____/8 = ____
1	7	12	16	24	26	34	36	Total

The CONTRIBUTION TO SOCIETY SCORE is found by adding responses to items:

____	____	____	____	____	____	____	____	____/8 = ____
6	15	18	22	33	35	39	42	Total

The FAMILY RELATIONSHIPS SCORE is found by adding responses to items:

____	____	____	____	____	____	____	____	____/8 = ____
3	8	10	11	20	25	31	41	Total

The PERSONAL FULFILLMENT SCORE is found by adding responses to items:

____	____	____	____	____	____	____	____	____/8 = ____
2	14	17	23	27	29	38	40	Total

The PROFESSIONAL FULFILLMENT SCORE is found by adding responses to items:

____	____	____	____	____	____/5 = ____
5	13	21	32	37	Total

The SECURITY SCORE is found by adding responses to items:

____	____	____	____	____	____/5 = ____
4	9	19	28	30	Total

To compare your scores with those of managerial men and women, please use the following norms.

NORMS:

	Women (n = 439)	Men (n = 317)
Status/Wealth	3.48	3.65
Social Contribution	4.04	4.07
Family Realtionships	4.44	4.28
Personal Fulfillment	4.60	4.43
Professional Fulfillment	4.21	4.15
Security	4.30	4.21

In what areas do your scores differ from those of managers? Why?

MARCUS DURON

Marcus Duron had forty minutes left on his lunch hour and decided that he needed to devote that time to thinking about the decision he faced. This was not going to be easy, but a decision had to be made.

Marcus, who was twenty-three, had graduated from the University of South Carolina with a major in international business and a minor in economics. During his college days, he spent a semester overseas in Madrid, Spain. He desired to work overseas or with a corporation that was involved internationally. After taking a few weeks' break after graduation, he had headed to New York City to start the interviewing process. He was surprised at his reception by organizations headquartered in New York City. He found people very friendly and helpful. He found the most useful information came from people who had similar interests and who had been searching for a job themselves just recently.

He eventually received a positive contact from a small merchant bank located in Taipei, Taiwan, R.O.C. The bank worked with small and medium-sized corporations that sought financial assistance for expansion. The bank offered to fly Marcus to Taipei for one week to take a good look at the situation before making a decision. Since he had never been to Asia before, he decided to make the trip. He found Taipei a stimulating but very expensive city. Many of his fellow co-workers commuted an hour each way to work and lived in small, compared to his standards, apartments with relatives to make their salary go further. Most people he met spoke fluent English and had been educated in North American colleges. The clients that visited the bank's offices also spoke English, but when he went out drinking with co-workers, they spoke Chinese. He felt that the most important step for him to take if he took the job was to learn the local language. At the end of the week, the bank offered him a job starting at eighteen thousand dollars. Marcus realized that with low taxes and big year-end bonuses, he might be able to live like his Asian co-workers.

To complicate his decision, he was engaged to be married to Linda Ratcliff. The wedding was planned for December 20. Linda was a commercial banker with a global bank. She had been with her bank for two years and loved living in Atlanta. Although she was now in a position that could call for her to move to any one of several domestic and foreign cities, she had yet to be approached regarding a transfer.

Linda had never lived overseas and did not like the prospects of living so far away from her home. She also had some major concerns about her career and if it would be derailed by her taking an assignment overseas. She would be far away from the "action." Linda especially liked the team environment at work and the close relations she had built with her customers. She also wanted her marriage to Marcus to work. She wanted to have a successful career and a great marriage.

QUESTIONS:

1. What are some issues facing both Marcus and Linda?
2. What would you recommend they do?

References

1. Adapted from Deutschman, A. What 25-Year-Olds Want. *Fortune,* August 27, 1990, 422–50.
2. Allen, N. J., and Meyer, J. P. Organizational Socialization Tactics: A Longitudinal Analysis of Links to Newcomers' Commitment and Role Orientation. *Academy of Management Journal,* 1990, *33,* 847–858.
3. Wanous, J. P. *Organizational Entry.* Reading, Mass.: Addison Wesley, 1981; Louis, M. R. Surprise and Sense Making: What Newcomers Experience in Entering Unfamiliar Organizational Settings. *Administrative Science Quarterly.* 1980, *25,* 226–251.
4. Wanous, J. P. The Entry of Newcomers into Organizations. In J. R. Hackman, E. E. Lawler, III, and L. W. Porter (eds.), *Perspectives on Behavior in Organizations.* 2d ed. New York: McGraw-Hill, 1983, 126–135.
5. Meglino, B. M., DeNisi, A. S., Youngblood, S. A., and Williams, K. K. Effects of Realistic Job Previews: A Comparison Using an Enhancement and a Reduction Preview. *Journal of Applied Psychology,* 1988, *73,* 259–266; Vandenberg, J., and Scarpello, V. The Matching Method: An Examination of the Processes Underlying Realistic Job Previews. *Journal of Applied Psychology,* 1990, *75,* 60–67.
6. Adapted from Buss, D. Job Tryouts without Pay Get More Testing in U.S. Auto Plants. *Wall Street Journal,* January 10, 1985, Section 2, 29.
7. Murray, T. J. PepsiCo's Fast Track. *Business Month,* June 1987, 50–52; Pepsi Expectations, *HR Reporter,* July 1987, 4–5.
8. VanMaanen, J. People Processing: Strategies of Organizational Socialization. *Organizational Dynamics,* Winter 1978, 18–36.
9. Feldman, D. C. *Managing Careers in Organizations.* Glenview, Ill.: Scott, Foresman, 1988.
10. Hall, D. T. *Careers in Organizations.* Pacific Palisades, Calif.: Goodyear, 1976.
11. For an excellent review of these, see Greenhaus, J. H., and Parasuraman, S. Vocational and Occupational Behavior: A Review. *Journal of Vocational Behavior,* 1986, *29,* 115–176.
12. Jelinek, M., and Adler, N. J. Women: World-Class Managers for Global Competition. *Academy of Management Executive,* 1988, *2,* 11–19. For other materials focusing on how cultural values affect career paths, see Jackofsky, E. F., Slocum, J. W., Jr., and McQuaid, S. J. Cultural Values and the CEO: Alluring Companions? *Academy of Management Executive,* 1988, *2,* 39–50; Arbona, C., and Novy, D. M. Career Aspirations and Expectations of Black, Mexican-American and White Students. *The Career Development Quarterly,* 1990, *39,* 231–239.
13. Sonnenfeld, J. A., and Peiperi, M. A. Staffing Policy as a Strategic Response: A Typology of Career Systems. *Academy of Management Review,* 1988, *13,* 588–600.

14. Granrose, C. S., and Portwood, J. D. Matching Individual Career Plans and Organizational Career Management. *Academy of Management Journal*, 1987, *30*, 699–720.

15. Sheridan, J. E., Slocum, J. W., Jr., Buda, R., and Thompson, R. Effects of Corporate Sponsorship and Departmental Power on Career Tournaments: A Study of Intra-organizational Mobility. *Academy of Management Journal*, 1990, *33*, 578–602.

16. Personal interview with Leonard Thomas and Shilpa Patel, June 3, 1991.

17. Holland, J. V. *Making Vocational Choices*. Englewood Cliffs, N.J.: Prentice-Hall, 1973.

18. Hyland, A. M., and Muchinsky, P. M. Assessment of the Structural Validity of Holland's Model with Job Analysis. *Journal of Applied Psychology*, 1991, *76*, 75–80.

19. Poole, M., Langan-Fox, J., and Omodei, M. Determining Career Orientation in Women from Different Social-Class Backgrounds. *Sex Roles*, 1990, *23*, 471–490.

20. Schein, E. H. The Individual, the Organization and the Career: A Conceptual Scheme. *Journal of Applied Behavioral Science*, 1971, *7*, 401–426.

21. This section is based primarily on the work of Don Super and his associates. For an overview, see Super, D. E. A Life-Span, Life-Space Approach to Career Development. *Journal of Vocational Behavior*, 1980, *16*, 282–298; Super, D. E., and Hall, T. D. Career Developments: Exploration and Planning. *Annual Review of Psychology*, 1978, *29*, 334–356.

22. Slocum, J. W., Jr., and Cron, W. L. Job Attitudes and Performance during Three Career Stages. *Journal of Vocational Behavior*, 1985, *26*, 126–145.

23. Kram, K. E. *Mentoring at Work: Developmental Relationships in Organizational Life*. Glenview, Ill.: Scott, Foresman, 1985.

24. Whitely, W., Dougherty, T. W., and Dreher, G. G. Relationship of Career Mentoring and Socioeconomic Origin to Mangers' and Professionals' Early Career Progress. *Academy of Management Journal*, 1991, *34*, 331–351. Bushardt, S. C., Fretwell, C. and Holdnak, B. J. The Mentor/Protege Relationship: A Biological Perspective. *Human Relations*, 1991, *44*, 619–639.

25. Cox, T., Jr. The Multicultural Organization. *The Academy of Management Executive*, May 1991, 34–47.

26. Ragins, B. R., and McFarlin, D. B. Perceptions of Mentor Roles in Cross-Gender Mentoring Relationships. *Journal of Vocational Behavior*, 1990, *37*, 321–339; Dreher, G. F., and Ash, R. A. A Comparative Study of Mentoring among Men and Women in Managerial, Professional, and Technological Positions. *Journal of Applied Psychology*, 1990, *75*, 539–546; Wilson, J. A., and Elman, N. S. Organizational Benefits of Mentoring. *The Academy of Management Executive*, November 1990, 88–94.

27. Ornstein, S., Cron, W. L., and Slocum, J. W., Jr. Life Stage versus Career Stage: A Comparative Test of the Theories of Levinson and Super. *Journal of Organizational Behavior*, 1989, *10*, 117–133.

28. Gattiker, U. E., and Larwood, L. Predictors for Career Achievement in the Corporate Hierarchy. *Human Relations*, 1990, *43*, 703–726.

29. Rosenbaum, J. E. Tournament Mobility: Career Patterns in a Corporation. *Administrative Science Quarterly*, 1979, *24*, 220–241.

30. O'Reilly, B. Is Your Company Asking Too Much? *Fortune*, March 12, 1990, 38–46; Stout, S. K., Slocum, J. W., Jr., and Cron, W. L. Career Transitions of Superiors and Subordinates. *Journal of Vocational Behavior*, 1987, *30*, 124–137.

31. McGill, M. *The 40-to-60 Year Old Male*. New York: Simon and Schuster, 1980; Ackerman, R. J. Career Developments and Transitions of Middle-Aged Women. *Psychology of Women Quarterly*, 1990, *14*, 513–530.

32. Slocum, J. W., Jr., Cron, W. L., Hansen, R., and Rawlings, S. Business Strategy and the Management of the Plateaued Performer. *Academy of Management Journal*, 1985, *28*, 133–154; Cron, W. L., and Slocum, J.W., Jr. Career Plateauing. In L. K. Jones (ed.), *The Encyclopedia of Career Decision and Work Issues*. Phoenix: Oryx Press, in press.

33. Feldman, D. C., and Weitz, B. A. Career Plateaus Reconsidered. *Journal of Management*, 1988, *14*, 69–80; Chao, G. T. Exploration of the Conceptualization and Measurement of Career Plateau: A Comparative Analysis. *Journal of Management*, 1990, *16*, 181–193.

34. Kirkpatrick, D. Is Your Career on Track? *Fortune*, July 2, 1990, 39–48. Russell, J. E. A. Career Development Interventions in Organizations. *Journal of Vocational Behavior*, 1991, *38*, 237–287.

35. Hanisch, K. A., and Hulin, C. L. Job Attitudes and Organizational Withdrawal: An Examination of Retirement and Other Voluntary Withdrawal Behaviors. *Journal of Vocational Behavior*, 1990, *36*, 60–78.

36. Richman, L. S. The New Middle Class: How It Lives. *Fortune*, August 13, 1990, 103–115.

37. Worthy, F. S. Asia's New Yuppies. *Fortune*, June 4, 1990, 223–235.

38. Adapted from Hoerr, J., and Nathans, L. Culture Shock at Home: Working for a Foreign Boss. *Business Week*, December 17, 1990, 80–84; Hoerr, J., and Zellner, W. A Japanese Import That's Not Selling. *Business Week*, February 26, 1990, 86–87.

39. Wheeler, K. G., and Miller, J. G. The Relation of Career and Family Factors to the Expressed Minimum Percentage Pay Increase Required for Relocation. *Journal of Management*. 1990, *16*, 825–834. Kirschenbaum, A. The Corporate Transfer:

Origin and Destination Factors in the Decision to Change Jobs. *Journal of Vocational Behavior,* 1991, *38,* 107–123.

40. Kanter, R. M. Transcending Business Boundaries: 12,000 World Managers View Change. *Harvard Business Review,* May-June 1991, 151–164.

41. Goff, S. J., Mount, M. K., and Jamison, R. L. Employer-Supported Child Care, Work/Family Conflict, and Absenteeism: A Field Study. *Personnel Psychology,* 1990, *43,* 739–810; Kossek, E. E. Diversity in Child Care Assistance Needs: Employee Problems, Preferences, and Work-Related Outcomes. *Personnel Psychology,* 1990, *43,* 769–791.

42. O'Reilly, B. Why Grade "A" Execs Get an "F" as Parents. *Fortune,* January 1, 1990, 36–46; Labich, K. Can Your Career Hurt Your Kids? *Fortune,* May 20, 1991, 38–44, 48, 52, 56; Deutschman, A. Pioneers of the New Balance. *Fortune,* May 20, 1991, 60–64, 68.

43. Fierman, J. Why Women Still Don't Hit the Top. *Fortune,* July 30, 1990, 40, 42, 46, 50, 54, 58, 62; Konrad, W. Welcome to the Woman-Friendly Company. *Business Week,* August 6, 1990, 48–55.

44. Nelson, D. L., Quick, J. C., Hitt, M. A., and Moesel, D. Politics, Lack of Career Progress, and Work/Home Conflict: Stress and Strain for Working Women. *Sex Roles,* 1990, *23,* 169–185.

45. Morrison, A. M., White, R. P., Van Velsor, E., and the Center for Creative Leadership. *Breaking Through the Glass Ceiling: Can Women Reach the Top of America's Largest Corporations?* Reading, Mass.: Addison-Wesley, 1987.

46. Kirkpatrick, D. The New Executive Unemployed. *Fortune,* April 8, 1991, 36–39, 42, 46–48; Siehl, C. J., Smith, D., and Omura, A. After the Merger: Should Executives Stay or Go? *The Academy of Management Executive,* February 1990, 50–60; Leana, C. R., and Feldman, D. C. When mergers Force Layoffs: Some Lessons about Managing the Human Resource Problems. *Human Resource Planning,* 1989, *12,* 123–140.

47. Kirkpatrick, *Fortune,* 38.

48. Kirkpatrick, *Fortune,* 42.

49. Personal interview with Daniel Weston, senior principal, King Chapman Broussard & Gallagher, Dallas, Texas, May 29, 1991.

50. Parker, B., and Chusmir, L. H. *Development and Validation of the Life Success Measures Scale.* Miami Florida International University, 1991. Used with permission.

CHAPTER 21

NATURE OF PLANNED ORGANIZATIONAL CHANGE

LEARNING OBJECTIVES

When you have finished studying this chapter, you should be able to:

- Identify the goals of planned organizational change.
- Discuss the sources of pressures on organizations to change.
- Explain reasons for individual and organizational resistance to change.
- Diagnose the pressures for and resistance to change in a work setting.
- Provide suggestions for overcoming resistance to change.
- Describe some general models or approaches for organizational change.

OUTLINE

THE ADAPTIVE ORGANIZATION

The adaptive organization is still more dream than reality, but organizations such as Apple Computer, Cypress Semiconductor, Levi Strauss, and Xerox are experimenting with new organizational arrangements designed to unleash employee creativity and make their organizations more competitive. Paul Allaire, CEO of Xerox, states: "We're never going to out-discipline the Japanese on quality. To win, we need to find ways to capture the creative and innovative spirit of the American worker. That's the real organizational challenge."

One objective of the new, adaptive organization is to eliminate the traditional, bureaucratic organization chart in favor of ever-changing networks of teams, projects, alliances, and coalitions. In the adaptive organization, employees will rely less on guidance from their boss. Individuals will continuously examine the work process and be charged with the responsibility to improve it, even if this means going outside the boundaries of their regular job. For example, at Xerox, a team of employees from accounting, administration, distribution, and sales developed a system that saves the company $200 million a year in inventory costs.

Much of the "structure" of the adaptive organization will be temporary, flexible, and determined more by what needs to be done than by traditional boundaries between functions, products, and levels of the hierarchy. Raymond Gilmartin, the CEO of Becton Dickinson, a producer of high-technology medical equipment, says: "Forget structures invented by guys at the top. You've got to let the *task* form the organization."

The adaptive organization might be likened to a network where managers function as switchboard operators—connecting and co-ordinating the activities of teams of employees and possibly even suppliers and customers. Cypress Semiconductor, a producer of specialty computer chips in San Jose, California, uses a computer system that keeps track of its fifteen hundred employees as they crisscross among different functions, projects, and teams. Apple is developing a computer network named "Spider" to help leaders form project teams. The Spider system is composed of a network of personal computers, a video-conferencing system, and a data base of employee records. Spider can tell a manager whether an employee is available for a project, as well as the employee's skills, experience, and current location. The manager can even contact the prospective new team member via the Spider system and talk to him or her in living color on the computer screen.

All the designs for an adaptive organization have one thing in common—flexibility. A scientist or marketing expert who has the knowledge and experience to be the leader on one project may turn around and be a follower on the next project. The adaptive organization will work like global construction firms (such as Bechtel or Brown & Root). These firms carefully gather selected groups of employees and outside contractors with the right skills for each new airport, dam, or refinery. Companies in stable, slow-growth industries, such as oil, paper, and forest products, might be better served sticking with traditional, hierarchical organizations. In contrast, organizations in fast-changing markets, such as computers, telecommunications, publishing, automobiles, and specialty steel, may need to create adaptive organizational forms to survive.[1]

A major challenge facing organizations is to manage change effectively.[2] When organizations fail to change in necessary ways, the costs of that failure may be quite high. General Motors, while currently making dramatic efforts to change, has lost a significant portion of its market share during the last decade (from over half to about one third of the U.S. domestic auto market). In many sectors of the economy, organizations must have the capacity to adapt quickly in order to survive. Often, the speed and complexity of change severely test the capabilities of managers and employees, as well as the adaptive capacity of the organization.

To a certain extent, all organizations exist in a changing environment and are themselves constantly changing. Increasingly, organizations that emphasize bureaucratic or mechanistic systems—with rigid hierarchies, high degrees of functional specialization, narrow and limited job descriptions, many written rules and procedures, and impersonal human relationships—respond inadequately to the demands for change they face from within and outside the organization. Organizations need structures that are flexible and adaptive and systems that both require and allow greater commitment and use of talent on the part of employees and managers.

While we may think that business organizations confront the most turbulent environments, the forces of change are not limited to the for-profit sector of the economy. Such organizations as schools, hospitals, governments, and religious institutions must also deal with rapid change. The proliferation of social demands, together with costs that threaten to exceed available resources, requires that these organizations also operate more effectively than ever before.

In this chapter, we examine the goals of planned organizational change, pressure for and resistance to change, and some models and processes for implementing organizational change. In Chapter 22, we present a number of specific approaches and techniques for making organizational changes.

GOALS OF PLANNED CHANGE

It is important to distinguish between change that inevitably happens to all organizations and change that is *planned* by members of an organization.[3] Our focus is primarily on intentional, goal-oriented organizational change. **Planned organizational change** refers to a set of activities and processes designed to change individuals, groups, and organization structure and processes.[4] Because management cannot control an organization's environment, they must continually introduce internal organizational changes that allow it to cope more effectively with new challenges. These challenges come from employees and from sources outside the firm, such as increased competition, advances in technology, new governmental legislation, and pressing social demands. Most frequently, organizations introduce change in reaction to these pressures. In some cases, however, they make changes in anticipation of future problems (for example, impending governmental regulations or a competitor introducing new products).

Planned organizational change represents the intentional attempt by managers and employees to improve the functioning of groups, departments, or an entire organization in some important way. Planned change efforts will always involve specific goals, such as higher productivity, new technology, greater employee motivation, more innovation, or increased market share. These and other improvement goals, however, rest on two basic underlying objectives: (1) to improve the capacity or ability of the organization to adapt to changes in its environment and (2) to change patterns of employee behaviors.

Improving Organizational Adaptability

Organizations need effective approaches and techniques to adapt to changing markets, labor supplies, expectations of society, legal requirements, new ideas, and so on. Organizations typically create departments or specialized staffs that plan for and implement needed changes. These adaptive departments or groups often have such names as product research, market research, long-range planning, strategic planning, research and development, public affairs, or organization development. These staff groups and departments may maintain contact with a wide variety of organizations, including government agencies, centers of research on the future, planning staffs of other companies, professional societies, and universities.

Interestingly, however, organizations are discovering that the departments that have traditionally been concerned with issues of organizational change may no longer provide sufficient adaptability. Most areas of organizations are increasingly being pressured to become more flexible and adaptive. For example, Table 21.1 lists several functions—such as manufacturing and marketing—and contrasts the "old" with the "new" emphasis. The ability to effectively manage organizational change is no longer the exclusive concern of specialized departments: all parts of the organization are challenged to become more adaptive. Since the entire organization must be concerned with change issues, organizational culture (see Chapter 15) plays an important role in the ability of organizations to adapt.

Organizations that cannot or will not adapt to changes in their environment will eventually die. Table 21.2 shows the survival rates for U.S. corporations. Historically, some 62 percent of U.S. organizations fail within the first five years of their existence; only 10 percent survive even twenty years.

Changing Individual Behaviors

The second major objective of planned organizational change is to change the behavior of individuals within the organization. An organization may not be able to change its strategy for adapting to its environment unless its members behave differently in their relationships with one another and their jobs. In the final analysis, organizations survive, grow, prosper, decline, or fail because of employee behaviors—the things that employees do or fail to do. The following In Practice provides an example of this observation.

TABLE 21.1 Changes in Basic Business Functions

Function	Old Emphasis	New Emphasis
Manufacturing	Capital and automation more important than people; volume, low cost, and efficiency more important than quality and responsiveness	Short production runs; fast product changeover; people, quality, and responsiveness most important
Marketing	Mass markets; mass advertising; lengthy market tests	Fragmented markets; market creation; small-scale market testing; speed
Financial control	Centralized; specialized staff reviews proposals, sets policy	Decentralized; financial specialists members of business teams; high spending authority at local level
Management information systems	Centralized information control; information hoarded for sake of "consistency"	Decentralized data processing; personal computer proliferation; multiple databases permitted
Research and development	Centralized; emphasis on big projects; cleverness more important than reliability and serviceability; innovation limited to new products and services	All activities/functions hotbeds for innovation; not limited to new products and services; emphasis on "portfolio" of small projects; speed

Source: Adapted from T. Peters, A World Turned Upside Down. *Academy of Management Executive,* 1987, *1,* 231–241; T. Peters, Prometheus Barely Unbound. *Academy of Management Executive,* 1990, 4(4), 70–84.

TABLE 21.2 Survival Rates for U.S. Corporations

Age in Years	Percentage Surviving to This Age
5	38
10	21
15	14
20	10
25	7
50	2
75	1
100	0.5

Source: Adapted from P. C. Nystrom and W. H. Starbuck. To Avoid Organizational Crises, Unlearn. *Organizational Dynamics,* Spring 1984, 54.

THE NONCHANGE PROGRAM

The new CEO of an international bank announced a companywide change program. The bank's traditional hierarchical organization seemed ill-suited to respond to serious challenges stemming from deregulation in the United States and increased global competition. The only solution was a fundamental change in how the company operated.

The CEO held a retreat with fifteen top executives of the bank. They carefully examined the organization's culture and purpose and drew up a new mission statement. Following the retreat, a new vice-president for human resources was recruited from another organization well-known for its excellent management. In a quick succession of moves, the bank adopted a new organizational structure, performance appraisal system and compensation plan, and training programs. The CEO implemented quarterly attitude surveys to track the progress of the change program.

All of these steps would seem to represent a textbook example of successful organizational change. Unfortunately, there was one major problem. Two years after the change program was started, virtually nothing in the way of actual changes in organizational behavior had occurred. The CEO wondered what had gone wrong.[5]

In this In Practice, the CEO and his top management team were correct about the necessity for change. But they were incorrect in assumptions they made concerning how to proceed. They mistakenly assumed that simply adopting a new mission statement, new programs, and a new structure would result in the new employee behaviors. Unless employee behaviors actually change, new programs and structures may have little impact on organizational effectiveness.

Behavior should be a primary target of planned organizational change.[6] Change programs must have an effect on employee roles, responsibilities, and working relationships. At some fundamental level, all organizational changes depend on changes in behavior. In Chapter 22, we examine a number of specific strategies and approaches for changing the behaviors of employees.

PRESSURES FOR CHANGE

Both advanced industrialized societies and developing countries are changing in a number of important ways that have significant impacts on organizations.[7] Consider the United States as an example. A little over one hundred years ago, the country's biggest industry was agriculture. A few decades later, manufacturing engaged the largest number of people. By

◆ *ACROSS CULTURES*

TWELVE THOUSAND WORLD MANAGERS VIEW CHANGE

 The *Harvard Business Review* recently collected data on a variety of organizational issues from almost twelve thousand managers throughout the world. The journal was assisted in this effort by twenty-five business publications located in twenty-five countries on six continents. Each publication reproduced the survey questionnaire in its own language.

The questionnaire examined a number of issues, but one strong theme particularly stood out in the survey results. Change is everywhere—regardless of country, culture, or organization. Managers reported a rapidly changing business environment. Figure 21.1 contains data from six countries showing the percentage of respondents' organizations that underwent a major restructuring during just the last two years. An incredible 71 per-

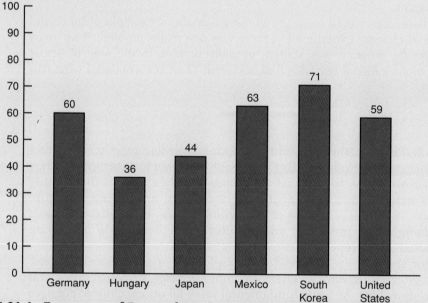

FIGURE 21.1   Percentage of Respondents Reporting a Major Restructuring in Their Organization

Source: Adapted from R. M. Kanter, Transcending Business Boundaries: 12,000 World Managers View Change. *Harvard Business Review,* May–June, 1991, 154.

continued

1991, 69 percent of the U.S. work force was involved in delivering services. Some experts predict that by the year 2000, more than 80 percent of the labor force may be employed in the service sector of the economy. The pressures on organizations for change seem to be accelerating.

Globalizing markets, instantaneous communications, travel at the speed of sound, political realignments, changing demographics, technological transfor-

continues

cent of South Korean firms were restructured during 1989 and 1990. Among the
six countries shown in Figure 21.1, Hungary had the smallest amount of organizational restructuring, at 36 percent. Even
this, however, is a significant amount of reorganization for any two-year period. Given
the dramatic political and economic
changes in Eastern Europe, we might expect to see this level of organizational re-

structuring continue in Hungary or even ac-
celerate.

Figure 21.2 summarizes results from the
same six countries with regard to international expansion. Almost half of German and
Japanese respondents' firms have expanded
their international operations during the
past two years. The United States trails, with
26 percent of the managers reporting such
increased globalization.[8]

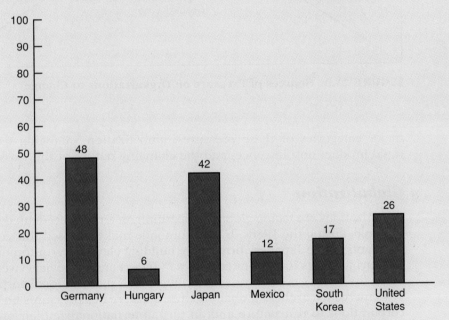

FIGURE 21.2 **Percentage of Respondents Reporting an International Expansion by Their Organization**

Source: Adapted from R. M. Kanter, Transcending Business Boundaries: 12,000 World Managers View Change. *Harvard Business Review,* May–June, 1991, 154.

mations in both products and production, corporate alliances, flattening
organizations—all these and more are changing the structure of the corporation.[9]

These **pressures for change** are a worldwide phenomenon, as we can
see in this chapter's Across Cultures.

There are, of course, an almost infinite variety of specific pressures on
organizations to change. As shown by Figure 21.3, we will explore four

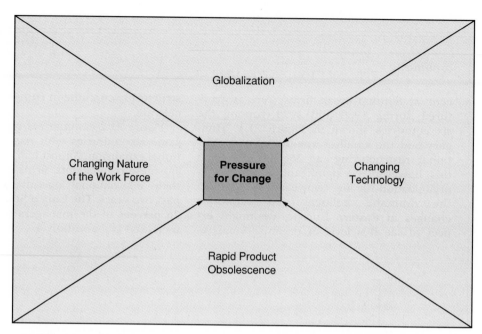

FIGURE 21.3 **Sources of Pressure on Organizations to Change**

major categories of these pressures: globalization, changing technology, rapid product obsolescence, and the changing nature of the work force.

Globalization

Organizations are facing global competition on an unprecedented scale. For example, during the 1980s, U.S. automobile makers closed thirteen assembly plants, while Japanese firms were building eleven new automobile manufacturing plants in the United States.[10] Increasingly, the heavyweight players in the world's economy are international or multinational corporations. The emergence of these global organizations creates pressures on domestic corporations to restructure and, in turn, internationalize their own operations. There is a global market for most products, but in order to compete effectively in it, firms often must transform their cultures, structures, and operations. Some effects of these changes were seen in Figures 21.1 and 21.2, which indicate the significant amounts of restructuring and internationalization occurring in organizations around the world.

The primary forces at work in **globalization** include:

- The recovery from World War II of the strong economies of Germany and Japan.
- The emergence of the "newly industrialized" countries, such as Korea, Taiwan, Singapore, and Spain.
- The dramatic shift from planned economies to market economies occurring in Eastern Europe, the Soviet Union, and, to a lesser extent, China.

- The emergence of new "power blocks" of international traders, such as EC 1992 (the scheduled economic unification of Europe involving currency, some governmental operations, lowered tariff barriers, and so on) and the "yen block" (Japan and its Pacific Rim trading partners).[11]

These powerful forces for globalization mean that organizations cannot pretend that the rest of the world does not exist. While successful strategies of globalization are not easy to implement, many organizations have been effective in moving outside their domestic markets. For example, Ford, Merck & Company, IBM, and Hewlett-Packard have strong, profitable operations in Europe. McDonald's Corporation, Walt Disney, Du Pont, and Amway have very successful Asian operations that include Japan. Amway, for example, sold over $500 million in housewares door to door in Japan in 1990.[12] The following In Practice describes the successful move toward globalization undertaken by Arco Chemical Company.

IN PRACTICE

ARCO CHEMICAL GOES GLOBAL

The headquarters for Arco Chemical Company is a three-hundred-acre campus in the horse country west of Philadelphia. This setting seems far removed from the political and economic changes occurring throughout the world. Yet, the lush, country-club atmosphere is deceiving, for any significant event anywhere in the world echoes through company headquarters.

Arco's shipments into China were stopped following the Tiananmen Square massacre in Beijing. Arco faces tough decisions about joint ventures in Eastern Europe as communism falls there. The reunification of Germany may mean stronger German competitors in the long run, in addition to new opportunities for sales. Events do not have to be earthshaking to send tremors through Arco's headquarters. Almost every world economic trend somehow affects Arco—from stronger Japanese competition, to rising or falling interest rates, to Korean government policy on financing joint ventures, to concern over the environment.

Although Arco risks being buffeted by world political and economic events, there are significant advantages in its globalization. The company has shed its less successful product lines so it can take advantage of its technological edge within its narrow niche around the world. This strategy has paid off: Arco Chemical rakes in more than one-third of its $2.66 billion in sales from abroad and makes about half of its new investment outside of the United States.

Arco Chemical went global partly because it was forced to. As an example, the company's engineering resins are sold to the auto industry. In the past, this meant selling exclusively to Detroit's Big Three in the U.S. market. This is no longer the case. "Today, we deal with Nissan, Toyota, Honda, Renault, Peugeot, and Volkswagen," says Jack Oppasser, vice-president for worldwide business management. "We're dealing with Nissan and Toyota in Japan and in the U.S. We're dealing with Ford and General Motors in the U.S. and in Europe." Arco has to be able to deliver a product anywhere in the world, Oppasser says, or else lose the business.[13]

Changing Technology

The rate of technological change is greater today than at any time in the past. Among the most dramatic technological changes in organizations is the rapid expansion of **information systems technology** (that is, complex networks of computers, telecommunications systems, and remote-controlled devices). As discussed in earlier chapters, the new information systems technology is having a profound impact on operations, power relationships in the organization, how managers and employees work, and even how firms develop and implement their strategies.[14]

For example, information technology might affect a J.C. Penney store manager who sees an attractive sweater at Neiman-Marcus. She buys the sweater, photographs it, and faxes the photograph to Penney buyers around the world. Soon, a buyer in Bangkok locates a factory that can produce the sweater. Within two weeks, thousands of replicas are on their way to Penney stores. Information technology permits an IBM engineer to ask colleagues around the world for help when confronted with a difficult problem. General Electric recently spent hundreds of millions of dollars to create its own private global phone network. Employees can now communicate directly with each other from anywhere in the world using just seven digits. Information technology allows CRSS, the giant architectural firm, to exchange drawings with its client 3M almost instantly. In an event of great historic (and perhaps symbolic) significance, the London Stock Exchange recently replaced its trading floor with a computer-telecommunications network.[15] The Spider system described in the Preview Case provides another example of information systems technology.

The latest frontier in the information technology arena is a computer application known as *virtual reality*. **Virtual reality** is created by a display and control technology that surrounds the user with an artificial environment that mimics real life. The user of virtual reality does not passively view a computer screen but rather becomes a participant in a three-dimensional setting. Boeing is investigating potential applications of virtual reality for the design and testing of aircraft. In 1991, Caterpillar started testing virtual reality models of its earthmovers to improve performance and driver visibility. Daniel Ling, leader of a research team on virtual reality at IBM, stated: "Virtual reality will eventually change the way people use computers. The applications are countless."[16]

The application of more sophisticated technology can change the nature of work performed at all levels of the organization. For example, the trend is toward greater use of robots in many manufacturing and assembly facilities. **Robots** are defined as "combinations of sophisticated microelectronic technology, usually involving a computer, and various mechanical devices that perform functions ordinarily ascribed to human beings and that operate with what appears to be almost human intelligence."[17] A new generation of robots is being developed that will employ *artificial intelligence:* this will be a complex mix of robots, computer hardware, and computer programs that possesses (at least to some extent) the abilities of knowing, reasoning, and understanding.[18]

Despite manufacturers' continuing interest in increased automation, there is some evidence that the frenzied push to find ways to utilize robots has slowed as organizations have realized their limitations. For example, in 1980, General Motors estimated that it would need twenty thousand robots by 1990. Actually, GM was using less than ten thousand that year.[19] In the new "script" for the factory of the future, robots will have a supporting part in the drama, but they have lost the lead role to a technology called computer-integrated manufacturing.

> Consider how Motorola, Inc., makes and sells its Bravo pocket pagers. On May 5, a salesman in Foster City, California, types an order into his Macintosh computer for 150 black Bravo pagers, specifies the unique code that will cause each pager to beep, and asks for delivery in two weeks. The order zips over phone lines to a mainframe computer in a new factory in Boynton Beach, Florida. The computer automatically schedules the 150 pagers for production May 15, orders the proper components, and, on the day after assembly, informs the shipping docks to express mail them to Pacific Telesis Group in California.[20]

Computer-integrated manufacturing (CIM) uses computer networks linking sales, production, and shipping. A CIM network is illustrated in Figure 21.4. This technology is designed to break down barriers between departments, to improve quality control, and to reduce inventory costs by creating a "just-in-time" manufacturing process. In addition, every employee (and their computers) involved can talk to each other and watch the process unfold as the product moves through the system. The earlier movement toward robots was designed to replace humans with machines and thus reduce labor costs. The major goal of CIM, however, is to improve competitiveness and adaptability by reducing the time it takes to turn ideas and sales into products and get these products to the customer.

Rapid Product Obsolescence

Fast-shifting consumer preferences, combined with frequent technological changes and innovations, have shortened the life cycle of many goods and services. You may have tried to buy a certain item only to find that the product or brand no longer exists. Approximately 55 percent of the items sold today did not exist ten years ago; of the products sold then, about 40 percent have been taken off the shelf. In the volatile pharmaceutical and electronics fields, some products become obsolete in as little as six months. The effects of rapid product obsolescence can be dramatic for companies that cannot adapt quickly enough. For example, Xerox introduced the first commercial fax machine in 1964. When fax machine popularity soared in the 1980s, competitors (largely Japanese) rapidly introduced a series of superior models. By 1989, Xerox had only 7 percent of U.S. fax sales. Raytheon developed the first microwave oven in 1947 and dominated the market in 1967, when the first household version was introduced. By 1991, however, 75 percent of the microwaves sold in the United States were made in Pacific Rim countries.[21]

As the pace of product obsolescence accelerates, employees may well participate in the creation of products with the knowledge that these products will remain on the market for only months. Almost every month, less expensive but more complex electronic equipment—stereos, VCRs, and per-

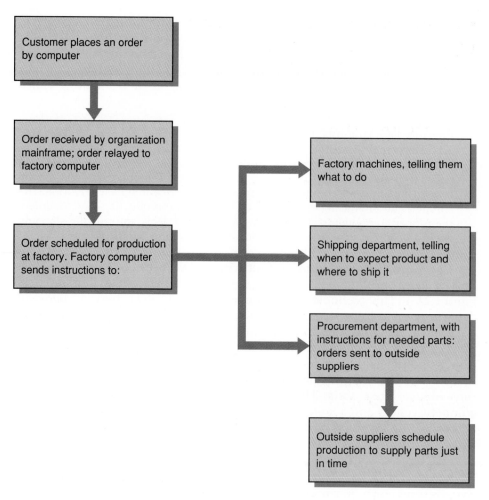

Figure 21.4   Computer-Integrated Manufacturing

Source: Adapted from S. K. Yoder, Putting It All Together. *The Wall Street Journal Reports: Workplace of the Future,* June 4, 1990, 24.

sonal computers—is introduced into the market, rendering older versions obsolete to some extent. Space exploration and development may be for the next century what computers, electronics, and aviation have been for this one. The commercialization of space would present opportunities for the development and marketing of new products and services. Manufacturing and materials processing performed in space may someday make some current products and processes obsolete.[22]

With product life cycles becoming shorter, organizations must shorten production lead times. The capacity to adapt rapidly to change is increased by using temporary or flexible structures to permit managers to assemble teams to develop ideas, determine strategies, and analyze decisions. Adaptive, temporary structures also enable the organization to react quickly to new information, facilitate transitions to new forms of operations, encourage broadly based and participative decision making, and develop potential future leaders.

Changing Nature of the Work Force

In addition to coping with globalization and rapid changes in technology, markets, and products, organizations must attract employees from a changing work force. As we noted in Chapter 1, the U.S. work force will be characterized by the following changes by the year 2000:

- The labor force will grow at only half the rate to which we are accustomed.
- A smaller percentage of the labor force will be under 35 years of age.
- The surge of women into the work force will continue at an increased rate; three in five new workers will be women.
- A larger proportion of new workers will be members of minority groups.
- The education level of the work force will continue to rise, and most new jobs will require at least some post-secondary education.[23]

The U.S. work force continues to grow older and more diverse in terms of gender and race. In Chapters 1 and 15, we explored the challenges facing organizations in terms of managing this cultural diversity. In addition, the dual-career family is rapidly becoming the norm, rather than the exception, in many advanced societies. Dual-career issues present difficult challenges for employees, as well as for organizations, as we discussed in Chapter 20. By 1995, over 60 percent of U.S. women will be employed full time outside the home. Also, the percentage of the work force that is minorities will continue to grow. Thus, equal opportunity pressures on hiring practices and promotion decisions will persist for some time to come.

The work force is increasingly better educated, less unionized, and characterized by changing values and aspirations. Changing values and expectations will not reduce the motivation to work but are altering, to a certain extent, the rewards that people seek from work and the balance they seek between work and other aspects of life. The **quality of work life**—the degree to which people are able to satisfy important personal needs through their work experiences—is an important goal for many, if not most, working women and men. More than ever before, employees desire pleasant working conditions, more participation in decisions that affect their jobs, and support facilities, such as day-care centers for their children. These and other changes put additional pressures on organizations to provide the opportunities that allow them to compete effectively in the labor market.

The pressures from a changing work force are not limited to U.S. organizations. A projection for the global work force for the year 2000 concluded:

- Women will enter the work force in great numbers, especially in the developing countries, where relatively few women have been employed to date.
- The average age of the world's work force will rise to around 35, especially in the developed countries.

- People worldwide will be increasingly well educated. The developing countries will produce a growing share of the world's high school and college graduates.[24]

Note the strong parallels between these conclusions and the description of changes in the U.S. labor market. While there will be differences among countries and regions, global organizations face many similar changes on a worldwide basis.

Not only will the composition and values of the work force continue to change, but interorganizational and international mobility also will increase. If an organization cannot meet an employee's need for vocational or personal development, the person may simply leave. Employees are likely to become less loyal to a particular organization. Their strongest ties will be to their profession or skill. People may be forced to change occupations several times during their working lives to adjust to changing economic conditions. As a result, it will become more common for individuals to have a variety of diverse occupations during their lifetime (see Chapter 20).

RESISTANCE TO CHANGE

Pressures on organizations to change are never-ending. It is also inevitable that change will be resisted, at least to some extent, by both individuals and organizations. **Resistance to change** is a baffling problem because it can take so many forms. Overt resistance may take the form of strikes, reduction in productivity, shoddy work, and even sabotage. Covert resistance may be expressed by increased tardiness and absenteeism, requests for transfers, resignations, loss of motivation, lower morale, and higher accident or error rates. One of the more damaging forms of resistance is lack of participation in and commitment to proposed changes by employees, even when they have opportunities to participate.[25] As shown by Figure 21.5, resistance to change stems from a variety of sources. Some of the sources may be traced to individuals, while others involve the nature and structure of organizations. It is important for managers and employees alike to understand the reasons for and sources of resistance to change.[26]

Individual Resistance to Change

Figure 21.5 shows five sources of individual resistance to change. These represent important sources, but they are not the only reasons why individuals may resist change at work.

Selective Perception   As we indicated in Chapter 4, people tend to perceive selectively those things that fit most comfortably into their current understanding of the world. Once individuals establish their understanding of reality, they resist changing it. Among other things, this means that some people tend to resist the possible impact of change on their lives by (1) reading or listening only to what they agree with, (2) conveniently forgetting any

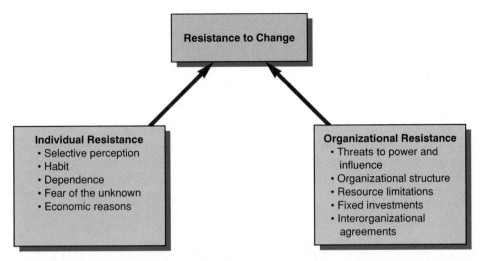

FIGURE 21.5   Sources of Resistance to Change

knowledge that could lead to other viewpoints, and (3) misunderstanding communication that, if correctly perceived, would not fit with their existing attitudes and values. For example, managers enrolled in management training programs are exposed to different managerial philosophies and techniques. They may ably discuss and answer questions about these philosophies, but they may carefully segregate in their minds the new approaches that they feel would not work in their job from those that they already practice.

Habit   Unless a situation changes dramatically, individuals may continue to respond to stimuli in their accustomed ways. An established habit may be a source of satisfaction for an individual because it allows the person to adjust to and cope with his or her world and provides a certain comfort and security. Whether a habit becomes a major source of resistance to change depends, to a certain extent, on whether individuals perceive advantages from changing some habitual behavior. For example, if an organization suddenly announced that all employees would immediately receive a 20 percent pay raise, few would object, even though this might bring about significant changes in their life-styles. However, if the organization announced that all employees could receive a 20 percent pay raise only if they switched from working from 9 to 5 to working during the evenings and nights, many would object. Employees would have to change many habits: when they slept, ate, interacted with their families, and so on.

Dependence   All human beings begin life dependent on others. Parents sustain life in the helpless infant and provide major satisfactions to their children. Thus, dependence is instilled in all people to a certain extent. Dependency is not a bad thing; indeed, to care deeply about other people is to allow yourself to be, in a sense, dependent on them. However, if carried to extremes, dependency on others can lead to resistance to change. People who are highly dependent on others often lack self-esteem (Chapter 3). They may resist change until those they depend on endorse the change and incorporate it into their behavior. For example, employees who are highly dependent on their boss for feedback on performance will probably not adopt any new techniques or methods unless the manager personally endorses them and indicates to the employees how these changes will improve performance.

Fear of the Unknown Confronting the unknown makes most people anxious. Each major change in a work situation carries with it an element of uncertainty. People starting a new job may be concerned about their ability to perform adequately. Women starting a second career after raising a family may be anxious about how they will fit in with other workers after a long absence from the work environment. An employee may wonder what might happen if he or she relocates to company headquarters in another state: "Would my family like it?" "Will I be able to find friends?" "What will top managers think of me if I refuse to relocate?" Uncertainty in such situations arises not only from the prospective change itself but also from the potential consequences of the change. In order to avoid both making more demanding types of decisions and the fear of the unknown, some employees may refuse promotions that require relocating or that require major changes in job duties and responsibilities.

Economic Reasons Money weighs heavily in people's considerations. They usually resist changes that could lower their income directly or indirectly. In a very real sense, employees have invested in the status quo in their jobs. That is, they have learned how to perform the work successfully, perhaps how to get good performance evaluations, how to interact with others, and so on. Changes in established work routines or job duties may threaten their economic security. Employees may fear that after changes are made, they will not be able to perform up to their previous standards and subsequently will not be as valuable to the organization, their boss, or their co-workers.

Organizational Resistance to Change

To a certain extent, it is the nature of organizations to resist change. Organizations are often most efficient when doing routine things and tend to perform more poorly, at least initially, when doing anything for the first time. To ensure operational efficiency and effectiveness, organizations may create strong defenses against change. Moreover, change often opposes vested interests and violates certain territorial rights or decision-making prerogatives that have been established and accepted over time. Figure 21.5 shows several of the more significant sources of organizational resistance to change.

Threats to Power and Influence Some people in organizations may view change as a threat to their power or influence. The control of something needed by other people, such as information or resources, is a source of power in organizations (see Chapter 16). Once a power position has been established, individuals or groups often resist changes that are perceived as reducing their power and influence. For example, programs to improve the quality of work life (QWL programs) in organizations tend to focus on nonmanagerial employees and are often perceived as increasing their power. As a result, managers and supervisors may resist such programs, as the following quotation indicates:

> I've killed myself for the last two years trying to get this QWL project going. I've attended meetings, had lots of one-to-ones, put in lots of extra time, and so forth. And the more I put in, the more the organization seemed to demand of me. I just couldn't take it any more. I am beginning to believe that all of this participation stuff is just a bunch of garbage that will never work in the long haul. I am not interested in improving someone else's QWL at my expense. There is just no way it will work![27]

This statement was made by a disgruntled middle manager who later resigned. He perceived (perhaps correctly) the QWL change program as a threat to his own position and power. Novel ideas or a new use for resources also can disrupt the power relationships among individuals and departments in an organization and therefore are often resisted.

Organization Structure   Organizations need stability and continuity in order to function effectively. Indeed, the very meaning of *organization* implies that a certain structure must be given to individual and group activities. Individuals must have assigned roles, established procedures for getting the job done, consistent ways of getting needed information, and so forth. However, this legitimate need for structure also can serve as a major resistance to change. Organizations may have narrowly defined jobs; clearly spelled-out lines of authority, responsibility, and accountability; and limited flows of information from the top to the bottom. The use of a rigid structure and an emphasis on the hierarchy of authority usually causes employees to use only specific channels of communication and to focus tightly on a narrow concept of their job duties and responsibilities. The more mechanistic the organization, typically the more numerous are the levels of the organization through which an idea must travel. This structure, then, increases the probability that any new idea will be screened out because it violates the status quo in the organization. Adaptive organizations, as described in the Preview Case, are designed to reduce the resistance to change created by rigid organizational structures.

Resource Limitations   While some organizations want to maintain the status quo, others would change if they had the available resources to do so. In general, change requires resources: capital, time, and people with the necessary skills. At any particular time, an organization's managers and employees may have identified a number of changes that could or should be made, but they may have to make difficult choices. Some desired changes may be deferred or abandoned because of resource limitations.

Fixed Investments   Resource limitations are not confined to organizations with insufficient assets. Wealthy organizations may experience difficulty and be unable to change because of fixed capital investments in assets that are not easily altered (such as equipment, buildings, and land).

The plight of the central business districts in many cities illustrates this resistance to change. Most larger cities developed before automobiles, so they cannot begin to accommodate today's traffic volumes and parking demands. The fixed investments in buildings, streets, and utilities are enormous and usually prevent rapid and substantial change. Therefore, the older central areas have experienced increasing difficulty in meeting the competition of suburban shopping centers.

Fixed investments are not always limited to physical assets; they also can be expressed in terms of people. For example, consider employees who no longer are making a significant contribution to an organization but have enough seniority to maintain their jobs. Unless they can be motivated to higher task performance or retrained for other positions, their salaries and fringe benefits represent, from the organization's perspective, fixed investments that cannot easily be changed.

Interorganizational Agreements   Agreements between organizations usually impose obligations on people that can restrain their behaviors. Labor negotiations and contracts are the most pertinent example. Some ways of doing things that were once considered major prerogatives of management (the right to hire and fire, task assignments, promotions, and so on) may become subject to negotiation and fixed in the negotiated contract. Other kinds of contracts also constrain organizations. For example, proponents of change may face delay because of arrangements with competitors, commitments to suppliers and other contractors, and pledges to public officials in return for licenses or permits. While agreements can be ignored or violated, the potential legal costs of such actions may be very expensive, lost customers may hesitate to buy the product again, and a lowered credit rating can be disastrous. In addition, appropriate concern for ethical implications may prevent individuals and organizations from ignoring agreements with others, whether those agreements are explicit or merely implied.

Overcoming Resistance to Change

Realistically, we should never expect resistance to change to cease completely. However, managers and employees can learn to identify and overcome much resistance to change and to become more effective change agents. Organizational members often encounter difficulty in clearly understanding situations that involve change. Analyzing a change problem can become quite complex because of the large number of variables to be considered. Kurt Lewin, a pioneering social psychologist, developed a way of looking at change that has proved to be highly useful to action-oriented managers and other employees.[28] Lewin saw change not as an event but as a dynamic balance of forces working in opposite directions. His approach, called **force field analysis,** suggests that any situation can be considered to be in a state of equilibrium resulting from a balance of forces constantly pushing against each other. Certain forces in the situation—various resistances to change—tend to maintain the status quo. At the same time, various pressures for change are acting opposite to these forces and are pushing for change. The combined effect of these two sets of forces results in the situation depicted in Figure 21.6, which shows the various sources of pres-

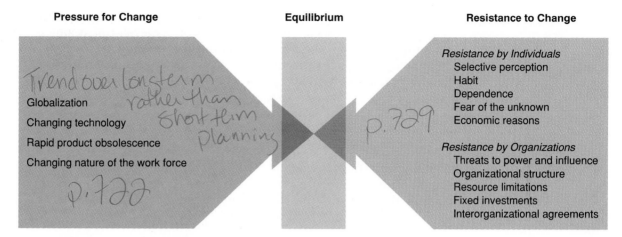

FIGURE 21.6   Force Field Analysis

sures for and resistance to change that we have discussed in the chapter.

In order to initiate change, a manager or other employee must act to modify the current equilibrium of forces. The manager might attempt to change the situation by:

- Increasing the strength of pressure for change.
- Reducing the strength of the resisting forces or removing them completely from the situation.
- Changing the direction of a force—that is, changing a resistance into a pressure for change.

Using this model to understand the processes of change has two primary benefits. First, managers and employees are required to analyze the current situation. By becoming skillful at diagnosing the forces pressing for and resisting change, individuals should be better able to understand the relevant aspects of any change situation. Second, the model highlights the factors that can be changed and those that cannot. Managers and employees often waste a great deal of time considering actions related to forces over which they have little, if any, control. When individuals direct their attention to those forces over which they do have some control, they increase the likelihood of selecting effective options to change the situation.

Careful analysis of a situation, however, does not guarantee successful change. For example, there is a natural tendency to increase the pressure for change in any situation in order to produce the desired change. While increasing such pressure may result in short-run changes, it may have a high cost: strong pressure on individuals and groups may disrupt and unbalance the organization. Often, the most effective way to make needed changes is to identify existing resistance to change and to focus efforts on removing or reducing as much resistance as possible.

An important part of Lewin's approach to changing behaviors consists of carefully managing and guiding change through a three-step process:

- **Unfreezing.** This step usually involves reducing those forces maintaining the organization's behavior at its present level. Unfreezing is sometimes accomplished by introducing information to show discrepancies between behaviors desired by employees and behaviors they currently exhibit.

- **Moving.** This step shifts the behavior of the organization or department to a new level. It involves developing new behaviors, values, and attitudes through changes in organizational structures and processes.

- **Refreezing.** This step stabilizes the organization at a new state of equilibrium. It is frequently accomplished through the use of supporting mechanisms that reinforce the new organizational state, such as organizational culture, norms, policies, and structures.[29]

Successful methods for dealing with resistance to change often include the following three features:

- *Empathy and support.* It is useful to understand how employees are experiencing change. This helps to identify those who are troubled by the change and understand the nature of their concerns. When employees feel that those managing change are open to their concerns, they are more willing to provide information. This, in turn, helps to establish collaborative problem solving, which may overcome barriers to change.

- *Communication.* As previously discussed, people are more likely to resist change when they are uncertain about its consequences. Effective communications can reduce gossip and unfounded fears. Adequate information helps employees prepare for change.

- *Participation and involvement.* Perhaps the single most effective strategy for overcoming resistance to change is to involve employees directly in planning and implementing change. Involvement in planning changes increases the probability that employee interests will be accounted for and thus lowers resistance to change. Involved employees are more committed to implementing the planned changes and more likely to ensure that they work.[30]

We can see the effects of communication and participation in the following In Practice description of a major organizational change at Xerox.

IN PRACTICE

OVERCOMING RESISTANCE AT XEROX

During the 1980s, Xerox faced a changing customer environment. Because of the rapid growth of information technology, a growing number of large customers were experiencing problems trying to coordinate their diverse data-processing operations. One solution was to move toward highly integrated, centralized, companywide information systems. In order to meet customer needs, vendors of information technology had to provide more integrated information products and more coordinated sales efforts. At the time, Xerox had seven different sales forces for its diverse duplicating and information-processing products. Past efforts to coordinate these selling efforts had been unsuccessful. An increasing number of customers were calling for "one face" to work with in terms of sales, service, and support.

Xerox responded to these changing customer demands by merging its office automation technologies into integrated products. The major problem for Xerox was integrating its diverse sales forces to sell the products and to meet customer demands. Fearing heavy resistance from the existing sales groups, Xerox decided to involve them directly in planning and implementing necessary changes. This not only would provide a diversity of input for the change but also would increase member commitment to it.

The company started the change effort with a public announcement from its president, David Kearns. He explained the need for change and the rationale for integrating the sales forces. Kearns then described what the change process would look like in bold and forthright terms. It would be guided by a task force composed of members from the various sales groups. These people would solicit input from other employees and would keep them informed about progress. Kearns strongly emphasized the importance of employees to the firm and the need to get them involved in the change process. Prior to the announcement, all key managers in the company were briefed about the change program so that they would be sensitive to employees' reactions and would provide coordinated responses.

Throughout the subsequent planning, implementation, and assessment phases of the change process, Xerox was extremely careful to communicate openly about what was going on and to involve employees in the changes. For example, during implementation, a videotape was created explaining the rationale, structure, and timing of specific changes in the sales force. Over the two years that were necessary to complete the changes, the open communication and employee involvement contributed to a relatively smooth and positively accepted change process. Sales and profits stayed close to business plans, employee turnover was negligible, and customers expressed satisfaction with Xerox's responsiveness to their needs.[31]

MODELS AND PROCESSES FOR ORGANIZATIONAL CHANGE

Many models and processes can be used to diagnose and introduce organizational change. We will consider four of these: a systems model of change, the process of innovation, the process of action research, and the applied behavioral science called organization development. These are among the most important and widely used approaches for initiating change in organizations.

A Systems Model of Change

The **systems model of change** describes the organization as five interacting variables that could serve as the focus of planned change: people, task, technology, structure, and strategy. The **people variable** applies to the individuals working within the organization, including their individual differences—personalities, attitudes, perceptions, attributions, problem-solving styles, needs, and motives. The **task variable** refers to the nature of the work itself—whether the job is simple or complex, novel or repetitive, standardized or unique. The **technology variable** encompasses the problem-solving methods and techniques, as well as the application of knowledge to various organizational processes. It includes such things as the use of information technology, robot and other automation, manufacturing processes, tools, and techniques (such as computer-integrated manufacturing). The **structure variable** is the systems of communication, authority, and responsibility in the organization, as described extensively in Chapter 18. Finally, the **strategy variable** refers to the planning process the organization engages in to determine its goals and how best to accomplish them. It typically consists of activities undertaken to identify appropriate organizational goals, as well as specific plans to acquire, allocate, and use resources in order to accomplish the organization's mission or goals.

As Figure 21.7 indicates, these five variables are highly interdependent. A change in any one variable usually results in a change in one or more of the others. For example, a change in the organization's strategic plan might dictate a structural change toward an adaptive or network organizational

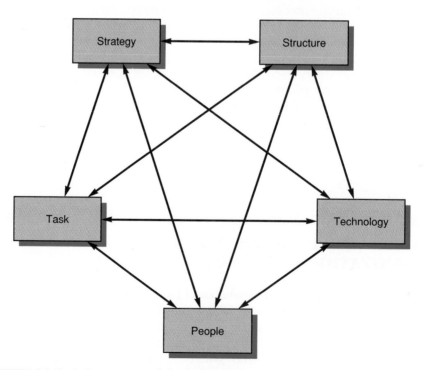

FIGURE 21.7   A Systems Model of Change.

form. This change, in turn, could result in the reassignment of people to certain organizational tasks. At the same time, the restructuring may also lead to a change in technology used in performing the tasks, which affects the attitudes and behaviors of the employees involved, and so on. An advantage of a systems approach to organizational change is that it helps managers and employees think through these kinds of interrelationships. A systems approach reminds us that we cannot change a part of the organization without, in some sense, changing the whole.

Organizational change can be introduced by altering these variables singly or in combination. However, all five are usually present in an organization-wide change process. A systems approach to change emphasizes the importance of understanding all five variables before making changes in any one of them. The systems model shown in Figure 21.7 provides the framework for examining specific approaches and techniques of organizational change in Chapter 22.

Innovation Processes

Innovation is the initiation or adoption of new products, services, processes, procedures, or ideas by an organization. The capacity to innovate is central to the ability of an organization to adapt to changes in its environment. The importance of innovation can readily be grasped by viewing Figure 21.8, which shows product orders at Hewlett-Packard. In 1989, for example, a significant majority of H-P's product orders came from products introduced since 1985. It would appear that Hewlett-Packard's sales growth would disappear if, at any point in time, the company failed to introduce

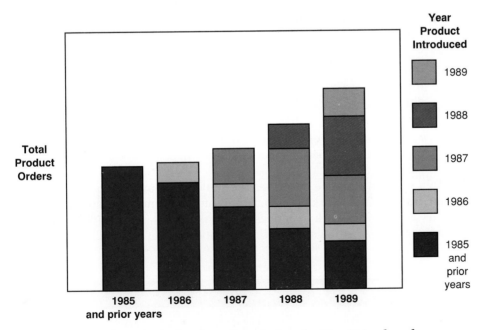

FIGURE 21.8 Hewlett-Packard Product Orders by Year Introduced

Source: Adapted from Hewlett-Packard, *1989 Annual Report;* T. Peters, Get Innovative or Get Dead. *California Management Review,* Fall 1990, 18.

sufficient new products. Recall our earlier discussion of rapid product obsolescence as a major source of pressure on organizations to change.

Many critics of U.S. industry argue that its most serious shortcoming in the face of increased global competition is a low rate of innovation.[32] The reasons put forward for an inability to generate sufficient innovation include: (1) an overemphasis on short-term profits, (2) an unwillingness to invest due to the high cost of capital, (3) government regulation, (4) resistance to change (including many of the issues discussed in this chapter), (5) rigid organizational structures and procedures that stifle new ideas, and (6) reward structures that punish creativity and risk taking. Others, however, have suggested that the central issues are ones of management philosophy, practices, and culture.

As an example of this latter view, consider the conclusions stemming from studies of innovation at the Xerox Palo Alto Research Center (PARC). Investigations of the organizational innovation process spanning the last twenty years at PARC suggest that effective innovation will occur only by creating "continuously innovating companies." Such an organization continuously "reinvents" itself and its products or services. The goals of this type of organization are quite similar, in many respects, to those of the adaptive organization described in the Preview Case.

Other conclusions regarding innovation from the studies at PARC include the following:

- Innovation in work practices is as important as innovation of new products.

- Innovation is everywhere in the organization, not just in research and development labs and research centers. Organizations need to learn how to identify these many innovations and share them throughout the system.

- Specialized research centers in the organization cannot just produce innovation; it must be "coproduced." Large numbers of employees must share a vision of the importance of innovation in order for changes to occur and be disseminated throughout the organization.

- The organization's ultimate innovation partner is the customer. Innovations, like everything else the organization does, must allow the organization to better meet customer needs.[33]

The following In Practice describes the philosophy and culture for innovation at Illinois Tool Works (ITW). Some of the points mentioned above—such as a focus on work practices and linking the innovation process to customer needs—can be seen in the operations of ITW.

IN PRACTICE

THE NUTS AND BOLTS OF INNOVATION

Illinois Tool Works is relatively unknown to the general public despite being a huge corporation with sales in excess of $2 billion per year. This obscurity stems from the products it produces, most of which are attached to or become part of somebody else's products. ITW is a manufacturer of nails, screws, bolts, strapping, wrapping, valves, capacitors, filters, and adhesives. It also manufactures tools and machines to apply these products. (One product many people would recognize is the plastic loops that hold six-packs together—ITW invented these.) ITW has a reputation for being extraordinarily innovative in a variety of relatively mundane areas. For the last three years, ITW has placed first in its industry in *Fortune* magazine's list of most admired companies. How has it done this?

The Illinois Tool Works factory in Elgin, Illinois—noisy, grimy and hot—hardly looks like a cutting-edge innovative operation. Yet, something little short of miraculous has taken place there. Productivity has been tripled in the last eight years, and the factory has regained market share previously lost to low-cost competitors. Across the entire company, ITW has lowered costs and prices, increased market share, and become dramatically more inventive. In addition, the firm has expanded internationally and now operates in more than thirty countries.

ITW's version of the adaptive organization might be described as an amoeba. When engineers and marketers develop a new product, the organization typically sets it up as a new entity. Currently, ITW has ninety product divisions, loosely arranged in nine groups. These divisions are usually small (less than $30 million in revenue) and autonomous. The corporation is highly decentralized, with divisions controlling their own manufacturing, marketing, and research and development. Employees work hard at staying in close touch with their customers and attribute much of the impetus for innovation to this philosophy. Employees spend as much time seeking innovative ways to organize their factories as they do focusing on product development. For example, ITW has found that in most of its factories, 80 percent of the business comes from 20 percent of the customers. These large customers only order a handful of products but do so in large quantities. The other 80 percent of the customers (the "small-batch guys") can dramatically reduce the productivity of the entire plant if all products are treated the same. The solution is segregation. The most sophisticated, high-speed, low inventory (such as "just-in-time" materials handling) manufacturing and assembly operations are used with the high-volume products. Other products are segregated into separate enclaves using procedures most appropriate for the product, volume, and so on. Another work system innovation at ITW is known as the "focused factory." Here, high-volume specialty products are spun off into separate small plants usually employing less than twenty-five people.[34]

Action Research

Action research is a data-based, problem-solving process of organizational change that closely follows the steps involved in the scientific method.[35] As such, it represents a powerful approach to organizational change. The process of action research consists of three essential steps:

- Gathering information about problems, concerns, and needed changes from the members of an organization.

- Organizing this information in some meaningful way and sharing it with the employees involved in the change effort.

- Planning and carrying out specific actions to correct identified problems.

The action-research sequence often includes an evaluation of the implemented actions. An organizational change program may go through repeated cycles of data gathering, information sharing, and action planning before its conclusion.

The strength of the action-research approach to change lies in (1) its careful diagnosis of the current situation in the organization and (2) its involvement of employees in the change process. Managers can effectively change an organization or group only if they understand the current situation, including what things are done well and what things need to be improved. In addition, employee involvement can present a powerful force for change for at least two reasons. First, people are more likely to implement and support a change that they have helped create. Second, once managers and employees have identified the need for change and have widely shared this information, the need becomes difficult for people to ignore. The pressure for change thus comes from within the group or department, rather than from outside. This internal pressure is a particularly powerful force for change.[36]

Organization Development

Organization development (OD) is a planned, systematic process of organizational change based on behavioral science technology, research, and theory.[37] As a field of behavioral science, it draws heavily from psychology, sociology, and anthropology. Organization development relies on information from motivation theory (Chapter 7), personality theory (Chapter 3), and learning theory (Chapter 6), as well as on research on group dynamics (Chapters 10 and 11), leadership (Chapter 12), power (Chapter 16), and organization design (Chapter 18). It is based on many well-established principles regarding the behaviors of individuals and groups in organizations. In short, OD rests on many of the facets of organizational behavior presented in this book.

Organization development is not a single technique but a collection of techniques that have a certain philosophy and body of knowledge in common. It comprises a set of actions undertaken to improve both organizational effectiveness and employee well-being.[38] The basic tenets that set OD apart from other organizational change approaches include:

- OD seeks to create self-directed change to which people are committed. The problems and issues to be solved are those identified by the organization members directly concerned.
- OD is a systemwide change effort. Making lasting changes that create a more effective organization requires an understanding of the entire organization. It is not possible to change part of the organization without changing the whole organization in some sense.
- OD typically places equal emphasis on solving immediate problems and the long-term development of an adaptive organization. The most effective change program is not just one that solves present problems but one that also prepares employees to solve future problems.

- OD places more emphasis than do other approaches on a collaborative process of data collection, diagnosis, and action for arriving at solutions to problems. Action research, discussed in the previous section, is a primary change process used in most OD programs.
- OD often leads to new organizational structure, job designs, and working relationships that break with traditional bureaucratic patterns.[39]

A recent survey of 110 of the Fortune 500 largest industrial corporations revealed that all but three of these organizations had viable OD change activities underway. Some 82 percent of these organizations considered their OD change programs to be effective.[40] Many of the techniques and methods for achieving organizational change described in Chapter 22 often make up part of an OD program.

SUMMARY

A rapidly changing world places many demands on managers and employees, including the need to plan for and manage organizational change effectively. Planned organizational change is the intentional attempt to alter the structure and processes of an organization in order to make it more effective and efficient. Organizational change requires adaptation by the organization as a whole and by individuals in the organization, who must alter their patterns of behavior.

Pressures for change stem from globalization, changing technology, rapid product obsolescence, and the changing nature of the work force. Individuals resist change through selective perception or through the effects of habit, dependence, fear of the unknown, and economic insecurities. Organizational resistances to change can be caused by a threat to power and influence, the organizational structure itself, resource limitations, fixed investments not easily altered, and interorganizational agreements.

Force field analysis can help managers and other employees diagnose and overcome resistance to change. The change process passes through three stages: unfreezing, moving, and refreezing. Managers must encourage pressures for change and discourage resistance to change. Resistance to change can be reduced through good communications and high levels of employee involvement in the change process.

The major variables in the systems model of change are people, task, technology, structure, and strategy. A systems approach to change recognizes the interdependent nature of these variables. Innovation processes are a crucial part of an organization's ability to adapt to changes in its environment. Successful change programs often utilize an action-research sequence of information gathering, feedback, and action planning. Organization development (OD) is a field of applied behavioral science that involves a planned, systematic approach to change and often includes the action-research process.

Key Words and Concepts

Action research	Quality of work life
Computer-integrated manufacturing	Refreezing
Force field analysis	Resistance to change
Globalization	Robots
Information systems technology	Strategy variable
Innovation	Structure variable
Moving	Systems model of change
Organization development	Task variable
People variable	Technology variable
Planned organizational change	Unfreezing
Pressures for change	Virtual reality

Discussion Questions

1. What are the basic objectives of planned organizational change?

2. Identify and explain the pressures for change on the college or university you are attending. For example, you might consider pressures in areas of funding, student life, and curriculum development, or other areas that you judge to be important.

3. Identify the major sources of individual resistance to change. Which have you had the most experience with? Explain.

4. Identify the major sources of organizational resistance to change. Which have you had the most experience with? Explain.

5. Based on your own work experience, use force field analysis to analyze some situation that needed changing. Start by describing the setting and situation. Then identify the major pressures and resistances to change operating in the situation.

6. Using the three-step process model of unfreezing, moving, and refreezing, describe some major behavioral change from your own experience.

7. Describe the five major systems variables that affect an organization's ability to achieve change. Provide an example to show how they are interrelated.

8. Suggest some reasons why innovation might be low in an organization. Explain why innovation is crucial in effective organizations.

9. Describe the process of action research. Suggest a situation in which it might be used effectively.

MANAGEMENT CASES AND EXERCISES

ATTITUDES TOWARD CHANGE

Use this questionnaire to assess your own attitudes toward change. As you answer the questions, think of your current job or a job you used to have. Respond to the questions using the scale below.

Strongly disagree	Disagree	Slightly disagree	Neither agree nor disagree	Slightly agree	Agree	Strongly agree
1	2	3	4	5	6	7

_____ **1.** I look forward to changes at work.

_____ **2.** I usually resist new ideas.

_____ **3.** Most employees benefit from change.

_____ **4.** I dislike change because management usually fails to support it.

_____ **5.** Change usually benefits the organization.

_____ **6.** Most changes are bad ideas.

_____ **7.** Change is necessary.

_____ **8.** I tend to use my power to resist change.

_____ **9.** I often suggest new approaches to things.

_____ **10.** I often feel less secure after changes in my job.

_____ **11.** Change usually helps improve unsatisfactory situations at work.

_____ **12.** I will go along with a change only when everyone else does.

_____ **13.** I try to stay aware of new ideas in areas related to my job.

_____ **14.** Change usually reduces my ability to control what goes on at work.

Scoring: Add the responses to questions 1 _____, 3_____, 5 _____, 7 _____, 9 _____, 11 _____, 13 _____ Total _____
Reverse the scores on questions 2, 4, 6, 8, 10, 12, and 14 (1 = 7, 2 = 6, 3 = 5, 4 = 4, 5 = 3, 6 = 2, 7 = 1). Now add these together: 2 ____, 4 ____, 6 ____, 8 ____, 10 ____, 12 _____, 14 _____ Total _____
TOTAL SCORE _____

Interpretation: Scores can range from 14 to 98. Scores from 70 to 98 indicate very positive attitudes toward change at work. Scores of 42 or below suggest relatively negative attitudes toward change. Scores from 43 to 69 suggest that you are somewhat ambivalent toward change.[41]

SYSTEMS ELECTRONICS CORPORATION

Systems Electronics Corporation (SEC) is a major producer and marketer of electronic products in the western United States. SEC had been predominately a producer of electronic components, such as transistors, used by other companies to make electronic products, such as industrial testing equipment. Because of the potential growth and profits in electronic products, SEC decided to expand its operations into the finished-goods market. It acquired and internally developed businesses for making electronic products. The new products used raw materials from the firm's original components business. Today, SEC has developed into an integrated producer and marketer of electronic products operating in both domestic and international markets.

Although SEC reaped substantial profits from its business expansion, top management felt that corporate profits were not reflecting the full potential that could result from the close technical relationship between the components business and the newer products businesses. The components business supplied raw materials to the products businesses, and full advantage was not being taken of the potential cost savings that could come from coordination among the businesses as they developed new products, processes, and markets. Top management believed that the businesses were not working well together because the heads of the businesses were not communicating effectively with one another. They often competed with each other and acted as though their own business was a separate company.

To speed the expansion of the company into the finished-goods markets, top management had selected aggressive managers to head each new business. They were given considerable freedom in decision making and were encouraged to move ahead and to get things done.

The major method of measuring and evaluating the operations of the businesses was the annual review carried out by top management. Heavy emphasis was placed on the business's actual return on investment against budget. The better the business performed on this measure, the greater were the compensation rewards to managers and the chances of gaining capital funds. In essence, the businesses competed with each other for financial rewards and capital funds.

Managerial methods and operating methods differed across the businesses, especially between the components business and the products businesses. The components business was more formalized and technically oriented than the latter businesses. It emphasized heavily the technical details of the production process and enforced a strict adherence to rules, procedures, and the formal hierarchy. The products businesses were more informal and focused mainly on marketing products. Decision making occurred at the lowest possible levels so the businesses could respond rapidly to product and market changes.

Managers characterized the company as aggressive and competitive and the relations between the businesses as conflictual. The businesses were often described as self-contained units that focused more on their own success than on the overall effectiveness of the company.[42]

QUESTIONS

1. Using the force field analysis techniques discussed in the chapter, analyze this case. Be specific about the pressures for change and the resistance to change likely to be encountered in this situation. Identify which types of pressure and resistance are likely to be the strongest.

2. Use the systems model of change to identify key variables that might be changed in order to increase the overall effectiveness of Systems Electronics Corporation.

3. What would you do to achieve greater coordination and communication among the separate businesses of SEC?

References

1. Based on Dumaine, B. The Bureaucracy Busters. *Fortune*, June 17, 1991, 36–50.
2. Carnall, C. A. *Managing Change in Organizations.* New York: Prentice Hall, 1990; McLennan, R. *Managing Organizational Change.* Englewood Cliffs, N.J.: Prentice-Hall, 1989; Woodman, R. W. and Pasmore, W. A. (eds.), *Research in Organizational Change and Development,* vol. 5. Greenwich, Conn.: JAI Press, 1991.
3. See, for example, Cummings, T. G., and Huse, E. F. *Organization Development and Change,* 4th ed. St. Paul: West, 1989, 46–63.
4. Goodman, P. S., and Kurke, L. B. Studies of Change in Organizations: A Status Report. In P. S. Goodman and Associates (eds.), *Change in Organizations.* San Francisco: Jossey-Bass, 1982, 4.
5. Adapted from Beer, M., Eisenstat, R. A., and Spector, B. Why Change Programs Don't Produce Change. *Harvard Business Review,* November-December 1990, 158.
6. Ibid., 158–166.
7. Doyle, F. P. People-Power: The Global Human Resource Challenge for the '90s. *Columbia Journal of World Business,* Spring/Summer 1990, 36–45; Offermann, L. R., and Gowing, M. K. Organizations of the Future. *American Psychologist,* 1990, *45,* 95–108.
8. Based on Kanter, R. M. Transcending Business Boundaries: 12,000 World Managers View Change. *Harvard Business Review,* May-June 1991, 151-164.
9. Kanter, Transcending Business Boundaries, 151.
10. Hitt, M. A., Hoskisson, R. E., and Harrison, J. S. Strategic Competitiveness in the 1990s: Challenges and Opportunities for U.S. Executives. *Academy of Management Executive,* 1991, *5*(2), 7–22.
11. Peters, T. Prometheus Barely Unbound. *Academy of Management Executive,* 1990, *4*(4), 70–84.
12. Wysocki, B. Going Global in the New World. *Wall Street Journal Reports: World Business,* September 21, 1990, 3.
13. Adapted from Wysocki, B. Chemical Reaction. *Wall Street Journal Reports: World Business,* September 21, 1990, 4.
14. Barry, B. Information Technology and Organizational Development. In R. W. Woodman and W. A. Pasmore (eds.), *Research in Organizational Change and Development,* vol. 3. Greenwich, Conn.: JAI, 1989, 213–231; Gerstein, M. S. *The Technology Connection: Strategy and Change in the Information Age.* Reading, Mass.: Addison-Wesley, 1987. Lederer, A. L., and Nath, R. Making Strategic Information Systems Happen. *Academy of Management Executive,* 1990, *4*(3), 76–83.
15. These examples are drawn from Peters, Prometheus Barely Unbound, 72–73.
16. Bylinsky, G. The Marvels of 'Virtual Reality.' *Fortune,* June 3, 1991, 138–142.
17. Foulkes, F. K., and Hirsch, J. L. People Make Robots Work. *Harvard Business Review,* January-February, 1984, 96.
18. Holloway, C., and Hand, H. H. Who's Running the Store Anyway? Artificial Intelligence. *Business Horizons,* March-April, 1988, 70–76.
19. Naj, A. K. How U.S. Robots Lost the Market to Japan in Factory Automation. *Wall Street Journal,* November 6, 1990, A1, A10.
20. Yoder, S. K. Putting It All Together. *Wall Street Journal Reports: Workplace of the Future,* June 4, 1990, 24.
21. Stewart, T. A. Lessons from U.S. Business Blunders. *Fortune,* April 23, 1990, 128.
22. Goodrich, J. N., Kitmacher, G. H., and Amtey, S. R. Business in Space: The New Frontier. *Business Horizons,* January-February, 1987, 75–84.
23. Redwood, A. Human Resources Management in the 1990s. *Business Horizons,* January-February, 1990, 74.
24. Johnston, W. B. Global Work Force 2000: The New World Labor Market. *Harvard Business Review,* March-April 1991, 115–127.
25. Neumann, J. E. Why People Don't Participate in Organizational Change. In R. W. Woodman and W. A. Pasmore (eds.), *Research in Organizational Change and Development,* vol. 3. Greenwich, Conn.: JAI Press, 1989, 181–212.
26. For additional perspectives on resistance to change, see Argyris, C. *Overcoming Organizational Defenses.* Boston: Allyn and Bacon, 1990; Argyris, C. Reasoning, Action Strategies, and Defensive Routines: The Case of OD Practitioners. In R. W. Woodman and W. A. Pasmore (eds.), *Research in Organizational Change and Development,* vol. 1. Greenwich, Conn.: JAI Press, 1987, 89–128; Spector, B. A. From Bogged Down to Fired Up: Inspiring Organizational Change. *Sloan Management Review,* Summer 1989, 29–34; Staw, B. M. Counterforces to Change. In P. S. Goodman and Associates (eds.), *Change in Organizations,* San Francisco: Jossey-Bass, 1982, 87–121.
27. Schlesinger, L. A., and Oshry, B. Quality of Work Life and the Manager: Muddle in the Middle. *Organizational Dynamics,* Summer 1984, 6.
28. Lewin, K. *Field Theory in Social Science.* New York: Harper & Row, 1951; Lewin, K. Frontiers in Group Dynamics. *Human Relations,* 1947, *1,* 5–41.
29. Cummings and Huse, *Organization Development and Change,* 47.
30. Ibid., 112.
31. Ibid., 112–113. Reprinted with permission.
32. See, for example, Stata, R. Organizational Learning—The Key to Management Innovation.

Sloan Management Review, Spring 1989, 63–73; Taylor, W. The Business of Innovation. *Harvard Business Review,* March-April, 1990, 97–106.

33. Brown, J. S. Research That Reinvents the Corporation. *Harvard Business Review,* January-February, 1991, 102–111.

34. Based on Henkoff, R. The Ultimate Nuts and Bolts Company. *Fortune,* July 16, 1990, 70–73.

35. For a description of action research, see French, W. L., and Bell, C. H. *Organization Development: Behavioral Science Interventions for Organization Improvement,* 4th ed. Englewood Cliffs, N.J.: Prentice-Hall, 1990, 98-111.

36. See, for example, the classic statement by Cartwright, D. Achieving Change in People: Some Applications of Group Dynamics Theory. *Human Relations,* 1951, *4,* 381–392.

37. Burke, W. W. *Organization Development: A Normative View.* Reading, Mass.: Addison-Wesley, 1987; Porras, J. I., and Silvers, R. C. Organization Development and Transformation. *Annual Review of Psychology,* 1991, *42,* 51–78; Woodman, R. W. Organizational Change and Development: New Arenas for Inquiry and Action. *Journal of Management,* 1989, *15,* 205–228.

38. Beer, M., and Walton, A. E. Organization Change and Development. *Annual Review of Psychology,* 1987, *38,* 339–367.

39. Beer, M. *Organization Change and Development: A Systems View.* Santa Monica, Calif.: Goodyear, 1980, 10.

40. McMahan, G. C., and Woodman, R. W. The Current Practice of Organization Development within the Firm: A Survey of the 500 Largest Industrials. Paper presented at the national meeting of the Academy of Management, Miami, August 1991.

41. Adapted from Dunham, R. B., Grube, J. A., Gardner, D. G., Cummings, L. L., and Pierce, J. L. The Development of an Attitude toward Change Instrument. Paper presented at the annual meeting of the Academy of Management, Washington, D. C., August 1989.

42. Cummings and Huse, *Organization Development and Change,* 72–73. Reprinted with permission.

CHAPTER 22

APPROACHES TO PLANNED ORGANIZATIONAL CHANGE

LEARNING OBJECTIVES

When you have finished studying this chapter, you should be able to:

- Discuss the importance of an accurate diagnosis of organizational problems prior to selecting an approach to organizational change.
- Identify and describe four people-focused approaches to organizational change.
- List and explain five approaches to organizational change that focus on task and technology.
- Describe structure- and strategy-focused approaches to organizational change.
- Discuss ethical issues in organizational change.

OUTLINE

THE 'NEW PLANT' REVOLUTION

For about twenty years, a quiet revolution has been occurring in the design and management of manufacturing facilities. These "revolutionary" plants go by a variety of names: high-involvement plants, new-design plants, high performance-high commitment work systems, quality-of-work-life organizations, productive workplaces, and the like. Procter & Gamble may have been the first company to design and build such a plant in the late 1960s. It was quickly followed by Sherwin-Williams, TRW, Mead Corporation, Cummins Engine, General Foods, Chaparral Steel, and Westinghouse, among others. In the 1980s, the pace accelerated, and by 1990, there were close to five hundred such facilities in operation in the United States and many more around the world, most notably in the Scandinavian countries and Japan. These new plants differ from more traditionally organized and managed facilities in a number of ways.

Selection. Emphasis is placed on providing job applicants with a great deal of information concerning the jobs they are applying for. This allows for a high degree of self-selection out of a culture and work environment that might not be a good fit for all individuals. Major portions of the selection process are typically handled by the production employees, rather than solely by a human resources staff.

Pay System. The most common approach in new design plants is "skill-based" pay. Under this pay system, individuals are paid according to how many skills they can learn and perform. This tends to create a flexible, highly trained work force and pro-motes the development of effective work teams.

Plant Physical Layout. High-involvement plants are characterized by few barriers or status differences between managerial and nonmanagerial employees. For example, managers and employees park in the same lots, eat in the same cafeteria, and so on.

Job Design. Employees typically have challenging work that involves doing a whole, identifiable task and having responsibility for controlling how it is done. The use of autonomous or self-managing work teams, quality circles, or other participative group structures is common.

Organization Design. High-involvement plants are characterized by very flat structures and wide spans of control. Often, a plant may have only two layers of management with work teams having considerable autonomy to manage themselves. These plants are also characterized by relatively small staff groups. Many "expert" staff functions, such as quality control, selection of new employees, inventory control, and production scheduling, are handled directly by the work teams.

Plant Culture. New-design plants are characterized by high degrees of participative management with decision-making responsibility pushed as low in the organization as possible. The competitive advantage of high-involvement plants stems from having employees who can solve problems, coordinate their work with the efforts of others, and manage the production process effectively.[1]

Managing organizational change presents complex challenges. It is very difficult, for example, to change a traditional manufacturing facility into a high-involvement plant as described in the Preview Case. Planned changes may not work, or they may have consequences different from those intended. When trying to improve organizational adaptability and employee behaviors, managers and employees must understand the nature of the changes needed and the likely effects of alternative approaches to bring about that change.

In Chapter 21, we discussed the pressures on organizations to change and individual and organizational resistance to change. In this chapter, we discuss specific approaches and techniques for changing organizations and employee behavior. Each of these approaches may be valuable under certain conditions. Organizational change can be difficult and costly. However, adaptive, flexible organizations have a competitive advantage over rigid, static ones. The choice for management over the long run is obvious: innovate and adapt or stagnate and die.

OVERVIEW OF CHANGE APPROACHES

Disagreement exists about the best approaches to organizational change. Many different approaches have been used successfully in organizational change efforts, but a successful approach in one organization may not necessarily work in another. Thus, we emphasize a contingency perspective. There is no single best approach to change, and no approach is likely to be effective under all circumstances.

In Chapter 21, we introduced a systems model of change consisting of five variables: people, task, technology, structure, and strategy. We use this systems model to organize approaches to change into three major categories: people-focused approaches, task- and technology-focused approaches, and structure- and strategy-focused approaches. Task and technology are presented together because the change programs that focus on these variables tend to affect both areas. We combine structure and strategy for similar reasons. A number of specific change strategies and techniques will be explored within each of these general categories. Although the chapter is organized as if each approach to organizational change were independent, nothing could be further from the truth. A well-managed and carefully coordinated combination of approaches is often needed for effective change. Successful organizational change programs typically use a variety of these approaches at the same time.

Relative Impact on Major System Variables

Table 22.1 summaries the change approaches discussed in this chapter, the primary focus of each approach, and the relative direct impact of each on the five major system variables: people, task, technology, structure, and strategy. Each approach is characterized as usually having a high, moderate, or low *direct* impact on each of the variables. Table 22.1 indicates a range for those approaches that frequently have different degrees of direct impact. For example, the direct impact of team building on the task variable can

TABLE 22.1   Comparison of Relative Direct Impact of Change Approaches on System Variables

	Relative Direct Impact on System Variables				
Change Approach	*People*	*Task*	*Technology*	*Structure*	*Strategy*
People Focus					
Survey feedback	High	Low to moderate	Low	Low to moderate	Low
Team building	High	Low to high	Low	Low to moderate	Low
Process consultation	High	Low to moderate	Low	Low	Low
Quality of work life	High	Low to moderate	Low to moderate	Low to moderate	Low to moderate
Task-Technology Focus					
Job design	Low to high	High	Low to high	Low	Low
Sociotechnical systems	High	Moderate to high	High	Low to moderate	Low to moderate
Quality circles	Low to moderate	Moderate to high	Low to high	Low	Low
High performance-high commitment work systems	High	Moderate to high	High	Moderate to high	Low to moderate
Continuous improvement programs	High	High	High	Low to high	Low to high
Structure-Strategy Focus					
Adaptive structures	High	Low to moderate	Low to moderate	High	Low to high
Strategic change	Low to high	Low to moderate	Low to high	High	High

vary from low to high, depending on the focus and goals of the team-building activities.

The direct impact shown in Table 22.1 represents the initial focus, or target, of the change effort.[2] Remember, however, that the systems perspective means that to change part of an organization, in the long run, is to change the whole. Thus, each change approach, if successful, will ultimately impact all five major system variables.

Organizational Diagnosis

The key contingency that influences the choice of approach or combination of approaches is the nature of the problem the organization is trying to solve. There is no one best way to identify the problems facing work groups, departments, or organizations. Nor is there any magic formula for matching specific change programs or approaches to specific problems or issues after they have been identified. It is clear, however, that a careful analysis must be made of the current situation and how it came into being. An accurate diagnosis of organizational problems is absolutely essential as a starting point for an effective organizational change program.[3] In a humorous way, the following In Practice suggests the importance of organizational diagnosis.

IN PRACTICE

THE CHAIRMAN'S RICE PUDDING

A senior manager was given the responsibility of examining all operations and procedures at corporate headquarters. She formed a task force to help with this review. The top executives of the organization had their own private kitchen and dining room. While this was not high on its list of priorities, eventually the task force got around to taking a look at the operation of this kitchen.

The task force discovered that two rice puddings were made every day at 12:15 P.M. and thrown away at 2:45 P.M. Mysteriously, the rice puddings were not listed on the dining room's menu. The kitchen's chef was questioned about this practice, and he admitted that, to the best of his knowledge, no one had ever eaten one of these puddings. Nor did he know why they were being made. He had been the chef for eight years, and the practice was in place when he joined the organization; he had simply continued it.

Intrigued, the task force decided to investigate the origin of this odd ritual. The explanation found was as follows. Seventeen years before, the then-chairman of the organization had, one day, strolled through the kitchen. In a conversation with the chef at the time, he had mentioned how much he liked rice pudding. The chef then instructed his kitchen staff to prepare two rice puddings each day but not to include them on the menu. When the chairman came to lunch, his waiter could then offer him a rice pudding. The second rice pudding was made in case anyone else in the chairman's lunch party should also request one.

This chairman apparently occasionally had a rice pudding. Four years later, the chairman retired. Thirteen years after his retirement, the rice puddings were still being made. By now, however, no one on the kitchen staff knew why they were doing this, nor did any of the patrons of the dining room know the pudding was available.[4]

All organizations have "rice puddings"—patterns of behavior and procedures that, at one time and place, made perfect sense but are no longer effective. Diagnosing needed change, in part, means uncovering the organization's "rice puddings." Four basic steps should be undertaken in **organizational diagnosis:**

- Recognizing and interpreting the problem and assessing the need for change.
- Determining the organization's readiness and capability for change.

- Identifying managerial and work force resources and motivations for change.
- Determining a change strategy and goals.[5]

Information needed to diagnose organizational problems may be gathered by questionnaires, interviews, observation, or from the firm's records. Some combination of these data-gathering methods is typically used.[6] A major advantage of the information-collecting process is that it increases awareness of the need for change on the part of both managers and employees. However, even when widespread agreement exists in an organization concerning the need for change, people may have different ideas about the approach to be used and when, where, and how it should be implemented. Therefore, some systematic attempt should be made to determine the initial focus of the change effort. For example, using the systems model, managers might begin by placing problems in people, task, technology, structure, or strategy categories. Regardless of the analytical scheme used, however, problems may not fit neatly into a single category.

Readiness for change   Any change program requires a careful assessment of individual and organizational capacity for change. Two important aspects of individual readiness for change are the degree of employee satisfaction with the status quo and the perceived personal risk from possible changes. The possible combinations of these considerations are shown in Figure 22.1. When employees are dissatisfied with the current situation and perceive little personal risk from a change, we would predict a high readiness for change. In contrast, when employees are satisfied with the status quo and perceive high personal risk in change, we would predict readiness for change to be relatively low.[7]

With regard to individual readiness for change, another critical variable is employee expectations regarding the change effort.[8] Expectations play a

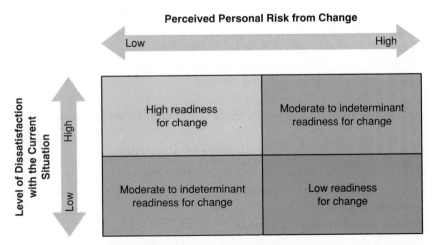

FIGURE 22.1   Employee Readiness for Change

Source: Adapted from Y. Zeira and J. Avedisian, Organizational Planned Change: Assessing the Chances for Success. *Organizational Dynamics,* Spring 1989, 37.

key role in behavior (see Chapters 4 and 7). If people expect that nothing of significance will change, regardless of the amount of time and effort they devote, this belief can act as a self-fulfilling prophecy. On the other hand, employee expectations for improvement might sometimes be unrealistically high, thus creating a situation where unfulfilled expectations make matters worse. Ideally, expectations regarding change should be positive yet realistic.

The various resistances to change described in Chapter 21 represent another important aspect of readiness for change. Both individual and organizational resistance to change must be diagnosed. In addition, the organization's capacity to make the change must be accurately assessed. Approaches that require a massive commitment of personal energy and organizational resources will probably fail if the organization has few resources and its people do not have the time or opportunity to implement the needed changes. Under such circumstances, the organization may benefit most from starting with a more modest, less-demanding approach. Then, as the organization develops the necessary resources and employee commitment, it can increase the depth and breadth of the change.

Principles of change   When managers and employees conduct an organizational diagnosis, they should recognize two important factors. First, organizational behavior is the product of many interacting forces. Therefore, what is observed or diagnosed—employee behaviors, problems, and the current state of the organization—has multiple causes. Trying to isolate single causes for complex problems can lead to simplistic change strategies that are usually ineffective. Second, much of the information gathered about an organization during a diagnosis will represent symptoms rather than causes of problems.[9] Needless to say, focusing change strategies on symptoms will not solve underlying problems. For example, in one organization, an awards program that recognized perfect attendance failed to reduce absenteeism because it failed to deal with the causes of the problem. Further careful diagnosis revealed that employees were absent from work because of pressures created by excessive work loads and an inefficient, frustrating set of procedures for doing their jobs. The awards offered were not sufficient to change employee behaviors and, more importantly, did not address the real problems of work overload and job design.

The importance of organizational diagnosis can be seen in the following practical principles of organizational change:

- You must understand something thoroughly before you try to change it.
- You cannot change just one element of a system.
- People resist anything they feel is punishment.
- People are reluctant to endure discomfort, even for the sake of possible gains.
- Change always generates stress.
- Participation in setting goals and devising strategies reduces resistance to change.
- Behavioral change comes in small steps.[10]

PEOPLE-FOCUSED APPROACHES TO CHANGE

People-focused approaches to change tend to rely a great deal on active involvement and participation by many members of the organization. If successful, people-focused approaches may improve individual and group processes in such areas as decision making, problem identification and solving, communication, working relationships, and the like. We examine four people-focused approaches to organizational change: survey feedback, team building, process consultation, and quality-of-work-life (QWL) programs.

Survey Feedback

Survey feedback consists of (1) collecting information (usually by questionnaire) from members of an organization or work group; (2) organizing the data into an understandable and useful form; and (3) feeding it back to the employees who generated the data.[11] Some or all of the employees then use this information as a basis for planning actions to deal with specific issues and problems. Survey feedback follows the action-research process described in Chapter 21. The primary objective of survey feedback is to improve the relationships among the members of groups or between departments through the discussion of common problems, rather than to introduce a specific change (such as a new computer system). Survey feedback is also frequently used as a diagnostic tool to identify group, department, and organizational problems. Because of its value in organizational diagnosis, survey feedback is often utilized as part of large-scale, long-term change programs in conjunction with other approaches and techniques.

Survey feedback usually begins with the commitment and endorsement of top management. Top managers or other employees may collaborate with outside consultants or human resource professionals in designing the questionnaire to be used. Employees in the survey feedback program then complete a standardized questionnaire. Generally, surveying members of the entire organization, or at least everyone in a department or work group, yields the best results. The questionnaire, which people often answer anonymously, may ask for employees' perceptions and attitudes about a wide range of issues, including communication processes, motivational incentives, decision-making practices, coordination among departments and individuals, job satisfaction, and so on. Table 22.2 contains a sample of items from a questionnaire that has been used in numerous survey feedback programs.

Typically, all employees receive a summary of the responses from the entire organization, department, or work group, as well as their own individual responses. Group discussion and problem-solving meetings are then held to discuss the data that were fed back. The groups involved need to have the discretion to consider and take action based on the survey findings and analysis. There are three alternatives for feedback of the data— employees can obtain the data (1) almost simultaneously; (2) in a "waterfall" pattern, with group meetings held at the highest organizational levels first, followed by group meetings at each succeeding lower level; or (3) in a

TABLE 22.2   Sample Questions in a Survey-Feedback Program

Instructions: To indicate how descriptive each statement is (or should be) of your situation, write a number in the blank beside each statement, based on the following scale:

1	2	3	4	5
To a very little extent	To a little extent	To some extent	To a great extent	To a very great extent

_____ 1. To what extent is this organization generally quick to use improved work methods?

_____ 2. To what extent does this organization have a real interest in the welfare and happiness of those who work here?

_____ 3. How much does this organization try to improve working conditions?

_____ 4. To what extent does this organization have clear-cut, reasonable goals and objectives?

_____ 5. To what extent are work activities sensibly organized in this organization?

_____ 6. In this organization, to what extent are decisions made at levels where the most adequate and accurate information is available?

_____ 7. When decisions are being made, to what extent are the people affected asked for their ideas?

_____ 8. People at all levels of an organization usually have know-how that could be of use to decision makers. To what extent is information widely shared in this organization so that those who make decisions have access to all available know-how?

_____ 9. To what extent do different units or departments plan together and coordinate their efforts?

How friendly and easy to approach are the people in your work group?

_____ 10. This is how it is _now_.

_____ 11. This is how I would _like_ it to be.

When you talk with people in your work group, to what extent do they pay attention to what you are saying?

_____ 12. This is how it is _now_.

_____ 13. This is how I would _like_ it to be.

To what extent are people in your work group willing to listen to your problems?

_____ 14. This is how it is _now_.

_____ 15. This is how I would _like_ it to be.

To what extent does your supervisor offer new ideas for solving job-related problems?

_____ 16. This is how it is _now_.

_____ 17. This is how I would _like_ it to be.

To what extent does your supervisor encourage the people who work for him or her to work as a team?

_____ 18. This is how it is _now_.

_____ 19. This is how I would _like_ it to be.

Source: Adapted with permission from J. C. Taylor, and D. G. Bowers, _Survey of Organizations: A Machine-Scored Standardized Questionnaire Instrument._ Ann Arbor: Institute for Social Research, the University of Michigan, 1972. No further reproduction in any form authorized without written permission of the copyright holders.

"bottom-up" fashion, with group meetings held first at the lowest participating levels of the organization.

A major strength of survey feedback is that it deals with managers and
employees in the context of their own jobs, problems, and work relationships. Thus, employees often perceive that the data generated and the process employed are highly relevant to their goals and concerns. Survey feedback can effectively meet both organizational goals and individual and
group needs. It does not usually bring about fundamental changes in organizational structure, task design, technology, or strategy. However, survey
feedback helps bring problems to the surface and clarifies issues, which, in
turn, may indicate the need for changes in structure, tasks, technology, or
strategy.

Team Building

Team building is a process by which members of a work group diagnose
how they work together and plan changes to improve their effectiveness.
Many different work groups comprise an organization, and much of its
success depends on how effectively people can work together as a team (see
Chapters 10 and 11).[12] Some interdependence among the group members
should exist before a group attempts team building. That is, the work of
team members must require group effort, and effective performance by one
group member must depend on that of the others. When such task interdependence does not exist, team building is inappropriate, and managers
should use other change programs.

Team building attempts to improve the effectiveness of work groups by
having group members focus on one or more of the following actions:

- Setting goals or priorities for the group.
- Analyzing or allocating the way work is performed.
- Examining the way the group is working.
- Examining relationships among the people doing the work.[13]

Team building usually follows a cycle similar to that shown in Figure
22.2. Team building begins when group members recognize a problem in
group functioning for which this approach seems appropriate. During the
team-building program, members of the work group contribute information
concerning their perceptions of issues, problems, and working relationships. Data may be gathered informally during group meetings or prior to
meetings using interviews or questionnaires. These data are analyzed, and
work group problems are diagnosed. Using problem diagnosis as the starting point, members of the group plan specific actions and assign individuals
to implement them. At some later stage, members of the team must evaluate
their progress and determine whether their action plans solved the problems. Note that the team-building cycle depicted in Figure 22.2 also includes
the action-research process described in Chapter 21.

Team building addresses immediate group problems and helps the
members learn how to deal with new problems on an ongoing basis. An
effective work group can recognize barriers to its own effectiveness and

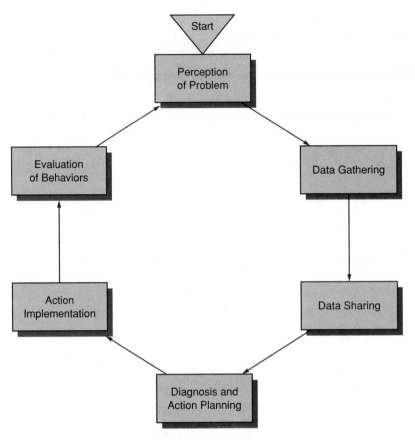

FIGURE 22.2   The Team-Building Cycle

design and carry out actions to remove those barriers. Team building has
resulted in many positive outcomes for work groups and organizations. As
a result of team-building programs, organizations have reported positive
changes in employee participation, involvement, job satisfaction and other
work attitudes, organizational climate, group decision-making and
problem-solving skills, and other aspects of group behavior.[14] Tom Tyrrell,
president of American Steel and Wire Company, gives team building a large
part of the credit for holding his organization together during a recent
downturn. When a major supplier was shut down by a strike, this independent steel producer had to stop its own production and lost $25 million in
orders. Tyrrell refused to lay off any employees and put teams to work
maintaining machinery, developing cost-cutting plans, and improving the
production process. In the last five years, American Steel's sales have quin-
tupled. In 1991, the firm was among the lowest-cost, highest-quality producers in the nation.[15]

   Team building frequently is an important part of an organization development (OD) program, as described in Chapter 21. Organization development practitioners place great value on collaborative behaviors in the process of organizational change. Many OD programs are based on the
assumption that widespread participation by employees is necessary to ef-

fect and sustain meaningful change in an organization. Increased involvement and participation are among the strongest expected outcomes of team building.[16] As such, team building often can provide a useful way to involve employees in an organizational change program and to increase collaborative behavior. The following In Practice provides an example of team building in a mining organization.

IN PRACTICE

BUILDING TEAMS TO IMPROVE MINE SAFETY

The U.S. Bureau of Mines selected a mine for a demonstration project designed to reduce mining accidents. The principal approach used was the organization development technique of team building. Problem-solving meetings involving a facilitator were held at every level of the organization—from the president and his staff down to the first-line supervisors and their crews. In addition to the usual team-building focus on increasing work team effectiveness, all teams examined safety issues.

As a result of the team-building program, a number of changes took place. The president and his top executives instituted new policies designed to monitor, evaluate, and reward mine safety. The performance appraisal system was redesigned to include safety performance. The vice-president for operations and his staff redesigned the organizational structure to change the reporting relationships of safety specialists and increased the authority in their roles. The mine manager and his management team and staff analyzed safety problems and accidents. They then set safety goals, changed safety procedures, established a safety incentive program, and developed ways to improve mining conditions. The first-line supervisors and their work crews identified hazardous conditions and work practices. They also developed a number of plans for immediate corrective actions when hazards appeared.

The team-building format involved everyone from the top to the bottom of the organization in problem solving, action planning, and taking action to increase employee safety. While everyone was involved in improving mine safety, program evaluators concluded that the greatest contributions (and benefits) came from the work teams actually in the mine. Mine safety is a complex and difficult problem. Yet, after two-and-one-half years of this program, results were a 50 percent reduction in lost-time injuries in the mine. A comparison mine, where team building was not used, suffered a 20 percent increase in lost-time injuries during the same time period. In addition, the team-building program resulted in gains in productivity and production quality and reduced costs and absenteeism.[17]

Process Consultation

Process consultation is guidance provided by a consultant to help members of an organization perceive, understand, and act on process events that occur in their work environment.[18] *Process events* are the ways in which employees do their work. Process events include the behaviors of people at meetings; formal and informal encounters among employees at work; and, in general, any of the behaviors involved in performing a task. In order to help you understand the concept of "process," Figure 22.3 indicates some of the differences between process and content when tasks or interpersonal relationships are changed.

Process consultation is characterized by the use of a skilled third party or facilitator who may be an outsider to the organization, such as an external behavioral science consultant, or a member of the organization, such as a human resource professional or a manager skilled in process activities.

Process consultation programs typically address one or more of the following areas of concern:

- *Communication.* Managers must understand the nature and style of the communication process in the organization and make this process as open and valid as possible. In particular, communication patterns in meetings can contribute to or reduce group effectiveness.

- *Leadership.* Process consultation can help a work group understand leadership styles and help individual managers adjust their style to better fit different situations. In addition, by understanding influence processes, members of a group can learn to rotate leadership according to individual expertise; this is an important group skill.

- *Decision making and problem solving.* Efficient decision-making and problem-solving processes are crucial for individual and group effectiveness in organizations. Managers must understand how decisions are made in their organizations and learn effective problem-solving behaviors.

- *Group norms and roles.* Managers should be aware of the processes by which employees take on certain roles in groups and organizations. In addition, process consultation can help a group examine the appropriateness of norms that influence individuals' behavior. It is possible to change norms by a conscious process.

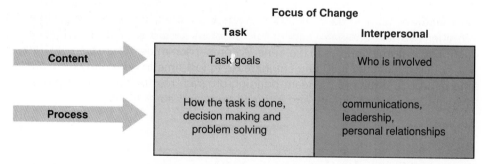

FIGURE 22.3 Some Examples of Differences between Content and Process

Source: Adapted from E. H. Schein, *Process Consultation,* vol. II. Reading, Mass.: Addison-Wesley, 1987, 40.

- *Conflict resolution.* How organizations resolve conflicts between individuals and groups is another important process. Process consultation provides an often effective approach to diagnosing, understanding, and resolving organizational conflict.[19]

Process consultation is often effective in changing attitudes and group
norms, improving interpersonal and decision-making skills, and increasing group cohesiveness and teamwork. There is little evidence that process consultation *directly* affects outcomes, such as task performance.
There is some evidence, however, that a reduction in conflict in labor-
management relations leads to improved organizational performance in
the long run.[20] The use of process consultation could contribute to this
outcome. Process consultation is seldom the sole component of an organizational change program; rather, it usually is used in combination with
other approaches.

Quality-of-Work-Life Programs

Quality-of-work-life (QWL) programs are activities undertaken by an organization for the purpose of improving important conditions that affect an
employee's experience with the organization. Conditions that may be the
focus of QWL programs include security, safety and health, participation in
decisions, opportunities to use and develop talents and skills, meaningful
work, control over work time or place, protection from arbitrary or unfair
treatment, and opportunities to satisfy social needs.[21]

Quality-of-work-life programs became increasingly popular during the
1980s in response to demands from organizational members for improvements in the quality of their work experiences.[22] In addition, QWL programs have been perceived as a way to increase productivity and quality of
output through greater involvement and participation by employees in decisions that affect their jobs. Such programs are typically broad-based and,
to a certain extent, lack the precise definition and focus of survey feedback
and team building.

Organizations with active QWL programs include GM, Ford, Chrysler,
Motorola, Honeywell, Westinghouse, Digital Equipment, Hewlett-Packard,
AT&T, Bethlehem Steel, Polaroid, and GE. Quality-of-work-life programs
may include a wide variety of specific techniques to improve conditions
affecting employee's work experiences, such as team building, job redesign,
participative management, quality circles, work environment improvements, and flextime or other alternative work schedule programs. **Flextime**
programs give employees some control over their own work schedules. For
example, employees might be allowed to begin work anytime between 7 and
9 A.M. and to stop work between 4 and 6 P.M., depending on their starting
times. Or employees might have the option of working a compressed work
schedule of four ten-hour days, instead of five eight-hour days.

In addition to flextime, **alternative work schedule** programs might
include the use of part-time employment, job sharing (where two individuals share the same job, each working part of the day or week), or work at
home. A recent survey of 259 companies found that 42 percent used flex-

time, 13 percent allowed compressed work schedules, 36 percent utilized part-time employees, 17 percent had some job sharing, and 9 percent had employees who were allowed to do at least a portion of their job at home.[23] Aetna Life and Casualty Company is using practically all of these alternative work schedule options with good results. Although the new flexibility has required some challenging adjustments, particularly from managers who have subordinates using these alternatives, on balance managers and employees are pleased. For Aetna, the availability of alternative work schedules has often meant retaining a highly valued employee who otherwise would have quit. One Aetna manager said, "We're not doing flexible work scheduling to be nice, but because it makes business sense."[24]

Quality-of-work-life programs usually have two major objectives: (1) improving the quality of work life for employees and (2) improving group or organizational productivity. Such programs encompass so many change activities that documenting their precise effects is difficult. However, considerable success has been reported in improving employee work attitudes, increasing levels of employee involvement, improving working conditions, and changing organizational culture. Improvements in productivity have also been reported, although the relationship between QWL programs and productivity changes is complex, often indirect, and not easily measured. For example, Figure 22.4 suggests that QWL programs have the potential for improving communication, coordination, motivation, and performance capabilities. These improvements, in turn, may translate into increased productivity.

QWL programs can have negative outcomes as well. For example, middle managers and first-line supervisors sometimes resist QWL programs, perceiving them as increasing employee participation at the expense of their management prerogatives. Unless such resistance is overcome, a QWL pro-

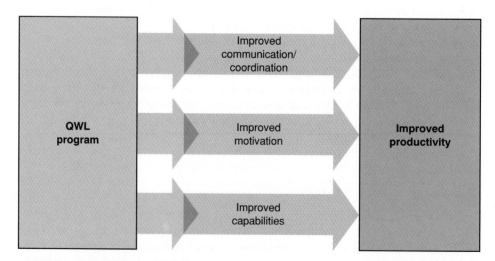

FIGURE 22.4 Potential Effects of QWL Programs on Productivity

Source: E. E. Lawler and G. E. Ledford. Productivity and the Quality of Work Life. *National Productivity Review:* Winter 1981–1982, 29. Reprinted with permission of the publisher. National Productivity Review, 33 West 60th St., New York, NY 10023.

gram may fail or be achieved at a high cost in terms of managerial or supervisory turnover.

TASK- AND TECHNOLOGY-FOCUSED APPROACHES TO CHANGE

The task-focused approach to change emphasizes making changes in the work of employees or groups, while the technology-focused approach concentrates on the technological processes and tools used to perform the work. In practice, task-focused and technology-focused approaches tend to overlap during organizational change efforts. We examine five approaches to organizational change that focus (at least initially) on task and technology: job design, sociotechnical systems, quality circles, high performance-high commitment work systems, and continuous improvement programs.

Job Design

Job design represents a deliberate, planned restructuring of the way work is performed in order to increase employee motivation, involvement, and efficiency—and ultimately improve performance. Job design encompasses a whole family of specific organizational change techniques, including job engineering, job rotation, job enlargement, job enrichment, and the redesign of core task characteristics, which we described fully in Chapter 17.

Each of these job design techniques has been found to be an effective approach to organizational change under certain conditions. All can positively affect task performance, absenteeism, turnover, and job satisfaction. Managers sometimes use specific job design approaches inappropriately, however. For example, job enrichment programs can fail if managers wrongly assume that all employees want enriched work and do not allow for differences in employee needs and values. Job design techniques are perhaps most successful in the context of a comprehensive organizational change program that examines the complex fit among the tasks to be performed, the types of technology used, the structure and culture of the organization or group, and the nature and characteristics of the people doing the work.[25] Recently, studies have shown improvements in the quality of work life and performance and reduced turnover and conflict in organizations that have involved employees in redesigning their own jobs.[26]

Sociotechnical Systems

The **sociotechnical systems** (STS) approach simultaneously focuses on changing both the technical and social aspects of the organization in order to optimize their relationship and thus to increase organizational effectiveness.[27] STS regards the organization as more than just a technical system for making products and providing services. Ultimately, the organization is a collection of human beings—a social system. Changes made in the technical system affect the social fabric of the organization. Thus, in order to manage organizational change effectively, managers must deal with both the social and technical aspects of that change.

Sociotechnical approaches to organizational change usually incorporate a major redesign of the way work is done (the task variable), in addition to emphasizing technological and social issues (the technology and people variables). The sociotechnical systems approach to job design was described in detail in Chapter 17.

From the perspective of organizational change, the idea of autonomous or self-managing work groups is a major contribution of sociotechnical systems theory. **Autonomous groups** or **self-managing teams** are work groups that are self-managing in terms of planning their work, controlling its pace and quality, and making many of the decisions traditionally reserved to management.[28] A self-managing team may determine its own job assignments, work schedules, and even the quantity and quality of its output. STS redesigns work groups to give them a greater measure of control over virtually all the resources and skills needed to produce a specific product or deliver a specific service to a customer.

Individuals in autonomous groups fully participate in task-related decision making and may, as a result, find their jobs to be more meaningful and satisfying. Productivity of autonomous groups is usually equal to or better than that of other types of groups. Other factors, such as labor-management relations, absenteeism, turnover, and cooperation among employees, may also improve. Such improvements should not be taken for granted, however, simply because work groups become more autonomous. For example, a recent study in two Australian minerals-processing plants indicated improvements in work attitudes (satisfaction and commitment) but *increased* absenteeism and turnover among the plant's autonomous groups.[29]

Sociotechnical approaches to organizational change were originally developed in England at the Tavistock Institute, and for many years, most took place in Europe. The Volvo Kalmar Plant in Sweden is a well-known European example of a successful sociotechnical change program. During the 1970s and 1980s, sociotechnical approaches have been used extensively in the United States and Canada to design, build, and manage new plants. The high-involvement plants described in the Preview Case typically incorporate many aspects of the STS approach.

Quality Circles

Quality circles are work groups, generally containing less than a dozen volunteers from the same work area, who meet regularly to monitor and solve job-related quality and/or production problems. Quality circles may also be utilized to improve working conditions, increase the level of employee involvement and commitment, and encourage employee self-development. As such, they are frequently an important component of QWL programs. Adapted initially from Japanese quality-control practices, their use has spread rapidly in the United States. The activities and focus of quality circles has been described as follows:

> The [quality circle] members receive training in problem solving, statistical quality control, and group process. Quality circles generally recommend solu-

tions for quality and productivity problems which management then may implement. A facilitator, usually a specially trained member of management, helps train circle members and ensures that things run smoothly. Typical objectives of QC programs include quality improvement, productivity enhancement, and employee involvement. Circles generally meet four hours a month on company time. Members may get recognition but rarely receive financial rewards.[30]

Quality circles typically have a narrower focus than many of the other change techniques described in this chapter. They also differ from other approaches in that management retains more control over the activities of the employees than is possible, or desirable, in most of the other approaches. The tight control and narrow focus have both advantages and disadvantages.

Although the effects of quality circles often are not carefully evaluated, evidence comparing expected to actual outcomes is beginning to accumulate.[31] So far, the results seem to be mixed. Productivity and quality gains—sometimes substantial—have been reported. For example, at Stanley Works, a New England manufacturer of tools and hardware, quality circles contributed to reducing the scrap rate from 15 percent to 3 percent.[32] Quality circles are often part of comprehensive QWL programs and can foster greater employee involvement in decision making and other aspects of work. However, a number of failures have also been reported. Quality circles often make their greatest contributions relatively quickly. Sustaining these initial successes over a period of time requires considerable energy and creating new challenges to maintain employee interest. Quality circles may not fit well into an organization's culture and are not likely to move the organization toward a highly participative culture if other changes are not made at the same time. Quality circles appear to cope successfully with only a limited range of problems; accurate diagnosis is essential to ensure that the problems facing the organization can be best addressed by this approach.

High Performance-High Commitment Work Systems

Early in 1983, Westinghouse opened the doors of its newest defense plant—the Westinghouse Electronic Assembly Plant (EAP) in College Station, Texas. The EAP manufactures printed wiring assemblies for various military radar systems. From the start, Westinghouse sought to apply innovative work practices at EAP. The goal was to create a participative management structure and work culture that would lead to a sense of ownership in the work force. Employees in the plant work in eight- to twelve-person teams responsible for their own performance appraisal, devising solutions to many production problems, doing some scheduling, and so on. All employees are on salary and earn pay raises based on skill testing. Notice the similarities between these characteristics and those of the high-involvement plants described in the Preview Case. The plant was designed using sociotechnical systems concepts and carefully integrates the semiautonomous work teams with advanced automated equipment and sophisticated workflow patterns. This blending of technology and teamwork creates a **high performance-high commitment** (HP-HC) **work system.** The EAP has received much favorable publicity and national recognition in the popular business press. Performance achievements in quality, productivity, and cycle time have resulted in Westinghouse awards for excellence. Manufacturing costs for circuit assemblies in the EAP are one half that of Westinghouse's traditional plants. In a comparable Baltimore plant, one worker builds one and a half electronic circuit assemblies per day. In the College Station EAP, each worker builds a dozen. The Westinghouse EAP is further described in a case study at the end of this chapter.

We introduced the concept of HP-HC work cultures in Chapter 15. High performance-high commitment work systems are designed to foster a work culture and design having the following characteristics:

- *Delegation.* People who have the most relevant and timely information or the most appropriate skills are given responsibility for decisions and actions.

- *Teamwork across boundaries.* All employees in the organization are focused on servicing the product and the customer for the product, rather than their function or department.

- *Empowerment.* Everyone is expected to accept and exercise the responsibility necessary to do their jobs and help others accomplish theirs. Providing opportunities to be responsible *empowers* people—the opposite of limiting roles and contributions. No one feels free to say, "It's not my job."

- *Integration of people and technology.* People are in charge of the technology, instead of the technology being in charge of the people.

- *A shared sense of purpose.* People in the work culture share a vision of the organization's purpose and the methods for accomplishing this purpose.[33]

An underlying assumption of this approach is that superior technology, efficient task design, congruent structure and processes, good planning, and the like are necessary—but not sufficient—for high performance. Individuals and work groups must be *committed* to make the technology, task design, structure, or strategy work. The HP-HC system is designed to manage human, technological, and financial resources efficiently and to more fully engage the talents and capacities of employees. These efficiencies are central to the ability to adapt and compete in a global economy.[34]

Continuous Improvement Programs

Continuous improvement programs (CIPs) are designed to harness employee experience and commitment to improving both the products or services and the work practices of the organization.[35] An underlying philosophy is that this improvement must be a continuing focus of managers and employees and not be limited to one-time programs or "quick-fix" solutions for productivity or quality problems. CIPs are sometimes called total quality control (TQC) or total quality management (TQM) programs. Such programs may be a key component of a comprehensive cultural change program (see Chapter 15).

The focus on quality and continuous improvement is considered crucial for effectively competing in the global economy. The U.S. government created the Malcolm Baldridge National Quality Award to honor organizations that attain "world-class" quality in their products, services, and operations. (The award is named after a Reagan administration secretary of commerce who was killed in a 1987 horse-riding accident.) In 1990, the winners of the Baldridge award were the Cadillac division of General Motors, the Rochester, Minnesota, computer plant of IBM, Federal Express, and Wallace Company, a small Houston pipe distributor. Cadillac, for example, moved from seventeenth place to fourth in consumer satisfaction (displacing Honda Motor Company), reduced warranty defects by 60 percent in three years, and increased productivity by 50 percent between 1986 and 1989.[36]

The examiners and judges look for eight critical factors in organizations competing for the Baldridge award. These factors, which follow, also provide insight into the key components of continuous improvement programs.

- A plan to keep improving all operations continuously.
- A system for measuring these improvements accurately.
- A strategic plan based on benchmarks that compare the company's performance with the world's best.
- A close partnership with suppliers and customers that feeds improvements back into the operation.
- A deep understanding of the customers so that their wants can be translated into products.
- A long-lasting relationship with customers, going beyond the delivery of the product to include sales, service, and ease of maintenance.
- A focus on preventing mistakes, rather than merely correcting them.
- A commitment to improving quality that runs from the top of the organization to the bottom.[37]

This chapter's Across Cultures describes the philosophy of continuous improvement at Toyota.

STRUCTURE- AND STRATEGY-FOCUSED APPROACHES TO CHANGE

Organizationwide change programs frequently have as their goals changes in organizational structure or design, strategy, and culture. Structure-focused approaches to change involve redefining positions or roles and relationships among positions and redesigning department, division, or organization structure. Strategy-focused approaches involve a reexamination of the organization's basic mission or goals, as well as the specific plans or strategies for attaining those goals. Many of the approaches presented in this chapter can be used to change organizational culture (see Chapter 15). Below, we discuss adaptive structures and examine issues of strategic change in organizations.

◆ *ACROSS CULTURES*

WHY TOYOTA KEEPS GETTING BETTER

 A key slogan at Toyota is *kaizen*, which means "continuous improvement." While many organizations strive for dramatic changes, Toyota seems to excel at doing lots of little things better and better. In 1990, Toyota had an astounding 43 percent of the new car sales in Japan and was the third-largest automaker in the world (behind General Motors and Ford). Projections are that Toyota will surpass Ford in worldwide sales by 1993.

Many industry observers and analysts consider Toyota as, simply, the best carmaker in the world—ranking it tops in quality, productivity, and efficiency. Its factories produce a wide range of models (fifty-nine different passenger cars, for example), all built with unequaled precision. The company originated just-in-time mass production and continues to be its leading practitioner.

Traditional mass production in the auto industry means that finished cars are produced in large quantities and shipped to dealers where they sit as inventory on their lots. Under Toyota's just-in-time system (as it works in Japan), a car is not built until an order is placed for it. Japanese dealers have on-line computers to order cars directly from the factory. The customer can get his or her built-to-order car in seven to ten days. This leads to considerable savings—the factory can carefully balance production with demand; the dealer has almost no inventory (just a collection of models for show). A key aspect of the Toyota just-in-time system is a carefully developed and managed network of some 230 suppliers that feed parts into this production system on command. The just-in-time system may sound simple in concept, but it took Toyota twenty years to perfect it.

Toyota has a total dedication to a philosophy of continuous improvement. Iwao Isomura, head of human resources, stated: "Our current success is the best reason to change things." Company personnel seem to exist in a state of permanent dissatisfaction. Shoichiro Toyoda, the company president, describes the dissatisfaction this way: "We felt we suffered from large corporation disease. It had become extremely difficult for top executives to convey their feelings to our workers. So we embarked on a cure. We have a saying: A large man has difficulty exercising his wits fully." Currently, Toyota is restructuring its management hierarchy, continuing to refine already elegant manufacturing processes, tinkering with its organizational culture, and developing a global strategy for the twenty-first century.[38]

Adaptive Structures

Organizational structure and its design characteristics were examined in Chapter 18. As organizations grow increasingly complex, they often need new ways of organizing their activities. They particularly need more flexible and adaptive designs than those of the traditional mechanistic system, with its rigid hierarchy and standardized procedures. Here, we explore three forms of organizational structure or design that characterize flexible, adaptive organizations: collateral organization, matrix organization, and network organization.

Collateral Organization   A **collateral organization** is a parallel, co-existing organization that can be used to supplement the existing formal organization. This organizational form (sometimes called parallel organization or parallel learning structures)[39] utilizes groups of people outside normal communication and authority channels to identify and solve difficult problems that the formal organization may be unwilling or unable to solve. A collateral organization has norms—ways of working together, making decisions, and solving problems—that are different from those of the rest of the organization. However, the collateral organization requires no new people, is carefully linked to the formal organization, and coexists with it.

Collateral organizations have the following characteristics:

- All communication channels are open and connected. Managers and employees freely communicate without being restricted to the formal channels of the organizational hierarchy.

- There is a rapid and complete exchange of relevant information on problems and issues. The outputs of the parallel learning structure are ideas, solutions to problems, and innovation.

- The norms in use encourage careful questioning and analysis of goals, assumptions, methods, alternatives, and criteria for evaluation.

- Managers can approach and enlist others in the organization to help solve a problem; they are not restricted to their formal subordinates.

- Mechanisms are developed to link the collateral and formal organization.[40]

Collateral designs have been successfully used by automobile manufacturers, banks, high technology firms, hospitals, research and development laboratories, and universities. Collateral organizations seem appealing, but improvements stemming from this approach are not yet well-documented. Perhaps a major advantage of the collateral form of organization is that it gives managers a way to match problems with organizational structures best suited to solve them. For example, the formal organization may best deal with routine production problems, whereas poorly structured or defined problems may best be handled by problem-solving groups operating outside the formal structure.

Some evidence suggests that the real advantages of collateral organizations may be other than in problem solving. Collateral organizations create more complex roles for employees. Employees interact with different people than they would in a group restricted to the formal hierarchy, and they interact with them in different ways—that is, the norms have been changed. These complex roles may provide more opportunities for individuals to be involved, engage in meaningful work, have control over their jobs, and gain needed satisfactions from their work. In addition, collateral organizations may be particularly good at developing managerial skills, coping with crises requiring decentralized decision making, and fostering organizational innovation.[41]

Matrix Organization Many organizations have turned to a matrix design to address the limitations of mechanistic or bureaucratic structures. As we described in Chapter 18, a **matrix organization** represents a balance between organizing resources according to products or functions, such as marketing, production, finance, human resources, and research and development.

A mutually beneficial relationship often exists between the matrix form of organization and the capacity to change. For example, many features of OD programs, such as an emphasis on collaborative behavior and the effective use of groups, are also important for implementing a matrix structure with its decentralized decision making and extensive use of temporary task forces and teams. In general, the matrix form helps to create a culture receptive to organizational improvement efforts.

Changing an organization to a matrix is never easy. Often, managers need a people-focused change strategy to facilitate the transition. For example, team building has successfully helped organizations introduce matrix structures. One senior executive put it this way: "The challenge is not so much to build a matrix structure as it is to create a matrix in the minds of our managers."[42]

The matrix design is appealing due to its flexibility and adaptability. It may be superior to other organizational forms when the organization uses complex technology, faces rapidly changing market conditions, and needs a high degree of cooperation among projects and functions. However, a matrix structure is costly to implement and maintain and can be extremely difficult to manage effectively, as we pointed out in Chapter 18.[43]

Network Organization The **network organization,** as described in Chapter 18, is a complex mosaic of lateral communication, decision making, and control processes. Although a network organization might have an organization chart showing the typical hierarchical authority and communication relationships, this chart cannot begin to capture the reality of this complex organizational form. Network organizations share some features of both matrix and collateral organizations yet place more emphasis on sophisticated information technologies to coordinate activities and perform work. Managers in a network organization function much like switchboard operators in terms of coordination and control. They can pull together temporary teams of employees to bring expertise to bear on projects and concerns as needed. The collaborative behaviors and attitudes characterizing the network organization are similar to those typical of the high performance-high commitment work system described earlier. As pointed out in Chapter 18, network organizations are increasingly utilized by global organizations that need this flexibility to function effectively in the international arena.

Strategic Change

At its most basic level, a strategy is a *plan*—some purposefully intended course of action to attain organizational goals.[44] **Strategic change** is planned organizational change designed to alter the organization's intended courses of action to attain its goals. Strategic change may include assessment and redefinition of the goals themselves.

A good example of a strategic change program is provided by the process of open systems planning. **Open systems planning** is designed to help an organization systematically assess its environment and develop a strategic response to it. It consists of the following steps:

- Assess the external environment in terms of its expectations and demands on the organization's behavior.

- Assess the organization's current response to these environmental demands.

- Identify the organization's core mission.

- Create a realistic scenario of future environmental demands and organizational responses.

- Create an ideal scenario of future environmental demands and organizational responses.

- Compare the present with the ideal future and prepare an action plan for reducing the discrepancy.[45]

Central to many approaches to strategic change, including open systems planning, is the concept of visioning.[46] In general, **visioning** refers to choosing a desired future state or condition for the organization. Visioning includes identifying and articulating for organizational members the central or core mission and goals of the system, as well as specifying, at least broadly, how the goals or future state is to be attained. In Chapter 12, we discussed how visioning is a crucial component of leadership; it is also a crucial aspect of most approaches to strategic organizational change.

Issues of strategic change need to be addressed in comprehensive organizational change programs.[47] The following In Practice describes strategic issues in managing change at BankAmerica.

IN PRACTICE

THE TURNAROUND AT BANKAMERICA

BankAmerica Corporation was the largest bank holding company in the world in 1981, when the U.S. banking industry changed significantly. The corporation had been very prosperous in the highly regulated banking industry, with annual profits increasing for eighteen years in a row. BankAmerica knew its world was about to change but did not fully appreciate how dramatic the changes would be from deregulation, increased competition, and an unstable global economy. The corporation was unable to respond rapidly enough to these changes and, by 1986, the company was on its knees:

- Accumulated net losses were $1.8 billion.
- Dividends on its common stock were suspended in November 1985.
- Another major bank was attempting a hostile takeover.
- Regulators were alarmed by the deteriorating capital situation and leaning heavily on the bank to make changes.

At this point, BankAmerica's ability to survive as an independent organization was in doubt. Faced with these challenges, BankAmerica undertook a strategic change program designed to turn the company around.

BankAmerica's strategic actions had several components. First, the entire business was reassessed. What had been successful in the past was no longer working, so new strategic objectives were developed. In line with its new strategic vision, both the organization of the bank and its approach to banking were restructured. For example, BankAmerica decided to concentrate on providing banking services to the western United States and, subsequently, reduced its banking services in other regions of the country. The new strategy also focused on reducing the bank's costs to be competitive in the rapidly changing financial services industry.

Another key component of BankAmerica's strategic plan was an emphasis on teamwork throughout the organization. The belief was that in order for the new strategy to be effective, every employee must feel personally involved in the change process, and responsible for an important part of the bank's recovery efforts. Because of the staff reductions that accompanied BankAmerica's reorganization, developing this sense of teamwork in the surviving employees was an especially difficult challenge. Clear communications of plans and intentions for change were particularly crucial in implementing the new strategy.

By 1990, BankAmerica had returned to profitability. Costs were cut dramatically, and revenues and market share were up. The bank's dividend to stockholders was reinstated in 1989. Without the fundamental change in strategy and operations, the bank could not have survived.[48]

ETHICAL ISSUES IN ORGANIZATIONAL CHANGE

Serious ethical issues can exist in any organizational change program, no matter how carefully managed it might be. Managers and employees need to be aware of potential ethical concerns during organizational change. Ethical issues may exist in four major areas: change approach selection, change target selection, managerial responsibilities, and manipulation.[49]

In this chapter, we have discussed a number of approaches to organizational change. Clearly, managers must choose the approach or combination of approaches deemed best for the situation. However, ethical issues could appear in the criteria used for selecting an approach. Does the manager or change agent have a vested interest in using a particular technique such that other alternatives do not receive a fair hearing? Do individuals involved in the organizational diagnosis have biases that might predetermine the problems identified and thus influence the change approach chosen?

What is to be the target of change? Which individuals, groups, or departments of the organization will the change effort focus on? Who will make this determination? These issues of change-target selection raise ethical concerns about participation in the change program. Which members of the firm participate in diagnosing, planning, and implementing the change and to what degree? To what extent can managers make choices about changing the behaviors of employees, and where should the line be drawn in this regard? Earlier in our discussion of power and political behavior, we pointed out that influencing the behavior of others is an appropriate managerial function. The conclusion was to use power fairly and appropriately to achieve the organization's legitimate goals. Similarly, the organization cannot change unless employees change their behavior. However, serious ethical concerns arise when managers attempt inappropriate change or make choices concerning what is to be changed that overstep the bounds of their legitimate roles.

A major ethical concern in the area of managerial responsibility involves whose goals and values are to guide the change effort. Whose vision guides the change? Whose values influence the adoption of goals and methods chosen to accomplish them? Organizational change is never value-neutral. The value systems of managers and employees always underlie assumptions about what the organization should be doing. Ethical concerns could arise if managers involved in the change process fail to recognize the potential problems associated with incompatible goals and values held by organizational members.

Finally, the area of manipulation concerns the fundamental question of power in the change process. It is difficult to make changes in organizations without some employees feeling manipulated in some way. Often, the organization needs to make changes that do, in fact, result in some individuals or groups being worse off after the change than they were before. Ethical issues exist concerning the degree of openness surrounding planned changes. To what extent should the organization disclose all aspects of the change in advance? To what degree do employees have the right to participate in, or at least be aware of, changes that affect them, even indirectly?

These are not easy questions. Managers and employees need some basis for recognizing the potential ethical concerns involved in organizational change, so that fair and informed choices can be made. As a starting point, organizations need to be sensitive to the very real potential for ethical problems during planned change programs.

SUMMARY

An accurate diagnosis of organizational problems is the starting point for any effective organizational change effort. Based on this diagnosis, managers may choose among a variety of change strategies. Often, a combination of approaches is most effective in bringing about changes in the organization. Managers and employees must understand the likely effects of various change approaches and carefully match change programs with the problems they are intended to solve.

If the initial focus of the change effort is to be directed toward the people variable, managers might choose to use survey feedback, team building, process consultation, or quality-of-work-life programs. When the initial focus is on task or technology, organizations would typically utilize job design, sociotechnical systems, quality circles, high performance-high commitment work systems, or continuous improvement programs. The latter two of these often involve significant changes in organizational culture. Structure-focused approaches to change might include creating more adaptive organizational structures, such as collateral, matrix, or network designs. Strategic change is often the focus of organizationwide change efforts. Open systems planning is one method of strategic change.

No approach to organizational change is likely to be successful unless it addresses several, if not all, of the people, task, technology, structure, and strategy variables. Comprehensive organizational change programs, regardless of their initial focus, often make simultaneous changes in several aspects of the organization. In practice, the approaches presented in this chapter are commonly used in combination to manage organizational change.

Managers and employees need to be aware of and knowledgeable about potential ethical issues that can arise during organizational change. Ethical issues could exist in selection of the change approach, selection of the change targets, managerial responsibilities for the goals selected, and potential manipulation of employees.

Key Words and Concepts

Alternative work schedule
Autonomous groups
Collateral organization
Continuous improvement programs
Flextime
High performance-high
  commitment work system
Job design
Matrix organization
Network organization
Open systems planning

Organizational diagnosis
Process consultation
Quality circles
Quality-of-work-life programs
Self-managing teams
Sociotechnical systems
Strategic change
Survey feedback
Team building
Visioning

Discussion Questions

1. Explain the importance of an accurate diagnosis of organizational problems prior to implementing a change program.

2. Is it always possible for employees to have a high level of participation in organizational change programs? Why or why not?

3. Using your own words, write a brief summary description of each of the four people-focused change approaches presented in this chapter.

4. Using your own words, write a brief summary description of each of the five task- and technology-focused change approaches presented in this chapter.

5. What are the similarities and differences between survey feedback and team building?

6. Compare and contrast quality-of-work-life programs and high performance-high commitment work systems.

7. Explain why both HP-HC work systems and continuous improvement programs may require significant changes in organizational culture to be effective.

8.   Based on your own experiences, describe an organization or group that needed change. Which of the change approaches presented would you use? Why?

UNDERSTANDING QUALITY SYSTEMS: THE WESTINGHOUSE CORPORATION

During the 1970s, the Westinghouse Defense and Electronics Group anticipated significant growth in its electronic defense business. To satisfy this growth requirement, a new satellite facility was built in College Station, Texas. The facility was named Westinghouse Electronic Assembly Plant (EAP) and was developed in response to a growing market in high-technology wiring assemblies. In addition, the plant was designed to provide a competitive advantage for Westinghouse Corporation by having a "factory of the future" in its assembly-plant system. The plant design team created a state-of-the-art assembly system that included modern management practices, advanced information systems, and the latest in engineering technologies. Due to the anticipated growth and competition in the electronics defense business, EAP would be required to handle a broad range of product lines, small lot sizes, a high rate of change in product design, and ever-increasing quality requirements.

In 1983, the 186,000-square-foot Westinghouse Electronic Assembly Plant opened its doors and began producing printed wiring assemblies. These "circuit board" assemblies are part of a larger component that the parent plant, Westinghouse-Baltimore, supplies to external customers for use in land-based and airborne radar systems. EAP employs more than five hundred people—approximately four hundred technicians, sixty professionals, and forty managers.

By industry standards, the plant's start up was relatively smooth. The investments in the latest equipment and team-concept management technologies seemed to be paying off as the learning curve and adjustment period leveled off. It was not too long before the plant seemed to operate in a rather efficient and productive manner.

As with any organization, change was inevitable. In the latter part of 1984, the U.S. government clamped down on all defense contractors. New compliance procedures were established for all military suppliers. A major competitor of the Westinghouse Defense and Electronic Group was shut down after the government completed its internal audit of its facilities and found major problems with the product- and process-quality systems of its suppliers. An inability to change internal quality systems was threatening the very survival of defense contractors.

Although EAP was producing "good" quality (roughly 90 percent meeting standards on the first time through), the new compliance procedures required substantial changes and improvements in work processes and procedures. In March 1985, the EAP management team asked each member to answer the question, "If you owned this business, how would you fix it?" Using the ideas of the management team, a committee was formed under the direction of Keith Hudspeth, then product line manager, to develop a plan of action for solving the quality problem at EAP.

Hudspeth and his team started their investigation by reevaluating the production process in the plant. A few key questions were formulated to guide this evaluation: 1) How do we change our system to comply with our new customer requirements?; 2) What information are our work teams currently using to manage their processes?; and 3) Are we, management, managing the proper business processes?

After some lengthy discussions with nonexempt technicians, first-line supervisors, and other management team members, some answers were developed to these questions. First, in order to change the system to comply with the new customer requirements, technicians must know what the new requirements are and how important they are to survival. Management must create an awareness of the problem with all employees. Second, the supervisors keep track of a variety of information concerning work team performance. Supervisors need to have the technicians involved and measuring the critical information of the business. The plant must get "back to the basics" in measuring performance. Finally, because the plant was so new, there was a tendency to continue with the same "close supervision" management style used for a start-up operation. Management has to realize that the plant is in full operation and to let the employees begin to manage the daily operations of the business.

With these issues on the table, Hudspeth's committee established three task teams consisting of a cross-section of managers, engineers, and technicians who were given the responsibility to propose a plan of attack for EAP. From all the information that Hudspeth and his team had previously gathered in their production system analysis, the issues for the new task teams were formalized:

1. A need existed for a system to allow EAP to relay the vision and goals of the customer requirements to all employees.
2. A need existed for a system to change the current internal measures and allow EAP employees to measure the important aspects of the business from the customer's viewpoint.
3. The plant needed a system that would allow employees to assume responsibility for their own destiny, and EAP must reward and recognize employee efforts in this direction.

Each task team was given an issue and was asked to report back to the committee with their ideas. This input would be incorporated into a total plan to resolve EAP's pressing concerns.[50]

QUESTIONS

1. Assume you are the Westinghouse team responsible for developing a comprehensive plan to resolve these issues. Ask yourself, "If I owned this business, how would I fix it?" Explain and defend your plan.

CHAPARRAL STEEL COMPANY

Texas Industries Incorporated (TXI) is in the cement and concrete business. It decided to start a steel company in Midlothian, Texas. To some observers, it was an odd decision. For years, the U.S. steel industry has been plagued with severe problems, including formidable competition from abroad, slack demand, high labor costs, aging mills, and rigorous antipollution laws that require huge investments in nonproductive equipment. The industry has often seemed incapable of change, in part because of an inability to generate adequate profits for investment in needed changes and in part because of rigid organizational structures and processes.

You would not know that steel is a declining industry from looking at Chaparral Steel Company. By 1988, the firm had doubled in size since its founding in 1975, and, despite low-cost competition in the international markets, the firm exports steel to Europe and Canada. Chaparral would sell to Japan as well if it could get an import permit. As described by the *Harvard Business Review:*

Chaparral is not your run-of-the-mill steel company. It is a minimill operation, 30 miles outside Dallas, with an enviable record for improving productivity and bringing new technology on-line. Its organization is lean and flexible, with virtually no barriers between laboratory and plant floor. True, its limited product line gives it strong advantages over fully integrated producers. But its real accomplishment—its openness to change—is not the result of its favored position in the steel industry. It comes, instead, from a deliberate, clearly defined vision of how a company, any company, can remain flexible.

One of Chaparral's objectives has been to make research a "line" function. The people who make the steel are responsible for keeping their production process on the cutting edge of technology. The plant is, in effect, the laboratory. This approach has paid off. By 1991, a unique casting process had been developed and tested by Chaparral's production employees. This process casts molten steel into beams that are so close to their final shape that milling stages needed by conventional casting processes have been eliminated. The reduction in costs stemming from this process allows Chaparral to produce construction beams at the lowest cost in the world.

Chaparral made everyone in the company a member of the sales department. In 1991, all nine hundred employees were responsible for making sales calls. The philosophy is that all employees—from telephone operators to rolling mill operators—should be concerned with customer relations. A customer having problems with one of Chaparral's products might be visited by a team of employees, including the person who sold the product, an employee from production, someone from metallurgy, and so on.

Employees of the firm are shareholders. Conversely, management is directly involved in the production process. Employees move a great deal from job to job in order to provide more flexibility in planning and operations and also to give them a broad understanding of the firm's activities. Chaparral is attempting to reduce the distinction between production and maintenance workers. The connecting link in all this is involvement and ownership. People are responsible for their own product and its quality.

Perhaps not being mired in the traditions, rigid organizational structures, and approaches

of the past is Chaparral's greatest advantage. As explained by Robert Rogers, president and chief executive officer of TXI, speaking to a *Wall Street Journal* reporter:

> We went into the carbon-steel business when everyone else was going out of it. The biggest advantage we had was that we didn't have any plant, didn't have any customers, didn't have any employees or management and we didn't really know anything about how to make steel.

Chaparral does not desire to become the new "Big Steel." But with its imaginative approaches, its willingness to try new things, and its flexible organization, it is certainly demonstrating how to be a highly competitive little steel.[51]

QUESTIONS:

1. List the ideas and concepts from this chapter that appear, in one form or another, in this case description.

2. Describe the strategy, structure, culture, and approach to managing change of Chaparral Steel Company.

3. Would you describe Chaparral Steel Company as a high performance-high commitment work system? Why or why not?

References

1. Lawler, E. E. The New Plant Revolution Revisited. *Organizational Dynamics*, Autumn 1990, 5–14; Woodman, R. W. Organizational Change and Development: New Arenas for Inquiry and Action. *Journal of Management*, 1989, *15*, 205–228. See also Lawler, E. E. *High-Involvement Management*. San Francisco: Jossey-Bass, 1986; Weisbord, M. R. *Productive Workplaces: Organizing and Managing for Dignity, Meaning, and Community*. San Francisco: Jossey-Bass, 1987.

2. For additional perspectives, see Porras, J. I., and Robertson, P. J. Organization Development Theory: A Typology and Evaluation. In R. W. Woodman and W. A. Pasmore (eds.), *Research in Organizational Change and Development*, vol. 1. Greenwich, Conn.: JAI Press, 1987, 1–57; Porras, J. I., and Silvers, R. C. Organization Development and Transformation. *Annual Review of Psychology*, 1991, *42*, 51–78; Mirvis, P. H. Organization Development: Part II—A Revolutionary Perspective. In W. A. Pasmore and R. W. Woodman (eds.), *Research in Organizational Change and Development*, vol. 4. Greenwich, Conn.: JAI Press, 1990, 1–66.

3. Burke, W. W. *Organization Development: A Normative View*. Reading, Mass.: Addison-Wesley, 1987, 80–110; Cummings, T. G., and Huse, E. F. *Organization Development and Change*, 4th ed. St. Paul: West, 1989, 64–87; Jackson, C. N., and Manning, M. R. (eds.), *Organization Development Annual Volume III: Diagnosing Client Organizations*. Alexandria, Va.: American Society for Training and Development, 1990; Weisbord, M. R. Towards a New Practice Theory of OD: Notes on Snapshooting and Moviemaking. In W. A. Pasmore and R. W. Woodman (eds.), *Research in Organizational Change and Development*, vol. 2. Greenwich, Conn.: JAI Press, 1988, 59–96.

4. Adapted from Carnall, C. A. *Managing Change in Organizations*. London: Prentice Hall, 1990, 68–69.

5. Beckhard, R. Strategies for Large System Change. *Sloan Management Review,* 1975, *16,* 43–55; Beckhard, R., and Harris, R. T. *Organizational Transitions: Managing Complex Change.* Reading, Mass.: Addison-Wesley, 1987, 29–44; Spector, B. A. From Bogged Down to Fired Up: Inspiring Organizational Change. *Sloan Management Review,* Summer 1989, 29–34.

6. Woodman, R. W. Issues and Concerns in Organizational Diagnosis. In C. N. Jackson and M. R. Manning (eds.), *Organization Development Annual Volume III: Diagnosing Client Organizations.* Alexandria, Va.: American Society for Training and Development, 1990, 5–10.

7. Zeira, Y., and Avedisian, J. Organizational Planned Change: Assessing the Chances for Success. *Organizational Dynamics,* Spring 1989, 31–45.

8. Eden, D. Creating Expectation Effects in OD: Applying Self-Fulfilling Prophecy. In W. A. Pasmore and R. W. Woodman (eds.), *Research in Organizational Change and Development,* Vol. 2. Greenwich, Conn.: JAI Press, 1988, 235–267; Pond, S. B., Armenakis, A. A., and Green, S. B. The Importance of Employee Expectations in Organizational Diagnosis. *Journal of Applied Behavioral Science,* 1984, *20,* 167–180; Woodman, R. W., Organizational Change and Development, 209–210; Woodman, R. W., and Tolchinsky, P. D. Expectation Effects: Implications for Organization Development Interventions. In D. D. Warrick (ed.), *Contemporary Organization Development: Current Thinking and Applications.* Glenview, Ill.: Scott, Foresman, 1985, 477–487.

9. Woodman, Issues and Concerns in Organizational Diagnosis, 7.

10. Sikes, W. Basic Principles of Change. In W. Sikes, A. B. Drexler, and J. Gant (eds.), *The Emerging Practice of Organization Development.* Alexandria, Va.: NTL Institute for Applied Behavioral Science, 1989, 179.

11. For descriptions of survey feedback and its effects, see Cummings and Huse, *Organization Development and Change,* 188–193; French, W. L., and Bell, C. H. *Organization Development: Behavioral Science Interventions for Organization Improvement,* 4th ed. Englewood Cliffs, N.J.: Prentice Hall, 1990, 169–172.

12. See, for example, Hirschhorn, L. *Managing in the New Team Environment.* Reading, Mass.: Addison-Wesley, 1991.

13. Beckhard, R. Optimizing Team Building Efforts. *Journal of Contemporary Business,* 1972, *1*(3), 23–32; Dyer, W. G. *Team Building: Issues and Alternatives,* 2d ed. Reading, Mass.: Addison-Wesley, 1987, 22–23.

14. Allender, M. C. Productivity Enhancement: A New Teamwork Approach. *National Productivity Review,* Spring 1984, 181–189; Sundstrom, E., DeMeuse, K. P., and Futrell, D. Work Teams: Applications and Effectiveness. *American Psycholo-*

gist, 1990, *45,* 120–133; Woodman, R. W., and Sherwood, J. J. The Role of Team Development in Organizational Effectiveness: A Critical Review. *Psychological Bulletin,* 1980, *88,* 166–186.

15. Rigdon, J. E. Team Builders Shine in Perilous Waters. *Wall Street Journal,* October 29, 1990, B1.

16. Woodman, R. W., and Sherwood, J. J. Effects of Team Development Intervention: A Field Experiment. *Journal of Applied Behavioral Science,* 1980, *16,* 211–227.

17. Adapted from French and Bell, *Organization Development,* 6–7.

18. Schein, E. H. *Process Consultation, Volume I: Its Role in Organization Development,* 2d ed. Reading, Mass.: Addison-Wesley, 1988, 11.

19. Burke, W. W. *Organization Development: Principles and Practices.* Boston: Little, Brown, 1982, 282–286; Cummings and Huse, *Organization Development and Change,* 161–170.

20. Cutcher-Gershenfeld, J. The Impact on Economic Performance of a Transformation in Workplace Relations. *Industrial and Labor Relations Review,* 1991, *44,* 241–260.

21. Pasmore, W. A. A Comprehensive Approach to Planning an OD/QWL Strategy. In D. D. Warrick (ed.), *Contemporary Organization Development: Current Thinking and Applications.* Glenview, Ill.: Scott, Foresman, 1985, 205.

22. Sashkin, M., and Burke, W. W. Organization Development in the 1980's. *Journal of Management,* 1987, *13,* 393–417.

23. Trost, C., and Hymowitz, C. Careers Start Giving in to Family Needs. *Wall Street Journal,* June 18, 1990, B1.

24. Hymowitz, C. As Aetna Adds Flextime, Bosses Learn to Cope. *Wall Street Journal,* June 18, 1990, B1, B5.

25. Griffin, R. W., and Woodman, R. W. Utilizing Task Redesign Strategies within Organization Development Programs. In D. D. Warrick (ed.), *Contemporary Organization Development: Current Thinking and Applications.* Glenview, Ill.: Scott, Foresman, 1985, 308–319.

26. Perlman, S. L. Employees Redesign Their Jobs. *Personnel Journal,* November 1990, 37–40.

27. Pasmore, W. A. *Designing Effective Organizations: The Sociotechnical Systems Perspective.* New York: Wiley, 1988; Shani, A. B., and Elliott, O. Sociotechnical Systems Design in Transition. In W. Sikes, A. B. Drexler, and J. Gants (eds.), *The Emerging Practice of Organization Development.* Alexandria, Va.: NTL Institute for Applied Behavioral Science, 1989, 187–198.

28. Manz, C. Beyond Self-Managing Work Teams: Toward Self-Leading Teams in the Workplace. In W. A. Pasmore and R. W. Woodman (eds.), *Research in Organizational Change and Development,* vol. 4. Greenwich, Conn.: JAI Press, 1990, 273–299.

29. Cordery, J. L., Mueller, W. S., and Smith, L. M. Attitudinal and Behavioral Effects of Autono-

mous Group Working: A Longitudinal Field Study. *Academy of Management Journal,* 1991, *34,* 464–476.

30. Lawler, E. E., and Mohrman, S. A. Quality Circles after the Fad. *Harvard Business Review,* January–February 1985, 66.

31. Adam, E. E. Quality Circle Performance. *Journal of Management,* 1991, *17,* 25–39; Griffin, R. W. Consequences of Quality Circles in an Industrial Setting: A Longitudinal Assessment. *Academy of Management Journal,* 1988, *31,* 338–358; Steel, R. P., and Lloyd, R. F. Cognitive, Affective, and Behavioral Outcomes of Participation in Quality Circles: Conceptual and Empirical Findings. *Journal of Applied Behavioral Science,* 1988, *24,* 1–17.

32. Calonius, E. Smart Moves by Quality Champs. *Fortune,* Spring/Summer 1991, 24.

33. Sherwood, J. J. Creating Work Cultures with Competitive Advantage. *Organizational Dynamics,* Winter 1988, 5–26.

34. Mohrman, S. A., and Cummings, T. G. *Self-Designing Organizations: Learning How to Create High Performance.* Reading, Mass.: Addison-Wesley, 1989; Woodman, Organizational Change and Development, 218–219.

35. Schroeder, D. M., and Robinson, A. G. America's Most Successful Export to Japan: Continuous Improvement Programs. *Sloan Management Review,* Spring 1991, 67–81; Vansina, L. S. Total Quality Control: An Overall Organizational Improvement Strategy. *National Productivity Review,* Winter 1989/1990, 59–73.

36. Main, J. How to Win the Baldridge Award. *Fortune,* April 23, 1990, 108.

37. Yoder, S. K., Fuchsberg, G., and Stertz, B. A. All That's Lacking Is Bert Parks Singing 'Cadillac, Cadillac.' *Wall Street Journal,* December 13, 1990, A1, A4.

38. Adapted from Taylor, A. Why Toyota Keeps Getting Better and Better and Better. *Fortune,* November 19, 1990, 66–79.

39. Bushe, G. R., and Shani, A. B. *Parallel Learning Structures: Increasing Innovation in Bureaucracies.* Reading, Mass.: Addison-Wesley, 1991.

40. Bushe, G. R., and Shani, A. B. Parallel Learning Structure Interventions in Bureaucratic Organizations. In W. A. Pasmore and R. W. Woodman (eds.), *Research in Organizational Change and Development,* vol. 4. Greenwich, Conn.: JAI Press, 1990, 167–194; Zand, D. E. Collateral Organization: A New Change Strategy. *Journal of Applied Behavioral Science,* 1974, *10,* 63–89.

41. Rubinstein, D., and Woodman, R. W. Spiderman and the Burma Raiders: Collateral Organization Theory in Action. *Journal of Applied Behavioral Science,* 1984, *20,* 1–21.

42. Bartlett, C. A., and Ghoshal, S. Matrix Management: Not a Structure, a Frame of Mind. *Harvard Business Review,* July–August 1990, 145.

43. Larson, E. W., and Gobeli, D. H. Matrix Management: Contradictions and Insights. *California Management Review,* Summer 1987, 126–138.

44. Mintzberg, H. The Strategy Concept I: Five Ps for Strategy. *California Management Review,* Fall 1987, 11–24.

45. Cummings and Huse, *Organization Development and Change,* 402–403.

46. See, for example, Barczak, G., Smith, C., and Wilemon, D. Managing Large-Scale Organizational Change. *Organizational Dynamics,* Autumn 1987, 23–35.

47. Bartunek, J. M., and Louis, M. R. The Interplay of Organizational Development and Organizational Transformation. In W. A. Pasmore and R. W. Woodman (eds.), *Research in Organizational Change and Development,* vol. 2. Greenwich, Conn.: JAI Press, 1988, 97–134; Jelinek, M., and Litterer, J. A. Why OD Must Become Strategic. In W. A. Pasmore and R. W. Woodman (eds.), *Research in Organizational Change and Development,* vol. 2. Greenwich, Conn.: JAI Press, 1988, 135–162; Johnson, R. A., Hoskisson, R. E., and Margulies, N. Corporate Restructuring: Implications for Organization Change and Development. In W. A. Pasmore and R. W. Woodman (eds.), *Research in Organizational Change and Development,* vol 4. Greenwich, Conn.: JAI Press, 1990, 141–166.

48. Adapted from Clausen, A. W. Strategic Issues in Managing Change: The Turnaround at BankAmerica Corporation. *California Management Review,* Winter 1990, 98–105.

49. Boccialetti, G. Organization Development Ethics and Effectiveness. In W. Sikes, A. B. Drexler, and J. Gants (eds.), *The Emerging Practice of Organization Development.* Alexandria, Va.: NTL Institute for Applied Behavioral Sciences, 1989, 83–92; Connor, P. E., and Lake, L. K. *Managing Organizational Change.* New York: Praeger, 1988, 171–175.

50. Case prepared by Gary C. McMahan during his tenure as Westinghouse Manufacturing Fellow, Department of Management, Texas A & M University, January 1990. Reprinted with permission.

51. Based on Forward, G. E., and Kantrow, A. M. Wide-Open Management at Chaparral Steel. *Harvard Business Review,* May–June 1986, 96–102; Melloan, G. Making Money Making Steel in Texas. *Wall Street Journal,* January 26, 1988, 37; Pare, T. P., The Big Threat to Big Steel's Future. *Fortune,* July 15, 1991, 106–108.

INTEGRATING CASES

AIRLINE FLIGHT CREDIT—YOURS OR MINE? AN ETHICAL QUESTION

Steve Robbins had just received a real "feather" for his professional cap. The university at which Steve was on the faculty was developing an educational exchange program with a university in Sweden. The exchange was to be negotiated and finalized at a meeting in conjunction with an international conference in Copenhagen, Denmark. Steve had been chosen as one of the four faculty members to attend the conference. Such a selection was a coveted position, and Steve was definitely pleased to have received the honor. Needless to say, he was looking forward to the trip, as well as the responsibility the university had placed upon him.

Steve, who had taught at Middleton State University for ten years, was a highly respected, tenured, full professor of business management. He had held several college- and universitywide committee positions, including being elected Faculty Senate president. Many felt the honor of being chosen to attend the Copenhagen conference was a well-deserved one.

As the time grew nearer to the departure date, Steve began making his travel plans. At this time, Steve was informed by his administration that, if he chose, he could take along his spouse, at his own expense. This new development pleased Wendy, Steve's wife, and Steve was glad he could share this experience with her. Anticipation and excitement was running high at the Robbins's household.

On the date of departure for Denmark, several of the faculty members and spouses drove together to the International Airport at Kansas City, from where their United Airlines flight was to depart. Flight 503 was to leave Kansas City at 8:10 A.M. and arrive in O'Hare Airport in Chicago at 9:00 A.M. The party boarded the flight, and all went according to schedule.

After the two-hour layover in Chicago, the Middleton State University party heard the boarding call for Flight 125, their nonstop flight to Copenhagen. When it was their turn, the group boarded the DC-10 that would take them to the international conference. Steve and Wendy had

noticed there was a rather large number of passengers waiting for the flight, and they speculated as to just how full the flight was booked. Their answer was quick in coming.

The airline attendant came into their section of the plane and announced that the flight was overbooked. The attendant went on to say that any passenger willing to get off the flight and take a later flight to Copenhagen would be compensated for his or her inconvenience. The later flight was scheduled to arrive in Copenhagen six hours after Flight 125. To compensate those passengers willing to take the later flight, United would "pay" each ticket holder the equivalent of flying credit worth one thousand dollars, which could be used for any destination to which United flew.

Steve and Wendy were very impressed with the generous offer. If they both got off Flight 125 and took the later flight, they could receive flying credit worth two thousand dollars. That was certainly enough to get them to Hawaii and back, which had been a long-standing item on their wish list! However, there were some catches.

The first catch simply involved timing. Steve was scheduled to register for the international conference between 1:00 P.M. and 4:00 P.M., with the dinner and conference sessions beginning at 4:30 P.M. The later flight, Flight 350, would not arrive in Copenhagen until 4:00 P.M., which would not allow for Steve to have time to pick up baggage and reach the conference center before the dinner was to begin.

A second factor to consider was an ethical issue. The couple had paid for Wendy's ticket, so if any benefits were to be gained from it, they undeniably belonged to Steve and Wendy. However, Middleton State University had purchased Steve's ticket. So, if Steve were to receive flying credit worth one thousand dollars because he got off the flight, would that flying credit belong to him or to Middleton State University?

Steve and Wendy decided to stay on Flight 125 as planned. However, two of the other faculty members and spouses from Middleton State

University decided to get off Flight 125, take the later flight, and receive the flying credit worth two thousand dollars. They tried to convince Steve and Wendy that being late was "not that big of a deal, and anyway, who would know?" But Steve and Wendy stayed with their decision to remain on Flight 125.

QUESTIONS

1. What factors should an employee in Steve's position consider when faced with such a situation?

2. Did Steve make the correct decision by staying on Flight 125? Why or why not?

3. If Steve and Wendy had decided to take the later flight and receive the flying credit, does the flying credit from Steve's ticket belong to them or to Middleton State? Why do you feel this way?

4. If Steve could have taken the later flight and still arrived at the international conference on time, would it have been a different situation?

5. If you were the president of Middleton State University, what would you say to Steve if he had opted to take the later flight and was therefore late to the conference that he had been sent to attend? What would you say to Steve, had the later flight not caused him to be late for the conference and he had opted to take it?

6. If Steve had been faced with the described situation on a return flight, rather than the flight to the conference, would a decision to take the later flight and receive the flight credit have been an ethical one?

Source: This case was prepared by Ron Stephens of Central Missouri State University and Melody Waller LaPreze of University of Missouri-Columbia and is intended to be used as a basis for class discussion, rather than to illustrate either effective or ineffective handling of the situation. The names of the institution, individuals, and locations have been disguised to preserve anonymity. All rights reserved to the authors. © 1990 by Ron Stephens and Melody Waller LaPreze. Presented and accipted by the refereed Midwest Society for Case Research. See R. A. Cook (ed.) *Annual Advances in Business Cases 1990*. South Bend, Ind.: Midwest Society for Case Research, 1990, 58–60. Used with permission.

WAS INDUSTRY JUST NOT HER THING?

Kim sat at her desk wondering what had gone wrong. Was the whole business world like what she had experienced? Had she been too naive? Had her degrees sold her short? Was she not aggressive enough to make it in the "real world"?

Kim had completed her bachelor's of science degree (*summa cum laude*) with a major in Industrial Arts at the end of the winter semester. True, she had selected an unusual major for a five-foot, one-inch-tall female who weighed slightly less than one-hundred pounds. Not every woman enjoyed welding, drafting, and electrical wiring; however, Kim had always excelled on aptitude tests in spacial relations, and so forth. Her dad's being an industrial arts teacher probably was a factor, and both of her parents had always encouraged her and her younger sister (her only sibling) to pursue their areas of interest and to disregard "typical" female/male roles and stereotypes.

Frankly, she had paid little attention to this until she encountered differential treatment by some of her college professors. She had vivid memories of the one who belittled her answers in class whenever possible; he seemed very frustrated when she consistently made the top score on his tests. She would never forget his response, "That is the kindergarten method. Now, Todd, can you give us the real solution to this problem?" Her answer had been correct but not phrased in the exact way that Dr. Young had wanted. Then, of course, she also recalled Dr. Brown's asking her if she were "serious about her major" after she topped his first test—and "how long she had studied" after she topped his second test. However, most of the professors had been very fair and equal in their attitudes and treatment of her. She chalked it up to some of the professors—such as Dr. Young—being married to women who were housewives, "wore double-knit suits, and picked them up for lunch." "Some men do want surrogate mothers in wives, don't they?" Kim thought.

Kim had interviewed with various firms, received offers, and selected the one (the Tardement Company) she considered "the best fit." Of course, influencing factors related to her personal life were involved. She had been married only a few months and her husband, Allen, was finishing his degree, so she had needed to locate within driving distance of the university. Even though Allen was three years older than she, his military service had slowed him down in completing college. Allen was majoring in manufacturing and construction; their romance had blossomed while working together on woodworking projects and trigonometry. She had met him in trig class.

Getting a position of employment that she wanted had been easy for Kim. She had been recruited by Tardement. They had selected her papers from the University Placement Office and had contacted her to come for an interview. Getting jobs while in high school and college had always been easy—generally, Kim had been asked to come for interviews because she had been recommended by someone else. Maybe job hunting had been too easy; maybe she had not really appreciated how some "pound the payment" hunting a position.

As a new employee, being the only female in the engineering department of Tardement really did not bother her. She soon realized, however, that this could cause some minor conflicts. With whom should she eat lunch? She went to the company cafeteria for lunch the first day and realized that she was the only female in the whole cafeteria who was not involved in serving food. So, the next day she brought her lunch and ate with the secretarial/clerical staff. However, their conversation was not related to the projects within the engineering department, as the conversation had been the day before. Even then, one guy kept discussing his golf game from the Saturday before—and she had felt a bit left out. She had "hit and missed" between the lunch options until Wendell, her co-worker and informal mentor in the engineering department, stopped by her desk and said, "You work in a men's department, come and have lunch with us." She had noticed that he made sure she was involved in discussion and was rather curt with one guy when he made a snide comment that she felt was directed toward her. She was more comfortable eating in the cafeteria because she had missed some of the work-related information sharing when she had eaten with the secretaries. However, some of the women suddenly seemed a bit cool when she spoke to them. How could she be in two places? Which was the right place for her?

She appreciated that Wendell had become somewhat of a mentor to her. He was older than her dad, had excellent credentials for his engineering position, was very well versed in his area, and exuded confidence. Lots of the other employees seemed to ask him questions related to projects or general company information. Kim was a bit surprised to learn that his wife was president of the Greens Cafeteria Company. Wendell did not mention this directly; he had mentioned that his wife could identify the source of every salad, dessert, and so on when they went out to eat. Kim had asked what she did. Wendell had appeared very matter-of-fact about his wife's position—no big deal. Kim was impressed.

Charlie, another older engineer, was also nice to her. She felt a bit sorry for Charlie as he always seemed to be in Wendell's shadow. Wendell had been with Tardement longer than Charlie and always seemed to get the really desirable job assignments. Mark rounded out the immediate work group. He was about Kim's age, had a two-year degree and limp blonde hair, was slightly built, and appeared to be rather passive.

Then there was David, the boss. David was a bachelor in his early thirties and the son of one of Kim's university professors. He was adamant about Kim's not being treated as a secretary to the point of forbidding her to touch a word processor—until the day his big report was due. Kim had typed her way through college and had a net speed of approximately ninety words a minute. Somehow waiting to get the small dab of typing required on her projects through the secretary's desk or the word processing department seemed a waste of time and energy. She could have whipped out the typing much faster than she could dictate or write directions for someone else to do it. The secretary's equipment was often available. However, David had been very definite that she was not to do her own typing—or anyone else's—until the day he got into a bind and really needed his report done. Kim had his typing done quickly and without error, which he seemed to appreciate. Kim couldn't really understand David's feelings—just because someone has keyboarding skills does not make one a "secretary."

At times, Kim wished David was married with three kids and a mortgage, instead of being a bachelor with a Corvette. He did not seem to have a very high regard for the women he dated. June, for example, was a manager with the company that Tardement contracted for cleaning the office, so she periodically was at the office. June seemed very possessive of David, indicating in subtle ways that an intimacy was involved. However, Kim sensed that David really preferred not to see June when she came to check on satisfaction with the service being given by her employees. June was attractive. Kim was surprised that she put up with David's attitude, but she seemed to accept it. Kim had heard that David had been "dumped" by a fiancée when he was a senior at the university and that he had taken it really hard. Maybe he was reluctant to put himself in a position of caring, fearing a repeat of the "dumping." Oh, well, that was his private life, Kim thought. These issues should be left at home and not brought to the job.

Kim had always considered herself to be outgoing, pleasant, and interested in people. She was really shocked when David called her in and suggested that she limit her conversations and interactions with the other employees. He also indicated that he had timed her walking to and from various areas in the office and felt that she should walk more rapidly and businesslike. Speak of being surprised. Kim had no idea that walking and thinking or musing over a project in hand could not go together. What else was he watching and timing if he had timed her walking?

David had been thoughtful and considerate in some ways. She recalled his taking her along when he was selecting a storage chest for the big layouts. Of course, she did have to be able to reach into the chest and lift out the layouts. But he had been very considerate that day. Then, the problem of the required steel-toed shoes had been reasonably solved. Tardement had no women's size five shoes for her to slip on for the occasional trips that she made out to the production floor. Her hard hat had been too big—but she could live with that, even if it almost covered her eyes. David and she had agreed that Tardement should not spend seventy-four dollars for her shoes; she would be sure to wear street shoes with solid toes on the trips to the floor—no open toes.

Ron, David's boss, seemed more tuned into equality than David. Kim recalled her disappointment when four men were being sent to the Mid-Western Engineering Conference in Dallas and David had explained to her that because of the added expense of a single room for her (the men were sharing), he was recommending that she attend the local meeting in Kansas City where lodging would not be necessary. She had not com-plained because she did not feel she dared—besides the other guys would probably have thought she was a whiner. However, Ron had canceled their trip because Kim was excluded.

Kim had tried to be a team player. She had passed on to David the union propaganda that Jackie had put on her desk. Jackie, a female member of a minority group, had been a real troublemaker. Kim remembered how difficult it had been the day the vice-president, Jim Sturgess, came down from Southmore and had called in a cross-section of employees to ask various questions and to see if any of the employees had questions. She recalled Jackie's saying that no females ate in the cafeteria. It had required real courage to raise her hand and say that she ate there daily. Sturgess had followed up on that immediately to see if she felt comfortable, if she were included in the conversations, how she had started going in, and why she thought she was the only female eating there. She had wondered if her tires would be slashed that evening, but the only results were cold stares from Jackie and some of her friends. The conversations sometimes stopped abruptly when she joined some of the women. She really did not have much to talk with them about anyhow. Their conversations centered on husbands (mainly their faults), kids, and cooking. Kim was still madly in love with her husband, did not want a family for several years, and preferred eating out to cooking. The only female that she really enjoyed talking with was Cheryl in purchasing. Cheryl had been promoted after her boss left and had done the job for several months. There was Diane in human resources, but one wondered what credentials she had for the job—it didn't seem to be getting along with the employees.

Once she was established at Tardement, Kim went to work on getting her master's degree. It has not been easy. David had been working on his for several years and had taken some of the courses she had. Kim's goal was to finish quickly, and Tardement picked up 80 percent of the tuition. However, some evenings David insisted she finish some project that kept her from attending her classes or made her late. Then she had asked for the professional leave day to take her comprehensive exams, but David had cancelled it. When she had tried to schedule it again, David had told her that they could not spare her right now. Thank goodness Dr. Winters, her advisor, would work with her. He had understood and said to call the morning of the day that she could come and he would have the test ready for her. She had scheduled a vacation day and had told no one where she was going. She resented this because the company pushed education in its employee handbook. She wondered if it was hard for David to see her completing her master's while his was still hanging. But that was his problem—not hers.

David gave a lot of lip service to equality, but he did not assign her the really big desirable projects: they went to Mark. The one she resented most was the big office layout project. She had just finished the plant layout and design and materials handling courses in her master's program, and Mark had a two-year degree from the community college. But he had brownnosing down to a T. He followed David around like a puppy—she wondered when he would carry in the paper and slippers in his mouth. Not her, no way!

Of course, salaries were a deep, dark secret. How well she remembered the day when she had figured out from the deduction percentages Mark was complaining about that his annual salary was between five and six thousand dollars more than hers and he had only six months' seniority on her. Her salary had not increased tremendously in six months. She did not resent whatever Wendell and Charlie made. They were good; Mark was not. Of course, he would probably be at Tardement until he died, being David's dog.

She wished just once that she could have looked David in the eye and told him everything she had wanted to. But Allen had to get through school, and her check had to supplement his Veterans' benefits. Oh, well, that was behind her now, she thought.

She remembered how overjoyed she had been when Dr. Winters had called asking if she was interested in a one-year position at the university as an instructor. She had jumped at the chance, even though the money and benefits were far from comparable to her job at Tardement. In rationalizing her decision to change, she realized that the experience in industry would be of benefit to her and to her students. For example, she recalled the hours she had spent lettering until she got the "9" exactly as the professor wanted it.

No one in industry took the time to make a curved "9"! She would be a better teacher since she had been in the "real world."

But she had to wonder: Had her experience been the "real world" of industry? If David had been middle-aged and married, would she have been able to feel successful? Were many people really trapped as Charlie, her colleague in the engineering department, seemed to be? Did he feel trapped? Did all passive employees like Mark get rewarded for their solicitous behavior toward supervisors? Was that really playing the game? Was she right in going back to academia? Should she have tried another company?

QUESTIONS

1. What are the most important areas of discrimination in this case?

2. Why was Kim willing to tolerate her situation as long as she did when she had always been successful in other endeavors? Do other employees of Tardement tolerate conditions of employment that they perhaps should not? Why?

3. Why was Kim not more assertive?

4. What management techniques would be most effective with Kim?

5. What changes would have contributed to Kim's success? How could Tardement have gained an effective long-term employee in Kim, instead of a turnover statistic? What changes would have contributed to Kim's having a positive attitude and deciding that "industry was her thing"?

6. How would an improved orientation program and an official mentoring assignment have helped Kim?

Source: This case was prepared by Fran Waller of Central Missouri State University and is intended to be used as a basis for class discussion, rather than to illustrate either effective or ineffective handling of the situation. Presented and accepted by the refereed Midwest Society for Case Research. All rights reserved to Fran Waller. Copyrighted © 1989 by Fran Waller. See L. L. Goulet (ed.), *Annual Advances in Business Cases 1989.* South Bend, Ind.: Midwest Society for Case Research, 1989, 639–643. Used with permission.

THE SHIFTLESS WORKER?

Charlie McManus, with a troubled look on his face, sat back in his chair and gazed out the window of his office past the plant to the surrounding mountains. It was a beautiful, sunny day, and he had hoped to be able to duck out by mid-afternoon and be somewhere far up Foster's Creek by 4:30 or so. He would rather be worrying some brook trout instead of worrying about the implications of a situation developing out in area 7.

He could not quite put his finger on it, but there seemed to be something going on out there. Reports of the failure of operators to complete all the necessary checks on their shifts and some indications of minor grumblings among the work force had him wondering if everything was all right in the area. As the manager of department B, he was thinking about whether or not he should try to get better information about what, if anything, was going on and intervene in some way or just let things ride unless something more definite came up. He continued to review in his mind the company and the situation with which he was dealing.

THE COMPANY

Lost River Processing, Inc., a wholly owned subsidiary plant of a large conglomerate, processes ore mined in the nearby mountains into an intermediate product serving as input material for a broad range of industrial processes. The plant's production output is sold to other plants owned by the parent conglomerate, as well as to outside purchasers.

The particular mineral business in which the company engages is highly competitive, with a number of strong competitors located around the country. Since the end product produced by all these plants has the basic characteristics of a commodity, it is important to strive to be a low-cost producer, especially under the current industry condition of overcapacity of production facilities. It is also important to maintain high quality standards because quality is a major factor in securing and maintaining highly sought sole-supplier relationships with customers, which are becoming more common in the industry.

The plant, located in Ashley Springs, Wyoming (population, forty-five hundred), has been an institution in the community for over forty years, employing approximately five hundred workers in operations that continue around the clock.

Most employees are from the surrounding rural, largely agricultural region. Many have grown up on farms and ranches in the area and still farm during their off time and on weekends. They tend to be a hard-working, independent, self-motivated work force in general, although there are some exceptions.

The plant has been nonunion for many years, and remaining so is an important objective of management. The chief advantage of the nonunion status as viewed by management is their flexibility to make changes as needed and as technological developments demand, without protracted negotiations or costly concessions to a union.

In seeking to continue its nonunion status, the company attempts to follow enlightened human resource practices and strives to maintain benefits and grant annual wage and salary increases comparable to those achieved by unions in directly competing firms in the area.

The plant manager for the last several years has been a very capable, yet friendly, unassuming, down-to-earth individual who relates very well with and has the respect of the work force.

For the past two or three years, the company has been cautiously restructuring its work force and adopting some new management practices in line with a decision to eliminate some layers of supervision and push decision making farther down in the organization. These moves are one response to the need for continually reducing costs in order to remain competitive.

Over the longer range, the plant is planning to move progressively toward an operation run on the concept of self-managed groups. Because the work force tends to have low turnover and be well trained and responsible, management feels this move is well founded and offers the potential for real savings.

The plant organization is structured (as shown in Figure 1) with operators in each area responsible to shift supervisors, who in turn report to department managers. The various department managers report to the superintendent in their functional area, who reports to the plant manager, the highest position at the plant site.

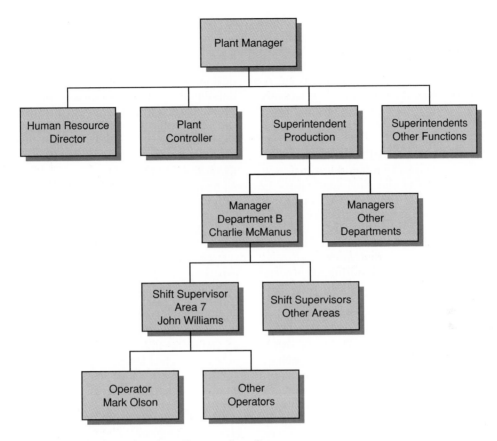

1. Organization Chart, Lost River Processing, Inc.

AREA 7

Area 7 is one of the processing areas falling under the supervision of the manager of department B, Charlie McManus. The area is worked by several crews assigned to assure coverage on an around-the-clock basis. The crews on each shift report to a shift supervisor, and the crews and supervisors rotate shifts monthly.

The supervisors are senior workers who have moved up to the position. Most have had eight or more years of experience in the plant before moving into their supervisory positions. As a result they are very knowledgeable about plant operations in their areas and also know all their fellow workers quite well.

There were, however, a few exceptions to this internal progression from experienced worker to supervisor within the plant. The parent corporation had operated a similar plant in South Carolina for many years. Increasing pressures to lower costs, combined with overcapacity in the

industry, made continued operation of the old plant uneconomic, and it was eventually closed a little over a year ago.

When the plant was closed, some supervisors who were not able to take early retirement or move to other nearby plants were offered transfers to the Wyoming plant. Four eventually elected to transfer and had arrived at the plant about one year ago. They were then placed in supervisory positions roughly equivalent to the positions they had held in South Carolina. Three of them were assigned to department B under Charlie McManus.

These new supervisors from the East had worked in an environment quite different from the Ashley Springs plant, with a quite different work force. The South Carolina plant had employed a racially mixed work force of relatively uneducated, predominantly rural people and had a turnover rate that was moderate to high by Ashley Springs standards. These workers were not highly trained and their supervisors tended to mange them quite closely. As a result, these supervisors had learned to be quite directive and spent a fair amount of their time making sure that their workers did what they had been assigned. These supervisors had subsequently brought these supervisory tendencies and practices with them to the West.

JOHN WILLIAMS, SUPERVISOR

John Williams, who was among the transferred supervisors, is one of the shift supervisors in area 7, responsible for several crews of operators involved in production work in that part of the plant. Among other duties, one of his crews is responsible for making sure that certain pumps are functioning properly, that several bins collecting by-products produced during the process are emptied on schedule, and that the work area is kept clean.

. John has been complaining to his manager Charlie, even asking for help on one occasion, that one of the operators on one of his crews, Mark Olson, has not been performing the job as well as John would like. Over the past several months, according to John, this worker has on occasion either simply failed to perform or performed very poorly several of his job responsibilities.

For example, the settling pond pumps are supposed to be checked every four hours, and certain readings written down. John mentioned that when assigned to this task, Mark does not check them this often and often fails to record the readings as required.

On the third shift, an operator is responsible for emptying the bins of coke and silica, which are produced as by-products, by performing a procedure called vactoring. On the second shift, the dryer bins are serviced in the same way. When assigned as the operator on these shifts, Mark reportedly often fails to vactor the appropriate bins as they should be.

Part of each operator's assigned responsibility is a clean-up area. As the supervisor, John usually has to call Mark's attention to his clean-up area before the monthly inspection.

John reported he has tried talking with Mark about his performance several times, but it hasn't seemed to make any difference. He recognizes that Mark is one of the more intelligent employees among his crew of operators. As such, John is certain Mark is capable of performing well, if he chooses to do the job right. John expressed his concern to Charlie that Mark "always seems to find new ways to screw up or just seems to forget to do certain aspects of his job assignments."

John indicated that Mark had also told him during one of the talks they have had that he doesn't really like his job very much and has been looking around for either a transfer within the plant or for some other opportunity outside the company.

MARK OLSON

As he tried to keep track of all employees in his department, Charlie had been following Mark Olson's progress with the company since he was hired. Mark had been working for the company for several years, and by most indications, it seemed to Charlie, it had generally been a good experience for him. In the course of their infrequent, informal chats, Mark had never given Charlie any indication that he was dissatisfied with his job, and until recently, his performance had always been rated quite highly. The job has no doubt become somewhat routine for Mark now that he has learned all the tasks performed by the crew, and shift work is not particularly enjoyable, but these are conditions everybody comes to terms with eventually. At the same time, the pay, the working conditions, and the company are pretty good.

One thing that has been bothering Mark—and some others, according to scuttlebutt Charlie has picked up in the department—has been the attitude of the new supervisors the company transferred in from back East. The crews' attitude is that these new people seem to have taken over the department, and all the day-to-day operations are being run by these "out of towners." "They treat us like a bunch of slaves, don't let us make decisions, and treat us like we're stupid" was one comment overheard in the shower room a few weeks ago.

Mark appeared to Charlie to be one example of an operator who has not been performing the job as well as he is capable of doing, perhaps partly in response to the attitude of these supervisors. Over the past several months, according to his supervisor, Mark has on occasion simply failed to perform, or performed poorly, several of his job responsibilities. Mark admitted to a friend, who mentioned it to Charlie, that he purposely chose random tasks to "forget" to do. "I'm acting like this to drive them crazy, and just waiting for a job bid," mark had told his friend in the human resource department.

Charlie ended his reverie and arose from the chair. He was still not sure if he was dealing with any real issue or just the usual griping and interpersonal problems heard among the crews. Still, these problems and comments seemed to be arising more frequently than before in department B, and he was concerned about young Mark Olson, for whom he had great hopes in the company.

What, if anything, should he do about the situation? Charlie wondered. In line with the downward delegation of authority in the plant, he generally did not intervene in cases of problem employees, but rather left resolution of such situations up to his supervisors. But in this case, he wondered if the supervisor might be part of the problem. He wasn't sure of just what he was dealing with here and didn't know if he should intervene in some way or not.

It was now 4:00, and Charlie headed out the door for the parking lot and his waiting pickup, gassed up and ready to go with his fly rod and some new Montana nymphs he was itching to try. He had decided to put in some good thinking time before tomorrow, when he would return with his decision.

QUESTIONS

1. What is your analysis of the situation faced by Charlie McManus? What are the key issues facing him?

2. How do you explain the behavior of the operator in this situation? Why do you think he is performing the way he is?

3. What do you think Charlie McManus should do? Explain in detail how you think he should proceed.

4. What do you think the supervisor John should do? How do you think the operator Mark will react to what you propose?

5. What are the implications of the short-term, operational decisions in this situation for the long-range strategic goals of the plant?

6. In this specific situation, the issue was an inappropriate supervisory style and its impact on worker behavior. What other issues are likely to arise in the transition from a traditional hiarachically structured unit to a group-oriented, self-managed organization? What managerial practices might be considered in dealing with them?

Source: This case was prepared by William E. Stratton of Idaho State University and is intended to be used as a basis for class discussion, rather than to illustrate either effective or ineffective handling of the situation. The names of the firm, individuals, and locations have been disguised to preserve the firm's anonymity. Presented and accepted by the refereed Midwest Society for Case Research. All rights reserved to the author. Copyright © 1990 by William E. Stratton. See R. A. Cook (ed.), *Annual Advances in Business Cases 1990* South Bend, Ind.: Midwest Society for Case Research, 1990, 610–615. Used with permission.

THE ROAD TO HELL

John Baker, chief engineer of the Caribbean Bauxite Company Limited of Barracania in the West Indies, was making his final preparations to leave the island. His promotion to production manager of Keso Mining Corporation near Winnipeg—one of Continental Ore's fast-expanding Canadian enterprises—had been announced a month before, and now everything had been attended to except the last vital interview with his successor, the able young Barracanian Matthew Rennalls. It was vital that this interview be a success and that Rennalls leave Baker's office uplifted and encouraged to face the challenge of his new job. A touch on the bell would have brought Rennalls walking into the room, but Baker delayed the moment and gazed thoughtfully through the window, considering just exactly what he was going to say and, more particularly, how he was going to say it.

Baker, an English expatriate, was forty-five years old and had served his twenty-three years with Continental Ore in many different places: the Far East, several countries of Africa; Europe; and for the last two years, the West Indies. He had not cared much for his previous assignment in Hamburg and was delighted when the West Indian appointment came through. Climate was not the only attraction. Baker had always preferred working overseas in what were called the "developing countries" because he felt he had an innate knack—more than most other expatriates working for Continental Ore—of knowing just how to get on with regional staff. After only twenty-four hours in Barracania, however, he realized that he would need all of his innate knack if he were to deal effectively with the problems in this field that now awaited him.

At his first interview with Glenda Hutchins, the production manager, the whole problem of Rennalls and his future was discussed. Then and there, it was made quite clear to Baker that one of his important tasks would be the grooming of Rennalls as his successor. Hutchins had pointed out that not only was Rennalls one of the brightest Barracanian prospects on the staff of Caribbean Bauxite—at London University, he had taken first-class honors in the B.Sc. engineering degree—but, being the son of the minister of finance and economic planning, he also had no small political pull.

Caribbean Bauxite had been particularly pleased when Rennalls decided to work for it, rather than for the government in which his father had such a prominent post. The company ascribed his action to the effect of its vigorous and liberal regionalization program that, since World War II, had produced eighteen Barracanians at the middle management level and had given Caribbean Bauxite a good lead in this respect over all other international concerns operating in Barracania. The success of this timely regionalization policy had led to excellent relations with the government—a relationship that gained added importance when Barracania, three years later, became independent, an occasion that encouraged a critical and challenging attitude toward the role foreign interests would play in the new Barracania. Hutchins, therefore, had little difficulty convincing Baker that the successful career development of Rennalls was of prime importance.

The interview with Hutchins was now two years in the past, and Baker, leaning back in his office chair, reviewed just how successful he had been in the grooming of Rennalls. What aspects of the latter's character had helped, and what had hindered? What about his own personality? How had that helped or hindered? The first item to go on the credit side, without question, would be the ability of Rennalls to master the technical aspects of his job. From the start, he had shown keenness and enthusiasm, and he had often impressed Baker with his ability in tackling new assignments and the constructive comments he invariably made in departmental discussions. He was popular with all ranks of Barracanian staff and had an ease of manner that stood him in good stead when dealing with his expatriate seniors.

Those were all assets, but what about the debit side? First and foremost was his racial consciousness. His four years at London University had accentuated this feeling and made him sensitive to any sign of condescension on the part of expatriates. Perhaps to give expression to this sentiment, as soon as he returned home from London, he threw himself into politics on behalf of the United Action Party, which was later to win the preindependence elections and provide the country with its first prime minister.

The ambitions of Rennalls—and he certainly was ambitious—did not, however, lie in politics. Staunch nationalist that he was, he saw that he could serve himself and his country best—was not bauxite responsible for nearly half the value of Barracania's export trade?—by putting his engineering talent to the best use possible. On this account, Hutchins found that she had an unexpectedly easy task in persuading Rennalls to give up his political work before entering the production department as an assistant engineer.

It was, Baker knew, Rennall's well-repressed sense of racial consciousness that had prevented their relationship from being as close as it should have been. On the surface, they could not have seemed more agreeable. Formality between the two was minimal. Baker was delighted to find that his assistant shared his own peculiar "shaggy dog" sense of humor, so jokes were continually being exchanged. They entertained one another at their houses and often played tennis together—and yet the barrier remained invisible, indefinable, but ever present. The existence of this screen between them was a constant source of frustration to Baker, since it indicated a weakness that he was loath to accept. If successful with people of all other nationalities, why not with Rennalls?

At least he had managed to break through to Rennalls more successfully than had any other expatriate. In fact, it was the young Barracanian's attitude—sometimes overbearing, sometimes cynical—toward other company expatriates that had been one of the subjects Baker raised last year when he discussed Rennall's staff report with him. Baker knew, too, that he would have to raise the same subject again in the forth-coming interview, because Martha Jackson, the senior person in charge of drafting, had complained only yesterday about the rudeness of Rennalls. With this thought in mind, Baker leaned forward and spoke into the intercom: "Would you come in, Matt, please? I'd like a word with you." Rennalls came in, and Baker held out a box and said, "Do sit down. Have a cigarette."

He paused while he held out his lighter and then went on. "As you know, Matt, I'll be off to Canada in a few days' time, and before I go, I thought it would be useful if we could have a final chat together. It is indeed with some deference that I suggest I can be of help. You will shortly be sitting in this chair doing the job I am now doing, but I, on the other hand, am ten years older, so perhaps you can accept the idea that I may be able to give you the benefit of my longer experience."

Baker saw Rennalls stiffen slightly in his chair as he made this point, so he added in explanation, "You and I have attended enough company courses to remember those repeated requests by the human resources manager to tell people how they are getting on as often as the convenient moment arises, and not just the automatic once a year when, by regulation, staff reports have to be discussed."

Rennalls nodded his agreement, so Baker went on, "I shall always remember the last job performance discussion I had with my previous boss back in Germany. She used what she called the 'plus and minus technique.' She firmly believed that when seniors seek to improve the work performance of their staff by discussion, their prime objective should be to make sure the latter leave the interview encouraged and inspired to improve. Any criticism, therefore, must be constructive and helpful. She said that one very good way to encourage a person—and I fully agree with her—is to discuss good points, the plus factors, as well as weak ones, the minus factors. So I thought, Matt, it would be a good idea to run our discussion along these lines."

Rennalls offered no comment, so Baker continued, "Let me say, therefore, right away, that as far as your own work performance is concerned, the pluses far outweigh the minuses. I have, for instance, been most impressed with the way you have adapted your considerable theoretical knowledge to master the practical techniques of your job—that ingenious method you used to get

air down to the fifth shaft level is a sufficient case in point. At departmental meetings, I have invariably found your comments well taken and helpful. In fact, you will be interested to know that only last week I reported to Ms. Hutchins that, from the technical point of view, she could not wish for a more able person to succeed to the position of chief engineer."

"That's very good indeed of you, John," cut in Rennalls with a smile of thanks. "My only worry now is how to live up to such a high recommendation."

"Of that I am quite sure," returned Baker, "especially if you can overcome the minus factor which I would like now to discuss with you. It is one that I have talked about before, so I'll come straight to the point. I have noticed that you are more friendly and get on better with your fellow Barracanians than you do with Europeans. In point of fact, I had a complaint only yesterday from Ms. Jackson, who said you had been rude to her—and not for the first time, either.

"There is, Matt, I am sure, no need for me to tell you how necessary it will be for you to get on well with expatriates, because until the company has trained sufficient men of your caliber, Europeans are bound to occupy senior positions here in Barracania. All this is vital to your future interests, so can I help you in any way?"

While Baker was speaking on this theme, Rennalls sat tensed in his chair, and it was some seconds before he replied. "It is quite extraordinary, isn't it, how one can convey an impression to others so at variance with what one intends? I can only assure you once again that my disputes with Jackson—and you may remember also Godson—have had nothing at all to do with the color of their skins. I promise you that if a Barracanian had behaved in an equally peremptory manner, I would have reacted in precisely the same way. And again, if I may say it within these four walls, I am sure I am not the only one who has found Jackson and Godson difficult. I could mention the names of several expatriates who have felt the same. However, I am really sorry to have created this impression of not being able to get on with Europeans—it is an entirely false one—and I quite realize that I must do all I can to correct it as quickly as possible. On your last point, regarding Europeans holding senior positions in the company for some time to come, I quite accept the situation. I know that Caribbean Bauxite—as it has been doing for many years now—will promote Barracanians as soon as their experience warrants it. And, finally, I would like to assure you, John—and my father thinks the same, too—that I am very happy in my work here and hope to stay with the company for many years to come."

Rennalls had spoken earnestly, and Baker, although not convinced by what he had heard, did not think he could pursue the matter further except to say, "All right, Matt, my impression may be wrong, but I would like to remind you about the truth of that old saying 'What is important is not what is true, but what is believed.' Let it rest at that."

But suddenly Baker knew that he did not want to "let it rest at that." He was disappointed once again at not being able to break through to Rennalls and at having again had to listen to his bland denial that there was any racial prejudice in his makeup.

Baker, who had intended to end the interview at this point, decided to try another tack. "To return for a moment to the plus and minus technique I was telling you about just now, there is another plus factor I forgot to mention. I would like to congratulate you not only on the caliber of your work but also on the ability you have shown in overcoming a challenge that I, as a European, have never had to meet.

"Continental Ore is, as you know, a typical commercial enterprise—admittedly a big one—that is a product of the economic and social environment of the United States and Western Europe. My ancestors have all been brought up in this environment for the past two or three hundred years, and I have, therefore, been able to live in a world in which commerce (as we know it today) has been part and parcel of my being. It has not been something revolutionary and new that has suddenly entered my life. In your case," went on Baker, "the situation is different, because you and your forebears have only had some fifty and not two or three hundred years. Again, Matt, let me congratulate you—and people like you—on having so successfully overcome this particular hurdle. It is for this very reason that I think the outlook for Barracania—and particularly Caribbean Bauxite—is so bright."

Rennalls had listened intently, and when Baker finished, he replied, "Well, once again, John, I have to thank you for what you have said, and, for my part, I can only say that it is gratifying to know that my own personal effort has been so much appreciated. I hope that more people will soon come to think as you do."

There was a pause, and, for a moment, Baker thought hopefully that he was about to achieve his long-awaited breakthrough. But Rennalls merely smiled back. The barrier remained unbreached. There were some five minutes' cheerful conversation about the contrast between the Caribbean and Canadian climates and whether the West Indies had any hope of beating England in the Fifth Test before Baker drew the interview to a close. Although he was as far as ever from knowing the real Rennalls, he was nevertheless glad that the interview had run along in this friendly manner and, particularly, that it had ended on such a cheerful note.

This feeling, however, lasted only until the following morning. Baker had some farewells to make, so he arrived at the office considerably later than usual. He had no sooner sat down at his desk than his secretary walked into the room with a worried frown on her face. Her words came fast. "When I arrived this morning, I found Mr. Rennalls already waiting at my door. He seemed very angry and told me that he had a vital letter to dictate that must be sent off without any delay. He was so worked up that he couldn't keep still and kept pacing about the room, which is most unlike him. He wouldn't even wait to read what he had dictated. Just signed the page where he thought the letter would end. It has been distributed, and your copy is in your tray."

Puzzled and feeling vaguely uneasy, Baker opened the envelope marked "confidential" and read the following letter:

14 August 1990

FROM: Assistant Engineer

TO: Chief Engineer Caribbean Bauxite Limited

SUBJECT: Assessment of Interview between Messrs. Baker and Rennalls

It has always been my practice to respect the advice given to me by seniors, so after our interview, I decided to give careful thought once again to its main points and to make sure that I had understood all that had been said. As I promised you at the time, I had every intention of putting your advice to the best effect.

It was not, therefore, until I had sat down quietly in my home yesterday evening to consider the interview objectively that its main purpose became clear. Only then did the full enormity of what you said dawn on me. The more I thought about it, the more convinced I was that I had hit upon the real truth—and the more furious I became. With a facility in the English language which I—a poor Barracanian—cannot hope to match, you had the audacity to insult me (and through me every Barracanian worth his salt) by claiming that our knowledge of modern living is only a paltry fifty years old, while yours goes back two hundred to three hundred years. As if your materialistic commercial environment could possibly be compared with the spiritual values of our culture! I'll have you know that if much of what I saw in London is representative of your most boasted culture, I hope fervently that it will never come to Barracania. By what right do you have the effrontery to condescend to us? After all, you Europeans think us barbarians, or, as you say amongst yourselves, we are "just down from the trees."

Far into the night I discussed this matter with my father, and he is as disgusted as I. He agrees with me that any company whose senior staff think as you do is no place for any Barracanian proud of his culture and race. So much for all the company claptrap and specious propaganda about regionalization and Barracania for the Barracanians.

I feel ashamed and betrayed. Please accept this letter as my resignation, which I wish to become effective immediately.

cc: Production Manager
Managing Director

QUESTIONS

1. What were Baker's intentions in the conversation with Rennalls? Were they fulfilled or not, and why?

2. Was Baker alert to nonverbal signals? What did both Baker and Rennalls communicate to one another by nonverbal means?

3. How did Baker's view of himself affect the impression he formed of Rennalls?

4. What kind of interpersonal relationship had existed between Baker and Rennalls prior to the conversation described in the case? Was the conversation consistent or inconsistent with that relationship?

5. What, if anything, could Baker or Rennalls have done before, during, or after the conversation to improve the situation?

6. How would you characterize the personality attributes of Baker and Rennalls?

7. What perceptual errors and attributions are evident?

Source: Prepared and adapted with permission from G. Evans, late of Shell International Petroleum Co. Ltd., London, for Shell-BP Petroleum Development Company of Nigeria, Limited.

FREIDA MAE JONES

Freida Mae Jones was born in her grandmother's Georgia farmhouse on June 1, 1949. She was the sixth of George and Ella Jones's ten children. Mr. and Mrs. Jones moved to New York City when Freida was four because they felt that the educational and career opportunities for their children would be better in the North. With the help of some cousins, they settled in a five-room apartment in the Bronx. George worked as a janitor at Lincoln Memorial Hospital, and Ella was a part-time housekeeper in a nearby neighborhood. George and Ella were conservative, strict parents. They kept a close watch on their children's activities and demanded they be home by a certain hour. The Joneses believed that because they were African-American, the children

would have to perform and behave better than their peers to be successful. They believed that their children's education would be the most important factor in their success as adults.

Freida entered Memorial High School, a racially integrated public school, in September 1963. Seventy percent of the student body was caucasian, 20 percent African-American, and 10 percent Hispanic. About 60 percent of the graduates went on to college. Of this 60 percent, 4 percent were African-American and Hispanic and all were male. In the middle of her senior year, Freida was the top student in her class. Following school regulations, Freida met with her guidance counselor to discuss her plans upon graduation. The counselor advised her to consider training in a "practical" field, such as housekeeping, cooking, or sewing, so that she could find a job.

George and Ella Jones were furious when Freida told them what the counselor had advised. Ella said, "Don't they see what they are doing. Freida is the top-rated student in her whole class and they are telling her to become a manual worker? She showed that she has a fine mind and can work better than any of her classmates, and still she is told not to become anybody in this world. It's really not any different in the North than back home in Georgia, except that they don't try to hide it down South. They want her to throw away her fine mind because she is an African-American girl and not a white boy. I'm going to go up to her school tomorrow and talk to the principal."

As a result of Mrs. Jones's visit to the principal, Freida was assisted in applying to ten Eastern colleges, each of which offered her full scholarships. In September 1966, Freida entered Wellesley College, an exclusive private women's college in Massachusetts. In 1970, Freida graduated *summa cum laude* in history. She decided to return to New York to teach grade school in the city's public school system. Freida was unable to obtain a full-time position, so she substituted. She also enrolled as a part-time student in Columbia University's Graduate School of Education. In 1975, she had attained her master of arts degree in teaching from Columbia but could not find a permanent teaching job. New York City was laying off teachers and had instituted a hiring freeze because of the city's financial problems.

Feeling frustrated about her future as a teacher, Freida decided to get an master's of business administration (MBA). She thought that there was more opportunity in business than in education. Churchill Business School, a small, prestigious school located in upstate New York, accepted Freida into its MBA program.

Freida completed her MBA in 1977 and accepted an entry-level position at the Industrialist World Bank of Boston in a fast-track management development program. The three-year program introduced her to all facets of bank operations, from teller to loan training and operations management. She was rotated to branch offices throughout New England. After completing the program, she became an assistant manager for branch operations in the West Springfield branch office.

During her second year in the program, Freida had met James Walker, an African-American, doctoral student in business administration at the University of Massachusetts. Her assignment to West Springfield precipitated their decision to get married. They originally anticipated that they would marry when James finished his doctorate and could move to Boston. Instead, they decided he would pursue a job in the Springfield–Hartford area.

Freida was not only the first African-American but also the first woman to hold an executive position in the West Springfield branch office. Throughout the training program, Freida felt somewhat uneasy, although she did very well. There were six other African-Americans in the program, five men and one woman, and she found support and comfort in sharing her feelings with them. The group spent much of their free time together. Freida had hoped that she would be located near one or more of the group when she went out into the "real world." She felt that although she was able to share her feelings about work with James, he did not have the full appreciation or understanding of her co-workers. However, the nearest group member was located one hundred miles away.

Freida's boss in Springfield was Stan Luboda, a fifty-five-year-old native New Englander. Freida felt that he treated her differently than he did the other trainees. He always tried to help her and took a lot of time (too much, according to Freida) explaining things to her. Freida felt that he was treating her like a child and not like an intelligent and able professional.

"I'm really getting frustrated and angry about what is happening at the bank," Freida said to her husband. "The people don't even realize it, but their prejudice comes through all the time. I feel as if I have to fight all the time just to start off even. Luboda gives Paul Cohen more responsibility than me, and we both started at the same time, with the same amount of training. He's meeting customers alone, and Luboda has accompanied me to each meeting I've had with a customer."

"I run into the same thing at school," said James. "The people don't even know that they are doing it. The other day I met with a professor on my dissertation committee. I've known and worked with him for over three years. He said he wanted to talk with me about a memo he had received. I asked him what it was about, and he said that the records office wanted to know about my absence during the spring semester. He said that I had to sign some forms. He had me confused with Martin Jordan, another African-American student. Then he realized that it wasn't me, but Jordan he wanted. All I could think was that we all must look alike to him. I was angry. Maybe it was an honest mistake on his part, but whenever something like that happens, and it happens often, it gets me really angry."

"Something like that happened to me," said Freida. "I was using the copy machine, and Luboda's secretary was talking to someone in the hall. She had just gotten a haircut and was saying that her hair was now like Freida's—short and kinky—and that she would have to talk to me about how to take care of it. Luckily, my back was to her. I bit my lip and went on with my business. Maybe she was trying to be cute, because I know she saw me standing there, but comments like that are not cute, they are racist."

"I don't know what to do," said James. "I try to keep things in perspective. Unless people interfere with my progress, I try to let it slide. I only have so much energy and it doesn't make sense to waste it on people who don't matter. But that doesn't make it any easier to function in a racist environment. People don't realize that they are being racist. But a lot of times their expectations of African-American people or women or whatever are different because of skin color or gender. They expect you to be different, although if you were to ask them, they would say that they don't. In fact, they would be highly offended if you implied that they were racist or sexist. They don't see themselves that way."

"Luboda is interfering with my progress," said Freida. "The kinds of experiences I have now will have a direct effect on my career advancement. If decisions are being made because I am African-American or a woman, then they are racially and sexually biased. It's the same kind of attitude that the guidance counselor had when I was in high school, although not as blatant."

In September 1980, Freida decided to speak to Luboda about his treatment of her. She met with him in his office. "Mr. Luboda, there is something that I would like to discuss with you, and I feel a little uncomfortable because I'm not sure how you will respond to what I am gong to say."

"I want you to feel that you can trust me," said Luboda. "I am anxious to help you in any way I can."

"I feel that you treat me differently than you treat the other people around here," said Freida. "I feel that you are overcautious with me, that you always try to help me, and never let me do anything on my own."

"I always try to help the new people around here," answered Luboda. "I'm not treating you any differently than I treat any other person. I think that you are being a little too sensitive. Do you think that I treat you differently because you are African-American?"

"The thought had occurred to me," said Freida. "Paul Cohen started here the same time that I did and he has much more responsibility than I do." (Cohen was already handling accounts on his own, while Freida had not yet been given that responsibility.)

"Freida, I know you are not a naive person," said Luboda. "You know the way the world works. There are some things which need to be taken more slowly than others. There are some assignments for which Cohen has been given more responsibility than you, and there are some assignments for which you are given more responsibility than Cohen. I try to put you where you do the most good."

"What you are saying is that Cohen gets the more visible, customer-contact assignments and I get the behind-the-scenes running of the operations assignments," said Freida. "I'm not naive, but I'm also not stupid either. Your decisions are unfair. Cohen's career will advance more quickly than mine because of the assignments that he gets."

"Freida, that is not true," said Luboda. "Your career will not be hurt because you are getting different responsibilities than Cohen. You both need the different kinds of experiences you are getting. And you have to face the reality of the banking business. We are in a conservative business. When we speak to customers we need to gain their confidence, and we put the best people for the job in the positions to achieve that end. If we don't get their confidence, they can go down the street to our competitors and do business with them. Their services are no different than ours. It's a competitive business in which you need every edge you have. It's going to take time for people to change some of their attitudes about whom they borrow money from or where they put their money. I can't change the way people feel. I am running a business, but believe me, I won't make any decisions that are detrimental to you or to the bank. There is an important place for you here at the bank. Remember, you have to use your skills to the best advantage of the bank as well as your career."

"So what you are saying is that all things being equal, except my gender and my race, that Cohen will get different treatment than me in terms of assignments," said Freida.

"You're making it sound like I am making a racist and sexist decision," said Luboda. "I'm making a business decision utilizing the resources at my disposal and the market situation in which I must operate. You know exactly what I am talking about. What would you do if you were in my position?"

QUESTIONS

1. What are the dominant attitudinal sets in this case? Are they valid?

2. How would you evaluate Freida Mae Jones's career planning efforts and career development?

3. Do you think Freida Mae Jones is being discriminated against? Explain.

4. If you were Luboda, what would you do?

5. If you were Freida Mae Jones, what would you do?

Source: M. R. Moser, Freida Mae Jones. *Journal of Management Case Studies*, 1985, *1*, 81–84. Used with permission. © Robert Randall, 320 Riverside Drive, N.Y., N.Y. 10025

RESISTANCE TO CHANGE?

Forest Park Hotels had been started as an outgrowth of a strategic planning process initiated by the board of directors of Golden Horizons, Inc. A desire to diversify out of a singular focus on "intermediate care" nursing home facilities resulted in an initial decision to explore the opportunities in hotel operations. Based upon extensive research, the development of a small chain of high-quality hotels appeared to provide a natural strategy for continued growth through diversification.

In just five years from the purchase of the first hotel, the chain had grown to six and was meeting both sales and profitability goals. The initial strategic plan adopted by the board had targeted the acquisition or construction of one hotel every twelve to eighteen months. According to Paul Halsey, CEO of Golden Horizons, "The growth of the Forest Park Hotel Division had happened at a faster rate than any of us had anticipated. Our positive cash flow allowed us to take advantage of some unique opportunities, both for construction and acquisition. If current operations continue at the present pace and attractive acquisitions become available, I would anticipate the continued rapid expansion of this division."

CENTRALIZATION

Rapid growth of the hotel division with properties located in Atlanta, Dallas, Orlando, Minneapolis, New Orleans, and St. Louis brought with it the need for many changes. A corporate office was formed for the hotel division, and professionals were hired from outside the organization to fill several key positions, providing the experience necessary to continue with the present plans for expansion. As the operating plans for the new division were established, the division vice-president, with the input and consensus of the hotel general managers, decided to centralize the accounting, marketing, and purchasing functions. These decisions were well-received, and immediate cost savings and operational improvements were noted.

However, a later decision implementing a centralized human resources program to achieve equity in the hiring, training, development, and compensation of the managerial and professional (exempt) employees had been difficult. Although the general managers had enjoyed the autonomy of making their own human resources decisions, they grudgingly realized, for both legal reasons and for the planned growth of the division to be successful, change was necessary. The unanticipated rapid growth of the hotel division had created the need to prepare employees for promotions and transfers to meet future human resource needs.

CENTRALIZED HUMAN RESOURCE PROGRAM IMPLEMENTED

Under the recently accepted human resource program, minimum qualifications for each position classified as being exempt from wage and hour regulations (including overtime provisions) were established through standardized job specifications. Training and development programs had also been outlined to prepare employees for promotions and transfers. A list of promotable employees was developed at each hotel and then forwarded to the division office to be compiled and shared with all of the general managers. In addition, minimum and maximum salary levels had been established for all exempt positions based on competitive salary and benefit surveys.

All of these guidelines had been developed by Chad Reynolds, division vice-president of human resources, and then sent to all general managers for possible changes before being officially adopted. When the proposed guidelines were sent to the hotels, the general managers had been instructed to work with the local human resource directors and other key members of their management teams in identifying any potential problems the guidelines could pose. After both formal and informal discussions between the vice-president of human resources, general managers, and local personnel directors, several modifications were made to the guidelines and the division vice-president endorsed the implementation of the following policy and procedures:

> To provide for the future human resource needs of the hotel division while ensuring equity in the hiring, transferring, promoting, and compensating of all exempt employees, the following procedures will be followed to maintain our status as an equal opportunity employer:

1. The corporate human resource office will assist the personnel manager and management staff in each hotel in maintaining the proper levels of staffing.
2. Initial exempt employee staffing requirements and subsequent changes can only be made with the prior approval of the division vice-president, the vice-president of human resources, and the general manager of the hotel making the request.
3. All job candidates must meet the minimum specifications set forth in the job description for each exempt position.
4. When qualified local candidates are not available, the costs of reasonable interviewing expenses including transportation will be reimbursed through the corporate human resource office.
5. Final approval must be obtained from the vice-president of human resources before

any job offers are extended, and all personnel records including payroll or exempt employees will be maintained in the corporate office.

Everyone appeared to understand and accept the new procedures as they were implemented. Some minor problems were encountered, but these had been quickly resolved to everyone's satisfaction. However, the first serious challenge to the new program came just six months after the program had been implemented.

REQUEST FOR AN EXCEPTION

The challenge came from the management team of the Atlanta hotel that had been acquired first and formed the foundation for the present chain. Not only was it the first hotel, but it was also managed by Jim Evans, the general manager with the longest tenure. Jim had earned an enviable record of success by managing the most profitable operation in the division. Jim knew he was facing a problem and had made several calls to Chad seeking an exception to the newly adopted guidelines.

The problem was in the culinary department, which was under the supervision of the hotel's food and beverage director, Joseph Langemier. Jim's personnel staff had been unable to fill a key position, evening sous chef, in the hotel's gourmet dining room.

As Chad read the following memo from Joseph, he sensed the frustration of the local hotel's management staff.

TO: Chad Reynolds

FROM: Joseph Langemier

RE: Human Resource Policies and Procedures

This is to follow up our conversation in which it seems we have differences of understanding as to the needs in the culinary department. After the resignation of George Deal, evening sous chef, the executive chef (Aaron Murphy) and I agreed to readjust our organizational structure with regard to the outstanding requisition to fill the sous chef position. We agreed to have the evening sous chef position currently held by George to be filled with a sous chef of perhaps not the same caliber in terms of years of experience, but rather by an individual with an excellent culinary background.

Because of my association with very good professionals in the past, I am in the position of recommending candidates from time to time. This has been the case with Walter Steiner. He may not have the years of supervisory experience you seem to feel necessary, but he definitely has the culinary background to qualify for the position of sous chef. With this in mind, I have asked Executive Chef Murphy to talk to Walter and determine his interest in being considered for the sous chef position. It was only after the executive chef talked to Walter that we recommended that he be flown from Baltimore to Atlanta to see the hotel and dining room and interview for the position.

He has indicated that he will not take less than the maximum amount specified in the salary range for the position since he is currently making just four thousand dollars less than this amount between wages and overtime. In addition, he has chosen not to be promoted in the past because he wanted to gain the experience of working for a first-class operation similar to the one he has been working for during the last two years.

By adhering to your human resource policies, we are punishing Walter by insisting on hiring a person with supervisory experience. Would he have been considered to be qualified for the current position if he had been a supervisor in a steak and potatoes-type restaurant? That would qualify him to meet your supervisory qualifications but not our culinary requirements. Your refusal to consider Walter for the job indicates that you do not understand the differences between a culinarian and a supervisor.

Chad realized the anger coming through in the memo because Joseph was aware that Chad had been a hotel food and beverage manager before moving into the human resource function and, as such, was very knowledgeable of culinary duties. After reading the memo, Chad decided to review the job description and gather more information before making any decisions.

Job Title: Sous Chef

General Description:

Assume full responsibility for the preparation, production, and presentation of quality food products for the dining room.

Duties and Responsibilities:

Supervise and coordinate all personnel under direct supervision.

Observe and train all food preparation workers in the preparation, portion control, and presentation of food items based on prescribed standards.

Requisition and maintain necessary supplies. Consult with executive chef on menu changes, work schedules, payroll, and personnel matters.

Assure adequate sanitation standards.

Other duties as assigned by the executive chef or executive sous chef.

Job Relationships:

Work under the direction of the executive chef and the executive sous chef. Supervise all preparation personnel in assigned location.

Job Specifications:

High school education; advanced training in food preparation, kitchen supervision, and sanitation preferred.

Minimum of two years' supervisory experience of food preparation in a full-service restaurant.

Must be knowledgeable of all basic cooking techniques, meats, and sauces.

Must be able to maintain rapport with superiors and subordinates.

Chad realized that Atlanta was experiencing a boom in new hotel construction that was resulting in an abnormally high turnover of skilled employees and upward pressure on salaries. In addition, the individual who had previously held the now-vacant position had been "lured" away by a new hotel as the executive sous chef (both a promotion in responsibility and title with a significant increase in pay). However, surveys completed by the Atlanta human resource staff within the last three months indicated the hotel had remained competitive in the salaries and benefits paid to comparable sous chefs. In fact, the salary guidelines established for the sous chef position in question were slightly above average for comparable hotels.

A review of the personnel files showed that the three sous chefs currently on staff met all minimum criteria set forth in the new human resource guidelines, and the open personnel requisition was for a person who would be in a comparable position. The fact that the position in question had now been vacant for one month and the hotel was entering its busiest season was puzzling since discussions with the local personnel manager indicated that two individuals meeting the guidelines had been screened and referred for interviews, but no interview comment forms had been returned. The personnel manager had also mentioned that Joseph and Walter had previously worked together and, based on some of Joseph's comments, they may have been "drinking buddies."

QUESTIONS

1. Describe the change process, problems encountered with implementing the planned change, and techniques used to promote change.

2. If one of the most experienced managers with a consistently profitable operation is requesting an exception to the guidelines, are there other underlying problems, or is he simply not accepting the new centralized human resource system?

3. How should Chad Reynolds respond to Joseph and the local management team?

4. What should Chad Reynolds do to prevent situations similar to this from happening again?

Source: The names of the parties, as well as all place names, in the case have been disguised. This case was prepared by Roy A. Cook of Fort Lewis College and Jeryl L. Nelson of Wayne State College as a basis for class discussion rather than to illustrate either effective or ineffective handling of an administrative situation. Presented to the Midwest Society for Case Research Workshop, 1989. All rights reserved to the authors. Copyright © 1989, Roy A. Cook and Jeryl L. Nelson. See L. L. Goulet (ed.), *Annual Advances in Business Cases, 1989* South Bend, Ind.: Midwest Society for Case Research, 1989, 539–544.

AUTHOR INDEX

ORGANIZATION AND SUBJECT INDEX